VISUAL BASIC® 2005
FOR PROGRAMMERS
SECOND EDITION

DEITEL® DEVELOPER SERIES

Deitel® Ser

How to Program Series

Advanced Java™ 2 Platform How to Program

C How to Program, 4/E

C++® How to Program, 5/E – Including Cyber Classroom

e-Business and e-Commerce How to Program

Internet and World Wide Web How to Program, 3/E

Java™ How to Program, 6/E – Including Cyber Classroom

Small C++® How to Program, 5/E – Including Cyber Classroom

Small Java™ How to Program, 6/E – Including Cyber Classroom

Perl How to Program

Python How to Program

Visual Basic® 2005 How to Program, 3/E

Visual C++® .NET How to Program

Visual C#® 2005 How to Program, 2/E

Wireless Internet & Mobile Business How to Program

XML How to Program

ies Page

Deitel® Developer Series

C# for Programmers, 2/e

Visual Basic® 2005 for Programmers, 2/e

Simply Series

Simply C++®: An Application-Driven
Tutorial Approach

Simply C#®: An Application-Driven
Tutorial Approach

Simply Java™ Programming: An
Application-Driven Tutorial
Approach

Simply Visual Basic® .NET: An
Application Driven Tutorial Approach
(Visual Studio .NET
2002 Edition)

Simply Visual Basic® .NET: An
Application Driven Tutorial
Approach (Visual Studio .NET
2003 Edition)

Also Available

SafariX Web Books
www.SafariX.com

To follow the Deitel publishing program, please register at:
www.deitel.com/newsletter/subscribe.html
for the free *DEITEL® BUZZ ONLINE* e-mail newsletter.

To communicate with the authors, send e-mail to:
deitel@deitel.com

For information on corporate on-site seminars offered by Deitel & Associates, Inc.
worldwide, visit:
www.deitel.com or write to deitel@deitel.com

For continuing updates on Prentice Hall/Deitel publications visit:
www.deitel.com,
www.prenhall.com/deitel or
www.InformIT.com/deitel

Many of the designations used by manufacturers and sellers to distinguish their products are claimed as trademarks. Where those designations appear in this book, and the publisher was aware of a trademark claim, the designations have been printed with initial capital letters or in all capitals.

The authors and publisher have taken care in the preparation of this book, but make no expressed or implied warranty of any kind and assume no responsibility for errors or omissions. No liability is assumed for incidental or consequential damages in connection with or arising out of the use of the information or programs contained herein.

The publisher offers excellent discounts on this book when ordered in quantity for bulk purchases or special sales, which may include electronic versions and/or custom covers and content particular to your business, training goals, marketing focus, and branding interests. For more information, please contact:

> U. S. Corporate and Government Sales
> (800) 382-3419
> corpsales@pearsontechgroup.com

For sales outside the U. S., please contact:

> International Sales
> international@pearsoned.com

Visit us on the Web: www.phptr.com

 This Book Is Safari Enabled

The Safari® Enabled icon on the cover of your favorite technology book means the book is available through Safari Bookshelf. When you buy this book, you get free access to the online edition for 45 days.

Safari Bookshelf is an electronic reference library that lets you easily search thousands of technical books, find code samples, download chapters, and access technical information whenever and wherever you need it.

To gain 45-day Safari Enabled access to this book:

- Go to http://www.prenhallprofessional.com/safarienabled
- Complete the brief registration form
- Enter the coupon code 2EEC-GH4D-5BSR-IDDQ-EMKU

If you have difficulty registering on Safari Bookshelf or accessing the online edition, please e-mail customer-service@safaribooksonline.com.

Library of Congress Cataloging-in-Publication Data

On file

Text printed in the United States on recycled paper at R.R . Donnelley in Crawfordsville, Indiana.
2nd printing, January 2007

VISUAL BASIC® 2005
FOR PROGRAMMERS
SECOND EDITION
DEITEL® DEVELOPER SERIES

Paul J. Deitel
Deitel & Associates, Inc.

Harvey M. Deitel
Deitel & Associates, Inc.

PRENTICE
HALL

Upper Saddle River, NJ • Boston • Indianapolis • San Francisco
New York • Toronto • Montreal • London • Munich • Paris • Madrid
Capetown • Sydney • Tokyo • Singapore • Mexico City

Trademarks

Microsoft®, Visual Studio®, Visual Basic® and Visual Web Developer™ are either trademarks or registered trademarks of Microsoft Corporation in the United States and/or other countries.

Object Management Group™, OMG™, Unified Modeling Language™ and UML™ are trademarks of Object Management Group, Inc.

To my wife Michelle and my daughter Jessica:
    You are the joys of my life.
Paul

To Barbara:
    I love you.
Harvey

Contents

9 Classes and Objects: A Deeper Look   302

10 Object-Oriented Programming: Inheritance   346

15 Multithreading 561

16 Strings, Characters and Regular Expressions 600

22 Web Services 941

23 Networking: Streams-Based Sockets and Datagrams 998

Preface

"Live in fragments no longer, only connect."
—Edgar Morgan Foster

Welcome to the world of Windows, Internet and Web programming with Visual Basic, Visual Studio 2005 and the .NET 2.0 platform! This book presents leading-edge computing technologies to software developers and IT professionals.

At Deitel & Associates, we write computer science textbooks for college students and professional books for software developers. We also teach this material in industry seminars at organizations worldwide.

This book was a joy to create. To start, we put the previous edition under the microscope:

- We audited our presentation against the most recent Microsoft Visual Basic Language Specification—Version 8—which can be downloaded from

  http://go.microsoft.com/fwlink/?LinkId=62990

- We fully updated the book to Visual Studio 2005 and .NET 2.0.

- All of the chapters have been significantly updated and upgraded.

- We changed to an early classes and objects pedagogy. Now readers build reusable classes starting with a very friendly treatment in Chapter 4.

- We updated our object-oriented presentation to use the latest version of the *UML (Unified Modeling Language)—UML™ 2.0*—the industry-standard graphical language for modeling object-oriented systems.

- We added an optional OOD/UML automated teller machine (ATM) case study in Chapters 1, 3–9 and 11. The case study includes a complete Visual Basic code implementation of the ATM in Appendix J.

- We added several multi-section, object-oriented programming case studies.

- We incorporated key new features of Microsoft's latest release of Visual Basic— Visual Basic 2005—and added discussions on generics, .NET remoting and debugging.

- We significantly enhanced our treatment of XML, ADO.NET, ASP.NET and Web services.

All of this has been carefully scrutinized by a substantial team of .NET industry developers, academic professionals and members of the Microsoft Visual Basic development team.

Who Should Read This Book

We have several Visual Basic publications, intended for different audiences. *Visual Basic 2005 for Programmers, 2/e*, is part of the *Deitel® Developer Series*, intended for professional software developers who want a deep treatment of a new technology with minimal introductory material. The book emphasizes achieving program clarity through the proven techniques of structured programming, object-oriented programming (OOP) and event-driven programming. It continues with upper-level topics such as XML, ASP.NET 2.0, ADO.NET 2.0 and Web services. Unlike our *How to Program Series* college textbooks, the *Deitel® Developer Series* books do not include the extensive pedagogic features and ancillary support materials required for college courses.

Visual Basic 2005 for Programmers, 2/e presents hundreds of complete, working Visual Basic programs and depicts their inputs and outputs in actual screen shots of running programs. This is our signature "live-code" approach—we present concepts in the context of complete working programs.

As you read this book, if you have questions, send an e-mail to deitel@deitel.com; we will respond promptly. For updates on this book and the status of Visual Basic software, and for the latest news on all Deitel publications and services, please visit www.deitel.com regularly and be sure to sign up for the free *Deitel® Buzz Online* e-mail newsletter at www.deitel.com/newsletter/subscribe.html. For more information about Visual Basic 2005, check out our Visual Basic resource center at www.deitel.com/VisualBasic. For a complete list of our resource centers, visit www.deitel.com/ResourceCenters.html.

Visual Basic 2005 for Programmers, 2/e Code Examples

You can download the book's source code from

> **www.deitel.com/books/vbforprogrammers2**

The examples are in ZIP archive files, so you'll need a ZIP archive tool such as WinZip (available from www.winzip.com) to extract the files. The examples are organized in an examples folder with a subfolder for each chapter (e.g., ch01, ch02, etc.). The example folders are named FigXX_YY, where XX represents the chapter number and YY represents the figure number. For examples that span multiple figures, the folder name has the format FigXX_YY_ZZ, where YY and ZZ represent the example's starting and ending figure numbers. We assume in our Chapter 1 "test-drive" instructions that you extract these examples to the C:\ folder on your computer.

Microsoft Visual Basic 2005 Express Edition Software

On November 7, 2005 Microsoft released its Visual Studio 2005 development tools, including the Visual Basic 2005 Express Edition. Per Microsoft's Web site, Microsoft Express Editions are "lightweight, easy-to-use and easy-to-learn tools for the hobbyist, novice and student developer." You may use Visual Basic 2005 Express (which is packaged with this book) or a complete version of Visual Studio 2005 to compile and execute the example programs. Visual Basic 2005 Express also can be downloaded from

> msdn.microsoft.com/vstudio/express/vb/

According to the Microsoft Express Editions FAQ page (msdn.microsoft.com/vstudio/express/support/faq/), "Effective April 19th, 2006, all Visual Studio 2005 Express Editions are free permanently. SQL Server 2005 Express Edition has always been and will continue to be a free download."

When you install this software, you will be asked if you wish to install the help documentation and SQL Server 2005 Express—we recommend that you choose to install both. Microsoft provides a dedicated forum for help using the Express edition:

>   forums.microsoft.com/msdn/ShowForum.aspx?ForumID=24

Other Software Requirements

For some examples in Chapter 17, Graphics and Multimedia, we use Microsoft Agent, which can be downloaded from

>   www.microsoft.com/msagent/downloads/default.asp

For Chapter 20, you will need SQL Server 2005 Express Edition, which is available at

>   msdn.microsoft.com/vstudio/express/sql/

Note that you *do not* need to download SQL Server 2005 Express separately if you select the option to install it during the Visual Basic 2005 Express installation.

Chapters 21 and 22 require either Visual Web Developer 2005 Express (or a complete version of Visual Studio 2005). Visual Web Developer 2005 Express is available at

>   msdn.microsoft.com/vstudio/express/vwd/

Like Visual Basic 2005 Express, the other express editions are free for download until November 6, 2006, after which Microsoft may charge a fee for these tools.

For Chapters 21 and 22, you may also want to install the IIS Web server to test the examples. For more information about installing IIS, please visit

>   www.microsoft.com/resources/documentation/windows/xp/all/proddocs/
>   en-us/iiiisin2.mspx?mfr=true

If you prefer not to (or cannot) install IIS, you can use the built-in test server in Visual Web Developer 2005 Express to test the examples in Chapters 21 and 22.

For updates on the software used in this book visit **www.deitel.com/books/vbforprogrammers2** or subscribe to our free e-mail newsletter at www.deitel.com/newsletter/subscribe.html. Also, be sure to check out our Visual Basic resource center (www.deitel.com/VisualBasic) frequently for new Visual Basic resources.

Features in *Visual Basic 2005 for Programmers, 2/e*

This new edition contains many new and enhanced features.

Updated for Visual Studio 2005, Visual Basic 2005 and .NET 2.0
We updated the entire text to reflect Microsoft's release of Visual Basic 2005. New items include:

- Screenshots updated to the Visual Studio 2005 IDE.

- Property accessors with different access modifiers.

- Viewing exception data with the Exception Assistant (a new feature of the Visual Studio 2005 Debugger).

- Using drag-and-drop techniques to create data-bound windows forms in ADO.NET 2.0.

- Using the IDE's **Data Sources** window to create application-wide data connections.

- Using a `BindingSource` to simplify the process of binding controls to an underlying data source in ADO.NET 2.0.

- Using a `BindingNavigator` to enable simple navigation, insertion, deletion and editing of database data on a Windows Form.

- Using the **Master Page Designer** to create a common look and feel for ASP.NET Web pages.

- Using Visual Studio 2005 smart tag menus to perform common programming tasks when new controls are dragged onto a Windows Form or ASP.NET Web page.

- Using Visual Web Developer's built-in Web server to test ASP.NET 2.0 applications and Web services.

- Using an `XmlDataSource` to bind XML data sources to a control.

- Using a `SqlDataSource` to bind a SQL Server database to a control or set of controls.

- Using an `ObjectDataSource` to bind a control to an object that serves as a data source.

- Using the ASP.NET 2.0 "login" and "create new user" controls to personalize access to Web applications.

- Using generics and generic collections to create general models of methods and classes that can be declared once, but used with many types of data.

- Using generic collections from the `Systems.Collections.Generic` namespace.

The My Namespace

One of the new Visual Basic features receiving attention is the My namespace, which makes many common .NET programming tasks more convenient in Visual Basic. Many of the My namespace's features are beyond the scope of this book. However, we've included extensive links to My namespace resources in our Visual Basic resource center

> `www.deitel.com/VisualBasic`

These resources include sample code, technical articles, whitepapers, webcasts, videos, presentations and more. For a quick overview of many My namespace features, check out

> `msdn.microsoft.com/library/en-us/dnvs05/html/mywalkthro.asp`

For a detailed introduction to the My namespace, check out the following 1-hour and 23-minute presentation from the 2005 Microsoft Professional Developers Conference:

```
microsoft.sitestream.com/pdc05/tln/tln414_files/default.htm#
    nopreload=1&autostart=0
```

New Interior Design

Working with the creative services team at Prentice Hall, we redesigned the interior styles for our *Deitel® Developer Series* books. In response to reader requests, we now place the key terms and the index's page reference for each defining occurrence in ***bold italic*** text for easier reference. We emphasize on-screen components in the **bold Helvetica** font (e.g., the **File** menu) and emphasize Visual Basic program text in the Lucida font (for example, Dim x As Integer = 5).

Syntax Shading

We syntax shade all the Visual Basic code, similar to the way most Visual Basic integrated-development environments and code editors syntax color code. This greatly improves code readability—an especially important goal, given that this book contains 16,200+ lines of code. Our syntax-shading conventions are as follows:

```
comments appear in italic
keywords appear in bold, italic
errors and ASP.NET delimiters appear in bold, black
constants and literal values appear in bold, gray
all other code appears in plain, black
```

Code Highlighting

Extensive code highlighting makes it easy for readers to spot each program's featured code segments—we place light rectangles around the key code.

Early Classes and Objects Approach

We still introduce basic object-technology concepts and terminology in Chapter 1. In the previous edition, we developed custom classes in Chapter 9, but in this edition, we start doing that in the completely new Chapter 4. Chapters 5–8 have been carefully rewritten with a very friendly "early classes and objects approach."

Carefully Tuned Treatment of Object-Oriented Programming in Chapters 9–11

This edition is clearer and more accessible—especially if you are new to object-oriented programming (OOP). We completely rewrote the OOP chapters, integrating an employee payroll class hierarchy case study and motivating interfaces with an accounts payable hierarchy.

Case Studies

We include many case studies, some spanning multiple sections and chapters:

- The GradeBook class in Chapters 4, 5, 6 and 8.
- The optional, OOD/UML ATM system in the Software Engineering sections of Chapters 1, 3–9 and 11 and Appendix J.
- The Time class in several sections of Chapter 9.

- The Employee payroll application in Chapters 10 and 11.
- The Guestbook ASP.NET application in Chapter 21.
- The secure book database ASP.NET application in Chapter 21.
- The blackjack Web service in Chapter 22.
- The airline reservation Web service in Chapter 22.

Integrated GradeBook Case Study

To reinforce our early classes presentation, we present an integrated case study using classes and objects in Chapters 4–6 and 8. We incrementally build a GradeBook class that represents an instructor's grade book and performs various calculations based on a set of student grades—finding the average, finding the maximum and minimum, and printing a bar chart. Our goal is to familiarize you with the important concepts of objects and classes through a real-world example of a substantial class.

The Unified Modeling Language (UML)—Using the UML 2.0 to Develop an Object-Oriented Design of an ATM

The Unified Modeling Language™ (UML™) has become the preferred graphical modeling language for designing object-oriented systems. All the UML diagrams in the book comply with the UML 2.0 specification. We use UML class diagrams to visually represent classes and their inheritance relationships, and we use UML activity diagrams to demonstrate the flow of control in each of Visual Basic's control statements.

This *Second Edition* includes a new, optional (but highly recommended) case study on object-oriented design using the UML. The case study was reviewed by a distinguished team of OOD/UML academic and industry professionals, including leaders in the field from Rational (the creators of the UML and now a division of IBM) and the Object Management Group (responsible for maintaining and evolving the UML). In the case study, we design and fully implement the software for a simple automated teller machine (ATM). The Software Engineering Case Study sections at the ends of Chapters 1, 3–9 and 11 present a carefully paced introduction to object-oriented design using the UML. We introduce a concise, simplified subset of the UML 2.0, then guide the reader through a first design experience intended for the novice object-oriented designer/programmer. The case study is not an exercise; rather, it is an end-to-end learning experience that concludes with a detailed walkthrough of the complete Visual Basic code. The Software Engineering Case Study sections help readers develop an object-oriented design to complement the object-oriented programming concepts they begin learning in Chapter 1 and implementing in Chapter 4. In the first of these sections at the end of Chapter 1, we introduce basic OOD concepts and terminology. In the optional Software Engineering Case Study sections at the ends of Chapters 3–6, we consider more substantial issues as we undertake a challenging problem with the techniques of OOD. We analyze a typical requirements document that specifies the system to be built, determine the classes needed to implement that system, determine the attributes the classes need to have, determine the behaviors the classes need to exhibit and specify how the classes must interact with one another to meet the system requirements. In Appendix J, we include a complete Visual Basic implementation of the object-oriented system that we design in the earlier chapters. We employ a carefully developed, incremental object-oriented design process to produce a UML model for our ATM system. From this design, we produce a substantial working Visual Basic implementation using key programming notions, including classes, objects, encapsulation, visibility, composition, inheritance and polymorphism.

Web Forms, Web Controls and ASP.NET 2.0

The .NET platform enables developers to create robust, scalable Web-based applications. Microsoft's .NET server-side technology, ASP.NET, allows programmers to build Web applications that respond to client requests. To enable interactive Web pages, server-side programs process information users input into HTML forms. ASP.NET provides enhanced visual programming capabilities, similar to those used in building Windows forms for desktop programs. Programmers can create Web pages visually, by dragging and dropping Web controls onto Web forms. Chapter 21, ASP.NET, Web Forms and Web Controls, introduces these powerful technologies.

Web Services and ASP.NET 2.0

Microsoft's .NET strategy embraces the Internet and Web as integral to software development and deployment. Web services technology enables information sharing, e-commerce and other interactions using standard Internet protocols and technologies, such as Hypertext Transfer Protocol (HTTP), Extensible Markup Language (XML) and Simple Object Access Protocol (SOAP). Web services enable programmers to package application functionality in a manner that turns the Web into a library of reusable software components. In Chapter 22, we present a Web service that allows users to manipulate huge integers—integers too large to be represented with Visual Basic's built-in data types. In this example, a user enters two huge integers and presses buttons to invoke Web services that add, subtract and compare the two integers. We also present a blackjack Web service and a database-driven airline reservation system.

Object-Oriented Programming

Object-oriented programming is the most widely employed technique for developing robust, reusable software. This text offers a rich treatment of Visual Basic's object-oriented programming features. Chapter 4 introduces how to create classes and objects. These concepts are extended in Chapter 9. Chapter 10 discusses how to create powerful new classes quickly by using inheritance to "absorb" the capabilities of existing classes. Chapter 11 familiarizes the reader with the crucial concepts of polymorphism, abstract classes, concrete classes and interfaces, which facilitate powerful manipulations among objects belonging to an inheritance hierarchy.

XML

Use of the Extensible Markup Language (XML) is exploding in the software-development industry and in the e-business community, and is pervasive in the .NET platform. Because XML is a platform-independent technology for describing data and for creating markup languages, XML's data portability integrates well with Visual Basic-based portable applications and services. Chapter 19 introduces XML, XML markup and the technologies, such as DTDs and Schema, which are used to validate XML documents' contents. We also explain how to manipulate XML documents programmatically using the Document Object Model (DOM™) and how to transform XML documents into other types of documents via Extensible Stylesheet Language Transformation (XSLT) technology.

ADO.NET 2.0

Databases store vast amounts of information that individuals and organizations must access to conduct business. As an evolution of Microsoft's ActiveX Data Objects (ADO) technology, ADO.NET represents a new approach for building applications that interact with databases. ADO.NET uses XML and an enhanced object model to provide developers with the tools they need to access and manipulate databases for large-scale, extensible, mission-critical multi-tier applications. Chapter 20 introduces the capabilities of ADO.NET and the Structured Query Language (SQL) to manipulate databases.

Visual Studio 2005 Debugger

In Appendix C, we explain how to use key debugger features, such as setting "breakpoints" and "watches," stepping into and out of methods, and examining the method call stack.

Teaching Approach

Visual Basic 2005 for Programmers, 2/e contains a rich collection of examples that have been tested on Windows XP. The book concentrates on the principles of good software engineering and stresses program clarity. We avoid arcane terminology and syntax specifications in favor of teaching by example. We are educators who teach leading-edge topics in industry classrooms worldwide. Dr. Harvey M. Deitel has 22 years of college teaching experience and 17 years of industry teaching experience. Paul Deitel has 14 years of industry teaching experience. The Deitels have taught courses at all levels to government, industry, military and academic clients of Deitel & Associates.

World Wide Web Access

All of the source-code examples for *Visual Basic 2005 for Programmers, 2/e,* are available for download from:

```
www.deitel.com/books/vbforprogrammers2/
www.prenhallprofessional.com/title/013225140X
```

Site registration is quick and easy. Download all the examples, then run each program as you read the corresponding text discussions. Making changes to the examples and immediately seeing the effects of those changes is a great way to enhance your Visual Basic learning experience.

Objectives

Each chapter begins with a statement of objectives. This lets you know what to expect and gives you an opportunity, after reading the chapter, to determine if you've met these objectives.

Quotations

The learning objectives are followed by quotations. Some are humorous, philosophical or offer interesting insights. We hope that you'll enjoy relating the quotations to the chapter material. Many of the quotations are worth a second look after reading the chapter.

Outline

The chapter outline helps you approach the material in a top-down fashion, so you can anticipate what is to come, and set a comfortable and effective learning pace.

16,232 Lines of Code in 215 Example Programs (with Program Outputs)

Our live-code programs range in size from just a few lines of code to substantial examples containing hundreds of lines of code (e.g., our ATM system implementation contains 597 lines of code). Each program is followed by screenshots of the outputs produced when the program is run, so you can confirm that the programs run as expected. Our programs demonstrate the diverse features of Visual Basic. The code is syntax shaded, with Visual Basic keywords, comments and other program text emphasized with variations of bold, italic and gray text. This makes reading the code easier, especially in the larger programs.

807 Illustrations/Figures

An abundance of charts, tables, line drawings, programs and program outputs is included. We model the flow of control in control statements with UML activity diagrams. UML class diagrams model the fields, constructors and methods of classes. We use additional types of UML diagrams throughout our optional OOD/UML ATM case study.

350 Programming Tips

We include programming tips to help readers focus on important aspects of program development. We highlight these tips as *Good Programming Practices, Common Programming Errors, Error-Prevention Tips, Look-and-Feel Observations, Performance Tips, Portability Tips* and *Software Engineering Observations*. These tips and practices represent the best we have gleaned from a combined six decades of programming, college teaching and professional training experience. The tips provide a basis on which to build good software.

Good Programming Practice 1.1

Good Programming Practices *call attention to techniques that will help you produce programs that are clearer, more understandable and more maintainable.*

Common Programming Error 1.1

Developers learning a language tend to make certain kinds of errors frequently. Pointing out these Common Programming Errors *reduces the likelihood that you'll make the same mistakes.*

Error-Prevention Tip 1.1

When we first designed this tip type, we thought the tips would contain suggestions for exposing bugs and removing them from programs. In fact, many of the tips describe aspects of Visual Basic that prevent bugs from getting into programs in the first place, thus simplifying the testing and debugging processes.

Look-and-Feel Observation 1.1

We provide Look-and-Feel Observations *to highlight graphical-user-interface conventions. These observations help you design attractive, user-friendly graphical user interfaces that conform to industry norms.*

Performance Tip 1.1

Programmers like to "turbo charge" their programs. We include Performance Tips *that highlight opportunities for improving program performance—making programs run faster or minimizing the amount of memory that they occupy.*

Portability Tip 1.1

We include Portability Tips *to help you write portable code and to explain how Visual Basic achieves its high degree of portability.*

Software Engineering Observation 1.1

The object-oriented programming paradigm necessitates a complete rethinking of the way we build software systems. Visual Basic is an effective language for achieving good software engineering. The Software Engineering Observations *highlight architectural and design issues that affect the construction of software systems, especially large-scale systems.*

Wrap-Up Section

Each chapter ends with a brief "wrap-up" section that recaps the chapter content and transitions to the next chapter.

Extensive Index

We have included an extensive index which is especially helpful when using the book as a reference.

"Double Indexing" of Visual Basic Live-Code Examples

Visual Basic 2005 for Programmers, 2/e has 215 live-code examples, which we have double indexed. For every source-code program in the book, we indexed the figure caption both alphabetically and as a subindex item under "Examples." This makes it easier to find examples using particular features.

A Tour of the Optional Case Study on Object-Oriented Design with the UML

In this section we tour the book's optional case study on object-oriented design with the UML. This tour previews the contents of the Software Engineering Case Study sections (in Chapters 1, 3–9, 11 and Appendix J). After completing this case study, you will be thoroughly familiar with an object-oriented design and implementation for a significant Visual Basic application.

The design presented in the ATM case study was developed at Deitel & Associates, Inc. and scrutinized by academic and industry professionals. Our primary goal was to create a simple design that would be clear to OOD and UML novices, while still demonstrating key OOD concepts and the related UML modeling techniques.

Section 1.9—(Only Required Section of the Case Study) Software Engineering Case Study: Introduction to Object Technology and the UML—introduces the object-oriented design case study with the UML. The section presents basic concepts and terminology of object technology, including classes, objects, encapsulation, inheritance and polymorphism. We discuss the history of the UML. This is the only required section of the case study.

Section 3.9—(Optional) Software Engineering Case Study: Examining the ATM Requirements Document—discusses a *requirements document* that specifies the requirements for a system that we will design and implement—the software for a simple automated teller machine (ATM). We investigate the structure and behavior of object-oriented systems in general. We discuss how the UML will facilitate the design process in subsequent Software Engineering Case Study sections by providing several additional types of diagrams to model our system. We include a list of URLs and book references on object-oriented design with the UML. We discuss the interaction between the ATM system and its user. Specifically, we investigate the scenarios that may occur between the user and the system itself— these are called *use cases*. We model these interactions, using UML *use case diagrams*.

Section 4.9—(Optional) Software Engineering Case Study: Identifying the Classes in the ATM Requirements Documents—begins to design the ATM system. We identify its classes by extracting the nouns and noun phrases from the requirements document. We arrange these classes into a UML class diagram that describes the class structure of our simulation. The class diagram also describes relationships, known as *associations*, among classes.

Section 5.14—(Optional) Software Engineering Case Study: Identifying Class Attributes in the ATM System—focuses on the attributes of the classes discussed in Section 3.9. A class contains both *attributes* (data) and *operations* (behaviors). As we see in later sections, changes in an object's attributes often affect the object's behavior. To determine the attributes for the classes in our case study, we extract the adjectives describing the nouns and noun phrases (which defined our classes) from the requirements document, then place the attributes in the class diagram we created in Section 3.9.

Section 6.11—(Optional) Software Engineering Case Study: Identifying Objects' States and Activities in the ATM System—discusses how an object, at any given time, occupies a specific condition called a *state*. A *state transition* occurs when the object receives a message to change state. The UML provides the *state machine diagram*, which identifies the set of possible states that an object may occupy and models that object's state transitions. An object also has an *activity*—the work it performs in its lifetime. The UML provides the *activity diagram*—a flowchart that models an object's activity. In this section, we use both types of diagrams to begin modeling specific behavioral aspects of our ATM system, such as how the ATM carries out a withdrawal transaction and how the ATM responds when the user is authenticated.

Section 7.20—(Optional) Software Engineering Case Study: Identifying Class Operations in the ATM System—identifies the operations, or services, of our classes. We extract from the requirements document the verbs and verb phrases that specify the operations for each class. We then modify the class diagram of Section 3.9 to include each operation with its associated class. At this point in the case study, we will have gathered all information possible from the requirements document. As future chapters introduce such topics as inheritance, we will modify our classes and diagrams.

Section 8.15—(Optional) Software Engineering Case Study: Collaboration Among Objects in the ATM System—provides a "rough sketch" of the model for our ATM system. In this section, we see how it works. We investigate the behavior of the simulation by discussing *collaborations*—messages that objects send to each other to communicate. The class operations that we discovered in Section 6.11 turn out to be the collaborations among the objects in our system. We determine the collaborations, then collect them into a *communication diagram*—the UML diagram for modeling collaborations. This diagram reveals which objects collaborate and when. We present a communication diagram of the collaborations among objects to perform an ATM balance inquiry. We then present the UML *sequence diagram* for modeling interactions in a system. This diagram emphasizes the chronological ordering of messages. A sequence diagram models how objects in the system interact to carry out withdrawal and deposit transactions.

Section 9.14—(Optional) Software Engineering Case Study: Starting to Program the Classes of the ATM System—takes a break from designing the behavior of our system. We begin the implementation process to emphasize the material discussed in Chapter 8. Using the UML class diagram of Section 3.9 and the attributes and operations discussed in Section 4.11 and Section 6.11, we show how to implement a class in Visual Basic from a design. We do not implement all classes—because we have not completed the design process. Working from our UML diagrams, we create code for the `Withdrawal` class.

Section 11.8—(Optional) Software Engineering Case Study: Incorporating Inheritance and Polymorphism into the ATM System—continues our discussion of object-oriented programming. We consider inheritance—classes sharing common characteristics may inherit attributes and operations from a "base" class. In this section, we investigate how our ATM system can benefit from using inheritance. We document our discoveries in a class diagram that models inheritance relationships—the UML refers to these relationships as *generalizations*. We modify the class diagram of Section 3.9 by using inheritance to group classes with similar characteristics. This section concludes the design of the model portion of our simulation. We implement this model in Visual Basic in Appendix J.

Appendix J—ATM Case Study Code—The majority of the case study involves designing the model (i.e., the data and logic) of the ATM system. In this appendix, we fully implement that model in Visual Basic, using all the UML diagrams we created. We apply the concepts of object-oriented design with the UML and object-oriented programming in Visual Basic that you learned in the chapters. By the end of this appendix, you will have completed the design and implementation of a real-world system, and should feel confident tackling larger systems, such as those that professional software engineers build.

Appendix K—UML 2: Additional Diagrams Types—Overviews the UML 2 diagram types not discussed the OOD/UML Case Study.

DEITEL® Buzz Online Free E-mail Newsletter

Our free e-mail newsletter, the *Deitel® Buzz Online*, includes commentary on industry trends and developments, links to free articles and resources from our published books and upcoming publications, product-release schedules, errata, challenges, anecdotes, information on our corporate instructor-led training courses and more. It's also a good way for you to keep posted about issues related to *Visual Basic 2005 for Programmers, 2/e*. To subscribe, visit

www.deitel.com/newsletter/subscribe.html

What's New at Deitel

Free Content Initiative. We are pleased to bring you guest articles and free tutorials selected from our current and forthcoming publications as part of our Free Content Initiative. In each issue of our *Deitel® Buzz Online* newsletter, we announce the latest additions to our free content library. Let us know what topics you'd like to see and let us know if you'd like to submit guest articles!

www.deitel.com/articles/

Resource Centers and the Deitel Internet Business Initiative. We have created many resource centers (at www.deitel.com/ResourceCenters.html) on such topics as Visual Basic, .NET, C#, C++, Java, AJAX, Ruby, PHP, Perl, Python, MySQL, RSS, XML, Web Services, Windows Vista, Google Analytics, Google Base, Google Video, Google AdSense, the Internet Business Initiative, Mash-Ups, Ning, Podcasting, Computer Games, Game Programming, Attention Economy, Affiliate Programs, Sudoku, Web 2.0, Search Engine Optimization and Skype, with many more coming. We announce new resource centers in each issue of the *Deitel® Buzz Online*.

Acknowledgments

It is a great pleasure to acknowledge the efforts of many people whose names may not appear on the cover, but whose hard work, cooperation, friendship and understanding were crucial to the production of the book. Many people at Deitel & Associates, Inc. devoted long hours to this project.

- Andrew B. Goldberg is a Computer Science graduate of Amherst College. Andrew co-authored the updates to Chapters 19–22. He co-designed and co-authored the new, optional OOD/UML ATM case study. He also co-authored Appendices J and K.

- Su Zhang holds B.Sc. and M.Sc. degrees in Computer Science from McGill University. Su contributed to Chapters 26 and 27 as well as Appendix J.

- Cheryl Yaeger graduated from Boston University with a bachelor's degree in Computer Science. Cheryl co-authored the updates to Chapters 3–14.

- Barbara Deitel, Chief Financial Officer at Deitel & Associates, Inc. applied copyedits to the book.

- Abbey Deitel, President of Deitel & Associates, Inc., and an Industrial Management graduate of Carnegie Mellon University, co-authored Chapter 1.

- Christi Kelsey, a graduate of Purdue University with a degree in business and a minor in information systems, co-authored Chapter 2, the Preface and Appendix C. She also worked closely with the production team at Prentice Hall coordinating virtually every aspect of the production of the book.

We would also like to thank three participants of our Honors Internship and Co-op programs who contributed to this publication—Nick Santos, a Computer Science major at Dartmouth College; Jeffrey Peng, a Computer Science major at Cornell University and William Chen, a Computer Science major at Cornell University.

We are fortunate to have worked on this project with the talented and dedicated team of publishing professionals at Pearson Education/PTG. We especially appreciate the extraordinary efforts of Mark Taub, Publishing Partner of Prentice Hall/PTR, and Marcia Horton, Editorial Director of Prentice Hall's Engineering and Computer Science Division. Jennifer Cappello and Dolores Mars did an extraordinary job recruiting the review team for this book and managing the review process. Sandra Schroeder did a wonderful job designing the book's cover. Vince O'Brien, Bob Engelhardt, Donna Crilly and Marta Samsel did a marvelous job managing the production of the book.

We'd like to give special thanks to Paul Vick, (Architect, Visual Basic) and author of the *Microsoft Visual Basic Language Specification, Version 8.0*, and Janie Schwark, Senior Business Manager, Division of Developer Marketing, both of Microsoft, for their special effort in working with us on this project.

Microsoft Reviewers
Corneliu Barsan, Microsoft
Dharmesh Chauhan, Microsoft
John Chen, Microsoft
Eric Gruber, Microsoft
Manish Jayaswal, Microsoft
Cameron McColl, Microsoft
Alexandre Moura, Microsoft
Baiju Nair, Microsoft
Cat Rambo, Microsoft
Thom Robbins, Microsoft
Chris Smith, Microsoft Compiler UI Team
Craig Vick, Microsoft

Industry Reviewers
Harlan Brewer, SES Consulting
Kunal Cheda, Computer Enterprises, Inc. U.S
James Huddleston, Independent Consultant
Terrell Hull, Independent Consultant
Amit Kalani, TechContent Corporation
Tysen Leckie, Edge Technologies
John Mueller, DataCon Services

Academic Reviewers
Karen Arlien, Bismarck State College
Robert Benavides, Collin County CC
Rekha Bhowmik, Winston-Salem State University
Chadi Boudiab, Georgia Perimeter College
Brian Larson, Modesto Junior College
Gavin Osborne, Saskatchewan Institute of Applied Science and Technology
Warren Wiltsie, Fairleigh Dickinson University

UML Case Study Reviewers
Scott Ambler, Ambysoft, Inc.
Rekha Bhowmik, Winston-Salem State University
Chadi Boudiab, Georgia Perimeter College
Brian Cook, Zurich North America
Sergio Davalos, University of Washington-Tacoma
Sujay Ghuge, Verizon IT
Manu Gupta, Patni Computer Systems
Terrell Hull, Independent Consultant
James Huddleston, Independent Consultant
Jeff Jones, Route Match Software
John Mueller, DataCon Services
Davyd Norris, Rational/IBM
Gavin Osborne, Saskatchewan Institute

Visual C# 2005 How to Program, 2/e and *C# for Programmers, 2/e* were written in parallel with this book and many of the comments from the C# review teams proved valuable to us in completing this book, so we wanted to acknowledge their contributions:

Microsoft Reviewers
George Bullock, Program Manager at Microsoft, `Microsoft.com` Community Team
Dharmesh Chauhan, Microsoft
Shon Katzenberger, Microsoft
Matteo Taveggia, Microsoft
Matt Tavis, Microsoft

Industry Reviewers
Alex Bondarev, Investor's Bank and Trust
Peter Bromberg, Senior Architect Merrill Lynch and C# MVP
Vijay Cinnakonda, TrueCommerce, Inc.
Jay Cook, Alcon Laboratories
Jeff Cowan, Magenic, Inc.
Ken Cox, Independent Consultant, Writer and Developer and ASP.NET MVP
Stochio Goutsev, Independent Consultant, writer and developer and C# MVP
James Huddleston, Independent Consultant
Rex Jaeschke, Independent Consultant and Editor of the *C# Standard ECMA-334,*
    2005, produced by committee Ecma TC39/TG2.
Saurabh Nandu, AksTech Solutions Pvt. Ltd.
Simon North, Quintiq BV
Mike O'Brien, State of California Employment Development Department
José Antonio González Seco, Andalucia's Parliament
Devan Shepard, XMaLpha Technologies
Pavel Tsekov, Caesar BSC
John Varghese, UBS
Stacey Yasenka, Software Developer at Hyland Software and C# MVP

Academic Reviewers
Rekha Bhowmik, California Lutheran University
Ayad Boudiab, Georgia Perimiter College
Harlan Brewer, SES Consulting
Sam Gill, San Francisco State University
Gavin Osborne, Saskatchewan Institute of Applied Science and Technology
Catherine Wyman, DeVry-Phoenix

And thanks to the many other members of the Microsoft team who answered our questions throughout this process:

Anders Hejlsburg, Technical Fellow (C#)
Brad Abrams, Lead Program Manager (.NET Framework)
Jim Miller, Software Architect (.NET Framework)
Joe Duffy, Program Manager (.NET Framework)

> Joe Stegman, Lead Program Manager (Windows Forms)
> Kit George, Program Manager (.NET Framework)
> Luca Bolognese, Lead Program Manager (C#)
> Luke Hoban, Program Manager (C#)
> Mads Torgersen, Program Manager (C#)
> Peter Hallam, Software Design Engineer (C#)
> Scott Nonnenberg, Program Manager (C#)
> Shamez Rajan, Program Manager (Visual Basic)

Well, there you have it! Visual Basic is a powerful programming language that will help you write programs quickly and effectively. Visual Basic scales nicely into the realm of enterprise systems development to help organizations build their business-critical and mission-critical information systems. As you read the book, we would sincerely appreciate your comments, criticisms, corrections and suggestions for improvement. Please address all correspondence to:

> deitel@deitel.com

We will respond promptly, and we will post corrections and clarifications on our Web site:

> www.deitel.com

We hope you enjoy reading *Visual Basic 2005 for Programmers, 2/e* as much as we enjoyed writing it!

> *Paul J. Deitel*
> *Harvey M. Deitel*

About the Authors

Paul J. Deitel, CEO and Chief Technical Officer of Deitel & Associates, Inc., is a graduate of the MIT's Sloan School of Management, where he studied Information Technology. Through Deitel & Associates, Inc., he has delivered programming language courses to industry clients, including IBM, Sun Microsystems, Dell, Lucent Technologies, Fidelity, NASA at the Kennedy Space Center, the National Severe Storm Laboratory, White Sands Missile Range, Rogue Wave Software, Boeing, Stratus, Cambridge Technology Partners, Open Environment Corporation, One Wave, Hyperion Software, Adra Systems, Entergy, CableData Systems, Nortel Networks and many more. Paul is one of the world's most experienced Java trainers, having taught about 100 professional Java courses. He has also lectured on C++ and Java for the Boston Chapter of the Association for Computing Machinery. He and his father, Dr. Harvey M. Deitel, are the world's best-selling programming language textbook authors.

   Dr. Harvey M. Deitel, Chairman and Chief Strategy Officer of Deitel & Associates, Inc., has 45 years of academic and industry experience in the computer field. Dr. Deitel earned B.S. and M.S. degrees from the Massachusetts Institute of Technology and a Ph.D. from Boston University. He has 20 years of college teaching experience, including earning tenure and serving as the Chairman of the Computer Science Department at Boston College before founding Deitel & Associates, Inc., with his son, Paul J. Deitel. He and Paul are the co-authors of several dozen books and multimedia packages and they are writing many more. With translations published in Japanese, German, Russian, Spanish, Traditional Chinese, Simplified Chinese, Korean, French, Polish, Italian, Portuguese, Greek, Urdu and Turkish, the Deitels' texts have earned international recognition. Dr. Deitel has delivered hundreds of professional seminars to major corporations, academic institutions, government organizations and the military.

About Deitel & Associates, Inc.

Deitel & Associates, Inc., is an internationally recognized corporate training and content-creation organization specializing in computer programming languages, Internet and World Wide Web software technology, object technology education and Internet business development. The company provides instructor-led courses on major programming languages and platforms, such as Java, Advanced Java, C, C++, C#, Visual C++, Visual Basic, XML, Perl, Python, object technology, and Internet and World Wide Web programming. The founders of Deitel & Associates, Inc., are Paul J. Deitel and Harvey M. Deitel. The company's clients include many of the world's largest computer companies, government agencies, branches of the military and business organizations. Through its 30-year publishing partnership with Prentice Hall, Deitel & Associates, Inc. publishes leading-edge programming textbooks, professional books, interactive multimedia *Cyber Classrooms*, *Complete Training Courses*, Web-based training courses and e-content for popular course management systems such as WebCT, Blackboard and Pearson's CourseCompass. Deitel & Associates, Inc., and the authors can be reached via e-mail at:

    deitel@deitel.com

To learn more about Deitel & Associates, Inc., its publications and its worldwide *Dive Into*® Series Corporate Training curriculum, see the last few pages of this book or visit:

    www.deitel.com

and subscribe to the free *Deitel*® *Buzz Online* e-mail newsletter at:

    www.deitel.com/newsletter/subscribe.html

Individuals wishing to purchase Deitel books, Cyber Classrooms, Complete Training Courses and Web-based training courses can do so through:

    www.deitel.com/books/index.html

Bulk orders by corporations, the government, the military and academic institutions should be placed directly with Prentice Hall.

1

Introduction to .NET, Visual Basic and Object Technology

The chief merit of language is clearness.
—Galen

High thoughts must have high language.
—Aristophanes

Our life is frittered away with detail. . . . Simplify, simplify.
—Henry David Thoreau

My object all sublime I shall achieve in time.
—W. S. Gilbert

Man is still the most extraordinary computer of all.
—John F. Kennedy

OBJECTIVES

In this chapter you will learn:

- The history of the Visual Basic programming language.

- Some basics of object technology.

- The history of the UML—the industry-standard object-oriented system modeling language.

- The history of the Internet and the World Wide Web.

- The motivation behind and an overview of Microsoft's .NET initiative, which involves the Internet in developing and using software systems.

- To test-drive a Visual Basic 2005 application that enables you to draw on the screen.

1.1 Introduction

Welcome to Visual Basic 2005! We have worked hard to provide you with accurate and complete information regarding this powerful computer programming language which, from this point forward, we shall refer to simply as Visual Basic. Visual Basic is appropriate for building substantial information systems. We hope that working with this book will be an informative, challenging and entertaining learning experience for you.

The core of this book emphasizes achieving program clarity through the proven techniques of object-oriented programming (OOP) and event-driven programming. The book presents hundreds of complete, working Visual Basic programs and depicts their inputs and outputs. We call this the *live-code approach.* All of the book's examples may be downloaded from www.deitel.com/books/vbforprogrammers2/index.html.

We hope that you will enjoy learning with *Visual Basic 2005 for Programmers, Second Edition.* As you proceed, if you have any questions, please send e-mail to

    deitel@deitel.com

To keep current with Visual Basic developments at Deitel & Associates and to receive updates to this textbook, please register for our free e-mail newsletter, the *Deitel® Buzz Online,* at

    www.deitel.com/newsletter/subscribe.html

1.2 Microsoft's Windows® Operating System

Microsoft Corporation became the dominant software company in the 1980s and 1990s. In 1981, Microsoft released the first version of its DOS operating system for the IBM Personal Computer (DOS is an acronym for "Disk Operating System"). In the mid-1980s, Microsoft developed the *Windows operating system*, a graphical user interface built on top of DOS. Microsoft released Windows 3.0 in 1990; this new version featured a user-friendly interface and rich functionality. The Windows operating system became incredibly popular after the 1993 release of Windows 3.1, whose successors, Windows 95 and

Windows 98, virtually cornered the desktop operating systems market by the late 1990s. These operating systems, which borrowed from many concepts (such as icons, menus and windows) popularized by early Apple Macintosh operating systems, enabled users to navigate multiple applications simultaneously. Microsoft entered the corporate operating systems market with the 1993 release of Windows NT®. Windows XP, which is based on the Windows NT operating system, was released in 2001 and combines Microsoft's corporate and consumer operating system lines. Windows is by far the world's most widely used operating system.

The biggest competitor to the Windows operating system is Linux. The name Linux derives from Linus, after Linus Torvalds, who developed Linux, and UNIX—the operating system upon which Linux is based; UNIX was developed at Bell Laboratories and was written in the C programming language. Linux is a free, open-source operating system, unlike Windows, which is proprietary (owned and controlled by Microsoft). The source code for Linux is freely available to users, and they can modify it to fit their needs.

1.3 Visual Basic

Visual Basic evolved from BASIC (Beginner's All-Purpose Symbolic Instruction Code), developed in the mid-1960s by Professors John Kemeny and Thomas Kurtz of Dartmouth College as a language for writing simple programs. BASIC's primary purpose was to familiarize novices with programming techniques.

The widespread use of BASIC on various types of computers led to many enhancements to the language. When Bill Gates founded Microsoft Corporation, he implemented BASIC on several early personal computers. With the development of the Microsoft Windows graphical user interface (GUI) in the late 1980s and the early 1990s, the natural evolution of BASIC was Visual Basic, introduced by Microsoft in 1991. Visual Basic makes the development of Windows applications convenient.

Until the first version of Visual Basic appeared in 1991, developing Microsoft Windows-based applications was a difficult and cumbersome process. Although Visual Basic is derived from the BASIC programming language, it is a distinctly different language that offers such powerful features as graphical user interfaces, event handling, object-oriented programming, and exception handling. Visual Basic is an event-driven language (i.e., the programs respond to user-initiated events such as mouse clicks and keystrokes). Also, it is a visual programming language in which programs are created using an Integrated Development Environment (IDE) in which you can write, run, test and debug Visual Basic programs conveniently.

The advancement of programming tools and consumer-electronic devices created many challenges. Integrating software components from diverse languages proved difficult. Developers also discovered they needed Web-based applications that could be accessed and used via the Internet. As programmable devices, such as personal digital assistants (PDAs) and cell phones, grew in popularity in the late 1990s, the need for these components to interact with others via the Internet rose dramatically. As a result of the popularity of mobile electronic devices, software developers realized that their clientele was no longer restricted to desktop users. Developers recognized the need for software accessible to anyone from almost any type of device.

To address these needs, Microsoft announced the introduction of its *.NET* (pro-nounced "dot-net") strategy in 2000. The .NET platform is one over which Web-based applications can be distributed to a variety of devices (such as PDAs and cell phones) and to desktop computers. The .NET platform enables programs created in different program-ming languages to communicate easily with each other.

Visual Basic offers powerful object-oriented programming capabilities, including a substantial library of components, allowing you to develop applications even faster. Also, Visual Basic applications can interact via the Internet, using industry standards such as XML, which is the subject of Chapter 19, and the XML-based Simple Object Access Pro-tocol (SOAP), which we discuss in Chapter 22, Web Services.

1.4 The Internet and the World Wide Web

The Internet was initiated almost four decades ago with funding supplied by the U.S. De-partment of Defense. Originally designed to connect the main computer systems of about a dozen universities and research organizations, its chief benefit proved early on to be the capability for quick and easy communication via what came to be known as electronic mail (e-mail). This is true even on today's Internet, with e-mail, instant messaging and file transfer facilitating communications among about a billion people worldwide. The Inter-net has exploded into one of the world's premier communication mechanisms and con-tinues to grow rapidly.

The World Wide Web allows computer users to locate and view multimedia-based documents on almost any subject over the Internet. The Web is a relatively recent devel-opment. In 1989, Tim Berners-Lee of CERN (the European Organization for Nuclear Research) began to develop a technology for sharing information via hyperlinked text doc-uments. Berners-Lee called his invention the HyperText Markup Language (HTML). He also wrote communication protocols to form the backbone of his new information system, which he referred to as the World Wide Web.

In the past, most computer applications ran on computers that were not connected to one another, whereas today's applications can be written to communicate among the world's computers. The Internet mixes computing and communications technologies. It makes our work easier. It makes information instantly and conveniently accessible world-wide. It enables individuals and small businesses to get worldwide exposure. It is changing the way business is done. People can search for the best prices on virtually any product or service. Special-interest communities can stay in touch with one another. Researchers can be made instantly aware of the latest breakthroughs. The Internet and the World Wide Web are surely among humankind's most profound creations. In Chapters 19–23, you will learn how to build Internet- and Web-based applications.

In 1994, Tim Berners-Lee founded an organization, called the *World Wide Web Consortium* (*W3C*), that is devoted to developing nonproprietary, interoperable technol-ogies for the World Wide Web. One of the W3C's primary goals is to make the Web uni-versally accessible—regardless of disabilities, language or culture.

The W3C (www.w3.org) is also a standardization organization. Web technologies standardized by the W3C are called Recommendations. Current W3C Recommendations include the *Extensible Markup Language* (*XML*). We introduce XML in Section 1.5 and present it in detail in Chapter 19, Extensible Markup Language (XML). It is the key technology underlying the next version of the Word Wide Web, sometimes called the "semantic Web." It is also one of the key technologies that underlies Web services, which we discuss in Chapter 22.

1.5 Extensible Markup Language (XML)

As the popularity of the Web exploded, HTML's limitations became apparent. HTML's lack of *extensibility* (the ability to change or add features) frustrated developers, and its ambiguous definition allowed erroneous HTML to proliferate. The need for a standardized, fully extensible and structurally strict language was apparent. As a result, XML was developed by the W3C.

Data independence, the separation of content from its presentation, is the essential characteristic of XML. Because XML documents describe data, any application conceivably can process them. Software developers are integrating XML into their applications to improve Web functionality and interoperability.

XML is not limited to Web applications. For example, it is increasingly being employed in databases—the structure of an XML document enables it to be integrated easily with database applications. As applications become more Web enabled, it is likely that XML will become the universal technology for data representation. All applications employing XML would be able to communicate with one another, provided that they could understand their respective XML markup schemes, or *vocabularies*.

The *Simple Object Access Protocol* (*SOAP*) is a technology for the transmission of objects (marked up as XML) over the Internet. Microsoft's .NET technologies (discussed in the next two sections) use XML and SOAP to mark up and transfer data over the Internet. XML and SOAP are at the core of .NET—they allow software components to interoperate (i.e., communicate easily with one another). Since SOAP's foundations are in XML and *HTTP* (*Hypertext Transfer Protocol*—the key communication protocol of the Web), it is supported on most types of computer systems. We discuss XML in Chapter 19, Extensible Markup Language (XML) and SOAP in Chapter 22, Web Services.

1.6 Microsoft's .NET

In 2000, Microsoft announced its *.NET initiative* (www.microsoft.com/net), a new vision for embracing the Internet and the Web in the development and use of software. One key aspect of .NET is its independence from a specific language or platform. Rather than being forced to use a single programming language, developers can create a .NET application in any .NET-compatible language. Programmers can contribute to the same software project, writing code in the .NET languages (such as Microsoft's Visual Basic, Visual C++, Visual C# and many others) in which they are most competent. Part of the initiative includes Microsoft's *ASP.NET* technology, which allows programmers to create applications for the Web. We discuss ASP.NET in Chapter 21, ASP.NET 2.0, Web Forms and Web Controls. We use ASP.NET technology in Chapter 22 to build applications that use Web Services.

The .NET architecture can exist on multiple platforms, not just Microsoft Windows–based systems, further extending the portability of .NET programs. One example is Mono (www.mono-project.com/Main_Page), an open-source project by Novell. Another is DotGNU Portable .NET (www.dotgnu.org).

A key component of the .NET architecture is *Web services*, which are reusable application software components that can be used over the Internet. Clients and other applications can use Web services as reusable building blocks. One example of a Web service is Dollar Rent a Car's reservation system.[1] An airline partner wanted to enable customers to make rental-car reservations from the airline's Web site. To do so, the airline needed to access Dollar's reservation system. In response, Dollar created a Web service that allows the airline to access Dollar's database and make reservations. Web services enable computers at the two companies to communicate over the Web, even though the airline uses UNIX systems and Dollar uses Microsoft Windows. Dollar could have created a one-time solution for that particular airline, but then would not have been able to reuse such a customized system. Dollar's Web service enables many airlines, hotels and travel companies to use its reservation system without creating a custom program for each relationship.

The .NET strategy extends the concept of software reuse to the Internet, allowing programmers and companies to concentrate on their specialties without having to implement every component of every application. Instead, companies can buy Web services and devote their resources to developing their own products. For example, a single application using Web services from various companies could manage bill payments, tax refunds, loans and investments. An online merchant could buy Web services for credit-card payments, user authentication, network security and inventory databases to create an e-commerce Web site.

1.7 The .NET Framework and the Common Language Runtime

The Microsoft *.NET Framework* is at the heart of the .NET strategy. This framework manages and executes applications and Web services, contains a class library (called the .NET Framework Class Library, or FCL), enforces security and provides many other programming capabilities. The details of the .NET Framework are found in the *Common Language Infrastructure (CLI)*, which contains information about the storage of data types (i.e., data that has predefined characteristics such as a date, percentage or currency amount), objects and so on. The CLI has been standardized by Ecma International (originally known as the European Computer Manufacturers Association), making it easier to create the .NET Framework for other platforms. This is like publishing the blueprints of the framework—anyone can build it by following the specifications.

The *Common Language Runtime (CLR)* is another central part of the .NET Framework—it executes .NET programs. Programs are compiled into machine-specific instructions in two steps. First, the program is compiled into *Microsoft Intermediate Language (MSIL)*, which defines instructions for the CLR. Code converted into MSIL from other languages and sources can be woven together by the CLR. The MSIL for an application's components is placed into the application's executable file. When the application executes, another compiler (known as the *just-in-time compiler* or *JIT compiler*) in the CLR translates the MSIL in the executable file into machine-language code (for a particular platform), then the machine-language code executes on that platform.

If the .NET Framework exists (and is installed) for a platform, that platform can run any .NET program. The ability of a program to run (without modification) across mul-

---

1. www.microsoft.com/resources/casestudies/CaseStudy.asp?CaseStudyID=11626

tiple platforms is known as *platform independence*. Code written once can be used on another type of computer without modification, saving both time and money. In addition, software can target a wider audience—previously, companies had to decide whether converting their programs to different platforms (sometimes called *porting*) was worth the cost. With .NET, porting programs is no longer an issue (at least once .NET itself has been made available on the platforms).

The .NET Framework also provides a high level of *language interoperability*. Programs written in different languages are all compiled into MSIL—the different parts can be combined to create a single unified program. MSIL allows the .NET Framework to be *language independent*, because .NET programs are not tied to a particular programming language. Any language that can be compiled into MSIL is called a *.NET-compliant language*. Figure 1.1 lists many of the programming languages that are available for the .NET platform (msdn.microsoft.com/netframework/technologyinfo/overview/default.aspx).

The .NET Framework Class Library (FCL) can be used by any .NET language. The FCL contains a variety of reusable components, saving programmers the trouble of creating new components. This book explains how to develop .NET software with Visual Basic.

1.8 Test-Driving a Visual Basic Application

In this section, you will "test-drive" a Visual Basic application that enables you to draw on the screen using the mouse. You will run and interact with the working application. You'll build a similar application in Chapter 13, Graphical User Interface Concepts: Part 1.

.NET programming languages	
APL	Oberon
COBOL	Oz
Component Pascal	Pascal
Curriculum	Perl
Eiffel	Python
Forth	RPG
Fortran	Scheme
Haskell	Smalltalk
Java	Standard ML
JScript	Visual Basic
Mercury	Visual C#
Mondrian	Visual C++

Fig. 1.1 | .NET languages.

The **Drawing** application allows you to draw with different brush sizes and colors. We use fonts to distinguish between IDE features (such as menu names and menu items) and other elements that appear in the IDE. Our convention is to emphasize IDE features (such as the **File** menu) in a bold sans-serif Helvetica font and to emphasize other elements, such as file names (e.g., Form1.vb), in a sans-serif Lucida font. The following steps show you how to test-drive the application.

1. *Checking your setup.* Confirm that you have installed Visual Basic 2005 Express or Visual Studio 2005 as discussed in the Preface.

2. *Locating the application directory.* Open Windows Explorer and navigate to the C:\examples\Ch01\Drawing directory.

3. *Running the Drawing application.* Now that you are in the correct directory, double click the file name Drawing.exe to run the application (Fig. 1.2).

   In Fig. 1.2, several graphical elements—called *controls*—are labeled. The controls include two GroupBoxes (in this case, **Color** and **Size**), seven RadioButtons and a Panel (these controls will be discussed in depth later in the text). The **Drawing** application allows you to draw with a red, blue, green or black brush of small, medium or large size. You will explore these options in this test-drive.

   You can use existing controls—which are objects—to get powerful applications running in Visual Basic much faster than if you had to write all of the code yourself. In this text, you will learn how to use many preexisting controls, and how to write your own program code to customize your applications.

   The brush's properties, selected in the RadioButtons (the small circles where you select an option by clicking the mouse) labeled **Black** and **Small**, are default settings, which are the initial settings you see when you first run the application. Programmers include default settings to provide reasonable choices which the application will use if the user chooses not to change the settings. You will now choose your own settings.

Fig. 1.2 | Visual Basic **Drawing** application.

4. *Changing the brush color.* Click the RadioButton labelled **Red** to change the color of the brush. Hold the mouse button down with the mouse pointer positioned anywhere on the white Panel, then drag the mouse to draw with the brush. Draw flower petals as shown in Fig. 1.3. Then click the RadioButton labeled **Green** to change the color of the brush again.

5. *Changing the brush size.* Click the RadioButton labeled **Large** to change the size of the brush. Draw grass and a flower stem as shown in Fig. 1.4.

6. *Finishing the drawing.* Click the RadioButton labeled **Blue**. Then click the RadioButton labeled **Medium**. Draw raindrops as shown in Fig. 1.5 to complete the drawing.

7. *Closing the application.* Click the *close box*, ⊠ to close your running application.

Fig. 1.3 | Drawing with a new brush color.

Fig. 1.4 | Drawing with a new brush size.

Fig. 1.5 | Finishing the drawing.

Additional Applications in **Visual Basic 2005 for Programmers, 2/e**
Figure 1.6 lists a few of the applications in the book's examples. We encourage you to run them. The examples folder for Chapter 1 contains all of the files required to run each application listed in Fig. 1.6. Simply double click the file names for any application you would like to run. [*Note:* The Garage.exe application assumes that the user inputs a value from 0 to 24.]

1.9 (Only Required Section of the Case Study) Software Engineering Case Study: Introduction to Object Technology and the UML

Now we begin our introduction to object orientation, a natural way of thinking about the world and writing computer programs. Chapters 1, 3–9 and 11 each end with a brief Software Engineering Case Study section in which we present a carefully paced introduction to object orientation. Our goal here is to help you develop an object-oriented way of thinking and to introduce you to the *Unified Modeling Language™ (UML™)*—a graphical language that allows people who design object-oriented software systems to use an industry-standard notation to represent them.

In this, the only required section of the case study (because it contains foundational information for all readers), we introduce basic object-oriented concepts and terminology. The optional case study sections in Chapters 3–9 and 11, and in Appendix J present an object-oriented design and implementation of the software for a simple automated teller machine (ATM) system. The Software Engineering Case Study sections at the ends of Chapters 3–8

- analyze a typical requirements document that describes a software system (the ATM) to be built
- determine the objects required to implement that system
- determine the attributes the objects will have
- determine the behaviors these objects will exhibit
- specify how the objects will interact with one another to meet the system requirements

Application name	File to execute
Parking Fees	`Garage.exe`
Tic Tac Toe	`TicTacToe.exe`
Drawing Stars	`DrawStars.exe`
Drawing Shapes	`DrawShapes.exe`
Drawing Polygons	`DrawPolygons.exe`

Fig. 1.6 | Examples of Visual Basic applications found in this book.

The Software Engineering Case Study sections at the ends of Chapters 9 and 11 modify and enhance the design presented in Chapters 3–8. Appendix J contains a complete, working Visual Basic implementation of the object-oriented ATM system.

Although our case study is a scaled-down version of an industry-level problem, we nevertheless cover many common industry practices. You will experience a solid introduction to object-oriented design with the UML. Also, you will sharpen your code-reading skills by touring a complete, straightforward and well-documented Visual Basic implementation of the ATM.

Basic Object Technology Concepts

We begin our introduction to object orientation with some key terminology. Everywhere you look in the real world you see *objects*—people, animals, plants, cars, planes, buildings, computers and so on. Humans think in terms of objects. Telephones, houses, traffic lights, microwave ovens and water coolers are just a few more objects we see around us every day.

We sometimes divide objects into two categories: animate and inanimate. Animate objects are "alive" in some sense—they move around and do things. Inanimate objects do not move on their own. Objects of both types, however, have some things in common. They all have *attributes* (e.g., size, shape, color and weight), and they all exhibit *behaviors* (e.g., a ball rolls, bounces, inflates and deflates; a baby cries, sleeps, crawls, walks and blinks; a car accelerates, brakes and turns; a towel absorbs water). We will study the kinds of attributes and behaviors that software objects have.

Humans learn about objects by studying their attributes and observing their behaviors. Different objects can have similar attributes and can exhibit similar behaviors. Comparisons can be made, for example, between babies and adults and between humans and chimpanzees.

Object-oriented design (OOD) models software in terms similar to those that people use to describe real-world objects. It takes advantage of class relationships, where objects of a certain class, such as a class of vehicles, have the same characteristics—cars, trucks, little red wagons and roller skates have much in common. OOD takes advantage of *inheritance* relationships, where new classes of objects are derived by absorbing characteristics of existing classes and adding unique characteristics of their own. An object of class "convertible" certainly has the characteristics of the more general class "automobile," but more specifically, the roof goes up and down.

Object-oriented design provides a natural and intuitive way to view the software design process—namely, modeling objects by their attributes, behaviors and interrelationships, just as we describe real-world objects. OOD also models communication between objects. Just as people send messages to one another (e.g., a sergeant commands a soldier to stand at attention), objects also communicate via messages. A bank account object may receive a message to decrease its balance by a certain amount because the customer has withdrawn that amount of money.

OOD *encapsulates* (i.e., wraps) attributes and *operations* (behaviors) into objects—an object's attributes and operations are intimately tied together. Objects have the property of *information hiding*. This means that objects may know how to communicate with one another across well-defined *interfaces,* but normally they are not allowed to know how other objects are implemented—implementation details are hidden within the objects themselves. You can drive a car effectively, for instance, without knowing the details of how engines, transmissions, brakes and exhaust systems work internally—as long as you know how to use the accelerator pedal, the brake pedal, the steering wheel and so on. Information hiding, as you will see, is crucial to good software engineering.

Languages like Visual Basic are *object oriented.* Programming in such a language is called *object-oriented programming (OOP),* and it allows computer programmers to conveniently implement an object-oriented design as a working software system. Languages like C, on the other hand, are *procedural,* so programming tends to be *action oriented.* In C, the unit of programming is the *function.* In Visual Basic, the unit of programming is the *class* from which objects are eventually *instantiated* (an OOP term for "created"). Visual Basic classes contain *methods* (Visual Basic's equivalent of C's functions) that implement operations, and data that implements attributes.

Classes, Fields and Methods

Visual Basic programmers concentrate on creating their own *user-defined types* called *classes.* Each class contains data as well as the set of methods that manipulate that data and provide services to *clients* (i.e., other classes that use the class). The data components of a class are called attributes or *fields.* For example, a bank account class might include an account number and a balance. The operation components of a class are called methods. For example, a bank account class might include methods to make a deposit (increase the balance), make a withdrawal (decrease the balance) and inquire what the current balance is. Programmers use built-in types and user-defined types as the "building blocks" for constructing new user-defined types (classes). The *nouns in a system specification* help the Visual Basic programmer determine the set of classes from which objects are created that work together to implement the system.

Classes are to objects as blueprints are to houses—a class is a "plan" for building objects of the class. Just as we can build many houses from one blueprint, we can instantiate (create) many objects from one class. You cannot cook meals in the kitchen of a blueprint, but you can cook meals in the kitchen of a house. You cannot sleep in the bedroom of a blueprint, but you can sleep in the bedroom of a house.

Classes can have relationships with other classes. For example, in an object-oriented design of a bank, the "bank teller" class needs to relate to other classes, such as the "customer" class, the "cash drawer" class, the "safe" class, and so on. These relationships are called *associations.*

Packaging software as classes makes it possible for future software systems to *reuse* the classes. Groups of related classes often are packaged as reusable *components*. Just as realtors often say that the three most important factors affecting the price of real estate are "location, location and location," people in the software development community often say that the three most important factors affecting the future of software development are "reuse, reuse and reuse."

Software Engineering Observation 1.1

Reuse of existing classes when building new classes and programs saves time, money and effort. Reuse also helps programmers build more reliable and effective systems, because existing classes and components often have gone through extensive testing, debugging and performance tuning.

Indeed, with object technology, you can build much of the new software you will need by combining existing classes, just as automobile manufacturers combine interchangeable parts. Each new class you create will have the potential to become a valuable software asset that you and other programmers can reuse to speed and enhance the quality of future software development efforts.

Introduction to Object-Oriented Analysis and Design (OOAD)

Soon you will be writing programs in Visual Basic. How will you create the code for your programs? Perhaps, like many programmers, you will simply turn on your computer and start typing. This approach may work for small programs (like the ones we present in the early chapters of the book), but what if you were asked to create a software system to control thousands of automated teller machines for a major bank? Or what if you were asked to work on a team of 1,000 software developers building the next generation of the U.S. air traffic control system? For projects so large and complex, you could not simply sit down and start writing programs.

To create the best solutions, you should follow a detailed process for *analyzing* your project's *requirements* (i.e., determining *what* your system is supposed to do) and developing a *design* that satisfies them (i.e., deciding *how* your system should do it). Ideally, you would go through this process and carefully review the design (and have your design reviewed by other software professionals) before writing any code. If this process involves analyzing and designing your system from an object-oriented point of view, it is called *object-oriented analysis and design* (*OOAD*). Experienced programmers know that proper analysis and design can save many hours by helping avoid an ill-planned system development approach that has to be abandoned partway through its implementation, possibly wasting considerable time, money and effort.

OOAD is the generic term for the process of analyzing a problem and developing an approach for solving it. Small problems like the ones discussed in the first few chapters of this book, do not require an exhaustive OOAD process. It may be sufficient, before you begin writing Visual Basic code, to write *pseudocode*—an informal text-based means of expressing program logic. Pseudocode is not actually a programming language, but we can use it as a kind of outline to guide us as we write our code.

As problems and the groups of people solving them increase in size, OOAD quickly becomes more appropriate than pseudocode. Ideally, a group should agree on a strictly defined process for solving its problem and a uniform way of communicating the results of that process to one another. Although many different OOAD processes exist, a single graphical language for communicating the results of *any* OOAD process has come into wide use. This language, known as the Unified Modeling Language (UML), was developed in the mid-1990s under the initial direction of three software methodologists: Grady Booch, James Rumbaugh and Ivar Jacobson.

History of the UML

In the 1980s, increasing numbers of organizations began using OOP to build their applications, and a need developed for a standard object-oriented analysis and design (OOAD) process. Many methodologists—including Grady Booch, James Rumbaugh and Ivar Jacobson—individually produced and promoted separate processes to satisfy this need. Each process had its own notation, or "language" (in the form of graphical diagrams), to convey the results of analysis (i.e., determining *what* a proposed system is supposed to do) and design (i.e., determining *how* a proposed system should be implemented to do what it is supposed to do).

By the early 1990s, different organizations were using their own unique processes and notations. At the same time, these organizations also wanted to use software tools that would support their particular processes. Software vendors found it difficult to provide tools for so many processes. A standard notation and standard process were needed.

In 1994, James Rumbaugh joined Grady Booch at Rational Software Corporation (now a division of IBM), and the two began working to unify their popular processes. They soon were joined by Ivar Jacobson. In 1996, the group released early versions of the UML to the software engineering community and requested feedback. Around the same time, an organization known as the Object Management Group™ (OMG™) invited submissions for a common modeling language. The OMG (www.omg.org) is a nonprofit organization that promotes the standardization of object-oriented technologies by issuing guidelines and specifications, such as the UML. Several corporations—among them HP, IBM, Microsoft, Oracle and Rational Software—had already recognized the need for a common modeling language. In response to the OMG's request for proposals, these companies formed the UML Partners—the consortium that developed the UML version 1.1 and submitted it to the OMG. The OMG accepted the proposal and, in 1997, assumed responsibility for the continuing maintenance and revision of the UML. We present the recently adopted UML 2 terminology and notation throughout this book.

What is the UML?

The *Unified Modeling Language* (*UML*) is the most widely used graphical representation scheme for modeling object-oriented systems. It has indeed unified the various popular notational schemes. Those who design systems use the language (in the form of diagrams, many of which we discuss throughout our ATM case study and other portions of the book) to model their systems.

An attractive feature of the UML is its flexibility. The UML is *extensible* (i.e., capable of being enhanced with new features) and is independent of any particular OOAD process. UML modelers are free to use various processes in designing systems, but all developers can now express their designs with one standard set of graphical notations.

The UML is a feature-rich graphical language. In our subsequent (and optional) Software Engineering Case Study sections on developing the software for an automated teller machine (ATM), we present a simple, concise subset of these features. We then use this subset to guide you through a first design experience with the UML. We sincerely hope you enjoy working through it.

Internet and Web UML Resources

For more information about the UML, refer to the following Web sites. For additional UML sites, please refer to the Internet and Web resources listed at the end of Section 3.9.

`www.uml.org`
This UML resource site from the Object Management Group (OMG) provides specification documents for the UML and other object-oriented technologies.

`www.ibm.com/software/rational/uml`
This is the UML resource page for IBM Rational—the successor to the Rational Software Corporation (the company that created the UML).

`www.uml.org/#Links-Tutorials`
The Object Management Group's list of recommended UML tutorials.

`bdn.borland.com/article/0,1410,31863,00.html`
A short tutorial on the UML from the Borland Developer Network.

Recommended Readings

The following books provide information about object-oriented design with the UML.

- Arlow, J., and I. Neustadt. *UML and the Unified Process: Practical Object-Oriented Analysis and Design, Second Edition.* London: Addison-Wesley, 2005.

- Fowler, M. *UML Distilled, Third Edition: A Brief Guide to the Standard Object Modeling Language.* Boston: Addison-Wesley, 2004.

- Rumbaugh, J., I. Jacobson and G. Booch. *The Unified Modeling Language User Guide, Second Edition.* Reading, MA: Addison-Wesley, 2005.

For additional books on the UML, please refer to the recommended readings listed at the end of Section 3.9, or visit `www.amazon.com`, `www.bn.com` and `www.informIT.com`. IBM Rational provides a recommended reading list for UML books at `www.ibm.com/software/rational/info/technical/books.jsp`.

Section 1.9 Self-Review Exercises

1.1 List three examples of real-world objects that we did not mention. For each object, list several attributes and behaviors.

1.2 Pseudocode is _____.
  a) another term for OOAD
  b) a programming language used to display UML diagrams
  c) an informal means of expressing program logic
  d) a graphical representation scheme for modeling object-oriented systems

1.3 The UML is used primarily to _____.
  a) test object-oriented systems
  b) design object-oriented systems
  c) implement object-oriented systems
  d) Both a and b

Answers to Section 1.9 Self-Review Exercises

1.1   [*Note:* Answers may vary.] a) A television's attributes include the size of the screen, the number of colors it can display, and its current channel and volume. A television turns on and off, changes channels, displays video and plays sounds. b) A coffee maker's attributes include the maximum volume of water it can hold, the time required to brew a pot of coffee and the temperature of the heating plate under the coffee pot. A coffee maker turns on and off, brews coffee and heats coffee. c) A turtle's attributes include its age, the size of its shell and its weight. A turtle crawls, retreats into its shell, emerges from its shell and eats vegetation.

1.2   c.

1.3   b.

1.10 Wrap-Up

This chapter introduced basic object technology concepts, including classes, objects, attributes and behaviors. We presented a brief history of Microsoft's Windows. We discussed the history of the Internet and the Web. We presented the history of Visual Basic programming and Microsoft's .NET initiative, which allows you to program Internet and Web-based applications using Visual Basic (and other languages). You learned the steps for executing a Visual Basic application. You test-drove a sample Visual Basic application similar to the types of applications you will learn to program in this book. You learned about the history and purpose of the UML—the industry-standard graphical language for modeling software systems. We launched our early objects and classes presentation with the first of our Software Engineering Case Study sections (and the only one which is required). The remaining (all optional) sections of the case study use object-oriented design and the UML to design the software for our simplified automated teller machine system. We present the complete Visual Basic code implementation of the ATM system in Appendix J.

In the next chapter, you will use the Visual Studio IDE (Integrated Development Environment) to create your first Visual Basic application using the techniques of visual programming. You will also learn about Visual Studio's help features.

1.11 Web Resources

Deitel & Associates Web Sites

www.deitel.com/books/vbforprogrammers2/index.html
The Deitel & Associates site for *Visual Basic 2005 for Programmers, Second Edition* includes links to the book's examples and other resources.

www.deitel.com
Please check this site for updates, corrections and additional resources for all Deitel publications.

www.deitel.com/newsletter/subscribe.html
Please visit this site to subscribe to the free *Deitel® Buzz Online* e-mail newsletter to follow the Deitel & Associates publishing program and to receive updates on Visual Basic 2005 and this book.

www.prenhallprofessional.com/title/013225140X
Prentice Hall's site for this *Deitel Developer Series* publication. Includes detailed product information, sample chapters and code downloads.

Microsoft Web Sites

`msdn.microsoft.com/vbasic/default.aspx`
The Microsoft Visual Basic Developer Center site includes product information, downloads, tutorials, chat groups and more. Includes case studies on companies using Visual Basic in their businesses.

`msdn.microsoft.com/vstudio/default.aspx`
Visit this site to learn more about Microsoft's Visual Studio products and resources.

`www.gotdotnet.com/`
This is the site for the Microsoft .NET Framework Community. It includes message boards, a resource center, sample programs and more.

`www.thespoke.net`
Students can chat, post their code, rate other students' code, create hubs and post questions at this site.

Resources

`www.w3.org`
The World Wide Web Consortium (W3C) develops technologies for the Internet and the Web. This site includes links to W3C technologies, news and frequently asked questions (FAQs).

`www.startvbdotnet.com/`
Intended for novices, this site includes tutorials and links to numerous Visual Basic resources.

`www.vbexplorer.com/VBExplorer/VBExplorer.asp`
Includes tutorials, downloads, tips, downloads, games and more.

`www.devx.com/vb/`
This Visual Basic developers' Web site include links to articles, downloads, demos and code.

`www.error-bank.com/`
The Error Bank is a collection of .NET errors, exceptions and solutions.

`www.vbdotnetforums.com/`
This site allows you to chat with other Visual Basic developers, including the Visual Basic team at Microsoft.

UML Resources

`www.uml.org`
This UML resource page from the Object Management Group (OMG) provides specification documents for the UML and other object-oriented technologies.

`www.ibm.com/software/rational/uml`
This is the UML resource page for IBM Rational—the successor to the Rational Software Corporation (the company that created the UML).

Visual Basic Games

`www.homestead.com/vbgames6/game.html`
Check out Visual Basic games or post your own at this site.

`www.vbexplorer.com/VBExplorer/vb_game_downloads.asp`
Download Visual Basic games and graphics from this site.

`www.codetoad.com/visual_basic/games/`
This programmers' resource site includes links to several Visual Basic games.

2

Introduction to the Visual Basic Express 2005 IDE

Seeing is believing.
—Proverb

Form ever follows function.
—Louis Henri Sullivan

Intelligence ... is the faculty of making artificial objects, especially tools to make tools.
—Henri-Louis Bergson

OBJECTIVES

In this chapter you will learn:

- The basics of the Visual Studio Integrated Development Environment (IDE) that assists you in writing, running and debugging your Visual Basic programs.

- Visual Studio's help features.

- Key commands contained in the IDE's menus and toolbars.

- The purpose of the various kinds of windows in the Visual Studio 2005 IDE.

- What visual programming is and how it simplifies and speeds program development.

- To create, compile and execute a simple Visual Basic program that displays text and an image using the Visual Studio IDE and the technique of visual programming.

2.1 Introduction

Visual Studio® 2005 is Microsoft's Integrated Development Environment (IDE) for creating, running and debugging programs (also called *applications*) written in a variety of .NET programming languages. In this chapter, we provide an overview of the Visual Studio 2005 IDE and demonstrate how to create a simple Visual Basic program by dragging and dropping predefined building blocks into place—a technique called *visual programming*.

2.2 Overview of the Visual Studio 2005 IDE

There are many versions of Visual Studio available. The book's examples are based on the *Microsoft Visual Basic 2005 Express Edition*, which supports only the Visual Basic programming language. Microsoft also offers a full version of Visual Studio 2005, which includes support for other languages in addition to Visual Basic, such as Visual C# and Visual C++. Our screen captures and discussions focus on the IDE of the Visual Basic 2005 Express Edition. We assume that you have some familiarity with Windows.

Again, we use fonts to distinguish between IDE features (such as menu names and menu items) and other elements that appear in the IDE. We emphasize IDE features in a sans-serif bold **Helvetica** font (e.g., **File** menu) and emphasize other elements, such as file names (e.g., `Form1.vb`) and property names (discussed in Section 2.4.3), in a sans-serif `Lucida` font.

Introduction to Microsoft Visual Basic 2005 Express Edition

To start Microsoft Visual Basic 2005 Express Edition in Windows XP, select **Start > All Programs > Microsoft Visual Basic 2005 Express Edition**. For Windows 2000 users, select **Start > Programs > Microsoft Visual Basic 2005 Express Edition**. Once the Express Edition begins execution, the **Start Page** displays (Fig. 2.1) Depending on your version of Visual Studio, your **Start Page** may look different. For new programmers unfamiliar with Visual Basic, the **Start Page** contains a list of links to resources in the Visual Studio 2005 IDE and on the Internet. From this point forward, we will refer to the Visual Studio 2005 IDE

New Project button   Start Page tab

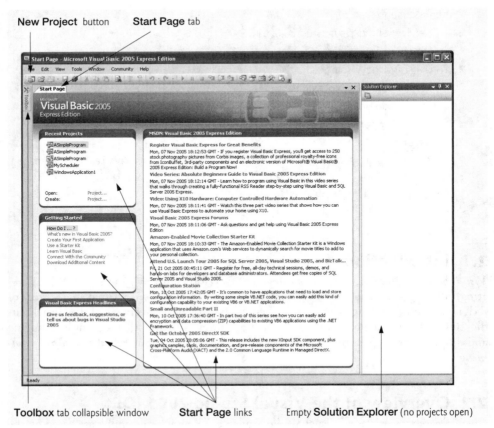

Toolbox tab collapsible window   Start Page links   Empty Solution Explorer (no projects open)

Fig. 2.1 | **Start Page** in Visual Basic 2005 Express Edition.

simply as "Visual Studio" or "the IDE." For experienced developers, this page provides links to the latest developments in Visual Basic (such as updates and bug fixes) and to information on advanced programming topics. Once you start exploring the IDE, you can return to the **Start Page** by selecting **View > Other Windows > Start Page**. We use the **>** character to indicate the selection of a menu command from a menu. For example, we use the notation **File > Open File** to indicate that you should select the **Open File** command from the **File** menu.

Links on the Start Page

The **Start Page** links are organized into sections—**Recent Projects**, **Getting Started**, **Visual Basic Express Headlines** and **MSDN: Visual Basic 2005 Express Edition**—that contain links to helpful programming resources. Clicking any link on the **Start Page** displays relevant information associated with the specific link. We refer to *single clicking* with the left mouse button as *selecting*, or *clicking*; we refer to double clicking with the left mouse button simply as *double clicking*.

The **Recent Projects** section contains information on projects you have recently created or modified. You can also open existing projects or create new ones by clicking the links in the section. The **Getting Started** section focuses on using the IDE for creating programs, learning Visual Basic, connecting to the Visual Basic developer community (i.e., other software developers with whom you can communicate through newsgroups and Web sites) and providing various development tools such as starter kits. For example, clicking the link **Use a Starter Kit** provides you with resources and links for building a simple screen saver application or a movie collection application. The screen saver application builds a screen saver that displays current news articles. The movie collection starter kit builds an application that lets you maintain a catalog of your DVDs and VHS movies, or the application can be changed to track anything else you might collect (e.g., CDs, video games).

The **Getting Started**, **Visual Basic Express Headlines** and **MSDN: Visual Basic 2005 Express Edition** sections provide links to information about programming in Visual Basic, including a tour of the language, new Visual Basic 2005 features and online courses. To access more extensive information on Visual Studio, you can browse the *MSDN* (*Microsoft Developer Network*) online library at msdn2.microsoft.com. The MSDN site contains articles, downloads and tutorials on technologies of interest to Visual Studio developers. You can also browse the Web from the IDE using Internet Explorer. To request a Web page, type its URL into the location bar (Fig. 2.2) and press the *Enter* key— your computer, of course, must be connected to the Internet. (If the location bar is not already displayed, select **View > Other Windows > Web Browser** or type *<Ctrl> <Alt> R*.) The Web page that you wish to view will appear as another *tab*, which you can select, inside the Visual Studio IDE (Fig. 2.2).

Requested Web page (URL in location bar drop-down menu)   Selected tab for requested Web page

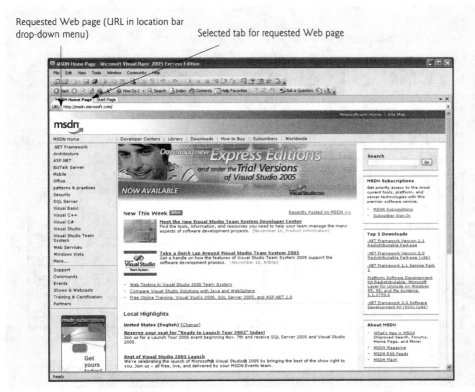

Fig. 2.2 | Displaying a Web page in Visual Studio.

Customizing the IDE and Creating a New Project

To begin programming in Visual Basic, you must create a new project or open an existing one. There are two ways to create a new project or open an existing project. You can select either **File > New Project…** or **File > Open Project…**, which creates a new project or opens an existing project, respectively. From the **Start Page**, under the **Recent Projects** section, you can also click the links **Create: Project…** or **Open: Project…**. A *project* is a group of related files, such as the Visual Basic code and any images that might make up a program. Visual Studio 2005 organizes programs into projects and *solutions*, which contain one or more projects. Multiple-project solutions are used to create large-scale programs. Each of the programs we create in this book consists of a single project.

Select **File > New Project…** or the **Create: Project…** link on the **Start Page** to display the ***New Project** dialog* (Fig. 2.3). *Dialogs* are windows that facilitate user-computer communication. We will discuss the detailed process of creating new projects momentarily.

Visual Studio provides templates for a variety of projects (Fig. 2.3). *Templates* are the project types users can create in Visual Basic—Windows applications, console applications and others (you will primarily use Windows applications and console applications in this textbook). Users can also create their own custom application templates. In this chapter, we build a **Windows Application**. We discuss the **Console Application** template in Chapter 3, Introduction to Visual Basic Programming. A *Windows application* is a program that executes within a Windows operating system (e.g., Windows 2000 or Windows XP) and typically has a *graphical user interface* (*GUI*)—the visual part of the program with which

Fig. 2.3 | **New Project** dialog.

the user interacts. Windows applications include Microsoft software products like Microsoft Word, Internet Explorer and Visual Studio; software products created by other vendors; and customized software that you and other programmers create. You will create many Windows applications in this text. [*Note:* Novell sponsors an open source project called *Mono* that enables developers to create .NET applications for Linux, Windows and Mac OS X. Mono is based on the Ecma standards for the Common Language Infrastructure (CLI). For more information on Mono, visit `www.mono-project.com`.]

By default, Visual Studio assigns the name **WindowsApplication1** to the new project and solution (Fig. 2.3). Soon you will change the name of the project and the location where it is saved. Click **OK** to display the IDE in *design view* (Fig. 2.4), which contains all the features necessary for you to begin creating programs. The design view portion of the IDE is also known as the *Windows Form Designer*.

The gray rectangle titled **Form1** (called a *Form*) represents the main window of the Windows application that you are creating. Visual Basic applications can have multiple Forms (windows); however, the applications you will create in this text use only one Form. Soon, you will learn how to customize the Form by adding controls (i.e., reusable components) to a program—in this example, you'll add a Label and a PictureBox (Fig. 2.27). A *Label* typically contains descriptive text (e.g., "Welcome to Visual Basic!"), and a *PictureBox* displays an image, such as the Deitel bug mascot. Visual Basic Express has 66 pre-existing controls you can use to build and customize your programs. Many of these controls are discussed and used throughout the book. Other controls are available from

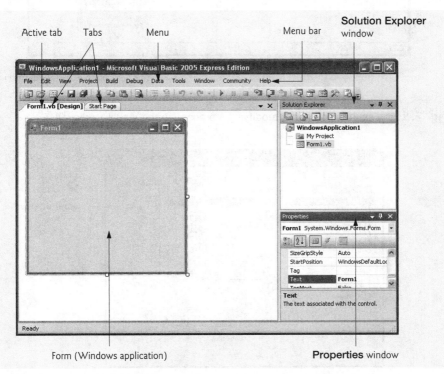

Fig. 2.4 | **Design** view of the IDE.

third parties. You can download several third party controls from msdn.microsoft.com/ vbasic/downloads/controls/default.aspx.

In this chapter, you will work with preexisting controls that are part of the FCL. As you place controls on the form, you'll be able to modify their properties (discussed in Section 2.4). For example, Fig. 2.5 shows where the Form's name can be modified in a text box and Fig. 2.6 shows a dialog in which a control's font properties can be modified.

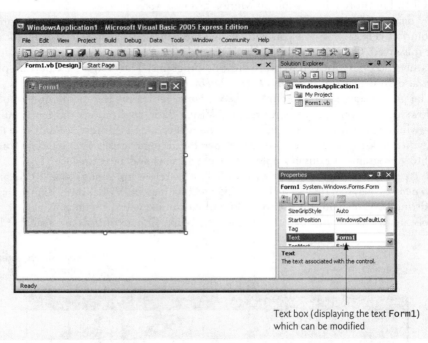

Text box (displaying the text Form1) which can be modified

Fig. 2.5 | Text box control for modifying a property in the Visual Studio IDE.

Fig. 2.6 | Dialog for modifying a control's font properties in the Visual Studio IDE.

Collectively, the Form and controls constitute the program's GUI. Users enter data (*inputs*) into the program by typing at the keyboard, by clicking the mouse buttons and in a variety of other ways. Programs use the GUI to display instructions and other information (*outputs*) for users to read. For example, the **New Project** dialog in Fig. 2.3 presents a GUI where the user clicks the mouse button to select a template type, then inputs a project name from the keyboard (note that the figure is still showing the default project name **WindowsApplication1** supplied by Visual Studio).

The name of each open document is listed on a tab—in Fig. 2.4, the open documents are **Form1.vb [Design]** and the **Start Page**. To view a document, click its tab. Tabs facilitate easy access to multiple open documents. The *active tab* (the tab of the document currently displayed in the IDE) is displayed in bold text (e.g., **Form1.vb [Design]** in Fig. 2.4) and is positioned in front of all the other tabs.

2.3 Menu Bar and Toolbar

Commands for managing the IDE and for developing, maintaining and executing programs are contained in *menus*, which are located on the *menu bar* of the IDE (Fig. 2.7). The set of menus displayed depends on what you are currently doing in the IDE.

Menus contain groups of related commands (also called *menu items*) that, when selected, cause the IDE to perform specific actions (e.g., open a window, save a file, print a file and execute a program). For example, new projects are created by selecting **File > New Project...**. The menus depicted in Fig. 2.7 are summarized in Fig. 2.8. In Chapter 14, Graphical User Interface Concepts: Part 2, we discuss how to create and add your own menus and menu items to your programs.

| File | Edit | View | Project | Build | Debug | Data | Format | Tools | Window | Community | Help |

Fig. 2.7 | Visual Studio menu bar.

Menu	Description
File	Contains commands for opening, closing, adding and saving projects, as well as printing project data and exiting Visual Studio.
Edit	Contains commands for editing programs, such as cut, copy, paste, undo, redo, delete, find and select.
View	Contains commands for displaying windows (e.g., **Solution Explorer**, **Toolbox**, **Properties** window) and for adding toolbars to the IDE.
Project	Contains commands for managing projects and their files.
Build	Contains commands for compiling programs.
Debug	Contains commands for debugging (i.e., identifying and correcting problems in programs) and running programs. Debugging is discussed in detail in Appendix C.

Fig. 2.8 | Summary of Visual Studio 2005 IDE menus. (Part 1 of 2.)

Menu	Description
Data	Contains commands for interacting with databases (i.e., organized collections of data stored on computers), which we discuss in Chapter 20, Databases, SQL and ADO.NET.
Format	Contains commands for arranging and modifying a form's controls. Note that the **Format** menu appears only when a GUI component is selected in **Design** view.
Tools	Contains commands for accessing additional IDE tools (e.g., the **Toolbox**) and options that enable customization of the IDE.
Window	Contains commands for arranging and displaying windows.
Community	Contains commands for sending questions directly to Microsoft, checking question status, sending feedback on Visual Basic and searching the Code-Zone developer center and the Microsoft developers community site.
Help	Contains commands for accessing the IDE's help features.

Fig. 2.8 | Summary of Visual Studio 2005 IDE menus. (Part 2 of 2.)

Rather than navigating the menus from the menu bar, you can access many of the more common commands from the *toolbar* (Fig. 2.9), which contains graphics, called *icons*, that graphically represent commands. By default, the standard toolbar is displayed

Fig. 2.9 | Standard Visual Studio toolbar.

when you run Visual Studio for the first time; it contains icons for the most commonly used commands, such as opening a file, adding an item to a project, save and run (Fig. 2.9). The icons that appear on the standard toolbar may vary depending on the version of Visual Studio you are using. Some commands are initially disabled (or unavailable to use). These commands are enabled by Visual Studio only when they are necessary. For example, Visual Studio enables the command for saving a file once you begin editing a file.

You can customize the IDE by adding more toolbars. Select **View > Toolbars** (Fig. 2.10). Each toolbar you select will be displayed with the other toolbars at the top of the Visual Studio window. To execute a command via the toolbar, click its icon. Some icons contain a down arrow that, when clicked, displays a related command or commands, as shown in Fig. 2.11.

It is difficult to remember what each of the icons on the toolbar represents. Positioning the mouse pointer over an icon highlights it and, after a brief pause, displays a description of the icon called a *tool tip* (Fig. 2.12). Tool tips help novice programmers become familiar with the IDE's features and serve as useful reminders for each toolbar icon's functionality.

2.4 Navigating the Visual Studio IDE

The IDE provides windows for accessing project files and customizing controls. In this section, we introduce several windows that you will use frequently when developing Visual Basic programs. These windows can be accessed via the toolbar icons (Fig. 2.13) or by selecting the name of the desired window in the **View** menu.

Visual Studio provides a space-saving feature called *auto-hide*. When auto-hide is enabled, a tab appears along either the left or right edge of the IDE window (Fig. 2.14). This tab contains one or more icons, each of which identifies a hidden window. Placing

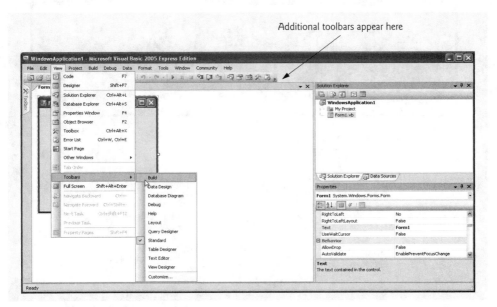

Fig. 2.10 | Adding the **Build** toolbar to the IDE.

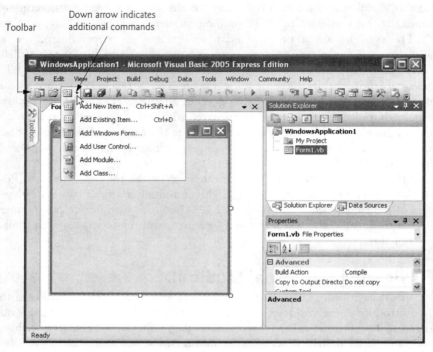

Fig. 2.11 | IDE toolbar icon showing additional command.

Fig. 2.12 | Tool tip demonstration.

Fig. 2.13 | Toolbar icons for three Visual Studio windows.

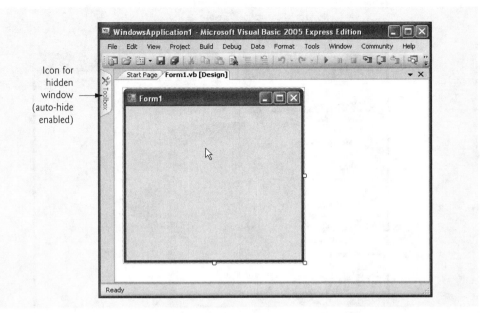

Icon for hidden window (auto-hide enabled)

Fig. 2.14 | Auto-hide feature demonstration.

the mouse pointer over one of these icons displays that window (Fig. 2.15). The window is hidden again when the mouse pointer is moved outside the window's area. To "pin down" a window (i.e., to disable auto-hide and keep the window open), click the pin icon. When auto-hide is enabled, the pin icon is horizontal (Fig. 2.15); when a window is "pinned down," the pin icon is vertical (Fig. 2.16).

The next few sections overview three of the main windows used in Visual Studio—the **Solution Explorer,** the **Properties** window and the **Toolbox**. These windows show information about the project and include tools that help you build your programs.

2.4.1 Solution Explorer

The *Solution Explorer* window (Fig. 2.17) provides access to all of the files in a solution. If the **Solution Explorer** window is not shown in the IDE, you can display it by clicking the Solution Explorer icon in the IDE (Fig. 2.13), by selecting **View > Solution Explorer** or by typing *<Ctrl> <Alt> L*. When Visual Studio is first run, the **Solution Explorer** is empty; there are no files to display. Once you open a new or existing solution, the **Solution Explorer** displays the contents of the solution.

The solution's *startup project* is the project that runs when the program executes. If you have multiple projects in a given solution, you can specify the startup project by right-clicking the project name in the **Solution Explorer** window, then selecting the **Set as StartUp Project**. For our single-project solution, the startup project is the only project (in this case, **WindowsApplication1**) and the project name appears in bold text in the **Solution Explorer** window. We discuss only single-project solutions in this text. For programmers using Visual Studio for the first time, the **Solution Explorer** window lists only the **My Project** and **Form1.vb** files (Fig. 2.17). The **Solution Explorer** window includes a toolbar that contains several icons.

Horizontal orientation for pin
icon when auto-hide is enabled

Toolbox
title bar

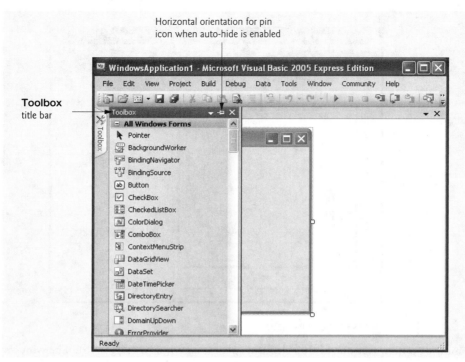

Fig. 2.15 | Displaying a hidden window when auto-hide is enabled.

Toolbox
"pinned down"

Vertical orientation for pin icon
when window is pinned down

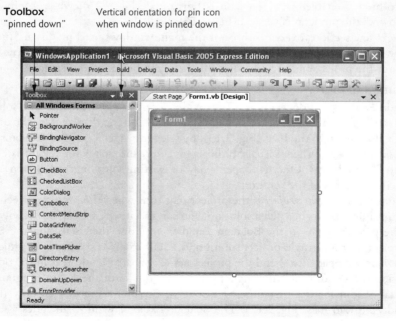

Fig. 2.16 | Disabling auto-hide ("pinning down" a window).

Show All Files icon

Toolbar
Startup project

Fig. 2.17 | **Solution Explorer** with an open project.

The Visual Basic file that corresponds to the form shown in Fig. 2.4 is named Form1.vb (selected in Fig. 2.17). Visual Basic files use the .vb filename extension, which is short for "Visual Basic."

By default, the IDE displays only files that you may need to edit—other files generated by the IDE are hidden. When clicked, the ***Show All Files icon*** (Fig. 2.17) displays all the files in the solution, including those generated by the IDE (Fig. 2.18). The plus and minus boxes that appear can be clicked to expand and collapse the project tree, respectively. Click the plus box to the left of **My Project** to display items grouped under the heading to the right of the plus box (Fig. 2.19); click the minus box to collapse the tree from its expanded state (Fig. 2.20). Other Visual Studio windows also use this plus-box/minus-box convention.

2.4.2 Toolbox

The **Toolbox** contains icons representing controls used to customize forms (Fig. 2.21). Using visual programming, programmers can "drag and drop" controls onto the form, which is faster and simpler than building them by writing GUI code (we discuss writing this type of code in Chapter 5, Control Statements: Part 1). Just as you do not need to know how to build an engine to drive a car, you do not need to know how to build controls to use them. Reusing pre-existing controls saves time and money when you develop programs. You will use the **Toolbox** when you create your first program later in the chapter.

Plus box
Minus box

Fig. 2.18 | **Solution Explorer** showing plus boxes and minus boxes for expanding and collapsing the tree to reveal or hide project files.

Minus box indicates that the file or folder is expanded (changed from plus box)

Fig. 2.19 | **Solution Explorer** expanding the **My Project** file after clicking its plus box.

Plus boxes indicate that the file or folder is collapsed (changed from minus

Fig. 2.20 | **Solution Explorer** collapsing all files after clicking any minus boxes.

The **Toolbox** groups the prebuilt controls into categories—**All Windows Forms, Common Controls, Containers, Menus & Toolbars, Data, Components, Printing, Dialogs** and **General** are listed in Fig. 2.21. Again, note the use of plus and minus boxes which can expand or collapse a group of controls. We discuss many of the **Toolbox**'s controls and their functionality throughout the book.

2.4.3 Properties Window

To display the **Properties** window if it is not visible, select **View > Properties Window**, click the **Properties** window icon shown in Fig. 2.13, or press the *F4* key. The ***Properties window*** displays the properties for the currently selected Form (Fig. 2.22), control or file in design view. ***Properties*** specify information about the form or control, such as its size, color and position. Each form or control has its own set of properties; a property's description is displayed at the bottom of the **Properties** window whenever that property is selected.

Figure 2.22 shows Form1's **Properties** window. The left column lists the form's properties; the right column displays the current value of each property. You can sort the properties either alphabetically (by clicking the ***Alphabetical icon***) or categorically (by clicking the ***Categorized icon***). The properties can be sorted alphabetically from A–Z or Z–A; sorting by category groups the properties according to their use (i.e., **Appearance, Behavior, Design**, etc.). Depending on the size of the **Properties** window, some of the properties may

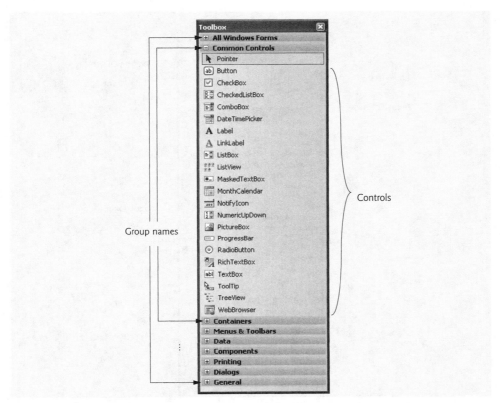

Fig. 2.21 | **Toolbox** window displaying controls for the **Common Controls** group.

be hidden from view on the screen. Users can scroll through the list of properties by *dragging* the *scrollbox* up or down inside the *scrollbar*, or by clicking the arrows at the top and bottom of the scrollbar. We show how to set individual properties later in this chapter.

The **Properties** window is crucial to visual programming; it allows you to modify a control's properties visually, without writing code. You can see which properties are available for modification and, in many cases, can learn the range of acceptable values for a given property. The **Properties** window displays a brief description of the selected property, helping you understand its purpose. A property can be set quickly using this window and no code needs to be written.

At the top of the **Properties** window is the *component selection drop-down list*, which allows you to select the form or control whose properties you wish to display in the **Properties** window (Fig. 2.22). Using the component selection drop-down list is an alternative way to display a form's or control's properties without selecting the actual form or control in the GUI.

2.5 Using Help

Visual Studio provides extensive help features. The ***Help menu*** commands are summarized in Fig. 2.23.

Fig. 2.22 │ **Properties** window.

Command	Description
How Do I?	Contains links to relevant topics, including how to upgrade programs and learn more about Web services, architecture and design, files and I/O, data, debugging and more.
Search	Finds help articles based on search keywords.
Index	Displays an alphabetized list of topics you can browse.
Contents	Displays a categorized table of contents in which help articles are organized by topic.

Fig. 2.23 │ **Help** menu commands.

Dynamic help (Fig. 2.24) is an excellent way to get information quickly about the IDE and its features. It provides a list of articles pertaining to the "current content" (i.e., the items around the location of the mouse cursor). To open the **Dynamic Help** window, select **Help > Dynamic Help**. Then, when you click a word or component (such as a form or a control), links to relevant help articles appear in the **Dynamic Help** window. The window lists help topics, code samples and "Getting Started" information. There is also a toolbar that provides access to the **How Do I?**, **Search**, **Index** and **Contents** help features.

Visual Studio also provides *context-sensitive help*, which is similar to dynamic help, except that it immediately displays a relevant help article rather than presenting a list of articles. To use context-sensitive help, click an item, such as the form, and press the *F1* key. Figure 2.25 displays help articles related to a form.

The **Help** options can be set in the **Options** dialog (accessed by selecting **Tools > Options...**). To display all the settings that you can modify (including the settings for the **Help** options), make sure that the **Show all settings** checkbox in the lower-left corner of the dialog is checked (Fig. 2.26). To change whether the **Help** is displayed in the IDE window or in a separate window, select **Help** on the left, then locate the **Show Help Using:** drop-down list on the right. Depending on your preference, selecting **External Help Viewer** displays a relevant help article in a separate window outside the IDE (some programmers like to view Web pages separately from the project on which they are working in the IDE); selecting **Integrated Help Viewer** displays a help article as a tabbed window inside the IDE.

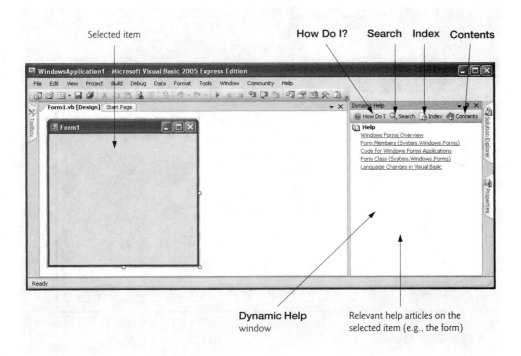

Fig. 2.24 | **Dynamic Help** window.

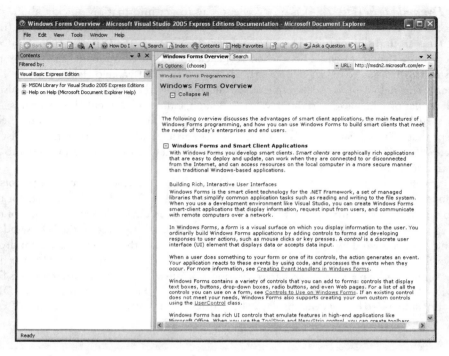

Fig. 2.25 | Using context-sensitive help.

Show all settings check box

Fig. 2.26 | **Options** dialog displaying **Help** settings.

2.6 Using Visual Programming to Create a Simple Program that Displays Text and an Image

In this section, we create a program that displays the text "Welcome to Visual Basic!" and an image of the Deitel & Associates bug mascot. The program consists of a single form that uses a Label and a PictureBox. Figure 2.27 shows the result of the program as it executes. The program and the bug image are available with this chapter's examples. You can download the examples from www.deitel.com/books/vbforprogrammers2/index.html. Please read the Before You Begin section of the Preface to ensure that you install the examples correctly on your computer.

To create the program whose output is shown in Fig. 2.27, you will not write a single line of program code. Instead, you will use the techniques of visual programming. Visual Studio processes programmer actions (such as mouse clicking, dragging and dropping) to generate program code. Chapter 3 begins our discussion of writing program code. Throughout the book, you produce increasingly substantial and powerful programs that usually include a combination of code written by you and code generated by Visual Studio. The generated code can be difficult for novices to understand—fortunately programmers rarely need to look at this code.

Visual programming is useful for building GUI-intensive programs that require a significant amount of user interaction. Visual programming cannot be used to create programs that do not have GUIs—you must write such code directly.

To create, run and terminate this first program, perform the following steps:

1. *Create the new project.* If a project is already open, close it by selecting **File > Close Solution**. A dialog asking whether to save the current project might appear. Click **Save** to save any changes. To create a new Windows application for the program, select **File > New Project...** to display the **New Project** dialog (Fig. 2.28). From the template options, select **Windows Application**. Name the project **ASimpleProgram** and click **OK**. [*Note:* File names must conform to certain rules. For example, file

Fig. 2.27 | Simple program executing.

Template types

Type in the project name

Fig. 2.28 | **New Project** dialog.

names cannot contain symbols (e.g., ?, :, *, <, >, # and %) or Unicode® control characters (Unicode is a special character set described in Appendix E). Also, file names cannot be system reserved names, such as "CON", "PRN", "AUX" and "COM1" or "." and "..", and cannot be longer than 256 characters in length.] We mentioned earlier in this chapter that you must set the directory in which the project will be saved. In the complete Visual Studio, you do this in the **New Project** dialog. To specify the directory in Visual Basic 2005 Express, select **File > Save All** to display the **Save Project** *dialog* (Fig. 2.29). To set the project location, click the **Browse...** button, which opens the **Project Location** *dialog* (Fig. 2.30). Navigate through the directories, select one in which to place the project (in our example, we use a directory named **My Projects**) and click **OK** to close the dialog. Click **Save** in the **Save Project** dialog (Fig. 2.29) to save the project and close the dialog.

Fig. 2.29 | **Save Project** dialog.

Fig. 2.30 | Setting the project location in the **Project Location** dialog.

When you first begin working in the IDE, it is in ***design mode*** (i.e., the program is being designed and is not executing). While the IDE is in design mode, programmers have access to all the environment windows (e.g., **Toolbox**, **Properties**), menus and toolbars, as you will see shortly.

2. *Set the text in the form's title bar.* The text in the form's title bar is determined by the form's ***Text property*** (Fig. 2.31). If the **Properties** window is not open, click the properties icon in the toolbar or select **View > Properties Window**. Click anywhere in the form to display the form's properties in the **Properties** window. Click in the textbox to the right of the Text property box and type "A Simple Program," as in Fig. 2.31. Press the *Enter* key (*Return* key) when finished; the form's title bar is updated immediately (Fig. 2.32).

Fig. 2.31 | Setting the form's Text property in the **Properties** window.

Fig. 2.32 | Form with enabled sizing handles.

3. *Resize the form.* Click and drag one of the form's ***enabled sizing handles*** (the small white squares that appear around the form, as shown in Fig. 2.32). Using the mouse, select the bottom-right sizing handle and drag it down and to the right to make the form larger (Fig. 2.33).

4. *Change the form's background color.* The ***BackColor property*** specifies a form's or control's background color. Clicking BackColor in the **Properties** window causes a down-arrow button to appear next to the value of the property (Fig. 2.34). When clicked, the down-arrow button displays a set of other options, which vary depending on the property. In this case, the arrow displays tabs for **Custom**, **Web** and **System** (the default). Click the ***Custom tab*** to display the *palette* (a grid of colors). Select the box that represents light blue. Once you select the color, the palette closes and the form's background color changes to light blue (Fig. 2.35).

Fig. 2.33 | Resized form.

Fig. 2.34 | Changing the form's BackColor property.

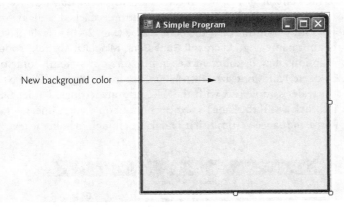

Fig. 2.35 | Form with new BackColor property applied.

5. *Add a Label control to the Form.* If the **Toolbox** is not already open, select **View > Toolbox** to display the set of controls you will use for creating your programs. For the type of program we are creating in this chapter, the typical controls we use will be located in either the **All Windows Forms** category of the **Toolbox** or the **Common Controls** group. If either group name is collapsed, expand it by clicking the plus sign (the **All Windows Forms** and **Common Controls** groups are shown in Fig. 2.21). Next, double click the Label control in the **Toolbox**. This action causes a label to appear in the upper-left corner of the form (Fig. 2.36). [*Note:* If the Form is behind the **Toolbox**, you may need to close the **Toolbox** to see the Label.] Although double clicking any **Toolbox** control places the control on the form, you also can "drag" controls from the **Toolbox** to the form (you may prefer dragging the control because you can position it wherever you want). Our Label displays the text **Label1** by default. Note that our Label's background color is the same as

the form's background color. When a control is added to the form, its BackColor property is set to the form's BackColor. You can change the Label's background color by changing its BackColor property.

6. *Customize the Label's appearance.* Select the Label by clicking it. Its properties now appear in the **Properties** window. The Label's Text property determines the text (if any) that the Label displays. The form and Label each have their own Text property—forms and controls can have the same types of properties (such as Back-Color, Text, etc.) without conflict. Set the Label's Text property to **Welcome to Visual Basic!**. Note that the Label resizes to fit all the typed text on one line. By default, the ***AutoSize property*** of the Label is set to True, which allows the Label to update its size to fit all of the text if necessary. Set the AutoSize property to False (Fig. 2.37) so that you can resize the Label on your own. Resize the Label (using the sizing handles) so that the text fits. Move the Label to the top center of the form by dragging it or by using the keyboard's left and right arrow keys to adjust its position (Fig. 2.38). Alternatively, when the Label is selected, you can center the Label control horizontally by selecting **Format > Center In Form > Horizontally**.

7. *Set the Label's font size.* To change the font type and appearance of the Label's text, select the value of the ***Font property***, which causes an ***ellipsis button*** (⬚) to appear next to the value (Fig. 2.39). When the ellipsis button is clicked, a dialog that provides additional values—in this case, the ***Font dialog*** (Fig. 2.40)—is displayed. You can select the font name (e.g., **Microsoft Sans Serif, MingLiU, Mistral, Modern No. 20**—the font options may be different depending on your system), font style (**Regular, Italic, Bold**, etc.) and font size (**16, 18, 20**, etc.) in this dialog. The text in the **Sample** area provides sample text with the selected font settings. Under **Size**, select **24** points and click **OK**. If the Label's text does not fit on a single line, it wraps to the next line. Resize the Label vertically if it's not large enough to hold the text.

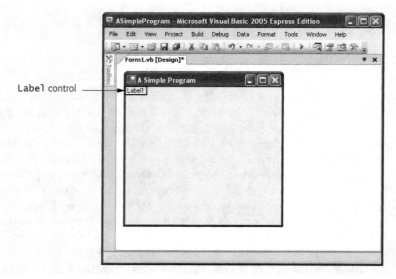

Label control

Fig. 2.36 | Adding a Label to the form.

Fig. 2.37 | Changing the Label's AutoSize property to False.

Fig. 2.38 | GUI after the form and Label have been customized.

Fig. 2.39 | **Properties** window displaying the Label's properties.

Current font

Font sample

Fig. 2.40 | **Font** dialog for selecting fonts, styles and sizes.

8. *Align the Label's text.* Select the Label's ***TextAlign*** property, which determines how the text is aligned within the Label. A three-by-three grid of buttons representing alignment choices is displayed (Fig. 2.41). The position of each button corresponds to where the text appears in the Label. For this program, set the TextAlign property to MiddleCenter in the three-by-three grid; this selection causes the text to appear centered in the middle of the Label, with equal spacing from the text to all sides of the Label. The other TextAlign values, such as TopLeft, TopRight, and BottomCenter, can be used to position the text anywhere within a Label. Certain alignment values may require that you resize the Label larger or smaller to better fit the text.

9. *Add a PictureBox to the form.* The PictureBox control displays images. The process involved in this step is similar to that of *Step 5*, in which we added a Label to the form. Locate the PictureBox in the **Toolbox** (Fig. 2.21) and double click it to add it to the form. When the PictureBox appears, move it underneath the Label, either by dragging it or by using the arrow keys (Fig. 2.42).

Text alignment options

Middle-center alignment option

Fig. 2.41 | Centering the Label's text.

Fig. 2.42 | Inserting and aligning a PictureBox.

10. *Insert an image.* Click the PictureBox to display its properties in the **Properties** window (Fig. 2.43). Locate the ***Image property***, which displays a preview of the image, if one exists. No picture has been assigned, so the value of the Image property displays **(none)**. Click the ellipsis button to display the **Select Resource dialog** (Fig. 2.44). This dialog is used to import files, such as images, to any program. Click the **Import...** button to browse for an image to insert. In our case, the picture is bug.png. In the dialog that appears, locate the image file, select it and click **OK**. The image is previewed in the **Select Resource** dialog (Fig. 2.45). Click **OK** to place the image in your program. Supported image formats include PNG (Portable Network Graphics), GIF (Graphic Interchange Format), JPEG (Joint Photographic Experts Group) and BMP (Windows bitmap). Creating a new image requires image-editing software, such as Jasc® Paint Shop Pro™ (www.jasc.com), Adobe® Photoshop™ Elements (www.adobe.com) or Microsoft Paint (provided with Windows). To size the image to the PictureBox, change the ***SizeMode property*** to ***StretchImage*** (Fig. 2.46), which scales the image to the size of the PictureBox. Resize the PictureBox, making it larger (Fig. 2.47).

Fig. 2.43 | Image property of the PictureBox.

Fig. 2.44 | **Select Resource** dialog to select an image for the PictureBox.

Image file name ⟶

Fig. 2.45 | **Select Resource** dialog displaying a preview of selected image.

SizeMode property ⟶

⟵ SizeMode property set to StretchImage

Fig. 2.46 | Scaling an image to the size of the PictureBox.

Fig. 2.47 | `PictureBox` displaying an image.

11. *Save the project.* Select **File > Save All** to save the entire solution. The solution file contains the name and location of its project, and the project file contains the names and locations of all the files in the project.

12. *Run the project.* Recall that up to this point we have been working in the IDE design mode (i.e., the program being created is not executing). In ***run mode***, the program is executing, and you can interact with only a few IDE features—features that are not available are disabled (grayed out). The text **Form1.vb [Design]*** in the project tab (Fig. 2.48) means that we are designing the form visually rather

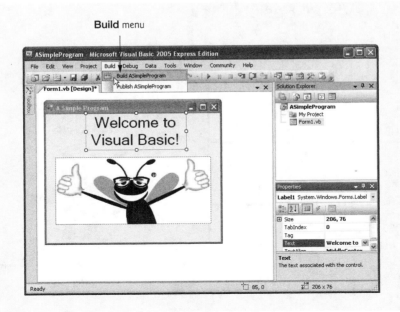

Fig. 2.48 | Building a solution.

than programmatically. If we had been writing code, the tab would have contained only the text **Form1.vb**. The * at the end of the text in the tab indicates that the file has been changed and should be saved. To run the program you must first build the solution. Select **Build > Build ASimpleProgram** to compile the project (Fig. 2.48). Once you build the solution (the IDE will display "**Build succeeded**" in the lower-left corner—also known as the status bar), select **Debug > Start Debugging** to execute the program (or you can select the *F5* key). Figure 2.49 shows the IDE in run mode (indicated by the title bar text **A Simple Program (Running) – Microsoft Visual Basic 2005 Express Edition**). Note that many toolbar icons and menus are disabled since they cannot be used while the program is running. The running program will appear in a separate window outside the IDE as shown in the lower-right portion of Fig. 2.49.

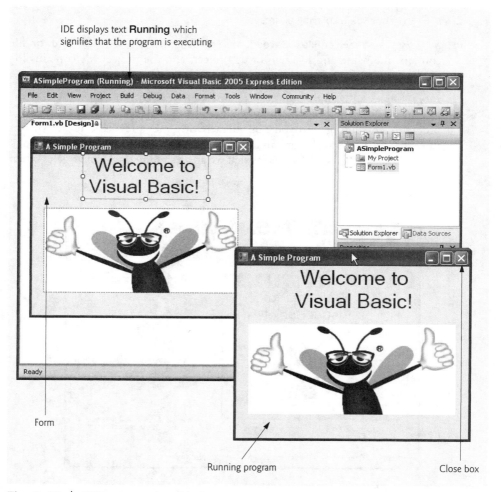

Fig. 2.49 | IDE in run mode, with the running program in the foreground.

13. *Terminate execution.* Click the running program's close box (the **X** in the top-right corner of the running program's window). This action stops the program's execution and returns the IDE to design mode.

2.7 Wrap-Up

In this chapter, we introduced key features of the Visual Studio Integrated Development Environment (IDE). You used the technique of visual programming to create a working Visual Basic program without writing a single line of code. Visual Basic programming is a mixture of the two styles—visual programming allows you to develop GUIs easily and avoid tedious GUI programming; conventional programming (which we introduce in Chapter 3) allows to specify the behavior of your programs.

You created a Visual Basic Windows application with one form. You worked with the **Solution Explorer**, **Toolbox** and **Properties** windows, which are essential to developing Visual Basic programs. The **Solution Explorer** window allows you to manage your solution's files visually. The **Toolbox** window contains a rich collection of controls for creating GUIs. The **Properties** window allows you to set the attributes of a form and controls.

You explored Visual Studio's help features, including the **Dynamic Help** window and the **Help** menu. The **Dynamic Help** window displays links related to the item that you select with the mouse. You also learned how to set **Help** options to display help resources internally or externally in a Web browser. We also demonstrated context-sensitive help.

You used visual programming to design the GUI portions of a program quickly and easily, by dragging and dropping controls (a `Label` and a `PictureBox`) onto a form or by double clicking controls in the **Toolbox**.

In creating the **ASimpleProgram** program, you used the **Properties** window to set the `Text` and `BackColor` properties of the form. You learned that `Label` controls display text and that `PictureBox`es display images. You displayed text in a `Label` and added an image to a `PictureBox`. You also worked with the `AutoSize`, `TextAlign` and `SizeMode` properties of a `Label`.

In the next chapter, we discuss "nonvisual," or "conventional," programming—you'll create your first programs that contain Visual Basic code that you write, instead of having Visual Studio write the code. You'll study console applications (programs that display only text and do not have a GUI). We'll discuss memory concepts, arithmetic, decision making and how to use a dialog to display a message.

2.8 Web Resources

`msdn.microsoft.com/vstudio`
Microsoft's Visual Studio site provides news, documentation, downloads and other resources.

`msdn.microsoft.com/vbasic/default.aspx`
This site provides information on the newest release of Visual Basic, including downloads, community information and resources.

`www.worldofdotnet.net`
This site offers Visual Studio news and links to newsgroups and other resources.

`www.vbi.org`
This site contains articles, reviews of books and software, documentation, downloads, links and searchable information on Visual Basic listed by subject.

www.devx.com/vb

This site has a dedicated zone for Visual Basic developers; it contains articles, opinions, newsgroups, code, tips and other resources discussing Visual Basic 2005.

www.visualbasicforum.com

This forum provides Visual Basic developers the opportunity to post their thoughts to the Visual Basic community, including opinions on new features, issues encountered, resource links and more.

Introduction to Visual Basic Programming

*Comment is free, but facts
are sacred.*
—C. P. Scott

*When faced with a decision,
I always ask, "What would
be the most fun?"*
—Peggy Walker

*Equality, in a social sense,
may be divided into that of
condition and that of rights.*
—James Fenimore Cooper

OBJECTIVES

In this chapter you will learn:

- To write simple Visual Basic programs using code rather than visual programming.
- To write statements that input data from the keyboard and output data to the screen.
- To declare and use data of various types.
- To store and retrieve data from memory.
- To use arithmetic operators to perform calculations.
- To use the precedence of arithmetic operators to determine the order in which operators are applied.
- To write decision-making statements.
- To use equality and relational operators to compare operands.
- To use message dialogs to display messages.

3.1 Introduction

In this chapter, we introduce Visual Basic programming with program code and present examples to demonstrate how programs can display messages and obtain information from the user at the keyboard for processing. The first two programs simply display text on the screen. The next obtains two numbers from the user, calculates their sum and displays the result. The accompanying discussion shows you how to perform various arithmetic calculations and save their results for later use. The fourth example demonstrates decision-making fundamentals by showing you how to compare two numbers in various ways, then display messages based on the comparison results. The final example demonstrates how to display text in a special window known as a message dialog.

We introduce *console applications*—that is, applications that do not have a graphical user interface. There are several types of Visual Basic projects (you have already seen Windows applications in Chapter 2); the console application is one of the simplest types. When a console application is executed in Visual Basic 2005 Express, its text output appears in the **Console window**. A console application can also be executed outside the IDE in a Windows **Command Prompt**. Programs can input and output information in a variety of ways. For example, in Chapter 2, we created a simple graphical user interface (GUI) for a Windows application, using visual programming techniques. We will briefly return to Windows applications in Chapter 5, Control Statements: Part 1 and Chapter 6, Control Statements: Part 2, respectively. These chapters provide a more detailed introduction to program development in Visual Basic. We discuss Windows applications in detail in Chapter 13, Graphical User Interface Concepts: Part 1 and Chapter 14, Graphical User Interface Concepts: Part 2.

3.2 Displaying a Line of Text

We begin by considering a simple program (Fig. 3.1) that displays a line of text. When this program runs, its output appears in a Command Prompt window. We show such output in

```
 1   ' Fig. 3.1: Welcome1.vb
 2   ' Simple Visual Basic program.
 3
 4   Module FirstWelcome
 5
 6      Sub Main()
 7
 8         Console.WriteLine("Welcome to Visual Basic!")
 9
10      End Sub ' Main
11
12   End Module ' FirstWelcome
```

```
Welcome to Visual Basic!
```

Fig. 3.1 | Simple Visual Basic program.

a blue box following the program listing. You will see what a Command Prompt window looks like later in this section, when we explain the process of creating a console application.

Analyzing the Program

This program illustrates several important Visual Basic features. For your convenience, all program listings in this text include line numbers—these are not part of the Visual Basic language. The line numbers help us refer to specific parts of a program. We will soon show how to display line numbers in program files. Each program is followed by one or more windows showing the program's execution output.

Line 1 of Fig. 3.1 begins with a *single-quote character* (') which indicates that the remainder of the line is a *comment*. Programmers insert comments in programs to improve the readability of the code—you can write anything you want in a comment. Comments can be placed either on their own lines (we call these "*full-line comments*") or at the end of a line of Visual Basic code (we call these "*end-of-line comments*"). The Visual Basic compiler ignores comments—they do not cause the computer to perform any actions when you run a program. The comment in line 1 simply indicates the figure number (Fig. 3.1) and the file name (Welcome1.vb) in which we stored this program. The comment in line 2 provides a brief description of the program. By convention, we begin every program in this manner (you can, of course, say anything you want in a comment).

Visual Basic console applications consist of pieces called *modules*, which are logical groupings of methods that simplify program organization. Lines 4–12 define our first module. These lines collectively are called a *module declaration*. We discuss the method in lines 6–10 momentarily—*methods* perform tasks and can return information when the tasks are completed. Every console application in Visual Basic consists of at least one module and one method in that module. In Chapter 7, Methods: A Deeper Look, we discuss methods in detail.

The word **Module** (line 4) is an example of a *keyword*. Keywords are words reserved for use by Visual Basic. A complete list of Visual Basic keywords is presented in Fig. 3.2. We discuss many of Visual Basic's keywords throughout this book. Visual Basic has a larger set of keywords than most other programming languages.

Visual Basic keywords			
AddHandler	AddressOf	Alias	And
AndAlso	Ansi	As	Assembly
Auto	Boolean	ByRef	Byte
ByVal	Call	Case	Catch
CBool	CByte	CChar	CDate
CDbl	CDec	Char	CInt
Class	CLng	CObj	Const
Continue	CSByte	CShort	CSng
CStr	CType	CUInt	CULng
CUShort	Date	Decimal	Declare
Default	Delegate	Dim	DirectCast
Do	Double	Each	Else
ElseIf	End	Enum	Erase
Error	Event	Exit	False
Finally	For	Friend	Function
Get	GetType	Global	GoTo
Handles	If	Implements	Imports
In	Inherits	Integer	Interface
Is	IsNot	Lib	Like
Long	Loop	Me	Mod
Module	MustInherit	MustOverride	MyBase
MyClass	Namespace	Narrowing	New
Next	Not	Nothing	NotInheritable
NotOverridable	Object	Of	On
Operator	Option	Optional	Or
OrElse	Overloads	Overridable	Overrides
ParamArray	Partial	Preserve	Private
Property	Protected	Public	RaiseEvent
ReadOnly	ReDim	REM	RemoveHandler
Resume	Return	SByte	Select
Set	Shadows	Shared	Short
Single	Static	Step	Stop
String	Structure	Sub	SyncLock
Then	Throw	To	True
Try	TryCast	TypeOf	UInteger

Fig. 3.2 | Keywords in Visual Basic. (Part 1 of 2.)

Visual Basic keywords			
ULong	*Unicode*	*Until*	*UShort*
Using	*When*	*While*	*Widening*
With	*WithEvents*	*WriteOnly*	*Xor*
The following are retained as keywords, although they are no longer supported in Visual Basic 2005			
EndIf	*GoSub*	*Let*	*Variant*	*Wend*

Fig. 3.2 | Keywords in Visual Basic. (Part 2 of 2.)

The name of the Module—FirstWelcome in line 4—is known as an ***identifier***, which is a series of characters consisting of letters, digits and underscores (_). Identifiers cannot begin with a digit and cannot contain spaces. Examples of valid identifiers are value1, FirstWelcome, xy_coordinate, _total and grossPay. The name 7Welcome is not a valid identifier because it begins with a digit, and the name input field is not a valid identifier because it contains a space.

Common Programming Error 3.1

Identifiers cannot be keywords, so it is an error, for example, to choose any of the words in Fig. 3.2 as a Module name. Though keywords cannot be used as identifiers, they can be used in strings and comments.

Visual Basic keywords and identifiers are not case sensitive—uppercase and lowercase letters are considered to be identical, which causes firstwelcome and FirstWelcome to be interpreted as the same identifier. Although keywords appear to be case sensitive, they are not. Visual Basic Express applies its "preferred" case (i.e., the casing used in Fig. 3.2) to each letter of a keyword, so when you type module and press the *Enter* key, Visual Basic changes the lowercase m to uppercase, as in Module, even though module would be perfectly correct.

Lines 3, 5, 7, 9 and 11 (Fig. 3.1) are blank lines. Blank lines, space characters and tab characters are used throughout a program to make it easier to read. Collectively, these are called whitespace characters.

Line 6 is present in all Visual Basic console applications. These begin executing at **Main**, which is known as the ***entry point of the program***. The keyword Sub that appears before Main indicates that Main is a method.

Note that lines 6–10 are indented three spaces relative to lines 4 and 12. Indentation improves program readability. We refer to spacing conventions that enhance program clarity as *Good Programming Practices*. We show how to set the indent size in Visual Basic Express shortly.

The keyword ***Sub*** (line 6) begins the body of the method declaration. The keywords ***End Sub*** (line 10) close the method declaration's body. The keyword Sub is short for "subroutine"—an early term for method. Note that the line of code (line 8) in the method body is indented three additional spaces to the right relative to lines 6 and 10. This emphasizes that line 8 is part of the Main method's body.

Good Programming Practice 3.1

Indent the entire body of each method declaration one additional "level" of indentation. This emphasizes the structure of the method, improving its readability. In this text, one level of indentation is set to three spaces—this keeps the code readable yet concise.

Using `Console.WriteLine` to Display Text

Line 8 in Fig. 3.1 does the "real work" of the program, displaying the phrase `Welcome to Visual Basic!` on the screen. Characters and the surrounding double quotes are called *strings*, *character strings* or *string literals*.

The entire line, including `Console.WriteLine` and its string in the parentheses, is called a *statement*. When this statement executes, it *displays* (or *prints*) the message `Welcome to Visual Basic!` in the **Console** window (Fig. 3.1).

Note that `Console.WriteLine` contains two identifiers (i.e., `Console` and `WriteLine`) separated by the *dot separator* (.). The identifier to the right of the dot separator is the *method name*, and the identifier to the left of the dot separator is the *class name* to which the method belongs. *Classes* organize groups of related methods and data; *methods* perform tasks and can return information when the tasks are completed. For instance, the **`Console` *class*** contains methods, such as **`WriteLine`**, that communicate with users via the **Console** window. The statement in line 8 is a method call—it invokes method `WriteLine` of class `Console`. In Fig. 3.1, the string in parentheses in line 8 is the argument to method `WriteLine`.

When method `WriteLine` completes its task, it positions the output cursor at the beginning of the next line in the **Console** window. Program execution terminates when the program encounters the keywords `End Sub` in line 10. The `Module` is a package that contains the program's methods; the methods contain the statements that perform the actions of the program.

3.3 Creating A Console Application in Visual Basic Express

Now that we have presented our first console application (Fig. 3.1), we provide a step-by-step explanation of how to create and run it using Visual Basic 2005 Express.

Creating the Console Application

Select **File > New Project...** to display the **New Project** dialog (Fig. 3.3). Click **Console Application** to ensure that it is selected in the section labeled **Visual Studio installed templates**. In the dialog's **Name** field, type `Welcome1`. Click **OK** to create the project. The IDE now contains the open console application, as shown in Fig. 3.4. Note that the editor window contains four lines of Visual Basic code provided by the IDE. The code coloring scheme used by the IDE is called *syntax-color highlighting* and helps you visually differentiate program elements. Keywords appear in blue and other text is black. When present, comments are colored green. In this book, we syntax shade our code similarly—bold italic for keywords, italic for comments, bold gray for literals and constants and black for other text. One example of a literal is the string passed to `Console.WriteLine` in line 8 of Fig. 3.1. You can customize the colors shown in the code editor by selecting **Tools > Options...** and clicking the **Show all settings** checkbox. Then click the plus sign, +, next to **Environment** and select **Fonts and Colors**. Here you can change the colors for various code elements.

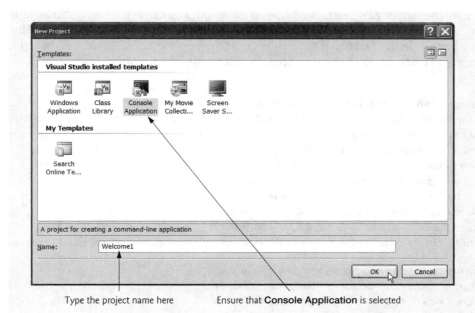

Type the project name here   Ensure that **Console Application** is selected

Fig. 3.3 | Creating a **Console Application** with the **New Project** dialog.

Editor window
(type your program code here)

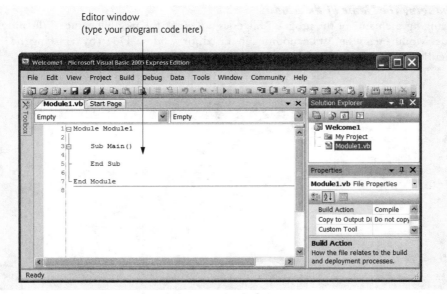

Fig. 3.4 | IDE with an open console application.

Modifying the Editor Settings to Display Line Numbers
Visual Basic 2005 Express provides many ways to personalize your coding experience. In this step, we specify how to change the settings so that your code matches that of this book.

To have the IDE display line numbers, select **Tools > Options...**. In the dialog that appears (Fig. 3.5), ensure that the **Show all settings** check box in the lower left corner of the dialog is unchecked. In the **Text Editor Basic** category of the left pane, select **Editor**. On the right, check the **Line Numbers** check box. Keep the **Options** dialog open for the next step.

Setting Code Indentation to Three Spaces per Indent

In the **Options** dialog that you opened in the previous step, enter **3** for both the **Tab Size** and **Indent Size** fields (Fig. 3.5). Any new code you add will now use three spaces for each level of indentation. Click **OK** to save your settings, close the dialog and return to the editor window. Note that lines 3 and 5 (Fig. 3.4) are still indented four spaces because this code was created before we changed the indentation settings. Go to line 3 and move the code back one space to conform to our new convention, then move the cursor to the next line of code. After you do this, line 5 updates its indentation to match that of line 3. As you create applications in this book, Visual Basic Express will often update code to conform to various code conventions and the latest settings specified in Visual Basic Express.

Changing the Name of the Program File

For programs in this book, we change the name of the program file (i.e., `Module1.vb`) to a more descriptive name for each application we develop. To rename the file, click `Module1.vb` in the **Solution Explorer** window. This displays the program file's properties in the **Properties** window (Fig. 3.6). Change the *File Name* property to `Welcome1.vb`.

Changing the Name of the Module

Changing the name of the program file does not affect the module name in the program code. Module names must be modified in the editor window. Do so by replacing the identifier `Module1` in the code with `FirstWelcome`.

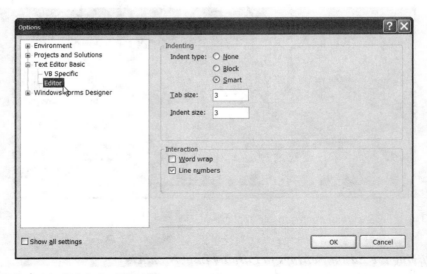

Fig. 3.5 | Modifying the IDE settings.

Fig. 3.6 | Renaming the program file in the **Properties** window.

Setting the Startup Object

Each Visual Basic project has a *startup object* that specifies where the application begins executing. Now that we have modified the name of the module where Main resides, we need to update the application's startup object as well. In the **Solution Explorer** window, double click the **My Project** item (near the top of Fig. 3.6). A page appears (Fig. 3.7) where you can set several properties of your application. Select **FirstWelcome** (our new module name) from the **Startup object** drop-down list.

Writing Code

Click the **Welcome1.vb** tab in the IDE to view the editor window. In the editor window (Fig. 3.4), add the comments from lines 1 and 2 of Fig. 3.1. Then type the code contained in line 8 of Fig. 3.1 between the lines Sub Main() and End Sub. After you type the class name and the dot separator (i.e., Console.), a window containing a scrollbar is displayed (Fig. 3.8). This IDE feature, called *IntelliSense*, lists a class's *members*, which include method names. Note that tabs (**All** and **Common**) are provided so that you can view either all available class members or only those that are commonly used. As you type characters, Visual Basic Express highlights the first member that matches all the characters typed, then displays a tool tip containing a description of that member. You can either type the complete member name (e.g., WriteLine), double click the member name in the member list or press the *Tab* key to complete the name. Once the complete name is provided, the *IntelliSense* window closes. When you type the open parenthesis character, (, after Console.WriteLine, the *Parameter Info* window is displayed (Fig. 3.9). This window contains information about the method's parameters. We'll see in Chapter 7 that there can be several versions of a method—that is, a class or module can define several methods that have the same name as long as they have different numbers and/or types of parameters.

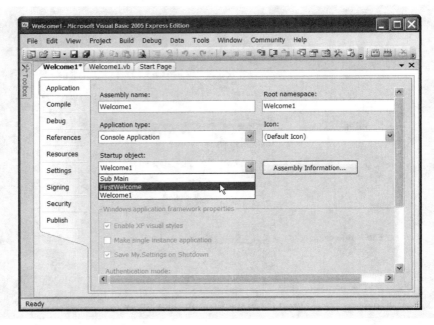

Fig. 3.7 | Setting the startup object.

Fig. 3.8 | *IntelliSense* feature of Visual Basic Express.

Generally, these methods all perform similar tasks, although they are not required to. The *Parameter Info* window indicates how many versions of the selected method are available and provides up and down arrows for scrolling through the different versions. For example,

Fig. 3.9 | *Parameter Info* window.

there are 18 versions of the WriteLine method—we use one of these 18 versions in our program. The *Parameter Info* window is one of the many features provided by the IDE that help you develop programs. The *Parameter Info* window is especially helpful when you want to see the different ways in which a method can be used. From the code in Fig. 3.1, we already know that we intend to display a string with WriteLine, so you can simply close the *Parameter Info* window by pressing the *Esc* key. Finish entering line 8, as well as the comments in lines 10 and 12 of Fig. 3.1.

Saving the Program

Select **File > Save All** to display the **Save Project** dialog (Fig. 3.10). In the **Location** text box, specify the directory where you want to save this project. We choose to save the project in the MyProjects directory on the C: drive. Select the **Create directory for Solution** check box, and click **Save**.

Compiling and Running the Program

You are now ready to compile and execute your program. To compile the program, select **Build > Build Welcome1**. This creates a new file (named Welcome1.exe, in the project's directory structure) that contains the Microsoft Intermediate Language (MSIL) code for the program. The *.exe file extension* indicates that the file is *executable*.

To execute this console application (i.e., Welcome1.exe), select **Debug > Start Debugging**, which invokes the Main method. The statement in line 8 of Main displays Welcome to Visual Basic!, however, the window disappears immediately. Figure 3.11 shows the results of the program's execution. To enable the window to remain on the screen so you can view the results, you can use the **Debug** menu's **Start Without Debugging** option. This

Fig. 3.10 | **Save Project** dialog.

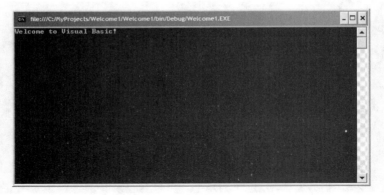

Fig. 3.11 | Executing the program shown in Fig. 3.1.

option is not in the menu by default, so you must add it. To do so, select **Tools > Customize....** In the **Commands** tab of the dialog that appears, select **Debug** from the **Categories** pane, then locate **Start Without Debugging** in the **Commands** pane. Drag the **Start Without Debugging** option over the **Debug** menu in the IDE (which will open the menu), then position the mouse just below the **Start / Continue** option and release the mouse button. Click **Close** to dismiss the **Customize** dialog. You can now execute the program using the select **Debug > Start Without Debugging** option. The window showing the results will remain on the screen until you press a key or click the window's close box. Leave the application open in Visual Basic Express, as we will return to it later in this section.

Running the Program from the Command Prompt

As we mentioned at the beginning of this chapter, you can execute applications outside the IDE in a **Command Prompt**. This is useful when you simply want to run an application rather than open it for modification. To open the **Command Prompt**, click the Windows **Start** button, then select **All Programs > Accessories > Command Prompt**. The window (Fig. 3.12) displays copyright information followed by a prompt that indicates the current directory. By default, the prompt specifies the current user's directory on the local machine

Default prompt displays when
Command Prompt is opened

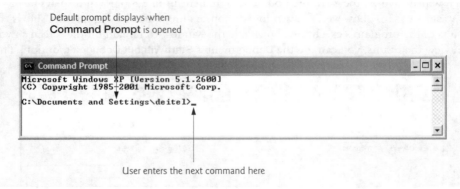

User enters the next command here

Fig. 3.12 | Executing the program shown in Fig. 3.1 from a **Command Prompt**.

(in our case, C:\Documents and Settings\deitel). On your machine, the folder name de-itel will be replaced with your username. A flashing cursor appears at the end of the prompt to indicate that the **Command Prompt** window is waiting for you to type a command. Enter the command cd (which stands for "change directory") followed by the directory where the application's .exe file is located (i.e., the bin\Release directory of your application). For example, the command cd C:\MyProjects\Welcome1\Welcome1\ bin\Release (Fig. 3.13) changes the current directory to the Welcome1 application's bin\Release directory. The next prompt displays the new directory followed by the flashing cursor. After changing to the proper directory, you can run the compiled application by entering the name of the .exe file (i.e., Welcome1.exe). The application will run to completion, then the prompt will display again, awaiting the next command. To close the **Command Prompt**, type exit and press *Enter*. [*Note:* Many environments show **Command Prompt** windows with black backgrounds and white text. We adjusted these settings in our environment to make our screen captures more readable.]

Syntax Errors, Error Messages and the Error List *Window*

Go back to the application in Visual Basic Express. When you type a line of code and press the *Enter* key, the IDE responds either by applying syntax-color highlighting or by generating a syntax error. When a syntax error occurs, the IDE underlines the error in blue and provides a description of the error in the ***Error List** window*. If the **Error List** window is not visible in the IDE, select **View > Error List** to display it. In Fig. 3.14, we intentionally omitted the first parenthesis in line 8. The first error contains the text "**Method arguments must be enclosed in parentheses.**" and specifies that the error is in column 25 of line 8. This informs the programmer that one or more parentheses are missing in line 8. The second error—"**End of statement expected.**"—specifies that this error is in column 50 of line 8. This error message appears when the compiler thinks that the line contains a complete statement, followed by the beginning of another statement. Visual Basic allows only one statement per line. Although we are attempting to include only one statement in line 8, the missing parenthesis causes the compiler to incorrectly assume that there is more than one statement on that line.

Fig. 3.13 | Executing the program shown in Fig. 3.1 from a **Command Prompt**.

Omitted parenthesis character (syntax error)

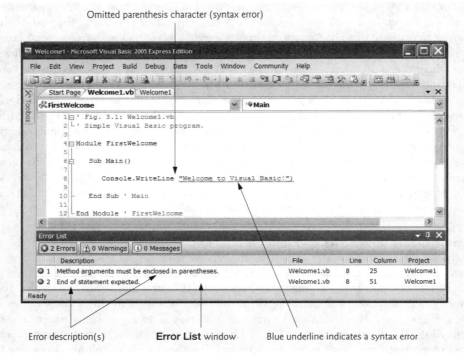

Error description(s)   **Error List** window   Blue underline indicates a syntax error

Fig. 3.14 | Syntax error indicated by the IDE.

Error-Prevention Tip 3.1

*One syntax error can lead to multiple entries in the **Error List** window. Each error that you address could eliminate several subsequent error messages when you recompile your program. So, when you see a particular error you know how to fix, correct it and recompile—this may make the other errors disappear.*

3.4 Displaying a Single Line of Text with Multiple Statements

The message `Welcome to Visual Basic!` can be displayed using multiple statements. Figure 3.15 uses two method calls to produce the same output as the program in Fig. 3.1.

Lines 8–9 of Fig. 3.15 display only one line of text in the **Console** window. The first statement calls `Console` method *`Write`* to display a string. Unlike `WriteLine`, `Write` does not position the output cursor at the beginning of the next line in the **Console** window after displaying its string. Instead, the next character displayed in the **Console** window appears immediately to the right of the last character displayed with `Write`. Thus, when line 9 executes, the first character displayed ("V") appears immediately after the last character displayed with `Write` (i.e., the space character after the word "to" in line 8). Each `Write` or `WriteLine` outputs its characters at the exact location where the previous `Write`'s or `WriteLine`'s output ended.

```
 1    ' Fig. 3.15: Welcome2.vb
 2    ' Displaying a line of text with multiple statements.
 3
 4    Module SecondWelcome
 5
 6       Sub Main()
 7
 8          Console.Write("Welcome to ")
 9          Console.WriteLine("Visual Basic!")
10
11       End Sub ' Main
12
13    End Module ' SecondWelcome
```

```
Welcome to Visual Basic!
```

Fig. 3.15 | Displaying a line of text with multiple statements.

3.5 Adding Integers

Our next program (Fig. 3.16) inputs two integers (whole numbers) entered at the keyboard by a user, computes the sum of these integers and displays the result. As the user enters each integer and presses the *Enter* key, the integer is read into the program and added to the total.

Lines 9–11 are declarations, which begin with keyword *Dim* (a contraction of the word "dimension"). The words number1, number2 and total are the names of variables. All variables must be declared before they can be used in a program. The declarations in lines 9–11 specify that the variables number1, number2 and total are data of type *Integer*; that is, these variables store integer values. Types already defined in Visual Basic, such as Integer, are known as *primitive types*. Primitive type names are keywords. The 15 primitive types are listed in Fig. 3.17 and discussed further in Chapter 7. Recall that keywords cannot be used as identifiers.

```
 1    ' Fig. 3.16: Addition.vb
 2    ' Addition program.
 3
 4    Module Addition
 5
 6       Sub Main()
 7
 8          ' variables used in the addition calculation
 9          Dim number1 As Integer
10          Dim number2 As Integer
11          Dim total As Integer
12
13          ' prompt for and read the first number from the user
14          Console.Write("Please enter the first integer: ")
15          number1 = Console.ReadLine()
16
```

Fig. 3.16 | Addition program that adds two integers entered by the user. (Part 1 of 2.)

```
17            ' prompt for and read the second number from the user
18            Console.Write("Please enter the second integer: ")
19            number2 = Console.ReadLine()
20
21            total = number1 + number2 ' add the numbers
22
23            Console.WriteLine("The sum is " & total) ' display the sum
24
25        End Sub ' Main
26
27    End Module ' Addition
```

```
Please enter the first integer: 45
Please enter the second integer: 72
The sum is 117
```

Fig. 3.16 | Addition program that adds two integers entered by the user. (Part 2 of 2.)

Primitive Types		
Boolean	*Byte*	*Char*
Date	*Decimal*	*Double*
Integer	*Long*	*SByte*
Short	*Single*	*String*
UInteger	*ULong*	*UShort*

Fig. 3.17 | Primitive types in Visual Basic.

A variable name can be any valid identifier. Variables of the same type can be declared in separate statements or they can be declared in one statement with each variable in the declaration separated by a comma. The latter format uses a comma-separated list of variable names.

Good Programming Practice 3.2

A common convention (and the one used in this book) is to have the first word in a variable-name identifier begin with a lowercase letter. Every word in the name after the first word should begin with a uppercase letter. For example, identifier firstNumber *has a capital* N *beginning its second word,* Number. *We use a similar convention for module names, except that the first letter of the first word is also capitalized. Although identifiers are not case sensitive, using these conventions helps make your programs more readable. In this book, we use widely adopted Visual Basic naming conventions.*

Good Programming Practice 3.3

Declaring each variable on a separate line allows for easy insertion of an end-of-line comment next to each declaration. We will follow this convention.

Line 14 prompts the user to enter the first of two integers that will be summed. Line 15 obtains the value entered by the user and assigns it to variable number1. The method **ReadLine** (line 15) causes the program to pause and wait for user input. After entering the integer via the keyboard, the user presses the *Enter* key to send the integer to the program.

Once the user has entered a number and pressed *Enter*, the number is assigned to variable number1 (line 15) by an assignment, =. Lines 18–19 prompt the user to enter a second integer and assign the entered value to number2.

Good Programming Practice 3.4

Place spaces on either side of a binary operator to make the operator stand out and improve the readability of the statement.

Technically, the user can send any character to the program as input. For this program, if the user types a non-integer value, such as "hello," a run-time error occurs (Fig. 3.18). Chapter 12, Exception Handling, discusses how to handle such errors to make programs more robust—that is, able to handle run-time errors and continue executing.

The assignment statement in line 21 (Fig. 3.16) calculates the sum of the Integer variables number1 and number2 and assigns the result to variable total. Line 23 displays the total of the two values. The argument to method WriteLine

```
"The sum is " & total
```

uses the ***string concatenation operator***, **&**, to combine the string literal "The sum is " and the value of the variable total (the Integer variable containing the sum calculated in line 21). The string concatenation operator combines two strings (i.e., to join them together). This operation results in a new, longer string. If an operand given to the string concatenation operator is a number (e.g., an integer), the program automatically creates a string representation of the number.

When reading or writing a program, you may find it difficult to match End Sub statements with their method declarations. For this reason, you may want to include an end-of-line comment after End Sub (indicating which method is ending), as we do in line 25. This practice is especially helpful when modules contain multiple methods.

Good Programming Practice 3.5

Follow a method's End Sub with an end-of-line comment containing the name of the method that the End Sub terminates.

Fig. 3.18 | Dialog displaying a run-time error.

3.6 Arithmetic

The arithmetic operators are summarized in Fig. 3.19. The asterisk (*) indicates multiplication, and the keyword *Mod* represents the *Mod operator* (also known as the *modulus* or *modulo operator*), which will be discussed shortly. Most of the arithmetic operators in Fig. 3.19 are binary operators. For example, the expression sum + value contains the binary operator + and the two operands sum and value. Visual Basic also provides unary operators that take only one operand. For example, unary versions of plus (+) and minus (–) are provided, so that programmers can write expressions such as +9 and –19.

Division Operators

Visual Basic has separate operators for integer division (the backslash, \) and floating-point division (the forward slash, /). Integer division takes two Integer operands and yields an Integer result; for example, the expression 7 \ 4 evaluates to 1, and the expression 17 \ 5 evaluates to 3. Any fractional part in an Integer division result simply is truncated (i.e., discarded)—no rounding occurs. When floating-point numbers such as 2.3456 and –845.7840 are used with the integer division operator, the numbers are first rounded to the nearest whole number, then divided. This means that, although 7.1 \ 4 evaluates to 1 as expected, the statement 7.7 \ 4 evaluates to 2, because 7.7 is rounded to 8 before the division occurs. To divide floating-point numbers without rounding the operands (which is normally what you want to do), use the floating-point division operator.

Common Programming Error 3.2

Using the integer division operator (\) when the floating-point division operator (/) is expected (i.e., when one or both of the operands is a floating-point value) can lead to incorrect results.

Error-Prevention Tip 3.2

Ensure that each integer division operator has only integer operands.

Visual Basic operation	Arithmetic operator	Algebraic expression	Visual Basic expression
Addition	+	$f + 7$	f + 7
Subtraction	–	$p - c$	p - c
Multiplication	*	bm	b * m
Division (floating point)	/	x/y or $\frac{x}{y}$ or $x \div y$	x / y
Division (integer)	\	none	v \ u
Modulus	Mod	$r \bmod s$	r Mod s
Exponentiation	^	q^p	q ^ p
Unary minus	–	$-e$	-e
Unary plus	+	$+g$	+g

Fig. 3.19 | Arithmetic operators.

Mod Operator

The Mod operator yields the remainder after division. The expression x Mod y yields the remainder after x is divided by y. Thus, 7 Mod 4 yields 3, and 17 Mod 5 yields 2. We will use this operator mostly with Integer operands, but it also can be used with other types. In later chapters, we consider interesting applications of the Mod operator, such as determining whether one number is a multiple of another.

Rules of Operator Precedence

Visual Basic applies the operators in arithmetic expressions in a precise sequence determined by the following rules of operator precedence, which are similar to those followed in algebra:

1. Exponentiation is applied first. If an expression contains several exponentiation operations, they are applied from left to right.

2. Unary plus and minus, + and - (also called *sign operations*), are applied next. If an expression contains several sign operations, they are applied from left to right. Sign operations + and - have the same level of precedence.

3. Multiplication and floating-point division operations are applied next. If an expression contains several multiplication and floating-point division operations, they are applied from left to right. Multiplication and floating-point division have the same level of precedence.

4. Integer division is applied next. If an expression contains several Integer division operations, they are applied from left to right.

5. Modulus operations are applied next. If an expression contains several modulus operations, they are applied from left to right.

6. Addition and subtraction operations are applied last. If an expression contains several addition and subtraction operations, they are applied from left to right. Addition and subtraction have the same level of precedence.

Operators in expressions contained within a pair of parentheses are evaluated before those that are outside a pair of parentheses. Parentheses can be used to group expressions and change the order of evaluation to occur *in any sequence desired by the programmer*. With nested parentheses, the operators contained in the innermost pair of parentheses are applied first.

The rules of operator precedence enable Visual Basic to apply operators in expressions in the correct order. When we say operators are applied from left to right, we are referring to the *associativity* of the operators. All binary operators in Visual Basic associate from left to right. If there are multiple operators, each with the same precedence, the order in which the operators are applied is determined by the operators' associativity. Figure 3.20 summarizes the rules of operator precedence. This table will be expanded as we introduce additional operators in subsequent chapters. Appendix A contains a complete operator-precedence chart.

Operator(s)	Operation	Order of evaluation (precedence)
^	Exponentiation	Evaluated first. If there are several such operators, they are evaluated from left to right.
+, −	Sign operations	Evaluated second. If there are several such operators, they are evaluated from left to right.
*, /	Multiplication and Division	Evaluated third. If there are several such operators, they are evaluated from left to right.
\	Integer division	Evaluated fourth. If there are several such operators, they are evaluated from left to right.
Mod	Modulus	Evaluated fifth. If there are several such operators, they are evaluated from left to right.
+, −	Addition and Subtraction	Evaluated sixth. If there are several such operators, they are evaluated from left to right.

Fig. 3.20 | Precedence of arithmetic operators.

3.7 Decision Making: Equality and Relational Operators

This section introduces Visual Basic's *If...Then* statement, which allows a program to make a decision based on the truth or falsity of some expression. The expression in an If...Then statement is called a *condition.* If the condition is met (i.e., the condition is true), the statement in the If...Then statement's body executes. If the condition is not met (i.e., the condition is false), the body statement is not executed. Conditions in If...Then statements can be formed by using the *equality operators* and *relational operators* (also called *comparison operators*), which are summarized in Fig. 3.21. The relational and equality operators all have the same level of precedence and associate from left to right.

Standard algebraic equality operator or relational operator	Visual Basic equality or relational operator	Example of Visual Basic condition	Meaning of Visual Basic condition
Equality operators			
=	=	x = y	x is equal to y
≠	<>	x <> y	x is not equal to y
Relational operators			
>	>	x > y	x is greater than y
<	<	x < y	x is less than y

Fig. 3.21 | Equality and relational operators. (Part 1 of 2.)

Standard algebraic equality operator or relational operator	Visual Basic equality or relational operator	Example of Visual Basic condition	Meaning of Visual Basic condition
≥	>=	x >= y	x is greater than or equal to y
≤	<=	x <= y	x is less than or equal to y

Fig. 3.21 | Equality and relational operators. (Part 2 of 2.)

Common Programming Error 3.3

It is a syntax error to reverse the symbols in the operators <>, >= and <= (as in ><, =>, =<).

The next example uses six If...Then statements to compare two numbers entered into a program by the user. If the condition in any of these statements is true, the output statement associated with that If...Then executes. The user enters these values, which are stored in variables number1 and number2, respectively. The comparisons are performed, and the results of the comparison are displayed in the **Console** window. The program and outputs are shown in Fig. 3.22.

```
1   ' Fig. 3.26: Comparison.vb
2   ' Using equality and relational operators.
3
4   Module Comparison
5
6      Sub Main()
7
8         ' declare Integer variables for user input
9         Dim number1 As Integer
10        Dim number2 As Integer
11
12        ' read first number from user
13        Console.Write("Please enter first integer: ")
14        number1 = Console.ReadLine()
15
16        ' read second number from user
17        Console.Write("Please enter second integer: ")
18        number2 = Console.ReadLine()
19
20        If number1 = number2 Then ' number1 is equal to number2
21           Console.WriteLine(number1 & " = " & number2)
22        End If
23
24        If number1 <> number2 Then ' number1 is not equal to number2
25           Console.WriteLine(number1 & " <> " & number2)
26        End If
27
```

Fig. 3.22 | Performing comparisons with equality and relational operators. (Part 1 of 2.)

```
28          If number1 < number2 Then ' number1 is less than number2
29              Console.WriteLine(number1 & " < " & number2)
30          End If
31
32          If number1 > number2 Then ' number1 is greater than number2
33              Console.WriteLine(number1 & " > " & number2)
34          End If
35
36          ' number1 is less than or equal to number2
37          If number1 <= number2 Then
38              Console.WriteLine(number1 & " <= " & number2)
39          End If
40
41          ' number1 is greater than or equal to number2
42          If number1 >= number2 Then
43              Console.WriteLine(number1 & " >= " & number2)
44          End If
45
46       End Sub ' Main
47
48    End Module ' Comparison
```

```
Please enter first integer: 1000
Please enter second integer: 2000
1000 <> 2000
1000 < 2000
1000 <= 2000
```

```
Please enter first integer: 515
Please enter second integer: 49
515 <> 49
515 > 49
515 >= 49
```

```
Please enter first integer: 333
Please enter second integer: 333
333 = 333
333 <= 333
333 >= 333
```

Fig. 3.22 | Performing comparisons with equality and relational operators. (Part 2 of 2.)

The If...Then statement in lines 20–22 compares the values of the variables number1 and number2 for equality. If the values are equal, the statement in line 21 outputs a string indicating that the two numbers are equal. Note that assignment and the equality operator both use the = symbol. When a condition is expected (such as after the If keyword in an If...Else statement), the = is used as an equality operator.

If number1 contains the value 333 and number2 contains the value 333, the expression in line 21 evaluates as follows: number1 is converted to a string and concatenated with the string " = ", then number2 is converted to a string and concatenated with the resulting string from the first concatenation. At this point, the string "333 = 333" is displayed by

WriteLine. As the program proceeds through the remaining If...Then statements (lines 24–44), additional strings are output by the WriteLine statements. For example, when given the value 333 for number1 and number2, the conditions in lines 37 and 42 also are true. Thus, the output displayed (in the third output of Fig. 3.22) is:

```
333 = 333
333 <= 333
333 >= 333
```

The table in Fig. 3.23 shows the precedence of the operators introduced in this chapter. The operators are displayed from top to bottom in decreasing order of precedence.

3.8 Using a Message Dialog to Display a Message

The programs discussed thus far display output in the **Console** window. Visual Basic programs often use message dialog windows to display output. Visual Basic provides class **MessageBox** for creating message dialogs. We use a message dialog in Fig. 3.24 to display the square root of 2. For this program to compile and execute, you must perform several steps discussed later in this section. Be sure to read the entire section as you create this example.

Note that in the output for Fig. 3.24, the square root of 2 is displayed with many digits to the right of the decimal point. In many applications, you won't need such precise output. In the next chapter, we demonstrate how to display only a few digits to the right of the decimal point.

Operators	Type
^	exponentiation
+ -	sign operations (unary)
* /	multiplication and floating-point division
\	Integer division
Mod	modulus
+ -	addition and subtraction (binary)
= <> < <= > >=	equality and relational

Fig. 3.23 | Precedence of the operators introduced in this chapter.

```
1    ' Fig. 3.28: SquareRoot.vb
2    ' Displaying the square root of 2 in a dialog.
3
4    Imports System.Windows.Forms ' Namespace containing class MessageBox
5
6    Module SquareRoot
7
```

Fig. 3.24 | Displaying text in a message dialog. (Part 1 of 2.)

```
 8      Sub Main()
 9
10          Dim root As Double = Math.Sqrt(2) ' calculate the square root of 2
11
12          ' display the results in a message dialog
13          MessageBox.Show("The square root of 2 is " & root, _
14             "The Square Root of 2")
15
16      End Sub ' Main
17
18  End Module ' SquareRoot
```

The Square Root of 2

The square root of 2 is 1.4142135623731

OK

Fig. 3.24 | Displaying text in a message dialog. (Part 2 of 2.)

Displaying a MessageBox

Figure 3.24 presents a program that creates a simple GUI (i.e., the message dialog). The .NET Framework Class Library (FCL) contains a rich collection of classes that can be used to construct GUIs. FCL classes are grouped by functionality into *namespaces*, which make it easier for programmers to find the classes needed to perform particular tasks. Line 4 is an *Imports statement* indicating that we are using the features provided by the namespace *System.Windows.Forms*, which contains windows-related classes (i.e., forms and dialogs). We will discuss this namespace in more detail after we discuss the code in this example.

Line 10 calls the *Sqrt* method of the *Math* class to compute the square root of 2. The value returned is a floating-point number, so we declare the variable root as type *Double*. Variables of type Double can store floating-point numbers. We declare and initialize root in a single statement.

Note the use of spacing in lines 13–14 of Fig. 3.24. To improve readability, long statements may be split over several lines using the *line-continuation character*, _ . Line 13 uses the line-continuation character to indicate that line 14 is a continuation of the preceding line. A single statement can contain as many line-continuation characters as necessary. At least one whitespace character must precede each line-continuation character.

Common Programming Error 3.4

Splitting a statement over several lines without including the line-continuation character is a syntax error.

Common Programming Error 3.5

Failure to precede the line-continuation character (_) with at least one whitespace character is a syntax error.

Common Programming Error 3.6

Placing anything, including comments, on the same line after a line-continuation character is a syntax error.

Common Programming Error 3.7

Splitting a statement in the middle of an identifier or string is a syntax error.

Good Programming Practice 3.6

If a single statement must be split across lines, choose breaking points that make sense, such as after a comma in a comma-separated list or after an operator in a lengthy expression. If a statement is split across two or more lines, indent all subsequent lines with one level of indentation.

Lines 13–14 (Fig. 3.24) call method ***Show*** of class MessageBox. This method takes a comma-separated argument list. The first argument is the string that is displayed in the message dialog. The second argument is the string that is displayed in the message dialog's title bar.

Good Programming Practice 3.7

Place a space after each comma in a method's argument list to make method calls more readable.

Analyzing the MessageBox

When executed, lines 13–14 (Fig. 3.24) display the message dialog shown in Fig. 3.25. The message dialog includes an **OK** button that allows the user to dismiss (i.e., close) the message dialog by clicking the button. After you dismiss the message dialog, the program reaches the end of Main and terminates. You can also dismiss the message dialog by clicking the dialog's close box—the button with an **X** in the dialog's upper-right corner. You will see various dialogs throughout this book, some with more buttons than the **OK** button and the close box. In Chapter 13, you'll see how to determine which button was pressed and have your application respond accordingly. For instance, you can have one action occur when the user clicks the **OK** button and a different action occur when the user clicks the close box. By default, these buttons simply dismiss the dialog.

If you create this example and enter the code in Fig. 3.24, you will notice that line 13 gives you the error **Name 'MessageBox' is not declared**. Some classes provided by Visual Basic (such as MessageBox) must be added to the project before they can be used in a program. These compiled classes are located in a file, called an ***assembly***, that has a *.dll*

Fig. 3.25 | Message dialog displayed by calling MessageBox.Show.

(*dynamic link library*) file extension. Information about the assembly our program must reference so that it can use class MessageBox can be found in the Visual Basic Express documentation—also called the *MSDN (Microsoft Developer Network) Documentation*. To locate this information, select **Help > Index**. This displays the Visual Basic Express documentation in a separate window that contains an **Index** dialog (Fig. 3.26).

Type the class name MessageBox in the **Look for:** box, and select the appropriate *filter*, which narrows the search to a subset of the documentation—we selected **Visual Basic Express** in Fig. 3.26. You should select whichever edition of Visual Basic you are using. Next, click the **about MessageBox class** link (Fig. 3.26) to display documentation for the MessageBox class (Fig. 3.27). The documentation lists the assembly that contains the class. Class MessageBox is located in assembly *System.Windows.Forms.dll*. Note that the file name is listed in Fig. 3.27 using lowercase letters. Uppercase and lowercase letters can be used interchangeably, because file names are not case sensitive.

Adding a Reference to an Assembly

We must *add a reference* to this assembly if we wish to use class MessageBox in our program. Visual Basic 2005 Express provides a simple process for adding a reference. To see

Fig. 3.26 | Obtaining documentation for a class by using the **Index** dialog.

Fig. 3.27 | Documentation for the MessageBox class.

which assemblies are currently referenced in a project, you need to view the project's **References** folder. To do this, click the **Show All Files** button of the **Solution Explorer** (Fig. 3.28), which displays any of the project's files that are normally hidden by the IDE. If you expand the **References** folder (i.e., click the **+** to the left of the folder name), you will see that **System.Windows.Forms** is not listed. It *is* listed in Fig. 3.29(c)—we will discuss this figure shortly.

To add a reference to an existing project, select **Project > Add Reference...** to display the ***Add Reference* dialog** (Fig. 3.29(a)). Scroll through the list of DLLs in the **.NET** tab and click `System.Windows.Forms.dll` to add it to the **References** folder, then click **OK**. Note that **System.Windows.Forms** was not originally listed in the **References** folder (Fig. 3.29(b)), but after we add the reference using the **Add Reference** dialog, it *is* listed (Fig. 3.29(c)).

Common Programming Error 3.8

Including a namespace with the `Imports` *statement without adding a reference to the proper assembly results in a compilation error.*

Now that the assembly `System.Windows.Forms.dll` is referenced, we can use the classes that are part of the assembly. The namespace that includes class `MessageBox`, `System.Windows.Forms`, also is specified with the `Imports` statement in line 4 of our code (Fig. 3.24). The `Imports` statement is not added to the program by Visual Basic 2005 Express; you must add this line to your code.

We did not have to add references to any of our previous programs because Visual Basic 2005 Express adds references to some assemblies when the project is created. The references added depend on the project type that you select in the **New Project** dialog. In addition, some assemblies do not need to be referenced. For example, class `Console` is located in the assembly ***mscorlib.dll***, but we did not need to reference this assembly explicitly to use it.

GUI Components and the System.Windows.Forms Namespace
The `System.Windows.Forms` namespace contains many classes that help Visual Basic programmers define graphical user interfaces (GUIs) for their applications. *GUI components* (such as `Button`s) facilitate both data entry by the user and presenting data outputs to the user. For example, Fig. 3.30 is an Internet Explorer window with a menu bar containing various menus, such as **File**, **Edit** and **View**. Below the menu bar is a tool bar that consists of buttons. Each button, when clicked, executes a task. Beneath the tool bar is a combo box in which the user can type the location of a Web site to visit. To the left of this combo

Fig. 3.28 | Viewing a project's references.

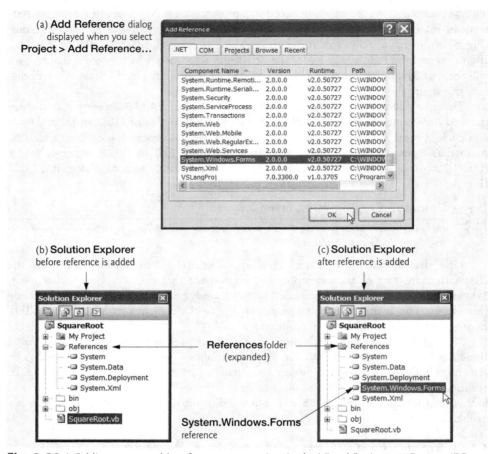

(a) **Add Reference** dialog displayed when you select **Project > Add Reference...**

(b) **Solution Explorer** before reference is added

(c) **Solution Explorer** after reference is added

References folder (expanded)

System.Windows.Forms reference

Fig. 3.29 | Adding an assembly reference to a project in the Visual Basic 2005 Express IDE.

box is a label that indicates the purpose of the text box (in this case, **Address**). The menus, buttons, text boxes and labels are part of Internet Explorer's GUI. They enable users to interact effectively with the Internet Explorer program. Visual Basic provides classes for creating the GUI components shown here. Other classes that create GUI components are described throughout this book (beginning in the next chapter), and covered in detail in Chapter 13, Graphical User Interface Concepts: Part 1 and Chapter 14, Graphical User Interface Concepts: Part 2.

3.9 (Optional) Software Engineering Case Study: Examining the ATM Requirements Document

Now we begin our optional object-oriented design and implementation case study. The "Software Engineering Case Study" sections at the ends of this and the next several chapters will ease you into object orientation. We will develop software for a simple automated teller machine (ATM) system, providing you with a concise, carefully paced, complete design and implementation experience. In Chapters 4–9 and 11, we will perform the various

Label   Button (displaying an icon)   Menu (e.g., **Help**)   Combo box   Menu bar   Tool bar

Fig. 3.30 | Internet Explorer window with GUI components.

steps of an object-oriented design (OOD) process using the UML, while relating these steps to the object-oriented concepts discussed in the chapters. Appendix J implements the ATM using Visual Basic object-oriented programming (OOP) techniques. We present the complete case study solution. This is not an exercise; rather, it is an end-to-end experience that concludes with a detailed walkthrough of the complete Visual Basic code that implements our design.

We begin our design process by presenting a *requirements document* that specifies the ATM system's purpose and *what* it must do. Throughout the case study, we refer to the requirements document to determine precisely what functionality the system must provide.

Requirements Document

A small local bank intends to install a new automated teller machine (ATM) to allow users (i.e., bank customers) to perform basic financial transactions (Fig. 3.31). For simplicity, each user can have only one account at the bank. ATM users should be able to view their account balance, withdraw cash (i.e., take money out of an account) and deposit funds (i.e., place money into an account).

The user interface of the automated teller machine contains the following hardware components:

- a screen that displays messages to the user;
- a keypad that receives numeric input from the user;
- a cash dispenser that dispenses cash to the user; and
- a deposit slot that receives deposit envelopes from the user.

The cash dispenser begins each day loaded with 500 $20 bills. [*Note:* Certain elements of the ATM described here simplify various aspects of a real ATM. For example, commercial

Fig. 3.31 | Automated teller machine user interface.

ATMs typically contain a device that reads a user's account number from an ATM card, whereas our ATM asks the user to type an account number on the keypad (which you will simulate with your personal computer's keypad). Also, commercial ATMs usually print a paper receipt at the end of a session, but all output from this ATM appears on the screen.]

The bank wants you to develop software to perform the financial transactions initiated by bank customers through the ATM. The bank will integrate the software with the ATM's hardware at a later time. The software should simulate the functionality of the hardware devices (e.g., cash dispenser, deposit slot) in software components, but it need not concern itself with how these devices perform their duties. The ATM hardware has not been developed yet, so instead of writing your software to run on the ATM, you should develop a first version of the software to run on a personal computer. This version should use the computer's monitor to simulate the ATM's screen, and the computer's keyboard to simulate the ATM's keypad.

An ATM session consists of authenticating a user (i.e., proving the user's identity) based on an account number and personal identification number (PIN), followed by creating and executing financial transactions. To authenticate a user and perform transactions, the ATM must interact with the bank's account information database. [*Note:* A database is an organized collection of data stored on a computer.] For each bank account, the database stores an account number, a PIN and a balance indicating the amount of money in the account. [*Note:* The bank plans to build only one ATM, so we do not need to worry about multiple ATMs accessing the database at the same time. Furthermore, we assume that the bank does not make any changes to the information in the database while a user is accessing the ATM other than those initiated by this ATM session itself. Also, any business system like an ATM faces reasonably complicated security issues that go well beyond the scope of this book—we make the simplifying assumption that the bank trusts the ATM to access and manipulate the information in the database without significant security measures.]

Upon approaching the ATM, the user should experience the following sequence of events (see Fig. 3.31):

1. The screen displays a welcome message and prompts the user to enter an account number.

2. The user enters a five-digit account number, using the keypad.

3. For authentication purposes, the screen prompts the user to enter the PIN (personal identification number) associated with the specified account number.

4. The user enters a five-digit PIN, using the keypad.

5. If the user enters a valid account number and the correct PIN for that account, the screen displays the main menu (Fig. 3.32). If the user enters an invalid account number or an incorrect PIN, the screen displays an appropriate message, then the ATM returns to *Step 1* to restart the authentication process.

After the ATM authenticates the user, the main menu (Fig. 3.32) displays a numbered option for each of the three types of transactions—balance inquiry (option 1), withdrawal (option 2) and deposit (option 3). The main menu also displays an option that allows the user to exit the system (option 4). The user then chooses either to perform a transaction (by entering 1, 2 or 3) or to exit the system (by entering 4). If the user enters an invalid option, the screen displays an error message, then redisplays the main menu.

If the user enters 1 to make a balance inquiry, the screen displays the user's account balance. To do so, the ATM must retrieve the balance from the bank's database.

Fig. 3.32 | ATM main menu.

The following actions occur when the user enters 2 to make a withdrawal:

1. The screen displays a menu (shown in Fig. 3.33) containing standard withdrawal amounts: $20 (option 1), $40 (option 2), $60 (option 3), $100 (option 4) and $200 (option 5). Option 6 allows the user to cancel the transaction.

2. The user enters a menu selection (1–6) using the keypad.

3. If the withdrawal amount chosen is greater than the user's account balance, the screen displays a message stating this and telling the user to choose a smaller amount. The ATM then returns to *Step 1*. If the withdrawal amount chosen is less than or equal to the user's account balance (i.e., an acceptable withdrawal amount), the ATM proceeds to *Step 4*. If the user chooses to cancel the transaction (option 6), the ATM displays the main menu (Fig. 3.32) and waits for user input.

4. If the cash dispenser contains enough cash to satisfy the request, the ATM proceeds to *Step 5*. Otherwise, the screen displays a message indicating the problem and telling the user to choose a smaller withdrawal amount. The ATM then returns to *Step 1*.

5. The ATM debits (reduces) the user's account balance in the bank's database by the withdrawal amount.

6. The cash dispenser dispenses the desired amount of money to the user.

7. The screen displays a message reminding the user to take the money.

The following actions occur when the user enters 3 (from the main menu) to make a deposit:

Fig. 3.33 | ATM withdrawal menu.

1. The screen prompts the user to enter a deposit amount or to type 0 (zero) to cancel the transaction.

2. The user enters a deposit amount or 0, using the keypad. [*Note:* The keypad does not contain a decimal point or a dollar sign, so the user cannot type a dollar amount (e.g., $147.25). Instead, the user must enter a deposit amount as a number of cents (e.g., 14725). The ATM then divides this number by 100 to obtain a number representing a dollar amount (e.g., $14725 \div 100 = 147.25$).]

3. If the user specifies a deposit amount, the ATM proceeds to *Step 4*. If the user cancels the transaction (by entering 0), the ATM displays the main menu (Fig. 3.32) and waits for user input.

4. The screen displays a message telling the user to insert a deposit envelope into the deposit slot.

5. If the deposit slot receives a deposit envelope within two minutes, the ATM credits (i.e., increases) the user's account balance in the bank's database by the deposit amount. [*Note:* This money is not immediately available for withdrawal. The bank first must verify the amount of cash in the deposit envelope, and any checks in the envelope must clear (i.e., money must be transferred from the check writer's account to the check recipient's account). When either of these events occurs, the bank appropriately updates the user's balance stored in database. This occurs independently of the ATM system.] If the deposit slot does not receive a deposit envelope within two minutes, the screen displays a message that the system has canceled the transaction due to inactivity. The ATM then displays the main menu and waits for user input.

After the system successfully executes a transaction, the system should redisplay the main menu (Fig. 3.32) so that the user can perform additional transactions. If the user chooses to exit the system (by entering option 4), the screen should display a thank you message, then display the welcome message for the next user.

Analyzing the ATM System

The preceding statement presented a simplified requirements document. Typically, such a document is the result of a detailed process of ***requirements gathering*** that might include interviews with potential users of the system and specialists in fields related to the system. For example, a systems analyst who is hired to prepare a requirements document for banking software (e.g., the ATM system described here) might interview people who have used ATMs and financial experts to gain a better understanding of *what* the software must do. The analyst would use the information gathered to compile a list of ***system requirements*** to guide systems designers.

The process of requirements gathering is a key task of the first stage of the software life cycle. The ***software life cycle*** specifies the stages through which software evolves from the time it is conceived to the time at which it is retired from use. These stages typically include analysis, design, implementation, testing, debugging, deployment, maintenance and retirement. Several software life cycle models exist, each with its own preferences and specifications for when and how often software engineers should perform the various stages. ***Waterfall models*** perform each stage once in succession, whereas ***iterative models*** may repeat one or more stages several times throughout a product's life cycle.

The analysis stage of the software life cycle focuses on precisely defining the problem to be solved. When designing any system, one must certainly *solve the problem right*, but of equal importance, one must *solve the right problem*. Systems analysts collect the requirements that indicate the specific problem to solve. Our requirements document describes our simple ATM system in sufficient detail that you do not need to go through an extensive analysis stage—it has been done for you.

To capture what a proposed system should do, developers often employ a technique known as *use case modeling*. This process identifies the *use cases* of the system, each of which represents a different capability that the system provides to its clients. For example, ATMs typically have several use cases, such as "View Account Balance," "Withdraw Cash," "Deposit Funds," "Transfer Funds Between Accounts" and "Buy Postage Stamps." The simplified ATM system we build in this case study requires only the first three use cases.

Each use case describes a typical scenario in which the user uses the system. You have already read descriptions of the ATM system's use cases in the requirements document. The lists of steps required to perform each type of transaction (i.e., balance inquiry, withdrawal and deposit) actually described the three use cases of our ATM—"View Account Balance," "Withdraw Cash" and "Deposit Funds."

Use Case Diagrams

We create a *use case diagram* to model the interactions between a system's clients (in this case study, bank customers) and the system. The goal is to show the kinds of interactions users have with a system without providing the details—these are shown in other UML diagrams (which we present throughout the case study). Use case diagrams are often accompanied by informal text that describes the use cases in more detail—like the text that appears in the requirements document. Use case diagrams are produced during the analysis stage of the software life cycle. In larger systems, use case diagrams are simple but indispensable tools that help system designers focus on satisfying the users' needs.

Figure 3.34 shows the use case diagram for our ATM system. The stick figure represents an *actor*, which defines the roles that an external entity—such as a person or another system—plays when interacting with the system. For our automated teller machine, the actor is a User who can view an account balance, withdraw cash and deposit funds using

Fig. 3.34 | Use case diagram for the ATM system from the User's perspective.

the ATM. The User is not an actual person, but instead comprises the roles that a real person—when playing the part of a User—can play while interacting with the ATM. Note that a use case diagram can include multiple actors. For example, the use case diagram for a real bank's ATM system might also include an actor named Administrator who refills the cash dispenser each day.

We identify the actor in our system by examining the requirements document, which states, "ATM users should be able to view their account balance, withdraw cash and deposit funds." The actor in each of the three use cases is simply the User who interacts with the ATM. An external entity—a real person—plays the part of the User to perform financial transactions. Figure 3.34 shows one actor, whose name, User, appears below the actor in the diagram. The UML models each use case as an oval connected to an actor with a solid line.

Systems designers must analyze the requirements document or a set of use cases, and design the system before programmers implement it in a particular programming language. During the analysis stage, systems designers focus on understanding the requirements document to produce a high-level specification that describes *what* the system is supposed to do. The output of the design stage—a ***design specification***—should specify *how* the system should be constructed to satisfy these requirements. In the next several "Software Engineering Case Study" sections, we perform the steps of a simple object-oriented design (OOD) process on the ATM system to produce a design specification containing a collection of UML diagrams and supporting text. Recall that the UML can be used with any OOD process. Many such processes exist, the best known of which is the Rational Unified Process™ (RUP) developed by Rational Software Corporation (now a division of IBM). RUP is a rich process for designing "industrial strength" applications. For this case study, we employ a simplified design process.

Designing the ATM System

We now begin the design stage of our ATM system. A ***system*** is a set of components that interact to solve a problem. For example, to perform the ATM system's designated tasks, our ATM system has a user interface (Fig. 3.31), contains software that executes financial transactions and interacts with a database of bank account information. ***System structure*** describes the system's objects and their interrelationships. ***System behavior*** describes how the system changes as its objects interact with one another. Every system has both structure and behavior—designers must specify both. There are several distinct types of system structures and behaviors. For example, the interactions among objects in the system differ from those between the user and the system, yet both constitute a portion of the system behavior.

The UML 2 specifies 13 diagram types for documenting system models. Each diagram type models a distinct characteristic of a system's structure or behavior—six diagram types relate to system structure; the remaining seven relate to system behavior. We list here only the six types of diagrams used in our case study—one of these (class diagrams) models system structure—the remaining five model system behavior. We overview the remaining seven UML diagram types in Appendix K, UML 2: Additional Diagram Types:

1. *Use case diagrams*, such as the one in Fig. 3.34, model the interactions between a system and its external entities (actors) in terms of use cases (system capabilities, such as "View Account Balance," "Withdraw Cash" and "Deposit Funds").

2. *Class diagrams*, which we discuss in Section 4.9, model the classes, or "building blocks," used in a system. Each noun or "thing" described in the requirements document is a candidate to be a class in the system (e.g., "account," "keypad"). Class diagrams help us specify the structural relationships between parts of the system. For example, the ATM system class diagram will, among other things, specify that the ATM is physically composed of a screen, a keypad, a cash dispenser and a deposit slot.

3. *State machine diagrams*, which we discuss in Section 6.11, model the ways in which an object changes state. An object's *state* is indicated by the values of all the object's attributes at a given time. When an object changes state, that object may subsequently behave differently in the system. For example, after validating a user's PIN, the ATM transitions from the "user not authenticated" state to the "user authenticated" state, at which point the ATM allows the user to perform financial transactions (i.e., view account balance, withdraw cash, deposit funds).

4. *Activity diagrams*, which we also discuss in Section 6.11, model an object's *activity*—the object's workflow (sequence of events) during program execution. An activity diagram models the actions the object performs and specifies the order in which it performs these actions. For example, an activity diagram shows that the ATM must obtain the balance of the user's account (from the bank's account information database) before the screen can display the balance to the user.

5. *Communication diagrams* (called *collaboration diagrams* in earlier versions of the UML) model the interactions among objects in a system, with an emphasis on *what* interactions occur. You'll see in Section 8.15 that these diagrams show which objects must interact to perform an ATM transaction. For example, the ATM must communicate with the bank's account information database to retrieve an account balance.

6. *Sequence diagrams* also model the interactions among the objects in a system, but unlike communication diagrams, they emphasize *when* interactions occur. You'll see in Section 8.15 that these diagrams help show the order in which interactions occur in executing a financial transaction. For example, the screen prompts the user to enter a withdrawal amount before cash is dispensed.

In Section 4.9, we continue designing our ATM system by identifying the classes from the requirements document. We accomplish this by extracting key nouns and noun phrases from the requirements document. Using these classes, we develop our first draft of the class diagram that models the structure of our ATM system.

Internet and Web Resources

The following URLs provide information on object-oriented design with the UML.

`www-306.ibm.com/software/rational/uml/`
Lists frequently asked questions about the UML, provided by IBM Rational.

`www.agilemodeling.com/essays/umlDiagrams.htm`
Provides in-depth descriptions and tutorials on each of the 13 UML 2 diagram types.

`www.borland.com/us/products/together/index.html`
Provides a free 30-day license to download a trial version of Borland® Together® Control-Center™—a software development tool that supports the UML.

`www-306.ibm.com/software/rational/offerings/design.html`
Provides information about IBM Rational software available for designing systems. Provides downloads of 30-day trial versions of several products, such as IBM Rational Rose® XDE (e Xtended Development Environment) Developer.

`www.embarcadero.com/products/describe/index.html`
Provides a 15-day trial license for the Embarcadero Technologies® UML modeling tool Describe.™

`www.ilogix.com/rhapsody/rhapsody.cfm`
Provides a free 30-day license to download a trial version of I-Logix Rhapsody®—a UML 2-based model-driven development environment.

`argouml.tigris.org`
Contains information and downloads for ArgoUML, a free open-source UML tool.

`www.objectsbydesign.com/books/booklist.html`
Lists books on the UML and object-oriented design.

`www.objectsbydesign.com/tools/umltools_byCompany.html`
Lists software tools that use the UML, such as IBM Rational Rose, Embarcadero Describe, Sparx Systems Enterprise Architect, I-Logix Rhapsody and Gentleware Poseidon for UML.

`www.ootips.org/ood-principles.html`
Provides answers to the question, "What makes a good object-oriented design?"

`www.cetus-links.org/oo_uml.html`
Introduces the UML and provides links to numerous UML resources.

Recommended Readings

The following books provide information on object-oriented design with the UML.

Ambler, S. *The Elements of the UML 2.0 Style*. New York: Cambridge University Press, 2005.

Booch, G. *Object-Oriented Analysis and Design with Applications*, Third Edition. Boston: Addison-Wesley, 2004.

Eriksson, H., et al. *UML 2 Toolkit*. Hoboken, N.J.: John Wiley & Sons, 2003.

Kruchten, P. *The Rational Unified Process: An Introduction*. Boston: Addison-Wesley, 2004.

Larman, C. *Applying UML and Patterns: An Introduction to Object-Oriented Analysis and Design*, Second Edition. Upper Saddle River, NJ: Prentice Hall, 2002.

Roques, P. *UML in Practice: The Art of Modeling Software Systems Demonstrated Through Worked Examples and Solutions*. Hoboken, N.J.: John Wiley & Sons, 2004.

Rosenberg, D., and K. Scott. *Applying Use Case Driven Object Modeling with UML: An Annotated e-Commerce Example*. Reading, MA: Addison-Wesley, 2001.

Rumbaugh, J., I. Jacobson and G. Booch. *The Complete UML Training Course*. Upper Saddle River, NJ: Prentice Hall, 2000.

Rumbaugh, J., I. Jacobson and G. Booch. *The Unified Modeling Language Reference Manual*. Reading, MA: Addison-Wesley, 1999.

Rumbaugh, J., I. Jacobson and G. Booch. *The Unified Software Development Process*. Reading, MA: Addison-Wesley, 1999.

Software Engineering Case Study Self-Review Exercises

3.1   Suppose we enabled a user of our ATM system to transfer money between two bank accounts. Modify the use case diagram of Fig. 3.34 to reflect this change.

3.2   _____ model the interactions among objects in a system with an emphasis on *when* these interactions occur.
  a) Class diagrams
  b) Sequence diagrams
  c) Communication diagrams
  d) Activity diagrams

3.3   Which of the following choices lists stages of a typical software life cycle in sequential order?
  a) design, analysis, implementation, testing
  b) design, analysis, testing, implementation
  c) analysis, design, testing, implementation
  d) analysis, design, implementation, testing

Answers to Software Engineering Case Study Self-Review Exercises

3.1   Figure 3.35 contains a use case diagram for a modified version of our ATM system that also allows users to transfer money between accounts.

3.2   b.

3.3   d.

3.10 Wrap-Up

We discussed many features of Visual Basic in this chapter, including displaying data on the screen, inputting data from the keyboard and declaring variables of primitive types `Integer` and `Double`. You used the `WriteLine`, `Write` and `ReadLine` methods of class `Console` to build simple interactive programs that input and output text. You learned how to use the arithmetic operators to perform calculations, and the order in which Visual Basic applies these operators (i.e., the rules of operator precedence). We demonstrated how Visual Basic's `If...Then` statement allows a program to perform actions based on a condition. You created conditions using the equality and relational operators. We demonstrated several features of Visual Basic 2005 Express, including creating console applications, modifying the IDE's settings and adding references to assemblies.

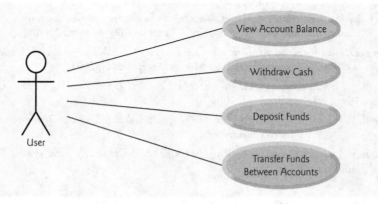

Fig. 3.35 | Use case diagram for a modified version of our ATM system that also allows Users to transfer money between accounts.

In the next chapter, we return to Visual Basic Windows applications that provide graphical user interfaces. The chapter begins our discussion of *structured programming*. We study how to specify and vary the order in which statements are executed—this is called *flow of control*. You'll use control statements to select between alternative actions based on the truth or falsity of a condition, or to perform actions repeatedly based on a condition. We present several case studies that demonstrate the types of repetition that can occur in Visual Basic programs.

3.11 Web Resources

www.developer.com/net/vb

The Visual Basic section of developer.com provides a rich collection of Visual Basic articles.

www.devx.com/dotnet

This site contains information about the .NET platform, with topics ranging from Visual Basic to ASP.NET. The site includes links to articles, books and current news.

www.vbcity.com

The vbCity site lists numerous links to articles, books and tutorials on Visual Basic. You can submit code and have it rated by other developers. The site also polls visitors on many Visual Basic topics and provides access to archives, which include code listings and news.

www.cyber-matrix.com/vb.htm

This site links to Visual Basic tutorials, books, tips and tricks, programming tools, magazines, news groups and more.

searchvb.techtarget.com

This site offers a search engine designed specifically to discover Visual Basic Web sites.

www.aewnet.com/root/dotnet/vbnet

The site links to demos, articles, tutorials and other Visual Basic sites. There is also a message board where you can start discussions on various topics.

4

Introduction to Classes and Objects

OBJECTIVES

In this chapter you will learn:

- What classes, objects, methods, instance variables and properties are.

- How to declare a class and use it to create an object.

- How to implement a class's behaviors as methods.

- How to implement a class's attributes as instance variables and properties.

- How to call an object's methods to make them perform their tasks.

- The differences between instance variables of a class and local variables of a method.

- How to use a constructor to ensure that an object's attributes are initialized when the object is created.

- The differences between value types and reference types.

- How to use properties to ensure that only valid data is placed in attributes.

Nothing can have value without being an object of utility.
—**Karl Marx**

You will see something new. Two things. And I call them Thing One and Thing Two.
—**Dr. Theodor Seuss Geisel**

Your public servants serve you right.
—**Adlai E. Stevenson**

*Knowing how to answer one who speaks,
To reply to one who sends a message.*
—**Amenemope**

4.1 Introduction

We introduced the basic terminology and concepts of object-oriented programming in Section 1.9. In Chapter 3, you began to use those concepts to create simple applications that displayed messages to the user, obtained information from the user, performed calculations and made decisions. One common feature of every application in Chapter 3 was that all the statements that performed tasks were located in method `Main`, in a module. Many of the applications you develop in this book will consist of one or more classes, each containing one or more methods. These classes will then be used in the module that contains `Main`. Industry applications can contain hundreds, or even thousands, of classes. In this chapter, we present a simple framework for organizing object-oriented applications in Visual Basic.

First, we motivate the notion of classes with a real-world example. Then we present five complete working applications to demonstrate creating and using your own classes. These examples begin our integrated case study on developing a grade-book class that instructors can use to maintain student test scores. This case study is enhanced over the next several chapters, culminating with the version presented in Chapter 8, Arrays.

4.2 Classes, Objects, Methods and Instance Variables

We will begin with a simple analogy to help you understand classes and their contents. Suppose you want to drive a car and make it go faster by pressing down on its accelerator pedal. What must happen before you can do this? Well, before you can drive a car, someone has to design the car. A car typically begins as engineering drawings, similar to the blueprints used to design a house. These engineering drawings include the design for an accelerator pedal to make the car go faster. The pedal "hides" the complex mechanisms that actually make the car go faster, just as the brake pedal "hides" the mechanisms that slow the car and the steering wheel "hides" the mechanisms that turn the car. This enables people with little or no knowledge of how engines work to easily drive a car.

Unfortunately, you cannot drive a car's engineering drawings. Before you can drive a car, the car must be built from the engineering drawings that describe it. A completed car has an actual accelerator pedal to make it go faster, but even that is not enough—the car will not accelerate on its own, so the driver must press the accelerator pedal.

Now let's use our car example to introduce the key programming concepts of this section. Performing a task in a program requires a method. The method describes the mechanisms that actually perform its tasks. The method hides these mechanisms from its user, just as the accelerator pedal of a car hides from the driver the complex mechanisms that make the car go faster. In Visual Basic, we begin by creating a program unit called a class to house a method, just as a car's engineering drawings house the design of an accelerator pedal. In a class, you provide one or more methods that are designed to perform the class's tasks. For example, a class that represents a bank account might contain many methods, including one to deposit money in the account, another to withdraw money from the account and a third to inquire what the current balance is.

Just as you cannot drive an engineering drawing of a car, you cannot "drive" a class. Just as someone has to build a car from its engineering drawings before you can actually drive it, you must build an object of a class before you can get a program to perform the tasks the class describes how to do. That is one reason Visual Basic is known as an object-oriented programming language.

When you drive a car, pressing its gas pedal sends a message to the car to perform a task—that is, to go faster. Similarly, you send *messages* to an object—each message is a method call and tells one of an object's methods to perform its task.

Thus far, we have used the car analogy to introduce classes, objects and methods. In addition to the capabilities a car provides, it also has many attributes, such as its color, the number of doors, the amount of gas in its tank, its current speed and its odometer reading (i.e., its total miles driven since it was built). Like the car's capabilities, its attributes are represented as part of a car's design in its engineering diagrams. As you drive a car, these attributes are always associated with the car. For example, each car knows how much gas is in its own gas tank, but not how much is in the tanks of other cars. Similarly, an object has attributes that are carried with it as it's used in a program. These attributes are specified in the object's class. For example, a bank account object has a balance attribute that represents the amount of money in the account. Each bank account object knows the balance in the account it represents, but not the balances of the other accounts in the bank. Attributes are specified by the class's *instance variables*.

This chapter presents five simple examples that demonstrate the concepts introduced in the context of the car analogy. The examples incrementally build a GradeBook class:

1. The first example presents a GradeBook class with one method that simply displays a welcome message when it is called. We show how to create an object of the class and call the method so that it displays the welcome message.

2. The second example modifies the first by allowing the method to receive a course name as an argument and display the name as part of the welcome message.

3. The third example shows how to store the course name in a GradeBook object. We show how to use the convenient notation of "properties" to set the course name in the object and obtain the course name from the object.

4. The fourth example demonstrates how the data in a GradeBook object can be initialized when the object is created—the initialization is performed by the class's constructor (a special type of method with the name New).

5. The last example enhances class GradeBook by introducing data validation, which ensures that data in an object adheres to a particular format or is in a proper value range. For example, a Date object should accept month values only in the range 1–12. In our GradeBook example, the property that sets the course name for a GradeBook object ensures that the course name is 25 or fewer characters. If not, the property uses only the first 25 characters of the course name and displays a warning message. Restrictions like this are common in information systems that have to display data in fixed-size boxes in a form on the screen.

The GradeBook examples in this chapter do not process or store grades. We begin processing grades with the version of class GradeBook in Chapter 5, Control Statements: Part 1, and we store grades in the version of GradeBook in Chapter 8, Arrays.

4.3 Declaring a Class with a Method and Instantiating an Object of a Class

We begin with an example that consists of class GradeBook (Fig. 4.1) and module GradeBookTest (Fig. 4.2). Class GradeBook (declared in file GradeBook.vb) displays a message on the screen (Fig. 4.2) welcoming the instructor to the grade-book application. Module GradeBookTest (declared in file GradeBookTest.vb) contains the Main method that instantiates (creates) and uses an object of class GradeBook. The class and module are placed in separate files for clarity, but it is possible to place them in the same file.

Adding a Class to a Visual Basic Project

For each example in this chapter, you will add a class to your console application. To do this, right click the project name in the **Solution Explorer** and select **Add > Class...** from the menu that appears. In the **Add New Item** dialog that appears, enter the name of your new file, in this case GradeBook.vb. A new file will be added to your project with an empty GradeBook class. Add the code from Fig. 4.1 to this file—we'll discuss this code shortly.

Class GradeBook

The GradeBook class declaration (Fig. 4.1) contains a DisplayMessage method (lines 5–7) that displays a message on the screen. Recall that a class is like a blueprint—we need to make an object of class GradeBook and call its method to get line 6 to execute and display its message. We do this in the Main method in Fig. 4.2.

The class declaration begins at line 3. The keyword *Public* is an *access modifier*. For now, we will simply declare every class Public. Every class declaration contains keyword

```
1    ' Fig. 4.1: GradeBook.vb
2    ' Class declaration with one method.
3    Public Class GradeBook
4        ' display a welcome message to the GradeBook user
5        Public Sub DisplayMessage()
6            Console.WriteLine("Welcome to the Grade Book!")
7        End Sub ' DisplayMessage
8    End Class ' GradeBook
```

Fig. 4.1 | Class declaration with one method.

Class followed immediately by the class's name. Every class's body ends with the keywords *End Class*, as in line 8 of class GradeBook.

Method DisplayMessage

Class GradeBook has one method—DisplayMessage (lines 5–7). The method declaration begins with keyword Public to indicate that the method is "available to the public"—that is, it can be called from outside the class declaration's body by methods of other classes or modules (these other classes and modules are called *clients of the class*). Keyword Sub indicates that this method will perform a task but will not return (i.e., give back) any information to its calling method when it completes its task. You have already used methods that return information—for example, in Chapter 3 you used Console method ReadLine to input an integer typed by the user at the keyboard. When ReadLine inputs a value, it returns that value for use in the program.

The name of the method, DisplayMessage, follows keyword Sub. By convention, method names begin with an uppercase letter and all subsequent words in the name begin with a capital letter (recall that Visual Basic is not case sensitive). The parentheses after the method name are used to indicate any *parameters*—additional information that is required by the method to perform its task (we discuss parameters in more detail in Section 4.4). An empty set of parentheses, as in line 5, indicates that this method does not require any additional information and does not need any parameters. We refer to the part of the method in line 5 as the *method header*. Like Main, method DisplayMessage ends with keywords End Sub.

The body of a method contains statements that perform the method's task. In this case, the method contains one statement (line 6) that displays the message "Welcome to the Grade Book!" in the **Console** window. After this statement executes, the method has completed its task.

Note that the DisplayMessage method declaration is similar to the declaration of Main. We discuss methods in depth in Chapter 7, Methods: A Deeper Look.

In Chapter 3, each module we declared had one method named Main. Class Grade-Book, likewise, has one method. Recall that Main is a special method that is required to begin the execution of every application. Main is called automatically by the runtime when you execute an application.

Using Class GradeBook

We will now use class GradeBook in an application. A Visual Basic project that contains only class GradeBook is not an application that can be executed because GradeBook does not contain Main. If you try to compile such a project, you will get the error message:

```
'Sub Main' was not found in 'GradeBook.GradeBookTest'.
```

This was not a problem in Chapter 3, because every application you created contained a Main method. To fix this problem for the GradeBook, either we must declare a separate class or module that contains Main, or we must place Main in class GradeBook. We use a separate module (GradeBookTest in this example) containing Main to test each new class we create in this chapter.

Module GradeBookTest

The GradeBookTest module declaration (Fig. 4.2; lines 3–12) contains the Main method (lines 5–11) that controls our application's execution. The module contains only a Main method, which is typical of many modules that begin an application's execution.

Lines 5–11 declare method Main. In this application, we would like to call class GradeBook's DisplayMessage method to display the welcome message in the **Console** window. Typically, you cannot call a method that belongs to another class until you create an object of that class. We begin by declaring variable gradeBook (line 7). Note that the variable's type is GradeBook—the class we declared in Fig. 4.1. Each new class you create becomes a new type in Visual Basic that can be used to declare variables and create objects. Programmers can declare new class types as needed; this is one reason why Visual Basic is known as an *extensible language.*

Variable gradeBook is initialized with the result of the *object creation expression* New GradeBook() (Fig. 4.2; line 7). Operator New creates a new object of the class specified to the right of the New keyword (i.e., GradeBook). The class name is followed by a set of parentheses. As you'll see in Section 4.7, those parentheses in combination with a class name represent a call to a *constructor*, a special type of method that is used only when an object is created to initialize the object's data. In that section you will see that arguments can be placed in the parentheses to specify initial values for the object's data. In this example, we simply leave the parentheses empty. When there are no arguments to be placed in the parentheses, Visual Basic allows for the parentheses to be omitted, as in the next example. Although Visual Basic is not case sensitive, it does allow us to create objects (e.g., grade-Book) with the "same" name as their class (e.g. GradeBook)—we do this throughout the book.

We can now use object gradeBook to call method DisplayMessage. Line 10 calls DisplayMessage (declared in lines 5–7 of Fig. 4.1) using variable gradeBook followed by a dot separator (.), the method name DisplayMessage and an empty set of parentheses. This call causes the DisplayMessage method to perform its task. This method call differs from the method calls in Chapter 3 that displayed information in the **Console** window—each of those method calls provided arguments that specified the data to display. At the

```
1    ' Fig. 4.2: GradeBookTest.vb
2    ' Create a GradeBook object and call its DisplayMessage method.
3    Module GradeBookTest
4        ' Main begins program execution
5        Sub Main()
6            ' initialize gradeBook to refer to a new GradeBook object
7            Dim gradeBook As New GradeBook()
8
9            ' call gradeBook's DisplayMessage method
10           gradeBook.DisplayMessage()
11       End Sub ' Main
12   End Module ' GradeBookTest
```

```
Welcome to the Grade Book!
```

Fig. 4.2 | Creating an object of class GradeBook and calling its DisplayMessage method.

beginning of line 10, "gradeBook." indicates that Main should use the object of class GradeBook that was created in line 7. The empty parentheses in line 5 of Fig. 4.1 indicate that method DisplayMessage has no parameters—that is, DisplayMessage does not require additional information to perform its task. For this reason, the method call (line 10 of Fig. 4.2) specifies an empty set of parentheses after the method name to indicate that no arguments are being passed to method DisplayMessage. When method Display-Message completes its task, Main continues executing at line 11, which is the end of method Main, so the program terminates.

UML Class Diagram for Class GradeBook

Figure 4.3 presents a *UML class diagram* for class GradeBook of Fig. 4.1. Recall from Section 1.9 that the UML is a graphical language that programmers use to represent their object-oriented systems in a standardized manner. In the UML, each class is modeled in a class diagram as a rectangle with three compartments. The top compartment contains the name of the class centered horizontally in boldface type. The middle compartment contains the class's *attributes*, which correspond to instance variables in Visual Basic. In Fig. 4.3, the middle compartment is empty because the version of class GradeBook in Fig. 4.1 does not have any attributes. The bottom compartment contains the class's *operations*, which correspond to methods in Visual Basic. The UML models an operation by listing its name followed by a set of parentheses. Class GradeBook has one method, DisplayMessage, so the bottom compartment of Fig. 4.3 lists the operation with this name. Method DisplayMessage does not require additional information to perform its tasks, so the parentheses following DisplayMessage in the class diagram are empty, just as they were in the method's declaration in line 5 of Fig. 4.1. The plus sign (+) in front of the operation name indicates that DisplayMessage is a public operation in the UML (because it is a Public method in Visual Basic). We will often use UML class diagrams to summarize a class's attributes and operations.

4.4 Declaring a Method with a Parameter

In our car analogy in Section 4.2, we discussed the fact that pressing a car's gas pedal sends a message to the car to perform a task—make the car go faster. But how fast should the car accelerate? The farther down you press the pedal, the faster the car accelerates. So the message to the car actually includes both the task to perform and additional information that helps the car perform the task. This additional information is known as a parameter (mentioned briefly in Section 4.3)—the value of the parameter helps the car determine how fast to accelerate. Similarly, a method can require one or more parameters that represent additional information it needs to perform its task. A method call supplies values—called ar-

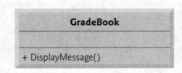

Fig. 4.3 | UML class diagram indicating that class GradeBook has a public DisplayMessage operation.

guments—for each of the method's parameters. For example, the method call to `Console.WriteLine` requires an argument that specifies the data to output in a Command Prompt window. Similarly, to deposit funds into a bank account, a `Deposit` method specifies a parameter that represents the deposit amount. When the `Deposit` method is called, the argument value representing the deposit amount is assigned to the method's parameter. The method then makes a deposit of that amount, increasing the balance in the bank account.

Our next example declares class `GradeBook` (Fig. 4.4) with a `DisplayMessage` method that displays the course name as part of the welcome message. (See the sample execution in Fig. 4.5.) The new `DisplayMessage` method requires a parameter that represents the course name to output (line 5).

Before discussing the new features of class `GradeBook`, let us see how the new class is used from the `Main` method of module `GradeBookTest` (Fig. 4.5). Line 7 initializes variable `gradeBook` to reference a new `GradeBook` object. Note that empty parentheses are

```vb
1   ' Fig. 4.4: GradeBook.vb
2   ' Class declaration with a method that has a parameter.
3   Public Class GradeBook
4       ' display a welcome message to the GradeBook user
5       Public Sub DisplayMessage(ByVal courseName As String)
6           Console.WriteLine( _
7               "Welcome to the grade book for " & vbCrLf & courseName & "!")
8       End Sub ' DisplayMessage
9   End Class ' GradeBook
```

Fig. 4.4 | Class declaration with one method that has a parameter.

```vb
1   ' Fig. 4.5: GradeBookTest.vb
2   ' Create a GradeBook object and call its DisplayMessage method.
3   Module GradeBookTest
4       ' Main begins program execution
5       Sub Main()
6           ' initialize gradeBook to reference a new gradeBook object
7           Dim gradeBook As New GradeBook()
8
9           ' prompt for the course name
10          Console.WriteLine("Please enter the course name:")
11
12          ' read the course name
13          Dim nameOfCourse As String = Console.ReadLine()
14
15          Console.WriteLine() ' output a blank line
16
17          ' call gradeBook's DisplayMessage method
18          ' and pass nameOfCourse as an argument
19          gradeBook.DisplayMessage(nameOfCourse)
20      End Sub ' Main
21  End Module ' GradeBookTest
```

Fig. 4.5 | Creating a `GradeBook` object and passing a `String` to its `DisplayMessage` method. (Part 1 of 2.)

```
Please enter the course name:
CS101 Introduction to Visual Basic Programming

Welcome to the grade book for
CS101 Introduction to Visual Basic Programming!
```

Fig. 4.5 | Creating a GradeBook object and passing a String to its DisplayMessage method. (Part 2 of 2.)

used in the object-creation expression (New GradeBook()), because no arguments need to be passed to create a GradeBook object. Line 10 prompts the user to enter a course name. Line 13 reads the name from the user and assigns it to the nameOfCourse variable, using method ReadLine to perform the input. The user types the course name and presses *Enter* to submit the course name to the program. Variable nameOfCourse is declared as a String (line 13). *String* is the type used for strings in Visual Basic, such as names, addresses, cities, states and product descriptions. Strings can consist of up to 2,147,483,648 (2^{31}) characters.

Line 19 calls gradeBook's DisplayMessage method. The argument nameOfCourse in parentheses is passed to method DisplayMessage so that it can perform its task. The value of variable nameOfCourse in Main (i.e., whatever course name the user types) becomes the value of method DisplayMessage's parameter courseName in line 5 of Fig. 4.4. When you execute this application, you will see that method DisplayMessage outputs a welcome message with the course name you type (Fig. 4.5).

More on Arguments and Parameters
When you declare a method, you must specify in the method's declaration whether the method requires data to perform its task. To do so, you place additional information in the method's *parameter list*, which is located in the parentheses that follow the method name. The parameter list may contain any number of parameters, including none at all. In Fig. 4.4, DisplayMessage's parameter list (line 5) declares that the method requires one parameter. Each parameter must specify a type and an identifier. In this case, the type String and the identifier courseName indicate that method DisplayMessage requires a String parameter named courseName in order to perform its task. At the time the method is called, the argument value in the call (in this case, the value of nameOfCourse in line 19 of Fig. 4.5) is assigned to the corresponding parameter in the method header (in this case, courseName in line 5 of Fig. 4.4). Then the method body uses the parameter courseName to access the value. Lines 6–7 of Fig. 4.4 display parameter courseName's value. The parameter variable's name (Fig. 4.4, line 5) can be the same or different from the argument variable's name (Fig. 4.5, line 19)—there is no conflict if the names are identical, because as we will see in Chapter 7, Methods: A Deeper Look, these names appear in different "scopes."

Note that the parameter declaration in the parameter list looks similar to a variable declaration, but uses keyword *ByVal* instead of Dim. ByVal specifies that the calling program should pass a copy of the value of the argument in the method call to the parameter, which can be used in the method body. Section 7.13 discusses argument-passing options in detail.

A method can specify multiple parameters by separating each from the next with a comma. The number of arguments in a method call must match the number of parameters in the called method's parameter list. Also, the argument types in the method call must be "consistent" with the types of the corresponding parameters in the method's declaration. In our example, the method call (line 19 of Fig. 4.5) passes one argument of type `String` (`nameOfCourse` is declared as a `String` in line 13 of Fig. 4.5) and the method declaration specifies one parameter of type `String` (line 5 in Fig. 4.4), so the type of the argument in the method call is identical to the type of the parameter in the method header.

Updated UML Class Diagram for Class GradeBook
The UML class diagram in Fig. 4.6 models class `GradeBook` of Fig. 4.4. Like Fig. 4.1, this `GradeBook` class contains public operation `DisplayMessage`. However, this version of `DisplayMessage` has a parameter. The UML models a parameter a bit differently from Visual Basic, by listing the parameter name in the parentheses following the operation name, followed by a colon and the parameter type. The UML has several data types that are similar to the Visual Basic types. For example, UML types `String` and `Integer` correspond to Visual Basic types `String` and `Integer`, respectively. Unfortunately, the UML does not provide types that correspond to every Visual Basic type. For this reason, and to avoid confusion between UML types and Visual Basic types, we use only Visual Basic types in our UML diagrams. Class `GradeBook`'s method `DisplayMessage` (Fig. 4.4) has a `String` parameter named `courseName`, so Fig. 4.6 lists `courseName : String` between the parentheses following `DisplayMessage`.

4.5 Instance Variables and Properties
In Chapter 3, we declared all of an application's variables in the `Main` method. Variables declared in the body of a particular method are local variables and can be used only in that method. When a method terminates, the values of its local variables are lost. In contrast, an object's attributes are carried with the object as it is used in a program. Such attributes exist before a method is called on the object, while the method is executing, and after the method completes execution.

Attributes are represented as variables in a class declaration. Such variables are called *instance variables* and are declared inside a class declaration but outside the bodies of the class's other members, such as methods (and properties, which are discussed later in this section). Each object of a class maintains its own copy of an instance variable—that is, each object (instance) of the class has a separate instance of the variable in memory. [*Note:* In Chapter 9, Classes and Objects: A Deeper Look, we discuss another type of variable called

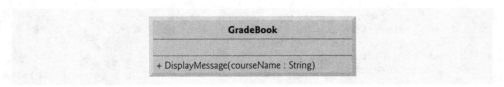

Fig. 4.6 | UML class diagram indicating that class `GradeBook` has a `DisplayMessage` operation with a `courseName` parameter of type `String`.

a Shared variable, where all objects of a class share one copy of the variable.] The following example demonstrates a GradeBook class that contains a courseNameValue instance variable to represent a particular GradeBook object's course name.

GradeBook Class with an Instance Variable and a Property

The next version of class GradeBook (Fig. 4.7) maintains the course name as instance variable courseNameValue (line 5) so that the course name can be used or modified at any time during an application's execution. The class also contains one method—DisplayMessage (lines 19–24)—and one property—CourseName (line 8–16). Recall from Chapter 2 that properties are used to manipulate an object's attributes. For example, in that chapter, we used a Label's Text property to specify the text to display on the Label. In this example, we use a property in code rather than in the **Properties** window of the IDE. To do this, we first declare a property as a member of the GradeBook class. As you'll soon see, the GradeBook's CourseName property can be used to store a course name in a GradeBook (in instance variable courseNameValue) or retrieve the GradeBook's course name (from instance variable courseNameValue). Method DisplayMessage—which now specifies no parameters—still displays a welcome message that includes the course name. However, the method now uses the CourseName property to obtain the course name from instance variable courseNameValue.

```vb
 1    ' Fig. 4.7: GradeBook.vb
 2    ' GradeBook class that contains instance variable courseNameValue
 3    ' and a property to get and set its value.
 4    Public Class GradeBook
 5        Private courseNameValue As String ' course name for this GradeBook
 6
 7        ' property CourseName
 8        Public Property CourseName() As String
 9            Get ' retrieve courseNameValue
10                Return courseNameValue
11            End Get
12
13            Set(ByVal value As String) ' set courseNameValue
14                courseNameValue = value ' store the course name in the object
15            End Set
16        End Property ' CourseName
17
18        ' display a welcome message to the GradeBook user
19        Public Sub DisplayMessage()
20            ' use property CourseName to display the
21            ' name of the course this GradeBook represents
22            Console.WriteLine("Welcome to the grade book for " _
23                & vbCrLf & CourseName & "!")
24        End Sub ' DisplayMessage
25    End Class ' GradeBook
```

Fig. 4.7 | GradeBook class that contains a courseNameValue instance variable and a CourseName property.

A typical instructor teaches more than one course, each with its own course name. Line 5 declares instance variable courseNameValue as a String. Line 5 is a declaration for an instance variable because it is in the body of the class (lines 4–25) but outside the bodies of the class's method (lines 19–24) and property (lines 8–16). Every GradeBook object requires its own copy of instance variable courseNameValue because each object represents a GradeBook for a different course. All the methods and properties of class GradeBook can directly manipulate its instance variable courseNameValue, but it is considered good practice for methods to use properties to manipulate instance variables (as we do in line 23 of method DisplayMessage)—we will see why in Section 4.8, Validating Data with Set Accessors in Properties.

Note that line 23 contains the identifier, *vbCrLf*, which is not declared explicitly in the program. Identifier vbCrLf is one of several predefined *constants* provided by Visual Basic. Constants contain values that programmers cannot modify. The constant vbCrLf represents a combination of the carriage return and linefeed characters. Outputting this constant's value causes subsequent text to display at the beginning of the next line. The effect of this constant is similar to calling Console.WriteLine().

Although not demonstrated in this example, Visual Basic also provides the *vbTab* constant, which represents a *Tab* character. Both the vbCrLf and vbTab constants are defined in the Constants module. To view the complete list of constants, select **Help > Index** and type **Constants module** in the **Look for** field. Then select **Constants module** from the index list to view all of Visual Basic's predefined constants.

Access Modifiers Public and Private

Most instance variable declarations are preceded with the access modifier Private (as in line 5 of Fig. 4.7). Variables, methods and properties that are declared Private are accessible only to methods and properties of the class in which they are declared. Note that the keyword Dim is replaced by Private in an instance variable declaration.

Declaring instance variables with access modifier Private is known as *information hiding*. When a program creates (instantiates) an object of class GradeBook, variable courseNameValue is encapsulated (hidden) in the object and can be accessed only by methods and properties of the object's class.

Software Engineering Observation 4.1

Precede every instance variable declaration, method declaration and property declaration with an access modifier. In most cases, instance variables should be declared Private, and methods and properties should be declared Public. If these modifiers are omitted, instance variables are Private by default, and methods and properties are Public by default. (We'll see in Section 9.2 that it is appropriate to declare certain methods and properties Private if they should be accessed only by other methods and properties of the class.)

Software Engineering Observation 4.2

Declaring the instance variables of a class as Private and the methods of the class as Public facilitates debugging, because problems with data manipulations are localized to the class's methods and properties.

Setting and Getting the Values of Private Instance Variables

How can we allow a program to manipulate a class's Private instance variables but ensure that they remain in a valid state? We need to provide controlled ways for programmers to "get" (i.e., retrieve) the value in an instance variable and "set" (i.e., modify) the value in an instance variable. For these purposes, programmers using languages other than Visual Basic normally use methods known as *get* and *set* methods. These methods typically are made Public, and provide ways for the client to access or modify Private data. Historically, these methods begin with the words "get" and "set"—in our class GradeBook for example, if we were to use such methods they might be called GetCourseNameValue and SetCourse-NameValue, respectively. Although it is possible to define methods with these names, Visual Basic properties provide a more elegant solution.

GradeBook Class with a Property

The GradeBook class's CourseName *property declaration* is located in lines 8–16 of Fig. 4.7. The property begins in line 8 with an access modifier (in this case, Public), followed by the keyword **Property**, the property's name—CourseName—and an empty set of parentheses. The keywords As String indicate that property CourseName represents a String (which in this example is the instance variable courseNameValue).

Properties contain *accessors* that handle the details of returning and modifying data. A property declaration can contain a **Get** *accessor*, a **Set** *accessor* or both. The Get accessor (lines 9–11) enables a client to read the value of Private instance variable courseName-Value; the Set accessor (lines 13–15) enables a client to modify courseNameValue.

After defining a property, you can use it like a variable in your code. For example, you can assign a value to a property using an assignment statement. This executes the code in the property's Set accessor to set the value of the corresponding instance variable. Similarly, referencing the property to use its value (for example, to display it on the screen) executes the code in the property's Get accessor to obtain the corresponding instance variable's value. We will demonstrate how to use properties in a program shortly. When we use properties in our examples, our convention is to append "Value" to instance variable names (e.g., courseNameValue). Visual Basic is not case sensitive, so we cannot have both an instance variable named courseName and a property named CourseName in the same class.

Get and Set Accessors

Let us look more closely at property CourseName's Get and Set accessors (Fig. 4.7). The Get accessor (lines 9–11) begins with the keyword **Get** and ends with the keywords **End Get**. The accessor's body contains a **Return statement**, which consists of the keyword **Return** followed by an expression. The expression's value is returned to the client code that references the property. In this example, the value of courseNameValue is returned when the property CourseName is referenced. For example, the following statement

```
Dim theCourseName As String = gradeBook.CourseName
```

executes property CourseName's Get accessor, which returns the value of instance variable courseNameValue. That value is then stored in variable theCourseName. Note that property CourseName can be used as simply as if it were an instance variable. The property notation allows the client to think of the property as the underlying data. Again, the client cannot directly manipulate instance variable courseNameValue because it is Private.

The Set accessor (lines 13–15) begins with the keyword **Set** and ends with the keywords **End Set**. Following the keyword Set in line 13 is a pair of parentheses enclosing the

Set accessor's parameter. When the property `CourseName` appears in an assignment statement, as in

```
gradeBook.CourseName = "CS100 Introduction to Computers"
```

the text `"CS100 Introduction to Computers"` is automatically passed to the parameter named `value` in line 13, and the `Set` accessor executes. Line 14 then stores `value` in instance variable `courseNameValue`. Set accessors do not return any data when they complete their tasks.

When you type the first line of a property declaration in the IDE and press *Enter*, the IDE creates empty `Get` and `Set` accessors for you. The parameter for the `Set` accessor is named `value` by default, so we use this parameter name in our examples. You can choose a different name if you like.

The statements inside the property's accessors at lines 10 and 14 (Fig. 4.7) each access `courseNameValue` even though it was declared (as `Private`) outside the accessors. We can use variable `courseNameValue` in the methods and properties of class `GradeBook` because `courseNameValue` is an instance variable of the class. The order in which methods and properties are declared in a class does not determine when they are called at execution time, so you can declare method `DisplayMessage` (which uses property `CourseName`) before you declare property `CourseName`. Within the property itself, the `Get` and `Set` accessors can appear in any order, and either accessor can be omitted. In Chapter 9, we discuss how to omit either a `Set` or `Get` accessor to create a "read-only" or "write-only" property, respectively.

Using Property CourseName in Method DisplayMessage

Method `DisplayMessage` (lines 19–24 of Fig. 4.7) does not receive any parameters. Lines 22–23 output a welcome message that includes the value of instance variable `courseNameValue`. We do not reference `courseNameValue` directly. Instead, we access property `CourseName` (line 23), which automatically executes the property's `Get` accessor, returning the value of `courseNameValue`.

GradeBookTest Module That Demonstrates Class GradeBook

Module `GradeBookTest` (Fig. 4.8) creates a `GradeBook` object and demonstrates property `CourseName`. Line 8 creates a `GradeBook` object that is referenced by variable `gradeBook` of type `GradeBook`. Lines 11–12 display the initial course name by referencing the object's `CourseName` property—this executes the property's `Get` accessor, which returns the value of `courseNameValue`. Note that the first line of the output does not contain a course name. Variables have a default initial value—a value provided by Visual Basic when the programmer does not specify the variable's initial value. The default value for numeric types like `Integer` is zero. As we will see in the next section, `String` is a reference type; the default value for reference types is ***Nothing***—a keyword which indicates that a variable does not yet refer to an object. When you display a `String` variable that contains the value `Nothing`, no text is displayed on the screen.

Line 15 prompts the user to enter a course name. Local `String` variable `theName` (declared in line 18) is initialized with the course name entered by the user, which is returned by the call to `Console.ReadLine()`. Line 20 assigns `theName` to the `gradeBook` object's `CourseName` property. When a value is assigned to `CourseName`, the value specified

```
 1   ' Fig. 4.8: GradeBookTest.vb
 2   ' Create and manipulate a GradeBook object.
 3   Module GradeBookTest
 4      ' Main begins program execution
 5      Sub Main()
 6         ' line 8 creates a GradeBook object that is referenced by
 7         ' variable gradeBook of type GradeBook
 8         Dim gradeBook As New GradeBook
 9
10         ' display initial value of property CourseName (invokes Get)
11         Console.WriteLine( _
12            "Initial course name is: " & gradeBook.CourseName & vbCrLf)
13
14         ' prompt for course name
15         Console.WriteLine("Please enter the course name:")
16
17         ' read course name
18         Dim theName As String = Console.ReadLine()
19
20         gradeBook.CourseName = theName ' set the CourseName (invokes Set)
21         Console.WriteLine() ' output a blank line
22
23         ' display welcome message including the course name (invokes Get)
24         gradeBook.DisplayMessage()
25      End Sub ' Main
26   End Module ' GradeBookTest
```

```
Initial course name is:

Please enter the course name:
CS101 Introduction to Visual Basic Programming

Welcome to the grade book for
CS101 Introduction to Visual Basic Programming!
```

Fig. 4.8 | Creating and manipulating a GradeBook object (invoking properties).

(in this case, theName) is assigned to parameter value (line 13 of Fig. 4.7) of CourseName's Set accessor (lines 13–15, Fig. 4.7). Then parameter value is assigned by the Set accessor to instance variable courseNameValue (line 14 of Fig. 4.7). Line 21 (Fig. 4.8) displays a blank line, then line 24 calls gradeBook's DisplayMessage method to display the welcome message containing the course name.

GradeBook's UML Class Diagram with a Property

Figure 4.9 contains an updated UML class diagram for the version of class GradeBook in Fig. 4.7. We model properties in the UML as attributes—the property (in this case, CourseName) is listed as a public attribute—as indicated by the plus (+) sign—preceded by the word "Property" in guillemets (« and »). Using descriptive words in guillemets (called *stereotypes* in the UML) helps distinguish properties from other attributes and operations. The UML indicates the type of the property by placing a colon and a type after the property name. The Get and Set accessors of the property are implied (otherwise, the

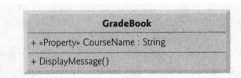

Fig. 4.9 | UML class diagram indicating that class `GradeBook` has a `courseNameValue` attribute of type `String`, one property and one method.

property would be inaccessible), so they are not listed in the UML diagram. In some cases, a property may require only a `Get` accessor to allow client code to retrieve the property's value. This is known as a "read-only" property. You can indicate this in a class diagram by placing the annotation {ReadOnly} after the property's type.

The diagram shows that class `GradeBook` also contains one `Public` method `Display-Message`, which the class diagram lists this operation in the third compartment. Recall that the plus (+) sign before an operation name indicates that the operation is `Public`.

When we demonstrated how to declare a property in Visual Basic code, you saw that we typically name a property the same as the instance variable it manipulates, but with a capital first letter (e.g., property `CourseName` manipulates instance variable `courseName`). A class diagram helps you design a class, so it is not required to show every implementation detail of the class. Since an instance variable that is manipulated by a property is really an implementation detail of that property, our class diagram does not show the `courseName-Value` instance variable. A programmer implementing the `GradeBook` class based on this class diagram would create the instance variable `courseNameValue` as part of the implementation process (as we did in Fig. 4.7).

In some cases, you may find it necessary to model the `Private` instance variables of a class, because they are not implementation details of properties. Like properties, instance variables are attributes of a class and are modeled in the middle compartment of a class diagram. The UML represents instance variables as attributes by listing the attribute name, followed by a colon and the attribute type. To indicate that an attribute is `private`, a class diagram would list a minus sign (–) before the attribute's name. For example, the instance variable `courseNameValue` in Fig. 4.7 would be modeled as "– courseNameValue : string"

Software Engineering with Properties and Set and Get Accessors
Using properties as described earlier in this section would seem to violate the notion of `Private` data. Although providing a property with `Get` and `Set` accessors may appear to be the same as making its corresponding instance variable `Public`, this is not the case. A `Public` instance variable can be read or written by any method in the program. If an instance variable is `Private`, the client code can access the instance variable only indirectly through the class's non-`Private` methods or properties. This allows the class to control the manner in which the data is set or returned. For example, `Get` and `Set` accessors can translate between the format of the data used by the client and the format stored in the `Private` instance variable.

Consider a `Clock` class that represents the time of day as a `Private Integer` instance variable `timeValue` containing the number of seconds since midnight. Suppose the class provides a `Time` property of type `String` to manipulate this instance variable. Although `Get` accessors typically return data exactly as it is stored in an object, they need not expose the data in this "raw" format. When a client refers to a `Clock` object's `Time` property, the property's `Get` accessor could use instance variable `timeValue` to determine the number of hours, minutes and seconds since midnight, then return the time as a `String` of the form `"HH:MM:SS"`. Similarly, suppose a `Clock` object's `Time` property is assigned a `String` of the form `"HH:MM:SS"`. Using the `String` capabilities presented in Section 4.8 and the method `Convert.ToInt32` presented in Section 7.10, the `Time` property's `Set` accessor could convert this `String` to an `Integer` number of seconds and store the result in the `Clock` object's `Private` instance variable `timeValue`. The `Time` property's `Set` accessor can also provide data validation capabilities that scrutinize attempts to modify the instance variable's value to ensure that the value it receives represents a valid time (e.g., `"12:30:45"` is valid but `"42:85:70"` is not). We demonstrate data validation in Section 4.8. So, although a property's accessors enable clients to manipulate `Private` data, they carefully control those manipulations and the object's `Private` data remains safely encapsulated (i.e., hidden) in the object. This is not possible with `Public` instance variables, which can easily be set by clients to invalid values.

Properties of a class should also be used by the class's own methods to manipulate the class's `Private` instance variables, even though the methods can directly access the `Private` instance variables. Accessing an instance variable via a property's accessors—as in the body of method `DisplayMessage` (Fig. 4.7, line 23)—creates a better, more robust class that is easier to maintain and less likely to malfunction. If we decide to change the representation of instance variable `courseNameValue` in some way, the declaration of method `DisplayMessage` will not require modification—only the bodies of property `CourseName`'s `Get` and `Set` accessors that directly manipulate the instance variable will need to change. For example, suppose that we want to represent the course name as two separate instance variables—`courseNumber` (e.g., `"CS101"`) and `courseTitle` (e.g., `"Introduction to Visual Basic Programming"`). The `DisplayMessage` method can still use property `CourseName`'s `Get` accessor to obtain the full course name to display as part of the welcome message. In this case, the `Get` accessor would need to build and return a `String` containing the `courseNumber` followed by the `courseTitle`. Method `DisplayMessage` would continue to display the complete course title "CS101 Introduction to Visual Basic Programming," because it is unaffected by the change to the class's instance variables.

Software Engineering Observation 4.3

Accessing Private *data through* Set *and* Get *accessors not only protects the instance variables from receiving invalid values, but also hides the internal representation of the instance variables from that class's clients. Thus, if representation of the data changes (often, to reduce the amount of required storage or to improve performance), only the properties' implementations need to change—the clients' implementations need not change as long as the services provided by the properties are preserved.*

4.6 Value Types and Reference Types

Data types in Visual Basic are divided into two categories—*value types* and *reference types*. A variable of a value type (such as `Integer`) simply contains a value of that type. For example, Fig. 4.10 shows an `Integer` variable named `count` that contains the value 7.

By contrast, a variable of a reference type (sometimes called a *reference*) contains the memory address where the data referred to by that variable is stored. Such a variable is said

Fig. 4.10 | Value type variable.

to *refer to an object* in the program. Line 8 of Fig. 4.8 creates a GradeBook object, places it in memory and stores the object's memory address in reference variable gradeBook of type GradeBook as shown in Fig. 4.11. Note that the GradeBook object is shown with its courseNameValue instance variable.

Reference type instance variables (such as gradeBook in Fig. 4.11) are initialized by default to the value Nothing. Except for type String, Visual Basic's primitive types are value types—String is a reference type. For this reason, the String variable courseName-Value is shown in Fig. 4.11 with an empty box representing the variable in memory.

A client of an object must use a reference to the object to *invoke* (i.e., call) the object's methods and access the object's properties. In Fig. 4.8, the statements in Main use variable gradeBook, which contains the GradeBook object's reference, to send messages to the GradeBook object. These messages are calls to methods (like DisplayMessage) or references to properties (like CourseName) that enable the program to interact with GradeBook objects. For example, the statement (in line 20)

```
gradeBook.CourseName = theName ' set the CourseName (invokes Set)
```

uses gradeBook to set the course name by assigning a value to property CourseName. This sends a message to the GradeBook object to invoke the CourseName property's Set accessor. The message includes as an argument the value (i.e., the value of theName, namely CS101 Introduction to Visual Basic Programming) that CourseName's Set accessor requires to perform its task. The Set accessor uses this information to set the courseNameValue instance variable. In Section 7.11, we discuss value types and reference types in detail.

4.7 Initializing Objects with Constructors

As mentioned in Section 4.5, when an object of class GradeBook (Fig. 4.7) is created, its instance variable courseNameValue is initialized to Nothing by default. What if you want to provide a course name when you create a GradeBook object? Each class you declare can

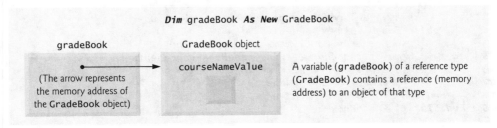

Fig. 4.11 | Reference type variable.

provide a constructor that can be used to initialize an object of the class when the object is created. In fact, Visual Basic requires a constructor call for every object that is created. The New keyword calls the class's constructor to perform the initialization. The constructor call is indicated by the class name followed by parentheses. For example, line 8 of Fig. 4.8 first uses New to create a GradeBook object. The lack of parentheses after "New GradeBook" indicates a call to the class's constructor that takes no arguments. By default, the compiler provides a *default constructor* with no parameters in any class that does not explicitly include a constructor.

When you declare a class, you can provide your own constructor to specify custom initialization for objects of your class. For example, a programmer might want to specify a course name for a GradeBook object when the object is created, as in

```
Dim gradeBook As New GradeBook( _
    "CS101 Introduction to Visual Basic Programming")
```

This passes the argument "CS101 Introduction to Visual Basic Programming" to the GradeBook object's constructor, which uses the argument value to initialize instance variable courseNameValue. The preceding statement requires that the class provide a constructor with a String parameter. Figure 4.12 contains a modified GradeBook class with such a constructor.

```vb
1  ' Fig. 4.12: GradeBook.vb
2  ' GradeBook class with a constructor to initialize the course name.
3  Public Class GradeBook
4     Private courseNameValue As String ' course name for this GradeBook
5
6     ' constructor initializes course name with String supplied as argument
7     Public Sub New(ByVal name As String)
8        CourseName = name ' initialize courseNameValue via property
9     End Sub ' New
10
11    ' property CourseName
12    Public Property CourseName() As String
13       Get ' retrieve courseNameValue
14          Return courseNameValue
15       End Get
16
17       Set(ByVal value As String) ' set courseNameValue
18          courseNameValue = value ' store the course name in the object
19       End Set
20    End Property ' CourseName
21
22    ' display a welcome message to the GradeBook user
23    Public Sub DisplayMessage()
24       ' use property CourseName to display the
25       ' name of the course this GradeBook represents
26       Console.WriteLine("Welcome to the grade book for " _
27          & vbCrLf & CourseName & "!")
28    End Sub ' DisplayMessage
29 End Class ' GradeBook
```

Fig. 4.12 | GradeBook class with a constructor that receives a course name.

Lines 7–9 declare the constructor for class GradeBook—a constructor must have the name New. As with the other methods we have declared, a constructor specifies in its parameter list the data it requires to perform its task. When you create a new object, this data is placed in the parentheses that follow the class name (as in lines 8–11 of Fig. 4.13). Line 7 (Fig. 4.12) indicates that class GradeBook's constructor has a parameter called name of type String.

Line 8 of the constructor's body assigns name to property CourseName. This causes the Set accessor of property CourseName to execute, which (in line 18) assigns parameter value to instance variable courseNameValue. You might be wondering why we bother using property CourseName—the constructor certainly could perform the assignment courseNameValue = name. In Section 4.8, we will modify the Set accessor of property CourseName to perform validation (in this case, to ensure that the courseNameValue is 25 or fewer characters in length). At that point the benefits of using property CourseName from the constructor will become clear.

Figure 4.13 demonstrates initializing GradeBook objects using this constructor. Lines 8–9 create and initialize a GradeBook object. The constructor of class GradeBook is called with the argument "CS101 Introduction to Visual Basic Programming" to initialize the course name. The object-creation expression in lines 8–9 returns a reference to the new object, which is assigned to variable gradeBook1. Lines 10–11 repeat this process for another GradeBook object, this time passing the argument "CS102 Data Structures in Visual Basic" to initialize the course name for gradeBook2. Lines 14–17 use each object's CourseName property to display the course names and show that they were initialized properly when the objects were created. The output confirms that each GradeBook maintains its own copy of instance variable courseNameValue.

```vb
1   ' Fig. 4.13: GradeBookTest.vb
2   ' GradeBook constructor used to specify the course name at the
3   ' time each GradeBook object is created.
4   Module GradeBookTest
5      ' Main begins program execution
6      Sub Main()
7         ' create GradeBook object
8         Dim gradeBook1 As New GradeBook( _
9            "CS101 Introduction to Visual Basic Programming")
10        Dim gradeBook2 As New GradeBook( _
11           "CS102 Data Structures in Visual Basic")
12
13        ' display initial value of CourseName for each GradeBook
14        Console.WriteLine( _
15           "gradeBook1 course name is: " & gradeBook1.CourseName)
16        Console.WriteLine( _
17           "gradeBook2 course name is: " & gradeBook2.CourseName)
18     End Sub ' Main
19  End Module ' GradeBookTest
```

```
gradeBook1 course name is: CS101 Introduction to Visual Basic Programming
gradeBook2 course name is: CS102 Data Structures in Visual Basic
```

Fig. 4.13 | Constructor used to initialize GradeBook objects.

Like other methods, constructors also can take arguments. However, an important difference between constructors and methods is that constructor declarations cannot return values (even though, as you know, each constructor does return a reference—to an object of its class type). Normally, constructors are declared Public. If a class does not include a constructor, the class's instance variables are initialized to their default values.

Error-Prevention Tip 4.1

Unless default initialization of your class's instance variables is acceptable, provide a constructor to ensure that these variables are properly initialized with meaningful values when each new object of your class is created.

Adding the Constructor to Class GradeBook's UML Class Diagram

The UML class diagram of Fig. 4.14 models the class GradeBook of Fig. 4.12, which has a constructor that has a name parameter of type String. Like operations, the UML models constructors in the third compartment of a class in a class diagram. To distinguish a constructor from a class's operations, the UML places the word "constructor" between guillemets (« and ») before the constructor's name (New). It is customary to list constructors before other operations in the third compartment.

4.8 Validating Data with Set Accessors in Properties

In Section 4.5, we introduced properties whose Set accessors allow clients of a class to modify the value of a Private instance variable. In Fig. 4.7, class GradeBook defines property CourseName's Set accessor to assign the value received in its parameter value to instance variable courseNameValue (line 14). This CourseName property does not ensure that courseNameValue contains valid data. In this section, we enhance our property to include data validation in its Set accessor. Property CourseName (Fig. 4.12) does not ensure that the course name adheres to any particular format or follows any other rules regarding what a "valid" course name is. Suppose that a university can display student transcripts in an online form that can hold course names of only 25 or fewer characters. If the university uses a system containing GradeBook objects to generate the transcripts, we might want class GradeBook to ensure that its courseNameValue never contains more than 25 characters. The program of Figs. 4.15–4.16 enhances class GradeBook's property CourseName to perform this validation.

GradeBook Class Definition

GradeBook's class definition in Fig. 4.15 contains all the same members as Fig. 4.12. Since the name and type of the property remain unchanged, clients of this class need not be

GradeBook
+ «Property» CourseName : String
+ «constructor» New(name : String)
+ DisplayMessage()

Fig. 4.14 | UML class diagram indicating that class GradeBook has a constructor that has a name parameter of type String.

```vbnet
1   ' Fig. 4.15: GradeBook.vb
2   ' GradeBook class with a property that performs validation.
3   Public Class GradeBook
4      Private courseNameValue As String ' course name for this GradeBook
5
6      ' constructor initializes CourseName with String supplied as argument
7      Public Sub New(ByVal name As String)
8         CourseName = name ' validate and store course name
9      End Sub ' New
10
11     ' property that gets and sets the course name; the Set accessor
12     ' ensures that the course name has at most 25 characters
13     Public Property CourseName() As String
14        Get ' retrieve courseNameValue
15           Return courseNameValue
16        End Get
17
18        Set(ByVal value As String) ' set courseNameValue
19           If value.Length <= 25 Then ' if value has 25 or fewer characters
20              courseNameValue = value ' store the course name in the object
21           End If
22
23           If value.Length > 25 Then ' if value has more than 25 characters
24              ' set courseNameValue to first 25 characters of value
25              ' start at 0, length of 25
26              courseNameValue = value.Substring(0, 25)
27
28              Console.WriteLine( _
29                 "Name """ & value & """ exceeds maximum length (25).")
30              Console.WriteLine( _
31                 "Limiting course name to first 25 characters." & vbCrLf)
32           End If
33        End Set
34     End Property ' CourseName
35
36     ' display a welcome message to the GradeBook user
37     Public Sub DisplayMessage()
38        ' this statement uses property CourseName to get the
39        ' name of the course this GradeBook represents
40        Console.WriteLine("Welcome to the grade book for " _
41           & vbCrLf & CourseName & "!")
42     End Sub ' DisplayMessage
43  End Class ' GradeBook
```

Fig. 4.15 | Method declarations for class GradeBook with a CourseName property that validates the length of instance variable courseNameValue.

changed when the definition of property CourseName is modified. This enables clients to take advantage of the improved GradeBook class without having to modify their own code.

Validating the Course Name with GradeBook Property CourseName
The enhancement to class GradeBook is in the definition of CourseName's Set accessor (Fig. 4.15, lines 18–33). The If...Then statement in lines 19–21 determines whether pa-

rameter `value` contains a valid course name (i.e., a `String` of 25 or fewer characters). If the course name is valid, line 20 stores it in instance variable `courseNameValue`. Note the expression `value.Length` in line 19. *Length* is a property of class `String` that returns the number of characters in the `String`. Parameter `value` is a `String` object, so the expression `value.Length` returns the number of characters in `value`. If `value.Length` is less than or equal to 25, `value` is valid and line 20 executes.

The `If...Then` statement in lines 23–32 handles the case in which `CourseName` receives an invalid course name (i.e., a name longer than 25 characters). Even if the `String` in parameter `value` is too long, we still want to leave the `GradeBook` object in a *consistent state*—that is, a state in which the object's instance variable `courseNameValue` contains a `String` of 25 or fewer characters. We choose to truncate (i.e., shorten) the specified course name and assign the first 25 characters of `value` to the `courseNameValue` instance variable (unfortunately, this could truncate the course name awkwardly). Class `String` provides method *Substring* that returns a new `String` object created by copying part of an existing `String` object. The call in line 26 (i.e., `value.Substring(0, 25)`) passes two integers (0 and 25) to `value`'s method `Substring`. These arguments indicate the portion of the string `value` that `Substring` should return. The first argument specifies the starting position in the original `String` from which characters are to be copied—the first character in every string is considered to be at position 0. The second argument specifies the number of characters to copy. Therefore, the call in line 26 returns a 25-character substring of `value` starting at position 0 (i.e., the first 25 characters in `value`). For example, if `value` holds `"CS101 Introduction to Visual Basic Programming"`, `Substring` returns `"CS101 Introduction to Vis"`. After the call to `Substring`, line 26 assigns the substring returned by `Substring` to `courseNameValue`. In this way, property `CourseName` ensures that `courseNameValue` is always assigned a string containing 25 or fewer characters. If the property has to truncate the course name to make it valid, lines 28–31 display a warning message. Note that line 29 displays a string of text that includes double quotes ("). Double quotes are normally used to delimit string literals, so to display double quotes in a string, you use two double quotes in a row.

Testing Class GradeBook

Figure 4.16 demonstrates the modified version of class `GradeBook` featuring validation. Lines 8–9 create a `GradeBook` object named `gradeBook1`. Note that the `GradeBook` constructor (lines 7–9 of Fig. 4.15) references property `CourseName` to initialize `courseNameValue`. In previous versions of the class, the benefit of referencing the property `CourseName` in the constructor was not evident. Now, however, the constructor takes advantage of the validation provided by the `Set` accessor of the `CourseName` property. The constructor simply assigns a value to `CourseName` rather than duplicate the `Set` accessor's validation code. When line 9 of Fig. 4.16 passes an initial course name of `"CS101 Introduction to Visual Basic Programming"` to the `GradeBook` constructor, the constructor passes this value to the `Set` accessor of `CourseName`, where the actual initialization occurs. This course name contains more than 25 characters, so the body of the second `If...Then` statement (lines 23–32 of Fig. 4.15) executes, causing `courseNameValue` to be initialized to the truncated 25-character course name `"CS101 Introduction to Vis"` (the truncated part of the `String` is syntax shaded in bold black in line 9 of Fig. 4.16). The output in Fig. 4.16 contains the warning message output by lines 28–31 of Fig. 4.15. Line 10 of Fig. 4.16 creates another

```vb
1    ' Fig. 4.16: GradeBookTest.vb
2    ' Create and manipulate a GradeBook object; illustrate validation.
3    Module GradeBookTest
4       ' Main begins program execution
5       Sub Main()
6          ' create two GradeBook objects;
7          ' initial course name of gradeBook1 is too long
8          Dim gradeBook1 As New GradeBook( _
9             "CS101 Introduction to Visual Basic Programming")
10         Dim gradeBook2 As New GradeBook("CS102 VB Data Structures")
11
12         ' display each GradeBook's course name (by invoking Get)
13         Console.WriteLine("gradeBook1's initial course name is: " & _
14            gradeBook1.CourseName)
15         Console.WriteLine("gradeBook2's initial course name is: " & _
16            gradeBook2.CourseName)
17         Console.WriteLine() ' display blank line
18
19         ' place in gradeBook1's course name a valid-length String
20         gradeBook1.CourseName = "CS101 VB Programming"
21
22         ' display each GradeBook's course name (by invoking Get)
23         Console.WriteLine( _
24            "gradeBook1's course name is: " & gradeBook1.CourseName)
25         Console.WriteLine( _
26            "gradeBook2's course name is: " & gradeBook2.CourseName)
27      End Sub ' Main
28   End Module ' GradeBookTest
```

```
Name "CS101 Introduction to Visual Basic Programming" exceeds maximum length
(25).
Limiting course name to first 25 characters.

gradeBook1's initial course name is: CS101 Introduction to Vis
gradeBook2's initial course name is: CS102 VB Data Structures

gradeBook1's course name is: CS101 VB Programming
gradeBook2's course name is: CS102 VB Data Structures
```

Fig. 4.16 | Creating and manipulating a GradeBook object in which the course name is limited to 25 characters in length.

GradeBook object called gradeBook2—the valid course name passed to the constructor contains fewer than 25 characters (it contains 24 characters to be exact).

Lines 13–16 of Fig. 4.16 display the truncated course name for gradeBook1 (we highlight this in bold black in the program output) and the course name for gradeBook2. Line 20 assigns a new value to gradeBook1's CourseName property, to change the course name in the GradeBook object to a shorter name that does not need to be truncated. Then lines 23–26 output the course names for the GradeBook objects again.

A class's Set accessors cannot return values that indicate a failed attempt to assign invalid data to objects of the class. Such return values could be useful to a class's clients for handling errors—clients could then take appropriate actions. Chapter 12 presents exception handling—a mechanism that can be used (among other things) to notify a class's clients of attempts to set objects of that class to inconsistent states. To keep the program of Figs. 4.15–4.16 simple at this early point in the book, the `CourseName` property's `Set` accessor in Fig. 4.15 prints an appropriate message on the screen and sets `courseName-Value` to the first 25 characters of the specified course name.

Set and Get Accessors with Different Access Modifiers

By default, the `Get` and `Set` accessors of a property have the same access as the property—in other words, for a `Public` property, the accessors also are `Public`. In Visual Basic, it is possible to declare the `Get` and `Set` accessors with different access modifiers. In this case, one of the accessors must have the same access as the property and the other must be more restrictive than the property. For example, in a `Public` property, the `Get` accessor might be `Public` and the `Set` accessor might be `Private`.

Error-Prevention Tip 4.2

The benefits of data integrity are not automatic simply because instance variables are made `Private`—the programmer must provide appropriate validity checking and report the errors.

Error-Prevention Tip 4.3

Set accessors that set the values of `Private` data should verify that the intended new values are proper; if they are not, the `Set` accessors should place the `Private` instance variables into an appropriately consistent state.

4.9 (Optional) Software Engineering Case Study: Identifying the Classes in the ATM Requirements Document

Now we begin designing the ATM system that we introduced in Chapter 3. In this section, we identify the classes that are needed to build the ATM system by analyzing the nouns and noun phrases that appear in the requirements document. We introduce UML class diagrams to model the relationships among these classes. This is an important first step in defining the structure of our system.

Identifying the Classes in a System

We begin our OOD process by identifying the classes required to build the ATM system. We will eventually describe these classes using UML class diagrams and implement these classes in Visual Basic. First, we review the requirements document of Section 3.9 and find key nouns and noun phrases to help us identify classes that comprise the ATM system. We may decide that some of the nouns and noun phrases are attributes of other classes in the system. We may also conclude that some of the nouns and noun phrases do not correspond to parts of the system and thus should not be modeled at all. Additional classes may become apparent as we proceed through the design process.

Figure 4.17 lists the nouns and noun phrases in the requirements document. We list them from left to right in the order in which they appear in the requirements document.

We create classes only for the nouns and noun phrases that have significance in the ATM system. We do not need to model "bank" as a class, because the bank is not a part of the ATM system—the bank simply wants us to build the ATM. "User" and "customer"

Nouns and noun phrases in the requirements document		
bank	money / funds	account number
ATM	screen	PIN
user	keypad	bank database
customer	cash dispenser	balance inquiry
transaction	$20 bill / cash	withdrawal
account	deposit slot	deposit
balance	deposit envelope	

Fig. 4.17 | Nouns and noun phrases in the requirements document.

also represent entities outside of the system—they are important because they interact with our ATM system, but we do not need to model them as classes in the ATM system itself. Recall that we modeled an ATM user (i.e., a bank customer) as the actor in the use case diagram of Fig. 3.34.

We do not model "$20 bill" or "deposit envelope" as classes. These are physical objects in the real world, but they are not part of what is being automated. We can adequately represent the presence of $20 bills in the system using an attribute of the class that models the cash dispenser. (We assign attributes to classes in Section 5.14.) For example, the cash dispenser maintains a count of the number of bills it contains. The requirements document does not say anything about what the system should do with deposit envelopes after it receives them. We can assume that simply acknowledging the receipt of an envelope—an operation performed by the class that models the deposit slot—is sufficient to represent the presence of an envelope in the system. (We assign operations to classes in Section 7.20.)

In our simplified ATM system, representing various amounts of "money," including the "balance" of an account, as attributes of other classes seems most appropriate. Likewise, the nouns "account number" and "PIN" represent significant pieces of information in the ATM system. They are important attributes of a bank account. They do not, however, exhibit behaviors. Thus, we can most appropriately model them as attributes of an account class.

Though the requirements document frequently describes a "transaction" in a general sense, we do not model the broad notion of a financial transaction at this time. Instead, we model the three types of transactions (i.e., "balance inquiry," "withdrawal" and "deposit") as individual classes. These classes possess specific attributes needed for executing the transactions they represent. For example, a withdrawal needs to know the amount of money the user wants to withdraw. A balance inquiry, however, does not require any additional data. Furthermore, the three transaction classes exhibit unique behaviors. A withdrawal includes dispensing cash to the user, whereas a deposit involves receiving a deposit envelope from the user. [*Note:* In Section 11.8, we "factor out" common features of all transactions into a general "transaction" class using the object-oriented concepts of abstract classes and inheritance.]

We determine the classes for our system based on the remaining nouns and noun phrases from Fig. 4.17. Each of these refers to one or more of the following:

- ATM
- screen
- keypad
- cash dispenser
- deposit slot
- account
- bank database
- balance inquiry
- withdrawal
- deposit

The elements of this list are likely to be classes we will need to implement our system, although it's too early in our process to claim that this list is complete.

We can now begin modeling the classes in our system based on the list we have created. We capitalize class names in the design process—a UML convention—as we will do when we write the actual Visual Basic code that implements our design. If the name of a class contains more than one word, we run the words together and capitalize each word (e.g., `MultipleWordName`). Using these conventions, we create classes ATM, `Screen`, `Keypad`, `CashDispenser`, `DepositSlot`, `Account`, `BankDatabase`, `BalanceInquiry`, `Withdrawal` and `Deposit`. We construct our system using all of these classes as building blocks. Before we begin building the system, however, we must gain a better understanding of how the classes relate to one another.

Modeling Classes

The UML enables us to model, via *class diagrams*, the classes in the ATM system and their interrelationships. Figure 4.18 represents class ATM. In the UML, each class is modeled as a rectangle with three compartments. The top compartment contains the name of the class, centered horizontally and appearing in boldface. The middle compartment contains the class's attributes (which we discuss in Section 5.14 and Section 6.11.) The bottom compartment contains the class's operations (which we discuss in Section 7.20). In Fig. 4.18 the middle and bottom compartments are empty, because we have not yet determined the ATM class's attributes and operations.

Class diagrams also show the relationships between the classes of the system. Figure 4.19 shows how classes ATM and `Withdrawal` relate to one another. For the

Fig. 4.18 | Representing a class in the UML using a class diagram.

Fig. 4.19 | Class diagram showing an association among classes.

moment, we choose to model only this subset of the ATM classes for simplicity. We present a more complete class diagram later in this section. Notice that the rectangles representing classes in this diagram are not subdivided into compartments. The UML allows the suppression of class attributes and operations in this manner, when appropriate, to create more readable diagrams. Such a diagram is said to be an *elided diagram*—one in which some information, such as the contents of the second and third compartments, is not modeled. We will place information in these compartments in Section 5.14 and Section 7.20.

In Fig. 4.19, the solid line that connects the two classes represents an *association*—a relationship between classes. The numbers near each end of the line are *multiplicity* values, which indicate how many objects of each class participate in the association. In this case, following the line from the ATM to the Withdrawal reveals that, at any given moment, one ATM object participates in an association with either zero or one Withdrawal objects— zero if the current user is not performing a transaction or has requested a different type of transaction, and one if the user has requested a withdrawal. The UML can model many types of multiplicity (Fig. 4.20).

An association can be named. For example, the word Executes above the line connecting classes ATM and Withdrawal in Fig. 4.19 indicates the name of that association. This part of the diagram reads "one object of class ATM executes zero or one objects of class Withdrawal." Note that association names are directional, as indicated by the filled arrowhead—so it would be improper, for example, to read the preceding association from right to left as "zero or one objects of class Withdrawal execute one object of class ATM."

Symbol	Meaning
0	None
1	One
m	An integer value
0..1	Zero or one
m, n	m or n
$m..n$	At least m, but not more than n
*	Any nonnegative integer (zero or more)
0..*	Zero or more (identical to *)
1..*	One or more

Fig. 4.20 | Multiplicity types.

The word `currentTransaction` at the `Withdrawal` end of the association line in Fig. 4.19 is a *role name*, which identifies the role the `Withdrawal` object plays in its relationship with the `ATM` object. A role name adds meaning to an association between classes by identifying the role a class plays in the context of an association. A class can play several roles in the same system. For example, in a college personnel system, a person may play the role of "professor" when relating to students. The same person may take on the role of "colleague" when participating in a relationship with another professor, and "coach" when coaching student athletes. In Fig. 4.19, the role name `currentTransaction` indicates that the `Withdrawal` object participating in the `Executes` association with an object of class `ATM` represents the transaction currently being processed by the ATM. In other contexts, a `Withdrawal` object may take on other roles (e.g., the previous transaction). Notice that we do not specify a role name for the `ATM` end of the `Executes` association. Role names in class diagrams are often omitted when the meaning of an association is clear without them.

In addition to indicating simple relationships, associations can specify more complex relationships, such as objects of one class being composed of objects of other classes. Consider a real-world automated teller machine. What "pieces" does a manufacturer put together to build a working ATM? Our requirements document tells us that the ATM is composed of a screen, a keypad, a cash dispenser and a deposit slot.

In Fig. 4.21, the solid diamonds attached to the association lines of class `ATM` indicate that class `ATM` has a *composition* relationship with classes `Screen`, `Keypad`, `CashDispenser` and `DepositSlot`. Composition implies a whole/part relationship. The class that has the composition symbol (the solid diamond) on its end of the association line is the whole (in this case, `ATM`), and the classes on the other end of the association lines are the parts—in this case, classes `Screen`, `Keypad`, `CashDispenser` and `DepositSlot`. The compositions in Fig. 4.21 indicate that an object of class `ATM` is formed from one object of class `Screen`, one object of class `CashDispenser`, one object of class `Keypad` and one object of class `DepositSlot`—the ATM "has a" screen, a keypad, a cash dispenser and a deposit slot. The *"has-a" relationship* defines composition. (We'll see in Section 11.8 that the "is-a" relationship defines inheritance.)

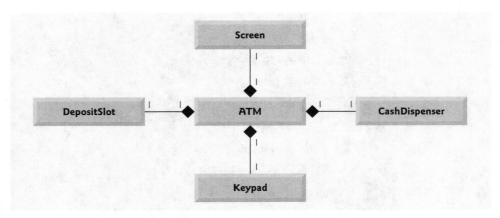

Fig. 4.21 | Class diagram showing composition relationships.

According to the UML specification, composition relationships have the following properties:

1. Only one class in the relationship can represent the whole (i.e., the diamond can be placed on only one end of the association line). For example, either the screen is part of the ATM or the ATM is part of the screen, but the screen and the ATM cannot both represent the whole in the relationship.

2. The parts in the composition relationship exist only as long as the whole, and the whole is responsible for creating and destroying its parts. For example, the act of constructing an ATM includes manufacturing its parts. Furthermore, if the ATM is destroyed, its screen, keypad, cash dispenser and deposit slot are also destroyed.

3. A part may belong to only one whole at a time, although the part may be removed and attached to another whole, which then assumes responsibility for the part.

The solid diamonds in our class diagrams indicate composition relationships that fulfill these three properties. If a "has-a" relationship does not satisfy one or more of these criteria, the UML specifies that hollow diamonds be attached to the ends of association lines to indicate *aggregation*—a weaker form of composition. For example, a personal computer and a computer monitor participate in an aggregation relationship—the computer "has a" monitor, but the two parts can exist independently, and the same monitor can be attached to multiple computers at once, thus violating the second and third properties of composition.

Figure 4.22 shows a class diagram for the ATM system. This diagram models most of the classes that we identified earlier in this section, as well as the associations between them that we can infer from the requirements document. [*Note:* Classes BalanceInquiry and Deposit participate in associations similar to those of class Withdrawal, so we have chosen to omit them from this diagram for simplicity. In Chapter 11, we expand our class diagram to include all the classes in the ATM system.]

Figure 4.22 presents a graphical model of the structure of the ATM system. This class diagram includes classes BankDatabase and Account, and several associations that were not present in either Fig. 4.19 or Fig. 4.21. The class diagram shows that class ATM has a *one-to-one relationship* with class BankDatabase—one ATM object authenticates users against one BankDatabase object. In Fig. 4.22, we also model the fact that the bank's database contains information about many accounts—one object of class BankDatabase participates in a composition relationship with zero or more Account objects. Recall from Fig. 4.20 that the multiplicity value 0..* at the Account end of the association between class BankDatabase and class Account indicates that zero or more objects of class Account take part in the association. Class BankDatabase has a *one-to-many relationship* with class Account—the BankDatabase can contain many Accounts. Similarly, class Account has a *many-to-one relationship* with class BankDatabase—there can be many Accounts in the BankDatabase. Recall from Fig. 4.20 that the multiplicity value * is identical to 0..*.

Figure 4.22 also indicates that if the user is performing a withdrawal, "one object of class Withdrawal accesses/modifies an account balance through one object of class Bank-Database." We could have created an association directly between class Withdrawal and class Account. The requirements document, however, states that the "ATM must interact with the bank's account information database" to perform transactions. A bank account contains sensitive information, and systems engineers must always consider the security of

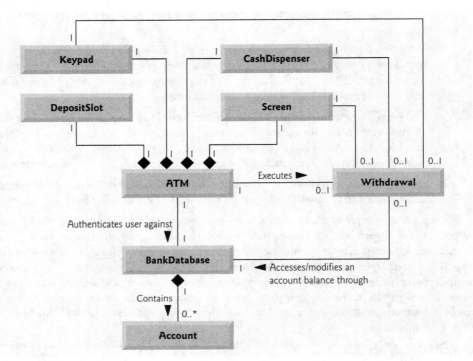

Fig. 4.22 | Class diagram for the ATM system model.

personal data when designing a system. Thus, only the `BankDatabase` can access and manipulate an account directly. All other parts of the system must interact with the database to retrieve or update account information (e.g., an account balance).

The class diagram in Fig. 4.22 also models associations between class `Withdrawal` and classes `Screen`, `CashDispenser` and `Keypad`. A withdrawal transaction includes prompting the user to choose a withdrawal amount and receiving numeric input. These actions require the use of the screen and the keypad, respectively. Furthermore, dispensing cash to the user requires access to the cash dispenser.

Classes `BalanceInquiry` and `Deposit`, though not shown in Fig. 4.22, take part in several associations with the other classes of the ATM system. Like class `Withdrawal`, each of these classes associates with classes `ATM` and `BankDatabase`. An object of class `Balance-Inquiry` also associates with an object of class `Screen` to display the balance of an account to the user. Class `Deposit` associates with classes `Screen`, `Keypad` and `DepositSlot`. Like withdrawals, deposit transactions require use of the screen and the keypad to display prompts and receive inputs, respectively. To receive a deposit envelope, an object of class `Deposit` associates with an object of class `DepositSlot`.

We have identified the classes in our ATM system, although we may discover others as we proceed with the design and implementation. In Section 5.14, we determine the attributes for each of these classes, and in Section 6.11, we use these attributes to examine how the system changes over time. In Section 7.20, we determine the operations of the classes in our system.

Software Engineering Case Study Self-Review Exercises

4.1   Suppose we have a class Car that represents a car. Think of some of the different pieces that a manufacturer would put together to produce a whole car. Create a class diagram (similar to Fig. 4.21) that models some of the composition relationships of class Car.

4.2   Suppose we have a class File that represents an electronic document in a stand-alone, non-networked computer represented by class Computer. What sort of association exists between class Computer and class File?

    a) Class Computer has a one-to-one relationship with class File.
    b) Class Computer has a many-to-one relationship with class File.
    c) Class Computer has a one-to-many relationship with class File.
    d) Class Computer has a many-to-many relationship with class File.

4.3   State whether the following statement is *true* or *false*, and if *false*, explain why: A UML class diagram in which a class's second and third compartments are not modeled is said to be an elided diagram.

4.4   Modify the class diagram of Fig. 4.22 to include class Deposit instead of class Withdrawal.

Answers to Software Engineering Case Study Self-Review Exercises

4.1   Figure 4.23 presents a class diagram that shows some of the composition relationships of a class Car.

4.2   c. In a computer network, this relationship could be many-to-many.

4.3   True.

4.4   Figure 4.24 presents a class diagram for the ATM including class Deposit instead of class Withdrawal (as in Fig. 4.22). Note that class Deposit does not associate with class CashDispenser, but does associate with class DepositSlot.

4.10 Wrap-Up

In this chapter, we presented the basic concepts of classes, objects, methods, instance variables and properties. You learned how to declare instance variables of a class to maintain separate data for each object of the class, and how to declare methods that operate on that data. You called methods and passed arguments to them. We explained the difference between a

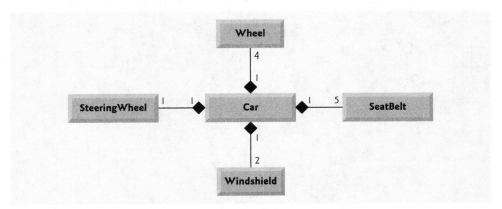

Fig. 4.23 | Class diagram showing some composition relationships of a class Car.

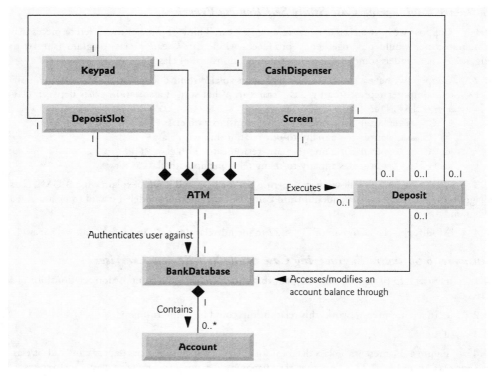

Fig. 4.24 | Class diagram for the ATM system model including class `Deposit`.

local variable of a method and an instance variable of a class. You used a class's constructor to specify the initial values for an object's instance variables. You saw how UML class diagrams model the constructors, operations, attributes and properties of classes. Finally, we demonstrated how `Set` accessors in properties can be used to validate an object's data and ensure that the object is maintained in a consistent state. In the next chapter we introduce control statements.

5

Control Statements: Part 1

Let's all move one place on.
—Lewis Carroll

The wheel is come full circle.
—William Shakespeare, *King Lear*

How many apples fell on Newton's head before he took the hint?
—Robert Frost

All the evolution we know of proceeds from the vague to the definite.
—Charles Sanders Peirce

OBJECTIVES

In this chapter you will learn:

- To use the `If...Then` and `If...Then...Else` selection statements to choose among alternative actions.

- To use the `While`, `Do While...Loop` and `Do Until...Loop` repetition statements to execute statements in a program repeatedly.

- To use the compound assignment operators to abbreviate assignment operations.

- To use counter-controlled repetition and sentinel-controlled repetition.

- To use nested control statements.

- To add Visual Basic code to a Windows application.

5.1 Introduction

In this chapter and the next, we present the theory and principles of structured programming with control statements—important in building and manipulating objects. In this chapter, we introduce Visual Basic's If...Then, If...Then...Else, While, Do While...Loop and Do Until...Loop control statements, five of the building blocks that allow programmers to specify the logic required for methods to perform their tasks. We devote a portion of the chapter (and Chapters 6 and 8) to further developing the GradeBook class introduced in Chapter 4. In particular, we add a method to the GradeBook class that uses control statements to calculate the average of a set of student grades. Another example demonstrates how to combine control statements by "stacking" and "nesting" to solve a particular problem. You will notice that some examples use classes and a test module to demonstrate a concept, while others use only a module. When it does not make sense to create a reusable class to demonstrate a simple concept, we write the code in the Main method of a module.

Throughout most of the chapter we use console applications to demonstrate new programming techniques. We devote one section to enhancing the Windows application you created in Chapter 2 to include your own Visual Basic code.

5.2 Control Structures

The 1960s research of Bohm and Jacopini demonstrated that all programs containing GoTo statements could be written without them and that all programs could be written in terms of only three *control structures*[1]—the *sequence structure*, the *selection structure*

---

1. C. Bohm and G. Jacopini, "Flow Diagrams, Turing Machines, and Languages with Only Two Formation Rules," *Communications of the ACM*, Vol. 9, No. 5, May 1966, pp. 366–371.

and the *repetition structure*. The term "control structures" comes from the field of computer science. When we introduce Visual Basic's implementation of control structures, we will refer to them as "control statements."

Sequence Structure in Visual Basic

The UML *activity diagram* in Fig. 5.1 illustrates a typical sequence structure in which two calculations are performed in order. Visual Basic lets us have as many actions as we want in a sequence structure. As we will soon see, anywhere a single action may be placed, we may place several actions in sequence.

The two statements in Fig. 5.1 involve adding a `grade` to a `total` variable and adding the value 1 to a `counter` variable. Such statements might appear in a program that takes the average of several student grades. To calculate an average, the total of the grades being averaged is divided by the number of grades. A counter variable would be used to keep track of the number of values being averaged. You'll see similar statements in the program in Section 5.9.

UML Activity Diagrams

Activity diagrams are part of the UML. An activity diagram models the *workflow* (also called the *activity*) of a portion of a software system. A workflow may include a portion of an algorithm, such as the sequence structure in Fig. 5.1. Activity diagrams are composed of special-purpose symbols, such as the *action state symbol* (a rectangle with its left and right sides replaced with arcs curving outward; there are two of these in Fig. 5.1), the *diamond symbol* (there are none in this figure) and the *small circle symbol*; these symbols are connected by *transition arrows*, which represent the flow of the activity.

Activity diagrams help programmers develop and represent algorithms. Activity diagrams clearly show how control structures operate.

Consider the sequence-structure activity diagram in Fig. 5.1. It contains two *action states* that represent actions to perform. Each action state contains an *action expression*—"add grade to total" or "add 1 to counter"—that specifies a particular action to perform. Other actions might include calculations or input/output operations. The transition arrows represent *transitions* that indicate the order in which the actions represented by the action states occur—the program that implements the activities illustrated by the activity diagram in Fig. 5.1 first adds `grade` to `total`, then adds 1 to `counter`.

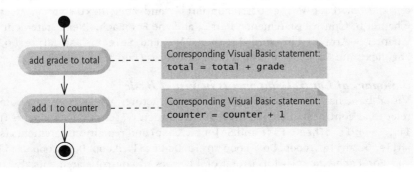

Fig. 5.1 | Sequence-structure activity diagram.

The solid circle symbol located at the top of the activity diagram represents the activity's *initial state*—the beginning of the workflow before the corresponding program performs the modeled activities. The solid circle surrounded by a hollow circle that appears at the bottom of the activity diagram represents the *final state*—the end of the workflow after the corresponding program performs its activities.

Figure 5.1 also includes rectangles with the upper-right corners folded over. These are called *notes* in the UML. Notes are optional explanatory remarks that describe the purpose of symbols in the diagram. Notes can be used in any UML diagram—not just activity diagrams. Figure 5.1 uses UML notes to show the Visual Basic code associated with each action state in the activity diagram. A dotted line connects each note with the element that the note describes. An activity diagram normally does not show the Visual Basic code that implements the activity. We use notes here for this purpose to illustrate how the diagram relates to Visual Basic code. For more information on the UML, visit www.uml.org.

Selection Statements in Visual Basic

Visual Basic provides three types of selection statements. The If...Then selection statement (which we introduced briefly in Chapter 3 and study in detail in Section 5.3) either performs (selects) an action (or sequence of actions) if a condition is true, or skips the action (or sequence of actions) if the condition is false. The If...Then...Else selection statement, which we introduce in Section 5.4, performs an action (or sequence of actions) if a condition is true, and performs a different action (or sequence of actions) if the condition is false. The Select...Case statement, which we introduce in Chapter 6, performs one of many different actions (or sequences of actions), depending on the value of an expression.

The If...Then statement is called a *single-selection statement* because it selects or ignores a single action (or a sequence of actions). The If...Then...Else statement is called a *double-selection statement* because it selects between two different actions (or sequences of actions). The Select...Case statement is called a *multiple-selection statement* because it selects among many different actions or sequences of actions.

Repetition Statements in Visual Basic

Visual Basic provides seven types of repetition statements (also called *looping statements* or *loops*) that enable programs to perform statements repeatedly based on the value of a condition. The repetition statements are the While, Do While...Loop, Do...Loop While, Do Until...Loop, Do...Loop Until, For...Next and the For Each...Next statements. (The repetition statements While, Do While...Loop and Do Until...Loop are covered in this chapter; the Do...Loop While, Do...Loop Until, and For...Next statements are covered in Chapter 6, Control Statements: Part 2; and the For Each...Next statement is covered in Chapter 8, Arrays.) The words If, Then, Else, End, Select, Case, While, Do, Until, Loop, For, Next and Each are all Visual Basic keywords (Fig. 3.2).

Summary of Control Statements in Visual Basic

Visual Basic has only three kinds of control structures, which from this point forward we refer to as control statements: the sequence structure, selection statements (three types—If...Then, If...Then...Else and Select...Case) and repetition statements (seven types—While, Do While...Loop, Do...Loop While, Do Until...Loop, Do...Loop Until, For...Next and For Each...Next)—for a total of 11 types of control statements. Every program is formed by combining as many of each type of control statement as is necessary. We can model each control statement as an activity diagram. Each diagram contains one initial state and one final state, which represent the control statement's entry point and exit point, respectively. These *single-entry/single-exit control statements* make it easy to build programs—the control statements are "attached" to one another by "connecting" the exit point of one control statement to the entry point of the next (which we accomplish simply by following one control statement immediately by another). This is similar to stacking building blocks, so we call it *control-statement stacking*. Section 5.10 shows an example of control-statement stacking. There is only one other way to connect control statements, and that is through *control-statement nesting*, where one control statement is placed inside another. We discuss control-statement nesting in Sections 5.11 and 5.12.

> **Software Engineering Observation 5.1**
>
> *Any Visual Basic program can be constructed from only 11 different types of control statements (sequence, three types of selection statements and seven types of repetition statements) combined in only two ways (control-statement stacking and control-statement nesting).*

5.3 If...Then Selection Statement

A selection statement chooses among alternative courses of action. For example, suppose that the passing grade on an examination is 60 (out of 100). Then the statement

```
If studentGrade >= 60 Then
    Console.WriteLine("Passed")
End If
```

outputs the string "Passed" if the student's grade is at least 60.

The preceding If...Then selection statement also could be written on a single line as

```
If studentGrade >= 60 Then Console.WriteLine("Passed")
```

In the multiple-line format, all statements (there can be many) in the body of the If...Then are executed if the condition is true. In the single-line format, only the statement immediately after the Then keyword is executed if the condition is true. Although writing the If...Then selection statement in the latter format saves space, some programmers feel that the organization of the statement is clearer when the multiple-line format is used.

Figure 5.2 is an activity diagram that illustrates the single-selection If...Then statement. It contains what is perhaps the most important symbol in an activity diagram—the

Fig. 5.2 | If...Then single-selection statement activity diagram.

diamond, or *decision symbol*, which indicates that a decision is to be made. A decision symbol indicates that the workflow will continue along a path determined by the symbol's associated *guard conditions*, which can be true or false. Each transition arrow emerging from a decision symbol has a guard condition (specified in square brackets above or next to the transition arrow). If a particular guard condition is true, the workflow enters the action state to which that transition arrow points. Exactly one of the guard conditions associated with a decision symbol must be true when a decision is made. In Fig. 5.2, if the grade is greater than or equal to 60, the program prints "Passed" to the screen, then transitions to the final state of this activity. If the grade is less than 60, the program immediately transitions to the final state without displaying a message.

Note that the If...Then statement is a single-entry/single-exit statement (as are all Visual Basic control statements). The activity diagrams for the remaining control statements also contain initial states, transition arrows, action states that indicate actions to perform, decision symbols (with associated guard conditions) that indicate decisions to be made, and final states.

5.4 If...Then...Else Selection Statement

As we have explained, the If...Then selection statement performs an indicated action (or sequence of actions) only when the condition evaluates to true; otherwise, the action (or sequence of actions) is skipped. The If...Then...Else selection statement allows you to specify that a different action (or sequence of actions) is to be performed when the condition is true than when the condition is false. For example, the Visual Basic statement

```
If studentGrade >= 60 Then
    Console.WriteLine("Passed")
Else
    Console.WriteLine("Failed")
End If
```

prints "Passed" if the student's grade is greater than or equal to 60, and prints "Failed" if the student's grade is less than 60. In either case, after printing occurs, the next statement in sequence executes.

Figure 5.3 illustrates the flow of control in the If...Then...Else statement. Once again, note that (besides the initial state, transition arrows and final state) the only other symbols in this activity diagram represent action states and decisions.

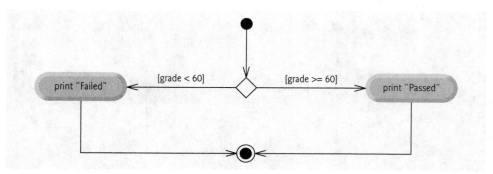

Fig. 5.3 | If...Then...Else double-selection statement activity diagram.

Nested *If...Then...Else Statements*

Nested If...Then...Else statements test for multiple conditions by placing `If...Then...Else` statements inside other `If...Then...Else` statements. For example, the following statement will print "A" for exam grades greater than or equal to 90, "B" for grades in the range 80–89, "C" for grades in the range 70–79, "D" for grades in the range 60–69 and "F" for all other grades.

```
If studentGrade >= 90 Then
    Console.WriteLine("A")
Else
    If studentGrade >= 80 Then
        Console.WriteLine("B")
    Else
        If studentGrade >= 70 Then
            Console.WriteLine("C")
        Else
            If studentGrade >= 60 Then
                Console.WriteLine("D")
            Else
                Console.WriteLine("F")
            End If
        End If
    End If
End If
```

If `studentGrade` is greater than or equal to 90, the first four conditions are true, but only the `Console.WriteLine` statement in the body of the first test is executed. After that particular `Console.WriteLine` executes, the `Else` part of the "outer" `If...Then...Else` statement is skipped, and the program proceeds with the next statement after the last `End If`.

Good Programming Practice 5.1

If there are several levels of indentation, each level should be indented additionally by the same amount of space; this gives programs a neatly structured appearance.

Some Visual Basic programmers prefer to write the preceding `If...Then...Else` statement using the *ElseIf keyword* as

```
If grade >= 90 Then
    Console.WriteLine("A")
ElseIf grade >= 80 Then
    Console.WriteLine("B")
ElseIf grade >= 70 Then
    Console.WriteLine("C")
ElseIf grade >= 60 Then
    Console.WriteLine("D")
Else
    Console.WriteLine("F")
End If
```

Both forms are equivalent, but the latter is popular because it avoids the deep indentation of the code. Such deep indentation often leaves little room on a line, forcing lines to be split and decreasing program readability.

5.5 While Repetition Statement

A *repetition statement* (also called a looping statement or a loop) allows you to specify that an action should be repeated, depending on the value of a condition (called the *loop-continuation condition*).

As an example of a **While** statement (sometimes more formally referred to as the While...End While statement), consider a program designed to find the first power of 3 larger than 100 (Fig. 5.4). In line 5, we take advantage of a Visual Basic feature that allows variable initialization to be incorporated into a declaration. When the While statement is entered (line 9), product is 3. Variable product is repeatedly multiplied by 3 (line 11), taking on the values 3, 9, 27, 81 and 243, successively. When product becomes 243, the condition product <= 100 in the While statement becomes false. This terminates the repetition with 243 as product's final value. Execution continues with the next statement after the keywords End While in line 12. [*Note:* If a While statement's condition is initially false, the body statement(s) are not performed.]

The UML activity diagram of Fig. 5.5 illustrates the flow of control that corresponds to the While statement shown in Fig. 5.4 (we have omitted the display of product each time through the loop at line 10). Once again, the symbols in the diagram (besides the initial state, transition arrows, a final state and three notes) represent an action state and a decision. This diagram also introduces the UML's *merge symbol*, which joins two flows of activity into one flow of activity. The UML represents both the merge symbol and the decision symbol as diamonds (this can be confusing). In this diagram, the merge symbol joins the transitions from the initial state and the action state, so they both flow into the decision that determines whether the loop should begin (or continue) executing. The decision and merge

```
 1    ' Fig. 5.4: PowersOfThree.vb
 2    ' Demonstration of While statement.
 3    Module PowersOfThree
 4       Sub Main()
 5          Dim product As Integer = 3
 6
 7          ' statement multiplies and displays product
 8          ' while product is less than or equal to 100
 9          While product <= 100
10             Console.Write(product & "   ")
11             product = product * 3 ' compute next power of 3
12          End While
13
14          Console.WriteLine() ' write blank line
15
16          ' print result
17          Console.WriteLine("First power of 3 " & _
18             "larger than 100 is " & product)
19       End Sub ' Main
20    End Module ' PowersOfThree
```

```
3  9  27  81
First power of 3 larger than 100 is 243
```

Fig. 5.4 | While repetition statement used to print powers of 3.

Fig. 5.5 | `While` repetition statement activity diagram.

symbols can be distinguished by the number of "incoming" and "outgoing" transition arrows. A decision symbol has one transition arrow pointing to the diamond and two or more transition arrows pointing out from the diamond to indicate possible transitions from that point. In addition, each transition arrow pointing out of a decision symbol has a guard condition next to it (exactly one of which must be true when a decision is made). A merge symbol has two or more transition arrows pointing to the diamond and only one transition arrow pointing from the diamond, to indicate multiple activity flows merging to continue the activity. Note that, unlike the decision symbol, the merge symbol does not have a counterpart in Visual Basic code. None of the transition arrows associated with a merge symbol have guard conditions.

The activity diagram of Fig. 5.5 clearly shows the repetition of the `While` statement discussed earlier in this section. The transition arrow emerging from the action state connects back to the merge, which transitions back to the decision that is tested each time through the loop until the guard condition `product > 100` becomes true. Then the `While` statement exits (reaches its final state) and control passes to the next statement in sequence in the program.

 Common Programming Error 5.1

Failure to provide the body of a `While` *statement with an action that eventually causes the loop-continuation condition to become false is a logic error. Normally, such a repetition statement never terminates, resulting in an* linfinite *loop.*

5.6 Do While…Loop Repetition Statement

The **Do While…Loop** repetition statement behaves like the `While` repetition statement. As an example of a Do While…Loop statement, consider another version of the program designed to find the first power of 3 larger than 100 (Fig. 5.6).

When the Do While…Loop statement is entered (line 9), the value of `product` is 3. The variable `product` is repeatedly multiplied by 3, taking on the values 3, 9, 27, 81 and 243, successively. When `product` becomes 243, the condition in the Do While…Loop statement, `product <= 100`, becomes false. This terminates the repetition, with the final value

```
 1    ' Fig. 5.6: DoWhile.vb
 2    ' Demonstration of the Do While...Loop statement.
 3    Module DoWhile
 4       Sub Main()
 5          Dim product As Integer = 3 ' initialize product
 6
 7          ' statement multiplies and displays the
 8          ' product while it is less than or equal to 100
 9          Do While product <= 100
10             Console.Write(product & "   ")
11             product = product * 3
12          Loop
13
14          Console.WriteLine() ' write blank line
15
16          ' print result
17          Console.WriteLine("First power of 3 " & _
18             "larger than 100 is " & product)
19       End Sub ' Main
20    End Module ' DoWhile
```

```
3   9   27   81
First power of 3 larger than 100 is 243
```

Fig. 5.6 | Do While...Loop repetition statement demonstration.

of product being 243. Program execution continues with the next statement after the Do While...Loop statement. Because the While and Do While...Loop statements behave in the same way, the activity diagram in Fig. 5.5 also illustrates the flow of control of the Do While...Loop repetition statement.

 Common Programming Error 5.2

Failure to provide the body of a Do While...Loop statement with an action that eventually causes the loop-continuation condition in the Do While...Loop to become false creates an infinite loop.

5.7 Do Until...Loop Repetition Statement

Unlike the While and Do While...Loop repetition statements, the **Do Until...Loop** repetition statement tests a condition for falsity for repetition to continue. Statements in the body of a Do Until...Loop are executed repeatedly as long as the condition (known as the *loop-termination condition*) evaluates to false. The program of Fig. 5.7 finds the first power of 3 larger than 100 by using a Do Until...Loop repetition statement.

Once again, the activity diagram of Fig. 5.5 illustrates the flow of control in the Do Until...Loop repetition statement shown in Fig. 5.7. This time, however, we focus on the leftmost guard condition—product > 100—the loop-termination condition for our control statement. Because we are using a Do Until...Loop statement, the statement's actions (lines 9–10) are performed when the statement's loop-termination condition is false (i.e., product is less than or equal to 100). When the loop-termination condition (product > 100, the leftmost guard condition) is true the statement exits.

```
 I   ' Fig. 5.7: DoUntil.vb
 2   ' Demonstration of the Do Until...Loop statement.
 3   Module DoUntil
 4      Sub Main()
 5         Dim product As Integer = 3
 6
 7         ' find first power of 3 larger than 100
 8         Do Until product > 100
 9            Console.Write(product & "   ")
10            product = product * 3
11         Loop
12
13         Console.WriteLine() ' write blank line
14
15         ' print result
16         Console.WriteLine("First power of 3 " & _
17            "larger than 100 is " & product)
18      End Sub ' Main
19   End Module ' DoUntil
```

```
3  9  27  81
First power of 3 larger than 100 is 243
```

Fig. 5.7 | Do Until...Loop repetition statement demonstration.

Common Programming Error 5.3

Failure to provide the body of a Do Until...Loop *statement with an action that eventually causes the loop-termination condition in the* Do Until...Loop *to become true creates an infinite loop.*

5.8 Compound Assignment Operators

Visual Basic provides several *compound assignment operators* for abbreviating assignment statements. For example, the statement

```
value = value + 3
```

can be abbreviated with the *addition assignment operator, +=* as

```
value += 3
```

The += operator adds the value of the right operand to the value of the left operand and stores the result in the left operand's variable. Any statement of the form

variable = variable operator expression

can be written in the form

variable operator= expression

where *operator* is one of the binary operators +, -, *, ^, &, / or \, and *variable* is an *lvalue* ("left value"). An *lvalue* is a variable or property that can appear on the left side of an assignment statement. We will learn how to declare constants in Section 7.16—constants cannot be *lvalues*. Figure 5.8 includes the compound assignment operators, sample expressions using these operators and explanations.

The =, +=, -=, *=, /=, \=, ^= and &= operators are always applied last in an expression. When an assignment statement is evaluated, the expression to the right of the operator is always evaluated first, then the value is assigned to the *lvalue* on the left. Figure 5.9 calculates a power of two using the exponentiation assignment operator. Lines 12 and 16 have the same effect on the variable result. Both statements raise result to the value of variable exponent. Note that the results of these two calculations are identical.

Compound assignment operator	Sample expression	Explanation	Assigns
Assume: c = 4, d = "He"			
+=	c += 7	c = c + 7	11 to c
-=	c -= 3	c = c - 3	1 to c
*=	c *= 4	c = c * 4	16 to c
/=	c /= 2	c = c / 2	2 to c
\=	c \= 3	c = c \ 3	1 to c
^=	c ^= 2	c = c ^ 2	16 to c
&=	d &= "llo"	d = d & "llo"	"Hello" to d

Fig. 5.8 | Compound assignment operators.

```
 1   ' Fig. 5.9: Assignment.vb
 2   ' Using a compound assignment operator to calculate a power of 2.
 3   Module Assignment
 4      Sub Main()
 5         Dim exponent As Integer ' power input by user
 6         Dim result As Integer = 2 ' number to raise to a power
 7
 8         ' prompt user for exponent
 9         Console.Write("Enter an integer exponent: ")
10         exponent = Console.ReadLine() ' input exponent
11
12         result ^= exponent ' same as result = result ^ exponent
13         Console.WriteLine("result ^= exponent: " & result)
14
15         result = 2 ' reset result to 2
16         result = result ^ exponent ' same as result ^= exponent
17         Console.WriteLine("result = result ^ exponent: " & result)
18      End Sub ' Main
19   End Module ' Assignment
```

Fig. 5.9 | Exponentiation using a compound assignment operator. (Part 1 of 2.)

```
Enter an integer exponent: 8
result ^= exponent: 256
result = result ^ exponent: 256
```

Fig. 5.9 | Exponentiation using a compound assignment operator. (Part 2 of 2.)

5.9 Counter-Controlled Repetition

Next, we modify the GradeBook class of Chapter 4 to solve two variations of a problem that averages student grades. Consider the following problem statement:

> *A class of 10 students took a quiz. The grades (integers in the range 0 to 100) for this quiz are available to you. Determine the class average on the quiz.*

The class average is equal to the sum of the grades divided by the number of students (10). The program for solving this problem must input each grade, keep track of the total of all grades input, perform the averaging calculation and print the result.

We use *counter-controlled repetition* to input and process the grades one at a time. This technique uses a counter to specify the number of times that a set of statements will execute. Counter-controlled repetition also is called *definite repetition* because the number of repetitions is known before the loop begins executing. In this example, repetition terminates when the counter exceeds 10. This section presents a version of class GradeBook (Fig. 5.10) that implements the algorithm in a method. The section then presents an application (Fig. 5.11) that demonstrates the algorithm in action.

```vb
1    ' Fig. 5.10: GradeBook.vb
2    ' GradeBook class that solves class-average problem using
3    ' counter-controlled repetition.
4    Public Class GradeBook
5       Private courseNameValue As String ' course name for this GradeBook
6
7       ' constructor initializes CourseName with String supplied as argument
8       Public Sub New(ByVal name As String)
9          CourseName = name ' validate and store course name
10      End Sub ' New
11
12      ' property that gets and sets the course name; the Set accessor
13      ' ensures that the course name has at most 25 characters
14      Public Property CourseName() As String
15         Get ' retrieve courseNameValue
16            Return courseNameValue
17         End Get
18
19         Set(ByVal value As String) ' set courseNameValue
20            If value.Length <= 25 Then ' if value has 25 or fewer characters
21               courseNameValue = value ' store the course name in the object
22            Else ' if name has more than 25 characters
23               ' set courseNameValue to first 25 characters of parameter name
24               ' start at 0, length of 25
25               courseNameValue = value.Substring(0, 25)
```

Fig. 5.10 | Counter-controlled repetition: Class-average problem. (Part 1 of 2.)

```
26
27                 Console.WriteLine( _
28                     "Course name (" & value & ") exceeds maximum length (25).")
29                 Console.WriteLine( _
30                     "Limiting course name to first 25 characters." & vbCrLf)
31             End If
32         End Set
33     End Property ' CourseName
34
35     ' display a welcome message to the GradeBook user
36     Public Sub DisplayMessage()
37         ' this statement uses property CourseName to get the
38         ' name of the course this GradeBook represents
39         Console.WriteLine("Welcome to the grade book for " _
40             & vbCrLf & CourseName & "!" & vbCrLf)
41     End Sub ' DisplayMessage
42
43     ' determine class average based on 10 grades entered by user
44     Public Sub DetermineClassAverage()
45         Dim total As Integer ' sum of grades entered by user
46         Dim gradeCounter As Integer ' number of grades input
47         Dim grade As Integer ' grade input by user
48         Dim average As Integer ' average of grades
49
50         ' initialization phase
51         total = 0 ' set total to zero
52         gradeCounter = 1 ' prepare to loop
53
54         ' processing phase
55         While gradeCounter <= 10 ' loop 10 times
56             ' prompt for and input grade from user
57             Console.Write("Enter grade: ") ' prompt for grade
58             grade = Console.ReadLine() ' input the next grade
59             total += grade ' add grade to total
60             gradeCounter += 1 ' add 1 to gradeCounter
61         End While
62
63         ' termination phase
64         average = total \ 10 ' integer division yields integer result
65
66         ' display total and average of grades
67         Console.WriteLine(vbCrLf & "Total of all 10 grades is " & total)
68         Console.WriteLine("Class average is " & average)
69     End Sub ' DetermineClassAverage
70 End Class ' GradeBook
```

Fig. 5.10 | Counter-controlled repetition: Class-average problem. (Part 2 of 2.)

Implementing Counter-Controlled Repetition in Class GradeBook

Class GradeBook (Fig. 5.10) contains a constructor (lines 8–10) that assigns a value to the class's property CourseName. Lines 14–33 and 36–41 declare property CourseName and method DisplayMessage, respectively. Lines 44–69 declare method DetermineClassAverage, which implements the class-averaging algorithm.

Lines 45–48 declare local variables total, gradeCounter, grade and average to be of type Integer. In this example, variable total accumulates the sum of the grades entered and gradeCounter counts the number of grades entered. Variable grade stores the most recent grade value entered (line 58).

Note that the declarations (in lines 45–48) appear in the body of method Determine-ClassAverage. Recall that variables declared in a method body are local variables and can be used only from their declaration until the end of the method declaration. A local variable's declaration must appear before the variable is used in that method. A local variable cannot be accessed outside the method in which it is declared. In Visual Basic, numeric variables are initialized by default to 0 when they are declared, unless another value is assigned to the variable in its declaration.

In the versions of class GradeBook in this chapter, we simply read and process a set of grades. The averaging calculation is performed in method DetermineClassAverage using local variables—we do not preserve any information about student grades in instance variables of the class. In versions of the class in Chapter 8, Arrays, we maintain the grades in memory using an instance variable that refers to an array. This allows a GradeBook object to perform various calculations on the same set of grades without requiring the user to enter the grades multiple times.

The assignments (in lines 51–52) initialize total to 0 and gradeCounter to 1. Line 55 indicates that the While statement should continue looping as long as the value of gradeCounter is less than or equal to 10. While this condition remains true, the While statement repeatedly executes the statements in its body (lines 57–60).

Line 57 displays the prompt "Enter grade: ". Line 58 reads the grade entered by the user and assigns it to the variable grade. Then line 59 adds the new grade entered by the user into the variable total.

Line 60 adds 1 to gradeCounter to indicate that the program has processed another grade and is ready to input the next grade from the user. Incrementing gradeCounter eventually causes it to exceed 10. At that point the While loop terminates because its condition (line 55) becomes false.

When the loop terminates, line 64 performs the averaging calculation and assigns its result to the variable average. Line 67 displays the text "Total of all 10 grades is " followed by variable total's value. Line 68 then displays the text "Class average is " followed by variable average's value. Method DetermineClassAverage returns control to the calling method (i.e., Main in GradeBookTest of Fig. 5.11) after reaching line 69.

Module GradeBookTest
Module GradeBookTest (Fig. 5.11) creates an object of class GradeBook (Fig. 5.10) and demonstrates its capabilities. Line 7 of Fig. 5.11 creates a new GradeBook object and assigns it to variable gradeBook. The string in line 7 is passed to the GradeBook constructor (lines 8–10 of Fig. 5.10). Line 9 calls gradeBook's DisplayMessage method to display a welcome message to the user. Line 10 then calls gradeBook's DetermineClassAverage method to allow the user to enter 10 grades, for which the method then calculates and prints the average, performing the algorithm shown in Fig. 5.10.

Notes on Integer Division
The averaging calculation performed by method DetermineClassAverage in response to the method call at line 10 in Fig. 5.11 produces an integer result. The program's output

```
 1    ' Fig. 5.11: GradeBookTest.vb
 2    ' Create GradeBook object and invoke its DetermineClassAverage method.
 3    Module GradeBookTest
 4       Sub Main()
 5          ' create GradeBook object gradeBook and
 6          ' pass course name to constructor
 7          Dim gradeBook As New GradeBook("CS101 Introduction to VB")
 8
 9          gradeBook.DisplayMessage() ' display welcome message
10          gradeBook.DetermineClassAverage() ' find average of 10 grades
11       End Sub ' Main
12    End Module ' GradeBookTest
```

```
Welcome to the grade book for
CS101 Introduction to VB!

Enter grade: 65
Enter grade: 78
Enter grade: 89
Enter grade: 67
Enter grade: 87
Enter grade: 98
Enter grade: 93
Enter grade: 85
Enter grade: 82
Enter grade: 100

Total of all 10 grades is 844
Class average is 84
```

Fig. 5.11 | Module `GradeBookTest` creates an object of class `GradeBook` (Fig. 5.10) and invokes its `DetermineClassAverage` method.

indicates that the sum of the grade values in the sample execution is 844, which, when divided by 10, should yield the floating-point number 84.4. However, the result of the calculation total \ 10 (line 64 of Fig. 5.10) is the integer 84, because the integer division operator is used. Recall that the integer division operator takes two integer operands and returns an integer result. We use the floating-point division operator in the next section to determine a floating-point average.

5.10 Sentinel-Controlled Repetition

Let us generalize Section 5.9's class-average problem. Consider the following problem:

> *Develop a class-averaging program that processes grades for an arbitrary number of students each time it is run.*

In the previous class-average example, the problem statement specified the number of students, so the number of grades (10) was known in advance. In this example, no indication is given of how many grades are to be input. The program must process an arbitrary number of grades. How can it determine when to stop the input of grades? How will it know when to calculate and print the class average?

One way to solve this problem is to use a special value called a ***sentinel value*** (also called a ***signal value***, a ***dummy value*** or a ***flag value***) to indicate "end of data entry." The user enters grades until all legitimate grades have been entered. The user then types the sentinel value to indicate that no more grades will be entered. Sentinel-controlled repetition is called ***indefinite repetition*** because the number of repetitions is not known before the loop begins its execution.

It is crucial to employ a sentinel value that cannot be confused with an acceptable input value. Grades on a quiz are nonnegative integers, so –1 is an acceptable sentinel value for this problem. A run of the class-average program might process a stream of inputs such as 95, 96, 75, 74, 89 and –1. The program would then compute and print the class average for the grades 95, 96, 75, 74 and 89. The sentinel value, –1, should not enter into the averaging calculation.

Common Programming Error 5.4

Choosing a sentinel value that is also a legitimate data value could result in a logic error that would cause a program to produce incorrect results.

Implementing Sentinel-Controlled Repetition in Class GradeBook

Figure 5.12 shows the Visual Basic class `GradeBook` containing the method `Determine-ClassAverage` that solves the class average problem with sentinel-controlled repetition. Although each grade is an integer, the averaging calculation is likely to produce a number with a decimal point—a real number or floating-point number. The type `Integer` cannot represent such a number, so this class uses type `Double` to do so.

In this example, we see that control statements may be stacked on top of one another (i.e., placed in sequence). The `While` statement (lines 60–67) is followed in sequence by an `If...Then...Else` statement (lines 70–80). Much of the code in this program is identical to the code in Fig. 5.10, so we concentrate on the new features and issues.

Line 48 declares `Double` variable `average`. This variable allows us to store the calculated class average as a floating-point number. We discuss floating-point numbers in more detail shortly. Line 52 initializes `gradeCounter` to 0, because no grades have been entered yet. Remember that this program uses sentinel-controlled repetition to input the grades from the user. To keep an accurate record of the number of grades entered, the program increments `gradeCounter` only when the user inputs a valid grade value. Recall that `Integer` variables are initialized to zero by default, so lines 51–52 can be omitted.

Program Logic for Sentinel-Controlled Repetition vs. Counter-Controlled Repetition

Compare the program logic for sentinel-controlled repetition in this application with that for counter-controlled repetition in Fig. 5.10. In counter-controlled repetition, each iteration (repetition) of the `While` statement (e.g., lines 55–61 of Fig. 5.10) reads a value from the user for the specified number of iterations. In sentinel-controlled repetition, the program reads the first value (lines 56–57 of Fig. 5.12) before reaching the `While`. This value determines whether the program's flow of control should enter the body of the `While`. If the condition of the `While` is false, the user entered the sentinel value, so the body of the `While` does not execute (i.e., no grades were entered). If, on the other hand, the condition is true, the body begins execution, and the loop adds the `grade` value to the `total` (line 61). Lines 65–66 in the loop's body input the next value from the user. Next, program control reaches the end of the `While` statement, so execution continues with the test of the

```vb
 1   ' Fig. 5.12: GradeBook.vb
 2   ' GradeBook class that solves class-average problem using
 3   ' sentinel-controlled repetition.
 4   Public Class GradeBook
 5      Private courseNameValue As String ' course name for this GradeBook
 6
 7      ' constructor initializes CourseName with String supplied as argument
 8      Public Sub New(ByVal name As String)
 9         CourseName = name ' validate and store course name
10      End Sub ' New
11
12      ' property that gets and sets the course name; the Set accessor
13      ' ensures that the course name has at most 25 characters
14      Public Property CourseName() As String
15         Get ' retrieve courseNameValue
16            Return courseNameValue
17         End Get
18
19         Set(ByVal value As String) ' set courseNameValue
20            If value.Length <= 25 Then ' if value has 25 or fewer characters
21               courseNameValue = value ' store the course name in the object
22            Else ' if name has more than 25 characters
23               ' set courseNameValue to first 25 characters of parameter name
24               ' start at 0, length of 25
25               courseNameValue = value.Substring(0, 25)
26
27               Console.WriteLine( _
28                  "Course name (" & value & ") exceeds maximum length (25).")
29               Console.WriteLine( _
30                  "Limiting course name to first 25 characters." & vbCrLf)
31            End If
32         End Set
33      End Property ' CourseName
34
35      ' display a welcome message to the GradeBook user
36      Public Sub DisplayMessage()
37         ' this statement uses property CourseName to get the
38         ' name of the course this GradeBook represents
39         Console.WriteLine("Welcome to the grade book for " _
40            & vbCrLf & CourseName & "!" & vbCrLf)
41      End Sub ' DisplayMessage
42
43      ' determine class average based on 10 grades entered by user
44      Public Sub DetermineClassAverage()
45         Dim total As Integer ' sum of grades entered by user
46         Dim gradeCounter As Integer ' number of grades input
47         Dim grade As Integer ' grade input by user
48         Dim average As Double ' average of all grades
49
50         ' initialization phase
51         total = 0 ' clear total
52         gradeCounter = 0 ' prepare to loop
53
```

Fig. 5.12 | Sentinel-controlled repetition: Class-average problem. (Part 1 of 2.)

```
54          ' processing phase
55          ' prompt for input and read grade from user
56          Console.Write("Enter grade or -1 to quit: ")
57          grade = Console.ReadLine()
58
59          ' sentinel-controlled loop where -1 is the sentinel value
60          While grade <> -1
61             total += grade ' add grade to total
62             gradeCounter += 1 ' add 1 to gradeCounter
63
64             ' prompt for and input next grade from user
65             Console.Write("Enter grade or -1 to quit: ") ' prompt
66             grade = Console.ReadLine() ' input next grade
67          End While
68
69          ' termination phase
70          If gradeCounter <> 0 Then ' if user entered at least one grade
71             ' calculate average of all grades entered
72             average = total / gradeCounter
73
74             ' display total and average (with two digits of precision)
75             Console.WriteLine(vbCrLf & "Total of the " & gradeCounter & _
76                " grades entered is " & total)
77             Console.WriteLine("Class average is {0:F}", average)
78          Else ' no grades were entered, so output appropriate message
79             Console.WriteLine("No grades were entered")
80          End If
81       End Sub ' DetermineClassAverage
82    End Class ' GradeBook
```

Fig. 5.12 | Sentinel-controlled repetition: Class-average problem. (Part 2 of 2.)

While's condition (line 60). The condition uses the most recent grade input by the user to determine whether the loop's body should execute again. Note that the value of variable grade is always input from the user immediately before the program tests the While condition. This allows the program to determine whether the value just input is the sentinel value *before* processing that value (i.e., adding it to the total). If the sentinel value is input, the loop terminates, and the program does not add −1 to the total.

Good Programming Practice 5.2

In a sentinel-controlled loop, the prompts requesting data entry should explicitly remind the user of the sentinel value.

After the loop terminates, the If...Then...Else statement at lines 70–80 executes. The condition at line 70 determines whether any grades were input. If none were input, the Else part (lines 78–79) of the If...Then...Else statement executes and displays the message "No grades were entered" and the method returns control to the calling method.

Floating-Point Numbers and Type Double

Although each grade entered is an integer, the averaging calculation is likely to produce a number with a decimal point (i.e., a floating-point number). The type Integer cannot represent floating-point numbers, so this program uses data type `Double` to store floating-point numbers.

Visual Basic provides two primitive types for storing floating-point numbers in memory—`Single` and `Double`. The primary difference between them is that `Double` variables can store numbers of larger magnitude and finer detail (i.e., more digits to the right of the decimal point—also known as the number's *precision*) than `Single` variables.

Floating-Point Number Precision and Memory Requirements

Variables of type `Single` represent *single-precision floating-point numbers* and have seven significant digits. Variables of type `Double` represent *double-precision floating-point numbers*. These require twice as much memory as `Single` variables and provide 15 significant digits—approximately double the precision of `Single` variables. For the range of values required by most programs, variables of type `Single` should suffice, but you can use `Double` to play it safe. In some applications, even variables of type `Double` will be inadequate—such applications are beyond the scope of this book. Most programmers represent floating-point numbers with type `Double`. In fact, Visual Basic treats all the floating-point numbers you type in a program's source code (such as 7.33 and 0.0975) as `Double` values by default. Such values in the source code are known as *floating-point literals*. See Section 7.11 for the ranges of values for `Single`s and `Double`s.

Implicitly Converting Between Primitive Types

If at least one grade was entered, line 72 of Fig. 5.12 calculates the average of the grades. Recall from Fig. 5.10 that we used the integer division operator to yield an integer result. Since we are now calculating a floating-point value, we use the floating-point division operator. But the operands of the division in line 72 are of type `Integer`. To perform a floating-point calculation with integer values, we must temporarily treat these values as floating-point numbers for use in the calculation.

The floating-point division operator is defined to operate on values of three types—`Single`, `Double` and `Decimal` (you will learn about type `Decimal` in Chapter 6). To ensure that the operator's operands are one of these three types, Visual Basic performs an operation called *implicit conversion* on selected operands. For example, in an expression using the floating-point division operator, if both operands are of type `Integer`, the operands will be *promoted* to `Double` values for use in the expression. In this example, the values of `total` and `gradeCounter` are promoted to type `Double`, then the floating-point division is performed and the result of the calculation is assigned to `average`. We'll say more about the implicit conversion rules in Section 7.9.

Formatting for Floating-Point Numbers

Line 77 outputs the class average. In this example, we decided to display the class average rounded to the nearest hundredth and to output the average with exactly two digits to the right of the decimal point. Note that the call to method `WriteLine` in line 77 uses the string "{0:F}" to indicate that the value of `average` should be displayed in the command prompt as a *fixed-point number*, (i.e., a number with a specified number of places after the decimal point). The numeric value that appears before the colon (in this case, 0) indicates which of `WriteLine`'s arguments will be formatted—0 specifies the first argument that occurs *after* the string is passed to `WriteLine`, namely `average`. Additional values can be inserted into the string to specify other arguments. If we had passed `total` as a third argument to method WriteLine and used the string "{1:F}" the value to be formatted would be total. The value after the colon (in this case, F) is known as a *format specifier*, which indicates how a value is to be formatted. The format specifier F indicates that a fixed-point number should (by default) be displayed with two decimal places. This can be changed by placing a numeric value after the format specifier. For example, the string "{0:F3}" would display a fixed-point value with three decimal places. Some of the more common format specifiers are summarized in Fig. 5.13. The format specifiers are case insensitive. Also, the format specifiers D and X can be used only with integer values.

 Good Programming Practice 5.3

When formatting with two positions to the right of the decimal point, some programmers prefer to use the format specifier F2 for clarity.

The three grades entered during the sample execution of module GradeBookTest (Fig. 5.14) total 257, which yields the average 85.666666…. The format specifier causes the output to be rounded to the specified number of digits. In this program, the average is rounded to the hundredths position and is displayed as 85.67.

5.11 Nested Control Statements

We have seen that control statements can be stacked on top of one another (in sequence). In this case study, we examine the only other structured way control statements can be combined, namely, through the nesting of one control statement within another.

Format Code	Description
C	Currency. Precedes the number with $, separates every three digits with commas and sets the number of decimal places to two.
E	Scientific notation. Displays one digit to the left of the decimal and six digits to the right of the decimal, followed by the character E and a three-digit integer representing the exponent of a power of 10. For example, 956.2 is formatted as 9.562000E+002.
F	Fixed point. Sets the number of decimal places to two.
G	General. Visual Basic chooses either E or F for you, depending on which representation generates a shorter string.
D	Decimal integer. Displays an integer as a whole number in standard base-10 format.
N	Number. Separates every three digits with a comma and sets the number of decimal places to two.
X	Hexadecimal integer. Displays the integer in hexadecimal (base-16) notation. We discuss hexadecimal notation in Appendix B.

Fig. 5.13 | Formatting codes for Strings.

```
 1    ' Fig. 5.14: GradeBookTest.vb
 2    ' Create GradeBook object and invoke its DetermineClassAverage method.
 3    Module GradeBookTest
 4       Sub Main()
 5          ' create GradeBook object gradeBook and
 6          ' pass course name to constructor
 7          Dim gradeBook As New GradeBook("CS101 Introduction to VB")
 8
 9          gradeBook.DisplayMessage() ' display welcome message
10          gradeBook.DetermineClassAverage() ' find average of grades
11       End Sub ' Main
12    End Module ' GradeBookTest
```

```
Welcome to the grade book for
CS101 Introduction to VB!

Enter grade or -1 to quit: 97
Enter grade or -1 to quit: 88
Enter grade or -1 to quit: 72
Enter grade or -1 to quit: -1

Total of the 3 grades entered is 257
Class average is 85.67
```

Fig. 5.14 | GradeBookTest module creates an object of class GradeBook (Fig. 5.12) and invokes its DetermineClassAverage method.

Consider the following problem statement:

A college offers a course that prepares students for the state licensing exam for real estate brokers. Last year, 10 of the students who completed this course took the licensing exam. The college wants to know how well its students did on the exam. You have been asked to write a program to summarize the results. You have been given a list of the 10 students. Next to each name is written a "P" if the student passed the exam and an "F" if the student failed the exam.

Your program should analyze the results of the exam as follows:

1. Input each exam result (i.e., a "P" or an "F"). Display the message "Enter result" on the screen each time the program requests another exam result.

2. Count the number of passes and failures.

3. Display a summary of the exam results, indicating the number of students who passed and the number who failed.

4. If more than eight students passed the exam, print the message "Raise tuition."

After reading the problem statement carefully, we make the following observations:

1. The program must process exam results for 10 students. A counter-controlled loop can be used because the number of test results is known in advance.

2. Each exam result is a string—either a "P" or an "F." Each time the program reads an exam result, the program must determine whether the input is a "P" or an "F."

We test for a "P" in our algorithm. If the input is not a "P," we assume it is an "F."

3. Two counters store the exam results—one counts the number of students who passed the exam and the other counts the number of students who failed.

4. After the program has processed all the exam results, it must determine whether more than eight students passed the exam.

The class that solves the preceding problem is shown in Fig. 5.15, and two sample executions appear in Fig. 5.16.

Lines 7–10 of Fig. 5.15 declare the variables that method ProcessExamResults of class Analysis uses to process the examination results. Several of these declarations use Visual Basic's ability to incorporate variable initialization into declarations (passes is initialized to 0, failures is initialized to 0 and student is initialized to 1). Looping programs may require initialization at the beginning of each repetition—such reinitialization would normally be performed by assignment statements rather than in declarations.

The While statement (lines 13–25) loops 10 times. During each iteration, the loop inputs and processes one exam result. Note that the If...Then...Else statement (lines 18–22) for processing each result is nested in the While statement. If the result is "P", the If...Then...Else statement increments passes; otherwise, it assumes the result is "F" and increments failures. Line 24 increments student before the loop condition is tested

```
1    ' Fig. 5.15: Analysis.vb
2    ' Analysis of examination results.
3    Public Class Analysis
4        ' input and analyze exam results
5        Public Sub ProcessExamResults()
6            ' initializing variables in declarations
7            Dim passes As Integer = 0 ' number of passes
8            Dim failures As Integer = 0 ' number of failures
9            Dim student As Integer = 1 ' student counter
10           Dim result As String ' one exam result (obtains value from user)
11
12           ' process 10 students using counter-controlled loop
13           While student <= 10
14               Console.Write("Enter result (P = pass, F = fail): ")
15               result = Console.ReadLine()
16
17               ' nested control statement
18               If result = "P" Then
19                   passes += 1 ' increment number of passes
20               Else
21                   failures += 1 ' increment number of failures
22               End If
23
24               student += 1 ' increment student counter
25           End While
26
```

Fig. 5.15 | Nested control statements: Examination-results problem. (Part 1 of 2.)

```
27        ' display exam results
28        Console.WriteLine( _
29           "Passed: " & passes & vbCrLf & "Failed: " & failures)
30
31        ' raise tuition if more than 8 students passed
32        If passes > 8 Then
33           Console.WriteLine("Raise tuition")
34        End If
35     End Sub ' ProcessExamResults
36  End Class ' Analysis
```

Fig. 5.15 | Nested control statements: Examination-results problem. (Part 2 of 2.)

again at line 13. After 10 values have been input, the loop terminates and lines 28–29 display the number of passes and the number of failures. The If...Then statement at lines 32–34 determines whether more than eight students passed the exam and, if so, outputs the message "Raise tuition".

AnalysisTest Module That Demonstrates Class Analysis

Module AnalysisTest (Fig. 5.16) creates an Analysis object (line 5) and invokes the object's ProcessExamResults method (line 6) to process a set of exam results entered by the user. Figure 5.16 shows the input and output from two sample executions of the program. During the first sample execution, the condition at line 32 of method ProcessExamResults in Fig. 5.15 is true—more than eight students passed the exam, so the program outputs a message indicating that the tuition should be raised.

```
1   ' Fig. 5.16: AnalysisTest.vb
2   ' Test program for class Analysis.
3   Module AnalysisTest
4      Sub Main()
5         Dim application As New Analysis() ' create Analysis object
6         application.ProcessExamResults() ' call method to process results
7      End Sub ' Main
8   End Module ' AnalysisTest
```

```
Enter result (P = pass, F = fail): P
Enter result (P = pass, F = fail): F
Enter result (P = pass, F = fail): P
Enter result (P = pass, F = fail): P
Enter result (P = pass, F = fail): P
Enter result (P = pass, F = fail): P
Enter result (P = pass, F = fail): P
Enter result (P = pass, F = fail): P
Enter result (P = pass, F = fail): P
Enter result (P = pass, F = fail): P
Passed: 9
Failed: 1
Raise tuition
```

Fig. 5.16 | Test program for class Analysis (Fig. 5.15). (Part 1 of 2.)

```
Enter result (P = pass, F = fail): P
Enter result (P = pass, F = fail): P
Enter result (P = pass, F = fail): P
Enter result (P = pass, F = fail): F
Enter result (P = pass, F = fail): F
Enter result (P = pass, F = fail): P
Enter result (P = pass, F = fail): P
Enter result (P = pass, F = fail): P
Enter result (P = pass, F = fail): P
Enter result (P = pass, F = fail): P
Passed: 8
Failed: 2
```

Fig. 5.16 | Test program for class Analysis (Fig. 5.15). (Part 2 of 2.)

5.12 Nested Repetition Statements

Let us present another complete example. We use nested repetition statements to solve the problem. Consider the following problem statement:

> Write a program that draws in the command prompt a filled square consisting solely of one type of character, such as the asterisk (*). The side of the square and the character to be used to fill the square should be entered by the user. The length of the side should not exceed 20 characters. If the user enters a value over 20, the message "Side is too large" should be printed.

Your program should draw the square as follows:

1. Input the side of the square.
2. Validate that the side is less than or equal to 20.
3. Use repetition to draw the square by printing only one fill character at a time.

After reading the problem statement, we make the following observations:

1. The program must draw *side* rows, each containing *side* fill characters, where *side* is the value entered by the user. Counter-controlled repetition should be used.
2. A test must be employed to ensure that the value of *side* is less than or equal to 20. If it is not, the message "Side is too large" should be printed.
3. Four variables should be used—one that represents the length of the side of the square, one that represents (as a String) the fill character to be used, one that represents the row in which the next symbol should appear and one that represents the column in which the next symbol should appear.

The Visual Basic class and test program that solve this problem are shown in Fig. 5.17 and 5.18.

```
1    ' Fig. 5.17: Box.vb
2    ' Class can be used to draw a square of a specified length, using
3    ' a specified fill character.
4    Public Class Box
5        Private sideValue As Integer ' length of side of square
```

Fig. 5.17 | Nested repetition statements used to print a square of symbols. (Part 1 of 2.)

```
 6        Private fillCharacterValue As String ' character used to draw square
 7
 8        ' property provides access to side length of box
 9        Public Property Side() As Integer
10           Get
11              Return sideValue ' return side length
12           End Get
13
14           Set(ByVal value As Integer)
15              sideValue = value ' modify side length
16           End Set
17        End Property ' Side
18
19        ' property provides access to fill character for drawing box
20        Public Property FillCharacter() As String
21           Get
22              Return fillCharacterValue ' return fill character
23           End Get
24
25           Set(ByVal value As String)
26              fillCharacterValue = value ' modify fill character
27           End Set
28        End Property ' FillCharacter
29
30        ' display box
31        Public Sub Display()
32           Dim row As Integer ' current row
33           Dim column As Integer ' current column
34
35           If Side <= 20 Then ' if true, then print the box
36              row = 1
37
38                 ' this While is nested inside the If in lines 35-55
39                 While row <= Side ' controls row being printed
40                    column = 1 ' prepare to print first character in the row
41
42                    ' this loop prints one row of the square
43                    ' and is nested inside the While in lines 39-52
44                    While column <= Side
45                       ' print fill character and a space
46                       Console.Write(FillCharacter & " ")
47                       column += 1 ' increment column
48                    End While
49
50                    Console.WriteLine() ' position cursor to next line
51                    row += 1 ' increment row
52                 End While
53           Else ' condition (Side <= 20) is false
54              Console.WriteLine("Side too large")
55           End If
56        End Sub ' Display
57     End Class ' Box
```

Fig. 5.17 | Nested repetition statements used to print a square of symbols. (Part 2 of 2.)

```
 1    ' Fig. 5.18: BoxTest.vb
 2    ' Program draws square by creating an object of class Box.
 3    Module BoxTest
 4       ' Main begins program execution
 5       Sub Main()
 6          Dim box As New Box()
 7
 8          ' obtain fill character and side length from user
 9          Console.Write("Enter fill character: ")
10          box.FillCharacter = Console.ReadLine()
11          Console.Write("Enter side length (must be 20 or less): ")
12          box.Side = Console.ReadLine()
13
14          box.Display() ' display box
15       End Sub ' Main
16    End Module ' BoxTest
```

```
Enter fill character: #
Enter side length (must be 20 or less): 8
# # # # # # # #
# # # # # # # #
# # # # # # # #
# # # # # # # #
# # # # # # # #
# # # # # # # #
# # # # # # # #
# # # # # # # #
```

```
Enter fill character: *
Enter side length (must be 20 or less): 5
* * * * *
* * * * *
* * * * *
* * * * *
* * * * *
```

```
Enter fill character: $
Enter side length (must be 20 or less): 37
Side too large
```

Fig. 5.18 | Using class Box to draw a square.

5.13 Visual Basic Programming in a Windows Application

In Chapter 2, we showed how to create a simple GUI application using visual programming—that is, defining the appearance of an application by dragging and dropping GUI controls onto a Form and setting properties in design mode without writing any program code. The application you created in Chapter 2 (Fig. 2.27) displayed text and an image, but did not perform any other actions. In Chapters 3, 4 and 5 we have focused on console applications, which do not provide a GUI but perform various actions, such as finding the average of several grades and displaying the results as text in the command prompt. Most Visual Basic programmers use a combination of visual programming and conventional programming techniques. In this section, you will see that when you build a GUI, Visual Basic code (which makes use of predefined FCL classes) is generated by the IDE to define that GUI. You will modify a GUI control's property programmatically, causing the text displayed on the Form to change at runtime. You will also add code to a GUI application to perform an action when the Form is loaded.

Before proceeding, load the project ASimpleProgram from your Chapter 4 examples folder into the IDE. This is the same program as the one you created in Chapter 2. Change the name of the file from Form1.vb to FrmASimpleProgram.vb to enhance clarity. Then double click this file in the **Solution Explorer** to open the file in design mode. Select the Form by clicking it. Notice in the **Properties** window that Visual Basic changed the Form's name to FrmASimpleProgram when you changed the name of the file from Form1.vb to FrmASimpleProgram.vb.

Next, let's change the name of the Form's controls for clarity. To do this, simply select the control, and modify the *Name* property (listed in the **Properties** window as **(Name)**), entering the new identifier you want to represent the control. Use this technique to change the name of the Label to lblWelcome and the name of the PictureBox to picBug. This enables us to easily identify the Form's controls in the program code.

Viewing Windows-Generated Code

Let us view the code that defines our Windows application. When you use visual programming to create a program's GUI, the IDE generates the Visual Basic code that defines how the GUI appears. The code that defines the GUI application is stored in two files—one to define the initial appearance of the GUI (e.g., the background color of the Form or the size of a Label), and one to define the behavior of the GUI (i.e., what happens when a Button is clicked or text is entered in a TextBox). Unlike a console application's code, a Windows application's program code is not displayed initially in the editor window. Once you open the file FrmASimpleProgram.vb in design mode, you can view the code by selecting **View > Code**. Figure 5.19 shows the code editor displaying the program code. This is the file that defines your GUI's behavior.

Note that FrmASimpleProgram.vb does not contain a Module. Instead Windows applications use classes. You have used FCL classes, such as Console and MessageBox, and you have created your own classes in Chapters 4 and 5.

The class declared in Fig. 5.19 is called FrmASimpleProgram and is currently empty, as we have not yet defined the application's behavior. Recall that the application's initial

Fig. 5.19 | IDE showing program code for ASimpleProgram.vb.

GUI appearance is defined in another file. To view that file, go into the **Solution Explorer** and click the **Show All Files** button. Then click the plus sign to the left of **FrmASimpleProgram.vb**, and double click **FrmASimpleProgram.Designer.vb**. The file is shown in Fig. 5.20.

This code appears complex (and especially so for this early in the book), but it is created for you by the IDE, and normally you will not edit it. It is important for novice programmers to be aware of the code that the IDE generates, even though much of the code is not explained until Chapters 9–14. This type of code is present in every Windows application. If the IDE did not provide the code, you would have to write it, which would require a considerable amount of time and would be an error-prone process.

Inheriting Predefined Functionality

Keyword **_Inherits_** (line 3 of Fig. 5.20) indicates that the class FrmASimpleProgram inherits existing pieces from another class. The class from which FrmASimpleProgram inherits— System.Windows.Forms.Form—appears to the right of the Inherits keyword. This is the class Form preceded by its namespace and a dot separator. The namespace and class name together form the class's *fully-qualified name*. In this inheritance relationship, Form is called the *base class*, and FrmASimpleProgram is called the *derived class*. This inheritance results in a FrmASimpleProgram class definition that has the attributes (data) and behaviors (methods) of class Form.

Every Windows application consists of at least one class that inherits from class ***Form***. A key benefit of inheriting from class Form is that someone else has previously defined everything about "what it means to be a Form." The Windows operating system expects every window, including Form, to have certain capabilities (attributes and behaviors).

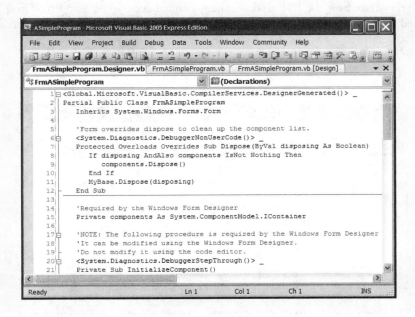

Fig. 5.20 | Windows Form Designer generated code.

However, because class Form already provides these capabilities, you do not need to "reinvent the wheel" by defining all those capabilities yourself. In fact, class Form has over 200 methods! The use of Inherits to absorb the capabilities of class Form enables you to create Forms quickly and easily.

When you created this application in Chapter 2, you used the **Properties** window to set properties for the Form, Label and PictureBox. Once a property was set, the Form or control was updated immediately. Forms and controls contain a set of default values for their properties, which are displayed initially in the **Properties** window when a Form or control is selected. These default values provide the initial characteristics of a Form or control. When a control (such as a Label) is first placed on the Form, the IDE adds code to the class's designer file (e.g., FrmASimpleProgram.Designer.vb) that creates the control and sets some of the control's property values, such as the name of the control and its location on the Form. Figure 5.21 shows the portion of ASimpleProgram.Designer.vb that sets the lblWelcome's Font, Location, Name, Size, TabIndex, Text and TextAlign properties. These lines specify property values that are set when the Label is first placed on the Form, or edited by you in the **Properties** window (your line numbers may differ if you have made your own changes to the original application). The control contains many more properties—those not set in the code contain their default values. Recall from Chapter 2 that you explicitly set values for the Label's Text and TextAlign properties. The values set in the **Properties** window are reflected in this code. Note that the code sets properties of control lblWelcome. Had we not updated the name of this control, every instance of the identifier lblWelcome would be replaced with its default name, in this case Label1.

Modifying Properties in Design View

The values assigned to the properties are based on the values in the **Properties** window. We now demonstrate how the IDE updates the generated code when a control's property is modified. While performing the steps in this section, you must switch between code view

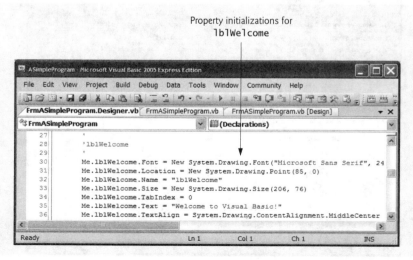

Fig. 5.21 | Property initializations generated by the Windows Form Designer for lblWelcome.

and design view. To switch views, select the corresponding tabs—**FrmASimpleProgram.vb** or **FrmASimpleProgram.Designer.vb** for code view (we will specify which file as necessary) and **FrmASimpleProgram.vb [Design]** for design view. Alternatively, you can select **View > Code** (for **FrmASimpleProgram.vb**) or **View > Designer** (for **FrmASimpleProgram.vb [Design]**). Now you will modify the application's code:

1. *Modifying the* `Label` *control's* `Text` *property using the* **Properties** *window.* If you have not already done so, switch to design view. Recall that properties can be changed in design view by clicking a `Form` or control to select the desired property, then modifying it in the **Properties** window. Select the `Label` (`lblWelcome`) control and change its `Text` property to "`Deitel and Associates`" (Fig. 5.22).

2. *Examining the change in code view.* Switch to code view (`ASimpleProgram.Design.vb`) and examine the code (Fig. 5.23). Note that the `Label`'s `Text` property is now assigned the text that you entered in the **Properties** window (line 35). When a property is changed in design mode, the Windows Form Designer updates the appropriate line of code for you in the class to reflect the new value. Once again, note that your code lines may be different.

Modifying Properties Programmatically

Now that you have seen how properties are updated in code in response to changes in the **Properties** window, we show how you can write code to modify a property. You'll also see how to specify code that executes when a GUI application loads.

Fig. 5.22 | **Properties** window used to set a property value.

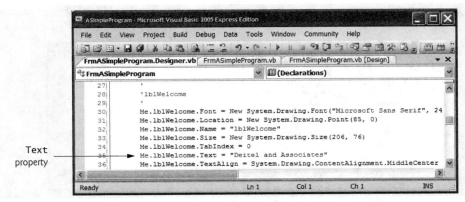

Fig. 5.23 | Windows Form Designer–generated code reflecting new property value.

1. *Adding an event handler to your application.* In the preceding steps, we set properties at design time. Often, however, it is necessary to modify a property while a program is running. For example, to display the result of a calculation, a `Label`'s text can be assigned a `String` containing the result. In the applications we have created so far, such code is located in `Main`. In Windows applications, you can create a method that executes when the `Form` loads into memory during program execution. Like `Main`, this method is invoked when the program is run. Double clicking the `Form` in design view adds a method named `FrmASimpleProgram_Load` to the class (Fig. 5.24). Be sure to double click the background of the `Form`, that is, the portion of the `Form` that is not covered with another control. Note that `FrmASimpleProgram_Load` is not part of the Windows Form Designer–generated code found in `ASimpleProgram.Designer.vb`; rather it is added by the IDE to the `FrmASimpleProgram.vb` file. This is because this method will be used to define the behavior of the application. Method `FrmASimpleProgram_Load` is a type of method known as an event handler. *Event handlers* respond to state changes in the GUI. Such state changes are known as *events*. Most events represent user actions, such as clicking a `Button` or entering text in a `TextBox`. In the event handler created here, the event is the loading of the `Form` when the application begins. When this event is *raised* (i.e., the event occurs), `FrmASimpleProgram_Load` is executed, performing any statements in its body (we will add a statement to this method shortly). Most of a GUI application's functionality is executed based on events. You will see many examples of events and event handling throughout this book.

2. *Changing the `Label`'s `Text` property at runtime.* Add the statement `lblWelcome.Text = "Visual Basic!"` to the body of the method declaration (Fig. 5.25). Note that we use the dot separator to access a property of `lblWelcome`. This is because GUI controls are actually objects, just like the objects you created and used in Chapter 4 and 5.

3. *Examining the results of the `FrmASimpleProgram_Load` method.* Switch back to design view. Note that the text in the `Label` is still "`Deitel and Associates`" and that the **Properties** window still displays the value "`Deitel and Associates`" as the `Label`'s `Text` property value. The code generated by the IDE has not changed either. Instead, the property value is changed in the `FrmASimpleProgram_Load`

Fig. 5.24 | Method `FrmASimpleProgram_Load` created when `Form` is double clicked.

Fig. 5.25 | Method `FrmASimpleProgram_Load` containing program code.

method, causing the property value to be updated at runtime. Select **Build > Build ASimpleProgram** then **Debug > Start** to run the program. Once the Form is displayed, the text in the Label reflects the property assignment in FrmASimpleProgram_Load (Fig. 5.26).

4. *Terminating program execution.* Click the close button to terminate program execution. Once again, notice that both the Label and the Label's Text property contain the text "Deitel and Associates". Remember that the event handler FrmASimpleProgram_Load changes the text to **Visual Basic!** only when the application runs.

This example combined conventional programming and visual programming. We provided a brief overview of the code that the IDE generates for a Windows application, and showed how to add code that performs actions when the application's Form loads. The topics covered in this section provide a basis for the more complex GUI applications that you'll create throughout this book. Our next GUI program appears in Chapter 7, which finds the maximum of three input values. The user enters input into TextBoxes then clicks a Button to indicate that the application should determine and display the maximum value.

Fig. 5.26 | Changing a property value at runtime.

5.14 (Optional) Software Engineering Case Study: Identifying Class Attributes in the ATM System

In Section 4.9, we began the first stage of an object-oriented design (OOD) for our ATM system—analyzing the requirements document and identifying the classes needed to implement the system. We listed the nouns and noun phrases in the requirements document and identified a separate class for each one that plays a significant role in the ATM system. We then modeled the classes and their relationships in a UML class diagram (Fig. 4.22). Classes have attributes (data) and operations (behaviors). Class attributes are implemented in Visual Basic programs as properties and instance variables (and Shared variables, as we will see in Section 9.10), and class operations are implemented as methods and properties. In this section, we determine many of the attributes needed in the ATM system. In Section 6.11, we examine how these attributes represent an object's state. In Section 7.20, we determine the operations for our classes.

Identifying Attributes

Consider the attributes of some real-world objects: A person's attributes include height, weight and whether the person is left-handed, right-handed or ambidextrous. A radio's attributes include its station setting, its volume setting and its AM or FM setting. A car's attributes include its speedometer and odometer readings, the amount of gas in its tank and what gear it is in. A personal computer's attributes include its manufacturer (e.g., Dell, Gateway, Sun, Apple or HP), type of screen (e.g., LCD or CRT), main memory size and hard disk size.

We can identify many attributes of the classes in our system by looking for descriptive words and phrases in the requirements document. For each one we find that plays a significant role in the ATM system, we create an attribute and assign it to one or more of the classes identified in Section 4.9. We also create attributes to represent any additional data that a class may need as such needs become clear throughout the design process.

Figure 5.27 lists the words or phrases from the requirements document that describe each class. For example, the requirements document describes the steps taken to obtain a "withdrawal amount," so we list "amount" next to class Withdrawal.

Class	Descriptive words and phrases
ATM	user is authenticated
BalanceInquiry	account number
Withdrawal	account number amount
Deposit	account number amount
BankDatabase	[no descriptive words or phrases]

Fig. 5.27 | Descriptive words and phrases from the ATM requirements document. (Part 1 of 2.)

Class	Descriptive words and phrases
Account	account number PIN balance
Screen	[no descriptive words or phrases]
Keypad	[no descriptive words or phrases]
CashDispenser	begins each day loaded with 500 $20 bills
DepositSlot	[no descriptive words or phrases]

Fig. 5.27 | Descriptive words and phrases from the ATM requirements document. (Part 2 of 2.)

Figure 5.27 leads us to create one attribute of class ATM. Class ATM maintains information about the state of the ATM. The phrase "user is authenticated" describes a state of the ATM (we discuss states in detail in Section 6.11), so we include userAuthenticated as a Boolean *attribute* (i.e., an attribute that has a value of either True or False). This attribute indicates whether the ATM has successfully authenticated the current user—userAuthenticated must be True for the system to allow the user to perform transactions and access account information. This attribute helps ensure the security of the data in the system.

Classes BalanceInquiry, Withdrawal and Deposit share one attribute. Each transaction involves an "account number" that corresponds to the account of the user making the transaction. We assign an integer attribute accountNumber to each transaction class to identify the account to which an object of the class applies.

Descriptive words and phrases in the requirements document also suggest some differences in the attributes required by each transaction class. The requirements document indicates that to withdraw cash or deposit funds, users must enter a specific "amount" of money to be withdrawn or deposited, respectively. Thus, we assign to classes Withdrawal and Deposit an attribute amount to store the value supplied by the user. The amounts of money related to a withdrawal and a deposit are defining characteristics of these transactions that the system requires for them to take place. In Visual Basic, monetary amounts are represented with type Decimal (which you will learn more about in Chapter 6). Note that class BalanceInquiry does not need additional data to perform its task—it requires only an account number to indicate the account whose balance should be retrieved.

Class Account has several attributes. The requirements document states that each bank account has an "account number" and a "PIN," which the system uses for identifying accounts and authenticating users. We assign to class Account two Integer attributes: accountNumber and pin. The requirements document also specifies that an account maintains a "balance" of the amount of money in the account, and that the money the user deposits does not become available for a withdrawal until the bank verifies the amount of cash in the deposit envelope and any checks in the envelope clear. An account must still record the amount of money that a user deposits, however. Therefore, we decide that an account should represent a balance using two attributes of type Decimal—availableBalance and `totalBalance`. Attribute `availableBalance` tracks the amount of money that a user can withdraw from the account. Attribute `totalBalance` refers to the total amount of money that the user has "on deposit" (i.e., the amount of money available, plus the amount of cash deposits waiting to be verified or checks waiting to clear). For example, suppose an ATM user deposits $50.00 in cash into an empty account. The `totalBalance` attribute would increase to $50.00 to record the deposit, but the `availableBalance` would remain at $0 until a bank employee counts the amount of cash in the envelope and confirms that it is correct. [*Note:* We assume that the bank updates the `availableBalance` attribute of the `Account` soon after the ATM transaction occurs, in response to confirming that $50 in cash was found in the deposit envelope. We assume that this update occurs through a transaction that a bank employee performs using some a bank system other than the ATM. Thus, we do not discuss this "external" transaction in our case study.]

Class `CashDispenser` has one attribute. The requirements document states that the cash dispenser "begins each day loaded with 500 $20 bills." The cash dispenser must keep track of the number of bills it contains to determine whether enough cash is on hand to satisfy withdrawal requests. We assign to class `CashDispenser` an integer attribute `billCount`, which is initially set to 500.

For real problems in industry, there is no guarantee that requirements documents will be rich enough and precise enough for the object-oriented systems designer to determine all the attributes or even all the classes. The need for additional classes, attributes and behaviors may become clear as the design process proceeds. As we progress through this case study, we too will continue to add, modify and delete information about the classes in our system.

Modeling Attributes

The class diagram in Fig. 5.28 lists some of the attributes for the classes in our system—the descriptive words and phrases in Fig. 5.27 helped us identify these attributes. For simplicity, Fig. 5.28 does not show the associations among classes—we showed these in Fig. 4.22. Systems designers commonly do this. Recall that in the UML, a class's attributes are placed in the middle compartment of the class's rectangle. We list each attribute's name and type separated by a colon (:), followed in some cases by an equal sign (=) and an initial value.

Consider the `userAuthenticated` attribute of class `ATM`:

```
userAuthenticated : Boolean = False
```

This attribute declaration contains three pieces of information about the attribute. The *attribute name* is `userAuthenticated`. The *attribute type* is `Boolean`. In Visual Basic, an attribute can be represented by a primitive type, such as `Boolean`, `Integer`, `Double` or `Decimal`, or a class type—as discussed in Chapter 4. We have chosen to model only primitive-type attributes in Fig. 5.28—we discuss the reasoning behind this decision shortly. For simplicity, we use Visual Basic primitive type names in our UML diagrams. These type names sometimes differ from those defined in the UML specification.

We can also indicate an initial value for an attribute. Attribute `userAuthenticated` in class `ATM` has an initial value of `False`. This indicates that the system initially does not consider the user to be authenticated. If an attribute has no initial value specified, only its name and type (separated by a colon) are shown. For example, the `accountNumber` attribute of class `BalanceInquiry` is an `Integer`. Here we show no initial value, because

Fig. 5.28 | Classes with attributes.

the value of this attribute is a number that we do not yet know. This number will be determined at execution time based on the account number entered by the current ATM user. Recall that Visual Basic initializes all instance variables to their default values.

Figure 5.28 does not contain attributes for classes Screen, Keypad and DepositSlot. These are important components of our system, for which our design process simply has not yet revealed any attributes.

Software Engineering Observation 5.2

Early in the design process classes often lack attributes (and operations). Such classes should not necessarily be eliminated, however, because attributes (and operations) may become evident in the later phases of design and implementation.

Note that Fig. 5.28 also does not include attributes for class BankDatabase. Recall that in Visual Basic, attributes can be represented by either primitive types or class types. We have chosen to include only primitive-type attributes in Fig. 5.28 (and in similar class diagrams throughout the case study). A class-type attribute is modeled more clearly as an association (in particular, a composition) between the class with the attribute and the attribute's own class. For example, the class diagram in Fig. 4.22 indicates that class Bank-Database participates in a composition relationship with zero or more Account objects. From this composition, we can determine that when we implement the ATM system in

Visual Basic, we will be required to create an attribute of class BankDatabase to hold zero or more Account objects. Similarly, we will assign attributes to class ATM that correspond to its composition relationships with classes Screen, Keypad, CashDispenser and DepositSlot. These composition-based attributes would be redundant if modeled in Fig. 5.28, because the compositions modeled in Fig. 4.22 already convey the fact that the database contains information about zero or more accounts and that an ATM is composed of a screen, keypad, cash dispenser and deposit slot. Software developers typically model these whole/part relationships as composition associations rather than as attributes required to implement the relationships. We show how such composition relationships are implemented in Section 9.7.

The class diagram in Fig. 5.28 provides a solid basis for the structure of our model, but the diagram is not complete. In Section 6.11, we identify the states and activities of the objects in the model, and in Section 7.20 we identify the operations that the objects perform. As we present more of the UML and object-oriented design, we will continue to strengthen the structure of our model.

Software Engineering Case Study Self-Review Exercises

5.1   We typically identify the attributes of the classes in our system by analyzing the _____ in the requirements document.
   a) nouns and noun phrases
   b) descriptive words and phrases
   c) verbs and verb phrases
   d) All of the above.

5.2   Which of the following is not an attribute of an airplane?
   a) length
   b) wingspan
   c) fly
   d) number of seats

5.3   Describe the meaning of the following attribute declaration of class CashDispenser in the class diagram in Fig. 5.28:

```
billCount : Integer = 500
```

Answers to Software Engineering Case Study Self-Review Exercises

5.1   b.

5.2   c. Fly is an operation or behavior of an airplane, not an attribute.

5.3   This declaration indicates that attribute billCount is an Integer with an initial value of 500; billCount keeps track of the number of $20 bills available in the CashDispenser at any given time.

5.15 Wrap-Up

In this chapter, we demonstrated two of Visual Basic's selection statements—the If...Then single-selection statement and the If...Then...Else double-selection statement. The If...Then statement is used to execute a set of one or more statements based on a condition—if the condition is true, the statements execute; if it is false, the statements are skipped. The If...Then...Else double-selection statement is used to execute one set of statements if a condition is true, and another set if the condition is false. We discussed the

`While` and `Do While...Loop` repetition statements, where a set of statements is executed repeatedly as long as a loop-continuation condition remains true. We discussed the `Do Until...Loop` repetition statement, where a set of statements is executed repeatedly as long as a loop-termination condition remains false. We used control-statement stacking to compute the average of a set of student grades with counter-controlled repetition and then with sentinel-controlled repetition, and we used control-statement nesting to analyze and make decisions based on a set of exam results, and also to display a square of fill characters. We introduced compound assignment operators, which can be used for abbreviating assignment statements. The chapter concluded with an introduction to adding event handlers to a GUI application. You modified a GUI application programmatically. In Chapter 6, Control Statements: Part 2, we present additional selection and repetition statements. In the next few chapters, we build Windows applications that interact more with the user.

6

Control Statements: Part 2

Who can control his fate?
—William Shakespeare,
Othello

*The used key is always
bright.*
—Benjamin Franklin

*Not everything that can be
counted counts, and not
every thing that counts can
be counted.*
—Albert Einstein

*Every advantage in the past
is judged in the light of the
final issue.*
—Demosthenes

OBJECTIVES

In this chapter you will learn:

■ The essentials of counter-controlled repetition.

■ To use the `For…Next`, `Do…Loop While` and `Do…Loop Until` repetition statements to execute statements in a program repeatedly.

■ To perform multiple selection using the `Select…Case` selection statement.

■ To use the `Exit` statement to break out of a repetition statement.

■ To use the `Continue` statement to break out of the current iteration of a repetition statement.

■ To use logical operators to form more complex conditions.

6.1 Introduction

In this chapter, we introduce Visual Basic's remaining control statements. We continue our early emphasis on object-oriented programming, presenting the next version of our GradeBook class. We demonstrate the For...Next, Select...Case, Do...Loop While and Do...Loop Until control statements. Through a series of short examples using While...End While and For...Next, we explore the essentials of counter-controlled repetition. We create a GradeBook class that uses a Select...Case multiple-selection statement to count the number of A, B, C, D and F grades in a set of letter grades entered by the user. We introduce the Exit and Continue program control statements. Finally, we discuss the logical operators, which enable you to use more powerful conditional expressions in control statements.

6.2 Essentials of Counter-Controlled Repetition

This section uses the While repetition statement introduced in Chapter 5 to highlight the elements required to perform counter-controlled repetition. Counter-controlled repetition requires

1. the *name* of a control variable (or loop counter) that is used to determine whether the loop continues to iterate
2. the *initial value* of the control variable
3. the *increment* (or *decrement*) by which the control variable is modified each time through the loop
4. the condition that tests for the *final value* of the control variable (i.e., whether looping should continue)

The example in Fig. 6.1 uses the four elements of counter-controlled repetition to display the even integers in the range 2–10. The declaration in line 5 *names* the control variable (counter), indicates that it is of type Integer, reserves space for it in memory and sets it to an *initial value* of 2.

Consider the While statement (lines 7–10). Line 8 displays the current value of counter, and line 9 *increments* the control variable by 2 to prepare for the next iteration (repetition) of the loop. The loop-continuation condition in the While statement (line 7) tests whether the value of the control variable is less than or equal to 10—the *final value* for which the condition is true. The body of the While is performed even when the control variable is 10. The loop terminates when the control variable exceeds 10 (i.e., when counter becomes 12, because the loop is incrementing by 2 each time).

6.3 For...Next Repetition Statement

Section 6.2 presented the essentials of counter-controlled repetition with the While statement. Visual Basic also provides the For...Next repetition statement, which specifies the counter-controlled repetition details in a single line of code. To illustrate the power of For...Next, we rewrite the program of Fig. 6.1 using the For...Next statement in Fig. 6.2.

The Main method of the program operates as follows: When the For...Next statement (lines 7–9) begins its execution, the control variable counter is declared as an Integer and initialized to 2, thus addressing the first two elements of counter-controlled repetition—control variable *name* and *initial value*. Next, the implied loop-continuation condition counter <= 10 is tested. The **To keyword** is required in the For...Next statement. The optional **Step keyword** specifies the increment (i.e., the amount that is added to counter each time the For...Next body is executed). If Step and the value following it are omitted, the increment defaults to 1. The increment of a For...Next statement could be negative, in which case it is a decrement, and the loop counts downwards.

```
 1    ' Fig. 6.1: WhileCounter.vb
 2    ' Using the While statement to demonstrate counter-controlled repetition.
 3    Module WhileCounter
 4       Sub Main()
 5          Dim counter As Integer = 2 ' name and initialize loop counter
 6
 7          While counter <= 10 ' test final value of loop counter
 8             Console.Write(counter & " ")
 9             counter += 2 ' increment counter
10          End While
11
12          Console.WriteLine()
13       End Sub ' Main
14    End Module ' WhileCounter
```

```
2 4 6 8 10
```

Fig. 6.1 | Counter-controlled repetition with the While...End While statement.

```
 1    ' Fig. 6.2: ForCounter.vb
 2    ' Using the For...Next statement for counter-controlled repetition.
 3   Module ForCounter
 4      Sub Main()
 5         ' initialization, repetition condition and
 6         ' incrementing are all included in For...Next statement
 7         For counter As Integer = 2 To 10 Step 2
 8            Console.Write(counter & " ")
 9         Next
10
11         Console.WriteLine()
12      End Sub ' Main
13   End Module ' ForCounter
```

```
2 4 6 8 10
```

Fig. 6.2 | Counter-controlled repetition with the For...Next statement.

In this example, the initial value of counter is 2, so the implied condition is satisfied (i.e., true), and the counter's value 2 is output in line 8. The required **Next** *keyword* marks the end of the For...Next repetition statement. When the Next keyword is reached, variable counter is incremented by the specified value of 2, and the loop begins again with the loop-continuation test.

At this point, the control variable is equal to 4. This value does not exceed the final value, so the program performs the body statement again. This process continues until the counter value of 10 has been printed and the control variable counter is incremented to 12, causing the (implied) loop-continuation test to fail and repetition to terminate. The program continues by performing the first statement after the For...Next statement. (In this case, method Main terminates, because the program reaches the End Sub statement at line 12.)

Error-Prevention Tip 6.1

Use a For...Next loop for counter-controlled repetition. Off-by-one errors (which occur when a loop is executed for one more or one less iteration than is necessary) tend to disappear, because the terminating value is clear.

For...Next Statement Header Components

Figure 6.3 takes a closer look at the For...Next statement from Fig. 6.2. The first line of the For...Next statement sometimes is called the *For...Next header*. Note that the For...Next header specifies each of the items needed for counter-controlled repetition with a control variable.

The general form of the For...Next statement is

> **For** *initialization* **To** *finalValue* **Step** *increment*
>   *statement*
> **Next**

Fig. 6.3 | For...Next header components.

where the *initialization* expression initializes the loop's control variable, *finalValue* determines whether the loop should continue executing (if the control variable is less than or equal to *finalValue*) and *increment* specifies the amount the control variable should be incremented each time through the loop. In most cases, the For...Next statement can be represented by an equivalent While statement, as follows:

```
initialization

While variable <= finalValue
    statement
    increment
End While
```

There is an exception to this rule, which we discuss in Section 6.9.

Note in Fig. 6.3 that the counter variable is both initialized and declared in the For...Next header. The counter variable may be declared before the For...Next statement. For example, the code in Fig. 6.2 could have been written as

```
Dim counter As Integer

For counter = 2 To 10 Step 2
    Console.Write(counter & " ")
Next
```

Although both forms are correct, declaring the control variable in the For...Next header is more clear and concise. The difference between the two forms is that if the *initialization* expression in the For...Next statement header declares the control variable (as we have done in Fig. 6.2), the control variable can be used only in the body of the For...Next statement—it will be unknown outside the For...Next statement. This restricted use of the control variable name is known as the variable's *scope*. The scope of a variable specifies where it can be used in a program. Scope is discussed in detail in Chapter 7, Methods: A Deeper Look. If the control variable is declared before the For...Next statement, it can be used from the point of declaration, inside the control statement and after it as well.

The starting value, ending value and increment portions of a For...Next statement can contain arithmetic expressions. The expressions are evaluated once (when the For...Next statement begins executing) and used as the starting value, ending value and increment of the For...Next statement's header. For example, assume that value1 = 2 and value2 = 10. The header

```
For j As Integer = value1 To 4 * value1 * value2 Step value2 \ value1
```

is equivalent to the header

```
For j As Integer = 2 To 80 Step 5
```

If the loop-continuation condition is initially false (e.g., if the starting value is greater than the ending value and the increment is positive), the For...Next's body is not performed. Instead, execution proceeds with the first statement after the For...Next statement.

The control variable frequently is printed or used in calculations in the For...Next body, but it does not have to be. It is common to use the control variable exclusively to control repetition and never mention it in the For...Next body.

Common Programming Error 6.1

Counter-controlled loops should not be controlled with floating-point variables. Floating-point values are represented only approximately in memory; this can lead to imprecise counter values and inaccurate tests for termination.

Error-Prevention Tip 6.2

Although the value of the control variable can be changed in the body of a For...Next loop, avoid doing so, because this practice can lead to subtle errors.

Common Programming Error 6.2

In nested For...Next loops, the use of the same control-variable name in more than one loop is a compilation error.

For Statement UML Activity Diagram

The activity diagram for the For...Next statement is similar to that of the While statement (Fig. 5.5). For example, the activity diagram of the For...Next statement

```
For counter As Integer = 1 To 10
    Console.WriteLine(counter)
Next
```

is shown in Fig. 6.4. This activity diagram makes it clear that the initialization occurs only once and that incrementing occurs *after* each execution of the body statement. Note that (besides an initial state, transition arrows, a merge, a final state and several notes) the diagram contains only action states and a decision.

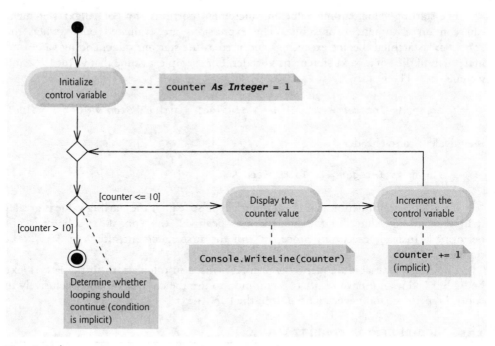

Fig. 6.4 | For...Next repetition statement activity diagram.

6.4 Examples Using the For...Next Statement

The following examples demonstrate different ways of varying the control variable in a For...Next statement. In each case, we write the appropriate For...Next header.

a) Vary the control variable from 1 to 100 in increments of 1.

   For i = 1 *To* 100 or *For* i = 1 *To* 100 *Step* 1

b) Vary the control variable from 100 to 1 in increments of -1 (decrements of 1).

   For i = 100 *To* 1 *Step* -1

c) Vary the control variable from 7 to 77 in increments of 7.

   For i = 7 *To* 77 *Step* 7

d) Vary the control variable from 20 to 2 in increments of -2 (decrements of 2).

   For i = 20 *To* 2 *Step* -2

e) Vary the control variable over the sequence of the following values: 2, 5, 8, 11, 14, 17, 20.

   For i = 2 *To* 20 *Step* 3

f) Vary the control variable over the sequence of the following values: 99, 88, 77, 66, 55, 44, 33, 22, 11, 0.

   For i = 99 *To* 0 *Step* -11

Application: Summing the Even Integers from 2 to 100

The next two examples demonstrate simple applications of the For...Next repetition statement. The program in Fig. 6.5 uses the For...Next statement to sum the even integers from 2 to 100. Remember that to use the MessageBox class you must add a reference to System.Windows.Forms.dll, as explained in Section 3.8.

Message Dialog Buttons and Icons

The version of method MessageBox.Show called in Fig. 6.5 (lines 14–16) is different from the version discussed in earlier examples in that it takes four arguments instead of two. The dialog in Fig. 6.5 is labeled to emphasize the effects of the four arguments. The first two arguments are Strings displayed in the dialog and the dialog's title bar, respectively. The third argument indicates which button(s) to display, and the fourth argument indicates an icon that appears to the left of the message. The documentation provided with the IDE includes the complete listing of *MessageBoxButtons* and *MessageBoxIcon* constants. The message dialog icon options are described in Fig. 6.6; the message dialog button options are described in Fig. 6.7, including how to display multiple buttons. Note that there are multiple icon constants that display the same icon. Sometimes using a different constant name improves program readability. For instance, it may make more sense to use the constant MessageBoxIcon.Warning to indicate that a warning is being displayed, while the constant MessageBoxIcon.Exclamation would be used to indicate that an unexpected result occurred. Both constants display the same icon, but the names used in the code are clearer based on context.

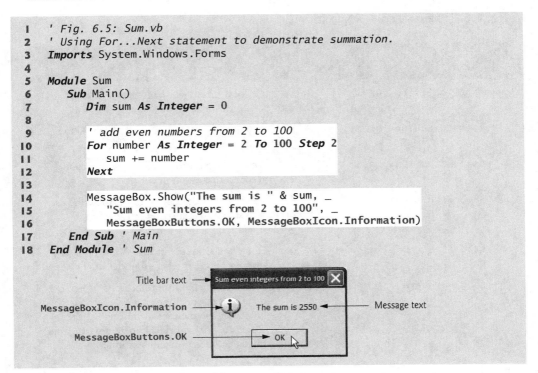

```vb
1   ' Fig. 6.5: Sum.vb
2   ' Using For...Next statement to demonstrate summation.
3   Imports System.Windows.Forms
4
5   Module Sum
6      Sub Main()
7         Dim sum As Integer = 0
8
9         ' add even numbers from 2 to 100
10        For number As Integer = 2 To 100 Step 2
11           sum += number
12        Next
13
14        MessageBox.Show("The sum is " & sum, _
15           "Sum even integers from 2 to 100", _
16           MessageBoxButtons.OK, MessageBoxIcon.Information)
17     End Sub ' Main
18  End Module ' Sum
```

Title bar text → Sum even integers from 2 to 100

MessageBoxIcon.Information → ⓘ The sum is 2550 ← — Message text

MessageBoxButtons.OK → OK

Fig. 6.5 | For...Next statement used for summation.

MessageBoxIcon constants	Icon	Description
MessageBoxIcon.Exclamation and MessageBoxIcon.Warning		Both constants display an icon containing an exclamation point. Typically used to caution the user against potential problems or display information that may be unexpected.
MessageBoxIcon.Information and MessageBoxIcon.Asterisk		Both constants display an icon containing the letter "i." Typically used to display information about the state of the application.
MessageBoxIcon.Question		This constant displays an icon containing a question mark. Typically used to ask the user a question.
MessageBoxIcon.Error, MessageBoxIcon.Stop and MessageBoxIcon.Hand		These constants display an icon containing an ∞ in a red circle. Typically used to alert the user of errors or critical situations.
MessageBoxIcon.None		This constant causes no icon to be displayed.

Fig. 6.6 | Message dialog icon constants.

MessageBoxButton constants	Description
MessageBoxButtons.OK	**OK** button. Allows the user to acknowledge a message. Included by default.
MessageBoxButtons.OKCancel	**OK** and **Cancel** buttons. Allow the user to either continue or cancel an operation.
MessageBoxButtons.YesNo	**Yes** and **No** buttons. Allow the user to respond to a question.
MessageBoxButtons.YesNoCancel	**Yes**, **No** and **Cancel** buttons. Allow the user to respond to a question or cancel an operation.
MessageBoxButtons.RetryCancel	**Retry** and **Cancel** buttons. Allow the user to retry or cancel an operation that has failed.
MessageBoxButtons.AbortRetryIgnore	**Abort**, **Retry** and **Ignore** buttons. When one of a series of operations has failed, these buttons allow the user to abort the entire sequence, retry the failed operation or ignore the failed operation and continue.

Fig. 6.7 | Message dialog button constants.

Application: Compound Interest Calculations

The next example computes compound interest using the For...Next statement. Consider the following problem statement:

A person invests $1000.00 in a savings account that yields 5% interest. Assuming that all the interest is left on deposit, calculate and print the amount of money in the account at the end of each year over a period of 10 years. To determine these amounts, use the following formula:

$$a = p \, (1 + r)^n$$

where

      p is the original amount invested (i.e., the principal)
      r is the annual interest rate (e.g., .05 stands for 5%)
      n is the number of years
      a is the amount on deposit at the end of the *n*th year.

This problem involves a loop that performs the indicated calculation for each of the 10 years that the money remains on deposit. The solution is shown in Fig. 6.8.

Lines 7–8 declare two Decimal variables. Type **Decimal** is used for monetary calculations. Line 9 declares rate as type Double. Variable principal is initialized to 1000.00 and rate is initialized to 0.05, (i.e., 5%). Variable output (line 12) will be used to store the output that we will eventually display in a message dialog.

```vb
1   ' Fig. 6.8: Interest.vb
2   ' Calculating compound interest.
3   Imports System.Windows.Forms
4
5   Module Interest
6      Sub Main()
7         Dim amount As Decimal ' dollar amounts on deposit
8         Dim principal As Decimal = 1000.00 ' amount invested
9         Dim rate As Double = 0.05 ' interest rate
10
11         ' amount after each year
12         Dim output As String = "Year" & vbTab & "Amount on deposit" & vbCrLf
13
14         ' calculate amount after each year
15         For year As Integer = 1 To 10
16            amount = principal * (1 + rate) ^ year
17            output &= _
18               (year & vbTab & String.Format("{0:C}", amount) & vbCrLf)
19         Next
20
21         ' display output
22         MessageBox.Show(output, "Compound Interest", _
23            MessageBoxButtons.OK, MessageBoxIcon.Information)
24      End Sub ' Main
25   End Module ' Interest
```

Fig. 6.8 | For...Next statement used to calculate compound interest. (Part 1 of 2.)

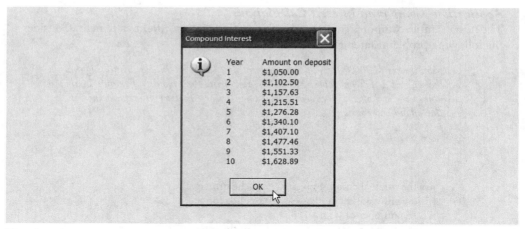

Fig. 6.8 | For...Next statement used to calculate compound interest. (Part 2 of 2.)

The For...Next statement (lines 15–19) iterates 10 times, varying control variable year from 1 to 10 in increments of 1. Line 16 performs the calculation from the problem statement

$$a = p (1 + r)^n$$

where a is the amount, p is the principal, r is the rate and n is the year.

Formatting Currency Output

Lines 17–18 append additional text to the end of String output. The text includes the current year value, a tab character (vbTab) to position to the second column, the result of the method call String.Format("{0:C}", amount) and, finally, a line feed (vbCrLf) to start the next output on the next line. Method **Format** of class String takes a formatted string and the values to be formatted as arguments, and returns the resulting text with the formatting applied. The first argument passed to Format is the format string. In Chapter 5, we used the format string "{0:F}" to print a floating-point number with two digits after the decimal. Line 18 uses the format string "{0:C}". The **C** (for "currency") format specifier indicates that its corresponding value (amount) should be displayed in monetary format—with a dollar sign to the left and commas in the proper locations. For example, the value 1334.50, when formatted using the C format specifier, will appear as "$1,334.50."

Type Decimal vs. Type Double

Variables amount and principal are declared as type Decimal. We do this because we are dealing with fractional parts of dollars and need a type that allows precise calculations with monetary amounts—Single and Double, because they only approximate values, do not. Using floating-point types, such as Single or Double, to represent dollar amounts (assuming that dollar amounts are displayed with two digits to the right of the decimal point) can cause errors. For example, two Double dollar amounts stored in the machine could be 14.234 (normally rounded to 14.23) and 18.673 (normally rounded to 18.67). When these amounts are added together, they produce the internal sum 32.907, which normally rounds to 32.91. Thus, the output could appear as

```
   14.23
 + 18.67
 ───────
   32.91
```

but a person adding the individual numbers as displayed would expect the sum to be 32.90. Therefore, it is inappropriate to use Single or Double for dollar amounts. You have been warned!

Error-Prevention Tip 6.3

Do not use variables of type Single or Double to perform precise monetary calculations. The imprecision of floating-point numbers can cause errors that result in incorrect monetary values. Use the type Decimal for monetary calculations.

Variable rate, of type Double, is used in the calculation 1 + rate, which appears as the left operand of the exponentiation operator. In fact, this calculation produces the same result each time through the loop, so performing the calculation in the body of the For...Next loop is wasteful.

Performance Tip 6.1

Avoid placing inside a loop the calculation of an expression whose value does not change each time through the loop. Such an expression should be evaluated only once and prior to the loop.

6.5 GradeBook Case Study: Select...Case Multiple-Selection Statement

Chapter 5 presented the If...Then single-selection statement and the If...Then...Else double-selection statement. Occasionally, an algorithm contains a series of decisions that test a variable or expression separately for each value that the variable or expression might assume. The algorithm then takes different actions based on those values. Visual Basic provides the **Select...Case** *multiple-selection statement* to handle such decision making.

GradeBook Class with Select...Case Statement to Count A, B, C, D and F Grades.

Figure 6.9 contains an enhanced version of the GradeBook class introduced in Chapter 4 and further developed in Chapter 5. The new version not only calculates the average of a set of numeric grades entered by the user, but uses a Select...Case statement to determine whether each grade is the equivalent of an A, B, C, D or F and to increment the appropriate grade counter. The class also displays a summary of the number of students who received each grade. An extra counter is used to display the number of students who received a perfect score of 100 on the exam. Figure 6.10 shows a sample execution of the GradeBookTest module that uses an object of class GradeBook to process a set of grades.

```
1    ' Fig. 6.9: GradeBook.vb
2    ' GradeBook class uses Select...Case statement to count letter grades.
3    Public Class GradeBook
4       Private courseNameValue As String ' name of course
```

Fig. 6.9 | GradeBook class uses Select...Case statement to count A, B, C, D and F grades. (Part 1 of 4.)

```
5     Private total As Integer ' sum of grades
6     Private gradeCounter As Integer ' number of grades entered
7     Private aCount As Integer ' count of A grades
8     Private bCount As Integer ' count of B grades
9     Private cCount As Integer ' count of C grades
10    Private dCount As Integer ' count of D grades
11    Private fCount As Integer ' count of F grades
12    Private perfectScoreCount As Integer ' count of perfect scores
13
14    ' constructor initializes course name;
15    ' Integer instance variables are initialized to 0 by default
16    Public Sub New(ByVal name As String)
17       CourseName = name ' initializes CourseName
18    End Sub ' New
19
20    ' property that gets and sets the course name; the Set accessor
21    ' ensures that the course name has at most 25 characters
22    Public Property CourseName() As String
23       Get ' retrieve courseNameValue
24          Return courseNameValue
25       End Get
26
27       Set(ByVal value As String) ' set courseNameValue
28          If value.Length <= 25 Then ' if value has 25 or fewer characters
29             courseNameValue = value ' store the course name in the object
30          Else ' if name has more than 25 characters
31             ' set courseNameValue to first 25 characters of parameter name
32             ' start at 0, length of 25
33             courseNameValue = value.Substring(0, 25)
34
35             Console.WriteLine( _
36                "Course name (" & value & ") exceeds maximum length (25).")
37             Console.WriteLine( _
38                "Limiting course name to first 25 characters." & vbCrLf)
39          End If
40       End Set
41    End Property ' CourseName
42
43    ' display a welcome message to the GradeBook user
44    Public Sub DisplayMessage()
45       Console.WriteLine("Welcome to the grade book for " _
46          & vbCrLf & CourseName & "!" & vbCrLf)
47    End Sub ' DisplayMessage
48
49    ' input arbitrary number of grades from user
50    Public Sub InputGrades()
51       Console.Write( _
52          "Enter the grades in the range 0-100, negative value to quit: ")
53       Dim grade As Integer = Console.ReadLine() ' input grade
54
```

Fig. 6.9 | GradeBook class uses Select...Case statement to count A, B, C, D and F grades. (Part 2 of 4.)

```vb
55        ' loop until user enters a sentinel value
56        While grade >= 0
57           total += grade ' add grade to total
58           gradeCounter += 1 ' increment number of grades
59
60           ' call method to increment appropriate counter
61           IncrementLetterGradeCounter(grade)
62
63           ' input next grade
64           Console.Write("Enter the grades in the range 0-100, " & _
65              "negative value to quit: ")
66           grade = Console.ReadLine()
67        End While
68     End Sub ' InputGrades
69
70     ' add 1 to appropriate counter for specified grade
71     Private Sub IncrementLetterGradeCounter(ByVal grade As Integer)
72        Select Case grade ' determine which grade was entered
73           Case 100 ' perfect score
74              perfectScoreCount += 1 ' increment perfectScoreCount
75              aCount += 1 ' increment aCount
76           Case 90 To 99 ' grade was between 90 and 99
77              aCount += 1 ' increment aCount
78           Case 80 To 89 ' grade was between 80 and 89
79              bCount += 1 ' increment bCount
80           Case 70 To 79 ' grade was between 70 and 79
81              cCount += 1 ' increment cCount
82           Case 60 To 69 ' grade was between 60 and 69
83              dCount += 1 ' increment dCount
84           Case Else ' grade was less than 60
85              fCount += 1 ' increment fCount
86        End Select
87     End Sub ' IncrementLetterGradeCounter
88
89     ' display a report based on the grades entered by user
90     Public Sub DisplayGradeReport()
91        Console.WriteLine(vbCrLf & "Grade Report:")
92
93        ' if user entered at least one grade
94        If (gradeCounter > 0) Then
95           ' calculate average of all grades entered
96           Dim average As Double = total / gradeCounter
97
98           ' output summary of results
99           Console.WriteLine("Total of the {0} grades entered is {1}", _
100             gradeCounter, total)
101          Console.WriteLine("Class average is {0:F2}", average)
102          Console.WriteLine("Number of students who received each grade:")
103          Console.WriteLine("A: " & aCount) ' display number of A grades
104          Console.WriteLine("B: " & bCount) ' display number of B grades
```

Fig. 6.9 | GradeBook class uses Select...Case statement to count A, B, C, D and F grades. (Part 3 of 4.)

```
105              Console.WriteLine("C: " & cCount) ' display number of C grades
106              Console.WriteLine("D: " & dCount) ' display number of D grades
107              Console.WriteLine("F: " & fCount) ' display number of F grades
108              Console.WriteLine(vbCrLf & "Number of students who received " & _
109                 "perfect scores: " & perfectScoreCount)
110          Else ' no grades were entered, so output appropriate message
111              Console.WriteLine("No grades were entered")
112          End If
113      End Sub ' DisplayGradeReport
114  End Class ' GradeBook
```

Fig. 6.9 | GradeBook class uses Select...Case statement to count A, B, C, D and F grades. (Part 4 of 4.)

Like earlier versions of the class, class GradeBook (Fig. 6.9) declares instance variable courseNameValue (line 4) and contains property CourseName (lines 22–41) and method DisplayMessage (lines 44–47), which access the course name and display a welcome message to the user, respectively. The class also contains a constructor (lines 16–18) that initializes the course name.

This version of class GradeBook declares instance variables total (line 5) and grade-Counter (line 6), which keep track of the sum of the grades entered by the user and the number of grades entered, respectively. Lines 7–11 declare counter variables for each grade category. Line 12 declares perfectScoreCount, a counter for the number of students who received a perfect score of 100 on the exam. The class maintains total, gradeCounter and the six counters as instance variables so that they can be used or modified in any of the class's methods. Note that the class's constructor (lines 16–18) sets only the course name; the remaining instance variables are Integers and are initialized to 0 by default.

This version of class GradeBook contains three additional methods—InputGrades, IncrementLetterGradeCounter and DisplayGradeReport. Method InputGrades (lines 50–68) reads an arbitrary number of integer grades from the user using sentinel-controlled repetition and updates instance variables total and gradeCounter. The method calls method IncrementLetterGradeCounter (lines 71–87) to update the appropriate letter-grade counter for each grade entered. Note that method IncrementLetterGradeCounter is declared Private—we will discuss why later in the section. Method DisplayGrade-Report (lines 90–113) outputs a report containing the total of all the grades entered, the average of the grades, the number of students who received each letter grade and the number of students who received a perfect score.

Let's examine these methods in more detail. Lines 51–53 in method InputGrades prompt the user to enter a grade, which is assigned to variable grade. In this example, we are using any negative number as a sentinel. The While statement (lines 56–67) executes if there is more data to input (i.e., if the grade is not a sentinel value).

Line 57 adds grade to total. Line 58 increments gradeCounter. The DisplayGrade-Report method uses these variables to compute the average. Line 61 calls method Incre-mentLetterGradeCounter to increment the appropriate letter-grade counter based on the numeric grade entered. Lines 64–66 prompt the user and input the next grade.

Method IncrementLetterGradeCounter uses a Select...Case statement (lines 72–86) to determine which counter to increment. In this example, we assume that the user

enters a valid grade in the range 0–100. A grade in the range 90–100 represents an A, 80–89 represents a B, 70–79 represents a C, 60–69 represents a D and 0–59 represents an F.
  Line 72

> `Select Case grade`

begins the Select...Case statement. The expression following the keywords Select Case (in this case, grade) is called the ***controlling expression***. The controlling expression is compared sequentially with each Case. If a matching Case is found, the code in the Case executes, then program control proceeds to the first statement after the Select...Case statement (line 87).

Common Programming Error 6.3

Duplicate Case statements are logic errors. At run time, the first matching Case is executed.

  The first Case statement (line 73) determines whether the value of grade is equal to 100. If this is true, the statements in lines 74–75 execute, incrementing both aCount (because a grade of 100 is an A) and perfectScoreCount. Note that a Case statement can specify multiple actions—in this case, incrementing both aCount and perfectScore-Count. The next Case statement (line 76) determines whether grade is between 90 and 99 inclusive. In this case, only aCount is incremented (line 77). Keyword To specifies the range; lines 78–83 use this keyword to present a series of similar Cases. Each case increments the appropriate counter.

Common Programming Error 6.4

If the value on the left side of the To keyword in a Case statement is larger than the value on the right side, the Case is ignored during program execution; this is probably a logic error.

  If no match occurs between the controlling expression's value and a Case label, the optional ***Case Else*** (lines 84–85) executes. We use the Case Else in this example to process all controlling-expression values that are less than 60, that is, all failing grades. If no match occurs and the Select...Case does not contain a Case Else, program control simply continues with the first statement after the Select...Case. Case Else commonly is used to deal with invalid input. When employed, the Case Else must be the last Case.
  The required ***End Select*** keywords terminate the Select...Case statement. Note that the body parts of the Select...Case statement are indented to emphasize structure and improve program readability.

Error-Prevention Tip 6.4

Provide a Case Else in Select...Case statements. Cases not handled in a Select...Case statement are ignored unless a Case Else is provided. The inclusion of a Case Else statement can facilitate the processing of exceptional conditions.

Types of Case Statements
Case statements also can use relational operators to determine whether the controlling expression satisfies a condition. For example

> `Case Is < 0`

uses keyword ***Is*** along with the relational operator, <, to test for values less than 0.

Multiple values can be tested in a `Case` statement where the values are separated by commas, as in

> **Case** 0, 5 **To** 9

which tests for the value 0 or values in the range 5–9.

GradeBookTest *Module That Demonstrates Class* GradeBook

Module `GradeBookTest` (Fig. 6.10) creates a `GradeBook` object (line 7). Line 9 invokes the object's `DisplayMessage` method to output a welcome message to the user. Line 10 invokes the object's `InputGrades` method to read grades from the user and keep track of the sum of all the grades entered and the number of grades. Recall that method `InputGrades` also calls method `IncrementLetterGradeCounter` to keep track of the number of students who received each letter grade. Line 11 invokes method `DisplayGradeReport` of class `GradeBook`, which outputs a report based on the grades entered (as in the sample execution in Fig. 6.10). Line 94 of class `GradeBook` (Fig. 6.9) determines whether the user entered at least one grade—this helps us avoid dividing by zero. If so, line 96 calculates the average of the grades. Lines 99–109 then output the totals of all the grades, the class average, the number of students who received each letter grade and the number of students who received a perfect score. If no grades were entered, line 111 outputs an appropriate message.

```
 1   ' Fig. 6.10: GradeBookTest.vb
 2   ' Create GradeBook object, input grades and display grade report.
 3   Module GradeBookTest
 4      Sub Main()
 5         ' create GradeBook object gradeBook1 and
 6         ' pass course name to constructor
 7         Dim gradeBook1 As New GradeBook("CS101 Introduction to VB")
 8
 9         gradeBook1.DisplayMessage() ' display welcome message
10         gradeBook1.InputGrades() ' read grades from user
11         gradeBook1.DisplayGradeReport() ' display report based on grades
12      End Sub ' Main
13   End Module ' GradeBookTest
```

```
Welcome to the grade book for
CS101 Introduction to VB!

Enter a grade in the range 0-100, negative value to quit: 99
Enter a grade in the range 0-100, negative value to quit: 92
Enter a grade in the range 0-100, negative value to quit: 45
Enter a grade in the range 0-100, negative value to quit: 57
Enter a grade in the range 0-100, negative value to quit: 63
Enter a grade in the range 0-100, negative value to quit: 71
Enter a grade in the range 0-100, negative value to quit: 76
Enter a grade in the range 0-100, negative value to quit: 85
Enter a grade in the range 0-100, negative value to quit: 90
Enter a grade in the range 0-100, negative value to quit: 100
Enter a grade in the range 0-100, negative value to quit: -1
```

(continued on next page...)

Fig. 6.10 | GradeBookTest creates a GradeBook object and invokes its methods. (Part 1 of 2.)

```
Grade Report:
Total of the 10 grades entered is 778
Class average is 77.80
Number of students who received each grade:
A: 4
B: 1
C: 2
D: 1
F: 2

Number of students who received a perfect score: 1
```

Fig. 6.10 | GradeBookTest creates a GradeBook object and invokes its methods. (Part 2 of 2.)

Note that module GradeBookTest (Fig. 6.10) does not directly call GradeBook method IncrementLetterGradeCounter (lines 71–87 of Fig. 6.9). This method is used exclusively by method InputGrades of class GradeBook to update the appropriate letter-grade counter as each new grade is entered by the user. Method IncrementLetterGrade-Counter exists solely to support the operation of class GradeBook's other methods and thus is declared Private. Methods declared Private can be called only by other members of the class in which the Private methods are declared. Such Private methods are commonly referred to as *utility methods* or *helper methods*.

Using the With Statement
The *With statement* allows you to make multiple references to the same object in a concise manner. For example, we can replace lines 9–11 of Fig. 6.10 (which all reference the same object, gradeBook1) with

```
With gradeBook1
    .DisplayMessage() ' display welcome message
    .InputGrades() ' read grades from user
    .DisplayGradeReport() ' display report based on grades
End With
```

These lines of code are collectively known as a *With statement block*. At the beginning of the block, we specify the object (gradeBook1) that we will be using in the block. The With statement allows you to access an object's members in the block without having to specify the name of the object before the dot separator, e.g., .DisplayMessage() instead of gradeBook1.DisplayMessage().

Select...Case Statement UML Activity Diagram
Figure 6.11 shows the UML activity diagram for the general Select...Case statement. Again, note that (besides an initial state, transition arrows, merges, a final state and several notes) the diagram contains only action states and decisions.

In Chapter 11, Object-Oriented Programming: Polymorphism, we present a more elegant method of implementing multiple-selection logic. We use a technique called polymorphism to create programs that are often clearer, more manageable, and easier to extend than programs that use Select...Case logic.

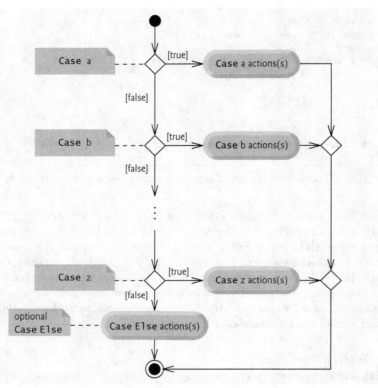

Fig. 6.11 | `Select...Case` multiple-selection statement UML activity diagram.

6.6 Do...Loop While Repetition Statement

The ***Do...Loop While*** repetition statement is similar to the `While` statement and `Do While...Loop` statement. In the `While` and `Do While...Loop` statements, the loop-continuation condition is tested at the *beginning* of the loop, before the body of the loop is performed. The `Do...Loop While` statement tests the loop-continuation condition *after* the loop body is performed; therefore, in a `Do...Loop While` statement, the loop body is always executed at least once. When a `Do...Loop While` statement terminates, execution continues with the statement after the `Loop While` clause. The program in Fig. 6.12 uses a `Do...Loop While` statement to output the values 1–5.

Lines 8–11 demonstrate the `Do...Loop While` statement. The first time that the statement is encountered, lines 9–10 are executed, displaying the value of `counter` (at this point, 1) then incrementing `counter` by 1. Then the condition in line 11 is evaluated. Variable `counter` is 2, which is less than or equal to 5; because the loop-continuation condition is met, the `Do...Loop While` statement executes again. In the fifth iteration of the statement, line 9 outputs the value 5, and line 10 increments `counter` to 6. At this point, the loop-continuation condition in line 11 evaluates to false, and the program exits the `Do...Loop While` statement.

```
 1   ' Fig. 6.12: DoLoopWhile.vb
 2   ' Demonstrating the Do...Loop While repetition statement.
 3   Module DoLoopWhile
 4      Sub Main()
 5         Dim counter As Integer = 1
 6
 7         ' print values 1 to 5
 8         Do
 9            Console.Write(counter & " ")
10            counter += 1
11         Loop While counter <= 5
12
13         Console.WriteLine()
14      End Sub ' Main
15   End Module ' DoLoopWhile
```

```
1 2 3 4 5
```

Fig. 6.12 | Do…Loop While repetition statement.

Do…Loop While *Statement UML Activity Diagram*

The Do…Loop While UML activity diagram (Fig. 6.14) illustrates the fact that the loop-continuation condition is not evaluated until after the statement body is executed at least once. Compare this activity diagram with that of the While statement (Fig. 5.5). Again, note that (besides an initial state, transition arrows, a merge, a final state and several notes) the diagram contains only action states and a decision.

6.7 Do…Loop Until Repetition Statement

The **Do…Loop Until** repetition statement is similar to the Do Until…Loop statement, except that the loop-termination condition is tested after the loop body is performed; therefore, the loop body executes at least once. When a Do…Loop Until terminates, execution continues with the statement after the Loop Until clause. Figure 6.13 uses a Do…Loop Until statement to print the numbers from 1 to 5.

```
 1   ' Fig. 6.13: DoLoopUntil.vb
 2   ' Using Do...Loop Until repetition statement.
 3   Module DoLoopUntil
 4      Sub Main()
 5         Dim counter As Integer = 1
 6
 7         ' print values 1 to 5
 8         Do
 9            Console.Write(counter & " ")
10            counter += 1
11         Loop Until counter > 5
```

Fig. 6.13 | Do…Loop Until repetition statement. (Part 1 of 2.)

```
12
13          Console.WriteLine()
14      End Sub ' Main
15   End Module ' DoLoopUntil
```

```
1 2 3 4 5
```

Fig. 6.13 | Do...Loop Until repetition statement. (Part 2 of 2.)

The Do...Loop Until statement activity diagram is the same as the one in Fig. 6.14. Note that the loop-termination condition (counter > 5) is not evaluated until after the body is executed at least once. If this condition is true, the statement exits. If the condition is false (i.e., the condition counter <= 5 is true), the loop continues executing.

 Error-Prevention Tip 6.5

In a counter-controlled loop, ensure that the control variable is incremented (or decremented) appropriately in the body of the loop to avoid an infinite loop.

6.8 Using the Exit Statement in Repetition Statements

The *Exit statement* can be used to alter a program's flow of control. There are many forms of the Exit statement, designed to exit different types of code blocks. In this section, we focus on using the Exit statement in repetition statements. The *Exit Do statement* can be

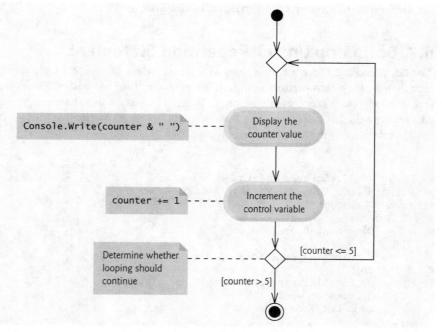

Fig. 6.14 | Do...Loop While repetition statement activity diagram.

executed in a Do While...Loop, Do...Loop While, Do Until...Loop or Do...Loop Until statement, to cause the program to exit immediately from that repetition statement. Similarly, the ***Exit For statement*** and the ***Exit While statement*** cause immediate exit from For...Next and While...End While loops, respectively. Execution continues with the first statement after the repetition statement. Figure 6.15 demonstrates the Exit For, Exit Do and Exit While statements in their respective repetition statements.

```vb
1   ' Fig. 6.15: ExitTest.vb
2   ' Using the Exit statement in repetition statements.
3   Module ExitTest
4      Sub Main()
5         Dim counter As Integer ' loop counter
6
7         ' exit For...Next statement
8         For counter = 1 To 10
9            ' skip remaining code in loop only if counter = 5
10           If counter = 5 Then
11              Exit For ' break out of loop
12           End If
13
14           Console.Write(counter & " ") ' output counter
15        Next
16
17        Console.WriteLine(vbCrLf & _
18           "Broke out of For...Next at counter = " & counter & vbCrLf)
19        counter = 1 ' reset counter
20
21        ' exit Do Until...Loop statement
22        Do Until counter > 10
23           ' skip remaining code in loop only if counter = 5
24           If counter = 5 Then
25              Exit Do ' break out of loop
26           End If
27
28           Console.Write(counter & " ") ' output counter
29           counter += 1 ' increment counter
30        Loop
31
32        Console.WriteLine(vbCrLf & _
33           "Broke out of Do Until...Loop at counter = " & counter & vbCrLf)
34        counter = 1 ' reset counter
35
36        ' exit While statement
37        While counter <= 10
38           ' skip remaining code in loop only if counter = 5
39           If counter = 5 Then
40              Exit While ' break out of loop
41           End If
42
43           Console.Write(counter & " ") ' output counter
44           counter += 1 ' increment counter
45        End While
```

Fig. 6.15 | Exit statement in repetition statements. (Part 1 of 2.)

```
46
47          Console.WriteLine( _
48             vbCrLf & "Broke out of While at counter = " & counter)
49      End Sub ' Main
50   End Module ' ExitTest
```

```
1 2 3 4
Broke out of For...Next at counter = 5

1 2 3 4
Broke out of Do Until...Loop at counter = 5

1 2 3 4
Broke out of While at counter = 5
```

Fig. 6.15 | Exit statement in repetition statements. (Part 2 of 2.)

The header of the For...Next statement (line 8) indicates that the body of the loop is to execute 10 times. During each execution, the If...Then statement (lines 10–12) determines whether the control variable, counter, is equal to 5. For the first four iterations of the loop (counter values 1–4), this condition is false, so program control proceeds to line 14, which displays the current value of counter. Once the value of counter reaches 5, the condition in line 10 evaluates to true, so the Exit For statement (line 11) executes, terminating the execution of the loop. Program control then proceeds to the output statement in lines 17–18, which displays the value of counter after the loop has been exited.

Line 19 resets the value of counter for the next repetition statement. The header of the Do Until...Loop statement (line 22) indicates that the loop should continue executing until counter is greater than 10. When counter has values in the range 1–4, the body of the If...Then statement (lines 24–26) is skipped, the current value of counter is displayed (line 28) and counter is incremented (line 29). However, when counter is 5, the Exit Do statement (line 25) executes, terminating the loop. Lines 32–33 display the value of counter after the loop has been exited. Note that the program does not increment counter (line 29) after the Exit Do statement executes.

Line 34 once again resets the value of counter for the next repetition statement. The header of the While statement (lines 37) indicates that the loop should continue executing while counter is less than or equal to 10. When counter is 5, the Exit While statement (line 40) executes, terminating execution of the While statement. Lines 47–48 display the value of counter after the loop has been exited.

The **Exit Select statement** can be used to exit a Select...Case statement. The **Exit Property statement** can be used to exit from a property. We encounter different forms of the Exit statement throughout the book.

6.9 Using the Continue Statement in Repetition Statements

The **Continue statement** skips the remaining statements in the loop body of a repetition statement and causes control to proceed to the next iteration of the loop. Like the Exit statement, Continue comes in many forms. The **Continue Do statement** can be executed in a Do While...Loop, Do...Loop While, Do Until...Loop or Do...Loop Until statement to cause the program to skip the remainder of the current iteration of that repetition statement. Similarly, the **Continue For statement** and **Continue While statement** cause the program to skip the remainder of the current iteration of For...Next and While loops, respectively. Unlike the Exit statement, the Continue statement is used to alter program control only in repetition statements.

When Continue For is encountered in a For...Next statement, execution continues with the statement's increment expression, then the program evaluates the loop-continuation test. When Continue is used in another type of repetition statement, the program evaluates the loop-continuation (or loop-termination) test immediately after the Continue statement executes. If a control variable's increment occurs in the loop after the Continue statement, the increment is skipped.

Figure 6.16 demonstrates the Continue For, Continue Do and Continue While statements in their respective repetition statements. Each repetition statement displays the values 1–4 and 6–10; the value 5 is skipped in each case using an appropriate form of the Continue statement.

```vb
1    ' Fig. 6.16: ContinueTest.vb
2    ' Using the Continue statement in repetition statements.
3    Module ContinueTest
4       Sub Main()
5          Dim counter As Integer ' loop counter
6
7          ' skipping an iteration of a For...Next statement
8          For counter = 1 To 10
9             If counter = 5 Then
10                Continue For ' skip to next iteration of loop if counter = 5
11            End If
12
13            Console.Write(counter & " ") ' output counter
14         Next
15
16         Console.WriteLine(vbCrLf & _
17            "Skipped printing in For...Next at counter = 5" & vbCrLf)
18         counter = 0 ' reset counter
19
20         ' skipping an iteration of a Do Until...Loop statement
21         Do Until counter >= 10
22            counter += 1 ' increment counter
23
24            If counter = 5 Then
25               Continue Do ' skip to next iteration of loop if counter = 5
26            End If
27
28            Console.Write(counter & " ") ' output counter
29         Loop
30
31         Console.WriteLine(vbCrLf & _
32            "Skipped printing in Do Until...Loop at counter = 5" & vbCrLf)
33         counter = 0 ' reset counter
```

Fig. 6.16 | Continue statement in repetition statements. (Part 1 of 2.)

```
34
35          ' skipping an iteration of a While statement
36          While counter < 10
37              counter += 1 ' increment counter
38
39              If counter = 5 Then
40                  Continue While ' skip to next iteration of loop if counter = 5
41              End If
42
43              Console.Write(counter & " ") ' output counter
44          End While
45
46          Console.WriteLine( _
47              vbCrLf & "Skipped printing in While at counter = 5")
48      End Sub ' Main
49  End Module ' ContinueTest
```

```
1 2 3 4 6 7 8 9 10
Skipped printing in For...Next at counter = 5

1 2 3 4 6 7 8 9 10
Skipped printing in Do Until...Loop at counter = 5

1 2 3 4 6 7 8 9 10
Skipped printing in While at counter = 5
```

Fig. 6.16 | Continue statement in repetition statements. (Part 2 of 2.)

The header of the For...Next statement (line 8) indicates that the body of the loop is to execute 10 times. During each execution, the If...Then statement (lines 9–11) determines whether the control variable, counter, is equal to 5. If it is not, line 13 displays the current value of counter and the repetition statement continues to iterate. When the value of counter reaches 5, the Continue For statement (line 10) executes, which terminates the current iteration of the loop, causing the display of the current value of counter to be skipped. The control variable is incremented, then the program evaluates the loop-continuation test. The value of counter is now 6, so the For...Next statement continues to loop, eventually printing the values 1–4 and 6–10.

Line 18 sets counter to 0, so that we can loop through the values 1–10 again, this time using a Do Until...Loop statement. Line 21 indicates that the loop is to continue executing until counter is greater than or equal to 10. Line 22 increments counter. The If...Then statement in lines 24–26 tests whether counter is 5. If it is, the Continue Do statement (line 25) executes, causing the display of the variable counter to be skipped. The program then immediately evaluates the loop-termination test (line 21). The value of counter is still 5, which is not greater than or equal to 10, so the loop continues. During the next iteration, the value of counter is incremented to 6, so the loop executes to completion, eventually displaying the values 1–4 and 6–10. We placed the increment at the beginning of the loop (line 22) so that it would not be skipped during the iteration when the Continue statement executes. If we had placed the increment after the If...Then statement, the value of counter would reach 5 and never be incremented in subsequent iterations. The If...Then condition would repeatedly evaluate to true, causing an infinite loop.

Line 33 once again sets `counter` to 0. The `While` statement in lines 36–44 executes while `counter` is less than 10. Once again, the increment appears at the beginning of the loop. When the value of `counter` is 5, the `If...Then` statement's condition (line 39) evaluates to true, and the `Continue While` statement (line 40) executes, terminating the current iteration of the `While` statement. Note that the `While` statement also displays only the values 1–4 and 6–10.

The `Exit` and `Continue` statements can be used in nested control statements. For instance, `Exit For` or `Continue For` can be used in a `While` statement, as long as the `While` statement is itself located in a `For...Next` statement. In such an example, the `Exit` or `Continue` statement would be applied to the proper control statement based on the keywords used in the `Exit` or `Continue` statement—in this example, the `For` keyword is used, so the `For...Next` statement is the control statement whose flow of control will be altered. If there are nested loops of the same type (e.g., a `For...Next` statement within a `For...Next` statement), the statement that immediately surrounds the `Exit` or `Continue` statement is the one affected.

In Section 6.3, we stated that `While` could be used in most cases in place of `For...Next`. The one exception occurs when the increment expression in the `While` follows a `Continue` statement. In this case, the increment does not execute before the program evaluates the repetition-continuation condition, so the `While` does not execute in the same manner as the `For...Next`.

6.10 Logical Operators

So far, we have studied only *simple conditions*, such as `count <= 10`, `total > 1000` and `number <> sentinelValue`. Each selection and repetition statement evaluated only one condition with one of the operators >, <, >=, <=, = and <>. To make a decision that relied on the evaluation of multiple conditions, we performed these tests in separate statements or in nested `If...Then` or `If...Then...Else` statements.

To handle multiple conditions more efficiently, Visual Basic provides *logical operators* that can be used to form complex conditions by combining simple ones. The logical operators are `And`, `Or`, `AndAlso`, `OrElse`, `Xor` and `Not`. We consider examples that use each of these operators.

Logical And Operator

Suppose we wish to ensure that two conditions are *both* true in a program before a certain path of execution is chosen. In such a case, we can use the logical *And* operator as follows:

```
If gender = "F" And age >= 65 Then
    seniorFemales += 1
End If
```

This `If...Then` statement contains two simple conditions. The condition `gender = "F"` determines whether a person is female and the condition `age >= 65` determines whether a person is a senior citizen. The two simple conditions are evaluated first, because the precedences of = and >= are both higher than the precedence of `And`. The `If...Then` statement then considers the combined condition

```
gender = "F" And age >= 65
```

This condition evaluates to true if and only if *both* simple conditions are true. When this combined condition is true, the seniorFemales count is incremented by 1. However, if either or both of the simple conditions are false, the program skips the increment and proceeds to the statement following the If...Then statement. The readability of the preceding combined condition can be improved by adding redundant (i.e., unnecessary) parentheses:

```
(gender = "F") And (age >= 65)
```

Figure 6.17 illustrates the effect of using the And operator with two expressions. The table lists all four possible combinations of true and false values for *expression1* and *expression2*. Such tables often are called ***truth tables.*** Visual Basic evaluates to true or false expressions that include relational operators, equality operators and logical operators.

Logical Or Operator

Now let us consider the **Or** operator. Suppose we wish to ensure that either *or* both of two conditions are true before we choose a certain path of execution. We use the Or operator as in the following program segment:

```
If (semesterAverage >= 90 Or finalExam >= 90) Then
    Console.WriteLine("Student grade is A")
End If
```

This statement also contains two simple conditions. The condition semesterAverage >= 90 is evaluated to determine whether the student deserves an "A" in the course because of an outstanding performance throughout the semester. The condition finalExam >= 90 is evaluated to determine whether the student deserves an "A" in the course because of an outstanding performance on the final exam. The If...Then statement then considers the combined condition

```
(semesterAverage >= 90 Or finalExam >= 90)
```

and awards the student an "A" if either or both of the conditions are true. Note that the text "Student grade is A" is *always* printed, unless both of the conditions are false. Figure 6.18 provides a truth table for the Or operator. The And operator has a higher precedence than the Or operator.

Logical AndAlso and OrElse Operators

The *logical AND operator with short-circuit evaluation* (**AndAlso**) and the *logical inclusive OR operator with short-circuit evaluation* (**OrElse**) are similar to the And and Or operators,

expression1	expression2	expression1 And expression2
False	False	False
False	True	False
True	False	False
True	True	True

Fig. 6.17 | Truth table for the logical And operator.

expression1	expression2	expression1 Or expression2
False	False	False
False	True	True
True	False	True
True	True	True

Fig. 6.18 | Truth table for the logical Or operator.

respectively, with one exception—an expression containing AndAlso or OrElse operators is evaluated only until its truth or falsity is known. For example, evaluation of the expression

```
(gender = "F" AndAlso age >= 65)
```

stops immediately if gender is not equal to "F" (i.e., the entire expression is false); the evaluation of the second expression is irrelevant because the first condition is false. Evaluation of the second condition occurs if and only if gender is equal to "F" (i.e., the entire expression could still be true if the condition age >= 65 is true). This performance feature for the evaluation of AndAlso and OrElse expressions is called *short-circuit evaluation.*

Performance Tip 6.2

In expressions using operator AndAlso, if the separate conditions are independent of one another, place the condition most likely to be false as the leftmost condition. In expressions using operator OrElse, make the condition most likely to be true the leftmost condition. Each of these suggestions can reduce a program's execution time.

Normally, the AndAlso and OrElse operators can be used in place of And and Or. An exception to this rule occurs when the right operand of a condition produces a *side effect* such as a modification of a variable's value or a required method call, as in the following program segment:

```
Console.WriteLine("How old are you?")
If (gender = "F" And Console.ReadLine() >= 65) Then
    Console.WriteLine("You are a female senior citizen.")
End If
```

Here, the And operator guarantees that the condition Console.ReadLine() >= 65 is evaluated, so ReadLine is called regardless of whether the overall expression is true or false. If operator AndAlso had been used, the call to Console.ReadLine might not be evaluated. It is better to write this code as two separate statements—a first that stores the result of Console.ReadLine() in a variable, and a second that uses the variable with either the operator AndAlso or the operator And in the condition.

Error-Prevention Tip 6.6

Avoid expressions with side effects in conditions, because side effects often cause subtle errors.

Logical Xor Operator

A condition containing the *logical exclusive OR* (**Xor**) operator is true if and only if one of its operands results in a true value and the other results in a false value. If both operands are true or both are false, the entire condition is false. Figure 6.19 presents a truth table for the logical exclusive OR operator (**Xor**). This operator always evaluates both of its operands (i.e., there is no short-circuit evaluation).

Logical Not Operator

The **Not** (logical negation) operator enables a programmer to "reverse" the meaning of a condition. Unlike the logical operators And, AndAlso, Or, OrElse and Xor, which each combine two conditions (i.e., these are all binary operators), the logical negation operator is a unary operator, requiring only one operand. The logical negation operator is placed before a condition to choose a path of execution if the original condition (without the logical negation operator) is false. The logical negation operator is demonstrated by the following program segment:

```
If Not (grade = sentinelValue) Then
    Console.WriteLine("The next grade is " & grade)
End If
```

The parentheses around the condition grade = sentinelValue are necessary because the logical negation operator (Not) has a higher precedence than the equality operator. Figure 6.20 provides a truth table for the logical negation operator.

In most cases, you can avoid using logical negation by expressing the condition differently with relational or equality operators. For example, the preceding statement can be written as follows:

expression1	expression2	expression1 Xor expression2
False	False	False
False	True	True
True	False	True
True	True	False

Fig. 6.19 | Truth table for the logical exclusive OR (Xor) operator.

expression	Not expression
False	True
True	False

Fig. 6.20 | Truth table for operator Not (logical negation).

```
If grade <> sentinelValue Then
   Console.WriteLine("The next grade is " & grade)
End If
```

This flexibility helps you express conditions more naturally.

Logical Operators Example

The application in Fig. 6.21 demonstrates the use of the logical operators by displaying their truth tables.

```
1   ' Fig. 6.21: LogicalOperators.vb
2   ' Using logical operators.
3   Module LogicalOperators
4      Sub Main()
5         ' display truth table for And
6         Console.WriteLine("And" & vbCrLf & _
7            "False And False: " & (False And False) & vbCrLf & _
8            "False And True: " & (False And True) & vbCrLf & _
9            "True And False: " & (True And False) & vbCrLf & _
10           "True And True: " & (True And True) & vbCrLf)
11
12        ' display truth table for Or
13        Console.WriteLine("Or" & vbCrLf & _
14           "False Or False: " & (False Or False) & vbCrLf & _
15           "False Or True: " & (False Or True) & vbCrLf & _
16           "True Or False: " & (True Or False) & vbCrLf & _
17           "True Or True: " & (True Or True) & vbCrLf)
18
19        ' display truth table for AndAlso
20        Console.WriteLine("AndAlso" & vbCrLf & _
21           "False AndAlso False: " & (False AndAlso False) & vbCrLf & _
22           "False AndAlso True: " & (False AndAlso True) & vbCrLf & _
23           "True AndAlso False: " & (True AndAlso False) & vbCrLf & _
24           "True AndAlso True: " & (True AndAlso True) & vbCrLf)
25
26        ' display truth table for OrElse
27        Console.WriteLine("OrElse" & vbCrLf & _
28           "False OrElse False: " & (False OrElse False) & vbCrLf & _
29           "False OrElse True: " & (False OrElse True) & vbCrLf & _
30           "True OrElse False: " & (True OrElse False) & vbCrLf & _
31           "True OrElse True: " & (True OrElse True) & vbCrLf)
32
33        ' display truth table for Xor
34        Console.WriteLine("Xor" & vbCrLf & _
35           "False Xor False: " & (False Xor False) & vbCrLf & _
36           "False Xor True: " & (False Xor True) & vbCrLf & _
37           "True Xor False: " & (True Xor False) & vbCrLf & _
38           "True Xor True: " & (True Xor True) & vbCrLf)
```

Fig. 6.21 | Logical operator truth tables. (Part 1 of 2.)

```
39
40             ' display truth table for Not
41             Console.WriteLine("Not" & vbCrLf & "Not False: " & _
42                (Not False) & vbCrLf & "Not True: " & (Not True) & vbCrLf)
43       End Sub ' Main
44    End Module ' LogicalOperators
```

```
And
False And False: False
False And True: False
True And False: False
True And True: True

Or
False Or False: False
False Or True: True
True Or False: True
True Or True: True

AndAlso
False AndAlso False: False
False AndAlso True: False
True AndAlso False: False
True AndAlso True: True

OrElse
False OrElse False: False
False OrElse True: True
True OrElse False: True
True OrElse True: True

Xor
False Xor False: False
False Xor True: True
True Xor False: True
True Xor True: False

Not
Not False: True
Not True: False
```

Fig. 6.21 | Logical operator truth tables. (Part 2 of 2.)

Lines 6–10 demonstrate operator And; lines 13–17 demonstrate operator Or. The remainder of method Main demonstrates the AndAlso, OrElse, Xor and Not operators. We use keywords *True* and *False* in the program to specify values of the Boolean type. Note that when a Boolean value is concatenated to a String, Visual Basic concatenates the string "False" or "True" based on the Boolean's value.

Summary of Operator Precedence
The chart in Fig. 6.22 displays the precedence of the operators introduced so far. The operators are shown from top to bottom in decreasing order of precedence.

Operators	Type
^	exponentiation
+ -	unary plus and minus
* /	multiplicative operators
\	integer division
Mod	modulus
+ -	additive operators
&	concatenation
< <= > >= = <>	relational and equality
Not	logical NOT
And AndAlso	logical AND
Or OrElse	logical inclusive OR
Xor	logical exclusive OR
= += -= *= /= \= ^= &=	assignment

Fig. 6.22 | Precedence of the operators discussed so far.

6.11 (Optional) Software Engineering Case Study: Identifying Objects' States and Activities in the ATM System

In Section 5.14, we identified many of the class attributes needed to implement the ATM system and added them to a class diagram (Fig. 5.28). In this section, we show how these attributes represent an object's state. We identify some key states that our objects may occupy and discuss how objects change state in response to various events occurring in the system. We also discuss the workflow, or *activities*, that objects perform in the ATM system. We present the activities of the BalanceInquiry and Withdrawal transaction objects.

State Machine Diagrams

Each object in a system goes through a series of discrete states. An object's current state is indicated by the values of the object's attributes at that time. *State machine diagrams* model key states of an object and show under what circumstances the object changes state. Unlike the class diagrams presented in earlier case study sections, which focused primarily on the system's structure, state machine diagrams model some of the system's behavior.

Figure 6.23 is a simple state machine diagram that models some of the states of an ATM object. The UML represents each state in a state machine diagram as a *rounded rectangle* with the name of the state placed inside it. A *solid circle* with an attached stick arrowhead designates the *initial state*. Recall that we modeled this state information as the Boolean attribute userAuthenticated in the class diagram of Fig. 5.28. This attribute is initialized to False, or the "User not authenticated" state, according to the state machine diagram.

Fig. 6.23 | State machine diagram for some of the states of the ATM object.

The arrows with stick arrowheads indicate *transitions* between states. An object can transition from one state to another in response to various events that occur in the system. The name or description of the event that causes a transition is written near the line that corresponds to the transition. For example, the ATM object changes from the "User not authenticated" state to the "User authenticated" state after the bank database authenticates the user. Recall from the requirements document that the database authenticates a user by comparing the account number and PIN entered by the user with those of the corresponding account in the database. If the database indicates that the user has entered a valid account number and the correct PIN, the ATM object transitions to the "User authenticated" state and changes its userAuthenticated attribute to a value of True. When the user exits the system by choosing the **Exit** option from the main menu, the ATM object returns to the "User not authenticated" state in preparation for the next ATM user.

Software Engineering Observation 6.1

Software designers do not generally create state machine diagrams showing every possible state and state transition for all attributes—there are simply too many of them. State machine diagrams typically show only the most important or complex states and state transitions.

Activity Diagrams

Like a state machine diagram, an activity diagram models aspects of system behavior. Unlike a state machine diagram, an activity diagram models an object's workflow (sequence of events) during program execution. An activity diagram models the actions the object will perform and in what order. Recall that we used UML activity diagrams to illustrate the flow of control for the control statements presented in Chapters 5 and 6.

The activity diagram in Fig. 6.24 models the actions involved in executing a Balance-Inquiry transaction. We assume that a BalanceInquiry object has already been initialized and assigned a valid account number (that of the current user), so the object knows which balance to retrieve. The diagram includes the actions that occur after the user selects a balance inquiry from the main menu and before the ATM returns the user to the main menu—a BalanceInquiry object does not perform or initiate these actions, so we do not model them here. The diagram begins with retrieving the available balance of the user's account from the database. Next, the BalanceInquiry retrieves the total balance of the account. Finally, the transaction displays the balances on the screen.

The UML represents an action in an activity diagram as an action state modeled by a rectangle with its left and right sides replaced by arcs curving outward. Each action state contains an action expression—for example, "get available balance of user's account from database"—that specifies an action to be performed. An arrow with a stick arrowhead connects two action states, indicating the order in which the actions represented by the action states occur. The solid circle (at the top of Fig. 6.24) represents the activity's initial state—the beginning of the workflow before the object performs the modeled actions. In this

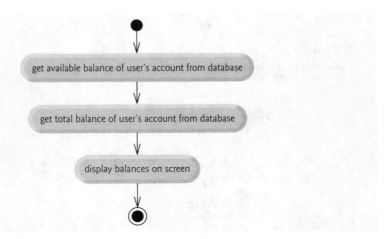

Fig. 6.24 | Activity diagram for a `BalanceInquiry` transaction.

case, the transaction first executes the "get available balance of user's account from database" action expression. Second, the transaction retrieves the total balance. Finally, the transaction displays both balances on the screen. The solid circle enclosed in an open circle (at the bottom of Fig. 6.24) represents the final state—the end of the workflow after the object performs the modeled actions.

Figure 6.25 shows a more complex activity diagram for a `Withdrawal` transaction. We assume that a `Withdrawal` object has been assigned a valid account number. We do not model the user selecting a withdrawal from the main menu or the ATM returning the user to the main menu because these are not actions performed by a `Withdrawal` object. The transaction first displays a menu of standard withdrawal amounts (Fig. 3.33) and an option to cancel the transaction. The transaction then inputs a menu selection from the user. The activity flow now arrives at a decision symbol to determine the next action based on the associated guard conditions. If the user cancels the transaction, the system displays an appropriate message and the cancellation flow reaches a merge symbol (at the bottom of the activity diagram), where this activity flow joins the transaction's other possible activity flows (which we discuss shortly). Note that a merge can have any number of incoming transition arrows, but only one outgoing transition arrow. The decision at the bottom of the diagram determines whether the transaction should repeat from the beginning. When the user has canceled the transaction, the guard condition "cash dispensed or user canceled transaction" is true, so control transitions to the activity's final state.

If the user selects a withdrawal amount from the menu, `amount` (an attribute of class `Withdrawal` originally modeled in Fig. 5.28) is set to the value chosen by the user. The transaction next gets the available balance of the user's account (i.e., the `availableBalance` attribute of the user's `Account` object) from the database. The activity flow then arrives at another decision. If the requested withdrawal amount exceeds the user's available balance, the system displays an error message informing the user of the problem. Control then merges with the other activity flows before reaching the decision at the bottom of the diagram. The guard decision "cash not dispensed and user did not cancel" is true, so the activity flow returns to the top of the diagram, and the transaction prompts the user to input a new amount.

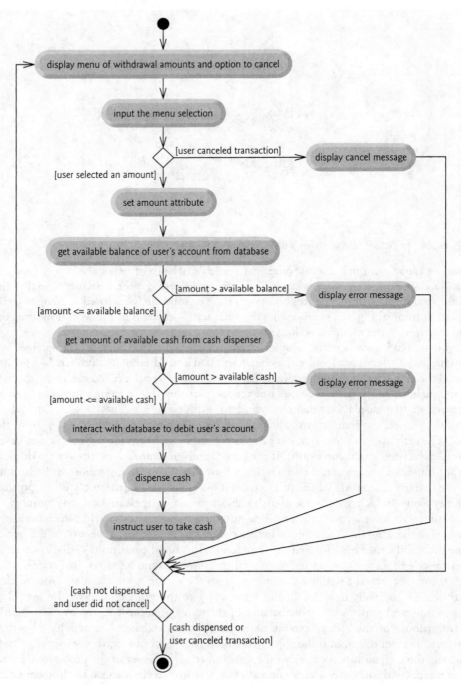

Fig. 6.25 | Activity diagram for a `Withdrawal` transaction.

If the requested withdrawal amount is less than or equal to the user's available balance, the transaction tests whether the cash dispenser has enough cash to satisfy the request. If it does not, the transaction displays an appropriate error message and passes through the merge before reaching the final decision. Cash was not dispensed, so the activity flow returns to the beginning of the activity diagram, and the transaction prompts the user to choose a new amount. If sufficient cash is available, the transaction interacts with the database to debit the user's account by the withdrawal amount (i.e., subtract the amount from both the `availableBalance` and `totalBalance` attributes of the user's `Account` object). The transaction then dispenses the desired amount of cash and instructs the user to take the cash. The main flow of activity next merges with the two error flows and the cancellation flow. In this case, cash was dispensed, so the activity flow reaches the final state.

We have taken the first steps in modeling the behavior of the ATM system and have shown how an object's attributes affect the object's activities. In Section 7.20, we investigate the operations of our classes to create a more complete model of the system's behavior.

Software Engineering Case Study Self-Review Exercises

6.1 State whether the following statement is *true* or *false*, and if *false*, explain why: State machine diagrams model structural aspects of a system.

6.2 An activity diagram models the _____ that an object performs and the order in which it performs them.
    a) actions
    b) attributes
    c) states
    d) state transitions

6.3 Based on the requirements document, create an activity diagram for a deposit transaction.

Answers to Software Engineering Case Study Self-Review Exercises

6.1 False. State machine diagrams model some of the behavior of a system.

6.2 a.

6.3 Figure 6.26 presents an activity diagram for a deposit transaction. The diagram models the actions that occur after the user chooses the deposit option from the main menu and before the ATM returns the user to the main menu. Recall that part of receiving a deposit amount from the user involves converting an integer number of cents to a dollar amount. Also recall that crediting an account by the deposit amount involves increasing only the `totalBalance` attribute of the user's `Account` object. The bank updates the `availableBalance` attribute of the user's `Account` object only after confirming the amount of cash in the deposit envelope and after the enclosed checks clear—this occurs independently of the ATM system.

6.12 Wrap-Up

In this chapter, we completed our introduction to control statements. Chapter 5 discussed the `If...Then`, `If...Then...Else`, `While...End While`, `Do While...Loop` and `Do Until...Loop` statements. Chapter 6 demonstrated the `For...Next`, `Select...Case`, `Do...Loop While` and `Do...Loop Until` statements. Any algorithm can be developed using combinations of the sequence structure (i.e., statements listed in the order in which they are to execute), the three types of selection statements—`If...Then`, `If...Then...Else` and `Select...Case`—and the seven types of repetition statements—`While...End While`, `Do`

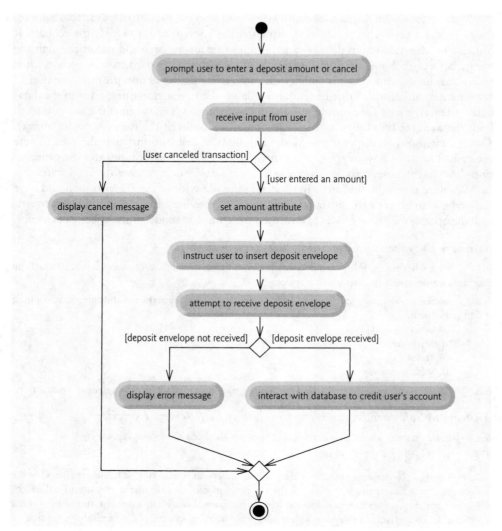

Fig. 6.26 | Activity diagram for a Deposit transaction.

While...Loop, Do Until...Loop, Do...Loop While, Do...Loop Until, For...Next and For Each...Next (which we discuss in Chapter 8). In Chapters 5 and 6, we discussed how you can combine these building blocks to utilize proven program-construction and problem-solving techniques. We demonstrated how to alter the flow of program control using the various Exit and Continue statements. We introduced the logical operators, which enable you to use more complex conditional expressions in control statements. In Chapter 7, we examine methods in greater depth. So far you have learned how to create methods in classes, and a Main method in a module. Chapter 7 introduces the different types of methods, including how and when to use each of them. You will learn how to use methods to organize a complex object-oriented program into small, manageable pieces.

7

Methods: A Deeper Look

The greatest invention of the
nineteenth century was the
invention of the method of
invention.
—Alfred North Whitehead

Form ever follows function.
—Louis Henri Sullivan

Call me Ishmael.
—Herman Melville, *Moby
Dick*

When you call me that,
smile!
—Owen Wister

O! call back yesterday, bid
time return.
—William Shakespeare

Answer me in one word.
—William Shakespeare

There is a point at which
methods devour themselves.
—Frantz Fanon

OBJECTIVES

In this chapter you will learn:

- To construct programs modularly from methods.

- That `Shared` methods are associated with a class rather than a specific instance of the class.

- To use common `Math` methods from the Framework Class Library.

- To create new methods.

- The mechanisms used to pass information between methods.

- Simulation techniques that employ random number generation.

- How the visibility of identifiers is limited to specific regions of programs.

- To write and use recursive methods (methods that call themselves).

7.1 Introduction

Experience has shown that the best way to develop and maintain a large program is to construct it from small, simple pieces. This technique is called *divide and conquer*. We introduced methods in Chapter 3. In this chapter, we study methods in greater depth. We emphasize how to declare and use methods to facilitate the design, implementation, operation and maintenance of large programs.

You'll see that it is possible for certain methods, called `Shared` methods, to be called without the need for an object of the class to exist. You'll declare a method with more than one parameter. You'll see how Visual Basic keeps track of which method is currently executing, how local variables of methods are maintained in memory and how a method knows where to return after it finishes executing.

We will take a brief diversion into simulation techniques with random-number generation and develop a version of the casino dice game called craps that will use most of the programming techniques you have learned to this point in the book. In addition, we will introduce two techniques for declaring constants in your programs.

You'll see that applications can have more than one method of the same name. This technique, called overloading, is used for convenience and clarity when implementing methods that perform similar tasks using different types or numbers of arguments. In certain situations, you can replace a series of overloaded method declarations with a single "generic" method—we study this powerful code reuse capability in Chapter 25, Generics.

7.2 Modules, Classes and Methods

Programs consist of many pieces, including modules and classes. These modules and classes are composed of smaller pieces called methods. You combine new modules and classes with "prepackaged" classes available in the .NET Framework Class Library (FCL) and in various other class libraries. Related classes are typically grouped into namespaces (and compiled into library files) so that they can be imported into programs and reused. You will learn how to package your own classes into class libraries in Section 9.13. The FCL provides a rich collection of classes and methods for performing common mathematical calculations (Chapter 3), error checking (Chapter 12), building sophisticated GUI applications (Chapters 13 and 14), string and character manipulations (Chapter 16), graphics (Chapter 17), input/output operations (Chapter 18), XML processing (Chapter 19), database manipulations (Chapter 20), creating applications for the Web (Chapters 21 and 22) and many other useful operations. This framework makes your job easier, because the methods provide many of the capabilities you need. In earlier chapters, we introduced some FCL classes, such as `Console`, which provides methods for inputting and outputting data and `MessageBox`, used to display message dialogs.

Software Engineering Observation 7.1

When possible, use .NET Framework classes and methods instead of writing new classes and methods. This reduces program development time and can prevent the introduction of errors.

Performance Tip 7.1

.NET Framework Class Library methods are written to perform efficiently.

You can create your own classes and methods to meet the unique requirements of a particular application. Two types of methods exist: *subroutines* and *functions*. We discuss the differences between subroutines and functions shortly. Throughout this book, the term "method" refers to both subroutines and functions unless otherwise noted.

You write methods to define specific tasks that a program may use one or more times during its execution. Although the same method can be executed from multiple points in a program, the actual statements that define the method are written only once.

Let's briefly review some of the basics of methods. A method is invoked (i.e., made to perform its designated task) by a method call. The method call specifies the method name and provides information (as arguments) that the *callee* (i.e, the method being called) requires to do its job. When the method completes its task, it returns control to the caller (i.e., the calling method). In some cases, the method also returns a result to the caller.

There are several motivations for dividing code into methods. First, the divide-and-conquer approach makes program development more manageable. Another motivation is software reusability—the ability to use existing methods as building blocks for new programs. When proper naming and definition conventions are applied, programs can be created from standardized pieces that accomplish specific tasks, to minimize the need for customized code. A third motivation is to avoid repeating code in a program—when code is packaged as a method, the code can be executed from various points in a program simply by calling the method.

Software Engineering Observation 7.2

To promote reusability, the capabilities of each method should be limited to the performance of a single, well-defined task, and the name of the method should express that task effectively.

Software Engineering Observation 7.3

If you cannot choose a concise method name that expresses the task performed by a method, the method could be attempting to perform too many diverse tasks. Consider dividing such a method into several smaller methods.

7.3 Subroutines: Methods That Do Not Return a Value

The programs presented earlier in the book each contain at least one method declaration that calls FCL methods (such as `Console.WriteLine`) to accomplish the program's tasks. All of the methods that you have defined so far, such as `DisplayMessage` in class `Grade-Book`, are known as subroutines—methods that perform tasks but do not return a value. Functions are methods that do return a value to the calling method. An example of a function that you have seen is `Console.ReadLine`, which returns to the caller the data entered by the user at the keyboard. We show how to declare functions in Section 7.4.

Consider the console application in Fig. 7.1, which uses a subroutine (invoked from the application's `Main` method) to print a worker's payment information.

The program contains two method declarations. Lines 4–10 define method `Main`, the subroutine that executes when the console application is loaded. Lines 13–16 define method `PrintPay`, a subroutine that executes when it is called from method `Main`.

`Main` makes four calls (lines 6–9) to subroutine `PrintPay`, causing `PrintPay` to execute four times. Although the method arguments in this example are constants, recall that arguments can also be variables or expressions. For example, the statement

```
PrintPay(employeeExtraHours, employeeWage * 1.5)
```

could be used to display payment information for an employee who is being paid time-and-a-half for working overtime—this statement calculates only the overtime portion of the person's pay.

When `Main` calls `PrintPay`, the program makes a copy of the value of each argument (e.g., 40 and 10.5 in line 6), and program control transfers to the first line of method `PrintPay`. Method `PrintPay` receives the copied values and stores them in the parameters hours and wage. Then `PrintPay` calculates hours * wage and displays the result, using the currency format (line 15). When the End Sub statement (line 16) is encountered, control is returned to the next statement in the calling method, `Main`.

The first line of method `PrintPay` (line 13) shows that `PrintPay` declares a `Double` parameter hours and a `Decimal` parameter wage. These parameters hold the values passed to `PrintPay` so that they can be accessed within this method. Note that the entire declaration of method `PrintPay` appears within the body of module `Payment`.

```
 1   ' Fig. 7.1: Payment.vb
 2   ' Subroutine that prints payment information.
 3   Module Payment
 4      Sub Main()
 5         ' call subroutine PrintPay 4 times
 6         PrintPay(40, 10.5)
 7         PrintPay(38, 21.75)
 8         PrintPay(20, 13)
 9         PrintPay(30, 14)
10      End Sub ' Main
11
12      ' print dollar amount earned in console window
13      Sub PrintPay(ByVal hours As Double, ByVal wage As Decimal)
14         ' pay = hours * wage
15         Console.WriteLine("The payment is {0:C}", hours * wage)
16      End Sub ' PrintPay
17   End Module ' Payment
```

```
The payment is $420.00
The payment is $826.50
The payment is $260.00
The payment is $420.00
```

Fig. 7.1 | Subroutine for printing payment information.

Subroutine Declarations

The format of a subroutine declaration is

> **Sub** *method-name(parameter-list)*
> *declarations and statements*
> **End Sub**

Subroutines in previous versions of Visual Basic were referred to as **Sub procedures** because of the use of keyword Sub. The *parameter-list* is a comma-separated list in which the subroutine declares each parameter variable's type and name. There must be one argument in the method call for each parameter in the method header (we will see an exception to this when we study Optional parameters in Section 7.18). The type of each argument must be consistent with its corresponding parameter's type, i.e., Visual Basic must be able to implicitly convert the value of the argument to a value of the parameter's type. For example, a parameter of type Double could receive a value of 7.35, 22 or –0.03546, but not "hello", because a Double variable cannot contain a String. In Section 7.9 we discuss this issue in detail. If a method does not receive any values, the parameter list is empty (i.e., the method name is followed by an empty set of parentheses).

Common Programming Error 7.1

Declaring a variable in the method's body with the same name as a parameter variable in the method header is a compilation error.

Error-Prevention Tip 7.1

Although it is allowable, an argument passed to a method should not have the same name as the corresponding parameter name in the method declaration. This prevents ambiguity that could lead to logic errors.

The declarations and statements in the method declaration form the method body. The method body contains code that performs actions, generally by manipulating or processing the method's parameters. The body of a method declared with Sub must be terminated with keywords End Sub. The method body is also referred to as a *block*. A block is a group of declarations and executable statements.

Control returns to the next statement in the caller when execution reaches the End Sub statement in the called method.

Software Engineering Observation 7.4

Method names tend to be verbs because methods typically perform actions. By convention, method names begin with an uppercase first letter. For example, a method that sends an e-mail message might be named SendMail.

Error-Prevention Tip 7.2

Small methods are easier to test, debug and understand than large methods.

Good Programming Practice 7.1

When a parameter is declared without a type, its type is assumed to be Object. Explicitly declaring a parameter's type improves program clarity.

7.4 Functions: Methods That Return a Value

Functions (known as *Function procedures* in earlier versions of Visual Basic) are methods that *return a value* to the caller (whereas subroutines do not). The console application in Fig. 7.2 uses the function Square to calculate the squares of the integers from 1–10.

The For...Next statement (lines 8–10) displays the results of squaring the integers from 1–10. Each iteration of the loop calculates and displays the square of control variable counter (line 9).

Function Square is invoked (line 9) with the expression Square(counter). When program control reaches this expression, the program calls Square (lines 14–16). At this point, the program makes a copy of the value of counter (the argument), and program control transfers to the first line of Square. Square receives the copy of counter's value and stores it in the parameter y. Line 15 is a *Return statement*, which terminates execution of the method and returns the result of y ^ 2 to the calling program. The result is returned to the point in line 9 where Square was invoked. Line 9 displays in the command prompt the value of counter and the value returned by Square. This process is repeated 10 times. Note that returning a value from a function is similar to returning a value from the Get accessor of a property.

Function Declarations

The format of a function declaration is

```
Function method-name(parameter-list) As return-type
    declarations and statements
End Function
```

The *method-name*, *parameter-list*, and *declarations and statements* in a function declaration behave like the corresponding elements in a subroutine declaration. In the function header, the *return-type* indicates the type of the result returned from the function to its caller. The statement

```
1    ' Fig. 7.2: SquareInteger.vb
2    ' Function that squares a number.
3    Module SquareInteger
4       Sub Main()
5          Console.WriteLine("Number" & vbTab & "Square")
6
7          ' square integers from 1 to 10
8          For counter As Integer = 1 To 10
9             Console.WriteLine(counter & vbTab & Square(counter))
10         Next
11      End Sub ' Main
12
13      ' function Square is executed when it is explicitly called
14      Function Square(ByVal y As Integer) As Integer
15         Return y ^ 2 ' return square of parameter value
16      End Function ' Square
17   End Module ' SquareInteger
```

```
Number   Square
1        1
2        4
3        9
4        16
5        25
6        36
7        49
8        64
9        81
10       100
```

Fig. 7.2 | Function for squaring an integer.

> **Return** *expression*

can occur anywhere in a function body and returns the value of *expression* to the caller. If necessary, Visual Basic attempts to convert the *expression* to the function's return-type. Functions Return exactly one value. When a Return statement is executed, control returns immediately to the point at which that function was invoked.

Common Programming Error 7.2

If the expression in a Return statement cannot be converted to the function's return-type, a run-time error is generated.

Common Programming Error 7.3

Failure to return a value from a function (e.g., by forgetting to provide a Return statement) causes the function to return the default value for the return-type, possibly producing incorrect output.

7.5 Shared Methods and Class Math

As you know, every class provides methods that perform common tasks on objects of the class. For example, to display the grade information in a GradeBook object, we defined and called method DisplayGradeReport (Section 6.5). Recall that when we call GradeBook methods such as DisplayGradeReport, we first need to create a GradeBook object.

Although most methods of a class execute in response to method calls on specific objects, this is not always the case. Sometimes a method performs a task that does not depend on the contents of an object. Such a method applies to the class in which it is declared and is known as a *Shared method* or a *class method*. It is not uncommon for a class to contain a group of convenient Shared methods to perform common tasks. For example, recall that we use method WriteLine of class Console throughout this book; method WriteLine is a Shared method.

Methods that are declared in modules are Shared by default. To declare a Shared method in a class, place the Shared modifier before the keyword Sub or Function in the method's header. To call a Shared method, specify the name of the class or module in which the method is declared, followed by the dot (.) separator and the method name, as in

ClassName.*methodName*(*arguments*)

We use various Math class Shared methods here. Class Math provides a collection of methods that enable you to perform common mathematical calculations. For example, you can calculate the square root of 900.0 with the Shared method call

```
Math.Sqrt(900.0)
```

which evaluates to and returns 30.0. Method Sqrt takes an argument of type Double and returns a result of type Double. To output the value of the preceding method call in the command prompt, you could write

```
Console.WriteLine(Math.Sqrt(900.0))
```

In this statement, the value that Sqrt returns becomes the argument to method Write-Line. Note that we did not create a Math object before calling method Sqrt. Most Math class methods are Shared and are therefore called by preceding the name of the method with the class name Math and a dot (.) separator.

Software Engineering Observation 7.5

It is not necessary to add an assembly reference to use the Math class methods in a program, because class Math is located in namespace System, which is implicitly added to all .NET applications.

Method arguments may be constants, variables or expressions. If c = 13.0, d = 3.0 and f = 4.0, then the statement

```
Console.WriteLine(Math.Sqrt(c + d * f))
```

calculates and prints the square root of 13.0 + 3.0 * 4.0 = 25.0—namely, 5.0. Figure 7.3 summarizes several Math class methods. In the figure, x and y are of type Double. Methods Min and Max have overloaded versions for several types. We discuss method overloading in Section 7.17.

Math Class Constants PI and E

Class Math also declares two commonly used mathematical constants: **Math.PI** and **Math.E**. The constant Math.PI (3.14159265358979323846) is the ratio of a circle's circumference to its diameter. The constant Math.E (2.7182818284590452354) is the base value for natural logarithms (calculated with Shared Math method Log). These values are declared in class Math with the modifiers Public and Const. Making them Public allows you to use the values in your own classes. Keyword **Const** declares a constant—a value that

Method	Description	Example
Abs(x)	returns the absolute value of x	Abs(23.7) is 23.7 Abs(0) is 0 Abs(-23.7) is 23.7
Ceiling(x)	rounds x to the smallest integer not less than x	Ceiling(9.2) is 10.0 Ceiling(-9.8) is -9.0
Cos(x)	returns the trigonometric cosine of x (x in radians)	Cos(0.0) is 1.0
Exp(x)	returns the exponential e^x	Exp(1.0) is approximately 2.71828182845905 Exp(2.0) is approximately 7.38905609893065
Floor(x)	rounds x to the largest integer not greater than x	Floor(9.2) is 9.0 Floor(-9.8) is -10.0
Log(x)	returns the natural logarithm of x (base e)	Log(2.7182818284590451) is approximately 1.0 Log(7.3890560989306504) is approximately 2.0
Max(x, y)	returns the larger value of x and y (also has versions for Single, Integer and Long values)	Max(2.3, 12.7) is 12.7 Max(-2.3, -12.7) is -2.3
Min(x, y)	returns the smaller value of x and y (also has versions for Single, Integer and Long values)	Min(2.3, 12.7) is 2.3 Min(-2.3, -12.7) is -12.7
Pow(x, y)	calculates x raised to the power y (x^y)	Pow(2.0, 7.0) is 128.0 Pow(9.0, .5) is 3.0
Sin(x)	returns the trigonometric sine of x (x in radians)	Sin(0.0) is 0.0
Sqrt(x)	returns the square root of x	Sqrt(9.0) is 3.0 Sqrt(2.0) is 1.4142135623731
Tan(x)	returns the trigonometric tangent of x (x in radians)	Tan(0.0) is 0.0

Fig. 7.3 | Math class methods.

cannot be changed after the variable is initialized. Both PI and E are declared Const because their values never change. Constants are implicitly Shared, so they can be accessed via the class name Math and a dot (.) separator, just like class Math's methods. Recall from Section 4.5 that when each object of a class maintains its own copy of an attribute, the variable that represents the attribute is also known as an instance variable—each object (instance) of the class has a separate instance of the variable in memory. There are also variables for which each object of a class does not have a separate instance of the variable. That is the case with Shared variables. When objects of a class containing Shared variables are created, all the objects of that class share one copy of the class's Shared variables. Together the Shared variables and instance variables represent the so-called *fields* of a class. You will learn more about Shared members in Section 9.10.

7.6 GradeBook Case Study: Declaring Methods with Multiple Parameters

Chapters 3–6 presented classes containing simple methods that had at most one parameter. Methods often need to receive more than one piece of information to perform their tasks. We now consider how to write methods with multiple parameters.

Declaring Method Maximum

The application in Figs. 7.4–7.5 uses a user-declared method called Maximum to determine and return the largest of three Integer values entered by the user. When the application begins execution, class GradeBookTest's Main method (lines 4–11 of Fig. 7.5) creates one object of class GradeBook (line 6) and uses this object to call method InputGrades (line 9). This method is declared in lines 43–57 of class GradeBook (Fig. 7.4). Lines 48–53 prompt the user to enter three Integer values and read them from the user. Line 56 calls method Maximum (declared in lines 60–76) to determine the largest of the three Integer arguments. When method Maximum returns the result to line 56, the program assigns Maximum's return value to instance variable maximumGrade. Then line 10 of Fig. 7.5 calls method DisplayGradeReport, which outputs the maximum value.

Consider method Maximum (lines 60–76). Lines 60–61 indicate that the method returns an Integer value, the method's name is Maximum and the method requires three Integer parameters (x, y and z) to accomplish its task. When a method has more than one parameter, the parameters are specified as a comma-separated list. When Maximum is called in line 56, the parameter x is initialized with the value of the argument grade1, the parameter y is initialized with the value of the argument grade2 and the parameter z is initialized with the value of the argument grade3. There must be one argument in the method call for each parameter (sometimes called a *formal parameter*) in the method declaration. Also, the type of each argument must be consistent with the type of the corresponding parameter.

```vb
1   ' Fig. 7.4: GradeBook.vb
2   ' Definition of class GradeBook that finds the maximum of three grades.
3   Public Class GradeBook
4       Private courseNameValue As String ' name of course
5       Private maximumGrade As Integer ' maximum of three grades
6
7       ' constructor initializes course name
8       Public Sub New(ByVal name As String)
9           CourseName = name ' initializes CourseName
10          maximumGrade = 0 ' this value will be replaced by maximum grade
11      End Sub ' New
12
```

Fig. 7.4 | User-declared method Maximum that has three Integer parameters. (Part 1 of 3.)

```vb
13      ' property that gets and sets the course name; the Set accessor
14      ' ensures that the course name has at most 25 characters
15      Public Property CourseName() As String
16         Get ' retrieve courseNameValue
17            Return courseNameValue
18         End Get
19
20         Set(ByVal value As String) ' set courseNameValue
21            If value.Length <= 25 Then ' if value has 25 or fewer characters
22               courseNameValue = value ' store the course name in the object
23            Else ' if name has more than 25 characters
24               ' set courseNameValue to first 25 characters of parameter name
25               ' start at 0, length of 25
26               courseNameValue = value.Substring(0, 25)
27
28               Console.WriteLine( _
29                  "Course name (" & value & ") exceeds maximum length (25).")
30               Console.WriteLine( _
31                  "Limiting course name to first 25 characters." & vbCrLf)
32            End If
33         End Set
34      End Property ' CourseName
35
36      ' display a welcome message to the GradeBook user
37      Public Sub DisplayMessage()
38         Console.WriteLine("Welcome to the grade book for " _
39            & vbCrLf & CourseName & "!" & vbCrLf)
40      End Sub ' DisplayMessage
41
42      ' input three grades from user
43      Public Sub InputGrades()
44         Dim grade1 As Integer ' first grade entered by user
45         Dim grade2 As Integer ' second grade entered by user
46         Dim grade3 As Integer ' third grade entered by user
47
48         Console.Write("Enter the first grade: ")
49         grade1 = Console.ReadLine()
50         Console.Write("Enter the second grade: ")
51         grade2 = Console.ReadLine()
52         Console.Write("Enter the third grade: ")
53         grade3 = Console.ReadLine()
54
55         ' store the maximum in maximumGrade
56         maximumGrade = Maximum(grade1, grade2, grade3)
57      End Sub ' InputGrades
58
59      ' returns the maximum of its three integer parameters
60      Function Maximum(ByVal x As Integer, ByVal y As Integer, _
61         ByVal z As Integer) As Integer
62
63         Dim maximumValue As Integer = x ' assume x is the largest to start
64
```

Fig. 7.4 | User-declared method Maximum that has three Integer parameters. (Part 2 of 3.)

```
65          ' determine whether y is greater than maximumValue
66          If (y > maximumValue) Then
67             maximumValue = y ' make y the new maximumValue
68          End If
69
70          ' determine whether z is greater than maximumValue
71          If (z > maximumValue) Then
72             maximumValue = z ' make z the new maximumValue
73          End If
74
75          Return maximumValue
76       End Function ' Maximum
77
78       ' display a report based on the grades entered by user
79       Public Sub DisplayGradeReport()
80          ' output maximum of grades entered
81          Console.WriteLine("Maximum of grades entered: " & maximumGrade)
82       End Sub ' DisplayGradeReport
83    End Class ' GradeBook
```

Fig. 7.4 | User-declared method Maximum that has three Integer parameters. (Part 3 of 3.)

```
1    ' Fig. 7.5: GradeBookTest.vb
2    ' Create a GradeBook object, input grades and display grade report.
3    Module GradeBookTest
4       Sub Main()
5          ' create GradeBook object
6          Dim gradeBook1 As New GradeBook("CS101 Introduction to VB")
7
8          gradeBook1.DisplayMessage() ' display welcome message
9          gradeBook1.InputGrades() ' read grades from user
10         gradeBook1.DisplayGradeReport() ' display report based on grades
11      End Sub ' Main
12   End Module ' GradeBookTest
```

```
Welcome to the grade book for
CS101 Introduction to VB!

Enter the first grade: 65
Enter the second grade: 87
Enter the third grade: 45
Maximum of grades entered: 87
```

```
Welcome to the grade book for
CS101 Introduction to VB!

Enter the first grade: 45
Enter the second grade: 65
Enter the third grade: 87
Maximum of grades entered: 87
```

Fig. 7.5 | Application to test class GradeBook's Maximum method. (Part 1 of 2.)

```
Welcome to the grade book for
CS101 Introduction to VB!

Enter the first grade: 87
Enter the second grade: 45
Enter the third grade: 65
Maximum of grades entered: 87
```

Fig. 7.5 | Application to test class `GradeBook`'s `Maximum` method. (Part 2 of 2.)

To determine the maximum value, we begin with the assumption that parameter x contains the largest value, so line 63 declares local variable `maximumValue` and initializes it with the value of parameter x. Of course parameter y or z may contain the actual largest value, so we must compare each of these values with `maximumValue`. The `If...Then` statement in lines 66–68 determines whether y is greater than `maximumValue`, and if so, line 67 assigns y to `maximumValue`. The `If...Then` statement in lines 71–73 determines whether z is greater than `maximumValue`, and if so, line 72 assigns z to `maximumValue`. At this point the largest of the three values resides in `maximumValue`, so line 75 returns that value to line 56. When program control returns to the point in the program where `Maximum` was called, `Maximum`'s parameters x, y and z are no longer accessible to the program—we will see why in Section 7.8. Note that methods can return at most one value, but the returned value could be a reference to an object that contains many values.

Note that `maximumGrade` is an instance variable in class `GradeBook`. Variables should be declared as instance variables of a class only if they are required for use in more than one method of the class or if the program should save their values between calls to the class's methods.

Implementing Method `Maximum` by Reusing Method `Math.Max`

Recall from Fig. 7.3 that class `Math` has a `Max` method that can determine the larger of two values. The entire body of our maximum method could also be implemented with two calls to `Math.Max`, as follows:

Return Math.Max(x, Math.Max(y, z))

The outer call to `Math.Max` specifies arguments x and `Math.Max(y, z)`. Before any method is called, all its arguments are evaluated to determine their values. If an argument is a method call, the method call is performed to determine its return value. So, in the preceding statement, `Math.Max(y, z)` is evaluated first to determine the maximum of y and z. Then the result is passed as the second argument to the other call to `Math.Max`, which returns the larger of its two arguments. Using `Math.Max` in this manner is a good example of software reuse—we find the largest of three values by reusing `Math.Max`, which finds the largest of two values. Note how concise this code is compared to lines 63–75 of Fig. 7.4.

7.7 Notes on Declaring and Using Methods

There are three ways to call a method:

1. Using a method name by itself to call another method of the same class or module—such as `Maximum(number1, number2, number3)` in line 56 of Fig. 7.4.

2. Using a variable that contains a reference to an object, followed by a dot (.) and the method name to call a method of the referenced object—such as the method call in line 10 of Fig. 7.5, `gradeBook1.DisplayGradeReport()`, which calls a method of class `GradeBook` from the `Main` method of module `GradeBookTest`.

3. Using the class or module name and a dot (.) to call a `Shared` method of a class or module (all methods of a module are implicitly `Shared`). One example of this is `Math.Sqrt(900.0)` in Section 7.5.

Note that a `Shared` method can call only other `Shared` methods of the same class directly (i.e., using the method name by itself) and can manipulate only `Shared` members in the same class directly. To access the class's non-`Shared` members, a `Shared` method must use a reference to an object of the class. Recall that `Shared` methods relate to the class, whereas non-`Shared` methods are associated with a specific instance (object) of the class and may manipulate the instance variables of that object. Many objects of a class, each with its own copies of the instance variables, may exist at the same time. Suppose a `Shared` method were to invoke a non-`Shared` method directly. How would the method know which object's instance variables to manipulate? What would happen if no objects of the class existed at the time the non-`Shared` method was invoked? Thus, a `Shared` method cannot access non-`Shared` members of the same class directly.

Control can be returned to the statement that calls a method by using the `Return` statement or by reaching the end of the method (`End Sub` or `End Function`). If the method does not return a result but uses a `Return` statement to return control to the calling method, the `Return` statement cannot include an expression. If the method does return a result, the statement

Return *expression*

evaluates the *expression*, then returns the result to the caller.

Common Programming Error 7.4

Declaring a method outside the body of a class or module declaration or inside the body of another method is a syntax error.

Common Programming Error 7.5

Omitting the return-value-type *in a method declaration, if that method is a function, is a syntax error.*

Common Programming Error 7.6

Redeclaring a method parameter as a local variable in the method's body is a compilation error.

Common Programming Error 7.7

Returning a value from a method that is a subroutine is a compilation error.

7.8 Method Call Stack and Activation Records

To understand how Visual Basic performs method calls, we first need to consider a data structure (i.e., collection of related data items) known as a *stack*. You can think of a stack as analogous to a pile of dishes. When a dish is placed on the pile, it is normally placed at the top (referred to as *pushing* the dish onto the stack). Similarly, when a dish is removed from the pile, it is normally removed from the top (referred to as *popping* the dish off the stack). Stacks are known as *last-in, first-out (LIFO) data structures*—the last item pushed (inserted) onto the stack is the first item popped (removed) from the stack.

When a program calls a method, the called method must know how to return to the correct location in its caller, so the return address in the calling method is pushed onto the *method call stack*. If a series of nested method calls occurs (e.g., method A calls method B, and method B calls method C), the successive return addresses are pushed onto the stack in last-in, first-out order so that each method can return to its caller.

The method call stack also contains the memory for the local variables used in each invocation of a method during a program's execution. A method's local variables also include its parameters. This data, stored as a portion of the method call stack, is known as the *activation record* or *stack frame* of the method call. When a method call is made, the activation record for that method call is pushed onto the method call stack. When the method returns to its caller, the activation record for the returning method call is popped off the stack and those local variables are no longer known to the program. If a local variable holding a reference to an object is the only variable in the program with a reference to that object, when the activation record containing that local variable is popped off the stack, the object can no longer be accessed by the program and it will eventually be deleted from memory by the CLR during garbage collection. We discuss garbage collection in Section 9.9.

Of course, the amount of memory in a computer is finite, so only a certain amount of memory can be used to store activation records on the method call stack. If more method calls occur than can have their activation records stored on the method call stack, an error known as a *stack overflow* occurs.

7.9 Implicit Argument Conversions

An important feature of argument passing is *implicit argument conversion*—converting an argument's value to a type that the method expects to receive in its corresponding parameter. Visual Basic supports both widening and narrowing conversions. A *widening conversion* occurs when an argument is converted to a parameter of another type that can hold more data, whereas a *narrowing conversion* occurs when there is potential for data loss during the conversion (i.e., a conversion to a parameter of a type that holds a smaller amount of data). Figure 7.6 lists the widening conversions supported by Visual Basic that occur between primitive types. In addition to the conversions in Fig. 7.6, all primitive type variables can be converted to type `Object` without losing data.

Type	Conversion types
`Boolean`	no possible widening conversions to other primitive types
`Byte`	`UShort`, `Short`, `UInteger`, `Integer`, `ULong`, `Long`, `Decimal`, `Single` or `Double`
`Char`	`String`

Fig. 7.6 | Widening conversions between primitive types. (Part 1 of 2.)

Type	Conversion types
Date	no possible widening conversions to other primitive types
Decimal	*Single* or *Double*
Double	no possible widening conversions to other primitive types
Integer	*Long*, *Decimal*, *Single* or *Double*
Long	*Decimal*, *Single* or *Double*
SByte	*Short*, *Integer*, *Long*, *Decimal*, *Single* or *Double*
Short	*Integer*, *Long*, *Decimal*, *Single* or *Double*
Single	*Double*
String	no possible widening conversions to other primitive types
UInteger	*ULong*, *Long*, *Decimal*, *Single* or *Double*
ULong	*Decimal*, *Single* or *Double*
UShort	*UInteger*, *Integer*, *ULong*, *Long*, *Decimal*, *Single* or *Double*

Fig. 7.6 | Widening conversions between primitive types. (Part 2 of 2.)

For example, the Math class method Sqrt can be called with an Integer argument, even though the method is defined in class Math with a Double parameter. The statement

```
Console.Write(Math.Sqrt(4))
```

correctly evaluates Math.Sqrt(4) and prints the value 2. Visual Basic implicitly converts the Integer argument 4 to the Double value 4.0 before the argument is passed to Math.Sqrt. In this case, the argument does not precisely correspond to the parameter type in the method declaration, so an implicit widening conversion changes the value to the proper type before the method is called. Visual Basic also performs narrowing conversions on arguments passed to methods. For example, if a Double variable containing the value 4.0 were passed to a method expecting an Integer variable, the value would be converted to 4. Some implicit narrowing conversions can cause runtime errors. In the next section, we discuss measures you can take to avoid such runtime errors. In Chapter 12, Exception Handling, we discuss how to handle the errors caused by failed narrowing conversions.

 Common Programming Error 7.8

Converting a primitive-type value to a value of another primitive type may change the value if the conversion is not a widening conversion. For example, converting a floating-point value to an integral value truncates any fractional part of the floating-point value (e.g., 4.7 becomes 4).

Conversions occur not only for values passed as arguments to methods, but also for expressions containing values of two or more types. In such expressions, the values' original types are maintained, while temporary copies of the values are converted for use in the expression. Each value is converted to the "widest" type in the expression (i.e., widening conversions are made until the values are of the same type as the "widest" type). For example, if `singleNumber` is of type `Single` and `integerNumber` is of type `Integer`, when Visual Basic evaluates the expression

```
singleNumber + integerNumber
```

the value of `integerNumber` is converted to type `Single` (the widest type in the expression), then added to `singleNumber`, producing a `Single` result.

7.10 Option Strict and Data-Type Conversions

Visual Basic provides several options for controlling the way the compiler handles types. These options can help you eliminate such errors as those caused by narrowing conversions. The first option is **Option Explicit**, which is set to **On** by default—it has been enabled in the programs we created in Chapters 2–6. **Option Explicit** forces you to explicitly declare all variables before they are used in a program. Forcing explicit declarations eliminates various errors. For example, when **Option Explicit** is set to **Off**, the compiler interprets misspelled variable names as new variables and implicitly declares them to be of type **Object**. (Class **Object** is the base type of all types in Visual Basic. We will discuss class **Object** in more detail in Chapter 10.) This creates subtle errors that can be difficult to debug. To set **Option Explicit** to **Off**, double click **My Project** in **Solution Explorer**. This opens a window that allows you to change the properties of the project. In this window, click the **Compile** tab (Fig. 7.7), then select the value **Off** from the **Option Explicit** drop-down list. If **Option Explicit** is **Off**, any undeclared variables are implicitly declared as being of type **Object**. Note that all variables have a type regardless of whether **Option Explicit** is **On**, so Visual Basic is known as a *strongly-typed language*.

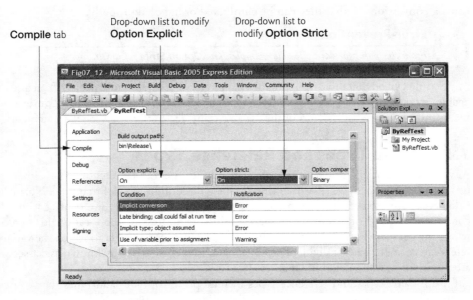

Fig. 7.7 | Modifying `Option Strict` and `Option Explicit`.

A second option, which defaults to **Off**, is **Option Strict**. Visual Basic provides **Option Strict** as a means of increasing program clarity and reducing debugging time. When set to **On, Option Strict** causes the compiler to check all conversions and requires you to perform an explicit conversion for all narrowing conversions that could cause data loss (e.g., conversion from `Double` to `Integer`) or program termination (e.g., conversion of a `String`, such as `"hello"`, to type `Integer`). To set **Option Strict** to **On**, double click **My Project** in the **Solution Explorer**—this opens a window that allows you to change the properties of the project. In that window, click the **Compile** tab and select the value **On** in the **Option Strict** drop-down list (Fig. 7.7). An *explicit conversion* is a conversion that uses a cast operator or a method to force a conversion to occur. In Chapter 11 we discuss using operators known as cast operators to perform explicit conversions. Explicit conversion enables you to "take control" from the compiler. You essentially say, "I know this conversion might cause loss of information, but for my purposes here, that's fine."

The methods of class **Convert** can be used to explicitly convert data from one type to another. The name of each conversion method is the word `To`, followed by the name of the type to which the method converts its argument. For instance, to convert a `String` input by the user to type `Double` (to be stored in variable `number` of type `Double`), we use the statement

```
number = Convert.ToDouble(Console.ReadLine())
```

Likewise, many of the primitive types have a `Parse` method that they can use for conversions. For instance, method **Double.Parse** converts a string representation of a number to a value of type `Double`.

When **Option Strict** is **Off** (as it has been for all the code examples so far in this book), Visual Basic performs such type conversions implicitly, and thus you may not realize that a narrowing conversion is being performed. If the data being converted is incompatible with the new type, a runtime error occurs. `Option Strict` draws your attention to narrowing conversions so that they can be eliminated or handled properly.

Error-Prevention Tip 7.3

From this point forward, all code examples have **Option Strict** *set to* **On**.

Setting **Option Strict** to **On** applies the change globally, to the entire project. You also can enable **Option Strict** within an individual code file by typing `Option Strict On`—`Option` statements must be placed at the start of the file above any declarations or `Imports` statements.

7.11 Value Types and Reference Types

As we discussed briefly in Chapter 4, all Visual Basic types can be categorized as either value types or reference types. A variable of a value type contains data of that type. Normally, value types are used for a single piece of data, such as an `Integer` or a `Double` value. By contrast, a variable of a reference type contains the address of the location in memory where the data referred to by that variable is stored. The actual object to which the variable refers can contain many individual pieces of data. Reference types are known as classes and are discussed in more detail in Chapters 9–11.

Both value types and reference types include primitive types and types that you can create. The primitive value types include the *integral types* (`Byte`, `SByte`, `Short`, `UShort`, `Integer`, `UInteger`, `Long` and `ULong`), the *floating-point types* (`Single` and `Double`) and types `Boolean`, `Date`, `Decimal` and `Char`. There is only one primitive reference type—`String`. Reference types can be created by declaring classes and modules, as well as interfaces and delegates, constructs that we will discuss in Chapters 11 and 13, respectively. The primitive reference type, `String`, actually represents the ***String*** class in the FCL. Value types can be created by declaring structures and enumerations. ***Structures***, like classes, define types that contain members such as methods and instance variables. ***Enumerations*** may only contain sets of integral values. The primitive value types are defined using structures. Most of these structures have the same name as the Visual Basic primitive type (type `Double` is defined by structure ***Double***), but others do not (type `Integer` is defined by structure ***Int32***). These structures are part of the FCL, which is used by several languages—as a result, the naming of types in the various .NET languages may not always be identical to their underlying classes and structures in the FCL. User-defined types are discussed in greater detail in Chapter 9, Classes and Objects: A Deeper Look; Chapter 10, Object-Oriented Programming: Inheritance and Chapter 16, Strings, Characters and Regular Expressions. Figure 7.8 lists the primitive types, which form the building blocks for more complicated types, such as the `GradeBook` type we have defined in several examples in this book.

Type	Size in bits	Values	Standard	Name of FCL class or structure
`Boolean`	16	***True*** or ***False***		`Boolean`
`Byte`	8	0 to 255		`Byte`
`SByte`	8	–128 to 127		`SByte`
`Char`	16	One Unicode character	(Unicode character set)	`Char`
`Date`	64	1 January 0001 to 31 December 9999 12:00:00 AM to 11:59:59 PM		`DateTime`
`Decimal`	128	1.0E–28 to 7.9E+28		`Decimal`
`Double`	64	±5.0E–324 to ±1.7E+308	(IEEE 754 floating point)	`Double`
`Integer`	32	–2,147,483,648 to 2,147,483,647		`Int32`
`Long`	64	–9,223,372,036,854,775,808 to 9,223,372,036,854,775,807		`Int64`
`Short`	16	–32,768 to 32,767		`Int16`
`Single`	32	±1.5E–45 to ±3.4E+38	(IEEE 754 floating point)	`Single`
`String`		0 to ~2000000000 Unicode characters	(Unicode character set)	`String`

Fig. 7.8 | Primitive types. (Part 1 of 2.)

Type	Size in bits	Values	Standard	Name of FCL class or structure
UInteger	32	0 to 4,294,967,295		UInt32
ULong	64	0 to 18,446,744,073,709,551,615		UInt64
UShort	16	0 to 65,535		UInt16

Fig. 7.8 | Primitive types. (Part 2 of 2.)

Each value type in the table is accompanied by its size in bits (there are 8 bits to a byte) and its range of values. To promote portability, Microsoft chose to use internationally recognized standards for character formats (Unicode®, www.unicode.org) and floating-point numbers (IEEE 754, grouper.ieee.org/groups/754/). We discuss the Unicode character formats in Appendix E, Unicode®. In the far right column of the table, we display the name of the structure or class that defines the primitive type. Note that these are the names used for the methods of class Convert that we discussed in the previous section. For instance, to convert a value to type Integer, the name of the proper Convert class method would be *Convert.ToInt32*, not Convert.ToInteger.

7.12 Framework Class Library Namespaces

As we have seen, the FCL contains many predefined classes that are grouped into namespaces. Throughout the text, we have used Imports statements to specify the namespaces used in a program. For example, a program includes the declaration

> *Imports* System.Windows.Forms

to specify that the program uses classes in this namespace, such as class MessageBox. This allows you to use the simple class name MessageBox, rather than the fully qualified class name System.Windows.Forms.MessageBox, in the code. A great strength of Visual Basic is the large number of classes in the FCL. Some key FCL namespaces are described in Fig. 7.9, which represents only a small portion of the reusable components in the FCL.

The set of namespaces available in the FCL is quite large. In addition to the namespaces summarized in Fig. 7.9, the FCL includes namespaces for complex graphics, Web services, printing, security and many other capabilities.

You can locate additional information about a predefined FCL class's methods in the Visual Studio .NET documentation by selecting **Help > Index**. In the window that appears there will be an index to the left. Enter .NET Framework in the **Filtered by** drop-down list, and enter the name of the class in the **Look for** field. You will be provided with links for general information about the class or for a listing of the class's members.

Good Programming Practice 7.2

The Visual Studio .NET documentation is easy to search and provides many details about each class. As you learn a class in this book, you should read about the class in the online documentation.

Namespace	Description
System.Windows.Forms	Contains the classes required to create and manipulate GUIs. (Various classes in this namespace are discussed in Chapter 13, Graphical User Interface Concepts: Part 1 and Chapter 14, Graphical User Interface Concepts: Part 2.)
System.IO	Contains classes that enable programs to input and output data. (You will learn more about this namespace in Chapter 18, Files and Streams.)
System.Data	Contains classes that enable programs to access and manipulate databases (i.e., an organized collection of data). (You will learn more about this namespace in Chapter 20, Database, SQL and ADO.NET.)
System.Web	Contains classes used for creating and maintaining Web applications, which are accessible over the Internet. (You will learn more about this namespace in Chapter 21, ASP.NET 2.0, Web Forms and Web Controls.)
System.Xml	Contains classes for creating and manipulating XML data. Data can be read from or written to XML files. (You will learn more about this namespace in Chapter 19, Extensible Markup Language (XML).)
System.Collections	Contains classes that define data structures for maintaining collections of data. (You will learn more about this namespace in Chapter 26, Collections.)
System.Net	Contains classes that enable programs to communicate via computer networks like the Internet. (You will learn more about this namespace in Chapter 23, Networking: Streams-Based Sockets and Datagrams.)
System.Text	Contains classes and interfaces that enable programs to manipulate characters and strings. (You will learn more about this namespace in Chapter 16, Strings, Characters and Regular Expressions.)
System.Threading	Contains classes that enable programs to perform several tasks concurrently, or at the same time. (You will learn more about this namespace in Chapter 15, Multithreading.)
System.Drawing	Contains classes that enable programs to perform basic graphics processing, such as displaying shapes and arcs. (You will learn more about this namespace in Chapter 17, Graphics and Multimedia.)

Fig. 7.9 | FCL namespaces (a subset).

7.13 Passing Arguments: Pass-by-Value vs. Pass-by-Reference

Arguments are passed in one of two ways: *pass-by-value* and *pass-by-reference*. When an argument is passed by value, the program makes a *copy* of the argument's value and passes the copy to the called method. With pass-by-value, changes to the called method's copy do not affect the original variable's value in the caller. In contrast, when an argument is passed by reference, the caller gives the called method the ability to access and modify the caller's original data directly. Figure 7.10 demonstrates passing value-type arguments by value and by reference.

The program passes three value-type variables, number1, number2 and number3, in different ways to methods SquareByValue (lines 36–42) and SquareByReference (lines 45–51). Keyword ByVal in the method header of SquareByValue (line 36) indicates that value-type arguments should be passed by value. A parameter declared with keyword ByVal is known as a *value parameter*. When number1 is passed to SquareByValue (line 10), a copy of the value stored in number1 (i.e., 2) is passed to the method. Therefore, the value of number1 in the calling method, Main, is not modified when parameter number is squared in method SquareByValue (line 39)—only the local copy stored in parameter number gets modified.

Method SquareByReference uses *keyword ByRef* (line 45) to receive its value-type parameter by reference. A parameter declared with keyword ByRef is known as a *reference parameter*. When Main calls SquareByReference (line 20), a reference to the value stored in number2 is passed, which gives SquareByReference direct access to the value stored in the original variable. Thus, the value stored in number2 after SquareByReference finishes executing is the same as the final value of parameter number.

```
 1    ' Fig. 7.10: ByRefTest.vb
 2    ' Demonstrates passing by value and by reference.
 3    Module ByRefTest
 4       Sub Main()
 5          Dim number1 As Integer = 2
 6
 7          Console.WriteLine("Passing a value-type argument by value:")
 8          Console.WriteLine("Before calling SquareByValue, " & _
 9             "number1 is {0}", number1)
10          SquareByValue(number1)   ' passes number1 by value
11          Console.WriteLine("After returning from SquareByValue, " & _
12             "number1 is {0}" & vbCrLf, number1)
13
14          Dim number2 As Integer = 2
15
16          Console.WriteLine("Passing a value-type argument" & _
17             " by reference:")
18          Console.WriteLine("Before calling SquareByReference, " & _
19             "number2 is {0}", number2)
20          SquareByReference(number2) ' passes number2 by reference
21          Console.WriteLine("After returning from " & _
22             "SquareByReference, number2 is {0}" & vbCrLf, number2)
```

Fig. 7.10 | ByVal and ByRef used to pass value-type arguments. (Part 1 of 2.)

```
23
24         Dim number3 As Integer = 2
25
26         Console.WriteLine("Passing a value-type argument" & _
27             " by reference, but in parentheses:")
28         Console.WriteLine("Before calling SquareByReference " & _
29             "using parentheses, number3 is {0}", number3)
30         SquareByReference((number3)) ' passes number3 by value
31         Console.WriteLine("After returning from " & _
32             "SquareByReference, number3 is {0}", number3)
33      End Sub ' Main
34
35      ' squares number by value (note ByVal keyword)
36      Sub SquareByValue(ByVal number As Integer)
37         Console.WriteLine("After entering SquareByValue, " & _
38             "number is {0}", number)
39         number *= number
40         Console.WriteLine("Before exiting SquareByValue, " & _
41             "number is {0}", number)
42      End Sub ' SquareByValue
43
44      ' squares number by reference (note ByRef keyword)
45      Sub SquareByReference(ByRef number As Integer)
46         Console.WriteLine("After entering SquareByReference" & _
47             ", number is {0}", number)
48         number *= number
49         Console.WriteLine("Before exiting SquareByReference" & _
50             ", number is {0}", number)
51      End Sub ' SquareByReference
52   End Module ' ByRefTest
```

```
Passing a value-type argument by value:
Before calling SquareByValue, number1 is 2
After entering SquareByValue, number is 2
Before exiting SquareByValue, number is 4
After returning from SquareByValue, number1 is 2

Passing a value-type argument by reference:
Before calling SquareByReference, number2 is 2
After entering SquareByReference, number is 2
Before exiting SquareByReference, number is 4
After returning from SquareByReference, number2 is 4

Passing a value-type argument by reference, but in parentheses:
Before calling SquareByReference using parentheses, number3 is 2
After entering SquareByReference, number is 2
Before exiting SquareByReference, number is 4
After returning from SquareByReference, number3 is 2
```

Fig. 7.10 | ByVal and ByRef used to pass value-type arguments. (Part 2 of 2.)

When arguments are enclosed in parentheses, (), the expression within the parentheses is evaluated. In line 30, the inner set of parentheses evaluates number3 to its value (2) and passes this value to the method, even if the method header includes keyword

ByRef. Thus, the value of number3 does not change after it is passed to SquareByReference (line 30) via parentheses.

Passing value-type arguments with keyword ByRef is useful when methods need to alter argument values directly. However, passing by reference can weaken security, because the called method can modify the caller's data. We discuss some of the more complex subtleties of passing arguments by value and by reference in Section 8.14.

When you pass a variable of a reference type to a method that declares the corresponding parameter ByVal, a copy of the variable's value is passed. In this case, the value is actually a reference to an object, so the method is able to modify the object in memory. Thus, reference-type variables passed with keyword ByVal are effectively passed by reference. Although Visual Basic allows you to use keyword ByRef with reference-type parameters, it is usually not necessary to do so except with type String. Although they technically are reference types, String arguments cannot be modified directly when passed with keyword ByVal, due to some subtle details of the String type, which we discuss in Chapter 16, Strings, Characters and Regular Expressions. We discuss passing reference types by reference in Section 8.14.

Error-Prevention Tip 7.4

When passing arguments by value, changes to the called method's copy do not affect the original variable's value. This prevents possible side effects that could hinder the development of correct and reliable software systems. Always pass value-type arguments by value unless you explicitly intend for the called method to modify the caller's data.

7.14 Scope of Declarations

You have seen declarations of various Visual Basic entities, such as classes, methods, variables and parameters. Declarations introduce names that are used to refer to such entities. A declaration's *Scope* is the portion of the program that can refer to the declared entity by its name without qualification. Such an entity is said to be "in scope" for that portion of the program. This section introduces several important scope issues.

The basic scopes are as follows:

1. *Block scope*—The scope of a variable declared in a block is from the point of the declaration to the end of the block (e.g., a variable declared in a control statement's body is in scope only until the end of that control statement).

2. *Method scope*—The scope of a method's local-variable declaration or parameter is from the point at which the declaration appears to the end of that method. This is similar to block scope.

3. *Module scope*—The scope of a class's members or a module's members is the entire body of the class or module. This enables non-Shared methods of a class to use all of the class's members. (Note that Shared methods of a class can access only the class's Shared variables and Shared methods.) All module members are implicitly Shared, so all methods of a module can access all variables and other methods of the module.

4. *Namespace scope*—Elements declared in a namespace (i.e., classes, modules, interfaces, delegates, enumerations, structures and other namespaces) are accessible to all

other elements in the same namespace. By default, all elements of a project are part of a namespace that uses the project's name. This enables, for example, a module method in the project to create an object of a class that is also part of the project.

Any block may contain variable declarations. If a local variable or parameter in a method has the same name as a field of the class, the field is "hidden" until the block terminates execution—this is called *shadowing*. In Chapter 9, we discuss how to access shadowed members. Keep in mind that although a variable may not be in scope, it may still exist. A variable's *lifetime* is the period during which the variable exists in memory. Some variables exist briefly, some are created and destroyed repeatedly, yet others are maintained through the entire execution of a program. Variables normally exist as long as their container exists—for instance, a local variable of a method will exist as long as the method itself exists in memory.

Error-Prevention Tip 7.5

Use different names for fields and local variables to help prevent subtle logic errors that occur when a method is called and a local variable of the method shadows a field of the same name in the class.

The application in Figs. 7.11 and 7.12 demonstrates scoping issues with fields and local variables. When the application begins execution, module ScopeTest's Main method (Fig. 7.12, lines 4–7) creates an object of class Scope (line 5) and calls the object's Begin method (line 6) to produce the program's output (shown in Fig. 7.12).

```vb
 1  ' Fig. 7.11: Scope.vb
 2  ' Scope class demonstrates instance and local variable scopes.
 3  Public Class Scope
 4     ' instance variable that is accessible to all methods of this class
 5     Private x As Integer = 1
 6
 7     ' method Begin creates and initializes local variable x and
 8     ' calls methods UseLocalVariable and UseInstanceVariable
 9     Public Sub Begin()
10        ' method's local variable x shadows instance variable x
11        Dim x As Integer = 5
12
13        Console.WriteLine("local x in method Begin is " & x)
14
15        UseLocalVariable() ' UseLocalVariable has local x
16        UseInstanceVariable() ' uses class Scope's instance variable x
17        UseLocalVariable() ' UseLocalVariable reinitializes local x
18        UseInstanceVariable() ' Scope's instance variable x retains value
19
20        Console.WriteLine(vbCrLf & "local x in method Begin is " & x)
21     End Sub ' Begin
22
23     ' create and initialize local variable x during each call
24     Sub UseLocalVariable()
25        Dim x As Integer = 25 ' initialized in each call
26
```

Fig. 7.11 | Scoping rules in a class. (Part 1 of 2.)

```
27          Console.WriteLine( _
28             vbCrLf & "local x on entering method UseLocalVariable is " & x)
29          x += 1 ' modifies this method's local variable x
30          Console.WriteLine("local variable x before exiting method " & _
31             "UseLocalVariable is " & x)
32       End Sub ' UseLocalVariable
33
34       ' modify class Scope's instance variable x during each call
35       Sub UseInstanceVariable()
36          Console.WriteLine(vbCrLf & "instance variable" & _
37             " x on entering method UseInstanceVariable is " & x)
38          x *= 10 ' modifies class Scope's instance variable x
39          Console.WriteLine("instance variable " & _
40             "x before exiting method UseInstanceVariable is " & x)
41       End Sub ' UseInstanceVariable
42    End Class ' Scope
```

Fig. 7.11 | Scoping rules in a class. (Part 2 of 2.)

```
1     ' Fig. 7.12: ScopeTest.vb
2     ' Testing class Scope.
3     Module ScopeTest
4        Sub Main()
5           Dim testScope As New Scope()
6           testScope.Begin()
7        End Sub ' Main
8     End Module ' ScopeTest
```

```
local x in method Begin is 5

local x on entering method UseLocalVariable is 25
local variable x before exiting method UseLocalVariable is 26

instance variable x on entering method UseInstanceVariable is 1
instance variable x before exiting method UseInstanceVariable is 10

local x on entering method UseLocalVariable is 25
local variable x before exiting method UseLocalVariable is 26

instance variable x on entering method UseInstanceVariable is 10
instance variable x before exiting method UseInstanceVariable is 100

local x in method Begin is 5
```

Fig. 7.12 | Module to test class Scope.

In class Scope, line 5 declares and initializes the instance variable x to 1. This instance variable is shadowed (hidden) in any block (or method) that declares a local variable named x. Method Begin (lines 9–21) declares a local variable x (line 11) and initializes it to 5. This local variable's value is output to show that the instance variable x (whose value is 1) is shadowed in method Begin. The program declares two other methods—UseLocal-Variable (lines 24–32) and UseInstanceVariable (lines 35–41)—that each take no arguments and do not return results. Method Begin calls each method twice (lines 15–18).

Method `UseLocalVariable` declares local variable x (line 25). When `UseLocalVariable` is first called (line 15), it creates local variable x and initializes it to 25 (line 25), outputs the value of x (lines 27–28), increments x (line 29) and outputs the value of x again (lines 30–31). When `UseLocalVariable` is called a second time (line 17), it recreates local variable x and reinitializes it to 25, so the output of each `UseLocalVariable` call is identical.

Method `UseInstanceVariable` does not declare any local variables. Therefore, when it refers to x, instance variable x (line 5) of the class is used. When method `UseInstanceVariable` is first called (line 16), it outputs the value (1) of instance variable x (lines 36–37), multiplies the instance variable x by 10 (line 38) and outputs the value (10) of instance variable x again (lines 39–40) before returning. The next time method `UseInstanceVariable` is called (line 18), the instance variable has its modified value, 10, so the method outputs 10, then 100. Finally, in method `Begin`, the program outputs the value of local variable x again (line 20) to show that none of the method calls modified `Begin`'s local variable x, because the methods all referred to variables named x in other scopes.

7.15 Case Study: Random Number Generation

We now take a brief and hopefully entertaining diversion into a popular programming application—simulation and game playing. In this and the next section, we develop a game-playing program with multiple methods. The program employs many of the control statements presented thus far in the book and introduces several new concepts.

There is something in the air of a gambling casino that invigorates people—from the high rollers at the plush mahogany-and-felt craps tables to the quarter poppers at the one-armed bandits. It is the element of chance, the possibility that luck will convert a pocketful of money into a mountain of wealth. Unfortunately, that rarely happens because the odds, of course, favor the casinos. The element of chance can be introduced through class ***Random*** (located in namespace `System`).

Class *Random* and Method `Next`
Consider the following statements:

```
Dim randomObject As New Random()
Dim randomNumber As Integer = randomObject.Next()
```

The first statement declares `randomObject` as a reference to an object of type `Random` and creates a new `Random` object.

The second statement declares `Integer` variable `randomNumber` and assigns to it the value returned by calling `Random` method ***Next***. Method `Next` generates a positive `Integer` value greater than or equal to zero and less than the constant ***Int32.MaxValue*** (2,147,483,647). If `Next` truly produces values at random, every value in this range has an equal chance (or *probability*) of being chosen when `Next` is called. The values returned by `Next` are actually *pseudo-random numbers*, or a sequence of values produced by a complex mathematical calculation. This calculation requires a *seed value*. If the seed value is different each time the program is run, the series of values will be different as well (so that the generated numbers are indeed random). When we create a `Random` object, the seed is based on the current time. Alternatively, we can pass a seed value as an argument in the parentheses after `New Random`. Passing in the same seed twice results in the same series of random numbers. Using the current time of day as the seed value is effective because the time is likely to change for each `Random` object we create.

The range of values produced by Next is often different from what is needed in a particular application. For example, a program that simulates coin-tossing might require only 0 for "heads" and 1 for "tails." A program that simulates the rolling of a six-sided die would require random integers in the range 1–6. Similarly, a program that randomly predicts the next type of spaceship (out of four possibilities) that flies across the horizon in a video game might require random integers from 1 to 4.

Scaling and Shifting of Random Numbers
By passing an argument to method Next as follows

```
value = 1 + randomObject.Next(6)
```

we can produce integers in the range 1–6. When a single argument is passed to Next, the values returned by Next will be in the range from 0 to (but not including) the value of that argument. This is called *scaling*. The number 6 is the *scaling factor*. We *shift* the range of numbers produced by adding 1 to our previous result, so that the return values are between 1 and 6 rather than 0 and 5.

Visual Basic simplifies the process of specifying a range of random numbers by allowing you to pass two arguments to Next. For example, the preceding statement also could be written as

```
value = randomObject.Next(1, 7)
```

Note that we must use 7 as the second argument to method Next to produce integers in the range from 1 to 6. The first argument indicates the minimum value in our desired range, whereas the second is equal to 1 + the maximum value desired. Figure 7.13 demonstrates the use of class Random and method Next by simulating 20 rolls of a six-sided die and showing the value of each roll. Note that all the values are in the range from 1 to 6, inclusive.

```
1   ' Fig. 7.13: RandomInteger.vb
2   ' Generating random integers.
3   Module RandomInteger
4      Sub Main()
5         Dim randomObject As New Random() ' create Random object
6         Dim randomNumber As Integer
7
8         ' generate 20 random numbers between 1 and 6
9         For i As Integer = 1 To 20
10           randomNumber = randomObject.Next(1, 7)
11           Console.Write(randomNumber & " ")
12
13           If i Mod 5 = 0 Then ' is i a multiple of 5?
14              Console.WriteLine()
15           End If
16        Next
17     End Sub ' Main
18  End Module ' RandomInteger
```

Fig. 7.13 | Random integers from 1 to 6 created by calling method Next of class Random. (Part 1 of 2.)

```
1 1 3 1 1
2 1 1 3 6
6 3 4 6 6
2 2 3 6 5
```

Fig. 7.13 | Random integers from 1 to 6 created by calling method Next of class Random. (Part 2 of 2.)

The program in Fig. 7.14 uses class Random to simulate rolling four six-sided dice. We then use some of the functionality from this program in another example (Fig. 7.16) to demonstrate that the numbers generated by Next occur with approximately equal likelihood.

Using Buttons on a GUI

Before we discuss the use of Random in this application, let us analyze the GUI controls we use and the flow of control in this example. The names of the GUI controls are indicated in the output of Fig. 7.14. In this example, we use four PictureBoxes. You used Picture-Boxes in Chapters 2 and 5. In these examples, you used the PictureBox's Image property to display an image. We will do the same, but set the control's Image property programmatically, so that different die images can be displayed based on the random numbers generated.

In this example, we also use our first Button control. Like the other controls we have used, the Button control can be simply dragged and dropped onto the Form from the **Toolbox**, and its sizing handles can be used to increase or decrease the size of the Button. The Text property of the Button has been set to **Roll** and the font size of the Button's text has been set to 12, using the same **Font** dialog as you would for Label controls. Name the control btnRoll. Recall that we have used prefixes for our other controls, to make identifying the type of control easier during coding. For Buttons, we will use the btn prefix.

```vb
1   ' Fig. 7.14: RollDice.vb
2   ' Rolling four dice.
3   Imports System.IO
4
5   Public Class FrmRollDice
6       ' declare Random object reference
7       Dim randomObject As New Random()
8
9       ' display results of four rolls
10      Private Sub btnRoll_Click(ByVal sender As System.Object, _
11          ByVal e As System.EventArgs) Handles btnRoll.Click
12          ' method randomly assigns a face to each die
13          DisplayDie(picDie1)
14          DisplayDie(picDie2)
15          DisplayDie(picDie3)
16          DisplayDie(picDie4)
17      End Sub ' btnRoll_Click
18
```

Fig. 7.14 | Demonstrating four die rolls with graphical output. (Part 1 of 2.)

```
19        ' get a random die image
20        Sub DisplayDie(ByVal picDie As PictureBox)
21            ' generate random integer in range 1 to 6
22            Dim face As Integer = randomObject.Next(1, 7)
23
24            ' load corresponding image
25            picDie.Image = Image.FromFile( _
26                Directory.GetCurrentDirectory & "\Images\die" & face & ".png")
27        End Sub ' DisplayDie
28    End Class ' FrmRollDice
```

Fig. 7.14 | Demonstrating four die rolls with graphical output. (Part 2 of 2.)

Creating a Click Event Handler

For this example, the random die images will be displayed whenever btnRoll is clicked. To enable such functionality, we need to add an event handler for our Button's **Click event**. To do so, simply double click the Button in design view. This will create the empty event handler in your code. In Chapter 5 we created an event handler for the Form's Load event, which is executed when the Form is loaded. An event handler for a Button's Click event executes whenever the Button is clicked. The event handler with code added to its body is defined in lines 10–17. The name of the event handler is btnRoll_Click. Note that the event handler is a subroutine—the event handler performs actions in response to an event, but does not return a value. The first argument to this method represents the object that is associated with the event; the second argument is an object that contains information about the event. Event-handler names created by the IDE normally begin with the object's name, followed by an underscore and the name of the event. From here on, if you see a method in an example named using this convention, you can assume that it is an event handler. Event handlers are discussed in more detail in Chapter 13.

Displaying Random Images in a PictureBox

The body of our event handler calls method DisplayDie four times, once for each PictureBox on the Form. Calling DisplayDie (lines 13–16) causes four dice to appear as if they are being rolled each time **Roll** is clicked. When this program runs, the dice images do not appear until the user clicks **Roll** for the first time.

Method `DisplayDie` specifies the correct image for the face value calculated by method `Next` (line 22). Note that we declare `randomObject` as an instance variable of `Frm-RollDice` (line 7). This allows the same Random object to be used each time `DisplayDie` executes. We set the `Image` property (line 25) to display one of the die images (the image is selected using random values) in the current `PictureBox` (passed as an argument). We set the property's value with an assignment statement (lines 25–26). Note that we specify the image to display through method *FromFile* in class *Image* (contained in the `System.Drawing` namespace). Method *GetCurrentDirectory* of class *Directory* (contained in the `System.IO` namespace) returns the current directory. Recall that when the application is compiled, an executable (`.exe` file) is created. This is the file that is executed when the application is run, so `GetCurrentDirectory` returns the location of this file. It is important to note that there are actually two `.exe` files created—one to execute when the application is run with debugging (located in the application's `bin\Debug` directory), and one to execute when the application is run without debugging (located in the application's `bin\Release` directory). Therefore, method `GetCurrentDirectory` can return different values based on how you run the application. We have added the images to both directories so that the application will run correctly with and without debugging. The graphics used in this example are located in the example's project directory. The examples for this book are available at `www.deitel.com/books/vbforprogrammers2`.

Importing a Namespace for an Entire Project
We include an `Imports` statement (line 3) for the namespace `System.IO` but not for `System.Drawing`. By default, Windows applications import several namespaces, including `System`, `System.Drawing`, and `System.Windows.Forms`. These namespaces are imported for the entire project, eliminating the need for `Imports` statements in individual project files. You can see which namespaces have been imported into a project by double clicking the **My Project** folder in the **Solution Explorer**, and then selecting **References** in the page that appears. You will be presented with a list of the application's references to assemblies in the **References** area of the window, and a list of the namespaces defined in those references in the **Imported namespaces** area (Fig. 7.15). The namespaces that have been checked are those that are imported for the entire project. Some of the namespaces imported by default are not used in this example. For instance, we do not yet use namespace `System.Collections`, which allows you to create collections of objects (see Chapter 26, Collections). Do not confuse importing namespaces for an entire application with adding references to an application. Adding a reference to an application causes a library (`.dll`) file to be included into your application. This compiled code can contain several namespaces. An `Imports` statement indicates that you will be using a specific namespace from a library file.

The Windows application in Fig. 7.16 enables the reader to repeatedly roll 12 dice to show that the numbers generated by class `Random` occur with approximately equal frequencies. The program displays the cumulative frequencies of each face in a `TextBox` control, and the die faces are displayed using 12 `PictureBoxes`.

The `TextBox` control is located toward the bottom of the GUI. This control can be used both for displaying data to the user and inputting data from the user. The data in the `TextBox` can be accessed and modified via the control's *Text property*. This TextBox's name is `txtDisplay` (we use the `txt` prefix for `TextBoxes`) and the font size has been set to

Fig. 7.15 | Imported namespaces in a project.

9. Finally, the TextBox's *Multiline property* has been set to True, so that multiple lines of text can be displayed.

Figure 7.16 contains two screenshots. The one on the left shows the program when it initially executes, and the one on the right shows the program after the user has clicked **Roll** over 200 times. If the values produced by method Next are indeed random, the frequencies of the face values (1–6) should be approximately the same (as Figure 7.16(b) illustrates).

```vb
 1    ' Fig. 7.16: RollTwelveDice.vb
 2    ' Rolling 12 dice with frequency chart.
 3    Imports System.IO
 4
 5    Public Class FrmRollTwelveDice
 6        Dim randomObject As New Random() ' generate random number
 7        Dim ones As Integer ' count of die face 1
 8        Dim twos As Integer ' count of die face 2
 9        Dim threes As Integer ' count of die face 3
10        Dim fours As Integer ' count of die face 4
11        Dim fives As Integer ' count of die face 5
12        Dim sixes As Integer ' count of die face 6
13
14        ' display result of twelve rolls
15        Private Sub btnRoll_Click(ByVal sender As System.Object, _
16            ByVal e As System.EventArgs) Handles btnRoll.Click
```

Fig. 7.16 | Random class used to simulate rolling 12 six-sided dice. (Part 1 of 3.)

```
17
18        ' assign random faces to 12 dice using DisplayDie
19        DisplayDie(picDie1)
20        DisplayDie(picDie2)
21        DisplayDie(picDie3)
22        DisplayDie(picDie4)
23        DisplayDie(picDie5)
24        DisplayDie(picDie6)
25        DisplayDie(picDie7)
26        DisplayDie(picDie8)
27        DisplayDie(picDie9)
28        DisplayDie(picDie10)
29        DisplayDie(picDie11)
30        DisplayDie(picDie12)
31
32        Dim total As Integer = ones + twos + threes + fours + fives + sixes
33        Dim output As String
34
35        ' display frequencies of faces
36        output = ("Face" & vbTab & vbTab & "Frequency" & vbTab & "Percent")
37        output &= (vbCrLf & "1" & vbTab & vbTab & ones & _
38           vbTab & vbTab & String.Format("{0:P}", ones / total))
39        output &= (vbCrLf & "2" & vbTab & vbTab & twos & vbTab & _
40           vbTab & String.Format("{0:P}", twos / total))
41        output &= (vbCrLf & "3" & vbTab & vbTab & threes & vbTab & _
42           vbTab & String.Format("{0:P}", threes / total))
43        output &= (vbCrLf & "4" & vbTab & vbTab & fours & vbTab & _
44           vbTab & String.Format("{0:P}", fours / total))
45        output &= (vbCrLf & "5" & vbTab & vbTab & fives & vbTab & _
46           vbTab & String.Format("{0:P}", fives / total))
47        output &= (vbCrLf & "6" & vbTab & vbTab & sixes & vbTab & _
48           vbTab & String.Format("{0:P}", sixes / total) & vbCrLf)
49        txtDisplay.Text = output
50     End Sub ' btnRoll_Click
51
52     ' display a single die image
53     Sub DisplayDie(ByVal picDie As PictureBox)
54        Dim face As Integer = randomObject.Next(1, 7)
55
56        picDie.Image = Image.FromFile(Directory.GetCurrentDirectory & _
57           "\Images\die" & face & ".png")
58
59        ' maintain count of die faces
60        Select Case face
61           Case 1 ' die face 1
62              ones += 1
63           Case 2 ' die face 2
64              twos += 1
65           Case 3 ' die face 3
66              threes += 1
67           Case 4 ' die face 4
68              fours += 1
```

Fig. 7.16 | Random class used to simulate rolling 12 six-sided dice. (Part 2 of 3.)

```
69              Case 5 ' die face 5
70                 fives += 1
71              Case 6 ' die face 6
72                 sixes += 1
73           End Select
74        End Sub ' DisplayDie
75     End Class ' FrmRollTwelveDice
```

Fig. 7.16 | Random class used to simulate rolling 12 six-sided dice. (Part 3 of 3.)

To show that the die rolls occur with approximately equal likelihood, the program in Fig. 7.16 has been modified to keep some simple statistics. We declare counters for each of the possible rolls in lines 7–12. Note that the counters are instance variables. Lines 37–49 display the frequency of each roll as percentages using the *P* format specifier.

As the program output demonstrates, method Next can be used to effectively simulate the rolling of a six-sided die. Over the course of many die rolls, each of the possible faces from 1–6 appears with equal likelihood, or approximately one-sixth of the time. Note that *no* Case Else is provided in the Select...Case statement (lines 60–73), because we know that the values generated are in the range 1–6. In Chapter 8, Arrays, we show the power of arrays by explaining how to replace the entire Select...Case statement in this program with a single-line statement.

Run the program several times and observe the results. Note that a different sequence of random numbers is obtained each time the program is executed, causing the resulting frequencies to vary.

7.16 Case Study: A Game of Chance

One of the most popular games of chance is a dice game known as "craps." The rules of the game are straightforward:

> *A player rolls two dice. Each die has six faces. Each face contains 1, 2, 3, 4, 5 or 6 spots. After the dice have come to rest, the sum of the spots on the two upward faces is calculated. If the sum is 7 or 11 on the first throw, the player wins. If the sum is 2, 3 or 12 on the first throw (called "craps"), the player loses (i.e., the "house" wins). If the sum is 4, 5, 6, 8, 9 or 10 on the first throw, that sum becomes the player's "point." To win, players must continue rolling the dice until they "make their point" (i.e., roll their point value). The player loses by rolling a 7 before making the point.*

The application in Fig. 7.17 simulates the game of craps.

The player must roll two dice on the first and all subsequent rolls. When executing the application, click the **Play** Button to play the game. The form displays the results of each roll. The screen captures depict the execution of two games. Figure 7.17(a) displays the Form before the game has begun, while Fig. 7.17(b) shows the application after the **Play** Button has been clicked. In this example, a 6 is rolled, which is made the point. We click **Roll** again and a 7 is rolled, causing us to lose the game (Fig. 7.17(c)). Figure 7.17(d) shows another example game, where the user wins by rolling a 7 on the first roll.

```vb
1  ' Fig. 7.17: CrapsGame.vb
2  ' Playing a craps game.
3  Imports System.IO
4
5  Public Class FrmCrapsGame
6     ' die-roll constants
7     Enum DiceNames
8        SNAKE_EYES = 2
9        TREY = 3
10       LUCKY_SEVEN = 7
11       CRAPS = 7
12       YO_LEVEN = 11
13       BOX_CARS = 12
14    End Enum
15
16    ' file-name and directory constants
17    Const FILE_PREFIX As String = "/images/die"
18    Const FILE_SUFFIX As String = ".png"
19
20    Dim myPoint As Integer ' total point
21    Dim myDie1 As Integer ' die1 face
22    Dim myDie2 As Integer ' die2 face
23    Dim randomObject As New Random() ' generate random number
24
25    ' begins new game and determines point
26    Private Sub btnPlay_Click(ByVal sender As System.Object, _
27       ByVal e As System.EventArgs) Handles btnPlay.Click
28
29       ' initialize variables for new game
30       myPoint = 0
```

Fig. 7.17 | Craps game using class Random. (Part 1 of 3.)

```vb
31          grpPoint.Text = "Point"
32          lblStatus.Text = ""
33
34          ' remove point-die images
35          picPointDie1.Image = Nothing
36          picPointDie2.Image = Nothing
37
38          Dim sum As Integer = RollDice() ' roll dice and calculate sum
39
40          ' check die roll
41          Select Case sum
42             Case DiceNames.LUCKY_SEVEN, DiceNames.YO_LEVEN
43                btnRoll.Enabled = False ' disable Roll button
44                lblStatus.Text = "You Win!!!"
45             Case DiceNames.SNAKE_EYES, DiceNames.TREY, DiceNames.BOX_CARS
46                btnRoll.Enabled = False ' disable Roll button
47                lblStatus.Text = "Sorry. You Lose."
48             Case Else
49                myPoint = sum
50                grpPoint.Text = "Point is " & sum
51                lblStatus.Text = "Roll Again!"
52                DisplayDie(picPointDie1, myDie1)
53                DisplayDie(picPointDie2, myDie2)
54                btnPlay.Enabled = False ' disable Play button
55                btnRoll.Enabled = True ' enable Roll button
56          End Select
57       End Sub ' btnPlay_Click
58
59       ' determines outcome of next roll
60       Private Sub btnRoll_Click(ByVal sender As System.Object, _
61          ByVal e As System.EventArgs) Handles btnRoll.Click
62
63          Dim sum As Integer = RollDice() ' roll dice and calculate sum
64
65          ' check outcome of roll
66          If sum = myPoint Then ' win
67             lblStatus.Text = "You Win!!!"
68             btnRoll.Enabled = False ' disable Roll button
69             btnPlay.Enabled = True ' enable Play button
70          ElseIf sum = DiceNames.CRAPS Then ' lose
71             lblStatus.Text = "Sorry. You Lose."
72             btnRoll.Enabled = False ' disable Roll button
73             btnPlay.Enabled = True ' enable Play button
74          End If
75       End Sub ' btnRoll_Click
76
77       ' display die image
78       Sub DisplayDie(ByVal picDie As PictureBox, _
79          ByVal face As Integer)
80          ' assign die image to picture box
81          picDie.Image = Image.FromFile(Directory.GetCurrentDirectory & _
82             FILE_PREFIX & face & FILE_SUFFIX)
83       End Sub ' DisplayDie
```

Fig. 7.17 | Craps game using class Random. (Part 2 of 3.)

```
84
85          ' generate random die rolls
86          Function RollDice() As Integer
87              ' determine random integer
88              myDie1 = randomObject.Next(1, 7)
89              myDie2 = randomObject.Next(1, 7)
90
91              ' display rolls
92              DisplayDie(picDie1, myDie1)
93              DisplayDie(picDie2, myDie2)
94
95              Return myDie1 + myDie2 ' return sum
96          End Function ' RollDice
97      End Class ' FrmCrapsGame
```

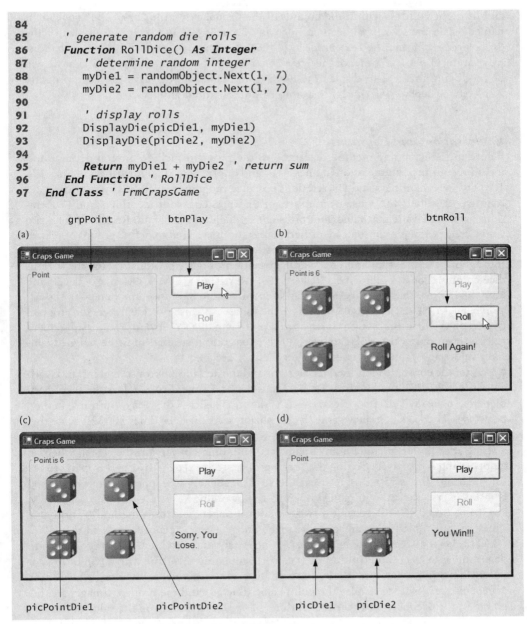

Fig. 7.17 | Craps game using class Random. (Part 3 of 3.)

This program introduces the **GroupBox** control, used to display the user's point. A GroupBox is a container used to group related controls. Within the GroupBox pointDice-Group, we add two PictureBoxes, which are controls that display images. A GroupBox can be dragged and dropped onto the Form the same way you would any other control. When adding other controls to a GroupBox (such as the two PictureBoxes in this example), drag and drop the controls within the bounds of the GroupBox on the Form. The GroupBox is named grpPoint. We use the prefix grp for GroupBoxes. We set the font size of the GroupBox to 9.75 and the **Text** *property* of the GroupBox to **Point**. This is the text that displays in the upper-left corner of the GroupBox. Note in the output of Fig. 7.17 that we will be modifying this text to display the user's point value. If you leave the Text property blank, the GroupBox will display as a simple border without any text.

Enumerations and Constants

Before introducing any method declarations, the program includes several declarations, including our first enumeration in lines 7–14 and our first constant identifiers in lines 17–18. Constant identifiers and Enumerations enhance program readability by providing descriptive identifiers for constant numbers or Strings. Constant identifiers and Enumerations help you ensure that values are consistent throughout a program. Recall that keyword Const creates a single constant identifier; Enumerations are used to define groups of related constants. In this case, we create Constant identifiers for the file names that are used throughout the program and create an Enumeration of descriptive names for the various dice combinations in craps (i.e., SNAKE_EYES, TREY, LUCKY_SEVEN, CRAPS, YO_LEVEN and BOX_CARS). Note that multiple enumeration members can have the same value—in this example, LUCKY_SEVEN and CRAPS both have the value 7. We use two identifiers for program clarity; on the first roll, a seven causes the player to win (LUCKY_SEVEN), and on subsequent rolls, a seven causes the player to lose (CRAPS). Constant identifiers must be assigned constant values and cannot be modified after they are declared.

After the constant-identifier declarations and the declarations for several instance variables (lines 20–23), method btnPlay_Click is declared (lines 26–57). It is the event handler for btnPlay's Click event. When the user clicks the **Play** button, method btnPlay_Click sets up a new game by initializing several values (lines 30–32). Note that line 32 sets our status Label's Text property to "". This is known as the *empty string* (i.e., a string that does not contain any characters). Nothing appears on the screen when an empty string is displayed. Setting the Image property of picPointDie1 and picPointDie2 to Nothing (lines 35–36) causes the PictureBoxes to appear blank. Method btnPlay_Click executes the game's opening roll by calling RollDice (line 38). Internally, RollDice (lines 86–96) generates two random numbers and calls method DisplayDie (lines 78–83), which loads an appropriate die image in the PictureBox passed to it.

The Select...Case statement (lines 41–56) analyzes the roll returned by RollDice to determine how play should continue (i.e., by terminating the game with a win or loss, or by enabling subsequent rolls). If the user does not win or lose on the first roll, the GroupBox's text is set to display the point value (line 50) and the property images are displayed in the GroupBox's PictureBoxes (lines 52–53). Depending on the value of the roll, Buttons **Roll** and **Play** become either enabled or disabled (lines 43, 46 and 54–55). Disabling a Button means that no action will be performed when the Button is clicked. Buttons can be enabled and disabled by setting the Button's **Enabled** *property* to True or False, respectively.

If button **Roll** is enabled, clicking it invokes method btnRoll_Click (lines 60–75), which executes an additional roll of the dice. Method btnRoll_Click then analyzes the roll, letting users know whether they have won or lost.

7.17 Method Overloading

Visual Basic provides several ways of allowing methods to have variable sets of parameters. *Method overloading* allows you to create multiple methods with the same name but different *signatures*—that is, different numbers and types of parameters, or with different orderings of the parameters (by type). When an overloaded method is called, the compiler selects the proper method by examining the number, types and order (by type) of the arguments. Often, method overloading is used to create several methods with the same name that perform similar tasks on different types of data.

 Good Programming Practice 7.3

Overloading methods that perform closely related tasks can make programs clearer.

The program in Fig. 7.18 uses overloaded method Square to calculate the square of both an Integer and a Double.

If the compiler looked only at method names during compilation, the code in Fig. 7.18 would be ambiguous—the compiler would not know how to differentiate between the two Square methods. The compiler uses a process known as *overload resolution* to determine which method to call. This process first searches for all methods that *could* be used on the basis of the number and type of arguments that are present. Although it might seem that only one method would match, it is important to remember that Visual Basic converts variables as necessary when they are passed as arguments. Once all matching methods are found, the compiler then selects the closest match.

Note that at line 12 we use method Convert.ToInt32, which converts its argument to a value of type Integer. This explicit conversion is needed because the exponent (∧) operator expects operands of type Double, and implicitly converts its operands to that type. This version of method Square returns an Integer value, so Convert.ToInt32 performs this conversion. Recall that because we are now using **Option Strict**, such conversion is required to compile the application.

In Fig. 7.18, the compiler might use the logical name "Square of Integer" for the Square method that specifies an Integer parameter (line 10) and "Square of Double" for the Square method that specifies a Double parameter (line 15). If a method ExampleSub's declaration begins as

```
Function ExampleSub(ByVal a As Integer, ByVal b As Double) _
    As Integer
```

```
1   ' Fig. 7.18: Overload2.vb
2   ' Using overloaded methods with identical signatures and
3   ' different return types.
4   Module Overload2
5      Sub Main() ' call Square methods with Integer and Double
6         Console.WriteLine("The square of Integer 7 is " & Square(7) & _
7            vbCrLf & "The square of Double 7.5 is " & Square(7.5))
8      End Sub ' Main
```

Fig. 7.18 | Syntax error generated from overloaded methods with identical parameter lists and different return types. (Part 1 of 2.)

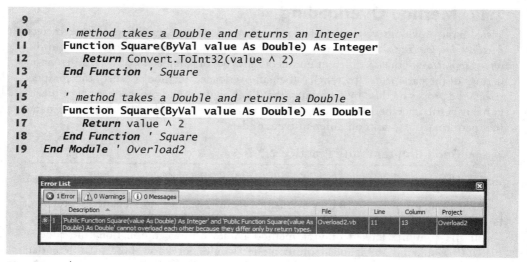

```
 9
10          ' method takes a Double and returns an Integer
11          Function Square(ByVal value As Double) As Integer
12             Return Convert.ToInt32(value ^ 2)
13          End Function ' Square
14
15          ' method takes a Double and returns a Double
16          Function Square(ByVal value As Double) As Double
17             Return value ^ 2
18          End Function ' Square
19       End Module ' Overload2
```

Fig. 7.18 | Syntax error generated from overloaded methods with identical parameter lists and different return types. (Part 2 of 2.)

the compiler might use the logical name "ExampleSub of Integer and Double." Similarly, if the parameters are specified as

```
Function ExampleSub(ByVal a As Double, ByVal b As Integer) _
   As Integer
```

the compiler might use the logical name "ExampleSub of Double and Integer." The order of the parameters (by type) is important to the compiler; it considers the preceding two ExampleSub methods to be distinct.

So far, the logical method names used by the compiler have not mentioned the methods' return types. This is because method calls cannot be distinguished by return type. The program in Fig. 7.18 illustrates the syntax error that is generated when two methods have the same signature and different return types. Overloaded methods with different parameter lists can have different return types. Overloaded methods need not have the same number of parameters.

Common Programming Error 7.9

Creating overloaded methods with identical parameter lists and different return types is a compilation error.

7.18 Optional Parameters

Methods can have *optional parameters*. Declaring a parameter as optional allows the calling method to vary the number of arguments to pass. Optional parameters specify a default value that is assigned to the parameter if the optional argument is not passed. Overloaded methods are generally more flexible than methods with optional parameters. For instance, you can specify different return types for overloaded methods.

You can create methods with one or more optional parameters. All optional parameters, however, must be placed to the right of the method's non-optional parameters.

Common Programming Error 7.10
Declaring a non-Optional parameter to the right of an Optional parameter is a syntax error.

When a parameter is declared as optional, the caller has the *option* of passing that particular argument. Optional parameters are specified in the method header with keyword **Optional**. For example, the method header

```
Sub ExampleMethod(ByVal value1 As Boolean, Optional _
    ByVal value2 As Integer = 0)
```

specifies the last parameter as Optional. Any call to ExampleMethod must pass at least one argument (the Boolean), or else a syntax error is generated. If the caller chooses, a second argument (the Integer) can be passed to ExampleMethod. Consider the following calls to ExampleMethod:

```
ExampleMethod()
ExampleMethod(True)
ExampleMethod(False, 10)
```

The first call to ExampleMethod generates a syntax error because a minimum of one argument is required for this method. The second call to ExampleMethod is valid because one argument (the Boolean) is being passed—the Optional argument, corresponding to parameter value2, is not specified in the method call. The last call to ExampleMethod also is valid: False is passed as the one required argument, and 10 is passed as the Optional argument.

In the call that passes only one argument (True) to ExampleMethod, parameter value2 defaults to 0, which is the value specified in the method header. Optional parameters must specify a *default value*, using the equals sign followed by the value. For example, the header for ExampleMethod sets 0 as the default value for value2. Default values can be used only with parameters declared as Optional.

Common Programming Error 7.11
Not specifying a default value for an Optional parameter is a syntax error.

The example in Fig. 7.19 demonstrates the use of optional parameters. The program calculates the result of raising a base to an exponent, both of which are specified by the

```
1   ' Fig. 7.19: Power.vb
2   ' Calculates the power of a value, demonstrates optional parameters.
3   Public Class FrmPower
4      ' reads input and displays result
5      Private Sub btnCalculate_Click(ByVal sender As System.Object, _
6         ByVal e As System.EventArgs) Handles btnCalculate.Click
7
8         Dim value As Integer
9
```

Fig. 7.19 | Optional argument demonstration with method Power. (Part 1 of 2.)

```
10          ' call version of Power depending on power input
11          If Not txtPower.Text = "" Then
12            value = Power(Convert.ToInt32(txtBase.Text), _
13              Convert.ToInt32(txtPower.Text))
14          Else
15            value = Power(Convert.ToInt32(txtBase.Text))
16            txtPower.Text = Convert.ToString(2)
17          End If
18
19          lblOutput.Text = Convert.ToString(value)
20        End Sub ' btnCalculate_Click
21
22        ' use iteration to calculate power
23        Function Power(ByVal base As Integer, _
24          Optional ByVal exponent As Integer = 2) As Integer
25
26          Dim total As Integer = 1 ' initialize total
27
28          For i As Integer = 1 To exponent ' calculate power
29            total *= base
30          Next
31
32          Return total ' return result
33        End Function ' Power
34      End Class ' FrmPower
```

Fig. 7.19 | Optional argument demonstration with method Power. (Part 2 of 2.)

user. Method `Power` (lines 23–33) specifies that its second parameter is `Optional`. If the user does not specify an exponent, the `Optional` argument is omitted, and the default parameter value, 2, is used.

In this example, we use `TextBox`es to input data from the user. When the **Calculate Power** `Button` is clicked, line 11 determines whether `txtPower` contains a value. If true (as in Fig. 7.19(a)), the values in the `TextBox`es are converted to `Integer`s and passed to `Power`. Otherwise, `txtBase`'s value is converted to an `Integer` and passed as the first of two arguments to `Power` in line 15. An example of this is shown in Fig. 7.19(b), where we clicked the **Calculate Power** `Button` without entering an exponent value. The second argument, 2, is provided by the compiler (using the default value of the `Optional` argument) and is not visible to you in the call. Line 16 displays the value 2 in `txtPower`, for clarity (Fig. 7.19(c)).

7.19 Recursion

It is sometimes useful for methods to call themselves—a ***recursive method*** is a method that calls itself either directly or indirectly (i.e., through another method). In this section, we present a simple example of recursion.

Let us first consider recursion conceptually. Recursive problem-solving approaches have a number of elements in common. A recursive method is called to solve a problem. The method actually knows how to solve only the simplest case(s)—the ***base case(s)***. If the method is called with a base case, it returns a result. If the method is called with a more complex problem, it divides the problem into two conceptual pieces—a piece that the method knows how to perform (i.e., base case), and a piece that it does not know how to perform. To make recursion feasible, the latter piece must resemble the original problem but be a slightly simpler or smaller version of it. The method invokes (calls) a fresh copy of itself to work on the smaller problem—this is referred to as a ***recursive call***, or ***recursion step***. The recursion step also normally includes the keyword `Return`, because its result will be combined with the portion of the problem that the method knew how to solve. Such a combination will form a result that will be passed back to the original caller.

The recursion step executes while the original call to the method is still "open" (i.e., has not finished executing). The recursion step can result in many more recursive calls, as the method divides each new subproblem into two conceptual pieces. As the method continues to call itself with slightly simpler versions of the original problem, the sequence of smaller and smaller problems must converge on a base case, so that the recursion can eventually terminate. At that point, the method recognizes the base case and returns a result to the previous copy of the method. A sequence of returns ensues up the line until the original method call returns the final result to the caller. As an example of these concepts, let us write a recursive program that performs a popular mathematical calculation.

Determining a Factorial Value Recursively

The factorial of a nonnegative integer n, written $n!$ (and read "n factorial"), is the product

$$n \cdot (n-1) \cdot (n-2) \cdot \ldots \cdot 1$$

with 1! equal to 1, and 0! defined as 1. For example, 5! is the product $5 \cdot 4 \cdot 3 \cdot 2 \cdot 1$, which is equal to 120.

The factorial of an integer `number` greater than or equal to 0 can be calculated *iteratively* (nonrecursively) using a `For...Next` statement, as follows:

```
Dim counter, factorial As Integer = 1

For counter = number To 1 Step -1
    factorial *= counter
Next
```

We arrive at a recursive definition of the factorial method by observing the following relationship:

$$n! = n \cdot (n - 1)!$$

For example, 5! is clearly equal to 5 · 4!, as is shown by the following:

$$5! = 5 \cdot 4 \cdot 3 \cdot 2 \cdot 1$$
$$5! = 5 \cdot (4 \cdot 3 \cdot 2 \cdot 1)$$
$$5! = 5 \cdot (4!)$$

A recursive evaluation of 5! would proceed as in Fig. 7.20. Figure 7.20(a) shows how the succession of recursive calls proceeds until 1! is evaluated to be 1, which terminates the recursion. Figure 7.20(b) depicts the values that are returned from each recursive call to its caller until the final value is calculated and returned.

The program in Fig. 7.21 recursively calculates and prints factorials. The recursive method `Factorial` (lines 19–25) first tests (line 20) to determine whether its terminating condition is true (i.e., `number` is less than or equal to 1). This determines whether the parameter is one of the base cases (0 or 1). If `number` is less than or equal to 1, `Factorial`

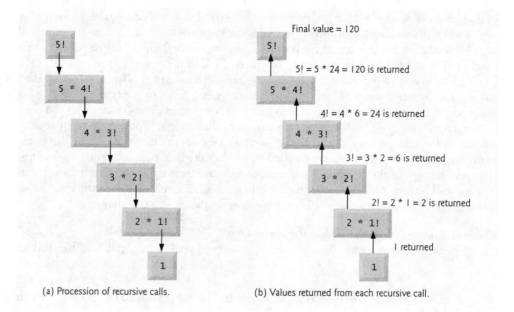

(a) Procession of recursive calls.　　　(b) Values returned from each recursive call.

Fig. 7.20 | Recursive evaluation of 5!.

```
 1   ' Fig. 7.21: Factorial.vb
 2   ' Calculating factorials using recursion.
 3   Public Class FrmFactorial
 4      ' calculate factorial
 5      Private Sub btnCalculate_Click(ByVal sender As System.Object, _
 6         ByVal e As System.EventArgs) Handles btnCalculate.Click
 7
 8         ' convert text in TextBox to Integer
 9         Dim value As Integer = Convert.ToInt32(txtInput.Text)
10         txtDisplay.Text = "" ' reset TextBox
11
12         ' call Factorial to perform calculation
13         For i As Integer = 0 To value
14            txtDisplay.Text &= i & "! = " & Factorial(i) & vbCrLf
15         Next
16      End Sub ' btnCalculate_Click
17
18      ' recursively generates factorial of number
19      Function Factorial(ByVal number As Integer) As Long
20         If number <= 1 Then ' base case
21            Return 1
22         Else
23            Return number * Factorial(number - 1)
24         End If
25      End Function ' Factorial
26   End Class ' FrmFactorial
```

Fig. 7.21 | Recursive factorial program.

returns 1, no further recursion is necessary and the method returns. If number is greater than 1, line 23 expresses the problem as the product of number and a recursive call to Factorial, evaluating the factorial of number - 1. Note that calculating Factorial(number - 1) is slightly simpler than the original calculation, Factorial(number).

We have set the output TextBox's *ScrollBars property* to Vertical, to display a vertical scrollbar. This allows us to display more outputs than will fit in the space allocated for the TextBox. Method Factorial (line 19) receives a parameter of type Integer and returns a result of type Long. Type *Long* is designed to store integer values in a range much larger than that of type Integer. As is seen in the output window of Fig. 7.21, factorial values grow quickly. We choose type Long to enable the program to calculate factorials greater than 12!. Unfortunately, the values produced by the Factorial method increase at such a rate that the range of even the Long type is quickly exceeded. This points to a weakness in most programming languages—they are not easily extended to handle the unique requirements of various applications, such as the evaluation of large factorials. Recall that Visual Basic is an extensible language—programmers with unique requirements can extend the language by defining new classes. You could create a HugeInteger class that would enable a program to calculate the factorials of arbitrarily large numbers— we create a HugeInteger class in Chapter 22, Web Services.

Common Programming Error 7.12

Forgetting to return a value from a recursive method can result in logic errors.

Common Programming Error 7.13

Omitting the base case or writing the recursion step so that it does not converge on the base case will cause infinite recursion, eventually exhausting memory. This is analogous to the problem of an infinite loop in an iterative (nonrecursive) solution.

7.20 (Optional) Software Engineering Case Study: Identifying Class Operations in the ATM System

In the Software Engineering Case Study sections at the ends of Chapters 4–6, we performed the first few steps in the object-oriented design of our ATM system. In Chapter 4, we identified the classes that we will likely need to implement and we created our first class diagram. In Chapter 5, we described some attributes of our classes. In Chapter 6, we examined our objects' states and modeled the objects' state transitions and activities. We now determine some of the class operations (or behaviors) needed to implement the ATM system.

Identifying Operations

An operation is a service that objects of a class provide to clients of the class. Consider the operations of some real-world objects. A radio's operations include setting its station and volume (typically invoked by a person adjusting the radio's controls). A car's operations include accelerating (invoked by the driver pressing the accelerator pedal), decelerating (invoked by the driver pressing the brake pedal or releasing the gas pedal), turning, and shifting gears. Software objects can offer operations as well—for example, a software graphics object might offer operations for drawing a circle, drawing a line, drawing a square and the like. A spreadsheet software object might offer operations like printing the spreadsheet, totaling the elements in a row or column and graphing information in the spreadsheet as a bar chart or pie chart.

We can derive many of the operations of the classes in our ATM system by examining the verbs and verb phrases in the requirements document. We then relate each of these to

Class	Verbs and verb phrases
ATM	executes financial transactions
BalanceInquiry	[none in the requirements document]
Withdrawal	[none in the requirements document]
Deposit	[none in the requirements document]
BankDatabase	authenticates a user, retrieves an account balance, credits an account by a deposit amount, debits an account by a withdrawal amount
Account	retrieves an account balance, credits an account by a deposit amount, debits an account by a withdrawal amount
Screen	displays a message to the user
Keypad	receives numeric input from the user
CashDispenser	dispenses cash, indicates whether it contains enough cash to satisfy a withdrawal request
DepositSlot	receives a deposit envelope

Fig. 7.22 | Verbs and verb phrases for each class in the ATM system.

particular classes in our system (Fig. 7.22). The verb phrases in Fig. 7.22 help us determine the operations of our classes.

Modeling Operations

To identify operations, we examine the verb phrases listed for each class in Fig. 7.22. The "executes financial transactions" phrase associated with class ATM implies that class ATM instructs transactions to execute. Therefore, classes BalanceInquiry, Withdrawal and Deposit each need an operation to provide this service to the ATM. We place this operation (which we have named Execute) in the third compartment of the three transaction classes in the updated class diagram of Fig. 7.23. During an ATM session, the ATM object will invoke the Execute operation of each transaction object to tell it to execute.

The UML represents operations (which are implemented as methods in Visual Basic) by listing the operation name, followed by a comma-separated list of parameters in parentheses, a colon and the return type:

operationName(parameter1, parameter2, ..., parameterN) : returnType

Each parameter in the comma-separated parameter list consists of a parameter name, followed by a colon and the parameter type:

parameterName : parameterType

For the moment, we do not list the parameters of our operations—we will identify and model the parameters of some of the operations shortly. For some of the operations, we do not yet know the return types, so we also omit them from the diagram. These omissions are perfectly normal at this point. As our design and implementation proceed, we will add the remaining return types.

Operations of Class BankDatabase and Class Account

Figure 7.22 lists the phrase "authenticates a user" next to class BankDatabase—the database is the object that contains the account information necessary to determine whether the account number and PIN entered by a user match those of an account held at the bank. Therefore, class BankDatabase needs an operation that provides an authentication service to the ATM. We place the operation AuthenticateUser in the third compartment of class BankDatabase (Fig. 7.23). However, an object of class Account, not class Bank-Database, stores the account number and PIN that must be accessed to authenticate a user, so class Account must provide a service to validate a PIN obtained through user input against a PIN stored in an Account object. Therefore, we add a ValidatePIN operation to class Account. Note that we specify a return type of Boolean for the AuthenticateUser and ValidatePIN operations. Each operation returns a value indicating either that the operation was successful in performing its task (i.e., a return value of True) or that it was not successful (i.e., a return value of False).

Fig. 7.23 | Classes in the ATM system with attributes and operations.

Figure 7.22 lists several additional verb phrases for class BankDatabase: "retrieves an account balance," "credits an account by a deposit amount" and "debits an account by a withdrawal amount." Like "authenticates a user," these phrases refer to services that the database must provide to the ATM, because the database holds all the account data used to authenticate a user and perform ATM transactions. However, Account objects actually perform the operations to which these phrases refer. Thus, class BankDatabase and class Account both need operations that correspond to each of these phrases. Recall from Section 4.9 that, because a bank account contains sensitive information, we do not allow the ATM to access accounts directly. The database acts as an intermediary between the ATM and the account data, preventing unauthorized access. As we will see in Section 8.15, class ATM invokes the operations of class BankDatabase, each of which in turn invokes operations (which are the Get accessors of ReadOnly properties) in class Account.

The phrase "retrieves an account balance" suggests that classes BankDatabase and Account each need an operation that gets the balance. However, recall that Fig. 5.28 specified two attributes in class Account to represent a balance—availableBalance and totalBalance. A balance inquiry requires access to both balance attributes so that it can display them to the user, but a withdrawal needs to check only the value of available-Balance. To allow objects in the system to obtain these balance attributes individually from a specific Account object in the BankDatabase, we add operations GetAvailable-Balance and GetTotalBalance to the third compartment of class BankDatabase (Fig. 7.23). We specify a return type of Decimal for each of these operations, because the balances which they retrieve are of type Decimal.

Once the BankDatabase knows which Account to access, the BankDatabase must be able to obtain each balance attribute individually from that Account. For this purpose, we could add operations GetAvailableBalance and GetTotalBalance to the third compartment of class Account (Fig. 7.23). However, in Visual Basic, simple operations such as getting the value of an attribute are typically performed by a property's Get accessor (at least when that particular class "owns" the underlying attribute). This design is for a Visual Basic application, so rather than modeling operations GetAvailableBalance and Get-TotalBalance, we model Decimal properties AvailableBalance and TotalBalance in class Account. Properties are placed in the second compartment of a class diagram. These properties replace the availableBalance and totalBalance attributes that we modeled for class Account in Fig. 5.28. Recall from Chapter 4 that a property's accessors are implied, thus they are not modeled in a class diagram. Figure 7.22 does not mention the need to set the balances, so Fig. 7.23 shows properties AvailableBalance and TotalBalance as ReadOnly properties (i.e., they have only Get accessors). To indicate a ReadOnly property, we follow the property's type with "{ReadOnly}."

You may be wondering why we modeled AvailableBalance and TotalBalance *properties* in class Account, but modeled GetAvailableBalance and GetTotalBalance *operations* in class BankDatabase. Since there can be many Account objects in the BankDatabase, the ATM must specify which Account to access when invoking BankDatabase operations GetAvailableBalance and GetTotalBalance. The ATM does this by passing an account number argument to each BankDatabase operation. The Get accessors of the properties you have seen in Visual Basic code cannot receive arguments. Thus, we modeled GetAvailableBalance and GetTotalBalance as operations in class BankDatabase so that we could specify parameters to which the ATM can pass arguments. Also, the underlying balance attributes are not owned by the BankDatabase, so Get accessors are not appropriate here. We discuss the parameters for the BankDatabase operations shortly.

The phrases "credits an account by a deposit amount" and "debits an account by a withdrawal amount" indicate that classes BankDatabase and Account must perform operations to update an account during a deposit and withdrawal, respectively. We therefore assign Credit and Debit operations to classes BankDatabase and Account. You may recall that crediting an account (as in a deposit) adds an amount only to the Account's total balance. Debiting an account (as in a withdrawal), on the other hand, subtracts the amount from both the total and available balances. We hide these implementation details inside class Account. This is a good example of encapsulation and information hiding.

If this were a real ATM system, classes BankDatabase and Account would also provide a set of operations to allow another banking system to update a user's account balance after either confirming or rejecting all or part of a deposit. Operation ConfirmDepositAmount, for example, would add an amount to the Account's available balance, thus making deposited funds available for withdrawal. Operation RejectDepositAmount would subtract an amount from the Account's total balance to indicate that a specified amount, which had recently been deposited through the ATM and added to the Account's total balance, was invalidated (or checks may have "bounced"). The bank would invoke operation Reject-DepositAmount after determining either that the user failed to include the correct amount of cash or that any checks did not clear (i.e., they "bounced"). While adding these operations would make our system more complete, we do not include them in our class diagrams or implementation because they are beyond the scope of the case study.

Operations of Class Screen

Class Screen "displays a message to the user" at various times in an ATM session. All visual output occurs through the screen of the ATM. The requirements document describes many types of messages (e.g., a welcome message, an error message, a thank-you message) that the screen displays to the user. The requirements document also indicates that the screen displays prompts and menus to the user. However, a prompt is really just a message describing what the user should input next, and a menu is essentially a type of prompt consisting of a series of messages (i.e., menu options) displayed consecutively. Therefore, rather than assign class Screen an individual operation to display each type of message, prompt and menu, we simply create one operation that can display any message specified by a parameter. We place this operation (DisplayMessage) in the third compartment of class Screen in our class diagram (Fig. 7.23). Note that we do not worry about the parameter of this operation at this time—we model the parameter momentarily.

Operations of Class Keypad

From the phrase "receives numeric input from the user" listed by class Keypad in Fig. 7.22, we conclude that class Keypad should perform a GetInput operation. Because the ATM's keypad, unlike a computer keyboard, contains only the numbers 0–9, we specify that this operation returns an integer value. Recall from the requirements document that in different situations the user may be required to enter a different type of number (e.g., an account number, a PIN, the number of a menu option, a deposit amount as a number of cents). Class Keypad simply obtains a numeric value for a client of the class—it does not determine whether the value meets any specific criteria. Any class that uses this operation must verify that the user enters appropriate numbers, and if not, display error messages via class

Screen). [*Note:* When we implement the system, we simulate the ATM's keypad with a computer keyboard, and for simplicity we assume that the user does not enter nonnumeric input using keys on the computer keyboard that do not appear on the ATM's keypad. In Chapter 16, Strings, Characters and Regular Expressions, you will learn how to examine inputs to determine if they are of particular types.]

Operations of Class `CashDispenser` and Class `DepositSlot`

Figure 7.22 lists "dispenses cash" for class `CashDispenser`. Therefore, we create operation `DispenseCash` and list it under class `CashDispenser` in Fig. 7.23. Class `CashDispenser` also "indicates whether it contains enough cash to satisfy a withdrawal request." Thus, we include `IsSufficientCashAvailable`, an operation that returns a value of type `Boolean`, in class `CashDispenser`. Figure 7.22 also lists "receives a deposit envelope" for class `DepositSlot`. The deposit slot must indicate whether it received an envelope, so we place the operation `IsDepositEnvelopeReceived`, which returns a `Boolean` value, in the third compartment of class `DepositSlot`. [*Note:* A real hardware deposit slot would most likely send the ATM a signal to indicate that an envelope was received. We simulate this behavior, however, with an operation in class `DepositSlot` that class ATM can invoke to find out whether the deposit slot received an envelope.]

Operations of Class ATM

We do not list any operations for class ATM at this time. We are not yet aware of any services that class ATM provides to other classes in the system. When we implement the system in Visual Basic (Appendix J), however, operations of this class, and additional operations of the other classes in the system, may become apparent.

Identifying and Modeling Operation Parameters

So far, we have not been concerned with the parameters of our operations—we have attempted to gain only a basic understanding of the operations of each class. Let's now take a closer look at some operation parameters. We identify an operation's parameters by examining what data the operation requires to perform its assigned task.

Consider class `BankDatabase`'s `AuthenticateUser` operation. To authenticate a user, this operation must know the account number and PIN supplied by the user. Thus we specify that operation `AuthenticateUser` takes integer parameters `userAccountNumber` and `userPIN`, which the operation must compare to the account number and PIN of an `Account` object in the database. We prefix these parameter names with "user" to avoid confusion between the operation's parameter names and the attribute names that belong to class `Account`. We list these parameters in the class diagram in Fig. 7.24 that models only class `BankDatabase`. [*Note:* It is perfectly normal to model only one class in a class diagram. In this case, we are most concerned with examining the parameters of this one class in particular, so we omit the other classes. In class diagrams later in the case study, in which parameters are no longer the focus of our attention, we omit the parameters to save space. Remember, however, that the operations listed in these diagrams still have parameters.]

Recall that the UML models each parameter in an operation's comma-separated parameter list by listing the parameter name, followed by a colon and the parameter type. Figure 7.24 thus specifies, for example, that operation `AuthenticateUser` takes two parameters—`userAccountNumber` and `userPIN`, both of type `Integer`.

BankDatabase
AuthenticateUser(userAccountNumber : Integer, userPIN : Integer) : Boolean GetAvailableBalance(userAccountNumber : Integer) : Decimal GetTotalBalance(userAccountNumber : Integer) : Decimal Credit(userAccountNumber : Integer, amount : Decimal) Debit(userAccountNumber : Integer, amount : Decimal)

Fig. 7.24 | Class BankDatabase with operation parameters.

Class BankDatabase operations GetAvailableBalance, GetTotalBalance, Credit and Debit also each require a userAccountNumber parameter to identify the account to which the database must apply the operations, so we include these parameters in the class diagram. In addition, operations Credit and Debit each require a Decimal parameter amount to specify the amount of money to be credited or debited, respectively.

The class diagram in Fig. 7.25 models the parameters of class Account's operations. Operation ValidatePIN requires only a userPIN parameter, which contains the user-specified PIN to be compared with the PIN associated with the account. Like their counterparts in class BankDatabase, operations Credit and Debit in class Account each require a Decimal parameter amount that indicates the amount of money involved in the operation. Note that class Account's operations do not require an account number parameter—each of these operations can be invoked only on the Account object in which they are executing, so including a parameter to specify an Account is unnecessary.

Figure 7.26 models class Screen with a parameter specified for operation Display-Message. This operation requires only a String parameter message that indicates the text to be displayed.

The class diagram in Fig. 7.27 specifies that operation DispenseCash of class Cash-Dispenser takes a Decimal parameter amount to indicate the amount of cash (in dollars) to be dispensed. Operation IsSufficientCashAvailable also takes a Decimal parameter amount to indicate the amount of cash in question.

Note that we do not discuss parameters for operation Execute of classes Balance-Inquiry, Withdrawal and Deposit, operation GetInput of class Keypad and operation IsDepositEnvelopeReceived of class DepositSlot. At this point in our design process, we cannot determine whether these operations require additional data to perform their

Account
accountNumber : Integer pin : Integer «property» AvailableBalance : Decimal {ReadOnly} «property» TotalBalance : Decimal {ReadOnly}
ValidatePIN(userPIN: Integer) : Boolean Credit(amount : Decimal) Debit(amount : Decimal)

Fig. 7.25 | Class Account with operation parameters.

Fig. 7.26 | Class `Screen` with an operation parameter.

Fig. 7.27 | Class `CashDispenser` with operation parameters.

tasks, so we leave their parameter lists empty. As we progress through the case study, we may decide to add parameters to these operations.

In this section, we have determined many of the operations performed by the classes in the ATM system. We have identified the parameters and return types of some of the operations. As we continue our design process, the number of operations belonging to each class may vary—we might find that new operations are needed or that some current ones are unnecessary—and we might determine that some of our class operations need additional parameters and different return types. Again, all of this is perfectly normal.

Software Engineering Case Study Self-Review Exercises

7.1   Which of the following is not a behavior?
   a)   reading data from a file
   b)   printing output
   c)   text output
   d)   obtaining input from the user

7.2   If you were to add to the ATM system an operation that returns the amount attribute of class `Withdrawal`, how and where would you specify this operation in the class diagram of Fig. 7.23?

7.3   Describe the meaning of the following operation listing that might appear in a class diagram for an object-oriented design of a calculator:

```
Add( x : Integer, y : Integer ) : Integer
```

Answers to Software Engineering Case Study Self-Review Exercises

7.1   c.

7.2   An operation that retrieves the amount attribute of class `Withdrawal` would typically be implemented as a `Get` accessor of a property of class `Withdrawal`. The following would replace attribute amount in the attribute (i.e., second) compartment of class `Withdrawal`:

```
«property» Amount : Decimal
```

7.3   This is an operation named `Add` that takes `Integer` parameters x and y and returns an `Integer` value. This operation would most likely sum its parameters x and y and return the result.

7.21 Wrap-Up

In this chapter, you studied methods in greater depth. We distinguished between subroutines and functions, and when to use each type of method. You saw the difference between non-Shared and Shared methods and how to call Shared methods by preceding the method name with the name of the class in which it appears and a dot (.). We declared named constants using both enumerations and constant variables. You saw that arguments can be implicitly converted to the type of their corresponding parameters. We demonstrated using **Option Strict**, which causes the compiler to check all conversions and requires you to perform explicit conversion for all narrowing conversions that could cause data loss or program termination. We discussed how Visual Basic performs method calls using a stack data structure. You used class Random to generate random numbers that can be used for simulations and game playing. You studied the scope of instance variables and local variables in classes and methods, respectively. You enhanced your GUI skills, using Picture-Boxes, GroupBoxes, Buttons and TextBoxes, and created event handlers for Buttons. Finally, you learned that multiple methods in one class can be overloaded by providing methods with the same name and different signatures. Such methods can be used to perform the same or similar tasks using different types or different numbers of parameters.

In Chapter 8, we discuss how to maintain lists and tables of data in arrays. You will see a more elegant implementation of the application that rolls a die several times and two enhanced versions of the GradeBook case study in Chapters 4–7.

8

Arrays

Now go, write it before them in a table,
and note it in a book.
—Isaiah 30:8

With sobs and tears he sorted out
Those of the largest size ...
—Lewis Carroll

Attempt the end, and never stand to doubt;
Nothing's so hard, but search will find it out.
—Robert Herrick

Begin at the beginning, ...
and go on till you come to the end: then stop.
—Lewis Carroll

To go beyond is as wrong as to fall short
—Confucius

OBJECTIVES

In this chapter you will learn:

■ To use the array data structure; arrays are objects.

■ How arrays are used to store, sort and search lists and tables of values.

■ To declare, initialize and refer to individual elements of arrays.

■ To pass arrays to methods using `ByVal` and `ByRef`.

■ To declare and manipulate multidimensional arrays, especially rectangular arrays and jagged arrays.

■ To create variable-length parameter lists.

■ To use the `For Each...Next` statement to iterate through the elements of arrays without using a loop counter.

8.1 Introduction

This chapter introduces basic concepts and features of data structures. *Arrays* are simple data structures consisting only of data items of the same type. Arrays normally are "static" entities, in that they typically remain the same size once they are created, although you can use the ReDim statement to resize an array at execution time. We begin by creating and accessing arrays; we then perform more complex manipulations of arrays, including searching and sorting. We discuss arrays with one dimension and with multiple dimensions. Chapter 24, Data Structures and Chapter 26, Collections introduce dynamic data structures, such as lists, queues, stacks and trees, which typically grow and shrink as programs execute. Chapter 26 also presents Visual Basic's predefined data structures, including lists, queues, stacks and trees.

8.2 Arrays

An array is a group of variables (called *elements*) containing values that all have the same type. Array names follow the same conventions that apply to other variable names. To refer to a particular element in an array, we specify the name of the array and the *position number* of the element to which we refer. Position numbers are values that indicate specific locations within arrays.

Figure 8.1 shows a logical representation of an integer array called c. This array contains 12 elements, any one of which can be referred to by giving the name of the array followed by the position number of the element in parentheses (). The first element in every array is the *zeroth element.* Thus, the elements of array c are c(0), c(1), c(2) and so on. The highest position number in array c is 11, which is 1 less than 12—the number of elements in the array.

The position number in parentheses more formally is called an *index* (or a *subscript*). An index must be a non-negative integer or integer expression. If a program uses an expression as an index, the expression is evaluated first to determine the index. For example, if variable value1 is equal to 5, and variable value2 is equal to 6, then the statement

```
c(value1 + value2) += 2
```

adds 2 to array element c(11). Note that an *indexed array name* (i.e., the array name followed by an index enclosed in parentheses) is an *lvalue*—it can be used on the left side of an assignment statement to place a new value into an array element.

Let us examine array c in Fig. 8.1 more closely. The name of the array is c. The 12 elements of the array are referred to as c(0) through c(11)—pronounced as "c sub zero" through "c sub 11," where "sub" derives from "subscript." The value of c(0) is -45, the value of c(1) is 6, the value of c(2) is 0, the value of c(7) is 62 and the value of c(11) is 78. Values stored in arrays can be employed in calculations. For example, to determine the total of the values contained in the first three elements of array c and then store the result in variable sum, we would write

```
sum = c(0) + c(1) + c(2)
```

Name of array, c

c(0)	-45
c(1)	6
c(2)	0
c(3)	72
c(4)	1543
c(5)	-89
c(6)	0
c(7)	62
c(8)	-3
c(9)	1
c(10)	6453
c(11)	78

Index (or subcript) of the element in array c

Fig. 8.1 | Array consisting of 12 elements.

To divide the value of c(6) by 2 and assign the result to the variable result, we would write

```
result = c(6) \ 2
```

 Common Programming Error 8.1

It is important to note the difference between the "seventh element of the array" and "array element seven." Array indices begin at 0, which means that the "seventh element of the array" has the index 6, whereas "array element seven" has the index 7 and is actually the eighth element of the array. This confusion is a common source of "off-by-one" errors. We will avoid such terminology; instead, we refer to all array elements simply by their indexed names—such as c(0) rather than "the first element of c."

Every array in Visual Basic "knows" its own length. The *length* of array c (i.e., 12) is determined by the following expression:

```
c.Length
```

All arrays have access to the methods and properties of class **System.Array**, including the **Length property**. For instance, method **GetUpperBound** returns the index of the last element in the array. Method GetUpperBound takes one argument indicating a dimension of the array (e.g., 0 for the first dimension, 1 for the second dimension, etc.). We discuss arrays with multiple dimensions in Section 8.9. For one-dimensional arrays, such as c, the argument passed to GetUpperBound is 0. For example, the expression

```
c.GetUpperBound(0)
```

returns 11. Note that the value returned by method GetUpperBound is one less than the value of the array's Length property.

8.3 Declaring and Allocating Arrays

Arrays occupy space in memory. The amount of memory required by an array depends on the length of the array and the size of the type of the elements in the array. To declare an array, provide the array's name and type. Either of the following statements can be used to declare the array in Fig. 8.1:

```
Dim c As Integer()
Dim c() As Integer
```

The parentheses that follow the type indicate that c is an array. Arrays can be declared to contain elements of any type; every element of the array is of that type. For example, every element of an Integer array contains an Integer value.

Before an array can be used, you must specify the size of the array and allocate memory for the array, using keyword New. Recall from Chapter 4 that keyword New creates an object. Arrays are objects in Visual Basic, so they too must be allocated using keyword New. The value stored in the array variable is actually a reference to the location in the computer's memory where the array object is stored. All non-primitive and non-structure type variables (such as arrays) are reference variables (normally called references).

The statement

```
c = New Integer(11) {}
```

allocates memory for the array c after it has been declared. In our example, the number 11 defines the upper bound for the array. *Array bounds* determine what indices can be used to access an element in the array. Here the array bounds are 0 (which is implicit in the preceding statement and is always the lower bound of every array) and 11—an index outside these bounds cannot be used to access elements in the array c. Note that the actual size of the array is one larger (12) than the upper bound specified in the allocation. We also can explicitly specify the array bounds, as in

```
c = New Integer(0 To 11) {}
```

The *explicit array bounds* specified in the preceding statement indicate that the lower bound of the array is 0 and the upper bound is 11. Note that the size of the array is still 12.

 Common Programming Error 8.2

Explicitly setting the lower bound of an array to a value other than 0 is a compilation error.

The required braces ({ and }) are called an *initializer list* and specify the initial values of the elements in the array. When the initializer list is empty, the elements in the array are initialized to the default value for the type of the elements of the array. Again, the default value is 0 for numeric primitive data-type variables, False for Boolean variables and Nothing for references. The initializer list also can contain a comma-separated list specifying the initial values of the elements in the array. For instance,

```
Dim numbers As Integer()
numbers = New Integer() {1, 2, 3, 6}
```

declares and allocates an array containing four Integer values. Visual Basic can determine the array bounds from the number of elements in the initializer list—it is not necessary to specify the upper bound of the array when a non-empty initializer list is present. When you explicitly state the upper bound and a non-empty initializer list, make sure that the upper bound of the array is one less than the number of elements in the initializer list; otherwise, a compilation error occurs.

The two preceding statements can be combined into a single statement, as in

```
Dim numbers As Integer() = New Integer() {1, 2, 3, 6}
```

8.4 Examples Using Arrays

This section presents several examples that demonstrate the declaration, allocation and initialization of arrays, as well as various common manipulations of array elements. The examples in this section use arrays that contain elements of type Integer.

8.4.1 Allocating an Array

The program in Fig. 8.2 uses the New operator to allocate an array of 10 Integer elements, which are initially zero (the default value for Integer variables). The program displays the array elements in tabular format in a console window.

```
 1   ' Fig. 8.2: CreateArray.vb
 2   ' Declaring and allocating an array.
 3   Module CreateArray
 4      Sub Main()
 5         Dim array As Integer() ' declare array variable
 6
 7         ' allocate memory for 10-element array using explicit array bounds
 8         array = New Integer(0 To 9) {}
 9
10         Console.WriteLine("Index " & vbTab & "Value")
11
12         ' display values in array
13         For i As Integer = 0 To array.GetUpperBound(0)
14            Console.WriteLine(i & vbTab & array(i))
15         Next
16
17         Console.WriteLine(vbCrLf & "The array contains " & _
18            array.Length & " elements.")
19      End Sub ' Main
20   End Module ' CreateArray
```

```
Index   Value
0       0
1       0
2       0
3       0
4       0
5       0
6       0
7       0
8       0
9       0

The array contains 10 elements.
```

Fig. 8.2 | Creating an array.

Line 5 declares array—a variable capable of storing a reference to an array of Integers. Line 8 allocates an array of 10 elements (with explicit array bounds 0 to 9) using New and assigns it to array. Line 10 displays the headings for the columns. The columns represent the index for each array element and the value of each array element, respectively.

Lines 13–15 use a For statement to display the index number (i) and the value of each array element (array(i)). We use zero-based counting (recall that array indices start at 0), so that the loop accesses every array element. Also note, in the header of the For statement, the expression array.GetUpperBound(0), used to retrieve the upper bound of the array (in this case, 9). The Length property (line 18) returns the number of elements in the array.

8.4.2 Initializing the Values in an Array

The program in Fig. 8.3 creates two integer arrays of 10 elements each and sets the values of the elements, using an initializer list and a For statement, respectively. The arrays are displayed in tabular format.

```vb
1    ' Fig. 8.3: InitArray.vb
2    ' Initializing arrays.
3    Module InitArray
4       Sub Main()
5          ' initializer list specifies the number of elements
6          ' and the value of each element
7          Dim array1 As Integer() = New Integer() _
8             {32, 27, 64, 18, 95, 14, 90, 70, 60, 37}
9
10         ' allocate array2 based on length of array1
11         Dim array2 As Integer() = New Integer(array1.GetUpperBound(0)) {}
12
13         ' set values in array2 by a calculation
14         For i As Integer = 0 To array2.GetUpperBound(0)
15            array2(i) = 2 + 2 * i ' generate 2, 4, 6, ..., 20
16         Next
17
18         Console.WriteLine("Index " & vbTab & "Array1" & vbTab & "Array2")
19
20         ' display values for both arrays side by side
21         For i As Integer = 0 To array1.GetUpperBound(0)
22            Console.WriteLine(i & vbTab & array1(i) & vbTab & array2(i))
23         Next
24      End Sub ' Main
25   End Module ' InitArray
```

```
Index   Array1  Array2
0       32      2
1       27      4
2       64      6
3       18      8
4       95      10
5       14      12
6       90      14
7       70      16
8       60      18
9       37      20
```

Fig. 8.3 | Initializing array elements with an array initializer and a For statement.

Lines 7–8 combine the declaration and allocation of array1 into one statement, allocate the 10 elements of array1 with New, and initialize the values in array1, using an initializer list. Line 11 declares and allocates array2, whose size is determined by the expression array1.GetUpperBound(0), meaning that array1 and array2, in this particular program, have the same upper bound (9) and the same size (10).

The For statement in lines 14–16 initializes the elements in array2 to the even integers 2, 4, 6, ..., 20. These numbers are generated by multiplying each successive value of the loop counter by 2 and adding 2 to the product. The For statement in lines 21–23 displays the values in the arrays.

8.4.3 Summing the Elements of an Array

Often, the elements of an array represent a series of values that are employed in a calculation. For example, if the elements of an array represent a group of students' exam grades, the instructor might wish to total the elements of the array, then calculate the class average for the exam. The program in Fig. 8.4 sums the values contained in a 10-element integer array.

Lines 5–6 declare, allocate and initialize the 10-element array `array`. Line 11, in the body of the `For` statement, performs the addition. Alternatively, the values supplied as initializers for `array` could have been read into the program. For example, the user could enter the values through a `TextBox`, or the values could be read from a file on disk. Information about reading values into a program from a file can be found in Chapter 18, Files and Streams.

8.4.4 Using Arrays to Analyze Survey Results

Our next example uses arrays to summarize data collected in a survey. Consider the following problem statement:

> *Forty students were asked to rate on a scale of 1 to 10 the quality of the food in the student cafeteria, with 1 being "awful" and 10 being "excellent." Place the 40 responses in an integer array and determine the frequency of each rating.*

This exercise represents a typical array-processing application (Fig. 8.5). We wish to summarize the number of responses of each type (i.e., 1–10). Array `responses` (lines 6–8) is a 40-element integer array containing the students' responses to the survey. Using an 11-element array `frequency`, we can count the number of occurrences of each response. We ignore `frequency(0)` because it is more natural to have a survey response of 1 result in `frequency(1)` being incremented rather than incrementing `frequency(0)`. We can use each response directly as an index on the `frequency` array. Each element of the array is used as a counter for one of the possible types of survey responses—`frequency(1)` counts the number of students who rated the food as 1, `frequency(2)` counts the number of students who rated the food as 2, and so on.

```
 1    ' Fig. 8.4: SumArray.vb
 2    ' Computing the sum of the elements in an array.
 3    Module SumArray
 4       Sub Main()
 5          Dim array As Integer() = New Integer() _
 6             {1, 2, 3, 4, 5, 6, 7, 8, 9, 10}
 7          Dim total As Integer = 0
 8
 9          ' sum the array element values
10          For i As Integer = 0 To array.GetUpperBound(0)
11             total += array(i)
12          Next
13
14          Console.WriteLine("Total of array elements: " & total)
15       End Sub ' Main
16    End Module ' SumArray
```

```
Total of array elements: 55
```

Fig. 8.4 | Computing the sum of the elements in an array .

```
 I    ' Fig. 8.5: StudentPoll.vb
 2    ' Using arrays to display poll results.
 3    Module StudentPoll
 4       Sub Main()
 5          ' student response array (more typically, input at run time)
 6          Dim responses As Integer() = New Integer() _
 7             {1, 2, 6, 4, 8, 5, 9, 7, 8, 10, 1, 6, 3, 8, 6, 10, 3, 8, 2, _
 8             7, 6, 5, 7, 6, 8, 6, 7, 5, 6, 6, 5, 6, 7, 5, 6, 4, 8, 6, 8, 10}
 9
10          ' response frequency array (indices 0 through 10)
11          Dim frequency As Integer() = New Integer(10) {}
12
13          ' count frequencies
14          For answer As Integer = 0 To responses.GetUpperBound(0)
15             frequency(responses(answer)) += 1
16          Next
17
18          Console.WriteLine("Rating " & vbTab & "Frequency ")
19
20          ' display output, ignore element 0 of frequency
21          For rating As Integer = 1 To frequency.GetUpperBound(0)
22             Console.WriteLine(rating & vbTab & frequency(rating))
23          Next
24       End Sub ' Main
25    End Module ' StudentPoll
```

```
Rating  Frequency
1       2
2       2
3       2
4       2
5       5
6       11
7       5
8       7
9       1
10      3
```

Fig. 8.5 | Simple student-poll analysis program.

The For statement (lines 14–16) reads the responses from the array responses one at a time and increments one of the 10 counters in the frequency array (frequency(1) to frequency(10); we ignore frequency(0) because the survey responses are limited to the range 1–10). The key statement in the loop appears in line 15. This statement increments the appropriate frequency counter as determined by the value of responses(answer).

Let us consider several iterations of the For statement. When the counter answer is 0, responses(answer) is the value of responses(0) (i.e., 1—see line 7). Therefore, frequency(responses(answer)) is interpreted as frequency(1), meaning that the counter frequency(1) is incremented by one. In evaluating the expression frequency(responses(answer)), Visual Basic starts with the value in the innermost set of parentheses (`answer`, currently 0). The value of `answer` is plugged into the expression, and Visual Basic evaluates the next set of parentheses (`responses(answer)`). That value is used as the index for the `frequency` array to determine which counter to increment (in this case, the 1 counter).

When `answer` is 1, `responses(answer)` is the value of `responses(1)` (i.e., 2—see line 7). As a result, `frequency(responses(answer))` is interpreted as `frequency(2)`, causing array element 2 to be incremented.

When `answer` is 2, `responses(answer)` is the value of `responses(2)` (i.e., 6—see line 7), so `frequency(responses(answer))` is interpreted as `frequency(6)`, causing array element 6 to be incremented, and so on. Note that, regardless of the number of responses processed in the survey, only an 11-element array (in which we ignore element zero) is required to summarize the results, because all the response values are between 1 and 10, and the index values for an 11-element array are 0–10. Note that, in the output in Fig. 8.5, the numbers in the frequency column correctly total 40 (the elements of the `frequency` array were initialized to zero when the array was allocated with `New`).

If the data contained the out-of-range value 13, the program would attempt to add 1 to `frequency(13)`. This is outside the bounds of the array. In languages like C and C++, such a dangerous out-of-bounds reference would be allowed. The program would "walk" past the end of the array to where it thought element number 13 was located and would add 1 to whatever happened to be stored at that memory location. This could modify another variable in the program, possibly causing incorrect results or even premature program termination. Visual Basic provides mechanisms that prevent accessing elements outside the bounds of arrays.

Common Programming Error 8.3

Referencing an element outside the array bounds is a runtime error.

Error-Prevention Tip 8.1

When a program is executed, array element indices are checked for validity (i.e., all indices must be greater than or equal to 0 and less than the length of the array). If an attempt is made to use an invalid index to access an element, Visual Basic generates an `IndexOutOfRangeException` exception. Exceptions are discussed in detail in Chapter 12, Exception Handling.

Error-Prevention Tip 8.2

When looping through an array, the array index should remain between 0 and the upper bound of the array (i.e., the value returned by method `GetUpperBound`). The initial and final values used in the repetition statement should prevent accessing elements outside this range.

8.4.5 Using Bar Charts to Display Array Data Graphically

Many programs present data to users in a visual or graphical format. For example, numeric values are often displayed as bars in a bar chart. In such a chart, longer bars represent proportionally larger numeric values. Figure 8.6 displays numeric data graphically by creating a bar chart that shows each numeric value as a bar of asterisks (*).

The program reads numbers from an array and graphs the information as a bar chart. Each number is printed, and a bar consisting of the corresponding number of asterisks is

```vb
 1   ' Fig. 8.6: BarChart.vb
 2   ' Using data to create bar chart.
 3   Module BarChart
 4      Sub Main()
 5         ' create data array
 6         Dim array1 As Integer() = New Integer() _
 7            {19, 3, 15, 7, 11, 9, 13, 5, 17, 1}
 8
 9         Console.WriteLIne("Element " & "Value " & vbTab & "Bar Chart")
10
11         ' display a bar of the bar chart for each element in the array
12         For i As Integer = 0 To array1.GetUpperBound(0)
13            Console.Write(i & vbTab & array1(i) & vbTab)
14
15            For j As Integer = 1 To array1(i)
16               Console.Write("*") ' display one asterisk
17            Next
18
19            Console.WriteLine()
20         Next
21      End Sub ' Main
22   End Module ' BarChart
```

```
Element Value   Bar Chart
0       19      ********************
1       3       ***
2       15      ***************
3       7       *******
4       11      ***********
5       9       *********
6       13      *************
7       5       *****
8       17      *****************
9       1       *
```

Fig. 8.6 | Bar chart printing program.

displayed beside the number. The nested For loops (lines 12–20) display the bars. Note the end value (array1(i)) of the inner For statement at line 15. Each time the inner For statement is reached (line 15), it counts from 1 to array1(i), using a value in array1 to determine the final value of the control variable j—the number of asterisks to display.

8.4.6 Using the Elements of an Array as Counters

Sometimes programs use a series of counter variables to summarize data, such as the results of a survey. In Chapter 7, we used a series of counters in our die-rolling program to track the number of occurrences of each face on a six-sided die as the program rolled the die 12 times. We indicated that there is a more elegant way of doing what we did in Fig. 7.16 for writing the dice-rolling program. An array version of this application is shown in Fig. 8.7. The images of the dice are included in this example's directory.

```vb
1    ' Fig. 8.7: RollDie.vb
2    ' Rolling 12 dice with frequency chart.
3    Imports System.IO
4
5    Public Class FrmRollDie
6       Dim randomNumber As Random = New Random()
7       Dim frequency As Integer() = New Integer(6) {}
8
9       ' event handler for btnRoll button
10      Private Sub btnRoll_Click(ByVal sender As System.Object, _
11         ByVal e As System.EventArgs) Handles btnRoll.Click
12
13         ' pass PictureBox to a method that assigns a face to each die
14         DisplayDie(picDie1)
15         DisplayDie(picDie2)
16         DisplayDie(picDie3)
17         DisplayDie(picDie4)
18         DisplayDie(picDie5)
19         DisplayDie(picDie6)
20         DisplayDie(picDie7)
21         DisplayDie(picDie8)
22         DisplayDie(picDie9)
23         DisplayDie(picDie10)
24         DisplayDie(picDie11)
25         DisplayDie(picDie12)
26
27         Dim total As Double = 0
28
29         ' total the die faces (used in percentage calculations)
30         For i As Integer = 1 To frequency.GetUpperBound(0)
31            total += frequency(i)
32         Next
33
34         txtDisplay.Text = "Face" & vbTab & "Frequency" & _
35            vbTab & "Percent" & vbCrLf
36
37         ' output frequency values
38         For i As Integer = 1 To frequency.GetUpperBound(0)
39            txtDisplay.Text &= i & vbTab & frequency(i) & _
40               vbTab & vbTab & String.Format("{0:N}", _
41               frequency(i) / total * 100) & "%" & vbCrLf
42         Next
43      End Sub ' btnRoll_Click
44
45      ' simulate roll, display proper image and increment frequency
46      Sub DisplayDie(ByVal picDie As PictureBox)
47         Dim face As Integer = 1 + randomNumber.Next(6)
48
49         ' set appropriate die image in Image property
50         picDie.Image = _
51            Image.FromFile(Directory.GetCurrentDirectory & _
52            "\Images\die" & face & ".png")
```

Fig. 8.7 | Using arrays to eliminate a Select Case statement. (Part 1 of 2.)

```
53          frequency(face) += 1 ' increment appropriate frequency counter
54      End Sub ' DisplayDie
55  End Class ' FrmRollDie
```

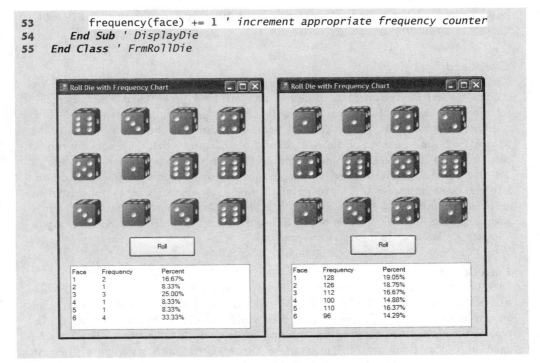

Fig. 8.7 | Using arrays to eliminate a Select Case statement. (Part 2 of 2.)

Lines 60–73 of Fig. 7.16 are replaced by line 53 of Fig. 8.7, which uses face's value as the index for array frequency to determine which element should be incremented during each iteration of the loop. The random number calculation at line 47 produces numbers from 1to 6 (the values for a six-sided die); thus, the frequency array must have seven elements to allow the index values 1–6. We ignore element 0 of array frequency. Lines 34–42 replace lines 36–49 from Fig. 7.16. We can loop through array frequency; therefore, we do not have to enumerate each line of text to display in the PictureBox, as we did in Fig. 7.16.

8.5 Case Study: Card Shuffling and Dealing Simulation

The examples in the chapter thus far have used arrays containing elements of primitive types. Recall from Section 8.2 that the elements of an array can be of either primitive types or reference types. This section uses random number generation and an array of reference-type elements, namely references to objects representing playing cards, to develop a class that simulates card shuffling and dealing. You can then use this class to implement applications that play specific card games.

First, we develop class Card (Fig. 8.8), which represents a playing card that has a face (e.g., "Ace", "Deuce", "Three", ..., "Jack", "Queen", "King") and a suit (e.g., "Hearts", "Diamonds", "Clubs", "Spades"). Next, we develop the DeckOfCards class (Fig. 8.9), which creates a deck of 52 playing cards in which each element is a Card object. We then build a test application DeckOfCardsTest (Fig. 8.10) that demonstrates class DeckOf-Cards's card shuffling and dealing capabilities.

Class Card

Class Card (Fig. 8.8) contains two String instance variables—face and suit—that are used to store references to the face name and suit name for a specific Card. The constructor for the class (lines 8–11) receives two Strings that it uses to initialize face and suit. Method ToString (lines 14–16) creates a String consisting of the face of the card, the String " of " and the suit of the card. Recall from Chapter 3 that the & operator can be used to concatenate (i.e., combine) several Strings to form one larger String. Card's ToString method can be invoked explicitly to obtain a string representation of a Card object (e.g., "Ace of Spades"). The ToString method of an object is called implicitly when an object is output as a String. For this behavior to occur, ToString must be declared with the header shown in line 14 of Fig. 8.8. We discuss the special method ToString in Chapter 9, Classes and Objects: A Deeper Look.

Class DeckOfCards

Class DeckOfCards (Fig. 8.9) declares an instance variable array named deck, which consists of Card objects (line 4). Like primitive-type array declarations, the declaration of an array of objects includes the name of the array variable, followed by the keyword As, the type of the elements in the array and parentheses (e.g., deck As Card()). Class DeckOf-Cards also declares an integer instance variable currentCard (line 5) representing the next Card to be dealt from the deck array and a named constant NUMBER_OF_CARDS (line 6) indicating the number of Cards in the deck (52).

The class's constructor instantiates the deck array (line 15) with upper bound NUMBER_OF_CARDS - 1. When first created, the elements of the deck array are Nothing by default, so the constructor uses a For statement (lines 20–22) to fill the deck array with Cards. This statement initializes control variable count to 0 and loops while count is less

```vb
1   ' Fig. 8.8: Card.vb
2   ' Card class represents a playing card.
3   Public Class Card
4      Private face As String ' face of card ("Ace", "Deuce", ...)
5      Private suit As String ' suit of card ("Hearts", "Diamonds", ...)
6
7      ' two-argument constructor initializes card's face and suit
8      Public Sub New(ByVal cardFace As String, ByVal cardSuit As String)
9         face = cardFace ' initialize face of card
10        suit = cardSuit ' initialize suit of card
11     End Sub ' New
12
13     ' return String representation of Card, Overrides defined in Ch 9
14     Public Overrides Function ToString() As String
15        Return face & " of " & suit
16     End Function ' ToString
17  End Class ' Card
```

Fig. 8.8 | Card class represents a playing card.

than or equal to deck.GetUpperBound(0), causing count to take on each integer value from 0 to 51 (the indices of the deck array). Each Card is instantiated and initialized with two Strings—one from the faces array (which contains the Strings "Ace" through "King") and one from the suits array (which contains the Strings "Hearts", "Diamonds", "Clubs" and "Spades"). The calculation count Mod 13 always results in a value from 0 to 12 (the 13 indices of the faces array in lines 11–12), and the calculation count \ 13 always results in a value from 0 to 3 (the four indices of the suits array in line 13). When the deck array is initialized, it contains the Cards with faces "Ace" through "King" in order for each suit.

```vb
1   ' Fig. 8.9: DeckOfCards.vb
2   ' DeckOfCards class represents a deck of playing cards.
3   Public Class DeckOfCards
4      Private deck As Card() ' array of Card objects
5      Private currentCard As Integer ' index of next Card to be dealt
6      Private Const NUMBER_OF_CARDS As Integer = 52 ' number of cards
7      Private randomNumbers As Random ' random number generator
8
9      ' constructor fills deck of Cards
10     Public Sub New()
11        Dim faces As String() = {"Ace", "Deuce", "Three", "Four", "Five", _
12           "Six", "Seven", "Eight", "Nine", "Ten", "Jack", "Queen", "King"}
13        Dim suits As String() = {"Hearts", "Diamonds", "Clubs", "Spades"}
14
15        deck = New Card(NUMBER_OF_CARDS - 1) {} ' create array of Cards
16        currentCard = 0 ' set currentCard so first Card dealt is deck(0)
17        randomNumbers = New Random() ' create random number generator
18
19        ' populate deck with Card objects
20        For count As Integer = 0 To deck.GetUpperBound(0)
21           deck(count) = New Card(faces(count Mod 13), suits(count \ 13))
22        Next
23     End Sub ' New
24
25     ' shuffle deck of Cards with simple one-pass algorithm
26     Public Sub Shuffle()
27        ' after shuffling, dealing should start at deck(0) again
28        currentCard = 0 ' reinitialize currentCard
29
30        ' for each Card, pick another random Card and swap them
31        For first As Integer = 0 To deck.GetUpperBound(0)
32           ' select a random number between 0 and 51
33           Dim second As Integer = randomNumbers.Next(NUMBER_OF_CARDS)
34
35           ' swap current Card with randomly selected Card
36           Dim temp As Card = deck(first)
37           deck(first) = deck(second)
38           deck(second) = temp
39        Next
40     End Sub ' Shuffle
```

Fig. 8.9 | DeckOfCards class represents a deck of playing cards that can be shuffled and dealt one at a time. (Part 1 of 2.)

```
41
42        ' deal one Card
43        Public Function DealCard() As Card
44            ' determine whether Cards remain to be dealt
45            If currentCard <= deck.GetUpperBound(0) Then
46                Dim lastCard = currentCard ' store current card number
47                currentCard += 1 ' increment current card number
48                Return deck(lastCard)
49            Else
50                Return Nothing
51            End If
52        End Function ' DealCard
53    End Class ' DeckOfCards
```

Fig. 8.9 | DeckOfCards class represents a deck of playing cards that can be shuffled and dealt one at a time. (Part 2 of 2.)

Method Shuffle (lines 26–40) shuffles the Cards in the deck. The method loops through all 52 Cards (array indices 0 to 51). For each Card, a number between 0 and 51 is picked randomly to select another Card (line 33). Next, the current Card object and the randomly selected Card object are swapped in the array (lines 36–38). The extra variable temp temporarily stores one of the two Card objects being swapped. The swap cannot be performed with only the two statements

```
deck(first) = deck(second)
deck(second) = deck(first)
```

If deck(first) is the "Ace" of "Spades" and deck(second) is the "Queen" of "Hearts", after the first assignment, both array elements contain the "Queen" of "Hearts" and the "Ace" of "Spades" is lost—hence, the extra variable temp is needed. After the For loop terminates, the Card objects are randomly ordered. Only 52 swaps are made in a single pass of the entire array, and the array of Card objects is shuffled!

Method DealCard (lines 43–52) deals one Card in the array. Recall that currentCard indicates the index of the next Card to be dealt (i.e., the Card at the top of the deck). Thus, line 45 compares currentCard to the upper bound (51) of the deck array. If the deck is not empty (i.e., currentCard is less than or equal to 51), line 46 assigns currentCard (the index of the card that will be returned) to temporary variable lastCard, line 47 increments currentCard to prepare for the next call to DealCard and line 48 returns deck(lastCard), which represents the top card of the deck for this call to DealCard. Otherwise, DealCard returns Nothing to indicate that the deck is empty.

Shuffling and Dealing Cards
The application in Fig. 8.10 demonstrates the card dealing and shuffling capabilities of class DeckOfCards (Fig. 8.9). Line 5 creates a DeckOfCards object named cards. Recall that the DeckOfCards constructor creates the deck with the 52 Card objects in order by suit and face. Line 6 invokes cards's Shuffle method to randomly rearrange the Card objects. The For statement in lines 9–13 deals all 52 Cards in the deck and prints them in four columns of 13 Cards each. Lines 10–12 deal and print four Card objects (on one line), each obtained by invoking cards's DealCard method. When Console.WriteLine outputs

```
 1   ' Fig. 8.10: DeckOfCardsTest.vb
 2   ' Card shuffling and dealing application.
 3   Module DeckOfCardsTest
 4      Sub Main()
 5         Dim cards As New DeckOfCards()
 6         cards.Shuffle() ' place Cards in random order
 7
 8         ' print all 52 Cards in the order in which they are dealt
 9         For i As Integer = 0 To 12
10            Console.WriteLine("{0, -18} {1, -18} {2, -18} {3, -18}", _
11               cards.DealCard(), cards.DealCard(), cards.DealCard(), _
12               cards.DealCard())
13         Next
14      End Sub ' Main
15   End Module ' DeckOfCardsTest
```

Five of Spades	Nine of Spades	Seven of Hearts	Eight of Clubs
Jack of Spades	Seven of Clubs	Queen of Spades	Ace of Diamonds
Ace of Clubs	Five of Hearts	Ten of Diamonds	Queen of Diamonds
Nine of Diamonds	Four of Hearts	Six of Spades	Six of Diamonds
Ace of Hearts	King of Spades	Jack of Diamonds	Seven of Spades
Four of Spades	Seven of Diamonds	Ten of Spades	Eight of Spades
Deuce of Spades	King of Diamonds	Deuce of Hearts	Nine of Hearts
Three of Clubs	King of Hearts	Six of Hearts	Queen of Hearts
Eight of Hearts	Ten of Hearts	Five of Clubs	King of Clubs
Five of Diamonds	Jack of Clubs	Jack of Hearts	Eight of Diamonds
Six of Clubs	Deuce of Clubs	Ace of Spades	Three of Hearts
Four of Diamonds	Ten of Clubs	Nine of Clubs	Three of Spades
Queen of Clubs	Deuce of Diamonds	Three of Diamonds	Four of Clubs

Fig. 8.10 | Card shuffling and dealing (all 52 cards are dealt).

a Card with the {0, -18} format specifier, the Card's ToString method (declared in lines 14–16 of Fig. 8.8) is implicitly invoked, and the result is output left justified (because of the minus sign in -18) in a field of width 18. Again, we explain ToString in detail in Chapter 9.

8.6 Passing an Array to a Method

To pass an array argument to a method, specify the name of the array without using parentheses. For example, if array hourlyTemperatures has been declared as

```
Dim hourlyTemperatures As Integer() = New Integer(24) {}
```

the method call

```
DayData(hourlyTemperatures)
```

passes array hourlyTemperatures to method DayData.

Every array object "knows" its own upper bound (i.e., the value returned by the method GetUpperBound), so when you pass an array object to a method, you do not need to pass the upper bound of the array as a separate argument.

For a method to receive an array through a method call, the method's parameter list must specify that an array will be received. For example, the method header for DayData might be written as

Sub DayData(**ByVal** temperatureData **As Integer**())

indicating that DayData expects to receive an Integer array in parameter temperatureData. In Visual Basic, arrays always are passed by reference, yet it is normally inappropriate to use keyword ByRef in the method definition header. We discuss this subtle (and somewhat complex) issue in more detail in Section 8.14.

Although entire arrays are always passed by reference, individual array elements can be passed in the same manner as simple variables of that type. For instance, array element values of primitive types, such as Integer, can be passed either by value or by reference, depending on the method definition. To pass an array element to a method, use the indexed name of the array element as an argument in the method call. The program in Fig. 8.11 demonstrates the difference between passing an entire array and passing an array element.

The For...Next statement in lines 12–14 displays the five elements of integer array array1 (line 5). Line 16 passes array1 to method ModifyArray (lines 42–46), which then multiplies each element by 2 (line 44). To illustrate that array1's elements were modified in the called method (i.e., as enabled by passing by reference), the For...Next statement in lines 20–22 displays the five elements of array1. As the output indicates, the elements of array1 are indeed modified by ModifyArray.

To show the value of array1(3) before the call to ModifyElementByVal, lines 24–27 display the value of array1(3). Line 29 invokes method ModifyElementByVal (lines 50–56) and passes array1(3). When array1(3) is passed by value, the Integer value in position 3 of array array1 (now an 8) is copied and is passed to method ModifyElementByVal, where it becomes the value of parameter element. Method ModifyElementByVal then multiplies element by 2 (line 53). The parameter element of ModifyElementByVal is a local variable that is destroyed when the method terminates. Thus, when control is returned to Main, the unmodified value of array1(3) is displayed.

```
1   ' Fig. 8.11: PassArray.vb
2   ' Passing arrays and individual array elements to methods.
3   Module PassArray
4      Sub Main()
5         Dim array1 As Integer() = New Integer() {1, 2, 3, 4, 5}
6
7         Console.WriteLine("EFFECTS OF PASSING AN ENTIRE ARRAY " & _
8            "BY REFERENCE:" & vbCrLf & vbCrLf & _
9            "The values of the original array are:")
10
11         ' display original elements of array1
12         For i As Integer = 0 To array1.GetUpperBound(0)
13            Console.Write("  " & array1(i))
14         Next
15
```

Fig. 8.11 | Passing arrays and individual array elements to methods. (Part 1 of 3.)

```vbnet
16          ModifyArray(array1) ' array is passed by reference
17          Console.WriteLine(vbCrLf & "The values of the modified array are:")
18
19          ' display modified elements of array1
20          For i As Integer = 0 To array1.GetUpperBound(0)
21             Console.Write("  " & array1(i))
22          Next
23
24          Console.WriteLine(vbCrLf & vbCrLf & _
25             "EFFECTS OF PASSING AN ARRAY ELEMENT BY VALUE:" & _
26             vbCrLf & vbCrLf & "array1(3) before ModifyElementByVal: " & _
27             array1(3))
28
29          ModifyElementByVal(array1(3)) ' array element passed by value
30          Console.WriteLine("array1(3) after ModifyElementByVal: " & _
31             array1(3))
32          Console.WriteLine(vbCrLf & "EFFECTS OF PASSING AN " & _
33             "ARRAY ELEMENT BY REFERENCE: " & vbCrLf & vbCrLf & _
34             "array1(3) before ModifyElementByRef: " & array1(3))
35
36          ModifyElementByRef(array1(3)) ' array element passed by reference
37          Console.WriteLine("array1(3) after ModifyElementByRef: " & _
38             array1(3))
39       End Sub ' Main
40
41       ' method modifies array it receives (note ByVal)
42       Sub ModifyArray(ByVal arrayParameter As Integer())
43          For j As Integer = 0 To arrayParameter.GetUpperBound(0)
44             arrayParameter(j) *= 2 ' double the array element
45          Next
46       End Sub ' ModifyArray
47
48       ' method modifies integer passed to it
49       ' original is not modified (note ByVal)
50       Sub ModifyElementByVal(ByVal element As Integer)
51          Console.WriteLine("Value received in ModifyElementByVal: " & _
52             element)
53          element *= 2 ' double the array element
54          Console.WriteLine("Value calculated in ModifyElementByVal: " & _
55             element)
56       End Sub ' ModifyElementByVal
57
58       ' method modifies integer passed to it
59       ' original is modified (note ByRef)
60       Sub ModifyElementByRef(ByRef element As Integer)
61          Console.WriteLine("Value received in ModifyElementByRef: " & _
62             element)
63          element *= 2 ' double the array element
64          Console.WriteLine("Value calculated in ModifyElementByRef: " & _
65             element)
66       End Sub ' ModifyElementByRef
67    End Module ' PassArray
```

Fig. 8.11 | Passing arrays and individual array elements to methods. (Part 2 of 3.)

```
EFFECTS OF PASSING AN ENTIRE ARRAY BY REFERENCE:

The values of the original array are:
   1   2   3   4   5
The values of the modified array are:
   2   4   6   8   10

EFFECTS OF PASSING AN ARRAY ELEMENT BY VALUE:

array1(3) before ModifyElementByVal: 8
Value received in ModifyElementByVal: 8
Value calculated in ModifyElementByVal: 16
array1(3) after ModifyElementByVal: 8

EFFECTS OF PASSING AN ARRAY ELEMENT BY REFERENCE:

array1(3) before ModifyElementByRef: 8
Value received in ModifyElementByRef: 8
Value calculated in ModifyElementByRef: 16
array1(3) after ModifyElementByRef: 16
```

Fig. 8.11 | Passing arrays and individual array elements to methods. (Part 3 of 3.)

Lines 32–38 demonstrate the effects of method ModifyElementByRef (lines 60–66). This method performs the same calculation as ModifyElementByVal, multiplying element by 2. In this case, array1(3) is passed by reference, meaning that the value of array1(3) displayed (lines 37–38) is the same as the value calculated in the method (i.e., the original value in the caller is modified by the called method).

 Common Programming Error 8.4

When passing an array to a method, including an empty pair of parentheses after the array name is a syntax error.

8.7 For Each...Next Repetition Statement

Visual Basic provides the *For Each...Next* repetition statement for iterating through the values in a data structure, such as an array, without using a loop counter. When used with one-dimensional arrays, For Each...Next behaves like a For...Next statement that iterates through the range of indices from 0 to the value returned by GetUpperBound(0). Instead of a counter, For Each...Next uses a variable to represent the value of each element. The program in Fig. 8.12 uses the For Each...Next statement to determine the minimum value in a one-dimensional array of grades.

The header of the For Each repetition statement (line 10) specifies an Integer variable (grade) and an array (gradeArray). The For Each statement iterates through all the elements in gradeArray, sequentially assigning each value to variable grade. The values are compared to variable lowGrade (line 11), which stores the lowest grade in the array.

For one-dimensional arrays, the repetition of the For Each...Next statement begins with the element whose index is zero, then iterates through all the indices. In this case, grade takes on the successive values as they are ordered in the initializer list in line 6. When

```
1    ' Fig. 8.12: ForEach.vb
2    ' Program uses For Each...Next to find the minimum grade.
3    Module ForEach
4       Sub Main()
5          Dim gradeArray As Integer() = New Integer() _
6             {77, 68, 86, 73, 98, 87, 89, 81, 70, 90, 86, 81}
7          Dim lowGrade As Integer = 100
8
9             ' use For Each...Next to find the minimum grade
10            For Each grade As Integer In gradeArray
11               If grade < lowGrade Then
12                  lowGrade = grade
13               End If
14            Next
15
16            Console.WriteLine("The minimum grade is: {0}", lowGrade)
17       End Sub ' Main
18    End Module ' ForEach
```

```
The minimum grade is: 68
```

Fig. 8.12 | Using For Each...Next with an array.

all the grades have been processed, lowGrade is displayed. Although many array calculations are handled best with a counter, For Each is useful when the indices of the elements are not important.

8.8 GradeBook Case Study: Using an Array to Store Grades

This section further evolves class GradeBook, introduced in Chapter 4 and expanded in Chapters 5–6. Recall that this class represents a grade book used by a professor to store and analyze a set of student grades. Previous versions of the class process a set of grades entered by the user, but do not maintain the individual grade values in instance variables of the class. Thus, repeat calculations require the user to reenter the same grades. One way to solve this problem would be to store each grade entered in an instance of the class. For example, we could create instance variables grade1, grade2, ..., grade10 in class GradeBook to store 10 student grades. However, the code to total the grades and determine the class average would be cumbersome, and the class would not be able to process any more than 10 grades at a time. In this section, we solve the problem by storing the grades in an array.

Storing Student Grades in an Array in Class GradeBook

The version of class GradeBook (Fig. 8.13) presented here uses an array of Integers to store the grades of several students on a single exam. This eliminates the need to repeatedly input the same set of grades. Array grades is declared as an instance variable in line 5—therefore, each GradeBook object maintains its own set of grades. The class's constructor (lines 8–11) has two parameters—the name of the course and an array of grades. When an application (e.g., class GradeBookTest in Fig. 8.14) creates a GradeBook object, the application passes an existing Integer array to the constructor, which assigns the array's reference to instance variable grades (line 10). The size of the array grades is determined by the class that passes the array to the constructor. Thus, a GradeBook object can process a variable number of grades. The grade values in the passed array could have been input from a user or read from a file on disk (as discussed in Chapter 18). In our test application, we simply initialize an array with a set of grade values (Fig. 8.14, lines 6–7). Once the grades are stored in instance variable grades of class GradeBook, all the class's methods can access the elements of grades as needed to perform various calculations.

Method ProcessGrades (lines 31–43) contains a series of method calls that result in the output of a report summarizing the grades. Line 32 calls method OutputGrades to print the contents of the array grades. Lines 124–127 in method OutputGrades use a For statement to output each student's grade. Lines 125–126 use counter variable student's value to output each grade next to a particular student number (see the output in

```vb
 1    ' Fig. 8.13: GradeBook.vb
 2    ' GradeBook class uses an array to store test grades.
 3    Public Class GradeBook
 4       Private courseNameValue As String ' name of course
 5       Private grades As Integer() ' array of student grades
 6
 7       ' two-argument constructor initializes courseNameValue and grades
 8       Public Sub New(ByVal name As String, ByVal gradesArray As Integer())
 9          CourseName = name ' initializes courseNameValue via property
10          grades = gradesArray ' store reference to gradesArray
11       End Sub ' New
12
13       ' property CourseName
14       Public Property CourseName() As String
15          Get
16             Return courseNameValue
17          End Get
18
19          Set(ByVal name As String)
20             courseNameValue = name
21          End Set
22       End Property ' Course Name
23
24       ' display a welcome message to the GradeBook user
25       Public Sub DisplayMessage()
26          Console.WriteLine("Welcome to the grade book for " & vbCrLf & _
27             CourseName & vbCrLf)
28       End Sub ' DisplayMessage
29
30       ' perform various operations on the data
31       Public Sub ProcessGrades()
32          OutputGrades() ' output grades array
33
```

Fig. 8.13 | GradeBook class using an array to store test grades. (Part 1 of 3.)

```vb
34          ' call method GetAverage to calculate the average grade
35          Console.WriteLine("Class average is {0:F2}", GetAverage())
36
37          ' call methods GetMinimum and GetMaximum
38          Console.WriteLine("Lowest grade is {0}", GetMinimum())
39          Console.WriteLine("Highest grade is {0}", GetMaximum())
40
41          ' call OutputBarChart to print grade distribution chart
42          OutputBarChart()
43      End Sub ' ProcessGrades
44
45      ' find minimum grade
46      Public Function GetMinimum() As Integer
47          Dim lowGrade As Integer = grades(0) ' assume grades(0) is smallest
48
49          ' loop through grades array
50          For Each grade As Integer In grades
51              ' if grade lower than lowGrade, assign it to lowGrade
52              If grade < lowGrade Then
53                  lowGrade = grade ' new lowest grade
54              End If
55          Next
56
57          Return lowGrade ' return lowest grade
58      End Function ' GetMinimum
59
60      ' find maximum grade
61      Public Function GetMaximum() As Integer
62          Dim highGrade As Integer = grades(0) ' assume grades(0) is largest
63
64          ' loop through grades array
65          For Each grade As Integer In grades
66              ' if grade greater than highGrade, assign it to highGrade
67              If grade > highGrade Then
68                  highGrade = grade ' new highest grade
69              End If
70          Next
71
72          Return highGrade ' return highest grade
73      End Function ' GetMaximum
74
75      ' determine average grade for test
76      Public Function GetAverage() As Double
77          Dim total As Integer = 0 ' initialize total
78
79          ' sum grades for one student
80          For Each grade As Integer In grades
81              total += grade
82          Next
83
84          ' return average of grades
85          Return (total / grades.Length)
86      End Function ' GetAverage
```

Fig. 8.13 | GradeBook class using an array to store test grades. (Part 2 of 3.)

```
 87
 88        ' output bar chart displaying grade distribution
 89        Public Sub OutputBarChart()
 90           Console.WriteLine(vbCrLf & "Grade distribution:")
 91
 92           ' stores frequency of grades in each range of 10 grades
 93           Dim frequency As Integer() = New Integer(10) {}
 94
 95           ' for each grade, increment the appropriate frequency
 96           For Each grade As Integer In grades
 97              frequency(grade \ 10) += 1
 98           Next
 99
100           ' for each grade frequency, print bar in chart
101           For count As Integer = 0 To frequency.GetUpperBound(0)
102              ' output bar label ( "00-09: ", ..., "90-99: ", "100: " )
103              If count = 10 Then
104                 Console.Write("{0, 5:D}: ", 100)
105              Else
106                 Console.Write("{0, 2:D2}-{1, 2:D2}: ", _
107                    count * 10, count * 10 + 9)
108              End If
109
110              ' print bar of asterisks
111              For stars As Integer = 0 To frequency(count) - 1
112                 Console.Write("*")
113              Next
114
115              Console.WriteLine() ' start a new line of output
116           Next
117        End Sub ' OutputBarChart
118
119        ' output the contents of the grades array
120        Public Sub OutputGrades()
121           Console.WriteLine("The grades are:" & vbCrLf)
122
123           ' output each student's grade
124           For student As Integer = 0 To grades.GetUpperBound(0)
125              Console.WriteLine("Student {0, 2:D}: {1, 3:D}", _
126                 student + 1, grades(student))
127           Next
128
129           Console.WriteLine()
130        End Sub ' OutputGrades
131  End Class ' GradeBook
```

Fig. 8.13 | GradeBook class using an array to store test grades. (Part 3 of 3.)

Fig. 8.14). Although array indices start at 0, a professor would typically number students starting at 1. Thus, lines 125–126 output student + 1 as the student number to produce grade labels "Student 1: ", "Student 2: ", and so on.

Method ProcessGrades next calls method GetAverage (line 35) to obtain the average of the grades in the array. Method GetAverage (lines 76–86) uses a For Each statement to total the values in array grades before calculating the average. The loop control variable declaration in the For Each's header (e.g., grade As Integer) indicates that for each iteration, the Integer variable grade takes on the next successive value in the array grades. The averaging calculation in line 85 uses grades.Length to determine the number of grades being averaged.

Lines 38–39 in method ProcessGrades call methods GetMinimum and GetMaximum to determine the lowest and highest grades of any student on the exam, respectively. Each of these methods uses a For Each statement to loop through array grades. Lines 50–55 in method GetMinimum loop through the array, and lines 52–54 compare each grade to lowGrade. If a grade is less than lowGrade, lowGrade is set to that grade. When line 57 executes, lowGrade contains the lowest grade in the array. Method GetMaximum (lines 61–73) works similarly to method GetMinimum.

Finally, line 42 in method ProcessGrades calls method OutputBarChart to print a distribution chart of the grade data using a technique similar to that in Fig. 8.6. Lines 96–98 calculate the frequency of grades in each category. Line 106 passes to the method Console.Write the format string "{0, 2:D2}-{1, 2:D2}", which indicates that arguments 0 and 1 (the first two arguments after the format string) should take the format D2 (base 10 decimal number format using two digits) for display purposes—thus, 8 would be converted to 08 and 10 would remain as 10. Recall that the number 2 before the colon indicates that the result should be output right justified in a field of width 2. The dash that separates the curly braces } and { is printed to display the range of the grades (see the output of Fig. 8.14).

Line 93 declares and creates array frequency of 11 Integers to store the frequency of grades in each grade category. For each grade in array grades, lines 96–98 increment the appropriate element of the frequency array. To determine which element to increment, line 97 divides the current grade by 10 using integer division. For example, if grade is 85, line 97 increments frequency[8] to update the count of grades in the range 80–89. Lines 101–116 next print the bar chart (see the output of Fig. 8.14) based on the values in the frequency array. Like lines 15–17 of Fig. 8.6, lines 111–113 of Fig. 8.13 use a value in array frequency to determine the number of asterisks to display in each bar.

Class GradeBookTest That Demonstrates Class GradeBook

The application in Fig. 8.14 creates an object of class GradeBook (Fig. 8.13) using the Integer array gradesArray (declared and initialized in lines 6–7). Lines 8–9 pass a course name and gradesArray to the GradeBook constructor. Line 10 displays a welcome message, and line 11 invokes the GradeBook object's ProcessGrades method. The output presents an analysis of the 10 grades in gradeBooks.

Software Engineering Observation 8.1

A test harness (or test application) is responsible for creating an object of the class being tested and providing it with data. This data could come from any of several sources. Test data can be placed directly into an array with an array initializer, it can be entered by the user at the keyboard, it can be read from a file (as you will see in Chapter 18), or it can arrive over a network (as you will see in Chapter 23). After passing this data to the class's constructor to instantiate the object, the test harness should call the object's methods to verify that they work properly.

```
 1   ' Fig. 8.14: GradeBookTest.vb
 2   ' Create GradeBook object using any array of grades.
 3   Module GradeBookTest
 4      Sub Main()
 5         ' array of student grades
 6         Dim gradesArray As Integer() = _
 7            {87, 68, 94, 100, 83, 78, 85, 91, 76, 87}
 8         Dim gradeBooks As New GradeBook( _
 9            "CS101 Introduction to Visual Basic Programming", gradesArray)
10         gradeBooks.DisplayMessage()
11         gradeBooks.ProcessGrades()
12      End Sub ' Main
13   End Module ' GradeBookTest
```

```
Welcome to the grade book for
CS101 Introduction to Visual Basic Programming

The grades are:

Student  1:  87
Student  2:  68
Student  3:  94
Student  4: 100
Student  5:  83
Student  6:  78
Student  7:  85
Student  8:  91
Student  9:  76
Student 10:  87

Class average is 84.90
Lowest grade is 68
Highest grade is 100

Grade distribution:
00-09:
10-19:
20-29:
30-39:
40-49:
50-59:
60-69: *
70-79: **
80-89: ****
90-99: **
  100: *
```

Fig. 8.14 | GradeBookTest creates a GradeBook object using an array of grades, then invokes method ProcessGrades to analyze them.

8.9 Rectangular Arrays

So far, we have discussed *one-dimensional* (or *single-subscripted*) arrays—arrays that contain one row of values. In this section, we introduce *multidimensional* (also called *multiple-subscripted*) arrays, which require two or more indices to identify particular elements. We concentrate on *two-dimensional* (also called *double-subscripted*) arrays, or arrays that contain multiple rows of values. There are two types of two-dimensional arrays—*rectangular* and *jagged*. We discuss jagged arrays in Section 8.12. Rectangular arrays often represent *tables* of values consisting of information arranged in *rows* and *columns*. Each row is the same size, and each column is the same size (hence the term "rectangular"). To identify a particular table element, we specify two indices—by convention, the first identifies the element's row, the second the element's column. Figure 8.15 illustrates a rectangular array, a, containing three rows and four columns. A rectangular array with m rows and n columns is called an *m-by-n array*; the array in Fig. 8.15 is referred to as a 3-by-4 array.

Every element in array a is identified in Fig. 8.15 by an element name of the form a(i, j), where a is the name of the array and i and j are the indices that uniquely identify the row and column of each element in array a. Array indices are zero-based, so the names of the elements in the first row all have a first index of 0; the names of the elements in the fourth column all have a second index of 3.

Declaring and Initializing Rectangular Arrays

A two-dimensional rectangular array numbers with two rows and two columns can be declared and initialized with

```
Dim numbers As Integer(,) = New Integer(1,1) {}

numbers(0, 0) = 1 ' leftmost element in row 0
numbers(0, 1) = 2 ' rightmost element in row 0
numbers(1, 0) = 3 ' leftmost element in row 1
numbers(1, 1) = 4 ' rightmost element in row 1
```

Alternatively, the initialization can be written on one line, as shown below:

```
Dim numbers As Integer(,) = New Integer(,) {{1, 2}, {3, 4}}
```

The values are grouped by row in braces, with 1 and 2 initializing numbers(0,0) and numbers(0,1), respectively, and 3 and 4 initializing numbers(1,0) and numbers(1,1), respectively. The compiler determines the number of rows by counting the number of subinitializer lists (represented by the sets of data in curly braces) in the main initializer list. Then the compiler determines the number of columns in each row by counting the

Fig. 8.15 | Two-dimensional array with three rows and four columns.

number of initializer values in the subinitializer list for that row. In rectangular arrays, each row has the same number of values.

The program in Fig. 8.16 demonstrates the initialization of a rectangular array (array1) and the use of nested For...Next loops to traverse the arrays (i.e., to manipulate every array element).

The program declares a rectangular array in method Main. The allocation of rectangular array1 (line 7) provides six initializers in two sublists. The first sublist initializes row 0 of the array to the values 1, 2 and 3; the second sublist initializes row 1 of the array to the values 4, 5 and 6.

The nested For...Next statements in lines 12–18 display the elements of rectangular array array1, traversing the array in two dimensions. The outer For...Next statement traverses the rows; the inner For...Next statement traverses the columns within a row. Each For...Next statement calls method GetUpperBound to obtain the upper bound of the dimension it traverses. Note that the dimensions are zero-based, meaning that the rows are dimension 0 (line 12) and the columns are dimension 1 (line 13).

8.10 GradeBook Case Study: Using a Rectangular Array

In Section 8.8, we presented class GradeBook (Fig. 8.13), which used a one-dimensional array to store student grades on a single exam. In most semesters, students take several exams. Professors are likely to want to analyze grades across the entire semester, both for a single student and for the class as a whole.

```vb
1    ' Fig. 8.16: RectangularArray.vb
2    ' Initializing a rectangular array.
3    Module RectangularArray
4       Sub Main()
5          ' create rectangular array
6          Dim array1 As Integer(,)
7          array1 = New Integer(,) {{1, 2, 3}, {4, 5, 6}}
8
9          Console.WriteLine("Values in rectangular array1 by row are ")
10
11         ' output array1 elements
12         For i As Integer = 0 To array1.GetUpperBound(0)
13            For j As Integer = 0 To array1.GetUpperBound(1)
14               Console.Write(array1(i, j) & "  ")
15            Next
16
17            Console.WriteLine()
18         Next
19      End Sub ' Main
20   End Module ' RectangularArray
```

```
Values in rectangular array1 by row are
1  2  3
4  5  6
```

Fig. 8.16 | Initializing a rectangular array.

*Storing Student Grades in a Rectangular Array in Class **GradeBook***

Figure 8.17 contains a version of class GradeBook that uses a rectangular array grades to store the grades of several students on multiple exams. Each row of the array represents a single student's grades for the entire course, and each column represents a grade on one of the exams the students took during the course. An application such as GradeBookTest (Fig. 8.18) passes the array as an argument to the GradeBook constructor. In this example, we use a 10-by-3 array containing ten students' grades on three exams. Five methods perform various array manipulations to process the grades. Each method is similar to its counterpart in the earlier one-dimensional array version of class GradeBook (Fig. 8.13). Method GetMinimum (lines 45–61) determines the lowest grade of any student for the semester. Method GetMaximum (lines 64–80) determines the highest grade of any student for the semester. Method GetAverage (lines 83–93) determines a particular student's semester average. Method OutputBarChart (lines 96–126) outputs a bar chart of the distribution of all student grades for the semester. Method OutputGrades (lines 129–156) outputs the rectangular array in a tabular format, along with each student's semester average.

Methods GetMinimum, GetMaximum, OutputBarChart and OutputGrades each loop through array grades by using nested For statements—for example, the nested For statement (lines 50–58) from the declaration of method GetMinimum. The outer For statement iterates through the rows of two-dimensional array grades. To find the lowest overall grade, the inner For statement compares the current array element to variable lowGrade. For example, on the first iteration of the outer For, row 0 of grades is used. The inner For statement then loops through elements in row 0 and compares each grade value with lowGrade. If a grade is less than lowGrade, lowGrade is set to that grade. On the second iteration of the outer For statement, row 1 of grades is used, and the elements of this row are compared with variable lowGrade. This repeats until all the rows of grades have been traversed. When execution of the nested statement is complete, lowGrade contains the lowest grade in the two-dimensional array. Method GetMaximum works similarly to method GetMinimum.

```vb
1   ' Fig. 8.17: GradeBook.vb
2   ' Grade book using a rectangular array to store grades.
3   Public Class GradeBook
4       Private courseNameValue As String ' name of course
5       Private grades As Integer(,) ' rectangular array of student grades
6
7       ' two-argument constructor initializes courseNameValue and Grades
8       Public Sub New(ByVal name As String, ByVal gradesArray As Integer(,))
9           CourseName = name ' initializes courseNameValue via property
10          grades = gradesArray ' store grades
11      End Sub ' New
12
13      ' property CourseName
14      Public Property CourseName() As String
15          Get
16              Return courseNameValue
17          End Get
18
```

Fig. 8.17 | GradeBook class using a rectangular array to store grades. (Part 1 of 4.)

```vb
19          Set(ByVal name As String)
20             courseNameValue = name
21          End Set
22       End Property ' Course Name
23
24       ' display a welcome message to the GradeBook user
25       Public Sub DisplayMessage()
26          Console.WriteLine("Welcome to the grade book for " & vbCrLf & _
27             CourseName & vbCrLf)
28       End Sub ' DisplayMessage
29
30       ' perform various operations on the data
31       Public Sub ProcessGrades()
32          OutputGrades() ' output grades array
33
34          ' call methods GetMinimum and GetMaximum
35          Console.WriteLine("Lowest grade in the grade book is {0}", _
36             GetMinimum())
37          Console.WriteLine("Highest grade in the grade book is {0}", _
38             GetMaximum())
39
40          ' call OutputBarChart to print grade distribution chart
41          OutputBarChart()
42       End Sub ' ProcessGrades
43
44       ' find minimum grade
45       Public Function GetMinimum() As Integer
46          ' assume first element of grades array is smallest
47          Dim lowGrade As Integer = grades(0,0)
48
49          ' loop through grades array
50          For i As Integer = 0 To grades.GetUpperBound(0)
51             ' loop through columns of current row
52             For j As Integer = 0 To grades.GetUpperBound(1)
53                ' if grade lower than lowGrade, assign it to lowGrade
54                If grades(i,j) < lowGrade Then
55                   lowGrade = grades(i,j) ' new lowest grade
56                End If
57             Next
58          Next
59
60          Return lowGrade ' return lowest grade
61       End Function ' GetMinimum
62
63       ' find maximum grade
64       Public Function GetMaximum() As Integer
65          ' assume first element of grades array is largest
66          Dim highGrade As Integer = grades(0,0)
67
68          ' loop through grades array
69          For i As Integer = 0 To grades.GetUpperBound(0)
70             ' loop through columns of current row
71             For j As Integer = 0 To grades.GetUpperBound(1)
```

Fig. 8.17 | GradeBook class using a rectangular array to store grades. (Part 2 of 4.)

```
72          ' if grade greater than highGrade, assign it to highGrade
73          If grades(i,j) > highGrade Then
74              highGrade = grades(i,j) ' new highest grade
75          End If
76      Next
77    Next
78
79    Return highGrade ' return highest grade
80  End Function ' GetMaximum
81
82  ' determine average grade for particular student's grades
83  Public Function GetAverage(ByVal row As Integer) As Double
84    Dim total As Integer = 0 ' initialize total
85
86      ' sum grades for one student
87      For column As Integer = 0 To grades.GetUpperBound(1)
88          total += grades(row, column)
89      Next
90
91      ' return average of grades
92      Return (total / (grades.GetUpperBound(1) + 1))
93  End Function ' GetAverage
94
95  ' output bar chart displaying grade distribution
96  Public Sub OutputBarChart()
97      Console.WriteLine(vbCrLf & "Overall grade distribution:")
98
99      ' stores frequency of grades in each range of 10 grades
100     Dim frequency As Integer() = New Integer(10) {}
101
102     ' for each grade, increment the appropriate frequency
103     For i As Integer = 0 To grades.GetUpperBound(0)
104         For j As Integer = 0 To grades.GetUpperBound(1)
105             frequency(grades(i,j) \ 10) += 1
106         Next
107     Next
108
109     ' for each grade frequency, print bar in chart
110     For count As Integer = 0 To frequency.GetUpperBound(0)
111         ' output bar label ( "00-09: ", ..., "90-99: ", "100: " )
112         If count = 10 Then
113             Console.Write("{0, 5:D}: ", 100)
114         Else
115             Console.Write("{0, 2:D2}-{1, 2:D2}: ", _
116                 count * 10, count * 10 + 9)
117         End If
118
119         ' print bar of asterisks
120         For stars As Integer = 0 To frequency(count) - 1
121             Console.Write("*")
122         Next
123
```

Fig. 8.17 | GradeBook class using a rectangular array to store grades. (Part 3 of 4.)

```
124              Console.WriteLine() ' start a new line of output
125           Next
126        End Sub ' OutputBarChart
127
128        ' output the contents of the grades array
129        Public Sub OutputGrades()
130           Console.WriteLine("The grades are:" & vbCrLf)
131           Console.Write("          ") ' align column heads
132
133           ' create a column heading for each of the tests
134           For test As Integer = 0 To grades.GetUpperBound(1)
135              Console.Write("Test {0:D}  ", test + 1)
136           Next
137
138           Console.WriteLine("Average") ' student average column heading
139
140           ' create rows/columns of text representing array grades
141           For student As Integer = 0 To grades.GetUpperBound(0)
142              Console.Write("Student {0, 2:D}", student + 1)
143
144              ' output student's grades
145              For counter As Integer = 0 To grades.GetUpperBound(1)
146                 Console.Write("{0, 8:D}", grades(student, counter))
147              Next
148
149              ' call method GetAverage to calculate student's average grade;
150              ' pass row of grades as the argument to GetAverage
151              Dim average As Double = GetAverage(student)
152              Console.WriteLine("{0, 9:F2}", average)
153           Next
154
155           Console.WriteLine()
156        End Sub ' OutputGrades
157     End Class ' GradeBook
```

Fig. 8.17 | GradeBook class using a rectangular array to store grades. (Part 4 of 4.)

Method OutputBarChart in Fig. 8.17 is nearly identical to the one in Fig. 8.13. However, to output the overall grade distribution for a whole semester, the method here uses a nested For statement (lines 103–107) to create the one-dimensional array frequency based on all the grades in the rectangular array. The rest of the code in each of the two OutputBarChart methods that displays the chart is identical.

Method OutputGrades (lines 129–156) also uses nested For statements to output values of the array grades, in addition to each student's semester average. The output in Fig. 8.18 shows the result, which resembles the tabular format of a professor's physical grade book. Lines 134–136 (Fig. 8.17) print the column headings for each test. We use a counter-controlled For statement here so that we can identify each test with a number. Similarly, the For statement in lines 141–153 first outputs a row label using a counter variable to identify each student (line 142). Although array indices start at 0, note that lines 135 and 142 output test + 1 and student + 1, respectively, to produce test and student numbers starting at 1 (see Fig. 8.18). The inner For statement in lines 145–147 loops through a specific row of array grades and outputs each student's test grades. Finally, line

151 obtains each student's semester average by passing the current row number (i.e., student) to method GetAverage.

Method GetAverage (lines 83–93) takes one argument—an integer which specifies the row number of a particular student. When line 151 calls GetAverage, the argument is student, which specifies that a particular row number of the rectangular array grades should be passed to GetAverage. Method GetAverage calculates the sum of the array elements, divides the total by the number of test results and returns the floating-point result as a Double value (line 92).

Class *GradeBookTest* That Demonstrates Class *GradeBook*

The application in Fig. 8.18 creates an object of class GradeBook (Fig. 8.17) using the rectangular array of Integers named gradesArray (declared and initialized in lines 6–9). Lines 11–12 pass a course name and gradesArray to the GradeBook constructor. Lines 13–14 then invoke gradeBooks's DisplayMessage and ProcessGrades methods to display a welcome message and obtain a report summarizing the students' grades for the semester, respectively.

```
1   ' Fig. 8.18: GradeBookTest.vb
2   ' Create GradeBook object using a rectangular array of grades.
3   Module GradeBookTest
4      Sub Main()
5         ' array of student grades
6         Dim gradesArray As Integer(,)
7         gradesArray = New Integer(,) {{87, 96, 70}, {68, 87, 90}, _
8            {94, 37, 90}, {100, 81, 82}, {83, 65, 85}, {78, 87, 65}, _
9            {85, 75, 83}, {91, 59, 100}, {76, 72, 84}, {87, 93, 73}}
10
11        Dim gradeBooks As New GradeBook( _
12           "CS101 Introduction to Visual Basic Programming", gradesArray)
13        gradeBooks.DisplayMessage()
14        gradeBooks.ProcessGrades()
15     End Sub ' Main
16  End Module ' GradeBookTest
```

```
Welcome to the grade book for
CS101 Introduction to Visual Basic Programming

The grades are:
            Test 1  Test 2  Test 3  Average
Student  1     87      96      70    84.33
Student  2     68      87      90    81.67
Student  3     94      37      90    73.67
Student  4    100      81      82    87.67
Student  5     83      65      85    77.67
Student  6     78      87      65    76.67
Student  7     85      75      83    81.00
Student  8     91      59     100    83.33
Student  9     76      72      84    77.33
Student 10     87      93      73    84.33
```
(continued on next page…)

Fig. 8.18 | Creating a GradeBook object using a rectangular array of grades, then invoking method processGrades to analyze them. (Part 1 of 2.)

```
Lowest grade in the grade book is 37
Highest grade in the grade book is 100

Overall grade distribution:
00-09:
10-19:
20-29:
30-39: *
40-49:
50-59: *
60-69: ***
70-79: ******
80-89: ***********
90-99: ******
  100: **
```

Fig. 8.18 | Creating a GradeBook object using a rectangular array of grades, then invoking method processGrades to analyze them. (Part 2 of 2.)

8.11 Variable-Length Parameter Lists

It is possible to create methods that receive a variable number of arguments, using keyword ***ParamArray***. The program in Fig. 8.19 calls programmer-defined method AnyNumberOfArguments three times, passing a different number of values each time. The values passed into method AnyNumberOfArguments are stored in one-dimensional Integer array array1, which is declared using ParamArray.

We call method AnyNumberOfArguments in lines 5–7, passing a different number of arguments each time. The method is defined in lines 11–29 and applies keyword Param-Array to array1 in line 11. The If statement in lines 15–28 determines whether the number of arguments passed to the method is zero. If not, lines 19–27 display array1's elements and their sum. All arguments passed to the ParamArray array must be of the same type as the array or a type that can be implicitly converted to the type of the array, otherwise a compilation error occurs (when **Option Strict** is **On**). Though we used an Integer array in this example, any type of array can be used.

```
1    ' Fig. 8.19: ParamArrayTest.vb
2    ' Using ParamArray to create variable-length parameter lists.
3    Module ParamArrayTest
4       Sub Main()
5          AnyNumberOfArguments()
6          AnyNumberOfArguments(2, 3)
7          AnyNumberOfArguments(7, 8, 9, 10, 11, 12)
8       End Sub ' Main
9
10       ' receives any number of arguments in array
11       Sub AnyNumberOfArguments(ByVal ParamArray array1 As Integer())
12          Dim total As Integer = 0
13
```

Fig. 8.19 | Creating variable-length parameter lists (Part 1 of 2).

```
14          ' check number of arguments
15          If array1.Length = 0 Then
16              Console.WriteLine("Method AnyNumberOfArguments" & _
17                  " received 0 arguments.")
18          Else
19              Console.Write("The total of ")
20
21              ' total array elements
22              For i As Integer = 0 To array1.GetUpperBound(0)
23                  Console.Write(array1(i) & " ")
24                  total += array1(i)
25              Next
26
27              Console.WriteLine("is {0}.", total)
28          End If
29      End Sub ' AnyNumberOfArguments
30  End Module ' ParamArrayTest
```

```
Method AnyNumberOfArguments received 0 arguments.
The total of 2 3 is 5.
The total of 7 8 9 10 11 12 is 57.
```

Fig. 8.19 | Creating variable-length parameter lists (Part 2 of 2.).

In the last chapter, we discussed method overloading. Programmers often prefer to use method overloading rather than write methods with variable-length parameter lists.

Common Programming Error 8.5

Attempting to declare a parameter variable to the right of the ParamArray array variable is a syntax error.

Common Programming Error 8.6

Using ByRef with ParamArray is a syntax error.

8.12 Jagged Arrays

Jagged arrays are maintained as arrays of arrays. Unlike rectangular arrays, rows in jagged arrays can be of different lengths. The program in Fig. 8.20 demonstrates the initialization of a jagged array (array1) and the use of nested For...Next loops to traverse the array.

The program declares a jagged array in method Main. The declaration and allocation of the jagged array array1 (line 6) create a jagged array of three arrays (specified by the 2 in the first set of parentheses after keyword Integer). Lines 7–9 initialize each subarray so that the first subarray contains the values 1 and 2, the second contains the value 3 and the last contains the values 4, 5 and 6.

The nested For...Next statements in lines 14–20 behave similarly to those that manipulate the rectangular array in Fig. 8.16. However, in a jagged array, the second dimension is actually an index into the one-dimensional array that represents the current row. In the example, the inner For...Next statement (lines 15–17) uses GetUpperBound with the argument 0 to determine the number of columns in each row. In this case, we call

```
 1    ' Fig. 8.20: JaggedArray.vb
 2    ' Initializing a jagged array.
 3    Module JaggedArray
 4       Sub Main()
 5          ' create jagged array
 6          Dim array1 As Integer()() = New Integer(2)() {} ' three rows
 7          array1(0) = New Integer() {1, 2} ' row 0 is a single array
 8          array1(1) = New Integer() {3} ' row 1 is a single array
 9          array1(2) = New Integer() {4, 5, 6} ' row 2 is a single array
10
11          Console.WriteLine("Values in jagged array1 by row are ")
12
13          ' output array1 elements
14          For i As Integer = 0 To array1.GetUpperBound(0)
15             For j As Integer = 0 To array1(i).GetUpperBound(0)
16                Console.Write(array1(i)(j) & "  ")
17             Next
18
19             Console.WriteLine()
20          Next
21       End Sub ' Main
22    End Module ' JaggedArray
```

```
Values in jagged array1 by row are
1  2
3
4  5  6
```

Fig. 8.20 | Initializing a jagged array .

GetUpperBound on a single row—array(i). Arrays of more than two dimensions can be traversed using one nested For...Next statement for each dimension.

8.13 Changing the Size of an Array at Execution Time: Using the ReDim Statement

The number of elements in an array can be changed at execution time. For example, when an array is used to store information about all the employees in a company, the size of the array would change when the company hires a new employee or when an employee leaves the company. The **ReDim** statement enables you to dynamically change the array size, but not the type of the array elements, nor the number of dimensions in the array. Figure 8.21 demonstrates the ReDim statement.

Line 6 creates and initializes a five-element array array. Line 7 creates a copy of the array named arrayCopy. Lines 10–12 display the size and elements of the original array. Line 15 uses a ReDim statement to change the upper bound of array to 6, so that the array now contains seven elements. The ReDim statement contains keyword ReDim, followed by the name of the array to be resized and the new upper bound in parentheses. The output of Fig. 8.21 shows that after the ReDim statement is executed, the size of the array is changed to 7 and the value of each element is reinitialized to the default value of the type of the array element (i.e., 0 for Integers). To save the original data stored in an array,

```
1   ' Fig. 8.21: ReDimTest.vb
2   ' Resize an array using the ReDim statement.
3   Module ReDimTest
4      Sub Main()
5         ' create and initialize a 5-element array
6         Dim array As Integer() = {1, 2, 3, 4, 5}
7         Dim arrayCopy As Integer() = array
8
9         ' display array length and the elements in array
10        Console.Write("The original array has {0} elements: ", _
11           array.Length)
12        DisplayArray(array)
13
14        ' change the size of the array without the Preserve keyword
15        ReDim array(6)
16
17        ' display new array length and the elements in array
18        Console.Write("New array (without Preserve) has {0} elements: ", _
19           array.Length)
20        DisplayArray(array)
21
22        ' change the size of the array with the Preserve keyword
23        ReDim Preserve arrayCopy(6)
24        arrayCopy(6) = 7 ' assign 7 to array element 6
25
26        ' display new array length and the elements in array
27        Console.Write("New array (with Preserve) has {0} elements: ", _
28           arrayCopy.Length)
29        DisplayArray(arrayCopy)
30     End Sub ' Main
31
32     ' display array elements
33     Sub DisplayArray(ByVal array As Integer())
34        For Each number As Integer In array
35           Console.Write("{0} ", number)
36        Next
37
38        Console.WriteLine()
39     End Sub ' DisplayArray
40  End Module ' ReDimTest
```

```
The original array has 5 elements: 1 2 3 4 5
New array (without Preserve) has 7 elements: 0 0 0 0 0 0 0
New array (with Preserve) has 7 elements: 1 2 3 4 5 0 7
```

Fig. 8.21 | Using ReDim statements to change the array size.

follow the ReDim keyword with the optional **Preserve** keyword. Line 23 uses Preserve in the ReDim statement to indicate that the existing array elements are to be preserved in the now larger array after the array is resized. If the new array is smaller than the original array, the existing elements that are outside the bounds of the new array are discarded. If the new array is larger than the original array, all the existing elements are preserved in the now larger array, and the extra elements are initialized to the default value of the type of the array element. For example, after line 23 is executed, the value of arrayCopy(5) is 0. Line 24 assigns the value 7 to arrayCopy(6), so that the now larger array arrayCopy contains elements 1, 2, 3, 4, 5, 0 and 7.

In Chapter 26, Collections, we introduce class ArrayList from the System.Collections namespace. An ArrayList is a dynamically resizable array-like data structure that mimics the functionality of conventional arrays. Additional ArrayList capabilities include inserting elements, searching for elements, removing elements and sorting elements.

8.14 Passing Arrays: ByVal vs. ByRef

A variable that "stores" an object, such as an array, does not actually store the object itself. Instead, the variable stores a reference to the object (i.e., the address of the location in the computer's memory where the object is stored). Recall that in Chapters 4–6, we discussed two types of variables—value types and reference types. The distinction between value-type variables and reference-type variables raises some subtle issues that you must understand to create secure, stable programs.

Effects of ByVal on Value-Type Parameters and Reference-Type Parameters
When used to declare a value-type parameter, keyword ByVal causes the value of the argument to be copied to a local variable in the method. Changes to the local variable are reflected in the local copy of the variable, but not in the original variable in the calling program. If the argument passed using keyword ByVal is of a reference type, the value copied is a reference to the original object in the computer's memory. Thus, reference types (like arrays and other objects) passed via keyword ByVal are actually passed by reference, meaning that changes made to the objects in called methods are actually made to the original objects in the callers.

> **Performance Tip 8.1**
>
> *Passing arrays and other objects by reference makes sense for performance reasons. If arrays were passed by value, a copy of each element would be passed. For large, frequently passed arrays, this would waste time and consume considerable storage for the copies of the arrays—both of these problems cause poor performance.*

Passing Reference Type Parameters Using ByRef
Visual Basic also allows methods to pass references with keyword ByRef. This is a subtle capability, which, if misused, can lead to problems. For instance, when a reference-type object like an array is passed with ByRef, the called method actually gains control over the original reference in the caller, allowing the called method to replace the reference with one to a different object or even with Nothing. Such behavior can lead to unpredictable effects, which can be disastrous in business-critical and mission-critical applications. The program in Fig. 8.22 demonstrates the subtle difference between passing a reference ByVal and passing a reference ByRef.

Lines 6–7 declare two Integer array variables, firstArray and firstArrayCopy (we make the copy so that we can determine whether the reference firstArray gets overwritten by method FirstDouble). Line 10 allocates an array containing Integer values 1,

2 and 3 and stores the array reference in variable `firstArray`. The assignment statement at line 11 copies the reference `firstArray` to the reference variable `firstArrayCopy`, causing these variables to reference the same array object. The `For...Next` statement in lines 17–19 prints the contents of `firstArray` before it is passed to method `FirstDouble` at line 21 so we can verify that this array is passed by reference (i.e., the called method indeed changes the array's contents in `Main`).

```vb
1    ' Fig. 8.22: ArrayReferenceTest.vb
2    ' Testing the effects of passing array references using ByVal and ByRef.
3    Module ArrayReferenceTest
4       Sub Main()
5          ' declare array references
6          Dim firstArray As Integer()
7          Dim firstArrayCopy As Integer()
8
9          ' allocate firstArray and copy its reference
10         firstArray = New Integer() {1, 2, 3}
11         firstArrayCopy = firstArray ' reference preceding array
12
13         Console.WriteLine("Passing an array reference using ByVal.")
14         Console.Write("Contents of firstArray before calling FirstDouble: ")
15
16         ' print contents of firstArray
17         For i As Integer = 0 To firstArray.GetUpperBound(0)
18            Console.Write(firstArray(i) & " ")
19         Next
20
21         FirstDouble(firstArray) ' pass firstArray using ByVal
22         Console.Write(vbCrLf & "Contents of firstArray after " & _
23            "calling FirstDouble: ")
24
25         ' print contents of firstArray
26         For i As Integer = 0 To firstArray.GetUpperBound(0)
27            Console.Write(firstArray(i) & " ")
28         Next
29
30         ' was reference to firstArray changed by FirstDouble?
31         If firstArray Is firstArrayCopy Then
32            Console.WriteLine(vbCrLf & "The references are equal.")
33         Else
34            Console.WriteLine(vbCrLf & "The references are not equal.")
35         End If
36
37         ' declare array references
38         Dim secondArray As Integer()
39         Dim secondArrayCopy As Integer()
40
41         ' allocate secondArray and copy its reference
42         secondArray = New Integer() {1, 2, 3}
43         secondArrayCopy = secondArray
```

Fig. 8.22 | Passing an array reference with `ByVal` and `ByRef`. (Part I of 3.)

```
44
45        Console.WriteLine(vbCrLf & "Passing an array " & _
46           "reference using ByRef.")
47        Console.Write("Contents of secondArray before " & _
48           "calling SecondDouble: ")
49
50        ' print contents of secondArray before method call
51        For i As Integer = 0 To secondArray.GetUpperBound(0)
52           Console.Write(secondArray(i) & " ")
53        Next
54
55        SecondDouble(secondArray) ' pass secondArray using ByRef
56        Console.Write(vbCrLf & "Contents of secondArray " & _
57           "after calling SecondDouble: ")
58
59        ' print contents of secondArray after method call
60        For i As Integer = 0 To secondArray.GetUpperBound(0)
61           Console.Write(secondArray(i) & " ")
62        Next
63
64        ' was reference secondArray changed by SecondDouble
65        If secondArray Is secondArrayCopy Then
66           Console.WriteLine(vbCrLf & "The references are equal.")
67        Else
68           Console.WriteLine(vbCrLf & "The references are not equal.")
69        End If
70     End Sub ' Main
71
72     ' method modifies elements of array and assigns
73     ' new reference (note ByVal)
74     Sub FirstDouble(ByVal array As Integer())
75        ' double each element value in caller's array
76        For i As Integer = 0 To array.GetUpperBound(0)
77           array(i) *= 2 ' double the ith element
78        Next
79
80        ' create a new array and assign its reference to the variable array
81        array = New Integer() {11, 12, 13}
82     End Sub ' FirstDouble
83
84     ' method modifies elements of array and assigns
85     ' new reference (note ByRef)
86     Sub SecondDouble(ByRef array As Integer())
87        ' double each element value in caller's array
88        For i As Integer = 0 To array.GetUpperBound(0)
89           array(i) *= 2 ' double the ith element
90        Next
91
92        ' create a new array and assign its reference to the variable array
93        array = New Integer() {11, 12, 13} ' lose the 2, 4, 6 array
94     End Sub ' SecondDouble
95  End Module ' ArrayReferenceTest
```

Fig. 8.22 | Passing an array reference with ByVal and ByRef. (Part 2 of 3.)

```
Passing an array reference using ByVal.
Contents of firstArray before calling FirstDouble: 1 2 3
Contents of firstArray after calling FirstDouble: 2 4 6
The references are equal.

Passing an array reference using ByRef.
Contents of secondArray before calling SecondDouble: 1 2 3
Contents of secondArray after calling SecondDouble: 11 12 13
The references are not equal.
```

Fig. 8.22 | Passing an array reference with ByVal and ByRef. (Part 3 of 3.)

The For...Next statement in method FirstDouble (lines 76–78) multiplies the values of all the elements in the array by 2. Line 81 allocates a new array containing the values 11, 12 and 13; the reference for this array then is assigned to parameter array (in an attempt to overwrite reference firstArray in Main—this, of course, does not happen, because the reference firstArray was passed ByVal). After method FirstDouble executes, the For...Next statement in lines 26–28 prints the contents of firstArray, demonstrating that the values of the elements have been changed by the method FirstDouble (and confirming that in Visual Basic arrays are always passed by reference). The If statement in lines 31–35 uses the Is operator to compare references firstArray (which we just attempted to overwrite) and firstArrayCopy. Visual Basic provides *operator Is* for comparing references to determine whether they are referencing the same object. The expression at line 31 is true if the operands to the binary operator Is reference the same object. In this case, the object represented is the array allocated in line 10—not the array allocated in method FirstDouble (line 81). Visual Basic also provides *operator IsNot* for comparing two references. If two references refer to the same objects, operator IsNot returns False; otherwise it returns True. Line 81 modifies only the parameter array, not the variable firstArray because firstArray was passed with keyword ByVal. We will see in a moment the effect of passing an array with keyword ByRef.

Lines 38–69 in method Main perform similar tests, using array variables secondArray and secondArrayCopy and method SecondDouble (lines 86–94). Method SecondDouble performs the same operations as FirstDouble, but receives its array argument with ByRef. In this case, the reference stored in secondArray after the method call is a reference to the array allocated at line 93 of SecondDouble, demonstrating that a reference passed with ByRef can be modified by the called method so that the reference actually points to a different object, in this case the array that is allocated in method SecondDouble. The If statement in lines 65–69 determines that secondArray and secondArrayCopy no longer represent the same array.

Software Engineering Observation 8.2

Using ByVal to receive a reference-type object parameter does not cause the object to pass by value—the object still passes by reference. ByVal causes only the object's reference to pass by value. This prevents a called method from overwriting a reference in the caller. In the vast majority of cases, protecting the caller's reference from modification is the desired behavior. If you encounter a situation where you truly want the called method to modify the caller's reference, pass the reference-type object ByRef.

8.15 (Optional) Software Engineering Case Study: Collaboration Among Objects in the ATM System

When two objects communicate with each other to accomplish a task, they are said to *collaborate*. A *collaboration* consists of an object of one class sending a *message* to an object of another class. Messages are sent in Visual Basic via method calls. In this section, we concentrate on the collaborations (interactions) among the objects in our ATM system.

In Section 7.20, we determined many of the operations of the classes in our system. In this section, we concentrate on the messages that invoke these operations. To identify the collaborations in the system, we return to the requirements document of Section 3.9. Recall that this document specifies the activities that occur during an ATM session (e.g., authenticating a user, performing transactions). The steps used to describe how the system must perform each of these tasks are our first indication of the collaborations in our system. As we proceed through this and the remaining Software Engineering Case Study sections, we may discover additional collaborations.

Identifying the Collaborations in a System

We begin to identify the collaborations in the system by carefully reading the sections of the requirements document that specify what the ATM should do to authenticate a user and to perform each transaction type. For each action or step described in the requirements document, we decide which objects in our system must interact to achieve the desired result. We identify one object as the sending object (i.e., the object that sends the message) and another as the receiving object (i.e., the object that offers that operation to clients of the class). We then select one of the receiving object's operations (identified in Section 7.20) that must be invoked by the sending object to produce the proper behavior. For example, the ATM displays a welcome message when idle. We know that an object of class Screen displays a message to the user via its DisplayMessage operation. Thus, we decide that the system can display a welcome message by employing a collaboration between the ATM and the Screen in which the ATM sends a DisplayMessage message to the Screen by invoking the DisplayMessage operation of class Screen. [*Note:* To avoid repeating the phrase "an object of class...," we refer to each object simply by using its class name preceded by an article (e.g., "a," "an" or "the")—for example, "the ATM" refers to an object of class ATM.]

Figure 8.23 lists the collaborations that can be derived from the requirements document. For each sending object, we list the collaborations in the order in which they are discussed in the requirements document. We list each collaboration involving a unique sender, message and recipient only once, even though the collaboration may occur several times during an ATM session. For example, the first row in Fig. 8.23 indicates that the ATM collaborates with the Screen whenever the ATM needs to display a message to the user.

Let's consider the collaborations in Fig. 8.23. Before allowing a user to perform any transactions, the ATM must prompt the user to enter an account number, then to enter a PIN. It accomplishes each of these tasks by sending a DisplayMessage message to the Screen. Both of these actions refer to the same collaboration between the ATM and the Screen, which is already listed in Fig. 8.23. The ATM obtains input in response to a prompt by sending a GetInput message to the Keypad. Next, the ATM must determine whether the user-specified account number and PIN match those of an account in the database. It does so by sending an AuthenticateUser message to the BankDatabase. Recall that the BankDatabase cannot authenticate a user directly—only the user's Account (i.e., the

An object of class...	sends the message...	to an object of class...
ATM	DisplayMessage	Screen
	GetInput	Keypad
	AuthenticateUser	BankDatabase
	Execute	BalanceInquiry
	Execute	Withdrawal
	Execute	Deposit
BalanceInquiry	GetAvailableBalance	BankDatabase
	GetTotalBalance	BankDatabase
	DisplayMessage	Screen
Withdrawal	DisplayMessage	Screen
	GetInput	Keypad
	GetAvailableBalance	BankDatabase
	IsSufficientCashAvailable	CashDispenser
	Debit	BankDatabase
	DispenseCash	CashDispenser
Deposit	DisplayMessage	Screen
	GetInput	Keypad
	IsDepositEnvelopeReceived	DepositSlot
	Credit	BankDatabase
BankDatabase	ValidatePIN	Account
	AvailableBalance (Get)	Account
	TotalBalance (Get)	Account
	Debit	Account
	Credit	Account

Fig. 8.23 | Collaborations in the ATM system.

Account that contains the account number specified by the user) can access the user's PIN to authenticate the user. Figure 8.23 therefore lists a collaboration in which the Bank-Database sends a ValidatePIN message to an Account.

After the user is authenticated, the ATM displays the main menu by sending a series of DisplayMessage messages to the Screen and obtains input containing a menu selection by sending a GetInput message to the Keypad. We have already accounted for these collaborations. After the user chooses a type of transaction to perform, the ATM executes the transaction by sending an Execute message to an object of the appropriate transaction class (i.e., a BalanceInquiry, a Withdrawal or a Deposit). For example, if the user chooses to perform a balance inquiry, the ATM sends an Execute message to a BalanceInquiry.

Further examination of the requirements document reveals the collaborations involved in executing each transaction type. A BalanceInquiry retrieves the amount of money available in the user's account by sending a GetAvailableBalance message to the BankDatabase, which sends a Get message to an Account's AvailableBalance property to access the available balance. Similarly, the BalanceInquiry retrieves the amount of money on deposit by sending a GetTotalBalance message to the BankDatabase, which sends a Get message to an Account's TotalBalance property to access the total balance on deposit. To display both measures of the user's balance at the same time, the BalanceInquiry sends DisplayMessage messages to the Screen.

A Withdrawal sends DisplayMessage messages to the Screen to display a menu of standard withdrawal amounts (i.e., $20, $40, $60, $100, $200). The Withdrawal sends a GetInput message to the Keypad to obtain the user's menu selection. Next, the Withdrawal determines whether the requested withdrawal amount is less than or equal to the user's account balance. The Withdrawal can obtain the amount of money available in the user's account by sending a GetAvailableBalance message to the BankDatabase. The Withdrawal then tests whether the cash dispenser contains enough cash by sending an IsSufficient-CashAvailable message to the CashDispenser. A Withdrawal sends a Debit message to the BankDatabase to decrease the user's account balance. The BankDatabase in turn sends the same message to the appropriate Account. Recall that debiting an Account decreases both the total balance and the available balance. To dispense the requested amount of cash, the Withdrawal sends a DispenseCash message to the CashDispenser. Finally, the Withdrawal sends a DisplayMessage message to the Screen, instructing the user to take the cash.

A Deposit responds to an Execute message first by sending a DisplayMessage message to the Screen to prompt the user for a deposit amount. The Deposit sends a GetInput message to the Keypad to obtain the user's input. The Deposit then sends a DisplayMessage message to the Screen to tell the user to insert a deposit envelope. To determine whether the deposit slot received an incoming deposit envelope, the Deposit sends an IsDepositEnvelopeReceived message to the DepositSlot. The Deposit updates the user's account by sending a Credit message to the BankDatabase, which subsequently sends a Credit message to the user's Account. Recall that crediting an Account increases the total balance but not the available balance.

Interaction Diagrams

Now that we have identified a set of possible collaborations between the objects in our ATM system, let us graphically model these interactions. The UML provides several types of *interaction diagrams* that model the behavior of a system by modeling how objects interact with one another. The *communication diagram* emphasizes *which objects* participate in collaborations. [*Note:* Communication diagrams were called *collaboration diagrams* in earlier versions of the UML.] Like the communication diagram, the *sequence diagram* shows collaborations among objects, but it emphasizes *when* messages are sent between objects.

Communication Diagrams

Figure 8.24 shows a communication diagram that models the ATM executing a Balance-Inquiry. Objects are modeled in the UML as rectangles containing names in the form objectName : ClassName. In this example, which involves only one object of each type, we disregard the object name and list only a colon followed by the class name. Specifying the name of each object in a communication diagram is recommended when modeling multiple objects of the same type. Communicating objects are connected with solid lines, and messages are passed between objects along these lines in the direction shown by arrows with filled arrowheads. The name of the message, which appears next to the arrow, is the name of an operation (i.e., a method) belonging to the receiving object—think of the name as a service that the receiving object provides to sending objects (its "clients").

Fig. 8.24 | Communication diagram of the ATM executing a `BalanceInquiry`.

The filled arrow in Fig. 8.24 represents a message—or *synchronous call*—in the UML and a method call in Visual Basic. This arrow indicates that the flow of control is from the sending object (the ATM) to the receiving object (a `BalanceInquiry`). Since this is a synchronous call, the sending object may not send another message, or do anything at all, until the receiving object processes the message and returns control (and possibly a return value) to the sending object. The sender just waits. For example, in Fig. 8.24, the ATM calls method `Execute` of a `BalanceInquiry` and may not send another message until `Execute` finishes and returns control to the ATM. [*Note:* If this were an *asynchronous call*, represented by a stick arrowhead, the sending object would not have to wait for the receiving object to return control—it would continue sending additional messages immediately following the asynchronous call. Such calls are beyond the scope of this book.]

Sequence of Messages in a Communication Diagram

Figure 8.25 shows a communication diagram that models the interactions among objects in the system when an object of class `BalanceInquiry` executes. We assume that the object's `accountNumber` attribute contains the account number of the current user. The collaborations in Fig. 8.25 begin after the ATM sends an `Execute` message to a `BalanceInquiry` (i.e., the interaction modeled in Fig. 8.24). The number to the left of a message name indicates the order in which the message is passed. The *sequence of messages* in a communication diagram progresses in numerical order from least to greatest. In

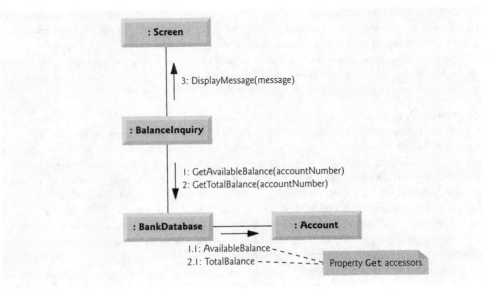

Fig. 8.25 | Communication diagram for executing a `BalanceInquiry`.

this diagram, the numbering starts with message 1 and ends with message 3. The Balance-Inquiry first sends a GetAvailableBalance message to the BankDatabase (message 1), then sends a GetTotalBalance message to the BankDatabase (message 2). Within the parentheses following a message name, we can specify a comma-separated list of the names of the arguments sent with the message (i.e., arguments in a Visual Basic method call)—the BalanceInquiry passes attribute accountNumber with its messages to the BankDatabase to indicate which Account's balance information to retrieve. Recall from Fig. 7.23 that operations GetAvailableBalance and GetTotalBalance of class BankDatabase each require a parameter to identify an account. The BalanceInquiry next displays the available balance and the total balance to the user by passing a DisplayMessage message to the Screen (message 3) that includes a parameter indicating the message to be displayed.

Note that Fig. 8.25 models two additional messages passing from the BankDatabase to an Account (message 1.1 and message 2.1). To provide the ATM with the two balances of the user's Account (as requested by messages 1 and 2), the BankDatabase must send Get messages to the Account's AvailableBalance and TotalBalance properties. A message passed within the handling of another message is called a *nested message*. The UML recommends using a decimal numbering scheme to indicate nested messages. For example, message 1.1 is the first message nested in message 1—the BankDatabase sends the Get message to the Account's AvailableBalance property during BankDatabase's processing of a GetAvailableBalance message. [*Note:* If the BankDatabase needed to pass a second nested message while processing message 1, the second message would be numbered 1.2.] A message may be passed only when all the nested messages from the previous message have been passed. For example, the BalanceInquiry passes message 3 to the Screen only after messages 2 and 2.1 have been passed, in that order.

The nested numbering scheme used in communication diagrams helps clarify precisely when and in what context each message is passed. For example, if we numbered the five messages in Fig. 8.25 using a flat numbering scheme (i.e., 1, 2, 3, 4, 5), someone looking at the diagram might not be able to determine that BankDatabase passes the Get message to an Account's AvailableBalance property (message 1.1) *during* the BankDatabase's processing of message 1, as opposed to *after* completing the processing of message 1. The nested decimal numbers make it clear that the Get message (message 1.1) is passed to an Account's AvailableBalance property within the handling of the GetAvailable-Balance message (message 1) by the BankDatabase.

Sequence Diagrams

Communication diagrams emphasize the participants in collaborations but model their timing a bit awkwardly. A sequence diagram helps model the timing of collaborations more clearly. Figure 8.26 shows a sequence diagram modeling the sequence of interactions that occur when a Withdrawal executes. The dotted line extending down from an object's rectangle is that object's *lifeline*, which represents the progression of time. Actions typically occur along an object's lifeline in chronological order from top to bottom—an action near the top of the sequence diagram is performed before one near the bottom.

Message passing in sequence diagrams is similar to message passing in communication diagrams. An arrow with a filled arrowhead extending from the sending object to the receiving object represents a message between two objects. The arrowhead points to an activation on the receiving object's lifeline. An *activation*, shown as a thin vertical rectangle, indicates that an object is executing. When an object returns control, a return message, represented as a

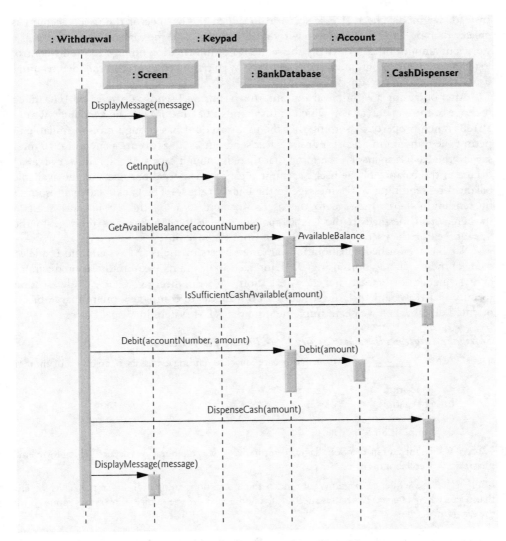

Fig. 8.26 | Sequence diagram that models a `Withdrawal` executing.

dashed line with a stick arrowhead, extends from the activation of the object returning control to the activation of the object that initially sent the message; to eliminate clutter, we omit the return-message arrows—the UML allows this practice to make diagrams more readable. Like communication diagrams, sequence diagrams can indicate message parameters between the parentheses following a message name.

The sequence of messages in Fig. 8.26 begins when a `Withdrawal` prompts the user to choose a withdrawal amount by sending a `DisplayMessage` message to the `Screen`. The `Withdrawal` then sends a `GetInput` message to the `Keypad`, which obtains input from the user. We have already modeled the control logic involved in a `Withdrawal` in the activity diagram of Fig. 6.25, so we do not show this logic in the sequence diagram of Fig. 8.26.

Instead, we model the best-case scenario in which the balance of the user's account is greater than or equal to the chosen withdrawal amount, and the cash dispenser contains a sufficient amount of cash to satisfy the request. For information on how to model control logic in a sequence diagram, please refer to the Web resources and recommended readings listed at the end of Section 3.9.

After obtaining a withdrawal amount, the `Withdrawal` sends a `GetAvailableBalance` message to the `BankDatabase`, which in turn sends a `Get` message to the `Account`'s `AvailableBalance` property. Assuming that the user's account has enough money available to permit the transaction, the `Withdrawal` next sends an `IsSufficientCashAvailable` message to the `CashDispenser`. Assuming that there is enough cash available, the `Withdrawal` decreases the balance of the user's account (i.e., both the total balance and the available balance) by sending a `Debit` message to the `BankDatabase`. The `BankDatabase` responds by sending a `Debit` message to the user's `Account`. Finally, the `Withdrawal` sends a `DispenseCash` message to the `CashDispenser` and a `DisplayMessage` message to the `Screen`, telling the user to remove the cash from the machine.

We have identified collaborations among objects in the ATM system and modeled some of these collaborations using UML interaction diagrams—communication diagrams and sequence diagrams. In the next Software Engineering Case Study section (Section 9.14), we enhance the structure of our model to complete a preliminary object-oriented design, then we begin implementing the ATM system in Visual Basic.

Software Engineering Case Study Self-Review Exercises

8.1 A(n) _____ consists of an object of one class sending a message to an object of another class.

    a) association
    b) aggregation
    c) collaboration
    d) composition

8.2 Which form of interaction diagram emphasizes *what* collaborations occur? Which form emphasizes *when* collaborations occur?

8.3 Create a sequence diagram that models the interactions among objects in the ATM system that occur when a `Deposit` executes successfully, and explain the sequence of messages modeled by the diagram.

Answers to Software Engineering Case Study Self-Review Exercises

8.1 c.

8.2 Communication diagrams emphasize *what* collaborations occur. Sequence diagrams emphasize *when* collaborations occur.

8.3 Figure 8.27 presents a sequence diagram that models the interactions between objects in the ATM system that occur when a `Deposit` executes successfully. Figure 8.27 indicates that a `Deposit` first sends a `DisplayMessage` message to the `Screen` (to ask the user to enter a deposit amount). Next the `Deposit` sends a `GetInput` message to the `Keypad` to receive the amount of the deposit from the user. The `Deposit` then prompts the user (to enter a deposit envelope) by sending a `DisplayMessage` message to the `Screen`. The `Deposit` next sends an `IsDepositEnvelopeReceived` message to the `DepositSlot` to confirm that the deposit envelope has been received by the ATM. Finally, the `Deposit` increases the total balance (but not the available balance) of the user's `Account` by sending a `Credit` message to the `BankDatabase`. The `BankDatabase` responds by sending the same message to the user's `Account`.

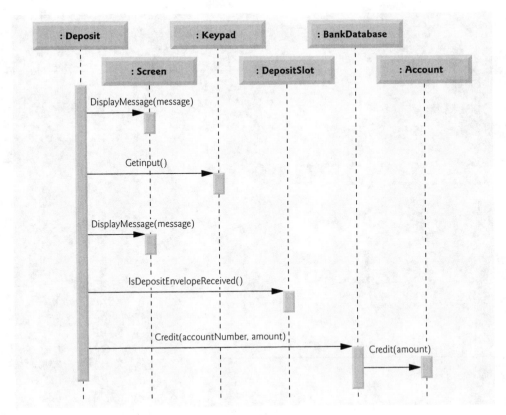

Fig. 8.27 | Sequence diagram that models a `Deposit` executing.

8.16 Wrap-Up

This chapter began our discussion of data structures, exploring the use of arrays to store data in and retrieve data from lists and tables of values. The chapter examples demonstrated how to declare an array, initialize an array and refer to individual elements of an array. We showed how to pass arrays to methods using `ByVal` and `ByRef`. We also showed how to use the `For Each...Next` statement to iterate through the values in an array without using an index. We explained how to declare and manipulate rectangular arrays and jagged arrays. We wrote methods that use variable-length parameter lists. Finally, we demonstrated how to use the `ReDim` statement to dynamically change an array's size.

Chapter 24, Data Structures introduces dynamic data structures, such as lists, queues, stacks and trees, that can grow and shrink as programs execute. Chapter 25, Generics, presents one of Visual Basic 2005's new features—generics—which provides the means to create general models of methods and classes that can be declared once but used with many different types. Chapter 26, Collections, introduces Visual Basic's predefined data structures, which you can use instead of building your own.

We have now introduced the basic concepts of classes, objects, control statements, methods and arrays. In Chapter 9, we take a deeper look at classes and objects.

9

Classes and Objects: A Deeper Look

My object all sublime
I shall achieve in time.
—W. S. Gilbert

Is it a world to hide virtues in?
—William Shakespeare,
Twelfth Night

This above all: to thine own self be true.
—William Shakespeare,
Hamlet

Don't be "consistent," but be simply true.
—Oliver Wendell Holmes, Jr.

OBJECTIVES

In this chapter you will learn:

- What class scope is and how it affects access to class members.

- To create overloaded constructors that can initialize objects of a class in a variety of ways.

- To use partial classes to enable one class to span multiple source-code files.

- How composition enables you to construct classes that are "made out of" other classes.

- To use Me to refer to the current object's members.

- How garbage collection eliminates most "memory leaks."

- How Shared class variables help conserve memory.

- How to create constant members with Const (at compile time) and ReadOnly (at runtime).

- To use the **Object Browser** to discover the capabilities of the classes in the Framework Class Library (FCL).

9.1 Introduction

In the preceding chapters, we introduced the basic concepts and terminology of object-oriented programming (OOP) in Visual Basic. This chapter takes a deeper look at classes. We introduce class scope and discuss how it affects where class members can be accessed. We demonstrate that constructors can be overloaded to allow clients to initialize objects of a class in several ways. We discuss how partial classes enable one class to span multiple source-code files. We explain composition—a capability that allows a class to have references to objects of other classes as members. We show how to use the Me reference to refer to the current object's members. The chapter presents garbage collection and discusses how it eliminates most "memory leaks." In addition, we discuss Shared class variables that are shared among all objects of a class. We then present the differences between constant members created with Const and ReadOnly. Finally, we show how to use the **Object Browser** to discover the capabilities of the classes in the Framework Class Library (FCL). Chapters 10 and 11 introduce inheritance and polymorphism, respectively—two key OOP technologies.

9.2 Time Class Case Study

We begin with a substantial application that uses most of the object-oriented programming concepts presented in Chapters 4 through 8. We introduce the Object class, the ultimate "ancestor" of all classes in Visual Basic. Also, we explain method ToString, which can be used to obtain a String representation of any Visual Basic object.

Time Class Declaration

The application consists of classes Time (Fig. 9.1) and FrmTimeTest (Fig. 9.2). Class Time contains the information needed to represent a specific time in two popular formats. Class FrmTimeTest represents a GUI for class Time.

```vb
1    ' Fig. 9.1: Time.vb
2    ' Represents time to clients in 12-hour and 24-hour clock formats.
3    Class Time
4       Inherits Object ' if omitted, Object is inherited implicitly
5
6       ' declare Integer instance variables for the hour, minute and second
7       Private hourValue As Integer ' 0 - 23
8       Private minuteValue As Integer ' 0 - 59
9       Private secondValue As Integer ' 0 - 59
10
11      ' Time constructor initializes instance variables
12      ' when a Time object is created
13      Public Sub New()
14         SetTime(12, 0, 0) ' initialize hour to noon; minute, second to 0
15      End Sub ' New
16
17      ' set a new time value using universal time, check validity of the
18      ' data, set invalid hour to noon, set invalid minute, second to zero
19      Public Sub SetTime(ByVal hh As Integer, _
20         ByVal mm As Integer, ByVal ss As Integer)
21         Hour = hh ' set hourValue using Hour property
22         Minute = mm ' set minuteValue using Minute property
23         Second = ss ' set secondValue using Second property
24      End Sub ' SetTime
25
26      ' property Hour
27      Public Property Hour() As Integer
28         Get ' return hourValue
29            Return hourValue
30         End Get
31
32         Set(ByVal value As Integer) ' set hourValue
33            If (value >= 0 AndAlso value < 24) Then ' in range 0-23
34               hourValue = value ' value is valid
35            Else ' value is invalid
36               hourValue = 12 ' set to default of noon
37            End If
38         End Set
39      End Property ' Hour
40
41      ' property Minute
42      Public Property Minute() As Integer
43         Get ' return minuteValue
44            Return minuteValue
45         End Get
46
```

Fig. 9.1 | Time class declaration maintains the time in 24-hour format. (Part 1 of 2.)

```
47          Set(ByVal value As Integer) ' set minuteValue
48             If (value >= 0 AndAlso value < 60) Then ' in range 0-59
49                minuteValue = value ' value is valid
50             Else ' value is invalid
51                minuteValue = 0 ' set to default of 0
52             End If
53          End Set
54       End Property ' Minute
55
56       ' property Second
57       Public Property Second() As Integer
58          Get ' return secondValue
59             Return secondValue
60          End Get
61
62          Set(ByVal value As Integer) ' set secondValue
63             If (value >= 0 AndAlso value < 60) Then ' in range 0-59
64                secondValue = value ' value is valid
65             Else ' value is invalid
66                secondValue = 0 ' set to default of 0
67             End If
68          End Set
69       End Property ' Second
70
71       ' convert Time to a String in universal-time (24-hour clock) format
72       Public Function ToUniversalString() As String
73          Return String.Format("{0}:{1:D2}:{2:D2}", Hour, Minute, Second)
74       End Function ' ToUniversalString
75
76       ' convert Time to a String in standard-time (12-hour clock) format
77       Public Overrides Function ToString() As String
78          Dim suffix As String ' AM or PM suffix
79          Dim standardHour As Integer ' a standard hour in the range 1-12
80
81          ' determine whether the 12-hour clock suffix should be AM or PM
82          If Hour < 12 Then
83             suffix = "AM" ' note space preceding AM
84          Else
85             suffix = "PM" ' note space preceding PM
86          End If
87
88          ' convert hour from universal-time format to standard-time format
89          If (Hour = 12 OrElse Hour = 0) Then
90             standardHour = 12
91          Else
92             standardHour = Hour Mod 12 ' 1 through 11, AM or PM
93          End If
94
95          Return String.Format("{0}:{1:D2}:{2:D2} {3}", _
96             standardHour, Minute, Second, suffix)
97       End Function ' ToString
98    End Class ' Time
```

Fig. 9.1 | Time class declaration maintains the time in 24-hour format. (Part 2 of 2.)

In Fig. 9.1, lines 3–4 begin the Time class declaration, indicating that class Time inherits from class ***Object*** of namespace System. Recall from Chapter 7 that it is not necessary to add an assembly reference for namespace System because it is implicitly added to all projects. Visual Basic programmers use inheritance to quickly create new classes from existing classes (and, as we will see in the next chapter, to organize groups of related classes). The Inherits keyword (line 4) followed by class name Object indicates that class Time inherits the attributes and behaviors of class Object. In fact, every class (except Object) inherits either directly or indirectly from Object. If you do not include line 4, the Visual Basic compiler includes it implicitly. A complete understanding of inheritance is not necessary to understand the concepts and programs in this chapter. We explore inheritance in detail in Chapter 10.

Lines 3 and 98 delimit with keywords Class and End Class, respectively, the ***body*** of the Time class declaration. Any information that we place in this body is contained within the class's scope. Class Time declares three Private Integer instance variables—hourValue, minuteValue and secondValue (lines 7–9)—that represent the time in universal-time format (24-hour clock format). We prefer to list the instance variables of a class first, so that, when reading the code, you see the name and type of each instance variable before it is used in the class's methods.

It is possible to have Private methods and Public instance variables. Private methods are called ***utility methods***, or ***helper methods***, because they can be called only by other methods of the class to support the operation of those methods. Using Public instance variables in a class is an uncommon and dangerous programming practice. Providing such access to a class's instance variables is unsafe; other parts of the program could accidentally or maliciously set these members to invalid values, producing potentially disastrous results.

Time Class Properties
Class Time (Fig. 9.1) declares properties Hour (lines 27–39), Minute (lines 42–54) and Second (lines 57–69) to access instance variables hourValue, minuteValue and secondValue, respectively. Each of these properties contains a Get accessor and a Set accessor. The Set accessors (lines 32–38, 47–53 and 62–68) strictly control the setting of the instance variables to ensure that they contain valid values. An attempt to set any instance variable to an incorrect value causes the instance variable to be set to its default value—12 (noon) for the hour and 0 for the minute and second—leaving the instance variable in a consistent state. Each Get accessor (lines 28–30, 43–45 and 58–60) returns the appropriate instance variable's value.

Time Class Methods
Class Time contains the following Public methods—the constructor New (lines 13–15), SetTime (lines 19–24), ToUniversalString (lines 72–74) and ToString (lines 77–97). Constructor New calls (in line 14) method SetTime (discussed shortly) with the hour value specified as 12, and the minute and second values specified as 0 to indicate that the default time should be noon. Visual Basic initializes Integer variables to 0 by default, so if we did not provide a constructor for class Time, instance variables hourValue, minuteValue and secondValue would each be initialized to 0, making the default time midnight. For some classes that would be fine, but we want our Time objects to be initialized to noon.

Constructors are implemented as Sub procedures, not as Functions, because Sub procedures cannot return values. Generally, constructors are declared Public. Private constructors are useful but are beyond the scope of the book. As we will see, a class can have many overloaded constructors—all share the same name, New, but each must have different numbers and/or types of parameters.

Method SetTime (lines 19–24) uses properties Hour, Minute and Second to ensure that instance variables hourValue, minuteValue and secondValue have valid values. For example, the hourValue must be greater than or equal to 0 and less than 24, because universal-time format represents hours as integers from 0 to 23. Similarly, both the minuteValue and secondValue must fall between 0 and 59. Any values outside these ranges are invalid and default to 12 for the hourValue or 0 for the minuteValue and secondValue, ensuring that a Time object always contains valid data; that is, the object remains in a consistent state. When a user calls SetTime with invalid arguments, the program should indicate that the attempted time setting was invalid. This can be done by "throwing an exception"—we discuss exception handling in Chapter 12.

Method ToUniversalString (lines 72–74) takes no arguments and returns a String in universal-time format, consisting of the Hour property value, two digits for the Minute property value and two digits for the Second property value. For example, if the time were 1:30:07 PM, method ToUniversalString would return the String "13:30:07". Note that format specifier D2 formats a single digit integer value with a leading 0.

Method *ToString* (lines 77–97) takes no arguments and returns a String in standard-time format, consisting of the Hour, Minute and Second property values separated by colons and followed by an AM or PM indicator (e.g., 1:27:06 PM). Lines 82–93 determine the proper formatting for the hour—hours from 0 to 11 print with AM, hours from 12 to 23 print with PM, hour 0 prints as 12 (midnight), hours 1–12 print as is and hours 13–23 print as 1–11 (PM).

Note that method ToString contains the keyword *Overrides* (line 77) in its declaration. Recall that every class in Visual Basic (such as class Time) inherits either directly or indirectly from class Object, which is the root of the class hierarchy. Section 10.7 summarizes class Object's seven methods, including method ToString, which returns a String representation of an object. The default implementation of ToString that every class inherits (directly or indirectly) from class Object returns the namespace and the class name of the object's class. This implementation is primarily a placeholder that can be overridden by a derived class to specify a more appropriate String representation of the data in a derived class object. For class Time, we choose to override (i.e., redefine) the ToString method to return a String which represents the Time object in standard-time (i.e., 12-hour clock) format.

After defining the class, we can use it as a type in declarations such as

```
Dim sunset As Time ' reference to object of class Time
```

Using the Time Class

Class FrmTimeTest (Fig. 9.2) provides a GUI for testing class Time. The GUI contains three text boxes in which the user can enter values for the Time object's Hour, Minute and Second properties, respectively. Class FrmTimeTest creates an object of class Time (line 4) and assigns its reference to variable time. When the object is instantiated, New allocates the memory for the Time object, then calls the Time constructor (method New in lines 13–15 of Fig. 9.1) to initialize the object's instance variables. The constructor invokes method SetTime of class Time to initialize each of the properties, setting the time to noon.

Common Programming Error 9.1

Using a reference (which, as you know, is initialized to the default value Nothing) before it refers to an actual object results in a NullReferenceException at execution time and causes the program to terminate prematurely. We discuss how to handle exceptions to make programs more robust in Chapter 12, Exception Handling.

```vb
1   ' Fig. 9.2: FrmTimeTest.vb
2   ' Demonstrates Properties.
3   Public Class FrmTimeTest
4      Dim time As New Time() ' construct Time with zero arguments
5
6      ' invoked when user clicks the Add 1 to Second button
7      Private Sub btnAddSecond_Click(ByVal sender As System.Object, _
8         ByVal e As System.EventArgs) Handles btnAddSecond.Click
9         time.Second = (time.Second + 1) Mod 60 ' add 1 to Second
10        txtSetSecond.Text = time.Second
11
12        ' add one minute if 60 seconds have passed
13        If time.Second = 0 Then
14           time.Minute = (time.Minute + 1) Mod 60 ' add 1 to Minute
15           txtSetMinute.Text = time.Minute
16
17           ' add one hour if 60 minutes have passed
18           If time.Minute = 0 Then
19              time.Hour = (time.Hour + 1) Mod 24 ' add 1 to Hour
20              txtSetHour.Text = time.Hour
21           End If
22        End If
23
24        UpdateDisplay() ' update the text in lblOutput1 and lblOutput2
25     End Sub ' btnAddSecond_Click
26
27     ' handle event when txtSetHour's text changes
28     Private Sub txtSetHour_TextChanged(ByVal sender As System.Object, _
29        ByVal e As System.EventArgs) Handles txtSetHour.TextChanged
30        time.Hour = txtSetHour.Text
31        UpdateDisplay() ' update the text in lblOutput1 and lblOutput2
32     End Sub ' txtSetHour_TextChanged
33
34     ' handle event when txtSetMinute's text changes
35     Private Sub txtSetMinute_TextChanged(ByVal sender As System.Object, _
36        ByVal e As System.EventArgs) Handles txtSetMinute.TextChanged
37        time.Minute = txtSetMinute.Text
38        UpdateDisplay() ' update the text in lblOutput1 and lblOutput2
39     End Sub ' txtSetMinute_TextChanged
40
41     ' handle event when txtSetSecond's text changes
42     Private Sub txtSetSecond_TextChanged(ByVal sender As System.Object, _
43        ByVal e As System.EventArgs) Handles txtSetSecond.TextChanged
```

Fig. 9.2 | Graphical user interface for class Time. (Part 1 of 2.)

```
44          time.Second = txtSetSecond.Text
45          UpdateDisplay() ' update the text in lblOutput1 and lblOutput2
46       End Sub ' txtSetSecond_Textchanged
47
48       ' update time display
49       Private Sub UpdateDisplay()
50          txtSetHour.Text = time.Hour
51          txtSetMinute.Text = time.Minute
52          txtSetSecond.Text = time.Second
53          lblOutput1.Text = ("Hour: " & time.Hour & "; Minute: " & _
54             time.Minute & "; Second: " & time.Second)
55          lblOutput2.Text = ("Standard time is: " & time.ToString() & _
56             "; Universal Time is: " & time.ToUniversalString())
57       End Sub ' UpdateDisplay
58    End Class ' FrmTimeTest
```

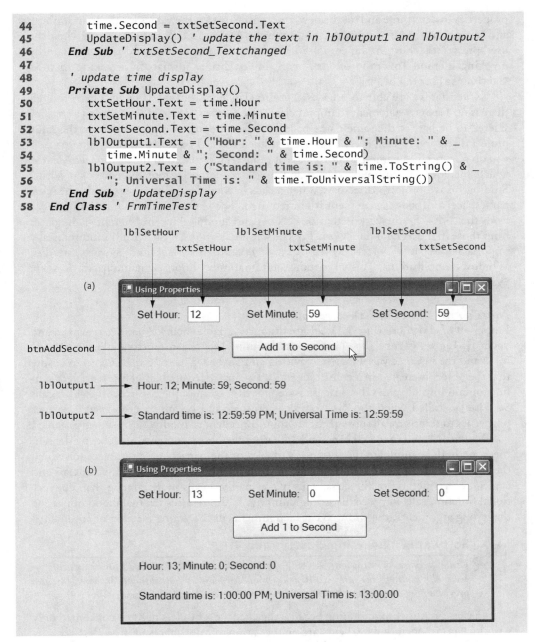

Fig. 9.2 | Graphical user interface for class Time. (Part 2 of 2.)

Lines 28–46 declare three methods that use the Time object's Hour, Minute and Second properties to alter the corresponding instance variable values. The GUI also contains a button that enables the user to increment the Second property value by 1 without having to use the corresponding text box. Method btnAddSecond_Click (lines 7–25) uses properties to determine and set the new time, ensuring that the values for the hour, minute and second are updated properly. For example, `23:59:59` becomes `00:00:00` when the user presses the button. Lines 55–56 display the time in standard-time format (by invoking method `ToString` of `Time`) and universal-time format (by invoking method `ToUniversalString` of `Time`).

Note that we are able to use class `Time` in class `FrmTimeTest` (Fig. 9.2) even though there is no `Imports` statement to import class `Time`. Classes `Time` and `FrmTimeTest` are considered to be part of the same namespace by default because we placed then in the same project directory. In fact, every class and module in Visual Basic is part of a namespace. If you do not specify a namespace for a class or module, it is placed in the *default namespace*, which includes the compiled classes and modules in the current directory—in Visual Studio, this is a project's directory. When a class or module uses another class in the same namespace, an `Imports` statement is not required. The reason we must import the classes from the .NET Framework is that our classes and modules are in different namespaces from those in the .NET Framework. For console applications, Visual Studio automatically imports namespaces `System`, `System.Data`, `System.Deployment` and `System.Xml`. For Windows applications, Visual Studio automatically imports namespaces `System`, `System.Deployment`, `System.Drawing` and `System.Windows.Forms`.

Notes on the Time Class Declaration

Lines 7–9 of class `Time` (Fig. 9.1) declare instance variables `hourValue`, `minuteValue` and `secondValue` as `Private`. The `Time` constructor initializes the instance variable `hourValue` to `12` and the instance variables `minuteValue` and `secondValue` to 0 (i.e., noon) to ensure that the object is created in a consistent state. The instance variables of a `Time` object cannot contain invalid values, because they are `Private`, because the constructor (which calls `SetTime`) is called when the `Time` object is created, and because method `SetTime` uses properties to scrutinize all subsequent attempts by a client to modify the instance variables.

Methods `ToUniversalString` and `ToString` take no arguments because, by default, these methods manipulate the instance variables of the particular `Time` object for which they are invoked. Any method of a class can access all the instance variables of the class and can call every method of the class. This makes method calls more concise than conventional function calls in procedural programming. It also reduces the likelihood of passing the wrong arguments, the wrong types of arguments or the wrong number of arguments.

Software Engineering Observation 9.1

Using an object-oriented programming approach often simplifies method calls by reducing, or even eliminating, the arguments that must be passed. This benefit of object-oriented programming derives from the encapsulation of instance variables within an object.

Classes simplify programming because the clients of the class need be concerned only with its `Public` operations. Clients are neither aware of, nor involved in, a class's implementation. Interfaces change less frequently than implementations. When an implementation changes, implementation-dependent code must change accordingly. By hiding the implementation, we eliminate the possibility that the clients of the class will become dependent on the class's implementation details.

You do not always have to create classes from scratch. Rather, you can derive classes by inheritance from other classes that provide capabilities required by the new classes.

Classes also can include references to objects of other classes as members—this is called composition. Such software reuse can greatly enhance your productivity. Section 9.7 discusses composition. Chapter 10 discusses inheritance.

9.3 Class Scope

In Section 7.16, we discussed method scope; now, we consider *class scope*. A class's instance variables and methods belong to its scope. Within a class's scope, class members are accessible to all of the class's methods and properties and can be referenced simply by name (without an object reference). Outside a class's scope, class members cannot be referenced directly by name. Those class members that are visible (such as `Public` members) can be accessed through a "handle" (i.e., members can be referenced via names of the form *objectReferenceName.memberName* or *ClassName.memberName* for `Shared` members). For example, line 56 of Fig. 9.2 accessess a `Time` object's method with the method call `time.ToUniversalString()`.

If a variable is defined in a method, only that method can access the variable (i.e., the variable is a local variable of that method). Such variables have block scope. If a method defines a local variable that has the same name as an instance variable, the local variable hides the instance variable in that method's scope—this is called shadowing. A shadowed instance variable can be accessed in a method of that class by preceding its name with the keyword `Me` and the dot separator, as in `Me.hourValue`. Section 9.8 discusses keyword `Me`.

9.4 Default and Parameterless Constructors

If a class does not define constructors, the compiler provides a default constructor. This constructor contains no code (i.e., the constructor body is empty) and takes no parameters. You can also provide a constructor—called a *parameterless constructor*—that contains code (but, again, takes no parameters), as we demonstrated in class `Time` (lines 13–15 of Fig. 9.1), and as we will see again in the next example. If you provide any constructors for a class, the compiler will not provide a default constructor for that class.

Common Programming Error 9.2

If `Public` constructors are provided for a class, but none of them is a parameterless constructor, and an attempt is made to call a constructor with no arguments to initialize an object of the class, a compilation error occurs. A constructor can be called with no arguments only if there are no constructors for the class (in which case the default constructor is called) or if the class includes a parameterless constructor provided by the programmer.

9.5 Time Class Case Study: Overloaded Constructors

Like methods, constructors of a class can be overloaded. To do so, provide a separate method declaration with the same name (`New`) for each version of the method but different numbers, types and/or orders of parameters.

Class *Time* with Overloaded Constructors

The `Time` constructor in Fig. 9.1 initialized `hourValue` to `12` and `minuteValue` and `secondValue` to `0` (i.e., noon) with a call to the class's `SetTime` method. Recall that the declaration in line 4 of Fig. 9.2 supplied no arguments to the `Time` class constructor. Suppose you would like to create `Time` objects with any legitimate hour, minute and/or second values. Class `Time` of Fig. 9.3 includes five overloaded constructors to provide several ways to initialize `Time` objects. Each constructor calls method `SetTime` of the `Time` object, which uses the `Set` accessors of properties `Hour`, `Minute` and `Second` to ensure that the object begins in a consistent state by setting out-of-range hour, minute and second values to 12, 0 and 0, respectively. The compiler invokes the appropriate constructor by matching the number, types and order of the arguments specified in the constructor call with the number, types and order of the parameters specified in each constructor method declaration.

```vb
1   ' Fig. 9.3: Time.vb
2   ' Represents time and contains overloaded constructors.
3   Class Time
4      ' declare Integer instance variables for the hour, minute and second
5      Private hourValue As Integer ' 0 - 23
6      Private minuteValue As Integer ' 0 - 59
7      Private secondValue As Integer ' 0 - 59
8
9      ' constructor initializes hour to 12, minute to 0 and second to 0
10     ' to ensure that each Time object starts in a consistent state
11     Public Sub New() ' parameterless constructor
12        SetTime(12) ' initialize hour to noon; minute and second to 0
13     End Sub ' New
14
15     ' Time constructor: hour supplied;
16     ' minute and second default to 0
17     Public Sub New(ByVal hh As Integer)
18        SetTime(hh) ' call SetTime with one argument
19     End Sub ' New
20
21     ' Time constructor: hour and minute supplied;
22     ' second defaults to 0
23     Public Sub New(ByVal hh As Integer, ByVal mm As Integer)
24        SetTime(hh, mm) ' call SetTime with two arguments
25     End Sub ' New
26
27     ' Time constructor: hour, minute and second supplied
28     Public Sub New(ByVal hh As Integer, _
29        ByVal mm As Integer, ByVal ss As Integer)
30        SetTime(hh, mm, ss) ' call SetTime with three arguments
31     End Sub ' New
32
33     ' Time constructor: another Time object supplied
34     Public Sub New(ByVal tt As Time)
35        SetTime(tt.Hour, tt.Minute, tt.Second)
36     End Sub ' New
37
38     ' set a new time value using universal time, check validity of the
39     ' data, set invalid hour to 12, set invalid minute/second to zero
40     Public Sub SetTime(Optional ByVal hh As Integer = 12, _
41        Optional ByVal mm As Integer = 0, Optional ByVal ss As Integer = 0)
42        Hour = hh ' set hourValue using the Hour property
```

Fig. 9.3 | Overloaded constructors and `Optional` arguments. (Part 1 of 3.)

```
43          Minute = mm ' set minuteValue using the Minute property
44          Second = ss ' set secondValue using the Second property
45       End Sub ' SetTime
46
47       ' property Hour
48       Public Property Hour() As Integer
49          Get ' return hourValue
50             Return hourValue
51          End Get
52
53          Set(ByVal value As Integer) ' set hourValue
54             If (value >= 0 AndAlso value < 24) Then ' in range 0-23
55                hourValue = value ' value is valid
56             Else ' value is invalid
57                hourValue = 12 ' set to default of noon
58             End If
59          End Set
60       End Property ' Hour
61
62       ' property Minute
63       Public Property Minute() As Integer
64          Get ' return minuteValue
65             Return minuteValue
66          End Get
67
68          Set(ByVal value As Integer) ' set minuteValue
69             If (value >= 0 AndAlso value < 60) Then ' in range 0-59
70                minuteValue = value ' value is valid
71             Else ' value is invalid
72                minuteValue = 0 ' set to default of 0
73             End If
74          End Set
75       End Property ' Minute
76
77       ' property Second
78       Public Property Second() As Integer
79          Get ' return secondValue
80             Return secondValue
81          End Get
82
83          Set(ByVal value As Integer) ' set secondValue
84             If (value >= 0 AndAlso value < 60) Then ' in range 0-59
85                secondValue = value ' value is valid
86             Else ' value is invalid
87                secondValue = 0 ' set to default of 0
88             End If
89          End Set
90       End Property ' Second
91
92       ' convert Time to a String in universal-time (24-hour clock) format
93       Public Function ToUniversalString() As String
94          Return String.Format("{0}:{1:D2}:{2:D2}", Hour, Minute, Second)
95       End Function ' ToUniversalString
```

Fig. 9.3 | Overloaded constructors and `Optional` arguments. (Part 2 of 3.)

```
96
97        ' convert Time to a String in standard-time (12-hour clock) format
98      Public Overrides Function ToString() As String
99         Dim suffix As String ' AM or PM suffix
100        Dim standardHour As Integer ' a standard hour in the range 1-12
101
102        ' determine whether the 12-hour clock suffix should be AM or PM
103        If Hour < 12 Then
104           suffix = " AM" ' note space preceding AM
105        Else
106           suffix = " PM" ' note space preceding PM
107        End If
108
109        ' convert hour from universal-time format to standard-time format
110        If (Hour = 12 OrElse Hour = 0) Then
111           standardHour = 12
112        Else
113           standardHour = Hour Mod 12 ' 1 through 11, AM or PM
114        End If
115
116        Return String.Format("{0}:{1:D2}:{2:D2}", standardHour, Minute, _
117           Second) & suffix
118     End Function ' ToString
119  End Class ' Time
```

Fig. 9.3 | Overloaded constructors and `Optional` arguments. (Part 3 of 3.)

Class Time's Constructors

Because most of the code in class Time is identical to that in Fig. 9.1, this section concentrates only on the overloaded constructors. Lines 11–13 define the parameterless constructor that calls SetTime (line 12), initializing the time to noon. Lines 17–19 define a Time constructor with a single Integer parameter, representing the hour. Lines 23–25 define a Time constructor with two Integer parameters, representing the hour and minute. Lines 28–31 define a Time constructor with three Integer parameters representing the hour, minute and second. Lines 34–36 define a Time constructor that receives a reference to another Time object. When this last constructor—sometimes called a *copy constructor*—is called, the values from the Time argument are copied to initialize the new object's hour-Value, minuteValue and secondValue. Class Time declares these values as Private (lines 5–7), but the new Time object's constructor obtains these values via the Public properties of its Time parameter by using the expressions tt.Hour, tt.Minute and tt.Second. In fact, line 35 could have accessed the argument Time object's instance variables directly with the expressions tt.hourValue, tt.minuteValue and tt.secondValue.

Software Engineering Observation 9.2

When one object of a class has a reference to another object of the same class, the first object can access all of the second object's data, methods and properties (including those that are Private).

Although the parameter to the constructor in lines 34–36 is passed by value, this does not make a copy of the Time object that is passed as the constructor's argument. Rather, it makes a copy of the reference to the Time object passed as the argument.

Software Engineering Observation 9.3

Visual Basic classes are reference types, so all Visual Basic objects are passed to methods by reference.

Note that each constructor receives a different number and/or different types of parameters. Also, recall that if a method has one or more Optional parameters, the caller has the option of passing a value for each parameter. Method SetTime declares three Optional parameters—hh, mm and ss (lines 40–41). Lines 12 and 18 call method SetTime with one argument, which indicates that the default values for the Optional minuteValue and secondValue parameters should be used. Line 24 calls method SetTime with two arguments, which indicates that the default value for the Optional parameter second-Value is used. Lines 30 and 35 call method SetTime with all three arguments, so that no default values are used.

Common Programming Error 9.3

A constructor can call other class methods that use instance variables not yet initialized. Using instance variables before they have been initialized can lead to logic errors.

Using Class Time's Overloaded Constructors

Figure 9.4 (TimeTest.vb) demonstrates class Time's overloaded constructors. Lines 6–11 create six Time objects that invoke various constructors of the class. Line 6 invokes the parameterless constructor by placing an empty set of parentheses after the class name. Lines 7–11 demonstrate passing arguments to the Time constructors. Line 7 invokes the constructor at lines 17–19 of Fig. 9.3. Line 8 invokes the constructor at lines 23–25 of Fig. 9.3. Lines 9–10 invoke the constructor at lines 28–31 of Fig. 9.3. Line 11 invokes the constructor at lines 34–36 of Fig. 9.3.

```
1   ' Fig. 9.4: TimeTest.vb
2   ' Overloading constructors.
3   Module TimeTest
4      Sub Main()
5         ' use overloaded constructors
6         Dim time1 As New Time() ' constructor with zero parameters
7         Dim time2 As New Time(2) ' constructor with one parameter
8         Dim time3 As New Time(21, 34) ' constructor with two parameters
9         Dim time4 As New Time(12, 25, 42) ' three valid arguments
10        Dim time5 As New Time(27, 74, 99) ' three invalid arguments
11        Dim time6 As New Time(time4) ' copy another Time object
12
13        ' invoke time1 methods
14        Console.WriteLine("Constructed with: " & vbCrLf & _
15           "time1: all arguments defaulted" & vbCrLf & vbTab & _
16           time1.ToUniversalString() & vbCrLf & vbTab & _
17           time1.ToString())
18        ' invoke time2 methods
19        Console.WriteLine( _
20           "time2: hour specified; minute and second defaulted" & _
21           vbCrLf & vbTab & time2.ToUniversalString() & _
```

Fig. 9.4 | Overloading constructors. (Part 1 of 2.)

```
22              vbCrLf & vbTab & time2.ToString())
23          ' invoke time3 methods
24          Console.WriteLine( _
25              "time3: hour and minute specified; second defaulted" & _
26              vbCrLf & vbTab & time3.ToUniversalString() & _
27              vbCrLf & vbTab & time3.ToString())
28          ' invoke time4 methods
29          Console.WriteLine("time4: hour, minute and second specified" & _
30              vbCrLf & vbTab & time4.ToUniversalString() & _
31              vbCrLf & vbTab & time4.ToString())
32          ' invoke time5 methods
33          Console.WriteLine( _
34              "time5: invalid hour, minute and second specified" & _
35              vbCrLf & vbTab & time5.ToUniversalString() & _
36              vbCrLf & vbTab & time5.ToString())
37          ' invoke time6 methods
38          Console.WriteLine( "time6: Time object copied from time4" & _
39              vbCrLf & vbTab & time6.ToUniversalString() & _
40              vbCrLf & vbTab & time6.ToString())
41      End Sub ' Main
42  End Module ' TimeTest
```

```
Constructed with:
time1: all arguments defaulted
       12:00:00
       12:00:00 PM
time2: hour specified; minute and second defaulted
       2:00:00
       2:00:00 AM
time3: hour and minute specified; second defaulted
       21:34:00
       9:34:00 PM
time4: hour, minute and second specified
       12:25:42
       12:25:42 PM
time5: invalid hour, minute and second specified
       12:00:00
       12:00:00 PM
time6: Time object copied from time4
       12:25:42
       12:25:42 PM
```

Fig. 9.4 | Overloading constructors. (Part 2 of 2.)

Each Time constructor can be written to include a copy of the appropriate statements from method SetTime. This might be slightly more efficient, because it eliminates the extra SetTime call. However, consider what would happen if you change the representation of the time from three Integer values (requiring 12 bytes of memory) to a single Integer value representing the total number of elapsed seconds since midnight (requiring only 4 bytes of memory). Placing identical code in the Time constructors and method Set-Time makes such a change in the class declaration more difficult. If the implementation of SetTime changes, the implementation of all the Time constructors would need to change accordingly. If, on the other hand, the Time constructors call method SetTime directly, any changes to the implementation of SetTime must be made only once, thus reducing the likelihood of a programming error when altering the implementation.

Software Engineering Observation 9.4

If a method of a class provides functionality required by a constructor (or other method) of the class, call that method from the constructor (or other method). This simplifies the maintenance of the code and reduces the likelihood of code errors.

9.6 Partial Classes

Visual Basic allows a class declaration to span multiple source-code files. The separate portions of the class declaration in each file are known as *partial classes*. We have already created applications that use partial classes—in each GUI application, the code that is auto-generated by the IDE (i.e., the code that declares and creates GUI components in the code-behind file) is marked with the *Partial modifier* and stored in a separate source file. For example, in the GUI application in Fig. 9.2, the lines 2–3 of the auto-generated partial class (stored in FrmTimeTest.Designer.vb) are:

```
Partial Public Class FrmTimeTest
    Inherits System.Windows.Forms.Form
```

which indicates that the code in this file is part of class FrmTimeTest. The partial class is stored in a file named FrmTimeTest.Designer.vb. To view the file FrmTimeTest.Designer.vb, click the **Show All Files** button on the **Solution Explorer** toolbar and then click the plus sign (+) to the left of the FrmTimeTest.vb in the **Solution Explorer** window.

When a class declaration specifies the Partial modifier, any class declarations with the same class name in the program will be combined with the partial class declaration to form a single class declaration at compile time. Partial classes must be declared in the same namespace and assembly. If members (e.g., instance variables, methods and properties) in one source file conflict with those in other source files, compilation errors will occur.

Error-Prevention Tip 9.1

When combining all partial classes, at least one class declaration must have a Partial modifier. Otherwise, a compilation error occurs.

Most of the classes you have seen to this point are small. In real applications, classes can grow to be quite large and might be developed by a team of programmers. Partial classes provide a convenient way to split a large class into small, manageable pieces. With partial classes, several developers can work on the same class at once.

9.7 Composition

A class can have references to objects of other classes as members. Such a capability is called *composition* and is sometimes referred to as a *has-a relationship*. For example, an object of class AlarmClock needs to know the current time and the time when it is supposed to sound its alarm, so it is reasonable to include two references to Time objects as members of the AlarmClock object.

Software Engineering Observation 9.5

One form of software reuse is composition, in which a class has as members references to objects of other classes.

Our example of composition contains two classes—Day (Fig. 9.5) and Employee (Fig. 9.6)—and module CompositionTest (Fig. 9.7) to demonstrate them. Class Day (Fig. 9.5) encapsulates information relating to a specific date. Lines 4–6 declare Integers monthValue, dayValue and yearValue. Lines 10–15 declare the constructor, which receives as parameters values for the month, day and year, then assigns these values to the class's properties to ensure that the parameter values are valid.

```vb
1   ' Fig. 9.5: Day.vb
2   ' Encapsulates month, day and year.
3   Class Day
4      Private monthValue As Integer ' 1-12
5      Private dayValue As Integer ' 1-31 based on month
6      Private yearValue As Integer ' any year (could validate)
7
8      ' constructor confirms proper value for month, then calls
9      ' method CheckDay to confirm proper value for day
10     Public Sub New(ByVal mm As Integer, _
11        ByVal dd As Integer, ByVal yy As Integer)
12        Month = mm
13        Day = dd
14        Year = yy
15     End Sub ' New
16
17     ' property Month
18     Public Property Month() As Integer
19        Get
20           Return monthValue
21        End Get
22
23        Set(ByVal mm As Integer)
24           ' ensure month value is valid (in the range 1-12)
25           If (mm > 0 AndAlso mm <= 12) Then
26              monthValue = mm
27           Else
28              monthValue = 1 ' to ensure consistent state
29
30              ' inform user of error
31              Console.WriteLine("Invalid month (" & mm & _
32                 ") set to 1.")
33           End If
34        End Set
35     End Property ' Month
36
37     ' property Day
38     Public Property Day() As Integer
39        Get
40           Return dayValue
41        End Get
42
```

Fig. 9.5 | Day class encapsulates day, month and year information. (Part 1 of 2.)

```
43          Set(ByVal dd As Integer)
44              dayValue = CheckDay(dd) ' validate dayPassed
45          End Set
46      End Property ' Day
47
48      ' property Year
49      Public Property Year() As Integer
50          Get
51              Return yearValue
52          End Get
53
54          Set(ByVal yy As Integer)
55              yearValue = yy
56          End Set
57      End Property ' Year
58
59      ' confirm proper day value based on month and year
60      Private Function CheckDay(ByVal testDayValue As Integer) As Integer
61          Dim daysPerMonth() As Integer = _
62              {0, 31, 28, 31, 30, 31, 30, 31, 31, 30, 31, 30, 31}
63
64          ' validate day
65          If (testDayValue > 0 AndAlso _
66              testDayValue <= daysPerMonth(Month)) Then
67              Return testDayValue
68          End If
69
70          ' check for leap year in February
71          If (Month = 2 AndAlso testDayValue = 29 AndAlso _
72              ((Year Mod 400 = 0) OrElse _
73              (Year Mod 4 = 0 AndAlso Year Mod 100 <> 0))) Then
74              Return testDayValue
75          End If
76
77          ' inform user of error
78          Console.WriteLine("Invalid day (" & testDayValue & ") set to 1. ")
79          Return 1 ' leave object in consistent state
80      End Function ' CheckDay
81
82      ' create string containing month/day/year format
83      Public Overrides Function ToString() As String
84          Return (Month & "/" & Day & "/" & Year)
85      End Function ' ToString
86  End Class ' Day
```

Fig. 9.5 | Day class encapsulates day, month and year information. (Part 2 of 2.)

The Set accessor (lines 23–34) of property Month ensures that the month value is in the range 1–12. The Set accessor (lines 43–45) of property Day invokes utility function CheckDay to validate the day value. The Year property does not perform the validation of the year value. We assume that the Year is a valid four-digit year, such as 2005; however, we could have validated the year as well.

Function CheckDay (lines 60–80) validates whether the day is correct based on the current Month and Year. Lines 65–68 determine whether the day is a valid day for the particular month. If not, lines 71–75 determine whether the Month is February, the day is 29 and the Year is a leap year. A year is a leap year if it is divisible by 400 (tested at line 72), or if it is divisible by 4 and not divisible by 100 (tested at line 73). If lines 71–75 do not return a correct value for day, line 79 returns 1 to maintain the date in a consistent state.

Using Class Day in Class Employee

Class Employee (Fig. 9.6) holds information relating to an employee's birthday and hire date using instance variables firstName, lastName, birthDate and hireDate (lines 4–7). Members birthDate and hireDate are references to Day objects, each of which contains instance variables month, day and year. In this example, class Employee is *composed of* two references to Day objects. The Employee constructor (lines 10–23) takes eight arguments (first, last, birthMonth, birthDay, birthYear, hireMonth, hireDay and hireYear). Line 19 passes arguments birthMonth, birthDay and birthYear to the Day constructor to create the birthDate object. Similarly, line 22 passes arguments hireMonth, hireDay and hireYear to the Day constructor to create the hireDate object.

Testing Class Employee

Module CompositionTest (Fig. 9.7) contains Main, which tests the classes in Figs. 9.5–9.6. Lines 5–6 instantiate an Employee object ("Bob Blue" with birthday 7/24/1949 and hire date 3/12/1988), and line 7 displays the Employee information to the user.

```vb
 1   ' Fig. 9.6: Employee.vb
 2   ' Represent employee name, birthday and hire date.
 3   Class Employee
 4       Private firstName As String
 5       Private lastName As String
 6       Private birthDate As Day ' member object reference
 7       Private hireDate As Day ' member object reference
 8
 9       ' Employee constructor
10       Public Sub New(ByVal first As String, ByVal last As String, _
11           ByVal birthMonth As Integer, ByVal birthDay As Integer, _
12           ByVal birthYear As Integer, ByVal hireMonth As Integer, _
13           ByVal hireDay As Integer, ByVal hireYear As Integer)
14
15           firstName = first
16           lastName = last
17
18           ' create Day instance for employee birthday
19           birthDate = New Day(birthMonth, birthDay, birthYear)
20
21           ' create Day instance for employee hire date
22           hireDate = New Day(hireMonth, hireDay, hireYear)
23       End Sub ' New
24
```

Fig. 9.6 | Employee class encapsulates employee name, birthday and hire date. (Part 1 of 2.)

```
25        ' return employee information as String
26        Public Overrides Function ToString() As String
27           Return (lastName & ", " & firstName & " Hired: " _
28              & hireDate.ToString() & " Birthday: " & birthDate.ToString())
29        End Function ' ToString
30     End Class ' Employee
```

Fig. 9.6 | Employee class encapsulates employee name, birthday and hire date. (Part 2 of 2.)

```
1    ' Fig. 9.7: CompositionTest.vb
2    ' Demonstrate an object with member object reference.
3    Module CompositionTest
4       Sub Main()
5          Dim employee As New Employee( _
6             "Bob", "Blue", 7, 24, 1949, 3, 12, 1988)
7          Console.WriteLine(employee.ToString())
8       End Sub ' Main
9    End Module ' CompositionTest
```

```
Blue, Bob Hired: 3/12/1988 Birthday: 7/24/1949
```

Fig. 9.7 | Composition demonstration.

9.8 Using the Me Reference to Access the Current Object

Every object of a class shares the class's method declarations. We have seen that an object's methods can manipulate the object's data. But how do methods know which object's instance variables to manipulate? Every object has access to itself through a reference called Me (a Visual Basic keyword). On every method call, the compiler passes an object's Me reference as an implicit argument to each of the object's non-Shared methods. The Me reference can then be used to access a particular object's members implicitly or explicitly. (Section 9.10 introduces Shared class members and explains why the Me reference is *not* implicitly passed to Shared methods.)

Class Time (Fig. 9.8) defines Private instance variables hour, minute and second (lines 4–6). The constructor (lines 9–14) receives three Integer arguments to initialize a Time object. For this example, we use parameter names (lines 9–10) that are identical to the class's instance variable names (lines 4–6). When a method has a parameter or local variable with the same name as one of the class's instance variables, the instance variable is shadowed (hidden) in the method's scope. However, the method can use the Me reference to refer explicitly to shadowed instance variables. Lines 11–13 of Fig. 9.8 demonstrate this feature.

Method BuildString (lines 17–20) returns a String created by a statement that uses the Me reference first explicitly then implicitly. Line 18 uses the Me reference explicitly to call method ToUniversalString, whereas line 19 calls the same method using the Me reference implicitly. Note that both lines generate identical outputs.

Error-Prevention Tip 9.2

For a method in which a parameter has the same name as an instance variable, use reference Me to access the instance variable explicitly; otherwise, the method parameter is referenced.

```
 1    ' Fig. 9.8: Time.vb
 2    ' Encapsulate time using Me reference.
 3    Class Time
 4       Private hour As Integer
 5       Private minute As Integer
 6       Private second As Integer
 7
 8       ' Time constructor
 9       Public Sub New(ByVal hour As Integer, _
10          ByVal minute As Integer, ByVal second As Integer)
11          Me.hour = hour ' set instance variable to parameter
12          Me.minute = minute ' set instance variable to parameter
13          Me.second = second ' set instance variable to parameter
14       End Sub ' New
15
16       ' create String using Me explicitly then implicitly
17       Public Function BuildString() As String
18          Return "Me.ToUniversalString(): " & Me.ToUniversalString() _
19             & vbCrLf & "ToUniversalString(): " & ToUniversalString()
20       End Function ' BuildString
21
22       ' convert to String in universal-time format
23       Public Function ToUniversalString() As String
24          Return String.Format("{0:D2}:{1:D2}:{2:D2}", hour, minute, second)
25       End Function ' ToUniversalString
26    End Class ' Time
```

Fig. 9.8 | Class using the Me reference.

Error-Prevention Tip 9.3

Avoid parameter names that conflict with instance variable names to prevent subtle, hard-to-find bugs.

Module MeTest (Fig. 9.9) demonstrates the Me reference. Line 5 instantiates a Time object. Line 6 invokes method BuildString, then displays the results to the user.

```
 1    ' Fig. 9.9: MeTest.vb
 2    ' Demonstrates Me reference.
 3    Module MeTest
 4       Sub Main()
 5          Dim time As New Time(12, 30, 19)
 6          Console.WriteLine(time.BuildString())
 7       End Sub ' Main
 8    End Module ' MeTest
```

```
Me.ToUniversalString(): 12:30:19
ToUniversalString(): 12:30:19
```

Fig. 9.9 | Me reference demonstration.

9.9 Garbage Collection

Every object you create uses various system resources, including the memory that holds the object itself. We need a disciplined way to give resources back to the system when they are no longer needed, so as to avoid "resource leaks." The Common Language Runtime (CLR) performs automatic *garbage collection* to reclaim the memory occupied by objects that are no longer in use. When there are no more references to an object, the object is *marked for garbage collection* by the CLR. The memory for such an object can be reclaimed when the runtime executes its *garbage collector*, which is responsible for retrieving the memory of objects that are no longer used, so that the memory can be used for other objects. Therefore, whereas memory leaks are common in other languages like C and C++ (because memory is not automatically reclaimed in those languages), they are much less likely in Visual Basic (but some can still happen in subtle ways). Resources like memory that are allocated and reclaimed by the CLR are known as *managed resources*.

Other types of resource leaks can occur. For example, an application could open a file on disk to modify the file's contents. If the application does not close the file, no other application may be allowed to use the file until the application that opened the file finishes. An application that no longer needs a file should close it immediately so that other programs can access the file. Resources like files, network connections and database connections that the *programmer* must manage are known as *unmanaged resources* (because they are not managed by the CLR). Such resources are typically scarce and should be released as soon as they are no longer needed by a program.

To help prevent resource leaks for unmanaged resources, the garbage collector calls a special method named *Finalize* on each object before it is removed from memory. Recall from Section 9.2 that all classes inherit the methods of class Object, one of which is Finalize. You will learn more about class Object in Chapter 10, Object-Oriented Programming: Inheritance. The Finalize method is called by the garbage collector to perform *termination housekeeping* on an object (such as releasing unmanaged resources used by the object) just before the garbage collector reclaims the object's memory. Method Finalize does not take parameters and does not return a value. In Section 9.10, we demonstrate a situation in which method Finalize is called by the garbage collector.

Unfortunately, Finalize is not ideal for releasing unmanaged resources because the garbage collector is unpredictable—it is not guaranteed to execute at a specified time. In some cases the garbage collector may *never* execute before a program terminates. Thus, it is unclear if, or when, method Finalize will be called. Unmanaged resources might not be released for a long time, which would prevent these scarce resources from being used by other programs. For this reason, most programmers should avoid method Finalize.

In Chapter 11, we discuss interfaces. As will be explained, an interface describes methods that a class must implement. The FCL provides interface IDisposable, which contains a method named Dispose that a client can invoke to immediately release the resources used by an object. When a program creates an object of a class that implements interface IDisposable, the client should call that object's Dispose method as soon as the client is done using the object. This ensures that the resources used by the object are released promptly so they can be reused. The following URL links to a Microsoft Developer Network (MSDN) TV interview describing IDisposable:

```
msdn.microsoft.com/msdntv/episode.aspx?xml=episodes/en/
    20030501CLRBA/manifest.xml
```

The following URL provides detailed information on memory management in .NET:

```
www.gotdotnet.com/team/libraries/whitepapers/resourcemanagement/
    resourcemanagement.aspx
```

Software Engineering Observation 9.6

A class that uses unmanaged resources, such as files on disk, should provide a method that clients of the class can call explicitly to release the resources. Many Visual Basic library classes provide Close *or* Dispose *methods for this purpose.*

9.10 Shared Class Members

Each object of a class has its own copy of all the instance variables of the class. However, in certain cases, all class objects should share only one copy of a particular variable. A program contains only one copy of a **Shared class variable** in memory, no matter how many objects of the class have been instantiated. A Shared class variable represents **class-wide information**—all class objects share the same piece of data. The declaration of a Shared member begins with the keyword Shared.

Let us use a video game example to explain the need for Shared class-wide data. Suppose we have a video game in which Martians attack other space creatures. A Martian tends to be brave and willing to attack other space creatures when it is aware that there are at least four other Martians present. If there are fewer than five Martians present, a Martian becomes cowardly. For this reason, each Martian must know the martianCount. We could endow class Martian with a martianCount instance variable. If we were to do this, then every Martian would have a separate copy of the instance variable, and every time we create a Martian, we would have to update the instance variable martianCount in every Martian. The redundant copies waste space, and updating those copies is time-consuming. Worse yet, while we are updating the individual copies of martianCount, there will be periods of time during which some of these copies have not yet been updated, so we could have inconsistent bravery behavior among the Martians. Instead, we declare martianCount to be Shared so that martianCount is class-wide data. Each Martian can then see the martianCount as if it were instance data of that Martian, but Visual Basic maintains only one copy of the Shared martianCount to save space. We also save time, in that the Martian constructor increments only the Shared martianCount—there is only one copy, so we do not have to increment separate copies of martianCount for each Martian object. This also prevents inconsistent bravery behavior among the Martians.

Performance Tip 9.1

When a single copy of the data will suffice, use Shared *class variables rather than instance variables to save storage and simplify program logic.*

Shared class members have class scope. A class's Public Shared members can be accessed through the class name using the dot separator (e.g., *className.sharedMemberName*). A class's Private Shared class members can be accessed by clients only indirectly through non-Private methods of the class. Shared class members are available as soon as the class is loaded into memory at execution time; like other variables with class scope, they exist for the duration of program execution, even when no objects of that class exist. To allow clients to access a Private Shared class member when no objects of the class exist, you must provide a non-Private Shared method or property.

Unlike non-Shared methods, a Shared method has no Me reference, because Shared class members exist independently of any class objects and even when there are no objects of that class. So a Shared method cannot access non-Shared class members.

Common Programming Error 9.4

Using the Me reference in a Shared method or Shared property is a compilation error.

Shared Constructors

When Shared variables require more complex initialization than can be accomplished in a Shared variable declaration, you can create a ***Shared constructor*** to initialize them. A Shared constructor is declared like an instance constructor, but is preceded by the Shared modifier and can be used only to initialize Shared variables. A Shared constructor is implicitly Public, must be declared with no parameters, cannot call other constructors of the class and is guaranteed to execute before a program creates any objects of the class or accesses any Shared class members. A class can have both a Shared constructor and a non-Shared parameterless constructor.

Common Programming Error 9.5

Explicitly declaring a Shared constructor Public is a compilation error, because a Shared constructor is Public implicitly.

Class Employee with Shared Variables

Class Employee (Fig. 9.10) demonstrates a Private Shared class variable and a Public Shared Property. The Shared class variable countValue is initialized to zero by default (line 6). It maintains a count of the number of Employee objects that have been instantiated and currently reside in memory, including objects that have already been marked for garbage collection but have not yet been reclaimed by the garbage collector.

When objects of class Employee exist, Shared member countValue can be used in any method of an Employee object—in this example, the constructor (lines 9–15) increments countValue (line 12) and method Finalize (lines 18–23) decrements countValue (line

```vb
1   ' Fig. 9.10: Employee.vb
2   ' Class Employee uses Shared variable.
3   Class Employee
4      Private firstNameValue As String ' employee first name
5      Private lastNameValue As String ' employee last name
6      Private Shared countValue As Integer ' Employee objects in memory
7
8      ' Employee constructor
9      Public Sub New(ByVal first As String, ByVal last As String)
10        firstNameValue = first
11        lastNameValue = last
12        countValue += 1 ' increment shared count of employees
13        Console.WriteLine("Employee object constructor for " & _
14           firstNameValue & " " & lastNameValue)
15     End Sub ' New
16
```

Fig. 9.10 | Employee class objects share Shared variable. (Part 1 of 2.)

```
17      ' finalizer method decrements Shared count of employees
18      Protected Overrides Sub Finalize()
19          countValue -= 1 ' decrement countValue
20          Console.WriteLine("Employee object finalizer for " & _
21              firstNameValue & " " & lastNameValue & "; count = " & _
22              countValue)
23      End Sub ' Finalize
24
25      ' return first name
26      Public ReadOnly Property FirstName() As String
27          Get
28              Return firstNameValue
29          End Get
30      End Property ' FirstName
31
32      ' return last name
33      Public ReadOnly Property LastName() As String
34          Get
35              Return lastNameValue
36          End Get
37      End Property ' LastName
38
39      ' property Count
40      Public Shared ReadOnly Property Count() As Integer
41          Get
42              Return countValue
43          End Get
44      End Property ' Count
45  End Class ' Employee
```

Fig. 9.10 | Employee class objects share Shared variable. (Part 2 of 2.)

19). (Note that method Finalize is declared using keywords Protected and Over-rides—method Finalize's header must contain these keywords, which we discuss in Chapters 10–11.) If no objects of class Employee exist, member countValue can be referenced through a call to Property Count (lines 40–44)—this Property is Shared, and therefore we do not have to instantiate an Employee object to call the Get method of the Property. Also, by declaring property Count as ReadOnly, we prevent clients from changing the value of countValue directly, thus ensuring that clients can change count-Value's value only under the tight control of class Employee's constructors and finalizer.

Testing Shared Variables

Module SharedTest (Fig. 9.11) demonstrates the Shared members of Fig. 9.10. Lines 5–6 use the ReadOnly Shared Property Count of class Employee to obtain the current value of countValue. No Employee objects exist yet, so we must call Count using the class name Employee. Lines 8–9 then instantiate two Employee objects, causing countValue to be incremented by 2. Lines 13–14 print the countValue by using ReadOnly Shared Property Count. Lines 17–21 display the names of the employees. Lines 24–25 set these objects' references to Nothing, so that employee1 and employee2 no longer refer to the Employee objects. This "marks" the objects for garbage collection, because there are no more references to these objects in the program.

Common Programming Error 9.6

A compilation error occurs if a Shared method calls an instance (non-Shared) method in the same class by using only the name of the method. Similarly, a compilation error occurs if a Shared method attempts to access an instance variable in the same class by using only the name of the variable.

```vb
 1    ' Fig. 9.11: SharedTest.vb
 2    ' Demonstrates Shared members.
 3    Module SharedTest
 4       Sub Main()
 5          Console.WriteLine("Employees before instantiation: " & _
 6             Employee.Count) ' Count is a Shared property
 7
 8          Dim employee1 As New Employee("Susan", "Baker") ' call constructor
 9          Dim employee2 As New Employee("Bob", "Blue") ' call constructor
10
11          ' output number of employees after instantiation
12          ' (use Shared property)
13          Console.WriteLine(vbCrLf & "Employees after instantiation " & _
14             "(via Employee.Count): " & Employee.Count)
15
16          ' display names of first and second employees (using properties)
17          Console.WriteLine(vbCrLf & "Display names of employees " & _
18             "(using properties)" & vbCrLf & "Employee 1: " & _
19             employee1.FirstName & " " & employee1.LastName & vbCrLf & _
20             "Employee 2: " & employee2.FirstName & " " & _
21             employee2.LastName & vbCrLf)
22
23          Console.WriteLine("Marking employees for garbage collection")
24          employee1 = Nothing ' mark employee1 for garbage collection
25          employee2 = Nothing ' mark employee2 for garbage collection
26
27          Console.WriteLine()
28          Console.WriteLine("Explicitly invoking the garbage collector")
29          System.GC.Collect() ' request garbage collection
30       End Sub ' Main
31    End Module ' SharedTest
```

```
Employees before instantiation: 0
Employee object constructor for Susan Baker
Employee object constructor for Bob Blue

Employees after instantiation (via Employee.Count): 2

Display names of employees (using properties)
Employee 1: Susan Baker
Employee 2: Bob Blue

Marking employees for garbage collection

Explicitly invoking the garbage collector
Employee object finalizer for Bob Blue; count = 1
Employee object finalizer for Susan Baker; count = 0
```

Fig. 9.11 | Shared class member demonstration.

Normally, the garbage collector is not invoked directly by the user. Either the garbage collector reclaims the memory for objects when it deems garbage collection is appropriate, or the operating system recovers the unneeded memory when the program terminates. Line 29 uses `Public Shared` method **Collect** from class **GC** (namespace `System`) to request that the garbage collector execute. Before the garbage collector releases the memory occupied by the two `Employee` objects, it invokes method `Finalize` for each `Employee` object, which decrements the `countValue` value by a total of 2.

The last two lines of the sample output show that the `Employee` object for Bob Blue was finalized before the `Employee` object for Susan Baker. However, the output of this program on your system could differ. The garbage collector is not guaranteed to collect objects in a specific order, nor is it guaranteed to run at all before the program terminates.

9.11 Const and ReadOnly Members

Visual Basic allows you to create constants—members whose values cannot change during program execution. To create a constant instance variable of a class, declare that member as either **Const** or **ReadOnly**. An instance variable declared as `Const` must be initialized in its declaration; an instance variable declared as `ReadOnly` can be initialized either in its declaration or in the class constructor. `Const` values must be initialized at compile time; whereas `ReadOnly` values are not initialized until runtime. Neither a `Const` nor a `ReadOnly` value can be modified once initialized.

 Error-Prevention Tip 9.4

If a variable's value should never change, making it a constant prevents it from changing. This helps eliminate errors that might occur if the value of the variable were to change.

 Common Programming Error 9.7

Declaring an instance variable as Const *but failing to initialize it in that declaration is a compilation error.*

 Common Programming Error 9.8

Assigning a value to a Const *instance variable is a compilation error.*

`Const` members must be initialized at compile time; thus, they can be initialized only to constant values, such as integers, string literals, characters and other `Const` members. Constant members with values that cannot be determined at compile time must be declared `ReadOnly`. Recall that a `ReadOnly` member can be assigned a value only once, either when it is declared or within the class's constructor (the `Shared` constructor for `Shared ReadOnly` members and a non-`Shared` constructor for non-`Shared ReadOnly` members).

 Common Programming Error 9.9

Declaring an instance variable as ReadOnly *and attempting to use it before it is initialized is a logic error.*

 Common Programming Error 9.10

A Shared ReadOnly *variable cannot be initialized in an instance constructor for that class, and a* ReadOnly *instance variable cannot be initialized in a* Shared *constructor for that class. Attempting to define a* ReadOnly *variable in an inappropriate constructor is a compilation error.*

Common Programming Error 9.11

Declaring a Const *member as* Shared *is a compilation error, because a* Const *member is* Shared *implicitly.*

Common Programming Error 9.12

Declaring a ReadOnly *member as* Const *is a compilation error, because these two keywords are not allowed to be combined in a variable declaration.*

Class CircleConstants *with* Const *and* ReadOnly *Instance Variables*

Class CircleConstants (Fig. 9.12) demonstrates constants. Line 4 creates constant PI using keyword Const and assigns to PI the Double value 3.14159—an approximation of π. We could have used pre-defined constant PI of class Math (Math.PI) as the value, but we wanted to demonstrate how you can create your own Const instance variables. The compiler must be able to determine a Const's value to be able to initialize a Const instance variable with that value. The value 3.14159 is acceptable (line 4), but the expression

```
Convert.ToDouble("3.14159")
```

generates a compilation error if used in place of that value. Although this expression uses a constant value (String literal "3.14159") as an argument and produces the same numeric value, a compilation error occurs, because the compiler cannot evaluate executable code (such as a method call). This restriction is lifted with ReadOnly members, which are initialized at runtime. Note that line 9 assigns the value of the constructor parameter radiusValue to ReadOnly member RADIUS at runtime. We could also have used a method call, such as Convert.ToDouble, to assign a value to this ReadOnly member.

Using Const and ReadOnly

Module ConstAndReadOnly (Fig. 9.13) demonstrates the Const and ReadOnly values. Line 5 creates a Random object that is used in line 8 to generate a random Integer in the range 1–20 that corresponds to a circle's radius. This enables each program execution to produce different output. The random value is passed to the CircleConstants constructor to initialize a CircleConstants object. Lines 11–13 access the ReadOnly variable RADIUS through a reference to object circle, and compute and display the circle's circumference.

```vb
1   ' Fig. 9.12: CircleConstants.vb
2   ' Encapsulate constants PI and radius.
3   Class CircleConstants
4      Public Const PI As Double = 3.14159 ' PI is a Const instance variable
5      Public ReadOnly RADIUS As Integer ' radius is uninitialized constant
6
7      ' constructor of class CircleConstants
8      Public Sub New(ByVal radiusValue As Integer)
9         RADIUS = radiusValue ' initialize ReadOnly constant
10     End Sub ' New
11  End Class ' CircleConstants
```

Fig. 9.12 | Constants used in class CircleConstants.

```
1   ' Fig. 9.13: ConstAndReadOnly.vb
2   ' Demonstrates Const and ReadOnly members.
3   Module ConstAndReadOnly
4      Sub Main()
5         Dim random As New Random() ' create Random object
6
7         ' create CircleConstants object with random radius
8         Dim circle As New CircleConstants(random.Next(1, 20))
9
10        ' calculate the circle's circumference
11        Console.WriteLine("Radius = " & circle.RADIUS & vbCrLf & _
12           "Circumference = " & String.Format("{0:F3}", _
13           2 * CircleConstants.PI * circle.RADIUS))
14     End Sub ' Main
15   End Module ' ConstAndReadOnly
```

```
Radius = 9
Circumference = 56.549
```

Fig. 9.13 | Const and ReadOnly class members demonstration.

This calculation employs the Public Const member PI, which we access in line 13 through its class name CircleConstants. Recall that Const members are implicitly Shared; thus we can access a Const member with its class name followed by the dot separator even when no objects of the class are present.

ReadOnly *and* WriteOnly *Properties*

Recall from Chapter 4 that not all properties need to have Get and Set accessors—a property with only a Get accessor is called a *read-only property* and must be declared using keyword ReadOnly; a property with only a Set accessor is called a *write-only property* and must be declared using keyword WriteOnly.

9.12 Object Browser

Now we present a feature that Visual Studio provides to facilitate the design of object-oriented applications—the **Object Browser**. The **Object Browser** lists all the libraries that are available to the application, including the Framework Class Library (FCL) classes and programmer-defined classes. Developers use the **Object Browser** to learn about the functionality provided by specific classes. To open the **Object Browser**, right click any Visual Basic class or method in the code editor and select **Go To Definition** (Figs. 9.14–9.15). Figure 9.16 shows the **Object Browser** after the user selects class Random in Fig. 9.14. Figure 9.17 shows the **Object Browser** after the user selects method Next of class Random in Fig. 9.15. The **Object Browser** lists all non-Private members provided by class Random in the upper-right portion of the window, which offers developers instant access to information regarding the services of the selected class. You can also view the details of method Next by clicking the method name in the upper-right portion of the windows in Figure 9.16.

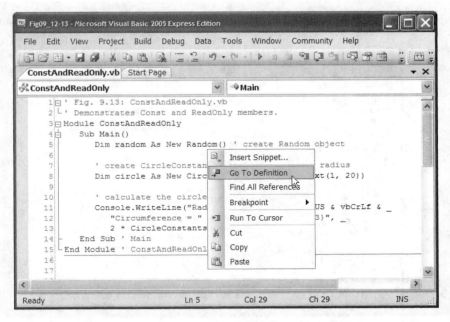

Fig. 9.14 | Invoking the **Object Browser** by right clicking class `Random` and selecting **Go To Definition**.

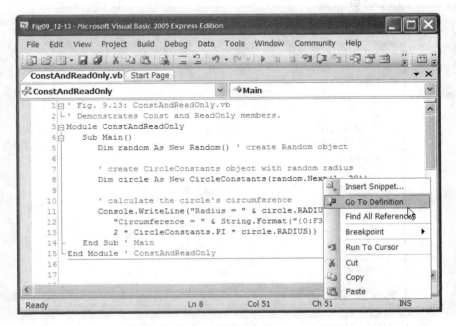

Fig. 9.15 | Invoking the **Object Browser** by right clicking method `Next` and selecting **Go To Definition**.

Classes available to the application are listed here   Non-**Private** members of the selected class are listed here   Details of a particular member are listed here (or a summary of the class if a specific member is not selected)

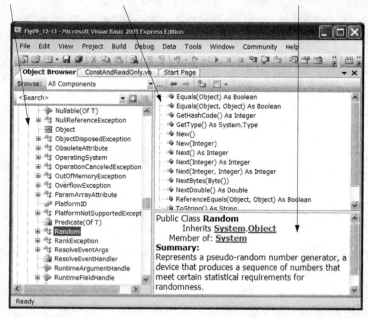

Fig. 9.16 | **Object Browser** when user selects class `Random` from the code editor.

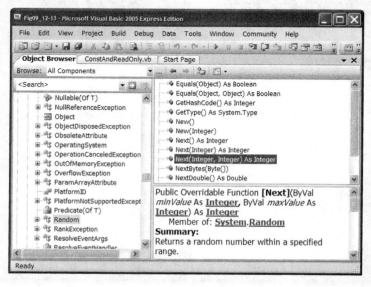

Fig. 9.17 | **Object Browser** when user selects class `Random`'s `Next` method from the code editor.

9.13 Time Class Case Study: Creating Class Libraries

We have seen that classes from preexisting libraries, such as .NET's Framework Class Library (FCL), can be imported into Visual Basic applications. Each class in the FCL belongs to a namespace that contains a group of related classes. Class libraries and namespaces facilitate software reuse by enabling applications to add classes from other namespaces (as we have done in most examples). This section demonstrates how to create your own class libraries for reuse.

Making a Class Reusable

Before a class can be imported into multiple applications, it must be placed in an assembly to make it reusable. The steps for creating an assembly are as follows:

1. Create a **Class Library** project.

2. Add the reusable class(es) to the project. [*Note:* You can also create reusable classes from scratch.]

3. Ensure that each reusable class is declared Public—only Public classes can be imported for use in other projects; non-Public classes are typically placed in a library to support the Public reusable classes in that library.

4. Compile the project to create the assembly that contains the reusable class(es).

5. In an application that requires the class library, add a reference to the class library. Then specify an Imports statement for the class library and use its class(es) in your application.

Next, we present the five steps in detail.

Step 1: Creating a Class Library Project

In this example, we'd like to place class Time of Fig. 9.1 into a class library to make it a reusable class. To create a class library in Visual Basic 2005 Express, select **File > New Project...** and choose **Class Library** from the list of templates, as shown in Fig. 9.18. Name your project TimeLibrary, then click **OK**.

When you create a **Class Library** project, Visual Basic automatically includes the file Class1.vb in the project. You can modify the Public class in this file to create a reusable class. However, we'll be using the file from the Time class in Fig. 9.1, so you can select Class1.vb in the **Solution Explorer** and press *Delete* to remove it from the project.

Step 2: Adding Class Time to the Project

Next, you must add the file that contains class Time to the project. Right click **TimeLibrary** in the **Solution Explorer**. In the menu that appears, select **Add > Existing Item...** to display the **Add Existing Item** dialog box. Locate the Time.vb file from Fig. 9.1, select it and click the **Add** button to add the file to this **Class Library** project. [*Note:* We assume that you downloaded the book's examples and placed them on your C:\ drive. If so, the file is located in the directory C:\examples\ch09\Fig09_01-02\TimeTest\.]

Step 3: Adding Class Time to the Project

Recall that only Public classes can be imported for use in other projects. Thus, you must add the Public access modifier to class Time to make it reusable. The new version of class Time is shown in Fig. 9.19. Notice that line 3 now contains Public.

Fig. 9.18 | Creating a **Class Library** Project.

```
1   ' Fig. 9.19: Time.vb
2   ' Represents time to clients in 12-hour and 24-hour clock formats.
3   Public Class Time
4      Inherits Object ' if not specified, compiler includes it implicitly
5
6      ' declare Integer instance variables for the hour, minute and second
7      Private hourValue As Integer ' 0 - 23
8      Private minuteValue As Integer ' 0 - 59
9      Private secondValue As Integer ' 0 - 59
10
11     ' Time constructor initializes instance variables
12     ' when a Time object is created
13     Public Sub New()
14        SetTime(12, 0, 0) ' initialize hour to noon; minute, second to 0
15     End Sub ' New
16
17     ' set a new time value using universal time, check validity of the
18     ' data, set invalid hour to noon, set invalid minute, second to zero
19     Public Sub SetTime(ByVal hh As Integer, _
20        ByVal mm As Integer, ByVal ss As Integer)
21        Hour = hh ' set hourValue using Hour property
22        Minute = mm ' set minuteValue using Minute property
23        Second = ss ' set secondValue using Second property
24     End Sub ' SetTime
25
```

Fig. 9.19 | Creating reusable class Time. (Part 1 of 3.)

```
26      ' property Hour
27      Public Property Hour() As Integer
28         Get ' return hourValue
29            Return hourValue
30         End Get
31
32         Set(ByVal value As Integer) ' set hourValue
33            If (value >= 0 AndAlso value < 24) Then ' in range 0-23
34               hourValue = value ' value is valid
35            Else ' value is invalid
36               hourValue = 12 ' set to default of noon
37            End If
38         End Set
39      End Property ' Hour
40
41      ' property Minute
42      Public Property Minute() As Integer
43         Get ' return minuteValue
44            Return minuteValue
45         End Get
46
47         Set(ByVal value As Integer) ' set minuteValue
48            If (value >= 0 AndAlso value < 60) Then ' in range 0-59
49               minuteValue = value ' value is valid
50            Else ' value is invalid
51               minuteValue = 0 ' set to default of 0
52            End If
53         End Set
54      End Property ' Minute
55
56      ' property Second
57      Public Property Second() As Integer
58         Get ' return secondValue
59            Return secondValue
60         End Get
61
62         Set(ByVal value As Integer) ' set secondValue
63            If (value >= 0 AndAlso value < 60) Then ' in range 0-59
64               secondValue = value ' value is valid
65            Else ' value is invalid
66               secondValue = 0 ' set to default of 0
67            End If
68         End Set
69      End Property ' Second
70
71      ' convert Time to a String in universal-time (24-hour clock) format
72      Public Function ToUniversalString() As String
73         Return String.Format("{0}:{1:D2}:{2:D2}", Hour, Minute, Second)
74      End Function ' ToUniversalString
75
76      ' convert Time to a String in standard-time (12-hour clock) format
77      Public Overrides Function ToString() As String
78         Dim suffix As String ' AM or PM suffix
```

Fig. 9.19 | Creating reusable class Time. (Part 2 of 3.)

```
79        Dim standardHour As Integer ' a standard hour in the range 1-12
80
81        ' determine whether the 12-hour clock suffix should be AM or PM
82        If Hour < 12 Then
83           suffix = "AM" ' note space preceding AM
84        Else
85           suffix = "PM" ' note space preceding PM
86        End If
87
88        ' convert hour from universal-time format to standard-time format
89        If (Hour = 12 OrElse Hour = 0) Then
90           standardHour = 12
91        Else
92           standardHour = Hour Mod 12 ' 1 through 11, AM or PM
93        End If
94
95        Return String.Format("{0}:{1:D2}:{2:D2} {3}", _
96           standardHour, Minute, Second, suffix)
97     End Function ' ToString
98  End Class ' Time
```

Fig. 9.19 | Creating reusable class `Time`. (Part 3 of 3.)

Step 4: Building the TimeLibrary

To create the assembly containing the reusable class, select **Build > Build TimeLibrary**. When you build a **Class Library** project, the compiler creates a *.dll file*, known as a *dynamic link library*—a type of assembly that you can reference from other applications. This assembly is located in the project's `bin\Release` directory. By default, the name of the file is the class library's name followed by the `.dll` extension—`TimeLibrary.dll` in this example. The assembly file contains the reusable class `Time`, which can now be imported into other projects. Save your project and remember where you saved it on your system, so you can locate the `TimeLibrary.dll` file in the next step. Note that class libraries are not executable, so if you attempt to execute the class library by selecting **Debug > Start**, you'll receive an error message.

Step 5: Create an Application, Add a Reference to the Class Library's Assembly and Import the Library's Namespace

Once the class is compiled and stored in an assembly, it can be imported into a program for reuse. Module `TimeLibraryTest` (Fig. 9.20) uses class `Time` from the assembly `TimeLibrary.dll` to create a `Time` object, set its time and display the time.

```
 1  ' Fig. 9.20: TimeLibraryTest.vb
 2  ' Demonstrating class Time in TimeLibrary.
 3  Imports TimeLibrary ' import namespace TimeLibrary
 4
 5  Module TimeLibraryTest
 6     Sub Main()
 7        Dim time As New Time() ' call Time constructor
```

Fig. 9.20 | Module `TimeLibraryTest` references `TimeLibrary.dll`. (Part 1 of 2.)

```
8
9        Console.WriteLine("The initial universal time is: " & _
10          time.ToUniversalString() & vbCrLf & _
11          "The initial standard time is: " & time.ToString())
12
13       time.SetTime(13, 27, 6) ' set time with valid settings
14       Console.WriteLine(vbCrLf & "Universal time after setTime is: " & _
15          time.ToUniversalString() & vbCrLf & _
16          "Standard time after setTime is: " & time.ToString())
17
18       time.SetTime(99, 99, 99) ' set time with invalid settings
19       Console.WriteLine(vbCrLf & _
20          "After attempting invalid settings: " & vbCrLf & _
21          "Universal time: " & time.ToUniversalString() & _
22          vbCrLf & "Standard time: " & time.ToString())
23    End Sub ' Main
24 End Module ' TimeLibraryTest
```

```
The initial universal time is: 12:00:00
The initial standard time is: 12:00:00 PM

Universal time after setTime is: 13:27:06
Standard time after setTime is: 1:27:06 PM

After attempting invalid settings:
Universal time: 12:00:00
Standard time: 12:00:00 PM
```

Fig. 9.20 | Module `TimeLibraryTest` references `TimeLibrary.dll`. (Part 2 of 2.)

When you create a **Class Library** project, the classes in that library are automatically placed in a namespace that has the same name as the library itself. Thus, class `Time` is located in namespace `TimeLibrary`—part of the assembly `TimeLibrary.dll`. Before you can use the classes in the namespace `TimeLibrary`, you must reference its assembly. Select **Project > Add Reference....** The **Add Reference** dialog that appears contains a list of class libraries from the .NET Framework. Some class libraries, like the one containing the `System` namespace, are so common that they are added to your application implicitly. Additional libraries can be selected from this dialog. In the dialog, click the **Browse** tab, then locate and select the `TimeLibrary.dll` file (located in the `bin\Release` directory of the `TimeLibrary` project we created in *Steps 1–4*) as shown in Fig. 9.21. Click **OK** to add the reference to the project.

After adding the reference, you can use keyword `Imports` followed by the namespace name `TimeLibrary` (line 3) to inform the compiler that you are using classes from this namespace. Module `TimeLibraryTest` and class `Time` are in different namespaces, so the `Imports` statement at line 3 allows module `TimeLibraryTest` to use class `Time`.

The `Imports` statement at line 3 is not required if you refer to class `Time` with its *fully qualified name*—`TimeLibrary.Time`—which includes the namespace name and the class name. For example, line 7 could be written as

Dim time *As New* TimeLibrary.Time()

Fig. 9.21 | Adding a Reference.

You can use this fully qualified name in your programs, or you can import the class and use its *simple name* (the unqualified class name—Time). If another namespace also contains a Time class, fully qualified class names can be used to distinguish between the two Time classes and prevent a *name conflict* (also called a *name collision*).

9.14 (Optional) Software Engineering Case Study: Starting to Program the Classes of the ATM System

In the Software Engineering Case Study sections in Chapters 1 and 3–8, we introduced the fundamentals of object orientation and developed an object-oriented design for our ATM system. In Chapters 4–8, we introduced object-oriented programming in Visual Basic. In Chapter 9, we took a deeper look at the details of programming with classes. We now begin implementing our object-oriented design by converting class diagrams to Visual Basic code. In the final Software Engineering Case Study section (Section 11.8), we modify the code to incorporate the object-oriented concepts of inheritance and polymorphism. We present the full Visual Basic code implementation in Appendix J.

Visibility

We now apply access modifiers to the members of our classes. In Chapter 9, we introduced access modifiers Public and Private. Access modifiers determine the *visibility* or accessibility of an object's attributes and operations to other objects. Before we can begin implementing our design, we must consider which attributes and methods of our classes should be Public and which should be Private.

In Chapter 9, we observed that attributes normally should be Private and that methods invoked by clients of a class should be Public. Methods that are called only by other methods of the class as "utility functions," however, should be Private. The UML employs *visibility markers* for modeling the visibility of attributes and operations. Public visibility is indicated by placing a plus sign (+) before an operation or an attribute; a minus sign (–) indicates private visibility. Figure 9.22 shows our updated class diagram with visibility markers included. [*Note:* We do not include any operation parameters in Fig. 9.22.

Fig. 9.22 | Class diagram with visibility markers.

This is perfectly normal. Adding visibility markers does not affect the parameters already modeled in the class diagrams of Figs. 7.24–7.27.]

Navigability

Before we begin implementing our design in Visual Basic, we introduce an additional UML notation. The class diagram in Fig. 9.23 further refines the relationships among classes in the ATM system by adding navigability arrows to the association lines. *Navigability arrows* (represented as arrows with stick arrowheads in the class diagram) indicate in which direction an association can be traversed and are based on the collaborations modeled in communication and sequence diagrams (see Section 8.15). When implementing a system designed using the UML, you use navigability arrows to help determine which objects need references to other objects. For example, the navigability arrow pointing from class ATM to class BankDatabase indicates that we can navigate from the former to the latter, thereby enabling the ATM to invoke the BankDatabase's operations. However, since Fig. 9.23 does not contain a navigability arrow pointing from class BankDatabase to

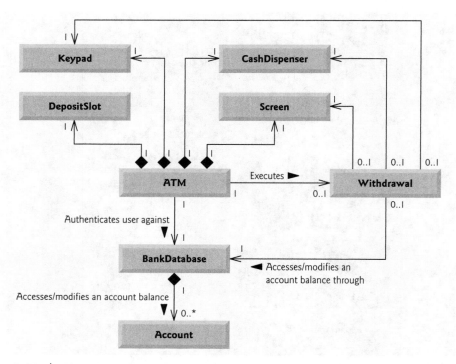

Fig. 9.23 | Class diagram with navigability arrows.

class ATM, the BankDatabase cannot access the ATM's operations. Note that associations in a class diagram that have navigability arrows at both ends or do not have navigability arrows at all indicate *bidirectional navigability*—navigation can proceed in either direction across the association.

Like the class diagram of Fig. 4.22, the one in Fig. 9.23 omits classes BalanceInquiry and Deposit to keep the diagram simple. The navigability of the associations in which these classes participate closely parallels the navigability of class Withdrawal's associations. Recall from Section 4.9 that BalanceInquiry has an association with class Screen. We can navigate from class BalanceInquiry to class Screen along this association, but we cannot navigate from class Screen to class BalanceInquiry. Thus, if we were to model class BalanceInquiry in Fig. 9.23, we would place a navigability arrow at class Screen's end of this association. Also recall that class Deposit associates with classes Screen, Keypad and DepositSlot. We can navigate from class Deposit to each of these classes, but not vice versa. We therefore would place navigability arrows at the Screen, Keypad and DepositSlot ends of these associations. [*Note:* We model these additional classes and associations in our final class diagram in Section 11.8, after we have simplified the structure of our system by incorporating the object-oriented concept of inheritance.]

Implementing the ATM System from Its UML Design
We are now ready to begin implementing the ATM system. We first convert the classes in the diagrams of Fig. 9.22 and Fig. 9.23 into Visual Basic code. This code will represent

the "skeleton" of the system. In Chapter 11, we modify the code to incorporate the object-oriented concept of inheritance. In Appendix J, ATM Case Study Code, we present the complete working Visual Basic code that implements our object-oriented design.

As an example, we begin to develop the code for class Withdrawal from our design of class Withdrawal in Fig. 9.22. We use this figure to determine the attributes and operations of the class. We use the UML model in Fig. 9.23 to determine the associations among classes. We follow the following four guidelines for each class:

1. Use the name located in the first compartment of a class in a class diagram to declare the class as a Public class with an empty parameterless constructor. We include this constructor simply as a placeholder to remind us that most classes will need one or more constructors. In Appendix J, when we complete a working version of this class, we add any necessary arguments and code to the body of the constructor. Class Withdrawal initially yields the code in Fig. 9.24. [*Note:* If we find that the class's instance variables require only default initialization, we will remove the empty parameterless constructor because it is unnecessary.]

2. Use the attributes located in the class's second compartment to declare the instance variables. The Private attributes accountNumber and amount of class Withdrawal yield the code in Fig. 9.25.

3. Use the associations described in the class diagram to declare references (or pointers, where appropriate) to other objects. According to Fig. 9.23, Withdrawal can access one object of class Screen, one object of class Keypad, one object of class CashDispenser and one object of class BankDatabase. Class Withdrawal must

```
 1   ' Class Withdrawal represents an ATM withdrawal transaction
 2   Public Class Withdrawal
 3      ' parameterless constructor
 4      Public Sub New()
 5         ' constructor body code
 6      End Sub ' New
 7   End Class ' Withdrawal
```

Fig. 9.24 | Initial Visual Basic code for class Withdrawal based on Figs. 9.22 and 9.23.

```
 1   ' Class Withdrawal represents an ATM withdrawal transaction
 2   Public Class Withdrawal
 3      ' attributes
 4      Private accountNumber As Integer ' account to withdraw funds from
 5      Private amount As Decimal ' amount to withdraw from account
 6
 7      ' parameterless constructor
 8      Public Sub New()
 9         ' constructor body code
10      End Sub ' New
11   End Class ' Withdrawal
```

Fig. 9.25 | Visual Basic code incorporating Private variables for class Withdrawal based on Figs. 9.22 and 9.23.

maintain references to these objects for sending messages to them, so lines 8–11 of Fig. 9.26 declare four references as Private instance variables. In the implementation of class Withdrawal in Appendix J, a constructor initializes these instance variables with references to the actual objects.

4. Use the operations located in the third compartment of Fig. 9.22 to declare the shells of the methods. If we have not yet specified a return type for an operation, we declare the method with keyword Sub. Refer to the class diagrams of Figs. 7.24–7.27 to declare any necessary parameters. Adding the Public operation Execute (which has an empty parameter list) in class Withdrawal yields the code in line 19 of Fig. 9.27. [*Note:* We code the bodies of methods when we implement the complete ATM system in Appendix J.]

```
 1    ' Class Withdrawal represents an ATM withdrawal transaction
 2    Public Class Withdrawal
 3       ' attributes
 4       Private accountNumber As Integer ' account to withdraw funds from
 5       Private amount As Decimal ' amount to withdraw
 6
 7       ' references to associated objects
 8       Private screenHandle As Screen ' ATM's screen
 9       Private keypadHandle As Keypad ' ATM's keypad
10       Private cashDispenserHandle As CashDispenser ' ATM's cash dispenser
11       Private bankDatabaseHandle As BankDatabase ' account info database
12
13       ' parameterless constructor
14       Public Sub New()
15          ' constructor body code
16       End Sub ' New
17    End Class ' Withdrawal
```

Fig. 9.26 | Visual Basic code incorporating Private reference handles for the associations of class Withdrawal based on Figs. 9.22 and 9.23.

```
 1    ' Class Withdrawal represents an ATM withdrawal transaction
 2    Public Class Withdrawal
 3       ' attributes
 4       Private accountNumber As Integer ' account to withdraw funds from
 5       Private amount As Decimal ' amount to withdraw
 6
 7       ' references to associated objects
 8       Private screenHandle As Screen ' ATM's screen
 9       Private keypadHandle As Keypad ' ATM's keypad
10       Private cashDispenserHandle As CashDispenser ' ATM's cash dispenser
11       Private bankDatabaseHandle As BankDatabase ' account info database
12
```

Fig. 9.27 | Visual Basic code incorporating method Execute in class Withdrawal based on Figs. 9.22 and 9.23. (Part I of 2.)

```
13        ' parameterless constructor
14        Public Sub New()
15           ' constructor body code
16        End Sub ' New
17
18        ' operations
19        Public Sub Execute()
20           ' Execute method body code
21        End Sub ' Execute
22     End Class ' Withdrawal
```

Fig. 9.27 | Visual Basic code incorporating method Execute in class Withdrawal based on Figs. 9.22 and 9.23. (Part 2 of 2.)

Software Engineering Observation 9.7

Many UML modeling tools can convert UML-based designs into Visual Basic code, considerably speeding the implementation process. For more information on these "automatic" code generators, refer to the Web resources listed at the end of Section 3.9.

This concludes our discussion of the basics of generating class files from UML diagrams. In the final Software Engineering Case Study section (Section 11.8), we demonstrate how to modify the code in Fig. 9.27 to incorporate the object-oriented concepts of inheritance and polymorphism in Chapter 11.

Software Engineering Case Study Self-Review Exercises

9.1 State whether the following statement is *true* or *false*, and if *false*, explain why: If an attribute of a class is marked with a minus sign (-) in a class diagram, the attribute is not directly accessible outside of the class.

9.2 In Fig. 9.23, the association between the ATM and the Screen indicates that:
  a) we can navigate from the Screen to the ATM
  b) we can navigate from the ATM to the Screen
  c) Both a and b; the association is bidirectional
  d) None of the above

9.3 Write Visual Basic code to begin implementing the design for class Account.

Answers to Software Engineering Case Study Self-Review Exercises

9.1 True. The minus sign (-) indicates private visibility. We've mentioned "friendship" as an exception to private visibility. Friendship is discussed in Chapter 10.

9.2 b.

9.3 The design for class Account yields the code in Fig. 9.28. Note that we include Private instance variables availableBalance and totalBalance to store the data that properties AvailableBalance and TotalBalance, and methods Credit and Debit will manipulate.

9.15 Wrap-Up

This chapter investigated the object-oriented programming concepts of classes, objects, methods and instance variables in more depth. The Time class case study presented a complete class declaration consisting of Private data, overloaded constructors for initializa-

```vbnet
 1    ' Represents a bank account.
 2    Public Class Account
 3       Private accountNumber As Integer ' account number
 4       Private pin As Integer ' PIN for authentication
 5       Private availableBalance As Decimal ' available withdrawal amount
 6       Private totalBalance As Decimal ' funds available + pending deposit
 7
 8       ' parameterless constructor
 9       Public Sub New()
10          ' constructor body code
11       End Sub ' New
12
13       ' validates user PIN
14       Public Function ValidatePIN() As Boolean
15          ' ValidatePIN method body code
16       End Function ' ValidatePIN
17
18       ' property AvailableBalance
19       Public ReadOnly Property AvailableBalance() As Decimal
20          ' AvailableBalance property body code
21       End Property ' AvailableBalance
22
23       ' property TotalBalance
24       Public ReadOnly Property TotalBalance() As Decimal
25          ' TotalBalance property body code
26       End Property ' TotalBalance
27
28       ' credits the account
29       Public Sub Credit()
30          ' Credit method body code
31       End Sub ' Credit
32
33       ' debits the account
34       Public Sub Debit()
35          ' Debit method body code
36       End Sub ' Debit
37    End Class ' Account
```

Fig. 9.28 | Visual Basic code for class `Account` based on Figs. 9.22 and 9.23.

tion flexibility, properties with `Set` and `Get` accessors for manipulating the class's data, and methods that returned `String` representations of a `Time` object in two different formats.

We showed how the `Me` reference is used implicitly in a class's non-`Shared` methods to access the class's instance variables and non-`Shared` methods. We also showed how to use the `Me` reference explicitly to access the class's shadowed instance variables explicitly.

You learned that a class can have references to objects of other classes as members—a concept known as composition. We discussed how garbage collection reclaims the memory of objects that are no longer needed. You learned how to execute the garbage collector to invoke the method `Finalize` on each object before it is removed from memory. We explained the motivation for `Shared` instance variables in a class, and demonstrated how to declare and use `Shared` variables and methods in your own classes. You learned how to declare and initialize `Const` and `ReadOnly` variables. We showed how to use the

Object Browser to learn the functionality provided by the classes of the Framework Class Library. We also showed how to create a class library for reuse and how to use the classes of the library in an application.

In the next chapter, we continue our discussion of classes by introducing a form of software reuse called inheritance. We will see that classes often share common attributes and behaviors. In such cases, it is possible to define those attributes and behaviors in a common "base" class and "inherit" those capabilities into new class declarations.

10

Object-Oriented Programming: Inheritance

*Say not you know
another entirely,
till you have divided an
inheritance with him.*
—Johann Kasper Lavater

*This method is to define as
the number of a class the
class of all classes similar to
the given class.*
—Bertrand Russell

*Good as it is to inherit
a library, it is better to
collect one.*
—Augustine Birrell

*Save base authority from
others' books.*
—William Shakespeare

OBJECTIVES

In this chapter you will learn:

- What inheritance is and how it promotes software reusability.

- The notions of base classes and derived classes.

- To use keyword `Inherits` to create a class that inherits attributes and behaviors from another class.

- To use the access modifier `Protected` in a base class to give derived class methods access to base class members.

- To access base class members from a derived class with `MyBase`.

- How constructors are used in inheritance hierarchies.

- To access the current object with `Me` and `MyClass`.

- The methods of class `Object`—the direct or indirect base class of all classes in Visual Basic.

10.1 Introduction

This chapter continues our discussion of object-oriented programming (OOP) by introducing one of its primary features, *inheritance*, a form of software reuse in which a new class is created by absorbing an existing class's members and embellishing them with new or modified capabilities. With inheritance, you can save time during program development by reusing proven and debugged high-quality software. This increases the likelihood that a system will be implemented effectively.

When creating a class, rather than declaring completely new members, you can designate that the new class will inherit the members of an existing class. The existing class is called the *base class*, and the new class is the *derived class*. (The Java programming language refers to the base class as the *superclass* and the derived class as the *subclass*.) A derived class can become the base class for future derived classes.

A derived class normally adds its own instance variables, Shared variables, properties and methods. Therefore, a derived class is more specific than its base class and represents a more specialized group of objects. Typically, the derived class exhibits the behaviors of its base class and additional behaviors that are specific to the derived class. [*Note:* A class's instance variables and Shared variables are referred to collectively as the class's *fields*.]

The *direct base class* is the class from which the derived class explicitly inherits. An *indirect base class* is inherited from two or more levels up in the *class hierarchy*. In Visual Basic, the class hierarchy begins with class Object (in namespace System), which *every* class in Visual Basic directly or indirectly *extends* (or "inherits from"). Section 10.7 lists the seven methods of class Object, which every other class inherits. In the case of *single inher-*

itance, a class is derived from one direct base class. Visual Basic, unlike C++, does not support multiple inheritance (which occurs when a class is derived from more than one direct base class). In Chapter 11, Object-Oriented Programming: Polymorphism, we explain how you can use `Interfaces` to realize many of the benefits of multiple inheritance while avoiding the associated problems.

We distinguish between the ***is-a relationship*** and the ***has-a relationship***. *Is-a* represents inheritance. In an *is-a* relationship, an object of a derived class also can be treated as an object of its base class. For example, a car *is a* vehicle. By contrast, the *has-a* relationship represents composition (see Chapter 9). In a *has-a* relationship, an object contains one or more object references as members. For example, a car *has a* steering wheel (and a car object has a reference to a steering wheel object).

New classes can inherit from classes in ***class libraries***. Organizations develop their own class libraries and can take advantage of others available worldwide. Some day, most new software will probably be constructed from ***standardized reusable components***, just as automobiles and most computer hardware items are constructed today. This will facilitate the development of more powerful, abundant and economical software.

10.2 Base Classes and Derived Classes

Often, an object of one class *is an* object of another class as well. For example, in geometry, a rectangle *is a* quadrilateral (as are squares, parallelograms and trapezoids). Thus, in Visual Basic, class `Rectangle` can be said to inherit from class `Quadrilateral`. In this context, class `Quadrilateral` is a base class and class `Rectangle` is a derived class. A rectangle *is a* specific type of quadrilateral, but it is incorrect to claim that every quadrilateral *is a* rectangle—the quadrilateral could be a parallelogram or some other shape. Figure 10.1 lists several simple examples of base classes and derived classes—note that base classes tend to be "more general" and derived classes tend to be "more specific."

Every derived class object *is an* object of its base class, and one base class can have many derived classes, so the set of objects represented by a base class is typically larger than the set of objects represented by any of its derived classes. For example, the base class `Vehicle` represents all vehicles, including cars, trucks, boats, bicycles and so on. By contrast, derived class `Car` represents a smaller, more specific subset of vehicles.

Inheritance relationships form tree-like hierarchical structures. A base class exists in a hierarchical relationship with its derived classes. When classes participate in inheritance

Base class	Derived classes
Student	GraduateStudent, UndergraduateStudent
Shape	Circle, Triangle, Rectangle
Loan	CarLoan, HomeImprovementLoan, MortgageLoan
Employee	Faculty, Staff
BankAccount	CheckingAccount, SavingsAccount

Fig. 10.1 | Inheritance examples.

relationships, they become "affiliated" with other classes. A class becomes either a base class, supplying members to other classes, or a derived class, inheriting its members from other classes. In some cases, a class is both a base class and a derived class.

CommunityMember *Inheritance Hierarchy*

Let's develop a sample class hierarchy (Fig. 10.2), also called an *inheritance hierarchy*. A university community has thousands of members, including employees, students and alumni. Employees are either faculty members or staff members. Faculty members are either administrators (such as deans and department chairpersons) or teachers. The hierarchy could contain many other classes. For example, students can be graduate or undergraduate students. Undergraduate students can be freshmen, sophomores, juniors or seniors.

Each arrow in the inheritance hierarchy diagram of Fig. 10.2 represents an *is-a* relationship. As we follow the arrows in this class hierarchy, we can state, for instance, that "an Employee *is a* CommunityMember" and "a Teacher *is a* Faculty member." Community-Member is the direct base class of Employee, Student and Alumnus, and is an indirect base class of all the other classes in the diagram. Starting from the bottom of the diagram, you can follow the arrows and apply the *is-a* relationship up to the topmost base class. For example, an Administrator *is a* Faculty member, *is an* Employee and *is a* Community-Member.

Shape *Inheritance Hierarchy*

Now consider the Shape inheritance hierarchy in Fig. 10.3. This hierarchy begins with base class Shape, which is inherited by derived classes TwoDimensionalShape and Three-DimensionalShape—Shapes are either TwoDimensionalShapes or ThreeDimensional-Shapes. The third level of the hierarchy contains some more specific types of TwoDimensionalShapes and ThreeDimensionalShapes. As in Fig. 10.2, we can follow the arrows from the bottom of the diagram to the topmost base class in this class hierarchy to identify several *is-a* relationships. For example, a Triangle *is a* TwoDimensionalShape and *is a* Shape, while a Sphere *is a* ThreeDimensionalShape and *is a* Shape. Note that this hierarchy could contain many other classes. For example, ellipses and trapezoids also are TwoDimensionalShapes, and cylinders also are ThreeDimensionalShapes.

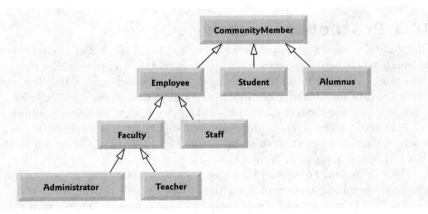

Fig. 10.2 | Inheritance hierarchy for university CommunityMembers.

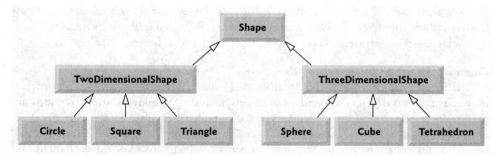

Fig. 10.3 | Inheritance hierarchy for Shapes.

Notes on Inheritance Relationships

Not every class relationship is an inheritance relationship. In Chapter 9, we discussed the *has-a* relationship, in which classes have members that are references to objects of other classes. Such relationships create classes by composition of existing classes. For example, given the classes Employee, BirthDate and TelephoneNumber, it is improper to say that an Employee *is a* BirthDate or that an Employee *is a* TelephoneNumber. However, an Employee *has a* BirthDate, and an Employee *has a* TelephoneNumber.

It is possible to treat base class objects and derived class objects similarly—their commonalities are expressed in the members of the base class. Objects of all classes that inherit a common base class can be treated as objects of that base class (i.e., such objects have an *is-a* relationship with the base class). However, base class objects cannot be treated as objects of their derived classes. For example, all cars are vehicles, but not all vehicles are cars (the other vehicles could be trucks, planes or bicycles, for example). Later in this chapter and in Chapter 11, we consider many examples that use the *is-a* relationship.

One problem with inheritance is that a derived class can inherit methods that it does not need or should not have. Even when a base class method is appropriate for a derived class, the derived class often needs a customized version of the method. In such cases, the derived class can ***override*** (redefine) the base class method with an implementation appropriate for the derived class, as we will see often in the chapter's code examples.

10.3 Protected Members

Chapter 9 discussed access modifiers Public and Private. A class's Public members are accessible wherever the program has a reference to an object of that class or one of its derived classes. A class's Private members are accessible only within the class itself. A base class's Private members are not inherited by its derived classes. This section introduces the access modifier Protected. In Section 10.8, we discuss the access modifier ***Friend***.

Protected access offers an intermediate level of access between Public and Private access. A base class's Protected members can be accessed only by members of that base class and by members of its derived classes.

All Public and Protected base class members retain their original access modifier when they become members of the derived class (i.e., Public members of the base class become Public members of the derived class, and Protected members of the base class become Protected members of the derived class).

Derived class methods can refer to `Public` and `Protected` members inherited from the base class simply by using the member names. When a derived class method overrides a base class method, the base class version can be accessed from the derived class by preceding the base class method name with keyword `MyBase` and a dot (`.`) separator. We discuss accessing overridden members of the base class in Section 10.4.

Software Engineering Observation 10.1

Derived class methods cannot directly access `Private` members of their base class. A derived class can change the state of `Private` base class instance variables only through non-`Private` methods provided in the base class and inherited by the derived class.

Software Engineering Observation 10.2

Declaring `Private` instance variables helps programmers test, debug and correctly modify systems. If a derived class could access its base class's `Private` instance variables, classes that inherit from that derived class could access the instance variables as well. This would propagate access to what should be `Private` instance variables, and the benefits of information hiding would be lost.

10.4 Relationship between Base Classes and Derived Classes

In this section, we use a business-oriented inheritance hierarchy containing types of employees in a company's payroll application to discuss the relationship between a base class and a derived class. Commission employees (who will be represented as objects of a base class) are paid a percentage of their sales, while base-salaried commission employees (who will be represented as objects of a derived class) receive a base salary plus a percentage of their sales. We divide our discussion of the relationship between commission employees and base-salaried commission employees into a carefully paced series of five examples:

1. In the first example, we create class `CommissionEmployee`, which contains as `Private` instance variables a first name, last name, social security number, commission rate (percentage) and gross (i.e., total) sales amount.

2. The second example defines class `BasePlusCommissionEmployee`, which contains as `Private` instance variables a first name, last name, social security number, commission rate, gross sales amount *and* a base salary. We create the class by writing every line of code that the class requires—we will soon see that it is much more efficient to create this class simply by inheriting from class `CommissionEmployee`, then adding appropriate attributes and behaviors.

3. The third example defines a new version of class `BasePlusCommissionEmployee` that inherits directly from class `CommissionEmployee` (i.e., a `BasePlusCommissionEmployee` *is a* `CommissionEmployee` who also has a base salary) and attempts to access class `CommissionEmployee`'s `Private` members—this results in compilation errors, because the derived class does not have access to the base class's `Private` data.

4. The fourth example shows that if `CommissionEmployee`'s data is declared as `Protected`, a new version of class `BasePlusCommissionEmployee` that inherits from class `CommissionEmployee` *can* access that data directly. For this purpose, we de-

fine a new version of class CommissionEmployee with Protected data. Both the inherited and noninherited BasePlusCommissionEmployee classes contain identical functionality, but we show how the version of BasePlusCommissionEmployee that inherits from class CommissionEmployee is easier to create and manage.

5. After we discuss the convenience of using protected data, we create the fifth example, which sets the CommissionEmployee data members back to Private to enforce good software engineering. This example demonstrates that derived class BasePlusCommissionEmployee can use base class CommissionEmployee's Public properties and methods to manipulate (in a carefully controlled manner) CommissionEmployee's Private data.

10.4.1 Creating and Using a CommissionEmployee Class

We begin by declaring class CommissionEmployee (Fig. 10.4). Lines 3–4 begin the class declaration and indicate that class CommissionEmployee *Inherits* from class Object (from namespace System). Visual Basic programmers use inheritance to create classes from existing classes. In fact, every class in Visual Basic (except Object) inherits from an existing class. Because class CommissionEmployee is derived from class Object, class CommissionEmployee inherits the methods of class Object—class Object does not have any fields. In fact, every Visual Basic class directly or indirectly inherits Object's methods. If a class does not specify that it inherits another class, the new class implicitly inherits Object. For this reason, programmers typically do not include "Inherits Object" in their code—we do so in this example for demonstration purposes, but then we omit "Inherits Object" in all subsequent examples.

The Public services of class CommissionEmployee include a constructor (lines 13–22), properties FirstName (lines 25–33), LastName (lines 36–44), SocialSecurityNumber (lines 47–55), GrossSales (lines 58–70) and CommissionRate (lines 73–85), and methods CalculateEarnings (lines 88–90) and ToString (lines 93–100). Lines 25–85 declare Public properties for manipulating the class's instance variables firstNameValue, lastNameValue, socialSecurityNumberValue, grossSalesValue and commissionRateValue (declared in lines 6–10). Class CommissionEmployee declares each of its instance variables as Private, so objects of other classes cannot directly access these variables. Properties GrossSales and CommissionRate validate their arguments before assigning the values to instance variables grossSalesValue and commissionRateValue, respectively.

```vb
1   ' Fig. 10.4: CommmissionEmployee.vb
2   ' CommissionEmployee class represents a commission employee.
3   Public Class CommissionEmployee
4       Inherits Object ' optional
5
6       Private firstNameValue As String ' first name
7       Private lastNameValue As String ' last name
8       Private socialSecurityNumberValue As String ' social security number
9       Private grossSalesValue As Decimal ' gross weekly sales
10      Private commissionRateValue As Decimal ' commission percentage
```

Fig. 10.4 | CommissionEmployee class represents an employee paid a percentage of gross sales. (Part 1 of 3.)

```
11
12      ' five-argument constructor
13      Public Sub New(ByVal first As String, ByVal last As String, _
14          ByVal ssn As String, ByVal sales As Decimal, ByVal rate As Decimal)
15
16          ' implicit call to Object constructor occurs here
17          FirstName = first
18          LastName = last
19          SocialSecurityNumber = ssn
20          GrossSales = sales ' validate and store gross sales
21          CommissionRate = rate ' validate and store commission rate
22      End Sub ' New
23
24      ' property FirstName
25      Public Property FirstName() As String
26          Get
27              Return firstNameValue
28          End Get
29
30          Set(ByVal first As String)
31              firstNameValue = first ' no validation
32          End Set
33      End Property ' FirstName
34
35      ' property LastName
36      Public Property LastName() As String
37          Get
38              Return lastNameValue
39          End Get
40
41          Set(ByVal last As String)
42              lastNameValue = last ' no validation
43          End Set
44      End Property ' LastName
45
46      ' property SocialSecurityNumber
47      Public Property SocialSecurityNumber() As String
48          Get
49              Return socialSecurityNumberValue
50          End Get
51
52          Set(ByVal ssn As String)
53              socialSecurityNumberValue = ssn ' no validation
54          End Set
55      End Property ' SocialSecurityNumber
56
57      ' property GrossSales
58      Public Property GrossSales() As Decimal
59          Get
60              Return grossSalesValue
61          End Get
```

Fig. 10.4 | CommissionEmployee class represents an employee paid a percentage of gross sales. (Part 2 of 3.)

```
62
63          Set(ByVal sales As Decimal)
64             If sales < 0.0 Then ' validate gross sales
65                grossSalesValue = 0
66             Else
67                grossSalesValue = sales
68             End If
69          End Set
70       End Property ' GrossSales
71
72       ' property CommissionRate
73       Public Property CommissionRate() As Decimal
74          Get
75             Return commissionRateValue
76          End Get
77
78          Set(ByVal rate As Decimal)
79             If rate > 0.0 AndAlso rate < 1.0 Then ' validate rate
80                commissionRateValue = rate
81             Else
82                commissionRateValue = 0
83             End If
84          End Set
85       End Property ' CommissionRate
86
87       ' calculate earnings
88       Public Function CalculateEarnings() As Decimal
89          Return commissionRateValue * grossSalesValue
90       End Function ' CalculateEarnings
91
92       ' return String representation of CommissionEmployee object
93       Public Overrides Function ToString() As String
94          Return ("commission employee: " & firstNameValue & " " & _
95             lastNameValue & vbCrLf & "social security number: " & _
96             socialSecurityNumberValue & vbCrLf & "gross sales: " & _
97             String.Format("{0:C}", grossSalesValue) & vbCrLf & _
98             "commission rate: " & String.Format("{0:F}", _
99             commissionRateValue))
100      End Function ' ToString
101   End Class ' CommissionEmployee
```

Fig. 10.4 | CommissionEmployee class represents an employee paid a percentage of gross sales. (Part 3 of 3.)

Constructors are not inherited, so class CommissionEmployee does not inherit class Object's constructor. However, class CommissionEmployee's constructor calls class Object's constructor implicitly. In fact, the first task of any derived class constructor is to call its direct base class's constructor, either explicitly or implicitly (if no constructor call is specified), to ensure that the instance variables inherited from the base class are initialized properly. The syntax for calling a base class constructor explicitly is discussed in Section 10.4.3. If the code does not include an explicit call to the base class constructor, Visual Basic implicitly calls the base class's default or parameterless constructor. The comment in line 16 of Fig. 10.4 indicates where the implicit call to the base class Object's default constructor is made (you do not need to write the code for this call). Object's default constructor does nothing. Note that even if a class does not have constructors, the default constructor that the compiler implicitly declares for the class will call the base class's default or parameterless constructor.

After the implicit call to Object's constructor occurs, lines 17–21 of Commission-Employee's constructor assign values to the class's instance variables. Note that we do not validate the values of arguments first, last and ssn before assigning them to the corresponding instance variables. We could validate the first and last names—perhaps by ensuring that they are of a reasonable length. Similarly, a social security number could be validated to ensure that it contains nine digits, with or without dashes (e.g., 123-45-6789 or 123456789).

Method CalculateEarnings (lines 88–90) calculates a CommissionEmployee's earnings. Line 89 multiplies the commissionRateValue by the grossSalesValue and returns the result.

Method ToString (lines 93–100) of class CommissionEmployee Overrides (redefines) class Object's ToString method. When invoked, CommissionEmployee's ToString method returns a String containing information about the CommissionEmployee. Without overriding ToString in class CommissionEmployee, the default implementation would return "CommissionEmployeeTest.CommissionEmployee", where CommissionEmployeeTest is the default namespace (which is the same as the project name).

A base class method must be declared *Overridable* if it is to be overridden in a derived class. Method ToString of class Object is declared Overridable, so derived class CommissionEmployee can override this method. To view the method header for ToString, select **Help > Index...**, and enter "Object.ToString method" in the search text box. The page displayed contains a description of method ToString, which includes the following header:

> **Public Overridable Function** ToString() *As String*

Common Programming Error 10.1
It is a compilation error to attempt to override a method that is not declared Overridable.

Common Programming Error 10.2
It is a compilation error to override a method with a method that has a different access modifier than the method being overridden.

Testing Class CommissionEmployee
Figure 10.5 tests class CommissionEmployee. Lines 6–7 instantiate a CommissionEmployee object and invoke CommissionEmployee's constructor (lines 13–22 of Fig. 10.4) to initialize it with "Sue" as the first name, "Jones" as the last name, "222-22-2222" as the social security number, 10000 as the gross sales amount and 0.06 as the commission rate. Lines 10–16 access CommissionEmployee's Public properties for output. Lines 18–19 change the values of properties GrossSales and CommissionRate. Lines 22–24 call CommissionEmployee's ToString method to output the string representation of the updated CommissionEmployee. Lines 27–28 display the CommissionEmployee's earnings, calculated by the object's CalculateEarnings method using the updated values of instance variables grossSalesValue and commissionRateValue.

```vb
 1   ' Fig. 10.5: CommissionEmployeeTest.vb
 2   ' Testing class CommissionEmployee.
 3   Module CommissionEmployeeTest
 4      Sub Main()
 5         ' instantiate CommissionEmployee object
 6         Dim employee As New CommissionEmployee( _
 7            "Sue", "Jones", "222-22-2222", 10000, 0.06D)
 8
 9         ' get commission employee data
10         Console.WriteLine("Employee information obtained by properties:" _
11            & vbCrLf & "First name is " & employee.FirstName & vbCrLf & _
12            "Last name is " & employee.LastName & vbCrLf & _
13            "Social Security Number is " & employee.SocialSecurityNumber)
14         Console.WriteLine("Gross sales is {0:C}", employee.GrossSales)
15         Console.WriteLine("Commission rate is {0:F}", _
16            employee.CommissionRate)
17
18         employee.GrossSales = 500 ' set gross sales
19         employee.CommissionRate = 0.1D ' set commission rate to 10%
20
21         ' get new employee information
22         Console.WriteLine(vbCrLf & _
23            "Updated employee information obtained by ToString: " & _
24            vbCrLf & employee.ToString() & vbCrLf)
25
26         ' display the employee's earnings
27         Console.WriteLine("Employee's earnings: {0:C}", _
28            employee.CalculateEarnings())
29      End Sub ' Main
30   End Module ' CommissionEmployeeTest
```

```
Employee information obtained by properties:
First name is Sue
Last name is Jones
Social Security Number is 222-22-2222
Gross sales is $10,000.00
Commission rate is 0.06

Updated employee information obtained by ToString:
commission employee: Sue Jones
social security number: 222-22-2222
gross sales: $500.00
commission rate: 0.10

Employee's earnings: $50.00
```

Fig. 10.5 | CommissionEmployee class test program.

10.4.2 Creating a BasePlusCommissionEmployee Class without Using Inheritance

We now discuss the second part of our introduction to inheritance by declaring and testing a completely new and independent class BasePlusCommissionEmployee (Fig. 10.6), which contains a first name, last name, social security number, gross sales amount, commission rate *and* base salary.

```vb
1   ' Fig. 10.6: BasePlusCommissionEmployee.vb
2   ' BasePlusCommissionEmployee class represents an employee that receives
3   ' a base salary in addition to a commission.
4   Public Class BasePlusCommissionEmployee
5      Private firstNameValue As String ' first name
6      Private lastNameValue As String ' last name
7      Private socialSecurityNumberValue As String ' social security number
8      Private grossSalesValue As Decimal ' gross weekly sales
9      Private commissionRateValue As Decimal ' commission percentage
10     Private baseSalaryValue As Decimal ' base salary per week
11
12     ' six-argument constructor
13     Public Sub New(ByVal first As String, ByVal last As String, _
14        ByVal ssn As String, ByVal sales As Decimal, _
15        ByVal rate As Decimal, ByVal salary As Decimal)
16
17        ' implicit call to Object constructor occurs here
18        FirstName = first
19        LastName = last
20        SocialSecurityNumber = ssn
21        GrossSales = sales ' validate and store gross sales
22        CommissionRate = rate ' validate and store commission rate
23        BaseSalary = salary ' validate and store base salary
24     End Sub ' New
25
26     ' property FirstName
27     Public Property FirstName() As String
28        Get
29           Return firstNameValue
30        End Get
31
32        Set(ByVal first As String)
33           firstNameValue = first ' no validation
34        End Set
35     End Property ' FirstName
36
37     ' property LastName
38     Public Property LastName() As String
39        Get
40           Return lastNameValue
41        End Get
42
43        Set(ByVal last As String)
44           lastNameValue = last ' no validation
45        End Set
46     End Property ' LastName
47
```

Fig. 10.6 | BasePlusCommissionEmployee class represents an employee who receives a base salary in addition to a commission. (Part 1 of 3.)

```
48      ' property SocialSecurityNumber
49      Public Property SocialSecurityNumber() As String
50         Get
51            Return socialSecurityNumberValue
52         End Get
53
54         Set(ByVal ssn As String)
55            socialSecurityNumberValue = ssn ' no validation
56         End Set
57      End Property ' SocialSecurityNumber
58
59      ' property GrossSales
60      Public Property GrossSales() As Decimal
61         Get
62            Return grossSalesValue
63         End Get
64
65         Set(ByVal sales As Decimal)
66            If sales < 0.0 Then ' validate gross sales
67               grossSalesValue = 0
68            Else
69               grossSalesValue = sales
70            End If
71         End Set
72      End Property ' GrossSales
73
74      ' property CommissionRate
75      Public Property CommissionRate() As Decimal
76         Get
77            Return commissionRateValue
78         End Get
79
80         Set(ByVal rate As Decimal)
81            If rate > 0.0 AndAlso rate < 1.0 Then ' validate rate
82               commissionRateValue = rate
83            Else
84               commissionRateValue = 0
85            End If
86         End Set
87      End Property ' CommissionRate
88
89      ' property BaseSalary
90      Public Property BaseSalary() As Decimal
91         Get
92            Return baseSalaryValue
93         End Get
94
95         Set(ByVal salary As Decimal)
96            If salary < 0.0 Then ' validate base salary
97               baseSalaryValue = 0
```

Fig. 10.6 | BasePlusCommissionEmployee class represents an employee who receives a base salary in addition to a commission. (Part 2 of 3.)

```
 98            Else
 99                baseSalaryValue = salary
100            End If
101        End Set
102    End Property ' BaseSalary
103
104        ' calculate earnings
105    Public Function CalculateEarnings() As Decimal
106        Return baseSalaryValue + (commissionRateValue * grossSalesValue)
107    End Function ' CalculateEarnings
108
109        ' return String representation of BasePlusCommissionEmployee object
110    Public Overrides Function ToString() As String
111        Return ("base-plus-commission employee: " & firstNameValue & " " & _
112            lastNameValue & vbCrLf & "social security number: " & _
113            socialSecurityNumberValue & vbCrLf & "gross sales: " & _
114            String.Format("{0:C}", grossSalesValue) & vbCrLf & _
115            "commission rate: " & String.Format("{0:F}", _
116            commissionRateValue) & vbCrLf & "base salary: " & _
117            String.Format("{0:C}", baseSalaryValue))
118    End Function ' ToString
119 End Class ' BasePlusCommissionEmployee
```

Fig. 10.6 | BasePlusCommissionEmployee class represents an employee who receives a base salary in addition to a commission. (Part 3 of 3.)

Defining Class BasePlusCommissionEmployee

Class BasePlusCommissionEmployee's Public services include a BasePlusCommissionEmployee constructor (lines 13–24), properties FirstName (lines 27–35), LastName (lines 38–46), SocialSecurityNumber (lines 49–57), GrossSales (lines 60–72), CommissionRate (lines 75–87) and BaseSalary (lines 90–102), and methods CalculateEarnings (lines 105–107) and ToString (lines 110–118). Lines 27–102 declare Public properties for the class's Private instance variables firstNameValue, lastNameValue, socialSecurityNumberValue, grossSalesValue, commissionRateValue and baseSalaryValue (declared in lines 5–10). These variables, properties and methods comprise all the necessary features of a base-salaried commission employee. Note the similarity between this class and class CommissionEmployee (Fig. 10.4)—in this example, we do not yet exploit that similarity.

Note that class BasePlusCommissionEmployee does not specify "Inherits Object," so the class implicitly inherits Object. Also, like class CommissionEmployee's constructor (lines 13–22 of Fig. 10.4), class BasePlusCommissionEmployee's constructor invokes class Object's default constructor implicitly, as noted in the comment in line 17 (Fig. 10.6).

Class BasePlusCommissionEmployee's CalculateEarnings method (lines 105–107) computes the earnings of a base-salaried commission employee. Line 106 returns the result of adding the base salary to the product of the commission rate and the gross sales. Class BasePlusCommissionEmployee overrides Object method ToString (lines 110–118) to return a String containing the BasePlusCommissionEmployee's information.

Testing Class BasePlusCommissionEmployee

Figure 10.7 tests class BasePlusCommissionEmployee. Lines 6–7 instantiate a BasePlusCommissionEmployee object and pass "Bob", "Lewis", "333-33-3333", 5000, 0.04 and

```
 1    ' Fig. 10.7: BasePlusCommissionEmployeeTest.vb
 2    ' Testing class BasePlusCommissionEmployee.
 3    Module BasePlusCommissionEmployeeTest
 4       Sub Main()
 5          ' instantite BasePlusCommissionEmployee object
 6          Dim employee As New BasePlusCommissionEmployee( _
 7             "Bob", "Lewis", "333-33-3333", 5000, 0.04D, 300)
 8
 9          ' get base-salaried commission employee data
10          Console.WriteLine("Employee information obtained by properties:" _
11             & vbCrLf & "First name is " & employee.FirstName & vbCrLf & _
12             "Last name is " & employee.LastName & vbCrLf & _
13             "Social Security Number is " & employee.SocialSecurityNumber)
14          Console.WriteLine("Gross sales is {0:C}", employee.GrossSales)
15          Console.WriteLine("Commission rate is {0:F}", _
16             employee.CommissionRate)
17          Console.WriteLine("Base salary is {0:C}", employee.BaseSalary)
18
19          employee.BaseSalary = 1000 ' set base salary
20
21          ' get new employee information
22          Console.WriteLine(vbCrLf & _
23             "Updated employee information obtained by ToString: " & _
24             vbCrLf & employee.ToString() & vbCrLf)
25
26          ' display the employee's earnings
27          Console.WriteLine("Employee's earnings: $" & _
28             employee.CalculateEarnings())
29       End Sub ' Main
30    End Module ' BasePlusCommissionEmployeeTest
```

```
Employee information obtained by properties:
First name is Bob
Last name is Lewis
Social Security Number is 333-33-3333
Gross sales is $5,000.00
Commission rate is 0.04
Base salary is $300.00

Updated employee information obtained by ToString:
base-plus-commission employee: Bob Lewis
social security number: 333-33-3333
gross sales: $5,000.00
commission rate: 0.04
base salary: $1,000.00

Employee's earnings: $1200.00
```

Fig. 10.7 | BasePlusCommissionEmployee test program.

300 to the constructor as the first name, last name, social security number, gross sales, commission rate and base salary, respectively. Lines 10–17 use BasePlus-CommissionEmployee's properties to retrieve the values of the object's instance variables for output. Line 19 changes the BaseSalary property. Property BaseSalary's Set accessor

(Fig. 10.6, lines 95–101) ensures that instance variable baseSalaryValue is not assigned a negative value, because an employee's base salary cannot be negative. Line 24 of Fig. 10.7 invokes the object's ToString method explicitly to get the object's string representation.

Exploring the Similarities between Class BasePlusCommissionEmployee and Class CommissionEmployee

Much of the code for class BasePlusCommissionEmployee (Fig. 10.6) is similar, if not identical, to the code for class CommissionEmployee (Fig. 10.4). For example, both classes contain Private instance variables firstNameValue, lastNameValue, socialSecurity-NumberValue, grossSalesValue and commissionRateValue, and properties FirstName, LastName, SocialSecurityNumber, GrossSales and CommissionRate to manipulate these variables. The BasePlusCommissionEmployee constructor is *almost* identical to that of class CommissionEmployee, except that BasePlusCommissionEmployee's constructor also sets the BaseSalary property. The other additions to class BasePlusCommissionEmployee are Private instance variable baseSalaryValue and property BaseSalary. Class Base-PlusCommissionEmployee's ToString method is nearly identical to that of class Commis-sionEmployee except that BasePlusCommissionEmployee's ToString also outputs the value of instance variable baseSalaryValue.

To form class BasePlusCommissionEmployee, we copied the code from class Commis-sionEmployee and pasted it into class BasePlusCommissionEmployee, then modified class BasePlusCommissionEmployee to include a base salary and methods that manipulate the base salary. This "copy-and-paste" approach is often error prone and time consuming. Worse yet, it can spread many physical copies of the same code throughout a system, creating a code-maintenance nightmare. Is there a way to "absorb" the instance variables and methods of one class in a way that makes them part of other classes without duplicating code? Indeed there is—using the elegant object-oriented programming technique of inheritance that we demonstrate in the next section.

Software Engineering Observation 10.3

Copying and pasting code from one class to another can spread errors among multiple source code files. To avoid duplicating code (and possibly errors), use inheritance, rather than the "copy-and-paste" approach, where you want one class to "absorb" the members of another class.

Software Engineering Observation 10.4

With inheritance, the common instance variables and methods of all the classes in the hierarchy ~~ *declared in a base class. When changes are required for these common features, software* ~~*bers need to make the changes only in the base class—derived classes then inherit the* ~~*Without inheritance, the changes would need to be made to all the source code files that* ~~ *of the code in question.*

~~mmissionEmployee–
~~Employee Inheritance Hierarchy

~~mmissionEmployee (Fig. 10.9), which inherits from class
~~). Class CommissionEmployee is almost identical to
~~CalculateEarnings (Fig. 10.8, lines 88–90) is now declared
~~ved class of CommissionEmployee can override method Calcu-
~~e an appropriate earnings calculation. A BasePlusCommission-

Employee object *is a* CommissionEmployee (because inheritance passes on the capabilities of class CommissionEmployee), but class BasePlusCommissionEmployee also has instance variable baseSalaryValue (Fig. 10.9, line 6). Note that Fig. 10.9 does not redeclare the base class instance variables (lines 6–10 of Fig. 10.8)—these are nevertheless present in the derived class (through inheritance). Even though they are present, they are declared Private in the base class, so as we will see in a moment, we will have to make special provision to access this base class information from the derived class. Keyword Inherits in line 4 of the class declaration (Fig. 10.9) indicates inheritance. As a derived class, BasePlusCommission-Employee inherits the Public (and Protected, if there were any) instance variables and methods of class CommissionEmployee. The constructor of class CommissionEmployee is not inherited. Thus, the Public services of BasePlusCommissionEmployee include its constructor (lines 9–16), Public methods and properties inherited from class Commission-Employee, property BaseSalary (lines 19–31), method CalculateEarnings (lines 34–37) and method ToString (lines 40–49).

```vb
 1    ' Fig. 10.8: CommmissionEmployee.vb
 2    ' CommissionEmployee class represents a commission employee.
 3    Public Class CommissionEmployee
 4        Inherits Object ' optional
 5
 6        Private firstNameValue As String ' first name
 7        Private lastNameValue As String ' last name
 8        Private socialSecurityNumberValue As String ' social security number
 9        Private grossSalesValue As Decimal ' gross weekly sales
10        Private commissionRateValue As Decimal ' commission percentage
11
12        ' five-argument constructor
13        Public Sub New(ByVal first As String, ByVal last As String, _
14            ByVal ssn As String, ByVal sales As Decimal, ByVal rate As Decimal)
15
16            ' implicit call to Object constructor occurs here
17            FirstName = first
18            LastName = last
19            SocialSecurityNumber = ssn
20            GrossSales = sales ' validate and store gross sales
21            CommissionRate = rate ' validate and store commission rate
22        End Sub ' New
23
24        ' property FirstName
25        Public Property FirstName() As String
26            Get
27                Return firstNameValue
28            End Get
29
30            Set(ByVal first As String)
31                firstNameValue = first ' no validation
32            End Set
33        End Property ' FirstName
34
```

Fig. 10.8 | CommissionEmployee class with Overridable method CalculateEar[...]
(Part 1 of 3.)

```
35         ' property LastName
36        Public Property LastName() As String
37           Get
38              Return lastNameValue
39           End Get
40
41           Set(ByVal last As String)
42              lastNameValue = last ' no validation
43           End Set
44        End Property ' LastName
45
46         ' property SocialSecurityNumber
47        Public Property SocialSecurityNumber() As String
48           Get
49              Return socialSecurityNumberValue
50           End Get
51
52           Set(ByVal ssn As String)
53              socialSecurityNumberValue = ssn ' no validation
54           End Set
55        End Property ' SocialSecurityNumber
56
57         ' property GrossSales
58        Public Property GrossSales() As Decimal
59           Get
60              Return grossSalesValue
61           End Get
62
63           Set(ByVal sales As Decimal)
64              If sales < 0.0 Then ' validate gross sales
65                 grossSalesValue = 0
66              Else
67                 grossSalesValue = sales
68              End If
69           End Set
70        End Property ' GrossSales
71
72         ' property CommissionRate
73        Public Property CommissionRate() As Decimal
74           Get
75              Return commissionRateValue
76           End Get
77
78           Set(ByVal rate As Decimal)
79              If rate > 0.0 AndAlso rate < 1.0 Then ' validate rate
80                 commissionRateValue = rate
81              Else
82                 commissionRateValue = 0
83              End If
84           End Set
85        End Property ' CommissionRate
```

Fig. 10.8 | CommissionEmployee class with Overridable method CalculateEarnings. (Part 2 of 3.)

```
86
87          ' calculate earnings
88          Public Overridable Function CalculateEarnings() As Decimal
89             Return commissionRateValue * grossSalesValue
90          End Function ' CalculateEarnings
91
92          ' return String representation of CommissionEmployee object
93          Public Overrides Function ToString() As String
94             Return ("commission employee: " & firstNameValue & " " & _
95                lastNameValue & vbCrLf & "social security number: " & _
96                socialSecurityNumberValue & vbCrLf & "gross sales: " & _
97                String.Format("{0:C}", grossSalesValue) & vbCrLf & _
98                "commission rate: " & String.Format("{0:F}", _
99                commissionRateValue))
100        End Function ' ToString
101     End Class ' CommissionEmployee
```

Fig. 10.8 | CommissionEmployee class with Overridable method CalculateEarnings. (Part 3 of 3.)

```
1       ' Fig. 10.9: BasePlusCommissionEmployee.vb
2       ' BasePlusCommissionEmployee inherits from class CommissionEmployee.
3       Public Class BasePlusCommissionEmployee
4          Inherits CommissionEmployee
5
6          Private baseSalaryValue As Decimal ' base salary per week
7
8          ' six-argument constructor
9          Public Sub New(ByVal first As String, ByVal last As String, _
10            ByVal ssn As String, ByVal sales As Decimal, _
11            ByVal rate As Decimal, ByVal salary As Decimal)
12
13            ' use MyBase to invoke CommissionEmployee constructor explicitly
14            MyBase.New(first, last, ssn, sales, rate)
15            BaseSalary = salary ' validate and store base salary
16         End Sub ' New
17
18         ' property BaseSalary
19         Public Property BaseSalary() As Decimal
20            Get
21               Return baseSalaryValue
22            End Get
23
24            Set(ByVal salary As Decimal)
25               If salary < 0.0 Then ' validate base salary
26                  baseSalaryValue = 0
27               Else
28                  baseSalaryValue = salary
29               End If
30            End Set
31         End Property ' BaseSalary
```

Fig. 10.9 | Private base class members cannot be accessed in a derived class. (Part 1 of 2.)

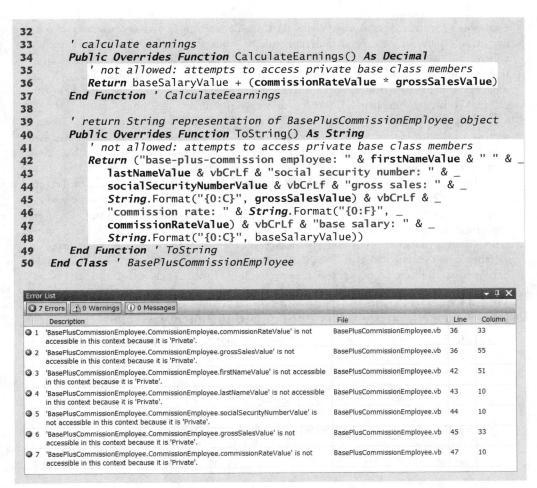

```
32
33          ' calculate earnings
34          Public Overrides Function CalculateEarnings() As Decimal
35             ' not allowed: attempts to access private base class members
36             Return baseSalaryValue + (commissionRateValue * grossSalesValue)
37          End Function ' CalculateEearnings
38
39          ' return String representation of BasePlusCommissionEmployee object
40          Public Overrides Function ToString() As String
41             ' not allowed: attempts to access private base class members
42             Return ("base-plus-commission employee: " & firstNameValue & " " & _
43                lastNameValue & vbCrLf & "social security number: " & _
44                socialSecurityNumberValue & vbCrLf & "gross sales: " & _
45                String.Format("{0:C}", grossSalesValue) & vbCrLf & _
46                "commission rate: " & String.Format("{0:F}", _
47                commissionRateValue) & vbCrLf & "base salary: " & _
48                String.Format("{0:C}", baseSalaryValue))
49          End Function ' ToString
50       End Class ' BasePlusCommissionEmployee
```

	Description	File	Line	Column
1	'BasePlusCommissionEmployee.CommissionEmployee.commissionRateValue' is not accessible in this context because it is 'Private'.	BasePlusCommissionEmployee.vb	36	33
2	'BasePlusCommissionEmployee.CommissionEmployee.grossSalesValue' is not accessible in this context because it is 'Private'.	BasePlusCommissionEmployee.vb	36	55
3	'BasePlusCommissionEmployee.CommissionEmployee.firstNameValue' is not accessible in this context because it is 'Private'.	BasePlusCommissionEmployee.vb	42	51
4	'BasePlusCommissionEmployee.CommissionEmployee.lastNameValue' is not accessible in this context because it is 'Private'.	BasePlusCommissionEmployee.vb	43	10
5	'BasePlusCommissionEmployee.CommissionEmployee.socialSecurityNumberValue' is not accessible in this context because it is 'Private'.	BasePlusCommissionEmployee.vb	44	10
6	'BasePlusCommissionEmployee.CommissionEmployee.grossSalesValue' is not accessible in this context because it is 'Private'.	BasePlusCommissionEmployee.vb	45	33
7	'BasePlusCommissionEmployee.CommissionEmployee.commissionRateValue' is not accessible in this context because it is 'Private'.	BasePlusCommissionEmployee.vb	47	10

Fig. 10.9 | Private base class members cannot be accessed in a derived class. (Part 2 of 2.)

Each derived class constructor must implicitly or explicitly call its base class constructor to ensure that the instance variables inherited from the base class are initialized properly. BasePlusCommissionEmployee's six-argument constructor (lines 9–16 of Fig. 10.9) explicitly calls class CommissionEmployee's five-argument constructor to initialize the base class portion of a BasePlusCommissionEmployee object (i.e., variables firstNameValue, last-NameValue, socialSecurityNumberValue, grossSalesValue and commissionRateValue). Line 14 in BasePlusCommissionEmployee's six-argument constructor invokes the CommissionEmployee's five-argument constructor (declared at lines 13–22 of Fig. 10.8) by using the *base class constructor call syntax*—keyword **MyBase**, followed by the dot (.) separator, followed by New and a set of parentheses containing the arguments to the base class constructor. The arguments first, last, ssn, sales and rate (which were received by the derived class constructor) are used to initialize base class members firstNameValue, last-NameValue, socialSecurityNumberValue, grossSalesValue and commissionRateValue, respectively. If the BasePlusCommissionEmployee constructor did not invoke Commission-

`Employee`'s constructor explicitly, Visual Basic would attempt to invoke class `Commission-Employee`'s parameterless or default constructor—but the class does not have such a constructor, so the compiler would issue an error. The explicit base class constructor call in line 14 (Fig. 10.9) *must* be the first statement in the derived class constructor's body. When a base class contains a default or parameterless constructor, you can use `MyBase.New()` to call that constructor explicitly, but this is unnecessary and is rarely done.

The compiler issues errors for line 36 of Fig. 10.9 because base class `CommissionEmployee`'s instance variables `commissionRateValue` and `grossSalesValue` are `Private`—derived class `BasePlusCommissionEmployee`'s methods are not allowed to access base class `CommissionEmployee`'s `Private` members. Note that we use bold black text in Fig. 10.9 (and elsewhere in the book) to indicate erroneous code. The compiler issues additional errors at lines 42–47 of `BasePlusCommissionEmployee`'s `ToString` method for the same reason. The errors in `BasePlusCommissionEmployee` could have been prevented by using the properties inherited from class `CommissionEmployee`. For example, line 36 could have used properties `CommissionRate` and `GrossSales` to access `CommissionEmployee`'s `Private` instance variables `commissionRateValue` and `grossSalesValue`, respectively. Lines 42–47 also could have used appropriate properties to retrieve the values of the base class's instance variables.

10.4.4 CommissionEmployee–BasePlusCommissionEmployee Inheritance Hierarchy Using Protected Instance Variables

To enable class `BasePlusCommissionEmployee` to directly access base class instance variables `firstNameValue`, `lastNameValue`, `socialSecurityNumberValue`, `grossSalesValue` and `commissionRateValue`, we can declare those members as `Protected` in the base class. As we discussed in Section 10.3, a base class's `Protected` members *are* inherited by all derived classes of that base class and are directly accessible by derived classes.

Defining Base Class CommissionEmployee with Protected Data

Class `CommissionEmployee` (Fig. 10.10) modifies Fig. 10.8 to declare instance variables `firstNameValue`, `lastNameValue`, `socialSecurityNumberValue`, `grossSalesValue` and

```
1    ' Fig. 10.10: CommmissionEmployee.vb
2    ' CommissionEmployee class represents a commission employee.
3    Public Class CommissionEmployee
4       Inherits Object ' optional
5
6       Protected firstNameValue As String ' first name
7       Protected lastNameValue As String ' last name
8       Protected socialSecurityNumberValue As String ' social security number
9       Protected grossSalesValue As Decimal ' gross weekly sales
10      Protected commissionRateValue As Decimal ' commission percentage
11
12      ' five-argument constructor
13      Public Sub New(ByVal first As String, ByVal last As String, _
14         ByVal ssn As String, ByVal sales As Decimal, ByVal rate As Decimal)
15
16         ' implicit call to Object constructor occurs here
17         FirstName = first
```

Fig. 10.10 | CommissionEmployee class with Protected instance variables. (Part 1 of 3.)

```vbnet
18          LastName = last
19          SocialSecurityNumber = ssn
20          GrossSales = sales ' validate and store gross sales
21          CommissionRate = rate ' validate and store commission rate
22       End Sub ' New
23
24       ' property FirstName
25       Public Property FirstName() As String
26          Get
27             Return firstNameValue
28          End Get
29
30          Set(ByVal first As String)
31             firstNameValue = first ' no validation
32          End Set
33       End Property ' FirstName
34
35       ' property LastName
36       Public Property LastName() As String
37          Get
38             Return lastNameValue
39          End Get
40
41          Set(ByVal last As String)
42             lastNameValue = last ' no validation
43          End Set
44       End Property ' LastName
45
46       ' property SocialSecurityNumber
47       Public Property SocialSecurityNumber() As String
48          Get
49             Return socialSecurityNumberValue
50          End Get
51
52          Set(ByVal ssn As String)
53             socialSecurityNumberValue = ssn ' no validation
54          End Set
55       End Property ' SocialSecurityNumber
56
57       ' property GrossSales
58       Public Property GrossSales() As Decimal
59          Get
60             Return grossSalesValue
61          End Get
62
63          Set(ByVal sales As Decimal)
64             If sales < 0.0 Then ' validate gross sales
65                grossSalesValue = 0
66             Else
67                grossSalesValue = sales
68             End If
69          End Set
70       End Property ' GrossSales
```

Fig. 10.10 | CommissionEmployee class with Protected instance variables. (Part 2 of 3.)

```
71
72          ' property CommissionRate
73          Public Property CommissionRate() As Decimal
74             Get
75                 Return commissionRateValue
76             End Get
77
78             Set(ByVal rate As Decimal)
79                 If rate > 0.0 AndAlso rate < 1.0 Then ' validate rate
80                     commissionRateValue = rate
81                 Else
82                     commissionRateValue = 0
83                 End If
84             End Set
85          End Property ' CommissionRate
86
87          ' calculate earnings
88          Public Overridable Function CalculateEarnings() As Decimal
89             Return commissionRateValue * grossSalesValue
90          End Function ' CalculateEarnings
91
92          ' return String representation of CommissionEmployee object
93          Public Overrides Function ToString() As String
94             Return ("commission employee: " & firstNameValue & " " & _
95                 lastNameValue & vbCrLf & "social security number: " & _
96                 socialSecurityNumberValue & vbCrLf & "gross sales: " & _
97                 String.Format("{0:C}", grossSalesValue) & vbCrLf & _
98                 "commission rate: " & String.Format("{0:F}", _
99                 commissionRateValue))
100         End Function ' ToString
101     End Class ' CommissionEmployee
```

Fig. 10.10 | CommissionEmployee class with Protected instance variables. (Part 3 of 3.)

commissionRateValue as Protected (Fig. 10.10, lines 6–10) rather than Private. The rest of the class declaration in Fig. 10.10 is identical to the one in Fig. 10.8.

We could have declared the base class CommissionEmployee's instance variables first-NameValue, lastNameValue, socialSecurityNumberValue, grossSalesvalue and commissionRateValue as Public to enable derived class BasePlusCommissionEmployee to access the base class instance variables. Doing this is dangerous because it allows unrestricted access to the instance variables, greatly increasing the chance of errors. With Protected base class instance variables, the derived class gains access to the instance variables, but classes that are not derived classes of this base class cannot access these variables directly.

Modifying Derived Class BasePlusCommissionEmployee
We now modify class BasePlusCommissionEmployee (Fig. 10.9) so that it inherits from the version of class CommissionEmployee in Fig. 10.10. Because class BasePlusCommissionEmployee inherits from this new version of class CommissionEmployee, objects of class BasePlusCommissionEmployee (Fig. 10.11) inherit CommissionEmployee's Protected instance variables firstNameValue, lastNameValue, socialSecurityNumberValue, grossSalesValue and commissionRateValue—all these variables are now Protected members

```vb
 1    ' Fig. 10.11: BasePlusCommissionEmployee.vb
 2    ' BasePlusCommissionEmployee inherits from class CommissionEmployee.
 3    Public Class BasePlusCommissionEmployee
 4       Inherits CommissionEmployee
 5
 6       Private baseSalaryValue As Decimal ' base salary per week
 7
 8       ' six-argument constructor
 9       Public Sub New(ByVal first As String, ByVal last As String, _
10          ByVal ssn As String, ByVal sales As Decimal, _
11          ByVal rate As Decimal, ByVal salary As Decimal)
12
13          ' use MyBase reference to CommissionEmployee constructor explicitly
14          MyBase.New(first, last, ssn, sales, rate)
15          BaseSalary = salary ' validate and store base salary
16       End Sub ' New
17
18       ' property BaseSalary
19       Public Property BaseSalary() As Decimal
20          Get
21             Return baseSalaryValue
22          End Get
23
24          Set(ByVal salary As Decimal)
25             If salary < 0.0 Then ' validate base salary
26                baseSalaryValue = 0
27             Else
28                baseSalaryValue = salary
29             End If
30          End Set
31       End Property ' BaseSalary
32
33       ' calculate earnings
34       Public Overrides Function CalculateEarnings() As Decimal
35          Return baseSalaryValue + (commissionRateValue * grossSalesValue)
36       End Function ' CalculateEarnings
37
38       ' return String representation of BasePlusCommissionEmployee object
39       Public Overrides Function ToString() As String
40          Return ("base-plus-commission employee: " & firstNameValue & " " & _
41             lastNameValue & vbCrLf & "social security number: " & _
42             socialSecurityNumberValue & vbCrLf & "gross sales: " & _
43             String.Format("{0:C}", grossSalesValue) & vbCrLf & _
44             "commission rate: " & String.Format("{0:F}", _
45             commissionRateValue) & vbCrLf & "base salary: " & _
46             String.Format("{0:C}", baseSalaryValue))
47       End Function ' ToString
48    End Class ' BasePlusCommissionEmployee
```

Fig. 10.11 | BasePlusCommissionEmployee inherits Protected instance variables from CommissionEmployee.

of BasePlusCommissionEmployee. As a result, the compiler does not generate errors when compiling line 35 of method CalculateEarnings and lines 40–45 of method ToString (so in Fig. 10.11 we have removed the two "not allowed" comments from Fig. 10.9 and we have changed all bold black text to black). If another class inherits BasePlusCommission-Employee, the new derived class also inherits the Protected members.

Class BasePlusCommissionEmployee does not inherit class CommissionEmployee's constructor. However, class BasePlusCommissionEmployee's six-argument constructor (lines 9–16) calls class CommissionEmployee's five-argument constructor explicitly. Base-PlusCommissionEmployee's constructor does this because CommissionEmployee does not provide a parameterless constructor that could be invoked implicitly and, more important, because arguments are being passed to the base class constructor.

Testing the Modified BasePlusCommissionEmployee Class

Figure 10.12 uses a BasePlusCommissionEmployee object to perform the same tasks that Fig. 10.7 performed on an object of the first version of class BasePlusCommissionEmploy-ee (Fig. 10.6). Note that the outputs of the two programs are identical. We declared the first class BasePlusCommissionEmployee without using inheritance and declared this version of BasePlusCommissionEmployee using inheritance—nevertheless, both classes provide the same functionality. Note that the code for class BasePlusCommissionEmployee (Fig. 10.11), which is 48 lines, is considerably shorter than the code for the noninherited version of the class (Fig. 10.6), which is 119 lines, because the inherited version absorbs much of its functionality from base class CommissionEmployee, whereas the noninherited version absorbs only class Object's functionality.

```vb
1   ' Fig. 10.12: BasePlusCommissionEmployeeTest.vb
2   ' Testing class BasePlusCommissionEmployee.
3   Module BasePlusCommissionEmployeeTest
4      Sub Main()
5         ' instantiate BasePlusCommissionEmployee object
6         Dim employee As New BasePlusCommissionEmployee( _
7            "Bob", "Lewis", "333-33-3333", 5000, 0.04D, 300)
8
9         ' get base-salaried commission employee data
10        Console.WriteLine("Employee information obtained by properties:" _
11           & vbCrLf & "First name is " & employee.FirstName & vbCrLf & _
12           "Last name is " & employee.LastName & vbCrLf & _
13           "Social Security Number is " & employee.SocialSecurityNumber)
14        Console.WriteLine("Gross sales is {0:C}", employee.GrossSales)
15        Console.WriteLine("Commission rate is {0:F}", _
16           employee.CommissionRate)
17        Console.WriteLine("Base salary is {0:C}", employee.BaseSalary)
18
19        employee.BaseSalary = 1000 ' set base salary
20
21        ' get new employee information
22        Console.WriteLine(vbCrLf & _
23           "Updated employee information obtained by ToString: " & _
24           vbCrLf & employee.ToString() & vbCrLf)
25
```

Fig. 10.12 | Protected base class members inherited into derived class BasePlusCommissionEmployee. (Part 1 of 2.)

```
26              ' display the employee's earnings
27              Console.WriteLine("Employee's earnings: $" & _
28                  employee.CalculateEarnings())
29      End Sub ' Main
30   End Module ' BasePlusCommissionEmployeeTest
```

```
Employee information obtained by properties:
First name is Bob
Last name is Lewis
Social Security Number is 333-33-3333
Gross sales is $5,000.00
Commission rate is 0.04
Base salary is $300.00

Updated employee information obtained by ToString:
base-plus-commission employee: Bob Lewis
social security number: 333-33-3333
gross sales: $5,000.00
commission rate: 0.04
base salary: $1,000.00

Employee's earnings: $1200.00
```

Fig. 10.12 | Protected base class members inherited into derived class
BasePlusCommissionEmployee. (Part 2 of 2.)

Notes on Using Protected Data

In this example, we declare base class instance variables as Protected so that derived classes can inherit and access them. Inheriting Protected instance variables slightly improves performance, because we can directly access the variables in the derived class without incurring the overhead of calling property Set or Get accessors. In most cases, however, it is better to use Private instance variables to encourage proper software engineering, and leave code optimization issues to the compiler. Your code will be easier to maintain, modify and debug.

Using Protected instance variables creates several potential problems. First, the derived class object can set an inherited variable's value directly without using a Set accessor. Therefore, a derived class object can assign an invalid value to the variable, thus leaving the object in an inconsistent state. For example, if we were to declare Commission-Employee's instance variable grossSalesValue as Protected, a derived class object could then assign a negative value to grossSalesValue. Another problem with using Protected instance variables is that derived class methods are more likely to be written so that they depend on the base class's data implementation. In practice, derived classes should depend only on the base class services (i.e., non-Private methods and properties) and not on the base class data implementation. With Protected instance variables in the base class, all the derived classes of the base class may need to be modified if the base class implementation changes. For example, if for some reason we were to change the names of instance variables firstNameValue and lastNameValue to first and last, then we would have to do so for all occurrences in which a derived class directly references base class instance variables firstNameValue and lastNameValue. In such a case, the software is said to be *fragile* or *brittle*, because a small change in the base class can "break" derived class implementations.

We should be able to change the base class implementation while still providing the same services to the derived classes. Of course, if the base class services change, we must reimplement our derived classes.

Software Engineering Observation 10.5

Use the Protected *access modifier on a method when a base class is to provide the method to its derived classes but not to other clients.*

10.4.5 CommissionEmployee–BasePlusCommissionEmployee Inheritance Hierarchy Using Private Instance Variables

We now reexamine our hierarchy once more, this time using better software engineering practices. Class CommissionEmployee (Fig. 10.13) declares instance variables firstName-Value, lastNameValue, socialSecurityNumberValue, grossSalesValue and commissionRateValue as Private (lines 4–8) and provides Public properties FirstName, LastName, SocialSecurityNumber, GrossSales and CommissionRate for manipulating these values. Note that methods CalculateEarnings (lines 86–88) and ToString (lines 91–97) use the class's properties to obtain the values of the Private instance variables. If we decide to change the instance variable names, the CalculateEarnings and ToString declarations will not require modification—only the bodies of the Get and Set accessors that directly manipulate the instance variables will need to change. These changes would occur solely within the base class—no changes to the derived class would be needed. Localizing the effects of changes is good software engineering. Derived class BasePlusCommissionEmployee (Fig. 10.14) inherits CommissionEmployee's non-Private properties and methods and can access the Private base class members via those properties and methods.

Software Engineering Observation 10.6

Declaring base class instance variables Private *(as opposed to* Protected*) enables the base class implementation of these instance variables to change without affecting derived class implementations.*

Error-Prevention Tip 10.1

When possible, do not include Protected *instance variables in a base class. Instead, include non-*Private *properties and methods that carefully access* Private *instance variables. This will ensure that objects of the derived classes of this base class maintain consistent states of the base class instance variables.*

```
1   ' Fig. 10.13: CommmissionEmployee.vb
2   ' CommissionEmployee class represents a commission employee.
3   Public Class CommissionEmployee
4      Private firstNameValue As String ' first name
5      Private lastNameValue As String ' last name
6      Private socialSecurityNumberValue As String ' social security number
7      Private grossSalesValue As Decimal ' gross weekly sales
8      Private commissionRateValue As Decimal ' commission percentage
```

Fig. 10.13 | CommissionEmployee class uses properties to manipulate its Private instance variables. (Part 1 of 3.)

```
9
10      ' five-argument constructor
11      Public Sub New(ByVal first As String, ByVal last As String, _
12         ByVal ssn As String, ByVal sales As Decimal, ByVal rate As Decimal)
13
14         ' implicit call to Object constructor occurs here
15         FirstName = first
16         LastName = last
17         SocialSecurityNumber = ssn
18         GrossSales = sales ' validate and store gross sales
19         CommissionRate = rate ' validate and store commission rate
20      End Sub ' New
21
22      ' property FirstName
23      Public Property FirstName() As String
24         Get
25            Return firstNameValue
26         End Get
27
28         Set(ByVal first As String)
29            firstNameValue = first ' no validation
30         End Set
31      End Property ' FirstName
32
33      ' property LastName
34      Public Property LastName() As String
35         Get
36            Return lastNameValue
37         End Get
38
39         Set(ByVal last As String)
40            lastNameValue = last ' no validation
41         End Set
42      End Property ' LastName
43
44      ' property SocialSecurityNumber
45      Public Property SocialSecurityNumber() As String
46         Get
47            Return socialSecurityNumberValue
48         End Get
49
50         Set(ByVal ssn As String)
51            socialSecurityNumberValue = ssn ' no validation
52         End Set
53      End Property ' SocialSecurityNumber
54
55      ' property GrossSales
56      Public Property GrossSales() As Decimal
57         Get
58            Return grossSalesValue
59         End Get
```

Fig. 10.13 | CommissionEmployee class uses properties to manipulate its Private instance variables. (Part 2 of 3.)

```
60
61        Set(ByVal sales As Decimal)
62          If sales < 0.0 Then ' validate gross sales
63            grossSalesValue = 0
64          Else
65            grossSalesValue = sales
66          End If
67        End Set
68      End Property ' GrossSales
69
70      ' property CommissionRate
71      Public Property CommissionRate() As Decimal
72        Get
73          Return commissionRateValue
74        End Get
75
76        Set(ByVal rate As Decimal)
77          If rate > 0.0 AndAlso rate < 1.0 Then ' validate rate
78            commissionRateValue = rate
79          Else
80            commissionRateValue = 0
81          End If
82        End Set
83      End Property ' CommissionRate
84
85      ' calculate earnings
86      Public Overridable Function CalculateEarnings() As Decimal
87        Return CommissionRate * GrossSales
88      End Function ' CalculateEarnings
89
90      ' return String representation of CommissionEmployee object
91      Public Overrides Function ToString() As String
92        Return ("commission employee: " & FirstName & " " & _
93          LastName & vbCrLf & "social security number: " & _
94          SocialSecurityNumber & vbCrLf & "gross sales: " & _
95          String.Format("{0:C}", GrossSales) & vbCrLf & _
96          "commission rate: " & String.Format("{0:F}", CommissionRate))
97      End Function ' ToString
98    End Class ' CommissionEmployee
```

Fig. 10.13 | CommissionEmployee class uses properties to manipulate its Private instance variables. (Part 3 of 3.)

Class BasePlusCommissionEmployee (Fig. 10.14) has several changes to its method implementations that distinguish it from class BasePlusCommissionEmployee (Fig. 10.11). Methods CalculateEarnings (Fig. 10.14, lines 34–36) and ToString (lines 39–42) both use property BaseSalary to obtain the base salary value, rather than accessing baseSalaryValue directly. If we decide to rename instance variable baseSalaryValue, only the bodies of property BaseSalary will need to change.

Class BasePlusCommissionEmployee's CalculateEarnings method (Fig. 10.14, lines 34–36) overrides class CommissionEmployee's CalculateEarnings method (Fig. 10.13, lines 86–88) to calculate the earnings of a base-salaried commission employee. The new

```
1    ' Fig. 10.14: BasePlusCommissionEmployee.vb
2    ' BasePlusCommissionEmployee inherits from class CommissionEmployee.
3    Public Class BasePlusCommissionEmployee
4        Inherits CommissionEmployee
5
6        Private baseSalaryValue As Decimal ' base salary per week
7
8        ' six-argument constructor
9        Public Sub New(ByVal first As String, ByVal last As String, _
10          ByVal ssn As String, ByVal sales As Decimal, _
11          ByVal rate As Decimal, ByVal salary As Decimal)
12
13          ' use MyBase reference to CommissionEmployee constructor explicitly
14          MyBase.New(first, last, ssn, sales, rate)
15          BaseSalary = salary ' validate and store base salary
16      End Sub ' New
17
18      ' property BaseSalary
19      Public Property BaseSalary() As Decimal
20          Get
21              Return baseSalaryValue
22          End Get
23
24          Set(ByVal salary As Decimal)
25              If salary < 0.0 Then ' validate base salary
26                  baseSalaryValue = 0
27              Else
28                  baseSalaryValue = salary
29              End If
30          End Set
31      End Property ' BaseSalary
32
33      ' calculate earnings
34      Public Overrides Function CalculateEarnings() As Decimal
35          Return BaseSalary + MyBase.CalculateEarnings()
36      End Function ' CalculateEarnings
37
38      ' return String representation of BasePlusCommissionEmployee object
39      Public Overrides Function ToString() As String
40          Return ("base-plus-" & MyBase.ToString() & vbCrLf & _
41              "base salary: " & String.Format("{0:C}", BaseSalary))
42      End Function ' ToString
43  End Class ' BasePlusCommissionEmployee
```

Fig. 10.14 | BasePlusCommissionEmployee class Inherits CommissionEmployee, which provides only Private instance variables.

version obtains the portion of the employee's earnings based on commission alone by calling CommissionEmployee's CalculateEarnings method with the expression MyBase.CalculateEarnings() (Fig. 10.14, line 35). BasePlusCommissionEmployee's CalculateEarnings method then adds the base salary to this value to calculate the total earnings of the derived-class employee. Note the syntax used to invoke an overridden base class method from a derived class—place the keyword MyBase and a dot (.) separator before the base class method name. By having BasePlusCommissionEmployee's Calculate-Earnings method invoke CommissionEmployee's CalculateEarnings method to calculate part of a BasePlusCommissionEmployee object's earnings, we avoid duplicating the code and reduce code maintenance problems.

 Common Programming Error 10.3

When a base class method is overridden in a derived class, the derived class version often calls the base class version to do a portion of the work. Failure to prefix the base class method name with the keyword MyBase and a dot (.) separator when referencing the base class's method causes the derived class method to call itself, creating an error called infinite recursion.

Similarly, BasePlusCommissionEmployee's ToString method (Fig. 10.14, lines 39–42) overrides class CommissionEmployee's ToString method (Fig. 10.13, lines 91–97) to return a string representation that is appropriate for a base-salaried commission employee. The derived class creates part of a BasePlusCommissionEmployee object's string representation (i.e., the string "base-plus-commission employee" and the values of class CommissionEmployee's Private instance variables) by appending "base-plus-" in front of the string returned by calling CommissionEmployee's ToString method with the expression MyBase.ToString() (Fig. 10.14, line 40). BasePlusCommissionEmployee's ToString method then outputs the remainder of a BasePlusCommissionEmployee object's string representation (i.e., the value of class BasePlusCommissionEmployee's base salary).

Figure 10.15 performs the same manipulations on a BasePlusCommissionEmployee object as did Fig. 10.7 and Fig. 10.12. Although each "base-salaried commission employee" class behaves identically, class BasePlusCommissionEmployee (Fig. 10.14) is the best engineered. By using inheritance and by calling methods that hide the data and ensure consistency, we have efficiently constructed a well-engineered class.

```vb
1   ' Fig. 10.15: BasePlusCommissionEmployeeTest.vb
2   ' Testing class BasePlusCommissionEmployee.
3   Module BasePlusCommissionEmployeeTest
4      Sub Main()
5         ' instantiate BasePlusCommissionEmployee object
6         Dim employee As New BasePlusCommissionEmployee( _
7            "Bob", "Lewis", "333-33-3333", 5000, 0.04D, 300)
8
9         ' get base-salaried commission employee data
10        Console.WriteLine("Employee information obtained by properties:" _
11           & vbCrLf & "First name is " & employee.FirstName & vbCrLf & _
12           "Last name is " & employee.LastName & vbCrLf & _
13           "Social Security Number is " & employee.SocialSecurityNumber)
14        Console.WriteLine("Gross sales is {0:C}", employee.GrossSales)
15        Console.WriteLine("Commission rate is {0:F}", _
16           employee.CommissionRate)
17        Console.WriteLine("Base salary is {0:C}", employee.BaseSalary)
18
19        employee.BaseSalary = 1000 ' set base salary
20
```

Fig. 10.15 | Base class Private instance variables are accessible to a derived class via the Public or Protected properties and methods inherited by the derived class. (Part 1 of 2.)

```
21          ' get new employee information
22          Console.WriteLine(vbCrLf & _
23              "Updated employee information obtained by ToString: " & _
24              vbCrLf & employee.ToString() & vbCrLf)
25
26          ' display the employee's earnings
27          Console.WriteLine("Employee's earnings: $" & _
28              employee.CalculateEarnings())
29      End Sub ' Main
30  End Module ' BasePlusCommissionEmployeeTest
```

```
Employee information obtained by properties:
First name is Bob
Last name is Lewis
Social Security Number is 333-33-3333
Gross sales is $5,000.00
Commission rate is 0.04
Base salary is $300.00

Updated employee information obtained by ToString:
base-plus-commission employee: Bob Lewis
social security number: 333-33-3333
gross sales: $5,000.00
commission rate: 0.04
base salary: $1,000.00

Employee's earnings: $1200.00
```

Fig. 10.15 | Base class `Private` instance variables are accessible to a derived class via the `Public` or `Protected` properties and methods inherited by the derived class. (Part 2 of 2.)

In this section, you studied five example programs that were carefully designed to teach key capabilities for good software engineering with inheritance. You learned how to use the keyword `Inherits` to create a derived class using inheritance, how to use `Protected` base class members to enable a derived class to access inherited base class instance variables and how to override base class methods to provide versions that are more appropriate for derived class objects. Also, you applied software engineering techniques from Chapter 9 and 10 to create classes that are easy to maintain, modify and debug.

10.5 Constructors in Derived Classes

As we explained in the preceding section, instantiating a derived class object begins a chain of constructor calls in which the derived class constructor, before performing its own tasks, invokes its direct base class's constructor either explicitly (via the `MyBase` reference) or implicitly (calling the base class's default or parameterless constructor). Similarly, if the base class is derived from another class (as is every class except `Object`), the base class constructor invokes the constructor of the next class up the hierarchy, and so on. The last constructor called in the chain is always the constructor for class `Object`. The original derived class constructor's body finishes executing last. Each base class's constructor manipulates the base class instance variables that the derived class object inherits. For example, let's reconsider the CommissionEmployee–BasePlusCommissionEmployee hierarchy from Figs. 10.13 and 10.14. When a program creates a BasePlusCommissionEmployee object, the BasePlusCommissionEmployee constructor is called. That constructor, before executing its full body code, immediately calls CommissionEmployee's constructor, which in turn calls Object's constructor. Class Object's constructor has an empty body, so it immediately returns control to the CommissionEmployee's constructor, which then initializes the Private instance variables of CommissionEmployee that are part of the BasePlusCommissionEmployee object. When the CommissionEmployee's constructor completes execution, it returns control to the BasePlusCommissionEmployee's constructor, which initializes the BasePlusCommissionEmployee object's baseSalaryValue.

Our next example revisits the commission employee hierarchy by redeclaring class CommissionEmployee (Fig. 10.16) and class BasePlusCommissionEmployee (Fig. 10.17) with each class's constructor printing a message when invoked, enabling us to observe the order in which the constructors in the hierarchy execute.

```vbnet
 1   ' Fig. 10.16: CommissionEmployee.vb
 2   ' CommissionEmployee class represents a commission employee.
 3   Public Class CommissionEmployee
 4      Private firstNameValue As String ' first name
 5      Private lastNameValue As String ' last name
 6      Private socialSecurityNumberValue As String ' social security number
 7      Private grossSalesValue As Decimal ' gross weekly sales
 8      Private commissionRateValue As Decimal ' commission percentage
 9
10      ' five-argument constructor
11      Public Sub New(ByVal first As String, ByVal last As String, _
12         ByVal ssn As String, ByVal sales As Decimal, ByVal rate As Decimal)
13
14         ' implicit call to Object constructor occurs here
15         FirstName = first
16         LastName = last
17         SocialSecurityNumber = ssn
18         GrossSales = sales ' validate and store gross sales
19         CommissionRate = rate ' validate and store commission rate
20         Console.WriteLine(vbCrLf & _
21            "CommissionEmployee constructor:" & vbCrLf & "{0}", Me)
22      End Sub ' New
23
24      ' property FirstName
25      Public Property FirstName() As String
26         Get
27            Return firstNameValue
28         End Get
29
30         Set(ByVal first As String)
31            firstNameValue = first ' no validation
32         End Set
33      End Property ' FirstName
34
```

Fig. 10.16 | CommissionEmployee's constructor outputs text. (Part 1 of 3.)

```
35        ' property LastName
36        Public Property LastName() As String
37           Get
38              Return lastNameValue
39           End Get
40
41           Set(ByVal last As String)
42              lastNameValue = last ' no validation
43           End Set
44        End Property ' LastName
45
46        ' property SocialSecurityNumber
47        Public Property SocialSecurityNumber() As String
48           Get
49              Return socialSecurityNumberValue
50           End Get
51
52           Set(ByVal ssn As String)
53              socialSecurityNumberValue = ssn ' no validation
54           End Set
55        End Property ' SocialSecurityNumber
56
57        ' property GrossSales
58        Public Property GrossSales() As Decimal
59           Get
60              Return grossSalesValue
61           End Get
62
63           Set(ByVal sales As Decimal)
64              If sales < 0.0 Then ' validate gross sales
65                 grossSalesValue = 0
66              Else
67                 grossSalesValue = sales
68              End If
69           End Set
70        End Property ' GrossSales
71
72        ' property CommissionRate
73        Public Property CommissionRate() As Decimal
74           Get
75              Return commissionRateValue
76           End Get
77
78           Set(ByVal rate As Decimal)
79              If rate > 0.0 AndAlso rate < 1.0 Then ' validate rate
80                 commissionRateValue = rate
81              Else
82                 commissionRateValue = 0
83              End If
84           End Set
85        End Property ' CommissionRate
86
```

Fig. 10.16 | CommissionEmployee's constructor outputs text. (Part 2 of 3.)

```
87         ' calculate earnings
88         Public Overridable Function CalculateEarnings() As Decimal
89            Return CommissionRate * GrossSales
90         End Function ' CalculateEarnings
91
92         ' return String representation of CommissionEmployee object
93         Public Overrides Function ToString() As String
94            Return ("commission employee: " & FirstName & " " & _
95               LastName & vbCrLf & "social security number: " & _
96               SocialSecurityNumber & vbCrLf & "gross sales: " & _
97               String.Format("{0:C}", GrossSales) & vbCrLf & _
98               "commission rate: " & String.Format("{0:F}", CommissionRate))
99         End Function ' ToString
100    End Class ' CommissionEmployee
```

Fig. 10.16 | CommissionEmployee's constructor outputs text. (Part 3 of 3.)

Class CommissionEmployee (Fig. 10.16) contains the same features as the version of the class shown in Fig. 10.13. We have modified the constructor (lines 11–22) to output text upon its invocation (lines 20–21). Note that outputting Me with the {0} format string (line 21) implicitly invokes the ToString method of the CommissionEmployee object being constructed to obtain the object's string representation.

Class BasePlusCommissionEmployee (Fig. 10.17) is almost identical to Fig. 10.14, except that BasePlusCommissionEmployee's constructor also outputs text when invoked (lines 16–17). Again, we output Me using the {0} format string (line 17) to implicitly invoke the ToString method, this time to obtain the BasePlusCommissionEmployee object's string representation.

```
1     ' Fig. 10.17: BasePlusCommissionEmployee.vb
2     ' BasePlusCommissionEmployee inherits from class CommissionEmployee.
3     Public Class BasePlusCommissionEmployee
4        Inherits CommissionEmployee
5
6        Private baseSalaryValue As Decimal ' base salary per week
7
8        ' six-argument constructor
9        Public Sub New(ByVal first As String, ByVal last As String, _
10          ByVal ssn As String, ByVal sales As Decimal, _
11          ByVal rate As Decimal, ByVal salary As Decimal)
12
13          ' use MyBase reference to CommissionEmployee constructor explicitly
14          MyBase.New(first, last, ssn, sales, rate)
15          BaseSalary = salary ' validate and store base salary
16          Console.WriteLine(vbCrLf & _
17             "BasePlusCommissionEmployee constructor:" & vbCrLf & "{0}", Me)
18       End Sub ' New
19
```

Fig. 10.17 | BasePlusCommissionEmployee's constructor outputs text. (Part 1 of 2.)

```
20        ' property BaseSalary
21        Public Property BaseSalary() As Decimal
22           Get
23              Return baseSalaryValue
24           End Get
25
26           Set(ByVal salary As Decimal)
27              If salary < 0.0 Then ' validate base salary
28                 baseSalaryValue = 0
29              Else
30                 baseSalaryValue = salary
31              End If
32           End Set
33        End Property ' BaseSalary
34
35        ' calculate earnings
36        Public Overrides Function CalculateEarnings() As Decimal
37           Return BaseSalary + MyBase.CalculateEarnings()
38        End Function ' earnings
39
40        ' return String representation of BasePlusCommissionEmployee object
41        Public Overrides Function ToString() As String
42           Return ("base-plus-" & MyBase.ToString() & vbCrLf & _
43              "base salary: " & String.Format("{0:C}", BaseSalary))
44        End Function ' ToString
45     End Class ' BasePlusCommissionEmployee
```

Fig. 10.17 | BasePlusCommissionEmployee's constructor outputs text. (Part 2 of 2.)

Figure 10.18 demonstrates the order in which constructors are called for objects of classes that are part of an inheritance hierarchy. Method Main begins by instantiating CommissionEmployee object employee1 (lines 6–7). Next, lines 10–11 instantiate BasePlusCommissionEmployee object employee2. This invokes the CommissionEmployee constructor, which prints output with the values passed from the BasePlusCommissionEmployee constructor, then performs the output specified in the BasePlusCommissionEmployee constructor.

```
1   ' Fig. 10.18: Constructor.vb
2   ' Display order in which base class and derived class constructors
3   ' and finalizers are called.
4   Module Constructor
5      Sub Main()
6         Dim employee1 As New CommissionEmployee( _
7            "Bob", "Lewis", "333-33-3333", 5000, 0.04D)
8         Console.WriteLine()
9
10        Dim employee2 As New BasePlusCommissionEmployee( _
11           "Lisa", "Jones", "555-55-5555", 2000, 0.06D, 800)
12     End Sub ' Main
13  End Module ' Constructor
```

Fig. 10.18 | Constructor call order using Me. (Part 1 of 2.)

```
CommissionEmployee constructor:
commission employee: Bob Lewis
social security number: 333-33-3333
gross sales: $5,000.00
commission rate: 0.04

CommissionEmployee constructor:
base-plus-commission employee: Lisa Jones
social security number: 555-55-5555
gross sales: $2,000.00
commission rate: 0.06
base salary: $0.00

BasePlusCommissionEmployee constructor:
base-plus-commission employee: Lisa Jones
social security number: 555-55-5555
gross sales: $2,000.00
commission rate: 0.06
base salary: $800.00
```

Fig. 10.18 | Constructor call order using Me. (Part 2 of 2.)

Analyzing the Output

The outputs of the CommissionEmployee constructor and BasePlusCommissionEmployee constructor calls each contain values for the first name, last name, social security number, gross sales, commission rate *and* base salary of the BasePlusCommissionEmployee. When constructing a BasePlusCommissionEmployee object, the Me reference used in the body of both the CommissionEmployee and BasePlusCommissionEmployee constructors refers to the BasePlusCommissionEmployee object being constructed. When a program invokes method ToString on an object, the version of ToString that executes is always the version defined in that object's class. This is an example of polymorphism, a key aspect of object-oriented programming that we discuss in detail in Chapter 11. Reference Me refers to the current BasePlusCommissionEmployee object being constructed, so BasePlusCommission-Employee's ToString method executes even when ToString is invoked from the body of class CommissionEmployee's constructor. This would not be the case if the Commission-Employee constructor were called to initialize a new CommissionEmployee object. When the CommissionEmployee constructor invokes method ToString for the BasePlusCommission-Employee being constructed, the program displays 0 for the BaseSalary value, because the BasePlusCommissionEmployee constructor's body has not yet initialized the BaseSalary. The BasePlusCommissionEmployee constructor output shows the proper BaseSalary value (i.e., 800.00), because this line is output after the BaseSalary is initialized.

Using MyClass in Class CommissionEmployee's Constructor

To force CommissionEmployee's ToString method to execute when the CommissionEmployee's constructor is called, we use the MyClass reference. Reference *MyClass* is similar to Me, except that a method call with MyClass always invokes the version of the method defined in that particular class—the method called is not affected by the runtime type of the object. For example, if we replace Me in line 21 of Fig. 10.16 with

```
MyClass.ToString()
```

then CommissionEmployee's ToString will be executed (even though the runtime type of the object is BasePlusCommissionEmployee). Thus, the output of the CommissionEmployee's constructor call will not display the base salary value (Fig. 10.19).

Recall that Shared class variables and Shared class methods exist independently of any class objects. They also exist when there are no objects of that class. Hence, the MyClass reference cannot be used in a Shared method because such a method can be called even when there are no objects of the corresponding class.

10.6 Software Engineering with Inheritance

Novice programmers sometimes have difficulty appreciating the scope of the problems faced by developers who work on large-scale software projects in industry. People experienced with such projects say that effective software reuse improves the software-development process. Object-oriented programming facilitates software reuse, potentially shortening development and maintenance efforts.

This section discusses customizing existing software with inheritance. When a new class inherits from an existing class, the new class inherits the non-Private members of the existing class. We can customize the new class to meet our needs by including additional members and by overriding base class members. Doing this does not require the derived class programmer to change the base class's source code. Visual Basic simply requires access to the base class's assembly file so that it can compile and execute any program that uses or inherits the base class. This is attractive to independent software vendors (ISVs) because they develop proprietary classes for sale or license and make them available to users in MSIL format. Users then can derive new classes from these library classes rapidly and without accessing the ISVs' proprietary source code.

Software Engineering Observation 10.7

Despite the fact that inheriting from a class does not require access to the class's source code, developers often insist on seeing the source code to see how the class is implemented. They want to ensure that they are extending a solid class that performs well and is implemented securely.

```
CommissionEmployee constructor:
commission employee: Bob Lewis
social security number: 333-33-3333
gross sales: $5,000.00
commission rate: 0.04

CommissionEmployee constructor:
commission employee: Lisa Jones
social security number: 555-55-5555
gross sales: $2,000.00
commission rate: 0.06

BasePlusCommissionEmployee constructor:
base-plus-commission employee: Lisa Jones
social security number: 555-55-5555
gross sales: $2,000.00
commission rate: 0.06
base salary: $800.00
```

Fig. 10.19 | Constructor call order using MyClass.

The availability of substantial class libraries helps deliver the maximum benefits of software reuse through inheritance. Application designers build their applications with these libraries, and library designers are compensated when their libraries are included with the applications. The standard Visual Basic class libraries tend to be general purpose. Many special-purpose class libraries exist and more are being created.

Software Engineering Observation 10.8

At the design stage in an object-oriented system, the designer often finds that certain classes are closely related. The designer should "factor out" common instance variables and methods and place them in a base class. Then the designer should use inheritance to develop derived classes, specializing them with capabilities beyond those inherited from the base class.

Performance Tip 10.1

If derived classes are larger than they need to be (i.e., contain too much functionality), memory and processing resources may be wasted. Extend the base class that contains the functionality that is closest to what you need.

Reading derived class declarations can be confusing, because inherited members are not declared explicitly in the derived classes, but are nevertheless present in them. A similar problem exists in documenting derived class members.

10.7 Class Object

As we have mentioned, all classes inherit directly or indirectly from the Object class (namespace System), so its seven methods are inherited by all other classes. Figure 10.20 summarizes Object's methods.

Method	Description
Equals	Compares two objects for equality; returns True if they are equal and False otherwise. The method takes any Object as an argument. When objects of a class must be compared for equality, the class should override method Equals to compare the contents of the two objects. The method's implementation should meet the following requirements: • It should return False if the argument is Nothing. • It should return True if an object is compared to itself, as in object1.Equals(object1). • It should return True only if both object1.Equals(object2) and object2.Equals(object1) would return True. • For three objects, if object1.Equals(object2) returns True and object2.Equals(object3) returns True, then object1.Equals(object3) should also return True. • A class that overrides Equals must also override GetHashCode to ensure that equal objects have identical hashcodes. The default Equals implementation determines only whether two references *refer to the same object* in memory.

Fig. 10.20 | Object methods that are inherited by all classes. (Part 1 of 2.)

Method	Description
Finalize	This Protected method (introduced in Section 9.9) is called by the garbage collector on an object just before the garbage collector reclaims the object's memory. It is not guaranteed that the garbage collector will reclaim an object, so it cannot be guaranteed that the object's Finalize method will execute. The method must specify an empty parameter list and must not return a value. The default implementation of this method is a placeholder that does nothing.
GetHashCode	A hashtable is a data structure that relates one object, called the key, to another object, called the value. We discuss class Hashtable in Chapter 26, Collections. When initially inserting a value into a hashtable, the key's GetHashCode method is called. The hashcode value returned is used by the hashtable to determine the location at which to insert the corresponding value. The key's hashcode is also used by the hashtable to locate the key's corresponding value.
GetType	Every object in Visual Basic knows its own type at execution time. Method GetType (used in Section 11.5) returns an object of class Type (namespace System) that contains information about the object's type, such as its class name (obtained from Type property FullName).
MemberwiseClone	This Protected method, which takes no arguments and returns an Object reference, makes a copy of the object on which it is called. The implementation of this method performs a *shallow copy*—instance variable values in one object are copied into another object of the same type. For reference types, only the references are copied.
ReferenceEquals	This Shared method takes two Object arguments and returns True if two objects are the same instance or if they are Nothing references. Otherwise, it returns False.
ToString	This method (introduced in Section 9.2) returns a String representation of an object. The default implementation of this method returns the namespace followed by a dot and the class name of the object's class.

Fig. 10.20 | Object methods that are inherited by all classes. (Part 2 of 2.)

We discuss most of Object's methods throughout this book (as indicated in the table). To learn more about these methods from the **Help** menu, select **Help > Index...**, and enter "Object class" in the search text box.

10.8 Friend Members

Another intermediate level of member access is Friend access. A class's Friend members can be accessed only by code in the same assembly. In a program or an assembly that consists of one class declaration, declaring a member with Friend access has no specific effect. However, if a program uses multiple classes from the same assembly, these classes can access each other's Friend members directly through references to objects of the appropriate classes. Unlike Public access, any other programs that are declared outside the assembly cannot access these Friend members. To access a non-Shared Friend member within the same assembly, you would first have to create an object of the class that declares the Friend member, then invoke the Friend member using the dot (.) separator. You can access a Friend member that is also Shared via the name of the class that declares the Friend member and a dot (.) separator. Note that you can also have Protected Friend members that are accessible both from code in the same assembly and by subclasses of the class in which the Protected Friend members are declared.

10.9 Wrap-Up

This chapter introduced inheritance—the ability to create a class by absorbing an existing class's members and embellishing them with new capabilities. Through a series of examples using an employee inheritance hierarchy, you learned the notions of base classes and derived classes and used keyword Inherits to create derived classes that inherit members from base classes. We introduced the access modifiers Protected and Friend. Derived class methods can access Protected base class members. Friend members are accessible to classes declared in the same assembly as the class that declares the Friend members. You learned how to access base class members with MyBase and how to access the current object with the Me and MyClass references. You also saw the order in which constructors are called for objects of classes that are part of an inheritance hierarchy. Finally, you learned about the methods of class Object—the direct or indirect base class of all classes.

In Chapter 11, Object-Oriented Programming: Polymorphism, we build on our discussion of inheritance by introducing polymorphism—an object-oriented concept that enables us to write programs that handle, in a simple and more general manner, objects of a wide variety of classes related by inheritance. After studying Chapter 11, you will be familiar with classes, objects, encapsulation, inheritance and polymorphism—the most essential aspects of object-oriented programming.

11

Object-Oriented Programming: Polymorphism

One Ring to rule them all,
One Ring to find them,
One Ring to bring them all
and in the darkness bind
them.
—J. R. R. Tolkien

General propositions do not
decide concrete cases.
—Oliver Wendell Holmes

A philosopher of imposing
stature doesn't think in a
vacuum. Even his most
abstract ideas are, to some
extent, conditioned by
what is or is not known
in the time when he lives.
—Alfred North Whitehead

Why art thou cast down,
O my soul?
—Psalms 42:5

OBJECTIVES

In this chapter you will learn:

- What polymorphism is.

- To use overridden methods to effect polymorphism.

- To distinguish between abstract and concrete classes.

- To declare abstract methods to create abstract classes.

- How polymorphism makes systems extensible and maintainable.

- To determine an object's type at execution time.

- To declare and implement interfaces.

11.1 Introduction

We now continue our study of object-oriented programming by explaining and demonstrating *polymorphism* with inheritance hierarchies. Polymorphism enables us to "program in the general" rather than "program in the specific." In particular, polymorphism enables us to write programs that process objects that share the same base class in a class hierarchy as simply as if they were all objects of the base class. Yet, as we send method calls in this general way, the specific objects "do the right thing."

Consider the following example of polymorphism. Suppose we create a program that simulates the movement of several types of animals for a biological study. Classes Fish, Frog and Bird represent the three types of animals under investigation. Imagine that each of these classes inherits base class Animal, which contains a method move and maintains the animal's current location as *x-y* coordinates. Each derived class implements method move. Our program maintains an array of references to objects of the various Animal derived classes. To simulate the animals' movements, the program sends each object the same message—move—once per second. However, each specific type of Animal responds to the move message in a unique way—a Fish might swim two feet, a Frog might jump three feet and a Bird might fly ten feet. The program issues the same move message to each animal object generically, but each object knows how to modify its *x-y* coordinates appropriately for its specific type of movement. Relying on each object to know how to "do the right thing" (i.e., what is appropriate for that type of object) in response to the same method call is the key concept of polymorphism. The same message (in this case, move) sent to a variety of objects has "many forms" of results—hence the term polymorphism.

With polymorphism, we can design and implement systems that are easily extensible—new classes can be added with little or no modification to the general portions of the program, as long as the new classes are part of the inheritance hierarchy that the program processes generically. The only parts of a program that must be altered to accommodate new classes are those that require direct knowledge of the new classes that you add to the hierarchy. For example, if we inherit from class Animal to create class Tortoise (which might respond to a move message by crawling one inch), we need to write only the Tortoise class (with a move method) and the part of the simulation that instantiates Tortoise objects. The portions of the simulation that process each Animal generically can remain the same.

This chapter has several key parts. First, we discuss common examples of polymorphism. We then provide a live-code example demonstrating polymorphic behavior. As you will soon see, you will use base class references to conveniently manipulate both base class objects and derived class objects polymorphically.

We then present a case study that revisits the employee hierarchy of Section 10.4.5. We develop a simple payroll application that polymorphically calculates the weekly pay of several different types of employees using each employee's CalculateEarnings method. Though the earnings of each type of employee are calculated in a specific way, polymorphism allows us to process the employees "in the general." We add two new classes to the hierarchy—SalariedEmployee (for people paid a fixed weekly salary) and HourlyEmployee (for people paid an hourly salary and "time-and-a-half" for overtime). We declare a common set of functionality for all the classes in the updated hierarchy in a so-called abstract class, Employee, from which classes SalariedEmployee, HourlyEmployee and CommissionEmployee inherit directly, and from which class BasePlusCommissionEmployee inherits indirectly. As you will see, when we invoke each employee's CalculateEarnings method off a base class Employee reference, the correct earnings calculation is performed due to Visual Basic's polymorphic capabilities.

Occasionally, when performing polymorphic processing, we need to program "in the specific." Our Employee case study demonstrates that a program can determine an object's type at execution time and act on that object accordingly. The case study uses these capabilities to determine whether a particular employee object *is a* BasePlusCommissionEmployee, and, in that specific case, we increase the employee's base salary by 10%.

The chapter continues with an introduction to interfaces. An interface describes a set of methods that can be called on an object, but does not provide concrete implementations for the methods. Programmers can declare classes that ***implement*** (i.e., declare the methods of) one or more interfaces. Each interface method must be declared in all the classes that implement the interface. Once a class implements an interface, all objects of that class have an *is-a* relationship with the interface type, and all objects of the class are guaranteed to provide the functionality described by the interface. This is true of all derived classes of that class as well.

Interfaces are particularly useful for assigning common functionality to possibly unrelated classes. This allows objects of unrelated classes to be processed polymorphically—objects of classes that implement the same interface can respond to the same method calls. To demonstrate creating and using interfaces, we modify our payroll application to create a general accounts payable application that can calculate payments due not only for company employees, but also for invoice amounts to be billed for purchased goods. As you will see, interfaces enable polymorphic capabilities similar to those possible with inheritance.

11.2 Polymorphic Video Game

Suppose we design a video game that manipulates objects of many different types, including objects of classes Martian, Venutian, Plutonian, SpaceShip and LaserBeam. Imagine that each class inherits from the common base class called SpaceObject, which contains method draw. Each derived class implements this method in a manner appropriate to that class. A screen-manager program maintains a collection (e.g., a SpaceObject array) of references to objects of the various classes. To refresh the screen, the screen manager periodically sends each object the same message—namely, draw. However, each object responds in a unique way. For example, a Martian object might draw itself in red with the appropriate number of antennae. A SpaceShip object might draw itself as a bright silver flying saucer. A LaserBeam object might draw itself as a bright red beam across the screen. The same message (in this case, draw) sent to a variety of objects has "many forms" of results.

A screen manager might use polymorphism to facilitate adding new classes to a system with minimal modifications to the system's code. Suppose that we want to add Mercurian objects to our video game. To do so, we must build a class Mercurian that inherits from SpaceObject and provides its own draw method implementation. When objects of class Mercurian appear in the SpaceObject collection, the screen manager code invokes method draw, exactly as it does for the other objects in the collection, regardless of their types. So the new Mercurian class simply "plugs right in" without any modification of the screen manager code by the programmer. Thus, without modifying the system (other than to build new classes and modify the code that creates new objects), programmers can use polymorphism to include types that were not envisioned when the system was created.

With polymorphism, calls to methods of the same method name, signature and return type can be used to cause different actions to occur, depending on the type of objects on which the method is invoked. This gives you tremendous expressive capability, as you will soon see.

Software Engineering Observation 11.1

Polymorphism promotes extensibility: Software that invokes polymorphic behavior is independent of the object types to which messages are sent. New object types that can respond to existing method calls can be incorporated into a system without requiring modification of the base system. Only client code that instantiates new objects must be modified to accommodate new types.

11.3 Demonstrating Polymorphic Behavior

Section 10.4 created a commission employee class hierarchy, in which class BasePlusCommissionEmployee inherited from class CommissionEmployee. The examples in that section manipulated CommissionEmployee and BasePlusCommissionEmployee objects by using references to them to invoke their methods. We aimed base class references at base class objects and derived class references at derived class objects. These assignments are natural and straightforward—base class references are intended to refer to base class objects, and derived class references are intended to refer to derived class objects. However, as you will soon see, some "crossover" assignments are possible.

In the next example, we aim a base class reference at a derived class object. We then show how invoking a method on a derived class object via a base class reference invokes the derived class functionality—*the type of the actual referenced object, not the type of the reference, determines which method is called.* This example demonstrates the key concept that an object of a derived class can be treated as an object of its base class, yet still "do the right thing." This enables various interesting manipulations. A program can create an array of base class references that refer to objects of many derived class types. This is allowed because each derived class object *is an* object of its base class. For instance, we can assign the reference of a BasePlusCommissionEmployee object to a base class CommissionEmployee variable because a BasePlusCommissionEmployee *is a* CommissionEmployee— so we can treat a BasePlusCommissionEmployee as a CommissionEmployee.

As you will learn later in the chapter, we cannot treat a base class object as a derived class object because a base class object is not an object of any of its derived classes. For example, we cannot assign the reference of a CommissionEmployee object to a derived class BasePlusCommissionEmployee variable because a CommissionEmployee is not a BasePlusCommissionEmployee—a CommissionEmployee does not have a baseSalary instance variable and does not have property BaseSalary. The *is-a* relationship applies only from a derived class to its direct (and indirect) base classes, but not vice versa.

The compiler *does* allow the assignment of a base class reference to a derived class variable if we explicitly cast the base class reference to the derived class type—a technique we discuss in detail in Section 11.5. Why would we ever want to perform such an assignment? A base class reference can be used to invoke only the methods declared in the base class— attempting to invoke derived-class-only methods through a base class reference results in compilation errors. If a program needs to perform a derived class-specific operation on a derived class object referenced by a base class variable, the program must first cast the base class reference to a derived class reference through a technique known as **downcasting**. This enables the program to invoke derived class methods that are not in the base class, but only off a derived class reference. We demonstrate downcasting in Section 11.5.

Figure 11.1 shows three ways to use base class and derived class variables to store references to base class and derived class objects. The first two are straightforward—as in Section 10.4, we assign a base class reference to a base class variable, and we assign a derived class reference to a derived class variable. Then we demonstrate the relationship between derived classes and base classes (i.e., the *is-a* relationship) by assigning a derived class reference to a base class variable. [*Note:* This program uses the CommissionEmployee and BasePlusCommissionEmployee classes from Fig. 10.13 and Fig. 10.14, respectively.]

In Fig. 11.1, lines 10–11 create a CommissionEmployee object and assign its reference to a CommissionEmployee variable. Lines 14–15 create a BasePlusCommissionEmployee object and assign its reference to a BasePlusCommissionEmployee variable. These assignments are natural—for example, a CommissionEmployee variable's primary purpose is to hold a reference to a CommissionEmployee object. Lines 18–20 use reference commissionEmployee1 to invoke ToString explicitly. Because commissionEmployee1 refers to a CommissionEmployee object, base class CommissionEmployee's version of ToString is called, as is evident from the output. Similarly, lines 24–26 use basePlusCommissionEmployee to invoke ToString explicitly on the BasePlusCommissionEmployee object. This invokes derived class BasePlusCommissionEmployee's version of ToString, as is also evident from the output.

Lines 29–30 then assign to a base class CommissionEmployee variable commissionEmployee2 the reference to derived class object basePlusCommissionEmployee, which

```vb
 1    ' Fig. 11.1: PolymorphismTest.vb
 2    ' Assigning base class and derived class references to base class and
 3    ' derived class variables.
 4   Module PolymorphismTest
 5      Sub Main()
 6         Dim commissionEmployee1 As CommissionEmployee
 7         Dim basePlusCommissionEmployee As BasePlusCommissionEmployee
 8
 9         ' assign base class reference to base class variable
10         commissionEmployee1 = New CommissionEmployee( _
11            "Sue", "Jones", "222-22-2222", 10000, 0.06D)
12
13         ' assign derived class reference to derived class variable
14         basePlusCommissionEmployee = New BasePlusCommissionEmployee( _
15            "Bob", "Lewis", "333-33-3333", 5000, 0.04D, 300)
16
17         ' invoke ToString on base class object using base class variable
18         Console.WriteLine("Call CommissionEmployee's ToString with " & _
19            "base class reference to base class object: " & vbCrLf & _
20            commissionEmployee1.ToString() & vbCrLf)
21
22         ' invoke ToString on derived class object using
23         ' derived class variable
24         Console.WriteLine("Call BasePlusCommissionEmployee's ToString " & _
25            "with derived class reference to derived class object: " & _
26            vbCrLf & basePlusCommissionEmployee.ToString() & vbCrLf)
27
28         ' assign derived class reference to base class variable
29         Dim commissionEmployee2 As CommissionEmployee = _
30            basePlusCommissionEmployee
31
32         ' invoke ToString on derived class object using base class variable
33         Console.WriteLine("Call BasePlusCommissionEmployee's ToString " & _
34            "with base class reference to derived class object: " & _
35            vbCrLf & commissionEmployee2.ToString())
36      End Sub ' Main
37   End Module ' PolymorphismTest
```

Fig. 11.1 | Assigning base class and derived class references to base class and derived class variables. (Part 1 of 2.)

```
Call CommissionEmployee's ToString with base class reference to base class
object:
commission employee: Sue Jones
social security number: 222-22-2222
gross sales: 10,000.00
commission rate: 0.06

Call BasePlusCommissionEmployee's ToString with derived class reference to
derived class object:
commission employee: Bob Lewis
social security number: 333-33-3333
gross sales: 5,000.00
commission rate: 0.04
base salary: 300.00

Call BasePlusCommissionEmployee's ToString with base class reference to
derived class object:
commission employee: Bob Lewis
social security number: 333-33-3333
gross sales: 5,000.00
commission rate: 0.04
base salary: 300.00
```

Fig. 11.1 | Assigning base class and derived class references to base class and derived class variables. (Part 2 of 2.)

lines 33–35 use to invoke method ToString. A base class variable that contains a reference to a derived class object and that is used to call a method (which is in both the base class and the derived class) actually calls the derived class version of the method (polymorphically). Hence, commissionEmployee2.ToString() in line 35 actually calls class BasePlusCommissionEmployee's ToString method. The compiler allows this "crossover" because an object of a derived class *is an* object of its base class (but not vice versa). When the compiler encounters a method call made through a variable, it determines whether the method can be called by checking the variable's class type. If that class contains the proper method declaration (or inherits one), the compiler allows the call to be compiled. At execution time, the type of the object to which the variable refers determines the actual version of the method to use. This is polymorphic behavior.

11.4 Abstract Classes and Methods

When we think of a class type, we assume that programs will create objects of that type. In some cases, however, it is useful to declare classes for which you never intend to instantiate objects. Such classes are called *abstract classes*. Because they are used only as base classes in inheritance hierarchies, we refer to them as *abstract base classes*. These classes cannot be used to instantiate objects, because, as we will soon see, abstract classes are incomplete. We demonstrate abstract classes in Section 11.5.

The purpose of an abstract class is primarily to provide an appropriate base class from which other classes can inherit and thus share a common design. In the Shape hierarchy of Fig. 10.3, for example, derived classes inherit the notion of what it means to be a Shape—possibly including common properties such as Location, Color and Border-

Thickness, and behaviors such as Draw, Move, Resize and ChangeColor. Classes that can be used to instantiate objects are called *concrete classes*. Such classes provide implementations of every method they declare (some of the implementations can be inherited). For example, we could derive concrete classes Circle, Square and Triangle from abstract base class TwoDimensionalShape. Similarly, we could derive concrete classes Sphere, Cube and Tetrahedron from abstract base class ThreeDimensionalShape. Abstract base classes are too general to create real objects—they specify only what is common among derived classes. We need to be more specific before we can create objects. For example, if you send the Draw message to abstract class TwoDimensionalShape, it knows that two-dimensional shapes should be *drawable*, but it does not know *what specific shape to draw*, so it cannot implement a real Draw method. Concrete classes provide the specifics that make it reasonable to instantiate objects.

Abstract Classes in Inheritance Hierarchies

Not all inheritance hierarchies contain abstract classes. However, programmers often write client code that uses only abstract base class types to reduce the client code's dependencies on a range of specific derived class types. For example, a programmer can write a method with a parameter of an abstract base class type. When called, such a method can be passed an object of any concrete class that directly or indirectly inherits the base class specified as the parameter's type.

Abstract classes sometimes constitute several levels of the hierarchy. For example, the Shape hierarchy of Fig. 10.3 begins with abstract class Shape. The next level of the hierarchy contains abstract classes TwoDimensionalShape and ThreeDimensionalShape. The next level of the hierarchy declares concrete classes for TwoDimensionalShapes (Circle, Square and Triangle) and ThreeDimensionalShapes (Sphere, Cube and Tetrahedron).

Declaring Abstract Classes and Abstract Methods

You make a class abstract by declaring it with keyword MustInherit. An abstract class normally contains one or more *abstract methods*. An abstract method is one with keyword **MustOverride** in its declaration, as in

```
Public MustOverride Sub Draw() ' abstract method
```

Abstract methods do not provide implementations. A class that contains any abstract methods must be declared as an abstract (i.e., MustInherit) class even if it contains some concrete (non-abstract) methods. Each concrete derived class of an abstract base class must provide concrete implementations of all the base class's abstract methods. Constructors and Shared methods cannot be inherited, so they cannot be declared MustOverride.

Software Engineering Observation 11.2

An abstract class declares common attributes and behaviors of the various classes in a class hierarchy. An abstract class typically contains one or more abstract methods that derived classes must override if the derived classes are to be concrete. The instance variables and concrete methods of an abstract class are subject to the normal rules of inheritance.

Common Programming Error 11.1

Attempting to instantiate an object of an abstract class is a compilation error.

Common Programming Error 11.2

Failure to implement a base class's abstract methods in a derived class is a compilation error unless the derived class is also declared MustInherit *(i.e., the derived class is also abstract).*

Although we cannot instantiate objects of abstract base classes, soon you will see that we *can* use abstract base classes to declare variables that can hold references to objects of any concrete classes derived from those abstract classes. Programs typically use such variables to manipulate derived class objects polymorphically.

Using Abstract Classes and Methods to Achieve Polymorphism

Consider another polymorphism application. A drawing program needs to display many shapes, including new shape types that you might add to the system even after writing the drawing program. The drawing program might need to display shapes, such as Circles, Triangles, Rectangles or others, that derive from abstract base class Shape. The drawing program uses Shape variables to manage the objects that are displayed. To draw any object in this inheritance hierarchy, the drawing program uses a base class Shape variable containing a reference to a derived class object to invoke the object's Draw method. This method is declared MustOverride in base class Shape, so each concrete derived class *must* implement method Draw in a manner specific to that shape. Each object in the Shape hierarchy "knows" how to draw itself. The drawing program does not have to worry about the type of each object or whether the drawing program has ever encountered objects of that type.

Polymorphism is particularly effective for implementing so-called layered software systems. Each of the physical devices in an operating system, for example, operates quite differently from the others. Even so, the same commands can be used to read or write data from and to the various devices. For each device, the operating system uses a piece of software called a device driver to control all communication between the system and the device. The write message sent to a device driver object needs to be interpreted specifically in the context of that driver and how it manipulates devices of that specific type. However, the write call itself really is no different from the write to any other device in the system—place some number of bytes from memory onto that device. An object-oriented operating system might use an abstract base class to provide an "interface" appropriate for all device drivers. Then, through inheritance from that abstract base class, derived classes are formed that all behave similarly. The device driver methods are declared as abstract methods in the abstract base class. The implementations of these abstract methods are provided in the concrete derived classes that correspond to the specific types of device drivers. New devices are always being developed, and often long after the operating system has been released. When you buy a new device, it comes with a device driver provided by the device vendor. The device is immediately operational after you connect it to your computer and install the driver. This is another nice example of how polymorphism makes systems extensible.

It is common in object-oriented programming to declare an *iterator class* that can traverse all the objects in a collection, such as an array (Chapter 8) or an ArrayList (Chapter 26, Collections). For example, a program can print an ArrayList of objects by creating an iterator object and using it to obtain the next list element each time the iterator is called. Iterators often are used in polymorphic programming to traverse a collection that contains references to objects from various levels of an inheritance hierarchy. (Chapter 26 presents a thorough treatment of ArrayLists, collections and iterators.) An ArrayList of objects of class TwoDimensionalShape, for example, could contain objects from derived classes Square, Circle, Triangle and so on. Calling method Draw for each TwoDimensionalShape object off a TwoDimensionalShape variable would polymorphically draw each object correctly on the screen.

11.5 Case Study: Payroll System Class Hierarchy Using Polymorphism

This section reexamines the CommissionEmployee–BasePlusCommissionEmployee hierarchy that we explored in Section 10.4. Now we use an abstract method and polymorphism to perform payroll calculations based on the type of employee. We create an enhanced employee hierarchy to solve the following problem:

> *A company pays its employees on a weekly basis. The employees are of four types: Salaried employees are paid a fixed weekly salary regardless of the number of hours worked, hourly employees are paid by the hour and receive overtime pay (1.5 times the regular hourly salary) for all hours worked in excess of 40 hours, commission employees are paid a percentage of their sales, and base-plus-commission employees receive a base salary plus a percentage of their sales. For the current pay period, the company has decided to reward base-plus-commission employees by adding 10% to their base salaries. The company wants to implement a Visual Basic application that performs its payroll calculations polymorphically.*

We use abstract class Employee to represent the general concept of an employee. The classes that inherit from Employee are SalariedEmployee, CommissionEmployee and HourlyEmployee. Class BasePlusCommissionEmployee inherits from CommissionEmployee. The UML class diagram in Fig. 11.2 shows our polymorphic employee inheritance hierarchy. Note that abstract class name Employee is italicized, as per UML convention; concrete class names are not italicized.

Abstract base class Employee declares the "interface" to the hierarchy—that is, the set of methods that a program can invoke on all Employee objects. We use the term "interface" here in a general sense to refer to the various ways programs can communicate with objects of any Employee derived class. Be careful not to confuse the general notion of an "interface" with the formal notion of a Visual Basic interface, the subject of Section 11.7. Each employee, regardless of the way his or her earnings are calculated, has a first name, a last

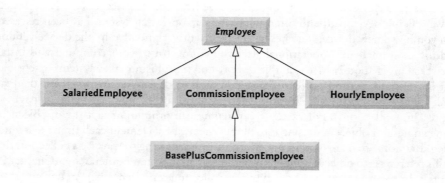

Fig. 11.2 | Employee hierarchy UML class diagram.

name and a social security number, so `Public` properties `FirstName`, `LastName` and `SocialSecurityNumber` appear in abstract base class `Employee`.

The following sections implement the `Employee` class hierarchy. The first five sections show the abstract base class `Employee` and the concrete derived classes `SalariedEmployee`, `CommissionEmployee`, `HourlyEmployee` and the indirectly derived concrete class `BasePlusCommissionEmployee`. The last section shows a test program that builds objects of these classes and processes the objects polymorphically.

11.5.1 Creating Abstract Base Class Employee

In this example, class `Employee` will provide methods `CalculateEarnings` and `ToString`, and properties that manipulate an `Employee`'s instance variables. A `CalculateEarnings` method certainly applies generically to all employees. But each earnings calculation depends on the employee's class. So we declare `CalculateEarnings` as `MustOverride` in base class `Employee` because a default implementation does not make sense for that method—there is not enough information to determine what amount `CalculateEarnings` should return. Each derived class overrides `CalculateEarnings` with an appropriate implementation. To calculate an employee's earnings, the program assigns to a base class `Employee` variable a reference to the employee's object, then invokes the `CalculateEarnings` method on that variable. We will maintain an array of `Employee` variables, each of which holds a reference to an `Employee` object (of course, there cannot be `Employee` objects because `Employee` is an abstract class—thanks to inheritance, however, all objects of all derived classes of `Employee` may nevertheless be thought of as `Employee` objects). The program iterates through the array and calls method `CalculateEarnings` for each `Employee` object. Visual Basic processes these method calls polymorphically. Including abstract method `CalculateEarnings` in class `Employee` forces every directly derived concrete class of `Employee` to override `CalculateEarnings`. This enables the designer of the class hierarchy to demand that each derived concrete class provide an appropriate pay calculation.

Method `ToString` in class `Employee` returns a `String` containing the first name, last name and social security number of the employee. As we will see, each derived class of `Employee` overrides method `ToString` to create a string representation of an object of that class that contains the employee's type (e.g., `"salaried employee:"`) followed by the rest of the employee's information.

The diagram in Fig. 11.3 shows the five classes of the hierarchy down the left side and methods `CalculateEarnings` and `ToString` across the top. For each class, the diagram shows the desired results of each method. [*Note:* We do not list base class `Employee`'s properties because they are not overridden in any of the derived classes—each of these properties is inherited and used "as is" by each of the derived classes.]

Class `Employee` (Fig. 11.4) includes a constructor that takes the first name, last name and social security number as arguments (lines 9–14); `Get` accessors that return the first name, last name and social security number (lines 18–20, 29–31 and 40–42, respectively); `Set` accessors that set the first name, last name and social security number (lines 22–24, 33–35 and 44–46, respectively); method `ToString` (lines 50–53), which returns the string representation of an `Employee`; and abstract (`MustOverride`) method `CalculateEarnings` (line 56), which must be implemented by concrete derived classes. Note that the `SocialSecurityNumber` property does not validate the social security number in this example. In business-critical applications, such validation should be provided.

	CalculateEarnings	ToString
Employee	MustOverride	*FirstName LastName* social security number: *SSN*
Salaried-Employee	*WeeklySalary*	salaried employee: *FirstName LastName* social security number: *SSN* weekly salary: *WeeklySalary*

Hourly-Employee	*If Hours <= 40*
	  Wage* Hours
	If Hours > 40
	  40 * *Wage* +
	  ((*Hours* - 40) *
	  Wage * 1.5)
		hourly employee: *FirstName LastName*
		social security number: *SSN*
		hourly wage: *Wage*; hours worked: *Hours*

Commission-Employee	*CommissionRate * GrossSales*	commission employee: *FirstName LastName* social security number: *SSN* gross sales: *GrossSales*; commission rate: *CommissionRate*
BasePlus-Commission-Employee	*(CommissionRate * GrossSales) + BaseSalary*	base-salaried commission employee: *FirstName LastName* social security number: *SSN* gross sales: *GrossSales*; commission rate: *CommissionRate*; base salary: *BaseSalary*

Fig. 11.3 | Polymorphic interface for the `Employee` hierarchy classes.

```vb
1    ' Fig. 11.4: Employee.vb
2    ' Employee abstract base class.
3    Public MustInherit Class Employee
4       Private firstNameValue As String
5       Private lastNameValue As String
6       Private socialSecurityNumberValue As String
7
8       ' three-argument constructor
9       Public Sub New(ByVal first As String, ByVal last As String, _
10         ByVal ssn As String)
11         FirstName = first
12         LastName = last
13         SocialSecurityNumber = ssn
14      End Sub ' New
15
16      ' property FirstName
17      Public Property FirstName() As String
18         Get
19            Return firstNameValue
20         End Get
```

Fig. 11.4 | Employee abstract base class. (Part 1 of 2.)

```vb
21
22        Set(ByVal first As String)
23            firstNameValue = first
24        End Set
25    End Property ' FirstName
26
27    ' property LastName
28    Public Property LastName() As String
29        Get
30            Return lastNameValue
31        End Get
32
33        Set(ByVal last As String)
34            lastNameValue = last
35        End Set
36    End Property ' LastName
37
38    ' property SocialSecurityNumber
39    Public Property SocialSecurityNumber() As String
40        Get
41            Return socialSecurityNumberValue
42        End Get
43
44        Set(ByVal ssn As String)
45            socialSecurityNumberValue = ssn
46        End Set
47    End Property ' SocialSecurityNumber
48
49    ' return String representation of Employee object
50    Public Overrides Function ToString() As String
51        Return (String.Format("{0} {1}", FirstName, LastName) & vbCrLf & _
52            "social security number: " & SocialSecurityNumber)
53    End Function ' ToString
54
55    ' abstract method overridden by derived class
56    Public MustOverride Function CalculateEarnings() As Decimal
57 End Class ' Employee
```

Fig. 11.4 | Employee abstract base class. (Part 2 of 2.)

Why did we decide to declare CalculateEarnings as a MustOverride method? It simply does not make sense to provide an implementation of this method in class Employee. We cannot calculate the earnings for a general Employee—we first must know the specific Employee type to determine the appropriate earnings calculation. By declaring this method MustOverride, we indicate that each concrete derived class *must* provide an appropriate CalculateEarnings implementation and that a program will be able to use base class Employee variables to invoke method CalculateEarnings polymorphically for any type of Employee.

11.5.2 Creating Concrete Derived Class SalariedEmployee

Class SalariedEmployee (Fig. 11.5) inherits class Employee (line 4) and overrides CalculateEarnings (lines 31–33), which makes SalariedEmployee a concrete class. The

```vb
 1    ' Fig. 11.5: SalariedEmployee.vb
 2    ' SalariedEmployee class inherits Employee
 3    Public Class SalariedEmployee
 4       Inherits Employee
 5
 6       Private weeklySalaryValue As Decimal ' employee's weekly salary
 7
 8       ' four-argument constructor
 9       Public Sub New(ByVal first As String, ByVal last As String, _
10          ByVal ssn As String, ByVal salary As Decimal)
11          MyBase.New(first, last, ssn) ' pass to Employee constructor
12          WeeklySalary = salary ' validate and store salary
13       End Sub ' New
14
15       ' property WeeklySalary
16       Public Property WeeklySalary() As Decimal
17          Get
18             Return weeklySalaryValue
19          End Get
20
21          Set(ByVal salary As Decimal)
22             If salary < 0.0 Then ' validate salary
23                weeklySalaryValue = 0
24             Else
25                weeklySalaryValue = salary
26             End If
27          End Set
28       End Property ' WeeklySalary
29
30       ' calculate earnings; override abstract method CalculateEarnings
31       Public Overrides Function CalculateEarnings() As Decimal
32          Return WeeklySalary
33       End Function ' CalculateEarnings
34
35       ' return String representation of SalariedEmployee object
36       Public Overrides Function ToString() As String
37          Return ("salaried employee: " & MyBase.ToString() & vbCrLf & _
38             String.Format("weekly salary {0:C}", WeeklySalary))
39       End Function ' ToString
40    End Class ' SalariedEmployee
```

Fig. 11.5 | SalariedEmployee class derived from class Employee.

class includes a constructor (lines 9–13) that takes a first name, a last name, a social security number and a weekly salary as arguments; a WeeklySalary property that has a Get accessor (lines 17–19) to return weeklySalaryValue's value and a Set accessor (lines 21–27) to assign a new non-negative value to instance variable weeklySalaryValue; a method CalculateEarnings (lines 31–33) to calculate a SalariedEmployee's earnings; and a method ToString (lines 36–39) that returns a String including the employee's type, namely, "salaried employee: ", followed by employee-specific information produced by base class Employee's ToString method, and the value of SalariedEmployee's WeeklySalary property. Class SalariedEmployee's constructor passes the first name, last name and social security number to base class `Employee`'s constructor (line 11). Method `CalculateEarnings` overrides abstract method `CalculateEarnings` of `Employee` with a concrete implementation that returns the `SalariedEmployee`'s weekly salary. If we do not implement `CalculateEarnings`, class `SalariedEmployee` must be declared `MustOverride`—otherwise, a compilation error occurs (and, of course, we want `SalariedEmployee` to be a concrete class).

`SalariedEmployee`'s `ToString` method (lines 36–39) overrides `Employee` method `ToString`. If class `SalariedEmployee` did not override `ToString`, the class would have inherited `Employee`'s `ToString` method. In that case, `SalariedEmployee`'s `ToString` method would simply return the employee's full name and social security number, which does not adequately represent a `SalariedEmployee`. To produce a complete string representation of a `SalariedEmployee`, the derived class's `ToString` method returns `"salaried employee: "` followed by the base class `Employee`-specific information (i.e., first name, last name and social security number) obtained by invoking the base class's `ToString` (line 37)—a nice example of code reuse. The string representation of a `SalariedEmployee` also contains the employee's weekly salary obtained from the `WeeklySalary` property.

11.5.3 Creating Concrete Derived Class HourlyEmployee

Class `HourlyEmployee` (Fig. 11.6) also inherits class `Employee` (line 4). The class includes a constructor (lines 10–16) that takes as arguments a first name, a last name, a social security number, an hourly wage and the number of hours worked. Lines 24–30 and 39–45

```vb
1   ' Fig. 11.6: HourlyEmployee.vb
2   ' HourlyEmployee class inherits Employee.
3   Public Class HourlyEmployee
4       Inherits Employee
5
6       Private wageValue As Decimal ' wage per hour
7       Private hoursValue As Decimal ' hours worked for week
8
9       ' five-argument constructor
10      Public Sub New(ByVal first As String, ByVal last As String, _
11          ByVal ssn As String, ByVal hourlyWage As Decimal, _
12          ByVal hoursWorked As Decimal)
13          MyBase.New(first, last, ssn) ' pass to Employee constructor
14          Wage = hourlyWage ' validate and store hourly wage
15          Hours = hoursWorked ' validate and store hours worked
16      End Sub ' New
17
18      ' property Wage
19      Public Property Wage() As Decimal
20          Get
21              Return wageValue
22          End Get
23
24          Set(ByVal hourlyWage As Decimal)
25              If hourlyWage < 0 Then ' validate hourly wage
26                  wageValue = 0
```

Fig. 11.6 | HourlyEmployee class derived from class `Employee`. (Part 1 of 2.)

```
27              Else
28                  wageValue = hourlyWage
29              End If
30          End Set
31      End Property ' Wage
32
33      ' property Hours
34      Public Property Hours() As Decimal
35          Get
36              Return hoursValue
37          End Get
38
39          Set(ByVal hoursWorked As Decimal)
40              If (hoursWorked >= 0.0) AndAlso (hoursWorked <= 168.0) Then
41                  hoursValue = hoursWorked ' valid weekly hours
42              Else
43                  hoursValue = 0
44              End If
45          End Set
46      End Property ' Hours
47
48      ' calculate earnings; override abstract method CalculageEarnings
49      Public Overrides Function CalculateEarnings() As Decimal
50          If Hours <= 40 Then ' no overtime
51              Return Wage * Hours
52          Else
53              Return 40 * Wage + ((Hours - 40) * Wage * 1.5D)
54          End If
55      End Function ' CalculateEarnings
56
57      ' return String representation of HourlyEmployee object
58      Public Overrides Function ToString() As String
59          Return ("hourly employee: " & MyBase.ToString() & vbCrLf & _
60              String.Format("hourly wage: {0:C}; hours worked: {1}", _
61              Wage, Hours))
62      End Function ' ToString
63  End Class ' HourlyEmployee
```

Fig. 11.6 | HourlyEmployee class derived from class Employee. (Part 2 of 2.)

declare Set accessors that assign new values to instance variables wageValue and hoursValue, respectively. The Set accessor of property Wage (lines 24–30) ensures that wageValue is non-negative, and the Set accessor of property Hours (lines 39–45) ensures that hoursValue is between 0 and 168 (the total number of hours in a week). Properties Wage and Hours also include Get accessors (lines 20–22 and 35–37) to return the values of wageValue and hoursValue, respectively. Method CalculateEarnings (lines 49–55) calculates an HourlyEmployee's earnings. Method ToString (lines 58–62) returns the employee's type, namely, "hourly employee: ", and employee-specific information, including the full name, the social security number, and the values of properties Wage and Hours. Note that the HourlyEmployee constructor, like the SalariedEmployee constructor, passes the first name, last name and social security number to the base class Employee constructor (line 13). In addition, method ToString calls base class method ToString (line 59) to obtain the Employee-specific information (i.e., first name, last name and social security number)—this is another nice example of code reuse.

11.5.4 Creating Concrete Derived Class CommissionEmployee

Class CommissionEmployee (Fig. 11.7) inherits class Employee (line 4). The class includes a constructor (lines 10–15) that takes a first name, a last name, a social security number, a sales amount and a commission rate; Get accessors (lines 19–21 and 34–36) that retrieve the values of instance variables grossSalesValue and commissionRateValue, respectively; Set accessors (lines 23–29 and 38–44) that assign new values to these instance variables; method CalculateEarnings (lines 48–50) to calculate a CommissionEmployee's earnings; and method ToString (lines 53–57), which returns the employee's type, namely, "commission employee: " and employee-specific information, including the full name and social security number, and the values of properties GrossSales and CommissionRate. The CommissionEmployee's constructor also passes the first name, last name and social security number to the Employee constructor (line 12) to initialize Employee's Private instance variables. Method ToString calls base class method ToString (line 54) to obtain the Employee-specific information (i.e., first name, last name and social security number).

```vb
1   ' Fig. 11.7: CommissionEmployee.vb
2   ' CommissionEmployee class inherits Employee.
3   Public Class CommissionEmployee
4      Inherits Employee
5
6      Private grossSalesValue As Decimal
7      Private commissionRateValue As Decimal
8
9      ' five-argument constructor
10     Public Sub New(ByVal first As String, ByVal last As String, _
11        ByVal ssn As String, ByVal sales As Decimal, ByVal rate As Decimal)
12        MyBase.New(first, last, ssn) ' pass to Employee constructor
13        GrossSales = sales ' validate and store gross sales
14        CommissionRate = rate ' validate and store commission rate
15     End Sub ' New
16
17     ' property GrossSales
18     Public Property GrossSales() As Decimal
19        Get
20           Return grossSalesValue
21        End Get
22
23        Set(ByVal sales As Decimal)
24           If sales < 0 Then ' validate gross sales
25              grossSalesValue = 0
26           Else
27              grossSalesValue = sales
28           End If
29        End Set
30     End Property ' GrossSales
31
```

Fig. 11.7 | CommissionEmployee class derived from Employee. (Part 1 of 2.)

```
32          ' property CommissionRate
33          Public Property CommissionRate() As Decimal
34             Get
35                Return commissionRateValue
36             End Get
37
38             Set(ByVal rate As Decimal)
39                If rate > 0.0 AndAlso rate < 1.0 Then ' validate commission rate
40                   commissionRateValue = rate
41                Else
42                   commissionRateValue = 0
43                End If
44             End Set
45          End Property ' CommissionRate
46
47          ' calculate earnings; override abstract method CalculateEarnings
48          Public Overrides Function CalculateEarnings() As Decimal
49             Return CommissionRate * GrossSales
50          End Function ' CalculateEarnings
51
52          ' return String representation of CommissionEmployee object
53          Public Overrides Function ToString() As String
54             Return ("commission employee: " & MyBase.ToString() & vbCrLf & _
55                String.Format("gross sales: {0:C}; commission rate: {1}", _
56                GrossSales, CommissionRate))
57          End Function ' ToString
58       End Class ' CommissionEmployee
```

Fig. 11.7 | CommissionEmployee class derived from Employee. (Part 2 of 2.)

11.5.5 Creating Indirect Concrete Derived Class BasePlusCommissionEmployee

Class BasePlusCommissionEmployee (Fig. 11.8) inherits class CommissionEmployee (line 4) and therefore is an indirect derived class of class Employee. Class BasePlusCommissionEmployee has a constructor (lines 9–14) that takes as arguments a first name, a last name, a social security number, a sales amount, a commission rate and a base salary. It then passes the first name, last name, social security number, sales amount and commission rate to the CommissionEmployee constructor (line 12) to initialize the inherited members. BasePlusCommissionEmployee also contains a property BaseSalary whose Set accessor (lines 22–28) assigns a new value to instance variable baseSalaryValue, and whose Get accessor (lines 18–20) returns baseSalaryValue. Method CalculateEarnings (lines 32–34) calculates a BasePlusCommissionEmployee's earnings. Note that line 33 in method CalculateEarnings calls base class CommissionEmployee's CalculateEarnings method to calculate the commission-based portion of the employee's earnings. This is another nice example of code reuse. BasePlusCommissionEmployee's ToString method (lines 37–40) creates a String representation of a BasePlusCommissionEmployee that contains "base-salaried", followed by the String obtained by invoking base class CommissionEmployee's ToString method (another example of code reuse), then the base salary. The result is a String beginning with "base-salaried commission employee" followed by the rest of the BasePlusCommissionEmployee's information. Recall that CommissionEmployee's

```
 1    ' Fig. 11.8: BasePlusCommissionEmployee.vb
 2    ' BasePlusCommissionEmployee class inherits CommissionEmployee.
 3   Public Class BasePlusCommissionEmployee
 4      Inherits CommissionEmployee
 5
 6      Private baseSalaryValue As Decimal ' base salary
 7
 8      ' six-argument constructor
 9      Public Sub New(ByVal first As String, ByVal last As String, _
10         ByVal ssn As String, ByVal sales As Decimal, _
11         ByVal rate As Decimal, ByVal salary As Decimal)
12         MyBase.New(first, last, ssn, sales, rate)
13         BaseSalary = salary
14      End Sub ' New
15
16      ' property BaseSalary
17      Public Property BaseSalary() As Decimal
18         Get
19            Return baseSalaryValue
20         End Get
21
22         Set(ByVal salary As Decimal)
23            If salary < 0 Then ' validate salary
24               baseSalaryValue = 0
25            Else
26               baseSalaryValue = salary
27            End If
28         End Set
29      End Property ' BaseSalary
30
31      ' calculate earnings; override method CalculateEarnings
32      Public Overrides Function CalculateEarnings() As Decimal
33         Return BaseSalary + MyBase.CalculateEarnings()
34      End Function ' CalculateEarnings
35
36      ' return String representation of BasePlusCommissionEmployee object
37      Public Overrides Function ToString() As String
38         Return ("base-salaried " & MyBase.ToString() & _
39            String.Format("; base salary: {0:C}", BaseSalary))
40      End Function ' ToString
41   End Class ' BasePlusCommissionEmployee
```

Fig. 11.8 | `BasePlusCommissionEmployee` derived from `CommissionEmployee`.

`ToString` method obtains the employee's first name, last name and social security number by invoking the `ToString` method of its base class (i.e., `Employee`)—another example of code reuse. Note that `BasePlusCommissionEmployee`'s `ToString` initiates a chain of method calls that spans all three levels of the `Employee` hierarchy.

11.5.6 Demonstrating Polymorphic Processing, Expression TypeOf...Is, TryCast and Downcasting

To test our `Employee` hierarchy, the program in Fig. 11.9 creates an object of each of the four concrete classes `SalariedEmployee`, `HourlyEmployee`, `CommissionEmployee` and

```
 1   ' Fig. 11.9: PayrollSystemTest.vb
 2   ' Employee hierarchy test program.
 3   Module PayrollSystemTest
 4      Sub Main()
 5         ' create derived class objects
 6         Dim salariedEmployee As New SalariedEmployee( _
 7            "John", "Smith", "111-11-1111", 800)
 8         Dim hourlyEmployee As New HourlyEmployee( _
 9            "Karen", "Price", "222-22-2222", 16.75D, 40)
10         Dim commissionEmployee As New CommissionEmployee( _
11            "Sue", "Jones", "333-33-3333", 10000, 0.06D)
12         Dim basePlusCommissionEmployee As New BasePlusCommissionEmployee( _
13            "Bob", "Lewis", "444-44-4444", 5000, 0.04D, 300)
14
15         ' display each employee's info non-polymorphically
16         Console.WriteLine("Employees processed individually:" & vbCrLf)
17         Console.WriteLine(salariedEmployee.ToString() & vbCrLf & _
18            String.Format("earned: {0:C}", _
19            salariedEmployee.CalculateEarnings()) & vbCrLf)
20         Console.WriteLine(hourlyEmployee.ToString() & vbCrLf & _
21            String.Format("earned: {0:C}", _
22            hourlyEmployee.CalculateEarnings()) & vbCrLf)
23         Console.WriteLine(commissionEmployee.ToString() & vbCrLf & _
24            String.Format("earned: {0:C}", _
25            commissionEmployee.CalculateEarnings()) & vbCrLf)
26         Console.WriteLine(basePlusCommissionEmployee.ToString() & _
27            vbCrLf & String.Format("earned: {0:C}", _
28            basePlusCommissionEmployee.CalculateEarnings()) & vbCrLf)
29
30         ' create four-element Employee array
31         Dim employees() As Employee = {salariedEmployee, hourlyEmployee, _
32            commissionEmployee, basePlusCommissionEmployee}
33
34         Console.WriteLine("Employees processed polymorphically:" & vbCrLf)
35
36         ' polymorphically process each element in array employees
37         For Each currentEmployee As Employee In employees
38            Console.WriteLine(currentEmployee.ToString())
39
40            ' determine if currentEmployee is a BasePlusCommissionEmployee
41            If (TypeOf currentEmployee Is BasePlusCommissionEmployee) Then
42
43               ' downcast Employee reference to BasePlusCommissionEmployee
44               Dim employee As BasePlusCommissionEmployee = _
45                  TryCast(currentEmployee, BasePlusCommissionEmployee)
46
47               employee.BaseSalary *= 1.1D
48               Console.WriteLine(String.Format( _
49                  "new base salary with 10% increase is: {0:C}", _
50                  employee.BaseSalary))
51            End If
52
```

Fig. 11.9 | Employee class hierarchy test program. (Part 1 of 3.)

```
53                Console.Write(String.Format("earned {0:C}", _
54                    currentEmployee.CalculateEarnings()) & vbCrLf & vbCrLf)
55         Next
56
57         ' get type name of each object in employees array
58         For i As Integer = 0 To employees.Length - 1
59             Console.WriteLine(String.Format("Employee {0} is a {1}", _
60                 i, employees(i).GetType().FullName))
61         Next
62     End Sub ' Main
63 End Module ' PayrollSystemTest
```

```
Employees processed individually:

salaried employee: John Smith
social security number: 111-11-1111
weekly salary $800.00
earned: $800.00

hourly employee: Karen Price
social security number: 222-22-2222
hourly wage: $16.75; hours worked: 40
earned: $670.00

commission employee: Sue Jones
social security number: 333-33-3333
gross sales: $10,000.00; commission rate: 0.06
earned: $600.00

base-salaried commission employee: Bob Lewis
social security number: 444-44-4444
gross sales: $5,000.00; commission rate: 0.04; base salary: $300.00
earned: $500.00

Employees processed polymorphically:

salaried employee: John Smith
social security number: 111-11-1111
weekly salary $800.00
earned $800.00

hourly employee: Karen Price
social security number: 222-22-2222
hourly wage: $16.75; hours worked: 40
earned $670.00

commission employee: Sue Jones
social security number: 333-33-3333
gross sales: $10,000.00; commission rate: 0.06
earned $600.00
```

(continued on next page...)

Fig. 11.9 | Employee class hierarchy test program. (Part 2 of 3.)

(continued from previous page...)

```
base-salaried commission employee: Bob Lewis
social security number: 444-44-4444
gross sales: $5,000.00; commission rate: 0.04; base salary: $300.00
new base salary with 10% increase is: $330.00
earned $530.00

Employee 0 is a PayrollSystem.SalariedEmployee
Employee 1 is a PayrollSystem.HourlyEmployee
Employee 2 is a PayrollSystem.CommissionEmployee
Employee 3 is a PayrollSystem.BasePlusCommissionEmployee
```

Fig. 11.9 | `Employee` class hierarchy test program. (Part 3 of 3.)

`BasePlusCommissionEmployee`. The program manipulates these objects, first via variables of each object's own type, then polymorphically, using an array of `Employee` variables. While processing the objects polymorphically, the program increases the base salary of each `BasePlusCommissionEmployee` by 10%—this requires that the program determine each object's type at execution time. Finally, the program polymorphically determines and outputs the type of each object in the `Employee` array. Lines 6–13 create objects of each of the four concrete `Employee` derived classes. Lines 16–28 output (non-polymorphically) the string representation and earnings of each of these objects.

Lines 31–32 create and initialize array `employees` with four `Employee`s. This statement is valid because, through inheritance, a `SalariedEmployee` *is an* `Employee`, an `HourlyEmployee` *is an* `Employee`, a `CommissionEmployee` *is an* `Employee` and a `BasePlusCommissionEmployee` *is an* `Employee`. Therefore, we can assign the references of `SalariedEmployee`, `HourlyEmployee`, `CommissionEmployee` and `BasePlusCommissionEmployee` objects to base class `Employee` variables, even though `Employee` is an abstract class.

Lines 37–55 iterate through array `employees` and invoke methods `ToString` and `CalculateEarnings` with `Employee` variable `currentEmployee`, which is assigned the reference to a different `Employee` in the array during each iteration. The output illustrates that the appropriate methods for each class are indeed invoked. All calls to method `ToString` and `CalculateEarnings` are resolved at execution time, based on the type of the object to which `currentEmployee` refers. This process is known as *late binding*. For example, line 38 explicitly invokes method `ToString` of the object to which `currentEmployee` refers. As a result of late binding, Visual Basic decides which class's `ToString` method to call at execution time rather than at compile time. Recall that only the methods of class `Employee` can be called via an `Employee` variable (and `Employee`, of course, includes the methods of class `Object`). (Section 10.7 discussed the set of methods that all classes inherit from class `Object`.) A base class reference can be used to invoke only methods of the base class, even though those method calls polymorphically invoke derived class method implementations when sent to derived class objects.

Using Expression TypeOf...Is to Determine Object Type

We perform special processing on `BasePlusCommissionEmployee` objects—as we encounter these objects, we increase their base salary by 10%. When processing objects polymorphically, we typically do not need to worry about the specifics, but to adjust the base salary, we do have to determine the specific type of Employee object at execution time. Line 41 uses a TypeOf...Is expression to determine whether a particular Employee object's type is BasePlusCommissionEmployee. The condition in line 41 is true if the object referenced by currentEmployee *is a* BasePlusCommissionEmployee. This would also be true for any object of a BasePlusCommissionEmployee derived class (if there are any) because of the *is-a* relationship a derived class has with its base class.

Using TryCast to Downcast from a Base Class to a Derived Class Type

Lines 44–45 use keyword *TryCast* to downcast currentEmployee from base class type Employee to derived class type BasePlusCommissionEmployee—this cast returns an object only if the object has an *is a* relationship with type BasePlusCommissionEmployee. The condition at line 41 ensures that this is the case. If the *is a* relationship does not exist, TryCast returns Nothing. This cast is required if we are to access derived class BasePlusCommissionEmployee property BaseSalary on the current Employee object—as you will see momentarily, attempting to invoke a derived-class-only method or property directly on a base class reference is a compilation error. Note that we did not need to use both TypeOf...Is and TryCast. We could have simply used TryCast, then tested the value of variable employee to ensure that it was not Nothing before attempting to execute the statements in lines 47–50. We used both here so that we could demonstrate the new Visual Basic 2005 TryCast keyword.

Common Programming Error 11.3

Assigning a base class variable to a derived class variable (without an explicit cast) is a compilation error.

Error-Prevention Tip 11.1

If at execution time the reference of a derived class object has been assigned to a variable of one of its direct or indirect base classes, it is acceptable to cast the reference stored in that base class variable back to a reference of the derived class type. Before performing such a cast, use the Typeof...Is expression to ensure that the object is indeed an object of an appropriate derived class type. You can then use TryCast to downcast from the base class type to the derived class type.

When downcasting an object, TryCast returns Nothing if at execution time the object being converted does not have an *is-a* relationship with the target type. An object can be cast only to its own type or to one of its base class types; otherwise, a compilation error occurs.

If the Typeof...Is expression in line 41 is True, the body of the If statement (lines 44–50) performs the special processing required for the BasePlusCommissionEmployee object. Using BasePlusCommissionEmployee variable employee, lines 47–50 access derived-class-only property BaseSalary to retrieve and update the employee's base salary with the 10% raise.

Lines 53–54 invoke method CalculateEarnings on currentEmployee, which calls the appropriate derived class object's CalculateEarnings method polymorphically. Note that obtaining the earnings of the SalariedEmployee, HourlyEmployee and CommissionEmployee polymorphically in lines 53–54 produces the same result as obtaining these employees' earnings non-polymorphically in lines 16–25. However, the earnings amount obtained for the BasePlusCommissionEmployee in lines 53–54 is higher than that obtained in lines 26–28, due to the 10% increase in its base salary.

Lines 58–61 display each employee's type as a string. Every object in Visual Basic knows its own class and can access this information through method GetType, which all classes inherit from class Object. Figure 10.20 lists the Object methods that are inherited directly or indirectly by all classes. Method GetType returns an object of class Type (namespace System), which contains information about the object's type, including its fully qualified class name. For more information on the Type class, please read msdn.microsoft.com/library/en-us/cpref/html/frlrfsystemtypeclasstopic.asp. Line 60 invokes method GetType on the object to get a Type object that represents the object's type at execution time. Then line 60 uses the FullName property of the object returned by GetType to get the class's name fully qualified name (see the last four lines of the program's output).

Notes on Downcasting
We avoid several compilation errors by downcasting an Employee variable to a BasePlusCommissionEmployee variable in lines 44–45. If we remove the cast expression from line 45 and attempt to assign Employee variable currentEmployee directly to BasePlusCommissionEmployee variable employee, we would receive a compilation error (when **Option Strict is On**). This error indicates that the attempt to assign the base class variable currentEmployee to derived class variable basePlusCommissionEmployee is not allowed. The compiler prevents this assignment because a CommissionEmployee is not a BasePlusCommissionEmployee—the *is-a* relationship applies only between the derived class and its base classes, not vice versa.

Similarly, if lines 47 and 50 were to use base class variable currentEmployee, rather than derived class variable employee, to access derived-class-only property BaseSalary, we would receive a compilation error on each of these lines. Attempting to invoke derivedclass-only methods and properties on a base class reference is not allowed. While lines 47 and 50 execute only if the Typeof...If expression in line 41 returns True to indicate that currentEmployee has been assigned a reference to a BasePlusCommissionEmployee object, we cannot attempt to invoke derived class BasePlusCommissionEmployee property BaseSalary on base class Employee reference currentEmployee. The compiler would generate errors in lines 47 and 50, because property BaseSalary is not a base class property and cannot be accessed using a base class variable. Although the actual method or property that is called depends on the object's type at execution time, a variable can be used to invoke only those methods and properties that are members of that variable's type, which the compiler verifies. Using a base class Employee variable, we can invoke only methods and properties found in class Employee (Fig. 11.4)—methods CalculateEarnings and ToString, and properties FirstName, LastName and SocialSecurityNumber.

11.5.7 Summary of the Allowed Assignments between Base Class and Derived Class Variables

Now that you have seen a complete application that processes diverse derived class objects polymorphically, we summarize what you can and cannot do with base class and derived class objects and variables. Although a derived class object also *is a* base class object, the two objects are nevertheless different. As discussed previously, derived class objects can be treated as if they are base class objects. However, the derived class can have additional derived-class-only members. For this reason, assigning a base class reference to a derived class variable is not allowed without a cast—such an assignment would leave the derived-class-only members undefined for the base class object.

We have discussed four ways to assign base class and derived class references to variables of base class and derived class types:

1. Assigning a base class reference to a base class variable is straightforward.

2. Assigning a derived class reference to a derived class variable is straightforward.

3. Assigning a derived class reference to a base class variable is safe, because the derived class object *is an* object of its base class. However, this reference can be used to refer only to base class members. Referring to a derived-class-only member through the base class variable is a compilation error.

4. Attempting to assign a base class reference to a derived class variable is a compilation error (when **Option Strict** is **On**). To avoid this error, the base class reference must be cast to a derived class type explicitly. At execution time, if the object to which the reference refers is not a derived class object, an exception will occur. (For more on exception handling, see Chapter 12, Exception Handling.) The `TypeOf...Is` expression can be used to ensure that such a cast is performed only if the object is a derived class object. Then a `TryCast` can be used to perform the downcast operation.

11.6 NotOverridable Methods and NotInheritable Classes

A method that is declared ***NotOverridable*** in a base class cannot be overridden in a derived class. A method that is declared `Overridable` in a base class can be declared `NotOverridable` in a derived class—this prevents overriding the method in classes that inherit from the derived class. All classes derived from the class that contains the `NotOverridable` method use that class's method implementation. Methods that are declared `Private` are implicitly `NotOverridable`.

A class that is declared ***NotInheritable*** cannot be a base class (i.e., a class cannot inherit from a `NotInheritable` class). All methods in a `NotInheritable` class are implicitly `NotOverridable`. A `NotInheritable` class is the opposite of a `MustInherit` class. A `NotInheritable` class is a concrete class that cannot act as a base class, whereas a `MustInherit` class is an abstract class that is intended as a base class. Class `String` is a `NotInheritable` class.

Common Programming Error 11.4

Attempting to inherit a `NotInheritable` class is a compilation error.

11.7 Case Study: Creating and Using Interfaces

Our next example reexamines the payroll system of Section 11.5. Suppose that the company involved wishes to perform several accounting operations in an accounts payable application In addition to calculating the earnings that must be paid to each employee, the company also wants to calculate the payment due on each of several invoices (i.e., bills for goods and services purchased). Though applied to unrelated things (i.e., employees and invoices), both operations have to do with obtaining some kind of payment amount. For an employee, the payment refers to the employee's earnings. For an invoice, the payment refers to the total cost of the goods and services listed on the invoice. Can we calculate such different things as the payments due for employees and invoices in a single application polymorphically? Does Visual Basic have a capability that forces possibly unrelated classes to implement a set of common methods (e.g., a method that calculates a payment amount)? Visual Basic interfaces offer exactly this capability.

Interfaces define and standardize the ways in which things such as people and systems can interact with one another. For example, the controls on a radio serve as an interface between radio users and a radio's internal components. The controls allow users to perform only a limited set of operations (e.g., changing the station, adjusting the volume, choosing between AM and FM), and different radios may implement the controls in different ways (e.g., using push buttons, dials, voice commands). The interface specifies *what* operations a radio permits users to perform but does not specify *how* the operations are implemented. Similarly, the interface between a driver and a car with a manual transmission includes the steering wheel, the gear shift, and the clutch, gas and brake pedals. This same interface is found in nearly all manual transmission cars, enabling someone who knows how to drive one particular manual transmission car to drive just about any manual transmission car. The components of each individual car may look a bit different, but the components' general purpose is the same—to allow people to drive the car.

Software objects also communicate via interfaces. A Visual Basic interface describes a set of methods that can be called on an object, to tell the object to perform some task or return some piece of information, for example. An interface is often used in place of a `Must-Inherit` class when there is no default implementation to inherit—that is, no instance variables and no default method and property implementations. The next example introduces an interface named `IPayable` to describe the functionality of any object that must be capable of being paid and thus must offer a method to determine the proper payment amount due. An *interface declaration* begins with the keyword `Interface` and can contain abstract methods and properties, but cannot contain instance variables, concreate methods or concrete properties. Unlike classes, interfaces may not specify any implementation details, such as concrete method declarations and instance variables. All members declared in an interface are implicitly `Public`, and may not specify an access modifier.

Common Programming Error 11.5

It is a compilation error to explicitly declare interface methods `Public`.

Common Programming Error 11.6

In Visual Basic, an `Interface` can be declared only as `Public` or `Friend`; the declaration of an `Interface` as `Private` or `Protected` is an error.

To use an interface, a concrete class must specify that it `Implements` the interface and must implement each method in the interface with the signature and return type specified in the interface declaration. A class that does not implement all the methods of the interface is an abstract class and must be declared `MustInherit`. Implementing an interface is like signing a contract with the compiler that states, "I will declare all the methods specified by the interface or I will declare my class `MustInherit`."

Common Programming Error 11.7

Failing to implement any method of an interface in a concrete class that Implements the interface results in a syntax error indicating that the class must be declared MustInherit.

An interface is typically used when unrelated classes need to share common methods and properties. This allows objects of unrelated classes to be processed polymorphically—objects of classes that implement the same interface have an *is-a* relationship with the interface type and can respond to the same method calls. Programmers can create an interface that describes the desired functionality, then implement this interface in any classes that require that functionality. For example, in the accounts payable application that we develop in the next several subsections, we implement interface IPayable in any class that must be able to calculate a payment amount (e.g., Employee, Invoice).

11.7.1 Developing an IPayable Hierarchy

To build an application that can determine payments for employees and invoices alike, we will first create interface IPayable. Interface IPayable contains method GetPayment-Amount, which returns a Decimal amount that must be paid for an IPayable object, and method ToString, which returns the String representation of an IPayable object. Method GetPaymentAmount is a general purpose version of the Employee hierarchy's CalculateEarnings method—method CalculateEarnings calculates a payment amount specifically for an Employee, while GetPaymentAmount can be applied more generally to unrelated objects. After declaring interface IPayable, we will introduce class Invoice, which implements interface IPayable. We then modify class Employee so that it, too, implements interface IPayable. Finally, we update Employee derived class SalariedEmployee to "fit" into the IPayable hierarchy (i.e., we rename SalariedEmployee method CalculateEarnings as GetPaymentAmount).

 Good Programming Practice 11.1

When declaring a method in an interface, choose a method name that describes the method's purpose in a general manner, because the method may be implemented by many unrelated classes.

Classes Invoice and Employee both represent things for which the company must be able to calculate a payment amount. Both classes implement IPayable, so a program can invoke method GetPaymentAmount on Invoice objects and Employee objects alike. As you will soon see, this enables the polymorphic processing of Invoices and Employees required for our accounts payable application.

The UML class diagram in Fig. 11.10 shows the class and interface hierarchy used in our accounts payable application. The hierarchy begins with interface IPayable. The UML distinguishes an interface from other classes by placing the word "interface" in guillemets (« ») above the interface name. The UML expresses the relationship between a class and an interface through an association known as a ***realization***. A class is said to "realize," or implement, an interface. A class diagram models a realization as a dashed arrow with a hollow arrowhead pointing from the implementing classes to the interface. The diagram in Fig. 11.10 indicates that class Invoice realizes (i.e., implements) interface IPayable. Class Employee also realizes interface IPayable, but it is not required to provide method implementations, because it is an abstract class (note that it appears in italics). Concrete class SalariedEmployee inherits from Employee and inherits its base class's

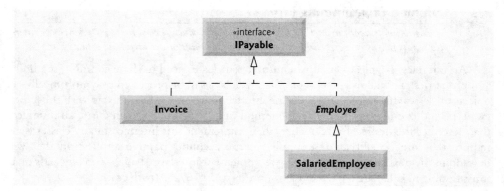

Fig. 11.10 | IPayable interface hierarchy UML class diagram.

realization relationship with interface IPayable, so SalariedEmployee must implement the method(s) of IPayable.

11.7.2 Declaring Interface IPayable

The declaration of interface IPayable begins in Fig. 11.11 at line 3. Interface IPayable contains Public methods GetPaymentAmount (line 4) and ToString (line 5). Note that the methods are not explicitly declared Public. Interface methods are implicitly Public. Also note that we explicitly declare the ToString method. Unlike a class, an interface does not inherit from Object, so it does not implicitly have a ToString method. You must explicitly declare ToString in the interface if a program must call this method through an IPayable variable. Interfaces can have any number of methods. Although methods GetPaymentAmount and ToString have no parameters, interface methods can have parameters.

11.7.3 Creating Class Invoice

We now create class Invoice (Fig. 11.12) to represent a simple invoice that contains billing information for only one kind of part. The class declares Private instance variables partNumberValue, partDescriptionValue, quantityValue and pricePerItemValue (in lines 6–9) that indicate the part number, a description of the part, the quantity of the part ordered and the price per item, respectively. Class Invoice also contains a constructor (lines 12–18), and properties PartNumber (lines 21–29), PartDescription(lines 32–40), Quantity (lines 43–55) and PricePerItem (lines 58–70) that manipulate the class's instance variables. Note that the Set accessors of properties Quantity and PricePerItem ensure that quantityValue and pricePerItemValue are assigned only non-negative values.

```
1    ' Fig. 11.11: IPayable.vb
2    ' IPayable interface declaration.
3    Public Interface IPayable
4        Function GetPaymentAmount() As Decimal ' calculate payment
5        Function ToString() As String ' display Payable object
6    End Interface ' IPayable
```

Fig. 11.11 | IPayable interface declaration.

Line 4 of Fig. 11.12 indicates that class `Invoice` implements interface `IPayable`. Class `Invoice` also implicitly inherits from `Object`. A derived class cannot inherit from more than one base class, but can inherit from a base class and implement zero or more interfaces. To implement more than one interface, use a comma-separated list of interface names after keyword `Implements` in the class declaration, as in:

```
Public Class ClassName
    Inherits BaseClassName
    Implements IFirstInterface, ISecondInterface, ...
```

```
 1   ' Fig. 11.12: Invoice.vb
 2   ' Invoice class implements IPayable.
 3   Public Class Invoice
 4       Implements IPayable
 5
 6       Private partNumberValue As String
 7       Private partDescriptionValue As String
 8       Private quantityValue As Integer
 9       Private pricePerItemValue As Decimal
10
11       ' four-argument constructor
12       Public Sub New(ByVal part As String, ByVal description As String, _
13           ByVal count As Integer, ByVal price As Decimal)
14           PartNumber = part
15           PartDescription = description
16           Quantity = count ' validate quantity
17           PricePerItem = price ' validate price per item
18       End Sub ' New
19
20       ' property PartNumber
21       Public Property PartNumber() As String
22           Get
23               Return partNumberValue
24           End Get
25
26           Set(ByVal part As String)
27               partNumberValue = part
28           End Set
29       End Property ' PartNumber
30
31       ' property PartDescription
32       Public Property PartDescription() As String
33           Get
34               Return partDescriptionValue
35           End Get
36
37           Set(ByVal description As String)
38               partDescriptionValue = description
39           End Set
40       End Property ' PartDescription
41
```

Fig. 11.12 | `Invoice` class that implements interface `IPayable`. (Part 1 of 2.)

```
42         ' property Quantity
43         Public Property Quantity() As Integer
44            Get
45                Return quantityValue
46            End Get
47
48            Set(ByVal count As Integer)
49                If count < 0 Then ' validate quantity
50                    quantityValue = 0
51                Else
52                    quantityValue = count
53                End If
54            End Set
55         End Property ' Quantity
56
57         ' property PricePerItem
58         Public Property PricePerItem() As Decimal
59            Get
60                Return pricePerItemValue
61            End Get
62
63            Set(ByVal price As Decimal)
64                If price < 0 Then ' validate price
65                    pricePerItemValue = 0
66                Else
67                    pricePerItemValue = price
68                End If
69            End Set
70         End Property ' PricePerItem
71
72         ' function required to carry out contract with interface IPayable
73         Public Function GetPaymentAmount() As Decimal _
74            Implements IPayable.GetPaymentAmount
75            Return Quantity * PricePerItem ' calculate total cost
76         End Function ' GetPaymentAmount
77
78         ' return String representation of Invoice object
79         Public Overrides Function ToString() As String _
80            Implements IPayable.ToString
81            Return ("invoice:" & vbCrLf & "part number: " & PartNumber & _
82                "(" & PartDescription & ")" & vbCrLf & "quantity: " & _
83                Quantity & vbCrLf & _
84                String.Format("price per item: {0:C}", PricePerItem))
85         End Function ' ToString
86      End Class ' Invoice
```

Fig. 11.12 | Invoice class that implements interface IPayable. (Part 2 of 2.)

Inherits *BaseClassName* is optional if the class implicitly inherits from class Object. All objects of a class that implements multiple interfaces have the *is-a* relationship with each implemented interface type.

Class Invoice implements the methods in interface IPayable. Method GetPayment-Amount is declared in lines 73–76. Line 74 contains keyword Implements followed by

IPayable.GetPaymentAmount to indicate that the method in lines 73–76 is the implementation of the interface's GetPaymentAmount method. Line 75 calculates the total payment required to pay the invoice by multiplying the values of quantityValue and pricePerItemValue (obtained through the appropriate properties) and returning the result.

Method ToString (lines 79–85) returns the String representation of an Invoice object. Recall that all classes directly or indirectly inherit from class Object. Therefore, class Invoice implicitly inherits Object's ToString method. However, we want to declare a customized ToString method in Invoice that returns a String containing the values of an Invoice's instance variables. Line 79 indicates that Invoice's ToString method overrides the one defined in base class Object. We also must satisfy the requirements of the IPayable interface, which Invoice implements. Line 80 contains the keyword Implements followed by IPayable.ToString to indicate that this version of ToString also serves as the required implementation of IPayable's ToString method. Note that it is possible for the same method to both override a method of a base class and implement a method of an interface. Implementing methods GetPaymentAmount and ToString in class Invoice satisfies the implementation requirement for the methods of interface IPayable—concrete class Invoice fulfills the interface contract with the compiler.

11.7.4 Modifying Class Employee to Implement Interface IPayable

We now modify class Employee to implement interface IPayable. Figure 11.13 contains the modified Employee class. This class declaration is identical to that of Fig. 11.4 with only three exceptions. First, line 4 of Fig. 11.13 indicates that class Employee now implements interface IPayable. Second, we must implement method ToString (lines 52–56) declared in the IPayable interface, which also overrides the version declared in base class Object. Third, since Employee now implements interface IPayable, we rename CalculateEarnings to GetPaymentAmount throughout the Employee hierarchy. As with method CalculateEarnings in the Employee class of Fig. 11.4, however, it does not make sense to implement method GetPaymentAmount in abstract class Employee because we cannot calculate the earnings payment owed to a general Employee—first we must know the specific type of Employee. In Fig. 11.4, we declared method CalculateEarnings as MustOverride for this reason, so class Employee had to be declared MustInherit. This forced each concrete Employee derived class to override CalculateEarnings with an implementation.

```
1   ' Fig. 11.13: Employee.vb
2   ' Employee abstract base class implements IPayable.
3   Public MustInherit Class Employee
4      Implements IPayable
5
6      Private firstNameValue As String
7      Private lastNameValue As String
8      Private socialSecurityNumberValue As String
9
10     ' three-argument constructor
11     Public Sub New(ByVal first As String, ByVal last As String, _
12        ByVal ssn As String)
13        FirstName = first
```

Fig. 11.13 | Employee class that implements interface IPayable. (Part 1 of 2.)

```
14              LastName = last
15              SocialSecurityNumber = ssn
16      End Sub ' New
17
18      ' property FirstName
19      Public Property FirstName() As String
20          Get
21              Return firstNameValue
22          End Get
23
24          Set(ByVal first As String)
25              firstNameValue = first
26          End Set
27      End Property ' FirstName
28
29      ' property LastName
30      Public Property LastName() As String
31          Get
32              Return lastNameValue
33          End Get
34
35          Set(ByVal last As String)
36              lastNameValue = last
37          End Set
38      End Property ' LastName
39
40      ' property SocialSecurityNumber
41      Public Property SocialSecurityNumber() As String
42          Get
43              Return socialSecurityNumberValue
44          End Get
45
46          Set(ByVal ssn As String)
47              socialSecurityNumberValue = ssn
48          End Set
49      End Property ' SocialSecurityNumber
50
51      ' return String representation of Employee object
52      Public Overrides Function ToString() As String _
53          Implements IPayable.ToString
54          Return (String.Format("{0} {1}", FirstName, LastName) & vbCrLf & _
55              "social security number: " & SocialSecurityNumber)
56      End Function ' ToString
57
58      ' Note: We do not implement IPayable function GetPaymentAmount here
59      Public MustOverride Function GetPaymentAmount() As Decimal _
60          Implements IPayable.GetPaymentAmount
61  End Class ' Employee
```

Fig. 11.13 | Employee class that implements interface IPayable. (Part 2 of 2.)

In Fig. 11.13, we handle this situation similarly. Recall that when a class implements an interface, the class makes a contract with the compiler stating either that the class will implement each of the methods in the interface or that the class will be declared MustInherit. If you choose the latter option, you must declare the interface methods as Must-Override in the abstract class. Any concrete derived class of the abstract class must implement the interface methods to fulfill the base class's contract with the compiler. If the derived class does not do so, it too must be declared MustInherit. As indicated in lines 59–60, class Employee of Fig. 11.13 does not implement method GetPaymentAmount, so the class is declared MustInherit (line 3). Each direct Employee derived class inherits the base class's contract to implement method GetPaymentAmount and thus must implement this method to become a concrete class from which objects can be instantiated. A class that inherits from one of Employee's concrete derived classes will inherit an implementation of GetPaymentAmount and thus will also be a concrete class.

11.7.5 Modifying Class SalariedEmployee for Use in the IPayable Hierarchy

Figure 11.14 contains a modified version of concrete class SalariedEmployee that inherits abstract class Employee and fulfills base class Employee's contract to implement interface IPayable's GetPaymentAmount method. This SalariedEmployee class is identical to that of Fig. 11.5, but this version implements method GetPaymentAmount (lines 32–34) instead of method CalculateEarnings. These methods contain the same functionality but have different names. Recall that IPayable's GetPaymentAmount method has a more general name to be applicable to possibly disparate classes. The remaining Employee derived classes (e.g., HourlyEmployee, CommissionEmployee and BasePlusCommissionEmployee) also must be modified to contain GetPaymentAmount methods in place of CalculateEarnings methods to reflect the fact that Employee now implements IPayable. We use only SalariedEmployee in our test program in this section.

```vb
1   ' Fig. 11.14: SalariedEmployee.vb
2   ' SalariedEmployee class inherits Employee, which implements IPayable.
3   Public Class SalariedEmployee
4      Inherits Employee
5
6      Private weeklySalaryValue As Decimal
7
8      ' four-argument constructor
9      Public Sub New(ByVal first As String, ByVal last As String, _
10        ByVal ssn As String, ByVal salary As Decimal)
11        MyBase.New(first, last, ssn) ' pass to Employee constructor
12        WeeklySalary = salary ' validate and store salary
13     End Sub ' New
14
15     ' property WeeklySalary
16     Public Property WeeklySalary() As Decimal
17        Get
18           Return weeklySalaryValue
19        End Get
20
```

Fig. 11.14 | SalariedEmployee class that implements interface IPayable methods GetPaymentAmount and ToString. (Part 1 of 2.)

```
21            Set(ByVal salary As Decimal)
22                If salary < 0 Then ' validate salary
23                    weeklySalaryValue = 0
24                Else
25                    weeklySalaryValue = salary
26                End If
27            End Set
28        End Property ' WeeklySalary
29
30        ' calculate earnings; implements interface IPayable method
31        ' GetPaymentAmount that was MustOverride in base class Employee
32        Public Overrides Function GetPaymentAmount() As Decimal
33            Return WeeklySalary
34        End Function ' GetPaymentAmount
35
36        ' return String representation of SalariedEmployee object
37        Public Overrides Function ToString() As String
38            Return ("salaried employee: " & MyBase.ToString() & vbCrLf & _
39                String.Format("weekly salary {0:C}", WeeklySalary))
40        End Function ' ToString
41    End Class ' SalariedEmployee
```

Fig. 11.14 | `SalariedEmployee` class that implements interface `IPayable` methods `GetPaymentAmount` and `ToString`. (Part 2 of 2.)

When a class implements an interface, the same *is-a* relationship as inheritance applies. For example, class `Employee` implements `IPayable`, so we can say that an `Employee` *is an* `IPayable`. Objects of any classes that inherit from `Employee` are also `IPayable` objects. `SalariedEmployee` objects, for instance, are `IPayable` objects. As with inheritance relationships, an object of a class that implements an interface may be thought of as an object of the interface type. Objects of any derived classes of the class that implements the interface can also be thought of as objects of the interface type. Thus, just as we can assign the reference of a `SalariedEmployee` object to a base class `Employee` variable, we can assign the reference of a `SalariedEmployee` object to an interface `IPayable` variable. `Invoice` implements `IPayable`, so an `Invoice` object also *is an* `IPayable` object, and we can assign the reference of an `Invoice` object to an `IPayable` variable.

Software Engineering Observation 11.3

Inheritance and interfaces are similar in their implementation of the is-a *relationship. An object of a class that implements an interface may be thought of as an object of that interface type. Objects of any derived classes of a class that implements an interface can also be thought of as objects of the interface type.*

Software Engineering Observation 11.4

The is-a *relationship that exists between derived classes and base classes, and between classes that implement interfaces and the interfaces themselves, holds when passing an object to a method. If a parameter has a base class type, it can receive either a base class or derived class reference as an argument. If a parameter has an interface type, it can receive a reference to an object of any class that implements the interface.*

11.7.6 Using Interface IPayable to Process Invoices and Employees Polymorphically

Module PayableInterfaceTest (Fig. 11.15) illustrates that interface IPayable can be used to process a set of Invoices and Employees polymorphically in a single application, even though these classes represent such different kinds of things.

Line 6 declares payableObjects and assigns to it an array of four IPayable variables. Lines 9 and 12 assign the references of Invoice objects to payableObjects(0) and payableObjects(2), respectively. Lines 10–11 and 13–14 assign the references of SalariedEmployee objects to payableObjects(1) and payableObjects(3), respectively. These assignments are allowed because an Invoice *is an* IPayable, and a SalariedEmployee *is an* Employee and an Employee *is an* IPayable. Lines 20–25 use a For Each...Next statement to polymorphically process each IPayable object in payableObjects, displaying the object as a String, along with the payment amount due. Line 22 invokes method ToString via an IPayable variable to get the String representation of each object. Line 24 invokes IPayable method GetPaymentAmount to obtain the payment amount for each object in payableObjects, regardless of the actual type of the object. The output reveals that the method calls in lines 22–24 invoke the appropriate class's implementation of methods ToString and GetPaymentAmount. For instance, when currentEmployee refers to an Invoice during the first iteration of the For Each loop, class Invoice's ToString and GetPaymentAmount methods execute.

Software Engineering Observation 11.5

Using a base class reference, you can polymorphically invoke any method specified in the base class declaration (and in class Object). Using an interface reference, you can polymorphically invoke any method specified in the interface declaration.

```
1    ' Fig. 11.15: PayableInterfaceTest.vb
2    ' Testing interface IPayable.
3    Module PayableInterfaceTest
4       Sub Main()
5          ' create four-element IPayable array
6          Dim payableObjects() As IPayable = New IPayable(3) {}
7
8          ' populate array with objects that implement IPayable
9          payableObjects(0) = New Invoice("01234", "seat", 2, 375)
10         payableObjects(1) = New SalariedEmployee( _
11            "John", "Smith", "111-11-1111", 800)
12         payableObjects(2) = New Invoice("56789", "tire", 4, 79.95D)
13         payableObjects(3) = New SalariedEmployee( _
14            "Lisa", "Barnes", "888-88-8888", 1200)
15
16         Console.WriteLine( _
17            "Invoices and Employees processed polymorphically:" & vbCrLf)
18
```

Fig. 11.15 | IPayable interface test program processing Invoices and Employees polymorphically. (Part 1 of 2.)

```
19          ' generically process each element in array payableObjects
20          For Each currentPayable As IPayable In payableObjects
21             ' output currentPayable and its appropriate payment amount
22             Console.WriteLine(currentPayable.ToString() & vbCrLf & _
23                String.Format("payment due: {0:C}", _
24                currentPayable.GetPaymentAmount()) & vbCrLf)
25          Next
26       End Sub ' Main
27    End Module ' PayableInterfaceTest
```

```
Invoices and Employees processed polymorphically:

invoice:
part number: 01234(seat)
quantity: 2
price per item: $375.00
payment due: $750.00

salaried employee: John Smith
social security number: 111-11-1111
weekly salary $800.00
payment due: $800.00

invoice:
part number: 56789(tire)
quantity: 4
price per item: $79.95
payment due: $319.80

salaried employee: Lisa Barnes
social security number: 888-88-8888
weekly salary $1,200.00
payment due: $1,200.00
```

Fig. 11.15 | IPayable interface test program processing Invoices and Employees polymorphically. (Part 2 of 2.)

11.7.7 Common Interfaces of the .NET Framework Class Library (FCL)

In this section, we overview several common interfaces found in the .NET class library. These interfaces are implemented and used in the same manner as the interfaces you create. Figure 11.16 overviews a few of the more popular interfaces of the .NET class library that we use in this book.

11.8 (Optional) Software Engineering Case Study: Incorporating Inheritance and Polymorphism into the ATM System

We now revisit our ATM system design to see how it might benefit from inheritance and polymorphism. To apply inheritance, we look for commonality among classes in the system. We create an inheritance hierarchy to model similar classes in an efficient and elegant manner that enables us to process objects of these classes polymorphically. We then modify our class diagram to incorporate the new inheritance relationships. Finally, we demonstrate how to translate the inheritance aspects of our updated design into Visual Basic code.

Interface	Description
IComparable	As you learned in Chapter 3, Visual Basic contains several comparison operators (e.g., <, <=, >, >=, =, <>) that allow you to compare primitive values. However, these operators cannot be used to compare objects. Interface IComparable is used to allow objects of a class that implements the interface to be compared to one another. The interface contains one method, CompareTo, that compares the object that calls the method to the object passed as an argument to the method. Classes must implement CompareTo such that it returns a value indicating whether the object on which it is invoked is less than (negative integer return value), equal to (0 return value) or greater than (positive integer return value) the object passed as an argument, using any criteria specified by the programmer. For example, if class Employee implements IComparable, its CompareTo method could compare Employee objects by their earnings amounts. Interface IComparable is commonly used for ordering objects in a collection such as an array. We use IComparable in Chapter 25, Generics and Chapter 26, Collections.
IComponent	Implemented by any class that represents a component, including Graphical User Interface (GUI) controls (such as buttons or labels). Interface IComponent defines the behaviors that components must implement. We discuss IComponent and many GUI controls that implement this interface in Chapter 13, Graphical User Interface Concepts: Part 1 and Chapter 14, Graphical User Interface Concepts: Part 2.
IEnumerator	Used for iterating through the elements of a collection (such as an array) one element at a time. Interface IEnumerator contains method MoveNext to move to the next element in a collection, method Reset to move to the position before the first element, and property Current to return the object at the current location. We use IEnumerator in Chapter 26, Collections.

Fig. 11.16 | Common interfaces of the .NET Class Library.

In Section 4.9, we encountered the problem of representing a financial transaction in the system. Rather than create one class to represent all transaction types, we created three distinct transaction classes—BalanceInquiry, Withdrawal and Deposit—to represent the transactions that the ATM system can perform. The class diagram of Fig. 11.17 shows the attributes and operations of these classes. Note that they have one private attribute (accountNumber) and one public operation (Execute) in common. Each class requires attribute accountNumber to specify the account to which the transaction applies. Each class contains operation Execute, which the ATM invokes to perform the transaction. Clearly, BalanceInquiry, Withdrawal and Deposit represent *types of* transactions. Figure 11.17 reveals commonality among the transaction classes, so using inheritance to factor out the common features seems appropriate for designing these classes. We place the common functionality in base class Transaction and derive classes BalanceInquiry, Withdrawal and Deposit from Transaction (Fig. 11.18).

The UML specifies a relationship called a *generalization* to model inheritance. Figure 11.18 is the class diagram that models the inheritance relationship between base class Transaction and its three derived classes. The arrows with triangular hollow arrow-

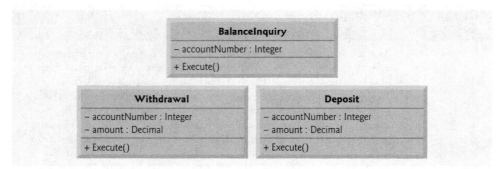

Fig. 11.17 | Attributes and operations of classes `BalanceInquiry`, `Withdrawal` and `Deposit`.

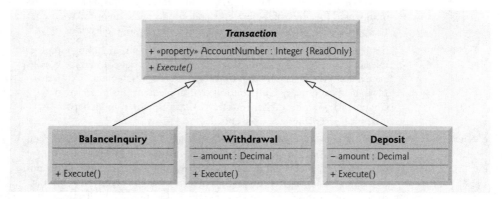

Fig. 11.18 | Class diagram modeling the generalization (i.e., inheritance) relationship between the base class `Transaction` and its derived classes `BalanceInquiry`, `Withdrawal` and `Deposit`.

heads indicate that classes `BalanceInquiry`, `Withdrawal` and `Deposit` are derived from class `Transaction` by inheritance. Class `Transaction` is said to be a generalization of its derived classes. The derived classes are said to be *specializations* of class `Transaction`.

In Fig. 11.17, you saw that classes `BalanceInquiry`, `Withdrawal` and `Deposit` share private `Integer` attribute `accountNumber`. We'd like to factor out this common attribute and place it in the base class `Transaction`. However, recall that a base class's private attributes are not accessible in derived classes. The derived classes of `Transaction` require access to attribute `accountNumber` so they can specify which `Account` to process in the `BankDatabase`. As you learned in Chapter 10, a derived class can access only the `Public` and `Protected` members of its base class. However, the derived classes in this case do not need to modify attribute `accountNumber`—they need only to access its value. For this reason, we have chosen to replace private attribute `accountNumber` in our model with the public `ReadOnly` property `AccountNumber`. Since this is a public `ReadOnly` property, it provides a only `Get` accessor to access the account number. Each derived class inherits this property, enabling the derived class to access its account number as needed to execute a transaction. We no longer list accountNumber in the second compartment of each derived class, because the three derived classes inherit property AccountNumber from Transaction.

According to Fig. 11.17, classes BalanceInquiry, Withdrawal and Deposit also share operation Execute, so base class Transaction should contain Public operation Execute. However, it does not make sense to implement Execute in class Transaction, because the functionality that this operation provides depends on the specific type of the actual transaction. We therefore declare Execute as an *abstract operation* in base class Transaction (i.e., it will become a MustOverride method in the Visual Basic implementation). This makes Transaction an abstract class (i.e., MustInherit class) and forces any class derived from Transaction that must be a concrete class (i.e., BalanceInquiry, Withdrawal and Deposit) to implement the operation Execute to make the derived class concrete. The UML requires that we place abstract class names and abstract operations in italics. Thus, in Fig. 11.18, Transaction and Execute appear in italics for the Transaction class; Execute is not italicized in derived classes BalanceInquiry, Withdrawal and Deposit. Each derived class overrides base class Transaction's Execute operation with an appropriate concrete implementation. Note that Fig. 11.18 includes operation Execute in the third compartment of classes BalanceInquiry, Withdrawal and Deposit, because each class has a different concrete implementation of the overridden operation.

As you learned in this chapter, a derived class can inherit "interface" and implementation from a base class. Compared to a hierarchy designed for implementation inheritance, one designed for interface inheritance tends to have its functionality lower in the hierarchy—a base class signifies one or more operations that should be defined by each class in the hierarchy, but the individual derived classes provide their own implementations of the operation(s). The inheritance hierarchy designed for the ATM system takes advantage of this type of inheritance, which provides the ATM with an elegant way to execute all transactions "in the general" (i.e., polymorphically). Each class derived from Transaction inherits some implementation details (e.g., property AccountNumber), but the primary benefit of incorporating inheritance into our system is that the derived classes share a common interface (e.g., abstract operation Execute). The ATM can aim a Transaction reference at any transaction, and when the ATM invokes the operation Execute through this reference, the version of Execute specific to that transaction runs automatically. For example, suppose a user chooses to perform a balance inquiry. The ATM aims a Transaction reference at a new object of class BalanceInquiry, which the Visual Basic compiler allows because a BalanceInquiry *is a* Transaction. When the ATM uses this reference to invoke Execute, BalanceInquiry's version of Execute is called.

This polymorphic approach also makes the system easily extensible. Should we wish to create a new transaction type (e.g., funds transfer or bill payment), we would simply create an additional Transaction derived class that overrides the Execute operation with a version appropriate for the new transaction type. We would need to make only minimal changes to the system code to allow users to choose the new transaction type from the main menu and for the ATM to instantiate and execute objects of the new derived class. The ATM could execute transactions of the new type using the current code, because it executes all transactions identically (through polymorphism).

As you learned earlier in the chapter, an abstract class like Transaction is one for which you never intend to (and, in fact, cannot) instantiate objects. An abstract class simply declares common attributes and behaviors for its derived classes in an inheritance hierarchy. Class Transaction defines the concept of what it means to be a transaction that has an account number and can be executed. You may wonder why we bother to include abstract operation Execute in class Transaction if Execute lacks a concrete implementation. Conceptually, we include this operation because it is the defining behavior of all transactions—executing. Technically, we must include operation Execute in base class Transaction so that the ATM (or any other class) can invoke each derived class's overridden version of this operation polymorphically via a Transaction reference.

Derived classes BalanceInquiry, Withdrawal and Deposit inherit property Account-Number from base class Transaction, but classes Withdrawal and Deposit contain the additional attribute amount that distinguishes them from class BalanceInquiry. Classes Withdrawal and Deposit require this additional attribute to store the amount of money that the user wishes to withdraw or deposit. Class BalanceInquiry has no need for such an attribute and requires only an account number to execute. Even though two of the three Transaction derived classes share the attribute amount, we do not place it in base class Transaction—we place only features common to *all* the derived classes in the base class, so that derived classes do not inherit unnecessary attributes (and operations).

Figure 11.19 presents an updated class diagram of our model that incorporates inheritance and introduces abstract base class Transaction. We model an association between class ATM and class Transaction to show that the ATM, at any given moment, either is exe-

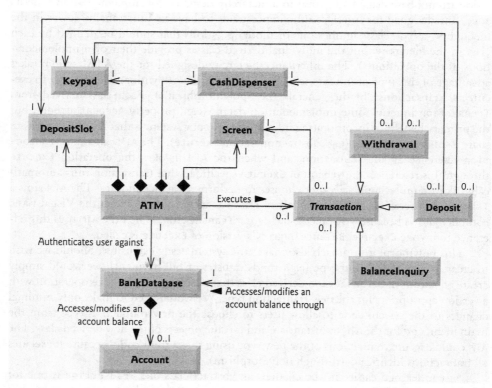

Fig. 11.19 | Class diagram of the ATM system (incorporating inheritance). Note that MustInherit class name Transaction appears in italics.

cuting a transaction or is not (i.e., zero or one objects of type Transaction exist in the system at a time). Because a Withdrawal is a type of Transaction, we no longer draw an association line directly between class ATM and class Withdrawal—derived class Withdrawal inherits base class Transaction's association with class ATM. Derived classes BalanceInquiry and Deposit also inherit this association, which replaces the previously omitted associations between classes BalanceInquiry and Deposit, and class ATM. Note again the use of triangular hollow arrowheads to indicate the specializations (i.e., derived classes) of class Transaction, as indicated in Fig. 11.18.

We also add an association between class Transaction and the BankDatabase (Fig. 11.19). All Transactions require a reference to the BankDatabase so they can access and modify account information. Each Transaction derived class inherits this reference, so we no longer model the association between class Withdrawal and the BankDatabase. Note that the association between class Transaction and the BankDatabase replaces the previously omitted associations between classes BalanceInquiry and Deposit, and the BankDatabase.

We include an association between class Transaction and the Screen because all Transactions display output to the user via the Screen. Each derived class inherits this association. Therefore, we no longer include the association previously modeled between Withdrawal and the Screen. Class Withdrawal still participates in associations with the CashDispenser and the Keypad, however—these associations apply to derived class Withdrawal but not to derived classes BalanceInquiry and Deposit, so we do not move these associations to base class Transaction.

Our class diagram incorporating inheritance (Fig. 11.19) also models classes Deposit and BalanceInquiry. We show associations between Deposit and both the DepositSlot and the Keypad. Note that class BalanceInquiry takes part in no associations other than those inherited from class Transaction—a BalanceInquiry interacts only with the BankDatabase and the Screen.

The class diagram of Fig. 9.22 showed attributes, properties and operations with visibility markers. Now we present a modified class diagram in Fig. 11.20 that includes abstract base class Transaction. This abbreviated diagram does not show inheritance relationships (these appear in Fig. 11.19), but instead shows the attributes and operations after we have employed inheritance in our system. Note that abstract class name Transaction and abstract operation name Execute in class Transaction appear in italics. To save space, as we did in Fig. 5.28, we do not include those attributes shown by associations in Fig. 11.19—we do, however, include them in the Visual Basic implementation in Appendix J. We also omit all operation parameters, as we did in Fig. 9.22—incorporating inheritance does not affect the parameters already modeled in Figs. 7.24–7.27.

Software Engineering Observation 11.6

A complete class diagram shows all the associations among classes, and all the attributes and operations for each class. When the number of class attributes, operations and associations is substantial (as in Fig. 11.19 and Fig. 11.20), a good practice that promotes readability is to divide this information between two class diagrams—one focusing on associations and the other on attributes and operations. When examining classes modeled in this fashion, it is crucial to consider both class diagrams to get a complete picture of the classes. For example, one must refer to Fig. 11.19 to observe the inheritance relationship between Transaction and its derived classes; that relationship is omitted from Fig. 11.20.

Fig. 11.20 | Class diagram after incorporating inheritance into the system.

Implementing the ATM System Design Incorporating Inheritance

In Section 9.14, we began implementing the ATM system design in Visual Basic. We now incorporate inheritance, using class Withdrawal as an example.

1. If a class A is a generalization of class B, then class B is derived from (and is a specialization of) class A. For example, abstract base class Transaction is a generalization of class Withdrawal. Thus, class Withdrawal is derived from (and is a specialization of) class Transaction. Figure 11.21 contains the shell of class Withdrawal, in which the class definition indicates the inheritance relationship between Withdrawal and Transaction (line 3).

2. If class A is an abstract class and class B is derived from class A, then class B must implement the abstract operations of class A if class B is to be a concrete class. For example, class Transaction contains abstract operation Execute, so class

```
 I    ' Class Withdrawal represents an ATM withdrawal transaction.
 2   Public Class Withdrawal
 3      Inherits Transaction
 4
 5   End Class ' Withdrawal
```

Fig. 11.21 | Visual Basic code for shell of class `Withdrawal`.

`Withdrawal` must implement this operation if we want to instantiate a `Withdrawal` object. Figure 11.22 contains the portions of the Visual Basic code for class `Withdrawal` that can be inferred from Fig. 11.19 and Fig. 11.20. Class `Withdrawal` inherits property `AccountNumber` from base class `Transaction`, so `Withdrawal` does not declare this property. Class `Withdrawal` also inherits references to the `Screen` and the `BankDatabase` from class `Transaction`, so we do not include these references in our code. Figure 11.20 specifies attribute `amount` and operation `Execute` for class `Withdrawal`. Line 6 of Fig. 11.22 declares an instance variable for attribute `amount`. Lines 16–18 declare the shell of a method for operation `Execute`. Recall that derived class `Withdrawal` must provide a concrete implementation of the `MustOverride` method `Execute` from base class `Transaction`. The `keypad` and `cashDispenser` references (lines 7–8) are instance variables whose need is apparent from class `Withdrawal`'s associations in Fig. 11.19—in the Visual Basic implementation of this class in Appendix J, a constructor initializes these references to actual objects.

We discuss the polymorphic processing of `Transactions` in Section J.2 of the ATM implementation. Class ATM performs the actual polymorphic call to method `Execute` at line 86 of Fig. J.1.

```
 I    ' Class Withdrawal represents an ATM withdrawal transaction.
 2   Public Class Withdrawal
 3      Inherits Transaction
 4
 5      ' attributes
 6      Private amount As Decimal ' amount to withdraw
 7      Private keypad As Keypad ' reference to keypad
 8      Private cashDispenser As CashDispenser ' reference to cash dispenser
 9
10      ' parameterless constructor
11      Public Sub New()
12         ' constructor body code
13      End Sub ' New
14
15      ' method that overrides Execute
16      Public Overrides Sub Execute()
17         ' Execute method body code
18      End Sub ' Execute
19   End Class ' Withdrawal
```

Fig. 11.22 | Visual Basic code for class `Withdrawal` based on Fig. 11.19 and Fig. 11.20.

ATM Case Study Wrap-Up

This concludes our object-oriented design of the ATM system. A complete Visual Basic implementation of the ATM system in 596 lines of code appears in Appendix J. This working implementation uses all of the key object-oriented programming concepts that we have covered to this point in the book, including classes, objects, encapsulation, visibility, composition, inheritance and polymorphism. The code is abundantly commented and conforms to the coding practices you've learned so far. Mastering this code is a wonderful capstone experience for you after studying the nine Software Engineering Case Study sections in Chapters 1, 3–9 and 11.

Software Engineering Case Study Self-Review Exercises

11.1 The UML uses an arrow with a _____ to indicate a generalization relationship.
a) solid filled arrowhead
b) triangular hollow arrowhead
c) diamond-shaped hollow arrowhead
d) stick arrowhead

11.2 State whether the following statement is *true* or *false*, and if *false*, explain why: The UML requires that we underline abstract class names and abstract operation names.

11.3 Write Visual Basic code to begin implementing the design for class Transaction specified in Fig. 11.19 and Fig. 11.20. Be sure to include Private references based on class Transaction's associations. Also be sure to include properties with Public Get accessors for any of the Private instance variables that the derived classes must access to perform their tasks.

Answers to Software Engineering Case Study Self-Review Exercises

11.1 b.

11.2 False. The UML requires that we italicize abstract class names and operation names.

11.3 The design for class Transaction yields the code in Fig. 11.23. In the implementation in Appendix J, a constructor initializes Private instance variables screenHandle and bankDatabaseHandle to actual objects, and ReadOnly properties ScreenReference and BankDatabaseReference access these instance variables. These properties allow classes derived from Transaction to access the ATM's screen and interact with the bank's database. Note that we use the word "Reference" in the names of the ScreenReference and BankDatabaseReference properties for clarity—we wanted to avoid property names that are the same as the class names Screen and BankDatabase, which can be confusing.

```
1    ' Abstract base class Transaction represents an ATM transaction.
2    Public MustInherit Class Transaction
3        Private accountNumberValue As Integer ' indicates account involved
4        Private screenHandle As Screen ' ATM's screen
5        Private bankDatabaseHandle As BankDatabase ' account info database
6
7        ' parameterless constructor
8        Public Sub New()
9            ' constructor body code
10       End Sub ' New
11
```

Fig. 11.23 | Visual Basic code for class Transaction based on Figs. 11.19 and 11.20. (Part 1 of 2.)

```
12        ' property AccountNumber
13        Public ReadOnly Property AccountNumber() As Integer
14           ' AccountNumber property body code
15        End Property ' AccountNumber
16
17        ' property Screen
18        Public ReadOnly Property ScreenReference() As Screen
19           ' ScreenReference property body code
20        End Property ' Screen
21
22        ' property BankDatabase
23        Public ReadOnly Property BankDatabaseReference() As BankDatabase
24           ' BankDatabaseReference property body code
25        End Property ' BankDatabase
26
27        ' perform the transaction (overridden by each derived class)
28        Public MustOverride Sub Execute()
29     End Class ' Transaction
```

Fig. 11.23 | Visual Basic code for class `Transaction` based on Figs. 11.19 and 11.20. (Part 2 of 2.)

11.9 Wrap-Up

In this chapter we discussed polymorphism, which enables you to "program in the general" rather than "program in the specific," and we showed how this makes programs more extensible. We began with an example of how polymorphism would allow a screen manager to display several "space" objects. We then demonstrated how base class and derived class references can be assigned to base class and derived class variables. We said that assigning base class references to base class variables is natural, as is assigning derived class references to derived class variables. We then discussed MustOverride methods (methods that do not provide an implementation) and MustInherit classes (abstract classes that typically have one or more MustOverride methods). You learned that abstract classes cannot be used to instantiate objects, whereas concrete classes can. We showed how abstract classes are used in an inheritance hierarchy. You learned that assigning derived class references to base class variables is natural because a derived class object *is an* object of its base class. You learned why assigning base class references to derived class variables is dangerous and why the compiler disallows such assignments (when **Option Strict** is **On**). We introduced late binding, which enables the proper methods to be called when objects at various levels of an inheritance hierarchy are referenced at execution time via base class variables. You also learned how to determine the type of an object at execution time by using a TypeOf...Is expression; you then can use TryCast to downcast from the base class type to the derived class type. You learned how interfaces even allow objects of unrelated classes to be processed polymorphically. Objects of classes that implement the same interface have an *is-a* relationship with the interface type. Finally, the chapter discussed how to declare and implement an interface.

You have studied classes, objects, encapsulation, inheritance, interfaces and polymorphism—the most essential aspects of object-oriented programming. In the next chapter, you will learn about exceptions, which are useful for handling errors during a program's execution, thus creating more robust programs.

12

Exception Handling

OBJECTIVES

In this chapter you will learn:

- What exceptions are and how they are handled.
- When to use exception handling.
- To use Try blocks to delimit code in which exceptions might occur.
- To Throw exceptions to indicate a problem.
- To use Catch blocks to specify exception handlers.
- To use the Finally block to release resources.
- The .NET exception class hierarchy.
- Exception properties.
- To create user-defined exceptions.

It is common sense to take a method and try it. If it fails, admit it frankly and try another. But above all, try something.
—Franklin Delano Roosevelt

O! throw away the worser part of it, And live the purer with the other half.
—William Shakespeare

If they're running and they don't look where they're going
I have to come out from somewhere and catch them.
—J. D. Salinger

And oftentimes excusing of a fault
Doth make the fault the worse by the excuse.
—William Shakespeare

O infinite virtue! com'st thou smiling from the world's great snare uncaught?
—William Shakespeare

12.1 Introduction

In this chapter, we introduce *exception handling*. An *exception* is an indication of a problem that occurs during a program's execution. The name "exception" comes from the fact that, although the problem can occur, it occurs infrequently. If the "rule" is that a statement normally executes correctly, then the occurrence of a problem represents the "exception to the rule." Exception handling enables you to create applications that can resolve (or handle) exceptions. In many cases, handling an exception allows a program to continue executing as if no problems were encountered. However, more severe problems may prevent a program from continuing normal execution, instead requiring the program to notify the user of the problem, then terminate in a controlled manner. The features presented in this chapter help you to write clear, *robust* and more *fault-tolerant programs* (i.e., programs that are able to deal with problems that may arise and continue executing). The style and details of Visual Basic exception handling are based in part on the work of Andrew Koenig and Bjarne Stroustrup in the C++ community. "Best practices" for exception handling in Visual Basic 2005 are specified in the Visual Studio documentation.[1]

 Error-Prevention Tip 12.1

Exception handling helps improve a program's fault tolerance.

This chapter begins with an overview of exception-handling concepts and demonstrations of basic exception-handling techniques. The chapter also overviews .NET's excep-

---

1. "Best Practices for Handling Exceptions [Visual Basic]," *.NET Framework Developer's Guide*, Visual Studio .NET Online Help (msdn2.microsoft.com/library/seyhszts(en-us,vs.80).aspx).

tion-handling class hierarchy. Programs typically request and release resources (such as files on disk) during program execution. Often, the supply of these resources is limited, or the resources can be used by only one program at a time. We demonstrate a part of the exception-handling mechanism that enables a program to use a resource, then guarantee that the resource will be released for use by other programs, even if an exception occurs. The chapter demonstrates several properties of class System.Exception (the base class of all exception classes) and discusses how you can create and use your own exception classes.

12.2 Exception Handling Overview

Programs frequently test conditions to determine how program execution should proceed. Consider the following pseudocode:

> *Perform a task*
>
> *If the preceding task did not execute correctly*
> > *Perform error processing*
>
> *Perform next task*
>
> *If the preceding task did not execute correctly*
> > *Perform error processing*
>
> ...

In this pseudocode, we begin by performing a task; then we test whether that task executed correctly. If not, we perform error processing. Otherwise, we continue with the next task. Although this form of error handling works, intermixing program logic with error-handling logic can make programs difficult to read, modify, maintain and debug—especially in large applications.

Exception handling enables you to remove error-handling code from the "main line" of the program's execution, improving program clarity and enhancing modifiability. You can decide to handle any exceptions you choose—all exceptions, all exceptions of a certain type or all exceptions of a group of related types (i.e., exception types that are related through an inheritance hierarchy). Such flexibility reduces the likelihood that errors will be overlooked, thus making programs more robust.

With programming languages that do not support exception handling, programmers often delay writing error-processing code and sometimes forget to include it. This results in less robust software products. Visual Basic enables you to deal with exception handling easily from the beginning of a project.

12.3 Example: Divide by Zero Without Exception Handling

First we demonstrate what happens when errors arise in a console application that does not use exception handling. Figure 12.1 inputs two integers from the user, then divides the first integer by the second using integer division to obtain an Integer result. In this example, we will see that an exception is ***thrown*** (i.e., an exception occurs) when a method detects a problem and is unable to handle it.

```vb
1    ' Fig. 12.1: DivideByZeroNoExceptionHandling.vb
2    ' An application that attempts to divide by zero.
3    Module DivideByZeroNoExceptionHandling
4       Sub Main()
5          ' get numerator and denominator
6          Console.Write("Please enter an integer numerator: ")
7          Dim numerator As Integer = Convert.ToInt32(Console.ReadLine())
8          Console.Write("Please enter an integer denominator: ")
9          Dim denominator As Integer = Convert.ToInt32(Console.ReadLine())
10
11         ' divide the two integers, then display the result
12         Dim result As Integer = numerator \ denominator
13         Console.WriteLine(vbCrLf & _
14            "Result: {0:D} \ {1:D} = {2:D}", numerator, denominator, result)
15      End Sub ' Main
16   End Module ' DivideByZeroNoExceptionHandling
```

```
Please enter an integer numerator: 100
Please enter an integer denominator: 7

Result: 100 \ 7 = 14
```

```
Please enter an integer numerator: 100
Please enter an integer denominator: 0

Unhandled Exception: System.DivideByZeroException:
   Attempted to divide by zero.
   at DivideByZeroNoExceptionHandling.Main()
      in C:\examples\ch12\Fig12_01\DivideByZeroNoExceptionHandling\
      DivideByZeroNoExceptionHandling.vb:line 12
```

```
Please enter an integer numerator: 100
Please enter an integer denominator: hello

Unhandled Exception: System.FormatException:
   Input string was not in a correct format.
   at System.Number.StringToNumber(String str, NumberStyles options,
      NumberBuffer& number, NumberFormatInfo info, Boolean parseDecimal)
   at System.Number.ParseInt32(String s, NumberStyles style,
      NumberFormatInfo info)
   at System.Convert.ToInt32(String value)
   at DivideByZeroNoExceptionHandling.Main()
      in C:\examples\ch12\Fig12_01\DivideByZeroNoExceptionHandling\
      DivideByZeroNoExceptionHandling.vb:line 9
```

Fig. 12.1 | Integer division without exception handling.

Running the Application

In most of the examples we have created so far, the application appears to run the same with or without debugging. As we discuss shortly, the example in Fig. 12.1 might cause errors, depending on the user's input. If you run this application using the **Debug > Start Debugging** menu option, the program pauses at the line where an exception occurs and allows you to analyze the current state of the program and debug it. We discuss the Exception Assistant in Section 12.4.3. We discuss debugging in detail in Appendix C.

In this example, we do not wish to debug the application; we simply want to see what happens when errors arise. For this reason, we execute this application from a Command Prompt window. Select **Start > All Programs > Accessories > Command Prompt** to open a Command Prompt window, then use the `cd` command to change to the application's `bin\Debug` directory. If this application resides in the directory `C:\examples\ch12\Fig12_01\DivideByZeroNoExceptionHandling` on your system, you would provide the `cd` command with the argument

```
C:\examples\ch12\Fig12_01\DivideByZeroNoExceptionHandling\bin\Debug
```

in the Command Prompt, then press *Enter* to change to the application's `Debug` directory. To execute the application, type

```
DivideByZeroNoExceptionHandling.exe
```

in the Command Prompt, then press *Enter*. If an error arises during execution, a dialog is displayed indicating that the application has encountered a problem and needs to close. The dialog also asks whether you'd like to send information about this error to Microsoft. Since we are creating this error for demonstration purposes, you should click **Don't Send**. [*Note:* On some systems a **Just-In-Time Debugging** dialog is displayed instead. If this occurs, simply click the **No** button to dismiss the dialog.] At this point, an error message describing the problem is displayed in the Command Prompt. We formatted the error messages in Fig. 12.1 for readability. [*Note:* Selecting **Debug > Start Without Debugging** (or *<Ctrl> F5*) to run the application from Visual Studio executes the application's so-called release version. The error messages produced by this version of the application may differ from those shown in Fig. 12.1 due to optimizations that the compiler performs to create an application's release version.]

Analyzing the Results

The first sample execution in Fig. 12.1 shows a successful division. In the second sample execution, the user enters 0 as the denominator. Note that several lines of information are displayed in response to the invalid input. This information—known as a *stack trace*—includes the exception name (`System.DivideByZeroException`) in a descriptive message indicating the problem that occurred and the path of execution that led to the exception, method by method. This information helps you debug a program. The first line of the error message specifies that a `DivideByZeroException` has occurred. When *division by zero* in integer arithmetic occurs, the CLR throws a ***DivideByZeroException*** (namespace System). The text after the name of the exception, "`Attempted to divide by zero,`" indicates that this exception occurred as a result of an attempt to divide by zero. Division by zero is not allowed in integer arithmetic. [*Note:* Division by zero with floating-point values is allowed. Such a calculation results in the value infinity, which is represented either by constant ***Double.PositiveInfinity*** or constant ***Double.NegativeInfinity***, depending on whether the numerator is positive or negative. These values are displayed as `Infinity` or

-Infinity. If both the numerator and denominator are zero, the result of the calculation is the constant ***Double.NaN*** ("not a number"), which is returned when a calculation's result is undefined.]

Each "at" line in the stack trace indicates a line of code in the method that was executing when the exception occurred. The "at" line contains the namespace, class name and method name in which the exception occurred (DivideByZeroNoExceptionHandling.Main), the location and name of the file in which the code resides (C:\examples\ch12\Fig12_01\DivideByZeroNoExceptionHandling\DivideByZeroNoException Handling.vb:line 12) and the line of code where the exception occurred. In this case, the stack trace indicates that the DivideByZeroException occurred when the program was executing line 12 of method Main. The first "at" line in the stack trace indicates the exception's ***throw point***—the initial point at which the exception occurred (i.e., line 12 in Main). This information makes it easy for you to see where the exception originated, and what method calls were made to get to that point in the program.

Now, let's look at a more detailed stack trace. In the third sample execution, the user enters the string "hello" as the denominator. This causes a FormatException, and another stack trace is displayed. Our earlier examples that input numeric values assumed that the user would input an integer value. However, a user could erroneously input a non-integer value. A ***FormatException*** (namespace System) occurs, for example, when Convert method ToInt32 receives a string that does not represent a valid integer. Starting from the last "at" line in the stack trace, we see that the exception was detected in line 9 of method Main. The stack trace also shows the other methods that led to the exception being thrown—Convert.ToInt32, Number.ParseInt32 and Number.StringToNumber. To perform its task, Convert.ToInt32 calls method Number.ParseInt32, which in turn calls Number.StringToNumber. The throw point occurs in Number.StringToNumber, as indicated by the first "at" line in the stack trace.

In Fig. 12.1, the program also terminates when exceptions occur and stack traces are displayed. This does not always happen—sometimes a program may continue executing even though an exception has occurred and a stack trace has been printed. In such cases, the application may produce incorrect results. The next section demonstrates how to handle exceptions to enable the program to run to normal completion.

12.4 Example: Handling DivideByZeroExceptions and FormatExceptions

Let us consider a simple example of exception handling. The application in Fig. 12.2 uses exception handling to process any DivideByZeroExceptions and FormatExceptions that might arise. The application displays two TextBoxes in which the user can type integers. When the user presses **Click To Divide**, the program invokes event handler btnDivide_Click (lines 6–33), which obtains the user's input, converts the input values to type Integer and divides the first number (numerator) by the second number (denominator). Assuming that the user provides integers as input and does not specify 0 as the denominator, btnDivide_Click displays the division result in lblOutput. However, if the user inputs a noninteger value or supplies 0 as the denominator, an exception occurs. This program demonstrates how to *catch* and *handle* (i.e., deal with) such exceptions—in this case, displaying an error message and allowing the user to enter another set of values.

Before we discuss the program's details in Sections 12.4.1–12.4.5, let's consider the sample output windows in Fig. 12.2. The window in Fig. 12.2(a) shows a successful calculation, in which the user enters the numerator 100 and the denominator 7. Note that the result (14) is an Integer, because integer division always yields an Integer result. The next two windows, Fig. 12.2(b and c), demonstrate the result of an attempt to divide by zero. In integer arithmetic, the CLR tests for division by zero and, if the denominator is

```vb
 1   ' Fig. 12.2: DivideByZeroTest.vb
 2   ' Exception handlers for FormatException and DivideByZeroException.
 3   Public Class frmDivideByZeroTest
 4      ' obtain 2 integers from the user
 5      ' and divide numerator by denominator
 6      Private Sub btnDivide_Click(ByVal sender As System.Object, _
 7         ByVal e As System.EventArgs) Handles btnDivide.Click
 8
 9         lblOutput.Text = "" ' clear Label lblOutput
10
11         ' retrieve user input and calculate quotient
12         Try
13            ' Convert.ToInt32 generates FormatException
14            ' if argument is not an integer
15            Dim numerator As Integer = Convert.ToInt32(txtNumerator.Text)
16            Dim denominator As Integer = Convert.ToInt32(txtDenominator.Text)
17
18            ' division generates DivideByZeroException
19            ' if denominator is 0
20            Dim result As Integer = numerator \ denominator
21
22            ' display result in lblOutput
23            lblOutput.Text = result.ToString()
24         Catch formatExceptionParameter As FormatException
25            MessageBox.Show("You must enter two integers.", _
26               "Invalid Number Format", MessageBoxButtons.OK, _
27               MessageBoxIcon.Error)
28         Catch divideByZeroExceptionParameter As DivideByZeroException
29            MessageBox.Show(divideByZeroExceptionParameter.Message, _
30               "Attempted to Divide by Zero", MessageBoxButtons.OK, _
31               MessageBoxIcon.Error)
32         End Try
33      End Sub ' btnDivide_Click
34   End Class ' frmDivideByZeroTest
```

(a)

Fig. 12.2 | FormatException and DivideByZeroException exception handlers. (Part 1 of 2.)

Fig. 12.2 | `FormatException` and `DivideByZeroException` exception handlers. (Part 2 of 2.)

zero, generates a `DivideByZeroException`. The program detects the exception and displays the error message dialog in Fig. 12.2(c) indicating the attempt to divide by zero. The last two output windows, Fig. 12.2(d) and Fig. 12.2(e), depict the result of inputting a non-`Integer` value—in this case, the user enters "hello" in the second `TextBox`, as shown in Fig. 12.2(d). When the user clicks **Click To Divide**, the program attempts to convert the input `Strings` into `Integer` values using method `Convert.ToInt32` (lines 15–16). If an argument passed to `Convert.ToInt32` cannot be converted to an `Integer` value, the method throws a `FormatException`. The program catches the exception and displays the error message dialog in Fig. 12.2(e) indicating that the user must enter two `Integers`.

12.4.1 Enclosing Code in a Try Block

Now we consider the user interactions and flow of control that yield the results shown in the sample output windows. The user inputs values into the `TextBoxes` that represent the numerator and denominator, then presses **Click To Divide**. At this point, the program invokes method `btnDivide_Click`. Line 9 assigns the empty string to `lblOutput` to clear any prior result in preparation for a new calculation. Lines 12–23 define a ***Try block*** enclosing the code that might throw exceptions, as well as the code that is skipped when an exception occurs. For example, the program should not display a new result in `lblOutput` (line 23) unless the calculation in line 20 completes successfully.

The two statements that read the `Integers` from the `TextBoxes` (lines 15–16) call method `Convert.ToInt32` to convert `Strings` to `Integer` values. This method throws a `FormatException` if it cannot convert its `String` argument to an `Integer`. If lines 15–16 convert the values properly (i.e., no exceptions occur), then line 20 divides the numerator by the denominator. If denominator is 0, line 20 causes the CLR to throw a `DivideByZeroException`. If line 20 does not cause an exception to be thrown, then the result is assigned to variable `result` and line 23 displays the result of the division.

12.4.2 Catching Exceptions

Exception-handling code appears in a *Catch block*. In general, when an exception occurs in a Try block, a corresponding Catch block catches the exception and handles it. The Try block in this example is followed by two Catch blocks—one that handles a Format-Exception (lines 24–27) and one that handles a DivideByZeroException (lines 28–31). A Catch block specifies an exception parameter representing the exception that the Catch block can handle. The Catch block can use the parameter's identifier (which is chosen by the programmer) to interact with a caught exception object. The type of the Catch's parameter is the type of the exception that the Catch block handles. Optionally, you can include a Catch block that does not specify an exception type or an identifier—such a Catch block catches all exception types. At least one Catch block or a *Finally block* (discussed in Section 12.6) must immediately follow a Try block.

In Fig. 12.2, the first Catch block (lines 23–27) catches FormatExceptions (thrown by method Convert.ToInt32), and the second Catch block (lines 28–31) catches Divide-ByZeroExceptions (thrown by the CLR). If an exception occurs, the program executes only the first matching Catch block. Both exception handlers in this example display an error message dialog. After either Catch block terminates, program control continues with the first statement after the last Catch block (the end of the method, in this example). We will soon take a deeper look at how this flow of control works in exception handling.

12.4.3 Uncaught Exceptions

An *uncaught exception* is an exception for which there is no matching Catch block. You saw the results of uncaught exceptions in the second and third outputs of Fig. 12.1. Recall that when exceptions occur in that example, the application terminates early (after displaying the exception's stack trace). The result of an uncaught exception depends on how you execute the program—Fig. 12.1 demonstrated the results of an uncaught exception when an application is executed in a Command Prompt. If you run the application from Visual Studio with debugging and the runtime environment detects an uncaught exception, the application pauses, and a window called the *Exception Assistant* appears indicating where the exception occurred, the type of the exception and links to helpful information on handling the exception. Figure 12.3 shows the Exception Assistant that is displayed if the user attempts to divide by zero in the application of Fig. 12.1.

12.4.4 Termination Model of Exception Handling

When a method called in a program or the CLR detects a problem, the method or the CLR throws an exception. Recall that the point in the program at which an exception occurs is called the throw point—this is an important location for debugging purposes (as we demonstrate in Section 12.7). If an exception occurs in a Try block (such as a Format-Exception being thrown as a result of the code in line 16 in Fig. 12.2), the Try block terminates immediately, and program control transfers to the first of the following Catch blocks in which the exception parameter's type matches the type of the thrown exception. In Fig. 12.2, the first Catch block catches FormatExceptions (which occur if input of an invalid type is entered); the second Catch block catches DivideByZeroExceptions (which occur if an attempt is made to divide by zero). After the exception is handled, program control does not return to the throw point because the Try block has expired (which also

Fig. 12.3 | Exception Assistant.

causes any of its local variables to go out of scope). Rather, control resumes after the last `Catch` block. This is known as the ***termination model of exception handling***. [*Note:* Some languages use the ***resumption model of exception handling***, in which after an exception is handled, control resumes just after the throw point.]

Common Programming Error 12.1

Logic errors can occur if you assume that after an exception is handled, control will return to the first statement after the throw point.

If no exceptions occur in the `Try` block, the program of Fig. 12.2 successfully completes the `Try` block by ignoring the `Catch` blocks in lines 24–27 and 28–31, and passing over line 32. Then the program executes the first statement following the `Try` and `Catch` blocks. In this example, the program reaches the end of event handler `btnDivide_Click` (line 33), so the method terminates, and the program awaits the next user interaction.

The `Try` block and its corresponding `Catch` and `Finally` blocks together form a ***Try statement***. It is important not to confuse the terms "Try block" and "Try statement"—the term "Try block" refers to the block of code following the keyword `Try` (but before any `Catch` or `Finally` blocks), while the term "Try statement" includes all the code from the opening `Try` keyword to the closing `End Try`. This includes the `Try` block, as well as any associated `Catch` blocks and `Finally` block, if there is one.

As with any other block of code, when a `Try` block terminates, local variables defined in the block go out of scope. If a `Try` block terminates due to an exception, the CLR searches for the first `Catch` block that can process the type of exception that occurred. The CLR locates the matching `Catch` by comparing the type of the thrown exception to each `Catch`'s parameter type. A match occurs if the types are identical or if the thrown exception's type is a derived class of the `Catch`'s parameter type. Once an exception is matched to a `Catch` block, the code in that block executes and the other `Catch` blocks in the `Try` statement are ignored.

12.4.5 Flow of Control When Exceptions Occur

In the sample output of Fig. 12.2(b), the user inputs 0 as the denominator. When the division in line 20 executes, a `DivideByZeroException` occurs. When the exception occurs, the Try block expires (terminates). Next, the CLR attempts to locate a matching Catch block. In this case, the first Catch block does not match—the exception type in the Catch-handler declaration is not the same as the type of the thrown exception, and FormatException is not a base class of DivideByZeroException. Therefore the program continues to search for a matching Catch block, which it finds in line 28. Line 29 displays the value of property *Message* of class Exception, which contains the error message. Note that our program never "sets" this error message attribute. This is done by the CLR when it creates the exception object.

In the sample output of Fig. 12.2(d), the user inputs hello as the denominator. When line 16 executes, Convert.ToInt32 cannot convert this String to an Integer, so Convert.ToInt32 throws a FormatException object to indicate that the method was unable to convert the String to an Integer. Once again, the Try block terminates, and the program attempts to locate a matching Catch block. A match occurs with the Catch block in line 24, so the exception handler executes and the program ignores all other exception handlers following the Try block.

Common Programming Error 12.2

Specifying a comma-separated list of parameters in a Catch block is a syntax error. A Catch block can have at most one parameter.

12.5 .NET Exception Hierarchy

In Visual Basic, the exception-handling mechanism allows only objects of class *Exception* (namespace System) and its derived classes to be thrown and caught. Visual Basic programs may interact with software components written in other .NET languages (such as C++) that do not restrict exception types. Such exceptions are wrapped by the CLR as Exception objects, so they can be caught by a Catch clause of type Exception.

This section overviews several of the .NET Framework's exception classes and focuses exclusively on exceptions that derive from class Exception. In addition, we discuss how to determine whether a particular method throws exceptions.

12.5.1 Classes ApplicationException and SystemException

Class *Exception* of namespace System is the base class of the .NET Framework exception class hierarchy. Two of the most important classes derived from Exception are *ApplicationException* and *SystemException*. ApplicationException is a base class that you can extend to create exception classes that are specific to their applications. We show how to create user-defined exception classes in Section 12.8. Programs can recover from most ApplicationExceptions and continue execution.

The CLR generates SystemExceptions, which can occur at any point during program execution. Many of these exceptions can be avoided if applications are coded properly. For example, if a program attempts to access an *out-of-range array index*, the CLR throws an exception of type *IndexOutOfRangeException* (a derived class of SystemException). Similarly, an exception occurs when a program uses an object reference to manipulate an object that does not yet exist (i.e., the reference has the value Nothing). Attempting to use a Nothing reference causes a *NullReferenceException* (another derived class of System-Exception). You saw earlier in this chapter that a DivideByZeroException occurs in integer division when a program attempts to divide by zero.

Other SystemException types thrown by the CLR include *OutOfMemoryException*, *StackOverflowException* and *ExecutionEngineException*. These are thrown when the something goes wrong that causes the CLR to become unstable. In some cases, such exceptions cannot even be caught. In general, it is best to simply log such exceptions (possibly by writing information about the problem to a file) then terminate your application.

A benefit of the exception class hierarchy is that a Catch block can catch exceptions of a particular type or—because of the *is-a* relationship of inheritance—can use a base-class type to catch exceptions in a hierarchy of related exception types. For example, Section 12.4.2 discussed the Catch block with no parameter, which catches exceptions of all types (including those that are not derived from Exception). A Catch block that specifies a parameter of type Exception can catch all exceptions that derive from Exception, because Exception is the base class of all exception classes. The advantage of this approach is that the exception handler can access the caught exception's information via the parameter in the Catch. We demonstrated accessing the information in an exception in line 29 of Fig. 12.2. We'll say more about accessing exception information in Section 12.7.

Using inheritance with exceptions enables a Catch block to catch related exceptions using a concise notation. A set of exception handlers could catch each derived-class exception type individually, but catching the base-class exception type is more concise. However, this technique makes sense only if the handling behavior is the same for a base class and all of its derived classes. Otherwise, catch each derived-class exception individually.

Common Programming Error 12.3

It is a compilation error if a Catch block that catches a base-class exception is placed before a Catch block for any of that class's derived-class types. If this were allowed, the base-class Catch block would catch all base-class and derived-class exceptions, so the derived-class exception handler would never execute.

12.5.2 Determining Which Exceptions a Method Throws

How do we determine that an exception might occur in a program? For methods of the .NET Framework classes, read the detailed descriptions of the methods in the online documentation (accessible through the IDE's **Help** menu). If a method throws an exception, its description contains a section called **Exceptions** that specifies the types of exceptions the method throws and briefly describes possible causes for the exceptions. For example, search for "Convert.ToInt32 method" in the **Index** of the Visual Studio online documentation (use the **.NET Framework** filter). Select the document entitled **Convert.ToInt32 Method**. In the document that describes the method, click the link **Convert.ToInt32(String)**. In the document that appears, the **Exceptions** section (near the bottom of the document) indicates that method Convert.ToInt32 throws two exception types—FormatException and OverflowException—and describes the reason why each might occur.

Software Engineering Observation 12.1

If a method throws exceptions, statements that invoke the method directly or indirectly should be placed in Try blocks, and those exceptions should be caught and handled.

It is more difficult to determine when the CLR throws exceptions. Such information appears in the *Visual Basic Language Specification 8.0* (http://go.microsoft.com/fwlink/?LinkId=62990). This document defines Visual Basic's syntax and specifies cases in which exceptions are thrown. Figure 12.2 demonstrated that the CLR throws a `Divide-ByZeroException` in integer arithmetic when a program attempts to divide by zero. Section 11.13.6 of the language specification discusses the division operator and when `DivideByZeroExceptions` occur.

12.6 Finally Block

Programs frequently request and release resources dynamically (i.e., at execution time). For example, a program that reads a file from disk first makes a file-open request (as we'll see in Chapter 18, Files and Streams). If that request succeeds, the program reads the contents of the file. Operating systems typically prevent more than one program from manipulating a file at once. Therefore, when a program finishes processing a file, the program should close the file (i.e., release the resource) so other programs can use it. If the file is not closed, a *resource leak* occurs. In such a case, the file resource is not available to other programs, possibly because a program using the file has not closed it.

In languages such as C and C++, in which the programmer (not the runtime) is responsible for dynamic memory management, the most common type of resource leak is a *memory leak*. A memory leak occurs when a program allocates memory (as Visual Basic programmers do via keyword `New`), but does not deallocate the memory when it is no longer needed. Normally, this is not an issue in Visual Basic, because the CLR garbage collects memory that is no longer needed by an executing program (Section 9.9). However, other kinds of resource leaks (such as unclosed files) can occur.

 Error-Prevention Tip 12.2

The CLR does not completely eliminate memory leaks. The CLR will not garbage collect an object until the program contains no more references to that object. Thus, memory leaks can occur if you inadvertently keep references to unwanted objects.

Moving Resource Release Code to a Finally Block

Typically, exceptions occur when processing resources that require explicit release. For example, a program that processes a file might receive `IOExceptions` during the processing. For this reason, file processing code normally appears in a `Try` block. Regardless of whether a program experiences exceptions while processing a file, the program should close the file when it is no longer needed. Suppose a program places all resource request and resource release code in a `Try` block. If no exceptions occur, the `Try` block executes normally and releases the resources after using them. However, if an exception occurs, the `Try` block may expire before the resource-release code can execute. We could duplicate all the resource release code in each of the `Catch` blocks, but this would make the code more difficult to modify and maintain. We could also place the resource release code after the `Try` statement; however, if the `Try` block terminates due to a return statement, code following the `Try` statement would never execute.

To address these problems, Visual Basic's exception handling mechanism provides the optional `Finally` block, which is guaranteed to execute regardless of whether the `Try` block executes successfully or an exception occurs. This makes the `Finally` block an ideal location in which to place resource-release code for resources that are acquired and manipulated in the corresponding `Try` block. If the `Try` block executes successfully, the `Finally` block executes immediately after the `Try` block terminates. If an exception occurs in the

Try block, the Finally block executes immediately after a Catch block completes. If the exception is not caught by a Catch block associated with the Try block, or if a Catch block associated with the Try block throws an exception itself, the Finally block executes before the exception is processed by the next enclosing Try block (if there is one). By placing the resource release code in a Finally block, we ensure that even if the program terminates due to an uncaught exception, the resource will be deallocated. Note that local variables in a Try block cannot be accessed in the corresponding Finally block. For this reason, variables that must be accessed in both a Try block and its corresponding Finally block should be declared before the Try block.

Error-Prevention Tip 12.3

A Finally block typically contains code to release resources acquired in the corresponding Try block, which makes the Finally block an effective mechanism for eliminating resource leaks.

Performance Tip 12.1

As a rule, resources should be released as soon as they are no longer needed in a program. This makes them available for reuse promptly.

If one or more Catch blocks follow a Try block, the Finally block is optional. However, if no Catch blocks follow a Try block, a Finally block must appear immediately after the Try block. If any Catch blocks follow a Try block, the Finally block (if there is one) appears after the last Catch block. Only whitespace and comments can separate the blocks in a Try statement.

Common Programming Error 12.4

Placing the Finally block before a Catch block is a syntax error.

Demonstrating the Finally Block

The application in Fig. 12.4 demonstrates that the Finally block always executes, regardless of whether an exception occurs in the corresponding Try block. The program consists of method Main (lines 5–37) and four other methods that Main invokes to demonstrate Finally. These methods are DoesNotThrowException (lines 40–51), ThrowException-WithCatch (lines 54–66), ThrowExceptionWithoutCatch (lines 69–81) and ThrowExceptionCatchRethrow (lines 84–103).

Line 8 of Main invokes method DoesNotThrowException. The Try block for this method outputs a message (line 43). Because the Try block does not throw any exceptions, program control ignores the Catch block (lines 44–45) and executes the Finally block (lines 46–47), which outputs a message. Program control continues with the first statement after end of the Finally block (line 50) which outputs a message indicating that the end of the method has been reached. Then, program control returns to line 11 of Main.

Throwing Exceptions Using the Throw Statement

Line 12 of Main invokes method ThrowExceptionWithCatch (lines 54–66), which begins in its Try block (lines 56–58) by outputting a message. Next, the Try block creates an Exception object and uses a ***Throw statement*** to throw the exception object (line 58). Executing the Throw statement indicates that an exception has occurred. So far you have caught exceptions thrown only by called methods. You can throw exceptions by using the

```
 1    ' Fig. 12.4: UsingExceptions.vb
 2    ' Using finally blocks.
 3    ' Demonstrate that finally always executes.
 4    Module UsingExceptions
 5       Sub Main()
 6          ' Case 1: No exceptions occur in called method
 7          Console.WriteLine("Calling DoesNotThrowException")
 8          DoesNotThrowException()
 9
10          ' Case 2: Exception occurs and is caught in called method
11          Console.WriteLine(vbCrLf & "Calling ThrowExceptionWithCatch")
12          ThrowExceptionWithCatch()
13
14          ' Case 3: Exception occurs, but is not caught in called method
15          ' because there is no catch block.
16          Console.WriteLine(vbCrLf & "Calling ThrowExceptionWithoutCatch")
17
18          ' call ThrowExceptionWithoutCatch
19          Try
20             ThrowExceptionWithoutCatch()
21          Catch
22             Console.WriteLine("Caught exception from " & _
23                "ThrowExceptionWithoutCatch in Main")
24          End Try
25
26          ' Case 4: Exception occurs and is caught in called method,
27          ' then rethrown to caller.
28          Console.WriteLine(vbCrLf & "Calling ThrowExceptionCatchRethrow")
29
30          ' call ThrowExceptionCatchRethrow
31          Try
32             ThrowExceptionCatchRethrow()
33          Catch
34             Console.WriteLine("Caught exception from " & _
35                "ThrowExceptionCatchRethrow in Main")
36          End Try
37       End Sub ' Main
38
39       ' no exceptions thrown
40       Sub DoesNotThrowException()
41          ' try block does not throw any exceptions
42          Try
43             Console.WriteLine("In DoesNotThrowException")
44          Catch
45             Console.WriteLine("This catch never executes")
46          Finally
47             Console.WriteLine("finally executed in DoesNotThrowException")
48          End Try
49
50          Console.WriteLine("End of DoesNotThrowException")
51       End Sub ' DoesNotThrowException
52
```

Fig. 12.4 | Finally always executes, regardless of whether an exception occurs. (Part 1 of 3.)

```vbnet
53      ' throws exception and catches it locally
54      Sub ThrowExceptionWithCatch()
55          ' try block throws exception
56          Try
57              Console.WriteLine("In ThrowExceptionWithCatch")
58              Throw New Exception("Exception in ThrowExceptionWithCatch")
59          Catch exceptionParameter As Exception
60              Console.WriteLine("Message: " & exceptionParameter.Message)
61          Finally
62              Console.WriteLine("finally executed in ThrowExceptionWithCatch")
63          End Try
64
65          Console.WriteLine("End of ThrowExceptionWithCatch")
66      End Sub ' ThrowExceptionWithCatch
67
68      ' throws exception and does not catch it locally
69      Sub ThrowExceptionWithoutCatch()
70          ' throw exception, but do not catch it
71          Try
72              Console.WriteLine("In ThrowExceptionWithoutCatch")
73              Throw New Exception("Exception in ThrowExceptionWithoutCatch")
74          Finally
75              Console.WriteLine("finally executed in " & _
76                  "ThrowExceptionWithoutCatch")
77          End Try
78
79          ' unreachable code; logic error
80          Console.WriteLine("End of ThrowExceptionWithoutCatch")
81      End Sub ' ThrowExceptionWithoutCatch
82
83      ' throws exception, catches it and rethrows it
84      Sub ThrowExceptionCatchRethrow()
85          ' try block throws exception
86          Try
87              Console.WriteLine("In ThrowExceptionCatchRethrow")
88              Throw New Exception("Exception in ThrowExceptionCatchRethrow")
89          Catch exceptionParameter As Exception
90              Console.WriteLine("Message: " & exceptionParameter.Message)
91
92              ' rethrow exception for further processing
93              Throw
94
95              ' code placed here would be unreachable; logic error
96          Finally
97              Console.WriteLine("finally executed in " & _
98                  "ThrowExceptionCatchRethrow")
99          End Try
100
101         ' any code placed here is never reached
102         Console.WriteLine("End of ThrowExceptionCatchRethrow")
103     End Sub ' ThrowExceptionCatchRethrow
104  End Module ' UsingExceptions
```

Fig. 12.4 | Finally always executes, regardless of whether an exception occurs. (Part 2 of 3.)

```
Calling DoesNotThrowException
In DoesNotThrowException
finally executed in DoesNotThrowException
End of DoesNotThrowException

Calling ThrowExceptionWithCatch
In ThrowExceptionWithCatch
Message: Exception in ThrowExceptionWithCatch
finally executed in ThrowExceptionWithCatch
End of ThrowExceptionWithCatch

Calling ThrowExceptionWithoutCatch
In ThrowExceptionWithoutCatch
finally executed in ThrowExceptionWithoutCatch
Caught exception from ThrowExceptionWithoutCatch in Main

Calling ThrowExceptionCatchRethrow
In ThrowExceptionCatchRethrow
Message: Exception in ThrowExceptionCatchRethrow
finally executed in ThrowExceptionCatchRethrow
Caught exception from ThrowExceptionCatchRethrow in Main
```

Fig. 12.4 | Finally always executes, regardless of whether an exception occurs. (Part 3 of 3.)

Throw statement. Just as with exceptions thrown by the FCL's methods and the CLR, this indicates to client applications that an error has occurred. A Throw statement specifies an object to be thrown. The operand of a Throw statement can be of type Exception or of any type derived from class Exception.

Common Programming Error 12.5

It is a compilation error if the argument of a Throw—an exception object—is not of class Exception or one of its derived classes.

The String passed to the constructor becomes the exception object's error message. When a Throw statement in a Try block executes, the Try block expires immediately, and program control continues with the first matching Catch block (lines 59–60) following the Try block. In this example, the type thrown (Exception) matches the type specified in the Catch, so line 60 outputs a message indicating the exception that occurred. Then, the Finally block (lines 61–62) executes and outputs a message. At this point, program control continues with the first statement after the end of the Finally block (line 65), which outputs a message indicating that the end of the method has been reached. Program control then returns to Main. In line 60, note that we use the exception object's Message property to retrieve the error message associated with the exception (i.e., the message passed to the Exception constructor). Section 12.7 discusses several properties of class Exception.

Lines 19–24 of Main define a Try statement in which Main invokes method ThrowExceptionWithoutCatch (lines 69–81). The Try block enables Main to catch any exceptions thrown by ThrowExceptionWithoutCatch. The Try block in lines 71–73 of ThrowExceptionWithoutCatch begins by outputting a message. Next, the Try block throws an Exception (line 73) and expires immediately.

Normally, program control would continue at the first Catch following this Try block. However, this Try block does not have any Catch blocks. Therefore, the exception is not caught in method ThrowExceptionWithoutCatch. Program control proceeds to the Finally block (lines 74–76), which outputs a message. At this point, program control returns to Main—any statements appearing after the Finally block (e.g., line 80) do not execute. In this example, such statements could cause logic errors, because the exception thrown in line 73 is not caught. In Main, the Catch block in lines 21–23 catches the exception and displays a message indicating that the exception was caught in Main.

Rethrowing Exceptions

Lines 31–36 of Main define a Try statement in which Main invokes method ThrowExceptionCatchRethrow (lines 84–103). The Try statement enables Main to catch any exceptions thrown by ThrowExceptionCatchRethrow. The Try statement in lines 86–99 of ThrowExceptionCatchRethrow begins by outputting a message. Next, the Try block throws an Exception (line 88). The Try block expires immediately, and program control continues at the first Catch (lines 89–95) following the Try block. In this example, the type thrown (Exception) matches the type specified in the Catch, so line 90 outputs the exception's message, which in this case indicates where the exception was thrown. Line 93 uses the Throw statement to *rethrow* the exception. This indicates that the Catch block performed partial processing of the exception and now is passing the exception back to the calling method (in this case, Main) for further processing.

You can also rethrow an exception with a version of the Throw statement which takes an operand that is the reference to the exception that was caught. It's important to note, however, that this form of Throw statement resets the throw point, so the original throw point's stack trace information is lost. Section 12.7 demonstrates using a Throw statement with an operand from a Catch block. In that section, you will see that after an exception is caught, you can create and throw a different type of exception object from the Catch block and you can include the original exception as part of the new exception object. Class library designers often do this to customize the exception types thrown from methods in their class libraries or to provide additional debugging information.

The exception handling in method ThrowExceptionCatchRethrow does not complete, because the the method rethrows the exception with the Throw statement in line 93. This causes method ThrowExceptionCatchRethrow to terminate and return control to Main. Once again, the Finally block (lines 96–98) executes and outputs a message before control returns to Main. When control returns to Main, the Catch block in lines 33–35 catches the exception and displays a message indicating that the exception was caught. Then the program terminates.

Returning After a Finally Block

Note that the next statement to execute after a Finally block terminates depends on the exception-handling state. If the Try block successfully completes, or if a Catch block catches and handles an exception, the program continues its execution with the next statement after the Finally block. However, if an exception is not caught, or if a Catch block rethrows an exception, program control continues in the next enclosing Try block, which could be in the calling method or in one of its callers. It also is possible to nest a Try statement in a Try block; in such a case, the outer Try statement's Catch blocks would process any exceptions that were not caught in the inner Try statement. If a Try block executes and has a corresponding Finally block, the Finally block executes even if the Try block terminates due to a Return statement—the Return occurs after executing the Finally block.

Common Programming Error 12.6

Throwing an exception from a Finally block can be dangerous. If an uncaught exception is awaiting processing when the Finally block executes, and the Finally block throws a new exception that is not caught in the Finally block, the first exception is lost, and the new exception is passed to the next enclosing Try block.

Error-Prevention Tip 12.4

When placing code that can throw an exception in a Finally block, always enclose the code in a Try statement that catches the appropriate exception types. This prevents the loss of any uncaught and rethrown exceptions that occur before the Finally block executes.

Software Engineering Observation 12.2

Do not place Try blocks around every statement that might throw an exception, because this can make programs difficult to read. It is better to place one Try block around a significant portion of code, and follow this Try block with Catch blocks that handle each of the possible exceptions. Then follow the Catch blocks with a single Finally block. Separate Try blocks should be used when it is important to distinguish between multiple statements that can throw the same exception type.

The Using Statement

Recall from earlier in this section that resource-release code should be placed in a Finally block to ensure that a resource is released, regardless of whether exceptions occurred when the resource was used in the corresponding Try block. An alternative notation—the **Using** statement—simplifies writing code in which you obtain a resource, use the resource in a Try block and release the resource in a corresponding Finally block. For example, a file-processing application (Chapter 18) could process a file with a Using statement to ensure that the file is closed properly when it is no longer needed. The resource must be an object that implements the IDisposable interface and therefore has a Dispose method. The general form of a Using statement is

```
Using exampleObject As New ExampleObject()
    exampleObject.SomeMethod()
End Using
```

where ExampleObject is a class that implements the IDisposable interface. This code creates an object of type ExampleObject and uses it in a statement, then calls its Dispose method to release any resources used by the object. The Using statement implicitly places the code in its body in a Try block with a corresponding Finally block that calls the object's Dispose method. For instance, the preceding code is equivalent to

```
Dim exampleObject As New ExampleObject()

Try
    exampleObject.SomeMethod()
Finally
    If Not (exampleObject Is Nothing) Then
        exampleObject.Dispose()
    End If
End Try
```

Note that the If statement ensures that exampleObject still references an object; otherwise, a NullReferenceException might occur. You can read more about the Using statement in Section 10.13 of the *Visual Basic Language Specification*.

12.7 Exception Properties

As we discussed in Section 12.5, exception types derive from class Exception, which has several properties. These frequently are used in error messages indicating a caught exception. Two important properties are Message and *StackTrace*.

Property Message stores the error message associated with an Exception object. This message can be a default message associated with the exception type or a customized message passed to an Exception object's constructor when the Exception object is thrown.

Property StackTrace contains a (normally lengthy) String that represents the *method-call stack*. Recall that the runtime environment at all times keeps a list of open method calls that have been made but have not yet returned. The StackTrace represents the series of methods that have not finished processing at the time the exception occurs.

Error-Prevention Tip 12.5

*A stack trace shows the complete method-call stack at the time an exception occurred. This enables you to view the series of method calls that led to the exception. Information in the stack trace includes the names of the methods on the call stack at the time of the exception, the names of the classes in which the methods are defined and the names of the namespaces in which the classes are defined. The IDE creates **program database (PDB) files** to maintain the debugging information for your projects. If the PDB file that contains the debugging information for the method is available, the stack trace also includes line numbers; the first line number indicates the throw point, and subsequent line numbers indicate the locations from which the methods in the stack trace were called.*

Property InnerException

Another property used frequently by class-library programmers is *InnerException*. Typically, class library programmers "wrap" exception objects caught in their code so they then can throw new exception types that are specific to their libraries. For example, a programmer implementing an accounting system might have some account-number processing code in which account numbers are input as Strings but represented as Integers in the code. Recall that a program can convert Strings to Integer values with Convert.ToInt32, which throws a FormatException when it encounters an invalid number format. When an invalid account number format occurs, the accounting system programmer might wish to employ a different error message than the default message supplied by FormatException or might wish to indicate a new exception type, such as InvalidAccountNumberFormatException. In such cases, the programmer would provide code to catch the FormatException, then create an appropriate type of Exception object in the Catch block and pass the original exception as one of the constructor arguments. The original exception object becomes the InnerException of the new exception object. When an InvalidAccountNumberFormatException occurs in code that uses the accounting system library, the Catch block that catches the exception can obtain a reference to the original exception via property InnerException. Thus the exception indicates both that the user specified an invalid account number and that the problem was an invalid number format.

If the InnerException property is Nothing, this indicates that the exception was not caused by another exception.

Other Exception Properties

Class Exception provides other properties, including *HelpLink*, *Source* and *TargetSite*. Property HelpLink specifies the location of the help file that describes the problem that occurred. This property is Nothing if no such file exists. Property Source specifies the name of the application where the exception occurred. Property TargetSite specifies the method where the exception originated.

Demonstrating Exception Properties and Stack Unwinding

Our next example (Fig. 12.5) demonstrates properties Message, StackTrace and Inner-Exception, and method ToString, of class Exception. In addition, the example introduces *stack unwinding*—when an exception is thrown but not caught in a particular scope, the method-call stack is "unwound," and an attempt is made to catch the exception in the next outer Try block. We keep track of the methods on the call stack as we discuss property StackTrace and the stack-unwinding mechanism. To see the proper stack trace, you should execute this program using steps similar to those presented in Section 12.3.

Program execution begins with Main, which becomes the first method on the method call stack. Line 9 of the Try block in Main invokes Method1 (declared in lines 29–31), which becomes the second method on the stack. If Method1 throws an exception, the Catch block in lines 10–24 handles the exception and outputs information about the exception that occurred. Line 30 of Method1 invokes Method2 (lines 34–36), which becomes the third method on the stack. Then line 35 of Method2 invokes Method3 (lines 39–48), which becomes the fourth method on the stack.

```vb
1    ' Fig. 12.5: Properties.vb
2    ' Stack unwinding and Exception class properties.
3    ' Demonstrates using properties Message, StackTrace and InnerException.
4    Module Properties
5       Sub Main()
6          ' call Method1; any Exception generated is caught
7          ' in the catch block that follows
8          Try
9             Method1()
10         Catch exceptionParameter As Exception
11            ' output the string representation of the Exception, then output
12            ' properties InnerException, Message and StackTrace
13            Console.WriteLine("exceptionParameter.ToString: " & _
14               vbCrLf & "{0}" & vbCrLf, _
15               exceptionParameter.ToString())
16            Console.WriteLine("exceptionParameter.Message: " & _
17               vbCrLf & "{0}" & vbCrLf, _
18               exceptionParameter.Message)
19            Console.WriteLine("exceptionParameter.StackTrace: " & _
20               vbCrLf & "{0}" & vbCrLf, _
21               exceptionParameter.StackTrace)
```

Fig. 12.5 | Exception properties and stack unwinding. (Part 1 of 3.)

```
22            Console.WriteLine("exceptionParameter.InnerException: " & _
23                vbCrLf & "{0}" & vbCrLf, _
24                exceptionParameter.InnerException.ToString())
25        End Try
26    End Sub ' Main
27
28    ' calls Method2
29    Sub Method1()
30        Method2()
31    End Sub ' Method1
32
33    ' calls Method3
34    Sub Method2()
35        Method3()
36    End Sub ' Method2
37
38    ' throws an Exception containing an InnerException
39    Sub Method3()
40        ' attempt to convert string to integer
41        Try
42            Convert.ToInt32("Not an integer")
43        Catch formatExceptionParameter As FormatException
44            ' wrap FormatException in new Exception
45            Throw New Exception("Exception occurred in Method3", _
46                formatExceptionParameter)
47        End Try
48    End Sub ' Method3
49 End Module ' Properties
```

```
exceptionParameter.ToString:
System.Exception: Exception occurred in Method3 --->
   System.FormatException: Input string was not in a correct format.
   at System.Number.StringToNumber(String str, NumberStyles options,
      NumberBuffer& number, NumberFormatInfo info, Boolean parseDecimal)
   at System.Number.ParseInt32(String s, NumberStyles style,
      NumberFormatInfo info)
   at System.Convert.ToInt32(String value)
   at Properties.Method3() in C:\examples\ch12\Fig12_04\Properties\
      Properties.vb:line 42
   --- End of inner exception stack trace ---
   at Properties.Method3() in C:\examples\ch12\Fig12_04\Properties\
      Properties.vb:line 45
   at Properties.Method2() in C:\examples\ch12\Fig12_04\Properties\
      Properties.vb:line 35
   at Properties.Method1() in C:\examples\ch12\Fig12_04\Properties\
      Properties.vb:line 30
   at Properties.Main() in C:\examples\ch12\Fig12_04\Properties\
      Properties.vb:line 9

exceptionParameter.Message:
Exception occurred in Method3
```

(continued on next page...)

Fig. 12.5 | Exception properties and stack unwinding. (Part 2 of 3.)

```
exceptionParameter.StackTrace:
    at Properties.Method3() in C:\examples\ch12\Fig12_04\Properties\
    Properties.vb:line 45
    at Properties.Method2() in C:\examples\ch12\Fig12_04\Properties\
    Properties.vb:line 35
    at Properties.Method1() in C:\examples\ch12\Fig12_04\Properties\
    Properties.vb:line 30
    at Properties.Main() in C:\examples\ch12\Fig12_04\Properties\
    Properties.vb:line 9

exceptionParameter.InnerException:
System.FormatException: Input string was not in a correct format.
    at System.Number.StringToNumber(String str, NumberStyles options,
    NumberBuffer& number, NumberFormatInfo info, Boolean parseDecimal)
    at System.Number.ParseInt32(String s, NumberStyles style,
    NumberFormatInfo info)
    at System.Convert.ToInt32(String value)
    at Properties.Method3() in C:\examples\ch12\Fig12_04\Properties\
    Properties.vb:line 42
```

Fig. 12.5 | Exception properties and stack unwinding. (Part 3 of 3.)

At this point, the method-call stack (from top to bottom) for the program is:

```
Method3
Method2
Method1
Main
```

The method called most recently (Method3) appears at the top of the stack; the first method called (Main) appears at the bottom. The Try statement (lines 41–47) in Method3 invokes Convert.ToInt32 (line 42), which attempts to convert a String to an Integer. At this point, Convert.ToInt32 becomes the fifth and final method on the call stack.

Throwing an Exception with an InnerException

Because the argument to Convert.ToInt32 is not in Integer format, line 42 throws a FormatException that is caught in line 43 of Method3. When the exception occurs, the call to Convert.ToInt32 terminates, so the method is removed (or unwound) from the method-call stack. The Catch block in Method3 then creates and throws an Exception object. The first argument to the Exception constructor is the custom error message for our example, "Exception occurred in Method3". The second argument is the InnerException—the FormatException that was caught. The StackTrace for this new exception object reflects the point at which the exception was thrown (line 45). Now Method3 terminates, because the exception thrown in the Catch block is not caught in the method body. Thus, control returns to the statement that invoked Method3 in the prior method in the call stack (Method2). This removes, or *unwinds*, Method3 from the method-call stack.

When control returns to line 35 in Method2, the CLR determines that line 35 is not in a Try block. Therefore the exception cannot be caught in Method2, and Method2 terminates. This unwinds Method2 from the call stack and returns control to line 30 in Method1.

Here again, line 30 is not in a Try block, so Method1 cannot catch the exception. The method terminates and is unwound from the call stack, returning control to line 9 in Main, which *is* located in a Try block. The Try block in Main expires and the Catch block (lines 10–24) catches the exception. The Catch block uses method ToString and properties Message, StackTrace and InnerException to create the output. Note that stack unwinding continues until a Catch block catches the exception or the program terminates.

Displaying Information About the Exception

The first block of output (which we reformatted for readability) in Fig. 12.5 contains the exception's String representation, which is returned from method ToString. The String begins with the name of the exception class followed by the Message property value. The next four items present the stack trace of the InnerException object. The remainder of the block of output shows the StackTrace for the exception thrown in Method3. Note that the StackTrace represents the state of the method-call stack at the throw point of the exception, rather than at the point where the exception eventually is caught. Each Stack-Trace line that begins with "at" represents a method on the call stack. These lines indicate the method in which the exception occurred, the file in which the method resides and the line number of the throw point in the file. Note that the inner-exception information includes the inner exception stack trace.

Error-Prevention Tip 12.6

When catching and rethrowing an exception, provide additional debugging information in the rethrown exception. To do so, create an Exception object containing more specific debugging information, then pass the original caught exception to the new exception object's constructor to initialize the InnerException property.

The next block of output (two lines) simply displays the Message property's value (Exception occurred in Method3) of the exception thrown in Method3.

The third block of output displays the StackTrace property of the exception thrown in Method3. Note that this StackTrace property contains the stack trace starting from line 45 in Method3, because that is the point at which the Exception object was created and thrown. The stack trace always begins with the exception's throw point.

Finally, the last block of output displays the String representation of the InnerException property, which includes the namespace and class name of the exception object, as well as its Message and StackTrace properties.

12.8 User-Defined Exception Classes

In many cases, you can use existing exception classes from the .NET Framework Class Library to indicate exceptions that occur in your programs. However, in some cases, you might wish to create new exception classes specific to the problems that occur in your programs. *User-defined exception classes* should derive directly or indirectly from class ApplicationException of namespace System.

Good Programming Practice 12.1

Associating each type of malfunction with an appropriately named exception class improves program clarity.

Software Engineering Observation 12.3

Before creating a user-defined exception class, investigate the existing exceptions in the .NET Framework Class Library to determine whether an appropriate exception type already exists.

Figures 12.6 and 12.7 demonstrate a user-defined exception class. Class Negative-NumberException (Fig. 12.6) is a user-defined exception class representing exceptions that occur when a program performs an illegal operation on a negative number, such as attempting to calculate its square root.

According to Microsoft's "Best Practices for Handling Exceptions [Visual Basic]," user-defined exceptions should extend class ApplicationException, have a class name that ends with "Exception" and define three constructors: a parameterless constructor; a constructor that receives a String argument (the error message); and a constructor that receives a String argument and an Exception argument (the error message and the inner exception object). Defining these three constructors makes your exception class more flexible, allowing other programmers to easily use and extend it.

NegativeNumberExceptions most frequently occur during arithmetic operations, so it seems logical to derive class NegativeNumberException from class Arithmetic-Exception. However, class ArithmeticException derives from class SystemException— the category of exceptions thrown by the CLR. Recall that user-defined exception classes should inherit from ApplicationException rather than SystemException.

Class SquareRootForm (Fig. 12.7) demonstrates our user-defined exception class. The application enables the user to input a numeric value, then invokes method SquareRoot (lines 6–14) to calculate the square root of that value. To perform this calculation, SquareRoot invokes class Math's Sqrt method, which receives a Double value as its argument. Normally, if the argument is negative, method Sqrt returns NaN. In this program, we would like to prevent the user from calculating the square root of a negative number. If the numeric value that the user enters is negative, the SquareRoot method throws a

```vb
1   ' Fig. 12.6: NegativeNumberException.vb
2   ' NegativeNumberException represents exceptions caused by
3   ' illegal operations performed on negative numbers.
4   Public Class NegativeNumberException : Inherits ApplicationException
5       ' default constructor
6       Public Sub New()
7           MyBase.New("Illegal operation for a negative number")
8       End Sub ' New
9
10      ' constructor for customizing error message
11      Public Sub New(ByVal messageValue As String)
12          MyBase.New(messageValue)
13      End Sub ' New
14
15      ' constructor for customizing the exception's error
16      ' message and specifying the InnerException object
17      Public Sub New(ByVal messageValue As String, ByVal inner As Exception)
18          MyBase.New(messageValue, inner)
19      End Sub ' New
20  End Class ' NegativeNumberException
```

Fig. 12.6 | ApplicationException derived class thrown when a program performs an illegal operation on a negative number.

NegativeNumberException (lines 9–10). Otherwise, SquareRoot invokes class Math's method Sqrt to compute the square root (line 12).

When the user inputs a value and clicks the **Calculate Square Root** button, the program invokes event handler SquareRootButton_Click (lines 17–37). The Try statement (lines 23–36) attempts to invoke SquareRoot using the value input by the user. If the user input is not a valid number, a FormatException occurs, and the Catch block in lines 28–31 processes the exception. If the user inputs a negative number, method SquareRoot throws a NegativeNumberException (lines 9–10); the Catch block in lines 32–35 catches and handles this type of exception.

```vb
1   ' Fig. 12.7: SquareRootTest.vb
2   ' Demonstrating a user-defined exception class.
3   Public Class frmSquareRootTest
4       ' computes square root of parameter; throws
5       ' NegativeNumberException if parameter is negative
6       Public Function SquareRoot(ByVal value As Double) As Double
7           ' if negative operand, throw NegativeNumberException
8           If value < 0 Then
9               Throw New NegativeNumberException( _
10                  "Square root of negative number not permitted")
11          Else
12              Return Math.Sqrt(value) ' compute square root
13          End If
14      End Function ' SquareRoot
15
16      ' obtain user input, convert to double, calculate square root
17      Private Sub btnSquareRoot_Click(ByVal sender As System.Object, _
18          ByVal e As System.EventArgs) Handles btnSquareRoot.Click
19
20          lblOutput.Text = "" ' clear lblOutput
21
22          ' catch any NegativeNumberException thrown
23          Try
24              Dim result As Double = _
25                  SquareRoot(Convert.ToDouble(txtInput.Text))
26
27              lblOutput.Text = result.ToString()
28          Catch formatExceptionParameter As FormatException
29              MessageBox.Show(formatExceptionParameter.Message, _
30                  "Invalid Number Format", MessageBoxButtons.OK, _
31                  MessageBoxIcon.Error)
32          Catch negativeNumberExceptionParameter As NegativeNumberException
33              MessageBox.Show(negativeNumberExceptionParameter.Message, _
34                  "Invalid Operation", MessageBoxButtons.OK, _
35                  MessageBoxIcon.Error)
36          End Try
37      End Sub ' btnSquareRoot_Click
38  End Class ' frmSquareRootTest
```

Fig. 12.7 | SquareRootForm class throws an exception if an error occurs when calculating the square root. (Part 1 of 2.)

Fig. 12.7 | `SquareRootForm` class throws an exception if an error occurs when calculating the square root. (Part 2 of 2.)

12.9 Wrap-Up

In this chapter, you learned how to use exception handling to deal with errors in an application. We showed how exception handling enables you to remove error-handling code from the "main line" of the program's execution. You saw exception handling in the context of a divide-by-zero example. You learned how to use Try blocks to enclose code that may throw an exception, and how to use Catch blocks to deal with exceptions that may arise. We discussed the termination model of exception handling, in which after an exception is handled, program control does not return to the throw point. We also discussed several important classes of the .NET Exception hierarchy, including ApplicationException (from which user-defined exception classes are derived) and SystemException. You learned how to use the Finally block to release resources whether or not an exception occurs, and how to throw and rethrow exceptions with the Throw statement. We also discussed how the Using statement can be used to automate the process of releasing a resource. You then learned how to obtain information about an exception using Exception properties Message, StackTrace and InnerException, and method ToString. You learned how to create your own exception classes. In the next two chapters, we present an in-depth treatment of graphical user interfaces. In these chapters and throughout the rest of the book, we use exception handling to make our examples more robust.

13

Graphical User Interface Concepts: Part 1

. . . The user should feel in control of the computer; not the other way around. This is achieved in applications that embody three qualities: responsiveness, permissiveness, and consistency.
—Apple Computer, Inc.

All the better to see you with, my dear.
—The Big Bad Wolf to Little Red Riding Hood

. . .the wisest prophets make sure of the event first.
—Horace Walpole

OBJECTIVES

In this chapter you will learn:

- Design principles of graphical user interfaces (GUIs).

- How to create graphical user interfaces.

- How to process events that are generated by user interactions with GUI controls.

- The namespaces that contain the classes for graphical user interface controls and event handling.

- How to create and manipulate Button, Label, RadioButton, CheckBox, TextBox, Panel and NumericUpDown controls.

- How to add descriptive ToolTips to GUI controls.

- How to process mouse and keyboard events.

13.1 Introduction

A graphical user interface (GUI) allows a user to interact visually with a program. A GUI (pronounced "GOO-ee") gives a program a distinctive look-and-feel.

Look-and-Feel Observation 13.1

Consistent user interfaces enable a user to learn new applications faster because the applications have the same look-and-feel.

As an example of a GUI, consider Fig. 13.1, which shows an Internet Explorer Web browser window containing various GUI controls. Near the top of the window, there is a menu bar containing the menus **File**, **Edit**, **View**, **Favorites**, **Tools** and **Help**. Below the menu bar is a set of buttons, each with a defined task in Internet Explorer, such as returning to the previously viewed Web page, printing the current page or refreshing the page. Below these buttons lies a combobox, in which users can type the locations of Web sites they wish to visit. To the left of the combobox is a label (**Address**) that indicates the combobox's purpose (in this case, entering the location of a Web site). Scrollbars are located at the right side and bottom of the window. Usually, scrollbars appear when a window contains more information than can be displayed in its viewable area. Scrollbars enable a user to view different portions of the window's contents. These controls form a user-friendly interface through which the user interacts with Internet Explorer.

GUIs are built from GUI controls (which are sometimes called *components* or *widgets*—short for *window gadgets*). GUI controls are objects that can display information

Label   Button   Menu   Title bar   Menu bar   Combobox   Scrollbars

Fig. 13.1 | GUI controls in an Internet Explorer window.

on the screen or enable users to interact with an application via the mouse, keyboard or some other form of input (such as voice commands). Several common GUI controls are listed in Fig. 13.2. In the sections that follow and in Chapter 14, Graphical User Interface Concepts: Part 2, we discuss each of these in detail. Chapter 14 also explores the features and properties of additional GUI controls.

Control	Description
Label	Displays images or uneditable text.
TextBox	Enables the user to enter data via the keyboard. Also can be used to display editable or uneditable text.
Button	Triggers an event when clicked with the mouse.
CheckBox	Specifies an option that can be selected (checked) or unselected (not checked).
ComboBox	Provides a drop-down list of items from which the user can make a selection either by clicking an item in the list or by typing in a box.
ListBox	Provides a list of items from which the user can make a selection by clicking an item in the list. Multiple elements can be selected.
Panel	A container in which controls can be placed and organized.
NumericUpDown	Enables the user to select from a range of numeric input values.

Fig. 13.2 | Some basic GUI controls.

13.2 Windows Forms

Windows Forms are used to create the GUIs for programs. A Form is a graphical element that appears on your computer's desktop; it can be a dialog, a window or an *MDI window* (*multiple document interface window*)—discussed in Chapter 14. A *component* is an instance of a class that implements the *IComponent interface*, which defines the behaviors that components must implement, such as how the component is loaded. A control, such as a Button or Label, has a graphical representation at runtime. Some components lack graphical representations (e.g., class Timer of namespace System.Windows.Forms—see Chapter 14). Such components are not visible at execution time.

Figure 13.3 displays the Windows Forms controls and components from the Visual Basic **Toolbox**. The controls and components are organized into categories by functionality. Selecting the category **All Windows Forms** at the top of the **Toolbox** allows you to view all the controls and components from the other tabs in one list (as shown in Fig. 13.3). In this chapter and the next, we discuss many of these controls and components. To add a control or component to a Form, select that control or component from the **Toolbox** and drag it onto the Form. To deselect a control or component, select the **Pointer** item in the **Toolbox** (the icon at the top of the list).

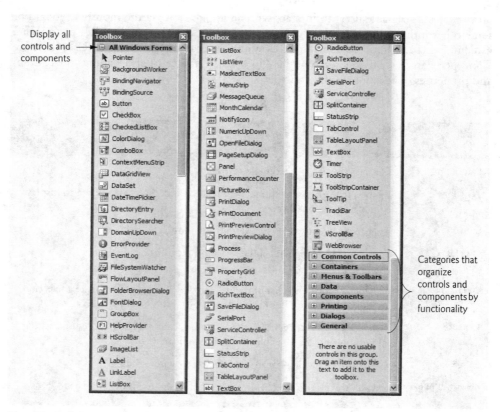

Fig. 13.3 | Components and controls for Windows Forms.

When there are several windows on the screen, the ***active window*** is the frontmost and has a highlighted title bar—typically darker than the other windows on the screen. A window becomes the active window when the user clicks somewhere inside it. The active window is said to "have the *focus*." For example, in Visual Studio the active window is the **Toolbox** when you are selecting an item from it, or the **Properties** window when you are editing a control's properties.

A Form is a ***container*** for controls and components. When you drag a control or component from the **Toolbox** onto the Form, Visual Studio generates code that instantiates the object and sets its basic properties to default values. This code is updated when the control or component's properties are modified in the IDE. If a control or component is removed from the Form, the generated code for that control is deleted. The generated code is placed by the IDE in a separate file using partial classes (introduced in Section 9.6). Although we could write this code ourselves, it is much easier to create and modify controls and components using the **Toolbox** and **Properties** windows and allow Visual Studio to handle the details. We introduced visual programming concepts in Chapter 2. In this chapter and the next, we use visual programming to build more substantial GUIs.

Each control or component we present in this chapter is located in namespace System.Windows.Forms. To create a Windows application, you generally create a Windows Form, set its properties, add controls to the Form, set their properties and implement event handlers (methods) that respond to events generated by the controls. Figure 13.4 lists common Form properties, methods and events.

Form properties, methods and an event	Description
Common Properties	
AcceptButton	Button that is clicked when *Enter* is pressed.
AutoScroll	Boolean value that allows or disallows scrollbars when needed.
CancelButton	Button that is clicked when the *Escape* key is pressed.
FormBorderStyle	Border style for the Form (e.g., none, single, three-dimensional).
Font	Font of text displayed on the Form, and the default font for controls added to the Form.
Text	Text in the Form's title bar.
Common Methods	
Close	Closes a Form and releases all resources, such as the memory used for the Form's controls and components. A closed Form cannot be reopened.
Hide	Hides a Form, but does not destroy the Form or release its resources.
Show	Displays a hidden Form.

Fig. 13.4 | Common Form properties, methods and an event. (Part 1 of 2.)

Form properties, methods and an event	Description
Common Event	
Load	Occurs before a Form is displayed to the user. The handler for this event is displayed in the Visual Studio editor when you double click the Form in the Visual Studio designer.

Fig. 13.4 | Common Form properties, methods and an event. (Part 2 of 2.)

When you create controls and event handlers, Visual Studio generates much of the GUI-related code. In visual programming, the IDE maintains GUI-related code and you write the bodies of the event handlers to indicate what actions the program should take when particular events occur.

13.3 Event Handling

Normally, a user interacts with an application's GUI to indicate the tasks that the application should perform. For example, when you write an e-mail in an e-mail application, clicking the **Send** button tells the application to send the e-mail to the specified e-mail addresses. GUIs are *event driven*. When the user interacts with a GUI component, the interaction—known as an *event*—drives the program to perform a task. Common events (user interactions) that might cause an application to perform a task include clicking a Button, typing in a TextBox, selecting an item from a menu, closing a window and moving the mouse. A method that performs a task in response to an event is called an *event handler*, and the overall process of responding to events is known as *event handling*. Event-handling methods don't return values, so they are implemented as Sub procedures.

13.3.1 A Simple Event-Driven GUI

The Form in the application of Fig. 13.5 contains a Button that a user can click to display a MessageBox. You have already created several GUI examples that execute an event handler in response to clicking a Button. In this example, we discuss Visual Studio's auto-generated code in more depth.

```
1   ' Fig. 13.5: FrmSimpleEventExample.vb
2   ' Using Visual Studio to create event handlers.
3   Public Class FrmSimpleEventExample
4       ' event handler for btnClickMe's Click event
5       Private Sub btnClickMe_Click(ByVal sender As System.Object, _
6           ByVal e As System.EventArgs) Handles btnClickMe.Click
7
8           MessageBox.Show("Button was clicked.")
9       End Sub ' btnClickMe_Click
10  End Class ' FrmSimpleEventExample
```

Fig. 13.5 | Simple event-handling example using visual programming. (Part 1 of 2.)

Fig. 13.5 | Simple event-handling example using visual programming. (Part 2 of 2.)

Using the techniques presented earlier in the book, create a Form containing a Button. First, create a new Windows application and add a Button to the Form. In the **Properties** window for the Button, set the (Name) property to btnClickMe and the Text property to Click Me. You'll notice that each variable name we create for a control starts with a three letter code that abbreviates the type of the control. For example, in the variable name btnClickMe, "btn" is an abbreviation for Button. This is a widely used naming practice in the Visual Basic community; however, a name such as clickMeButton would also suffice.

When the user clicks the Button in this example, we want the application to respond by displaying a MessageBox. To do this, you must create an event handler for the Button's Click event. You can create this event handler by double clicking the Button on the Form, which declares the following empty event handler in the program code:

> *Private Sub* btnClickMe_Click(*ByVal* sender *As* System.Object, _
>   *ByVal* e *As* System.EventArgs) *Handles* btnClickMe.Click
>
> **End Sub**

By convention, Visual Basic names the event-handler method as *controlName_eventName* (e.g., btnClickMe_Click). The btnClickMe_Click event handler executes when the user clicks the btnClickMe control.

Each event handler receives two parameters. The first—an Object reference named sender—is a reference to the object that generated the event. The second is a reference to an event arguments object (typically named e) of type System.EventArgs (or one of its derived classes). This object contains information about the event that occurred. System.EventArgs is the base class of all classes that represent event information.

Software Engineering Observation 13.1

Event handlers do not return values—they are designed to execute code based on an action and return control to the main program.

Good Programming Practice 13.1

Use the event-handler naming convention controlName_eventName *so that your method names will be meaningful. Such names tell users what event a method handles for what control. This convention is not required, but it makes your code easier to read, understand, modify and maintain.*

To display a MessageBox in response to the event, insert the statement

    MessageBox.Show("Button was clicked.")

in the event handler's body. The resulting event handler appears in lines 5–9 of Fig. 13.5. When you execute the application and click the Button, a MessageBox appears displaying the text "Button was clicked".

13.3.2 Another Look at the Visual Studio Generated Code

Visual Studio generates the code that creates and initializes the GUI you build in the GUI design window. This auto-generated code is placed in the `Designer.vb` file of the `Form` (`FrmSimpleEventExample.Designer.vb` in this example). You can open this file by expanding the node for the file you are currently working in (`FrmSimpleEventExample.vb`) and double clicking the file name that ends with `Designer.vb`. (You might need to click the **Show All Files** button first.) Figures 13.6 and 13.7 show this file's contents.

```
FrmSimpleEventExample.Designer.vb
FrmSimpleEventExample                                    (Declarations)
 1  <Global.Microsoft.VisualBasic.CompilerServices.DesignerGenerated()> _
 2  Partial Class FrmSimpleEventExample
 3      Inherits System.Windows.Forms.Form
 4
 5      'Form overrides dispose to clean up the component list.
 6      <System.Diagnostics.DebuggerNonUserCode()> _
 7      Protected Overrides Sub Dispose(ByVal disposing As Boolean)
 8          If disposing AndAlso components IsNot Nothing Then
 9              components.Dispose()
10          End If
11          MyBase.Dispose(disposing)
12      End Sub
13
14      'Required by the Windows Form Designer
15      Private components As System.ComponentModel.IContainer
16
```

Fig. 13.6 | First half of the Visual Studio generated code file.

```
FrmSimpleEventExample                                    (Declarations)
17      'NOTE: The following procedure is required by the Windows Form Designer
18      'It can be modified using the Windows Form Designer.
19      'Do not modify it using the code editor.
20      <System.Diagnostics.DebuggerStepThrough()> _
21      Private Sub InitializeComponent()
22          Me.btnClickMe = New System.Windows.Forms.Button
23          Me.SuspendLayout()
24          '
25          'btnClickMe
26          '
27          Me.btnClickMe.Location = New System.Drawing.Point(84, 28)
28          Me.btnClickMe.Name = "btnClickMe"
29          Me.btnClickMe.Size = New System.Drawing.Size(75, 29)
30          Me.btnClickMe.TabIndex = 1
31          Me.btnClickMe.Text = "Click Me"
32          '
33          'FrmSimpleEventExample
34          '
35          Me.AutoScaleDimensions = New System.Drawing.SizeF(6.0!, 13.0!)
36          Me.AutoScaleMode = System.Windows.Forms.AutoScaleMode.Font
37          Me.ClientSize = New System.Drawing.Size(242, 84)
38          Me.Controls.Add(Me.btnClickMe)
39          Me.Name = "FrmSimpleEventExample"
40          Me.Text = "Simple Event Example"
41          Me.ResumeLayout(False)
42
43      End Sub
44      Friend WithEvents btnClickMe As System.Windows.Forms.Button
45
46  End Class
```

Fig. 13.7 | Second half of the Visual Studio generated code file.

Now that you have studied classes and objects in detail, this code will be easier to understand. Since this code is created and maintained by Visual Studio, you generally don't need to look at it. In fact, you do not need to understand most of the code shown here to build GUI applications. However, we now take a closer look to help you understand how GUI applications work.

The auto-generated code that defines the GUI is actually part of the Form's class—in this case, FrmSimpleEventExample. Line 2 of Fig. 13.6 uses the Partial modifier, which allows this class to be split among multiple files. Line 44 declares as an instance variable of class FrmSimpleEventExample the Button control btnClickMe that we created in **Design** mode. By default, all variable declarations for controls created through Visual Basic's design window have a Friend access modifier. The code also includes the Dispose method for releasing resources (lines 7–12) and method InitializeComponent (lines 21–43), which contains the code that creates the Button, then sets some of the Button's and the Form's properties. The property values correspond to the values set in the **Properties** window for each control. Note that Visual Studio adds comments to the code that it generates, as in lines 24–26.

When the application begins executing, its Form is created, and the Form's InitializeComponent method is called automatically to establish such properties as the Form's title and size, and the location, size and text for each control. Visual Studio also uses the code in this method to create the GUI you see in design view. Changing the code in InitializeComponent may prevent Visual Studio from displaying the GUI properly.

Error-Prevention Tip 13.1

*The code generated by building a GUI in **Design** mode is not meant to be modified directly, and doing so can make an application function incorrectly. You should modify control properties through the **Properties** window.*

13.3.3 Delegates and the Event-Handling Mechanism

The control that generates an event is known as the *event sender*. An event-handling method—known as the *event receiver*—responds to a particular event that a control generates. When the event occurs, the event sender calls its event receiver to perform a task (i.e., to "handle the event").

The .NET event-handling mechanism allows you to choose your own names for event-handling methods. However, each event-handling method must declare the proper parameters to receive information about the event it handles. Since you can choose your own method names, an event sender such as a Button cannot know in advance which method will respond to its events. So we need a mechanism to indicate which method is the event receiver for an event.

Delegates

Event handlers are connected to a control's events via special objects called *delegates*. A delegate object holds a reference to a method. The method's signature must match the signature specified by the delegate type's declaration. GUI controls have predefined delegates that correspond to every event they can generate. For example, the delegate for a Button's Click event is of type EventHandler (namespace System). If you look at this type in the online help documentation, you will see that it is declared as follows:

> *Public Delegate Sub* EventHandler(sender *As* Object, e *As* EventArgs)

where Object and EventArgs are classes from the System namespace. This uses the *Delegate* keyword to declare a delegate type named EventHandler, which can hold a reference to a method that does not return a value and receives two parameters—one of type Object (the event sender) and one of type EventArgs. If you compare the delegate declaration with btnClickMe_Click's header (Fig. 13.5, lines 5–6), you will see that this event handler indeed meets the requirements of the EventHandler delegate. Note that the preceding declaration actually creates an entire class for you. The details of this special class's declaration are handled by the compiler.

Indicating the Method That a Delegate Should Call

An event sender uses a delegate object like a method call. Since each event handler must have the same signature as the control's delegate for a particular event, the event sender can simply "call" the appropriate delegate when an event occurs. For example, a Button calls its Click delegate in response to a click. The delegate's job is to invoke the appropriate event-handler method. To enable the btnClickMe_Click method to be called when the user clicks the Button, Visual Basic inserts the clause

> *Handles* *controlName* . *eventName*

following the event handler's parameter list. For example, Handles btnClickMe.Click in line 6 of Fig. 13.5 indicates that btnClickMe_Click will be called when the user clicks the btnClickMe control (i.e., when the button's Click event occurs). The *Handles clause*, which is added by Visual Studio when you double click the Button control in **Design** mode, causes Visual Basic to "register" your event handler as the method to call in response to the event. You can also manually add and remove event handlers at runtime by using the AddHandler and RemoveHandler statements (see msdn2.microsoft.com/en-us/library/6yyk8z93.aspx).

13.3.4 Other Ways to Create Event Handlers

In all the GUI applications you have created so far, you double clicked a control on the Form to create an event handler for that control. This technique creates an event handler for a control's *default event*—the event most frequently used with that control. Typically, controls can generate many different types of events, and each type can have its own event handler. For instance, you have already created Click event handlers for Buttons by double clicking a Button in design view (Click is the default event for a Button). However your application can also provide an event handler for a Button's MouseHover event, which occurs when the mouse pointer remains positioned over the Button. We now discuss how to create an event handler for an event that is not a control's default event.

Using the Properties Window to Create Event Handlers

You can create additional event handlers through the **Properties** window. If you select a control on the Form, then click the **Events** icon (the lightning bolt icon in Fig. 13.8) in the **Properties** window, all the events for that control are listed in the window. You can double click an event's name to display the event handler in the editor. If the event handler does not already exist, it will be created. You can also select an event, then use the drop-down list to its right to choose an existing method that will be used as the event handler for that

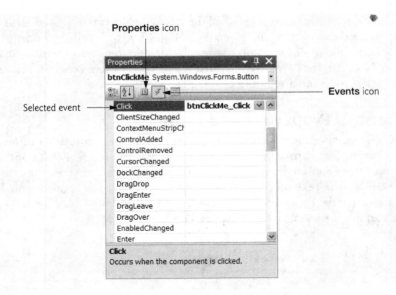

Fig. 13.8 | Viewing events for a `Button` control in the **Properties** window.

event. The methods that appear in this drop-down list are the class's methods that have the proper signature to be an event handler for the selected event. You can return to viewing the properties of a control by selecting the **Properties** icon (Fig. 13.8).

13.3.5 Locating Event Information

Read the Visual Studio documentation to learn about the different events raised by a control. To do this, select **Help > Index**. In the window that appears, select **.NET Framework** in the **Filtered by** drop-down list and enter the name of the control's class in the **Index** window. To ensure that you are selecting the proper class, enter the fully qualified class name as shown in Fig. 13.9 for class `System.Windows.Forms.Button`. Once you select a con-

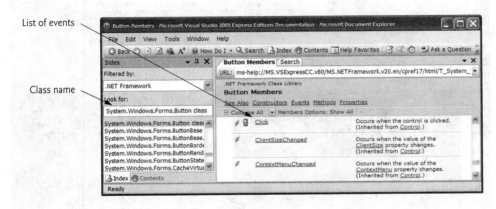

Fig. 13.9 | List of `Button` events.

trol's class in the documentation, a list of all the class's members is displayed. This list includes the events that the class can generate. In Fig. 13.9, we scrolled to class `Button`'s events. Click the name of an event to view its description and examples of its use (Fig. 13.10). Note that the `Click` event is listed as a member of class `Control`, because class `Button`'s `Click` event is inherited from class `Control`.

13.4 Control Properties and Layout

This section overviews properties that are common to many controls. Controls derive from class **_Control_** (namespace `System.Windows.Forms`). Figure 13.11 lists some of class `Control`'s properties and methods. The properties shown here can be set for many controls. For example, the `Text` property specifies the text that appears on a control. The location of this text varies depending on the control. In a Windows Form, the text appears in the title bar, but the text of a `Button` appears on its face.

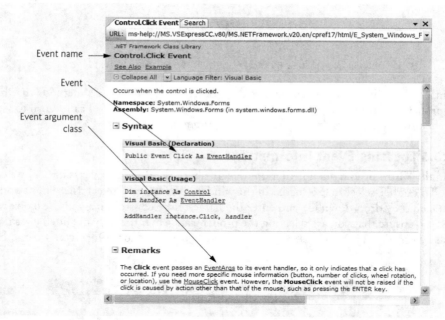

Fig. 13.10 | `Click` event details.

Class `Control` properties and methods	Description
Common Properties	
`BackColor`	The control's background color.

Fig. 13.11 | Class `Control` properties and methods. (Part 1 of 2.)

Class Control properties and methods	Description
BackgroundImage	The control's background image.
Enabled	Specifies whether the control is enabled (i.e., whether the user can interact with it). Typically, portions of a disabled control appear "grayed out" as a visual indication to the user that the control is disabled.
Focused	Indicates whether the control has the focus.
Font	The Font used to display the control's text.
ForeColor	The control's foreground color. This usually determines the color of the text in the Text property.
TabIndex	The tab order of the control. When the *Tab* key is pressed, the focus transfers between controls based on the tab order. You can set this order.
TabStop	If True, then a user can give focus to this control via the *Tab* key.
Text	The text associated with the control. The location and appearance of the text vary depending on the type of control.
Visible	Indicates whether the control is visible.
Common Methods	
Focus	Acquires the focus.
Hide	Hides the control (sets the Visible property to False).
Show	Shows the control (sets the Visible property to True).

Fig. 13.11 | Class Control properties and methods. (Part 2 of 2.)

The **Focus** method transfers the focus to a control and makes it the ***active control***. When you press the *Tab* key in an executing Windows application, controls receive the focus in the order specified by their **TabIndex** property. This property is set by Visual Studio based on the order in which controls are added to a Form, but you can modify this property to change the tabbing order. TabIndex is helpful for users who enter information in many controls, such as a set of TextBoxes that represent a user's name, address and telephone number. The user can enter information, then quickly select the next control by pressing the *Tab* key.

The **Enabled** property indicates whether the user can interact with a control to generate an event. If a control is disabled, it is often because an option is unavailable to the user at that time. For example, text editor applications often disable the "paste" command until the user copies some text. In most cases, a disabled control's text appears in gray (rather than in black). You can also hide a control from the user without disabling the control by setting the Visible property to False or by calling method Hide. In each case, the control still exists but is not visible on the Form.

You can use anchoring and docking to specify the layout of controls inside a container (such as a Form). *Anchoring* causes controls to remain at a fixed distance from the sides of the container even when the container is resized. Anchoring enhances the user experience. For example, if the user expects a control to appear in a certain corner of the application, anchoring ensures that the control will always be in that corner—even if the user resizes the Form. *Docking* attaches a control to a container such that the control stretches across an entire side. For example, a button docked to the top of a container stretches across the entire top of that container regardless of the container's width.

When parent containers are resized, anchored controls are moved (and possibly resized) so that the distance from the sides to which they are anchored does not vary. By default, most controls are anchored to the top-left corner of the Form. To see the effects of anchoring a control, create a simple Windows application that contains two Buttons. Anchor one control to the right and bottom sides by setting the **Anchor** property as shown in Fig. 13.12. Leave the other control unanchored. Execute the application and enlarge the Form. Note that the Button anchored to the bottom-right corner is always the same distance from the Form's bottom-right corner (Fig. 13.13), but that the other control stays its original distance from the top-left corner of the Form.

Sometimes, it is desirable for a control to span an entire side of the Form, even when the Form is resized. For example, a control such as a status bar typically should remain at the bottom of the Form. Docking allows a control to span an entire side (left, right, top or

Fig. 13.12 | Manipulating the **Anchor** property of a control.

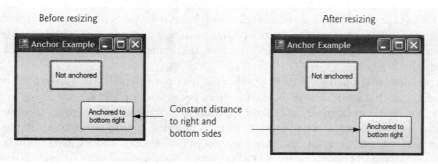

Fig. 13.13 | Anchoring demonstration.

bottom) of its parent container or to fill the entire container. When the parent control is resized, the docked control resizes as well. In Fig. 13.14, a Button is docked at the top of the Form (spanning the top portion). When the Form is resized, the Button is resized to the Form's new width. Forms have a ***Padding*** property that specifies the distance between the docked controls and the Form edges. This property specifies four values (one for each side), and each value is set to 0 by default. Some common control-layout properties are summarized in Fig. 13.15.

The Anchor and Dock properties of a Control are set with respect to the Control's parent container, which could be a Form or another parent container (such as a Panel; discussed in Section 13.6). The minimum and maximum Form (or other Control) sizes can be set via properties ***MinimumSize*** and ***MaximumSize***, respectively. Both are of type ***Size***,

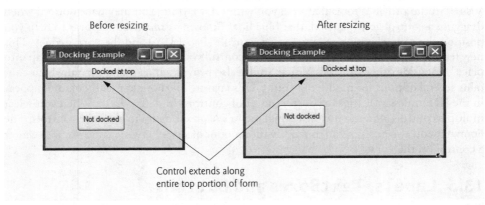

Fig. 13.14 | Docking a Button to the top of a Form.

Control layout properties	Description
Anchor	Causes a control to remain at a fixed distance from the side(s) of the container even when the container is resized.
Dock	Allows a control to span one side of its container or to fill the entire container.
Padding	Sets the space between a container's edges and docked controls. The default is 0, causing the control to appear flush with the container's sides.
Location	Specifies the location (as a set of coordinates) of the upper-left corner of the control, in relation to its container.
Size	Specifies the size of the control in pixels as a Size object, which has properties Width and Height.
MinimumSize, MaximumSize	Indicate the minimum and maximum sizes of a Control, respectively.

Fig. 13.15 | Control layout properties.

which has properties *Width* and *Height* to specify the size of the Form. Properties Mini-mumSize and MaximumSize allow you to design the GUI layout for a given size range. The user cannot make a Form smaller than the size specified by property MinimumSize and cannot make a Form larger than the size specified by property MaximumSize. To set a Form to a fixed size (where the Form cannot be resized by the user), set its minimum and max-imum sizes to the same values or set its FormBorderStyle property to FixedSingle.

Look-and-Feel Observation 13.2

For resizable Forms, ensure that the GUI layout appears consistent across various Form sizes.

Using Visual Studio To Edit a GUI's Layout

Visual Studio provides tools that help you with GUI layout. You may have noticed when dragging a control across a Form, that blue lines (known as *snap lines*) appear to help you position the control with respect to other controls (Fig. 13.16) and the Form's edges. This new feature of Visual Studio 2005 makes the control you are dragging appear to "snap into place" alongside other controls. Visual Studio also provides the **Format** menu, which con-tains several options for modifying your GUI's layout. The **Format** menu does not appear in the IDE unless you select a control (or set of controls) in design view. When you select multiple controls, you can use the **Format** menu's **Align** submenu to align the controls. The **Format** menu also enables you to modify the amount of space between controls or to center a control on the Form.

13.5 Labels, TextBoxes and Buttons

Labels provide text information (as well as optional images) and are defined with class La-bel (a derived class of Control). A Label displays text that the user cannot directly mod-ify. A Label's text can be changed programmatically by modifying the Label's Text property. Figure 13.17 lists common Label properties.

A textbox (class TextBox) is an area in which text can be displayed by a program or the user can type text via the keyboard. A *password TextBox* is a TextBox that hides the information entered by the user. As the user types characters, the password TextBox masks the user input by displaying a character you specify (usually *). If you set the *Password-Char* property, the TextBox becomes a password TextBox. Users often encounter both

Fig. 13.16 | Snap lines in Visual Studio 2005.

Common Label properties	Description
Font	The font of the text on the Label.
Text	The text on the Label.
TextAlign	The alignment of the Label's text on the control—horizontally (left, center or right) and vertically (top, middle or bottom).

Fig. 13.17 | Common Label properties.

types of TextBoxes when logging into a computer or Web site—the username TextBox allows users to input their usernames; the password TextBox allows users to enter their passwords. Figure 13.18 lists the common properties and a common event of TextBoxes.

A button is a control that the user clicks to trigger a specific action or to select an option in a program. As you will see, a program can use various button types, such as *checkboxes* and *radio buttons.* All the button classes derive from ***ButtonBase*** (namespace System.Windows.Forms), which defines common button features. In this section, we dis-

TextBox properties and an event	Description
Common Properties	
AcceptsReturn	If True in a multiline TextBox, pressing *Enter* in the TextBox creates a new line. If False, pressing *Enter* is the same as pressing the default Button on the Form. The default Button is the one assigned to a Form's AcceptButton property.
Multiline	If True, the TextBox can span multiple lines. The default value is False.
PasswordChar	When this property is set to a character, the TextBox becomes a password box, and the specified character masks each character the user types. If no character is specified, the TextBox displays the typed text.
ReadOnly	If True, the TextBox has a gray background, and its text cannot be edited. The default value is False.
ScrollBars	For multiline textboxes, this property indicates which scrollbars appear (None, Horizontal, Vertical or Both).
Text	The TextBox's text content.
Common Event	
TextChanged	Generated when the text changes in a TextBox (i.e., when the user adds or deletes characters). When you double click the TextBox control in **Design** mode, an empty event handler for this event is generated.

Fig. 13.18 | TextBox properties and an event.

cuss class Button, which typically enables a user to issue a command to an application. Figure 13.19 lists common properties and a common event of class Button.

Look-and-Feel Observation 13.3

Although Labels, TextBoxes and other controls can respond to mouse clicks, Buttons are more natural for this purpose.

Figure 13.20 uses a TextBox, a Button and a Label. When the user clicks the **Show Me** Button, this application retrieves the text that the user typed in the password TextBox and displays it in a Label. Normally, we would not display this text—the purpose of password TextBoxes is to hide the text being entered by the user. When the user clicks the **Show Me** Button, this application retrieves the text that the user typed in the password TextBox and displays it in another TextBox.

First, create the GUI by dragging the controls (a TextBox, a Button and a Label) onto the Form. Once the controls are positioned, change their names in the **Properties** window

Button properties and an event	Description
Common Properties	
Text	Specifies the text displayed on the Button face.
FlatStyle	Modifies a Button's appearance—attribute Flat (for the Button to display without a three-dimensional appearance), Popup (for the Button to appear flat until the user moves the mouse pointer over the Button), Standard (three-dimensional) and System, where the Button's appearance is controlled by the operating system. The default value is Standard.
Common Event	
Click	Generated when the user clicks the Button. When you double click a Button in design view, an empty event handler for this event is created.

Fig. 13.19 | Button properties and an event.

```
 1    ' Fig. 13.20: FrmLabelTextBoxButtonTest.vb
 2    ' Using a TextBox, Label and Button to display
 3    ' the hidden text in a password TextBox.
 4    Public Class FrmLabelTextBoxButtonTest
 5       ' event handler for btnDisplayPassword's Click event
 6       Private Sub btnDisplayPassword_Click(ByVal sender As System.Object, _
 7          ByVal e As System.EventArgs) Handles btnDisplayPassword.Click
 8          ' display the text that the user typed
 9          lblDisplayPassword.Text = txtInputPassword.Text
10       End Sub ' btnDisplayPassword_Click
11    End Class ' FrmLabelTextBoxButtonTest
```

Fig. 13.20 | Program to display hidden text in a password box. (Part 1 of 2.)

Fig. 13.20 | Program to display hidden text in a password box. (Part 2 of 2.)

from the default values—textBox1, button1 and label1—to the more descriptive names lblDisplayPassword, btnDisplayPassword and txtInputPassword. The (Name) property in the **Properties** window enables us to change the variable name for a control. Visual Studio creates the necessary code and places it in method InitializeComponent of the partial class in the file FrmLabelTextButtonTest.Designer.vb.

We then set btnDisplayPassword's Text property to "Show Me" and clear the Text of lblDisplayPassword and txtInputPassword so that they are blank when the program begins executing. The BorderStyle property of lblDisplayPassword is set to Fixed3D, giving our Label a three-dimensional appearance. The BorderStyle property of all Text-Boxes is set to Fixed3D by default. The password character for txtInputPassword is set by assigning the asterisk character (*) to the PasswordChar property. This property accepts only one character.

We create an event handler for btnDisplayPassword by double clicking this control in **Design** mode. We add line 9 to the event handler's body. When the user clicks the **Show Me** Button in the executing application, line 9 obtains the text entered by the user in txtInputPassword and displays the text in lblDisplayPassword.

13.6 GroupBoxes and Panels

GroupBoxes and *Panels* arrange controls on a GUI. GroupBoxes and Panels are typically used to group several controls of similar functionality or several controls that are related in a GUI. All of the controls in a GroupBox or Panel move together when the GroupBox or Panel is moved.

The primary difference between these two controls is that GroupBoxes can display a caption (i.e., text) and do not include scrollbars, whereas Panels can include scrollbars and do not include a caption. GroupBoxes have thin borders by default; Panels can be set so

GroupBox properties	Description
Controls	The set of controls that the GroupBox contains.
Text	Specifies the caption text displayed at the top of the GroupBox.

Fig. 13.21 | GroupBox properties.

Panel properties	Description
AutoScroll	Indicates whether scrollbars appear when the Panel is too small to display all of its controls. The default value is False.
BorderStyle	Sets the border of the Panel. The default value is None; other options are Fixed3D and FixedSingle.
Controls	The set of controls that the Panel contains.

Fig. 13.22 | Panel properties.

that they also have borders by changing their BorderStyle property. Figures 13.21–13.22 list the common properties of GroupBoxes and Panels, respectively.

Look-and-Feel Observation 13.4

Panels and GroupBoxes can contain other Panels and GroupBoxes for more complex layouts.

Look-and-Feel Observation 13.5

You can organize a GUI by anchoring and docking controls inside a GroupBox or Panel. The GroupBox or Panel can then be anchored or docked inside a Form. This divides controls into functional "groups" that can be arranged easily.

To create a GroupBox, drag its icon from the **Toolbox** onto the Form. Then drag new controls from the **Toolbox** into the GroupBox. These controls are added to the GroupBox's **Controls** property and become part of the GroupBox. The GroupBox's Text property specifies the caption.

To create a Panel, drag its icon from the **Toolbox** onto the Form. You can then add controls directly to the Panel by dragging them from the **Toolbox** onto the Panel. To enable the scrollbars, set the Panel's AutoScroll property to True. If the Panel is resized and cannot display all of its controls, scrollbars appear (Fig. 13.23). The scrollbars can be used to view all the controls in the Panel—both at design time and at execution time. In Fig. 13.23, we set the Panel's BorderStyle property to FixedSingle so that you can see the Panel in the Form.

The program in Fig. 13.24 uses a GroupBox and a Panel to arrange Buttons. When these Buttons are clicked, their event handlers change the text on a Label.

The GroupBox (named grpMain) has two Buttons—btnHi (which displays the text **Hi**) and btnBye (which displays the text **Bye**). The Panel (named pnlMain) also has two Buttons, btnLeft (which displays the text **Far Left**) and btnRight (which displays the text **Far Right**). The pnlMain has its AutoScroll property set to True, allowing scrollbars to appear when the contents of the Panel require more space than the Panel's visible area. The Label (named lblMessage) is initially blank. To add controls to grpMain or pblMain, Visual Studio calls method Add of each container's Controls property. This code is placed in the partial class located in the file FrmGroupBoxPanelExample.Designer.vb.

The event handlers for the four Buttons are located in lines 5–26. We added a line in each event handler (lines 7, 13, 19 and 25) to change the text of lblMessage to indicate which Button the user pressed.

Fig. 13.23 | Creating a Panel with scrollbars.

```
 I    ' Fig. 13.24: FrmGroupboxPanelExample.vb
 2    ' Using GroupBoxes and Panels to hold Buttons.
 3    Public Class FrmGroupBoxPanelExample
 4       ' event handler for btnHi's Click event
 5       Private Sub btnHi_Click(ByVal sender As System.Object, _
 6          ByVal e As System.EventArgs) Handles btnHi.Click
 7          lblMessage.Text = "Hi pressed" ' change text in Label
 8       End Sub ' btnHi_Click
 9
10       ' event handler for btnBye's Click event
11       Private Sub btnBye_Click(ByVal sender As System.Object, _
12          ByVal e As System.EventArgs) Handles btnBye.Click
13          lblMessage.Text = "Bye pressed" ' change text in Label
14       End Sub ' btnBye_Click
15
16       ' event handler for btnLeft's Click event
17       Private Sub btnLeft_Click(ByVal sender As System.Object, _
18          ByVal e As System.EventArgs) Handles btnLeft.Click
19          lblMessage.Text = "Far left pressed" ' change text in Label
20       End Sub ' btnLeft_Click
21
22       ' event handler for btnRIght's Click event
23       Private Sub btnRight_Click(ByVal sender As System.Object, _
24          ByVal e As System.EventArgs) Handles btnRight.Click
25          lblMessage.Text = "Far right pressed" ' change text in Label
26       End Sub ' btnRight_Click
27    End Class ' FrmGroupBoxPanelExample
```

Fig. 13.24 | Using GroupBoxes and Panels to arrange Buttons. (Part I of 2.)

Fig. 13.24 | Using GroupBoxes and Panels to arrange Buttons. (Part 2 of 2.)

13.7 CheckBoxes and RadioButtons

Visual Basic has two types of *state buttons* that can be in the on/off or true/false states—*CheckBoxes* and *RadioButtons*. Like class Button, classes CheckBox and RadioButton are derived from class ButtonBase.

CheckBoxes

A CheckBox is a small square that either is blank or contains a check mark. When the user clicks a CheckBox to select it, a check mark appears in the box. If the user clicks the CheckBox again to deselect it, the check mark is removed. Any number of CheckBoxes can be selected at a time. A list of common CheckBox properties and events appears in Fig. 13.25.

CheckBox properties and events	Description
Common Properties	
Checked	Indicates whether the CheckBox is checked (contains a check mark) or unchecked (blank). This property returns a Boolean value.
CheckState	Indicates whether the CheckBox is checked or unchecked with a value from the CheckState enumeration (Checked, Unchecked or Indeterminate). Indeterminate is used when it is unclear whether the state should be Checked or Unchecked. For example, in Microsoft Word, when you select a paragraph that contains several character formats, then go to **Format > Font**, some of the CheckBoxes appear in the Indeterminate state. When CheckState is set to Indeterminate, the CheckBox is usually shaded.
Text	Specifies the text displayed to the right of the CheckBox.

Fig. 13.25 | CheckBox properties and events. (Part I of 2.)

CheckBox properties and events	Description
Common Events	
CheckedChanged	Generated when the Checked property changes. This is a CheckBox's default event. When a user double clicks the CheckBox control in design view, an empty event handler for this event is generated.
CheckStateChanged	Generated when the CheckState property changes.

Fig. 13.25 | CheckBox properties and events. (Part 2 of 2.)

The program in Fig. 13.26 allows the user to select CheckBoxes to change a Label's font style. The event handler for one CheckBox applies bold, and the event handler for the other applies italic. If both CheckBoxes are selected, the font style is set to bold and italic. Initially, neither CheckBox is checked.

```
 1   ' Fig. 13.26: FrmCheckBoxTest.vb
 2   ' Using CheckBoxes to toggle italic and bold styles.
 3   Public Class FrmCheckBoxTest
 4      ' toggle the font style between bold and
 5      ' not bold based on the current setting
 6      Private Sub chkBold_CheckedChanged(ByVal sender As System.Object, _
 7         ByVal e As System.EventArgs) Handles chkBold.CheckedChanged
 8         lblOutput.Font = _
 9            New Font(lblOutput.Font.Name, lblOutput.Font.Size, _
10               lblOutput.Font.Style Xor FontStyle.Bold)
11      End Sub ' chkBold_CheckedChanged
12
13      ' toggle the font setting between italic and
14      ' not italic based on the current setting
15      Private Sub chkItalic_CheckedChanged(ByVal sender As System.Object, _
16         ByVal e As System.EventArgs) Handles chkItalic.CheckedChanged
17         lblOutput.Font = _
18            New Font(lblOutput.Font.Name, lblOutput.Font.Size, _
19               lblOutput.Font.Style Xor FontStyle.Italic)
20      End Sub ' chkItalic_CheckedChanged
21   End Class ' FrmCheckBoxTest
```

Fig. 13.26 | Using CheckBoxes to change font styles. (Part 1 of 2.)

Fig. 13.26 | Using CheckBoxes to change font styles. (Part 2 of 2.)

The chkBold has its Text property set to Bold. The chkItalic has its Text property set to Italic. The Text property of lblOutput is set to Watch the font style change. After creating the controls, we define their event handlers. Double clicking the CheckBoxes at design time creates empty CheckedChanged event handlers.

To change the font style on a Label, you must set its Font property to a new **Font object** (lines 8–10 and 17–19). The Font constructor that we use here takes the font name, size and style as arguments. The first two arguments—lblOutput.Font.Name and lblOutput.Font.Size—use lblOutput's original font name and size. The style is specified with a member of the **FontStyle enumeration**, which contains Regular, Bold, Italic, Strikeout and Underline. (The Strikeout style displays text with a line through it.) A Font object's **Style** property is read-only, so it can be set only when the Font object is created.

Styles can be combined via **bitwise operators**—operators that perform manipulations on bits of information. All data is represented in the computer as combinations of 0s and 1s. Each 0 or 1 represents a bit. FontStyle has a System.FlagAttribute, meaning that the FontStyle bit values are selected in a way that allows us to combine different FontStyle elements to create compound styles, using bitwise operators. These styles are not mutually exclusive, so we can combine different styles and remove them without affecting the combination of previous FontStyle elements. We can combine these various font styles using either the Or operator or the Xor operator. When the Or operator is applied to two bits, if at least one bit of the two has the value 1, then the result is 1. Combining styles using the Or operator works as follows. Assume that FontStyle.Bold is represented by bits 01 and that FontStyle.Italic is represented by bits 10. When we use the Or operator to combine the styles, we obtain the bits 11.

```
01  =  Bold
10  =  Italic
--
11  =  Bold and Italic
```

The Or operator helps create style combinations. However, what happens if we want to undo a style combination, as we did in Fig. 13.26?

The Xor operator enables us to combine styles and to undo existing style settings. When Xor is applied to two bits, if both bits have the same value, then the result is 0. If both bits are different, then the result is 1.

Combining styles using Xor works as follows. Assume, again, that FontStyle.Bold is represented by bits 01 and that FontStyle.Italic is represented by bits 10. When we use Xor on both styles, we obtain the bits 11.

```
01  =   Bold
10  =   Italic
--
11  =   Bold and Italic
```

Now suppose that we would like to remove the FontStyle.Bold style from the previous combination of FontStyle.Bold and FontStyle.Italic. The easiest way to do so is to reapply the Xor operator to the compound style and FontStyle.Bold.

```
11  =   Bold and Italic
01  =   Bold
--
10  =   Italic
```

This is a simple example. The advantages of using bitwise operators to combine FontStyle values become more evident when we consider that there are five different FontStyle values (Bold, Italic, Regular, Strikeout and Underline), resulting in 16 different FontStyle combinations. Using bitwise operators to combine font styles greatly reduces the amount of code required to check all possible font combinations.

In Fig. 13.26, we need to set the FontStyle so that the text appears in bold if it was not bold originally, and vice versa. Note that line 10 uses the Xor operator to do this. If lblOutput.Font.Style is bold, then the resulting style is not bold. If the text is originally italic, the resulting style is bold and italic rather than just bold. The same applies for FontStyle.Italic in line 19.

If we did not use bitwise operators to compound FontStyle elements, we would have to test for the current style and change it accordingly. For example, in event handler chkBold_CheckChanged, we could test for the regular style and make it bold, test for the bold style and make it regular, test for the italic style and make it bold italic, and test for the italic bold style and make it italic. This is cumbersome because for every new style we add, we double the number of combinations. Adding a CheckBox for underline would require testing eight additional styles. Adding a CheckBox for strikeout would require testing 16 additional styles.

RadioButtons

Radio buttons (defined with class RadioButton) are similar to CheckBoxes in that they also have two states—*selected* and *not selected* (also called *deselected*). However, RadioButtons normally appear as a *group*, in which only one RadioButton can be selected at a time. Selecting one RadioButton in the group forces all the others to be deselected. Therefore, RadioButtons are used to represent a set of *mutually exclusive* options (i.e., a set in which multiple options cannot be selected at the same time).

 Look-and-Feel Observation 13.6

Use RadioButtons when the user should choose only one option in a group.

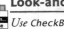 **Look-and-Feel Observation 13.7**

Use CheckBoxes when the user should be able to choose multiple options (or no options at all) in a group.

All RadioButtons added to a container are part of the same group. To separate them into several groups, the RadioButtons must be added to GroupBoxes or Panels. The common properties and a common event of class RadioButton are listed in Fig. 13.27.

Software Engineering Observation 13.2

Forms, GroupBoxes and Panels act as logical groups for RadioButtons. The RadioButtons within each group are mutually exclusive to each other, but not to those in different logical groups.

The program in Fig. 13.28 uses RadioButtons to enable users to select options for a MessageBox. After selecting the desired attributes, the user presses the **Display** Button to display the MessageBox. A Label in the lower-left corner shows the result of the MessageBox (i.e., which Button the user clicked—**Yes**, **No**, **Cancel**, etc.).

To store the user's choices, we create and initialize the iconType and buttonType objects (lines 5–6). Object iconType is of type MessageBoxIcon, and can have values Asterisk, Error, Exclamation, Hand, Information, None, Question, Stop and Warning. The sample output shows only the Error, Exclamation, Information and Question icons.

RadioButton properties and an event	Description
Common Properties	
Checked	Indicates whether the RadioButton is checked.
Text	Specifies the RadioButton's text.
Common Event	
CheckedChanged	Generated every time the RadioButton is checked or unchecked. When you double click a RadioButton control in design view, an empty event handler for this event is generated.

Fig. 13.27 | RadioButton properties and an event.

```
1   ' Fig. 13.28: FrmRadioButtonsTest.vb
2   ' Using RadioButtons to set message window options.
3   Public Class FrmRadioButtonsTest
4      ' create variables that store the user's choice of options
5      Private iconType As MessageBoxIcon
6      Private buttonType As MessageBoxButtons
7
8      ' set button type to OK
9      Private Sub radOk_CheckedChanged(ByVal sender As System.Object, _
10         ByVal e As System.EventArgs) Handles radOk.CheckedChanged
11         buttonType = MessageBoxButtons.OK
12      End Sub ' radOk_CheckedChanged
13
```

Fig. 13.28 | Using RadioButtons to set message-window options. (Part 1 of 4.)

```
14        ' set button type to OKCancel
15        Private Sub radOkCancel_CheckedChanged(ByVal sender As System.Object, _
16           ByVal e As System.EventArgs) Handles radOkCancel.CheckedChanged
17           buttonType = MessageBoxButtons.OKCancel
18        End Sub ' radOkCancel_CheckedChanged
19
20        ' set button type to AbortRetryIgnore
21        Private Sub radAbortRetryIgnore_CheckedChanged( _
22           ByVal sender As System.Object, ByVal e As System.EventArgs) _
23           Handles radAbortRetryIgnore.CheckedChanged
24           buttonType = MessageBoxButtons.AbortRetryIgnore
25        End Sub ' radAbortRetryIgnore_CheckedChanged
26
27        ' set button type to YesNoCancel
28        Private Sub radYesNoCancel_CheckedChanged( _
29           ByVal sender As System.Object, ByVal e As System.EventArgs) _
30           Handles radYesNoCancel.CheckedChanged
31           buttonType = MessageBoxButtons.YesNoCancel
32        End Sub ' radYesNoCancel_CheckedChanged
33
34        ' set button type to YesNo
35        Private Sub radYesNo_CheckedChanged(ByVal sender As System.Object, _
36           ByVal e As System.EventArgs) Handles radYesNo.CheckedChanged
37           buttonType = MessageBoxButtons.YesNo
38        End Sub ' radYesNo_CheckedChanged
39
40        ' set button type to RetryCancel
41        Private Sub radRetryCancel_CheckedChanged( _
42           ByVal sender As System.Object, ByVal e As System.EventArgs) _
43           Handles radRetryCancel.CheckedChanged
44           buttonType = MessageBoxButtons.RetryCancel
45        End Sub ' radRetryCancel_CheckedChanged
46
47        ' set icon type to Asterisk
48        Private Sub radAsterisk_CheckedChanged(ByVal sender As System.Object, _
49           ByVal e As System.EventArgs) Handles radAsterisk.CheckedChanged
50           iconType = MessageBoxIcon.Asterisk
51        End Sub ' radAsterisk_CheckedChanged
52
53        ' set icon type to Error
54        Private Sub radError_CheckedChanged(ByVal sender As System.Object, _
55           ByVal e As System.EventArgs) Handles radError.CheckedChanged
56           iconType = MessageBoxIcon.Error
57        End Sub ' radError_CheckedChanged
58
59        ' set icon type to Exclamation
60        Private Sub radExclamation_CheckedChanged( _
61           ByVal sender As System.Object, ByVal e As System.EventArgs) _
62           Handles radExclamation.CheckedChanged
63           iconType = MessageBoxIcon.Exclamation
64        End Sub ' radExclamation_CheckedChanged
65
```

Fig. 13.28 | Using RadioButtons to set message-window options. (Part 2 of 4.)

```
66      ' set icon type to Hand
67      Private Sub radHand_CheckedChanged(ByVal sender As System.Object, _
68         ByVal e As System.EventArgs) Handles radHand.CheckedChanged
69         iconType = MessageBoxIcon.Hand
70      End Sub ' radHand_CheckedChanged
71
72      ' set icon type to Information
73      Private Sub radInformation_CheckedChanged( _
74         ByVal sender As System.Object, ByVal e As System.EventArgs) _
75         Handles radInformation.CheckedChanged
76         iconType = MessageBoxIcon.Information
77      End Sub ' radInformation_CheckedChanged
78
79      ' set icon type to Question
80      Private Sub radQuestion_CheckedChanged(ByVal sender As System.Object, _
81         ByVal e As System.EventArgs) Handles radQuestion.CheckedChanged
82         iconType = MessageBoxIcon.Question
83      End Sub ' radQuestion_CheckedChanged
84
85      ' set icon type to Stop
86      Private Sub radStop_CheckedChanged(ByVal sender As System.Object, _
87         ByVal e As System.EventArgs) Handles radStop.CheckedChanged
88         iconType = MessageBoxIcon.Stop
89      End Sub ' radStop_CheckedChanged
90
91      ' set icon type to Warning
92      Private Sub radWarning_CheckedChanged(ByVal sender As System.Object, _
93         ByVal e As System.EventArgs) Handles radWarning.CheckedChanged
94         iconType = MessageBoxIcon.Warning
95      End Sub ' radWarning_CheckedChanged
96
97      ' display MessageBox and Button user pressed
98      Private Sub btnDisplay_Click(ByVal sender As System.Object, _
99         ByVal e As System.EventArgs) Handles btnDisplay.Click
100        ' display MessageBox and store
101        ' the value of the Button that was pressed
102        Dim result As DialogResult = MessageBox.Show( _
103           "This is your Custom MessageBox.", _
104           "Custon MessageBox", buttonType, iconType, 0, 0)
105
106        ' check to see which Button was pressed in the MessageBox
107        ' change text displayed accordingly
108        Select Case result
109           Case Windows.Forms.DialogResult.OK
110              lblDisplay.Text = "OK was pressed"
111           Case Windows.Forms.DialogResult.Cancel
112              lblDisplay.Text = "Cancel was pressed"
113           Case Windows.Forms.DialogResult.Abort
114              lblDisplay.Text = "Abort was pressed"
115           Case Windows.Forms.DialogResult.Retry
116              lblDisplay.Text = "Retry was pressed"
117           Case Windows.Forms.DialogResult.Ignore
118              lblDisplay.Text = "Ignore was pressed"
```

Fig. 13.28 | Using RadioButtons to set message-window options. (Part 3 of 4.)

```
119              Case Windows.Forms.DialogResult.Yes
120                 lblDisplay.Text = "Yes was pressed"
121              Case Windows.Forms.DialogResult.No
122                 lblDisplay.Text = "No was pressed"
123          End Select
124       End Sub ' btnDisplay_Click
125    End Class ' FrmRadioButtonsTest
```

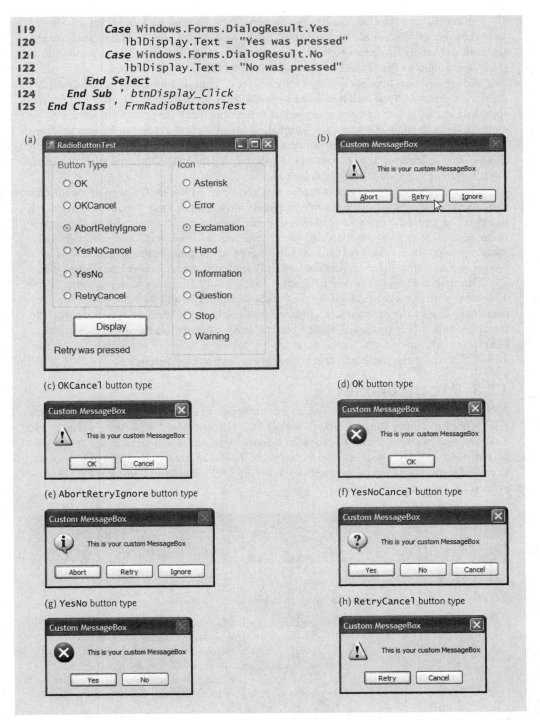

Fig. 13.28 | Using RadioButtons to set message-window options. (Part 4 of 4.)

Object `buttonType` is of type `MessageBoxButtons`, and can have values `Abort-RetryIgnore`, `OK`, `OKCancel`, `RetryCancel`, `YesNo` and `YesNoCancel`. The name indicates the options that are presented to the user in the `MessageBox`. The sample output windows show `MessageBox`es for all of the `MessageBoxButtons` enumeration values.

We created two `GroupBox`es, one for each set of enumeration values. The `GroupBox` captions are **Button Type** and **Icon**. The `GroupBox`es contain `RadioButton`s for the corresponding enumeration options, and the `RadioButton`s' `Text` properties are set appropriately. Because the `RadioButton`s are grouped, only one `RadioButton` can be selected from each `GroupBox`. There is also a `Button` (`btnDisplay`) labeled **Display**. When a user clicks this `Button`, a customized `MessageBox` is displayed. A `Label` (`lblDisplay`) displays which `Button` the user pressed in the `MessageBox`.

The event handler for each `RadioButton` handles the `CheckedChanged` event for that `RadioButton`. When a `RadioButton` contained in the **Button Type** `GroupBox` is checked, the checked `RadioButton`'s corresponding event handler sets `buttonType` to the appropriate value. Lines 9–45 contain the event handling for these `RadioButton`s. Similarly, when the user checks the `RadioButton`s belonging to the **Icon** `GroupBox`, the event handlers associated with these events (lines 48–95) set `iconType` to its corresponding value.

The `btnDisplay_Click` event handler (lines 98–124) creates a `MessageBox` (lines 102–104) with options specified by the values of `iconType` and `buttonType`. When the user clicks one of the `MessageBox`'s buttons, the result of the message box is returned to the application. This result is a value from the ***DialogResult* enumeration** that contains `Abort`, `Cancel`, `Ignore`, `No`, `None`, `OK`, `Retry` or `Yes`. The `Select Case` statement in lines 108–123 tests for the result and sets `lblDisplay.Text` appropriately.

13.8 PictureBoxes

A `PictureBox` displays an image. The image can be one of several formats, such as bitmap, GIF (Graphics Interchange Format) and JPEG. (Images are discussed in Chapter 17, Graphics and Multimedia.) A `PictureBox`'s `Image` property specifies the image that is displayed, and the `SizeMode` property indicates how the image is displayed (`Normal`, `StretchImage`, `Autosize` or `CenterImage`). Figure 13.29 describes common `PictureBox` properties and a common event.

PictureBox properties and an event	Description
Common Properties	
`Image`	Sets the image to display in the `PictureBox`.
`SizeMode`	Enumeration that controls image sizing and positioning. Values are `Normal` (default), `StretchImage`, `AutoSize` and `CenterImage`. `Normal` places the image in the top-left corner of the `PictureBox`; `CenterImage` puts the image in the middle. Both options truncate the image if it is too large. `StretchImage` resizes the image to fit in the `PictureBox`. `AutoSize` resizes the `PictureBox` to fit the image.

Fig. 13.29 | `PictureBox` properties and an event. (Part 1 of 2.)

PictureBox properties and an event	Description
Common Event	
Click	Occurs when the user clicks the control. Double clicking this control design mode generates an empty event handler for this event.

Fig. 13.29 | PictureBox properties and an event. (Part 2 of 2.)

Figure 13.30 uses a PictureBox named picImage to display one of three bitmap images—image0, image1 or image2. These images are located in the project's bin/Debug and bin/Release directories in the subdirectory images. Whenever a user clicks the **Next Image** Button, the image changes to the next image in sequence. When the last image is displayed and the user clicks the **Next Image** Button, the first image is displayed again. Event handler btnNext_Click (lines 10–17) uses Integer variable imageNum to store the number of the image we want to display. We then set the Image property of picImage to an Image (lines 15–16).

13.9 ToolTips

In Chapter 2, we discussed tool tips—the helpful text that appears when the mouse hovers over a GUI control. The tool tips displayed in Visual Studio serve as useful reminders of each toolbar icon's functionality. Many programs use tool tips to remind users of each control's purpose. For example, Microsoft Word has tool tips that help users determine the purpose of the application's icons. This section demonstrates how to use the ***ToolTip component*** to add tool tips to your applications. Figure 13.31 describes common properties and a common event of class ToolTip.

```vb
 1    ' Fig. 13.30: FrmPictureBoxTest.vb
 2    ' Using a PictureBox to display images.
 3    Imports System.IO
 4
 5    Public Class FrmPictureBoxTest
 6       ' determines which image is displayed
 7       Private imageNum As Integer = -1
 8
 9       ' change image whenever Next Button is clicked
10       Private Sub btnNext_Click(ByVal sender As System.Object, _
11          ByVal e As System.EventArgs) Handles btnNext.Click
12          imageNum = (imageNum + 1) Mod 3 ' imageNum cycles from 0 to 2
13
14          ' create Image object from file, display in PicutreBox
15          picImage.Image = Image.FromFile(Directory.GetCurrentDirectory() & _
16             "\images\image" & imageNum & ".bmp")
17       End Sub ' btnNext_Click
18    End Class ' FrmPictureBoxTest
```

Fig. 13.30 | Using a PictureBox to display images. (Part 1 of 2.)

Fig. 13.30 | Using a PictureBox to display images. (Part 2 of 2.)

ToolTip properties and an event	Description
Common Properties	
AutoPopDelay	The amount of time (in milliseconds) that the tool tip appears while the mouse is over a control.
InitialDelay	The amount of time (in milliseconds) that a mouse must hover over a control before a tool tip appears.
ReshowDelay	The amount of time (in milliseconds) between which two different tool tips appear (when the mouse is moved from one control to another).

Fig. 13.31 | ToolTip properties and an event. (Part 1 of 2.)

ToolTip properties and an event	Description
Common Event	
Draw	Raised when the tool tip is displayed. This event allows programmers to modify the appearance of the tool tip.

Fig. 13.31 | ToolTip properties and an event. (Part 2 of 2.)

When you add a ToolTip component from the **Toolbox**, it appears in the *component tray*—the gray region below the Form in **Design** mode. Once a ToolTip is added to a Form, a new property appears in the **Properties** window for the Form's other controls. This property appears in the **Properties** window as **ToolTip on**, followed by the name of the ToolTip component. For instance, if our Form's ToolTip were named helpfulToolTip, you would set a control's **ToolTip on helpfulToolTip** property value to specify the control's tool tip text. Figure 13.32 demonstrates the ToolTip component. For this example, we create a GUI containing two Labels so that we can demonstrate a different tool tip for each Label. To make the sample outputs clearer, we set the BorderStyle property of each Label to FixedSingle, which displays a solid border. Since there is no event-handling code in this example, the class in Fig. 13.32 is empty.

In this example, we named the ToolTip component labelsToolTip. Figure 13.33 shows the ToolTip in the component tray. We set the tool tip text for the first Label to "First Label" and the tool tip text for the second Label to "Second Label." Figure 13.34 demonstrates setting the tool tip text for the first Label.

13.10 NumericUpDown Control

At times, we will want to restrict a user's input choices to a specific range of numeric values. This is the purpose of the *NumericUpDown control*. This control appears as a TextBox, with two small Buttons on the right side—one with an up arrow and one with a down

```
 1    ' Fig. 13.32: FrmToolTipExample.vb
 2    ' Demonstrating the ToolTip component.
 3    Public Class FrmToolTipDemonstration
 4        ' no event handlers needed for this example
 5    End Class
```

Fig. 13.32 | Demonstrating the ToolTip component.

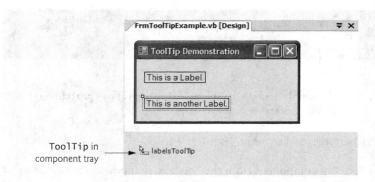

Fig. 13.33 | ToolTip component in the component tray.

Fig. 13.34 | Setting a control's tool tip text.

arrow. By default, a user can type numeric values into this control as if it were a TextBox or click the up and down arrows to increase or decrease the value in the control, respectively. The largest and smallest values in the range are specified with the *Maximum* and *Minimum* properties, respectively (both of type Decimal). The *Increment* property (also of type Decimal) specifies by how much the current number in the control changes when the user clicks the control's up and down arrows. Figure 13.35 describes common properties and a common event of class NumericUpDown.

NumericUpDown properties and an event	Description
Common Properties	
Increment	Specifies by how much the current number in the control changes when the user clicks the control's up and down arrows.

Fig. 13.35 | NumericUpDown properties and an event. (Part 1 of 2.)

NumericUpDown properties and an event	Description
Maximum	Largest value in the control's range.
Minimum	Smallest value in the control's range.
UpDownAlign	Modifies the alignment of the up and down Buttons on the NumericUpDown control. This property can be used to display these Buttons to either the left or the right of the control.
Value	The numeric value currently displayed in the control.
Common Event	
ValueChanged	This event is raised when the value in the control is changed. It is the default event for the NumericUpDown control.

Fig. 13.35 | NumericUpDown properties and an event. (Part 2 of 2.)

Figure 13.36 demonstrates using a NumericUpDown control for a GUI that calculates interest rate. The calculations performed in this application are similar to those performed in Fig. 6.8. TextBoxes are used to input the principal and interest rate amounts, and a NumericUpDown control is used to input the number of years for which we want to calculate interest.

```
1   ' Fig. 13.36: FrmInterestCalculator.vb
2   ' Demonstrating the NumericUpDown control.
3   Public Class FrmInterestCalculator
4
5      Private Sub btnCalculate_Click(ByVal sender As System.Object, _
6         ByVal e As System.EventArgs) Handles btnCalculate.Click
7         ' declare variables to store user input
8         Dim principal As Decimal ' store principal
9         Dim rate As Double ' store interest rate
10        Dim year As Integer ' store number of years
11        Dim amount As Decimal ' store amount
12
13        ' retrieve user input
14        principal = Convert.ToDecimal(txtPrincipal.Text)
15        rate = Convert.ToDouble(txtInterest.Text)
16        year = Convert.ToInt32(updYear.Value)
17
18        ' set output header
19        txtDisplay.Text = "Year" & vbTab & "Amount on Deposit" & vbCrLf
20
21        ' calculate amount after each year and append to output
22        For yearCounter As Integer = 1 To year
23           amount = principal * Convert.ToDecimal( _
24              Math.Pow(1 + rate / 100, yearCounter))
```

Fig. 13.36 | Demonstrating the NumericUpDown control. (Part 1 of 2.)

```
25                txtDisplay.Text &= (yearCounter & vbTab & _
26            String.Format("{0:C}", amount) & vbCrLf)
27       Next
28     End Sub ' btnCalculate_Click
29   End Class ' FrmInterestCalculator
```

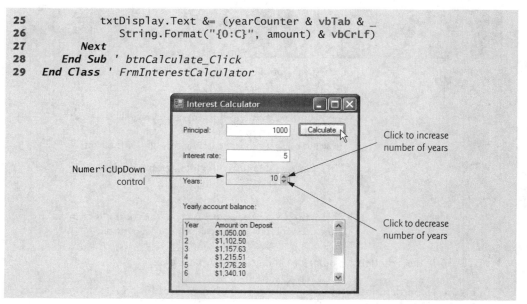

Fig. 13.36 | Demonstrating the NumericUpDown control. (Part 2 of 2.)

For the NumericUpDown control named updYear, we set the Minimum property to 1 and the Maximum property to 10. We left the Increment property's default value (1). These settings specify that users can enter a number of years in the range 1 to 10 in increments of 1. If we had set the Increment to 0.5, we could also input values such as 1.5 or 2.5. We set the NumericUpDown's **ReadOnly** *property* to True to indicate that the user cannot type a number into the control to make a selection. Thus, the user must click the up and down arrows (or use the arrow keys on the keyboard) to modify the value in the control. By default, the ReadOnly property is set to False. The output for this application is displayed in a multiline read-only TextBox with a vertical scrollbar so that the user can scroll through the entire output.

13.11 Mouse-Event Handling

This section explains how to handle *mouse events*, such as *clicks*, *presses* and *moves*, which are generated when the user interacts with a control via the mouse. Mouse events can be handled for any control that derives from class System.Windows.Forms.Control. For most mouse events, information about the event is passed to the event-handling method through an object of class *MouseEventArgs*, and the delegate used to create the mouse-event handlers is *MouseEventHandler*. Each mouse-event-handling method for these events requires an Object and a MouseEventArgs object as arguments.

Class MouseEventArgs contains information related to the mouse event, such as the mouse pointer's *x*- and *y*-coordinates, the mouse button pressed (Right, Left or Middle) and the number of times the mouse was clicked. Note that the *x*- and *y*-coordinates of the MouseEventArgs object are relative to the control that generated the event—that is point *(0,0)* represents the upper-left corner of the control where the mouse event occurred. Several common mouse events are described in Fig. 13.37.

Mouse events and event arguments	
Mouse Events with Event Argument of Type `EventArgs`	
MouseEnter	Occurs when the mouse cursor enters the control's boundaries.
MouseLeave	Occurs when the mouse cursor leaves the control's boundaries.
Mouse Events with Event Argument of Type `MouseEventArgs`	
MouseDown	Occurs when a mouse button is pressed while the mouse cursor is within a control's boundaries.
MouseHover	Occurs when the mouse cursor hovers within the control's boundaries.
MouseMove	Occurs when the mouse cursor is moved while in the control's boundaries.
MouseUp	Occurs when a mouse button is released when the cursor is within the control's boundaries.
Class `MouseEventArgs` *Properties*	
Button	Specifies which mouse button was pressed (Left, Right, Middle or none).
Clicks	The number of times the mouse button was clicked.
X	The *x*-coordinate within the control where the event occurred.
Y	The *y*-coordinate within the control where the event occurred.

Fig. 13.37 | Mouse events and event arguments.

Figure 13.38 uses mouse events to draw on a Form. Whenever the user drags the mouse (i.e., moves the mouse while a mouse button is pressed), small circles appear on the Form at the position where each mouse event occurs during the drag operation.

Line 4 declares variable shouldPaint, which determines whether to draw on the Form. We want to draw only while the mouse button is pressed (i.e., held down). Thus, when the user clicks or holds down a mouse button, the system generates a MouseDown event, and the event handler FrmPainter_MouseDown (lines 7–11) sets shouldPaint to True. When the user releases the mouse button, the system generates a MouseUp event, shouldPaint is set to False in the FrmPainter_MouseUp event handler (lines 14–18) and the program stops drawing. Unlike MouseMove events, which occur continuously as the user moves the mouse, the system generates a MouseDown event only when a mouse button is first pressed and generates a MouseUp event only when a mouse button is released.

```
1   ' Fig 13.38: FrmPainter.vb
2   ' Using the mouse to draw on a Form.
3   Public Class FrmPainter
4       Private shouldPaint As Boolean = False ' determines whether to paint
5
```

Fig. 13.38 | Using the mouse to draw on a Form. (Part 1 of 2.)

```
6        ' should paint when mouse button is pressed down
7        Private Sub FrmPainter_MouseDown(ByVal sender As System.Object, _
8           ByVal e As System.Windows.Forms.MouseEventArgs) _
9           Handles MyBase.MouseDown
10          shouldPaint = True
11       End Sub ' FrmPainter_MouseDown
12
13       ' stop painting when mouse button is released
14       Private Sub FrmPainter_MouseUp(ByVal sender As System.Object, _
15          ByVal e As System.Windows.Forms.MouseEventArgs) _
16          Handles MyBase.MouseUp
17          shouldPaint = False
18       End Sub ' FrmPainter_MouseUp
19
20       ' draw circle whenever mouse moves with its button held down
21       Private Sub FrmPainter_MouseMove(ByVal sender As System.Object, _
22          ByVal e As System.Windows.Forms.MouseEventArgs) _
23          Handles MyBase.MouseMove
24          ' check if mouse button is being pressed
25          If (shouldPaint) Then
26             ' draw a circle where the mouse pointer is present
27             Dim g As Graphics = CreateGraphics()
28             g.FillEllipse( _
29                New SolidBrush(Color.BlueViolet), e.X, e.Y, 4, 4)
30             g.Dispose()
31          End If
32       End Sub ' FrmPainter_MouseMove
33    End Class ' FrmPainter
```

Fig. 13.38 | Using the mouse to draw on a Form. (Part 2 of 2.)

Whenever the mouse moves over a control, the MouseMove event for that control occurs. Inside the FrmPainter_MouseMove event handler (lines 21–32), the program draws only if shouldPaint is True (i.e., a mouse button is pressed). Line 27 calls inherited Form method CreateGraphics to create a **Graphics** object that allows the program to draw on the Form. Class Graphics provides methods that draw various shapes. For example, lines 28–29 use method **FillEllipse** to draw a circle. The first parameter to method Fill-Ellipse in this case is an object of class **SolidBrush**, which specifies the solid color that will fill the shape. The color is provided as an argument to class SolidBrush's constructor. Type **Color** contains many predefined color constants—we selected Color.BlueViolet. FillEllipse draws an oval in a bounding rectangle that is specified by the *x*- and *y*-coordinates of its upper-left corner, its width and its height—the final four arguments to the method. The *x*- and *y*-coordinates represent the location of the mouse event and can be taken from the mouse-event arguments (e.X and e.Y). To draw a circle, we set the width and height of the bounding rectangle so that they are equal—in this example, both are 4 pixels. Line 30 invokes the Graphics object's Dispose method to return the Graphics object's resources back to the system. Graphics, SolidBrush and Color are all part of the System.Drawing namespace. We discuss class Graphics and its methods in depth in Chapter 17, Graphics and Multimedia.

13.12 Keyboard-Event Handling

Key events occur when keyboard keys are pressed and released. Such events can be handled for any control that inherits from System.Windows.Forms.Control. There are three key events—KeyPress, KeyUp and KeyDown. The **KeyPress** event occurs when the user presses a key that represents an ASCII character. The specific key can be determined with property **KeyChar** of the event handler's **KeyPressEventArgs** argument. ASCII is a 128-character set of alphanumeric symbols, a full listing of which can be found in Appendix D.

The KeyPress event does not indicate whether *modifier keys* (e.g., *Shift, Alt* and *Ctrl*) were pressed when a key event occurred. If this information is important, the **KeyUp** or **KeyDown** events can be used. The **KeyEventArgs** argument for each of these events contains information about modifier keys. Often, modifier keys are used in conjunction with the mouse to select or highlight information. Figure 13.39 lists important key-event information. Several properties return values from the **Keys** *enumeration*, which provides constants that specify the various keys on a keyboard. Like the FontStyle enumeration (Section 13.7), the Keys enumeration has the System.FlagAttribute, so the enumeration's constants can be combined to indicate multiple keys pressed at the same time.

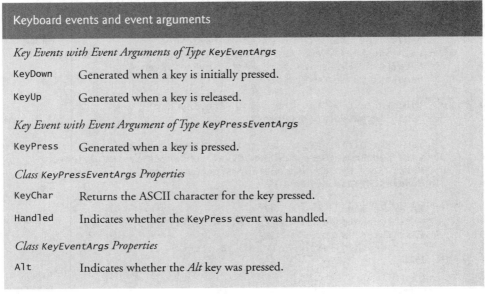

Keyboard events and event arguments
Key Events with Event Arguments of Type KeyEventArgs
KeyDown	Generated when a key is initially pressed.
KeyUp	Generated when a key is released.
Key Event with Event Argument of Type KeyPressEventArgs
KeyPress	Generated when a key is pressed.
Class KeyPressEventArgs Properties
KeyChar	Returns the ASCII character for the key pressed.
Handled	Indicates whether the KeyPress event was handled.
Class KeyEventArgs Properties
Alt	Indicates whether the *Alt* key was pressed.

Fig. 13.39 | Keyboard events and event arguments. (Part 1 of 2.)

Keyboard events and event arguments	
Control	Indicates whether the *Ctrl* key was pressed.
Shift	Indicates whether the *Shift* key was pressed.
Handled	Indicates whether the event was handled.
KeyCode	Returns the key code for the key as a value from the Keys enumeration. This does not include modifier-key information. It is used to test for a specific key.
KeyData	Returns the key code for a key combined with modifier information as a Keys value. This property contains all the information about the pressed key.
KeyValue	Returns the key code as an int, rather than as a value from the Keys enumeration. This property is used to obtain a numeric representation of the pressed key. The int value is known as a Windows virtual key code.
Modifiers	Returns a Keys value indicating any pressed modifier keys (*Alt*, *Ctrl* and *Shift*). This property is used to determine modifier-key information only.

Fig. 13.39 | Keyboard events and event arguments. (Part 2 of 2.)

Figure 13.40 demonstrates the use of the key-event handlers to display a key pressed by a user. The program is a Form with two Labels that displays the pressed key on one Label and modifier-key information on the other.

```
1   ' Fig. 13.40: FrmKeyDemo.vb
2   ' Displaying information about the key the user pressed.
3   Public Class FrmKeyDemo
4
5      ' display the character pressed using KeyChar
6      Private Sub FrmKeyDemo_KeyPress(ByVal sender As System.Object, _
7         ByVal e As System.Windows.Forms.KeyPressEventArgs) _
8         Handles MyBase.KeyPress
9
10        lblChar.Text = "Key pressed: " & e.KeyChar
11     End Sub ' FrmKeyDemo_KeyPress
12
13     ' display modifier keys, key code, key data and key value
14     Private Sub FrmKeyDemo_KeyDown(ByVal sender As System.Object, _
15        ByVal e As System.Windows.Forms.KeyEventArgs) _
16        Handles MyBase.KeyDown
17
18        If e.Alt Then ' key is Alt
19           lblKeyInfo.Text = "Alt: Yes" & vbCrLf
20        Else ' key is not Alt
21           lblKeyInfo.Text = "Alt: No" & vbCrLf
22        End If
23
```

Fig. 13.40 | Demonstrating keyboard events. (Part 1 of 2.)

```
24        If e.Shift Then ' key is Shift
25            lblKeyInfo.Text &= "Shift: Yes" & vbCrLf
26        Else ' key is not Shift
27            lblKeyInfo.Text &= "Shift: No" & vbCrLf
28        End If
29
30        If e.Control Then ' key is Control
31            lblKeyInfo.Text &= "Control: Yes" & vbCrLf
32        Else ' key is not Control
33            lblKeyInfo.Text &= "Control: No" & vbCrLf
34        End If
35
36        ' diplay key code, key data and key value
37        lblKeyInfo.Text &= "KeyCode: " & e.KeyCode.ToString() & vbCrLf & _
38            "KeyData: " & e.KeyData.ToString() & vbCrLf & _
39            "KeyValue: " & e.KeyValue.ToString()
40    End Sub ' FrmKeyDemo_KeyDown
41
42    ' clear Labels when keys are released
43    Private Sub FrmKeyDemo_KeyUp(ByVal sender As System.Object, _
44        ByVal e As System.Windows.Forms.KeyEventArgs) Handles MyBase.KeyUp
45
46        lblChar.Text = ""
47        lblKeyInfo.Text = ""
48    End Sub ' FrmKeyDemo_KeyUp
49 End Class ' FrmKeyDemo
```

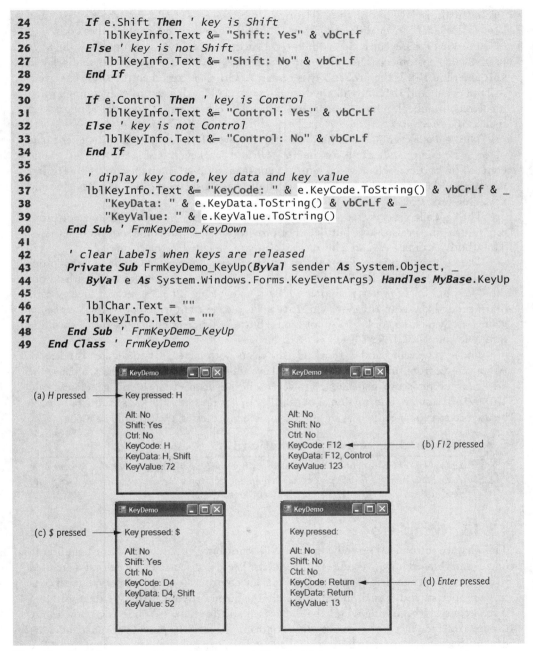

Fig. 13.40 | Demonstrating keyboard events. (Part 2 of 2.)

Initially, the two Labels (lblChar and lblKeyInfo) contain "Just Press" and "A Key...". Control lblChar displays the character value of the key pressed, whereas lblKeyInfo displays information relating to the pressed key. Because the KeyDown and KeyPress events convey different information, the Form (FrmKeyDemo) handles both.

The KeyPress event handler (lines 6–11) accesses the KeyChar property of the Key-PressEventArgs object. This returns the pressed key as a Char, which we then display in lblChar (line 10). If the pressed key is not an ASCII character, then the KeyPress event will not occur, and lblChar will not display any text. ASCII is a common encoding format for letters, numbers, punctuation marks and other characters. It does not support keys such as the *function keys* (like *F1*) or the modifier keys (*Alt*, *Ctrl* and *Shift*).

The KeyDown event handler (lines 14–40) displays information from its KeyEventArgs object. The event handler tests for the *Alt*, *Shift* and *Ctrl* keys by using the Alt, Shift and Control properties, each of which returns a Boolean value—True if the corresponding key is pressed and False otherwise. The event handler then displays the KeyCode, KeyData and KeyValue properties.

The KeyCode property returns a Keys enumeration value (line 37). The KeyCode property returns the pressed key, but does not provide any information about modifier keys. Thus, both a capital "A" and a lowercase "a" are represented as the *A* key.

The KeyData property (line 38) also returns a Keys enumeration value, but this property includes data about modifier keys. Thus, if "A" is input, the KeyData shows that both the *A* key and the *Shift* key were pressed. Lastly, KeyValue (line 39) returns the key code of the pressed key as an Integer. This Integer is the *key code*, which provides an Integer value for a wide range of keys and for mouse buttons. The key code is useful when one is testing for non-ASCII keys (such as *F12*).

The KeyUp event handler (lines 43–48) clears both Labels when the key is released. As we can see from the output, non-ASCII keys are not displayed in lblChar, because the KeyPress event is not generated. However, the KeyDown event is still generated, and lblKeyInfo displays information about the key that is pressed. The Keys enumeration can be used to test for specific keys by comparing the key pressed to a specific KeyCode.

Software Engineering Observation 13.3

To make a control react when a particular key is pressed (such as Enter*), handle a key event for that control and test for the pressed key. To allow a* Button *to be clicked when the user presses the* Enter *key on a* Form*, set the* Form*'s* AcceptButton *property.*

13.13 Wrap-Up

This chapter introduced several common GUI controls. We discussed event handling in detail, and showed how to create event handlers. We also discussed how delegates are used to connect event handlers to the events of specific controls. You learned how to use a control's properties and Visual Studio to specify the layout of your GUI. We demonstrated several controls, beginning with Labels, Buttons and TextBoxes. You learned how to use GroupBoxes and Panels to organize other controls. We demonstrated CheckBoxes and RadioButtons, which are state buttons that allow users to select among several options. We displayed images in PictureBox controls, displayed helpful text on a GUI with ToolTip components and specified a range of input values for users with a NumericUpDown control. We then demonstrated how to handle mouse and keyboard events. The next chapter introduces additional GUI controls. You will learn how to add menus to your GUIs and create Windows applications that display multiple Forms.

Graphical User Interface Concepts: Part 2

I claim not to have controlled events, but confess plainly that events have controlled me.
—Abraham Lincoln

Capture its reality in paint!
—Paul Cézanne

An actor entering through the door, you've got nothing. But if he enters through the window, you've got a situation.
—Billy Wilder

But, soft! what light through yonder window breaks? It is the east, and Juliet is the sun!
—William Shakespeare

OBJECTIVES

In this chapter you will learn:

■ To create menus, tabbed windows and multiple document interface (MDI) programs.

■ To use the `ListView` and `TreeView` controls for displaying information.

■ To create hyperlinks using the `LinkLabel` control.

■ To display lists of information in `ListBox` and `ComboBox` controls.

■ To input date and time data with the `DateTimePicker`.

■ To create custom controls.

14.1 Introduction

This chapter continues our study of GUIs. We begin our discussion with menus, which present users with logically organized commands (or options). We show how to develop menus with the tools provided by Visual Studio. Next, we discuss how to input and display dates and times using the MonthCalendar and DateTimePicker controls. We also introduce LinkLabels—powerful GUI components that enable the user to visit one of several destinations, such as a file on the current machine or a Web page, by simply clicking the mouse.

We demonstrate how to manipulate a list of values via a ListBox and how to combine several checkboxes in a CheckedListBox. We also create drop-down lists using ComboBoxes and display data hierarchically with a TreeView control. You'll also learn two other GUI components—tab controls and multiple document interface (MDI) windows. These components enable you to create real-world programs with sophisticated GUIs.

Visual Studio provides a large set of GUI components, several of which are discussed in this (and the preceding) chapter. Visual Studio also enables you to design custom controls and add them to the **ToolBox**, as we demonstrate in the last example of this chapter. The techniques presented in this chapter form the groundwork for creating more substantial GUIs and custom controls.

14.2 Menus

Menus provide groups of related commands for Windows applications. Although commands vary between applications, some—such as **Open** and **Save**—are common to many applications. Menus organize commands without "cluttering" the application's user interface.

In Fig. 14.1, an expanded menu from Visual Basic 2005 Express lists various commands (called *menu items*), plus *submenus* (menus within a menu). Menu items are typically displayed down and indented to the right of the top-level menu, but they can be displayed to the left if there is not enough space to the right. The menu that contains a menu item is called the menu item's *parent menu*. A menu item that contains a submenu is considered to be the parent of the submenu.

All menu items can have *Alt* key shortcuts (also called *access shortcuts* or *hotkeys*), which are accessed by pressing *Alt* and the underlined letter (for example, *Alt F* typically expands the **File** menu). Menus that are not top-level menus can have shortcut keys as well (combinations of *Ctrl, Shift, Alt, F1, F2*, letter keys, etc.). Some menu items display check marks, usually indicating that multiple options on the menu can be selected at once.

To create a menu, open the **Toolbox** and drag a *MenuStrip* control onto the Form. This creates a menu bar across the top of the Form (below the title bar) and places a MenuStrip icon in the component tray. To select the MenuStrip, click this icon. You can now use **Design** mode to create and edit menus for your application. Menus, like other controls, have properties and events, which can be accessed through the **Properties** window.

To add menu items to the menu, click the **Type Here** TextBox (Fig. 14.2) and type the menu item's name. This action adds an entry to the menu of type *ToolStripMenuItem*. After you press the *Enter* key, the menu item name is added to the menu. Additional **Type Here** TextBoxes appear, allowing you to add items underneath or to the right of the original menu item (Fig. 14.3).

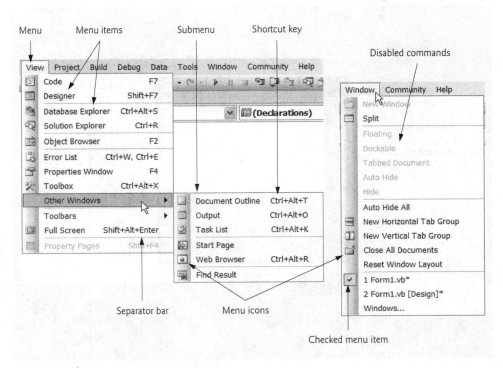

Fig. 14.1 | Menus, submenus, menu items and menu icons.

Type menu name in **TextBox**

Main menu bar

MenuStrip icon

Fig. 14.2 | Editing menus in Visual Studio.

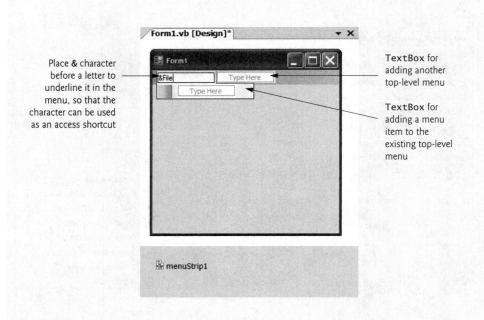

Place & character before a letter to underline it in the menu, so that the character can be used as an access shortcut

TextBox for adding another top-level menu

TextBox for adding a menu item to the existing top-level menu

Fig. 14.3 | Adding **ToolStripMenuItems** to a **MenuStrip**.

To create an *access shortcut* (or *keyboard shortcut*), type an ampersand (&) before the character to be underlined. For example, to create the **File** menu item with the letter **F** underlined, type &File. To display an ampersand, type &&. To add other shortcut keys (like those shown in Fig. 14.1) for menu items, set the ***ShortcutKeys*** property of the appropriate ToolStripMenuItems. To do this, select the down arrow to the right of this property in the **Properties** window. In the window that appears (Fig. 14.4), use the Check-Boxes and drop-down list to select the shortcut keys. When you are finished, click elsewhere on the screen. You can hide the shortcut keys by setting property ***ShowShortcutKeys*** to False, and you can modify how the control keys are displayed in the menu item by modifying property ***ShortcutKeyDisplayString***.

Look-and-Feel Observation 14.1

Buttons can have access shortcuts. Place the & symbol immediately before the desired character in the Button's text. To press the button by using its access key in the running application, press Alt and the underlined character.

You can remove a menu item by selecting it and pressing the *Delete* key. Menu items can be grouped logically by *separator bars*, which are inserted by right clicking a menu item and selecting **Insert > Separator** or by typing "-" for the text of a menu item.

You can also add TextBoxes and ComboBoxes (drop-down lists) as menu items. When adding an item in **Design** mode, you may have noticed that before you click to enter text for a new item, you are provided with a drop-down list. Clicking the down arrow (Fig. 14.5) allows you to select the type of item to add—**MenuItem** (of type ToolStrip-MenuItem, the default), **ComboBox** (of type ToolStripComboBox) and **TextBox** (of type ToolStripTextBox). We focus on ToolStripMenuItems. [*Note:* If you view this drop-down list for menu items that are not on the top level, a fourth option appears, allowing you to insert a separator bar.]

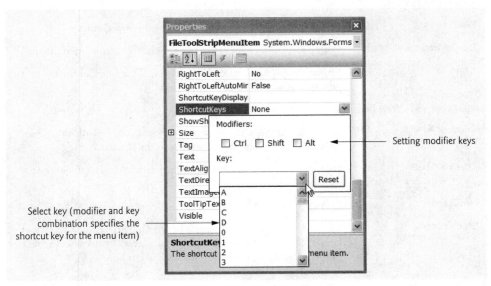

Fig. 14.4 | Setting a menu item's shortcut keys.

Fig. 14.5 | Menu item options.

ToolStripMenuItems generate a Click event when selected. To create an empty Click event handler, double click the menu item in **Design** mode. Common actions in response to these events include displaying dialogs and setting application properties. Common menu properties and a common event of MenuStrip and ToolStripMenuItem are summarized in Fig. 14.6.

MenuStrip and ToolStripMenuItem properties and an event	Description
MenuStrip Properties	
MenuItems	Contains the top-level menu items for this MenuStrip.
HasChildren	Indicates whether MenuStrip has any child controls (menu items).
RightToLeft	Causes text to display from right to left. This is useful for languages that are read from right to left.
ToolStripMenuItem Properties	
Checked	Indicates whether a menu item is checked. The default value is False, meaning that the menu item is unchecked.
CheckOnClick	Indicates that a menu item should appear checked or unchecked as the item is clicked.
MenuItems	Lists the submenu items for a particular menu item.
ShortcutKey-DisplayString	Specifies text that should appear beside a menu item for a shortcut key. If left blank, the key names are displayed. Otherwise, the text in this property is displayed for the shortcut key.

Fig. 14.6 | MenuStrip and ToolStripMenuItem properties and an event. (Part 1 of 2.)

MenuStrip and ToolStripMenuItem properties and an event	Description
ShortcutKeys	Specifies the shortcut key for the menu item.
ShowShortcutKeys	Indicates whether a shortcut key is shown beside the menu item text. The default is True, which displays the shortcut key.
Text	Specifies the menu item's text. To create an *Alt* access shortcut, precede a character with & (e.g., &File to specify a menu named **File** with the letter **F** underlined).
Common ToolStripMenuItem Event	
Click	Generated when an item is clicked or a shortcut key is used to select a menu item.

Fig. 14.6 | MenuStrip and ToolStripMenuItem properties and an event. (Part 2 of 2.)

Look-and-Feel Observation 14.2

It is a convention to place an ellipsis (...) after the name of a menu item that, when selected, displays a dialog (e.g. **Save As...**). *A menu item that causes an immediate action without prompting the user for more information (e.g.,* **Save**) *should not have an ellipsis following its name.*

Class FrmMenuTest (Fig. 14.7) creates a simple menu on a Form. The Form has a top-level **File** menu with menu items **About** (which displays a MessageBox) and **Exit** (which terminates the program). The program also includes a **Format** menu, which contains menu items that change the format of the text on a Label. The **Format** menu has submenus **Color** and **Font**, which change the color and font of the text on a Label.

```vb
1   ' Fig. 14.7: FrmMenuTest.vb
2   ' Using Menus to change font colors and styles.
3   Public Class FrmMenuTest
4
5      ' display MessageBox when About MenuItem is selected
6      Private Sub aboutToolStripMenuItem_Click( _
7         ByVal sender As System.Object, ByVal e As System.EventArgs) _
8         Handles aboutToolStripMenuItem.Click
9
10        MessageBox.Show("This is an example" & vbCrLf & "of using menus.", _
11           "About", MessageBoxButtons.OK, MessageBoxIcon.Information)
12     End Sub ' aboutToolStripMenuItem_Click
13
14     ' exit program when Exit MenuItem is selected
15     Private Sub exitToolStripMenuItem_Click( _
16        ByVal sender As System.Object, ByVal e As System.EventArgs) _
17        Handles exitToolStripMenuItem.Click
18
```

Fig. 14.7 | Menus for changing text font and color. (Part 1 of 4.)

```
19          Application.Exit()
20      End Sub ' exitToolStripMenuItem_Click
21
22      ' reset checkmarks for Color MenuItems
23      Private Sub ClearColor()
24          ' clear all checkmarks
25          blackToolStripMenuItem.Checked = False
26          blueToolStripMenuItem.Checked = False
27          redToolStripMenuItem.Checked = False
28          greenToolStripMenuItem.Checked = False
29      End Sub ' ClearColor
30
31      ' update Menu state and color display black
32      Private Sub blackToolStripMenuItem_Click( _
33          ByVal sender As System.Object, ByVal e As System.EventArgs) _
34          Handles blackToolStripMenuItem.Click
35
36          ClearColor() ' reset checkmarks for Color MenuItems
37          lblDisplay.ForeColor = Color.Black ' set Color to Black
38          blackToolStripMenuItem.Checked = True
39      End Sub ' blackToolStripMenuItem_Click
40
41      ' update Menu state and color display blue
42      Private Sub blueToolStripMenuItem_Click( _
43          ByVal sender As System.Object, ByVal e As System.EventArgs) _
44          Handles blueToolStripMenuItem.Click
45
46          ClearColor() ' reset checkmarks for Color MenuItems
47          lblDisplay.ForeColor = Color.Blue ' set Color to Blue
48          blueToolStripMenuItem.Checked = True
49      End Sub ' blueToolStripMenuItem_Click
50
51      ' update Menu state and color display red
52      Private Sub redToolStripMenuItem_Click( _
53          ByVal sender As System.Object, ByVal e As System.EventArgs) _
54          Handles redToolStripMenuItem.Click
55
56          ClearColor() ' reset checkmarks for Color MenuItems
57          lblDisplay.ForeColor = Color.Red ' set Color to Red
58          redToolStripMenuItem.Checked = True
59      End Sub ' redToolStripMenuItem_Click
60
61      ' update Menu state and color display green
62      Private Sub greenToolStripMenuItem_Click( _
63          ByVal sender As System.Object, ByVal e As System.EventArgs) _
64          Handles greenToolStripMenuItem.Click
65
66          ClearColor() ' reset checkmarks for Color MenuItems
67          lblDisplay.ForeColor = Color.Green ' set Color to Green
68          greenToolStripMenuItem.Checked = True
69      End Sub ' greenToolStripMenuItem_Click
70
```

Fig. 14.7 | Menus for changing text font and color. (Part 2 of 4.)

```vbnet
71      ' reset checkmarks for Font MenuItems
72      Private Sub ClearFont()
73         timesToolStripMenuItem.Checked = False
74         courierToolStripMenuItem.Checked = False
75         comicToolStripMenuItem.Checked = False
76      End Sub ' ClearFont
77
78      ' update Menu state and set Font to Times New Roman
79      Private Sub timesToolStripMenuItem_Click( _
80         ByVal sender As System.Object, ByVal e As System.EventArgs) _
81         Handles timesToolStripMenuItem.Click
82
83         ClearFont() 'reset checkmarks for Font MenuItems
84         timesToolStripMenuItem.Checked = True
85
86         ' set Times New Roman font
87         lblDisplay.Font = _
88            New Font("Times New Roman", 14, lblDisplay.Font.Style)
89      End Sub ' timesToolStripMenuItem_Click
90
91      ' update Menu state and set Font to Courier New
92      Private Sub courierToolStripMenuItem_Click( _
93         ByVal sender As System.Object, ByVal e As System.EventArgs) _
94         Handles courierToolStripMenuItem.Click
95
96         ClearFont() ' reset checkmarks for Font MenuItems
97         courierToolStripMenuItem.Checked = True
98
99         ' set Courier font
100        lblDisplay.Font = _
101           New Font("Courier New", 14, lblDisplay.Font.Style)
102     End Sub ' courierToolStripMenuItem_Click
103
104     ' update Menu state and set Font to Comic Sans MS
105     Private Sub comicToolStripMenuItem_Click( _
106        ByVal sender As System.Object, ByVal e As System.EventArgs) _
107        Handles comicToolStripMenuItem.Click
108
109        ClearFont() ' reset checkmarks for Font MenuItems
110        comicToolStripMenuItem.Checked = True
111
112        ' set Comic Sans MS font
113        lblDisplay.Font = _
114           New Font("Comic Sans MS", 14, lblDisplay.Font.Style)
115     End Sub ' comicToolStripMenuItem_Click
116
117     ' toggle checkmark and toggle bold style
118     Private Sub boldToolStripMenuItem_Click( _
119        ByVal sender As System.Object, ByVal e As System.EventArgs) _
120        Handles boldToolStripMenuItem.Click
121        ' toggle menu item checkmark
122        boldToolStripMenuItem.Checked = Not boldToolStripMenuItem.Checked
123
```

Fig. 14.7 | Menus for changing text font and color. (Part 3 of 4.)

```
124        ' use Xor to toggle bold, keep all other styles
125        lblDisplay.Font = New Font(lblDisplay.Font.FontFamily, 14, _
126           lblDisplay.Font.Style Xor FontStyle.Bold)
127     End Sub ' boldToolStripMenuItem_Click
128
129     ' toggle checkmark and toggle italic style
130     Private Sub italicToolStripMenuItem_Click( _
131        ByVal sender As System.Object, ByVal e As System.EventArgs) _
132        Handles italicToolStripMenuItem.Click
133        ' toggle menu item checkmark
134     italicToolStripMenuItem.Checked = _
135        Not italicToolStripMenuItem.Checked
136
137        ' use Xor to toggle italic, keep all other styles
138        lblDisplay.Font = New Font(lblDisplay.Font.FontFamily, 14, _
139           lblDisplay.Font.Style Xor FontStyle.Italic)
140     End Sub ' italicToolStripMenuItem_Click
141  End Class ' FrmMenuTest
```

Fig. 14.7 | Menus for changing text font and color. (Part 4 of 4.)

To create this GUI, begin by dragging the MenuStrip from the **ToolBox** onto the Form. Then use **Design** mode to create the menu structure shown in the sample outputs. The **File** menu (fileToolStripMenuItem) has menu items **About** (aboutToolStripMenuItem) and **Exit** (exitToolStripMenuItem); the **Format** menu (formatToolStripMenuItem) has two submenus. The first submenu, **Color** (colorToolStripMenuItem), contains menu items **Black** (blackToolStripMenuItem), **Blue** (blueToolStripMenuItem), **Red** (redToolStrip-MenuItem) and **Green** (greenToolStripMenuItem). The second submenu, **Font** (fontTool-StripMenuItem), contains menu items **Times New Roman** (timesToolStripMenuItem), **Courier New** (courierToolStripMenuItem), **Comic Sans MS** (comicToolStripMenuItem), a separator bar (dashToolStripMenuItem), **Bold** (boldToolStripMenuItem) and **Italic** (italicToolStripMenuItem).

The **About** menu item in the **File** menu displays a MessageBox when clicked (lines 6–12). The **Exit** menu item closes the application through Shared method *Exit* of class *Application* (line 19). Class Application's Shared methods control program execution. Method Exit causes our application to terminate.

We made the items in the **Color** submenu (**Black, Blue, Red** and **Green**) mutually exclusive—the user can select only one at a time (we explain how we did this shortly). To indicate that a menu item is selected, we will set each **Color** menu item's *Checked* property to True. This causes a check to appear to the left of a menu item.

Each **Color** menu item has its own Click event handler. The event handler for color **Black** is blackToolStripMenuItem_Click (lines 32–39). Similarly, the event handlers for colors **Blue, Red** and **Green** are blueToolStripMenuItem_Click (lines 42–49), redToolStripMenuItem_Click (lines 52–59) and greenToolStripMenuItem_Click (lines 62–69), respectively. The **Color** menu items must be mutually exclusive, so each event handler calls method ClearColor (lines 23–29) before setting its corresponding Checked property to True. Method ClearColor sets the Checked property of each color MenuItem to False, effectively preventing more than one menu item from being selected at a time. In the designer, we initially set the **Black** menu item's Checked property to True, because at the start of the program, the text on the Form is black.

Software Engineering Observation 14.1

The mutual exclusion of menu items is not enforced by the MenuStrip. You must program this behavior.

The **Font** menu contains three menu items for fonts (**Times New Roman, Courier New** and **Comic Sans MS**) and two menu items for font styles (**Bold** and **Italic**). We added a separator bar between the font and font-style menu items to indicate that these are separate options. A Font object can specify only one font at a time but can set multiple styles at once (e.g., a font can be both bold and italic). We set the font menu items to display checks. As with the **Color** menu, we must enforce mutual exclusion of these items in our event handlers.

Event handlers for font menu items **Times New Roman, Courier New** and **Comic Sans MS** are timesToolStripMenuItem_Click (lines 79–89), courierToolStripMenu-Item_Click (lines 92–102) and comicToolStripMenuItem_Click (lines 105–115), respectively. These event handlers behave in a manner similar to that of the event handlers for the **Color** menu items. Each event handler clears the Checked properties for all the font menu items by calling method ClearFont (lines 72–76), then sets to True the Checked property of the menu item that raised the event. This enforces the mutual exclusion of the font menu items. In the designer, we initially set the **Times New Roman** menu item's Checked property to True, because this is the original font for the text on the Form. The event handlers for the **Bold** and **Italic** menu items (lines 118–127 and 130–140) use the Xor operator to combine font styles, as we discussed in Chapter 13.

14.3 MonthCalendar Control

Many applications manipulate dates and times. The .NET Framework provides two controls that allow an application to retrieve date and time information—MonthCalendar and DateTimePicker (Section 14.4).

The *MonthCalendar* control (Fig. 14.8) displays a monthly calendar on the Form. The user can select a date from the currently displayed month or can use the provided links to navigate to another month. When a date is selected, it is highlighted. Multiple dates can be selected by clicking dates on the calendar while holding down the *Shift* key. The default event for this control is *DateChanged*, which is generated when a new date is selected. Properties are provided that allow you to modify the appearance of the calendar, how many dates can be selected at once, and the minimum and maximum dates that may be selected. MonthCalendar properties and a common event are summarized in Fig. 14.9.

Current day is outlined

Selected day is highlighted

Fig. 14.8 | MonthCalendar control.

MonthCalendar properties and an event	Description
MonthCalendar Properties	
FirstDayOfWeek	Sets which day of the week is the first displayed for each week in the calendar.
MaxDate	The last date that can be selected.
MaxSelectionCount	The maximum number of dates that can be selected at once.
MinDate	The first date that can be selected.

Fig. 14.9 | MonthCalendar properties and an event. (Part 1 of 2.)

MonthCalendar properties and an event	Description
MonthlyBoldedDates	An array of dates that will displayed in bold in the calendar.
SelectionEnd	The last of the dates selected by the user.
SelectionRange	The dates selected by the user.
SelectionStart	The first of the dates selected by the user.
Common MonthCalendar Event	
DateChanged	Generated when a date is selected in the calendar.

Fig. 14.9 | MonthCalendar properties and an event. (Part 2 of 2.)

14.4 DateTimePicker Control

The *DateTimePicker* control (see output of Fig. 14.11) is similar to the MonthCalendar control, but displays the calendar when the user clicks the down arrow. The DateTime-Picker can be used to retrieve date and time information from the user. The DateTime-Picker is also more customizable than a MonthCalendar control—more properties are provided to edit the look-and-feel of the drop-down calendar. Property *Format* specifies the user's selection options using the *DateTimePickerFormat* enumeration. The values in this enumeration are *Long* (displays the date in long format, as in **Friday, July 1, 2005**), *Short* (displays the date in short format, as in **7/1/2005**), *Time* (displays a time value, as in **11:48:02 PM**) and *Custom* (indicates that a custom format will be used). If value Custom is used, the display in the DateTimePicker is specified using property *CustomFormat*. The default event for this control is *ValueChanged*, which occurs when the selected value (whether a date or a time) is changed. DateTimePicker properties and a common event are summarized in Fig. 14.10.

DateTimePicker properties and an event	Description
DateTimePicker Properties	
CalendarForeColor	Sets the text color for the calendar.
CalendarMonth-Background	Sets the calendar's background color.
CustomFormat	Sets the custom format string for the user's options.
Format	Sets the format of the date and/or time used for the user's options.
MaxDate	The maximum date and time that can be selected.

Fig. 14.10 | DateTimePicker properties and an event. (Part 1 of 2.)

DateTimePicker properties and an event	Description
MinDate	The minimum date and time that can be selected.
ShowCheckBox	Indicates whether a CheckBox should be displayed to the left of the selected date and time.
ShowUpDown	Used to indicate that the control should have up and down Buttons. This is helpful for instances when the DateTimePicker is used to select a time—the Buttons can be used to increase or decrease hour, minute and second values.
Value	The data selected by the user.
Common DateTimePicker Event	
ValueChanged	Generated when the Value property changes, including when the user selects a new date or time.

Fig. 14.10 | DateTimePicker properties and an event. (Part 2 of 2.)

Figure 14.11 demonstrates using the DateTimePicker control to select an item's drop-off date. Many companies use such functionality. For instance, several online DVD-rental companies specify the day a movie is sent out, and the estimated time that the movie will arrive at your home. In this application, the user selects a drop-off day, and then an estimated arrival date is displayed. The date is always two days after drop off, three days if a Sunday is reached (mail is not delivered on Sunday).

```vb
1   ' Fig. 14.11: FrmDateTimePickerForm.vb
2   ' Using a DateTimePicker to select a drop off date.
3   Public Class FrmDateTimePickerTest
4      ' set DateTimePicker's MinDate and MaxDate properties
5      Private Sub FrmDateTimePickerTest_Load(ByVal sender As System.Object, _
6         ByVal e As System.EventArgs) Handles MyBase.Load
7         ' user cannot select days before today
8         dropOffDateTimePicker.MinDate = DateTime.Today
9
10        ' user can select days up to one year from now
11        dropOffDateTimePicker.MaxDate = DateTime.Today.AddYears(1)
12     End Sub ' FrmDateTimePickerTest_Load
13
14     ' display delivery date
15     Private Sub dropOffDateTimePicker_ValueChanged( _
16        ByVal sender As System.Object, ByVal e As System.EventArgs) _
17        Handles dropOffDateTimePicker.ValueChanged
18
19        Dim dropOffDate As DateTime = dropOffDateTimePicker.Value
20
```

Fig. 14.11 | Demonstrating DateTimePicker. (Part 1 of 2.)

```
21          ' add an extra day when items are dropped off Friday-Sunday
22          If dropOffDate.DayOfWeek = DayOfWeek.Friday Or _
23             dropOffDate.DayOfWeek = DayOfWeek.Saturday Or _
24             dropOffDate.DayOfWeek = DayOfWeek.Sunday Then
25             ' estimate three days for delivery
26             lblOutput.Text = dropOffDate.AddDays(3).ToLongDateString()
27          Else ' otherwise estimate only two days for delivery
28             lblOutput.Text = dropOffDate.AddDays(2).ToLongDateString()
29          End If
30       End Sub ' dateTimePickerDropOff_ValueChanged
31    End Class ' FrmDateTimePickerTest
```

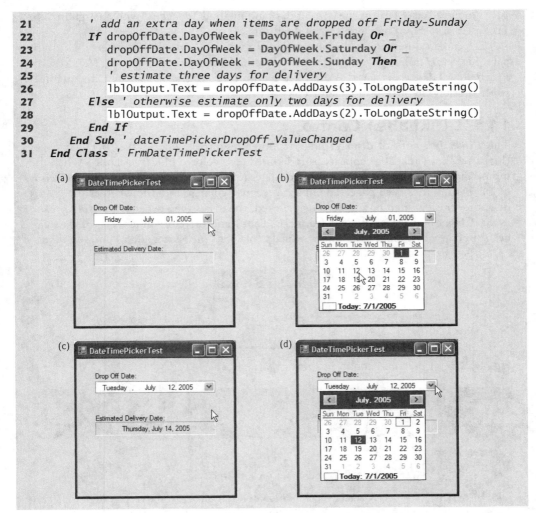

Fig. 14.11 | Demonstrating DateTimePicker. (Part 2 of 2.)

The DateTimePicker (dropOffDateTimePicker) has its Format property set to Long, so the user can select a date and not a time in this application. When the user selects a date, the ValueChanged event occurs. The event handler for this event (lines 15–30) first retrieves the selected date from the DateTimePicker's *Value* property (line 19). Lines 22–24 use the DateTime structure's *DayOfWeek* property to determine the day of the week on which the selected date falls. The day values are represented using the *DayOfWeek* enumeration. Lines 26 and 28 use DateTime's *AddDays* method to increase the date by three days or two days, respectively. Then a string representing the delivery date is obtained by calling method *ToLongDateString*.

In this application, we do not want the user to be able to select a drop-off day before the current day, or one that is more than a year into the future. To enforce this, we set the DateTimePicker's *MinDate* and *MaxDate* properties when the Form is loaded (lines 8 and

11). Property Today returns the current day, and method ***AddYears*** (with an argument of 1) is used to specify a date one year in the future.

Let's take a closer look at the output. This application begins by displaying the current date (Fig. 14.11(a)). In Fig. 14.11(b), we select the 12th of July. In Fig. 14.11(c), the estimated arrival date is displayed as the 14th. Figure 14.11(d) shows that the 12th, after it is selected, is highlighted in the calendar.

14.5 LinkLabel Control

The ***LinkLabel*** control displays links to other resources, such as files or Web pages (Fig. 14.12). A LinkLabel appears as underlined text (colored blue by default). When the mouse moves over the link, the pointer changes to a hand; this is similar to the behavior of a hyperlink in a Web page. The link can change color to indicate whether the link is new, previously visited or active. When clicked, the LinkLabel generates a ***LinkClicked*** event. Class LinkLabel is derived from class Label and therefore inherits all of class Label's functionality. Figure 14.13 lists several LinkLabel properties and a common event.

Fig. 14.12 | LinkLabel control in running program.

LinkLabel properties and an event	Description
Common Properties	
ActiveLinkColor	Specifies the color of the link when clicked.
LinkArea	Specifies which portion of text in the LinkLabel is part of the link.
LinkBehavior	Specifies the link's behavior, such as how the link appears when the mouse is placed over it.
LinkColor	Specifies the original color of all links before they have been visited. The default color is set by the system, but is usually blue.
LinkVisited	If True, the link appears as though it has been visited (its color is changed to that specified by property VisitedLinkColor). The default value is False.
Text	Specifies the control's text.
UseMnemonic	If True, the & character can be used in the Text property to create a shortcut (similar to the *Alt* shortcut in menus).

Fig. 14.13 | LinkLabel properties and an event. (Part 1 of 2.)

LinkLabel properties and an event	Description
VisitedLinkColor	Specifies the color of visited links. The default color is set by the system, but is usually purple.
Common Event (event argument type is LinkLabelLinkClickedEventArgs)	
LinkClicked	Generated when the link is clicked.

Fig. 14.13 | LinkLabel properties and an event. (Part 2 of 2.)

Look-and-Feel Observation 14.3

A LinkLabel is the preferred control for indicating that the user can click a link to jump to a resource such as a Web page, though other controls can perform similar tasks.

Class FrmLinkLabelTest (Fig. 14.14) uses three LinkLabels to link to the C: drive, the Deitel Web site (www.deitel.com) and the Notepad application, respectively. The Text properties of the LinkLabel's lnklblCDrive, lnklblDeitel and lnklblNotepad describe each link's purpose.

```vb
 1  ' Fig. 14.14: FrmLinkLabelTest.vb
 2  ' Using LinkLabels to create hyperlinks.
 3  Public Class FrmLinkLabelTest
 4     ' browse C:\ drive
 5     Private Sub lnklblCDrive_LinkClicked(ByVal sender As System.Object, _
 6        ByVal e As System.Windows.Forms.LinkLabelLinkClickedEventArgs) _
 7        Handles lnklblCDrive.LinkClicked
 8
 9        lnklblCDrive.LinkVisited = True ' change LinkColor after click
10        System.Diagnostics.Process.Start("C:\")
11     End Sub ' lnklblCDrive_LinkClicked
12
13     ' browse www.deitel.com in Internet Explorer
14     Private Sub lnklblDeitel_LinkClicked(ByVal sender As System.Object, _
15        ByVal e As System.Windows.Forms.LinkLabelLinkClickedEventArgs) _
16        Handles lnklblDeitel.LinkClicked
17
18        lnklblDeitel.LinkVisited = True ' change LinkColor after click
19        System.Diagnostics.Process.Start( _
20           "IExplore", "http://www.deitel.com")
21     End Sub ' lnklblDeitel_LinkClicked
22
23     ' run the Notepad application
24     Private Sub lnklblNotepad_LinkClicked(ByVal sender As System.Object, _
25        ByVal e As System.Windows.Forms.LinkLabelLinkClickedEventArgs) _
26        Handles lnklblNotepad.LinkClicked
27
```

Fig. 14.14 | LinkLabels used to link to a drive, a Web page and an application. (Part 1 of 2.)

```
28        lnklblNotepad.LinkVisited = True ' change LinkColor after click
29        System.Diagnostics.Process.Start("notepad")
30    End Sub ' lnklblNotepad_LinkClicked
31 End Class ' FrmLinkLabelTest
```

Fig. 14.14 | LinkLabels used to link to a drive, a Web page and an application. (Part 2 of 2.)

The event handlers for the LinkLabels call method *Start* of class *Process* (namespace *System.Diagnostics*), which allows you to execute other programs from an application. Method Start can take one argument, the file to open (a String), or two arguments, the application to run and its command-line arguments (two Strings). Method Start's arguments can be in the same form as if they were provided for input to the Windows **Run** command (**Start > Run...**). For applications that are known to Windows (such as Notepad), full path names are not required, and the .exe extension often can be omitted. To open a file that has a file type that Windows recognizes, simply use the file's full path name. The Windows operating system must be able to use the application associated with the given file's extension to open the file.

The event handler for lnklblCDrive's LinkClicked event browses the C: drive (lines 5–11). Line 9 sets the LinkVisited property to True, which changes the link's color from blue to purple (the LinkVisited colors can be configured through the **Properties** window in Visual Studio). The event handler then passes "C:\" to method Start (line 10), which opens a **Windows Explorer** window.

The event handler for lnklblDeitel's LinkClicked event (lines 14–21) opens the Web page www.deitel.com in Internet Explorer. We achieve this by passing the Web page address as a String (lines 19–20), which opens Internet Explorer. Line 18 sets the LinkVisited property to True.

The event handler for lnklblNotepad's LinkClicked event (lines 24–30) opens the Notepad application. Line 28 sets the LinkVisited property to True so that the link appears as a visited link. Line 29 passes the argument "notepad" to method Start, which runs notepad.exe. Note that in line 29, the .exe extension is not required—Windows can determine whether it recognizes the argument given to method Start as an executable file.

14.6 ListBox Control

The *ListBox* control allows the user to view and select from multiple items in a list. The *CheckedListBox* control (Section 14.7) extends a ListBox by including CheckBoxes next to each item in the list. This allows users to place checks on multiple items at once, as is possible with CheckBox controls. (Users also can select multiple items from a ListBox by setting the ListBox's *SelectionMode* property, which is discussed shortly.) Figure 14.15 displays a ListBox and a CheckedListBox. In both controls, scrollbars appear if the number of items exceeds the ListBox's viewable area.

Figure 14.16 lists common ListBox properties and methods, and a common event. The SelectionMode property determines the number of items that can be selected. This property has the possible values *None*, *One*, *MultiSimple* and *MultiExtended* (from the *SelectionMode* enumeration)—the differences among these settings are explained in Fig. 14.16. The *SelectedIndexChanged* event occurs when the user selects a new item.

Both the ListBox and CheckedListBox have properties Items, SelectedItem and SelectedIndex. Property *Items* returns all the list items as a collection. Collections are a common way of managing lists of Objects in the .NET framework. Many .NET GUI components (e.g., ListBoxes) use collections to expose lists of internal objects (e.g., items contained within a ListBox). We discuss collections further in Chapter 26. The collection returned by property Items is represented as an object of type *ObjectCollection*. Property *SelectedItem* returns the ListBox's currently selected item. If the user can select multiple items, use collection *SelectedItems* to obtain all the selected items as a collection.

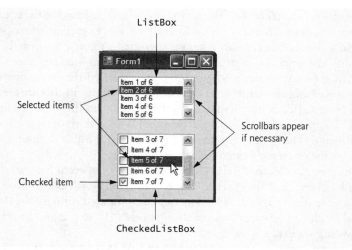

Fig. 14.15 | ListBox and CheckedListBox on a Form.

ListBox properties, methods and an event	Description
Common Properties	
Items	The collection of items in the ListBox.
MultiColumn	Indicates whether the ListBox can break a list into multiple columns, which eliminates vertical scrollbars from the display.
SelectedIndex	Returns the index of the selected item, or -1 if no items have been selected. If the user selects multiple items, this property returns only one of the selected indices. For this reason, if multiple items are selected, you should use property SelectedIndices.
SelectedIndices	Returns a collection containing the indices of all selected items.
SelectedItem	Returns a reference to the selected item. If multiple items are selected, it returns the item with the lowest index number.
SelectedItems	Returns a collection of the selected item(s).
SelectionMode	Determines the number of items that can be selected and the means through which multiple items can be selected. Values None, One, MultiSimple (multiple selection allowed) or MultiExtended (multiple selection allowed using a combination of arrow keys or mouse clicks and *Shift* and *Ctrl* keys).
Sorted	Indicates whether items are sorted alphabetically. Setting this property's value to True sorts the items. The default value is False.

Fig. 14.16 | ListBox properties, methods and an event. (Part 1 of 2.)

ListBox properties, methods and an event	Description
Common Methods	
ClearSelected	Deselects all items in the ListBox.
GetSelected	Takes an index as an argument, and returns True if the corresponding item is selected.
Common Event	
SelectedIndexChanged	Generated when the selected index changes.

Fig. 14.16 | ListBox properties, methods and an event. (Part 2 of 2.)

Property ***SelectedIndex*** returns the index of the selected item—if there could be more than one, use property ***SelectedIndices***. If no items are selected, property SelectedIndex returns -1. Method ***GetSelected*** takes an index and returns True if the corresponding item is selected.

To add items to a ListBox or to a CheckedListBox, we must add objects to its Items collection. This can be accomplished by calling method Add to add a String to the ListBox's or CheckedListBox's Items collection. For example, we could write

```
myListBox.Items.Add( myListItem )
```

to add String *myListItem* to ListBox *myListBox*. To add multiple objects, you can either call method Add multiple times or call method AddRange to add an array of objects. Classes ListBox and CheckedListBox each call the submitted object's ToString method to determine the Label for the corresponding object's entry in the list. This allows you to add non-String objects to a ListBox or a CheckedListBox that later can be returned through properties SelectedItem and SelectedItems.

Alternatively, you can add items to ListBoxes and CheckedListBoxes visually by examining the Items property in the **Properties** window. Clicking the ellipsis button opens the **String Collection Editor**, which contains a text area for adding items; each item appears on a separate line (Fig. 14.17). Visual Studio then writes code to add these Strings to the Items collection inside method InitializeComponent in the Form's Designer.vb file.

Fig. 14.17 | String Collection Editor.

Figure 14.18 uses class FrmListBoxTest to add, remove and clear items from ListBox lstDisplay. Class FrmListBoxTest uses TextBox txtInput to allow the user to enter new items. When the user clicks the **Add** Button, the new item appears in lstDisplay. Similarly, if the user selects an item and clicks **Remove**, the item is deleted. When clicked, **Clear** deletes all entries in lstDisplay. The user terminates the application by clicking **Exit**.

The btnAdd_Click event handler (lines 6–11) calls method *Add* of the ListBox's Items collection. This method takes an Object as the item to add to lstDisplay. In this case, the Object used is the text entered by the user—txtInput.Text (line 9). After the item is added, txtInput.Text is cleared (line 10).

The btnRemove_Click event handler (lines 14–21) uses method *RemoveAt* to remove an item from the ListBox. Lines 18–20 first use property SelectedIndex to determine which index is selected. If SelectedIndex is not –1 (i.e., an item is selected) line 19 removes the item that corresponds to the selected index.

```vb
 1    ' Fig. 14.18: FrmListBoxTest.vb
 2    ' Program to add, remove and clear ListBox items
 3    Public Class FrmListBoxTest
 4       ' add to lstDisplay the item the user enters in txtInput,
 5       ' then clear txtInput
 6       Private Sub btnAdd_Click(ByVal sender As System.Object, _
 7          ByVal e As System.EventArgs) Handles btnAdd.Click
 8
 9          lstDisplay.Items.Add(txtInput.Text)
10          txtInput.Clear()
11       End Sub ' btnAdd_Click
12
13       ' remove an item from lstDisplay if one is selected
14       Private Sub btnRemove_Click(ByVal sender As System.Object, _
15          ByVal e As System.EventArgs) Handles btnRemove.Click
16
17          ' if an item is selected, remove that item
18          If lstDisplay.SelectedIndex <> -1 Then
19             lstDisplay.Items.RemoveAt(lstDisplay.SelectedIndex)
20          End If
21       End Sub ' btnRemove_Click
22
23       ' clear all the items in lstDisplay
24       Private Sub btnClear_Click(ByVal sender As System.Object, _
25          ByVal e As System.EventArgs) Handles btnClear.Click
26
27          lstDisplay.Items.Clear()
28       End Sub ' btnClear_Click
29
30       ' terminate the application
31       Private Sub btnExit_Click(ByVal sender As System.Object, _
32          ByVal e As System.EventArgs) Handles btnExit.Click
33
34          Application.Exit()
35       End Sub ' btnExit_Click
36    End Class ' FrmListBoxTest
```

Fig. 14.18 | Program that adds, removes and clears ListBox items. (Part 1 of 2.)

Fig. 14.18 | Program that adds, removes and clears ListBox items. (Part 2 of 2.)

The btnClear_Click event handler (lines 24–28) calls method ***Clear*** of the Items collection (line 27) to remove all the entries in lstDisplay. Finally, event handler btnExit_Click (lines 31–35) terminates the application by calling method Application.Exit (line 34).

14.7 CheckedListBox Control

The CheckedListBox control derives from class ListBox and includes a CheckBox next to each item. As in ListBoxes, items can be added via methods Add and AddRange or through the **String Collection Editor**. CheckedListBoxes imply that multiple items can be selected, and the only possible values for the SelectionMode property are None and One. One allows multiple selection, because CheckBoxes imply that there are no logical restrictions on the items—the user can select as many items as required. Thus, the only choice is whether to give the user multiple selection or no selection at all. This keeps the CheckedListBox's behavior consistent with that of CheckBoxes. Figure 14.19 lists some common properties, a common method and a common event of class CheckedListBox.

Common Programming Error 14.1

*The IDE displays an error message if you attempt to set the SelectionMode property to MultiSimple or MultiExtended in the **Properties** window of a CheckedListBox. If this value is set programmatically, a runtime error occurs.*

CheckedListBox properties, methods and an event	Description
Common Properties	*(All the ListBox properties, methods and events are inherited by CheckedListBox.)*
CheckedItems	Contains the collection of items that are checked. This is distinct from the selected item, which is highlighted (but not necessarily checked). There can be at most one selected item at any given time.
CheckedIndices	Returns indices for all checked items.
SelectionMode	Determines how many items can be checked. The only possible values are One (allows multiple checks to be placed) or None (does not allow any checks to be placed).
Common Method	
GetItemChecked	Takes an index and returns True if the corresponding item is checked.
Common Event (Event arguments ItemCheckEventArgs)	
ItemCheck	Generated when an item is checked or unchecked.
ItemCheckEventArgs Properties	
CurrentValue	Indicates whether the current item is checked or unchecked. Possible values are Checked, Unchecked and Indeterminate.
Index	Returns the zero-based index of the item that changed.
NewValue	Specifies the new state of the item.

Fig. 14.19 | CheckedListBox properties, a method and an event.

Event ***ItemCheck*** occurs when a user checks or unchecks a CheckedListBox item. Event argument properties CurrentValue and NewValue return CheckState values for the current and new state of the item, respectively. A comparison of these values allows you to determine whether the CheckedListBox item was checked or unchecked. The CheckedListBox control inherits the SelectedItems and SelectedIndices properties from class ListBox. It also includes properties CheckedItems and CheckedIndices, which return information about the checked items and indices.

In Fig. 14.20, class FrmCheckedListBoxTest uses a CheckedListBox and a ListBox to display a user's book selections. The CheckedListBox allows the user to select multiple titles. In the **String Collection Editor**, we added items for some Deitel books—C++, Java, Visual Basic, Internet & WWW, Perl, Python, Wireless Internet and Advanced Java (the acronym HTP stands for "How to Program"). The ListBox (named lstDisplay) displays the user's selections.

When the user checks or unchecks an item in chklstInput, an ItemCheck event occurs and event handler chklstItem_ItemCheck (lines 5–20) executes. An If...Else statement (lines 15–19) determines whether the user checked or unchecked an item in the

```
 1    ' Fig. 14.20: FrmCheckedListBoxTest.vb
 2    ' Using the checked ListBox to add items to a display ListBox
 3    Public Class FrmCheckedListBoxTest
 4       ' add an item to or remove an item from lstDisplay
 5       Private Sub chklstItem_ItemCheck( _
 6          ByVal sender As System.Object, _
 7          ByVal e As System.Windows.Forms.ItemCheckEventArgs) _
 8          Handles chklstItem.ItemCheck
 9
10          ' obtain selected item
11          Dim item As String = chklstItem.SelectedItem.ToString()
12
13          ' if the selected item is checked add it to lstDisplay;
14          ' otherwise, remove it from lstDisplay
15          If e.NewValue = CheckState.Checked Then
16             lstDisplay.Items.Add(item)
17          Else
18             lstDisplay.Items.Remove(item)
19          End If
20       End Sub ' chklstItem_ItemCheck
21    End Class ' FrmCheckedListBoxTest
```

Fig. 14.20 | CheckedListBox and ListBox used in a program to display a user selection. (Part 1 of 2.)

Fig. 14.20 | CheckedListBox and ListBox used in a program to display a user selection. (Part 2 of 2.)

CheckedListBox. Line 15 uses the ItemCheckEventArgs property NewValue to determine whether the item is being checked (CheckState.Checked). If the user checks an item, line 16 adds the checked entry to lstDisplay. If the user unchecks an item, line 18 removes the corresponding item from lstDisplay. This event handler was created by selecting the CheckedListBox in **Design** mode, viewing the control's events in the **Properties** window and double clicking the ItemCheck event.

14.8 ComboBox Control

The **ComboBox** control combines TextBox features with a *drop-down list*—a GUI component that contains a list from which a value can be selected. A ComboBox usually appears as a TextBox with a down arrow to its right. By default, the user can enter text into the Text-Box or click the down arrow to display a list of predefined items. If a user chooses an element from this list, that element is displayed in the TextBox. If the list contains more elements than can be displayed in the drop-down list, a scrollbar appears. The maximum number of items that a drop-down list can display at one time is set by property **MaxDropDownItems**. Figure 14.21 shows a sample ComboBox in three different states.

As with the ListBox control, you can add objects to collection Items programmatically, using methods Add and AddRange, or visually, with the **String Collection Editor**. Figure 14.22 lists common properties and a common event of class ComboBox.

Look-and-Feel Observation 14.4

Use a ComboBox to save space on a GUI. It has the disadvantage, however, that unlike with a ListBox, the user cannot see available items without expanding the drop-down list.

Fig. 14.21 | ComboBox demonstration.

ComboBox properties and an event	Description
Common Properties	
DropDownStyle	Determines the ComboBox type. Value Simple means that the text portion is editable, and the list portion is always visible. Value DropDown (the default) means that the text portion is editable, but the user must click an arrow button to see the list portion. Value DropDownList means that the text portion is not editable, and the user must click the arrow button to see the list portion.
Items	The collection of items in the ComboBox control.
MaxDropDownItems	Specifies the maximum number of items (between 1 and 100) that the drop-down list can display. If the number of items exceeds the maximum number of items to display, a scrollbar appears.
SelectedIndex	Returns the index of the selected item, or –1 if there is no selected item.
SelectedItem	Returns a reference to the selected item.
Sorted	Indicates whether items are sorted alphabetically. Setting this property's value to True sorts the items. The default is False.
Common Event	
SelectedIndexChanged	Generated when the selected index changes (such as when a different item is selected). This is the default event when control is double clicked in the designer.

Fig. 14.22 | ComboBox properties and an event.

Property ***DropDownStyle*** determines the type of ComboBox and is represented as a value of the ***ComboBoxStyle*** enumeration, which contains values Simple, DropDown and DropDownList. Option ***Simple*** does not display a drop-down arrow. Instead, a scrollbar appears next to the control, allowing the user to select a choice from the list. The user also can type in a selection. Style ***DropDown*** (the default) displays a drop-down list when the down arrow is clicked (or the down-arrow key is pressed). The user can type a new item in the ComboBox. The last style is ***DropDownList***, which displays a drop-down list but does not allow the user to type in the ComboBox.

The ComboBox control has properties ***Items*** (a collection), ***SelectedItem*** and ***SelectedIndex***, which are similar to the corresponding properties in ListBox. There can be at most one selected item in a ComboBox. If no items are selected, then SelectedIndex is –1. When the selected item changes, a ***SelectedIndexChanged*** event occurs.

Class FrmComboBoxTest (Fig. 14.23) allows users to select a shape to draw—circle, ellipse, square or pie (in both filled and unfilled versions)—by using a ComboBox. The ComboBox in this example is uneditable, so the user cannot type in the ComboBox.

Look-and-Feel Observation 14.5

Make lists (such as ComboBoxes) editable only if the program is designed to accept user-submitted elements. Otherwise, the user might try to enter a custom item that is improper for the purposes of your application.

After creating ComboBox cboImage, make it uneditable by setting its DropDownStyle to DropDownList in the **Properties** window. Next, add items Circle, Square, Ellipse, Pie, Filled Circle, Filled Square, Filled Ellipse and Filled Pie to the Items collection using the **String Collection Editor**. Whenever the user selects an item from cboImage,

```vb
1   ' Fig. 14.23: FrmComboBoxTest.vb
2   ' Using ComboBox to select a shape to draw.
3   Public Class FrmComboBoxTest
4      ' get index of selected shape, then draw the shape
5      Private Sub cboImage_SelectedIndexChanged( _
6         ByVal sender As System.Object, ByVal e As System.EventArgs) _
7         Handles cboImage.SelectedIndexChanged
8         ' create graphics object, Pen and SolidBrush
9         Dim myGraphics As Graphics = MyBase.CreateGraphics()
10
11         ' create Pen using color DarkRed
12         Dim myPen As Pen = New Pen(Color.DarkRed)
13
14         ' create SolidBrush using color DarkRed
15         Dim mySolidBrush As SolidBrush = New SolidBrush(Color.DarkRed)
16
17         ' clear drawing area setting it to color white
18         myGraphics.Clear(Color.White)
19
20         ' find index, draw proper shape
21         Select Case cboImage.SelectedIndex
22            Case 0 ' case Circle is selected
23               myGraphics.DrawEllipse(myPen, 50, 50, 150, 150)
24            Case 1 ' case Rectangle is selected
25               myGraphics.DrawRectangle(myPen, 50, 50, 150, 150)
26            Case 2 ' case Ellipse is selected
27               myGraphics.DrawEllipse(myPen, 50, 85, 150, 115)
28            Case 3 ' case Pie is selected
29               myGraphics.DrawPie(myPen, 50, 50, 150, 150, 0, 45)
30            Case 4 ' case Filled Circle is selected
31               myGraphics.FillEllipse(mySolidBrush, 50, 50, 150, 150)
32            Case 5 ' case Filled Rectangle is selected
33               myGraphics.FillRectangle(mySolidBrush, 50, 50, 150, 150)
34            Case 6 ' case Filled Ellipse is selected
35               myGraphics.FillEllipse(mySolidBrush, 50, 85, 150, 115)
36            Case 7 ' case Filled Pie is selected
37               myGraphics.FillPie(mySolidBrush, 50, 50, 150, 150, 0, 45)
38         End Select
39
40         myGraphics.Dispose() ' release the Graphics object
41      End Sub ' cboImage_SelectedIndexChanged
42   End Class ' FrmComboBoxTest
```

Fig. 14.23 | ComboBox used to draw a selected shape. (Part 1 of 2.)

Fig. 14.23 | ComboBox used to draw a selected shape. (Part 2 of 2.)

a SelectedIndexChanged event occurs and event handler cboImage_SelectedIndex-Changed (lines 5–41) executes. Lines 9–15 create a Graphics object, a Pen and a Solid-Brush, which are used to draw on the Form. The Graphics object (line 9) allows a pen or brush to draw on a component using one of several Graphics methods. The Pen object (line 12) is used by methods DrawEllipse, DrawRectangle and DrawPie (lines 23, 25, 27 and 29) to draw the outlines of their corresponding shapes. The SolidBrush object (line 15) is used by methods FillEllipse, FillRectangle and FillPie (lines 31, 33, 35 and 37) to fill their corresponding solid shapes. Line 18 colors the entire Form White, using Graphics method *Clear*. These methods are discussed in greater detail in Chapter 17.

The application draws a shape based on the selected item's index. The Select Case statement (lines 21–38) uses cboImage.SelectedIndex to determine which item the user selected. Graphics method *DrawEllipse* (line 23) takes a Pen, the x- and y-coordinates of the center and the width and height of the ellipse to draw. The origin of the coordinate system is in the upper-left corner of the Form; the x-coordinate increases to the right, and the y-coordinate increases toward the bottom of the Form. A circle is a special case of an ellipse with equal width and height. Line 23 draws a circle. Line 27 draws an ellipse that has different values for width and height.

Class Graphics method *DrawRectangle* (line 25) takes a Pen, the x- and y-coordinates of the upper-left corner and the width and height of the rectangle to draw. Method *DrawPie* (line 29) draws a pie as a portion of an ellipse. The ellipse is bounded by a rectangle. Method DrawPie takes a Pen, the x- and y-coordinates of the upper-left corner of the rectangle, its width and height, the start angle (in degrees) and the sweep angle (in degrees) of the pie. Angles increase clockwise. The *FillEllipse* (lines 31 and 35), *Fill-Rectangle* (line 33) and *FillPie* (line 37) methods are similar to their unfilled counterparts, except that they take a SolidBrush instead of a Pen. Some of the drawn shapes are illustrated in the screen shots of Fig. 14.23.

14.9 TreeView Control

The *TreeView* control displays *nodes* hierarchically in a *tree*. Traditionally, nodes are objects that contain values and can refer to other nodes. A *parent node* contains *child nodes*, and the child nodes can be parents to other nodes. Two child nodes that have the same parent node are considered *sibling nodes*. A tree is a collection of nodes, usually organized in a hierarchical manner. The first parent node of a tree is the *root* node (a TreeView can have multiple roots). For example, the file system of a computer can be represented as a tree. The top-level directory (perhaps C:\) would be the root, each subfolder of C:\ would be a child node and each child folder could have its own children. TreeView controls are useful for displaying hierarchal information, such as the file structure that we just mentioned. We cover nodes and trees in greater detail in Chapter 24, Data Structures. Figure 14.24 displays a sample TreeView control on a Form.

A parent node can be expanded or collapsed by clicking the plus box or minus box to its left. Nodes without children do not have these boxes.

The nodes in a TreeView are instances of class *TreeNode*. Each TreeNode has a *Nodes collection* (type *TreeNodeCollection*), which contains a list of other TreeNodes—known as its children. The Parent property returns a reference to the parent node (or Nothing if the node is a root node). Figure 14.25 and Fig. 14.26 list the common properties of Tree-Views and TreeNodes, common TreeNode methods and a common TreeView event.

Fig. 14.24 | TreeView displaying a sample tree.

TreeView properties and an event	Description
Common Properties	
CheckBoxes	Indicates whether CheckBoxes appear next to nodes. A value of True displays CheckBoxes. The default value is False.

Fig. 14.25 | TreeView properties and an event. (Part 1 of 2.)

TreeView properties and an event	Description
ImageList	Specifies an ImageList object containing the node icons. An *Image-List* object is a collection that contains Image objects.
Nodes	Lists the collection of TreeNodes in the control. It contains methods Add (adds a TreeNode object), Clear (deletes the entire collection) and Remove (deletes a specific node). Removing a parent node deletes all of its children.
SelectedNode	The selected node.
Common Event (Event arguments TreeViewEventArgs)	
AfterSelect	Generated after selected node changes.

Fig. 14.25 | TreeView properties and an event. (Part 2 of 2.)

TreeNode properties and methods	Description
Common Properties	
Checked	Indicates whether the TreeNode is checked (CheckBoxes property must be set to True in the parent TreeView).
FirstNode	Specifies the first node in the Nodes collection (i.e., the first child in the tree).
FullPath	Indicates the path of the node, starting at the root of the tree.
ImageIndex	Specifies the index of the image shown when the node is deselected.
LastNode	Specifies the last node in the Nodes collection (i.e., the last child in the tree).
NextNode	Next sibling node.
Nodes	Collection of TreeNodes contained in the current node (i.e., all the children of the current node). The Nodes collection has methods Add (adds a TreeNode object), Clear (deletes the entire collection) and Remove (deletes a specific node). Removing a parent node deletes all of its children.
Parent	Parent node of the current node.
PrevNode	Previous sibling node.
SelectedImageIndex	Specifies the index of the image to use when the node is selected.
Text	Specifies the TreeNode's text.

Fig. 14.26 | TreeNode properties and methods. (Part 1 of 2.)

TreeNode properties and methods	Description
Common Methods	
Collapse	Collapses a node.
Expand	Expands a node.
ExpandAll	Expands all the children of a node.
GetNodeCount	Returns the number of child nodes.

Fig. 14.26 | TreeNode properties and methods. (Part 2 of 2.)

To add nodes to the TreeView visually, click the ellipsis next to the Nodes property in the **Properties** window. This opens the **TreeNode Editor** (Fig. 14.27), which displays an empty tree representing the TreeView. There are Buttons to create a root, and to add or delete a node. To the right are the properties of current node. Here you can rename the node.

To add nodes programmatically, first create a root node. Create a new TreeNode object and pass it a String to display. Then call method Add to add this new TreeNode to the TreeView's Nodes collection. Thus, to add a root node to TreeView *myTreeView*, write

myTreeView.Nodes.Add(*rootLabel*)

Fig. 14.27 | TreeNode Editor.

where *myTreeView* is the `TreeView` to which we are adding nodes, and *rootLabel* is the text to display in *myTreeView*. To add children to a root node, add new `TreeNodes` to its `Nodes` collection. We select the appropriate root node from the `TreeView` by writing

> *myTreeView*.`Nodes(`*myIndex*`)`

where *myIndex* is the root node's index in *myTreeView*'s `Nodes` collection. We add nodes to child nodes through the same process by which we added root nodes to *myTreeView*. To add a child to the root node at index *myIndex*, write

> *myTreeView*.`Nodes(`*myIndex*`)`.`Nodes.Add(`*childNodeText*`)`

Class `FrmTreeViewDirectoryStructure` (Fig. 14.28) uses a `TreeView` to display the contents of a directory chosen by the user. A `TextBox` and a `Button` are used to specify the directory. First, enter the full path of the directory you want to display. Then click the `Button` to set the specified directory as the root node in the `TreeView`. Each subdirectory of this directory becomes a child node. This layout is similar to the one used in **Windows Explorer**. Folders can be expanded or collapsed by clicking the plus or minus boxes that appear to their left.

```vb
1   ' Fig. 14.28: FrmTreeViewDirectoryStructure.vb
2   ' Using TreeView to display directory structure.
3   Imports System.IO
4
5   Public Class FrmTreeViewDirectoryStructure
6      ' clear treDirectory, then call PopulateTreeView
7      Private Sub btnEnter_Click(ByVal sender As System.Object, _
8         ByVal e As System.EventArgs) Handles btnEnter.Click
9
10        treDirectory.Nodes.Clear() ' clear all nodes
11
12        ' if the directory specified by the user exists, fill in the
13        ' TreeView; otherwise, display an error message
14        If (Directory.Exists(txtInput.Text)) Then
15           ' add full path name to directoryTreeView
16           treDirectory.Nodes.Add(txtInput.Text)
17
18           ' insert subfolders
19           PopulateTreeView(txtInput.Text, treDirectory.Nodes(0))
20        Else ' display error MessageBox if directory not found
21           MessageBox.Show(txtInput.Text & " could not be found.", _
22              "Directory Not Found", MessageBoxButtons.OK, _
23              MessageBoxIcon.Error)
24        End If
25     End Sub ' btnEnter
26
27     ' populate current node with subdirectories
28     Private Sub PopulateTreeView( _
29        ByVal directoryValue As String, ByVal parentNode As TreeNode)
30        ' array stores all subdirectories in the directory
31        Dim directoryArray As String() = _
32           Directory.GetDirectories(directoryValue)
```

Fig. 14.28 | TreeView used to display directories. (Part 1 of 2.)

```
33
34            ' populate current node with subdirectories
35            Try
36                ' check to see if any subdirectories are present
37                If directoryArray.Length <> 0 Then
38                    ' for every subdirectory, create new TreeNode,
39                    ' add as a child of current node and recursively
40                    ' populate child nodes with subdirectories
41                    For Each directory As String In directoryArray
42                        ' obtain last part of path name from the full path name
43                        ' by finding the last occurence of "\" and returning the
44                        ' part of the path name that comes after this occurrence
45                        Dim directoryName As String = directory.Substring( _
46                            directory.LastIndexOf("\") + 1)
47
48                        ' create TreeNode for current directory
49                        Dim myNode As TreeNode = New TreeNode(directoryName)
50
51                        ' add current directory node to parent node
52                        parentNode.Nodes.Add(myNode)
53
54                        ' recursively populate every subdirectory
55                        PopulateTreeView(directory, myNode)
56                    Next
57                End If
58            Catch e As UnauthorizedAccessException
59                parentNode.Nodes.Add("Access denied")
60            End Try
61        End Sub ' PopulateTreeView
62    End Class ' FrmTreeViewDirectoryStructure
```

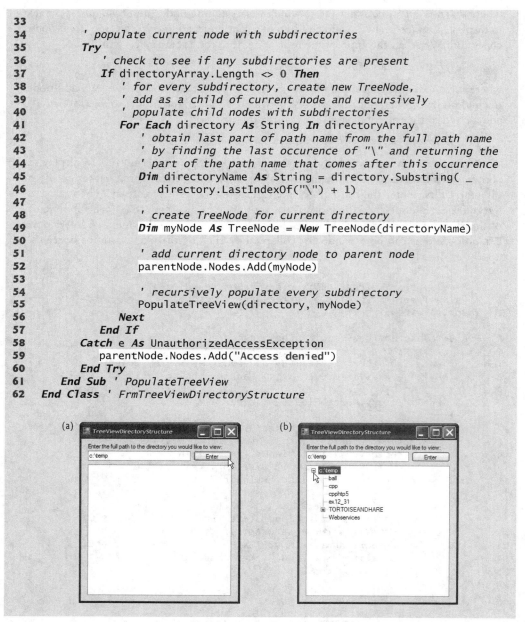

Fig. 14.28 | TreeView used to display directories. (Part 2 of 2.)

When the user clicks the btnEnter, all the nodes in treDirectory are cleared (line 10). Then the path entered in txtInput is used to create the root node. Line 16 adds the directory to treDirectory as the root node, and line 19 calls method PopulateTreeView (lines 28–61), which receives as arguments a directory (as a String) and a parent node (as a TreeNode). Method `PopulateTreeView` then creates child nodes corresponding to the subdirectories of the directory it receives as an argument.

PopulateTreeView (lines 28–61) obtains a list of subdirectories, using method **Get-Directories** of class `Directory` (namespace `System.IO`) in lines 31–32. Method `GetDirectories` receives the current directory (as a `String`) and returns an array of `Strings` representing its subdirectories. If a directory is not accessible for security reasons, an `UnauthorizedAccessException` is thrown. Lines 58–59 catch this exception and add a node containing "`Access Denied.`"

If there are accessible subdirectories, lines 45–46 use the `Substring` method to increase readability by shortening the full path name to just the directory name. Next, each `String` in the `directoryArray` is used to create a new child node (line 49). We use method `Add` (line 52) to add each child node to the parent. `PopulateTreeView` calls itself recursively on each subdirectory (line 55), which eventually populates the `TreeView` with the entire directory structure. Note that our recursive algorithm may cause a delay when the program loads directories with many subdirectories. However, once the folder names are added to the appropriate `Nodes` collection, they can be expanded and collapsed without delay. In the next section, we present an alternative algorithm to solve this problem.

14.10 ListView Control

The **ListView** control is similar to a `ListBox` in that both display lists from which the user can select one or more items (an example of a `ListView` can be found in Fig. 14.31). The important difference between the two classes is that a `ListView` can display icons next to the list items (controlled by its `ImageList` property). Property **MultiSelect** (a `Boolean`) determines whether multiple items can be selected. `CheckBoxes` can be included by setting property **CheckBoxes** (a `Boolean`) to `True`, making the `ListView` similar in appearance to a `CheckedListBox`. The **View** property specifies the layout of the `ListBox`. Property **Activation** determines the method by which the user selects a list item. Figure 14.29 presents some of the `ListView` class's common properties and its `ItemActivate` event.

ListView properties and an event	Description
Common Properties	
Activation	Determines how the user activates an item. This property takes a value in the `ItemActivation` enumeration. Possible values are `OneClick` (single-click activation), `TwoClick` (double-click activation, item changes color when selected) and `Standard` (double-click activation, item does not change color).
CheckBoxes	Indicates whether items appear with `CheckBoxes`. `True` displays `CheckBoxes`. The default is `False`.
LargeImageList	Specifies the `ImageList` containing large icons for display.
Items	Returns the collection of `ListViewItems` in the control.

Fig. 14.29 | ListView properties and an event. (Part 1 of 2.)

ListView properties and an event	Description
MultiSelect	Determines whether multiple selection is allowed. The default is True, which enables multiple selection.
SelectedItems	Gets the collection of selected items.
SmallImageList	Specifies the ImageList containing small icons for display.
View	Determines appearance of ListViewItems. Possible values are LargeIcon (large icon displayed, items can be in multiple columns), SmallIcon (small icon displayed, items can be in multiple columns), List (small icons displayed, items appear in a single column), Details (like List, but multiple columns of information can be displayed per item) and Tile (large icons displayed, information provided to right of icon, valid only in Windows XP or later).
Common Event	
ItemActivate	Generated when an item in the ListView is activated. Does not contain the specifics of the item activated.

Fig. 14.29 | ListView properties and an event. (Part 2 of 2.)

ListView allows you to define the images used as icons for ListView items. To display images, an ImageList component is required. Create one by dragging it to a Form from the **ToolBox**. Then select the ***Images*** property in the **Properties** window to display the **Image Collection Editor** (Fig. 14.30). Here you can browse for images that you wish to add to the ImageList, which contains an array of Images. Once the images have been defined, set property SmallImageList of the ListView to the new ImageList object. Property ***SmallImageList*** specifies the image list for the small icons. Property ***LargeImageList*** sets the ImageList for large icons. The items in a ListView are each of type ***ListViewItem***. Icons for the ListView items are selected by setting the item's ***ImageIndex*** property to the appropriate index.

Fig. 14.30 | **Image Collection Editor** window for an ImageList component.

Class FrmListViewTest (Fig. 14.31) displays files and folders in a ListView, along with small icons representing each file or folder. If a file or folder is inaccessible because of permission settings, a MessageBox appears. The program scans the contents of the directory as it browses, rather than indexing the entire drive at once.

```vb
' Fig. 14.31: FrmListViewTest.vb
' Displaying directories and their contents in ListView.
Imports System.IO

Public Class FrmListViewTest
   ' store current directory
   Private currentDirectory As String = Directory.GetCurrentDirectory()

   ' display files/subdirectories of current directory
   ' (i.e., the one from which the application is executed)
   Private Sub FrmListViewTest_Load(ByVal sender As Object, _
      ByVal e As System.EventArgs) Handles Me.Load
      ' set Image list
      Dim folderImage As Image = Image.FromFile( _
         currentDirectory & "\images\folder.bmp")

      Dim fileImage As Image = Image.FromFile( _
         currentDirectory & "\images\file.bmp")

      fileFolder.Images.Add(folderImage)
      fileFolder.Images.Add(fileImage)

      ' load current directory into browserListView
      LoadFilesInDirectory(currentDirectory)
      lblDisplay.Text = currentDirectory
   End Sub ' FrmListViewTest_Load

   ' browse directory user clicked or go up one level
   Private Sub lvwBrowser_Click(ByVal sender As System.Object, _
      ByVal e As System.EventArgs) Handles lvwBrowser.Click
      ' ensure an item is selected
      If lvwBrowser.SelectedItems.Count <> 0 Then
         ' if first item selected, go up one level
         If lvwBrowser.Items(0).Selected Then
            ' create DirectoryInfo object for directory
            Dim directoryObject As DirectoryInfo = _
               New DirectoryInfo(currentDirectory)

            ' if directory has parent, load it
            If directoryObject.Parent IsNot Nothing Then
               LoadFilesInDirectory(directoryObject.Parent.FullName)
               lblDisplay.Text = currentDirectory
            End If
         Else ' selected directory or file
            ' directory or file chosen
            Dim chosen As String = lvwBrowser.SelectedItems(0).Text
```

Fig. 14.31 | ListView displaying files and folders. (Part 1 of 3.)

```
47
48                    ' if item selected is directory, load selected directory
49               If Directory.Exists(currentDirectory & "\" & chosen) Then
50                   ' if currently in C:\, do not need '\'; otherwise we do
51                   If currentDirectory = "C:\" Then
52                       LoadFilesInDirectory(currentDirectory & chosen)
53                   Else
54                       LoadFilesInDirectory(currentDirectory & "\" & chosen)
55                   End If
56
57                   ' update displayLabel
58                   lblDisplay.Text = currentDirectory
59               End If
60           End If
61       End If
62   End Sub ' lvwBrowser_Click
63
64   ' display files/subdirectories of current directory
65   Private Sub LoadFilesInDirectory( _
66       ByVal currentDirectoryValue As String)
67       ' load directory information and display
68       Try
69           ' clear ListView and set first item
70           lvwBrowser.Items.Clear()
71           lvwBrowser.Items.Add("Go Up One Level")
72
73           ' update current directory
74           currentDirectory = currentDirectoryValue
75           Dim newCurrentDirectory As DirectoryInfo = _
76               New DirectoryInfo(currentDirectory)
77
78           ' put files and directories into arrays
79           Dim directoryArray As DirectoryInfo() = _
80               newCurrentDirectory.GetDirectories()
81           Dim fileArray As FileInfo() = newCurrentDirectory.GetFiles()
82
83           ' add directory names to ListView
84           For Each dir As DirectoryInfo In directoryArray
85               ' add directory to ListView
86               Dim newDirectoryItem As ListViewItem = _
87                   lvwBrowser.Items.Add(dir.Name)
88
89               newDirectoryItem.ImageIndex = 0 ' set directory image
90           Next
91
92           ' add file names to ListView
93           For Each file As FileInfo In fileArray
94               ' add file to ListView
95               Dim newFileItem As ListViewItem = _
96                   lvwBrowser.Items.Add(file.Name)
97
```

Fig. 14.31 | ListView displaying files and folders. (Part 2 of 3.)

```
98                     newFileItem.ImageIndex = 1 ' set file image
99             Next
100         Catch e As UnauthorizedAccessException
101             MessageBox.Show("Warning: Some files may not be " & _
102                 "visible due to permission settings", _
103                 "Attention", 0, MessageBoxIcon.Warning)
104         End Try
105     End Sub ' LoadFilesInDirectory
106 End Class ' FrmListViewTest
```

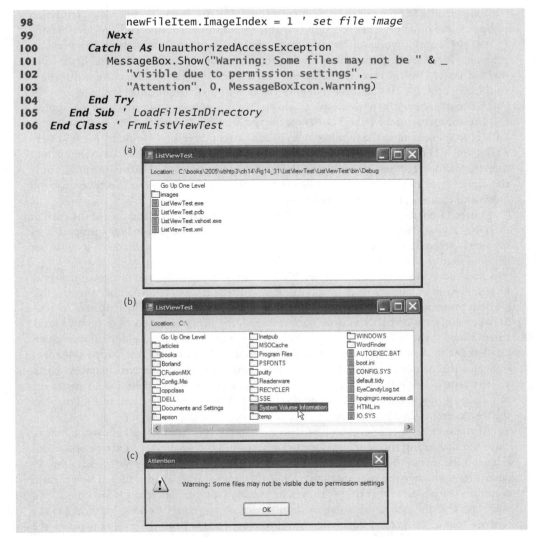

Fig. 14.31 | ListView displaying files and folders. (Part 3 of 3.)

To display icons beside list items, create an ImageList for the ListView lvwBrowser. First, drag and drop an ImageList on the Form and open the **Image Collection Editor.** Select our two simple bitmap images, provided in the bin\Debug and bin\Release folders of this example—one for a folder (array index 0) and the other for a file (array index 1). Then set the object lvwBrowser property SmallImageList to the new ImageList in the **Properties** window.

Method LoadFilesInDirectory (lines 65–105) populates lvwBrowser with the directory passed to it (currentDirectoryValue). It clears lvwBrowser and adds the element "Go Up One Level". When the user clicks this element, the program attempts to move up one level (we see how shortly). The method then creates a DirectoryInfo object initialized with the String currentDirectory (lines 75–76). If you do not have permission to browse the directory, an exception is thrown (and caught in line 100). Method Load-FilesInDirectory works differently from method PopulateTreeView in the previous program (Fig. 14.28). Rather than loading the names of all the folders on the hard drive, method LoadFilesInDirectory loads only the names of folders in the current directory. In this example, we also load the names of the files in the current directory.

Class *DirectoryInfo* (namespace System.IO) makes it easy to browse or manipulate the directory structure. Method *GetDirectories* (line 80) returns an array of Directory-Info objects containing the subdirectories of the current directory. Similarly, method *Get-Files* (line 81) returns an array of class *FileInfo* objects containing the files in the current directory. Property *Name* (of both class DirectoryInfo and class FileInfo) contains only the directory or file name, such as temp instead of C:\myfolder\temp. To access the full name and location, use property *FullName*.

Lines 84–90 and lines 93–99 iterate through the subdirectories and files of the current directory and add them to lvwBrowser. Lines 89 and 98 set the ImageIndex properties of the newly created items. If an item is a directory, we set its icon to a directory icon (index 0); if an item is a file, we set its icon to a file icon (index 1).

Method lvwBrowser_Click (lines 29–62) responds when the user clicks control lvw-Browser. Line 32 checks whether anything is selected. If a selection has been made, line 34 determines whether the user chose the first item in lvwBrowser. The first item in lvw-Browser is always **Go Up One Level**; if it is selected, the program attempts to go up a level. Lines 36–37 create a DirectoryInfo object for the current directory. Line 40 tests property Parent to ensure that the user is not at the root of the directory tree. Property *Parent* indicates the parent directory as a DirectoryInfo object; if no parent directory exists, Parent returns the value Nothing. If a parent directory does exist, then line 41 passes the full name of the parent directory to method LoadFilesInDirectory, and line 42 displays the new current directory's name.

If the user did not select the first item in lvwBrowser, lines 44–60 allow the user to continue navigating through the directory structure. Line 46 creates String chosen and assigns it the text of the selected item (the first item in collection SelectedItems). Line 49 determines whether the user selected a valid directory (rather than a file). The program combines variables currentDirectory and chosen (the new directory), separated by a backslash (\), and passes this value to class Directory's method *Exists*. Method Exists returns True if its String parameter is a directory. In this case, the program passes the directory's name to method LoadFilesInDirectory. If the current directory is C:\, a backslash is not needed to separate currentDirectory and chosen (line 52). However, other directories must be separated by a backslash (line 54). Finally, lblDisplay is updated with the new directory (line 58).

This program loads quickly, because it displays the names of only the directories and files in the current directory. This means that a small delay may occur each time you choose another directory. However, changes that occur in the directory structure while this program executes will appear when you reload a directory. The previous program (Fig. 14.28) may have a large initial delay as it loads an entire directory structure, but the program displays directory contents with no delay once the directory structure is loaded. Also, that program does not dynamically show directory structure changes—you would need to execute the program again. Trade-offs of this kind are typical in the software world.

Software Engineering Observation 14.2

When designing applications that run for long periods of time, you might choose a large initial delay to improve performance throughout the rest of the program. However, in applications that run for only short periods, developers often prefer fast initial loading times and small delays after each action.

14.11 TabControl Control

The *TabControl* control creates tabbed windows, such as the ones we have seen in Visual Studio (Fig. 14.32). Tabs allow you to organize more complex GUIs. TabControls contain *TabPage* objects on which you can place controls, similar to Panels and GroupBoxes. Figure 14.33 depicts a sample TabControl.

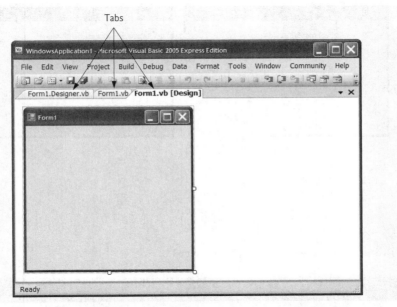

Fig. 14.32 | Tabbed windows in Visual Studio.

Fig. 14.33 | TabControl with TabPages example.

You can add TabControls visually by dragging and dropping them onto a Form in **Design** mode. To add TabPages in **Design** mode, right click the TabControl and select **Add Tab** (Fig. 14.34). Alternatively, click the ***TabPages*** property in the **Properties** window, and add tabs in the dialog that appears. To change a tab label, set the ***Text*** property of the TabPage. Note that clicking the tabs selects the TabControl—to select the TabPage, click the control area underneath the tabs. You can add controls to the TabPage by dragging and dropping items from the **ToolBox**. To view different TabPages (in **Design** mode or when the program is running), simply click the appropriate tab. When a TabPage is clicked at execution time, it generates a Click event. To create the event handler for this event, double click the body of a TabPage in **Design** mode. Common properties and a common event of TabControls are described in Fig. 14.35.

Fig. 14.34 | TabPages added to a TabControl.

TabControl properties and an event	Description
Common Properties	
ImageList	Specifies images to be displayed on tabs.
ItemSize	Specifies the tab size.
Multiline	Indicates whether multiple rows of tabs can be displayed.
SelectedIndex	Index of the selected TabPage.
SelectedTab	The selected TabPage.
TabCount	Returns the number of tab pages.

Fig. 14.35 | TabControl properties and an event. (Part 1 of 2.)

TabControl properties and an event	Description
TabPages	Collection of TabPages within the TabControl.
Common Event	
SelectedIndexChanged	Generated when SelectedIndex changes (i.e., another TabPage is selected).

Fig. 14.35 | TabControl properties and an event. (Part 2 of 2.)

You can add controls to a TabPage object and add TabPages to a TabControl object programmatically, with statements like

```
myTabPage.Controls.Add(myControl)
myTabControl.Controls.Add(myTabPage)
```

These statements call method Add of the Controls collection. The first statement adds a control to TabPage *myTabPage*, and the second statement adds *myTabPage* to TabControl *myTabControl*. Alternatively, you can use method AddRange to add an array of controls or TabPages to a TabPage or TabControl, respectively.

Class FrmUsingTabs (Fig. 14.36) uses a TabControl to display various options related to the text on a label (**Color, Size** and **Message**). The last TabPage displays an **About** message, which describes how TabControls are used.

The TabControl tbcTextOptions and the TabPages tbpColor, tbpSize, tbpMessage and tbpAbout are created in the designer (as described previously). The tbpColor contains three RadioButtons for the colors black (radBlack), red (radRed) and green (radGreen). This TabPage is displayed in Fig. 14.36(a). The CheckChanged event handler for each RadioButton updates the color of the text in lblDisplay (lines 8, 15 and 22). The tbp-Size (Fig. 14.36(b)) has three RadioButtons, corresponding to font sizes 12 (radSize12), 16 (radSize16) and 20 (radSize20), which change the font size of lblDisplay—lines 29, 36 and 43, respectively. The tbpMessage (Fig. 14.36(c)) contains two RadioButtons for the messages **Hello!** (radHello) and **Goodbye!** (radGoodbye). The two RadioButtons determine the text on lblDisplay (lines 50 and 57, respectively). The tbpAbout (Fig. 14.36(d)) contains a Label (lblMessage) describing the purpose of TabControls.

```vb
1    ' Fig. 14.36: FrmUsingTabs.vb
2    ' Using TabControl to display various font settings.
3    Public Class FrmUsingTabs
4       ' event handler for Black RadioButton
5       Private Sub radBlack_CheckedChanged(ByVal sender As System.Object, _
6          ByVal e As System.EventArgs) Handles radBlack.CheckedChanged
7
8          lblDisplay.ForeColor = Color.Black ' change font color to black
9       End Sub ' radBlack_CheckedChanged
```

Fig. 14.36 | TabControl used to display various font settings. (Part 1 of 3.)

```
10
11        ' event handler for Red RadioButton
12        Private Sub radRed_CheckedChanged(ByVal sender As System.Object, _
13          ByVal e As System.EventArgs) Handles radRed.CheckedChanged
14
15            lblDisplay.ForeColor = Color.Red ' change font color to red
16        End Sub ' radRed_CheckedChanged
17
18        ' event handler for Green RadioButton
19        Private Sub radGreen_CheckedChanged(ByVal sender As System.Object, _
20          ByVal e As System.EventArgs) Handles radGreen.CheckedChanged
21
22            lblDisplay.ForeColor = Color.Green ' change font color to green
23        End Sub ' radGreen_CheckedChanged
24
25        ' event handler for 12 point RadioButton
26        Private Sub radSize12_CheckedChanged(ByVal sender As System.Object, _
27          ByVal e As System.EventArgs) Handles radSize12.CheckedChanged
28            ' change font size to 12
29            lblDisplay.Font = New Font(lblDisplay.Font.Name, 12)
30        End Sub ' radSize12_CheckedChanged
31
32        ' event handler for 16 point RadioButton
33        Private Sub radSize16_CheckedChanged(ByVal sender As System.Object, _
34          ByVal e As System.EventArgs) Handles radSize16.CheckedChanged
35            ' change font size to 16
36            lblDisplay.Font = New Font(lblDisplay.Font.Name, 16)
37        End Sub ' radSize16_CheckedChanged
38
39        ' event handler for 20 point RadioButton
40        Private Sub radSize20_CheckedChanged(ByVal sender As System.Object, _
41          ByVal e As System.EventArgs) Handles radSize20.CheckedChanged
42            ' change font size to 20
43            lblDisplay.Font = New Font(lblDisplay.Font.Name, 20)
44        End Sub ' radSize20_CheckedChanged
45
46        ' event handler for Hello! RadioButton
47        Private Sub radHello_CheckedChanged(ByVal sender As System.Object, _
48          ByVal e As System.EventArgs) Handles radHello.CheckedChanged
49
50            lblDisplay.Text = "Hello!" ' change text to Hello!
51        End Sub ' radHello_CheckedChanged
52
53        ' event handler for Goodbye! RadioButton
54        Private Sub radGoodbye_CheckedChanged(ByVal sender As System.Object, _
55          ByVal e As System.EventArgs) Handles radGoodbye.CheckedChanged
56
57            lblDisplay.Text = "Goodbye!" ' change text to Goodbye!
58        End Sub ' radGoodbye_CheckedChanged
59    End Class ' FrmUsingTabs
```

Fig. 14.36 | TabControl used to display various font settings. (Part 2 of 3.)

Fig. 14.36 | TabControl used to display various font settings. (Part 3 of 3.)

> **Software Engineering Observation 14.3**
>
> *A TabPage can act as a container for a single logical group of RadioButtons, enforcing their mutual exclusivity. To place multiple RadioButton groups inside a single TabPage, group the RadioButtons within Panels or GroupBoxes and attach these containers to the TabPage.*

14.12 Multiple Document Interface (MDI) Windows

In previous chapters, we have built only *single document interface (SDI)* applications. Such programs (including Microsoft's Notepad and Paint) can support only one open window or document at a time. SDI applications usually have limited abilities—Paint and Notepad, for example, have limited image- and text-editing features. To edit multiple documents, the user must execute another instance of the SDI application.

Most recent applications have *multiple document interfaces (MDIs)*, which allow users to edit multiple documents at once—for example, graphics applications like Jasc PaintShop Pro and Adobe Photoshop allow you to edit multiple images at once. MDI programs also tend to be more complex—PaintShop Pro and Photoshop have a greater number of image-editing features than does Paint.

The main application window of an MDI program is called the *parent window*, and each window inside the application is referred to as a *child window*. Although an MDI application can have many child windows, there is only one parent window. Furthermore, a maximum of one child window can be active at once. Child windows cannot be parents themselves and cannot be moved outside their parent. In all other ways (closing, minimizing, resizing, etc.), a child window behaves like any other window. A child window's functionality can be different from the functionality of other child windows of the parent. For example, one child window might allow the user to edit images, another might allow the user to edit text and a third might display network traffic graphically, but all could belong to the same MDI parent. Figure 14.37 depicts a sample MDI application.

To create an MDI Form, create a new Form and set its **IsMdiContainer** property to True. The Form changes appearance, as in Fig. 14.38.

Next, create a child Form class to be added to the Form. To do this, right click the project in the **Solution Explorer**, select **Add > Windows Form...** and name the file. Edit the

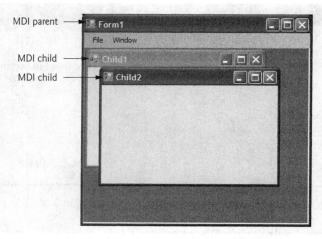

Fig. 14.37 | MDI parent window and MDI child windows.

Fig. 14.38 | SDI and MDI forms.

Form as you like. To add the child Form to the parent, we must create a new child Form object, set its **MdiParent** property to the parent Form and call the child Form's Show method. In general, to add a child Form to a parent, you would write

```
Dim childForm As New ChildFormClass()
childForm.MdiParent = parentForm
childForm.Show()
```

In most cases, the parent Form creates the child, so the *parentForm* reference is Me. The code to create a child usually resides in an event handler, which creates a new window in response to a user action. Menu selections (such as **File > New > Window**) are commonly used to create new child windows.

Class Form property **MdiChildren** returns an array of child Form references. This is useful if the parent window wants to check the status of all its children (for example, ensuring that all are saved before the parent closes). Property **ActiveMdiChild** returns a reference to the active child window; it returns Nothing if there are no active child windows. Other features of MDI windows are described in Fig. 14.39.

MDI Form properties, a method and an event	Description
Common MDI Child Properties	
IsMdiChild	Indicates whether a Form is an MDI child. If True, the Form is an MDI child (read-only property).
MdiParent	Specifies the MDI parent Form of the child.
Common MDI Parent Properties	
ActiveMdiChild	Returns the Form that is the currently active MDI child (returns Nothing if no children are active).
IsMdiContainer	Indicates whether a Form can be an MDI parent. If True, the Form can be an MDI parent. The default value is False.
MdiChildren	Returns the MDI children as an array of Forms.
Common Method	
LayoutMdi	Arranges child forms in an MDI parent Form. The method takes as a parameter an MdiLayout enumeration constant (ArrangeIcons, Cascade, TileHorizontal or TileVertical). Figure 14.42 depicts the effects of these values.
Common Event	
MdiChildActivate	Generated when an MDI child is closed or activated.

Fig. 14.39 | MDI parent and MDI child properties, a method and an event.

Child windows can be minimized, maximized and closed independently of each other and the parent window. Figure 14.40 shows two images—one containing two minimized child windows and a second containing a maximized child window. When the parent is minimized or closed, the child windows are minimized or closed as well. Note that the title bar in Fig. 14.40(b) is **Form1 - [Child2]**. When a child window is maximized, its title bar text is inserted into the parent window's title bar. When a child window is minimized or maximized, its title bar displays a restore icon, which can be used to return the child window to its previous size (i.e., its size before it was minimized or maximized).

Visual Basic provides a property that helps track which child windows are open in an MDI container. Property *MdiWindowListItem* of class MenuStrip specifies which menu, if any, displays a list of open child windows. When a new child window is opened, an entry is added to the list (as in the first screen of Figure 14.41). If nine or more child windows are open, the list includes the option **More Windows...**, which allows the user to select a window from a list in a dialog.

 Good Programming Practice 14.1

When creating MDI applications, include a menu that displays a list of the open child windows. This helps the user select a child window quickly, rather than having to search for it in the parent window.

MDI containers allow you to organize child windows by calling method *LayoutMdi* of the parent Form. Method LayoutMdi receives as its argument one of the *MdiLayout* enumeration constants—*ArrangeIcons*, *Cascade*, *TileHorizontal* and *TileVertical*. *Tiled windows* completely fill the parent and do not overlap; such windows can be arranged horizontally (value TileHorizontal) or vertically (value TileVertical). *Cascaded windows* (value Cascade) overlap—each is the same size and displays a visible title bar, if possible. Value ArrangeIcons arranges the icons for any minimized child windows. If minimized windows are scattered around the parent window, value ArrangeIcons orders them neatly at the bottom-left corner of the parent window. Figure 14.42 illustrates the values of the MdiLayout enumeration.

Fig. 14.40 | Minimized and maximized child windows.

Child windows list

Nine or more child
windows enables the
More Windows... option

Fig. 14.41 | MenuStrip property MdiWindowListItem example.

Class FrmUsingMDI (Fig. 14.43) demonstrates MDI windows. Class FrmUsingMDI uses
three instances of child FrmChild (Fig. 14.44), each containing a PictureBox that displays
an image. The parent MDI Form contains menus that enable users to create and arrange
child Forms.

FrmUsingMDI
Figure 14.43 presents class FrmUsingMDI—the application's MDI parent Form. This Form,
which is created first, contains two top-level menus. The first of these menus, **File** (file-
ToolStripMenuItem), contains both an **Exit** item (exitToolStripMenuItem) and a **New**
submenu (newToolStripMenuItem) consisting of items for each child window. The second
menu, **Window** (windowToolStripMenuItem), provides options for laying out the MDI
children, plus a list of the active MDI children.

In the **Properties** window, we set the Form's IsMdiContainer property to True,
making the Form an MDI parent. In addition, we set the MenuStrip's MdiWindowListItem
property to windowToolStripMenuItem so that the **Window** menu can list the open MDI
child windows.

Fig. 14.42 | MdiLayout enumeration values.

```
1   ' Fig. 14.43: FrmUsingMDI.vb
2   ' MDI parent and child windows.
3   Public Class FrmUsingMDI
4      ' create Child 1 window when child1ToolStripMenuItem is clicked
5      Private Sub child1ToolStripMenuItem_Click( _
6         ByVal sender As System.Object, ByVal e As System.EventArgs) _
7         Handles child1ToolStripMenuItem.Click
8         ' create new child
9         Dim child As New FrmChild("Child 1", "\images\vcsharphtp2_238h.jpg")
10        child.MdiParent = Me ' set parent
11        child.Show() ' display child
12     End Sub ' child1ToolStripMenuItem_Click
```

Fig. 14.43 | MDI parent-window class. (Part 1 of 3.)

```vb
13
14        ' create Child 2 window when child2ToolStripMenuItem is clicked
15        Private Sub child2ToolStripMenuItem_Click( _
16           ByVal sender As System.Object, ByVal e As System.EventArgs) _
17           Handles child2ToolStripMenuItem.Click
18           ' create new child
19           Dim child As New FrmChild("Child 2", "\images\vcsharpfp2_238h.jpg")
20           child.MdiParent = Me ' set parent
21           child.Show() ' display child
22        End Sub ' child2ToolStripMenuItem_Click
23
24        ' create Child 3 window when child3ToolStripMenuItem is clicked
25        Private Sub child3ToolStripMenuItem_Click( _
26           ByVal sender As System.Object, ByVal e As System.EventArgs) _
27           Handles child3ToolStripMenuItem.Click
28           ' create new child
29           Dim child As New FrmChild("Child 3", "\images\vbhtp3_238h.jpg")
30           child.MdiParent = Me ' set parent
31           child.Show() ' display child
32        End Sub ' child3ToolStripMenuItem_Click
33
34        ' exit application
35        Private Sub exitToolStripMenuItem_Click( _
36           ByVal sender As System.Object, ByVal e As System.EventArgs) _
37           Handles exitToolStripMenuItem.Click
38
39           Application.Exit()
40        End Sub ' exitToolStripMenuItem_Click
41
42        ' set Cascade layout
43        Private Sub cascadeToolStripMenuItem_Click( _
44           ByVal sender As System.Object, ByVal e As System.EventArgs) _
45           Handles cascadeToolStripMenuItem.Click
46
47           Me.LayoutMdi(MdiLayout.Cascade)
48        End Sub ' cascadeToolStripMenuItem_Click
49
50        ' set TileHorizontal layout
51        Private Sub tileHorizontalToolStripMenuItem_Click( _
52           ByVal sender As System.Object, ByVal e As System.EventArgs) _
53           Handles tileHorizontalToolStripMenuItem.Click
54
55           Me.LayoutMdi(MdiLayout.TileHorizontal)
56        End Sub ' tileHorizontalToolStripMenuItem_Click
57
58        ' set TileVertical layout
59        Private Sub tileVerticalToolStripMenuItem_Click( _
60           ByVal sender As System.Object, ByVal e As System.EventArgs) _
61           Handles tileVerticalToolStripMenuItem.Click
62
63           Me.LayoutMdi(MdiLayout.TileVertical)
64        End Sub ' tileVerticalToolStripMenuItem_Click
65     End Class ' FrmUsingMDI
```

Fig. 14.43 | MDI parent-window class. (Part 2 of 3.)

Fig. 14.43 | MDI parent-window class. (Part 3 of 3.)

The **Cascade** menu item's (cascadeToolStripMenuItem) event handler (lines 43–48) cascades the child windows by calling the parent Form's LayoutMdi method with the argument MdiLayout.Cascade (line 47). The **Tile Horizontal** menu item's (tileHorizontalToolStripMenuItem) event handler (lines 51–56) arranges the child windows horizontally by calling the parent Form's LayoutMdi method with the argument MdiLayout.TileHorizontal (line 55). Finally, the **Tile Vertical** menu item's (tileVerticalToolStripMenuItem) event handler (lines 59–64) arranges the child windows vertically by calling the parent Form's LayoutMdi method with the argument MdiLayout.TileVertical (line 63).

FrmChild
At this point, the application is still incomplete—we must define the MDI child class. To do this, right click the project in the **Solution Explorer** and select **Add > Windows Form…**. Then name the new class in the dialog as FrmChild (Fig. 14.44). Next, add a PictureBox (picDisplay) to FrmChild. In the constructor, line 8 sets the title bar text. Lines 11–12 set picDisplay's Image property to an Image by using method FromFile (a Shared method of class Image).

```
 1   ' Fig. 14.44: FrmChild.vb
 2   ' Child window of MDI parent.
 3   Imports System.IO
 4
 5   Public Class FrmChild
 6      Public Sub New(ByVal title As String, ByVal fileName As String)
 7         InitializeComponent() ' ensure that Designer generated code executes
 8         Text = title ' set title text
 9
10         ' set image to display in pictureBox
11         picDisplay.Image = Image.FromFile( _
12            Directory.GetCurrentDirectory() & fileName)
13      End Sub ' New
14   End Class ' FrmChild
```

Fig. 14.44 | MDI child FrmChild.

The parent MDI Form (Fig. 14.43) creates new child windows using class FrmChild. The event handlers in lines 5–32 create a new child Form corresponding to the menu item clicked. Lines 9, 19 and 29 create new instances of FrmChild. Lines 10, 20 and 30 set each child's MdiParent property to the parent Form (Me). Lines 11, 21 and 31 call method Show to display each child Form.

14.13 Visual Inheritance

Chapter 10 discussed how to create classes by inheriting from other classes. We have also used inheritance to create Forms that display a GUI, by deriving our new Form classes from class System.Windows.Forms.Form (the code that indicates the inheritance relationship appears in the Form's Designer.vb file). This is an example of *visual inheritance*. The derived Form class contains the functionality of its Form base class, including any base-class properties, methods, variables and controls. The derived class also inherits all visual aspects—such as size, component layout, spacing between GUI components, colors and fonts—from its base class.

Visual inheritance enables you to achieve visual consistency across your applications by giving them a common look-and-feel. This also reduces the learning curve as your users move between applications. For example, you could define a base Form that contains a product's logo, a specific background color, a predefined menu bar and other elements. You then could use the base Form throughout an application for uniformity and branding.

Class FrmVisualInheritance (Fig. 14.45) derives from Form. The output depicts the workings of the Form. The GUI contains two Labels with the text **Bugs, Bugs, Bugs** and **Copyright 2006, by Deitel & Associates, Inc.**, as well as one Button displaying the text **Learn More**. When a user presses the **Learn More** Button, the event handler btnLearnMore_Click (lines 5–12) displays a MessageBox that provides some informative text.

To allow other Forms to inherit from FrmVisualInheritance, we must package it as a class library in a .dll file. To do so, right click the project name in the **Solution Explorer** and select **Properties**, then choose the **Application** tab. In the **Application type** drop-down list, change **Windows Application** to **Class Library**. Building the project produces the .dll. The name of the solution that contains FrmVisualInheritance becomes parts of the class's fully qualified name—in this case, VisualInheritance.FrmVisualInheritance.

```
1   ' Fig. 14.45: FrmVisualInheritance.vb
2   ' Base Form for use with visual inheritance.
3   Public Class FrmVisualInheritance
4       ' display MessageBox when Button is clicked
5       Private Sub btnLearnMore_Click(ByVal sender As System.Object, _
6           ByVal e As System.EventArgs) Handles btnLearnMore.Click
7
8           MessageBox.Show( _
9               "Bugs, Bugs, Bugs is a product of deitel.com", _
10              "Learn More", MessageBoxButtons.OK, _
11              MessageBoxIcon.Information)
12      End Sub ' btnLearnMore_Click
13  End Class ' FrmVisualInheritance
```

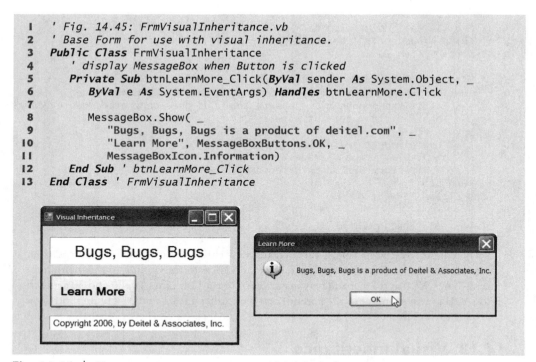

Fig. 14.45 | Class `FrmVisualInheritance`, which inherits from class `Form`, contains a Button (**Learn More**).

To visually inherit from `FrmVisualInheritance`, first create a new Windows application. In this application, add a reference to the `.dll` you just created (located in the `bin/Release` folder of the solution containing Fig. 14.45). Then open the `Designer.vb` file for the new application's `Form` and modify the line

> *Inherits* System.Windows.Forms.Form

to indicate that the application's `Form` should inherit from class `FrmVisualInheritance` instead. The `Inherits` line in the `Designer.vb` file should now appear as follows:

> *Inherits* VisualInheritance.FrmVisualInheritance

Note that you must either specify `FrmVisualInheritance`'s fully qualified name or use an `Imports` declaration to indicate that the new application uses classes from the namespace `VisualInheritance`. In **Design** view, the new application's `Form` now displays the inherited controls of the base class `FrmVisualInheritance` (as shown in Fig. 14.46). You can now add more components to the `Form`.

Class `FrmVisualInheritanceTest` (Fig. 14.47) derives from `FrmVisualInheritance` (Fig. 14.45). The GUI contains the components inherited from `FrmVisualInheritance` and a `Button` with the text **About this Program**. When the user presses this `Button`, the event handler `btnAbout_Click` (lines 5–12) displays another `MessageBox` providing different informative text.

Fig. 14.46 | Form demonstrating visual inheritance.

```
 1    ' Fig. 14.47: FrmVisualInheritanceTest.vb
 2    ' Derived Form using visual inheritance.
 3    Public Class FrmVisualInheritanceTest
 4       ' display MessageBox when Button is clicked
 5       Private Sub btnAbout_Click(ByVal sender As System.Object, _
 6          ByVal e As System.EventArgs) Handles btnAbout.Click
 7
 8          MessageBox.Show( _
 9             "This program was created by Deitel & Associates", _
10             "About this Program", MessageBoxButtons.OK, _
11             MessageBoxIcon.Information)
12       End Sub ' btnAbout_Click
13    End Class ' FrmVisualInheritanceTest
```

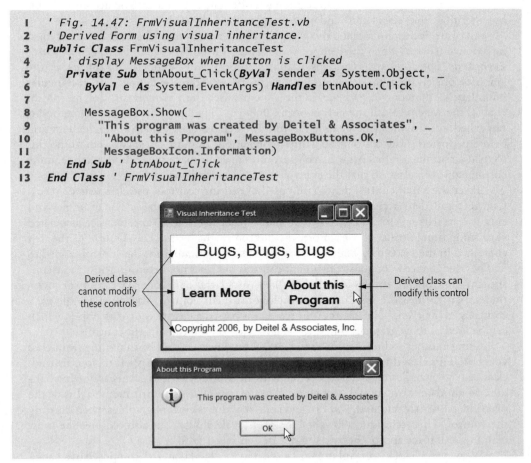

Fig. 14.47 | Class FrmVisualInheritanceTest, which inherits from class
FrmVisualInheritance, contains an additional Button.

Figure 14.47 demonstrates that the components, their layouts and the functionality of base-class FrmVisualInheritance (Fig. 14.45) are inherited by FrmVisualInheritance-Test. If a user clicks the button **Learn More**, the base class event handler btnLearnMore_Click displays a MessageBox. FrmVisualInheritance uses a Private access modifier to declare its controls (in its Designer.vb file), so class FrmVisualInheritanceTest cannot modify the inherited controls.

14.14 User-Defined Controls

The .NET Framework allows you to create *custom controls*. These custom controls appear in the user's **Toolbox** and can be added to Forms, Panels or GroupBoxes in the same way that we add Buttons, Labels and other predefined controls. The simplest way to create a custom control is to derive a class from an existing control, such as a Label. This is useful if you want to add functionality to an existing control rather than reimplement the existing control to include the desired functionality. For example, you can create a new type of Label that behaves like a normal Label but has a different appearance. You accomplish this by inheriting from class Label and overriding method OnPaint.

All controls contain method *OnPaint*, which the system calls when a component must be redrawn (such as when the component is resized). Method OnPaint is passed a *Paint-EventArgs* object, which contains graphics information—property *Graphics* is the graphics object used to draw, and property *ClipRectangle* defines the rectangular boundary of the control. Whenever the system raises the Paint event, polymorphism enables the system to call the new control's OnPaint. The base class's OnPaint method is not called, so you must call it explicitly from the derived class's OnPaint implementation before performing any customized painting operation. In most cases, you want to do this to ensure that the original painting code executes in addition to the code you define in the custom control's class, so that the control will be displayed correctly.

To create a new control that is composed of existing controls, use class *UserControl*. Controls added to a custom control are called *constituent controls*. For example, you could create a UserControl composed of a Button, a Label and a TextBox, each associated with some functionality (for example, the Button might set the Label's text to the text contained in the TextBox). The UserControl acts as a container for the controls added to it. The UserControl contains constituent controls but does not determine how these constituent controls are displayed. Method OnPaint of the UserControl cannot be overridden. To control the appearance of each constituent control, you must handle each control's Paint event. The Paint event handler is passed a PaintEventArgs object, which can be used to draw graphics (lines, rectangles, etc.) on the constituent controls.

Using another technique, you can create a brand new control by inheriting from class Control. This class does not define any specific behavior; that task is left to you. Instead, class Control handles the items associated with all controls, such as events and sizing handles. Method OnPaint should contain a call to the base class's OnPaint method. Inside the overridden OnPaint method, you can add code that draws custom graphics when drawing the control. This technique allows for the greatest flexibility, but also requires the most planning. All three approaches are summarized in Fig. 14.48.

We create a "clock" control in Fig. 14.49. This is a UserControl composed of a Label and a Timer—whenever the Timer raises an event (once per second in this example), the Timer's event handler updates the Label to reflect the current time.

Custom control techniques and PaintEventArgs properties	Description
Custom Control Techniques	
Inherit from Windows Forms control	You can do this to add functionality to a pre-existing control. If you override method OnPaint, call the base class's OnPaint method. Note that you only can add to the original control's appearance, not redesign it.
Create a UserControl	You can create a UserControl composed of multiple pre-existing controls (e.g., to combine their functionality). Note that you cannot override the OnPaint methods of custom controls. Instead, you must place drawing code in a Paint event handler. Again, note that you only can add to the original control's appearance, not redesign it
Inherit from class Control	Define a brand-new control. Override method OnPaint, then call base class method OnPaint and include methods to draw the control. With this method you can customize control appearance and functionality.
PaintEventArgs Properties	
Graphics	The graphics object of the control. It is used to draw on the control.
ClipRectangle	Specifies the rectangle indicating the boundary of the control.

Fig. 14.48 | Custom control creation.

```
 1    ' Fig. 14.49: ClockUserControl.vb
 2    ' User-defined control with a timer and a Label.
 3    Public Class ClockUserControl
 4       ' update label for each clock tick
 5       Private Sub tmrClock_Tick(ByVal sender As System.Object, _
 6          ByVal e As System.EventArgs) Handles tmrClock.Tick
 7          ' get current time (Now), convert to String
 8          lblDisplay.Text = DateTime.Now.ToLongTimeString()
 9       End Sub ' tmrClock_Tick
10    End Class ' ClockUserControl
```

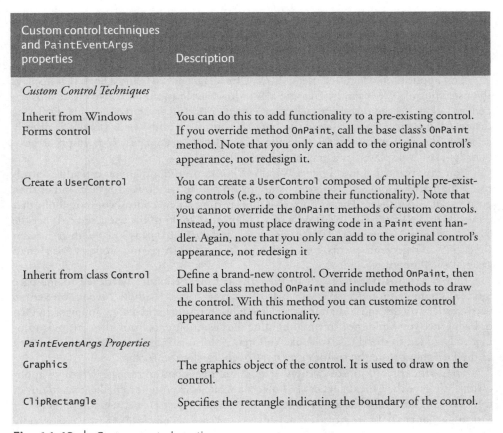

Fig. 14.49 | UserControl-defined clock.

Timers (System.Windows.Forms namespace) are invisible components that reside on a Form, generating *Tick* events at set intervals. The interval is set by the Timer's *Interval* property, which defines the number of milliseconds (thousandths of a second) between events. By default, timers are disabled and do not generate events.

This application contains a user control (ClockUserControl) and a Form that displays the user control. We begin by creating a Windows application. Next, we create a User-Control class for the project by selecting **Project > Add User Control...**. This displays a dialog from which we can select the type of control to add—**User Control** is already selected. We then name the file (and the class) ClockUserControl. Our empty ClockUserControl is displayed as a gray rectangle.

You can treat this control like a Windows Form, meaning that you can add controls using the **ToolBox** and set properties using the **Properties** window. However, rather than creating an application's Form, you are simply creating a new control composed of other controls. Add a Label (lblDisplay) and a Timer (tmrClock) to the UserControl. Set the Timer's Interval property to 1000 milliseconds and set lblDisplay's text with each event (lines 5–9). To generate events, tmrClock must be enabled by setting property Enabled to True in the **Properties** window.

Line 8 sets lblDisplay's text to the current time. Structure *DateTime* (namespace System) contains property *Now*, which is the current time. Method *ToLongTimeString* converts Now to a String containing the current hour, minute and second followed by AM or PM. Once you build the project containing the custom user control, the control is automatically added to the IDE's **Toolbox**. You may need to switch to the application's Form in the Designer before the custom user control appears in the **Toolbox**.

To use the custom control, simply drag it onto the Form and run the Windows application. We gave the ClockUserControl object a white background to make it stand out in the Form. Figure 14.49 shows the output of FrmUserControlTest, which contains our ClockUserControl. There are no event handlers in FrmUserControlTest, so we show only the code for ClockUserControl.

Sharing Custom Controls with Other Developers

Visual Studio allows you to share custom controls with other developers. To create a User-Control that can be exported to other solutions, do the following:

1. Create a new **Class Library** project.

2. Delete the file Class1.vb that is initially provided with the project.

3. Right click the project in the **Solution Explorer** and select **Add > User Control...**. In the dialog that appears, name the user control file and click **Add**.

4. In the project, add controls and functionality to the UserControl (Fig. 14.50).

5. Build the project. Visual Studio creates a .dll file for the UserControl in the solution's bin/Release directory. The file is not executable; class libraries are used to define classes that are reused in other executable applications.

6. Create a new Windows application.

7. In the new Windows application, right click the **Toolbox** and select **Choose Items...**. In the **Choose Toolbox Items** dialog that appears, click **Browse...** and locate the .dll file for the class library you created in *Steps 1–5*. The item will then

appear in the **Choose Toolbox Items** dialog (Fig. 14.51). If it is not already checked, check this item. Click **OK** to add the item to the **Toolbox**. This control can now be added to the Form as if it were any other control (Fig. 14.52).

Fig. 14.50 | Custom-control creation.

Fig. 14.51 | Custom control added to the **ToolBox**.

Fig. 14.52 | Custom control added to a Form.

14.15 Wrap-Up

Many of today's commercial applications provide GUIs that are easy to use and manipulate. The demand for user-friendly GUIs makes sophisticated GUI design an essential programming skill. Visual Studio's IDE makes GUI development quick and easy. In Chapter 13, we presented basic GUI development techniques. In Chapter 14, we demonstrated how to create menus that provide users easy access to an application's functionality. You learned the `DateTimePicker` and `MonthCalendar` controls, which allow users to input date and time values. We used `LinkLabels` to link the user to an application or a Web page. You used several controls that provide lists of data to the user—`ListBoxes`, `CheckedListBoxes` and `ListViews`. We used the `ComboBox` control to create drop-down lists, and the `TreeView` control to display data in hierarchical form. We then introduced complex GUIs that use tabbed windows and multiple document interfaces. The chapter concluded with demonstrations of visual inheritance and creating custom controls.

The next chapter explores multithreading, which enables you to create applications in which several activities can proceed in parallel.

15

Multithreading

*The most general definition
of beauty. . .Multeity in
Unity.*
—Samuel Taylor Coleridge

Learn to labor and to wait.
—Henry Wadsworth
Longfellow

*The world is moving so fast
these days that the man who
says it can't be done is
generally interrupted by
someone doing it.*
—Elbert Hubbard

*Do not block the way of
inquiry.*
—Charles Sanders Peirce

*A person with one watch
knows what time it is; a
person with two watches is
never sure.*
—Proverb

OBJECTIVES

In this chapter you will learn:

■ What threads are and why they are useful.

■ How threads enable you to implement and manage concurrent activities.

■ The life cycle of a thread.

■ Thread priorities and scheduling.

■ To create and execute `Thread`s.

■ Thread synchronization.

■ What producer/consumer relationships are and how they are implemented with multithreading.

■ To ensure that the User Interface thread performs all GUI modifications that are initiated by other threads in a Windows application.

15.1 Introduction

It would be nice if we could perform one action at a time and perform it well, but that is usually difficult to do. The human body performs a great variety of operations *in parallel*—or, as we will say throughout this chapter, *concurrently*. Respiration, blood circulation, digestion, walking and talking, for example, can occur concurrently. All the senses—sight, touch, smell, taste and hearing—can be employed at once. Computers, too, perform operations concurrently—compiling a program, sending a file to a printer and receiving electronic mail messages can all occur in parallel.

Ironically, most programming languages do not enable programmers to specify concurrent activities. Rather, programming languages generally provide only a simple set of control statements that enable programmers to perform one action at a time, proceeding to the next action after the previous one has finished. Historically, the type of concurrency that computers perform today has generally been implemented as operating-system "primitives" available only to highly experienced "systems programmers."

The Ada programming language, developed by the United States Department of Defense, made concurrency primitives widely available to defense contractors building military command-and-control systems. However, Ada has not been widely used in academia and commercial industry.

The FCL provides concurrency primitives. You specify that applications contain "threads of execution," each of which designates a portion of a program that may execute concurrently with other threads—this capability is called *multithreading*. Multithreading is available to all .NET programming languages, including Visual Basic, Visual C# and Visual C++. The FCL's multithreading capabilities are located in the *System.Threading* namespace.

Performance Tip 15.1

A problem with single-threaded applications is that lengthy activities must complete before other activities can begin. In a multithreaded application, threads can be distributed across multiple processors (if they are available) so that multiple tasks are performed concurrently, allowing the application to operate more efficiently. Multithreading can also increase performance on single-processor systems that simulate concurrency—when one thread cannot proceed, another can use the processor.

This chapter discusses many applications of *concurrent programming*. When programs download large files, such as audio clips or video clips over the Internet, users do not want to wait until an entire clip downloads before starting the playback. To solve this problem, we can put multiple threads to work—one thread downloads a clip, while another plays the clip. These activities proceed concurrently. To avoid choppy playback, we *synchronize* the threads so that the player thread does not begin until there is a sufficient amount of the clip in memory to keep the player thread busy.

Another example of multithreading is the CLR's automatic *garbage collection*. C and C++ require programmers to explicitly reclaim dynamically allocated memory. The CLR's garbage-collector thread reclaims dynamically allocated memory that is no longer needed.

Good Programming Practice 15.1

Set an object reference to Nothing *when the program no longer needs that object. This enables the garbage collector to determine at the earliest possible moment that the object can be garbage collected. If such an object has other references to it, that object cannot be collected. Note that you still cannot predict when, or if, the garbage collector will actually reclaim the memory.*

Writing multithreaded programs can be tricky. Although the human mind can perform functions concurrently, people find it difficult to jump between parallel "trains of thought." To see why multithreading can be difficult to program and understand, try the following experiment: Open three books to page 1 and try reading the books concurrently. Read a few words from the first book, then read a few words from the second book, then read a few words from the third book, then loop back and read the next few words from the first book, etc. After this experiment, you will appreciate the challenges of multi-threading—switching between books, reading briefly, remembering your place in each book, moving the book you are reading closer so you can see it, pushing aside books you are not reading and, amid all this chaos, trying to comprehend the content of the books!

15.2 Thread States: Life Cycle of a Thread

At any time, a thread is said to be in one of several *thread states* that are illustrated in the UML state diagram of Fig. 15.1. This section discusses these states and the transitions between states. Two classes critical for multithreaded applications are *Thread* and Monitor, both of the System.Threading namespace. This section also discusses several methods of classes Thread and Monitor that cause state transitions. Several of the terms introduced here are discussed in detail in later sections.

A Thread object begins its life cycle in the *Unstarted* state when the program creates the object and passes a *ThreadStart* delegate to the object's constructor. (For more information on delegates, see Chapter 13.) The ThreadStart delegate, which specifies the actions the thread will perform during its life cycle, must be initialized with a method that takes no arguments and does not return a value. [*Note:* .NET 2.0 also includes a Parame-terizedThreadStart delegate to which you can pass a method that takes arguments. For more information on this delegate, visit the site msdn2.microsoft.com/en-us/library/system.threading.parameterizedthreadstart.aspx.] The thread remains in the *Unstarted* state until the Thread's *Start* method is called, which places the thread in the *Running* state and immediately returns control to the method that called Start. Then the newly *Running* thread and any other threads in the program can execute concurrently on a multiprocessor system or share the processor on a system with a single processor.

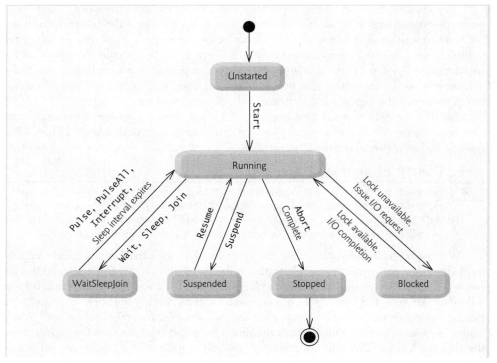

Fig. 15.1 | Thread life cycle.

While in the *Running* state, the thread may not actually be executing all the time. The thread executes in the *Running* state only when the operating system assigns a processor to the thread. When a *Running* thread receives a processor for the first time, the thread begins executing the method specified by its ThreadStart delegate.

A *Running* thread enters the ***Stopped*** (or ***Aborted***) state when its ThreadStart delegate terminates, which normally indicates that the thread has completed its task. Note that a program can force a thread into the *Stopped* state by calling Thread method Abort on the appropriate Thread object. Method Abort throws a ThreadAbortException in the thread, normally causing the thread to terminate. When a thread is in the *Stopped* state and there are no references to the thread object, the garbage collector can remove the thread object from memory. [*Note:* Internally, when a thread's Abort method is called, the thread actually enters the ***AbortRequested*** state before entering the *Stopped* state. The thread remains in the *AbortRequested* state while waiting to receive the pending ThreadAbortException. When Abort is called, a thread in the *WaitSleepJoin*, *Suspended* or *Blocked* state resides in its current state and the *AbortRequested* state, and cannot receive the ThreadAbortException until it leaves its current state.]

A thread is considered to be ***Blocked*** if it is unable to use a processor, even if one is available. For example, a thread becomes blocked when it issues an input/output (I/O) request. The thread is blocked from executing by the operating system until it can complete the thread's I/O request. At that point, the thread returns to the *Running* state so that it can resume execution. Another case in which a thread becomes blocked is in thread synchronization (Section 15.5). A thread being synchronized must acquire a lock on an object by calling Monitor method **Enter**. If a lock is not available, the thread is blocked until the desired lock becomes available. [*Note: Blocked* is not an actual state in .NET. It is a conceptual state that describes a thread that is not *Running*.]

There are three ways in which a *Running* thread enters the *WaitSleepJoin* state. If a thread encounters code that it cannot execute yet, the thread can call Monitor method **Wait** to enter the *WaitSleepJoin* state (we'll present several examples of this in this chapter). Once in this state, a thread returns to the *Running* state when another thread invokes Monitor method **Pulse** or **PulseAll**. Method Pulse moves the next waiting thread back to the *Running* state. Method PulseAll moves all waiting threads back to the *Running* state.

A *Running* thread can call Thread method **Sleep** to enter the *WaitSleepJoin* state for a period of milliseconds specified as the argument to Sleep. A sleeping thread returns to the *Running* state when its designated sleep time expires. Sleeping threads cannot use a processor even if one is available.

Any thread that enters the *WaitSleepJoin* state by calling Monitor method Wait or by calling Thread method Sleep also leaves the *WaitSleepJoin* state and returns to the *Running* state if the sleeping or waiting Thread's **Interrupt** method is called by another thread in the program. The Interrupt method causes a ThreadInterruptionException to be thrown in the interrupted thread.

A thread that cannot continue executing until another thread terminates is called the dependent thread. The dependent thread calls the other thread's **Join** method to "join" the two threads. When two threads are "joined," the dependent thread leaves the *WaitSleepJoin* state and re-enters the *Running* state when the other thread finishes execution (enters the *Stopped* state).

If a *Running* Thread's **Suspend** method is called, the *Running* thread enters the *Suspended* state. A *Suspended* thread returns to the *Running* state when another thread in the program invokes the *Suspended* thread's **Resume** method. [*Note:* Internally, when a thread's Suspend method is called, the thread actually enters the *SuspendRequested* state before entering the *Suspended* state. The thread remains in the *SuspendRequested* state while waiting to respond to the Suspend request. A thread that is in the *WaitSleepJoin* state or is blocked when its Suspend method is called resides in its current state and the *SuspendRequested* state, and cannot respond to the Suspend request until it leaves its current state.] Methods Suspend and Resume are now deprecated and should not be used. In Section 15.9, we show how to emulate these methods using thread synchronization.

If a thread's **IsBackground** property is set to True, the thread resides in the *Background* state (not shown in Fig. 15.1). A thread can reside in the *Background* state and any other state simultaneously. A process cannot terminate until all *foreground threads* (threads not in the *Background* state) finish executing and enter the *Stopped* state. However, if the only threads remaining in a process are *Background threads*, the CLR terminates each thread by invoking its Abort method, and the process terminates.

15.3 Thread Priorities and Thread Scheduling

Every thread has a priority in the range between ThreadPriority.Lowest and Thread-Priority.Highest. These values come from the *ThreadPriority* enumeration (namespace System.Threading), which consists of the values *Lowest*, *BelowNormal*, *Normal*, *AboveNormal* and *Highest*. By default, each thread has priority Normal.

The Windows operating system supports a concept called *timeslicing* that enables threads of equal priority to share a processor. Without timeslicing, each thread in a set of equal-priority threads runs to completion (unless the thread leaves the *Running* state and enters the *WaitSleepJoin*, *Suspended* or *Blocked* state) before the thread's peers get a chance to execute. With timeslicing, each thread receives a brief burst of processor time, called a *quantum*, during which the thread can execute. At the completion of the quantum, even if the thread has not finished executing, the processor is taken away from that thread and given to the next thread of equal priority, if one is available.

The job of the *thread scheduler* is to keep the highest-priority thread running at all times and, if there is more than one highest-priority thread, to ensure that all such threads execute for a quantum in round-robin fashion. Figure 15.2 illustrates the *multilevel priority queue* for threads. In Fig. 15.2, assuming a single-processor computer, threads A and B each execute for a quantum in round-robin fashion until both threads complete execution. This means that A gets a quantum of time to run. Then B gets a quantum. Then A gets another quantum. Then B gets another quantum. This continues until one thread completes. The processor then devotes all its power to the thread that remains (unless another thread of that priority is started). Next, thread C runs to completion. Threads D, E and F each execute for a quantum in round-robin fashion until they all complete execution. This process continues until all the threads run to completion. Depending on the operating system, new higher-priority threads could postpone—possibly indefinitely—the execution of lower-priority threads. Such *indefinite postponement* often is referred to more colorfully as *starvation*.

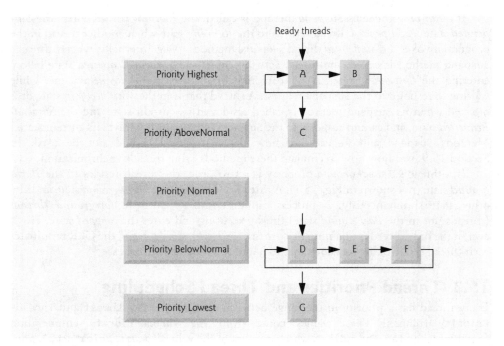

Fig. 15.2 | Thread-priority scheduling.

A thread's priority can be adjusted through the thread's `Priority` property, which accepts values from the `ThreadPriority` enumeration. If the value specified is not one of the valid thread-priority constants, an `ArgumentException` occurs.

A thread executes until it dies, becomes *Blocked* for I/O (or some other reason), calls `Sleep`, calls `Monitor` method `Wait` or `Join`, is preempted by a thread of higher priority or has its *quantum expire*. A thread with a higher priority than the *Running* thread can become *Running* (and hence preempt the first *Running* thread) if a sleeping thread wakes up, if I/O completes for a thread that *Blocked* for that I/O, if either `Pulse` or `PulseAll` is called on an object on which `Wait` was called, if a thread is `Resumed` from the *Suspended* state or if a thread to which the high-priority thread was joined completes.

15.4 Creating and Executing Threads

Figure 15.3 shows how to construct `Thread` objects and demonstrates class `Thread`'s `Shared` method *`Sleep`*. The program creates three threads of execution, each with the default priority `Normal`. Each thread displays a message indicating that it is going to sleep for a random interval of from 0 to 5000 milliseconds, then goes to sleep. When each thread awakens, it displays its name, indicates that it is done sleeping, terminates and enters the *Stopped* state. You will see that method `Main` (i.e., the `Main` *thread of execution*) terminates

```vb
1   ' Fig. 15.3: ThreadTester.vb
2   ' Multiple threads printing at different intervals.
3   Imports System.Threading
4
5   Module ThreadTester
6      Sub Main()
7         ' Create and name each thread. Use MessagePrinter's
8         ' Print method as argument to ThreadStart delegate.
9         Dim printer1 As New MessagePrinter
10        Dim thread1 As New Thread(New ThreadStart( _
11           AddressOf printer1.Print))
12        thread1.Name = "thread1"
13
14        Dim printer2 As New MessagePrinter
15        Dim thread2 As New Thread(New ThreadStart( _
16           AddressOf printer2.Print))
17        thread2.Name = "thread2"
18
19        Dim printer3 As New MessagePrinter
20        Dim thread3 As New Thread(New ThreadStart( _
21           AddressOf printer3.Print))
22        thread3.Name = "thread3"
23
24        Console.WriteLine("Starting threads in Main")
25
26        ' call each thread's Start method to place each
27        ' thread in Running state
28        thread1.Start()
29        thread2.Start()
30        thread3.Start()
```

Fig. 15.3 | Threads sleeping and printing. (Part 1 of 2.)

```
31
32            Console.WriteLine("Threads started, Main ends" & vbCrLf)
33        End Sub ' Main
34
35        ' Print method of this class used to control threads
36        Class MessagePrinter
37            Private sleepTime As Integer
38            Private Shared random As New Random
39
40            ' constructor to initialize a MessagePrinter object
41            Sub New()
42                ' pick random sleep time between 0 and 5 seconds
43                sleepTime = random.Next(5001)
44            End Sub ' New
45
46            ' method Print controls thread that prints messages
47            Public Sub Print()
48                ' obtain reference to currently executing thread
49                Dim current As Thread = Thread.CurrentThread
50
51                ' indicate that thread is going to sleep
52                Console.WriteLine(current.Name & " going to sleep for " & _
53                    sleepTime & " milliseconds")
54                Thread.Sleep(sleepTime) ' sleep for sleepTime milliseconds
55
56                ' display the thread's name
57                Console.WriteLine(current.Name + " done sleeping")
58            End Sub ' Print
59        End Class ' MessagePrinter
60    End Module ' ThreadTester
```

```
Starting threads in Main
thread1 going to sleep for 1603 milliseconds
thread2 going to sleep for 2355 milliseconds
thread3 going to sleep for 285 milliseconds
Threads started, Main ends

thread3 done sleeping
thread1 done sleeping
thread2 done sleeping
```

```
Starting threads in Main
thread1 going to sleep for 4245 milliseconds
thread2 going to sleep for 1466 milliseconds
Threads started, Main ends

thread3 going to sleep for 1929 milliseconds
thread2 done sleeping
thread3 done sleeping
thread1 done sleeping
```

Fig. 15.3 | Threads sleeping and printing. (Part 2 of 2.)

before the application terminates. The program consists of method Main (lines 6–33), which creates the three threads, and class MessagePrinter (lines 36–59), which defines a Print method containing the actions each thread will perform.

Objects of class MessagePrinter control the life cycle of each of the three threads created in class ThreadTester's Main method. Class MessagePrinter consists of instance variable sleepTime (line 37), Shared variable random (line 38), a constructor (lines 41–44) and a Print method (lines 47–58). Variable sleepTime stores a random integer value chosen when a new MessagePrinter object's constructor is called. Each thread controlled by a MessagePrinter object sleeps for the amount of time specified by the corresponding MessagePrinter object's sleepTime.

The MessagePrinter constructor (lines 41–44) initializes sleepTime to a random number of milliseconds from 0 up to, but not including, 5001 (i.e., from 0 to 5000).

Method Print begins by obtaining a reference to the currently executing thread (line 49) via class Thread's Shared property **CurrentThread**. The currently executing thread is the one that invoked method Print. Next, lines 52–53 display a message indicating the name of the currently executing thread and stating that the thread is going to sleep for a certain number of milliseconds. Note that line 52 uses the currently executing thread's **Name** property to obtain the thread's name (set in method Main when each thread is created). Line 54 invokes Shared Thread method Sleep to place the thread in the *WaitSleep-Join* state. At this point, the thread loses the processor, and the system allows another thread to execute if one is ready to run. When the thread awakens, it re-enters the *Running* state and waits to be assigned a processor by the thread scheduler. When the Message-Printer object enters the *Running* state again, line 57 outputs the thread's name in a message indicating that the thread is done sleeping, and method Print terminates.

Module ThreadTester's Main method (lines 6–33) creates three MessagePrinter objects (lines 9, 14 and 19). Lines 10–11, 15–16 and 20–21 create and initialize three Thread objects. Each Thread's constructor receives as an argument a ThreadStart delegate. A ThreadStart delegate represents a method with no arguments and no return value that specifies the actions a thread will perform. Lines 10–11 initialize the ThreadStart delegate for thread1 with printer1's Print method. The AddressOf operator creates a delegate that references a specific method—in this case printer1.Print. When thread1 enters the *Running* state for the first time, thread1 will invoke printer1's Print method to perform the tasks specified in method Print's body. Thus, thread1 will print its name, display the amount of time for which it will go to sleep, sleep for that amount of time, wake up and display a message indicating that the thread is done sleeping. At that point, method Print will terminate. A thread completes its task when the method specified by its ThreadStart delegate terminates, at which point the thread enters the *Stopped* state. When thread2 and thread3 enter the *Running* state for the first time, they invoke the Print methods of printer2 and printer3, respectively. Threads thread2 and thread3 perform the same tasks as thread1 by executing the Print methods of the objects to which printer2 and printer3 refer (each of which has its own randomly chosen sleep time). Lines 12, 17 and 22 set each Thread's Name property, which we use for output purposes.

Error-Prevention Tip 15.1

Naming threads helps in the debugging of a multithreaded program. Visual Studio .NET's debugger provides a **Threads** *window that displays the name of each thread and enables you to view the execution of any thread in the program.*

Lines 28–30 invoke each Thread's Start method to place the threads in the *Running* state. Method Start returns immediately from each invocation, then line 32 outputs a message indicating that the threads were started, and the Main thread of execution terminates. The program itself does not terminate, however, because there are still non-background threads that are alive (i.e., the threads are *Running* and have not yet reached the *Stopped* state). The program will not terminate until its last non-background thread dies. When the system assigns a processor to a thread, the thread enters the *Running* state and calls the method specified by the thread's ThreadStart delegate. In this program, each thread invokes method Print of the appropriate MessagePrinter object to perform the tasks discussed previously.

Note that the sample outputs for this program show each thread and the thread's sleep time in milliseconds as the thread goes to sleep. The thread with the shortest sleep time normally awakens first, then indicates that it is done sleeping and terminates. In Section 15.8, we discuss multithreading issues that could prevent the thread with the shortest sleep time from awakening first. Notice in the second sample output that thread1 and thread2 were able to report their sleep times before Main could output its final message. This means that the main thread's quantum ended before it could finish executing Main, and thread1 and thread2 each got a chance to execute.

15.5 Thread Synchronization and Class Monitor

Often, multiple threads of execution manipulate shared data. If threads with access to shared data simply read that data, then any number of threads can access the data simultaneously without problems. However, when multiple threads share data and the data is modified by one or more of the threads, then indeterminate results may occur. If one thread is in the process of updating the data and another thread tries to update it too, the data will reflect only the later update. If the data is an array or other data structure in which the threads could update separate parts of the data concurrently, it is possible that part of the data will reflect the information from one thread while another part of the data will reflect information from another thread. When this happens, the program has difficulty determining when the data has been updated properly.

The problem can be solved by giving one thread at a time exclusive access to code that manipulates the shared data. During this time, other threads wishing to manipulate the data are kept waiting. When the thread with exclusive access to the data completes its data manipulations, one of the waiting threads is allowed to proceed. In this fashion, each thread accessing the shared data excludes all other threads from doing so simultaneously. This is called *mutual exclusion* or *thread synchronization*.

Visual Basic programmers use the .NET Framework's *monitors* to perform synchronization. Class **Monitor** provides the methods for *locking objects* to implement synchronized access to shared data. Locking an object means that only one thread can access that object at a time. When a thread wishes to acquire exclusive control over an object, the thread invokes the Monitor method Enter to *acquire the lock* on the data object. Each object has a *SyncBlock* that maintains the state of the object's lock. Methods of class Monitor use the data in an object's SyncBlock to determine the state of the lock for that object. After acquiring the lock for an object, a thread can manipulate that object's data. While the object is locked, all other threads attempting to acquire the lock on that object are blocked from acquiring the lock—such threads enter the *Blocked* state. When the thread that locked the shared object no longer requires the lock, that thread invokes `Monitor` method **Exit** to release the lock. This updates the SyncBlock of the shared object to indicate that the lock for the object is available again. At this point, if there is a thread that was previously blocked from acquiring the lock on the shared object, that thread acquires the lock to begin its processing of the object. If all threads with access to an object attempt to acquire the object's lock before manipulating the object, only one thread at a time will be allowed to manipulate the object. This helps ensure the integrity of the data.

Error-Prevention Tip 15.2

All code that modifies a shared object should first lock the object to ensure that only one thread at a time has access to the shared object.

Common Programming Error 15.1

Deadlock occurs when a waiting thread (let us call this thread1) cannot proceed because it is waiting (either directly or indirectly) for another thread (let us call this thread2) to proceed, while simultaneously thread2 cannot proceed because it is waiting (either directly or indirectly) for thread1 to proceed. Two threads are waiting for each other, so the actions that would enable either thread to continue execution never occur.

Visual Basic provides another means of manipulating an object's lock—the **SyncLock** statement. Wrapping a block of code in `SyncLock... End SyncLock`, as in

```
SyncLock objectReference
    ' code that requires synchronization goes here
End SyncLock
```

obtains the lock on the object to which the *objectReference* refers; thus, only one thread at a time can execute the code in a `SyncLock` statement. The *objectReference* is the same reference that normally would be passed to `Monitor` methods `Enter`, `Exit`, `Pulse` and `PulseAll`. When a `SyncLock` statement terminates for any reason, Visual Basic releases the lock on the object to which the *objectReference* refers. We explain `SyncLock` further in Section 15.8.

If a thread that owns the lock on an object determines that it cannot continue with its task until some condition is satisfied, the thread should call `Monitor` method `Wait` and pass as an argument the object on which the thread will wait until the thread can perform its task. Calling method `Monitor.Wait` from a thread releases the lock the thread has on the object that `Wait` receives as an argument and places that thread in the *WaitSleepJoin* state for that object. A thread in the *WaitSleepJoin* state of a specific object leaves that state when a separate thread invokes `Monitor` method `Pulse` or `PulseAll` with that object as an argument. Method `Pulse` transitions the object's first waiting thread from the *WaitSleepJoin* state to the *Running* state. Method `PulseAll` transitions all threads in the object's *WaitSleepJoin* state to the *Running* state. The transition to the *Running* state enables the thread (or threads) to get ready to continue executing.

There is a difference between threads waiting to acquire an object's lock and threads waiting in an object's *WaitSleepJoin* state. Threads that call `Monitor` method `Wait` with an object as an argument are placed in that object's *WaitSleepJoin* state. Threads that are simply waiting to acquire the lock enter the conceptual *Blocked* state and wait until the object's lock becomes available. Then a *Blocked* thread can acquire the object's lock.

`Monitor` methods `Enter`, `Exit`, `Wait`, `Pulse` and `PulseAll` all take a reference to an object—usually the keyword `Me`—as their argument.

Common Programming Error 15.2

A thread in the WaitSleepJoin *state cannot re-enter the* Running *state to continue execution until a separate thread invokes* Monitor *method* Pulse *or* PulseAll *with the appropriate object as an argument. If this does not occur, the waiting thread will wait forever—essentially the equivalent of deadlock.*

Error-Prevention Tip 15.3

When multiple threads manipulate a shared object using monitors, ensure that if one thread calls Monitor *method* Wait *to enter the* WaitSleepJoin *state for the shared object, a separate thread eventually will call* Monitor *method* Pulse *to transition the thread waiting on the shared object back to the* Running *state. If multiple threads may be waiting for the shared object, a separate thread can call* Monitor *method* PulseAll *as a safeguard to ensure that all waiting threads have another opportunity to perform their tasks. If this is not done, indefinite postponement or deadlock could occur.*

Performance Tip 15.2

Synchronization to achieve correctness in multithreaded programs can make programs run more slowly, as a result of monitor overhead and the frequent transitioning of threads between the Running, WaitSleepJoin *and* Running *states. There is not much to say, however, for highly efficient but incorrect multithreaded programs!*

15.6 Producer/Consumer Relationship without Thread Synchronization

In a *producer/consumer relationship*, the *producer* portion of an application generates data and the *consumer* portion of the application uses that data. In a multithreaded producer/consumer relationship, a *producer thread* calls a *produce method* to generate data and place it in a shared region of memory called a *buffer*. A *consumer thread* calls a *consume method* to read the data. If the producer wishes to put the next data in the buffer but determines that the consumer has not yet read the previous data from the buffer, the producer thread should call Wait. Otherwise, the consumer would never see the previous data, which would be lost to that application. When the consumer thread reads the data, it should call Pulse to allow a waiting producer to proceed, since there is now free space in the buffer. If a consumer thread finds the buffer empty or finds that the previous data has already been read, the consumer should call Wait. Otherwise, the consumer might read "garbage" from the buffer or might process a previous data item more than once—each of these possibilities results in a logic error in the application. When the producer places the next data into the buffer, the producer should call Pulse to allow the consumer thread to proceed and read that data.

Let us consider how logic errors can arise if we do not synchronize access among multiple threads manipulating shared data. Consider a producer/consumer relationship in which a producer thread writes a sequence of numbers (we use 1–10) into a *shared buffer*—a memory location shared between multiple threads. The consumer thread reads this data from the shared buffer, then displays the data. We display in the program's output the values that the producer writes (produces) and the consumer reads (consumes). Figures 15.4–15.8 demonstrate a producer thread and a consumer thread accessing a single shared Integer variable without any synchronization. The producer thread writes to the variable; the consumer thread reads from it. We would like each value the producer thread writes to the shared variable to be consumed exactly once by the consumer thread. However, the threads in this example are not synchronized. Therefore, data can be lost if the producer places new data in the variable before the consumer consumes the previous data. Also, data can be incorrectly repeated if the consumer consumes data again before the producer produces the next value. If the consumer attempts to read before the producer produces the first value, the consumer reads garbage. To show these possibilities, the consumer thread in the example keeps a total of all the values it reads. The producer thread produces values from 1 to 10. If the consumer reads each value produced once and only once, the total will be 55. However, when you execute this program several times, you'll see that the total is rarely, if ever, 55. Also, to emphasize our point, the producer and consumer threads in the example each sleep for random intervals of up to three seconds between performing their tasks. Thus, we do not know exactly when the producer thread will attempt to write a new value, nor do we know when the consumer thread will attempt to read a value.

The program consists of interface `IBuffer` (Fig. 15.4), three classes—`Producer` (Fig. 15.5), `Consumer` (Fig. 15.6), `UnsynchronizedBuffer` (Fig. 15.7), and one module—`UnsynchronizedBufferTest` (Fig. 15.8). Interface `IBuffer` declares an `Integer` property called `Buffer`. Any implementation of `IBuffer` must provide a `Get` and a `Set` accessor for this property to allow the producer and consumer to access the shared data stored in the buffer.

Class `Producer` (Figure 15.5) consists of instance variable `sharedLocation` (line 8) of type `IBuffer`, instance variable `randomSleepTime` (line 9) of type `Random`, a constructor (lines 12–15) to initialize the instance variables and a `Produce` method (lines 18–28). The constructor initializes instance variable `sharedLocation` to refer to the `IBuffer` object received from method `Main` as the parameter `sharedBuffer`. The producer thread in this program executes the tasks specified in method `Produce` of class `Producer`. The `For` statement in method `Produce` (lines 21–24) loops ten times. Each iteration of the loop first invokes `Thread` method `Sleep` to place the producer thread in the *WaitSleepJoin* state for a random time interval between 0 and 3 seconds. When the thread awakens, line 23 assigns the value of control variable `count` to `sharedLocation`'s `Buffer` property. When the loop completes, lines 26–27 display a line of text in the console window indicating that the thread has finished producing data and the thread is terminating. The `Produce` method then terminates, and the producer thread enters the *Stopped* state.

Class `Consumer` (Figure 15.6) consists of instance variable `sharedLocation` (line 8) of type `IBuffer`, instance variable `randomSleepTime` (line 9) of type `Random`, a constructor (lines 12–15) to initialize the instance variables and a `Consume` method (lines 18–31). The constructor initializes `sharedLocation` to refer to the `IBuffer` object received from `Main` as the parameter `shared`. The consumer thread in this program performs the tasks specified in class `Consumer`'s `Consume` method. The method contains a for statement (lines 23–

```
1    ' Fig. 15.4: IBuffer.vb
2    ' Interface for a shared Integer buffer.
3    Public Interface IBuffer
4       Property Buffer() As Integer ' property to access the buffer
5    End Interface ' IBuffer
```

Fig. 15.4 | `IBuffer` interface used in producer/consumer examples.

```
1    ' Fig. 15.5: Producer.vb
2    ' Producer produces ten integer values in the shared buffer.
3    Imports System.Threading
4
5    ' class Producer's Produce method controls a thread that
6    ' stores values from 1 to 10 in sharedLocation
7    Public Class Producer
8        Private sharedLocation As IBuffer
9        Private randomSleepTime As Random
10
11       ' constructor
12       Public Sub New(ByVal sharedBuffer As IBuffer, ByVal random As Random)
13           sharedLocation = sharedBuffer
14           randomSleepTime = random
15       End Sub ' New
16
17       ' store values 1-10 in object sharedLocation
18       Public Sub Produce()
19           ' sleep for random interval up to 3000 milliseconds
20           ' then set sharedLocation's Buffer property
21           For count As Integer = 1 To 10
22               Thread.Sleep(randomSleepTime.Next(1, 3001))
23               sharedLocation.Buffer = count
24           Next count
25
26           Console.WriteLine(Thread.CurrentThread.Name & " done producing." & _
27               vbCrLf & "Terminating " & Thread.CurrentThread.Name & ".")
28       End Sub ' Produce
29   End Class ' Producer
```

Fig. 15.5 | `Producer` represents the producer thread in a producer/consumer relationship.

26) that loops ten times. Each iteration of the loop invokes `Thread` method `Sleep` to put the consumer thread into the *WaitSleepJoin* state for a random time interval between 0 and 3 seconds. Next, line 25 gets the value of `sharedLocation`'s `Buffer` property and adds the value to variable `sum`. When the loop completes, lines 28–30 display a line in the console window indicating the sum of all values read. Again, ideally the total should be 55, but because access to the shared data is not synchronized, this sum will almost never appear. The `Consume` method then terminates, and the consumer thread enters the *Stopped* state.

We use method `Sleep` in this example's threads to emphasize the fact that in multithreaded applications, it is unclear when each thread will perform its task and for how long it will perform that task when it has the processor. Normally, these thread-scheduling issues are the job of the computer's operating system. In this program, our thread's tasks are quite simple—for the producer, loop ten times and perform an assignment statement; for the consumer, loop ten times and add a value to variable `sum`. Without the `Sleep` method call, and if the producer executes first, the producer would most likely complete its task before the consumer ever gets a chance to execute. If the consumer executes first, it would consume –1 ten times, then terminate before the producer could produce the first real value.

Class `UnsynchronizedBuffer` (Figure 15.7) implements interface `IBuffer` (line 7) and consists of instance variable `bufferValue` (line 10) and property `Buffer` (lines 13–24),

```
1   ' Fig. 15.6: Consumer.vb
2   ' Consumer consumes ten integer values from the shared buffer.
3   Imports System.Threading
4
5   ' class Consumer's Consume method controls a thread that
6   ' loops ten times and reads a value from sharedLocation
7   Public Class Consumer
8      Private sharedLocation As IBuffer
9      Private randomSleepTime As Random
10
11     ' constructor
12     Public Sub New(ByVal sharedBuffer As IBuffer, ByVal random As Random)
13        sharedLocation = sharedBuffer
14        randomSleepTime = random
15     End Sub ' New
16
17     ' read sharedLocation's value ten times
18     Public Sub Consume()
19        Dim sum As Integer = 0
20
21        ' sleep for random interval up to 3000 milliseconds then
22        ' add sharedLocation's Buffer property value to sum
23        For count As Integer = 1 To 10
24           Thread.Sleep(randomSleepTime.Next(1, 3001))
25           sum += sharedLocation.Buffer ' consume
26        Next count
27
28        Console.WriteLine(Thread.CurrentThread.Name & _
29           " read values totaling: " & sum & "." & vbCrLf & _
30           "Terminating " & Thread.CurrentThread.Name & ".")
31     End Sub ' Consume
32  End Class ' Consumer
```

Fig. 15.6 | Consumer represents the consumer thread in a producer/consumer relationship.

which provides Get and Set accessors. Property Buffer's accessors do not synchronize access to instance variable bufferValue. Note that each accessor uses class Thread's Shared property CurrentThread to obtain a reference to the currently executing thread, then uses that thread's Name property to obtain the thread's name for output purposes.

```
1   ' Fig. 15.7: UnsynchronizedBuffer.vb
2   ' An unsynchronized shared buffer implementation.
3   Imports System.Threading
4
5   ' this class represents a single shared Integer
6   Public Class UnsynchronizedBuffer
7      Implements IBuffer
8
```

Fig. 15.7 | UnsynchronizedBuffer maintains the shared integer variable accessed by a producer thread and a consumer thread via property Buffer. (Part 1 of 2.)

```
9        ' buffer shared by producer and consumer threads
10       Private bufferValue As Integer = -1
11
12       ' property Buffer
13       Public Property Buffer() As Integer Implements IBuffer.Buffer
14          Get
15             Console.WriteLine(Thread.CurrentThread.Name & _
16                " reads " & bufferValue)
17             Return bufferValue
18          End Get
19          Set(ByVal value As Integer)
20             Console.WriteLine(Thread.CurrentThread.Name & _
21                " writes " & value)
22             bufferValue = value
23          End Set
24       End Property ' Buffer
25    End Class ' UnsynchronizedBuffer
```

Fig. 15.7 | UnsynchronizedBuffer maintains the shared integer variable accessed by a producer thread and a consumer thread via property Buffer. (Part 2 of 2.)

Module UnsynchronizedBufferTest (Figure 15.8) defines a Main method (lines 9–33) that instantiates a shared UnsynchronizedBuffer object (line 11) and a Random object (line 14) for generating random sleep times. These are used as arguments to the constructors for the objects of classes Producer (line 17) and Consumer (line 18). The UnsynchronizedBuffer object contains the data that will be shared between the producer and consumer threads. Because UnsynchronizedBuffer implements the IBuffer interface, the Producer and Consumer constructors can each take an UnsynchronizedBuffer object and assign it to their respective IBuffer variables named sharedLocation. Lines 22–24 create and name producerThread. The ThreadStart delegate for producerThread specifies that the thread will execute method Produce of object producer. Lines 26–28 create and name the consumerThread. The ThreadStart delegate for the consumerThread specifies that the thread will execute method Consume of object consumer. Finally, lines 31–32 place the two threads in the *Running* state by invoking each thread's Start method, then the thread executing Main terminates.

Ideally, we would like every value produced by the Producer object to be consumed exactly once by the Consumer object. However, when we study the first output of Fig. 15.8, we see (in bold black text) that the consumer retrieved a value (-1) before the producer ever placed a value in the shared buffer and that the values 2, 3 and 5 were consumed twice each. The consumer finished executing before the producer had an opportunity to produce the

```
1    ' Fig. 15.8: UnsynchronizedBufferTest.vb
2    ' Showing multiple threads modifying a shared object
3    ' without synchronization.
4    Imports System.Threading
5
6    ' this module creates producer and consumer threads
7    Module UnsynchronizedBufferTest
```

Fig. 15.8 | Producer and consumer threads accessing a shared object without synchronization. (Part 1 of 3.)

```vb
8        ' create producer and consumer threads and start them
9    Sub Main()
10       ' create shared object used by threads
11       Dim sharedBuffer As New UnsynchronizedBuffer
12
13       ' Random object used by each thread
14       Dim random As New Random
15
16       ' create Producer and Consumer objects
17       Dim producer As New Producer(sharedBuffer, random)
18       Dim consumer As New Consumer(sharedBuffer, random)
19
20       ' create threads for producer and consumer and set
21       ' delegates for each thread
22       Dim producerThread As New Thread(New ThreadStart( _
23          AddressOf producer.Produce))
24       producerThread.Name = "Producer"
25
26       Dim consumerThread As New Thread(New ThreadStart( _
27          AddressOf consumer.Consume))
28       consumerThread.Name = "Consumer"
29
30       ' start each thread
31       producerThread.Start()
32       consumerThread.Start()
33    End Sub ' Main
34 End Module ' UnsynchronizedBufferTest
```

```
Consumer reads -1
Producer writes 1
Consumer reads 1
Producer writes 2
Consumer reads 2
Consumer reads 2
Producer writes 3
Consumer reads 3
Consumer reads 3
Producer writes 4
Consumer reads 4
Producer writes 5
Consumer reads 5
Consumer reads 5
Producer writes 6
Consumer reads 6
Consumer read values totaling: 30.
Terminating Consumer.
Producer writes 7
Producer writes 8
Producer writes 9
Producer writes 10
Producer done producing.
Terminating Producer.
```

Fig. 15.8 | Producer and consumer threads accessing a shared object without synchronization. (Part 2 of 3.)

```
Producer writes 1
Producer writes 2
Consumer reads 2
Consumer reads 2
Producer writes 3
Producer writes 4
Consumer reads 4
Consumer reads 4
Producer writes 5
Consumer reads 5
Producer writes 6
Consumer reads 6
Producer writes 7
Consumer reads 7
Producer writes 8
Consumer reads 8
Producer writes 9
Producer writes 10
Producer done producing.
Terminating Producer.
Consumer reads 10
Consumer reads 10
Consumer read values totaling: 58.
Terminating Consumer.
```

Fig. 15.8 | Producer and consumer threads accessing a shared object without synchronization. (Part 3 of 3.)

values 7, 8, 9 and 10. Therefore, those four values were lost, and an incorrect sum resulted. In the second output, we see that the value 1 was lost, because the values 1 and 2 were produced before the consumer thread could read the value 1. The values 3 and 9 were also lost and the values 4 and 10 were consumed twice each, also resulting in an incorrect sum. This example clearly demonstrates that access to shared data by concurrent threads must be controlled carefully; otherwise, a program may produce incorrect results.

To solve the problems of lost data and data consumed more than once in the previous example, we will (in Figs. 15.9–15.10) synchronize the access of the concurrent producer and consumer threads to the code that manipulates the shared data by using Monitor class methods Enter, Wait, Pulse and Exit. When a thread uses synchronization to access a shared object, the object is *locked*, and thus no other thread can acquire the lock for that shared object at the same time.

15.7 Producer/Consumer Relationship with Thread Synchronization

Figures 15.9–15.10 demonstrate a producer and a consumer accessing a shared cell of memory with synchronization, so that the producer always goes first, the consumer consumes only after the producer produces a value and the producer produces a new value only after the consumer consumes the previous value produced. This examples reuses interface IBuffer (Fig. 15.4) and classes Producer (Fig. 15.5) and Consumer (Fig. 15.6) from the previous example. [*Note:* In this example, we demonstrate synchronization with class Monitor's Enter and Exit methods. In the next example, we demonstrate the same concepts via a lock block.]

Class SynchronizedBuffer (Figure 15.9) implements interface IBuffer and contains two instance variables—bufferValue (line 9) and occupiedBufferCount (line 12). Also, property Buffer's Get (lines 16–57) and Set (lines 58–88) accessors now use methods of class Monitor to synchronize access to instance variable bufferValue. Thus, each object of class SynchronizedBuffer has a SyncBlock to maintain synchronization. Instance variable occupiedBufferCount is known as a *condition variable*—property Buffer's accessors use this int in conditions to determine whether it is the producer's turn to perform a task or the consumer's turn to perform a task. If occupiedBufferCount is 0, property Buffer's Set accessor can place a value into variable bufferValue, because the variable currently does not contain information—but this means that property Buffer's Get accessor cannot read the value of bufferValue. If occupiedBufferCount is 1, the Buffer property's Get accessor can read a value from variable bufferValue, because the variable does contain information, but property Buffer's Set accessor cannot place a value into bufferValue.

As in the previous example, the producer thread performs the tasks specified in the producer object's Produce method. When line 23 of Fig. 15.5 sets the value of shared-Location's property Buffer, the producer thread invokes the Set accessor at lines 58–88 of Fig. 15.9. Line 60 invokes Monitor method Enter with the argument Me to acquire the lock on the SynchronizedBuffer object. The If statement (lines 64–70) determines

```vb
1    ' Fig. 15.9: SynchronizedBuffer.vb
2    ' A synchronized shared buffer implementation.
3    Imports System.Threading
4
5    ' this class represents a single shared int
6    Public Class SynchronizedBuffer
7       Implements IBuffer
8       ' buffer shared by producer and consumer threads
9       Private bufferValue As Integer = -1
10
11      ' occupiedBufferCount maintains count of occupied buffers
12      Private occupiedBufferCount As Integer = 0
13
14      ' property Buffer
15      Property Buffer() As Integer Implements IBuffer.Buffer
16         Get
17            ' obtain lock on this object
18            Monitor.Enter(Me)
19
20            ' if there is no data to read, place invoking
21            ' thread in WaitSleepJoin state
22            If occupiedBufferCount = 0 Then
23               Console.WriteLine( _
24                  Thread.CurrentThread.Name & " tries to read.")
25               DisplayState("Buffer empty. " & _
26                  Thread.CurrentThread.Name & " waits.")
27               Monitor.Wait(Me) ' enter WaitSleepJoin state
28            End If
```

Fig. 15.9 | SynchronizedBuffer synchronizes access to a shared integer. (Part 1 of 3.)

```vb
29
30              ' indicate that producer can store another value
31              ' because consumer is about to retrieve a buffer value
32              occupiedBufferCount -= 1
33
34              DisplayState(Thread.CurrentThread.Name & " reads " & bufferValue)
35
36              ' tell waiting thread (if there is one) to
37              ' become ready to execute (Running state)
38              Monitor.Pulse(Me)
39
40              ' Get copy of buffer before releasing lock.
41              ' It is possible that the producer could be
42              ' assigned the processor immediately after the
43              ' monitor is released and before the return
44              ' statement executes. In this case, the producer
45              ' would assign a new value to buffer before the
46              ' return statement returns the value to the
47              ' consumer. Thus, the consumer would receive the
48              ' new value. Making a copy of buffer and
49              ' returning the copy ensures that the
50              ' consumer receives the proper value.
51              Dim bufferCopy As Integer = bufferValue
52
53              ' release lock on this object
54              Monitor.Exit(Me)
55
56          Return bufferCopy
57       End Get
58       Set(ByVal value As Integer)
59              ' acquire lock for this object
60              Monitor.Enter(Me)
61
62              ' if there are no empty locations, place invoking
63              ' thread in WaitSleepJoin state
64              If occupiedBufferCount = 1 Then
65                 Console.WriteLine( _
66                    Thread.CurrentThread.Name & " tries to write.")
67                 DisplayState("Buffer full. " & _
68                    Thread.CurrentThread.Name & " waits.")
69                 Monitor.Wait(Me) ' enter WaitSleepJoin state
70              End If
71
72              ' set new buffer value
73              bufferValue = value
74
75              ' indicate consumer can retrieve another value
76              ' because producer has just stored a buffer value
77              occupiedBufferCount += 1
78
79              DisplayState(Thread.CurrentThread.Name & _
80                 " writes " & bufferValue)
81
```

Fig. 15.9 | SynchronizedBuffer synchronizes access to a shared integer. (Part 2 of 3.)

```
82              ' tell waiting thread (if there is one) to
83              ' become ready to execute (Running state)
84              Monitor.Pulse(Me)
85
86              ' release lock on this object
87              Monitor.Exit(Me)
88         End Set
89     End Property ' Buffer
90
91     ' display current operation and buffer state
92     Public Sub DisplayState(ByVal operation As String)
93         Console.WriteLine("{0,-35}{1,-9}{2}" & vbCrLf, operation, _
94             bufferValue, occupiedBufferCount)
95     End Sub ' DisplayState
96 End Class ' SynchronizedBuffer
```

Fig. 15.9 | `SynchronizedBuffer` synchronizes access to a shared integer. (Part 3 of 3.)

whether occupiedBufferCount is 1. If this condition is True, lines 65–66 output a message indicating that the producer thread is trying to write a value, and lines 67–68 invoke method DisplayState (lines 92–95) to output another message indicating that the buffer is full and the producer thread is waiting. Line 69 invokes Monitor method Wait with the argument Me to place the calling thread (i.e., the producer) in the *WaitSleepJoin* state for the SynchronizedBuffer object. This also releases the lock on the SynchronizedBuffer object. The *WaitSleepJoin* state for an object is maintained by that object's SyncBlock. Now another thread can invoke an accessor method of the SynchronizedBuffer object's Buffer property.

The producer thread remains in the *WaitSleepJoin* state until the thread is notified by the consumer's call to Monitor method Pulse that it may proceed—at which point the thread returns to the *Running* state and waits for the system to assign a processor to the thread. When the thread returns to the *Running* state, the thread implicitly reacquires the lock on the SynchronizedBuffer object, and the Set accessor continues executing with the next statement after Wait. Line 73 assigns value to bufferValue. Line 77 increments the occupiedBufferCount to indicate that the shared buffer now contains a value (i.e., a consumer can read the value, and a producer cannot yet put another value there). Lines 79–80 invoke method DisplayState to output a line to the console window indicating that the producer is writing a new value into the bufferValue. Line 84 invokes Monitor method Pulse with the SynchronizedBuffer object (Me) as an argument. If there are any waiting threads in that object's SyncBlock, the first waiting thread enters the *Running* state, indicating that the thread can now attempt its task again (as soon as the thread is assigned a processor). The Pulse method returns immediately. Line 87 invokes Monitor method Exit to release the lock on the SynchronizedBuffer object, and the Set accessor returns to its caller (i.e., the Produce method of the Producer).

Common Programming Error 15.3

Forgetting to release the lock on an object when the lock is no longer needed is a logic error. This will prevent the other threads in your program from acquiring the lock to proceed with their tasks. These threads will be forced to wait (unnecessarily, because the lock is no longer needed). Such waiting can lead to deadlock and indefinite postponement.

The Get and Set accessors are implemented similarly. As in the previous example, the consumer thread performs the tasks specified in the consumer object's Consume method. The consumer thread gets the value of the SynchronizedBuffer object's Buffer property (line 25 of Fig. 15.6) by invoking the Get accessor in lines 16–57 of Fig. 15.9. Line 18 invokes Monitor method Enter to acquire the lock on the SynchronizedBuffer object.

The If statement in lines 22–28 determines whether occupiedBufferCount is 0. If this condition is True, lines 23–24 output a message indicating that the consumer thread is trying to read a value, and lines 25–26 invoke method DisplayState to output another message indicating that the buffer is empty and the consumer thread is waiting. Line 27 invokes Monitor method Wait with the argument Me to place the calling thread (i.e., the consumer) in the *WaitSleepJoin* state for the SynchronizedBuffer object and releases the lock on the object. Now another thread can invoke an accessor method of the Synchronized-nizedBuffer object's Buffer property.

The consumer thread object remains in the *WaitSleepJoin* state until the thread is notified by the producer's call to Monitor method Pulse that it may proceed—at which point the thread returns to the *Running* state and waits for the system to assign a processor to the thread. When the thread reenters the *Running* state, the thread implicitly reacquires the lock on the SynchronizedBuffer object, and the Get accessor continues executing with the next statement after Wait. Line 32 decrements occupiedBufferCount to indicate that the shared buffer is now empty (i.e., a consumer cannot read the value, but a producer can place another value into the shared buffer), line 34 outputs a line to the console window indicating the value the consumer is reading and line 38 invokes Monitor method Pulse with the SynchronizedBuffer object as an argument. If there are any waiting threads in that object's SyncBlock, the first waiting thread enters the *Running* state, indicating that the thread can now attempt its task again (as soon as the thread is assigned a processor). The Pulse method returns immediately. Line 51 gets a copy of bufferValue before releasing the lock. This is necessary because it is possible that the producer could be assigned the processor immediately after the lock is released (line 54) and before the Return statement executes (line 56). In this case, the producer would assign a new value to bufferValue before the Return statement returns the value to the consumer and the consumer would receive the new value. Making a copy of bufferValue and returning the copy ensures that the consumer receives the proper value. Line 54 invokes Monitor method Exit to release the lock on the SynchronizedBuffer object, and the Get accessor returns bufferCopy to its caller.

Class SynchronizedBufferTest (Fig. 15.10) is nearly identical to class Unsynchro-nizedBufferTest (Fig. 15.8). SynchronizedBufferTest's Main method declares shared-Buffer as an object of class SynchronizedBuffer (line 10) and also displays header information for the output (lines 16–18).

Study the two sample outputs in Fig. 15.10. Observe that every integer produced is consumed exactly once—no values are lost and no values are consumed more than once. This occurs because the producer and consumer cannot perform tasks unless it is "their turn." The producer must go first; the consumer must wait if the producer has not produced since the consumer last consumed; and the producer must wait if the consumer has not yet consumed the value the producer most recently produced. Execute this program several times to confirm that every integer produced is consumed once. Notice the lines indicating when the producer and consumer must wait to perform their respective tasks.

```
 1    ' Fig. 15.10: SynchronizedBufferTest.vb
 2    ' Showing multiple threads modifying a shared object with synchronization.
 3    Imports System.Threading
 4
 5    ' this module creates producer and consumer threads
 6    Module SynchronizedBufferTest
 7       ' create producer and consumer threads and start them
 8       Sub Main()
 9          ' create shared object used by threads
10          Dim sharedBuffer As New SynchronizedBuffer
11
12          ' Random object used by each thread
13          Dim random As New Random
14
15          ' output column heads and initial buffer state
16          Console.WriteLine("{0,-35}{1,-9}{2}" & vbCrLf, _
17             "Operation", "Buffer", "Occupied Count")
18          sharedBuffer.DisplayState("Initial state")
19
20          ' create Producer and Consumer objects
21          Dim producer As New Producer(sharedBuffer, random)
22          Dim consumer As New Consumer(sharedBuffer, random)
23
24          ' create threads for producer and consumer and set
25          ' delegates for each thread
26          Dim producerThread As New Thread(New ThreadStart( _
27             AddressOf producer.Produce))
28          producerThread.Name = "Producer"
29
30          Dim consumerThread As New Thread(New ThreadStart( _
31             AddressOf consumer.Consume))
32          consumerThread.Name = "Consumer"
33
34          ' start each thread
35          producerThread.Start()
36          consumerThread.Start()
37       End Sub ' Main
38    End Module ' SynchronizedBufferTest
```

Operation	Buffer	Occupied Count
Initial state	-1	0
Producer writes 1	1	1
Consumer reads 1	1	0
Consumer tries to read. Buffer empty. Consumer waits.	1	0

(continued on next page...)

Fig. 15.10 | Producer and consumer threads accessing a shared object with synchronization.
(Part 1 of 4.)

Producer writes 2	2	1
Consumer reads 2	2	0
Producer writes 3	3	1
Producer tries to write. Buffer full. Producer waits.	3	1
Consumer reads 3	3	0
Producer writes 4	4	1
Consumer reads 4	4	0
Consumer tries to read. Buffer empty. Consumer waits.	4	0
Producer writes 5	5	1
Consumer reads 5	5	0
Producer writes 6	6	1
Consumer reads 6	6	0
Producer writes 7	7	1
Consumer reads 7	7	0
Producer writes 8	8	1
Producer tries to write. Buffer full. Producer waits.	8	1
Consumer reads 8	8	0
Producer writes 9	9	1
Consumer reads 9	9	0
Consumer tries to read. Buffer empty. Consumer waits.	9	0
Producer writes 10	10	1
Producer done producing. Terminating Producer. Consumer reads 10	10	0
Consumer read values totaling: 55. Terminating Consumer.		

Fig. 15.10 | Producer and consumer threads accessing a shared object with synchronization. (Part 2 of 4.)

Operation	Buffer	Occupied Count
Initial state	-1	0
Consumer tries to read. Buffer empty. Consumer waits.	-1	0
Producer writes 1	1	1
Consumer reads 1	1	0
Consumer tries to read. Buffer empty. Consumer waits.	1	0
Producer writes 2	2	1
Consumer reads 2	2	0
Producer writes 3	3	1
Consumer reads 3	3	0
Producer writes 4	4	1
Producer tries to write. Buffer full. Producer waits.	4	1
Consumer reads 4	4	0
Producer writes 5	5	1
Producer tries to write. Buffer full. Producer waits.	5	1
Consumer reads 5	5	0
Producer writes 6	6	1
Consumer reads 6	6	0
Producer writes 7	7	1
Consumer reads 7	7	0
Producer writes 8	8	1
Consumer reads 8	8	0
Consumer tries to read. Buffer empty. Consumer waits.	8	0
Producer writes 9	9	1

(continued on next page…)

Fig. 15.10 | Producer and consumer threads accessing a shared object with synchronization. (Part 3 of 4.)

```
Consumer reads 9                        9       0

Consumer tries to read.
Buffer empty. Consumer waits.           9       0

Producer writes 10                     10       1

Consumer reads 10                      10       0

Producer done producing.
Terminating Producer.
Consumer read values totaling: 55.
Terminating Consumer.
```

Fig. 15.10 | Producer and consumer threads accessing a shared object with synchronization. (Part 4 of 4.)

15.8 Producer/Consumer Relationship: Circular Buffer

Figures 15.9–15.10 use thread synchronization to guarantee that two threads manipulate data in a shared buffer correctly. However, the application may not perform optimally. If the two threads operate at different speeds, one will spend more (or most) of its time waiting. For example, in Fig. 15.9 we shared a single integer between the two threads. If the producer thread produces values faster than the consumer can consume them, then the producer thread waits for the consumer, because there are no other locations in memory to place the next value. Similarly, if the consumer consumes faster than the producer can produce values, the consumer waits until the producer places the next value in the shared location in memory. Even when we have threads that operate at the same relative speeds, they may become "out of sync" over a period of time, causing one of the threads to wait for the other. We cannot make assumptions about the relative speeds of concurrently executing threads. There are too many interactions that occur with the operating system, the network, the user and other components, which can cause the threads to operate at different speeds. When this happens, threads wait. When threads wait, programs can become less productive, user-interactive programs can become less responsive and network applications can suffer longer delays because the processor is not used efficiently.

To minimize the waiting for threads that share resources and operate at the same relative speeds, we can implement a *circular buffer* that provides extra locations in which the producer can place values (if it "gets ahead" of the consumer) and from which the consumer can retrieve those values (while it is "catching up" to the producer). Let us assume the buffer is implemented as an array. The producer and consumer work from the beginning of the array. When either thread reaches the end of the array, it simply returns to the first element of the array to perform its next task. If the producer temporarily produces values faster than the consumer can consume them, the producer can write additional values in the extra buffers (if cells are available; otherwise, the producer must, once again, wait). This enables the producer to perform its task even though the consumer is not ready to receive the current value being produced. Similarly, if the consumer consumes faster than the producer produces new values, the consumer can read additional values from the buffer (if there are any; otherwise, the consumer must, once again, wait) and thus "catch up" to the producer. This enables the consumer to perform its task even though the producer is not ready to produce additional values.

A circular buffer would be inappropriate if the producer and consumer operate at different speeds. If the consumer always executes faster than the producer, then a buffer with one location is sufficient. Additional locations would waste memory. If the producer always executes faster, a buffer with an infinite number of locations would be required to absorb the extra production.

The key to using a circular buffer is to define it with enough extra cells to handle the anticipated "extra" production. If, over a period of time, we determine that the producer often produces as many as three more values than the consumer can consume, we can define a buffer of at least three cells to handle the extra production. We do not want the buffer to be too small, because that would cause threads to wait more; we do not want the buffer to be too large, because that would waste memory.

Performance Tip 15.3

Even when using a circular buffer, it is possible that a producer thread could fill the buffer. This would force the producer thread to wait until a consumer consumes a value to free an element in the buffer. Similarly, if the buffer is empty, the consumer thread must wait until the producer produces another value. The key to using a circular buffer is to optimize the buffer size to minimize the amount of thread wait time.

Figures 15.11–15.12 demonstrate a producer and a consumer accessing a circular buffer (in this case, a shared array of three elements) with synchronization. In this version of the producer/consumer relationship, the consumer consumes a value only when the array is not empty, and the producer produces a value only when the array is not full. This example reuses interface IBuffer (Fig. 15.4) and classes Producer (Fig. 15.5) and Consumer (Fig. 15.6). The statements that created and started the thread objects in the Main methods of class UnsynchronizedBufferTest in Fig. 15.8 and SynchronizedBufferTest in Fig. 15.10 now appear in module CircularBufferTest (Fig. 15.12).

The most significant changes occur in class CircularBuffer (Fig. 15.11), which now contains four instance variables. Array buffers (line 9) is a three-element integer array that represents the circular buffer. Variable occupiedBufferCount is the condition variable that can be used to determine whether a producer can write in the circular buffer (i.e., occupiedBufferCount is less than the number of elements in array buffers) and whether a consumer can read from the circular buffer (i.e., occupiedBufferCount is greater than 0). Variable readLocation (line 15) indicates the position from which the next value can be read by a consumer. Variable writeLocation (line 16) indicates the next location in which a value can be placed by a producer.

The Set accessor (Fig. 15.11, lines 52–81) of property Buffer performs the same tasks that it did in Fig. 15.9, with a few modifications. Rather than using Monitor methods Enter and Exit to acquire and release the lock on the CircularBuffer object, we use a block of code preceded by keyword SyncLock to lock the CircularBuffer object. As program control enters the SyncLock block, the currently executing thread acquires the lock (assuming the lock is currently available) on the CircularBuffer object (i.e., Me). When program control reaches End SyncLock, the thread releases the lock automatically.

```vb
1    ' Fig. 15.11: CircularBuffer.vb
2    ' A circular shared buffer for the producer/consumer relationship.
3    Imports System.Threading
4
5    ' implement the an array of shared integers with synchronization
6    Public Class CircularBuffer
7       Implements IBuffer
8       ' each array element is a buffer
9       Private buffers As Integer() = {-1, -1, -1}
10
11      ' occupiedBufferCount maintains count of occupied buffers
12      Private occupiedBufferCount As Integer = 0
13
14      ' variable that maintain read and write buffer locations
15      Private readLocation As Integer = 0
16      Private writeLocation As Integer = 0
17
18      ' property Buffer
19      Public Property Buffer() As Integer Implements IBuffer.Buffer
20         Get
21            ' lock this object while getting value from buffers array
22            SyncLock (Me)
23               ' if there is no data to read, place invoking thread
24               ' in WaitSleepJoin state
25               If occupiedBufferCount = 0 Then
26                  Console.Write(vbCrLf & "All buffers empty. " & _
27                     Thread.CurrentThread.Name & " waits.")
28                  Monitor.Wait(Me) ' enter the WaitSleepJoin state
29               End If
30
31               ' obtain value at current readLocation
32               Dim readValue As Integer = buffers(readLocation)
33
34               Console.Write(vbCrLf & Thread.CurrentThread.Name & _
35                  " reads " & buffers(readLocation) & " ")
36
37               ' just consumed a value, so decrement
38               ' number of occupied buffers
39               occupiedBufferCount -= 1
40
41               ' update readLocation for future read operation, then
42               ' add current state to output
43               readLocation = (readLocation + 1) Mod buffers.Length
44               CreateStateOutput()
45
46               ' return waiting thread (if there is one) to Running state
47               Monitor.Pulse(Me)
48
49               Return readValue
50            End SyncLock
51         End Get
```

Fig. 15.11 | CircularBuffer synchronizes access to a circular buffer containing three slots. (Part 1 of 3.)

```vb
52          Set(ByVal value As Integer)
53              ' lock this object while setting value in buffers array
54              SyncLock (Me)
55                  ' if there are no empty locations, place invoking thread
56                  ' in WaitSleepJoin state
57                  If occupiedBufferCount = buffers.Length Then
58                      Console.Write(vbCrLf & "All buffers full. " & _
59                          Thread.CurrentThread.Name & " waits.")
60                      Monitor.Wait(Me) ' enter the WaitSleepJoin state
61                  End If
62
63                  ' place value in writeLocation of buffers
64                  buffers(writeLocation) = value
65
66                  Console.Write(vbCrLf & Thread.CurrentThread.Name & _
67                      " writes " & buffers(writeLocation) & " ")
68
69                  ' just produced a value, so increment
70                  ' number of occupied buffers
71                  occupiedBufferCount += 1
72
73                  ' update writeLocation for future write operation,
74                  ' then add current state to output
75                  writeLocation = (writeLocation + 1) Mod buffers.Length
76                  CreateStateOutput()
77
78                  ' return waiting thread (if there is one) to Running state
79                  Monitor.Pulse(Me)
80              End SyncLock
81          End Set
82      End Property ' Buffer
83
84      ' create state output
85      Public Sub CreateStateOutput()
86          ' display first line of state information
87          Console.Write("(buffers occupied: " & _
88              occupiedBufferCount & ")" & vbCrLf & "buffers: ")
89
90          For i As Integer = 0 To (buffers.Length - 1)
91              Console.Write(" " & String.Format("{0,2}", buffers(i)) & "  ")
92          Next (i)
93
94          Console.WriteLine()
95
96          ' display second line of state information
97          Console.Write("          ")
98
99          For i As Integer = 0 To (buffers.Length - 1)
100             Console.Write("---- ")
101         Next (i)
102
```

Fig. 15.11 | CircularBuffer synchronizes access to a circular buffer containing three slots. (Part 2 of 3.)

```
103              Console.WriteLine()
104
105              ' display third line of state information
106              Console.Write("          ")
107
108              ' display readLocation (R) and writeLocation (W) indicators
109              ' below appropriate buffer locations
110              For i As Integer = 0 To (buffers.Length - 1)
111                 If i = writeLocation And writeLocation = readLocation Then
112                    Console.Write(" WR ")
113                 ElseIf i = writeLocation Then
114                    Console.Write(" W  ")
115                 ElseIf i = readLocation Then
116                    Console.Write("  R ")
117                 Else
118                    Console.Write("    ")
119                 End If
120              Next (i)
121
122              Console.WriteLine()
123           End Sub ' CreateStateOutput
124        End Class ' CircularBuffer
```

Fig. 15.11 | CircularBuffer synchronizes access to a circular buffer containing three slots. (Part 3 of 3.)

Common Programming Error 15.4

When using class Monitor's Enter and Exit methods to manage an object's lock, Exit must be called explicitly to release the lock. If an exception occurs in a method before Exit can be called and the exception is not caught, the method could terminate without calling Exit. If so, the lock is not released. To avoid this error, place code that could throw exceptions in a try block, and place the call to Exit in the corresponding finally block to ensure that the lock is released.

Software Engineering Observation 15.1

Using a SyncLock block to manage the lock on a synchronized object eliminates the possibility of forgetting to relinquish the lock with a call to Monitor method Exit. Visual Basic implicitly calls Monitor method Exit when a SyncLock block terminates for any reason. Thus, even if an exception occurs in the block, the lock will be released.

The If statement in lines 57–61 in the Set accessor determines whether the producer must wait (i.e., all buffers are full). If the producer thread must wait, lines 58–59 output text indicating that the producer is waiting to perform its task, and line 60 invokes Monitor method Wait to place the producer thread in the *WaitSleepJoin* state. When execution continues at line 64 after the If statement, the value from the producer is placed in the circular buffer at location writeLocation. Next, lines 66–67 output a message containing the value produced. Line 71 increments occupiedBufferCount, because there is now one more value in the buffer that the consumer can read. Then, line 75 updates writeLocation for the next call to the Set accessor of property Buffer. The output continues at line 76 by invoking method CreateStateOutput (declared in lines 85–123), which outputs the number of occupied buffers, the contents of the buffers and the current write-Location and readLocation. Finally, line 79 invokes Monitor method Pulse to indicate that a thread waiting on the CircularBuffer object (if there is a waiting thread) should transition to the *Running* state. Note that End SyncLock (line 80) causes the thread to release the lock on the CircularBuffer object.

The Get accessor (lines 20–51) of property Buffer also performs the same tasks in this example that it did in Fig. 15.9, with a few minor modifications. Once again, we use a SyncLock block to acquire and release the lock on the CircularBuffer object, rather than using Monitor methods Enter and Exit. The If statement in lines 25–29 in the Get accessor determines whether the consumer must wait (i.e., all buffers are empty). If the consumer thread must wait, lines 26–27 indicate that the consumer is waiting to perform its task, and line 28 invokes Monitor method Wait to place the consumer thread in the *WaitSleepJoin* state. When execution continues in line 32 after the If statement, read-Value is assigned the value at location readLocation in the circular buffer. Lines 34–35 output the value consumed. Line 39 decrements the occupiedBufferCount, because the buffer now contains one more position in which the producer thread can place a value. Then, line 43 updates readLocation for the next call to the Get accessor of Buffer. Line 44 invokes method CreateStateOutput to output the number of occupied buffers, the contents of the buffers and the current writeLocation and readLocation. Finally, line 47 invokes method Pulse to transition the next thread waiting for the CircularBuffer object in the *Running* state, and line 49 returns the consumed value to the calling method.

In Fig. 15.12, line 9 now declares sharedBuffer as a CircularBuffer object, and line 16 displays the initial state of the shared buffer space. The outputs for this example include the current occupiedBufferCount, the contents of the buffers and the current write-Location and readLocation. In the output, the letters W and R represent the current writeLocation and readLocation, respectively. Note that after the third value is placed in the third element of the buffer, the fourth value is inserted at the beginning of the array. This provides the circular buffer effect.

```vb
1    ' Fig. 15.12: CircularBufferTest.vb
2    ' Implementing the producer/consumer relationship with a circular buffer.
3    Imports System.Threading
4
5    Module CircularBufferTest
6       ' create producer and consumer threads and start them
7       Sub Main()
8          ' create shared object used by threads
9          Dim sharedBuffer As New CircularBuffer()
10
11         ' Random object used by each thread
12         Dim random As New Random()
13
14         ' display shared state before producer and consumer
15         ' threads begin execution
16         sharedBuffer.CreateStateOutput()
```

Fig. 15.12 | Producer and consumer threads accessing a circular buffer. (Part 1 of 4.)

```vbnet
17
18          ' create Producer and Consumer objects
19          Dim producer As New Producer(sharedBuffer, random)
20          Dim consumer As New Consumer(sharedBuffer, random)
21
22          ' create threads for producer and consumer and set
23          ' delegates for each thread
24          Dim producerThread As New Thread(New ThreadStart( _
25             AddressOf producer.Produce))
26          producerThread.Name = "Producer"
27
28          Dim consumerThread As New Thread(New ThreadStart( _
29             AddressOf consumer.Consume))
30          consumerThread.Name = "Consumer"
31
32          ' start each thread
33          producerThread.Start()
34          consumerThread.Start()
35       End Sub ' Main
36    End Module ' CircularBufferTest
```

```
(buffers occupied: 0)
buffers:  -1    -1    -1
          ---- ---- ----
           WR

All buffers empty. Consumer waits.
Producer writes 1 (buffers occupied: 1)
buffers:   1    -1    -1
          ---- ---- ----
           R    W

Consumer reads 1 (buffers occupied: 0)
buffers:   1    -1    -1
          ---- ---- ----
                WR

Producer writes 2 (buffers occupied: 1)
buffers:   1     2    -1
          ---- ---- ----
                R    W

Consumer reads 2 (buffers occupied: 0)
buffers:   1     2    -1
          ---- ---- ----
                     WR

All buffers empty. Consumer waits.
Producer writes 3 (buffers occupied: 1)
buffers:   1     2     3
          ---- ---- ----
           W           R
```

Fig. 15.12 | Producer and consumer threads accessing a circular buffer. (Part 2 of 4.)

```
Consumer reads 3 (buffers occupied: 0)
buffers:    1    2    3
           ---- ---- ----
            WR

All buffers empty. Consumer waits.
Producer writes 4 (buffers occupied: 1)
buffers:    4    2    3
           ---- ---- ----
            R    W

Producer writes 5 (buffers occupied: 2)
buffers:    4    5    3
           ---- ---- ----
            R         W

Consumer reads 4 (buffers occupied: 1)
buffers:    4    5    3
           ---- ---- ----
                 R    W

Producer writes 6 (buffers occupied: 2)
buffers:    4    5    6
           ---- ---- ----
            W    R

Producer writes 7 (buffers occupied: 3)
buffers:    7    5    6
           ---- ---- ----
                 WR

All buffers full. Producer waits.
Consumer reads 5 (buffers occupied: 2)
buffers:    7    5    6
           ---- ---- ----
                 W    R

Consumer reads 6 (buffers occupied: 1)
buffers:    7    5    6
           ---- ---- ----
                 R    W

Producer writes 8 (buffers occupied: 2)
buffers:    7    8    6
           ---- ---- ----
                 R         W

Consumer reads 7 (buffers occupied: 1)
buffers:    7    8    6
           ---- ---- ----
                 R    W

Consumer reads 8 (buffers occupied: 0)
buffers:    7    8    6
           ---- ---- ----
                      WR
```

Fig. 15.12 | Producer and consumer threads accessing a circular buffer. (Part 3 of 4.)

```
Producer writes 9 (buffers occupied: 1)
buffers:   7     8     9
         ---- ---- ----
           W         R

Producer writes 10 (buffers occupied: 2)
buffers:  10     8     9
         ---- ---- ----
           W         R
Producer done producing.
Terminating Producer.

Consumer reads 9 (buffers occupied: 1)
buffers:  10     8     9
         ---- ---- ----
           R    W

Consumer reads 10 (buffers occupied: 0)
buffers:  10     8     9
         ---- ---- ----
              WR
Consumer read values totaling: 55.
Terminating Consumer.
```

Fig. 15.12 | Producer and consumer threads accessing a circular buffer. (Part 4 of 4.)

15.9 Multithreading with GUIs

The nature of multithreaded programming prevents you from knowing exactly when a thread will execute. GUI controls are not *thread safe*—if multiple threads manipulate a control, the results may not be correct. To ensure that threads manipulate controls in a thread-safe manner, all interactions with them should be performed by the *User Interface thread* (also known as the *UI thread*)—the thread that creates and maintains the GUI. Class Control provides method Invoke to help with this process. Method Invoke specifies GUI processing statements that the UI thread should execute. The method receives as its arguments a Delegate representing a method that will modify the GUI and an optional array of objects representing the parameters to the method. At some point after Invoke is called, the UI thread will execute the method represented by the Delegate, passing to the contents of the object array as the method's arguments.

Our next example (Figs. 15.13–15.14) uses separate threads to modify the content displayed in a Windows GUI. This example also demonstrates how to use thread synchronization to *suspend* a thread (i.e., temporarily prevent it from executing) and to *resume* a suspended thread. The GUI for the application contains three Labels and three Check-Boxes. Each thread in the program displays random characters in a particular Label. The user can temporarily suspend a thread by clicking the appropriate CheckBox and can resume the thread's execution by clicking the same CheckBox again.

Class RandomLetters (Fig. 15.13) contains method Run (lines 28–49), which takes no arguments and does not return any values. Line 30 uses Shared Thread property current-Thread to determine the currently executing thread, then uses the thread's Name property to get the thread's name. Each executing thread is assigned a name that includes the number of the thread in the Main method (see the output of Fig. 15.14). Lines 32–48 are an infinite loop, which is in a separate thread from the main thread. When the application window is closed in this example, all the threads created by the main thread are closed as well, including threads (such as this one) that are executing infinite loops. In each iteration of the loop, the thread sleeps for a random interval from 0 to 1 second (line 34).

```vb
1   ' Fig. 15.13: RandomLetters.vb
2   ' Writes a random letter to a label
3   Imports System.Threading
4
5   Public Class RandomLetters
6       Private Shared generator As New Random() ' for random letters
7       Private suspended As Boolean = False ' true if thread is suspended
8       Private output As Label ' Label for output
9       Private threadName As String ' name of the current thread
10
11      ' constructor
12      Public Sub New(ByVal label As Label)
13          output = label
14      End Sub ' New
15
16      ' delegate that allows method DisplayCharacter to be called
17      ' in the thread that creates and maintains the GUI
18      Delegate Sub DisplayDelegate(ByVal displayChar As Char)
19
20      ' method DisplayCharacter sets the Label's Text property
21      ' in a thread-safe manner
22      Private Sub DisplayCharacter(ByVal displayChar As Char)
23          ' output character in Label
24          output.Text = threadName + ": " + displayChar
25      End Sub ' DisplayCharacter
26
27      ' place random characters in GUI
28      Public Sub Run()
29          ' get name of executing thread
30          threadName = Thread.CurrentThread.Name
31
32          While True ' infinite loop; will be terminated from outside
33              ' sleep for up to 1 second
34              Thread.Sleep(generator.Next(1001))
35
36              SyncLock Me ' obtain lock
37                  While suspended ' loop until not suspended
38                      Monitor.Wait(Me) ' suspend thread execution
39                  End While
40              End SyncLock
41
42              ' select random uppercase letter
43              Dim displayChar As Char = ChrW(generator.Next(26) + 65)
44
```

Fig. 15.13 | Class RandomLetters outputs random letters and can be suspended. (Part 1 of 2.)

```
45              ' display character on corresponding Label
46              output.Invoke(New DisplayDelegate(AddressOf DisplayCharacter), _
47                 New Object() {displayChar})
48          End While
49      End Sub ' Run
50
51      ' change the suspended/running state
52      Public Sub Toggle()
53          suspended = Not suspended ' toggle bool controlling state
54
55          ' change label color on suspend/resume
56          If suspended Then
57              output.BackColor = Color.Red
58          Else
59              output.BackColor = Color.LightGreen
60          End If
61
62          SyncLock Me ' obtain lock
63              If Not suspended Then ' if thread resumed
64                  Monitor.Pulse(Me)
65              End If
66          End SyncLock
67      End Sub ' Toggle
68  End Class ' RandomLetters
```

Fig. 15.13 | Class RandomLetters outputs random letters and can be suspended. (Part 2 of 2.)

When the thread awakens, line 36 locks this RandomLetters object. so we can determine whether the thread has been suspended (i.e., the user clicked the corresponding CheckBox). Lines 37–39 loop while the Boolean variable suspended remains True. Line 38 calls Monitor method Wait on this RandomLetters object to temporarily release the lock and place this thread into the *WaitSleepJoin* state. When this thread is Pulsed (i.e., the user clicks the corresponding CheckBox again), it moves back to the *Running* state. If suspended is False, the thread resumes execution. If suspended is still True, the loop executes again and the thread re-enters the *WaitSleepJoin* state.

Line 43 generates a random uppercase character. Lines 46–47 call method Invoke passing to it a New DisplayDelegate containing the method DisplayCharacter and a New array of Objects that contains the randomly generated letter. Line 18 declares a Delegate type named DisplayDelegate, which represents methods that take a Char argument and do not return a value. Method DisplayCharacter (lines 22–25) meets those requirements—it receives a Char parameter named displayChar and does not return a value. The call to Invoke in lines 46–47 will cause the UI thread to call DisplayCharacter with the randomly generated letter as the argument. At that time, line 24 will replace the text in the Label associated with this RandomLetters object with the name of the Thread executing this RandomLetters object's GenerateRandomCharacters method and the randomly generated letter.

When the user clicks the CheckBox to the right of a Label, the corresponding thread should be suspended (temporarily prevented from executing) or resumed (allowed to continue executing). Suspending and resuming a thread can be implemented by using thread synchronization and `Monitor` methods `Wait` and `Pulse`. Lines 52–67 declare method `Toggle`, which will change the suspended/resumed state of the current thread. Line 53 reverses the value of `Boolean` variable `suspended`. Lines 56–60 change the background color of the `Label` by assigning a color to `Label` property `BackColor`. If the thread is suspended, the background color will be `Color.Red`. If the thread is running, the background color will be `Color.LightGreen`. Method `Toggle` is called from the event handler in Fig. 15.14, so its tasks will be performed in the UI thread—thus, there is no need to use `Invoke` for lines 57 and 59. Line 62 locks this `RandomLetters` object so we can determine whether the thread should resume execution. If so, line 64 calls method `Pulse` on this `RandomLetters` object to alert the thread that was placed in the *WaitSleepJoin* state by the `Wait` method call in line 38.

Note that the `If` statement in line 63 does not have an associated `Else`. If this condition fails, it means that the thread has just been suspended. When this happens, a thread executing in line 37 will enter the `while` loop and line 38 will suspend the thread with a call to method `Wait`.

Class `frmGUIThreads` (Fig. 15.14) displays three `Label`s and three `CheckBox`es. A separate thread of execution is associated with each `Label` and `CheckBox` pair. Each thread randomly displays letters from the alphabet in its corresponding `Label` object. Lines 14, 21 and 28 create three new `RandomLetters` objects. Lines 15–16, 22–23 and 29–30 create three new `Thread`s that will execute the `RandomLetters` objects' `GenerateRandomCharacters` methods. Lines 17, 24 and 31 assign each `Thread` a name, and lines 18, 25 and 32 `Start` the `Thread`s.

```vb
1    ' Fig. 15.14: frmGUIThreads.vb
2    ' Demonstrates using threads in a GUI
3    Imports System.Threading
4
5    Public Class frmGUIThreads
6       Private letter1 As RandomLetters ' first randomLetters object
7       Private letter2 As RandomLetters ' second randomLetters object
8       Private letter3 As RandomLetters ' third randomLetters object
9
10      Private Sub frmGUIThreads_Load(ByVal sender As System.Object, _
11         ByVal e As System.EventArgs) Handles MyBase.Load
12
13         ' create first thread
14         letter1 = New RandomLetters(lblThread1)
15         Dim firstThread As New Thread(New ThreadStart( _
16            AddressOf letter1.Run))
17         firstThread.Name = "Thread 1"
18         firstThread.Start()
19
20         ' create second thread
21         letter2 = New RandomLetters(lblTread2)
22         Dim secondThread As New Thread(New ThreadStart( _
23            AddressOf letter2.Run))
24         secondThread.Name = "Thread 2"
25         secondThread.Start()
```

Fig. 15.14 | GUIThreads demonstrates multithreading in a GUI application. (Part 1 of 2.)

```
26
27        ' create third thread
28        letter3 = New RandomLetters(lblThread3)
29        Dim thirdThread As New Thread(New ThreadStart( _
30           AddressOf letter3.Run))
31        thirdThread.Name = "Thread 3"
32        thirdThread.Start()
33     End Sub ' frmGUIThreads_Load
34
35     ' close all threads associated with this application
36     Private Sub frmGUIThreads_FormClosing(ByVal sender As System.Object, _
37        ByVal e As System.Windows.Forms.FormClosingEventArgs) _
38        Handles MyBase.FormClosing
39        System.Environment.Exit(System.Environment.ExitCode)
40     End Sub ' frmGUIThreads_FormClosing
41
42     Private Sub chkThread_CheckedChanged(ByVal sender As System.Object, _
43        ByVal e As System.EventArgs) Handles chkThread1.CheckedChanged, _
44        chkThread3.CheckedChanged, chkThread2.CheckedChanged
45        If sender.Equals(chkThread1) Then
46           letter1.Toggle()
47        ElseIf sender.Equals(chkThread2) Then
48           letter2.Toggle()
49        ElseIf sender.Equals(chkThread3) Then
50           letter3.Toggle()
51        End If
52     End Sub ' chkThread_CheckedChanged
53  End Class ' frmGUIThreads
```

Fig. 15.14 | GUIThreads demonstrates multithreading in a GUI application. (Part 2 of 2.)

If the user clicks the **Suspended** CheckBox next to a Label, event handler chkThread_CheckedChanged (lines 42–52) determines which CheckBox was clicked and calls its associated RandomLetters object's Toggle method to suspend or resume the thread.

Lines 36–40 define the frmGUIThreads_FormClosing event handler, which calls method Exit of class System.Environment with the ExitCode property as an argument. This causes all other threads in this application to terminate. Otherwise, only the UI thread would be terminated when the user closes this application; Thread1, Thread2 and Thread3 would continue executing forever.

15.10 Wrap-Up

In this chapter, you learned the capabilities of the .NET framework that enable you to specify concurrent tasks in your programs. We discussed how to create threads of execution using class Thread and ThreadStart delegates—both from the System.Threading namespace.

We discussed several applications of concurrent programming. In particular, you learned about problems that may occur when multiple threads share the same data. To emphasize these issues, we presented an unsynchronized example of the producer/consumer relationship in which a producer thread placed values in a shared buffer and a consumer thread consumed those values. We then demonstrated the producer/consumer relationship again and showed how to synchronize threads using the capabilities of class `Monitor`. This ensured that the shared data was accessed and manipulated properly by the producer and consumer threads. You also learned how to enable threads to operate more efficiently by using a circular buffer that provided extra locations in which the producer could place values and from which the consumer could retrieve those values.

Next, you learned that GUI components are not thread safe, so all changes to GUI components should be performed in the user interface thread that creates and maintains the GUI. We showed how to use `Control` method `Invoke` and a delegate to allow a thread to specify the tasks the user interface thread should perform on GUI components. This enabled multiple threads to modify GUI components in a thread-safe manner. In the next chapter, you will learn about the .NET framework's string, character and regular expression processing capabilities.

16

Strings, Characters and Regular Expressions

OBJECTIVES

In this chapter you will learn:

■ To create and manipulate immutable character String objects of class `String`.

■ To create and manipulate mutable character String objects of class `StringBuilder`.

■ To manipulate character objects of structure `Char`.

■ To use regular expressions in conjunction with classes `Regex` and `Match`.

*The chief defect of Henry King
Was chewing little bits of string.*
—Hilaire Belloc

*Vigorous writing is concise. A
sentence should contain no
unnecessary words, a paragraph
no unnecessary sentences.*
—William Strunk, Jr.

*I have made this letter longer
than usual, because I lack the
time to make it short.*
—Blaise Pascal

*The difference between the
almost-right word and the right
word is really a large matter—
it's the difference between the
lightning bug and the lightning.*
—Mark Twain

Mum's the word.
—Miguel de Cervantes

16.1 Introduction

This chapter introduces the FCL's string and character processing capabilities, and demonstrates how to use regular expressions to search for patterns in text. The techniques presented in this chapter can be employed in text editors, word processors, page-layout software, computerized typesetting systems and other kinds of text-processing software. Previous chapters presented some basic string-processing capabilities. In this chapter, we discuss in detail the text-processing capabilities of class `String` and type `Char` from the `System` namespace and class `StringBuilder` from the `System.Text` namespace.

We begin with an overview of the fundamentals of characters and strings in which we discuss character literals and string literals. We then provide examples of class `String`'s many constructors and methods. The examples demonstrate how to determine the length of strings, copy strings, access individual characters in strings, search strings, obtain substrings from larger strings, compare strings, concatenate strings, replace characters in strings and convert strings to uppercase or lowercase letters.

Next we introduce class `StringBuilder`, which is used to build strings dynamically. We demonstrate `StringBuilder` capabilities for determining and specifying the size of a `StringBuilder` object, as well as appending, inserting, removing and replacing characters in a `StringBuilder` object. We then introduce the character-testing methods of the `Char` structure that enable a program to determine whether a character is a digit, a letter, a lowercase letter, an uppercase letter, a punctuation mark or a symbol other than a punctuation mark. Such methods are useful for validating individual characters in user input. In addition, type Char provides methods for converting a character to uppercase or lowercase.

The chapter concludes with a discussion of regular expressions. We discuss classes Regex and Match from the System.Text.RegularExpressions namespace as well as the symbols that are used to form regular expressions. We then demonstrate how to find patterns in a string, match entire strings to patterns, replace characters in a string that match a pattern and split strings at delimiters specified as a pattern.

16.2 Fundamentals of Characters and Strings

Characters are the fundamental building blocks of Visual Basic source code. Every program is composed of characters that, when grouped together meaningfully, create a sequence that the compiler interprets as instructions describing how to accomplish a task. In addition to normal characters, a program also can contain *character literals*, also called *character constants*. A character literal is a character that is represented internally as an integer value, called a *character code*. For example, the integer value 97 corresponds to the character literal "a"c, and the integer value 122 corresponds to the character literal "z"c. The letter c following the closing double quote is Visual Basic's syntax for a character literal. Character literals are established according to the *Unicode character set*, an international character set that contains many more symbols and letters than the ASCII character set (listed in Appendix D). To learn more about Unicode, see Appendix E.

A string is a series of characters treated as a single unit. These characters can be uppercase letters, lowercase letters, digits and various *special characters*: +, -, *, /, $ and others. A string is an object of class String in the System namespace. We write *string literals*, also called *string constants*, as sequences of characters in double quotation marks, as follows:

```
"John Q. Doe"
"9999 Main Street"
"Waltham, Massachusetts"
"(201) 555-1212"
```

A declaration can assign a String literal to a String variable. The declaration

```
Dim color As String = "blue"
```

initializes String variable color to refer to the String literal object "blue".

Performance Tip 16.1

If there are multiple occurrences of the same String literal in an application, a single copy of the String literal object will be referenced from each location in the program that uses that String literal. It is possible to share the object in this manner because String literal objects are implicitly constant. Such sharing conserves memory.

Common Programming Error 16.1

Assigning Nothing to a String variable can lead to logic errors if you attempt to compare Nothing to an empty String. The keyword Nothing is a null reference, not an empty String (which is a String that is of length 0 and contains no characters).

16.3 String Constructors

Class String provides eight constructors for initializing Strings. Figure 16.1 demonstrates three of the constructors.

Lines 6–7 declare the String variables originalString, string1, string2, string3 and string4. Lines 8–9 allocate the Char array characterArray, which contains nine characters. Line 12 assigns the String literal "Welcome to VB programming!" to variable originalString. Line 13 sets string1 to refer to the same String literal as originalString.

Line 14 assigns a new String to string2, using the String constructor that takes a character array as an argument. The new String contains a copy of the characters in array characterArray.

Software Engineering Observation 16.1

In most cases, it is not necessary to make a copy of an existing String. All Strings are immutable—their character contents cannot be changed after they are created. Also, if there are one or more references to a String (or any object, for that matter), the object cannot be reclaimed by the garbage collector. When a new value is assigned to a String variable, the variable simply refers to a different String object in memory.

Line 15 assigns a new String to string3, using the String constructor that takes a Char array and two Integer arguments. The second argument specifies the starting index

```vb
1    ' Fig. 16.1: StringConstructor.vb
2    ' Demonstrating String class constructors.
3
4    Module StringConstructor
5       Sub Main()
6          Dim originalString, string1, string2, _
7             string3, string4 As String
8          Dim characterArray() As Char = _
9             {"b"c, "i"c, "r"c, "t"c, "h"c, " "c, "d"c, "a"c, "y"c}
10
11         ' string initialization
12         originalString = "Welcome to VB programming!"
13         string1 = originalString
14         string2 = New String(characterArray)
15         string3 = New String(characterArray, 6, 3)
16         string4 = New String("C"c, 5)
17
18         Console.WriteLine("string1 = " & """" & string1 & """" & _
19            vbCrLf & "string2 = " & """" & string2 & """" & vbCrLf & _
20            "string3 = " & """" & string3 & """" & vbCrLf & _
21            "string4 = " & """" & string4 & """" & vbCrLf)
22      End Sub ' Main
23   End Module ' StringConstructor
```

```
string1 = "Welcome to VB programming!"
string2 = "birth day"
string3 = "day"
string4 = "CCCCC"
```

Fig. 16.1 | String constructors.

position (the *offset*) from which characters in the array are to be copied. The third argument specifies the number of characters (the *count*) to be copied from the specified starting position in the array. The new String contains a copy of the specified characters in the array. If the offset or count causes the program to access an element outside the character array's bounds, an ArgumentOutOfRangeException is thrown.

Line 16 assigns a new String to string4, using the String constructor that takes as arguments a character and an Integer specifying the number of times to repeat that character in the String. Lines 18–21 output the contents of variables string1, string2, string3 and string4.

16.4 String Indexer, Length Property and CopyTo Method

Figure 16.2 uses the String indexer to access individual characters in a String, and demonstrates String property Length, which returns the length of the String. The program also uses String method CopyTo to copy a specified number of characters from a String into a Char array. This application determines the length of a String, reverses the order of the characters in the String and copies a series of characters from the String to a character array.

```
1    ' Fig. 16.2: StringMethods.vb
2    ' Using the indexer, property Length and method CopyTo
3    ' of class String.
4
5    Module StringMethods
6       Sub Main()
7          Dim string1 As String
8          Dim characterArray() As Char
9
10         string1 = "hello there"
11         characterArray = New Char(5) {}
12
13         ' output string1
14         Console.WriteLine("string1: """ & string1 & """")
15
16         ' test Length property
17         Console.WriteLine("Length of string1: " & string1.Length)
18
19         ' loop through characters in string1 and display reversed
20         Console.Write("The string reversed is: ")
21
22         Dim i As Integer
23
24         For i = string1.Length - 1 To 0 Step -1
25            Console.Write(string1(i))
26         Next i
27
28         ' copy characters from string1 into characterArray
29         string1.CopyTo(0, characterArray, 0, 5)
30         Console.Write(vbCrLf & "The character array is: ")
```

Fig. 16.2 | String indexer, Length property and CopyTo method. (Part 1 of 2.)

```
31
32          For i = 0 To characterArray.Length - 1
33              Console.Write(characterArray(i))
34          Next i
35
36          Console.WriteLine(vbCrLf)
37      End Sub ' Main
38  End Module ' StringMethods
```

```
string1: "hello there"
Length of string1: 11
The string reversed is: ereht olleh
The character array is: hello
```

Fig. 16.2 | String indexer, Length property and CopyTo method. (Part 2 of 2.)

Line 17 uses String property Length to determine the number of characters in string1. Like arrays, Strings always know their own size.

Lines 24–26 output the characters of string1 in reverse order using the String indexer, which treats a String as an array of Chars and returns the character at a specific index in the String. The indexer receives an integer argument as the index and returns the character at that index. As with arrays, the first element of a String is considered to be at position 0.

Common Programming Error 16.2

Attempting to access a character that is outside the bounds of a String (i.e., an index less than 0 or an index greater than or equal to the String's length) results in an IndexOutOfRangeException.

Line 29 uses String method CopyTo to copy the characters of a String (string1) into a character array (characterArray). CopyTo's first argument is the index from which the method begins copying characters in the String. The second argument is the character array into which the characters are copied. The third argument is the index specifying the starting location at which the method begins placing the copied characters into the character array. The last argument is the number of characters that the method will copy from the String. Lines 32–34 output the Char array contents one character at a time.

16.5 Comparing Strings

The next two examples demonstrate the various methods for comparing Strings. To understand how one String can be "greater than" or "less than" another String, consider the process of alphabetizing a series of last names. The reader would, no doubt, place "Jones" before "Smith", because the first letter of "Jones" comes before the first letter of "Smith" in the alphabet. The alphabet is more than just a set of 26 letters—it is an ordered list of characters in which each letter occurs in a specific position. For example, Z is more than just a letter of the alphabet; Z is specifically the 26th letter of the alphabet.

Computers can order characters alphabetically because the characters are represented internally as Unicode numeric codes. When comparing two Strings, the string comparison methods simply compare the numeric codes of the characters in the Strings.

Comparing Strings with = and String Methods Equals and CompareTo

Class String provides several ways to compare Strings. Figure 16.3 demonstrates method Equals, method CompareTo and the equality operator (=).

The condition in the If statement (line 18) uses String method Equals to compare string1 and the String literal "hello" to determine whether they are equal. Method Equals (inherited by String from class Object) tests any two objects for equality (i.e., whether the objects have the same contents). The method returns True if the objects are equal and False otherwise. In this instance, the preceding condition returns True because string1 references the String literal object "hello". Method Equals uses a *lexicographical comparison*—the integer Unicode values that represent each character in each String are compared. Comparing "hello" with "HELLO" would return False because the

```
1    ' Fig. 16.3: StringCompare.vb
2    ' Comparing Strings
3
4    Module StringCompare
5       Sub Main()
6          Dim string1 As String = "hello"
7          Dim string2 As String = "good bye"
8          Dim string3 As String = "Happy Birthday"
9          Dim string4 As String = "happy birthday"
10
11         ' output values of four strings
12         Console.WriteLine("string1 = """" & string1 & """" & vbCrLf & _
13            "string2 = """" & string2 & """" & vbCrLf & _
14            "string3 = """" & string3 & """" & vbCrLf & _
15            "string4 = """" & string4 & "" & vbCrLf)
16
17         ' test for equality using Equals method
18         If string1.Equals("hello") Then
19            Console.WriteLine("string1 equals ""hello""")
20         Else
21            Console.WriteLine("string1 does not equal ""hello""")
22         End If
23
24         ' test for equality with =
25         If string1 = "hello" Then
26            Console.WriteLine("string1 equals ""hello""")
27         Else
28            Console.WriteLine("string1 does not equal ""hello""")
29         End If
30
31         ' test for equality comparing case
32         If String.Equals(string3, string4) Then ' static method
33            Console.WriteLine("string3 equals string4")
34         Else
35            Console.WriteLine("string3 does not equal string4")
36         End If
37
```

Fig. 16.3 | String test to determine equality. (Part 1 of 2.)

```
38        ' test CompareTo
39        Console.WriteLine(vbCrLf & "string1.CompareTo( string2 ) is " & _
40           string1.CompareTo(string2) & vbCrLf & _
41           "string2.CompareTo( string1 ) is " & _
42           string2.CompareTo(string1) & vbCrLf & _
43           "string1.CompareTo( string1 ) is " & _
44           string1.CompareTo(string1) & vbCrLf & _
45           "string3.CompareTo( string4 ) is " & _
46           string3.CompareTo(string4) & vbCrLf & _
47           "string4.CompareTo( string3 ) is " & _
48           string4.CompareTo(string3) & vbCrLf)
49     End Sub ' Main
50 End Module ' StringCompare
```

```
string1 = "hello"
string2 = "good bye"
string3 = "Happy Birthday"
string4 = "happy birthday"

string1 equals "hello"
string1 equals "hello"
string3 does not equal string4

string1.CompareTo( string2 ) is 1
string2.CompareTo( string1 ) is -1
string1.CompareTo( string1 ) is 0
string3.CompareTo( string4 ) is 1
string4.CompareTo( string3 ) is -1
```

Fig. 16.3 | String test to determine equality. (Part 2 of 2.)

numeric representations of lowercase letters are different from the numeric representations of corresponding uppercase letters.

The condition in the second If statement (line 25) uses the equality operator (=) to compare string1 with the String literal "hello" for equality. In Visual Basic, the equality operator also uses a lexicographical comparison to compare two Strings. Thus, the condition in the If statement evaluates to True because the values of string1 and "hello" are equal.

Line 32 compares string3 and string4 for equality to illustrate that comparisons are indeed case sensitive. Shared method Equals is used to compare the values of two Strings. "Happy Birthday" does not equal "happy birthday", so the condition of the If statement fails, and the message "string3 does not equal string4" is output (line 35).

Lines 39–48 use String method CompareTo to compare Strings. Method CompareTo returns 0 if the Strings are equal, -1 if the String that invokes CompareTo is less than the String passed as an argument and 1 if the String that invokes CompareTo is greater than the String passed as an argument. Method CompareTo uses a lexicographical comparison.

Note that CompareTo considers string3 to be larger than string4. The only difference between these two Strings is that string3 contains two uppercase letters in positions where string4 contains lowercase letters.

Using String Methods StartsWith and EndsWith

The application in Fig. 16.4 shows how to test whether a String begins or ends with a given String. Method StartsWith determines whether a String starts with the String passed to it as an argument. Method EndsWith determines whether a String ends with the String passed to it as an argument. Class StringStartEnd's Main method defines an array of Strings (called strings), which contains "started", "starting", "ended" and "ending". The remainder of method Main tests the elements of the array to determine whether they start or end with a particular set of characters.

Line 11 uses method StartsWith, which takes a String argument. The condition in the If statement determines whether the String at index i of the array starts with the characters "st". If so, the method returns True, and lines 12–13 output a message.

Line 21 uses method EndsWith, which also takes a String argument. The condition in the If statement determines whether the String at index i of the array ends with the characters "ed". If so, the method returns True, and lines 22–23 output a message.

```vb
 1    ' Fig. 16.4: StringStartEnd.vb
 2    ' Demonstrating StartsWith and EndsWith methods.
 3
 4    Module StringStartEnd
 5       Sub Main()
 6          Dim strings As String() = _
 7             {"started", "starting", "ended", "ending"}
 8
 9          ' test every string to see if it starts with "st"
10          For i As Integer = 0 To strings.Length - 1
11             If strings(i).StartsWith("st") Then
12                Console.WriteLine( _
13                   """" & strings(i) & """" & " starts with ""st""")
14             End If
15          Next i
16
17          Console.WriteLine("")
18
19          ' test every string to see if it ends with "ed"
20          For i As Integer = 0 To strings.Length - 1
21             If strings(i).EndsWith("ed") Then
22                Console.WriteLine( _
23                   """" & strings(i) & """" & " ends with ""ed""")
24             End If
25          Next i
26
27          Console.WriteLine("")
28       End Sub ' Main
29    End Module ' StringStartEnd
```

```
"started" starts with "st"
"starting" starts with "st"

"started" ends with "ed"
"ended" ends with "ed"
```

Fig. 16.4 | StartsWith and EndsWith methods.

16.6 Locating Characters and Substrings in Strings

In many applications, it is necessary to search for a character or set of characters in a String. For example, a programmer creating a word processor would want to provide capabilities for searching through documents. Figure 16.5 demonstrates some of the many versions of String methods IndexOf, IndexOfAny, LastIndexOf and LastIndexOfAny, which search for a specified character or substring in a String. This example searches the String letters which is initialized with "abcdefghijklmabcdefghijklm" (line 6).

```
1    ' Fig. 16.5: StringIndexMethods.vb
2    ' Using String searching methods.
3
4    Module StringIndexMethods
5       Sub Main()
6          Dim letters As String = "abcdefghijklmabcdefghijklm"
7          Dim searchLetters As Char() = {"c"c, "a"c, "$"c}
8
9          ' test IndexOf to find a character in a string
10         Console.WriteLine("First 'c' is located at index " & _
11            letters.IndexOf("c"c))
12         Console.WriteLine("First 'a' starting at 1 is located at index " _
13            & letters.IndexOf("a"c, 1))
14         Console.WriteLine("First '$' in the 5 positions starting at 3 " & _
15            "is located at index " & letters.IndexOf("$"c, 3, 5))
16
17         ' test LastIndexOf to find a character in a string
18         Console.WriteLine(vbCrLf & "Last 'c' is located at index " & _
19            letters.LastIndexOf("c"c))
20         Console.WriteLine("Last 'a' up to position 25 is located at " & _
21            "index " & letters.LastIndexOf("a"c, 25))
22         Console.WriteLine("Last '$' in the 5 positions starting at 15 " & _
23            "is located at index " & letters.LastIndexOf("$"c, 15, 5))
24
25         ' test IndexOf to find a substring in a string
26         Console.WriteLine(vbCrLf & _
27            "First ""def"" is located at index " & letters.IndexOf("def"))
28         Console.WriteLine("First ""def"" starting at 7 is located at " & _
29            "index " & letters.IndexOf("def", 7))
30         Console.WriteLine("First ""hello"" in the 15 positions " & _
31            "starting at 5 is located at index " & _
32            letters.IndexOf("hello", 5, 15))
33
34         ' test LastIndexOf to find a substring in a string
35         Console.WriteLine(vbCrLf & "Last ""def"" is located at index " & _
36            letters.LastIndexOf("def"))
37         Console.WriteLine("Last ""def"" up to position 25 is located " & _
38            "at index" & letters.LastIndexOf("def", 25))
39         Console.WriteLine("Last ""hello"" in the 15 positions " & _
40            "ending at 20 is located at index " & _
41            letters.LastIndexOf("hello", 20, 15))
42
```

Fig. 16.5 | Searching for characters and substrings in Strings. (Part 1 of 2.)

```
43            ' test IndexOfAny to find first occurrence of character in array
44            Console.WriteLine(vbCrLf & "First 'c', 'a' or '$' is " & _
45               "located at index " & letters.IndexOfAny(searchLetters))
46            Console.WriteLine("First 'c', 'a' or '$' starting at 7 is " & _
47               "located at index " & letters.IndexOfAny(searchLetters, 7))
48            Console.WriteLine("First 'c', 'a' or '$' in the 5 positions " & _
49               "starting at 7 is located at index " & _
50               letters.IndexOfAny(searchLetters, 7, 5))
51
52            ' test LastIndexOfAny to find last occurrence of character
53            ' in array
54            Console.WriteLine(vbCrLf & "Last 'c', 'a' or '$' is " & _
55               "located at index " & letters.LastIndexOfAny(searchLetters))
56            Console.WriteLine("Last 'c', 'a' or '$' up to position 1 is " & _
57               "located at index " & letters.LastIndexOfAny(searchLetters, 1))
58            Console.WriteLine("Last 'c', 'a' or '$' in the 5 positions " & _
59               "ending at 25 is located at index " & _
60               letters.LastIndexOfAny(searchLetters, 25, 5))
61      End Sub ' Main
62   End Module ' StringIndexMethods
```

```
First 'c' is located at index 2
First 'a' starting at 1 is located at index 13
First '$' in the 5 positions starting at 3 is located at index -1

Last 'c' is located at index 15
Last 'a' up to position 25 is located at index 13
Last '$' in the 5 positions starting at 15 is located at index -1

First "def" is located at index 3
First "def" starting at 7 is located at index 16
First "hello" in the 15 positions starting at 5 is located at index -1

Last "def" is located at index 16
Last "def" up to position 25 is located at index 16
Last "hello" in the 15 positions ending at 20 is located at index -1

First 'c', 'a' or '$' is located at index 0
First 'c', 'a' or '$' starting at 7 is located at index 13
First 'c', 'a' or '$' in the 5 positions starting at 7 is located at index -1

Last 'c', 'a' or '$' is located at index 15
Last 'c', 'a' or '$' up to position 1 is located at index 0
Last 'c', 'a' or '$' in the 5 positions ending at 25 is located at index -1
```

Fig. 16.5 | Searching for characters and substrings in Strings. (Part 2 of 2.)

Lines 11, 13 and 15 use method IndexOf to locate the first occurrence of a character in a String. If it finds a character, IndexOf returns the index of the specified character in the String; otherwise, IndexOf returns –1. Line 13 uses a version of method IndexOf that takes two arguments—the character to search for and the starting index in the String at which the search should begin. The method does not examine any characters before the starting index (in this case, 1). Line 15 uses another version of method IndexOf that takes three arguments—the character to search for, the index at which to start searching and the number of characters to search.

Lines 19, 21 and 23 use method `LastIndexOf` to locate the last occurrence of a character in a `String`. Method `LastIndexOf` searches from the end of the `String` toward the beginning. If it finds the character, `LastIndexOf` returns the index of the specified character in the `String`; otherwise, `LastIndexOf` returns –1. There are three versions of `LastIndexOf`. Line 19 uses the version of method `LastIndexOf` that takes as an argument the character for which to search. Line 21 uses the version of method `LastIndexOf` that takes two arguments—the character for which to search and the highest index from which to begin searching backward for the character. The expression in line 23 uses a third version of method `LastIndexOf` that takes three arguments—the character for which to search, the starting index from which to start searching backward and the number of characters (the portion of the `String`) to search.

Lines 26–41 use versions of `IndexOf` and `LastIndexOf` that take a `String` instead of a character as the first argument. These versions of the methods perform identically to the ones described above except that they search for sequences of characters (or substrings) that are specified by their `String` arguments.

Lines 44–60 use methods `IndexOfAny` and `LastIndexOfAny`, which take an array of characters as the first argument. These versions of the methods also perform identically to those described above except that they return the index of the first occurrence of any of the characters in the character array argument.

Common Programming Error 16.3

In the overloaded methods `LastIndexOf` and `LastIndexOfAny` that take three parameters, the second argument must be greater than or equal to the third argument; otherwise, an exception occurs. This might seem counterintuitive, but remember that the search moves from the end of the string toward the beginning.

16.7 Extracting Substrings from `Strings`

Class `String` provides two `Substring` methods, which are used to create a new `String` by copying part of an existing `String`. Each method returns a new `String`. Figure 16.6 demonstrates both methods.

Line 11 uses the `Substring` method that takes one `Integer` argument. The argument specifies the starting index from which the method copies characters in the original `String`. The substring returned contains a copy of the characters from the starting index to the end of the `String`. If the index specified in the argument is outside the bounds of the `String`, an `ArgumentOutOfRangeException` occurs.

The second version of method `Substring` (line 15) takes two `Integer` arguments. The arguments specify the starting index from which to copy characters and the length of the substring to copy. The substring returned contains a copy of the specified characters from the original `String`. If the starting index plus the length is greater than the number of characters in the `String`, an `ArgumentOutOfRangeException` occurs.

```
1   ' Fig. 16.6: SubString.vb
2   ' Demonstrating the String Substring method.
3
```

Fig. 16.6 | Substrings generated from `Strings`. (Part 1 of 2.)

```
4   Module SubString
5     Sub Main()
6       Dim letters As String = "abcdefghijklmabcdefghijklm"
7       Dim output As String = ""
8
9       ' invoke Substring method and pass it one parameter
10      Console.WriteLine("Substring from index 20 to end is """ & _
11        letters.Substring(20) & """")
12
13      ' invoke Substring method and pass it two parameters
14      Console.WriteLine("Substring from index 0 of length 6 is """ & _
15        letters.Substring(0, 6) & """")
16    End Sub ' Main
17  End Module ' SubString
```

```
Substring from index 20 to end is "hijklm"
Substring from index 0 of length 6 is "abcdef"
```

Fig. 16.6 | Substrings generated from Strings. (Part 2 of 2.)

16.8 Concatenating Strings

Like the & operator, the String class's Shared method Concat (Fig. 16.7) can be used to concatenate two Strings. The method returns a new String containing the combined characters from both original Strings. Line 13 appends the characters from string2 to the end of a copy of string1, using method Concat. The original Strings are not modified.

```
1   ' Fig. 16.7: SubConcatenation.vb
2   ' Demonstrating String class Concat method.
3
4   Module StringConcatenation
5     Sub Main()
6       Dim string1 As String = "Happy "
7       Dim string2 As String = "Birthday"
8
9       Console.WriteLine("string1 = """ & string1 & """" & _
10        vbCrLf & "string2 = """ & string2 & """")
11      Console.WriteLine(vbCrLf & _
12        "Result of string.Concat( string1, string2 ) = " & _
13        String.Concat(string1, string2))
14      Console.WriteLine("string1 after concatenation = " & string1)
15    End Sub ' Main
16  End Module ' StringConcatenation
```

```
string1 = "Happy "
string2 = "Birthday"

Result of string.Concat( string1, string2 ) = Happy Birthday
string1 after concatenation = Happy
```

Fig. 16.7 | Concat Shared method.

16.9 Miscellaneous String Methods

Class String provides several methods that return modified copies of Strings. Figure 16.8 demonstrates String methods Replace, ToLower, ToUpper and Trim. None of these methods modifies the original String.

Line 18 uses String method Replace to return a new String, replacing every occurrence in string1 of character 'e' with character 'E'. Method Replace takes two arguments—a Char for which to search and another Char with which to replace all matching

```vb
 1  ' Fig. 16.8: StringMethods2.vb
 2  ' Demonstrating String methods Replace, ToLower, ToUpper, Trim,
 3  ' and ToString.
 4
 5  Module StringMethods2
 6     Sub Main()
 7        Dim string1 As String = "cheers!"
 8        Dim string2 As String = "GOOD BYE "
 9        Dim string3 As String = "   spaces   "
10
11        Console.WriteLine("string1 = """ & string1 & """" & vbCrLf & _
12           "string2 = """ & string2 & """" & vbCrLf & _
13           "string3 = """ & string3 & """")
14
15        ' call method Replace
16        Console.WriteLine( _
17           vbCrLf & "Replacing ""e"" with ""E"" in string1: """ & _
18           string1.Replace("e"c, "E"c) & """")
19
20        ' call ToLower and ToUpper
21        Console.WriteLine(vbCrLf & "string1.ToUpper() = """ & _
22           string1.ToUpper() & """" & vbCrLf & "string2.ToLower() = """ & _
23           string2.ToLower() & """")
24
25        ' call Trim method
26        Console.WriteLine( _
27           vbCrLf & "string3 after trim = """ & string3.Trim() & """")
28
29        Console.WriteLine(vbCrLf & "string1 = """ & string1 & """")
30     End Sub ' Main
31  End Module ' StringMethods2
```

```
string1 = "cheers!"
string2 = "GOOD BYE "
string3 = "   spaces   "

Replacing "e" with "E" in string1: "chEErs!"

string1.ToUpper() = "CHEERS!"
string2.ToLower() = "good bye "

string3 after trim = "spaces"

string1 = "cheers!"
```

Fig. 16.8 | String methods Replace, ToLower, ToUpper and Trim.

occurrences of the first argument. This method is also overloaded to receive two String parameters. If there are no occurrences of the first argument in the String, the method returns the original String.

String method ToUpper returns a new String (line 22) that replaces any lowercase letters in string1 with their uppercase equivalent. If there are no characters to convert to uppercase, the method returns the original String. Line 23 uses String method ToLower to return a new String in which any uppercase letters in string2 are replaced by their lowercase equivalents. As with ToUpper, if there are no characters to convert to lowercase, method ToLower returns the original String.

Line 27 uses String method Trim to remove all whitespace characters that appear at the beginning and end of a String. The method returns a new String that contains the original String, but omits leading or trailing whitespace characters. Another version of method Trim takes a character array and returns a String that does not contain the characters in the array argument at the start or end of the String. Line 29 demonstrates that string1 did not change.

16.10   Class **StringBuilder**

The String class provides many capabilities for processing Strings. However, a String's contents can never change. Operations that seem to concatenate Strings are in fact creating new Strings (e.g., the &= operator creates a new String and assigns it to the String variable on the left side of the operator).

The next several sections discuss the features of class StringBuilder (namespace System.Text), used to create and manipulate dynamic string information—that is, mutable strings. Every StringBuilder can store the number of characters specified by its capacity. Exceeding the capacity of a StringBuilder makes the capacity expand to accommodate the additional characters. As we will see, members of class StringBuilder, such as methods Append and AppendFormat, can be used for concatenation like the operators &, and &= for class String.

Performance Tip 16.2

Objects of class String are constant strings, whereas object of class StringBuilder are mutable sequences of characters. The CLR can perform certain optimizations with Strings (such as referring to one String with many variables) because it knows the Strings will not change.

Performance Tip 16.3

When you have a choice between using a String or a StringBuilder to represent a sequence of characters, always use a String if the contents of the object will not change. When appropriate, using Strings instead of StringBuilder objects improves performance.

Class StringBuilder provides six overloaded constructors. Class StringBuilderConstructor (Fig. 16.9) demonstrates three of them.

Line 9 employs the parameterless StringBuilder constructor to create a StringBuilder that contains no characters and has a default initial capacity of 16 characters. Line 10 uses the StringBuilder constructor that takes an Integer argument to create a StringBuilder that contains no characters and has the initial capacity specified in the Integer argument (i.e., 10). Line 11 uses the StringBuilder constructor that takes a String argument to create a StringBuilder containing the characters of the String argument. The

```
 1    ' Fig. 16.9: StringBuilderConstructor.vb
 2    ' Demonstrating StringBuilder class constructors.
 3    Imports System.Text
 4
 5    Module StringBuilderConstructor
 6       Sub Main()
 7          Dim buffer1, buffer2, buffer3 As StringBuilder
 8
 9          buffer1 = New StringBuilder()
10          buffer2 = New StringBuilder(10)
11          buffer3 = New StringBuilder("hello")
12
13          Console.WriteLine("buffer1 = """ & buffer1.ToString() & """")
14          Console.WriteLine("buffer2 = """ & buffer2.ToString() & """")
15          Console.WriteLine("buffer3 = """ & buffer3.ToString() & """")
16       End Sub ' Main
17    End Module ' StringBuilderConstructor
```

```
buffer1 = ""
buffer2 = ""
buffer3 = "hello"
```

Fig. 16.9 | StringBuilder class constructors.

initial capacity is the smallest power of two greater than or equal to the number of characters in the argument String, with a minimum of 16. Lines 13–15 use StringBuilder method ToString to obtain String representations of the StringBuilders' contents.

16.11 Length and Capacity Properties, EnsureCapacity Method and Indexer of Class StringBuilder

Class StringBuilder provides the Length and Capacity properties to return the number of characters currently in a StringBuilder and the number of characters that a StringBuilder can store without allocating more memory, respectively. These properties also can increase or decrease the length or the capacity of the StringBuilder.

Method EnsureCapacity allows you to reduce the number of times a StringBuilder's capacity must be increased. Method EnsureCapacity doubles the StringBuilder instance's current capacity. If this doubled value is greater than the value you wish to ensure, that value becomes the new capacity. Otherwise, EnsureCapacity alters the capacity by making it equal to the requested number. For example, if the current capacity is 17 and we wish to make it 40, 17 multiplied by 2 is not greater than or equal to 40, so the call will result in a new capacity of 40. If the current capacity is 23 and we wish to make it 40, 23 will be multiplied by 2 to result in a new capacity of 46. Both 40 and 46 are greater than or equal to 40, so a capacity of 40 is indeed ensured by method EnsureCapacity. Figure 16.10 demonstrates these methods and properties.

The program contains one StringBuilder, called buffer. Line 7 uses the String-Builder constructor that takes a String argument to instantiate a StringBuilder and initialize its value to "Hello, how are you?". Lines 10–12 output the content, length and capacity of the StringBuilder. In the output window, note that the capacity of the

```vb
1    ' Fig. 16.10: StringBuilderFeatures.vb
2    ' Demonstrating some features of class StringBuilder.
3    Imports System.Text
4
5    Module StringBuilderFeatures
6       Sub Main()
7          Dim buffer As New StringBuilder("Hello, how are you?")
8
9          ' use Length and Capacity properties
10         Console.WriteLine( _
11            "buffer = " & buffer.ToString() & vbCrLf & "Length = " & _
12            buffer.Length & vbCrLf & "Capacity = " & buffer.Capacity)
13
14         buffer.EnsureCapacity(75) ' ensure a capacity of at least 75
15         Console.WriteLine(vbCrLf & "New capacity = " & buffer.Capacity)
16
17         ' truncate StringBuilder by setting Length property
18         buffer.Length = 10
19         Console.Write(vbCrLf & "New length = " & _
20            buffer.Length & vbCrLf & "buffer = ")
21
22         ' use StringBuilder indexer
23         For i As Integer = 0 To buffer.Length - 1
24            Console.Write(buffer(i))
25         Next i
26
27         Console.WriteLine()
28      End Sub ' Main
29   End Module ' StringBuilderFeatures
```

```
buffer = Hello, how are you?
Length = 19
Capacity = 32

New capacity = 75

New length = 10
buffer = Hello, how
```

Fig. 16.10 | StringBuilder size manipulation.

StringBuilder is initially 32. Remember, the StringBuilder constructor that takes a String argument creates a StringBuilder object with an initial capacity that is the smallest power of two greater than or equal to the number of characters in the String passed as an argument.

Line 14 expands the capacity of the StringBuilder to a minimum of 75 characters. The current capacity (32) multiplied by two is less than 75, so method EnsureCapacity increases the capacity to 75. If new characters are added to a StringBuilder so that its length exceeds its capacity, the capacity grows to accommodate the additional characters in the same manner as if method EnsureCapacity had been called.

Line 18 uses property Length to set the length of the StringBuilder to 10. If the specified length is less than the current number of characters in the StringBuilder, the contents of the StringBuilder are truncated to the specified length. If the specified length is greater than the number of characters currently in the StringBuilder, null characters (characters with the numeric representation 0) are appended to the StringBuilder until the total number of characters in the StringBuilder is equal to the specified length. Lines 23–25 use the StringBuilder indexer to output the characters in the StringBuilder one character at a time.

16.12 Append and AppendFormat Methods of Class StringBuilder

Class StringBuilder provides 19 overloaded Append methods for appending values of various types to the end of a StringBuilder's contents. There are versions of this method for each of the primitive types and for character arrays, Strings and Objects. Remember that method ToString produces a String representation of any Object, so any Object's string representation can be appended to a StringBuilder. Each of the methods takes an argument, converts it to a String and appends it to the StringBuilder. Figure 16.11 demonstrates several Append methods.

```vb
1  ' Fig. 16.11: StringBuilderAppend.vb
2  ' Demonstrating StringBuilder Append methods.
3  Imports System.Text
4
5  Module StringBuilderAppend
6     Sub Main()
7        Dim objectValue As Object = "hello"
8        Dim stringValue As String = "good bye"
9        Dim characterArray As Char() = {"a"c, "b"c, "c"c, "d"c, "e"c, "f"c}
10       Dim booleanValue As Boolean = True
11       Dim characterValue As Char = "Z"c
12       Dim integerValue As Integer = 7
13       Dim longValue As Long = 1000000
14       Dim floatValue As Single = 2.5F ' F indicates that 2.5 is a float
15       Dim doubleValue As Double = 33.333
16       Dim buffer As New StringBuilder()
17
18       ' use method Append to append values to buffer
19       buffer.Append(objectValue)
20       buffer.Append("  ")
21       buffer.Append(stringValue)
22       buffer.Append("  ")
23       buffer.Append(characterArray)
24       buffer.Append("  ")
25       buffer.Append(characterArray, 0, 3)
26       buffer.Append("  ")
27       buffer.Append(booleanValue)
28       buffer.Append("  ")
29       buffer.Append(characterValue)
30       buffer.Append("  ")
31       buffer.Append(integerValue)
32       buffer.Append("  ")
```

Fig. 16.11 | Append methods of StringBuilder. (Part 1 of 2.)

```
33          buffer.Append(longValue)
34          buffer.Append("   ")
35          buffer.Append(floatValue)
36          buffer.Append("   ")
37          buffer.Append(doubleValue)
38
39          Console.WriteLine("buffer = " & buffer.ToString() & vbCrLf)
40      End Sub ' Main
41  End Module ' StringBuilderAppend
```

```
buffer = hello   good bye   abcdef   abc   True   Z   7   1000000   2.5   33.333
```

Fig. 16.11 | Append methods of `StringBuilder`. (Part 2 of 2.)

Lines 19–37 use 10 different overloaded `Append` methods to append the `String` representations of the variables created in lines 7–16 to the end of the `StringBuilder`. `Append` behaves similarly to the `&` operator, which is used to concatenate `Strings`.

Class `StringBuilder` also provides method `AppendFormat`, which converts a `String` to a specified format, then appends it to the `StringBuilder`. The example in Fig. 16.12 demonstrates this method.

```
1   ' Fig. 16.12: StringBuilderAppendFormat.vb
2   ' Demonstrating method AppendFormat.
3   Imports System.Text
4
5   Module StringBuilderAppendFormat
6      Sub Main()
7         Dim buffer As New StringBuilder()
8         Dim string1, string2 As String
9
10         ' formatted string
11         string1 = "This {0} costs: {1:C}." & vbCrLf
12
13         ' string1 argument array
14         Dim objectArray(2) As Object
15
16         objectArray(0) = "car"
17         objectArray(1) = 1234.56
18
19         ' append to buffer formatted string with argument
20         buffer.AppendFormat(string1, objectArray)
21
22         ' formatted string
23         string2 = "Number:{0:d3}." & vbCrLf & _
24            "Number right aligned with spaces:{0, 4}." & vbCrLf & _
25            "Number left aligned with spaces:{0, -4}."
26
27         ' append to buffer formatted string with argument
28         buffer.AppendFormat(string2, 5)
29
```

Fig. 16.12 | `StringBuilder`'s `AppendFormat` method. (Part 1 of 2.)

```
30            ' display formatted strings
31            Console.WriteLine(buffer.ToString())
32        End Sub ' Main
33    End Module ' StringBuilderAppendFormat
```

```
This car costs: $1,234.56.
Number:005.
Number right aligned with spaces:    5.
Number left aligned with spaces:5    .
```

Fig. 16.12 | StringBuilder's AppendFormat method. (Part 2 of 2.)

Line 11 creates a String that contains formatting information. The information enclosed within the braces specifies how to format a specific piece of information. Formats have the form {X[,Y][:FormatString]}, where X is the number of the argument to be formatted, counting from zero. Y is an optional argument, which can be positive or negative, indicating how many characters should be in the formatted String. If the resulting String has fewer characters than the number Y, the String will be padded with spaces to make up for the difference. A positive integer aligns the String to the right; a negative integer aligns it to the left. The optional FormatString applies a particular format to the argument—currency, decimal or scientific, among others. In this case, {0} means that the first argument's String representation will be included in the formatted String. {1:C} specifies that the second argument will be formatted as a currency value.

Line 20 shows a version of AppendFormat that takes two parameters—a String specifying the format and an array of objects to serve as the arguments to the format String. The argument referred to by {0} is in the object array at index 0.

Lines 23–25 define another String used for formatting. The first format {0:D3}, specifies that the first argument will be formatted as a three-digit decimal, meaning any number that has fewer than three digits will have leading zeros, so the total number of formatted digits will be 3. The next format, {0, 4}, specifies that the formatted String should have four characters and should be right aligned. The third format, {0, -4}, specifies that the String should be aligned to the left. For more formatting options, please refer to the online help documentation.

Line 28 uses a version of AppendFormat that takes two parameters—a String containing a format and an object to which the format is applied. In this case, the object is the number 5. The output of Fig. 16.12 displays the result of applying these versions of AppendFormat with their respective arguments.

16.13 Insert, Remove and Replace Methods of Class StringBuilder

Class StringBuilder provides 18 overloaded Insert methods to allow values of various types to be inserted at any position in a StringBuilder. There are versions of Insert for each of the primitive types and for character arrays, Strings and Objects. Each version takes its second argument, converts it to a String and inserts the String into the String-Builder at the index specified by the first argument. The index must be greater than or equal to 0 and less than the length of the StringBuilder; otherwise, an ArgumentOutOf-RangeException occurs.

Class `StringBuilder` also provides method `Remove` for deleting characters in a `StringBuilder`. Method `Remove` takes two arguments—the index at which to begin deletion and the number of characters to delete. The sum of the starting subscript and the number of characters to be deleted must always be less than the `StringBuilder`'s length; otherwise, an `ArgumentOutOfRangeException` occurs. Figure 16.13 demonstrates the `Insert` and `Remove` methods. Lines 20–37 use nine different overloaded `Insert` methods to insert the `String` representations of the variables created in lines 7–17 at index 0 in the `StringBuilder`.

```vb
 1   ' Fig. 16.13: StringBuilderInsertRemove.vb
 2   ' Insert and Remove methods of class StringBuilder.
 3   Imports System.Text
 4
 5   Module StringBuilderInsertRemove
 6      Sub Main()
 7         Dim objectValue As Object = "hello"
 8         Dim stringValue As String = "good bye"
 9         Dim characterArray As Char() = _
10            {"a"c, "b"c, "c"c, "d"c, "e"c, "f"c}
11         Dim booleanValue As Boolean = True
12         Dim characterValue As Char = "K"c
13         Dim integerValue As Integer = 7
14         Dim longValue As Long = 10000000
15         Dim floatValue As Single = 2.5F ' F indicates that 2.5 is a float
16         Dim doubleValue As Double = 33.333
17         Dim buffer As New StringBuilder()
18
19         ' insert values into buffer
20         buffer.Insert(0, objectValue)
21         buffer.Insert(0, "   ")
22         buffer.Insert(0, stringValue)
23         buffer.Insert(0, "   ")
24         buffer.Insert(0, characterArray)
25         buffer.Insert(0, "   ")
26         buffer.Insert(0, booleanValue)
27         buffer.Insert(0, "   ")
28         buffer.Insert(0, characterValue)
29         buffer.Insert(0, "   ")
30         buffer.Insert(0, integerValue)
31         buffer.Insert(0, "   ")
32         buffer.Insert(0, longValue)
33         buffer.Insert(0, "   ")
34         buffer.Insert(0, floatValue)
35         buffer.Insert(0, "   ")
36         buffer.Insert(0, doubleValue)
37         buffer.Insert(0, "   ")
38
39         Console.WriteLine("buffer after inserts: " & vbCrLf & _
40            buffer.ToString() & vbCrLf)
41
42         buffer.Remove(10, 1) ' delete 2 in 2.5
```

Fig. 16.13 | `StringBuilder` text insertion and removal. (Part 1 of 2.)

```
43            buffer.Remove(4, 4) ' delete .333 in 33.333
44
45            Console.WriteLine("buffer after Removes:" & vbCrLf & _
46                buffer.ToString())
47                    ' Main
48                ' StringBuilderInsertRemove
```

```
buffer after inserts:
  33.333  2.5  10000000  7  K  True  abcdef  good bye  hello

buffer after Removes:
  33  .5  10000000  7  K  True  abcdef  good bye  hello
```

Fig. 16.13 | `StringBuilder` text insertion and removal. (Part 2 of 2.)

Another useful `StringBuilder` method is `Replace`, which searches for a specified `String` or character and substitutes another `String` or character in its place. Figure 16.14 demonstrates `Replace`.

Line 13 uses method `Replace` to replace all instances of the `String` `"Jane"` with the `String` `"Greg"` in `builder1`. An overloaded version of this method takes two characters as parameters and replaces each occurrence of the first character with the second character. Line 14 uses an overload of `Replace` that takes four parameters—two characters and two `Integers`. The method replaces all instances of the first character with the second char-

```
 1    ' Fig. 16.14: StringBuilderReplace.vb
 2    ' Demonstrating method Replace.
 3    Imports System.Text
 4
 5    Module StringBuilderReplace
 6       Sub Main()
 7          Dim builder1 As New StringBuilder("Happy Birthday Jane")
 8          Dim builder2 As New StringBuilder("good bye greg")
 9
10          Console.WriteLine("Before replacements:" & vbCrLf & _
11              builder1.ToString() & vbCrLf & builder2.ToString())
12
13          builder1.Replace("Jane", "Greg")
14          builder2.Replace("g"c, "G"c, 0, 5)
15
16          Console.WriteLine(vbCrLf & "After replacements:" & vbCrLf & _
17              builder1.ToString() & vbCrLf & builder2.ToString())
18       End Sub ' Main
19    End Module ' StringBuilderReplace
```

```
Happy Birthday Jane
good bye greg

After replacements:
Happy Birthday Greg
Good bye greg
```

Fig. 16.14 | `StringBuilder` text replacement.

acter, beginning at the index specified by the first Integer and continuing for a count specified by the second Integer. In this case, Replace looks at only five characters, starting with the character at index 0. As the output illustrates, this version of Replace replaces g with G in the word "good", but not in "greg"—the gs in "greg" are not in the range indicated by the Integer arguments (i.e., between indexes 0 and 4).

16.14 Char Methods

Visual Basic provides a type called a *structure* that is similar to a class. Although structures and classes are comparable in many ways, structures represent value types. Like classes, structures include methods and properties. Both use the same access modifiers (such as Public, Protected and Private) and access members via the member access operator (.). Classes are created by using the keyword Class, but structures are created using the keyword *Structure*.

Many of the primitive types that we have used in this book are actually aliases for different structures. For instance, an Integer is defined by structure System.Int32, a Long by System.Int64 and so on. These structures derive from class *ValueType*, which in turn derives from class Object. In this section, we present structure *Char*, which is the structure for characters.

Most Char methods are Shared, take at least one character argument and perform either a test or a manipulation on the character. We present several of these methods in the next example. Figure 16.15 demonstrates Shared methods that test characters to determine whether they are of a specific character type and Shared methods that perform case conversions on characters.

This Windows application contains a prompt, a TextBox in which the user can input a character, a button that the user can press after entering a character and a second TextBox that displays the output of our analysis. When the user clicks the **Analyze Character** button, event handler btnAnalyze_Click (lines 7–28) converts the entered data from a String to a Char, using method Convert.ToChar (line 11).

Line 15 uses Char method IsDigit to determine whether character is a digit. If so, the method returns True; otherwise, it returns False. Line 16 uses Char method IsLetter to determine whether character is a letter. Line 18 uses Char method IsLetterOrDigit to determine whether character is a letter or a digit.

```
1    ' Fig. 16.15: SharedCharMethods.vb
2    ' Demonstrates Shared character testing methods
3    ' from Char structure
4
5    Public Class SharedCharMethods
6        ' handle btnAnalyze_Click
7        Private Sub btnAnalyze_Click( ByVal sender As System.Object, _
8            ByVal e As System.EventArgs) Handles btnAnalyze.Clickstructure
9
10           If txtInput.Text.Length > 0 Then
11               ' convert string entered to type char
12               Dim character As Char = Convert.ToChar(txtInput.Text)
13               Dim output As String
```

Fig. 16.15 | Char's Shared character-testing and case-conversion methods. (Part 1 of 2.)

```
14
15          output = "is digit: " & Char.IsDigit(character) & vbCrLf
16          output &= "is letter: " & Char.IsLetter(character) & vbCrLf
17          output &= "is letter or digit: " & _
18             Char.IsLetterOrDigit(character) & vbCrLf
19          output &= "is lowercase: " & Char.IsLower(character) & vbCrLf
20          output &= "is uppercase: " & Char.IsUpper(character) & vbCrLf
21          output &= "to uppercase: " & Char.ToUpper(character) & vbCrLf
22          output &= "to lowercase: " & Char.ToLower(character) & vbCrLf
23          output &= "is punctuation: " & _
24             Char.IsPunctuation(character) & vbCrLf
25          output &= "is symbol: " & Char.IsSymbol(character)
26          txtOutput.Text = output
27       End If
28    End Sub ' btnAnalyze_Click
29 End Class ' SharedCharMethods
```

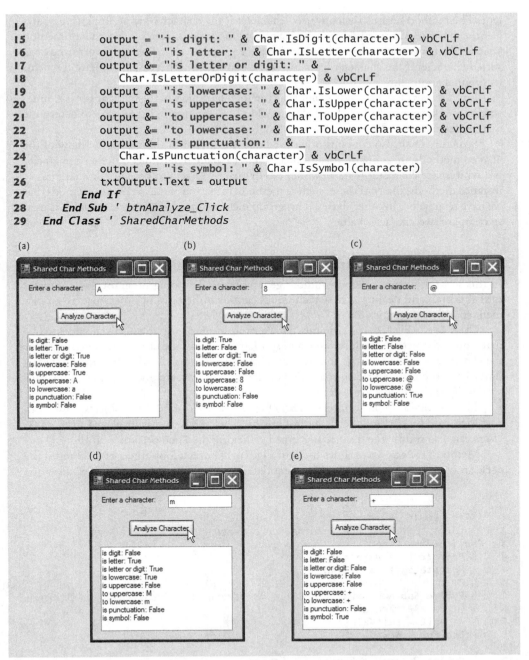

Fig. 16.15 | Char's Shared character-testing and case-conversion methods. (Part 2 of 2.)

Line 19 uses Char method IsLower to determine whether character is a lowercase letter. Line 20 uses Char method IsUpper to determine whether character is an uppercase letter. Line 21 uses Char method ToUpper to convert character to its uppercase equivalent. The method returns the converted character if the character has an uppercase equivalent; otherwise, the method returns its original argument. Line 22 uses Char method ToLower to convert character to its lowercase equivalent. The method returns the converted character if the character has a lowercase equivalent; otherwise, the method returns its original argument.

Line 24 uses Char method IsPunctuation to determine whether character is a punctuation mark, such as "!", ":" or ")". Line 24 uses Char method IsSymbol to determine whether character is a symbol, such as "+", "=" or "^".

Structure Char also contains other methods not shown in this example. Many of the Shared methods are similar—for instance, IsWhiteSpace determines whether a character is a whitespace character (e.g., newline, tab or space). Char also contains several Public instance methods; many of these, such as methods ToString and Equals, are methods that we have seen before in other classes. This group includes method CompareTo, which is used to compare two character values.

16.15 Card Shuffling and Dealing Simulation

In this section, we use random-number generation to develop a program that simulates card shuffling and dealing. These techniques can form the basis of programs that implement specific card games.

Class Card (Fig. 16.16) contains two String instance variables—face and suit—that store references to the face value and suit name of a specific card. The constructor for the class receives two Strings that it uses to initialize face and suit. Method ToString (lines 12–14) creates a String consisting of the face of the card and the suit of the card to identify the card when it is dealt.

The DeckForm application (Fig. 16.17) creates a deck of 52 Card objects. Users can deal each card by clicking the **Deal Card** button. Each dealt card is displayed in a Label. Users can also shuffle the deck at any time by clicking the **Shuffle Cards** button.

Method frmDeck_Load (lines 8–22 of Fig. 16.17) uses a loop (lines 19–21) to fill the deck array with Cards. Each Card is instantiated and initialized with two Strings—one

```
1   ' Fig. 16.16: Card.vb
2   ' Stores suit and face information on each card.
3   Public Class Card
4       Private face As String
5       Private suit As String
6
7       Public Sub New(ByVal faceValue As String, ByVal suitValue As String)
8           face = faceValue
9           suit = suitValue
10      End Sub ' New
11
12      Public Overrides Function ToString() As String
13          Return face & " of " & suit
14      End Function ' ToString
15  End Class ' Card
```

Fig. 16.16 | Card class.

from the faces array (Strings "Ace" through "King") and one from the suits array ("Hearts", "Diamonds", "Clubs" or "Spades"). The calculation i Mod 13 always results in a value from 0 to 12 (the 13 subscripts of the faces array), and the calculation i \ 13 always results in an Integer value from 0 to 3 (the four subscripts in the suits array). The initialized deck array contains the cards with faces Ace through King for each suit.

When the user clicks the **Deal Card** button, event handler btnDeal_Click (lines 25–39) invokes method DealCard (defined in lines 62–73) to get the next card in the deck array. If the deck is not empty, the method returns a Card object reference; otherwise, it returns Nothing. If the reference is not Nothing, lines 33–34 display the Card in lblDisplay and display the card number in lblStatus. If DealCard returns Nothing, the String

```vb
 1    ' Fig. 16.17: DeckForm.vb
 2    ' Simulating card shuffling and dealing.
 3    Public Class frmDeck
 4       Private deck(51) As Card ' deck of 52 cards
 5       Private currentCard As Integer ' count which card was just dealt
 6
 7       ' handles form at load time
 8       Private Sub frmDeck_Load( ByVal sender As System.Object, _
 9          ByVal e As System.EventArgs) Handles MyBase.Load
10
11          Dim faces As String() = _
12             {"Ace", "Deuce", "Three", "Four", "Five", "Six", "Seven", _
13             "Eight", "Nine", "Ten", "Jack", "Queen", "King"}
14          Dim suits As String() = {"Hearts", "Diamonds", "Clubs", "Spades"}
15
16          currentCard = -1 ' no cards have been dealt
17
18          ' initialize deck
19          For i As Integer = 0 To deck.Length - 1
20             deck(i) = New Card(faces(i Mod 13), suits(i \ 13))
21          Next i
22       End Sub ' frmDeck_Load
23
24    ' deal a card
25       Private Sub btnDeal_Click( ByVal sender As System.Object, _
26          ByVal e As System.EventArgs) Handles btnDeal.Click
27
28          Dim dealt As Card = DealCard()
29
30          ' if dealt card is Nothing, then no cards left
31          ' player must shuffle cards
32          If Not (dealt Is Nothing) Then
33             lblDisplay.Text = dealt.ToString()
34             lblStatus.Text = "Card #: " & currentCard
35          Else
36             lblDisplay.Text = "NO MORE CARDS TO DEAL"
37             lblStatus.Text = "Shuffle cards to continue"
38          End If
39       End Sub ' btnDeal_Click
40
```

Fig. 16.17 | Card shuffling and dealing simulation. (Part 1 of 3.)

```vb
41      ' shuffle cards
42      Private Sub Shuffle()
43          Dim randomNumber As New Random()
44          Dim temporaryValue As Card
45
46          currentCard = -1
47
48          ' swap each card with randomly selected card (0-51)
49          For i As Integer = 0 To deck.Length - 1
50              Dim j As Integer = randomNumber.Next(52)
51
52              ' swap cards
53              temporaryValue = deck(i)
54              deck(i) = deck(j)
55              deck(j) = temporaryValue
56          Next i
57
58          btnDeal.Enabled = True ' shuffled deck can now deal cards
59      End Sub ' Shuffle
60
61      ' deal a card if the deck is not empty
62      Private Function DealCard() As Card
63          ' if there is a card to deal then deal it;
64          ' otherwise, signal that cards need to be shuffled by
65          ' disabling dealButton and returning Nothing
66          If currentCard + 1 < deck.Length Then
67              currentCard += 1 ' increment count
68              Return deck(currentCard) ' return new card
69          Else
70              btnDeal.Enabled = False ' empty deck cannot deal cards
71              Return Nothing ' do not return a card
72          End If
73      End Function ' DealCard
74
75      ' handles btnShuffle Click
76      Private Sub btnShuffle_Click( ByVal sender As System.Object, _
77          ByVal e As System.EventArgs) Handles btnShuffle.Click
78
79          lblDisplay.Text = "SHUFFLING..."
80          Shuffle()
81          lblDisplay.Text = "DECK IS SHUFFLED"
82      End Sub ' btnShuffle_Click
83  End Class ' frmDeck
```

Fig. 16.17 | Card shuffling and dealing simulation. (Part 2 of 3.)

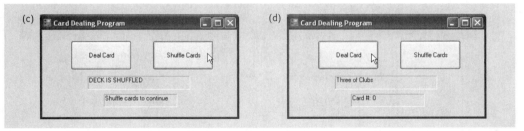

Fig. 16.17 | Card shuffling and dealing simulation. (Part 3 of 3.)

"NO MORE CARDS TO DEAL" is displayed in lblDisplay, and the String "Shuffle cards to continue" is displayed in lblStatus.

When the user clicks the **Shuffle Cards** button, event handler btnShuffle_Click (lines 76–82) invokes method Shuffle (defined in lines 42–59) to shuffle the cards. The method loops through all 52 cards (array subscripts 0–51). For each card, the method randomly picks a number between 0 and 51. Then the current Card object and the randomly selected Card object are swapped in the array. To shuffle the cards, method Shuffle makes a total of only 52 swaps during a single pass of the entire array. When the shuffling is complete, lblDisplay displays the String "DECK IS SHUFFLED".

16.16 Regular Expressions and Class RegEx

Regular expressions are specially formatted Strings used to find (and possibly replace) patterns in text. They can be useful during information validation, to ensure that data is in a particular format. For example, a United States ZIP code must consist of five digits, and a last name must start with a capital letter. Compilers use regular expressions to validate the syntax of programs. If the program code does not match the regular expression, the compiler indicates that there is a syntax error.

The .NET Framework provides several classes to help developers recognize and manipulate regular expressions. Class Regex (of the System.Text.RegularExpressions namespace) represents an immutable regular expression. Regex *method* Match returns an object of *class* Match that represents a single regular-expression match. Regex also provides method Matches, which finds all matches of a regular expression in an arbitrary String and returns an object of the class MatchCollection object containing all the Matches. A collection is a data structure similar to an array and can be used with a For Each statement to iterate through the collection's elements. We discuss collections in more detail in Chapter 26, Collections. To use class Regex, add an Imports statement for the package System.Text.RegularExpressions.

Regular Expression Character Classes

The table in Fig. 16.18 specifies some *character classes* that can be used with regular expressions. Do not confuse a character class with a Visual Basic class declaration. A character class is simply an escape sequence that represents a group of characters that might appear in a String.

A *word character* is any alphanumeric character or underscore. A whitespace character is a space, a tab, a carriage return, a newline or a form feed. A digit is any numeric character. Regular expressions are not limited to the character classes in Fig. 16.18. As you

Character class	Matches	Character class	Matches
\d	any digit	\D	any non-digit
\w	any word character	\W	any non-word character
\s	any whitespace	\S	any non-whitespace

Fig. 16.18 | Character classes.

will see in our first example, regular expressions can use other notations to search for complex patterns in `Strings`.

16.16.1 Regular Expression Example

The program in Fig. 16.19 tries to match birthdays to a regular expression. For demonstration purposes, the expression matches only birthdays that do not occur in April and that belong to people whose names begin with "J".

Line 8 creates a `Regex` object and passes a regular-expression pattern string to the `Regex` constructor. The first character in the regular expression, "J", is a literal character. Any `String` matching this regular expression is required to start with "J". In a regular expression, the dot character "." matches any single character except a newline character. When the dot character is followed by an asterisk, as in ".*", the regular expression

```vb
 1    ' Fig. 16.19: RegexMatches.vb
 2    ' Demonstrating Class Regex.
 3    Imports System.Text.RegularExpressions
 4
 5    Module RegexMatches
 6       Sub Main()
 7          ' create regular expression
 8          Dim expression As New Regex("J.*\d[0-35-9]-\d\d-\d\d")
 9
10          Dim string1 As String = "Jane's Birthday is 05-12-75" & vbCrLf & _
11             "Dave's Birthday is 11-04-68" & vbCrLf & _
12             "John's Birthday is 04-28-73" & vbCrLf & _
13             "Joe's Birthday is 12-17-77"
14
15          ' match regular expression to string and
16          ' print out all matches
17          For Each myMatch As Match In expression.Matches(string1)
18             Console.WriteLine(myMatch)
19          Next myMatch
20       End Sub ' Main
21    End Module ' RegexMatches
```

```
Jane's Birthday is 05-12-75
Joe's Birthday is 12-17-77
```

Fig. 16.19 | Regular expressions checking birthdays.

matches any number of unspecified characters except newlines. In general, when the regular-expression operator "*" is applied to a pattern, the pattern will match zero or more occurrences. By contrast, applying the regular-expression operator "+" to a pattern causes the pattern to match one or more occurrences. For example, both "A*" and "A+" will match "A", but only "A*" will match an empty String.

As indicated in Fig. 16.18, "\d" matches any numeric digit. To specify sets of characters other than those that belong to a predefined character class, characters can be listed in square brackets, []. For example, the pattern "[aeiou]" matches any vowel. Ranges of characters are represented by placing a dash (-) between two characters. In the example, "[0-35-9]" matches only digits in the ranges specified by the pattern—any digit between 0 and 3 or between 5 and 9; therefore, it matches any digit except 4. You can also specify that a pattern should match anything other than the characters in the brackets. To do so, place ^ as the first character in the brackets. It is important to note that "[^4]" is not the same as "[0-35-9]"; "[^4]" matches any non-digit and digits other than 4.

Although the "-" character indicates a range when it is enclosed in square brackets, instances of the "-" character outside grouping expressions are treated as literal characters. Thus, the regular expression in line 8 searches for a String that starts with the letter "J", followed by any number of characters, followed by a two-digit number (of which the second digit cannot be 4), followed by a dash, another two-digit number, a dash and another two-digit number.

Lines 17–19 use a For Each statement to iterate through the MatchCollection returned by the expression object's Matches method, which received string1 as an argument. The elements in the MatchCollection are Match objects, so the For Each statement declares variable myMatch to be of type Match. For each Match, line 18 outputs the text that matched the regular expression. The output in Fig. 16.19 indicates the two matches that were found in string1. Note that both matches conform to the pattern specified by the regular expression.

Quantifiers

The asterisk (*) in line 8 of Fig. 16.19 is more formally called a *quantifier*. Figure 16.20 lists various quantifiers that you can place after a pattern in a regular expression and the purpose of each quantifier.

Quantifier	Matches
*	Matches zero or more occurrences of the preceding pattern.
+	Matches one or more occurrences of the preceding pattern.
?	Matches zero or one occurrences of the preceding pattern.
{n}	Matches exactly n occurrences of the preceding pattern.
{n,}	Matches at least n occurrences of the preceding pattern.
{n,m}	Matches between n and m (inclusive) occurrences of the preceding pattern.

Fig. 16.20 | Quantifiers used in regular expressions.

We have already discussed how the asterisk (*) and plus (+) quantifiers work. The question mark (?) quantifier matches zero or one occurrences of the pattern that it quantifies. A set of braces containing one number ({n}) matches exactly n occurrences of the pattern it quantifies. We demonstrate this quantifier in the next example. Including a comma after the number enclosed in braces matches at least n occurrences of the quantified pattern. The set of braces containing two numbers ({n,m}) matches between n and m occurrences (inclusively) of the pattern it qualifies. All of the quantifiers are *greedy*—they will match as many occurrences of the pattern as possible until the pattern fails to make a match. If a quantifier is followed by a question mark (?), the quantifier becomes *lazy* and will match as few occurrences as possible as long as there is a successful match.

16.16.2 Validating User Input with Regular Expressions

The Windows application in Fig. 16.21 presents a more involved example that uses regular expressions to validate name, address and telephone number information input by a user.

When a user clicks the **OK** button, the program checks to make sure that none of the fields is empty (lines 10–13). If one or more fields are empty, the program displays a message to the user (lines 15–16) that all fields must be filled in before the program can validate the input information. Line 17 calls txtLastName's Focus method so that the user can begin typing in that TextBox. The program then exits the event handler (line 18). If there are no empty fields, lines 22–88 validate the user input. Lines 22–29 validate the last name by calling Shared method Match of class Regex, passing both the string to validate and the regular expression as arguments. Method Match returns a Match object. This object contains a Success property that indicates whether method Match's first argument matched the pattern specified by the regular expression in the second argument. If the value of Success is False (i.e., there was no match), lines 25–26 display an error message, line 27 sets the focus back to txtLastName so that the user can retype the input, and line 28 terminates the event handler. If there is a match, the event handler proceeds to validate the first name. This process continues for each TextBox's contents until the event handler validates the user input in all the TextBoxes or until a validation fails. If all of the fields contain valid information, the program displays a message dialog stating this, and the program terminates when the user dismisses the dialog.

```
1    ' Fig. 16.21: Validate.vb
2    ' Validate user information using regular expressions.
3    Imports System.Text.RegularExpressions
4
5    Public Class frmValidate
6       ' handles btnOk Click event
7       Private Sub btnOk_Click(ByVal sender As System.Object, _
8          ByVal e As System.EventArgs) Handles btnOk.Click
9          ' ensures no TextBoxes are empty
10         If txtLastName.Text = "" Or txtFirstName.Text = "" Or _
11            txtAddress.Text = "" Or txtCity.Text = "" Or _
12            txtState.Text = "" Or txtZipCode.Text = "" Or _
13            txtPhone.Text = "" Then
```

Fig. 16.21 | Validating user information using regular expressions. (Part 1 of 4.)

```
14           ' display popup box
15           MessageBox.Show("Please fill in all fields", "Error", _
16              MessageBoxButtons.OK, MessageBoxIcon.Error)
17           txtLastName.Focus() ' set focus to txtLastName
18           Return
19        End If
20
21        ' if last name format invalid show message
22        If Not Regex.Match(txtLastName.Text, _
23           "^[A-Z][a-zA-Z]*$").Success Then
24           ' last name was incorrect
25           MessageBox.Show("Invalid last name", "Message", _
26              MessageBoxButtons.OK, MessageBoxIcon.Error)
27           txtLastName.Focus()
28           Return
29        End If
30
31        ' if first name format invalid show message
32        If Not Regex.Match(txtFirstName.Text, _
33           "^[A-Z][a-zA-Z]*$").Success Then
34           ' first name was incorrect
35           MessageBox.Show("Invalid first name", "Message", _
36              MessageBoxButtons.OK, MessageBoxIcon.Error)
37           txtFirstName.Focus()
38           Return
39        End If
40
41        ' if address format invalid show message
42        If Not Regex.Match(txtAddress.Text, _
43           "^[0-9]+\s+([a-zA-Z]+|[a-zA-Z]+\s[a-zA-Z]+)$").Success Then
44           ' address was incorrect
45           MessageBox.Show("Invalid address", "Message", _
46              MessageBoxButtons.OK, MessageBoxIcon.Error)
47           txtAddress.Focus()
48           Return
49        End If
50
51        ' if state format invalid show message
52        If Not Regex.Match(txtCity.Text, _
53           "^([a-zA-Z]+|[a-zA-Z]+\s[a-zA-Z]+)$").Success Then
54           ' city was incorrect
55           MessageBox.Show("Invalid city", "Message", _
56              MessageBoxButtons.OK, MessageBoxIcon.Error)
57           txtCity.Focus()
58           Return
59        End If
60
61        ' if state format invalid show message
62        If Not Regex.Match(txtState.Text, _
63           "^([a-zA-Z]+|[a-zA-Z]+\s[a-zA-Z]+)$").Success Then
64           ' state was incorrect
65           MessageBox.Show("Invalid state", "Message", _
66              MessageBoxButtons.OK, MessageBoxIcon.Error)
```

Fig. 16.21 | Validating user information using regular expressions. (Part 2 of 4.)

```
67              txtState.Focus()
68              Return
69          End If
70
71          ' if zip code format invalid show message
72          If Not Regex.Match(txtZipCode.Text, "^\d{5}$").Success Then
73              ' zip was incorrect
74              MessageBox.Show("Invalid zip code", "Message", _
75                  MessageBoxButtons.OK, MessageBoxIcon.Error)
76              txtZipCode.Focus()
77              Return
78          End If
79
80          ' if phone number format invalid show message
81          If Not Regex.Match(txtPhone.Text, _
82              "^[1-9]\d{2}-[1-9]\d{2}-\d{4}$").Success Then
83              ' phone number was incorrect
84              MessageBox.Show("Invalid phone number", "Message", _
85                  MessageBoxButtons.OK, MessageBoxIcon.Error)
86              txtPhone.Focus()
87              Return
88          End If
89
90          ' information is valid, signal user and exit application
91          Me.Hide() ' hide main window while MessageBox displays
92          MessageBox.Show("Thank You!", "Information Correct", _
93              MessageBoxButtons.OK, MessageBoxIcon.Information)
94          Application.Exit()
95      End Sub ' btnOk_Click
96  End Class ' frmValidate
```

Fig. 16.21 | Validating user information using regular expressions. (Part 3 of 4.)

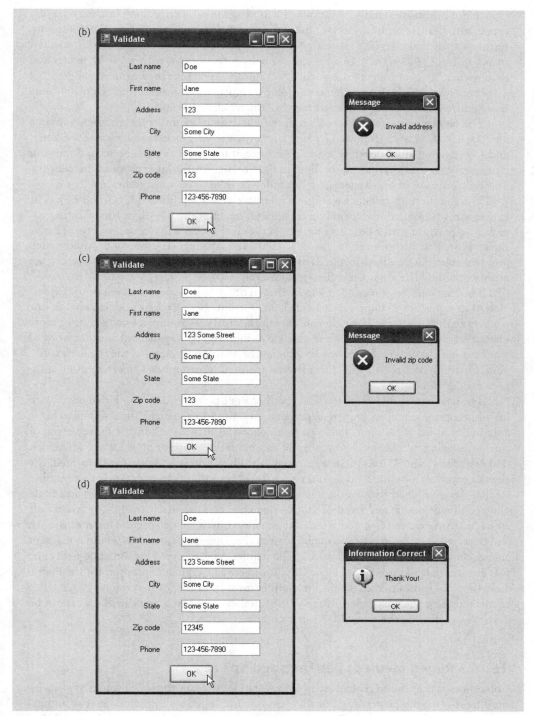

Fig. 16.21 | Validating user information using regular expressions. (Part 4 of 4.)

In the previous example, we searched a `String` for substrings that matched a regular expression. In this example, we want to ensure that the entire `String` in each `TextBox` conforms to a particular regular expression. For example, we want to accept "Smith" as a last name, but not "9@Smith#". In a regular expression that begins with a "^" character and ends with a "$" character, the characters "^" and "$" represent the beginning and end of a `String`, respectively. These characters force a regular expression to return a match only if the entire `String` being processed matches the regular expression.

The regular expression in line 23 uses the square bracket and range notation to match an uppercase first letter, followed by letters of any case—a-z matches any lowercase letter, and A-Z matches any uppercase letter. The * quantifier signifies that the second range of characters may occur zero or more times in the `String`. Thus, this expression matches any `String` consisting of one uppercase letter followed by zero or more additional letters.

The notation \s matches a single whitespace character (lines 43, 53 and 63). The expression \d{5}, used in the **Zip** (zip code) field, matches any five digits (line 72). In general, an expression with a positive integer x in the curly braces will match any x consecutive digits. Note that without the "^" and "$" characters, the regular expression would match any five consecutive digits in the `String`. By including the "^" and "$" characters, we ensure that only five-digit zip codes are allowed.

The character "|" (lines 43, 53 and 63) matches the expression to its left or the expression to its right. For example, Hi (John|Jane) matches both Hi John and Hi Jane. In line 43, we use the character "|" to indicate that the address can contain a word of one or more characters *or* a word of one or more characters followed by a space and another word of one or more characters. Note the use of parentheses to group parts of the regular expression. Quantifiers may be applied to patterns enclosed in parentheses to create more complex regular expressions.

The **Last name** and **First name** fields both accept `String`s of any length that begin with an uppercase letter. The regular expression for the **Address** field (line 43) matches a number of at least one digit, followed by a space and then either one or more letters, or one or more letters followed by a space and another series of one or more letters. Therefore, "10 Broadway" and "10 Main Street" are both valid addresses. As currently formed, the regular expression in line 43 does not match an address that does not start with a number or that has more than two words. The regular expressions for the **City** (line 53) and **State** (line 63) fields match any word of at least one character or, alternatively, any two words of at least one character if the words are separated by a single space. This means both Waltham and West Newton would match. Again, these regular expressions would not accept names that have more than two words. The regular expression for the **Zip code** field (line 72) ensures that the zip code is a five-digit number. The regular expression for the **Phone** field (line 82) indicates that the phone number must be of the form xxx-yyy-yyyy, where the xs represent the area code and the ys the number. The first x and the first y cannot be zero, as specified by the range [1-9] in each case.

16.16.3 Regex methods `Replace` and `Split`

Sometimes it is useful to replace parts of one `String` with another or to split a `String` according to a regular expression. For this purpose, the `Regex` class provides `Shared` and instance versions of methods `Replace` and `Split`, which are demonstrated in Fig. 16.22.

```vb
 1    ' Fig. 16.22: RegexSubstitution.vb
 2    ' Using Regex method Replace.
 3    Imports System.Text.RegularExpressions
 4
 5    Module RegexSubstitution
 6       Sub Main()
 7          Dim testString1 As String = _
 8             "This sentence ends in 5 stars *****"
 9          Dim output As String = ""
10          Dim testString2 As String = "1, 2, 3, 4, 5, 6, 7, 8"
11          Dim testRegex1 As New Regex("\d")
12          Dim result() As String
13
14          Console.WriteLine("Original string: " & testString1)
15          testString1 = Regex.Replace(testString1, "\*", "^")
16          Console.WriteLine("^ substituted for *: " & testString1)
17          testString1 = Regex.Replace(testString1, "stars", "carets")
18          Console.WriteLine("""carets"" substituted for ""stars"": " & _
19             testString1)
20          Console.WriteLine("Every word replaced by ""word"": " & _
21             Regex.Replace(testString1, "\w+", "word"))
22          Console.WriteLine(vbCrLf & "Original string: " & testString2)
23          Console.WriteLine("Replace first 3 digits by ""digit"": " & _
24             testRegex1.Replace(testString2, "digit", 3))
25          Console.Write("string split at commas [")
26
27          result = Regex.Split(testString2, ",\s")
28
29          For Each resultString As String In result
30             output &= """" & resultString & """, "
31          Next resultString
32
33          ' Delete ", " at the end of output string
34          Console.WriteLine(output.Substring(0, output.Length - 2) + "]")
35       End Sub ' Main
36    End Module ' RegexSubstitution
```

```
Original string: This sentence ends in 5 stars *****
^ substituted for *: This sentence ends in 5 stars ^^^^^
"carets" substituted for "stars": This sentence ends in 5 carets ^^^^^
Every word replaced by "word": word word word word word word ^^^^^

Original string: 1, 2, 3, 4, 5, 6, 7, 8
Replace first 3 digits by "digit": digit, digit, digit, 4, 5, 6, 7, 8
string split at commas ["1", "2", "3", "4", "5", "6", "7", "8"]
```

Fig. 16.22 | Regex methods `Replace` and `Split`.

Method `Replace` replaces text in a `String` with new text wherever the original `String` matches a regular expression. We use two versions of this method in Fig. 16.22. The first version (line 15) is `Shared` and takes three parameters—the `String` to modify, the `String` containing the regular expression to match and the replacement String. Here, Replace replaces every instance of "*" in testString1 with "^". Note that the regular expression ("*") precedes character * with a backslash, \. Normally, * is a quantifier indicating that a regular expression should match any number of occurrences of a preceding pattern. However, in line 15, we want to find all occurrences of the literal character *; to do this, we must escape character * with a \. By escaping a special regular-expression character with a \, we tell the regular-expression matching engine to find the actual character * rather than use it as a quantifier. Line 17 replaces every occurrence of "stars" in testString1 with "carets". Line 21 replaces every word in testString1 with "word".

The second version of method Replace (line 24) is an instance method that uses the regular expression passed to the constructor for testRegex1 (line 11) to perform the replacement operation. Line 11 instantiates testRegex1 with argument "\d". The call to instance method Replace in line 24 takes three arguments—a String to modify, a String containing the replacement text and an Integer specifying the number of replacements to make. In this case, line 24 replaces the first three instances of a digit ("\d") in testString2 with the text "digit".

Method Split divides a String into several substrings. The original String is broken at delimiters that match a specified regular expression. Method Split returns an array containing the substrings. In line 27, we use the Shared version of method Split to separate a String of comma-separated integers. The first argument is the String to split; the second argument is the regular expression that represents the delimiter. The regular expression ",\s*" separates the substrings at each comma. By matching any whitespace characters (\s* in the regular expression), we eliminate extra spaces from the resulting substrings.

16.17 Wrap-Up

In this chapter, you learned about the FCL's string and character processing capabilities. We overviewed the fundamentals of characters and strings. You saw how to determine the length of strings, copy strings, access the individual characters in strings, search strings, obtain substrings from larger strings, compare strings, concatenate strings, replace characters in strings and convert strings to uppercase or lowercase letters.

We showed how to use class StringBuilder to build sequences of characters dynamically. You learned how to determine and specify the size of a StringBuilder object, and how to append, insert, remove and replace characters in a StringBuilder object. We then introduced the character-testing methods of type Char that enable a program to determine whether a character is a digit, a letter, a lowercase letter, an uppercase letter, a punctuation mark or a symbol other than a punctuation mark, and the methods for converting a character to uppercase or lowercase.

Finally, we discussed classes Regex and Match from the System.Text.Regular-Expressions namespace. We also discussed the symbols that are used to form regular expressions. You learned how to find patterns in a string and match entire strings to patterns with Regex method Match, how to replace characters in a string with Regex method Replace and how to split strings at delimiters with Regex method Split. In the next chapter, you will learn how to add graphics and other multimedia capabilities to your Windows applications.

17

Graphics and Multimedia

One picture is worth ten thousand words.
—Chinese proverb

Treat nature in terms of the cylinder, the sphere, the cone, all in perspective.
—Paul Cezanne

Nothing ever becomes real till it is experienced—even a proverb is no proverb to you till your life has illustrated it.
—John Keats

A picture shows me at a glance what it takes dozens of pages of a book to expound.
—Ivan Sergeyevich Turgenev

OBJECTIVES

In this chapter you will learn:

- To understand graphics contexts and graphics objects.
- To manipulate colors and fonts.
- To understand and use GDI+ `Graphics` methods to draw lines, rectangles, `String`s and images.
- To use class `Image` to manipulate and display images.
- To draw complex shapes from simple shapes with class `GraphicsPath`.
- To use Windows Media Player to play audio or video in a Visual Basic application.
- To use Microsoft Agent to add interactive animated characters to a Visual Basic application.

17.1 Introduction

In this chapter, we overview the FCL's tools for drawing two-dimensional shapes and for controlling colors and fonts. The FCL supports graphics that enable programmers to visually enhance their Windows applications. The many sophisticated drawing capabilities are part of namespace System.Drawing and the other namespaces that make up the .NET resource *GDI+*. GDI+ is an application programming interface (API) that provides classes for creating two-dimensional vector graphics (a way to describe graphics that makes them easy to manipulate with high-performance techniques), manipulating fonts and inserting images.

We begin with an introduction to the .NET framework's drawing capabilities. We then present more powerful drawing capabilities, such as changing the styles of the lines used to draw shapes and controlling the colors and patterns of the filled shapes.

Later in this chapter, we explore techniques for manipulating images and creating smooth animations. We also discuss class Image, which can store and manipulate images of various formats. We explain how to combine the graphical rendering capabilities covered in the early sections of the chapter with those for image manipulation. The chapter ends with several multimedia examples in which you build an animation, use the Windows Media Player control and use Microsoft Agent—a technology for adding interactive animated characters to applications or Web pages.

17.2 Drawing Classes and the Coordinate System

Figure 17.1 depicts a portion of namespace *System.Drawing*, including several graphics classes and structures covered in this chapter. Namespaces System.Drawing and *System.Drawing.Drawing2D* contain the most commonly used GDI+ components.

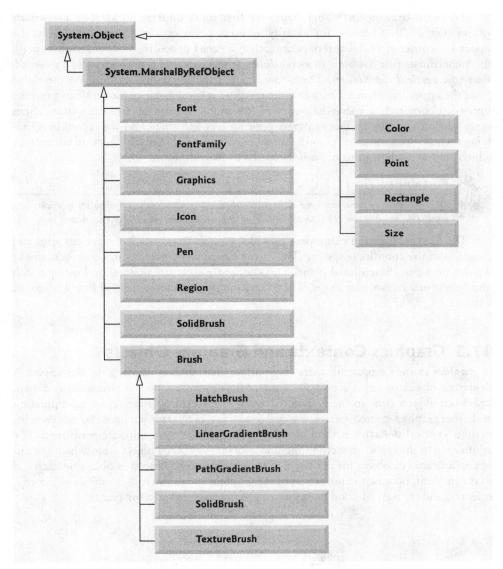

Fig. 17.1 | System.Drawing namespace's classes and structures.

Class **Graphics** contains methods used for drawing Strings, lines, rectangles and other shapes on a Control. The drawing methods of class Graphics usually require a **Pen** or **Brush** object to render a specified shape. The Pen draws shape outlines; the Brush draws solid objects.

The **Color** structure contains numerous Shared properties that set the colors of various graphical components, plus methods that allow users to create new colors. Class **Font** contains properties that define unique fonts. Class **FontFamily** contains methods for obtaining font information.

To begin drawing in Visual Basic, we first must understand GDI+'s *coordinate system* (Fig. 17.2), a scheme for identifying every point on the screen. By default, the upper-left corner of a GUI component (such as a `Panel` or a `Form`) has the coordinates (0, 0). A coordinate pair has both an *x-coordinate* (the *horizontal coordinate*) and a *y-coordinate* (the *vertical coordinate*). The *x*-coordinate is the horizontal distance (to the right) from the upper-left corner. The *y*-coordinate is the vertical distance (downward) from the upper-left corner. The *x-axis* defines every horizontal coordinate, and the *y-axis* defines every vertical coordinate. Programmers position text and shapes on the screen by specifying their (*x, y*) coordinates. Coordinate units are measured in pixels ("picture elements"), which are the smallest units of *resolution* on a display monitor.

 Portability Tip 17.1

Different display monitors have different resolutions, so the density of pixels on monitors will vary. This might cause the sizes of graphics to appear different on different monitors.

The `System.Drawing` namespace provides several structures that represent sizes and locations in the coordinate system. The ***Point*** structure represents the *x-y* coordinates of a point on a two-dimensional plane. The ***Rectangle*** structure defines the loading width and height of a rectangular shape. The `Size` structure represents the width and height of a shape.

17.3 Graphics Contexts and Graphics Objects

A *graphics context* represents a drawing surface that enables drawing on the screen. A `Graphics` object manages a graphics context by controlling how information is drawn. `Graphics` objects contain methods for drawing, font manipulation, color manipulation and other graphics-related actions. Every derived class of `System.Windows.Forms.Form` inherits a virtual ***OnPaint*** method in which most graphics operations are performed. The arguments to the `OnPaint` method include a ***PaintEventArgs*** object from which we can obtain a `Graphics` object for the `Form`. We must obtain the `Graphics` object on each call to the method, because the properties of the graphics context that the graphics object represents could change. Method `OnPaint` triggers the `Control`'s ***Paint*** event.

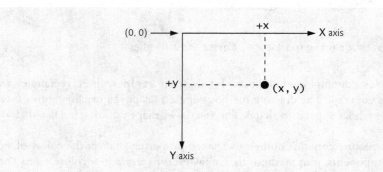

Fig. 17.2 | GDI+ coordinate system. Units are measured in pixels.

When drawing on a Form, you can override method OnPaint to retrieve a Graphics object from argument PaintEventArgs or to create a new Graphics object associated with the appropriate surface. We demonstrate these drawing techniques later in the chapter.

To override the inherited OnPaint method, use the following method header:

> **Protected Overrides Sub** OnPaint(PaintEventArgs e)

Next, extract the incoming Graphics object from argument PaintEventArg, as in:

> **Dim** graphicsObject **As** Graphics = e.Graphics

Variable graphicsObject can now be used to draw shapes and Strings on the Form.

Calling the OnPaint method raises the Paint event. Instead of overriding the OnPaint method, programmers can add an event handler for the Paint event. Visual Studio .NET generates the Paint event handler in this form:

> **Protected Sub** MyEventHandler_Paint(_
>   **ByVal** sender **As** Object, **ByVal** e As PaintEventArgs)

Programmers seldom call the OnPaint method directly, because drawing graphics is an ***event-driven process***. An event—such as covering, uncovering or resizing a window—calls the OnPaint method of that Form. Similarly, when any control (such as a TextBox or Label) is displayed, that control's OnPaint method is called.

You can force a call to OnPaint by calling a Control's ***Invalidate*** method. This method refreshes a control and implicitly repaints all its graphical components. Class Control has several overloaded Invalidate methods that allow programmers to update portions of a control.

Performance Tip 17.1

Calling the Invalidate method to refresh the Control can be inefficient if only a small portion of a Control needs refreshing. Calling Invalidate with a Rectangle parameter refreshes only the area designated by the rectangle. This improves program performance.

Controls, such as Labels and Buttons, do not have their own graphics contexts, but you can create them. To draw on a control, first create a graphics object by invoking the control's CreateGraphics method, as in:

> Dim *graphicsObject* **As** Graphics = *controlName*.CreateGraphics();

Now you can use the methods provided in class Graphics to draw on the control.

17.4 Color Control

Colors can enhance a program's appearance and help convey meaning. For example, a red traffic light indicates stop, yellow indicates caution and green indicates go. Structure Color defines methods and constants used to manipulate colors.

Every color can be created from a combination of alpha, red, green and blue components (called ***ARGB values***). All four ARGB components are Bytes that represent integer values in the range 0 to 255. The alpha value determines the opacity of the color. For example, the alpha value 0 represents a transparent color, and the value 255 represents an opaque color. Alpha values between 0 and 255 result in a weighted blending effect of the color's *RGB value* with that of any background color, causing a semitransparent effect. The first number in the RGB value defines the amount of red in the color, the second defines the amount of green and the third defines the amount of blue. The larger the value, the greater the amount of that color. Programmers can choose from almost 17 million colors. If a computer cannot display all these colors, it will display the color closest to the one specified. Figure 17.3 summarizes some predefined Color constants (all are Public and Shared), and Fig. 17.4 describes several Color methods and properties. For a complete list of the predefined Color constants, methods and properties, see Color structure's online documentation (msdn2.microsoft.com/en-us/library/system.drawing.color).

Constants in structure Color	RGB value	Constants in structure Color	RGB value
Orange	255, 200, 0	White	255, 255, 255
Pink	255, 175, 175	Gray	128, 128, 128
Cyan	0, 255, 255	DarkGray	64, 64, 64
Magenta	255, 0, 255	Red	255, 0, 0
Yellow	255, 255, 0	Green	0, 255, 0
Black	0, 0, 0	Blue	0, 0, 255

Fig. 17.3 | Color structure Shared constants and their RGB values.

Structure Color methods and properties	Description
Common Methods	
FromArgb	A Shared method that creates a color based on red, green and blue values expressed as ints from 0 to 255. The overloaded version allows specification of alpha, red, green and blue values.
FromName	A Shared method that creates a color from a name, passed as a String.
Common Properties	
A	A byte between 0 and 255, representing the alpha component.
R	A byte between 0 and 255, representing the red component.
G	A byte between 0 and 255, representing the green component.
B	A byte between 0 and 255, representing the blue component.

Fig. 17.4 | Color structure members.

The table in Fig. 17.4 describes two ***FromArgb*** method calls. One takes three `Integer` arguments, and one takes four `Integer` arguments (all argument values must be between 0 and 255, inclusive). Both take `Integer` arguments specifying the amount of red, green and blue. The overloaded version also allows the user to specify the alpha component; the three-argument version defaults the alpha to 255 (opaque). Both methods return a `Color` object. `Color` properties ***A***, ***R***, ***G*** and ***B*** return bytes that represent `Integer` values from 0 to 255, corresponding to the amounts of alpha, red, green and blue, respectively.

Programmers draw shapes and `Strings` with `Brushes` and `Pens`. A `Pen`, which functions similarly to an ordinary pen, is used to draw lines. Most drawing methods require a `Pen` object. The overloaded `Pen` constructors allow programmers to specify the colors and widths of the lines they wish to draw. The `System.Drawing` namespace also provides a `Pens` class containing predefined `Pens`.

All classes derived from `MustInherit` class `Brush` define objects that color the interiors of graphical shapes. For example, the `SolidBrush` constructor takes a `Color` object—the color to draw. In most `Fill` methods, `Brushes` fill a space with a color, pattern or image. Figure 17.5 summarizes various `Brushes` and their functions.

Manipulating Colors

Figure 17.6 demonstrates several of the methods and properties described in Fig. 17.4. It displays two overlapping rectangles, allowing you to experiment with color values, color names and alpha values (for transparency).

Class	Description
HatchBrush	Fills a region with a pattern. The pattern is defined by a member of the ***HatchStyle enumeration***, a foreground color (with which the pattern is drawn) and a background color.
LinearGradientBrush	Fills a region with a gradual blend of one color to another. Linear gradients are defined along a line. They can be specified by the two colors, the angle of the gradient and either the width of a rectangle or two points.
SolidBrush	Fills a region with one color that is specified by a `Color` object.
TextureBrush	Fills a region by repeating a specified `Image` across the surface.

Fig. 17.5 | Classes that derive from class `Brush`.

```
1    ' Fig 17.6: FrmShowColors.vb
2    ' Color value and alpha demonstration.
3    Public Class FrmShowColors
4        ' color for back rectangle
5        Private backgroundColor As Color = Color.Wheat
6
```

Fig. 17.6 | Color value and alpha demonstration. (Part 1 of 3.)

```vbnet
 7          ' color for front rectangle
 8          Private foregroundColor As Color = Color.FromArgb(100, 0, 0, 255)
 9
10          ' override Form's OnPaint method
11          Protected Overrides Sub OnPaint(ByVal e As PaintEventArgs)
12             Dim graphicsObject As Graphics = e.Graphics ' get graphics object
13
14             ' create text brush
15             Dim textBrush As New SolidBrush(Color.Black)
16
17             ' create solid brush
18             Dim brush As New SolidBrush(Color.White)
19
20             ' draw white background
21             graphicsObject.FillRectangle(brush, 4, 4, 275, 180)
22
23             ' display name of backColor
24             graphicsObject.DrawString( _
25                BackColor.Name, Me.Font, textBrush, 40, 5)
26
27             ' set brush color and display back rectangle
28             brush.Color = backgroundColor
29             graphicsObject.FillRectangle(brush, 45, 20, 150, 120)
30
31             ' display Argb values of front color
32             graphicsObject.DrawString("Alpha: " & foregroundColor.A & _
33                " Red: " & foregroundColor.R & " Green: " & _
34                foregroundColor.G & " Blue: " & foregroundColor.B, Me.Font, _
35                textBrush, 55, 165)
36
37             ' set brush color and display front rectangle
38             brush.Color = foregroundColor
39             graphicsObject.FillRectangle(brush, 65, 35, 170, 130)
40          End Sub ' OnPaint
41
42          ' change Form's background color
43          Private Sub btnColorName_Click(ByVal sender As System.Object, _
44             ByVal e As System.EventArgs) Handles btnColorName.Click
45             ' set backColor to color specified in text box
46             backgroundColor = Color.FromName(txtColorName.Text)
47             Invalidate() ' refresh Form
48          End Sub ' btnColorName_Click
49
50          ' change Form's foreground color
51          Private Sub btnColorValue_Click(ByVal sender As System.Object, _
52             ByVal e As System.EventArgs) Handles btnColorValue.Click
53             ' obtain new front color from text boxes
54             foregroundColor = Color.FromArgb( _
55                Convert.ToInt32(txtAlpha.Text), Convert.ToInt32(txtRed.Text), _
56                Convert.ToInt32(txtGreen.Text), Convert.ToInt32(txtBlue.Text))
57             Invalidate() ' refresh Form
58          End Sub ' btnColorValue_Click
59       End Class ' FrmShowColors
```

Fig. 17.6 | Color value and alpha demonstration. (Part 2 of 3.)

Fig. 17.6 | Color value and alpha demonstration. (Part 3 of 3.)

When the application begins executing, its Form is displayed. This results in a call to FrmShowColors's OnPaint method to paint the Form's contents. Line 12 gets a reference to PaintEventArgs e's Graphics object and assigns it to graphicsObject. Lines 15 and 18 create a black and a white SolidBrush for drawing solid shapes on the Form. Class *SolidBrush* derives from MustInherit class Brush, so a SolidBrush can be passed to any method that expects a Brush parameter.

Line 21 uses Graphics method FillRectangle to draw a solid white rectangle using the SolidBrush created in line 18. FillRectangle takes as parameters a Brush, the *x*- and *y*-coordinates of the rectangle's upper-left corner, and the width and height of the rectangle. Lines 24–25 display the Name property of BackColor with Graphics method *DrawString*. There are several overloaded DrawString methods; the version demonstrated in lines 24–25 takes as arguments the String to display, the display Font, the Brush to use for drawing and the *x*- and *y*-coordinates of the location for the String's first character.

Lines 28–29 assign the backgroundColor value to brush's Color property and display a rectangle. Lines 32–35 extract and display foregroundColor's ARGB values and draw a string containing those values. Lines 38–39 assign the foregroundColor value to brush's Color property, then draw a filled rectangle in the foregroundColor that overlaps the rectangle drawn at line 29.

Button event handler btnColorName_Click (lines 43–48) uses class Color's Shared method *FromName* to create a new Color object from the color name that a user enters in a TextBox. This Color is assigned to backgroundColor (line 46). Then line 47 invokes the Form's Invalidate method to indicate that the Form should be repainted, which results in a call to OnPaint to update the Form on the screen.

Button event handler btnColorValue_Click (lines 51–58) uses Color method FromArgb to construct a new Color object from the ARGB values that a user specifies via TextBoxes, then assigns the newly created Color to foregroundColor. Line 57 invokes the Form's Invalidate method to indicate that the Form should be repainted, which results in a call to OnPaint to update the Form on the screen.

Changing the alpha value of the foregroundColor from 0 to 255, makes the effects of alpha blending apparent. The sample output shows that the red back rectangle blends with the blue front rectangle to create purple where they overlap. Note that you cannot modify an existing Color object. To use a different color, create a new Color object.

Using the ColorDialog to Select Colors from a Color Palette

The predefined GUI component **ColorDialog** is a dialog box that allows users to select from a palette of available colors or to create custom colors. Figure 17.7 demonstrates the ColorDialog. When a user selects a color and presses **OK**, the application retrieves the user's selection via the ColorDialog's **Color** property.

The GUI for this application contains two Buttons. The btnBackgroundColor allows the user to change the Form's background color. The btnTextColor allows the user to change the button text colors. Line 5 creates a Private Shared ColorDialog named colorChooser, which is used in the event handlers for both Buttons.

Lines 8–17 define the btnBackgroundColor_Click event handler. The method sets the ColorDialog's **FullOpen** property to True (line 11), so the dialog displays all available

```vb
1   ' Fig. 17.7: FrmShowColorsComplex.vb
2   ' ColorDialog used to change background and text color.
3   Public Class FrmShowColorsComplex
4      ' create ColorDialog object
5      Private Shared colorChooser As New ColorDialog()
6
7      ' change background color
8      Private Sub btnBackgroundColor_Click(ByVal sender As System.Object, _
9         ByVal e As System.EventArgs) Handles btnBackgroundColor.Click
10        ' show ColorDialog and get result
11        colorChooser.FullOpen = True
12        Dim result As DialogResult = colorChooser.ShowDialog()
13
14        If result = Windows.Forms.DialogResult.OK Then
15           Me.BackColor = colorChooser.Color ' set background color
16        End If
17     End Sub ' btnBackgroundColor_Click
18
19     ' change text color
20     Private Sub btnTextColor_Click(ByVal sender As System.Object, _
21        ByVal e As System.EventArgs) Handles btnTextColor.Click
22        ' get chosen color
23        Dim result As DialogResult = colorChooser.ShowDialog()
24
25        If result = Windows.Forms.DialogResult.OK Then
26           ' assign forecolor to result of dialog
27           btnBackgroundColor.ForeColor = colorChooser.Color
28           btnTextColor.ForeColor = colorChooser.Color
29        End If
30     End Sub ' btnTextColor_Click
31  End Class ' FrmShowColorsComplex
```

Fig. 17.7 | ColorDialog used to change background and text color. (Part 1 of 2.)

Fig. 17.7 | ColorDialog used to change background and text color. (Part 2 of 2.)

colors, as shown in the screen capture in Fig. 17.7. When FullOpen is False, the dialog shows only the color swatches. Line 12 invokes colorChooser's ShowDialog method to display the dialog. The dialog's Color property stores the user's selection. If the user clicks **OK**, line 15 modifies the background color of the form by setting its BackColor property to the dialog's Color property.

Lines 20–30 define the btnTextColor_Click event handler. If the user clicks **OK** in the dialog, lines 27–28 set the text color of both buttons to the selected color.

Users are not restricted to the ColorDialog's 48 color swatches. To create a custom color, users can click anywhere in the ColorDialog's large rectangle, which displays various color shades. Adjust the slider, hue and other features to refine the color. When finished, click the **Add to Custom Colors** button, which adds the custom color to a square in the **Custom Colors** section of the dialog. Clicking **OK** sets the Color property of the Color-Dialog to that color.

17.5 Font Control

This section introduces methods and constants related to font control. The properties of Font objects cannot be modified. If you need a different Font, you must create a new Font object. There are many overloaded versions of the Font constructor for initializing Font objects. Some properties of class Font are summarized in Fig. 17.8.

Note that the *Size* property returns the font size as measured in design units, whereas *SizeInPoints* returns the font size as measured in points (the more common measurement). *Design units* allow the font size to be specified in one of several units of measurement, such as inches or millimeters. Some versions of the Font constructor accept a *GraphicsUnit* argument. GraphicsUnit is an enumeration that allows you to specify the unit of measurement that describes the font size. Members of the GraphicsUnit enumeration include *Point* (1/72 inch), *Display* (1/75 inch), *Document* (1/300 inch), *Millimeter*, *Inch* and *Pixel*. If this argument is provided, the Size property contains the size of the font as measured in the specified design unit, and the SizeInPoints property contains the corresponding size of the font in points. For example, if we create a Font having size 1 and specify the unit of measurement as GraphicsUnit.Inch, the Size property will be 1 and the SizeInPoints property will be 72, because there are 72 points in an inch. The default measurement for the font size is GraphicsUnit.Point (thus, the Size and SizeInPoints properties will be equal).

Class Font has several constructors. Most require a font name, which is a String representing a font currently supported by the system. Common fonts include *Microsoft SansSerif* and *Serif*. Most Font constructors also require as arguments the *font size* and *font style*. The font style is specified with a constant from the *FontStyle* enumeration (*Bold*, *Italic*, *Regular*, *Strikeout* and *Underline*, or a combination of these). You can combine font styles with the Or operator, as in FontStyle.Italic Or FontStyle.Bold, which makes a font both italic and bold. Graphics method *DrawString* sets the current drawing font—the font in which the text displays—to its Font argument.

Property	Description
Bold	Returns True if the font is bold.
FontFamily	Returns the font's FontFamily—a grouping structure to organize fonts and define their similar properties.
Height	Returns the height of the font.
Italic	Returns True if the font is italic.
Name	Returns the font's name as a String.
Size	Returns a float value indicating the current font size measured in design units (design units are any specified unit of measurement for the font).
SizeInPoints	Returns a float value indicating the current font size measured in points.
Strikeout	Returns True if the font is in strikeout format.
Underline	Returns True if the font is underlined.

Fig. 17.8 | Font class read-only properties.

Common Programming Error 17.1

Specifying a font that is not available on a system is a logic error. If this occurs, the system's default font is substituted.

Drawing Strings in Different Fonts

The program in Fig. 17.9 displays text in different fonts and sizes. The program uses the Font constructor to initialize the Font objects (lines 11, 15, 19 and 23). Each call to the Font constructor passes a font name (e.g., Arial, Times New Roman, Courier New or Tahoma) as a String, a font size (a float) and a FontStyle object (style). Graphics method DrawString sets the font and draws the text at the specified location. Note that line 7 creates a DarkBlue SolidBrush object (brush). All Strings drawn with that brush appear in DarkBlue.

```vb
1    ' Fig. 17.9 FrmUsingFonts.vb
2    ' Fonts and FontStyles.
3    Public Class FrmUsingFonts
4       ' demonstrate various font and style settings
5       Protected Overrides Sub OnPaint(ByVal paintEvent As PaintEventArgs)
6          Dim graphicsObject As Graphics = paintEvent.Graphics
7          Dim brush As New SolidBrush(Color.DarkBlue)
8
9          ' arial, 12 pt bold
10         Dim style As FontStyle = FontStyle.Bold
11         Dim arial As New Font("Arial", 12, style)
12
13         ' times new roman, 12 pt regular
14         style = FontStyle.Regular
15         Dim timesNewRoman As New Font("Times New Roman", 12, style)
16
17         ' courier new, 16 pt bold and italic
18         style = FontStyle.Bold Or FontStyle.Italic
19         Dim courierNew As New Font("Courier New", 16, style)
20
21         ' tahoma, 18 pt strikeout
22         style = FontStyle.Strikeout
23         Dim tahoma As New Font("Tahoma", 18, style)
24
25         graphicsObject.DrawString(arial.Name & _
26            " 12 point bold.", arial, brush, 10, 10)
27
28         graphicsObject.DrawString(timesNewRoman.Name & _
29            " 12 point plain.", timesNewRoman, brush, 10, 30)
30
31         graphicsObject.DrawString(courierNew.Name & _
32            " 16 point bold and italic.", courierNew, brush, 10, 50)
33
34         graphicsObject.DrawString(tahoma.Name & _
35            " 18 point strikeout.", tahoma, brush, 10, 70)
36      End Sub ' OnPaint
37   End Class ' FrmUsingFonts
```

Fig. 17.9 | Fonts and FontStyles. (Part 1 of 2.)

Fig. 17.9 | Fonts and FontStyles. (Part 2 of 2.)

Font Metrics

You can determine precise information about a font's ***metrics*** (or properties), such as ***height***, ***descent*** (the amount characters dip below the baseline), ***ascent*** (the amount characters rise above the baseline) and ***leading*** (the difference between the ascent of one line and the descent of the previous line). Figure 17.10 illustrates these font metrics.

Class FontFamily defines characteristics common to a group of related fonts. Class FontFamily provides several methods used to determine the font metrics shared by members of a particular family. These methods are summarized in Fig. 17.11.

Fig. 17.10 | Font metrics illustration.

Method	Description
GetCellAscent	Returns an Integer representing the ascent of a font as measured in design units.
GetCellDescent	Returns an Integer representing the descent of a font as measured in design units.
GetEmHeight	Returns an Integer representing the height of a font as measured in design units.
GetLineSpacing	Returns an Integer representing the distance between two consecutive lines of text as measured in design units.

Fig. 17.11 | FontFamily methods that return font-metric information.

The program in Fig. 17.12 displays the metrics of two fonts. Line 10 creates Font object arial and sets it to 10-point Arial font. Line 11 uses Font property FontFamily to obtain object arial's FontFamily object. Lines 14–15 output the String representation of the font. Lines 17–27 then use methods of class FontFamily to obtain the ascent, descent, height and leading of the font and draw strings containing this information. Lines 30–50 repeat the process for font sansSerif, a Font object derived from the MS Sans Serif FontFamily.

```
1   ' Fig 17.12: FrmUsingFontMetrics.vb
2   ' Displaying font metric information
3   Public Class FrmUsingFontMetrics
4      ' displays font information
5      Protected Overrides Sub OnPaint(ByVal paintEvent As PaintEventArgs)
6         Dim graphicsObject As Graphics = paintEvent.Graphics
7         Dim brush As New SolidBrush(Color.DarkBlue)
8
9         ' Arial font metrics
10        Dim arial As New Font("Arial", 10)
11        Dim family As FontFamily = arial.FontFamily
12
13        ' display Arial font metrics
14        graphicsObject.DrawString("Current Font: " & _
15           arial.ToString(), arial, brush, 10, 10)
16
17        graphicsObject.DrawString("Ascent: " & _
18           family.GetCellAscent(FontStyle.Regular), arial, brush, 10, 30)
19
20        graphicsObject.DrawString("Descent: " & _
21           family.GetCellDescent(FontStyle.Regular), arial, brush, 10, 50)
22
23        graphicsObject.DrawString("Height: " & _
24           family.GetEmHeight(FontStyle.Regular), arial, brush, 10, 70)
25
26        graphicsObject.DrawString("Leading: " & _
27           family.GetLineSpacing(FontStyle.Regular), arial, brush, 10, 90)
28
29        ' display Sans Serif font metrics
30        Dim sanSerif As New Font("Microsoft Sans Serif", _
31           12, FontStyle.Italic)
32        family = sanSerif.FontFamily
33
34        graphicsObject.DrawString("Current Font: " & _
35           sanSerif.ToString(), sanSerif, brush, 10, 130)
36
37        graphicsObject.DrawString("Ascent: " & _
38           family.GetCellAscent(FontStyle.Regular), _
39           sanSerif, brush, 10, 150)
40
41        graphicsObject.DrawString("Descent: " & _
42           family.GetCellDescent(FontStyle.Regular), _
43           sanSerif, brush, 10, 170)
```

Fig. 17.12 | FontFamily class used to obtain font-metric information. (Part 1 of 2.)

```
44
45          graphicsObject.DrawString("Height: " & _
46             family.GetEmHeight(FontStyle.Regular), sanSerif, brush, 10, 190)
47
48          graphicsObject.DrawString("Leading: " & _
49             family.GetLineSpacing(FontStyle.Regular), _
50             sanSerif, brush, 10, 210)
51      End Sub ' OnPaint
52   End Class ' FrmUsingFontMetrics
```

UsingFontMetrics

Current Font: [Font: Name=Arial, Size=10, Units=3, GdiCharSet=1, GdiVerticalFont=False]
Ascent: 1854
Descent: 434
Height: 2048
Leading: 2355

Current Font: [Font: Name=Microsoft Sans Serif, Size=12, Units=3, GdiCharSet=1, GdiVerticalFont=False]
Ascent: 1888
Descent: 430
Height: 2048
Leading: 2318

Fig. 17.12 | FontFamily class used to obtain font-metric information. (Part 2 of 2.)

17.6 Drawing Lines, Rectangles and Ovals

This section presents Graphics methods for drawing lines, rectangles and ovals. Each of the drawing methods has several overloaded versions. Methods that draw hollow shapes typically require as arguments a Pen and four ints. Methods that draw solid shapes typically require as arguments a Brush and four ints. The first two Integer arguments represent the coordinates of the upper-left corner of the shape (or its enclosing area), and the last two ints indicate the shape's (or enclosing area's) width and height. Figure 17.13 summarizes several Graphics methods and their parameters. [*Note:* Many of these methods are overloaded—consult the online Graphics class documentation for a complete listing (msdn2.microsoft.com/en-us/library/system.drawing.graphics).]

Graphics Drawing Methods and Descriptions

DrawLine(*ByVal* p *As* Pen, *ByVal* x1 *As Integer*, *ByVal* y1 *As Integer*, _
   ByVal x2 *As Integer*, *ByVal* y2 *As Integer*)
Draws a line from (x1, y1) to (x2, y2). The Pen determines the line's color, style and width.

DrawRectangle(*ByVal* p *As* Pen, *ByVal* x *As Integer*, *ByVal* y *As Integer*, _
   ByVal width *As Integer*, *ByVal* height *As Integer*)
Draws a rectangle of the specified width and height. The top-left corner of the rectangle is at point (x, y). The Pen determines the rectangle's color, style and border width.

Fig. 17.13 | Graphics methods that draw lines, rectangles and ovals. (Part 1 of 2.)

> **Graphics Drawing Methods and Descriptions**
>
> FillRectangle(*ByVal* b *As* Brush, *ByVal* x *As Integer*, *ByVal* y *As Integer*, _
>   *ByVal* width *As Integer*, *ByVal* height *As Integer*)
> Draws a solid rectangle of the specified width and height. The top-left corner of the rectangle is at point (x, y). The Brush determines the fill pattern inside the rectangle.
>
> DrawEllipse(*ByVal* p *As* Pen, *ByVal* x *As Integer*, *ByVal* y *As Integer*, _
>   *ByVal* width *As Integer*, *ByVal* height *As Integer*)
> Draws an ellipse inside a bounding rectangle of the specified width and height. The top-left corner of the bounding rectangle is located at (x, y). The Pen determines the color, style and border width of the ellipse.
>
> FillEllipse(*ByVal* b *As* Brush, *ByVal* x *As Integer*, *ByVal* y *As Integer*, _
>   *ByVal* width *As Integer*, *ByVal* height *As Integer*)
> Draws a filled ellipse inside a bounding rectangle of the specified width and height. The top-left corner of the bounding rectangle is located at (x, y). The Brush determines the pattern inside the ellipse.

Fig. 17.13 | Graphics methods that draw lines, rectangles and ovals. (Part 2 of 2.)

The application in Fig. 17.14 draws lines, rectangles and ellipses. In this application, we also demonstrate methods that draw filled and unfilled shapes.

```vb
1   ' Fig. 17.14: FrmLinesRectanglesOvals.vb
2   ' Demonstrating lines, rectangles and ovals.
3   Public Class FrmLinesRectanglesOvals
4      ' override Form OnPaint method
5      Protected Overrides Sub OnPaint(ByVal paintEvent As PaintEventArgs)
6         ' get graphics object
7         Dim g As Graphics = paintEvent.Graphics
8         Dim brush As New SolidBrush(Color.Blue)
9         Dim pen As New Pen(Color.Black)
10
11        ' create filled rectangle
12        g.FillRectangle(brush, 90, 30, 150, 90)
13
14        ' draw lines to connect rectangles
15        g.DrawLine(pen, 90, 30, 110, 40)
16        g.DrawLine(pen, 90, 120, 110, 130)
17        g.DrawLine(pen, 240, 30, 260, 40)
18        g.DrawLine(pen, 240, 120, 260, 130)
19
20        ' draw top rectangle
21        g.DrawRectangle(pen, 110, 40, 150, 90)
22
23        ' set brush to red
24        brush.Color = Color.Red
25
```

Fig. 17.14 | Demonstration of methods that draw lines, rectangles and ellipses. (Part 1 of 2.)

```
26              ' draw base Ellipse
27              g.FillEllipse(brush, 280, 75, 100, 50)
28
29              ' draw connecting lines
30              g.DrawLine(pen, 380, 55, 380, 100)
31              g.DrawLine(pen, 280, 55, 280, 100)
32
33              ' draw Ellipse outline
34              g.DrawEllipse(pen, 280, 30, 100, 50)
35          End Sub ' OnPaint
36      End Class ' FrmLinesRectanglesOvals
```

Fig. 17.14 | Demonstration of methods that draw lines, rectangles and ellipses. (Part 2 of 2.)

Methods *FillRectangle* and *DrawRectangle* (lines 12 and 21) draw rectangles on the screen. For each method, the first argument specifies the drawing object to use. The FillRectangle method uses a Brush object (in this case, an instance of SolidBrush—a class that derives from Brush), whereas the DrawRectangle method uses a Pen object. The next two arguments specify the coordinates of the upper-left corner of the *bounding rectangle*, which represents the area in which the rectangle will be drawn. The fourth and fifth arguments specify the rectangle's width and height. Method DrawLine (lines 15–18) takes a Pen and two pairs of ints, specifying the start and end of a line. The method then draws a line, using the Pen object.

Methods *FillEllipse* and *DrawEllipse* (lines 27 and 34) each provide overloaded versions that take five arguments. In both methods, the first argument specifies the drawing object to use. The next two arguments specify the upper-left coordinates of the bounding rectangle representing the area in which the ellipse will be drawn. The last two arguments specify the bounding rectangle's width and height, respectively. Figure 17.15 depicts an

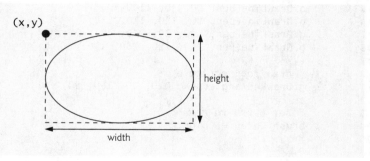

Fig. 17.15 | Ellipse bounded by a rectangle.

ellipse bounded by a rectangle. The ellipse touches the midpoint of each of the four sides of the bounding rectangle. The bounding rectangle is not displayed on the screen.

17.7 Drawing Arcs

Arcs are portions of ellipses and are measured in degrees, beginning at a *starting angle* and continuing for a specified number of degrees called the *arc angle*. An arc is said to *sweep* (traverse) its arc angle, beginning from its starting angle. Arcs that sweep in a clockwise direction are measured in positive degrees, whereas arcs that sweep in a counterclockwise direction are measured in negative degrees. Figure 17.16 depicts two arcs. Note that the arc at the left of the figure sweeps upward from zero degrees to approximately −110 degrees. Similarly, the arc at the right of the figure sweeps downward from zero degrees to approximately 110 degrees.

Note the dashed boxes around the arcs in Fig. 17.16. Each arc is drawn as part of an oval (the rest of which is not visible). When drawing an oval, we specify the oval's dimensions in the form of a bounding rectangle that encloses the oval. The boxes in Fig. 17.16 correspond to these bounding rectangles. The Graphics methods used to draw arcs— **DrawArc**, **DrawPie** and **FillPie**—are summarized in Fig. 17.17.

The program in Fig. 17.18 draws six images (three arcs and three filled pie slices) to demonstrate the arc methods listed in Fig. 17.17. To illustrate the bounding rectangles that determine the sizes and locations of the arcs, the arcs are displayed inside red rectangles that have the same *x-y* coordinates, width and height arguments as those that define the bounding rectangles for the arcs.

Fig. 17.16 | Positive and negative arc angles.

Graphics methods and descriptions

Note: Many of these methods are overloaded—consult the documentation for a complete listing.

```
DrawArc(ByVal p As Pen, ByVal x As Integer, ByVal y As Integer, _
    ByVal width As Integer, ByVal height As Integer, _
    ByVal startAngle As Integer, ByVal sweepAngle As Integer)
```
Draws an arc beginning from angle startAngle (in degrees) and sweeping sweepAngle degrees. The ellipse is defined by a bounding rectangle of width, height and upper-left corner (x,y). The Pen determines the color, border width and style of the arc.

Fig. 17.17 | Graphics methods for drawing arcs. (Part 1 of 2.)

Graphics methods and descriptions

DrawPie(*ByVal* p As Pen, *ByVal* x *As Integer*, *ByVal* y *As Integer*, _
   ByVal width *As Integer*, *ByVal* height *As Integer*, _
   ByVal startAngle *As Integer*, *ByVal* sweepAngle *As Integer*)
Draws a pie section of an ellipse beginning from angle startAngle (in degrees) and sweeping sweepAngle degrees. The ellipse is defined by a bounding rectangle of width, height and upper-left corner (x,y). The Pen determines the color, border width and style of the arc.

FillPie(*ByVal* b As Brush, *ByVal* x *As Integer*, *ByVal* y *As Integer*, _
   ByVal width *As Integer*, *ByVal* height *As Integer*, _
   ByVal startAngle *As Integer*, *ByVal* sweepAngle *As Integer*)
Functions similarly to DrawPie, except draws a solid arc (i.e., a sector). The Brush determines the fill pattern for the solid arc.

Fig. 17.17 | Graphics methods for drawing arcs. (Part 2 of 2.)

```
 1    ' Fig. 17.18: FrmDrawingArcs.vb
 2    ' Drawing various arcs on a Form.
 3    Public Class FrmDrawArcs
 4       ' draw arcs
 5       Private Sub FrmDrawArcs_Paint(ByVal sender As Object, _
 6          ByVal e As System.Windows.Forms.PaintEventArgs) Handles Me.Paint
 7          ' get graphics object
 8          Dim graphicsObject As Graphics = e.Graphics
 9          Dim rectangle1 As New Rectangle(15, 35, 80, 80)
10          Dim brush1 As New SolidBrush(Color.Firebrick)
11          Dim pen1 As New Pen(brush1, 1)
12          Dim brush2 As New SolidBrush(Color.DarkBlue)
13          Dim pen2 As New Pen(brush2, 1)
14
15          ' start at 0 and sweep 360 degrees
16          graphicsObject.DrawRectangle(pen1, rectangle1)
17          graphicsObject.DrawArc(pen2, rectangle1, 0, 360)
18
19          ' start at 0 and sweep 110 degrees
20          rectangle1.Location = New Point(100, 35)
21          graphicsObject.DrawRectangle(pen1, rectangle1)
22          graphicsObject.DrawArc(pen2, rectangle1, 0, 110)
23
24          ' start at 0 and sweep -270 degrees
25          rectangle1.Location = New Point(185, 35)
26          graphicsObject.DrawRectangle(pen1, rectangle1)
27          graphicsObject.DrawArc(pen2, rectangle1, 0, -270)
28
29          ' start at 0 and sweep 360 degrees
30          rectangle1.Location = New Point(15, 120)
31          rectangle1.Size = New Size(80, 40)
32          graphicsObject.DrawRectangle(pen1, rectangle1)
33          graphicsObject.FillPie(brush2, rectangle1, 0, 360)
34
```

Fig. 17.18 | Drawing various arcs on a Form. (Part 1 of 2.)

```
35            ' start at 270 and sweep -90 degrees
36            rectangle1.Location = New Point(100, 120)
37            graphicsObject.DrawRectangle(pen1, rectangle1)
38            graphicsObject.FillPie(brush2, rectangle1, 270, -90)
39
40            ' start at 0 and sweep -270 degrees
41            rectangle1.Location = New Point(185, 120)
42            graphicsObject.DrawRectangle(pen1, rectangle1)
43            graphicsObject.FillPie(brush2, rectangle1, 0, -270)
44      End Sub ' FrmDrawArcs_Paint
45  End Class ' FrmDrawArcs
```

Fig. 17.18 | Drawing various arcs on a Form. (Part 2 of 2.)

Lines 9–13 create the objects that we need to draw arcs—a Graphics object, a Rectangle, SolidBrushes and Pens. Lines 16–17 then draw a rectangle and an arc inside the rectangle. The arc sweeps 360 degrees, forming a circle. Line 20 changes the location of the Rectangle by setting its Location property to a new Point. The Point constructor takes as arguments the *x*- and *y*-coordinates of the new point. The Location property determines the upper-left corner of the Rectangle. After drawing the rectangle, the program draws an arc that starts at 0 degrees and sweeps 110 degrees. Because the angles increase in a clockwise direction, the arc sweeps downward. Lines 25–27 perform similar functions, except that the specified arc sweeps –270 degrees. The Size property of a Rectangle determines the arc's height and width.

Line 31 sets the Size property to a new Size object, which changes the size of the rectangle. The remainder of the program is similar to the portions described above, except that a SolidBrush is used with method FillPie. The resulting arcs, which are filled, can be seen in the bottom half of the sample output (Fig. 17.18).

17.8 Drawing Polygons and Polylines

Polygons are multisided shapes. There are several Graphics methods used to draw polygons—*DrawLines* draws a series of connected lines, *DrawPolygon* draws a closed polygon and *FillPolygon* draws a solid polygon. These methods are described in Fig. 17.19. The program in Fig. 17.20 allows users to draw polygons and connected lines via the methods listed in Fig. 17.19.

Method	Description
DrawLines	Draws a series of connected lines. The coordinates of each point are specified in an array of Point objects. If the last point is different from the first point, the figure is not closed.
DrawPolygon	Draws a polygon. The coordinates of each point are specified in an array of Point objects. If the last point is different from the first point, those two points are connected to close the polygon.
FillPolygon	Draws a solid polygon. The coordinates of each point are specified in an array of Point objects. If the last point is different from the first point, those two points are connected to close the polygon.

Fig. 17.19 | Graphics methods for drawing polygons.

```
1   ' Fig. 17.20: FrmDrawPolygons.vb
2   ' Demonstrating polygons.
3   Public Class FrmDrawPolygons
4      ' contains list of polygon vertices
5      Private points As New ArrayList()
6
7      ' initialize default pen and brush
8      Private pen As New Pen(Color.DarkBlue)
9      Private brush As New SolidBrush(Color.DarkBlue)
10
11     ' draw panel mouse down event handler
12     Private Sub pnlDraw_MouseDown(ByVal sender As Object, _
13        ByVal e As System.Windows.Forms.MouseEventArgs) _
14        Handles pnlDraw.MouseDown
15        ' add mouse position to vertex list
16        points.Add(New Point(e.X, e.Y))
17        pnlDraw.Invalidate() ' refresh panel
18     End Sub ' FrmDrawPolygons_MouseDown
19
20     ' draw panel Paint event handler
21     Private Sub pnlDraw_Paint(ByVal sender As Object, _
22        ByVal e As System.Windows.Forms.PaintEventArgs) _
23        Handles pnlDraw.Paint
24        ' get graphics object for panel
25        Dim graphicsObject As Graphics = e.Graphics
26
27        ' if arraylist has 2 or more points, display shape
28        If points.Count > 1 Then
29           ' get array for use in drawing functions
30           Dim pointArray As Point() = _
31              CType(points.ToArray(points(0).GetType()), Point())
32
```

Fig. 17.20 | Polygon-drawing demonstration. (Part 1 of 3.)

```vbnet
33              If radLineOption.Checked Then
34                  graphicsObject.DrawLines(pen, pointArray)
35              ElseIf radPolygonOption.Checked Then
36                  graphicsObject.DrawPolygon(pen, pointArray)
37              ElseIf radFilledPolygonOption.Checked Then
38                  graphicsObject.FillPolygon(brush, pointArray)
39              End If
40          End If
41      End Sub ' pnlDraw_Paint
42
43      ' clear all points in the polygon
44      Private Sub btnClear_Click(ByVal sender As System.Object, _
45          ByVal e As System.EventArgs) Handles btnClear.Click
46          points.Clear() ' remove points
47          pnlDraw.Invalidate() ' refresh panel
48      End Sub ' btnClear_Click
49
50      ' change pen and brush colors
51      Private Sub btnColor_Click(ByVal sender As System.Object, _
52          ByVal e As System.EventArgs) Handles btnColor.Click
53          ' create new color dialog
54          Dim dialogColor As New ColorDialog()
55
56          ' show dialog and obtain result
57          Dim result As DialogResult = dialogColor.ShowDialog()
58
59          ' return if user cancels
60          If result = Windows.Forms.DialogResult.Cancel Then
61              Return
62          End If
63
64          pen.Color = dialogColor.Color ' set pen to color
65          brush.Color = dialogColor.Color ' set brush
66          pnlDraw.Invalidate() ' refresh panel
67      End Sub ' btnColor_Click
68
69      ' cause Paint event
70      Private Sub radLineOption_CheckedChanged( _
71          ByVal sender As System.Object, ByVal e As System.EventArgs) _
72          Handles radLineOption.CheckedChanged
73
74          pnlDraw.Invalidate() ' refresh panel
75      End Sub ' radLineOption
76
77      ' cause Paint event
78      Private Sub radPolygonOption_CheckedChanged( _
79          ByVal sender As System.Object, ByVal e As System.EventArgs) _
80          Handles radPolygonOption.CheckedChanged
81
82          pnlDraw.Invalidate() ' refresh panel
83      End Sub ' radPolygonOption
84
```

Fig. 17.20 | Polygon-drawing demonstration. (Part 2 of 3.)

```
85          ' cause Paint event
86       Private Sub radFilledPolygonOption_CheckedChanged( _
87          ByVal sender As System.Object, ByVal e As System.EventArgs) _
88          Handles radFilledPolygonOption.CheckedChanged
89
90          pnlDraw.Invalidate() ' refresh panel
91       End Sub ' radFilledPolygonOption
92    End Class ' FrmDrawPolygons
```

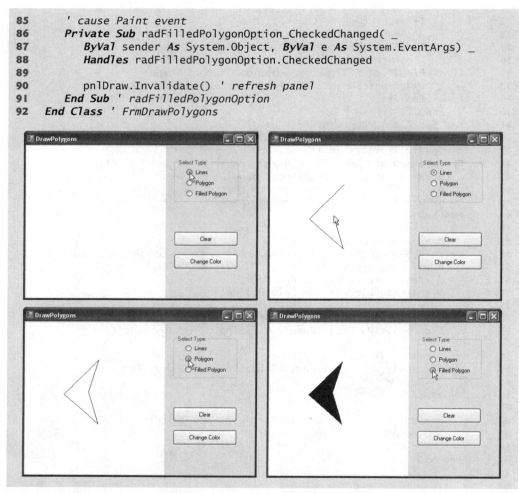

Fig. 17.20 | Polygon-drawing demonstration. (Part 3 of 3.)

To allow the user to specify a variable number of points, line 5 declares *ArrayList* points as a container for our Point objects. An ArrayList is similar to an array, but an ArrayList can grow dynamically to accommodate more elements. Lines 8–9 declare the Pen and Brush used to color our shapes. The MouseDown event handler (lines 12–18) for pnlDraw stores mouse-click locations in points with ArrayList method *Add* (line 16). The event handler then calls method Invalidate of pnlDraw (line 17) to ensure that the panel refreshes to accommodate the new point. Method pnlDraw_Paint (lines 21–41) handles the Panel's Paint event. It obtains the Panel's Graphics object (line 25) and, if the ArrayList points contains two or more Points (line 28), displays the polygon with the method the user selected via the GUI radio buttons (lines 33–39). In lines 30–31, we extract an array from the ArrayList via method *ToArray*. Method ToArray can take a single argument to determine the type of the returned array; we obtain the type from the first element in the ArrayList by calling the element's GetType method.

Note that line 31 uses Visual Basic's ***CType*** function to convert the Object array returned by ToArray into an array of type Point. This is required because implicit conversions are not allowed if **Option Strict** is turned on (as is the case in this chapter). A conversion performed with the CType function is also known as a ***cast operation***.

Method btnClear_Click (lines 44–48) handles the **Clear** button's Click event by calling ArrayList method ***Clear*** (causing the old list to be erased) and refreshing the display. Event handler btnColor_Click (51–67) allows the user to select a new drawing color with a ColorDialog, using the techniques demonstrated in Fig. 17.7. Lines 70–91 define the event handlers for each radio button's CheckedChanged event. Each method invalidates pnlDraw to ensure that the panel is repainted to reflect the selected shape type.

17.9 **Advanced Graphics Capabilities**

The FCL offers many other graphics capabilities. The Brush hierarchy, for example, also includes ***HatchBrush***, ***LinearGradientBrush***, ***PathGradientBrush*** and ***TextureBrush***.

Gradients, Line Styles and Fill Patterns

The program in Fig. 17.21 demonstrates several graphics features, such as dashed lines, thick lines and the ability to fill shapes with various patterns. These represent just a few of the additional capabilities of the System.Drawing namespace.

Lines 7–73 define the DrawShapesForm Paint event handler. Lines 14–15 create a LinearGradientBrush (namespace System.Drawing.Drawing2D) object named linearBrush to enable users to draw with a color gradient. The LinearGradientBrush used in this example takes four arguments—a Rectangle, two Colors and a member of enumeration LinearGradientMode. Linear gradients are defined along a line that determines the gradient endpoints. This line can be specified either by the starting and ending points or by the diagonal of a rectangle. The first argument, Rectangle drawArea1, represents the endpoints of the linear gradient—the upper-left corner is the starting point, and the bottom-right corner is the ending point. The second and third arguments specify the colors the gradient will use. In this case, the color of the ellipse will gradually change from Color.Blue to Color.Yellow. The last argument, a type from the enumeration ***Linear-GradientMode***, specifies the linear gradient's direction. In our case, we use ***LinearGradientMode.ForwardDiagonal***, which creates a gradient from the upper-left to the lower-right corner. We then use Graphics method FillEllipse in line 18 to draw an ellipse with linearBrush; the color gradually changes from blue to yellow, as described above.

```
1    ' Fig. 17.21: FrmDrawShapes.vb
2    ' Drawing various shapes on a Form.
3    Imports System.Drawing.Drawing2D
4
5    Public Class FrmDrawShapes
6       ' draw various shapes on Form
7       Private Sub FrmDrawShapes_Paint(ByVal sender As Object, _
8          ByVal e As System.Windows.Forms.PaintEventArgs) Handles Me.Paint
9          ' references to object we will use
10         Dim graphicsObject As Graphics = e.Graphics
11
```

Fig. 17.21 | Shapes drawn on a form. (Part 1 of 3.)

```vb
12          ' ellipse rectangle and gradient brush
13          Dim drawArea1 As New Rectangle(5, 35, 30, 100)
14          Dim linearBrush As New LinearGradientBrush(drawArea1, Color.Blue, _
15              Color.Yellow, LinearGradientMode.ForwardDiagonal)
16
17          ' draw ellipse filled with a blue-yellow gradient
18          graphicsObject.FillEllipse(linearBrush, 5, 30, 65, 100)
19
20          ' pen and location for red outline rectangle
21          Dim thickRedPen As New Pen(Color.Red, 10)
22          Dim drawArea2 As New Rectangle(80, 30, 65, 100)
23
24          ' draw thick rectangle outline in red
25          graphicsObject.DrawRectangle(thickRedPen, drawArea2)
26
27          ' bitmap texture
28          Dim textureBitmap As New Bitmap(10, 10)
29
30          ' get bitmap graphics
31          Dim graphicsObject2 As Graphics = Graphics.FromImage(textureBitmap)
32
33          ' brush and pen used throughout program
34          Dim solidColorBrush As New SolidBrush(Color.Red)
35          Dim coloredPen As New Pen(solidColorBrush)
36
37          ' fill textureBitmap with yellow
38          solidColorBrush.Color = Color.Yellow
39          graphicsObject2.FillRectangle(solidColorBrush, 0, 0, 10, 10)
40
41          ' draw small black rectangle in textureBitmap
42          coloredPen.Color = Color.Black
43          graphicsObject2.DrawRectangle(coloredPen, 1, 1, 6, 6)
44
45          ' draw small blue rectangle in textureBitmap
46          solidColorBrush.Color = Color.Blue
47          graphicsObject2.FillRectangle(solidColorBrush, 1, 1, 3, 3)
48
49          ' draw small red square in textureBitmap
50          solidColorBrush.Color = Color.Red
51          graphicsObject2.FillRectangle(solidColorBrush, 4, 4, 3, 3)
52
53          ' create textured brush and
54          ' display textured rectangle
55          Dim texturedBrush As New TextureBrush(textureBitmap)
56          graphicsObject.FillRectangle(texturedBrush, 155, 30, 75, 100)
57
58          ' draw pie-shaped arc in white
59          coloredPen.Color = Color.White
60          coloredPen.Width = 6
61          graphicsObject.DrawPie(coloredPen, 240, 30, 75, 100, 0, 270)
62
63          ' draw lines in green and yellow
64          coloredPen.Color = Color.Green
```

Fig. 17.21 | Shapes drawn on a form. (Part 2 of 3.)

```
65          coloredPen.Width = 5
66          graphicsObject.DrawLine(coloredPen, 395, 30, 320, 150)
67
68          ' draw a rounded, dashed yellow line
69          coloredPen.Color = Color.Yellow
70          coloredPen.DashCap = DashCap.Round
71          coloredPen.DashStyle = DashStyle.Dash
72          graphicsObject.DrawLine(coloredPen, 320, 30, 395, 150)
73     End Sub ' FrmDrawShapes_Paint
74 End Class ' FrmDrawShapes
```

Fig. 17.21 | Shapes drawn on a form. (Part 3 of 3.)

In line 21, we create Pen object thickRedPen. We pass to thickRedPen's constructor Color.Red and Integer argument 10, indicating that we want thickRedPen to draw red lines that are 10 pixels wide.

Line 28 creates a new *Bitmap* image, which initially is empty. Class Bitmap can produce images in color and gray scale; this particular Bitmap is 10 pixels wide and 10 pixels tall. Method *FromImage* (line 31) is a Shared member of class Graphics and retrieves the Graphics object associated with an Image, which may be used to draw on an image. Lines 38–51 draw on the Bitmap a pattern consisting of black, blue, red and yellow rectangles and lines. A TextureBrush is a brush that fills the interior of a shape with an image rather than a solid color. In lines 55–56, TextureBrush object textureBrush fills a rectangle with our Bitmap. The TextureBrush constructor used in line 55 takes as an argument an image that defines its texture.

Next, we draw a pie-shaped arc with a thick white line. Lines 59–60 set coloredPen's color to White and modify its width to be 6 pixels. We then draw the pie on the form by specifying the Pen, the x-coordinate, y-coordinate, the width and height of the bounding rectangle and the start and sweep angles.

Lines 64–66 draw a 5-pixel-wide green line. Finally, lines 70–71 use enumerations *DashCap* and *DashStyle* (namespace System.Drawing.Drawing2D) to specify settings for a dashed line. Line 70 sets the *DashCap* property of coloredPen (not to be confused with the DashCap enumeration) to a member of the DashCap enumeration. The DashCap enumeration specifies the styles for the start and end of a dashed line. In this case, we want both ends of the dashed line to be rounded, so we use *DashCap.Round*. Line 71 sets the *DashStyle* property of coloredPen (not to be confused with the DashStyle enumeration) to *DashStyle.Dash*, indicating that we want our line to consist entirely of dashes.

General Paths
Our next example demonstrates a *general path*. A general path is a shape constructed from straight lines and complex curves. An object of class *GraphicsPath* (namespace Sys-

tem.Drawing.Drawing2D) represents a general path. The GraphicsPath class provides functionality that enables the creation of complex shapes from vector-based primitive graphics objects. A GraphicsPath object consists of figures defined by simple shapes. The start point of each vector-graphics object (such as a line or an arc) added to the path is connected by a straight line to the endpoint of the previous object. When called, the **Close-Figure** method attaches the final vector-graphic object endpoint to the initial starting point for the current figure by a straight line, then starts a new figure. Method StartFigure begins a new figure within the path without closing the previous figure.

The program in Fig. 17.22 draws general paths in the shape of five-pointed stars. Lines 15–16 define two Integer arrays, representing the x- and y-coordinates of the points in the star, and line 19 defines GraphicsPath object star. A loop (lines 22–25) then creates lines to connect the points of the star and adds these lines to star. We use Graphics-Path method **AddLine** to append a line to the shape. The arguments of AddLine specify the coordinates for the line's endpoints; each new call to AddLine adds a line from the previous point to the current point. Line 27 uses GraphicsPath method CloseFigure to complete the shape.

```vb
1    ' Fig. 17.22: FrmDrawStars.vb
2    ' Using paths to draw stars on the form.
3    Imports System.Drawing.Drawing2D
4
5    Public Class FrmDrawStars
6       ' create path and draw stars along it
7       Private Sub FrmDrawStars_Paint(ByVal sender As Object, _
8          ByVal e As System.Windows.Forms.PaintEventArgs) Handles Me.Paint
9
10         Dim graphicsObject As Graphics = e.Graphics
11         Dim random As New Random()
12         Dim brush As New SolidBrush(Color.DarkMagenta)
13
14         ' x and y points of the path
15         Dim xPoints As Integer() = {55, 67, 109, 73, 83, 55, 27, 37, 1, 43}
16         Dim yPoints As Integer() = {0, 36, 36, 54, 96, 72, 96, 54, 36, 36}
17
18         ' create graphics path for star
19         Dim star As New GraphicsPath()
20
21         ' create star from series of points
22         For i As Integer = 0 To 8 Step 2
23            star.AddLine(xPoints(i), yPoints(i), _
24               xPoints(i + 1), yPoints(i + 1))
25         Next
26
27         star.CloseFigure() ' close the shape
28
29         ' translate the origin to (150, 150)
30         graphicsObject.TranslateTransform(150, 150)
31
```

Fig. 17.22 | Paths used to draw stars on a form. (Part 1 of 2.)

```
32          ' rotate the origin and draw stars in random colors
33          For i As Integer = 1 To 18
34              graphicsObject.RotateTransform(20)
35
36              brush.Color = Color.FromArgb(random.Next(200, 255), _
37                  random.Next(255), random.Next(255), random.Next(255))
38
39              graphicsObject.FillPath(brush, star)
40          Next
41      End Sub ' FrmDrawStars_Paint
42  End Class ' FrmDrawStars
```

Fig. 17.22 | Paths used to draw stars on a form. (Part 2 of 2.)

Line 30 sets the origin of the Graphics object. The arguments to method TranslateTransform indicate that the origin should be translated to the coordinates (150, 150). The loop in lines 33–40 draws the star 18 times, rotating it around the origin. Line 34 uses Graphics method *RotateTransform* to move to the next position on the form; the argument specifies the rotation angle in degrees. Graphics method FillPath (line 39) then draws a filled version of the star with the Brush created in lines 36–37. The application determines the SolidBrush's color randomly, using Random method Next.

17.10 Introduction to Multimedia

The FCL offers many convenient ways to include images and animations in programs. People who entered the computing field decades ago used computers primarily to perform arithmetic calculations. As the discipline evolves, we are realizing the importance of computers' data-manipulation capabilities. We are seeing many exciting new three-dimensional applications. Multimedia programming is an entertaining and innovative field, but one that presents many challenges

Multimedia applications demand extraordinary computing power. Today's ultrafast processors make multimedia-based applications commonplace. As the market for multimedia explodes, users are purchasing the faster processors, larger memories and wider communications bandwidths needed to support multimedia applications. This benefits the computer and communications industries, which provide the hardware, software and services fueling the multimedia revolution.

In the remaining sections of this chapter, we introduce basic image processing and other multimedia features and capabilities. Section 17.11 discusses how to load, display and scale images; Section 17.12 demonstrates image animation; Section 17.13 presents the video capabilities of the Windows Media Player control; and Section 17.14 explores Microsoft Agent technology.

17.11 Loading, Displaying and Scaling Images

Visual Basic's multimedia capabilities include graphics, images, animations and video. Previous sections demonstrated vector-graphics capabilities; this section presents image manipulation. The application in Fig. 17.23 loads an Image (System.Drawing namespace), then allows the user to scale the Image to a specified width and height.

Line 4 declares Image variable image. Line 11 in the Form's Load event handler uses Shared Image method **FromFile** to load an image from a file on disk. Line 12 uses the Form's **CreateGraphics** method to create a Graphics object for drawing on the Form. Method CreateGraphics is inherited from class Control. When you click the **Set Button**,

```
1   ' Fig. 17.23: FrmDisplayLogo.vb
2   ' Displaying and resizing an image
3   Public Class FrmDisplayLogo
4      Private imageValue As Image
5      Private graphicsObject As Graphics
6
7      ' load image and obtain Graphics object
8      Private Sub FrmDisplayLogo_Load(ByVal sender As Object, _
9         ByVal e As System.EventArgs) Handles Me.Load
10
11        imageValue = Image.FromFile("images\Logo.gif")
12        graphicsObject = Me.CreateGraphics()
13     End Sub ' FrmDisplayLogo_Load
14
15     ' get new width and height of image, then redraw it
16     Private Sub btnSet_Click(ByVal sender As System.Object, _
17        ByVal e As System.EventArgs) Handles btnSet.Click
18        ' get user input
19        Dim Width As Integer = Convert.ToInt32(widthTextBox.Text)
20        Dim Height As Integer = Convert.ToInt32(heightTextBox.Text)
21
22        ' if dimensions specified are too large
23        ' display problem
24        If Width > 375 Or Height > 225 Then
25           MessageBox.Show(" Height or Width too large")
26           Return
27        End If
28
29        ' clear the Form then draw the image
30        graphicsObject.Clear(Me.BackColor)
31        graphicsObject.DrawImage(imageValue, 5, 5, Width, Height)
32     End Sub ' btnSet_Click
33  End Class ' FrmDisplayLogo
```

Fig. 17.23 | Image resizing. (Part 1 of 2.)

Fig. 17.23 | Image resizing. (Part 2 of 2.)

lines 24–27 validate the width and height to ensure that they are not too large. If the parameters are valid, line 30 calls Graphics method *Clear* to paint the entire Form in the current background color. Line 31 calls Graphics method *DrawImage*, passing as arguments the image to draw, the x-coordinate of the image's upper-left corner, the y-coordinate of the image's upper-left corner, the width of the image and the height of the image. If the width and height do not correspond to the image's original dimensions, the image is scaled to fit the new width and height.

17.12 Animating a Series of Images

The next example animates a series of images stored in an array. The application uses the same technique to load and display Images as shown in Fig. 17.23.

The animation in Fig. 17.24 uses a PictureBox, which contains the images that we animate. We use a Timer to cycle through the images and display a new image every 50 milliseconds. Variable count keeps track of the current image number and increases by 1 every time we display a new image. The array includes 30 images (numbered 0–29); when the application reaches image 29, it returns to image 0. The 30 images are located in the images folder inside the project's bin/Debug and bin/Release directories.

```
1    ' Fig. 17.24: FrmLogoAnimator.vb
2    ' Program that animates a series of images.
3    Public Class FrmLogoAnimator
4       Private images(29) As Image
5       Private count As Integer = -1
6
7       ' load images
8       Private Sub FrmLogoAnimator_Load(ByVal sender As Object, _
9          ByVal e As System.EventArgs) Handles Me.Load
10
11         For i As Integer = 0 To images.Length - 1
12            images(i) = Image.FromFile("images\deitel" & i & ".gif")
13         Next
14
15         picLogo.Image = images(0) ' display first image
16
17          ' set PictureBox to be the same size as Image
18         picLogo.Size = picLogo.Image.Size
19       End Sub ' FrmLogoAnimator_Load
20
21       ' display new image every 50 milliseconds
22       Private Sub timer_Tick(ByVal sender As System.Object, _
23          ByVal e As System.EventArgs) Handles timer.Tick
24
25         count = (count + 1) Mod images.Length ' increment counter
26         picLogo.Image = images(count) ' display next image
27       End Sub ' timer_Tick
28    End Class ' FrmLogoAnimator
```

Fig. 17.24 | Animation of a series of images.

Lines 11–13 load each of 30 images and place them in an array of Images (declared in line 4). Line 15 places the first image in the PictureBox. Line 18 modifies the size of the PictureBox so that it is equal to the size of the Image it is displaying. The event handler for timer's Tick event (line 22–27) responds to each event by displaying the next image from the array.

Performance Tip 17.2

It is more efficient to load an animation's frames as one image than to load each image separately. (A painting program, such as Adobe Photoshop® or Jasc® Paint Shop Pro™, can be used to combine the animation's frames into one image.) If the images are being loaded separately from the Web, each loaded image requires a separate connection to the site on which the images are stored; this process can result in poor performance.

Chess Example

The following chess example demonstrates techniques for two-dimensional *collision detection*, selecting single frames from a multiframe image, and *regional invalidation*, refreshing only the parts of the screen that have changed, to increase performance. Two-dimensional collision detection enables a program to detect whether two shapes overlap or whether a point is contained within a shape. In the next example, we demonstrate the simplest form of collision detection, which determines whether a point (the mouse-click location) is contained within a rectangle (a chess-piece image).

Class `ChessPiece` (Fig. 17.25) represents the individual chess pieces. Lines 5–12 define a `Public` enumeration of constants that identify each chess-piece type. The constants also serve to identify the location of each piece in the chess-piece image file. `Rectangle` object `targetRectangle` (line 18) identifies the image location on the chessboard. The x and y properties of the rectangle are assigned in the `ChessPiece` constructor, and all chess-piece images have a width and height of 75 pixels.

```vb
1    ' Fig. 17.25 : ChessPiece.cs
2    ' Class that represents chess piece attributes.
3    Public Class ChessPiece
4       ' define chess-piece type constants
5       Public Enum Types
6          KING
7          QUEEN
8          BISHOP
9          KNIGHT
10         ROOK
11         PAWN
12      End Enum ' Types
13
14      Private currentType As Integer ' this object's type
15      Private pieceImage As Bitmap ' this object's image
16
17      ' default display location
18      Private targetRectangle As New Rectangle(0, 0, 75, 75)
19
20      ' constructor
21      Public Sub New(ByVal type As Integer, ByVal xLocation As Integer, _
22         ByVal yLocation As Integer, ByVal sourceImage As Bitmap)
23
24         currentType = type ' set current type
25         targetRectangle.X = xLocation ' set current x location
26         targetRectangle.Y = yLocation ' set current y location
27
28         ' obtain pieceImage from section of sourceImage
29         pieceImage = sourceImage.Clone( _
30            New Rectangle(type * 75, 0, 75, 75), _
31            System.Drawing.Imaging.PixelFormat.DontCare)
32      End Sub ' New
33
```

Fig. 17.25 | Class that represents chess-piece attributes. (Part 1 of 2.)

```
34        ' draw chess piece
35        Public Sub Draw(ByVal graphicsObject As Graphics)
36           graphicsObject.DrawImage(pieceImage, targetRectangle)
37        End Sub ' end method Draw
38
39        ' obtain this piece's location rectangle
40        Public Function GetBounds() As Rectangle
41           Return targetRectangle
42        End Function ' end method GetBounds
43
44        ' set this piece's location
45        Public Sub SetLocation( _
46           ByVal xLocation As Integer, ByVal yLocation As Integer)
47
48           targetRectangle.X = xLocation
49           targetRectangle.Y = yLocation
50        End Sub ' end method SetLocation
51     End Class ' ChessPiece
```

Fig. 17.25 | Class that represents chess-piece attributes. (Part 2 of 2.)

The ChessPiece constructor (lines 21–32) receives the chess-piece type, its x and y location and the Bitmap containing all chess-piece images. Rather than loading the chess-piece image within the class, we allow the calling class to pass the image. This increases the flexibility of the class by allowing the user to change images. Lines 29–31 extract a sub-image that contains only the current piece's bitmap data. Our chess-piece images are defined in a specific manner: One image contains six chess-piece images, each defined within a 75-pixel block, resulting in a total image size of 450-by-75. We obtain a single image via Bitmap's Clone method, which allows us to specify a rectangle-image location and the desired pixel format. The location is a 75-by-75 pixel block with its upper-left corner x equal to 75 * type, and the corresponding y equal to 0. For the pixel format, we specify constant DontCare, causing the format to remain unchanged.

Method Draw (lines 35–37) causes the ChessPiece to draw pieceImage in the targetRectangle using the Graphics object passed as Draw's argument. Method GetBounds (lines 40–52) returns the targetRectangle object for use in collision detection, and method SetLocation (lines 45–50) allows the calling class to specify a new piece location.

Class FrmChessGame (Fig. 17.26) defines the game and graphics code for our chess game. Lines 4–8 define instance variables the program requires. ArrayList chessTile (line 4) stores the board tile images. ArrayList chessPieces (line 5) stores all active ChessPiece objects, and Integer selectedIndex (line 6) identifies the index in chessPieces of the currently selected piece. The board (line 7) is an 8-by-8, two-dimensional Integer array corresponding to the squares of a chess board. Each board element is an integer from 0 to 3 that corresponds to an index in chessTile and is used to specify the chessboard-square image. Const TILESIZE (line 8) defines the size of each tile in pixels.

The chess game GUI consists of Form ChessGame, the area in which we draw the tiles; Panel pieceBox, the area in which we draw the pieces (note that pieceBox's background color is set to "transparent"); and a Menu that allows the user to begin a new game. Although the pieces and tiles could have been drawn on the same form, doing so would decrease performance. We would be forced to refresh the board and all the pieces every time we refreshed the control.

```vb
1    ' Fig. 17.26: FrmChessGame.vb
2    ' Chess Game graphics code.
3    Public Class FrmChessGame
4        Private chessTile As New ArrayList() ' for tile images
5        Private chessPieces As New ArrayList() ' for chess pieces
6        Private selectedIndex As Integer = -1 ' index for selected piece
7        Private board(,) As Integer = New Integer(7, 7) {} ' board array
8        Private Const TILESIZE As Integer = 75 ' chess tile size in pixels
9
10       ' load tile bitmaps and reset game
11       Private Sub FrmChessGame_Load(ByVal sender As Object, _
12           ByVal e As System.EventArgs) Handles Me.Load
13           ' load chess board tiles
14           chessTile.Add(Bitmap.FromFile("images\lightTile1.png"))
15           chessTile.Add(Bitmap.FromFile("images\lightTile2.png"))
16           chessTile.Add(Bitmap.FromFile("images\darkTile1.png"))
17           chessTile.Add(Bitmap.FromFile("images\darkTile2.png"))
18
19           ResetBoard() ' initialize board
20           Invalidate() ' refresh form
21       End Sub ' FrmChessGame_Load
22
23       ' initialize pieces to start and rebuild board
24       Private Sub ResetBoard()
25           Dim current As Integer = -1
26           Dim piece As ChessPiece
27           Dim random As New Random()
28           Dim light As Boolean = False
29           Dim type As Integer
30
31           chessPieces.Clear() ' ensure empty arraylist
32
33           ' load whitepieces image
34           Dim whitePieces As Bitmap = _
35               CType(Image.FromFile("images\whitePieces.png"), Bitmap)
36
37           ' load blackpieces image
38           Dim blackPieces As Bitmap = _
39               CType(Image.FromFile("images\blackPieces.png"), Bitmap)
40
41           ' set whitepieces to be drawn first
42           Dim selected As Bitmap = whitePieces
43
44           ' traverse board rows in outer loop
45           For row As Integer = 0 To board.GetUpperBound(0)
46               ' if at bottom rows, set to black pieces images
47               If row > 5 Then
48                   selected = blackPieces
49               End If
```

Fig. 17.26 | Chess-game code. (Part 1 of 6.)

```
50
51              ' traverse board columns in inner loop
52              For column As Integer = 0 To board.GetUpperBound(1)
53                 ' if first or last row, organize pieces
54                 If row = 0 OrElse row = 7 Then
55                    Select Case column
56                       Case 0, 7 ' set current piece to rook
57                          current = ChessPiece.Types.ROOK
58                       Case 1, 6 ' set current piece to knight
59                          current = ChessPiece.Types.KNIGHT
60                       Case 2, 5 ' set current piece to bishop
61                          current = ChessPiece.Types.BISHOP
62                       Case 3 ' set current piece to king
63                          current = ChessPiece.Types.KING
64                       Case 4 ' set current piece to queen
65                          current = ChessPiece.Types.QUEEN
66                    End Select
67
68                    ' create current piece at start position
69                    piece = New ChessPiece(current, _
70                       column * TILESIZE, row * TILESIZE, selected)
71
72                    chessPieces.Add(piece) ' add piece to arraylist
73                 End If
74
75                 ' if second or seventh row, organize pawns
76                 If row = 1 OrElse row = 6 Then
77                    piece = New ChessPiece(ChessPiece.Types.PAWN, _
78                       column * TILESIZE, row * TILESIZE, selected)
79                    chessPieces.Add(piece) ' add piece to arraylist
80                 End If
81
82                 type = random.Next(0, 2) ' determine board piece type
83
84                 If light Then ' set light tile
85                    board(row, column) = type
86                    light = False
87                 Else ' set dark tile
88                    board(row, column) = type + 2
89                    light = True
90                 End If
91              Next column
92
93           light = Not light ' account for new row tile color switch
94        Next row
95     End Sub ' ResetBoard
96
97     ' display board in form OnPaint event
98     Private Sub FrmChessGame_Paint(ByVal sender As Object, _
99        ByVal e As System.Windows.Forms.PaintEventArgs) Handles Me.Paint
100       Dim graphicsObject As Graphics = e.Graphics ' obtain graphics object
101       graphicsObject.TranslateTransform(0, 24) ' adjust origin
102
```

Fig. 17.26 | Chess-game code. (Part 2 of 6.)

```
103           For row As Integer = 0 To board.GetUpperBound(0)
104              For column As Integer = 0 To board.GetUpperBound(1)
105                 ' draw image specified in board array
106                 graphicsObject.DrawImage( _
107                    CType(chessTile(board(row, column)), Image), _
108                    New Point(TILESIZE * column, (TILESIZE * row)))
109              Next column
110           Next row
111        End Sub ' FrmChessGame_Paint
112
113        ' return index of piece that intersects point
114        ' optionally exclude a value
115        Private Function CheckBounds(ByVal pointValue As Point, _
116           ByVal exclude As Integer) As Integer
117           Dim rectangleValue As Rectangle ' current bounding rectangle
118
119           For i As Integer = 0 To chessPieces.Count - 1
120              ' get piece rectangle
121              rectangleValue = GetPiece(i).GetBounds()
122
123              ' check if rectangle contains point
124              If rectangleValue.Contains(pointValue) And i <> exclude Then
125                 Return i
126              End If
127           Next
128
129           Return -1
130        End Function ' CheckBounds
131
132        ' handle picBoard Paint event
133        Private Sub picBoard_Paint(ByVal sender As Object, _
134           ByVal e As System.Windows.Forms.PaintEventArgs) _
135           Handles picBoard.Paint
136           ' draw all pieces
137           For i As Integer = 0 To chessPieces.Count - 1
138              GetPiece(i).Draw(e.Graphics)
139           Next
140        End Sub ' picBoard_Paint
141
142        ' handle picBoard MouseDown event
143        Private Sub picBoard_MouseDown(ByVal sender As Object, _
144           ByVal e As System.Windows.Forms.MouseEventArgs) _
145           Handles picBoard.MouseDown
146           ' determine selected piece
147           selectedIndex = CheckBounds(New Point(e.X, e.Y), -1)
148        End Sub ' picBoard_MouseDown
149
150        ' if piece is selected, move it
151        Private Sub picBoard_MouseMove(ByVal sender As Object, _
152           ByVal e As System.Windows.Forms.MouseEventArgs) _
153           Handles picBoard.MouseMove
154
```

Fig. 17.26 | Chess-game code. (Part 3 of 6.)

```
155        If selectedIndex > -1 Then
156            Dim region As New Rectangle(e.X - TILESIZE * 2, _
157                e.Y - TILESIZE * 2, TILESIZE * 4, TILESIZE * 4)
158
159            ' set piece center to mouse
160            GetPiece(selectedIndex).SetLocation( _
161                e.X - TILESIZE \ 2, e.Y - TILESIZE \ 2)
162
163            picBoard.Invalidate(region) ' refresh region
164        End If
165    End Sub ' picBoard_MouseMove
166
167    ' on mouse up deselect piece and remove taken piece
168    Private Sub picBoard_MouseUp(ByVal sender As Object, _
169        ByVal e As System.Windows.Forms.MouseEventArgs) _
170        Handles picBoard.MouseUp
171
172        Dim remove As Integer = -1
173
174        ' if chess piece was selected
175        If selectedIndex > -1 Then
176            Dim current As New Point(e.X, e.Y)
177            Dim newPoint As New Point( _
178                current.X - (current.X Mod TILESIZE), _
179                current.Y - (current.Y Mod TILESIZE))
180
181            ' check bounds with point, exclude selected piece
182            remove = CheckBounds(current, selectedIndex)
183
184            ' snap piece into center of closest square
185            GetPiece(selectedIndex).SetLocation(newPoint.X, newPoint.Y)
186            selectedIndex = -1 ' deselect piece
187
188            ' remove taken piece
189            If remove > -1 Then
190                chessPieces.RemoveAt(remove)
191            End If
192        End If
193
194        picBoard.Invalidate() ' ensure artifact removal
195    End Sub ' picBoard_MouseUp
196
197    ' helper function to convert
198    ' ArrayList object to ChessPiece
199    Private Function GetPiece(ByVal i As Integer) As ChessPiece
200        Return CType(chessPieces(i), ChessPiece)
201    End Function ' GetPiece
202
203    ' handle NewGame menu option click
204    Private Sub newGameItem_Click(ByVal sender As System.Object, _
205        ByVal e As System.EventArgs) Handles newGameItem.Click
206
```

Fig. 17.26 | Chess-game code. (Part 4 of 6.)

```
207        ResetBoard() ' reinitialize board
208        Invalidate() ' refresh form
209     End Sub ' newGameItem_Click
210   End Class ' FrmChessGame
```

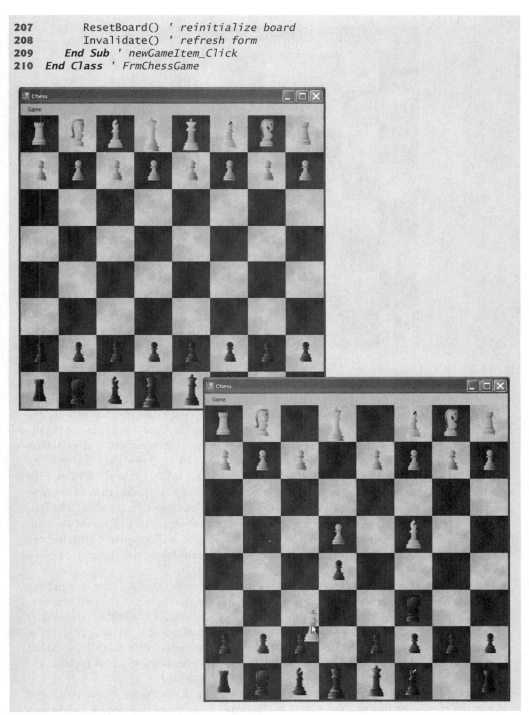

Fig. 17.26 | Chess-game code. (Part 5 of 6.)

Fig. 17.26 | Chess-game code. (Part 6 of 6.)

The ChessGame_Load event handler (lines 11–21) loads four tile images into chessTile—two light tiles and two dark tiles for variety. It then calls method ResetBoard to refresh the Form and begin the game. Method ResetBoard (lines 24–95) clears chessPieces, loads images for both the black and the white chess-piece sets and creates Bitmap selected to define the currently selected Bitmap set. Lines 45–94 loop through the board's 64 positions, setting the tile color and piece for each tile. Lines 47–49 cause the currently selected image to switch to the blackPieces after the fifth row. If the row counter is on the first or last row, lines 55–66 add a new piece to chessPieces. The type of the piece is based on the current column we are initializing. Pieces in chess are positioned in the following order, from left to right: rook, knight, bishop, queen, king, bishop, knight and rook. Lines 76–80 add a new pawn at the current location if the current row is second or seventh.

A chessboard is defined by alternating light and dark tiles across a row in a pattern where the color that starts each row is equal to the color of the last tile of the previous row. Lines 82–90 assign the current board-tile color to an element in the board array. Based on the alternating value of Boolean variable light and the results of the random operation in line 82, we assign an Integer to the board to determine the color of that tile—0 and 1 represent light tiles; 2 and 3 represent dark tiles. Line 93 inverts the value of light at the end of each row to maintain the staggered effect of a chessboard.

Method FrmChessGame_Paint (lines 98–111) handles the Form's Paint event and draws the tiles according to their values in the board array. Since the default height of a MenuStrip is 24 pixels, we use the *TranslateTransform* method of class Graphics to shift the origin of the Form down 24 pixels (line 101). This shift prevents the top row of tiles from being hidden behind the MenuStrip. Method picBoard_Paint (lines 133–140), which handles the Paint event for the picBoard Panel, iterates through each element of the chessPieces ArrayList and calls its Draw method.

The picBoard MouseDown event handler (lines 143–148) calls CheckBounds (declared in lines 115–130) with the location of the mouse to determine whether the user has selected a piece.

The picBoard MouseMove event handler (lines 151–165) moves the selected piece with the mouse. Lines 156–157 define a region of the Panel that spans two tiles in every direction from the pointer. As mentioned previously, Invalidate is slow. This means that the picBoard MouseMove event handler might be called several times before the Invalidate method completes. If a user working on a slow computer moves the mouse quickly, the application could leave behind *artifacts*. An artifact is any unintended visual abnormality in a graphical program. By causing the program to refresh a two-square rectangle, which should suffice in most cases, we achieve a significant performance enhancement over an entire component refresh during each MouseMove event. Lines 160–161 set the selected piece location to the mouse-cursor position, adjusting the location to center the image on the mouse. Line 163 invalidates the region defined in lines 156–157 so that it will be refreshed.

Lines 168–195 define the picBoard MouseUp event handler. If a piece has been selected, lines 175–192 determine the index in chessPieces of any piece collision, remove the collided piece, snap (align) the current piece to a valid location and deselect the piece. We check for piece collisions to allow the chess piece to "take" other chess pieces. Line 182 checks whether any piece (excluding the currently selected piece) is beneath the current mouse location. If a collision is detected, the returned piece index is assigned to remove. Line 185 determine the closest valid chess tile and "snaps" the selected piece to that location. If remove contains a positive value, line 190 removes the object at that index from the chessPieces ArrayList. Finally, the entire Panel is invalidated in line 194 to display the new piece location and remove any artifacts created during the move.

Method CheckBounds (lines 115–130) is a collision-detection helper method; it iterates through ArrayList chessPieces and returns the index of any piece's rectangle that contains the point passed to the method (the mouse location, in this example). CheckBounds uses Rectangle method Contains to determine whether a point is in the Rectangle. Method CheckBounds optionally can exclude a single piece index (to ignore the selected index in the picBoard MouseUp event handler, in this example).

Lines 199–201 define helper function GetPiece, which simplifies the conversion from objects in ArrayList chessPieces to ChessPiece types. Event handler newGameItem_Click (lines 204–209) handles the NewGame menu-item click event, calls RefreshBoard to reset the game and invalidates the entire form.

17.13 Windows Media Player

The *Windows Media Player control* enables an application to play video and sound in many *multimedia formats*. These include *MPEG (Motion Pictures Experts Group)* audio and video, *AVI (audio-video interleave)* video, *WAV (Windows wave-file format)* audio and *MIDI (Musical Instrument Digital Interface)* audio. Users can find pre-existing audio and video on the Internet, or they can create their own files, using available sound and graphics packages.

The application in Fig. 17.27 demonstrates the Windows Media Player control. To use this control, you must add the control to the **Toolbox**. First select **Tools > Choose Toolbox Items...** to display the **Choose Toolbox Items** dialog. Click the **COM components** tab, then scroll down and select the option **Windows Media Player**. Click the **OK** button to dismiss the dialog. The Windows Media Player control now appears at the bottom of the **Toolbox**.

The Windows Media Player control provides several buttons that allow the user to play the current file, pause, stop, play the previous file, rewind, forward and play the next file. The control also includes a volume control and trackbars to select a specific position in the media file.

```vb
1    ' Fig. 17.27: FrmMediaPlayer.vb
2    ' Windows Media Player control used to play media files.
3    Public Class FrmMediaPlayer
4       ' open new media file in Windows Media Player
5       Private Sub openItem_Click(ByVal sender As System.Object, _
6          ByVal e As System.EventArgs) Handles openItem.Click
7
8          openMediaFileDialog.ShowDialog()
9
10         ' load and play the media clip
11         player.URL = openMediaFileDialog.FileName
12      End Sub ' openItem_Click
13
14      ' exit program when exit menu item is clicked
15      Private Sub exitItem_Click(ByVal sender As System.Object, _
16         ByVal e As System.EventArgs) Handles exitItem.Click
17
18         Application.Exit()
19      End Sub ' exitItem_Click
20   End Class ' FrmMediaPlayer
```

Fig. 17.27 | Windows Media Player demonstration. (Part 1 of 2.)

Fig. 17.27 | Windows Media Player demonstration. (Part 2 of 2.)

Our application provides a **File** menu containing the **Open** and **Exit** menu items. When a user chooses **Open** from the **File** menu, event handler openItem_Click (lines 5–12) executes. An OpenFileDialog box displays (line 8) to allow the user to select a file. The program then sets the URL property of the player (the Windows Media Player control object of type *AxMediaPlayer*) to the name of the file chosen by the user. The URL property specifies the file that Windows Media Player is currently using.

The exitItem_Click event handler (lines 15–19) executes when the user selects **Exit** from the **File** menu. This event handler simply calls Application method Exit to terminate the application. We provide sample audio and video files in the directory that contains this example.

17.14 Microsoft Agent

Microsoft Agent is a technology used to add *interactive animated characters* to Windows applications or Web pages. Microsoft Agent characters can speak and respond to user input via speech recognition and synthesis. Microsoft employs its Agent technology in applications such as Word, Excel and PowerPoint. Agents in these programs aid users in finding answers to questions and in understanding how the applications function.

The Microsoft Agent control provides programmers with access to four predefined characters—*Genie* (a genie), *Merlin* (a wizard), *Peedy* (a parrot) and *Robby* (a robot). Each character has a unique set of animations that programmers can use in their applications to illustrate different points and functions. For instance, the Peedy character-animation set includes different flying animations, which the programmer might use to move Peedy on the screen. Microsoft provides basic information on Agent technology at

www.microsoft.com/msagent

Microsoft Agent technology enables users to interact with applications and Web pages through speech, the most natural form of human communication. To understand speech, the control uses a *speech-recognition engine*—an application that translates vocal sound input from a microphone to language that the computer understands. The Microsoft Agent control also uses a *text-to-speech engine*, which generates characters' spoken responses. A text-to-speech engine is an application that translates typed words into audio sound that users hear through headphones or speakers connected to a computer. Microsoft provides speech-recognition and text-to-speech engines for several languages at

> www.microsoft.com/msagent/downloads/user.asp

Programmers can even create their own animated characters with the help of the *Microsoft Agent Character Editor* and the *Microsoft Linguistic Sound Editing Tool*. These products are available free for download from

> www.microsoft.com/msagent/downloads/developer.asp

This section introduces the basic capabilities of the Microsoft Agent control. For complete details on downloading this control, visit

> www.microsoft.com/msagent/downloads/user.asp

The following example, Peedy's Pizza Palace, was developed by Microsoft to illustrate the capabilities of the Microsoft Agent control. Peedy's Pizza Palace is an online pizza shop where users can place their orders via voice input. The Peedy character interacts with users by helping them choose toppings and calculating the totals for their orders. You can view this example at

> www.microsoft.com/agent2/sdk/samples/html/peedypza.htm

To run the example, you must go to www.microsoft.com/msagent/downloads/user.asp and download and install the Peedy character file, a text-to-speech engine and a speech-recognition engine.

When the window opens, Peedy introduces himself (Fig. 17.28), and the words he speaks appear in a cartoon bubble above his head. Note that Peedy's animations correspond to the words he speaks.

Programmers can synchronize character animations with speech output to illustrate a point or to convey a character's mood. For instance, Fig. 17.29 depicts Peedy's *Pleased* animation. The Peedy character-animation set includes 85 different animations, each of which is unique to the Peedy character.

Look-and-Feel Observation 17.1

Agent characters remain on top of all active windows while a Microsoft Agent application is running. Their motions are not limited by the boundaries of the browser or the application window.

Peedy also responds to input from the keyboard and mouse. Figure 17.30 shows what happens when a user clicks Peedy with the mouse pointer. Peedy jumps up, ruffles his feathers and exclaims, "Hey, that tickles!" or "Be careful with that pointer!" Users can relocate Peedy on the screen by dragging him with the mouse. However, even when the user moves Peedy to a different part of the screen, he continues to perform his preset animations and location changes.

Bubble contains text equivalent to words Peedy speaks

Fig. 17.28 | Peedy introducing himself when the window opens.

Fig. 17.29 | Peedy's *Pleased* animation.

Pointer clicking
Peedy

Fig. 17.30 | Peedy's reaction when he is clicked.

Many location changes involve animations. For instance, Peedy can hop from one screen location to another, or he can fly (Fig. 17.31).

Once Peedy completes the ordering instructions, a tool tip appears beneath him indicating that he is listening for a voice command (Fig. 17.32). You can enter the type of pizza to order either by speaking the style name into a microphone or by clicking the radio button corresponding to your choice.

Fig. 17.31 | Peedy flying animation.

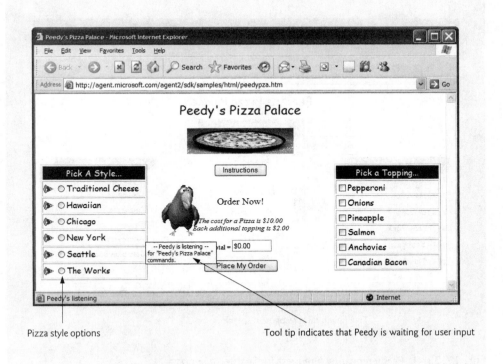

Fig. 17.32 | Peedy waiting for speech input.

If you choose speech input, a box appears below Peedy displaying the words that Peedy "heard" (i.e., the words translated to the program by the speech-recognition engine). Once he recognizes your input, Peedy gives you a description of the selected pizza. Figure 17.33 shows what happens when you choose **Seattle** as the pizza style.

Peedy then asks you to choose additional toppings. Again, you can either speak or use the mouse to make a selection. Checkboxes corresponding to toppings that come with the selected pizza style are checked for you. Figure 17.34 shows what happens when you choose anchovies as an additional topping. Peedy makes a wisecrack about your choice.

You can submit the order either by pressing the **Place My Order** button or by speaking "Place order" into the microphone. Peedy recounts the order while writing down the order items on his notepad (Fig. 17.35). He then calculates the figures on his calculator and reports the total price (Fig. 17.36).

Creating an Application That Uses Microsoft Agent
[*Note:* Before running this example, you must first download and install the Microsoft Agent control, a speech-recognition engine, a text-to-speech engine and the four character definitions from the Microsoft Agent Web site, as we discussed at the beginning of this section.]

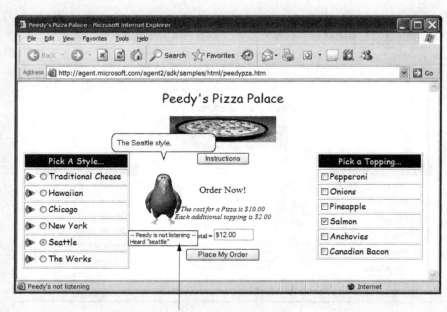

Tool tip indicates recognized speech

Fig. 17.33 | Peedy repeating a request for Seattle-style pizza.

Fig. 17.34 | Peedy repeating a request for anchovies as an additional topping.

Fig. 17.35 | Peedy recounting the order.

Fig. 17.36 | Peedy calculating the total.

The following example (Fig. 17.37) demonstrates how to build a simple application with the Microsoft Agent control. This application contains two drop-down lists from which the user can choose an Agent character and a character animation. When the user chooses from these lists, the chosen character appears and performs the selected animation. The application uses speech recognition and synthesis to control the character animations and speech—you can tell the character which animation to perform by pressing the *Scroll Lock* key, then speaking the animation name into a microphone.

The example also allows you to switch to a new character by speaking its name and creates a custom command, MoveToMouse. In addition, when you press the **Speak** Button, the characters speak any text that you typed in the TextBox.

To use the Microsoft Agent control, you must add it to the **Toolbox**. Select **Tools > Choose Toolbox Items...** to display the **Choose Toolbox Items** dialog. In the dialog, select the **COM Components** tab, then scroll down and select the **Microsoft Agent Control 2.0** option. When this option is selected properly, a small check mark appears in the box to the left of the option. Click **OK** to dismiss the dialog. The icon for the Microsoft Agent control now appears at the bottom of the **Toolbox**. Drag the **Microsoft Agent Control 2.0** control onto your Form and name the object mainAgent.

In addition to the Microsoft Agent object mainAgent (of type *AxAgent*) that manages the characters, you also need a variable of type *IAgentCtlCharacter* to represent the current character. We create this variable, named speaker, in line 11.

```vb
1    ' Fig. 17.28: FrmAgent.vb
2    ' Microsoft Agent demonstration.
3    Imports System.IO
4
5    Public Class FrmAgent
6       ' current agent object
7       Private speaker As AgentObjects.IAgentCtlCharacter
8
9       ' parameterless constructor
10      Public Sub New()
11         InitializeComponent()
12
13         ' initialize the characters
14         Try
15            ' load characters into agent object
16            mainAgent.Characters.Load("Genie", _
17               "C:\windows\msagent\chars\Genie.acs")
18            mainAgent.Characters.Load("Merlin", _
19               "C:\windows\msagent\chars\Merlin.acs")
20            mainAgent.Characters.Load("Peedy", _
21               "C:\windows\msagent\chars\Peedy.acs")
22            mainAgent.Characters.Load("Robby", _
23               "C:\windows\msagent\chars\Robby.acs")
24
25            ' set current character to Genie and show him
26            speaker = mainAgent.Characters("Genie")
27            GetAnimationNames() ' obtain an animation name list
28            speaker.Show(0) ' display Genie
29            cboCharacter.SelectedText = "Genie"
30         Catch fileNotFound As FileNotFoundException
31            MessageBox.Show("Invalid character location", _
32               "Error", MessageBoxButtons.OK, MessageBoxIcon.Error)
33         End Try
34      End Sub ' New
35
```

Fig. 17.37 | Microsoft Agent demonstration. (Part 1 of 5.)

```vb
36      ' event handler for Speak Button
37      Private Sub btnSpeak_Click(ByVal sender As System.Object, _
38         ByVal e As System.EventArgs) Handles btnSpeak.Click
39         ' if TextBox is empty, have the character ask
40         ' user to type the words into the TextBox otherwise,
41         ' have the character say the words in the TextBox
42         If txtSpeech.Text = "" Then
43            speaker.Speak("Please, type the words you want me to speak", "")
44         Else
45            speaker.Speak(txtSpeech.Text, "")
46         End If
47      End Sub ' btnSpeak_Click
48
49      ' event handler for Agent control's ClickEvent
50      Private Sub mainAgent_ClickEvent(ByVal sender As Object, _
51         ByVal e As AxAgentObjects._AgentEvents_ClickEvent) _
52         Handles mainAgent.ClickEvent
53
54         speaker.Play("Confused")
55         speaker.Speak("Why are you poking me?", "")
56         speaker.Play("RestPose")
57      End Sub ' mainAgent_ClickEvent
58
59      ' ComboBox changed event, switch active agent character
60      Private Sub cboCharacter_SelectedIndexChanged( _
61         ByVal sender As System.Object, ByVal e As System.EventArgs) _
62         Handles cboCharacter.SelectedIndexChanged
63
64         ChangeCharacter(cboCharacter.Text)
65      End Sub ' cboCharacter_SelectedIndexChanged
66
67      ' utility method to change characters
68      Private Sub ChangeCharacter(ByVal name As String)
69         speaker.StopAll("Play")
70         speaker.Hide(0)
71         speaker = mainAgent.Characters(Name)
72
73         ' regenerate animation name list
74         GetAnimationNames()
75         speaker.Show(0)
76      End Sub ' ChangeCharacter
77
78      ' get animation names and store in ArrayList
79      Private Sub GetAnimationNames()
80         ' ensure thread safety
81         SyncLock (Me)
82            ' get animation names
83            Dim enumerator As IEnumerator = mainAgent.Characters( _
84               speaker.Name).AnimationNames.GetEnumerator()
85
86            Dim voiceString As String
87
```

Fig. 17.37 | Microsoft Agent demonstration. (Part 2 of 5.)

```
88          ' clear cboActions
89          cboActions.Items.Clear()
90          speaker.Commands.RemoveAll()
91
92          ' copy enumeration to ArrayList
93          While enumerator.MoveNext()
94              ' remove underscores in speech string
95              voiceString = enumerator.Current.ToString()
96              voiceString = voiceString.Replace("_", "underscore")
97
98              cboActions.Items.Add(enumerator.Current)
99
100             ' add all animations as voice enabled commands
101             speaker.Commands.Add(enumerator.Current.ToString(), _
102                 enumerator.Current, voiceString, True, False)
103         End While
104
105         ' add custom command
106         speaker.Commands.Add("MoveToMouse", "MoveToMouse", _
107             "MoveToMouse", True, True)
108     End SyncLock
109 End Sub ' GetAnimationNames
110
111 ' user selects new action
112 Private Sub cboActions_SelectedIndexChanged( _
113     ByVal sender As System.Object, ByVal e As System.EventArgs) _
114     Handles cboActions.SelectedIndexChanged
115
116     speaker.StopAll("Play")
117     speaker.Play(cboActions.Text)
118     speaker.Play("RestPose")
119 End Sub ' cboActions_SelectedIndexChanged
120
121 ' event handler for Agent commands
122 Private Sub mainAgent_Command(ByVal sender As Object, _
123     ByVal e As AxAgentObjects._AgentEvents_CommandEvent) _
124     Handles mainAgent.Command
125     ' get UserInput object
126     Dim command As AgentObjects.IAgentCtlUserInput = _
127         CType(e.userInput, AgentObjects.IAgentCtlUserInput)
128
129     ' change character if user speaks character name
130     If command.Voice = "Peedy" OrElse command.Voice = "Robby" OrElse _
131         command.Voice = "Merlin" OrElse command.Voice = "Genie" Then
132         ChangeCharacter(command.Voice)
133         Return
134     End If
135
136     ' send agent to mouse
137     If command.Voice = "MoveToMouse" Then
138         speaker.MoveTo( _
139             Convert.ToInt16(Windows.Forms.Cursor.Position.X - 60), _
140             Convert.ToInt16(Windows.Forms.Cursor.Position.Y - 60), 5)
```

Fig. 17.37 | Microsoft Agent demonstration. (Part 3 of 5.)

```
141              Return
142          End If
143
144          ' play new animation
145          speaker.StopAll("Play")
146          speaker.Play(command.Name)
147       End Sub ' mainAgent_Command
148   End Class ' FrmAgent
```

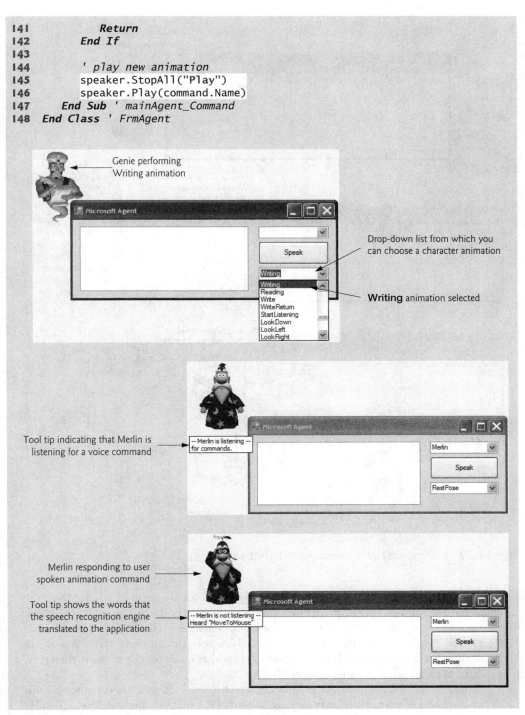

Genie performing
Writing animation

Drop-down list from which you
can choose a character animation

Writing animation selected

Tool tip indicating that Merlin is
listening for a voice command

Merlin responding to user
spoken animation command

Tool tip shows the words that
the speech recognition engine
translated to the application

Fig. 17.37 | Microsoft Agent demonstration. (Part 4 of 5.)

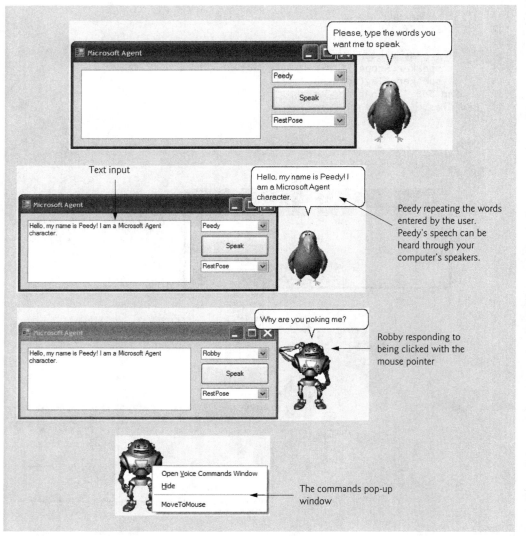

Fig. 17.37 | Microsoft Agent demonstration. (Part 5 of 5.)

When you execute this program, class `FrmAgent`'s constructor (lines 10–34) loads the character descriptions for the predefined animated characters (lines 16–23). If the specified location of the characters is incorrect, or if any character is missing, a `FileNotFound-Exception` is thrown. By default, the character descriptions are stored in `C:\Windows\msagent\chars`. If your system uses another name for the `Windows` directory, you'll need to modify the paths in lines 16–23.

Lines 26–28 set Genie as the default character, obtain all animation names via our utility method `GetAnimationNames` and call `IAgentCtlCharacter` method **_Show_** to display the character. We access characters through property **_Characters_** of `mainAgent`, which contains all the characters that have been loaded. We use the indexer of the `Characters` property to specify the name of the character we wish to load (Genie).

Responding to the Agent Control's `ClickEvent`

When a user clicks the character (i.e., pokes it with the mouse), event handler `mainAgent_ClickEvent` (lines 50–57) executes. First, `speaker` method *`Play`* plays an animation. This method accepts as an argument a `String` representing one of the predefined animations for the character (a list of animations for each character is available at the Microsoft Agent Web site; each character provides over 70 animations). In our example, the argument to `Play` is `"Confused"`—this animation is defined for all four characters, each of which expresses this emotion in a unique way. The character then speaks, `"Why are you poking me?"` via a call to method `Speak`. Finally, we play the `RestPose` animation, which returns the character to its neutral, resting pose.

Obtaining a Character's List of Animations and Defining Its Commands

The list of valid commands for a character is contained in property `Commands` of the `IAgentCtlCharacter` object (`speaker`, in this example). The commands for an Agent character can be viewed in the **Commands** pop-up window, which displays when the user right clicks an Agent character (the last screenshot in Fig. 17.37). Method `Add` of property `Commands` adds a new command to the command list. Method `Add` takes three `String` arguments and two `Boolean` arguments. The first `String` argument identifies the name of the command, which we use to identify the command programmatically. The second `String` defines the command name as it appears in the **Commands** pop-up window. The third `String` defines the voice input that triggers the command. The first `Boolean` specifies whether the command is active, and the second `Boolean` indicates whether the command is visible in the **Commands** pop-up window. A command is triggered when the user selects the command from the **Commands** pop-up window or speaks the voice input into a microphone. Command logic is handled in the `Command` event handler of the `AxAgent` control (`mainAgent`, in this example). In addition, Agent defines several global commands that have predefined functions (for example, speaking a character name causes that character to appear).

Method `GetAnimationNames` (lines 79–109) fills the `cboActions` ComboBox with the current character's animation listing and defines the valid commands that can be used with the character. The method contains a `SyncLock` block to prevent errors resulting from rapid character changes. The method uses an `IEnumerator` (lines 83–84) to obtain the current character's animations. Lines 89–90 clear the existing items in the ComboBox and the character's `Commands` property. Lines 93–103 iterate through all the items in the animation-name enumerator. For each animation, line 95 assigns the animation name to `String` `voiceString`. Line 96 removes any underscore characters (_) and replaces them with the `String` `"underscore"`; this changes the `String` so that a user can pronounce and employ it as a command activator. Line 98 adds the animation's name to the `cboActions` ComboBox. The `Add` method of the `Commands` property (lines 101–102) adds a new command to the current character. In this example, we add every animation name as a command. Each call to `Add` receives the animation name as both the name of the command and the string that appears in the **Commands** pop-up window. The third argument is the voice command, and the last two arguments enable the command but indicate that it is not available via the **Commands** pop-up window. Thus, the command can be activated only by voice input. Lines 106–107 create a new command, named `MoveToMouse`, which is visible in the **Commands** pop-up window.

Responding to Selections from the `cboActions` ComboBox

After the `GetAnimationNames` method has been called, the user can select a value from the `cboActions` ComboBox. Event handler `cboActions_SelectedIndexChanged` (lines 112–119) stops any current animation, then plays the animation that the user selects from the ComboBox, followed by the `RestPose` animation.

Speaking the Text Typed by the User

You can also type text in the `TextBox` and click **Speak**. This causes event handler `btnSpeak_Click` (line 37–47) to call `speaker` method `Speak`, supplying as an argument the text in `speechTextBox`. If the user clicks **Speak** without providing text, the character speaks, `"Please, type the words you want me to speak"`.

Changing Characters

At any point in the program, the user can choose a different character from the `cboChar-acters` ComboBox. When this happens, the `SelectedIndexChanged` event handler for `cbo-Characters` (lines 60–65) executes. The event handler calls method `ChangeCharacter` (declared in lines 68–76) with the text in the `cboCharacters` as an argument. Method `ChangeCharacter` stops any current animation, then calls the `Hide` method of `speaker` (line 70) to remove the current character from view. Line 71 assigns the newly selected character to `speaker`, line 74 generates the character's animation names and commands, and line 75 displays the character via a call to method `Show`.

Responding to Commands

Each time a user presses the *Scroll Lock* key and speaks into a microphone or selects a command from the **Commands** pop-up window, event handler `mainAgent_Command` (lines 122–147) is called. This method receives an argument of type `AxAgentObjects._AgentEvents_CommandEvent`, which contains a single property, `userInput`. This property returns an `Object` that can be converted to type `AgentObjects.IAgentCtlUserInput`. Lines 126–127 assigns the `userInput` object to an `IAgentCtlUserInput` object named `command`, which is used to identify the command, so that the program can respond appropriately. Lines 130–134 use method `ChangeCharacter` to change the current Agent character if the user speaks a character name. Microsoft Agent always will show a character when a user speaks its name; however, by controlling the character change, we can ensure that only one Agent character is displayed at a time. Lines 137–142 move the character to the current mouse location if the user invokes the `MoveToMouse` command. Agent method ***MoveTo*** takes *x*- and *y*-coordinate arguments and moves the character to the specified screen position, applying appropriate movement animations. For all other commands, we `Play` the command name as an animation in line 146.

17.15 Wrap-Up

This chapter began with an introduction to the .NET framework's drawing capabilities. We then presented more powerful drawing capabilities, such as changing the styles of the lines used to draw shapes and controlling the colors and patterns of filled shapes.

Next, you learned techniques for manipulating images and creating smooth animations. We discussed class `Image`, which can store and manipulate images of various formats. We explained how to combine the graphical rendering capabilities covered in the early sections of the chapter with those for image manipulation.

You also learned how to incorporate the Windows Media Player control in an application to play audio or video. Finally, we demonstrated Microsoft Agent—a technology for adding interactive animated characters to applications or Web pages—then showed how to incorporate Microsoft Agent in an application to add speech synthesis and recognition capabilities. In the next chapter, we discuss file-processing techniques that enable programs to store and retrieve data from persistent storage, such as your computer's hard disk. We also explore several types of streams included in Visual Studio .NET.

18

Files and Streams

OBJECTIVES

In this chapter you will learn:

- To create, read, write and update files.

- The .NET framework streams class hierarchy.

- To use classes `File` and `Directory` to obtain information about files and directories on your computer.

- To become familiar with sequential-access file processing.

- To use classes `FileStream`, `StreamReader` and `StreamWriter` to read text from and write text to files.

- To use classes `FileStream` and `BinaryFormatter` to read objects from and write objects to files.

Consciousness ... does not appear to itself chopped up in bits. ... A "river" or a "stream" are the metaphors by which it is most naturally described.
—William James

I read part of it all the way through.
—Samuel Goldwyn

I can only assume that a "Do Not File" document is filed in a "Do Not File" file.
—Senator Frank Church
Senate Intelligence
Subcommittee Hearing, 1975

18.1 Introduction

Variables and arrays offer only temporary storage of data—the data is lost when a local variable "goes out of scope" or when the program terminates. By contrast, files (and databases, which we cover in Chapter 20, Database, SQL and ADO.NET) are used for long-term retention of large amounts of data, even after the program that created the data terminates. Data maintained in files is often called *persistent data*. Computers store files on *secondary storage devices*, such as magnetic disks, optical disks and magnetic tapes. In this chapter, we explain how to create, update and process data files.

We begin with an overview of the data hierarchy from bits to files. Next, we overview some of the FCL's file-processing classes. We then present two examples that show how you can determine information about the files and directories on your computer. The remainder of the chapter shows how to write to and read from text files that are human readable and binary files that store entire objects in binary format.

18.2 Data Hierarchy

Ultimately, all data items that computers process are reduced to combinations of 0s and 1s. This occurs because it is simple and economical to build electronic devices that can assume two stable states—one state represents 0 and the other represents 1. It is remarkable that the impressive functions performed by computers involve only the most fundamental manipulations of 0s and 1s!

The smallest data item that computers support is called a *bit* (short for "*binary digit*"—a digit that can assume one of two values). Each data item, or bit, can assume either the value 0 or the value 1. Computer circuitry performs various simple bit manipulations, such as examining the value of a bit, setting the value of a bit and reversing a bit (from 1 to 0 or from 0 to 1).

Programming with data in the low-level form of bits is cumbersome. It is preferable to program with data in forms such as *decimal digits* (i.e., 0, 1, 2, 3, 4, 5, 6, 7, 8 and 9), *letters* (i.e., the uppercase letters A–Z and the lowercase letters a–z) and *special symbols* (i.e., $, @, %, &, *, (,), -, +, ", :, ?, / and many others). Digits, letters and special symbols are referred to as *characters*. The set of all characters used to write programs and represent data items on a particular computer is called that computer's **character set**. Because computers can process only 0s and 1s, every character in a computer's character set is represented as a pattern of 0s and 1s. **Bytes** are composed of eight bits. Visual Basic uses the **Unicode character set** (www.unicode.org) in which each character is composed of two bytes. Programmers create programs and data items with characters; computers manipulate and process these characters as patterns of bits.

Just as characters are composed of bits, fields are composed of characters. A *field* is a group of characters that conveys meaning. For example, a field consisting of uppercase and lowercase letters can represent a person's name.

Data items processed by computers form a **data hierarchy** (Fig. 18.1), in which data items become larger and more complex in structure as we progress up the hierarchy from bits to characters to fields to larger data aggregates.

Typically, a *record* (which can be represented as a Class) is composed of several related fields. In a payroll system, for example, a record for a particular employee might include the following fields:

1. Employee identification number

2. Name

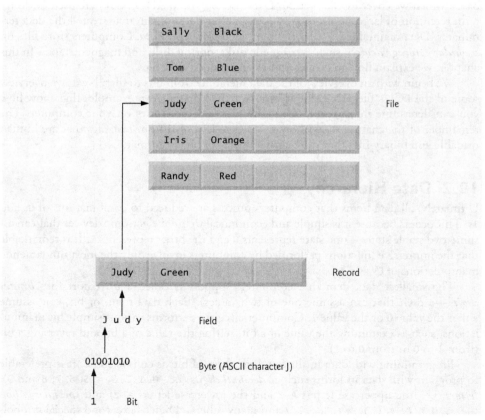

Fig. 18.1 | Data hierarchy.

3. Address

4. Hourly pay rate

5. Number of exemptions claimed

6. Year-to-date earnings

7. Amount of taxes withheld

In the preceding example, each field is associated with the same employee. A data file is a group of related records.[1] A company's payroll file normally contains one record for each employee. A payroll file for a small company might contain only 22 records, whereas one for a large company might contain 100,000 records. Companies typically have many files, some containing millions, billions or even trillions of characters of information.

To facilitate the retrieval of specific records from a file, at least one field in each record is chosen as a *record key*, which identifies a record as belonging to a particular person or entity and distinguishes that record from all others. For example, in a payroll record, the employee identification number normally would be the record key.

There are many ways to organize records in a file. A common organization is called a *sequential file,* in which records typically are stored in order by a record-key field. In a payroll file, records usually are placed in order by employee identification number. The first employee record in the file contains the lowest employee identification number, and subsequent records contain increasingly higher ones.

Most businesses use many different files to store data. For example, a company might have payroll files, accounts-receivable files (listing money due from clients), accounts-payable files (listing money due to suppliers), inventory files (listing facts about all the items handled by the business) and many other files. Related files often are stored in a *database.* A collection of programs designed to create and manage databases is called a *database management system (DBMS)*. We discuss databases in Chapter 20.

18.3 Files and Streams

Visual Basic views a file as a sequential *stream* of bytes (Fig. 18.2). Depending on the operating system, each file ends either with an *end-of-file marker* or at a specific byte number that is recorded in a system-maintained administrative data structure. For example, the Windows keeps track of the number of bytes in a file. When you open a file from a Visual Basic program, an object is created and a stream is associated with the object. When a program executes, the runtime environment creates three stream objects that are accessible via properties `Console.Out`, `Console.In` and `Console.Error`, respectively. These objects facilitate communication between a program and a particular file or device. `Console.In` refers to the *standard input stream object*, which enables a program to input data from the keyboard. `Console.Out` refers to the *standard output stream object*, which enables a program to output data to the screen. `Console.Error` refers to the *standard error stream object*, which enables a program to output error messages to the screen. We have been using `Console.Out` and `Console.In` in our console applications—`Console` methods `Write` and

---

1. Generally, a file can contain arbitrary data in arbitrary formats. In some operating systems, a file is viewed as nothing more than a collection of bytes, and any organization of the bytes in a file (such as organizing the data into records) is a view created by the application programmer.

Fig. 18.2 | Visual Basic's view of an n-byte file.

WriteLine use Console.Out to perform output, and Console methods Read and ReadLine use Console.In to perform input.

There are many file-processing classes in the FCL. The System.IO namespace includes stream classes such as *StreamReader* (for text input from a file), *StreamWriter* (for text output to a file) and *FileStream* (for both input from and output to a file). These stream classes inherit from the MustInherit classes *TextReader*, *TextWriter* and *Stream*, respectively. Actually, properties Console.In and Console.Out are of type TextReader and TextWriter, respectively. The system creates objects of TextReader and TextWriter classes to initialize Console properties Console.In and Console.Out.

MustInherit class Stream provides functionality for representing streams that are made of bytes. Classes FileStream, MemoryStream and BufferedStream (all in namespace System.IO) inherit from class Stream. Class FileStream can be used to write data to and read data from files. Class *MemoryStream* enables the transfer of data directly to and from memory—this is much faster than reading from and writing to external devices. Class *BufferedStream* uses buffering to transfer data to or from a stream. *Buffering* is an I/O performance-enhancement technique, in which each output operation is directed to a region in memory, called a *buffer*, that is large enough to hold the data from many output operations. Then actual transfer to the output device is performed more efficiently in one large *physical output operation* each time the buffer fills. The output operations directed to the output buffer in memory are often called *logical output operations*. Buffering can also be used to speed input operations by initially reading more data than is required into a buffer, so that subsequent reads get data from memory rather than an external device.

In this chapter, we use key stream classes to implement file processing programs that create and manipulate sequential-access files. In Chapter 23, Networking: Streams-Based Sockets and Datagrams, we use stream classes to implement networking applications.

18.4 Classes File and Directory

Information is stored in files, which are organized in directories. Classes File and Directory enable programs to manipulate files and directories on disk. Class *File* can determine information about files and can be used to open files for reading or writing. We discuss techniques for writing to and reading from files in subsequent sections.

Figure 18.3 lists several of class File's Shared methods for manipulating and determining information about files. We demonstrate several of these methods in Fig. 18.5.

Class *Directory* provides capabilities for manipulating directories. Figure 18.4 lists some of class Directory's Shared methods for directory manipulation. Figure 18.5 demonstrates several of these methods, as well. The *DirectoryInfo* object returned by method *CreateDirectory* contains information about a directory. Much of the information contained in class DirectoryInfo also can be accessed via the methods of class Directory.

File class Shared methods and descriptions	
AppendText	Returns a `StreamWriter` that appends text to an existing file or creates a file if one does not exist.
Copy	Copies a file to a new file.
Create	Creates a file and returns its associated `FileStream`.
CreateText	Creates a text file and returns its associated `StreamWriter`.
Delete	Deletes the specified file.
Exists	Returns `True` if the specified file exists and `False` otherwise.
GetCreationTime	Returns a `DateTime` object representing when the file was created.
GetLastAccessTime	Returns a `DateTime` object representing when the file was last accessed.
GetLastWriteTime	Returns a `DateTime` object representing when the file was last modified.
Move	Moves the specified file to a specified location.
Open	Returns a `FileStream` associated with the specified file and equipped with the specified read/write permissions.
OpenRead	Returns a read-only `FileStream` associated with the specified file.
OpenText	Returns a `StreamReader` associated with the specified file.
OpenWrite	Returns a read/write `FileStream` associated with the specified file.

Fig. 18.3 | `File` class `Shared` methods (partial list).

Directory class Shared methods and descriptions	
CreateDirectory	Creates a directory and returns its associated `DirectoryInfo` object.
Delete	Deletes the specified directory.
Exists	Returns `True` if the specified directory exists and `False` otherwise.
GetDirectories	Returns a `String` array containing the names of the subdirectories in the specified directory.
GetFiles	Returns a `String` array containing the names of the files in the specified directory.
GetCreationTime	Returns a `DateTime` object representing when the directory was created.
GetLastAccessTime	Returns a `DateTime` object representing when the directory was last accessed.

Fig. 18.4 | `Directory` class `Shared` methods. (Part 1 of 2.)

Directory class Shared methods and descriptions	
GetLastWriteTime	Returns a DateTime object representing when items were last written to the directory.
Move	Moves the specified directory to a specified location.

Fig. 18.4 | Directory class Shared methods. (Part 2 of 2.)

Demonstrating Classes File and Directory

Class FrmFileTest (Fig. 18.5) uses File and Directory methods to access file and directory information. This Form contains the control txtInput, in which the user enters a file or directory name. For each key that the user presses while typing in the TextBox, the program calls event handler txtInput_KeyDown (lines 8–58). If the user presses the *Enter* key (line 12), this method displays either the file's or the directory's contents, depending on the text the user input. (If the user does not press the *Enter* key, this method returns without displaying any content.) Line 19 uses File method Exists to determine whether the user-specified text is the name of an existing file. If so, line 22 invokes Private method GetInformation (lines 61–80), which calls File methods GetCreationTime (line 69), GetLastWriteTime (line 73) and GetLastAccessTime (line 77) to access file information. When method GetInformation returns, line 27 instantiates a StreamReader for reading text from the file. The StreamReader constructor takes as an argument a String containing the name of the file to open. Line 28 calls StreamReader method ReadToEnd to read the entire contents of the file as a String, then appends the String to txtOutput.

```
1    ' Fig 18.5: FrmFileTest.vb
2    ' Using classes File and Directory.
3    Imports System.IO
4
5    ' displays contents of files and directories
6    Public Class FrmFileTest
7       ' invoked when user presses key
8       Private Sub txtInput_KeyDown(ByVal sender As System.Object, _
9          ByVal e As System.Windows.Forms.KeyEventArgs) _
10         Handles txtInput.KeyDown
11         ' determine whether user pressed Enter key
12         If e.KeyCode = Keys.Enter Then
13            Dim fileName As String ' name of file or directory
14
15            ' get user-specified file or directory
16            fileName = txtInput.Text
17
18            ' determine whether fileName is a file
19            If File.Exists(fileName) Then
20               ' get file's creation date,
21               ' modification date, etc.
22               txtOutput.Text = GetInformation(fileName)
```

Fig. 18.5 | Testing classes File and Directory. (Part 1 of 3.)

```vbnet
23
24                    ' display file contents through StreamReader
25                    Try
26                       ' obtain reader and file contents
27                       Dim stream As New StreamReader(fileName)
28                       txtOutput.Text &= stream.ReadToEnd()
29                       ' handle exception if StreamReader is unavailable
30                    Catch ex As System.IO.IOException
31                       MessageBox.Show("Error reading from file", "File Error", _
32                          MessageBoxButtons.OK, MessageBoxIcon.Error)
33                    End Try
34                    ' determine whether fileName is a directory
35                 ElseIf Directory.Exists(fileName) Then
36                    Dim directoryList() As String ' array for directories
37
38                    ' get directory's creation date,
39                    ' modification date, etc.
40                    txtOutput.Text = GetInformation(fileName)
41
42                    ' obtain file/directory list of specified directory
43                    directoryList = Directory.GetDirectories(fileName)
44
45                    txtOutput.Text &= vbCrLf & vbCrLf & _
46                       "Directory contents:" & vbCrLf
47
48                    ' output directoryList contents
49                    For Each directoryName As String In directoryList
50                       txtOutput.Text &= directoryName & vbCrLf
51                    Next
52                 Else
53                    ' notify user that neither file nor directory exists
54                    MessageBox.Show(txtInput.Text & " does not exist", _
55                       "File Error", MessageBoxButtons.OK, MessageBoxIcon.Error)
56                 End If
57              End If
58           End Sub ' txtInput_KeyDown
59
60           ' get information on file or directory
61           Private Function GetInformation(ByVal fileName As String) As String
62              Dim information As String
63
64              ' output that file or directory exists
65              information = fileName & " exists" & vbCrLf & vbCrLf
66
67              ' output when file or directory was created
68              information &= "Created: " & _
69                 File.GetCreationTime(fileName) & vbCrLf
70
71              ' output when file or directory was last modified
72              information &= "Last modified: " & _
73                 File.GetLastWriteTime(fileName) & vbCrLf
74
```

Fig. 18.5 | Testing classes File and Directory. (Part 2 of 3.)

```
75              ' output when file or directory was last accessed
76              information &= "Last accessed: " & _
77                  File.GetLastAccessTime(fileName) & vbCrLf & vbCrLf
78
79          Return information
80      End Function ' GetInformation
81  End Class ' FrmFileTest
```

Fig. 18.5 | Testing classes File and Directory. (Part 3 of 3.)

If line 19 determines that the user-specified text is not a file, line 35 determines whether it is a directory using Directory method ***Exists***. If the user specified an existing directory, line 40 invokes method GetInformation to access the directory information. Line 43 calls Directory method ***GetDirectories*** to obtain a String array containing the names of subdirectories in the specified directory. Lines 49–51 display each element in the String array. If line 35 determines that the user-specified text is not a directory name, lines 54–55 notify the user (via a MessageBox) that the name the user entered does not exist as a file or directory.

Finding Directories with Regular Expressions

We now consider another example that uses the FCL's file- and directory-manipulation capabilities. Class FrmFileSearch (Fig. 18.6) uses classes File and Directory, and regular-expression capabilities, to report the number of files of each file type that exist in the specified directory path. The program also serves as a "clean-up" utility—when a file that has the .bak filename extension (i.e., a backup file) is encountered, the program displays a MessageBox asking the user whether that file should be removed, then responds appropriately to the user's input.

When the user presses the *Enter* key or clicks the **Search Directory** button, the program invokes method btnSearch_Click (lines 26–58), which searches recursively through the directory path that the user provides. If the user inputs text in the TextBox, line 31 calls Directory method Exists to determine whether that text is a valid directory path and name. If not, lines 39–40 notify the user of the error.

If the user specifies a valid directory, line 48 passes the directory name as an argument to Private method SearchDirectory (lines 61–134). This method locates files that match the regular expression defined in lines 67–68. This regular expression matches any sequence of numbers or letters followed by a period and one or more letters. Note the substring of format (?<extension>\w+) in the argument to the Regex constructor (line 68). This indicates that the part of the string that matches \w+ (i.e., the filename extension that appears after a period in the file name) should be placed in the regular-expression variable named extension. This variable's value is retrieved later from Match object matchResult to obtain the filename extension so that we can summarize the types of files in the directory.

```vb
 1  ' Fig 18.6: FrmFileSearch.vb
 2  ' Using regular expressions to determine file types.
 3  Imports System.IO
 4  Imports System.Text.RegularExpressions
 5  Imports System.Collections.Specialized
 6
 7  Public Class FrmFileSearch
 8     Dim currentDirectory As String = Directory.GetCurrentDirectory()
 9     Dim directoryList() As String ' subdirectories
10     Dim fileArray() As String
11
12     ' store extensions found and number found
13     Dim found As New NameValueCollection()
14
15     ' invoked when user types in text box
16     Private Sub txtInput_KeyDown(ByVal sender As System.Object, _
17        ByVal e As System.Windows.Forms.KeyEventArgs) _
18        Handles txtInput.KeyDown
19        ' determine whether user pressed Enter
20        If e.KeyCode = Keys.Enter Then
21           btnSearch_Click(sender, e)
22        End If
23     End Sub ' txtInput_KeyDown
24
25     ' invoked when user clicks "Search Directory" button
26     Private Sub btnSearch_Click(ByVal sender As System.Object, _
27        ByVal e As System.EventArgs) Handles btnSearch.Click
28        ' check for user input; default is current directory
29        If txtInput.Text <> "" Then
30           ' verify that user input is valid directory name
31           If Directory.Exists(txtInput.Text) Then
32              currentDirectory = txtInput.Text
```

Fig. 18.6 | Regular expression used to determine file types. (Part 1 of 4.)

```
33
34                   ' reset input text box and update display
35                   lblDirectory.Text = _
36                      "Current Directory:" & vbCrLf & currentDirectory
37               Else
38                   ' show error if user does not specify valid directory
39                   MessageBox.Show("Invalid Directory", "Error", _
40                       MessageBoxButtons.OK, MessageBoxIcon.Error)
41               End If
42           End If
43
44           ' clear text boxes
45           txtInput.Text = ""
46           txtOutput.Text = ""
47
48           SearchDirectory(currentDirectory) ' search directory
49
50           ' summarize and print results
51           For Each current As String In found
52               txtOutput.Text &= "* Found " & found(current) & _
53                   " " & current & " files." & vbCrLf
54           Next current
55
56           ' clear output for new search
57           found.Clear()
58       End Sub ' btnSearch_Click
59
60       ' search directory using regular expression
61       Private Sub SearchDirectory(ByVal currentDirectory As String)
62           ' for file name without directory path
63           Try
64               Dim fileName As String = ""
65
66               ' regular expression for extensions matching pattern
67               Dim regularExpression As New Regex( _
68                   "[a-zA-Z0-9]+\.(?<extension>\w+)")
69
70               ' stores regular-expression match result
71               Dim matchResult As Match
72
73               Dim fileExtension As String ' holds file extensions
74
75               ' number of files with given extension in directory
76               Dim extensionCount As Integer
77
78               ' get directories
79               directoryList = Directory.GetDirectories(currentDirectory)
80
81               ' get list of files in current directory
82               fileArray = Directory.GetFiles(currentDirectory)
83
```

Fig. 18.6 | Regular expression used to determine file types. (Part 2 of 4.)

```
84              ' iterate through list of files
85              For Each myFile As String In fileArray
86                  ' remove directory path from file name
87                  fileName = myFile.Substring(myFile.LastIndexOf("\") + 1)
88
89                  ' obtain result for regular-expression search
90                  matchResult = regularExpression.Match(fileName)
91
92                  ' check for match
93                  If matchResult.Success Then
94                      fileExtension = matchResult.Result("${extension}")
95                  Else
96                      fileExtension = "[no extension]"
97                  End If
98
99                  ' store value from container
100                 If found(fileExtension) Is Nothing Then
101                     found.Add(fileExtension, "1")
102                 Else
103                     extensionCount = Int32.Parse(found(fileExtension)) + 1
104                     found(fileExtension) = extensionCount.ToString()
105                 End If
106
107                 ' search for backup( .bak ) files
108                 If fileExtension = "bak" Then
109                     ' prompt user to delete ( .bak ) file
110                     Dim result As DialogResult = MessageBox.Show( _
111                         "Found backup file " & fileName & ". Delete?", _
112                         "Delete Backup", MessageBoxButtons.YesNo, _
113                         MessageBoxIcon.Question)
114
115                     ' delete file if user clicked 'yes'
116                     If result = Windows.Forms.DialogResult.Yes Then
117                         File.Delete(myFile)
118                         extensionCount = Int32.Parse(found("bak")) - 1
119                         found("bak") = extensionCount.ToString()
120                     End If
121                 End If
122             Next myFile
123
124             ' recursive call to search files in subdirectory
125             For Each myDirectory As String In directoryList
126                 SearchDirectory(myDirectory)
127             Next myDirectory
128             ' handle exception if files have unauthorized access
129         Catch ex As UnauthorizedAccessException
130             MessageBox.Show("Some files may not be visible" & _
131                 " due to permission settings", "Warning", _
132                 MessageBoxButtons.OK, MessageBoxIcon.Information)
133         End Try
134     End Sub ' SearchDirectory
135 End Class ' FrmFileSearch
```

Fig. 18.6 | Regular expression used to determine file types. (Part 3 of 4.)

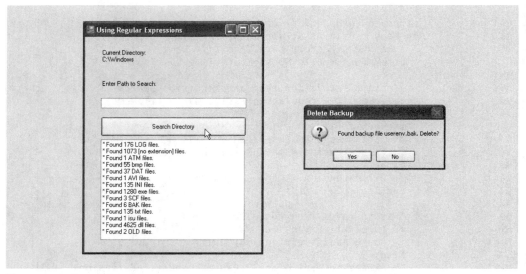

Fig. 18.6 | Regular expression used to determine file types. (Part 4 of 4.)

Line 79 calls Directory method GetDirectories to retrieve the names of all the sub-directories that belong to the current directory. Line 82 calls Directory method *GetFiles* to store in String array fileArray the names of the files in the current directory. The loop in lines 85–122 searches for all files with extension .bak. The loop at lines 125–127 then calls SearchDirectory recursively (line 126) for each subdirectory in the current directory. Line 87 eliminates the directory path, so the program can test only the file name when using the regular expression. Line 90 uses Regex method Match to match the regular expression with the file name, then assigns the result to Match object matchResult. If the match is successful, line 94 uses Match method Result to assign to fileExtension the value of the regular-expression variable extension from object matchResult. If the match is unsuccessful, line 96 sets fileExtension to "[no extension]".

Class FrmFileSearch uses an instance of class NameValueCollection (declared in line 13) to store each filename-extension type and the number of files for each type. A *Name-ValueCollection* (namespace System.Collections.Specialized) contains a collection of key-value pairs of Strings, and provides method Add to add a key-value pair to the collection. The indexer for this class can index according to the order in which the items were added or according to the keys. Line 100 uses NameValueCollection found to determine whether this is the first occurrence of the filename extension (the expression returns Nothing if the collection does not contain a key-value pair for the specified fileExtension). If this is the first occurrence, line 101 adds that extension to found as a key with the value 1. Otherwise, line 103 increments the value associated with the extension in found to indicate another occurrence of the file extension, and line 104 assigns the new value to the key-value pair.

Line 108 determines whether fileExtension equals "bak"—that is, whether the file is a backup file. If so, lines 110–113 prompt the user to indicate whether the file should be deleted; if the user clicks **Yes** (line 116), lines 117–119 delete the file and decrement the value for the "bak" file type in found.

Lines 125–127 call method `SearchDirectory` for each subdirectory. Using recursion, we ensure that the program performs the same logic for finding .bak files in each subdirectory. After each subdirectory has been checked for .bak files, method `SearchDirectory` completes, and lines 51–54 display the results.

18.5 Creating a Sequential-Access Text File

Visual Basic imposes no structure on files. Thus, the concept of a "record" does not exist in Visual Basic files. This means that you must structure files to meet the requirements of your applications. In the next few examples, we use text and special characters to organize our own concept of a "record."

Class FrmBankUI

The following examples demonstrate file processing in a bank-account maintenance application. These programs have similar user interfaces, so we used the Visual Studio `Form` designer to create reusable base class `FrmBankUI` (Fig. 18.7), which encapsulates the common GUI components (see the screen capture in Fig. 18.7). Class `FrmBankUI` contains four `Label`s and four `TextBox`es. Method `ClearTextBoxes` (lines 17–27) clears the `TextBox`es' contents. Method `SetTextBoxValues` (lines 30–49) sets the text in the `TextBox`es. Method `GetTextBoxValues` (lines 52–66) gets the values from the `TextBox`es.

```
 1    ' Fig. 18.7: FrmBankUI.vb
 2    ' A reusable Windows Form for the examples in this chapter.
 3
 4    Public Class FrmBankUI
 5       ' number of TextBoxes on Form
 6       Protected TextBoxCount As Integer = 4
 7
 8       ' enumeration constants specify TextBox indices
 9       Public Enum TextBoxIndices
10          ACCOUNT
11          FIRST
12          LAST
13          BALANCE
14       End Enum ' TextBoxIndices
15
16       ' clear all TextBoxes
17       Public Sub ClearTextBoxes()
18          ' iterate through every Control on form
19          For i As Integer = 0 To Controls.Count - 1
20             Dim myControl As Control = Controls(i) ' get control
21             ' determine whether Control is TextBox
22             If TypeOf myControl Is TextBox Then
23                ' clear Text property (set to empty string)
24                myControl.Text = ""
25             End If
26          Next i
27       End Sub ' ClearTextBoxes
28
```

Fig. 18.7 | Base class for GUIs in our file-processing applications. (Part 1 of 2.)

```vbnet
29      ' set text box values to string array values
30      Public Sub SetTextBoxValues(ByVal values() As String)
31         ' determine whether string array has correct length
32         If values.Length <> TextBoxCount Then
33            ' throw exception if not correct length
34            Throw New ArgumentException( _
35               "There must be " & (TextBoxCount + 1) & _
36               " strings in the array")
37            ' set array values if array has correct length
38         Else
39            ' set array values to text box values
40            txtAccount.Text = _
41               values(Convert.ToInt32(TextBoxIndices.ACCOUNT))
42            txtFirstName.Text = _
43               values(Convert.ToInt32(TextBoxIndices.FIRST))
44            txtLastName.Text = _
45               values(Convert.ToInt32(TextBoxIndices.LAST))
46            txtBalance.Text = _
47               values(Convert.ToInt32(TextBoxIndices.BALANCE))
48         End If
49      End Sub ' SetTextBoxValues
50
51      ' return text box values as string array
52      Public Function GetTextBoxValues() As String()
53         Dim values(TextBoxCount) As String
54
55         ' copy text box fields to string array
56         values(Convert.ToInt32(TextBoxIndices.ACCOUNT)) = _
57            txtAccount.Text
58         values(Convert.ToInt32(TextBoxIndices.FIRST)) = _
59            txtFirstName.Text
60         values(Convert.ToInt32(TextBoxIndices.LAST)) = _
61            txtLastName.Text
62         values(Convert.ToInt32(TextBoxIndices.BALANCE)) = _
63            txtBalance.Text
64
65         Return values
66      End Function ' GetTextBoxValues
67   End Class ' FrmBankUI
```

Fig. 18.7 | Base class for GUIs in our file-processing applications. (Part 2 of 2.)

To reuse class FrmBankUI, you must compile the GUI into a DLL (we called it Bank-Library) as described in Section 14.13. We provide the BankLibrary with the examples for this chapter. When you copy these examples to your system, you might need to delete the reference to BankLibrary and add it again, since the library most likely will reside in a different location on your system.

Class Record

Figure 18.8 contains class Record, which Fig. 18.9, Fig. 18.11 and Fig. 18.12 use to maintain the data in each record that is written to or read from a file. This class also belongs to the BankLibrary DLL, so it is located in the same project as class FrmBankUI.

Class Record contains Private instance variables accountValue, firstNameValue, lastNameValue and balanceValue (lines 6–9), which collectively represent all the information for a record. The parameterless constructor (lines 12–14) sets these members by

```
 1   ' Fig. 18.8: Record.vb
 2   ' Class that represents a data record.
 3   Imports System.Text
 4
 5   Public Class Record
 6      Private accountValue As Integer
 7      Private firstNameValue As String
 8      Private lastNameValue As String
 9      Private balanceValue As Decimal
10
11      ' parameterless constructor sets members to default values
12      Public Sub New()
13         MyClass.New(0, "", "", 0D)
14      End Sub ' New
15
16      ' overloaded constructor sets members to parameter values
17      Public Sub New(ByVal account As Integer, _
18         ByVal firstName As String, ByVal lastName As String, _
19         ByVal balance As Decimal)
20
21         accountValue = account
22         firstNameValue = firstName
23         lastNameValue = lastName
24         balanceValue = balance
25      End Sub ' New
26
27      ' property that gets and sets Account
28      Public Property Account() As Integer
29         Get
30            Return accountValue
31         End Get
32         Set(ByVal value As Integer)
33            accountValue = value
34         End Set
35      End Property ' Account
36
```

Fig. 18.8 | Record for sequential-access file-processing applications. (Part 1 of 2.)

```
37          ' property that gets and sets FirstName
38          Public Property FirstName() As String
39             Get
40                Return firstNameValue
41             End Get
42             Set(ByVal value As String)
43                firstNameValue = value
44             End Set
45          End Property ' FirstName
46
47          ' property that gets and sets LastName
48          Public Property LastName() As String
49             Get
50                Return lastNameValue
51             End Get
52             Set(ByVal value As String)
53                lastNameValue = value
54             End Set
55          End Property ' LastName
56
57          ' property that gets and sets Balance
58          Public Property Balance() As Decimal
59             Get
60                Return balanceValue
61             End Get
62             Set(ByVal value As Decimal)
63                balanceValue = value
64             End Set
65          End Property ' Balance
66       End Class ' Record
```

Fig. 18.8 | Record for sequential-access file-processing applications. (Part 2 of 2.)

calling the four-argument constructor with 0 for the account number, empty strings ("") for the first and last names and 0D for the balance. The four-argument constructor (lines 17–25) sets these members to the specified parameter values. Class Record also provides properties Account (lines 28–35), FirstName (lines 38–45), LastName (lines 48–55) and Balance (lines 58–65) for accessing each record's account number, first name, last name and balance, respectively.

Using a Character Stream to Create an Output File

Class FrmCreateFile (Fig. 18.9) uses instances of class Record to create a sequential-access file that might be used in an accounts-receivable system—a program that organizes data regarding money owed by a company's credit clients. For each client, the program obtains an account number and the client's first name, last name and balance (i.e., the amount of money that the client owes to the company for previously received goods and services). The data obtained for each client constitutes a record for that client. In this application, the account number is used as the record key—files are created and maintained in account-number order. This program assumes that the user enters records in account-number order. However, a comprehensive accounts-receivable system would provide a sorting capability so that the user could enter the records in any order.

```vb
 1    ' Fig. 18.9: FrmCreateFile.vb
 2    ' Creating a sequential-access file.
 3    Imports System.IO
 4    Imports BankLibrary ' imports classes from Figs. 18.7 and 18.8
 5
 6    Public Class FrmCreateFile
 7       Private fileWriter As StreamWriter ' writes data to text file
 8       Private output As FileStream ' maintains connection to file
 9
10       ' event handler for Save Button
11       Private Sub btnSave_Click(ByVal sender As System.Object, _
12          ByVal e As System.EventArgs) Handles btnSave.Click
13          ' create dialog box enabling user to save file
14          Dim fileChooser As New SaveFileDialog()
15          Dim result As DialogResult = fileChooser.ShowDialog()
16          Dim fileName As String ' name of file to save data
17
18          fileChooser.CheckFileExists = False ' allow user to create file
19
20          ' exit event handler if user clicked "Cancel"
21          If result = Windows.Forms.DialogResult.Cancel Then
22             Return
23          End If
24
25          fileName = fileChooser.FileName ' get specified file name
26
27          ' show error if user specified invalid file
28          If fileName = "" Or fileName Is Nothing Then
29             MessageBox.Show("Invalid File Name", "Error", _
30                MessageBoxButtons.OK, MessageBoxIcon.Error)
31          Else
32             ' save file via FileStream if user specified valid file
33             Try
34                ' open file with write access
35                output = New FileStream( _
36                   fileName, FileMode.OpenOrCreate, FileAccess.Write)
37
38                ' sets file to where data is written
39                fileWriter = New StreamWriter(output)
40
41                ' disable Save button and enable Enter button
42                btnSave.Enabled = False
43                btnEnter.Enabled = True
44                ' handle exception if there is a problem opening the file
45             Catch ex As IOException
46                ' notify user if file does not exist
47                MessageBox.Show("Error opening file", "Error", _
48                   MessageBoxButtons.OK, MessageBoxIcon.Error)
49             End Try
50          End If
51       End Sub ' btnSave_Click
52
```

Fig. 18.9 | Creating and writing to a sequential-access file. (Part 1 of 4.)

```vb.net
53       ' event handler for Enter Button
54       Private Sub btnEnter_Click(ByVal sender As System.Object, _
55          ByVal e As System.EventArgs) Handles btnEnter.Click
56          ' store TextBox values string array
57          Dim values As String() = GetTextBoxValues()
58
59          ' Record containing TextBox values to serialize
60          Dim record As New Record()
61
62          ' determine whether TextBox account field is empty
63          If values(TextBoxIndices.ACCOUNT) <> "" Then
64             ' store TextBox values in Record and serialize Record
65             Try
66                ' get account number value from TextBox
67                Dim accountNumber As Integer = _
68                   Int32.Parse(values(TextBoxIndices.ACCOUNT))
69
70                ' determine whether accountNumber is valid
71                If accountNumber > 0 Then
72                   ' store TextBox fields in Record
73                   record.Account = accountNumber
74                   record.FirstName = values(TextBoxIndices.FIRST)
75                   record.LastName = values(TextBoxIndices.LAST)
76                   record.Balance = _
77                      Decimal.Parse(values(TextBoxIndices.BALANCE))
78
79                   ' write Record to file, fields separated by commas
80                   fileWriter.WriteLine( _
81                      record.Account & "," & record.FirstName & "," & _
82                      record.LastName & "," & record.Balance)
83                Else
84                   ' notify user if invalid account number
85                   MessageBox.Show("Invalid Account Number", "Error", _
86                      MessageBoxButtons.OK, MessageBoxIcon.Error)
87                End If
88                ' notify user if error occurs in serialization
89             Catch ex As IOException
90                MessageBox.Show("Error Writing to File", "Error", _
91                   MessageBoxButtons.OK, MessageBoxIcon.Error)
92                ' notify user if error occurs regarding parameter format
93             Catch ex As FormatException
94                MessageBox.Show("Invalid Format", "Error", _
95                   MessageBoxButtons.OK, MessageBoxIcon.Error)
96             End Try
97          End If
98
99          ClearTextBoxes() ' clear TextBox values
100      End Sub ' btnEnter_Click
101
102      ' event handler for Exit Button
103      Private Sub btnExit_Click(ByVal sender As System.Object, _
104         ByVal e As System.EventArgs) Handles btnExit.Click
```

Fig. 18.9 | Creating and writing to a sequential-access file. (Part 2 of 4.)

```
105         ' determine whether file exists
106         If output IsNot Nothing Then
107            Try
108               fileWriter.Close() ' close StreamWriter
109               output.Close() ' close file
110               ' notify user of error closing file
111            Catch ex As IOException
112               MessageBox.Show("Cannot close file", "Error", _
113                  MessageBoxButtons.OK, MessageBoxIcon.Error)
114            End Try
115         End If
116
117         Application.Exit()
118      End Sub ' btnExit_Click
119   End Class ' FrmCreateFile
```

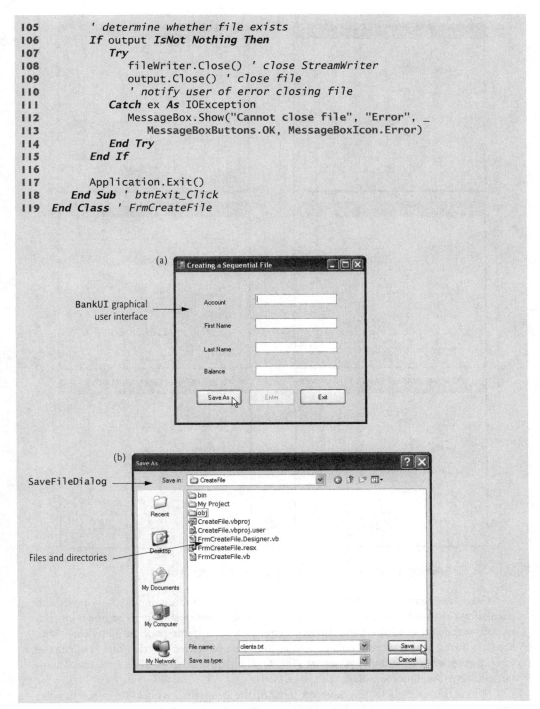

Fig. 18.9 | Creating and writing to a sequential-access file. (Part 3 of 4.)

Fig. 18.9 | Creating and writing to a sequential-access file. (Part 4 of 4.)

Class FrmCreateFile either creates or opens a file (depending on whether one exists), then allows the user to write records to that file. The Imports statement in line 4 enables us to use the classes of the BankLibrary namespace; this namespace contains class Frm-BankUI, from which class FrmCreateFile inherits (specified in the file FrmCreate-File.Designer.vb). Class FrmCreateFile's GUI enhances that of class FrmBankUI with buttons **Save As**, **Enter** and **Exit**.

When the user clicks the **Save As** button, the program invokes the event handler btnSave_Click (lines 11–51). Line 14 instantiates a *SaveFileDialog* object (namespace System.Windows.Forms). Objects of this class are used for selecting files (see the second screen in Fig. 18.9). Line 15 calls SaveFileDialog method ***ShowDialog*** to display the dialog. When displayed, a SaveFileDialog prevents the user from interacting with any other window in the program until the user closes the SaveFileDialog by clicking either **Save** or **Cancel**. Dialogs that behave in this manner are called ***modal dialogs***. The user selects the appropriate drive, directory and file name, then clicks **Save**. Method ShowDialog returns a DialogResult specifying which button (**Save** or **Cancel**) the user clicked to close the dialog. This is assigned to DialogResult variable result (line 15). Line 21 tests whether the user clicked **Cancel** by comparing this value to Windows.Forms.DialogResult.Cancel. If the values are equal, method btnSave_Click returns (line 22). Otherwise, line 25 uses SaveFileDialog property FileName to obtain the user-selected file.

You can open files to perform text manipulation by creating objects of class FileStream. In this example, we want the file to be opened for output, so lines 35–36 create a FileStream object. The FileStream constructor that we use receives three arguments—a String containing the path and name of the file to open, a constant describing how to open the file and a constant describing the file permissions. The constant FileMode.OpenOrCreate (line 36) indicates that the FileStream object should open the file if the file exists and create the file if it does not exist. There are other FileMode constants describing how to open files; we introduce these constants as we use them in examples. The constant FileAccess.Write (from the ***FileAccess enumeration***) indicates that the program can only perform write operations with the FileStream object. There are two other constants for the third constructor parameter—FileAccess.Read for read-only access and FileAccess.ReadWrite for both read and write access. The StreamWriter object (line 39) is constructed with a FileStream argument that specifies the file to which the StreamWriter will output text. Class StreamWriter belongs to the System.IO namespace. Line 45 catches an ***IOException*** if there is a problem opening the file or creating the StreamWriter. If so, the program displays an error message (lines 47–48). If no exception occurs, the file is open for writing.

 Common Programming Error 18.1

Failure to open a file before attempting to reference it in a program is a logic error.

After typing information in each TextBox, the user clicks the **Enter** button, which calls event handler btnEnter_Click (lines 54–100) to save the data from the TextBoxes into the user-specified file. If the user entered a valid account number (i.e., an integer greater than zero), lines 73–77 store the TextBox values in an object of type Record (created in line 60). If the user entered invalid data in one of the TextBoxes (such as non-numeric characters in the **Balance** field), the program throws a FormatException. The Catch block in lines 93–95 handles such exceptions by notifying the user (via a MessageBox) of the improper format.

If the user entered valid data, lines 80–82 write the record to the file by invoking method WriteLine of the StreamWriter object that was created at line 39. Method WriteLine writes a sequence of characters to a file. We separate each field with a comma in this example, and we place each record on its own line in the file.

When the user clicks the **Exit** button, event handler btnExit_Click (lines 103–118) exits the application. Line 108 closes the StreamWriter, line 109 closes the FileStream, then line 117 terminates the program. Note that the call to method Close is located in a

Try block. Method *Close* throws an IOException if the file or stream cannot be closed properly. In this case, it is important to notify the user that the information in the file or stream might be corrupted.

Performance Tip 18.1

Close each file explicitly when the program no longer needs to reference the file. This can reduce resource usage in programs that continue executing long after they finish using a specific file. The practice of explicitly closing files also improves program clarity.

Performance Tip 18.2

Releasing resources explicitly when they are no longer needed makes them immediately available for reuse by other programs, thus improving resource utilization.

In the sample execution for the program in Fig. 18.9, we entered information for the five accounts shown in Fig. 18.10. The program does not depict how the data records are rendered in the file. To verify that the file has been created successfully, we create a program in the next section to read and display the file. Since this is a text file, you can open it in any text editor to see its contents.

18.6 Reading Data from a Sequential-Access Text File

The preceding section demonstrated how to create a file for use in sequential-access applications. In this section, we discuss how to read (or retrieve) data sequentially from a file.

Class FrmReadSequentialAccessFile (Fig. 18.11) reads records from the file created in Fig. 18.9, then displays the contents of each record. Much of the code in this example is similar to that in Fig. 18.9, so we discuss only the unique aspects of the application.

Account Number	First Name	Last Name	Balance
100	Nancy	Brown	-25.54
200	Stacey	Dunn	314.33
300	Doug	Barker	0.00
400	Dave	Smith	258.34
500	Sam	Stone	34.98

Fig. 18.10 | Sample data for the program in Fig. 18.9.

```
1  ' Fig. 18.11: FrmReadSequentialAccessFile.vb
2  ' Reading a sequential-access file.
3  Imports System.IO
4  Imports BankLibrary ' imports classes from Figs. 18.7 and 18.8
5
6  Public Class FrmReadSequentialAccessFile
7      Private input As FileStream ' maintains connection to a file
```

Fig. 18.11 | Reading sequential-access files. (Part 1 of 4.)

```vbnet
8      Private fileReader As StreamReader ' reads data from a text file
9
10     ' invoked when user clicks the Open button
11     Private Sub btnOpen_Click(ByVal sender As System.Object, _
12        ByVal e As System.EventArgs) Handles btnOpen.Click
13        ' create dialog box enabling user to open file
14        Dim fileChooser As New OpenFileDialog()
15        Dim result As DialogResult = fileChooser.ShowDialog()
16        Dim fileName As String ' name of file containing data
17
18        ' exit event handler if user clicked Cancel
19        If result = Windows.Forms.DialogResult.Cancel Then
20           Return
21        End If
22
23        fileName = fileChooser.FileName ' get specified file name
24        ClearTextBoxes()
25
26        ' show error if user specified invalid file
27        If fileName = "" Or fileName Is Nothing Then
28           MessageBox.Show("Invalid File Name", "Error", _
29              MessageBoxButtons.OK, MessageBoxIcon.Error)
30        Else
31           ' create FileStream to obtain read access to file
32           input = New FileStream(fileName, FileMode.Open, FileAccess.Read)
33
34           ' set file from where data is read
35           fileReader = New StreamReader(input)
36
37           btnOpen.Enabled = False ' disable Open File button
38           btnNext.Enabled = True ' enable Next Record button
39        End If
40     End Sub ' btnOpen_Click
41
42     ' invoked when user clicks Next button
43     Private Sub btnNext_Click(ByVal sender As System.Object, _
44        ByVal e As System.EventArgs) Handles btnNext.Click
45
46        Try
47           ' get next record available in file
48           Dim inputRecord As String = fileReader.ReadLine()
49
50           ' will store individual pieces of data
51           Dim inputFields() As String
52
53           If inputRecord IsNot Nothing Then
54              inputFields = inputRecord.Split(","c)
55
56              Dim record As New Record(Convert.ToInt32( _
57                 inputFields(0)), inputFields(1), inputFields(2), _
58                 Convert.ToDecimal(inputFields(3)))
59
```

Fig. 18.11 | Reading sequential-access files. (Part 2 of 4.)

```
60              ' copy string array values to TextBox values
61              SetTextBoxValues(inputFields)
62          Else
63              fileReader.Close() ' close StreamReader
64              input.Close() ' close FileStream if no Records in file
65              btnOpen.Enabled = True ' enable Open File button
66              btnNext.Enabled = False ' disable Next Record button
67              ClearTextBoxes()
68
69              ' notify user if no Records in file
70              MessageBox.Show("No more records in file", "", _
71                  MessageBoxButtons.OK, MessageBoxIcon.Information)
72          End If
73      Catch ex As IOException
74          MessageBox.Show("Error Reading from File", "Error", _
75              MessageBoxButtons.OK, MessageBoxIcon.Error)
76      End Try
77  End Sub ' btnNext_Click
78 End Class ' FrmReadSequentialAccessFile
```

Fig. 18.11 | Reading sequential-access files. (Part 3 of 4.)

(c)
Reading a Sequential File

Account	100
First Name	Nancy
Last Name	Brown
Balance	-25.54

Open File   Next Record

(d)
Reading a Sequential File

Account	200
First Name	Stacey
Last Name	Dunn
Balance	314.33

Open File   Next Record

(e)
Reading a Sequential File

Account	300
First Name	Doug
Last Name	Barker
Balance	0.00

Open File   Next Record

(f)
Reading a Sequential File

Account	400
First Name	Dave
Last Name	Smith
Balance	258.34

Open File   Next Record

(g)
Reading a Sequential File

Account	500
First Name	Same
Last Name	Stone
Balance	34.98

Open File   Next Record

(h)

No more records in file

OK

Fig. 18.11 | Reading sequential-access files. (Part 4 of 4.)

When the user clicks the **Open File** button, the program calls event handler `btnOpen_Click` (lines 11–40). Line 14 creates an ***OpenFileDialog***, and line 15 calls its ***ShowDialog*** method to display the **Open** dialog (see the second screenshot in Fig. 18.11). The behavior and GUI for the **Save** and **Open** dialog types are identical, except that **Save** is replaced by **Open**. If the user inputs a valid file name, line 32 creates a `FileStream` object and assigns it to reference `input`. We pass constant `FileMode.Open` as the second argument to the `FileStream` constructor to indicate that the `FileStream` should open the file if it exists and throw a `FileNotFoundException` if the file does not exist. In the last example (Fig. 18.9), we wrote text to the file using a `FileStream` object with write-only access. In this example (Fig. 18.11), we specify read-only access to the file by passing constant `FileAccess.Read` as the third argument to the `FileStream` constructor (line 32). This `FileStream` object is used to create a `StreamReader` object in line 35. The `FileStream` object specifies the file from which the `StreamReader` object will read text.

Error-Prevention Tip 18.1

Open a file with the `FileAccess.Read` file-open mode if the contents of the file should not be modified. This prevents unintentional modification of the contents.

When the user clicks the **Next Record** button, the program calls event handler `btnNext_Click` (lines 43–77), which reads the next record from the user-specified file. (The user must click **Next Record** after opening the file to view the first record.) Line 48 calls `StreamReader` method `ReadLine` to read the next record. If an error occurs while reading the file, an `IOException` is thrown (caught at line 73), and the user is notified (line 74–75). Otherwise, line 53 determines whether `StreamReader` method `ReadLine` returned `Nothing` (i.e., there is no more text in the file). If not, line 54 uses method `Split` of class `String` to separate the stream of characters that was read from the file into strings that represent the `Record`'s properties. Recall that the fields of each record are separated by commas. These properties are then stored by constructing a `Record` object using the properties as arguments (lines 56–58). Line 61 displays the `Record` values in the `TextBox`es by invoking method `SetTextBoxes`, which was inherited from class `FrmBankUI`. If `ReadLine` returns `Nothing`, the program closes both the `StreamReader` object (line 63) and the `FileStream` object (line 64), then notifies the user that there are no more records (lines 70–71).

18.7 Case Study: A Credit-Inquiry Program

To retrieve data sequentially from a file, programs normally start from the beginning of the file, reading consecutively until the desired data is found. It sometimes is necessary to process a file sequentially several times (from the beginning of the file) during the execution of a program. A `FileStream` object can reposition its *file-position pointer* (which contains the byte number of the next byte to be read from or written to the file) to any position in the file. When a `FileStream` object is opened, its file-position pointer is set to byte position 0 (i.e., the beginning of the file)

We now present a program that builds on the concepts employed in Fig. 18.11. Class `FrmCreditInquiry` (Fig. 18.12) is a credit-inquiry program that enables a credit manager to search for and display account information for customers with credit balances (i.e., customers to whom the company owes money), zero balances (i.e., customers who do not owe the company money) and debit balances (i.e., customers who owe the company money for previously received goods and services). We use a `RichTextBox` in the program to display the account information. `RichTextBox`es provide more functionality than regular `TextBox`es—for example, `RichTextBox`es offer method `Find` for searching individual strings and method `LoadFile` for displaying file contents. Classes `RichTextBox` and `TextBox` both

inherit from MustInherit class System.Windows.Forms.TextBoxBase. We chose a Rich-
TextBox in this example because it displays multiple lines of text by default, whereas a regular TextBox displays only one. Alternatively, we could have specified that a TextBox
object display multiple lines of text by setting its Multiline property to True.

```vb
1   ' Fig. 18.12: FrmCreditInquiry.vb
2   ' Read a file sequentially and display contents based on
3   ' account type specified by user (credit, debit or zero balances).
4   Imports System.IO
5   Imports BankLibrary
6
7   Public Class FrmCreditInquiry
8      Private input As FileStream ' maintains the connection to the file
9      Private fileReader As StreamReader ' reads data from text file
10
11     ' name of file that stores credit, debit and zero balances
12     Private fileName As String
13
14     ' invoked when user clicks Open File button
15     Private Sub btnOpen_Click(ByVal sender As System.Object, _
16        ByVal e As System.EventArgs) Handles btnOpen.Click
17        ' create dialog box enabling user to open file
18        Dim fileChooser As New OpenFileDialog()
19        Dim result As DialogResult = fileChooser.ShowDialog()
20
21        ' exit event handler if user clicked Cancel
22        If result = Windows.Forms.DialogResult.Cancel Then
23           Return
24        End If
25
26        fileName = fileChooser.FileName ' get name from user
27
28        ' show error if user specified invalid file
29        If fileName = "" Or fileName Is Nothing Then
30           MessageBox.Show("Invalid File Name", "Error", _
31              MessageBoxButtons.OK, MessageBoxIcon.Error)
32        Else
33           ' create FileStream to obtain read access to file
34           input = New FileStream(fileName, FileMode.Open, FileAccess.Read)
35
36           ' set file from where data is read
37           fileReader = New StreamReader(input)
38
39           ' enable all GUI buttons, except for Open File button
40           btnOpen.Enabled = False
41           btnCredit.Enabled = True
42           btnDebit.Enabled = True
43           btnZero.Enabled = True
44        End If
45     End Sub ' btnOpen_Click
46
```

Fig. 18.12 | Credit-inquiry program. (Part 1 of 5.)

```vbnet
47      ' invoked when user clicks credit balances,
48      ' debit balances or zero balances button
49      Private Sub getBalances_Click( _
50         ByVal sender As System.Object, ByVal e As System.EventArgs) _
51         Handles btnCredit.Click, btnZero.Click, btnDebit.Click
52         ' convert sender explicitly to object of type button
53         Dim senderButton As Button = CType(sender, Button)
54
55         ' get text from clicked Button, which stores account type
56         Dim accountType As String = senderButton.Text
57
58         ' read and display file information
59         Try
60            ' go back to the beginning of the file
61            input.Seek(0, SeekOrigin.Begin)
62
63            txtDisplay.Text = "The accounts are:" & vbCrLf
64
65            ' traverse file until end of file
66            While True
67               ' will store individual pieces of data
68               Dim inputFields() As String
69
70               Dim record As Record ' store each Record as file is read
71               Dim balance As Decimal ' store each Record's balance
72
73               ' get next Record available in file
74               Dim inputRecord As String = fileReader.ReadLine()
75
76               ' when at the end of file, exit method
77               If inputRecord Is Nothing Then
78                  Return
79               End If
80
81               inputFields = inputRecord.Split(","c) ' parse input
82
83               ' create Record from input
84               record = New Record(Convert.ToInt32( _
85                  inputFields(0)), inputFields(1), inputFields(2), _
86                  Convert.ToDecimal(inputFields(3)))
87
88               ' store record's last field in balance
89               balance = record.Balance
90
91               ' determine whether to display balance
92               If ShouldDisplay(balance, accountType) Then
93                  ' display record
94                  Dim output As String = _
95                     record.Account & vbTab & _
96                     record.FirstName & vbTab & _
97                     record.LastName & vbTab
98
```

Fig. 18.12 | Credit-inquiry program. (Part 2 of 5.)

```
99                     ' display balance with correct monetary format
100                     output &= String.Format("{0:F}", balance) & vbCrLf
101
102                     txtDisplay.Text &= output ' copy output to screen
103                  End If
104               End While
105               ' handle exception when file cannot be read
106            Catch ex As IOException
107               MessageBox.Show("Cannot Read File", "Error", _
108                  MessageBoxButtons.OK, MessageBoxIcon.Error)
109            End Try
110      End Sub ' getBalances_Click
111
112      ' determine whether to display given record
113      Private Function ShouldDisplay(ByVal balance As Decimal, _
114         ByVal accountType As String) As Boolean
115
116         If balance > 0 Then
117            ' display credit balances
118            If accountType = "Credit Balances" Then
119               Return True
120            End If
121         ElseIf balance < 0 Then
122            ' display debit balances
123            If accountType = "Debit Balances" Then
124               Return True
125            End If
126         Else ' balance = 0
127            ' display zero balances
128            If accountType = "Zero Balances" Then
129               Return True
130            End If
131         End If
132
133         Return False
134      End Function ' ShouldDisplay
135
136      ' invoked when user clicks Done button
137      Private Sub btnDone_Click(ByVal sender As System.Object, _
138         ByVal e As System.EventArgs) Handles btnDone.Click
139         ' determine whether file exists
140         If input IsNot Nothing Then
141            ' close file and StreamReader
142            Try
143               input.Close()
144               fileReader.Close()
145               ' handle exception if FileStream does not exist
146            Catch ex As IOException
147               ' notify user of error closing file
148               MessageBox.Show("Cannot close file", "Error", _
149                  MessageBoxButtons.OK, MessageBoxIcon.Error)
150            End Try
151         End If
```

Fig. 18.12 | Credit-inquiry program. (Part 3 of 5.)

```
152
153        Application.Exit()
154    End Sub ' btnDone_Click
155 End Class ' FrmCreditInquiry
```

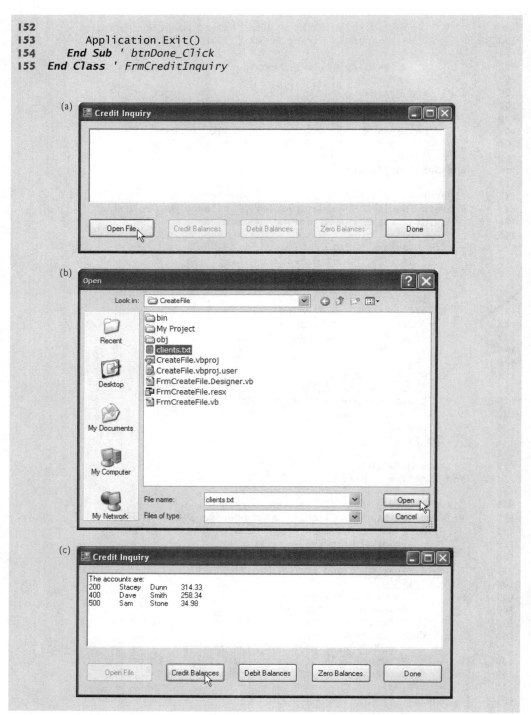

Fig. 18.12 | Credit-inquiry program. (Part 4 of 5.)

Fig. 18.12 | Credit-inquiry program. (Part 5 of 5.)

The program displays buttons that enable a credit manager to obtain credit information. The **Open File** button opens a file for gathering data. The **Credit Balances** button displays a list of accounts that have credit balances, the **Debit Balances** button displays a list of accounts that have debit balances and the **Zero Balances** button displays a list of accounts that have zero balances. The **Done** button exits the application.

When the user clicks the **Open File** button, the program calls the event handler btnOpen_Click (lines 15–45). Line 18 creates an OpenFileDialog, and line 19 calls its ShowDialog method to display the **Open** dialog, in which the user selects the file to open. Line 34 creates a FileStream object with read-only file access and assigns it to reference input. Line 37 creates a StreamReader object that we use to read text from the FileStream.

When the user clicks **Credit Balances**, **Debit Balances** or **Zero Balances**, the program invokes method getBalances_Click (lines 49–110). To create a single method that handles the events for multiple Buttons, select the Click event in the **Properties** window for one of the Buttons, type the name you wish to use for the event handler and press *Enter*. Then modify the Handles clause for the method so that it is followed by a comma separated list of the events the method handles, as shown in line 51. Line 53 uses Visual Basic's **CType** function to convert the sender parameter's type, which is an Object reference, to type Button. The sender parameter represents the control that generated the event. This conversion allows the event handler to use the properties and methods of the Button the user pressed. A conversion performed with the CType function is also known as a *cast operation*. Line 56 obtains the Button object's text, which the program uses to determine which type of accounts to display. Line 61 uses FileStream method **Seek** to reset the file-position pointer back to the beginning of the file. `FileStream` method `Seek` allows you to reset the file-position pointer by specifying the number of bytes it should be offset from the file's beginning, end or current position. The part of the file you want to be offset from is chosen using constants from the **SeekOrigin** enumeration. In this case, our stream is offset by 0 bytes from the file's beginning (`SeekOrigin.Begin`). Lines 66–104 loop using `Private` method `ShouldDisplay` (lines 113–134) to determine whether to display each record in the file. The loop obtains each record by repeatedly calling `StreamReader` method `ReadLine` (line 74) and splitting the text into tokens that are used to initialize object `record` (lines 81–86). Line 77 determines whether the end of the file has been reached. If so, the program returns from method `getBalances_Click` (line 78).

18.8 Serialization

Section 18.5 demonstrated how to write the individual fields of a `Record` object to a text file, and Section 18.6 demonstrated how to read those fields from a file and place their values in a `Record` object in memory. In the examples, `Record` was used to aggregate the information for one record. When the instance variables for a `Record` were output to a disk file, certain information was lost, such as the type of each value. For instance, if the value `"3"` is read from a file, there is no way to tell whether the value came from an `Integer`, a `String` or a `Decimal`. We have only data, not type information, on disk. If the program that is going to read this data "knows" what object type the data corresponds to, then the data can be read directly into objects of that type. For example, in Fig. 18.9, we know that we are inputting an `Integer` (the account number), followed by two `Strings` (the first and last names) and a `Decimal` (the balance). We also know that these values are separated by commas, with only one record on each line. Thus we are able to parse the strings and convert the account number to an `Integer` and the balance to a `Decimal`. Sometimes it would be easier to read or write entire objects. .NET provides such a mechanism, called *object serialization*. A *serialized object* is an object represented as a sequence of bytes that includes the object's data, as well as information about the object's type and the types of data stored in the object. After a serialized object has been written to a file, it can be read from the file and *deserialized*—that is, the type information and bytes that represent the object and its data can be used to recreate the object in memory.

Class **BinaryFormatter** (namespace **System.Runtime.Serialization.Formatters. Binary**) enables entire objects to be written to or read from a stream. `BinaryFormatter` method **Serialize** writes an object's representation to a file. `BinaryFormatter` method **Deserialize** reads this representation from a file and reconstructs the original object. Both methods throw a **SerializationException** if an error occurs during serialization or deserialization. Both methods require a `Stream` object (e.g., the `FileStream`) as a parameter so that the `BinaryFormatter` can access the correct stream. As you will see in Chapter 23, Networking: Streams-Based Sockets and Datagrams, serialization can be used to transmit objects between applications over a network.

In Sections 18.9 and 18.10, we create and manipulate sequential-access files using object serialization. Object serialization is performed with byte-based streams, so the sequential files created and manipulated will be binary files. Binary files are not human readable. For this reason, we write a separate application that reads and displays serialized objects.

18.9 Creating a Sequential-Access File Using Object Serialization

We begin by creating and writing serialized objects to a sequential-access file. In this section, we reuse much of the code from Section 18.5, so we focus only on the new features.

Defining the RecordSerializable Class

Let us begin by modifying our Record class (Fig. 18.8) so that objects of this class can be serialized. Class RecordSerializable (Fig. 18.13) is marked with the **<Serializable()>** attribute (line 5), which indicates to the CLR that objects of class RecordSerializable can be serialized. The classes for objects that we wish to write to or read from a stream must include this attribute in their declarations or must implement interface **ISerializable** (from namespace System.Runtime.Serialization). The remainder of class RecordSerializable is identical to class Record (Fig. 18.8).

```vb
 I    ' Fig. 18.13: RecordSerializable.vb
 2    ' Serializable class that represents a data record.
 3
 4    <Serializable()> _
 5    Public Class RecordSerializable
 6       Private accountValue As Integer
 7       Private firstNameValue As String
 8       Private lastNameValue As String
 9       Private balanceValue As Decimal
10
II       ' default constructor sets members to default values
12       Public Sub New()
13          MyClass.New(0, "", "", 0D)
14       End Sub ' New
15
16       ' overloaded constructor sets members to parameter values
17       Public Sub New(ByVal account As Integer, ByVal firstName As String, _
18          ByVal lastName As String, ByVal balance As Decimal)
19
20          account = account
21          firstNameValue = firstName
22          lastNameValue = lastName
23          balanceValue = balance
24       End Sub ' New
25
26       ' property Account
27       Public Property Account() As Integer
28          Get
29             Return accountValue
30          End Get
31          Set(ByVal value As Integer)
32             accountValue = value
33          End Set
34       End Property ' Account
35
```

Fig. 18.13 | RecordSerializable class for serializable objects. (Part I of 2.)

```
36          ' property FirstName
37          Public Property FirstName() As String
38             Get
39                Return firstNameValue
40             End Get
41             Set(ByVal value As String)
42                firstNameValue = value
43             End Set
44          End Property ' FirstName
45
46          ' property LastName
47          Public Property LastName() As String
48             Get
49                Return lastNameValue
50             End Get
51             Set(ByVal value As String)
52                lastNameValue = value
53             End Set
54          End Property ' LastName
55
56          ' property Balance
57          Public Property Balance() As Decimal
58             Get
59                Return balanceValue
60             End Get
61             Set(ByVal value As Decimal)
62                balanceValue = value
63             End Set
64          End Property ' Balance
65       End Class ' RecordSerializable
```

Fig. 18.13 | `RecordSerializable` class for serializable objects. (Part 2 of 2.)

In a class that is marked with the `<Serializable()>` attribute or that implements interface `ISerializable`, you must ensure that every instance variable of the class is also serializable. All simple-type variables and `String`s are serializable. For variables of reference types, you must check the class declaration (and possibly its base classes) to ensure that the type is serializable. By default, array objects are serializable. However, if the array contains references to other objects, those objects may or may not be serializable.

Using a Serialization Stream to Create an Output File

Now let's create a sequential-access file with serialization (Fig. 18.14). Line 10 creates a `BinaryFormatter` for writing serialized objects. Lines 38–39 open the `FileStream` to which this program writes the serialized objects. The `String` argument `fileName` that is passed to the `FileStream`'s constructor represents the name and path of the file to be opened. This specifies the file to which the serialized objects will be written.

 Common Programming Error 18.2

It is a logic error to open an existing file for output when the user wishes to preserve the file—the original file's contents will be lost.

```vb
 1    ' Fig 18.14: FrmCreateFile.vb
 2    ' Creating a sequential-access file using serialization.
 3    Imports System.IO
 4    Imports System.Runtime.Serialization.Formatters.Binary
 5    Imports System.Runtime.Serialization
 6    Imports BankLibrary
 7
 8    Public Class FrmCreateFile
 9       ' object for serializing Records in binary format
10       Private formatter As New BinaryFormatter()
11       Private output As FileStream ' stream for writing to a file
12
13       ' handler for btnSave_Click
14       Private Sub btnSave_Click(ByVal sender As System.Object, _
15          ByVal e As System.EventArgs) Handles btnSave.Click
16          ' create dialog box enabling user to save file
17          Dim fileChooser As New SaveFileDialog()
18          Dim result As DialogResult = fileChooser.ShowDialog()
19          Dim fileName As String ' name of file to save data
20
21          fileChooser.CheckFileExists = False ' allow user to create file
22
23          ' exit event handler if user clicked "Cancel"
24          If result = Windows.Forms.DialogResult.Cancel Then
25             Return
26          End If
27
28          fileName = fileChooser.FileName ' get specified file name
29
30          ' show error if user specified invalid file
31          If fileName = "" Or fileName Is Nothing Then
32             MessageBox.Show("Invalid File Name", "Error", _
33                MessageBoxButtons.OK, MessageBoxIcon.Error)
34          Else
35             ' save file via FileStream if user specified valid file
36             Try
37                ' open file with write access
38                output = New FileStream( _
39                   fileName, FileMode.OpenOrCreate, FileAccess.Write)
40
41                ' disable Save button and enable Enter button
42                btnSave.Enabled = False
43                btnEnter.Enabled = True
44                ' handle exception if there is a problem opening the file
45             Catch ex As IOException
46                ' notify user if file does not exist
47                MessageBox.Show("Error opening file", "Error", _
48                   MessageBoxButtons.OK, MessageBoxIcon.Error)
49             End Try
50          End If
51       End Sub ' btnSave_Click
52
```

Fig. 18.14 | Sequential file created using serialization. (Part 1 of 4.)

```
53      ' handler for btnEnter_Click
54      Private Sub btnEnter_Click(ByVal sender As System.Object, _
55         ByVal e As System.EventArgs) Handles btnEnter.Click
56         ' store TextBox values string array
57         Dim values As String() = GetTextBoxValues()
58
59         ' Record containing TextBox values to serialize
60         Dim record As New RecordSerializable()
61
62         ' determine whether TextBox account field is empty
63         If values(TextBoxIndices.ACCOUNT) <> "" Then
64            ' store TextBox values in Record and serialize Record
65            Try
66               ' get account number value from TextBox
67               Dim accountNumber As Integer = _
68                  Int32.Parse(values(TextBoxIndices.ACCOUNT))
69
70               ' determine whether accountNumber is valid
71               If accountNumber > 0 Then
72                  ' store TextBox fields in Record
73                  record.Account = accountNumber
74                  record.FirstName = _
75                     values(TextBoxIndices.FIRST)
76                  record.LastName = _
77                     values(TextBoxIndices.LAST)
78                  record.Balance = _
79                     Decimal.Parse(values(TextBoxIndices.BALANCE))
80
81                  ' write Record to FileStream ( serialize object )
82                  formatter.Serialize(output, record)
83               Else
84                  ' notify user if invalid account number
85                  MessageBox.Show("Invalid Account Number", "Error", _
86                     MessageBoxButtons.OK, MessageBoxIcon.Error)
87               End If
88            ' notify user if error occurs in serialization
89            Catch ex As SerializationException
90               MessageBox.Show("Error Writing to File", "Error", _
91                  MessageBoxButtons.OK, MessageBoxIcon.Error)
92            ' notify user if error occurs regarding parameter format
93            Catch ex As FormatException
94               MessageBox.Show("Invalid Format", "Error", _
95                  MessageBoxButtons.OK, MessageBoxIcon.Error)
96            End Try
97         End If
98
99         ClearTextBoxes() ' clear TextBox values
100     End Sub ' btnEnter_Click
101
102     ' handler for btnSave_Click
103     Private Sub btnExit_Click(ByVal sender As System.Object, _
104        ByVal e As System.EventArgs) Handles btnExit.Click
```

Fig. 18.14 | Sequential file created using serialization. (Part 2 of 4.)

```
105          ' determine whether file exists
106          If output IsNot Nothing Then
107             ' close file
108             Try
109                output.Close()
110                ' notify user of error closing file
111             Catch ex As IOException
112                MessageBox.Show("Cannot close file", "Error", _
113                   MessageBoxButtons.OK, MessageBoxIcon.Error)
114             End Try
115          End If
116
117          Application.Exit()
118       End Sub ' btnEnter_Click
119    End Class ' FrmCreateFile
```

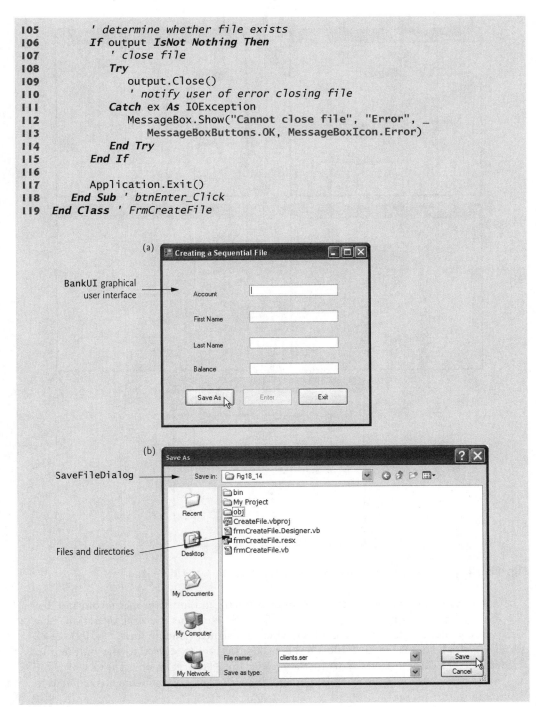

Fig. 18.14 | Sequential file created using serialization. (Part 3 of 4.)

Fig. 18.14 | Sequential file created using serialization. (Part 4 of 4.)

This program assumes that data is input correctly and in the proper record-number order. Event handler `btnEnter_Click` (lines 54–100) performs the write operation. Line 60 creates a `RecordSerializable` object, which is assigned values in lines 73–79. Line 82 calls method `Serialize` to write the `RecordSerializable` object to the output file. Method `Serialize` receives as its first argument the `FileStream` object into which the `BinaryFormatter` writes its second argument. Note that only one statement is required to write the entire object.

In the sample execution for the program in Fig. 18.14, we entered information for five accounts—the same information shown in Fig. 18.10. The program does not show

how the data records actually appear in the file. Remember that we are now using binary files, which are not human readable. To verify that the file was created successfully, the next section presents a program to read the file's contents and deserialize the objects.

18.10 Reading and Deserializing Data from a Sequential-Access Text File

The preceding section showed how to create a sequential-access file using object serialization. In this section, we discuss how to read serialized objects sequentially from a file.

Figure 18.15 reads and displays the contents of the file created by the program in Fig. 18.14. Line 10 creates the `BinaryFormatter` that will be used to read objects. The program opens the file for input by creating a `FileStream` object (line 35). The name of the file to open is specified as the first argument to the `FileStream` constructor.

```vb
1   ' Fig. 18.15: FrmReadSequentialAccessFile.vb
2   ' Reading a sequential-access file using deserialization.
3   Imports System.IO
4   Imports System.Runtime.Serialization.Formatters.Binary
5   Imports System.Runtime.Serialization
6   Imports BankLibrary
7
8   Public Class FrmReadSequentialAccessFile
9       ' object for deserializing Record in binary format
10      Private reader As New BinaryFormatter()
11      Private input As FileStream ' stream for reading from a file
12
13      ' invoked when user clicks Open button
14      Private Sub btnOpen_Click(ByVal sender As System.Object, _
15          ByVal e As System.EventArgs) Handles btnOpen.Click
16          ' create dialog box enabling user to open file
17          Dim fileChooser As New OpenFileDialog()
18          Dim result As DialogResult = fileChooser.ShowDialog()
19          Dim fileName As String ' name of file containing data
20
21          ' exit event handler if user clicked Cancel
22          If result = Windows.Forms.DialogResult.Cancel Then
23              Return
24          End If
25
26          fileName = fileChooser.FileName ' get specified file name
27          ClearTextBoxes()
28
29          ' show error if user specified invalid file
30          If fileName = "" Or fileName Is Nothing Then
31              MessageBox.Show("Invalid File Name", "Error", _
32                  MessageBoxButtons.OK, MessageBoxIcon.Error)
33          Else
34              ' create FileStream to obtain read access to file
35              input = New FileStream(fileName, FileMode.Open, FileAccess.Read)
36
```

Fig. 18.15 | Sequential file read using deserialzation. (Part 1 of 4.)

```
37                 btnOpen.Enabled = False ' disable Open File button
38                 btnNext.Enabled = True ' enable Next Record button
39             End If
40         End Sub ' btnOpen_Click
41
42         ' invoked when user clicks Next button
43         Private Sub btnNext_Click(ByVal sender As System.Object, _
44             ByVal e As System.EventArgs) Handles btnNext.Click
45             ' deserialize Record and store data in TextBoxes
46             Try
47                 ' get next RecordSerializable available in file
48                 Dim record As RecordSerializable = _
49                     CType(reader.Deserialize(input), RecordSerializable)
50
51                 ' store Record values in temporary string array
52                 Dim values() As String = { _
53                     record.Account.ToString(), record.FirstName.ToString(), _
54                     record.LastName.ToString(), record.Balance.ToString()}
55
56                 ' copy string array values to TextBox values
57                 SetTextBoxValues(values)
58                 ' handle exception when there are no Records in file
59             Catch ex As SerializationException
60                 input.Close() ' close FileStream if no Records in file
61                 btnOpen.Enabled = True ' enable Open File button
62                 btnNext.Enabled = False ' disable Next Record button
63
64                 ClearTextBoxes()
65
66                 ' notify user if no Records in file
67                 MessageBox.Show("No more records in file", "", _
68                     MessageBoxButtons.OK, MessageBoxIcon.Information)
69             End Try
70         End Sub ' btnNext_Click
71     End Class ' FrmReadSequentialAccessFile
```

Fig. 18.15 | Sequential file read using deserialzation. (Part 2 of 4.)

Fig. 18.15 | Sequential file read using deserialzation. (Part 3 of 4.)

Fig. 18.15 | Sequential file read using deserialzation. (Part 4 of 4.)

The program reads objects from a file in event handler `btnNext_Click` (lines 43–70). We use method `Deserialize` (of the `BinaryFormatter` created in line 10) to read the data (lines 48–49). Note that we cast the result of `Deserialize` to type `RecordSerializable` (line 49)—this cast is necessary because `Deserialize` returns a reference of type `object` and we need to access properties that belong to class `RecordSerializable`. If an error occurs during deserialization, a `SerializationException` is thrown, and the `FileStream` object is closed (line 60).

18.11 Wrap-Up

In this chapter, you learned how to use file processing to manipulate persistent data. You learned that data is stored in computers as 0s and 1s, and that combinations of these values are used to form bytes, fields, records and eventually files. We overviewed the differences between character-based and byte-based streams, as well as several file-processing classes from the `System.IO` namespace. You used class `File` to manipulate files and class `Directory` to manipulate directories. Next, you learned how to use sequential-access file processing to manipulate records in text files. We then discussed the differences between text-file processing and object serialization, and used serialization to store entire objects in and retrieve entire objects from files.

In Chapter 19, Extensible Markup Language (XML), we present Extensible Markup Language (XML)—a widely supported technology for describing data. Using XML, we can describe any type of data, such as mathematical formulas, music and financial reports. We demonstrate how to describe data with XML and how to write programs that can process XML encoded data. XML is having an important impact on the development of Web applications, which we discuss in detail in Chapters 21 and 22.

19

Extensible
Markup
Language
(XML)

*Knowing trees, I understand
the meaning of patience.
Knowing grass, I can
appreciate persistence.*
—Hal Borland

*Like everything
metaphysical, the harmony
between thought and reality
is to be found in the
grammar of the language.*
—Ludwig Wittgenstein

*I played with an idea, and
grew willful; tossed it into
the air; transformed it; let it
escape and recaptured it;
made it iridescent with
fancy, and winged it with
paradox.*
—Oscar Wilde

OBJECTIVES

In this chapter you will learn:

- To mark up data using XML.

- How XML namespaces help provide unique XML element and attribute names.

- To create DTDs and schemas for specifying and validating the structure of an XML document.

- To create and use simple XSL style sheets to render XML document data.

- To retrieve and modify XML data programmatically using .NET Framework classes.

- To validate XML documents against schemas using class `XmlReader`.

- To transform XML documents into XHTML using class `XslCompiledTransform`.

19.1 Introduction

The *Extensible Markup Language* (*XML*) was developed in 1996 by the *World Wide Web Consortium's* (*W3C's*) XML Working Group. XML is a widely supported *open technology* (i.e., nonproprietary technology) for describing data that has become the standard format for data exchanged between applications over the Internet.

The .NET Framework uses XML extensively. The Framework Class Library provides many XML-related classes, and much of Visual Studio's internal implementation also employs XML. Sections 19.2–19.6 introduce XML and XML-related technologies— XML namespaces for providing unique XML element and attribute names, and Document Type Definitions (DTDs) and XML Schemas for validating XML documents. These sections are required to support the use of XML in Chapters 20–22. Sections 19.7– 19.10 present additional XML technologies and key .NET Framework classes for creating and manipulating XML documents programmatically—this material is optional but recommended if you plan to use XML in your own Visual Basic applications.

19.2 XML Basics

XML permits document authors to create *markup* (i.e., a text-based notation for describing data) for virtually any type of information. This enables document authors to create entirely new markup languages for describing any type of data, such as mathematical formulas, software-configuration instructions, chemical molecular structures, music, news, recipes and financial reports. XML describes data in a way that both human beings and computers can understand.

Figure 19.1 is a simple XML document that describes information for a baseball player. We focus on lines 5–11 to introduce basic XML syntax. You will learn about the other elements of this document in Section 19.3.

XML documents contain text that represents content (i.e., data), such as John (line 6 of Fig. 19.1), and *elements* that specify the document's structure, such as firstName (line 6 of Fig. 19.1). XML documents delimit elements with *start tags* and *end tags*. A start tag

```
 1    <?xml version = "1.0"?>
 2    <!-- Fig. 19.1: player.xml -->
 3    <!-- Baseball player structured with XML -->
 4
 5    <player>
 6        <firstName>John</firstName>
 7
 8        <lastName>Doe</lastName>
 9
10        <battingAverage>0.375</battingAverage>
11    </player>
```

Fig. 19.1 | XML that describes a baseball player's information.

consists of the element name in *angle brackets* (e.g., <player> and <firstName> in lines 5 and 6, respectively). An end tag consists of the element name preceded by a *forward slash* (/) in angle brackets (e.g., </firstName> and </player> in lines 6 and 11, respectively). An element's start and end tags enclose text that represents a piece of data (e.g., the firstName of the player—John—in line 6, which is enclosed by the <firstName> start tag and </firstName> end tag). Every XML document must have exactly one *root element* that contains all the other elements. In Fig. 19.1, player (lines 5–11) is the root element.

Some XML-based markup languages include XHTML (Extensible HyperText Markup Language—HTML's replacement for marking up Web content), MathML (for mathematics), VoiceXML™ (for speech), CML (Chemical Markup Language—for chemistry) and XBRL (Extensible Business Reporting Language—for financial data exchange). These markup languages are called XML *vocabularies* and provide a means for describing particular types of data in standardized, structured ways.

Massive amounts of data are currently stored on the Internet in a variety of formats (e.g., databases, Web pages, text files). Based on current trends, it is likely that much of this data, especially that which is passed between systems, will soon take the form of XML. Organizations see XML as the future of data encoding. Information technology groups are planning ways to integrate XML into their systems. Industry groups are developing custom XML vocabularies for most major industries that will allow computer-based business applications to communicate in common languages. For example, Web services, which we discuss in Chapter 22, allow Web-based applications to exchange data seamlessly through standard protocols based on XML.

The next generation of the Internet and World Wide Web is being built on a foundation of XML, which enables the development of more sophisticated Web-based applications. XML allows you to assign meaning to what would otherwise be random pieces of data. As a result, programs can "understand" the data they manipulate. For example, a Web browser might view a street address listed on a simple HTML Web page as a string of characters without any real meaning. In an XML document, however, this data can be clearly identified (i.e., marked up) as an address. A program that uses the document can recognize this data as an address and provide links to a map of that location, driving directions from that location or other location-specific information. Likewise, an application can recognize names of people, dates, ISBN numbers and any other type of XML-encoded data. Based on this data, the application can present users with other related information, providing a richer, more meaningful user experience.

Viewing and Modifying XML Documents

XML documents are highly portable. Viewing or modifying an XML document—which is a text file that ends with the *.xml* filename extension—does not require special software, although many software tools exist, and new ones are frequently released that make it more convenient to develop XML-based applications. Any text editor that supports ASCII/Unicode characters can open XML documents for viewing and editing. Also, most Web browsers can display XML documents in a formatted manner that shows the XML's structure. We demonstrate this using Internet Explorer in Section 19.3. One important characteristic of XML is that it is both human readable and machine readable.

Processing XML Documents

Processing an XML document requires software called an *XML parser* (or *XML processor*). A parser makes the document's data available to applications. While reading the contents of an XML document, a parser checks that the document follows the syntax rules specified by the W3C's XML Recommendation (www.w3.org/XML). XML syntax requires a single root element, a start tag and end tag for each element, and properly nested tags (i.e., the end tag for a nested element must appear before the end tag of the enclosing element). Furthermore, XML is case sensitive, so the proper capitalization must be used in elements. A document that conforms to this syntax is a *well-formed XML document*, and is syntactically correct. We present fundamental XML syntax in Section 19.3. If an XML parser can process an XML document successfully, that XML document is well formed. Parsers can provide access to XML-encoded data in well-formed documents only.

Often, XML parsers are built into software such as Visual Studio or available for download over the Internet. Popular parsers include *Microsoft XML Core Services* (*MSXML*), the Apache Software Foundation's *Xerces* (xml.apache.org) and the opensource *Expat XML Parser* (expat.sourceforge.net). In this chapter, we use MSXML.

Validating XML Documents

An XML document can optionally reference a *Document Type Definition* (*DTD*) or a *schema* that defines the proper structure of the XML document. When an XML document references a DTD or a schema, some parsers (called *validating parsers*) can read the DTD/schema and check that the XML document follows the structure defined by the DTD/schema. If the XML document conforms to the DTD/schema (i.e., the document has the appropriate structure), the XML document is *valid*. For example, if in Fig. 19.1 we were referencing a DTD that specifies that a player element must have firstName, lastName and battingAverage elements, then omitting the lastName element (line 8 in Fig. 19.1) would cause the XML document player.xml to be invalid. However, the XML document would still be well formed, because it follows proper XML syntax (i.e., it has one root element, and each element has a start tag and an end tag). By definition, a valid XML document is well formed. Parsers that cannot check for document conformity against DTDs/schemas are *nonvalidating parsers*—they determine only whether an XML document is well formed, not whether it is valid.

We discuss validation, DTDs and schemas, as well as the key differences between these two types of structural specifications, in Sections 19.5 and 19.6. For now, note that schemas are XML documents themselves, whereas DTDs are not. As you will learn in Section 19.6, this difference presents several advantages in using schemas over DTDs.

 Software Engineering Observation 19.1

DTDs and schemas are essential for business-to-business (B2B) transactions and mission-critical systems. Validating XML documents ensures that disparate systems can manipulate data structured in standardized ways and prevents errors caused by missing or malformed data.

Formatting and Manipulating XML Documents

XML documents contain only data, not formatting instructions, so applications that process XML documents must decide how to manipulate or display each document's data. For example, a PDA (personal digital assistant) may render an XML document differently than a wireless phone or a desktop computer. You can use *Extensible Stylesheet Language (XSL)* to specify rendering instructions for different platforms. We discuss XSL in Section 19.7.

XML-processing programs can also search, sort and manipulate XML data using technologies such as XSL. Some other XML-related technologies are XPath (XML Path Language—a language for accessing parts of an XML document), XSL-FO (XSL Formatting Objects—an XML vocabulary used to describe document formatting) and XSLT (XSL Transformations—a language for transforming XML documents into other documents). We present XSLT in Section 19.7. We also introduce XPath in Section 19.7, then discuss it in greater detail in Section 19.8.

19.3 Structuring Data

In this section and throughout this chapter, we create our own XML markup. XML allows you to describe data precisely in a well-structured format.

XML Markup for an Article

In Fig. 19.2, we present an XML document that marks up a simple article using XML. The line numbers shown are for reference only and are not part of the XML document.

```
1   <?xml version = "1.0"?>
2   <!-- Fig. 19.2: article.xml -->
3   <!-- Article structured with XML -->
4
5   <article>
6      <title>Simple XML</title>
7
8      <date>May 5, 2005</date>
9
10     <author>
11        <firstName>John</firstName>
12        <lastName>Doe</lastName>
13     </author>
14
15     <summary>XML is pretty easy.</summary>
16
```

Fig. 19.2 | XML used to mark up an article. (Part I of 2.)

```
17      <content>
18          In this chapter, we present a wide variety of examples that use XML.
19      </content>
20  </article>
```

Fig. 19.2 | XML used to mark up an article. (Part 2 of 2.)

This document begins with an *XML declaration* (line 1), which identifies the document as an XML document. The *version attribute* specifies the XML version to which the document conforms. The current XML standard is version 1.0. Though the W3C released a version 1.1 specification in February 2004, this newer version is not yet widely supported. The W3C may continue to release new versions as XML evolves to meet the requirements of different fields.

Portability Tip 19.1

Documents should include the XML declaration to identify the version of XML used. A document that lacks an XML declaration might be assumed to conform to the latest version of XML—when it does not, errors could result.

Common Programming Error 19.1

Placing whitespace characters before the XML declaration is an error.

XML comments (lines 2–3), which begin with <!-- and end with -->, can be placed almost anywhere in an XML document. XML comments can span to multiple lines—an end marker on each line is not needed; the end marker can appear on a subsequent line as long as there is exactly one end marker (-->) for each begin marker (<!--). Comments are used in XML for documentation purposes. Line 4 is a blank line. As in a Visual Basic program, blank lines, whitespaces and indentation are used in XML to improve readability. Later you will see that the blank lines are normally ignored by XML parsers.

Common Programming Error 19.2

In an XML document, each start tag must have a matching end tag; omitting either tag is an error. Soon, you will learn how such errors are detected.

Common Programming Error 19.3

XML is case sensitive. Using different cases for the start tag and end tag names for the same element is a syntax error.

In Fig. 19.2, `article` (lines 5–20) is the root element. The lines that precede the root element (lines 1–4) are the XML *prolog*. In an XML prolog, the XML declaration must appear before the comments and any other markup.

The elements we used in the example do not come from any specific markup language. Instead, we chose the element names and markup structure that best describe our particular data. You can invent elements to mark up your data. For example, element `title` (line 6) contains text that describes the article's title (e.g., `Simple XML`). Similarly, `date` (line 8), `author` (lines 10–13), `firstName` (line 11), `lastName` (line 12), `summary` (line 15) and `content` (lines 17–19) contain text that describes the date, author, the author's first name, the author's last name, a summary and the content of the document, respectively. XML element names can be of any length and may contain letters, digits, underscores, hyphens and periods. However, they must begin with either a letter or an underscore, and they should not begin with "xml" in any combination of uppercase and lowercase letters (e.g., XML, Xml, xMl) as this is reserved for use in the XML standards.

Common Programming Error 19.4

Using a whitespace character in an XML element name is an error.

Good Programming Practice 19.1

XML element names should be meaningful to humans and should not use abbreviations.

XML elements are *nested* to form hierarchies—with the root element at the top of the hierarchy. This allows document authors to create parent/child relationships between data. For example, elements title, date, author, summary and content are nested within article. Elements firstName and lastName are nested within author. Figure 19.21 shows the hierarchy of Fig. 19.2.

Common Programming Error 19.5

Nesting XML tags improperly is a syntax error. For example, <x><y>hello</x></y> is an error, because the </y> tag must precede the </x> tag.

Any element that contains other elements (e.g., article or author) is a *container element*. Container elements also are called *parent elements*. Elements nested inside a container element are *child elements* (or children) of that container element.

Viewing an XML Document in Internet Explorer

The XML document in Fig. 19.2 is simply a text file named article.xml. This document does not contain formatting information for the article. This is because XML is a technology for describing the structure of data. Formatting and displaying data from an XML document are application-specific issues. For example, when the user loads article.xml in Internet Explorer (IE), MSXML (Microsoft XML Core Services) parses and displays the document's data. Internet Explorer uses a built-in *style sheet* to format the data. Note that the resulting format of the data (Fig. 19.3) is similar to the format of the listing in Fig. 19.2. In Section 19.7, we show how to create style sheets to transform your XML data into various formats suitable for display.

Note the minus sign (–) and plus sign (+) in the screen shots of Fig. 19.3. Although these symbols are not part of the XML document, Internet Explorer places them next to every container element. A minus sign indicates that Internet Explorer is displaying the container element's child elements. Clicking the minus sign next to an element collapses that element (i.e., causes Internet Explorer to hide the container element's children and replace the minus sign with a plus sign). Conversely, clicking the plus sign next to an element expands that element (i.e., causes Internet Explorer to display the container element's children and replace the plus sign with a minus sign). This behavior is similar to viewing the directory structure using Windows Explorer. In fact, a directory structure often is modeled as a series of tree structures, in which the *root* of a tree represents a drive letter (e.g., C:), and *nodes* in the tree represent directories. Parsers often store XML data as tree structures to facilitate efficient manipulation, as discussed in Section 19.8.

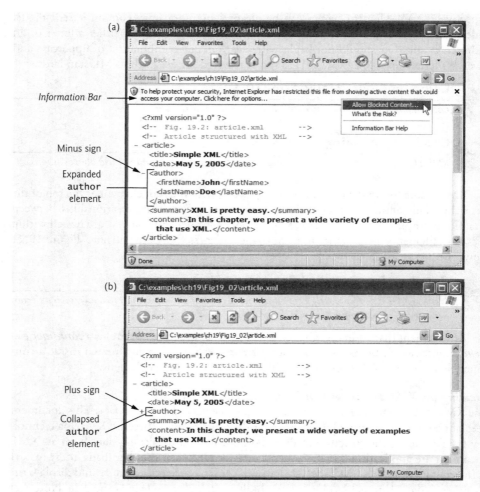

Fig. 19.3 | `article.xml` displayed by Internet Explorer.

[*Note:* In Windows XP Service Pack 2, by default Internet Explorer displays all the XML elements in expanded view, and clicking the minus sign (Fig. 19.3(a) does not do anything. So by default, Windows will not be able to collapse the element. To enable this functionality, right click the *Information Bar* just below the **Address** field and select **Allow Blocked Content....** Then click **Yes** in the popup window that appears.]

XML Markup for a Business Letter

Now that we have seen a simple XML document, let's examine a more complex XML document that marks up a business letter (Fig. 19.4). Again, we begin the document with the XML declaration (line 1) that states the XML version to which the document conforms.

Line 5 specifies that this XML document references a DTD. Recall from Section 19.2 that DTDs define the structure of the data for an XML document. For example, a DTD specifies the elements and parent-child relationships between elements permitted in an XML document.

```
1   <?xml version = "1.0"?>
2   <!-- Fig. 19.4: letter.xml -->
3   <!-- Business letter marked up as XML -->
4
5   <!DOCTYPE letter SYSTEM "letter.dtd">
6
7   <letter>
8      <contact type = "sender">
9         <name>Jane Doe</name>
10        <address1>Box 12345</address1>
11        <address2>15 Any Ave.</address2>
12        <city>Othertown</city>
13        <state>Otherstate</state>
14        <zip>67890</zip>
15        <phone>555-4321</phone>
16        <flag gender = "F" />
17     </contact>
18
19     <contact type = "receiver">
20        <name>John Doe</name>
21        <address1>123 Main St.</address1>
22        <address2></address2>
23        <city>Anytown</city>
24        <state>Anystate</state>
25        <zip>12345</zip>
26        <phone>555-1234</phone>
27        <flag gender = "M" />
28     </contact>
29
30     <salutation>Dear Sir:</salutation>
31
32     <paragraph>It is our privilege to inform you about our new database
33        managed with XML. This new system allows you to reduce the
34        load on your inventory list server by having the client machine
35        perform the work of sorting and filtering the data.
36     </paragraph>
37
38     <paragraph>Please visit our Web site for availability
39        and pricing.
40     </paragraph>
41
42     <closing>Sincerely,</closing>
43     <signature>Ms. Jane Doe</signature>
44  </letter>
```

Fig. 19.4 | Business letter marked up as XML.

Error-Prevention Tip 19.1

An XML document is not required to reference a DTD, but validating XML parsers can use a DTD to ensure that the document has the proper structure.

Portability Tip 19.2

Validating an XML document helps guarantee that independent developers will exchange data in a standardized form that conforms to the DTD.

The DTD reference (line 5) contains three items, the name of the root element that the DTD specifies (letter); the keyword **SYSTEM** (which denotes an *external DTD*—a DTD declared in a separate file, as opposed to a DTD declared locally in the same file); and the DTD's name and location (i.e., letter.dtd in the current directory). DTD document filenames typically end with the *.dtd* extension. We discuss DTDs and letter.dtd in detail in Section 19.5.

Several tools (many of which are free) validate documents against DTDs and schemas (discussed in Section 19.5 and Section 19.6, respectively). Microsoft's *XML Validator* is available free of charge from the **Download Sample** link at

```
msdn.microsoft.com/archive/en-us/samples/internet/
xml/xml_validator/default.asp
```

This validator can validate XML documents against both DTDs and Schemas. To install it, run the downloaded executable file xml_validator.exe and follow the steps to complete the installation. Once the installation is successful, open the validate_js.htm file located in your XML Validator installation directory in IE to validate your XML documents. We installed the XML Validator at C:\XMLValidator (Fig. 19.5). The output (Fig. 19.6) shows the results of validating the document using Microsoft's XML Validator. Visit www.w3.org/XML/Schema for a list of additional validation tools.

Root element letter (lines 7–44 of Fig. 19.4) contains the child elements contact, contact, salutation, paragraph, paragraph, closing and signature. In addition to being placed between tags, data also can be placed in *attributes*—name-value pairs that appear within the angle brackets of start tags. Elements can have any number of attributes (separated by spaces) in their start tags. The first contact element (lines 8–17) has an attribute named type with *attribute value* "sender", which indicates that this contact element identifies the letter's sender. The second contact element (lines 19–28) has attribute type with value "receiver", which indicates that this contact element identifies

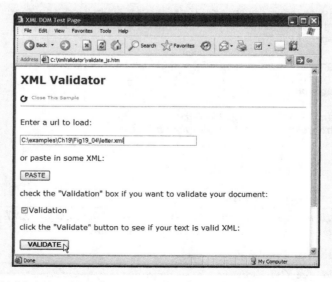

Fig. 19.5 | Validating an XML document with Microsoft's XML Validator.

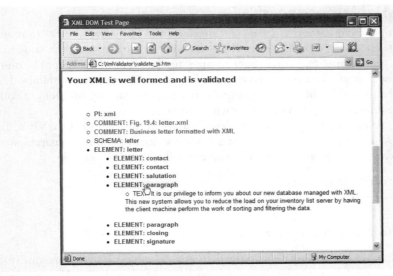

Fig. 19.6 | Validation result using Microsoft's XML Validator.

the letter's recipient. Like element names, attribute names are case sensitive, can be any length, may contain letters, digits, underscores, hyphens and periods, and must begin with either a letter or an underscore character. A `contact` element stores various items of information about a contact, such as the contact's name (represented by element `name`), address (represented by elements `address1`, `address2`, `city`, `state` and `zip`), phone number (represented by element `phone`) and gender (represented by attribute `gender` of element `flag`). Element `salutation` (line 30) marks up the letter's salutation. Lines 32–40 mark up the letter's body using two `paragraph` elements. Elements `closing` (line 42) and `signature` (line 43) mark up the closing sentence and the author's "signature," respectively.

Common Programming Error 19.6

Failure to enclose attribute values in double (" ") or single (' ') quotes is a syntax error.

Line 16 introduces the *empty element* `flag`. An empty element is one that does not contain any content. Instead, an empty element sometimes contains data in attributes. Empty element `flag` contains an attribute that indicates the gender of the contact (represented by the parent `contact` element). Document authors can close an empty element either by placing a slash immediately preceding the right angle bracket, as shown in line 16, or by explicitly writing an end tag, as in line 22

```
<address2></address2>
```

Note that the `address2` element in line 22 is empty because there is no second part to this contact's address. However, we must include this element to conform to the structural rules specified in the XML document's DTD—`letter.dtd` (which we present in Section 19.5). This DTD specifies that each `contact` element must have an `address2` child element (even if it is empty). In Section 19.5, you will learn how DTDs indicate that certain elements are required while others are optional.

19.4 XML Namespaces

XML allows document authors to create custom elements. This extensibility can result in *naming collisions* among elements in an XML document that each have the same name. For example, we may use the element book to mark up data about a Deitel publication. A stamp collector may use the element book to mark up data about a book of stamps. Using both of these elements in the same document could create a naming collision, making it difficult to determine which kind of data each element contains.

An XML *namespace* is a collection of element and attribute names. Like Visual Basic namespaces, XML namespaces provide a means for document authors to unambiguously refer to elements with the same name (i.e., prevent collisions). For example,

> `<subject>`Math`</subject>`

and

> `<subject>`Cardiology`</subject>`

use element subject to mark up data. In the first case, the subject is something one studies in school, whereas in the second case, the subject is a field of medicine. Namespaces can differentiate these two subject elements. For example

> `<school:subject>`Math`</school:subject>`

and

> `<medical:subject>`Cardiology`</medical:subject>`

Both school and medical are *namespace prefixes*. A document author places a namespace prefix and colon (:) before an element name to specify the namespace to which that element belongs. Document authors can create their own namespace prefixes using virtually any name except the reserved namespace prefix xml. In the next subsections, we demonstrate how document authors ensure that namespaces are unique.

Common Programming Error 19.7

Attempting to create a namespace prefix named xml in any mixture of uppercase and lowercase letters is a syntax error—the xml namespace prefix is reserved for internal use by XML itself.

Differentiating Elements with Namespaces

Figure 19.7 demonstrates namespaces. In this document, namespaces differentiate two distinct elements—the file element related to a text file and the file document related to an image file.

Lines 6–7 use the XML-namespace reserved attribute *xmlns* to create two namespace prefixes—text and image. Each namespace prefix is bound to a series of characters called a *Uniform Resource Identifier (URI)* that uniquely identifies the namespace. Document authors create their own namespace prefixes and URIs. A URI is a way to identifying a resource, typically on the Internet. Two popular types of URI are *Uniform Resource Name (URN)* and *Uniform Resource Locator (URL)*.

To ensure that namespaces are unique, document authors must provide unique URIs. In this example, we use the text urn:deitel:textInfo and urn:deitel:imageInfo as

```
 1   <?xml version = "1.0"?>
 2   <!-- Fig. 19.7: namespace.xml -->
 3   <!-- Demonstrating namespaces -->
 4
 5   <text:directory
 6      xmlns:text = "urn:deitel:textInfo"
 7      xmlns:image = "urn:deitel:imageInfo">
 8
 9      <text:file filename = "book.xml">
10         <text:description>A book list</text:description>
11      </text:file>
12
13      <image:file filename = "funny.jpg">
14         <image:description>A funny picture</image:description>
15         <image:size width = "200" height = "100" />
16      </image:file>
17   </text:directory>
```

```
C:\examples\ch19\Fig19_07\namespace.xml

File   Edit   View   Favorites   Tools   Help

  Back          x   ↻   ⌂   Search   Favorites   ◯   ◯ · ◯ · ◯   W   · ◯   ◯

Address   C:\examples\ch19\Fig19_07\namespace.xml                              Go

<?xml version="1.0" ?>
<!-- Fig. 19.7: namespace.xml   -->
<!-- Demonstrating namespaces   -->
- <text:directory xmlns:text="urn:deitel:textInfo" xmlns:image="urn:deitel:imageInfo">
  - <text:file filename="book.xml">
      <text:description>A book list</text:description>
    </text:file>
  - <image:file filename="funny.jpg">
      <image:description>A funny picture</image:description>
      <image:size width="200" height="100" />
    </image:file>
  </text:directory>

  Done                                                        My Computer
```

Fig. 19.7 | XML namespaces demonstration.

URIs. These URIs employ the URN scheme frequently used to identify namespaces. Under this naming scheme, a URI begins with `"urn:"`, followed by a unique series of additional names separated by colons.

Another common practice is to use URLs, which specify the location of a file or a resource on the Internet. For example, `www.deitel.com` is the URL that identifies the home page of the Deitel & Associates Web site. Using URLs guarantees that the namespaces are unique because the domain names (e.g., `www.deitel.com`) are guaranteed to be unique. For example, lines 5–7 could be rewritten as

```
<text:directory
    xmlns:text = "http://www.deitel.com/xmlns-text"
    xmlns:image = "http://www.deitel.com/xmlns-image">
```

where URLs related to the Deitel & Associates, Inc. domain name serve as URIs to identify the `text` and `image` namespaces. The parser does not visit these URLs, nor do these URLs need to refer to actual Web pages. They each simply represent a unique series of characters used to differentiate URI names. In fact, any string can represent a namespace. For example, our `image` namespace URI could be `hgjfkdlsa4556`, in which case our prefix assignment would be

> `xmlns:image = "hgjfkdlsa4556"`

Lines 9–11 use the `text` namespace prefix for elements `file` and `description`. Note that the end tags must also specify the namespace prefix `text`. Lines 13–16 apply namespace prefix `image` to the elements `file`, `description` and `size`. Note that attributes do not require namespace prefixes (although they can have them), because each attribute is already part of an element that specifies the namespace prefix. For example, attribute `filename` (line 9) is implicitly part of namespace `text` because its element (i.e., `file`) specifies the `text` namespace prefix.

Specifying a Default Namespace

To eliminate the need to place namespace prefixes in each element, document authors may specify a *default namespace* for an element and its children. Figure 19.8 demonstrates using a default namespace (`urn:deitel:textInfo`) for element `directory`.

```
 1   <?xml version = "1.0"?>
 2   <!-- Fig. 19.8: defaultnamespace.xml -->
 3   <!-- Using default namespaces -->
 4
 5   <directory xmlns = "urn:deitel:textInfo"
 6       xmlns:image = "urn:deitel:imageInfo">
 7
 8       <file filename = "book.xml">
 9          <description>A book list</description>
10       </file>
11
12       <image:file filename = "funny.jpg">
13          <image:description>A funny picture</image:description>
14          <image:size width = "200" height = "100" />
15       </image:file>
16   </directory>
```

Fig. 19.8 | Default namespace demonstration.

Line 5 defines a default namespace using attribute `xmlns` with a URI as its value. Once we define this default namespace, child elements belonging to the namespace need not be qualified by a namespace prefix. Thus, element `file` (lines 8–10) is in the default namespace `urn:deitel:textInfo`. Compare this to lines 8–10 of Fig. 19.7, where we had to prefix the `file` and `description` element names with the namespace prefix `text`.

The default namespace applies to the `directory` element and all elements that are not qualified with a namespace prefix. However, we can use a namespace prefix to specify a different namespace for particular elements. For example, the `file` element in lines 12–15 includes the `image` namespace prefix, indicating that this element is in the `urn:deitel:imageInfo` namespace, not the default namespace.

Namespaces in XML Vocabularies

XML-based languages, such as XML Schema (Section 19.6), Extensible Stylesheet Language (XSL) (Section 19.7) and BizTalk (`www.microsoft.com/biztalk`), often use namespaces to identify their elements. Each of these vocabularies defines special-purpose elements that are grouped in namespaces. These namespaces help prevent naming collisions between predefined elements and user-defined elements.

19.5 Document Type Definitions (DTDs)

Document Type Definitions (DTDs) are one of two main types of documents you can use to specify XML document structure. Section 19.6 presents W3C XML Schema documents, which provide an improved method of specifying XML document structure.

Software Engineering Observation 19.2

XML documents can have many different structures, and for this reason an application cannot be certain whether a particular document it receives is complete, ordered properly, and not missing data. DTDs and schemas (Section 19.6) solve this problem by providing an extensible way to describe XML document structure. Applications should use DTDs or schemas to confirm whether XML documents are valid.

Software Engineering Observation 19.3

*Many organizations and individuals are creating DTDs and schemas for a broad range of applications. These collections—called **repositories**—are available free for download from the Web (e.g., `www.xml.org`, `www.oasis-open.org`).*

Creating a Document Type Definition

Figure 19.4 presented a simple business letter marked up with XML. Recall that line 5 of `letter.xml` references a DTD—`letter.dtd` (Fig. 19.9). This DTS specifies the business letter's element types and attributes, and their relationships to one another.

A DTD describes the structure of an XML document and enables an XML parser to verify whether an XML document is valid (i.e., whether its elements contain the proper attributes and appear in the proper sequence). DTDs allow users to check document structure and to exchange data in a standardized format. A DTD expresses the set of rules for document structure using an EBNF (Extended Backus-Naur Form) grammar. [*Note:* EBNF grammars are commonly used to define programming languages. For more information on EBNF grammars, please see `en.wikipedia.org/wiki/EBNF` or `www.garshol.priv.no/download/text/bnf.html`.]

```
 1   <!-- Fig. 19.9: letter.dtd      -->
 2   <!-- DTD document for letter.xml -->
 3
 4   <!ELEMENT letter ( contact+, salutation, paragraph+,
 5      closing, signature )>
 6
 7   <!ELEMENT contact ( name, address1, address2, city, state,
 8      zip, phone, flag )>
 9   <!ATTLIST contact type CDATA #IMPLIED>
10
11   <!ELEMENT name ( #PCDATA )>
12   <!ELEMENT address1 ( #PCDATA )>
13   <!ELEMENT address2 ( #PCDATA )>
14   <!ELEMENT city ( #PCDATA )>
15   <!ELEMENT state ( #PCDATA )>
16   <!ELEMENT zip ( #PCDATA )>
17   <!ELEMENT phone ( #PCDATA )>
18   <!ELEMENT flag EMPTY>
19   <!ATTLIST flag gender (M | F) "M">
20
21   <!ELEMENT salutation ( #PCDATA )>
22   <!ELEMENT closing ( #PCDATA )>
23   <!ELEMENT paragraph ( #PCDATA )>
24   <!ELEMENT signature ( #PCDATA )>
```

Fig. 19.9 | Document Type Definition (DTD) for a business letter.

Common Programming Error 19.8

For documents validated with DTDs, any document that uses elements, attributes or relationships not explicitly defined by a DTD is an invalid document.

Defining Elements in a DTD

The **ELEMENT *element type declaration*** in lines 4–5 defines the rules for element letter. In this case, letter contains one or more contact elements, one salutation element, one or more paragraph elements, one closing element and one signature element, in that sequence. The *plus sign* (+) *occurrence indicator* specifies that the DTD allows one or more occurrences of an element. Other occurence indicators include the *asterisk* (*), which indicates an optional element that can occur zero or more times, and the *question mark* (?), which indicates an optional element that can occur at most once (i.e., zero or one occurrence). If an element does not have an occurrence indicator, the DTD allows exactly one occurrence.

The contact element type declaration (lines 7–8) specifies that a contact element contains child elements name, address1, address2, city, state, zip, phone and flag— in that order. The DTD requires exactly one occurrence of each of these elements.

Defining Attributes in a DTD

Line 9 uses the **ATTLIST *attribute-list declaration*** to define an attribute named type for the contact element. Keyword **#IMPLIED** specifies that if the parser finds a contact element without a type attribute, the parser can choose an arbitrary value for the attribute or can ignore the attribute. Either way the document will still be valid (if the rest of the document is valid)—a missing type attribute will not invalidate the document. Other keywords that can be used in place of #IMPLIED in an ATTLIST declaration include **#REQUIRED** and **#FIXED**. Keyword #REQUIRED specifies that the attribute must be present in the element, and keyword #FIXED specifies that the attribute (if present) must have the given fixed value. For example,

```
<!ATTLIST address zip CDATA #FIXED "01757">
```

indicates that attribute zip (if present in element address) must have the value 01757 for the document to be valid. If the attribute is not present, then the parser, by default, uses the fixed value that the ATTLIST declaration specifies.

Character Data vs. Parsed Character Data
Keyword **CDATA** (line 9) specifies that attribute type contains *character data* (i.e., a string). A parser will pass such data to an application without modification.

Software Engineering Observation 19.4

DTD syntax cannot describe an element's (or attribute's) type. For example, a DTD cannot specify that a particular element or attribute can contain only integer data.

Keyword **#PCDATA** (line 11) specifies that an element (e.g., name) may contain *parsed character data* (i.e., data that is processed by an XML parser). Elements with parsed character data cannot contain markup characters, such as less than (<), greater than (>) or ampersand (&). The document author should replace any markup character in a #PCDATA element with the character's corresponding *character entity reference*. For example, the character entity reference < should be used in place of the less-than symbol (<), and the character entity reference > should be used in place of the greater-than symbol (>). A document author who wishes to use a literal ampersand should use the entity reference & instead—parsed character data can contain ampersands (&) only for inserting entities. See Appendix H, XHTML Special Characters for a list of other character entity references.

Common Programming Error 19.9

Using markup characters (e.g., <, > and &) in parsed character data is an error. Use character entity references (e.g., <, > and & instead).

Defining Empty Elements in a DTD
Line 18 defines an empty element named flag. Keyword **EMPTY** specifies that the element does not contain any data between its start and end tags. Empty elements commonly describe data via attributes. For example, flag's data appears in its gender attribute (line 19). Line 19 specifies that the gender attribute's value must be one of the enumerated values (M or F) enclosed in parentheses and delimited by a vertical bar (|) meaning "or." Note that line 19 also indicates that gender has a default value of M.

Well-Formed Documents vs. Valid Documents
In Section 19.3, we demonstrated how to use the Microsoft XML Validator to validate an XML document against its specified DTD. The validation revealed that the XML document letter.xml (Fig. 19.4) is well formed and valid—it conforms to letter.dtd (Fig. 19.9). Recall that a well-formed document is syntactically correct (i.e., each start tag

has a corresponding end tag, the document contains only one root element, etc.), and a valid document contains the proper elements with the proper attributes in the proper sequence. An XML document cannot be valid unless it is well formed.

When a document fails to conform to a DTD or a schema, the Microsoft XML Validator displays an error message. For example, the DTD in Fig. 19.9 indicates that a `contact` element must contain the child element `name`. A document that omits this child element is still well formed, but is not valid. In such a scenario, Microsoft XML Validator displays the error message shown in Fig. 19.10.

19.6 W3C XML Schema Documents

In this section, we introduce schemas for specifying XML document structure and validating XML documents. Many developers in the XML community believe that DTDs are not flexible enough to meet today's programming needs. For example, DTDs lack a way of indicating what specific type of data (e.g., numeric, text) an element can contain and DTDs are not themselves XML documents. These and other limitations have led to the development of schemas.

Unlike DTDs, schemas do not use EBNF grammar. Instead, schemas use XML syntax and are actually XML documents that programs can manipulate. Like DTDs, schemas are used by validating parsers to validate documents.

In this section, we focus on the W3C's *XML Schema* vocabulary (note the capital "S" in "Schema"). We use the term XML Schema in the rest of the chapter whenever we refer to W3C's XML Schema vocabulary. For the latest information on XML Schema, visit www.w3.org/XML/Schema. For tutorials on XML Schema concepts beyond what we present here, visit www.w3schools.com/schema/default.asp.

A DTD describes an XML document's structure, not the content of its elements. For example,

> *<quantity>*5*</quantity>*

contains character data. If the document that contains element `quantity` references a DTD, an XML parser can validate the document to confirm that this element indeed does contain PCDATA content. However, the parser cannot validate that the content is numeric; DTDs do not provide this capability. So, unfortunately, the parser also considers

> *<quantity>*hello*</quantity>*

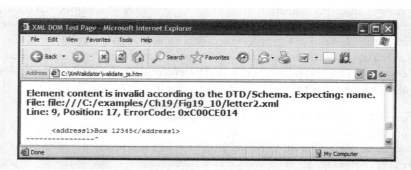

Fig. 19.10 | XML Validator displaying an error message.

to be valid. An application that uses the XML document containing this markup should test that the data in element quantity is numeric and take appropriate action if it is not.

XML Schema enables schema authors to specify that element quantity's data must be numeric or, even more specifically, an integer. A parser validating the XML document against this schema can determine that 5 conforms and hello does not. An XML document that conforms to a schema document is *schema valid*, and one that does not conform is *schema invalid*. Schemas are XML documents and therefore must themselves be valid.

Validating Against an XML Schema Document

Figure 19.11 shows a schema-valid XML document named book.xml, and Fig. 19.12 shows the pertinent XML Schema document (book.xsd) that defines the structure for book.xml. By convention, schemas use the *.xsd* extension. We used an online XSD schema validator provided by Microsoft at

> apps.gotdotnet.com/xmltools/xsdvalidator

to ensure that the XML document in Fig. 19.11 conforms to the schema in Fig. 19.12. To validate the schema document itself (i.e., book.xsd) and produce the output shown in Fig. 19.12, we used an online XSV (XML Schema Validator) provided by the W3C at

> www.w3.org/2001/03/webdata/xsv

These tools are free and enforce the W3C's specifications regarding XML Schemas and schema validation. Section 19.12 lists several online XML Schema validators.

```
 1   <?xml version = "1.0"?>
 2   <!-- Fig. 19.11: book.xml -->
 3   <!-- Book list marked up as XML -->
 4
 5   <deitel:books xmlns:deitel = "http://www.deitel.com/booklist">
 6      <book>
 7         <title>Visual Basic 2005 How to Program, 3/e</title>
 8      </book>
 9
10      <book>
11         <title>Visual C# 2005 How to Program</title>
12      </book>
13
14      <book>
15         <title>Java How to Program, 6/e</title>
16      </book>
17
18      <book>
19         <title>C++ How to Program, 5/e</title>
20      </book>
21
22      <book>
23         <title>Internet and World Wide Web How to Program, 3/e</title>
24      </book>
25   </deitel:books>
```

Fig. 19.11 | Schema-valid XML document describing a list of books.

```
 1   <?xml version = "1.0"?>
 2   <!-- Fig. 19.12: book.xsd          -->
 3   <!-- Simple W3C XML Schema document -->
 4
 5   <schema xmlns = "http://www.w3.org/2001/XMLSchema"
 6      xmlns:deitel = "http://www.deitel.com/booklist"
 7      targetNamespace = "http://www.deitel.com/booklist">
 8
 9      <element name = "books" type = "deitel:BooksType"/>
10
11      <complexType name = "BooksType">
12         <sequence>
13            <element name = "book" type = "deitel:SingleBookType"
14               minOccurs = "1" maxOccurs = "unbounded"/>
15         </sequence>
16      </complexType>
17
18      <complexType name = "SingleBookType">
19         <sequence>
20            <element name = "title" type = "string"/>
21         </sequence>
22      </complexType>
23   </schema>
```

Schema validation report for file:/usr/local/XSV/xsvlog/tmpIY3T...

Address http://www.w3.org/2001/03/webdata/xsv#

Schema validating with XSV 2.10-1 of 2005/04/22 13:10:49

- **Target**: file:/usr/local/XSV/xsvlog/tmpIY3Tc3uploaded
  (Real name: C:\examples\ch19\Fig19_11_12\book.xsd)
- **docElt**: {http://www.w3.org/2001/XMLSchema}schema
- Validation was strict, starting with type [Anonymous]
- The schema(s) used for schema-validation had no errors
- No schema-validity problems were found in the target

Fig. 19.12 | XML Schema document for book.xml.

Figure 19.11 contains markup describing several Deitel books. The books element (line 5) has the namespace prefix deitel, indicating that the books element is a part of the http://www.deitel.com/booklist namespace. Note that we declare the namespace prefix deitel in line 5.

Creating an XML Schema Document

Figure 19.12 presents the XML Schema document that specifies the structure of book.xml (Fig. 19.11). This document defines an XML-based language (i.e., a vocabulary) for writing XML documents about collections of books. The schema defines the elements, attributes and parent-child relationships that such a document can (or must) include. The schema also specifies the type of data that these elements and attributes may contain.

Root element *schema* (Fig. 19.12, lines 5–23) contains elements that define the structure of an XML document such as `book.xml`. Line 5 specifies as the default namespace the standard W3C XML Schema namespace URI—*http://www.w3.org/2001/XMLSchema*. This namespace contains predefined elements (e.g., root element `schema`) that comprise the XML Schema vocabulary—the language used to write an XML Schema document.

Portability Tip 19.3

W3C XML Schema authors specify URI http://www.w3.org/2001/XMLSchema when referring to the XML Schema namespace. This namespace contains predefined elements that comprise the XML Schema vocabulary. Specifying this URI ensures that validation tools correctly identify XML Schema elements and do not confuse them with those defined by document authors.

Line 6 binds the URI `http://www.deitel.com/booklist` to namespace prefix `deitel`. As we discuss momentarily, the schema uses this namespace to differentiate names created by us from names that are part of the XML Schema namespace. Line 7 also specifies `http://www.deitel.com/booklist` as the *targetNamespace* of the schema. This attribute identifies the namespace of the XML vocabulary that this schema defines. Note that the `targetNamespace` of `book.xsd` is the same as the namespace referenced in line 5 of `book.xml` (Fig. 19.11). This is what "connects" the XML document with the schema that defines its structure. When an XML schema validator examines `book.xml` and `book.xsd`, it will recognize that `book.xml` uses elements and attributes from the `http://www.deitel.com/booklist` namespace. The validator also will recognize that this namespace is the namespace defined in `book.xsd` (i.e., the schema's `targetNamespace`). Thus the validator knows where to look for the structural rules for the elements and attributes used in `book.xml`.

Defining an Element in XML Schema

In XML Schema, the *element* tag (line 9) defines an element to be included in an XML document that conforms to the schema. In other words, `element` specifies the actual *elements* that can be used to mark up data. Line 9 defines the `books` element, which we use as the root element in `book.xml` (Fig. 19.11). Attributes *name* and *type* specify the element's name and type, respectively. An element's type indicates the data that the element may contain. Possible types include XML Schema–defined types (e.g., `string`, `double`) and user-defined types (e.g., `BooksType`, which is defined in lines 11–16). Figure 19.13 lists several of XML Schema's many built-in types. For a complete list of built-in types, see Section 3 of the specification found at www.w3.org/TR/xmlschema-2.

In this example, `books` is defined as an element of type `deitel:BooksType` (line 9). `BooksType` is a user-defined type (lines 11–16) in the `http://www.deitel.com/booklist` namespace and therefore must have the namespace prefix `deitel`. It is not an existing XML Schema type.

Two categories of type exist in XML Schema—*simple types* and *complex types*. Simple and complex types differ only in that simple types cannot contain attributes or child elements and complex types can.

A user-defined type that contains attributes or child elements must be defined as a complex type. Lines 11–16 use element *complexType* to define `BooksType` as a complex type that has a child element named `book`. The `sequence` element (lines 12–15) allows you to specify the sequential order in which child elements must appear. The `element` (lines 13–14) nested within the `complexType` element indicates that a `BooksType` element (e.g.,

XML Schema type(s)	Description	Ranges or Structures	Examples
string	A character string.		"hello"
boolean	True or false.	true, false	true
decimal	A decimal numeral.	$i * (10^n)$, where i is an integer and n is an integer that is less than or equal to zero.	5, -12, -45.78
float	A floating-point number.	$m * (2^e)$, where m is an integer whose absolute value is less than 2^{24} and e is an integer in the range -149 to 104. Plus three additional numbers: positive infinity, negative infinity and not-a-number (NaN).	0, 12, -109.375, NaN
double	A floating-point number.	$m * (2^e)$, where m is an integer whose absolute value is less than 2^{53} and e is an integer in the range -1075 to 970. Plus three additional numbers: positive infinity, negative infinity and not-a-number (NaN).	0, 12, -109.375, NaN
long	A whole number.	-9223372036854775808 to 9223372036854775807, inclusive.	1234567890, -1234567890
int	A whole number.	-2147483648 to 2147483647, inclusive.	1234567890, -1234567890
short	A whole number.	-32768 to 32767, inclusive.	12, -345
date	A date consisting of a year, month and day.	yyyy-mm with an optional dd and an optional time zone, where yyyy is four digits long and mm and dd are two digits long.	2005-05-10
time	A time consisting of hours, minutes and seconds.	hh:mm:ss with an optional time zone, where hh, mm and ss are two digits long.	16:30:25-05:00

Fig. 19.13 | Some XML Schema types.

books) can contain child elements named book of type deitel:SingleBookType (defined in lines 18–22). Attribute **_minOccurs_** (line 14), with value 1, specifies that elements of type BooksType must contain a minimum of one book element. Attribute **_maxOccurs_** (line 14), with value **unbounded**, specifies that elements of type BooksType may have any number of book child elements.

Lines 18–22 define the complex type SingleBookType. An element of this type contains a child element named title. Line 20 defines element title to be of simple type string. Recall that elements of a simple type cannot contain attributes or child elements. The schema end tag (</schema>, line 23) declares the end of the XML Schema document.

A Closer Look at Types in XML Schema

Every element in XML Schema has a type. Types include the built-in types provided by XML Schema (Fig. 19.13) or user-defined types (e.g., SingleBookType in Fig. 19.12).

Every simple type defines a *restriction* on an XML Schema-defined type or a restriction on a user-defined type. Restrictions limit the possible values that an element can hold.

Complex types are divided into two groups—those with *simple content* and those with *complex content*. Both can contain attributes, but only complex content can contain child elements. Complex types with simple content must extend or restrict some other existing type. Complex types with complex content do not have this limitation. We demonstrate complex types with each kind of content in the next example.

The schema document in Fig. 19.14 creates both simple types and complex types. The XML document in Fig. 19.15 (laptop.xml) follows the structure defined in Fig. 19.14 to describe parts of a laptop computer. A document such as laptop.xml that conforms to a schema is known as an *XML instance document*—the document is an instance (i.e., example) of the schema.

Line 5 declares the default namespace to be the standard XML Schema namespace—any elements without a prefix are assumed to be in the XML Schema namespace. Line 6

```
1   <?xml version = "1.0"?>
2   <!-- Fig. 19.14: computer.xsd -->
3   <!-- W3C XML Schema document   -->
4
5   <schema xmlns = "http://www.w3.org/2001/XMLSchema"
6       xmlns:computer = "http://www.deitel.com/computer"
7       targetNamespace = "http://www.deitel.com/computer">
8
9       <simpleType name = "gigahertz">
10          <restriction base = "decimal">
11              <minInclusive value = "2.1"/>
12          </restriction>
13      </simpleType>
14
15      <complexType name = "CPU">
16          <simpleContent>
17              <extension base = "string">
18                  <attribute name = "model" type = "string"/>
19              </extension>
20          </simpleContent>
21      </complexType>
22
```

Fig. 19.14 | XML Schema document defining simple and complex types. (Part 1 of 2.)

```
23        <complexType name = "portable">
24         <all>
25            <element name = "processor" type = "computer:CPU"/>
26            <element name = "monitor" type = "int"/>
27            <element name = "CPUSpeed" type = "computer:gigahertz"/>
28            <element name = "RAM" type = "int"/>
29         </all>
30         <attribute name = "manufacturer" type = "string"/>
31       </complexType>
32
33       <element name = "laptop" type = "computer:portable"/>
34     </schema>
```

Fig. 19.14 | XML Schema document defining simple and complex types. (Part 2 of 2.)

```
1    <?xml version = "1.0"?>
2    <!-- Fig. 19.15: laptop.xml            -->
3    <!-- Laptop components marked up as XML -->
4
5    <computer:laptop xmlns:computer = "http://www.deitel.com/computer"
6       manufacturer = "IBM">
7
8       <processor model = "Centrino">Intel</processor>
9       <monitor>17</monitor>
10      <CPUSpeed>2.4</CPUSpeed>
11      <RAM>256</RAM>
12    </computer:laptop>
```

Fig. 19.15 | XML document using the laptop element defined in computer.xsd.

binds the namespace prefix computer to the namespace http://www.deitel.com/computer. Line 7 identifies this namespace as the targetNamespace—the namespace being defined by the current XML Schema document.

To design the XML elements for describing laptop computers, we first create a simple type in lines 9–13 using the *simpleType* element. We name this simpleType gigahertz because it will be used to describe the clock speed of the processor in gigahertz. Simple types are restrictions of a type typically called a *base type*. For this simpleType, line 10 declares the base type as decimal, and we restrict the value to be at least 2.1 by using the *minInclusive* element in line 11.

Next, we declare a complexType named CPU that has *simpleContent* (lines 16–20). Remember that a complex type with simple content can have attributes but not child elements. Also recall that complex types with simple content must extend or restrict some XML Schema type or user-defined type. The *extension* element with attribute *base* (line 17) sets the base type to string. In this complexType, we extend the base type string with an attribute. The *attribute* element (line 18) gives the complexType an attribute of type string named model. Thus an element of type CPU must contain string text (because the base type is string) and may contain a model attribute that is also of type string.

Lastly we define type portable, which is a complexType with complex content (lines 23–31). Such types are allowed to have child elements and attributes. The element *all* (lines 24–29) encloses elements that must each be included once in the corresponding XML instance document. These elements can be included in any order. This complex type holds four elements—processor, monitor, CPUSpeed and RAM. They are given types CPU, int, gigahertz and int, respectively. When using types CPU and gigahertz, we must include the namespace prefix computer, because these user-defined types are part of the computer namespace (http://www.deitel.com/computer)—the namespace defined in the current document (line 7). Also, portable contains an attribute defined in line 30. The attribute element indicates that elements of type portable contain an attribute of type string named manufacturer.

Line 33 declares the actual element that uses the three types defined in the schema. The element is called laptop and is of type portable. We must use the namespace prefix computer in front of portable.

We have now created an element named laptop that contains child elements processor, monitor, CPUSpeed and RAM, and an attribute manufacturer. Figure 19.15 uses the laptop element defined in the computer.xsd schema. Once again, we used an online XSD schema validator (apps.gotdotnet.com/xmltools/xsdvalidator) to ensure that this XML instance document adheres to the schema's structural rules.

Line 5 declares namespace prefix computer. The laptop element requires this prefix because it is part of the http://www.deitel.com/computer namespace. Line 6 sets the laptop's manufacturer attribute, and lines 8–11 use the elements defined in the schema to describe the laptop's characteristics.

This section introduced W3C XML Schema documents for defining the structure of XML documents, and we validated XML instance documents against schemas using an online XSD schema validator. Section 19.9 demonstrates programmatically validating XML documents against schemas using .NET Framework classes. This allows you to ensure that a Visual Basic program manipulates only valid documents—manipulating an invalid document that is missing required pieces of data could cause errors in the program.

19.7 (Optional) Extensible Stylesheet Language and XSL Transformations

Extensible Stylesheet Language (*XSL*) documents specify how programs are to render XML document data. XSL is a group of three technologies—*XSL-FO* (*XSL Formatting Objects*), *XPath* (*XML Path Language*) and *XSLT* (*XSL Transformations*). XSL-FO is a vocabulary for specifying formatting, and XPath is a string-based language of expressions used by XML and many of its related technologies for effectively and efficiently locating structures and data (such as specific elements and attributes) in XML documents.

The third portion of XSL—XSL Transformations (XSLT)—is a technology for transforming XML documents into other documents—i.e., transforming the structure of the XML document data to another structure. XSLT provides elements that define rules for transforming one XML document to produce a different XML document. This is useful when you want to use data in multiple applications or on multiple platforms, each of which may be designed to work with documents written in a particular vocabulary. For example, XSLT allows you to convert a simple XML document to an *XHTML* (*Extensible HyperText Markup Language*) document that presents the XML document's data (or a subset of the data) formatted for display in a Web browser. (See Fig. 19.16 for a sample "before" and "after" view of such a transformation.) XHTML is the W3C technical recommendation that replaces HTML for marking up Web content. For more information on XHTML, see Appendix F, Introduction to XHTML: Part 1, and Appendix G, Introduction to XHTML: Part 2, and visit www.w3.org.

Transforming an XML document using XSLT involves two tree structures—the *source tree* (i.e., the XML document to be transformed) and the *result tree* (i.e., the XML document to be created). XPath is used to locate parts of the source tree document that match *templates* defined in an *XSL style sheet*. When a match occurs (i.e., a node matches a template), the matching template executes and adds its result to the result tree. When there are no more matches, XSLT has transformed the source tree into the result tree. The XSLT does not analyze every node of the source tree; it selectively navigates the source tree using XPath's select and match attributes. For XSLT to function, the source tree must be properly structured. Schemas, DTDs and validating parsers can validate document structure before using XPath and XSLTs.

A Simple XSL Example

Figure 19.16 lists an XML document that describes various sports. The output shows the result of the transformation (specified in the XSLT template of Fig. 19.17) rendered by Internet Explorer 6.

```
 1   <?xml version = "1.0"?>
 2   <?xml:stylesheet type = "text/xsl" href = "sports.xsl"?>
 3
 4   <!-- Fig. 19.16: sports.xml -->
 5   <!-- Sports Database -->
 6
 7   <sports>
 8      <game id = "783">
 9         <name>Cricket</name>
10
11         <paragraph>
12            More popular among commonwealth nations.
13         </paragraph>
14      </game>
15
16      <game id = "239">
17         <name>Baseball</name>
18
19         <paragraph>
20            More popular in America.
21         </paragraph>
22      </game>
23
24      <game id = "418">
25         <name>Soccer (Futbol)</name>
26
27         <paragraph>
28            Most popular sport in the world.
29         </paragraph>
30      </game>
31   </sports>
```

Fig. 19.16 | XML document that describes various sports. (Part 1 of 2.)

Fig. 19.16 | XML document that describes various sports. (Part 2 of 2.)

To perform transformations, an XSLT processor is required. Popular XSLT processors include Microsoft's MSXML and the Apache Software Foundation's *Xalan 2* (xml.apache.org). The XML document shown in Fig. 19.16 is transformed into an XHTML document by MSXML when the document is loaded in Internet Explorer. MSXML is both an XML parser and an XSLT processor.

Line 2 (Fig. 19.16) is a *processing instruction* (*PI*) that references the XSL style sheet sports.xsl (Fig. 19.17). A processing instruction is embedded in an XML document and provides application-specific information to whichever XML processor the application uses. In this particular case, the processing instruction specifies the location of an XSLT document with which to transform the XML document. The characters **<?** and **?>** (line 2, Fig. 19.16) delimit a processing instruction, which consists of a *PI target* (e.g., xml:stylesheet) and a *PI value* (e.g., type = "text/xsl" href = "sports.xsl"). The PI value's type attribute specifies that sports.xsl is a text/xsl file (i.e., a text file containing XSL content). The href attribute specifies the name and location of the style sheet to apply—in this case, sports.xsl in the current directory.

Software Engineering Observation 19.5

XSL enables document authors to separate data presentation (specified in XSL documents) from data description (specified in XML documents).

Figure 19.17 shows the XSL document for transforming the structured data of the XML document of Fig. 19.16 into an XHTML document for presentation. By convention, XSL documents have the filename extension **.xsl**.

Lines 6–7 begin the XSL style sheet with the **stylesheet** start tag. Attribute **version** specifies the XSLT version to which this document conforms. Line 7 binds namespace prefix **xsl** to the W3C's XSLT URI (i.e., http://www.w3.org/1999/XSL/Transform).

Lines 9–12 use element **xsl:output** to write an XHTML document type declaration (DOCTYPE) to the result tree (i.e., the XML document to be created). The DOCTYPE identifies XHTML as the type of the resulting document. Attribute method is assigned "xml", which indicates that XML is being output to the result tree. (Recall that XHTML is a type of XML.) Attribute **omit-xml-declaration** specifies whether the transformation should write the XML declaration to the result tree. In this case, we do not want to omit the XML declaration, so we assign to this attribute the value "no". Attributes doctype-system and doctype-public write the DOCTYPE DTD information to the result tree.

```
 1   <?xml version = "1.0"?>
 2   <!-- Fig. 19.17: sports.xsl -->
 3   <!-- A simple XSLT transformation -->
 4
 5   <!-- reference XSL style sheet URI -->
 6   <xsl:stylesheet version = "1.0"
 7      xmlns:xsl = "http://www.w3.org/1999/XSL/Transform">
 8
 9      <xsl:output method = "xml" omit-xml-declaration = "no"
10         doctype-system =
11            "http://www.w3c.org/TR/xhtml1/DTD/xhtml1-strict.dtd"
12         doctype-public = "-//W3C//DTD XHTML 1.0 Strict//EN"/>
13
14      <xsl:template match = "/"> <!-- match root element -->
15
16      <html xmlns = "http://www.w3.org/1999/xhtml">
17         <head>
18            <title>Sports</title>
19         </head>
20
21         <body>
22            <table border = "1" bgcolor = "wheat">
23               <thead>
24                  <tr>
25                     <th>ID</th>
26                     <th>Sport</th>
27                     <th>Information</th>
28                  </tr>
29               </thead>
30
31               <!-- insert each name and paragraph element value -->
32               <!-- into a table row. -->
33               <xsl:for-each select = "/sports/game">
34                  <tr>
35                     <td><xsl:value-of select = "@id"/></td>
36                     <td><xsl:value-of select = "name"/></td>
37                     <td><xsl:value-of select = "paragraph"/></td>
38                  </tr>
39               </xsl:for-each>
40            </table>
41         </body>
42      </html>
43
44      </xsl:template>
45   </xsl:stylesheet>
```

Fig. 19.17 | XSLT that creates elements and attributes in an XHTML document.

XSLT uses *templates* (i.e., *xsl:template* elements) to describe how to transform particular nodes from the source tree to the result tree. A template is applied to nodes that are specified in the required match attribute. Line 14 uses the *match* attribute to select the *document root* (i.e., the conceptual part of the document that contains the root element and everything below it) of the XML source document (i.e., sports.xml). The XPath character / (a forward slash) always selects the document root. Recall that XPath is a string-based language used to locate parts of an XML document easily. In XPath, a leading forward slash specifies that we are using *absolute addressing* (i.e., we are starting from the root and defining paths down the source tree). In the XML document of Fig. 19.16, the child nodes of the document root are the two processing instruction nodes (lines 1–2), the two comment nodes (lines 4–5) and the sports element node (lines 7–31). The template in Fig. 19.17, line 14, matches a node (i.e., the root node), so the contents of the template are now added to the result tree.

The MSXML processor writes the XHTML in lines 16–29 (Fig. 19.17) to the result tree exactly as it appears in the XSL document. Now the result tree consists of the DOCTYPE definition and the XHTML code from lines 16–29. Lines 33–39 use element *xsl:for-each* to iterate through the source XML document, searching for game elements. The xsl:for-each element is similar to Visual Basic's For Each statement. Attribute *select* is an XPath expression that specifies the nodes (called the *node set*) on which the xsl:for-each operates. Again, the first forward slash means that we are using absolute addressing. The forward slash between sports and game indicates that game is a child node of sports. Thus, the xsl:for-each finds game nodes that are children of the sports node. The XML document sports.xml contains only one sports node, which is also the document root node. After finding the elements that match the selection criteria, the xsl:for-each processes each element with the code in lines 34–38 (these lines produce one row in a table each time they execute) and places the result of lines 34–38 in the result tree.

Line 35 uses element *value-of* to retrieve attribute id's value and place it in a td element in the result tree. The XPath symbol @ specifies that id is an attribute node of the context node game. Lines 36–37 place the name and paragraph element values in td elements and insert them in the result tree. When an XPath expression has no beginning forward slash, the expression uses *relative addressing*. Omitting the beginning forward slash tells the *xsl:value-of select* statements to search for name and paragraph elements that are children of the context node, not the root node. Due to the last XPath expression selection, the current context node is game, which indeed has an id attribute, a name child element and a paragraph child element.

Using XSLT to Sort and Format Data

Figure 19.18 presents an XML document (sorting.xml) that marks up information about a book. Note that several elements of the markup describing the book appear out of order (e.g., the element describing Chapter 3 appears before the element describing Chapter 2). We arranged them this way purposely to demonstrate that the XSL style sheet referenced in line 5 (sorting.xsl) can sort the XML file's data for presentation purposes.

```
1   <?xml version = "1.0"?>
2   <!-- Fig. 19.18: sorting.xml -->
3   <!-- XML document containing book information -->
4
5   <?xml:stylesheet type = "text/xsl" href = "sorting.xsl"?>
6
7   <book isbn = "999-99999-9-X">
8      <title>Deitel&apos;s XML Primer</title>
```

Fig. 19.18 | XML document containing book information. (Part 1 of 2.)

```
9
10      <author>
11         <firstName>Jane</firstName>
12         <lastName>Blue</lastName>
13      </author>
14
15      <chapters>
16         <frontMatter>
17            <preface pages = "2" />
18            <contents pages = "5" />
19            <illustrations pages = "4" />
20         </frontMatter>
21
22         <chapter number = "3" pages = "44">Advanced XML</chapter>
23         <chapter number = "2" pages = "35">Intermediate XML</chapter>
24         <appendix number = "B" pages = "26">Parsers and Tools</appendix>
25         <appendix number = "A" pages = "7">Entities</appendix>
26         <chapter number = "1" pages = "28">XML Fundamentals</chapter>
27      </chapters>
28
29      <media type = "CD" />
30   </book>
```

Fig. 19.18 | XML document containing book information. (Part 2 of 2.)

Figure 19.19 presents an XSL document (sorting.xsl) for transforming sorting.xml (Fig. 19.18) to XHTML. Recall that an XSL document navigates a source tree and builds a result tree. In this example, the source tree is XML, and the output tree is XHTML. Line 14 of Fig. 19.19 matches the root element of the document in Fig. 19.18. Line 15 outputs an html start tag to the result tree. The <xsl:apply-templates/> element (line 16) specifies that the XSLT processor is to apply the xsl:templates defined in this XSL document to the current node's (i.e., the document root's) children. The content from the applied templates is output in the html element that ends at line 17. Lines 21–84 specify a template that matches element book. The template indicates how to format the information contained in book elements of sorting.xml (Fig. 19.18) as XHTML.

```
1   <?xml version = "1.0"?>
2   <!-- Fig. 19.19: sorting.xsl -->
3   <!-- Transformation of book information into XHTML -->
4
5   <xsl:stylesheet version = "1.0"
6      xmlns:xsl = "http://www.w3.org/1999/XSL/Transform">
7
8      <!-- write XML declaration and DOCTYPE DTD information -->
9      <xsl:output method = "xml" omit-xml-declaration = "no"
10         doctype-system = "http://www.w3.org/TR/xhtml11/DTD/xhtml11.dtd"
11         doctype-public = "-//W3C//DTD XHTML 1.1//EN"/>
12
```

Fig. 19.19 | XSL document that transforms sorting.xml into XHTML. (Part 1 of 3.)

```
13    <!-- match document root -->
14    <xsl:template match = "/">
15       <html xmlns = "http://www.w3.org/1999/xhtml">
16          <xsl:apply-templates/>
17       </html>
18    </xsl:template>
19
20    <!-- match book -->
21    <xsl:template match = "book">
22       <head>
23          <title>ISBN <xsl:value-of select = "@isbn"/> -
24             <xsl:value-of select = "title"/></title>
25       </head>
26
27       <body>
28          <h1 style = "color: blue"><xsl:value-of select = "title"/></h1>
29          <h2 style = "color: blue">by
30             <xsl:value-of select = "author/lastName"/>,
31             <xsl:value-of select = "author/firstName"/></h2>
32
33          <table style = "border-style: groove; background-color: wheat">
34
35             <xsl:for-each select = "chapters/frontMatter/*">
36                <tr>
37                   <td style = "text-align: right">
38                      <xsl:value-of select = "name()"/>
39                   </td>
40
41                   <td>
42                      ( <xsl:value-of select = "@pages"/> pages )
43                   </td>
44                </tr>
45             </xsl:for-each>
46
47             <xsl:for-each select = "chapters/chapter">
48                <xsl:sort select = "@number" data-type = "number"
49                   order = "ascending"/>
50                <tr>
51                   <td style = "text-align: right">
52                      Chapter <xsl:value-of select = "@number"/>
53                   </td>
54
55                   <td>
56                      <xsl:value-of select = "text()"/>
57                      ( <xsl:value-of select = "@pages"/> pages )
58                   </td>
59                </tr>
60             </xsl:for-each>
61
62             <xsl:for-each select = "chapters/appendix">
63                <xsl:sort select = "@number" data-type = "text"
64                   order = "ascending"/>
```

Fig. 19.19 | XSL document that transforms `sorting.xml` into XHTML. (Part 2 of 3.)

```
65                    <tr>
66                        <td style = "text-align: right">
67                            Appendix <xsl:value-of select = "@number"/>
68                        </td>
69
70                        <td>
71                            <xsl:value-of select = "text()"/>
72                            ( <xsl:value-of select = "@pages"/> pages )
73                        </td>
74                    </tr>
75                </xsl:for-each>
76            </table>
77
78            <br /><p style = "color: blue">Pages:
79            <xsl:variable name = "pagecount"
80                select = "sum(chapters//*/@pages)"/>
81            <xsl:value-of select = "$pagecount"/>
82            <br />Media Type: <xsl:value-of select = "media/@type"/></p>
83        </body>
84    </xsl:template>
85 </xsl:stylesheet>
```

Fig. 19.19 | XSL document that transforms `sorting.xml` into XHTML. (Part 3 of 3.)

Lines 23–24 create the title for the XHTML document. We use the book's ISBN (from attribute `isbn`) and the contents of element `title` to create the string that appears in the browser window's title bar (**ISBN 999-99999-9-X - Deitel's XML Primer**).

Line 28 creates a header element that contains the book's title. Lines 29–31 create a header element that contains the book's author. Because the context node (i.e., the current node being processed) is `book`, the XPath expression `author/lastName` selects the author's last name, and the expression `author/firstName` selects the author's first name.

Line 35 selects each element (indicated by an asterisk) that is a child of element `frontMatter`. Line 38 calls *node-set function **name*** to retrieve the current node's element name (e.g., `preface`). The current node is the context node specified in the `xsl:for-each` (line 35). Line 42 retrieves the value of the `pages` attribute of the current node.

Line 47 selects each `chapter` element. Lines 48–49 use element ***xsl:sort*** to sort chapters by number in ascending order. Attribute ***select*** selects the value of attribute `number` in context node `chapter`. Attribute ***data-type***, with value `"number"`, specifies a numeric sort, and attribute ***order***, with value `"ascending"`, specifies ascending order. Attribute `data-type` also accepts the value `"text"` (line 63), and attribute `order` also accepts the value `"descending"`. Line 56 uses *node-set function **text*** to obtain the text between the `chapter` start and end tags (i.e., the name of the chapter). Line 57 retrieves the value of the `pages` attribute of the current node. Lines 62–75 perform similar tasks for each appendix.

Lines 79–80 use an *XSL variable* to store the value of the book's total page count and output the page count to the result tree. Attribute ***name*** specifies the variable's name (i.e., `pagecount`), and attribute `select` assigns a value to the variable. Function ***sum*** (line 80) totals the values for all `page` attribute values. The two slashes between `chapters` and `*` indicate a *recursive descent*—the MSXML processor will search for elements that contain an attribute named `pages` in all descendant nodes of `chapters`. The XPath expression

```
//*
```

selects all the nodes in an XML document. Line 81 retrieves the value of the newly created XSL variable `pagecount` by placing a dollar sign in front of its name.

Summary of XSL Style Sheet Elements
This section's examples used several predefined XSL elements to perform various operations. Figure 19.20 lists these elements and several other commonly used XSL elements. For more information on these elements and XSL in general, see www.w3.org/Style/XSL.

Element	Description
`<xsl:apply-templates>`	Applies the templates of the XSL document to the children of the current node.
`<xsl:apply-templates match = "`*expression*`">`	Applies the templates of the XSL document to the children of *expression*. The value of the attribute match (i.e., *expression*) must be an XPath expression that specifies elements.
`<xsl:template>`	Contains rules to apply when a specified node is matched.
`<xsl:value-of select = "`*expression*`">`	Selects the value of an XML element and adds it to the output tree of the transformation. The required `select` attribute contains an XPath expression.
`<xsl:for-each select = "`*expression*`">`	Applies a template to every node selected by the XPath specified by the `select` attribute.

Fig. 19.20 | XSL style sheet elements. (Part 1 of 2.)

Element	Description
`<xsl:sort select = "`*expression*`">`	Used as a child element of an `<xsl:apply-templates>` or `<xsl:for-each>` element. Sorts the nodes selected by the `<xsl:apply-template>` or `<xsl:for-each>` element so that the nodes are processed in sorted order.
`<xsl:output>`	Has various attributes to define the format (e.g., XML, XHTML), version (e.g., 1.0, 2.0), document type and media type of the output document. This tag is a top-level element—it can be used only as a child element of an `xml:stylesheet`.
`<xsl:copy>`	Adds the current node to the output tree.

Fig. 19.20 | XSL style sheet elements. (Part 2 of 2.)

This section introduced Extensible Stylesheet Language (XSL) and showed how to create XSL transformations to convert XML documents from one format to another. We showed how to transform XML documents to XHTML documents for display in a Web browser. Recall that these transformations are performed by MSXML, Internet Explorer's built-in XML parser and XSLT processor. In most business applications, XML documents are transferred between business partners and are transformed to other XML vocabularies programmatically. In Section 19.10, we demonstrate how to perform XSL transformations using the `XslCompiledTransform` class provided by the .NET Framework.

19.8 (Optional) Document Object Model (DOM)

Although an XML document is a text file, retrieving data from the document using traditional sequential file processing techniques is neither practical nor efficient, especially for adding and removing elements dynamically.

Upon successfully parsing a document, some XML parsers store document data as tree structures in memory. Figure 19.21 illustrates the tree structure for the root element of the document `article.xml` discussed in Fig. 19.2. This hierarchical tree structure is called a *Document Object Model (DOM) tree*, and an XML parser that creates this type of structure is known as a *DOM parser*. Each element name (e.g., `article`, `date`, `firstName`) is represented by a node. A node that contains other nodes (called *child nodes* or children) is called a *parent node* (e.g., `author`). A parent node can have many children, but a child node can have only one parent node. Nodes that are peers (e.g., `firstName` and `lastName`) are called *sibling nodes*. A node's *descendant nodes* include its children, its children's children and so on. A node's *ancestor nodes* include its parent, its parent's parent and so on.

The DOM tree has a single *root node*, which contains all the other nodes in the document. For example, the root node of the DOM tree that represents `article.xml` (Fig. 19.2) contains a node for the XML declaration (line 1), two nodes for the comments (lines 2–3) and a node for the XML document's root element `article` (line 5).

Classes for creating, reading and manipulating XML documents are located in the FCL namespace *System.Xml*. This namespace also contains additional namespaces that provide other XML-related operations.

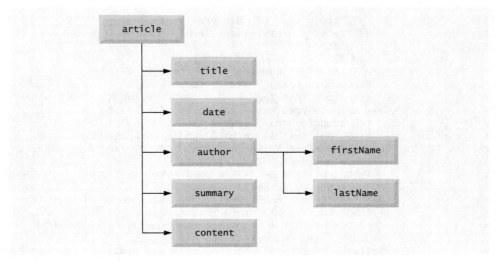

Fig. 19.21 | Tree structure for the document `article.xml` of Fig. 19.2.

Reading an XML Document with an XmlReader

In this section, we present several examples that use DOM trees. Our first example, the program in Fig. 19.22, loads the XML document presented in Fig. 19.2 and displays its data in a text box. This example uses class *XmlReader* to iterate through each node in the XML document.

```
 1  ' Fig. 19.22: FrmXmlReaderTest.vb
 2  ' Reading an XML document.
 3  Imports System.Xml
 4
 5  Public Class FrmXmlReaderTest
 6     ' read XML document and display its content
 7     Private Sub FrmXmlReaderTest_Load(ByVal sender As System.Object, _
 8        ByVal e As System.EventArgs) Handles MyBase.Load
 9        ' create the XmlReader object
10        Dim settings As New XmlReaderSettings()
11        Dim reader As XmlReader = XmlReader.Create("article.xml", settings)
12
13        Dim depth As Integer = -1 ' tree depth is -1, no indentation
14
15        While reader.Read() ' display each node's content
16           Select Case (reader.NodeType)
17              Case XmlNodeType.Element ' XML Element, display its name
18                 depth += 1 ' increase tab depth
19                 TabOutput(depth) ' insert tabs
20                 txtOutput.Text &= "<" & reader.Name & ">" & vbCrLf
21
```

Fig. 19.22 | XmlReader iterating through an XML document. (Part 1 of 2.)

```
22              ' if empty element, decrease depth
23              If reader.IsEmptyElement Then
24                  depth -= 1
25              End If
26          Case XmlNodeType.Comment ' XML Comment, display it
27              TabOutput(depth) ' insert tabs
28              txtOutput.Text &= "<!--" & reader.Value & "-->" & vbCrLf
29          Case XmlNodeType.Text ' XML Text, display it
30              TabOutput(depth) ' insert tabs
31              txtOutput.Text &= vbTab & reader.Value & vbCrLf
32          Case XmlNodeType.XmlDeclaration ' XML Declaration, display it
33              TabOutput(depth) ' insert tabs
34              txtOutput.Text &= "<?" & reader.Name & " " & _
35                  reader.Value & "?>" & vbCrLf
36          Case XmlNodeType.EndElement ' XML EndElement, display it
37              TabOutput(depth) ' insert tabs
38              txtOutput.Text &= "</" & reader.Name & ">" & vbCrLf
39              depth -= 1 ' decrement depth
40          End Select
41      End While
42  End Sub ' FrmXmlReaderTest_Load
43
44  ' insert tabs
45  Private Sub TabOutput(ByVal number As Integer)
46      For i As Integer = 1 To number
47          txtOutput.Text &= vbTab
48      Next
49  End Sub ' TabOutput
50 End Class ' FrmXmlReaderTest
```

Fig. 19.22 | XmlReader iterating through an XML document. (Part 2 of 2.)

Line 3 imports the System.Xml namespace, which contains the XML classes used in this example. Class XmlReader is a MustInherit class that defines the interface for reading

XML documents. We cannot create an XmlReader object directly. Instead, we must invoke XmlReader's Shared method **Create** to obtain an XmlReader reference (line 11). Before doing so, however, we must prepare an XmlReaderSettings object that specifies how we would like the XmlReader to behave (line 10). In this example, we use the default settings of the properties of an XmlReaderSettings object. Later, you will learn how to set certain properties of the XmlReaderSettings class to instruct the XmlReader to perform validation, which it does not do by default. The Shared method Create receives as arguments the name of the XML document to read and an XmlReaderSettings object. In this example the XML document article.xml (Fig. 19.2) is opened when method Create is invoked in line 11. Once the XmlReader is created, the XML document's contents can be read programmatically.

Method **Read** of XmlReader reads one node from the DOM tree. By calling this method in the loop condition (line 15), reader reads all the document nodes. The Select Case statement (lines 16–40) processes each node. Either the Name property (lines 20, 34 and 38), which contains the node's name, or the Value property (lines 28 and 31), which contains the node's data, is formatted and concatenated to the String assigned to the TextBox's Text property. The XmlReader's NodeType property specifies whether the node is an element, comment, text, XML declaration or end element. Note that each Case specifies a node type using **XmlNodeType** enumeration constants. For example, XmlNode-Type.Element (line 17) indicates the start tag of an element.

The displayed output emphasizes the structure of the XML document. Variable depth (line 13) maintains the number of tab characters to indent each element. We increment the depth each time the program encounters an Element and decrement it each time the program encounters an EndElement or empty element. We use a similar technique in the next example to emphasize the tree structure of the XML document being displayed.

Displaying a DOM Tree Graphically in a TreeView Control
XmlReaders do not provide features for displaying their content graphically. In this example, we display an XML document's contents using a **TreeView** control. We use class **TreeNode** to represent each node in the tree. Class TreeView and class TreeNode are part of the System.Windows.Forms namespace. TreeNodes are added to the TreeView to emphasize the structure of the XML document.

The program in Fig. 19.23 demonstrates how to manipulate a DOM tree programmatically to display it graphically in a TreeView control. The GUI for this application contains a TreeView control named treeXML (declared in FrmXmlDom.Designer.vb). The application loads letter.xml (Fig. 19.24) into an XmlReader (line 17), then displays the document's tree structure in the TreeView control. [*Note:* The version of letter.xml in Fig. 19.24 is nearly identical to the one in Fig. 19.4, except that Fig. 19.24 does not reference a DTD as line 5 of Fig. 19.4 does.]

In FrmXmlDom's Load event handler (lines 9–22), lines 13–14 create an XmlReaderSettings object and set its **IgnoreWhitespace** property to True so that the insignificant whitespaces in the XML document are ignored. Line 17 then invokes Shared XmlReader method Create to parse and load letter.xml.

Line 18 creates the TreeNode tree (declared in line 6). This TreeNode is used as a graphical representation of a DOM tree node in the TreeView control. Line 19 assigns the XML document's name (i.e., letter.xml) to tree's Text property. Line 20 calls method

Add to add the new `TreeNode` to the `TreeView`'s `Nodes` collection. Line 21 calls our `Private` method `BuildTree` to update the `TreeView` so that it displays the complete DOM tree.

```vb
1   ' Fig. 19.23: FrmXmlDom.vb
2   ' Demonstrates DOM tree manipulation.
3   Imports System.Xml
4
5   Public Class FrmXmlDom
6      Private tree As TreeNode ' TreeNode reference
7
8      ' initialize instance variables
9      Private Sub FrmXmlDom_Load(ByVal sender As Object, _
10        ByVal e As EventArgs) Handles MyBase.Load
11        ' create Xml ReaderSettings and
12        ' set the IgnoreWhitespace property
13        Dim settings As New XmlReaderSettings()
14        settings.IgnoreWhitespace = True
15
16        ' create XmlReader object
17        Dim reader As XmlReader = XmlReader.Create("letter.xml", settings)
18        tree = New TreeNode() ' instantiate TreeNode
19        tree.Text = "letter.xml" ' assign name to TreeNode
20        treeXml.Nodes.Add(tree) ' add TreeNode to TreeView control
21        BuildTree(reader, tree) ' build node and tree hierarchy
22     End Sub ' FrmXmlDom_Load
23
24      ' construct TreeView based on DOM tree
25      Private Sub BuildTree(ByVal reader As XmlReader, _
26        ByVal treeNode As TreeNode)
27        ' treeNode to add to existing tree
28        Dim newNode As New TreeNode()
29
30        While reader.Read()
31           ' build tree based on node type
32           Select Case reader.NodeType
33              Case XmlNodeType.Text ' add Text node's value to tree
34                 newNode.Text = reader.Value
35                 treeNode.Nodes.Add(newNode)
36              Case XmlNodeType.EndElement ' move up tree
37                 treeNode = treeNode.Parent
38              Case XmlNodeType.Element ' add element name and traverse tree
39                 ' determine whether element contains information
40                 If Not reader.IsEmptyElement Then
41                    newNode.Text = reader.Name ' assign node text
42                    treeNode.Nodes.Add(newNode) ' add newNode as child
43                    treeNode = newNode ' set treeNode to last child
44                 Else ' do not traverse empty elements
45                    ' assign NodeType string to newNode and add it to tree
46                    newNode.Text = reader.NodeType.ToString()
47                    treeNode.Nodes.Add(newNode)
48                 End If
```

Fig. 19.23 | DOM structure of an XML document displayed in a `TreeView`. (Part 1 of 2.)

```
49              Case Else ' all other types, display node type
50                   newNode.Text = reader.NodeType.ToString()
51                   treeNode.Nodes.Add(newNode)
52           End Select
53
54           newNode = New TreeNode()
55       End While
56
57       ' update TreeView control
58       treeXml.ExpandAll() ' expand tree nodes in TreeView
59       treeXml.Refresh() ' force TreeView to update
60   End Sub ' BuildTree
61 End Class ' FrmXmlDom
```

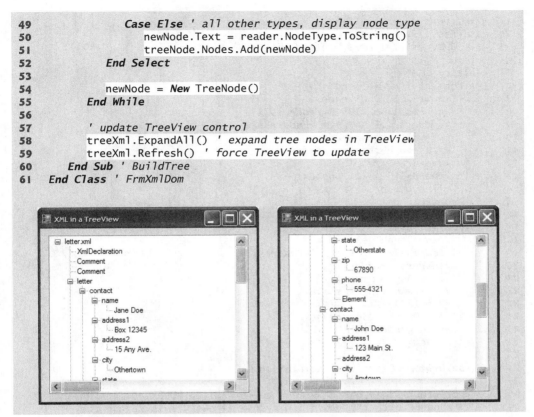

Fig. 19.23 | DOM structure of an XML document displayed in a TreeView. (Part 2 of 2.)

Method BuildTree (lines 25–60) receives an XmlReader for reading the XML document and a TreeNode referencing the current location in the tree (i.e., the TreeNode most recently added to the TreeView control). Line 28 declares TreeNode reference newNode, which will be used for adding new nodes to the TreeView. Lines 30–55 iterate through each node in the XML document's DOM tree.

The Select Case statement in lines 32–52 adds a node to the TreeView, based on the XmlReader's current node. When a text node is encountered, the Text property of the new TreeNode—newNode—is assigned the current node's value (line 34). Line 35 adds this TreeNode to treeNode's node list (i.e., adds the node to the TreeView control).

Line 36 matches an EndElement node type. This Case moves up the tree to the current node's parent because the end of an element has been encountered. Line 37 accesses treeNode's *Parent* property to retrieve the node's current parent.

Line 38 matches Element node types. Each non-empty Element NodeType (line 40) increases the depth of the tree; thus, we assign the current reader.Name to the newNode's Text property and add the newNode to treeNode's node list (lines 41–42). Line 43 assigns the newNode's reference to treeNode to ensure that treeNode refers to the last child TreeNode in the node list. If the current Element node is an empty element (line 44), we assign to the newNode's Text property the string representation of the NodeType (line 46).

```
 1   <?xml version = "1.0"?>
 2   <!-- Fig. 19.24: letter.xml -->
 3   <!-- Business letter formatted with XML -->
 4
 5   <letter>
 6      <contact type = "sender">
 7         <name>Jane Doe</name>
 8         <address1>Box 12345</address1>
 9         <address2>15 Any Ave.</address2>
10         <city>Othertown</city>
11         <state>Otherstate</state>
12         <zip>67890</zip>
13         <phone>555-4321</phone>
14         <flag gender = "F" />
15      </contact>
16
17      <contact type = "receiver">
18         <name>John Doe</name>
19         <address1>123 Main St.</address1>
20         <address2></address2>
21         <city>Anytown</city>
22         <state>Anystate</state>
23         <zip>12345</zip>
24         <phone>555-1234</phone>
25         <flag gender = "M" />
26      </contact>
27
28      <salutation>Dear Sir:</salutation>
29
30      <paragraph>It is our privilege to inform you about our new database
31         managed with XML. This new system allows you to reduce the
32         load on your inventory list server by having the client machine
33         perform the work of sorting and filtering the data.
34      </paragraph>
35
36      <paragraph>Please visit our Web site for availability
37         and pricing.
38      </paragraph>
39
40      <closing>Sincerely,</closing>
41      <signature>Ms. Doe</signature>
42   </letter>
```

Fig. 19.24 | Business letter marked up as XML.

Next, the newNode is added to the treeNode node list (line 47). The default case (lines 49–51) assigns the string representation of the node type to the newNode Text property, then adds the newNode to the TreeNode node list.

After the entire DOM tree is processed, the TreeNode node list is displayed in the TreeView control (lines 58–59). TreeView method **ExpandAll** causes all the nodes of the tree to be displayed. TreeView method **Refresh** updates the display to show the newly added TreeNodes. Note that while the application is running, clicking nodes (i.e., the + or − boxes) in the TreeView either expands or collapses them.

Locating Data in XML Documents with XPath

Although XmlReader includes methods for reading and modifying node values, it is not the most efficient means of locating data in a DOM tree. The Framework Class Library provides class *XPathNavigator* in the *System.Xml.XPath* namespace for iterating through node lists that match search criteria, which are written as XPath expressions. Recall that XPath (XML Path Language) provides a syntax for locating specific nodes in XML documents effectively and efficiently. XPath is a string-based language of expressions used by XML and many of its related technologies (such as XSLT, discussed in Section 19.7).

Figure 19.25 uses an XPathNavigator to navigate an XML document and uses a TreeView control and TreeNode objects to display the XML document's structure. In this example, the TreeNode node list is updated each time the XPathNavigator is positioned to a new node, rather than displaying the entire DOM tree at once. Nodes are added to and deleted from the TreeView to reflect the XPathNavigator's location in the DOM tree. Figure 19.26 shows the XML document sports.xml that we use in this example. [*Note:* The versions of sports.xml presented in Fig. 19.26 and Fig. 19.16 are nearly identical. In the current example, we do not want to apply an XSLT, so we omit the processing instruction found in line 2 of Fig. 19.16.]

```vb
 1    ' Fig. 19.25: FrmPathNavigator.vb
 2    ' Demonstrates class XPathNavigator.
 3    Imports System.Xml.XPath
 4
 5    Public Class FrmPathNavigator
 6       Private xPath As XPathNavigator ' navigator to traverse document
 7       Private document As XPathDocument ' document for use by XPathNavigator
 8       Private tree As TreeNode ' TreeNode used by TreeView control
 9
10       ' initialize variables and TreeView control
11       Private Sub FrmPathNavigator_Load(ByVal sender As Object, _
12          ByVal e As EventArgs) Handles MyBase.Load
13          document = New XPathDocument("sports.xml") ' load XML document
14          xPath = document.CreateNavigator() ' create navigator
15          tree = New TreeNode() ' create root node for TreeNodes
16
17          tree.Text = xPath.NodeType.ToString() ' root
18          treePath.Nodes.Add(tree) ' add tree
19
20          ' update TreeView control
21          treePath.ExpandAll() ' expand tree node in TreeView
22          treePath.Refresh() ' force TreeView update
23          treePath.SelectedNode = tree ' highlight root
24       End Sub ' FrmPathNavigator_Load
25
26       ' process btnSelect_Click event
27       Private Sub btnSelect_Click(ByVal sender As Object, _
28          ByVal e As EventArgs) Handles btnSelect.Click
29          Dim iterator As XPathNodeIterator ' enables node iteration
30
```

Fig. 19.25 | XPathNavigator navigating selected nodes. (Part 1 of 5.)

```
31          Try ' get specified node from ComboBox
32              iterator = xPath.Select(cboSelect.Text) ' select specified node
33              DisplayIterator(iterator) ' display selection
34          Catch argumentException As XPathException
35              MessageBox.Show(argumentException.Message, "Error", _
36                  MessageBoxButtons.OK, MessageBoxIcon.Error)
37          End Try
38      End Sub ' btnSelect_Click
39
40      ' traverse to first child on btnFirstChild_Click event
41      Private Sub btnFirstChild_Click(ByVal sender As Object, _
42          ByVal e As EventArgs) Handles btnFirstChild.Click
43          Dim newTreeNode As TreeNode
44
45          ' move to first child
46          If xPath.MoveToFirstChild() Then
47              newTreeNode = New TreeNode() ' create new node
48
49              ' set node's Text property to either navigator's name or value
50              DetermineType(newTreeNode, xPath)
51              tree.Nodes.Add(newTreeNode) ' add nodes to TreeNode node list
52              tree = newTreeNode ' assign tree newTreeNode
53
54              ' update TreeView control
55              treePath.ExpandAll() ' expand node in TreeView
56              treePath.Refresh() ' force TreeView to update
57              treePath.SelectedNode = tree ' highlight root
58          Else ' node has no children
59              MessageBox.Show("Current Node has no children.", _
60                  "", MessageBoxButtons.OK, MessageBoxIcon.Information)
61          End If
62      End Sub ' btnFirstChild_Click
63
64      ' traverse to node's parent on btnParent_Click event
65      Private Sub btnParent_Click(ByVal sender As Object, _
66          ByVal e As EventArgs) Handles btnParent.Click
67          ' move to parent
68          If xPath.MoveToParent() Then
69              tree = tree.Parent
70
71              ' get number of child nodes, not including sub trees
72              Dim count As Integer = tree.GetNodeCount(False)
73
74              ' remove all children
75              For i As Integer = 0 To count - 1
76                  tree.Nodes.Remove(tree.FirstNode) ' remove child node
77              Next
78
79              ' update TreeView control
80              treePath.ExpandAll() ' expand node in TreeView
81              treePath.Refresh() ' force TreeView to update
82              treePath.SelectedNode = tree ' highlight root
```

Fig. 19.25 | XPathNavigator navigating selected nodes. (Part 2 of 5.)

```
83           Else ' if node has no parent (root node)
84               MessageBox.Show("Current node has no parent.", "", _
85                   MessageBoxButtons.OK, MessageBoxIcon.Information)
86           End If
87       End Sub ' btnParent_Click
88
89       ' find next sibling on btnNext_Click event
90       Private Sub btnNext_Click(ByVal sender As Object, _
91           ByVal e As EventArgs) Handles btnNext.Click
92           ' declare and initialize two TreeNodes
93           Dim newTreeNode As TreeNode = Nothing
94           Dim newNode As TreeNode = Nothing
95
96           ' move to next sibling
97           If xPath.MoveToNext() Then
98               newTreeNode = tree.Parent ' get parent node
99               newNode = New TreeNode() ' create new node
100
101              ' decide whether to display current node
102              DetermineType(newNode, xPath)
103              newTreeNode.Nodes.Add(newNode) ' add to parent node
104
105              tree = newNode ' set current position for display
106
107              ' update TreeView control
108              treePath.ExpandAll() ' expand node in TreeView
109              treePath.Refresh() ' force TreeView to update
110              treePath.SelectedNode = tree ' highlight root
111          Else ' node has no additional siblings
112              MessageBox.Show("Current node is last sibling.", "", _
113                  MessageBoxButtons.OK, MessageBoxIcon.Information)
114          End If
115      End Sub ' btnNext_Click
116
117      ' get previous sibling on btnPrevious_Click
118      Private Sub btnPrevious_Click(ByVal sender As Object, _
119          ByVal e As EventArgs) Handles btnPrevious.Click
120          Dim parentTreeNode As TreeNode = Nothing
121
122          ' move to previous sibling
123          If xPath.MoveToPrevious() Then
124
125              parentTreeNode = tree.Parent ' get parent node
126              parentTreeNode.Nodes.Remove(tree) ' delete current node
127              tree = parentTreeNode.LastNode ' move to previous node
128
129              ' update TreeView control
130              treePath.ExpandAll() ' expand tree node in TreeView
131              treePath.Refresh() ' force TreeView to update
132              treePath.SelectedNode = tree ' highlight root
```

Fig. 19.25 | XPathNavigator navigating selected nodes. (Part 3 of 5.)

```
133        Else ' if current node has no previous siblings
134           MessageBox.Show("Current node is first sibling.", "", _
135              MessageBoxButtons.OK, MessageBoxIcon.Information)
136        End If
137     End Sub ' btnPrevious_Click
138
139     ' print values for XPathNodeIterator
140     Private Sub DisplayIterator(ByVal iterator As XPathNodeIterator)
141        txtSelect.Clear()
142
143        ' display selected node's values
144        While iterator.MoveNext()
145           txtSelect.Text &= iterator.Current.Value.Trim() & vbCrLf
146        End While
147     End Sub ' DisplayIterator
148
149     ' determine if TreeNode should display current node name or value
150     Private Sub DetermineType(ByVal node As TreeNode, _
151        ByVal xPath As XPathNavigator)
152
153        Select Case xPath.NodeType ' determine NodeType
154           Case XPathNodeType.Element ' if Element, get its name
155              ' get current node name, and remove whitespaces
156              node.Text = xPath.Name.Trim()
157           Case Else ' obtain node values
158              ' get current node value and remove whitespaces
159              node.Text = xPath.Value.Trim()
160        End Select
161     End Sub ' DetermineType
162  End Class ' FrmPathNavigator
```

Fig. 19.25 | XPathNavigator navigating selected nodes. (Part 4 of 5.)

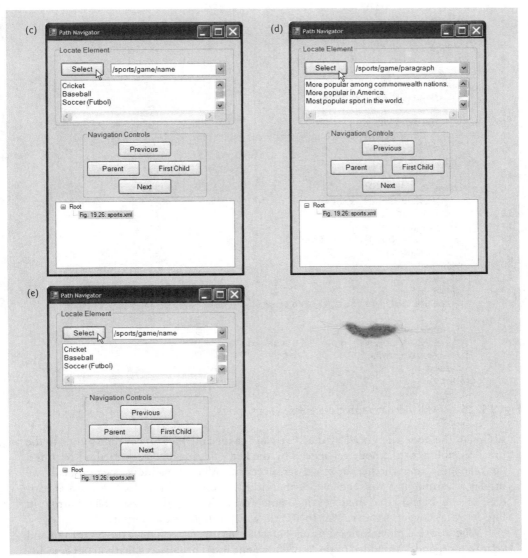

Fig. 19.25 | XPathNavigator navigating selected nodes. (Part 5 of 5.)

The program of Fig. 19.25 loads XML document sports.xml (Fig. 19.26) into an **XPathDocument** object by passing the document's file name to the XPathDocument constructor (line 13). Method **CreateNavigator** (line 14) creates and returns an XPathNavigator reference to the XPathDocument's tree structure.

The navigation methods of XPathNavigator are **MoveToFirstChild** (line 46), **MoveToParent** (line 68), **MoveToNext** (line 97) and **MoveToPrevious** (line 123). Each method performs the action that its name implies. Method MoveToFirstChild moves to the first child of the node referenced by the XPathNavigator, MoveToParent moves to the parent node of the node referenced by the XPathNavigator, MoveToNext moves to the next

```
 1   <?xml version = "1.0"?>
 2   <!-- Fig. 19.26: sports.xml -->
 3   <!-- Sports Database        -->
 4
 5   <sports>
 6     <game id = "783">
 7         <name>Cricket</name>
 8
 9         <paragraph>
10             More popular among commonwealth nations.
11         </paragraph>
12     </game>
13
14     <game id = "239">
15         <name>Baseball</name>
16
17         <paragraph>
18             More popular in America.
19         </paragraph>
20     </game>
21
22     <game id = "418">
23         <name>Soccer (Futbol)</name>
24
25         <paragraph>
26             Most popular sport in the world.
27         </paragraph>
28     </game>
29   </sports>
```

Fig. 19.26 | XML document that describes various sports.

sibling of the node referenced by the XPathNavigator and MoveToPrevious moves to the previous sibling of the node referenced by the XPathNavigator. Each method returns a Boolean indicating whether the move was successful. Whenever a move operation fails, we display a warning in a MessageBox. Furthermore, each method is called in the event handler of the button that matches its name (e.g., clicking the **First Child** button in Fig. 19.25(a) triggers btnFirstChild_Click, which calls MoveToFirstChild).

Whenever we move forward using XPathNavigator, as with MoveToFirstChild and MoveToNext, nodes are added to the TreeNode node list. The Private method Determine-Type (lines 150–161) determines whether to assign the Node's **Name** property or **Value** property to the TreeNode (lines 156 and 159). Whenever MoveToParent is called, all the children of the parent node are removed from the display. Similarly, a call to MoveToPrevious removes the current sibling node. Note that the nodes are removed only from the TreeView, not from the tree representation of the document.

The btnSelect_Click event handler (lines 27–38) corresponds to the **Select** button. XPathNavigator method Select (line 32) takes search criteria in the form of either an **XPathExpression** or a String that represents an XPath expression, and returns as an XPathNodeIterator object any node that matches the search criteria. Figure 19.27 summarizes the XPath expressions provided by this program's combo box. We show the result of some of these expressions in Figs. 19.25(b)–(d).

XPath Expression	Description
/sports	Matches all sports nodes that are child nodes of the document root node.
/sports/game	Matches all game nodes that are child nodes of sports, which is a child of the document root.
/sports/game/name	Matches all name nodes that are child nodes of game. The game is a child of sports, which is a child of the document root.
/sports/game/paragraph	Matches all paragraph nodes that are child nodes of game. The game is a child of sports, which is a child of the document root.
/sports/game [name='Cricket']	Matches all game nodes that contain a child element whose name is Cricket. The game is a child of sports, which is a child of the document root.

Fig. 19.27 | XPath expressions and descriptions.

Method DisplayIterator (defined in lines 140–147) appends the node values from the given XPathNodeIterator to the txtSelect TextBox. Note that we call String method Trim to remove unnecessary whitespace. Method *MoveNext* (line 144) advances to the next node, which property *Current* (line 145) can access.

19.9 (Optional) Schema Validation with Class XmlReader

Recall from Section 19.6 that schemas provide a means for specifying XML document structure and validating XML documents. Such validation helps an application determine whether a particular document it receives is complete, ordered properly and not missing any data. In Section 19.6, we used an online XSD schema validator to verify that an XML document conforms to an XML Schema. In this section, we show how to perform the same type of validation programmatically using classes provided by the .NET Framework.

Validating an XML Document Programmatically

Class XmlReader can validate an XML document as it reads and parses the document. In this example, we demonstrate how to activate such validation. The program in Fig. 19.28 validates an XML document that the user chooses—either book.xml (Fig. 19.11) or fail.xml (Fig. 19.29)—against the XML Schema document book.xsd (Fig. 19.12).

```vb
1   ' Fig. 19.28: FrmValidationTest.vb
2   ' Validating XML documents against schemas.
3   Imports System.Xml
4   Imports System.Xml.Schema ' contains XmlSchemaSet class
```

Fig. 19.28 | Schema-validation example. (Part 1 of 2.)

```vb.net
5
6  Public Class FrmValidationTest
7     Private schemas As XmlSchemaSet ' schemas to validate against
8     Private valid As Boolean = True ' validation result
9
10    ' handle Validate Button Click event
11    Private Sub btnValidate_Click(ByVal sender As Object, _
12       ByVal e As EventArgs) Handles btnValidate.Click
13       schemas = New XmlSchemaSet() ' create the XmlSchemaSet class
14
15       ' add the schema to the collection
16       schemas.Add("http://www.deitel.com/booklist", "book.xsd")
17
18       ' set the validation settings
19       Dim settings As New XmlReaderSettings()
20       settings.ValidationType = ValidationType.Schema
21       settings.Schemas = schemas
22       AddHandler settings.ValidationEventHandler, _
23          AddressOf ValidationError
24
25       ' create the XmlReader object
26       Dim reader As XmlReader = XmlReader.Create(cboFiles.Text, settings)
27
28       ' parse the file
29       While reader.Read()
30          ' empty body
31       End While
32
33       If valid Then ' check validation result
34          lblConsole.Text = "Document is valid"
35       End If
36
37       valid = True ' reset variable
38       reader.Close() ' close reader stream
39    End Sub ' btnValidate_Click
40
41    ' event handler for validation error
42    Private Sub ValidationError(ByVal sender As Object, _
43       ByVal arguments As ValidationEventArgs)
44       lblConsole.Text = arguments.Message
45       valid = False ' validation failed
46    End Sub ' ValidationError
47 End Class ' FrmValidationTest
```

Fig. 19.28 | Schema-validation example. (Part 2 of 2.)

```
 1   <?xml version = "1.0"?>
 2   <!-- Fig. 19.29: fail.xml                           -->
 3   <!-- XML file that does not conform to schema book.xsd -->
 4
 5   <deitel:books xmlns:deitel = "http://www.deitel.com/booklist">
 6      <book>
 7         <title>Visual Basic 2005 How to Program, 3/e</title>
 8      </book>
 9
10      <book>
11         <title>Visual C# 2005 How to Program</title>
12      </book>
13
14      <book>
15         <title>Java How to Program, 6/e</title>
16      </book>
17
18      <book>
19         <title>C++ How to Program, 5/e</title>
20         <title>Internet and World Wide Web How to Program, 3/e</title>
21      </book>
22
23      <book>
24         <title>XML How to Program</title>
25      </book>
26   </deitel:books>
```

Fig. 19.29 | XML file that does not conform to the XML Schema document in Fig. 19.12.

Line 7 declares *XmlSchemaSet* variable schemas. An object of class XmlSchemaSet stores a collection of schemas against which an XmlReader can validate. Line 13 assigns a new XmlSchemaSet object to variable schemas, and line 16 calls this object's *Add* method to add a schema to the collection. Method Add receives as arguments a namespace URI that identifies the schema (http://www.deitel.com/booklist) and the name and location of the schema file (book.xsd in the current directory).

Lines 19–21 create and set the properties of an XmlReaderSettings object. Line 20 sets the XmlReaderSettings object's *ValidationType property* to the value *Validation-Type.Schema*, indicating that we want the XmlReader to perform validation with a schema as it reads an XML document. Line 21 sets the XmlReaderSettings object's *Schemas property* to schemas. This property sets the schema(s) used to validate the document read by the XmlReader.

Lines 22–23 register method `ValidationError` with the `settings` object's *Valida-tionEventHandler*. Method `ValidationError` (lines 42–46) is called if the document being read is found to be invalid or an error occurs (e.g., the document cannot be found). Failure to register a method with `ValidationEventHandler` causes an exception (`XmlEx-ception`) to be thrown when the XML document is found to be invalid or missing.

After setting the `ValidationType` property, `Schemas` property and `Validation-EventHandler` of the `XmlReaderSettings` object, we are ready to create a validating `Xml-Reader`. Line 26 creates an `XmlReader` that reads the file selected by the user from the `cboFiles` ComboBox and validates it against the `book.xsd` schema.

Validation is performed node-by-node by calling method `Read` of the `XmlReader` object (line 29). Because we set `XmlReaderSettings` property `ValidationType` to `Vali-dationType.Schema`, each call to `Read` validates the next node in the document. The loop terminates either when all the nodes have been validated or when a node fails validation.

Detecting an Invalid XML Document

The program in Fig. 19.28 validates the XML document `book.xml` (Fig. 19.12) against the `book.xsd` (Fig. 19.11) schema successfully. However, when the user selects the XML document of Fig. 19.29, validation fails—the `book` element in lines 18–21 contains more than one `title` element. When the program encounters the invalid node, it calls method `ValidationError` (lines 42–46 of Fig. 19.28), which displays a message explaining why validation failed.

19.10 (Optional) XSLT with Class XslCompiledTransform

Recall from Section 19.7 that XSLT elements define rules for converting one type of XML document to another type of XML document. We showed how to transform XML documents into XHTML documents and displayed these in Internet Explorer. The XSLT processor included in Internet Explorer (i.e., MSXML) performed the transformations.

Performing an XSL Transformation in Visual Basic Using the .NET Framework

Figure 19.30 applies the style sheet `sports.xsl` (Fig. 19.17) to `sports.xml` (Fig. 19.26) programmatically. The result of the transformation is written to an XHTML file on disk and displayed in a text box. Figure 19.30(c) shows the resulting XHTML document (`sports.html`) when you view it in Internet Explorer.

Line 5 imports for the *System.Xml.Xsl* namespace, which contains class *XslCom-piledTransform* for applying XSLT style sheets to XML documents. Line 7 declares `XslCompiledTransform` reference `transformer`. An object of this type serves as an XSLT processor (like MSXML in earlier examples) to transform XML data from one format to another.

```
 1    ' Fig. 19.30: FrmTransformTest.vb
 2    ' Applying an XSLT style sheet to an XML document.
 3    Imports System.Xml.Xsl ' contains class XslCompiledTransform
 4
```

Fig. 19.30 | XSLT style sheet applied to an XML document. (Part 1 of 2.)

```vb
5  Public Class FrmTransformTest
6     ' applies the transformation
7     Private transformer As XslCompiledTransform
8
9     ' initialize variables
10    Private Sub FrmTransformTest_Load(ByVal sender As Object, _
11       ByVal e As EventArgs) Handles MyBase.Load
12       transformer = New XslCompiledTransform() ' create transformer
13       transformer.Load("sports.xsl") ' load and compile the style sheet
14    End Sub ' FrmTransformTest_Load
15
16    ' transform XML data on Transform XML Button Click event
17    Private Sub btnTransform_Click(ByVal sender As Object, _
18       ByVal e As EventArgs) Handles btnTransform.Click
19       ' perform the transformation and store the result in new file
20       transformer.Transform("sports.xml", "sports.html")
21
22       ' read and display the XHTML document's text in a Textbox
23       txtConsole.Text = System.IO.File.ReadAllText("sports.html")
24    End Sub ' btnTransform_Click
25 End Class ' FrmTransformTest
```

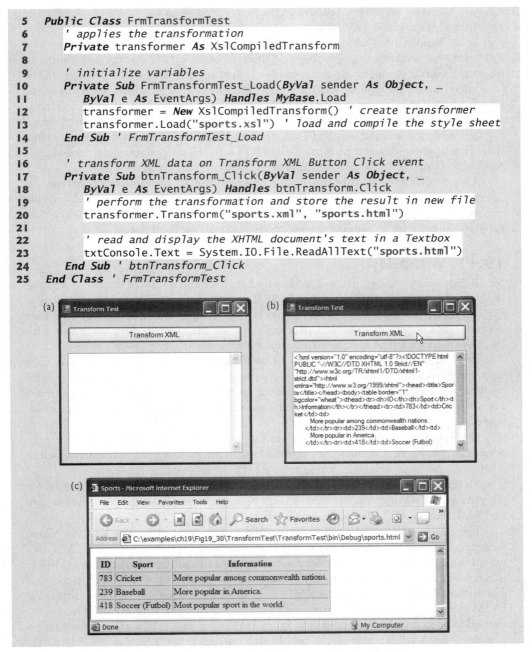

Fig. 19.30 | XSLT style sheet applied to an XML document. (Part 2 of 2.)

In event handler FrmTransformTest_Load (lines 10–14), line 12 creates a new XslCompiledTransform object. Then line 13 calls the XslCompiledTransform object's **Load** method, which parses and loads the style sheet that this application uses. This method takes an argument specifying the name and location of the style sheet—sports.xsl (Fig. 19.17) located in the current directory.

Event handler btnTransform_Click (lines 17–24) calls method *Transform* of class XslCompiledTransform to apply the style sheet (sports.xsl) to sports.xml (line 20). This method takes two String arguments—the first specifies the XML file to which the style sheet should be applied, and the second specifies the file in which the result of the transformation should be stored on disk. Thus the Transform method call in line 20 transforms sports.xml to XHTML and writes the result to disk as the file sports.html. Figure 19.30(c) shows the new XHTML document rendered in Internet Explorer. Note that the output is identical to that of Fig. 19.16—in the current example, though, the XHTML is stored on disk rather than generated dynamically by MSXML.

After applying the transformation, the program displays the content of the new file sports.html in the txtConsole TextBox, as shown in Fig. 19.30(b). Line 23 obtains the text of the file by passing its name to method ReadAllText of the System.IO.File class provided by the FCL to simplify file-processing tasks on the local system.

19.11 Wrap-Up

In this chapter, we studied Extensible Markup Language and several of its related technologies. We began by discussing some basic XML terminology, introducing the concepts of markup, XML vocabularies and XML parsers (validating and nonvalidating). We then demonstrated how to describe and structure data in XML, illustrating these points with examples marking up an article and a business letter.

The chapter discussed the concept of an XML namespace. You learned that each namespace has a unique name that provides a means for document authors to unambiguously refer to elements with the same name (i.e., prevent naming collisions). We presented examples of defining two namespaces in the same document, as well as setting the default namespace for a document.

We also discussed how to create DTDs and schemas for specifying and validating the structure of an XML document. We showed how to use various tools to confirm whether XML documents are valid (i.e., conform to a DTD or schema).

The chapter demonstrated how to create and use XSL documents to specify rules for converting XML documents between formats. Specifically, you learned how to format and sort XML data as XHTML for display in a Web browser.

The final sections of the chapter presented more advanced uses of XML in Visual Basic applications. We demonstrated how to retrieve and display data from an XML document using various FCL classes. We illustrated how a Document Object Model (DOM) tree represents each element of an XML document as a node in the tree. The chapter also demonstrated reading data from an XML document using the XmlReader class, displaying DOM trees graphically and locating data in XML documents with XPath. Finally, we showed how to use .NET Framework classes XmlReader and XslCompiledTransform to perform schema validation and XSL transformations, respectively.

In Chapter 20, we begin our discussion of databases, which organize data in such a way that the data can be selected and updated quickly. We introduce Structured Query Language (SQL) for writing simple database queries (i.e., searches) and ADO.NET for manipulating information in a database through Visual Basic. You will learn how to create XML documents based on data in a database.

19.12 Web Resources

www.w3.org/XML

The W3C (World Wide Web Consortium) facilitates the development of common protocols to ensure interoperability on the Web. Its XML page includes information about upcoming events, publications, software, discussion groups and the latest developments in XML.

www.xml.org

xml.org is a reference for XML, DTDs, schemas and namespaces.

www.w3.org/Style/XSL

This W3C site provides information on XSL, including such topics as XSL development, learning XSL, XSL-enabled tools, the XSL specification, FAQs and XSL history.

www.w3.org/TR

This is the W3C technical reports and publications site. It contains links to working drafts, proposed recommendations and other resources.

www.xmlbooks.com

This site provides a list of XML books recommended by Charles Goldfarb, one of the original designers of GML (General Markup Language), from which SGML, HTML and XML were derived.

www.xml-zone.com

The DevX XML Zone is a complete resource for XML information. This site includes FAQs, news, articles and links to other XML sites and newsgroups.

wdvl.internet.com/Authoring/Languages/XML

The Web Developer's Virtual Library XML site includes tutorials, FAQs, the latest news and extensive links to XML sites and software downloads.

www.xml.com

This site provides the latest news and information about XML, conference listings, links to XML Web resources organized by topic, tools and other resources.

msdn.microsoft.com/xml/default.aspx

The MSDN XML Development Center features articles on XML, Ask-the-Experts chat sessions, samples, demos, newsgroups and other helpful information.

www.oasis-open.org/cover/xml.html

This site includes links to several FAQs, online resources, industry initiatives, demos, conferences and tutorials.

www-106.ibm.com/developerworks/xml

The IBM developerWorks XML site is a great resource for developers that provides news, tools, a library, case studies and information about XML-related events and standards.

www.devx.com/projectcool/door/7051

The Project Cool DevX site includes several tutorials covering introductory through advanced XML topics.

www.ucc.ie/xml

This site provides a detailed XML FAQ. Developers can read responses to some popular questions or submit their own questions through the site.

www.w3.org/XML/Schema

This W3C site provides information on XML Schema, including links, tools, resources and the XML Schema specification.

tools.decisionsoft.com/schemaValidate.html

DecisionSoft provides a free online XML Schema validator from DecisionSoft.

www.sun.com/software/xml/developers/multischema/

The Web page for downloading the Sun Multi-Schema XML Validator (MSV), which validates XML documents against several kinds of schemas.

`en.wikipedia.org/wiki/EBNF`
This site provides detailed information about Extended Backus-Naur Form (EBNF).

`www.garshol.priv.no/download/text/bnf.html`
This site introduces Backus-Naur Form (BNF) and EBNF, and discusses the differences between these notations.

`www.w3schools.com/schema/default.asp`
This site provides an XML Schema tutorial.

`www.w3.org/2001/03/webdata/xsv`
This is an online tool for validating XML Schema documents.

`apps.gotdotnet.com/xmltools/xsdvalidator`
This is an online tool for validating XML documents against an XML Schema.

`www.w3.org/TR/xmlschema-2`
This is part 2 of the W3C XML Schema specification, which defines the types allowed in an XML Schema.

Database, SQL and ADO.NET

It is a capital mistake to theorize before one has data.
—Arthur Conan Doyle

Now go, write it before them in a table, and note it in a book, that it may be for the time to come for ever and ever.
—Holy Bible, Isaiah 30:8

Get your facts first, and then you can distort them as much as you please.
—Mark Twain

I like two kinds of men: domestic and foreign.
—Mae West

OBJECTIVES

In this chapter you will learn:

■ The relational database model.

■ To write basic database queries in SQL.

■ To add data sources to projects.

■ To use the IDE's drag-and-drop capabilities to display database tables in applications.

■ To use the classes of namespaces `System.Data` and `System.Data.SqlClient` to manipulate databases.

■ To use ADO.NET's disconnected object model to store data from a database in local memory.

■ To create XML documents from data sources.

20.1 Introduction

A *database* is an organized collection of data. Many strategies exist for organizing data to facilitate easy access and manipulation. A *database management system* (*DBMS*) provides mechanisms for storing, organizing, retrieving and modifying data for many users. Database management systems allow access to and storage of data independently of the internal representation of the data.

Today's most popular database systems are *relational databases*. A language called *SQL*—pronounced "sequel," or as its individual letters—is the international standard language used almost universally with relational databases to perform *queries* (i.e., to request information that satisfies given criteria) and to manipulate data. In this book, we pronounce SQL as "sequel."

Some popular *relational database management systems* (*RDBMS*) are Microsoft SQL Server, Oracle, Sybase, IBM DB2 and PostgreSQL. We provide URLs for these systems in Section 20.11, Web Resources. MySQL (www.mysql.com) is an increasingly popular open-source RDBMS that can be downloaded and used freely by non-commercial users. You may also be familiar with Microsoft Access—a relational database system that is part of Microsoft Office. In this chapter, we use *Microsoft SQL Server 2005 Express*—a version of SQL Server 2005 that is installed when you install Visual Basic 2005 Express. We will refer to SQL Server 2005 Express simply as SQL Server from this point forward.

A programming language connects to and interacts with a relational database via a *database interface*—software that facilitates communication between a database management system and a program. Visual Basic programs communicate with databases and manipulate their data through *ADO.NET*. The current version of ADO.NET is 2.0. Section 20.5 presents an overview of ADO.NET's object model and the relevant namespaces and classes that allow you to work with databases. However, as you will learn in subsequent sections, most of the work required to communicate with a database using ADO.NET 2.0 is performed by the IDE itself. You will work primarily with the IDE's visual programming tools and wizards, which simplify connecting to and manipulating a database. Throughout this chapter, we refer to ADO.NET 2.0 simply as ADO.NET.

This chapter introduces general concepts of relational databases and SQL, then explores ADO.NET and the IDE's tools for accessing data sources. The examples in Sections 20.6–20.9 demonstrate how to build applications that use databases to store information. In the next two chapters, you will see other practical database applications. Chapter 21, ASP.NET 2.0, Web Forms and Web Controls, presents a Web-based bookstore case study that retrieves user and book information from a database. Chapter 22, Web Services, uses a database to store airline reservation data for a Web service (i.e., a software component that can be accessed remotely over a network).

20.2 Relational Databases

A *relational database* is a logical representation of data that allows the data to be accessed independently of its physical structure. A relational database organizes data in *tables*. Figure 20.1 illustrates a sample Employees table that might be used in a personnel system. The table stores the attributes of employees. Tables are composed of *rows* and *columns* in which values are stored. This table consists of six rows and five columns. The Number column of each row in this table is the table's *primary key*—a column (or group of columns) in a table that requires a unique value that cannot be duplicated in other rows. This guarantees that a primary key value can be used to uniquely identify a row. A primary key that is composed of two or more columns is known as a *composite key*. Good examples of primary key columns in other applications are an employee ID number in a payroll system and a part number in an inventory system—values in each of these columns are guaranteed to be unique. The rows in Fig. 20.1 are displayed in order by primary key. In this case, the rows are listed in increasing (ascending) order, but they could also be listed in decreasing (descending) order or in no particular order at all. As we will demonstrate in an upcoming example, programs can specify ordering criteria when requesting data from a database.

Each column represents a different data attribute. Rows are normally unique (by primary key) within a table, but some column values may be duplicated between rows. For example, three different rows in the Employees table's Department column contain the number 413, indicating that these employees work in the same department.

Different database users are often interested in different data and different relationships among the data. Most users require only subsets of the rows and columns. To obtain these subsets, programs use SQL to define queries that select subsets of the data from a table. For example, a program might select data from the Employees table to create a query result that shows where each department is located, in increasing order by Department number (Fig. 20.2). SQL queries are discussed in Section 20.4. In Section 20.7, you will learn how to use the IDE's **Query Builder** to create SQL queries.

Table Employees

	Number	Name	Department	Salary	Location
	23603	Jones	413	1100	New Jersey
	24568	Kerwin	413	2000	New Jersey
Row	34589	Larson	642	1800	Los Angeles
	35761	Myers	611	1400	Orlando
	47132	Neumann	413	9000	New Jersey
	78321	Stephens	611	8500	Orlando

Primary key   Column

Fig. 20.1 | Employees table sample data.

Department	Location
413	New Jersey
611	Orlando
642	Los Angeles

Fig. 20.2 | Result of selecting distinct `Department` and `Location` data from the `Employees` table.

20.3 Relational Database Overview: Books Database

We now overview relational databases in the context of a simple `Books` database. The database stores information about some recent Deitel publications. First, we overview the tables of the `Books` database. Then we introduce database concepts, such as how to use SQL to retrieve information from the `Books` database and to manipulate the data. We provide the database file—`Books.mdf`—with the examples for this chapter (downloadable from www.deitel.com/books/vbforprogrammers2/). SQL Server database files typically end with the `.mdf` ("master data file") filename extension. Section 20.6 explains how to use this file in an application.

Authors Table of the Books Database

The database consists of three tables: `Authors`, `AuthorISBN` and `Titles`. The `Authors` table (described in Fig. 20.3) consists of three columns that maintain each author's unique ID number, first name and last name, respectively. Figure 20.4 contains the data from the `Authors` table. We list the rows in order by the table's primary key—`AuthorID`. You will learn how to sort data by other criteria (e.g., in alphabetical order by last name) using SQL's `ORDER BY` clause in Section 20.4.3.

Titles Table of the Books Database

The `Titles` table (described in Fig. 20.5) consists of four columns that maintain information about each book in the database, including the ISBN, title, edition number and copyright year. Figure 20.6 contains the data from the `Titles` table.

Column	Description
AuthorID	Author's ID number in the database. In the Books database, this integer column is defined as an *identity* column, also known as an *autoincremented* column—for each row inserted in the table, the AuthorID value is increased by 1 automatically to ensure that each row has a unique AuthorID. This is the primary key.
FirstName	Author's first name (a string).
LastName	Author's last name (a string).

Fig. 20.3 | Authors table of the Books database.

AuthorID	FirstName	LastName
1	Harvey	Deitel
2	Paul	Deitel
3	Andrew	Goldberg
4	David	Choffnes

Fig. 20.4 | Data from the Authors table of the Books database.

Column	Description
ISBN	ISBN of the book (a string). The table's primary key. ISBN is an abbreviation for "International Standard Book Number"—a numbering scheme that publishers worldwide use to give every book a unique identification number.
Title	Title of the book (a string).
EditionNumber	Edition number of the book (an integer).
Copyright	Copyright year of the book (a string).

Fig. 20.5 | Titles table of the Books database.

ISBN	Title	Edition-Number	Copy-right
0131426443	C How to Program	4	2004
0131450913	Internet & World Wide Web How to Program	3	2004

Fig. 20.6 | Data from the Titles table of the Books database. (Part 1 of 2.)

ISBN	Title	Edition-Number	Copy-right
0131483986	Java How to Program	6	2005
0131525239	Visual C# 2005 How to Program	2	2006
0131828274	Operating Systems	3	2004
0131857576	C++ How to Program	5	2005
0131869000	Visual Basic 2005 How to Program	3	2006

Fig. 20.6 | Data from the `Titles` table of the `Books` database. (Part 2 of 2.)

AuthorISBN *Table of the Books Database*

The `AuthorISBN` table (described in Fig. 20.7) consists of two columns that maintain ISBNs for each book and their corresponding authors' ID numbers. This table associates authors with their books. The `AuthorID` column is a *foreign key*—a column in this table that matches the primary key column in another table (i.e., `AuthorID` in the `Authors` table). The `ISBN` column is also a foreign key—it matches the primary key column (i.e., `ISBN`) in the `Titles` table. Together the `AuthorID` and `ISBN` columns in this table form a composite primary key. Every row in this table uniquely matches one author to one book's ISBN. Figure 20.8 contains the data from the `AuthorISBN` table of the `Books` database.

Column	Description
AuthorID	The author's ID number, a foreign key to the `Authors` table.
ISBN	The ISBN for a book, a foreign key to the `Titles` table.

Fig. 20.7 | `AuthorISBN` table of the `Books` database.

AuthorID	ISBN	AuthorID	ISBN
1	0131869000	2	0131450913
1	0131525239	2	0131426443
1	0131483986	2	0131857576
1	0131857576	2	0131483986
1	0131426443	2	0131525239
1	0131450913	2	0131869000
1	0131828274	3	0131450913
2	0131828274	4	0131828274

Fig. 20.8 | Data from the `AuthorISBN` table of `Books`.

Foreign Keys

Foreign keys can be specified when creating a table. A foreign key helps maintain the ***Rule of Referential Integrity***—every foreign key value must appear as another table's primary key value. This enables the DBMS to determine whether the AuthorID value for a particular row of the AuthorISBN table is valid. Foreign keys also allow related data in multiple tables to be selected from those tables—this is known as *joining* the data. (You will learn how to join data using SQL's INNER JOIN operator in Section 20.4.4.) There is a ***one-to-many relationship*** between a primary key and a corresponding foreign key (e.g., one author can write many books). This means that a foreign key can appear many times in its own table, but can appear only once (as the primary key) in another table. For example, the ISBN 0131450913 can appear in several rows of AuthorISBN (because this book has several authors), but can appear only once in Titles, where ISBN is the primary key.

Entity-Relationship Diagram for the Books Database

Figure 20.9 is an ***entity-relationship (ER) diagram*** for the Books database. This diagram shows the tables in the database and the relationships among them. The first compartment in each box contains the table's name. The names in italic font are primary keys (e.g., *AuthorID* in the Authors table). A table's primary key uniquely identifies each row in the table. Every row must have a value in the primary key column, and the value of the key must be unique in the table. This is known as the ***Rule of Entity Integrity***. Note that the names AuthorID and ISBN in the AuthorISBN table are both italic—together these form a composite primary key for the AuthorISBN table.

 Common Programming Error 20.1

Not providing a value for every column in a primary key breaks the Rule of Entity Integrity and causes the DBMS to report an error.

 Common Programming Error 20.2

Providing the same value for the primary key in multiple rows breaks the Rule of Entity Integrity and causes the DBMS to report an error.

The lines connecting the tables in Fig. 20.9 represent the relationships among the tables. Consider the line between the Authors and AuthorISBN tables. On the Authors end of the line, there is a 1, and on the AuthorISBN end, there is an infinity symbol (∞). This indicates a one-to-many relationship—for each author in the Authors table, there can be an arbitrary number of ISBNs for books written by that author in the AuthorISBN table

Fig. 20.9 | Entity-relationship diagram for the Books database.

(i.e., an author can write any number of books). Note that the relationship line links the AuthorID column in the Authors table (where AuthorID is the primary key) to the AuthorID column in the AuthorISBN table (where AuthorID is a foreign key)—the line between the tables links the primary key to the matching foreign key.

Common Programming Error 20.3

Providing a foreign-key value that does not appear as a primary-key value in another table breaks the Rule of Referential Integrity and causes the DBMS to report an error.

The line between the Titles and AuthorISBN tables illustrates a one-to-many relationship—a book can be written by many authors. Note that the line between the tables links the primary key ISBN in table Titles to the corresponding foreign key in table AuthorISBN. The relationships in Fig. 20.9 illustrate that the sole purpose of the AuthorISBN table is to provide a many-to-many relationship between the Authors and Titles tables—an author can write many books, and a book can have many authors.

20.4 SQL

We now overview SQL in the context of the Books database. Later in the chapter, you will build Visual Basic applications that execute SQL queries and access their results using ADO.NET technology. Though the Visual Basic IDE provides visual tools that hide some of the SQL used to manipulate databases, it is nevertheless important to understand SQL basics. Knowing the types of operations you can perform will help you develop more advanced database-intensive applications.

Figure 20.10 lists some common *SQL keywords* used to form complete *SQL statements*—we discuss these keywords in the next several subsections. Other SQL keywords exist, but they are beyond the scope of this text. For additional information on SQL, please refer to the URLs listed in Section 20.11, Web Resources.

SQL keyword	Description
SELECT	Retrieves data from one or more tables.
FROM	Specifies the tables involved in a query. Required in every query.
WHERE	Specifies optional criteria for selection that determine the rows to be retrieved, deleted or updated.
ORDER BY	Specifies optional criteria for ordering rows (e.g., ascending, descending).
INNER JOIN	Specifies optional operator for merging rows from multiple tables.
INSERT	Inserts rows in a specified table.
UPDATE	Updates rows in a specified table.
DELETE	Deletes rows from a specified table.

Fig. 20.10 | Common SQL keywords.

20.4.1 Basic SELECT Query

Let us consider several SQL queries that retrieve information from database Books. A SQL *query* "selects" rows and columns from one or more tables in a database. Such selections are performed by queries with the ***SELECT*** keyword. The basic form of a ***SELECT query*** is

> ***SELECT*** * ***FROM*** *tableName*

in which the asterisk (*) indicates that all the columns from the *tableName* table should be retrieved. For example, to retrieve all the data in the Authors table, use

> ***SELECT*** * ***FROM*** Authors

Note that the rows of the Authors table are not guaranteed to be returned in any particular order. You will learn how to specify criteria for sorting rows in Section 20.4.3.

Most programs do not require all the data in a table. To retrieve only specific columns from a table, replace the asterisk (*) with a comma-separated list of the column names. For example, to retrieve only the columns AuthorID and LastName for all the rows in the Authors table, use the query

> ***SELECT*** AuthorID, LastName ***FROM*** Authors

This query returns only the data listed in Fig. 20.11.

20.4.2 WHERE Clause

When users search a database for rows that satisfy certain *selection criteria* (formally called *predicates*), only rows that satisfy the selection criteria are selected. SQL uses the optional ***WHERE clause*** in a query to specify the selection criteria for the query. The basic form of a query with selection criteria is

> ***SELECT*** *columnName1*, *columnName2*, ... ***FROM*** *tableName* ***WHERE*** *criteria*

For example, to select the Title, EditionNumber and Copyright columns from table Titles for which the Copyright date is more recent than 2004, use the query

> ***SELECT*** Title, EditionNumber, Copyright
> ***FROM*** Titles
> ***WHERE*** Copyright > '2004'

Figure 20.12 shows the result of the preceding query.

AuthorID	LastName
1	Deitel
2	Deitel
3	Goldberg
4	Choffnes

Fig. 20.11 | AuthorID and LastName data from the Authors table.

Title	EditionNumber	Copyright
Java How to Program	6	2005
Visual C# 2005 How to Program	2	2006
C++ How to Program	5	2005
Visual Basic 2005 How to Program	3	2006

Fig. 20.12 | Titles with copyright dates after 2004 from table `Titles`.

The WHERE clause criteria can contain the relational operators <, >, <=, >=, = (equality), <> (inequality) and LIKE, as well as the logical operators AND, OR and NOT (discussed in Section 20.4.6). Operator **LIKE** is used for *pattern matching* with wildcard characters *percent* (**%**) and *underscore* (**_**). Pattern matching allows SQL to search for strings that match a given pattern.

A pattern that contains a percent character (%) searches for strings that have zero or more characters at the percent character's position in the pattern. For example, the following query locates the rows of all the authors whose last names start with the letter D:

```
SELECT AuthorID, FirstName, LastName
FROM Authors
WHERE LastName LIKE 'D%'
```

The preceding query selects the two rows shown in Fig. 20.13, because two of the four authors in our database have a last name starting with the letter D (followed by zero or more characters). The % in the WHERE clause's LIKE pattern indicates that any number of characters can appear after the letter D in the LastName column. Note that the pattern string is surrounded by single-quote characters.

An underscore (_) in the pattern string indicates a single wildcard character at that position in the pattern. For example, the following query locates the rows of all the authors whose last names start with any character (specified by _), followed by the letter h, followed by any number of additional characters (specified by %):

```
SELECT AuthorID, FirstName, LastName
FROM Authors
WHERE LastName LIKE '_h%'
```

The preceding query produces the row shown in Fig. 20.14, because only one author in our database has a last name that contains the letter h as its second letter.

AuthorID	FirstName	LastName
1	Harvey	Deitel
2	Paul	Deitel

Fig. 20.13 | Authors from the `Authors` table whose last names start with D.

AuthorID	FirstName	LastName
4	David	Choffnes

Fig. 20.14 | The only author from the `Authors` table whose last name contains h as the second letter.

20.4.3 ORDER BY Clause

The rows in the result of a query can be sorted into ascending or descending order by using the optional *ORDER BY clause*. The basic form of a query with an ORDER BY clause is

> **SELECT** *columnName1*, *columnName2*, ... **FROM** *tableName* **ORDER BY** *column* **ASC**
> **SELECT** *columnName1*, *columnName2*, ... **FROM** *tableName* **ORDER BY** *column* **DESC**

where **ASC** specifies ascending order (lowest to highest), **DESC** specifies descending order (highest to lowest) and *column* specifies the column on which the sort is based. For example, to obtain the list of authors in ascending order by last name (Fig. 20.15), use the query

```
SELECT AuthorID, FirstName, LastName
FROM Authors
ORDER BY LastName ASC
```

The default sorting order is ascending, so ASC is optional in the preceding query.

To obtain the same list of authors in descending order by last name (Fig. 20.16), use the query

```
SELECT AuthorID, FirstName, LastName
FROM Authors
ORDER BY LastName DESC
```

Multiple columns can be used for sorting with an ORDER BY clause of the form

> **ORDER BY** *column1 sortingOrder*, *column2 sortingOrder*, ...

where *sortingOrder* is either ASC or DESC. Note that the *sortingOrder* does not have to be identical for each column. For example, the query

```
SELECT Title, EditionNumber, Copyright
FROM Titles
ORDER BY Copyright DESC, Title ASC
```

AuthorID	FirstName	LastName
4	David	Choffnes
1	Harvey	Deitel
2	Paul	Deitel
3	Andrew	Goldberg

Fig. 20.15 | Authors from table `Authors` in ascending order by `LastName`.

AuthorID	FirstName	LastName
3	Andrew	Goldberg
1	Harvey	Deitel
2	Paul	Deitel
4	David	Choffnes

Fig. 20.16 | Authors from table `Authors` in descending order by `LastName`.

returns the rows of the `Titles` table sorted first in descending order by copyright date, then in ascending order by title (Fig. 20.17). This means that rows with higher `Copyright` values are returned before rows with lower `Copyright` values, and any rows that have the same `Copyright` values are sorted in ascending order by title.

The `WHERE` and `ORDER BY` clauses can be combined in one query. For example, the query

```
SELECT ISBN, Title, EditionNumber, Copyright
FROM Titles
WHERE Title LIKE '%How to Program'
ORDER BY Title ASC
```

returns the `ISBN`, `Title`, `EditionNumber` and `Copyright` of each book in the `Titles` table that has a `Title` ending with "How to Program" and sorts them in ascending order by `Title`. The query results are shown in Fig. 20.18.

20.4.4 Merging Data from Multiple Tables: INNER JOIN

Database designers typically *normalize* databases—i.e., split related data into separate tables to ensure that a database does not store redundant data. For example, the `Books` database has tables `Authors` and `Titles`. We use an `AuthorISBN` table to store "links"

Title	EditionNumber	Copyright
Visual Basic 2005 How to Program	3	2006
Visual C# 2005 How to Program	2	2006
C++ How to Program	5	2005
Java How to Program	6	2005
C How to Program	4	2004
Internet & World Wide Web How to Program	3	2004
Operating Systems	3	2004

Fig. 20.17 | Data from `Titles` in descending order by `Copyright` and ascending order by `Title`.

ISBN	Title	EditionNumber	Copyright
0131426443	C How to Program	4	2004
0131857576	C++ How to Program	5	2005
0131450913	Internet & World Wide Web How to Program	3	2004
0131483986	Java How to Program	6	2005
0131869000	Visual Basic 2005 How to Program	3	2006
0131525239	Visual C# 2005 How to Program	2	2006

Fig. 20.18 | Books from table `Titles` whose titles end with `How to Program` in ascending order by `Title`.

between authors and titles. If we did not separate this information into individual tables, we would need to include author information with each entry in the `Titles` table. This would result in the database storing duplicate author information for authors who wrote more than one book.

Often, it is desirable to merge data from multiple tables into a single result. This is referred to as joining the tables, and is specified by an ***INNER JOIN operator*** in the query. An INNER JOIN merges rows from two tables by testing for matching values in a column that is common to the tables. The basic form of an INNER JOIN is:

> **SELECT** *columnName1, columnName2, …*
> **FROM** *table1* **INNER JOIN** *table2*
>   **ON** *table1.columnName = table2.columnName*

The ***ON clause*** of the INNER JOIN specifies the columns from each table that are compared to determine which rows are merged. For example, the following query produces a list of authors accompanied by the ISBNs for books written by each author:

> **SELECT** FirstName, LastName, ISBN
> **FROM** Authors **INNER JOIN** AuthorISBN
>   **ON** Authors.AuthorID = AuthorISBN.AuthorID
> **ORDER BY** LastName, FirstName

The query combines the `FirstName` and `LastName` columns from table `Authors` and the ISBN column from table `AuthorISBN`, sorting the results in ascending order by `LastName` and `FirstName`. Note the use of the syntax *tableName.columnName* in the ON clause. This syntax (called a ***qualified name***) specifies the columns from each table that should be compared to join the tables. The "*tableName.*" syntax is required if the columns have the same name in both tables. The same syntax can be used in any query to distinguish columns that have the same name in different tables.

Common Programming Error 20.4

In a SQL query, failure to qualify names for columns that have the same name in two or more tables is an error.

As always, the query can contain an ORDER BY clause. Figure 20.19 depicts the results of the preceding query, ordered by LastName and FirstName.

20.4.5 INSERT Statement

The *INSERT statement* inserts a row into a table. The basic form of this statement is

> *INSERT INTO* tableName (columnName1, columnName2, ..., columnNameN)
> *VALUES* (value1, value2, ..., valueN)

where *tableName* is the table in which to insert the row. The *tableName* is followed by a comma-separated list of column names in parentheses (this list is not required if the INSERT operation specifies a value for every column of the table in the correct order). The list of column names is followed by the SQL keyword *VALUES* and a comma-separated list of values in parentheses. The values specified here must match up with the columns specified after the table name in both order and type (e.g., if *columnName1* is supposed to be the FirstName column, then *value1* should be a string in single quotes representing the first name). Always explicitly list the columns when inserting rows—if the order of the columns in the table changes, using only VALUES may cause an error. The INSERT statement

> *INSERT INTO* Authors (FirstName, LastName)
> *VALUES* ('Sue', 'Smith')

FirstName	LastName	ISBN
David	Choffnes	0131828274
Harvey	Deitel	0131869000
Harvey	Deitel	0131525239
Harvey	Deitel	0131483986
Harvey	Deitel	0131857576
Harvey	Deitel	0131426443
Harvey	Deitel	0131450913
Harvey	Deitel	0131828274
Paul	Deitel	0131869000
Paul	Deitel	0131525239
Paul	Deitel	0131483986
Paul	Deitel	0131857576
Paul	Deitel	0131426443
Paul	Deitel	0131450913
Paul	Deitel	0131828274
Andrew	Goldberg	0131450913

Fig. 20.19 | Authors and ISBNs for their books in ascending order by LastName and FirstName.

inserts a row into the Authors table. The statement indicates that the values 'Sue' and 'Smith' are provided for the FirstName and LastName columns, respectively.

We do not specify an AuthorID in this example because AuthorID is an identity column in the Authors table (see Fig. 20.3). For every row added to this table, SQL Server assigns a unique AuthorID value that is the next value in an autoincremented sequence (i.e., 1, 2, 3 and so on). In this case, Sue Smith would be assigned AuthorID number 5. Figure 20.20 shows the Authors table after the INSERT operation. Not every DBMS supports identity or autoincremented columns.

Common Programming Error 20.5

It is an error to specify a value for an identity column.

Common Programming Error 20.6

SQL uses the single-quote (') character to delimit strings. To specify a string containing a single quote (e.g., O'Malley) in a SQL statement, there must be two single quotes in the position where the single-quote character appears in the string (e.g., 'O''Malley'). The first of the two single-quote characters acts as an escape character for the second. Not escaping single-quote characters in a string that is part of a SQL statement is a syntax error.

20.4.6 UPDATE Statement

An **UPDATE** *statement* modifies data in a table. The basic form of the UPDATE statement is

> **UPDATE** *tableName*
> **SET** *columnName1 = value1* , *columnName2 = value2* , … , *columnNameN = valueN*
> **WHERE** *criteria*

where *tableName* is the table to update. The *tableName* is followed by keyword **SET** and a comma-separated list of column name-value pairs in the format *columnName = value*. The optional WHERE clause provides criteria that determine which rows to update. Though not required, the WHERE clause is typically used, unless a change is to be made to every row. The UPDATE statement

> **UPDATE** Authors
> **SET** LastName = 'Jones'
> **WHERE** LastName = 'Smith' **AND** FirstName = 'Sue'

AuthorID	FirstName	LastName
1	Harvey	Deitel
2	Paul	Deitel
3	Andrew	Goldberg
4	David	Choffnes
5	Sue	Smith

Fig. 20.20 | Table Authors after an INSERT operation.

updates a row in the Authors table. Keyword *AND* is a logical operator that, like the Visual Basic And operator, returns true *if and only if* both of its operands are true. Thus, the preceding statement assigns to LastName the value Jones for the row in which LastName is equal to Smith *and* FirstName is equal to Sue. [*Note:* If there are multiple rows with the first name "Sue" and the last name "Smith," this statement modifies all such rows to have the last name "Jones."] Figure 20.21 shows the Authors table after the UPDATE operation has taken place. SQL also provides other logical operators, such as *OR* and *NOT*, which behave like their Visual Basic counterparts.

20.4.7 DELETE Statement

A *DELETE statement* removes rows from a table. The basic form of a DELETE statement is

> *DELETE FROM* tableName *WHERE* criteria

where *tableName* is the table from which to delete. The optional WHERE clause specifies the criteria used to determine which rows to delete. The DELETE statement

```
DELETE FROM Authors
WHERE LastName = 'Jones' AND FirstName = 'Sue'
```

deletes the row for Sue Jones in the Authors table. DELETE statements can delete multiple rows if the rows all meet the criteria in the WHERE clause. Figure 20.22 shows the Authors table after the DELETE operation has taken place.

AuthorID	FirstName	LastName
1	Harvey	Deitel
2	Paul	Deitel
3	Andrew	Goldberg
4	David	Choffnes
5	Sue	Jones

Fig. 20.21 | Table Authors after an UPDATE operation.

AuthorID	FirstName	LastName
1	Harvey	Deitel
2	Paul	Deitel
3	Andrew	Goldberg
4	David	Choffnes

Fig. 20.22 | Table Authors after a DELETE operation.

SQL Wrap-Up

This concludes our SQL introduction. We demonstrated several commonly used SQL keywords, formed SQL queries that retrieved data from databases and formed other SQL statements that manipulated data in a database. Next, we introduce the ADO.NET object model, which allows Visual Basic applications to interact with databases. As you will see, ADO.NET objects manipulate databases using SQL statements like those presented here.

20.5 ADO.NET Object Model

The *ADO.NET object model* provides an API for accessing database systems programmatically. ADO.NET was created for the .NET framework to replace Microsoft's ActiveX Data Objects™ (ADO) technology. As will be discussed in the next section, the IDE features visual programming tools that simplify the process of using a database in your projects. While you may not need to work directly with many ADO.NET objects to develop simple applications, basic knowledge of how the ADO.NET object model works is important for understanding data access in Visual Basic.

Namespaces `System.Data`, `System.Data.OleDb` and `System.Data.SqlClient`

Namespace **`System.Data`** is the root namespace for the ADO.NET API. The other important ADO.NET namespaces, **`System.Data.OleDb`** and **`System.Data.SqlClient`**, contain classes that enable programs to connect with and manipulate *data sources*—locations that contain data, such as a database or an XML file. Namespace `System.Data.OleDb` contains classes that are designed to work with any data source, whereas `System.Data.SqlClient` contains classes that are optimized to work with Microsoft SQL Server databases. The chapter examples manipulate SQL Server 2005 Express databases, so we use the classes of namespace `System.Data.SqlClient`. SQL Server 2005 Express is provided with Visual Basic 2005 Express. It can also be downloaded from `msdn.microsoft.com/vstudio/express/sql/default.aspx`.

An object of class **`SqlConnection`** (namespace `System.Data.SqlClient`) represents a connection to a data source—specifically a SQL Server database. A `SqlConnection` object keeps track of the location of the data source and any settings that specify how the data source is to be accessed. A connection is either *active* (i.e., open and permitting data to be sent to and retrieved from the data source) or *closed*.

An object of class **`SqlCommand`** (namespace `System.Data.SqlClient`) represents a SQL command that a DBMS can execute on a database. A program can use `SqlCommand` objects to manipulate a data source through a `SqlConnection`. The program must open the connection to the data source before executing one or more `SqlCommand`s and close the connection once no further access to the data source is required. A connection that remains active for some length of time to permit multiple data operations is known as a *persistent connection*.

Class **`DataTable`** (namespace `System.Data`) represents a table of data. A `DataTable` contains a collection of **`DataRows`** that represent the table's data. A `DataTable` also has a collection of **`DataColumns`** that describe the columns in a table. `DataRow` and `DataColumn` are both located in namespace `System.Data`. An object of class **`System.Data.DataSet`**, which consists of a set of `DataTables` and the relationships among them, represents a *cache* of data—data that a program stores temporarily in local memory. The structure of a `DataSet` mimics the structure of a relational database.

ADO.NET's Disconnected Model

An advantage of using class DataSet is that it is *disconnected*—the program does not need a persistent connection to the data source to work with data in a DataSet. Instead, the program connects to the data source to *populate the DataSet* (i.e., fill the DataSet's Data-Tables with data), but disconnects from the data source immediately after retrieving the desired data. The program then accesses and potentially manipulates the data stored in the DataSet. The program operates on this local cache of data, rather than the original data in the data source. If the program makes changes to the data in the DataSet that need to be permanently saved in the data source, the program reconnects to the data source to perform an update then disconnects promptly. Thus the program does not require any active, persistent connection to the data source.

An object of class *SqlDataAdapter* (namespace System.Data.SqlClient) connects to a SQL Server data source and executes SQL statements to both populate a DataSet and update the data source based on the current contents of a DataSet. A SqlDataAdapter maintains a SqlConnection object that it opens and closes as needed to perform these operations using SqlCommands. We demonstrate populating DataSets and updating data sources later in this chapter.

20.6 Programming with ADO.NET: Extracting Information from a Database

In this section, we demonstrate how to connect to a database, query the database and display the result of the query. You will notice that there is little code in this section. The IDE provides visual programming tools and wizards that simplify accessing data in your projects. These tools establish database connections and create the ADO.NET objects necessary to view and manipulate the data through GUI controls. The example in this section connects to the SQL Server Books database that we have discussed throughout this chapter. The Books.mdf file that contains the database can be found with the chapter's examples (www.deitel.com/books/vbforprogrammers2).

20.6.1 Displaying a Database Table in a DataGridView

This example performs a simple query on the Books database that retrieves the entire Authors table and displays the data in a *DataGridView* (a control from namespace System.Windows.Forms that can display a data source in a GUI—see the sample outputs in Fig. 20.32 later in this section). First, we demonstrate how to connect to the Books database and include it as a data source in your project. Once the Books database is established as a data source, you can display the data from the Authors table in a DataGridView simply by dragging and dropping items in the project's **Design** view.

Step 1: Creating the Project

Create a new Windows Application named DisplayTable. Change name of the Form to FrmDisplayTable and change the source file name to FrmDisplayTable.vb. Then set the Form's **Text** property to Display Table.

Step 2: Adding a Data Source to the Project

To interact with a data source (e.g., a database), you must add it to the project using the **Data Sources** *window*, which lists the data that your project can access. Open the **Data**

Sources window (Fig. 20.23) by selecting **Data > Show Data Sources** or by clicking the tab to the right of the tab for the **Solution Explorer**. In the **Data Sources** window, click **Add New Data Source...** to open the ***Data Source Configuration Wizard*** (Fig. 20.24). This wizard guides you through connecting to a database and choosing the parts of the database to use in your project.

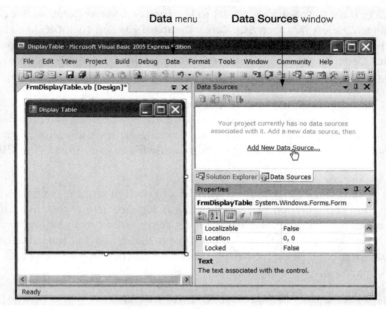

Fig. 20.23 | Adding a data source to a project.

Fig. 20.24 | Choosing the data source type in the **Data Source Configuration Wizard**.

Step 3: Choosing the Data Source Type to Add to the Project

The first screen of the **Data Source Configuration Wizard** (Fig. 20.24) asks you to choose the data source type you wish to include in the project. Select **Database** and click **Next >**.

Step 4: Adding a New Database Connection

You must next choose the connection that will be used to connect to the database (i.e., the actual *source* of the data). Click **New Connection...** to open the **Add Connection** dialog (Fig. 20.25). If the **Data Source** is not set to **Microsoft SQL Server Database File (SqlClient)**, click **Change...**, select **Microsoft SQL Server Database File** and click **OK**. In the **Add Connection** dialog, click **Browse...**, locate the `Books.mdf` database file on your computer, select it and click **Open**. You can click **Test Connection** to verify that the IDE can connect to the database through SQL Server. Click **OK** to create the connection.

Step 5: Choosing the `Books.mdf` Data Connection

Now that you have created a connection to the `Books.mdf` database, you can select and use this connection to access the database. Click **Next >** to set the connection, then click **Yes** when asked whether you want to move the database file to your project (Fig. 20.26).

Step 6: Saving the Connection String

The next screen (Fig. 20.27) asks you whether you want to save the connection string to the application configuration file. A *connection string* specifies the path to a database file on disk, as well as some additional settings that determine how to access the database. Saving the connection string in a configuration file makes it easy to change the connection settings at a later time. Leave the default selections and click **Next >** to proceed.

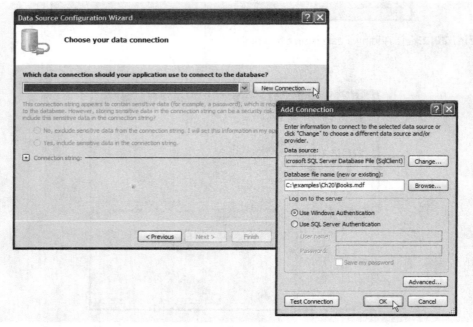

Fig. 20.25 | Adding a new data connection.

Fig. 20.26 | Choosing the Books.mdf data connection.

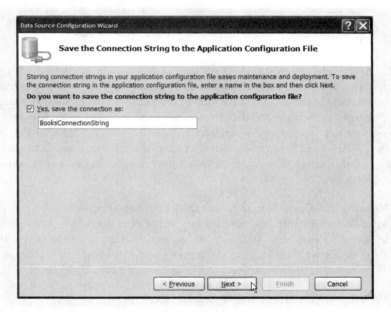

Fig. 20.27 | Saving the connection string to the application configuration file.

Step 7: Selecting the Database Objects to Include in Your DataSet

The IDE retrieves information about the database you selected and prompts you to select the database objects (i.e., the parts of the database) that you want your project to be able to access (Fig. 20.28). Recall that programs typically access a database's contents through a cache of the data, which is stored in a DataSet. In response to your selections in this screen, the IDE will generate a class derived from System.Data.DataSet that is designed

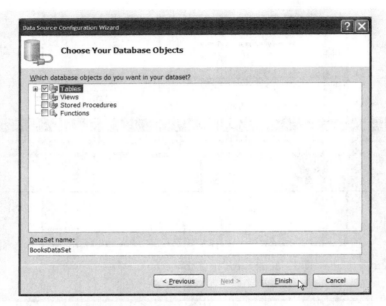

Fig. 20.28 | Choosing the database objects to include in the `DataSet`.

specifically to store data from the `Books` database. Click the checkbox to the left of **Tables** to indicate that the custom `DataSet` should cache (i.e., locally store) the data from all the tables in the `Books` database—`Authors`, `AuthorISBN` and `Titles`. [*Note:* You can also expand the **Tables** node to select specific tables. The other database objects listed do not contain any data in our sample `Books` database and are beyond the scope of the book.] By default, the IDE names the `DataSet` `BooksDataSet`, though it is possible to specify a different name in this screen. Finally, click **Finish** to complete the process of adding a data source to the project.

Step 8: Viewing the Data Source in the *Data Sources* Window
Notice that a **BooksDataSet** node now appears in the **Data Sources** window (Fig. 20.29) with child nodes for each table in the `Books` database—these nodes represent the `Data-Tables` of the `BooksDataSet`. Expand the **Authors** node and you will see the table's columns—the `DataSet`'s structure mimics that of the actual `Books` database.

Step 9: Viewing the Database in the *Solution Explorer*
`Books.mdf` is now listed as a node in the **Solution Explorer** (Fig. 20.30), indicating that the database is part of this project. In addition, the **Solution Explorer** now lists a new node named `BooksDataSet.xsd`. You learned in Chapter 19 that a file with the `.xsd` extension is an XML Schema document, which specifies the structure of a set of XML documents. The IDE uses an XML Schema document to represent a `DataSet`'s structure, including the tables that comprise the `DataSet` and the relationships among them. When you added the `Books` database as a data source, the IDE created the `BooksDataSet.xsd` file based on the structure of the `Books` database. The IDE then generated class `BooksDataSet` from the schema (i.e., structure) described by the `.xsd` file.

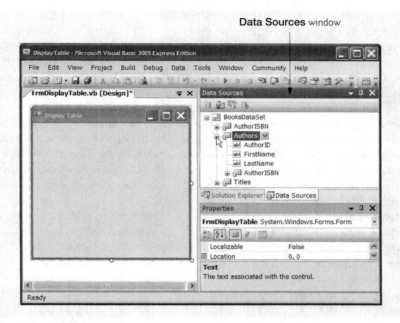

Fig. 20.29 | Viewing a data source listed in the **Data Sources** window.

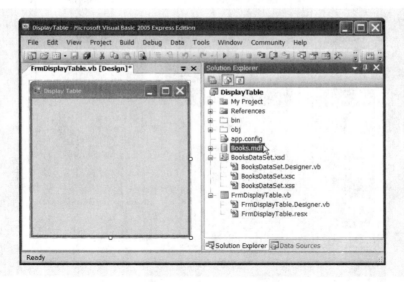

Fig. 20.30 | Viewing a database listed in the **Solution Explorer**.

Displaying the Authors Table

Now that you have added the Books database as a data source, you can display the data from the database's Authors table in your program. The IDE provides design tools that allow you to display data from a data source on a Form without writing any code. Simply drag and drop items from the **Data Sources** window onto a Form, and the IDE generates the GUI controls and code necessary to display the selected data source's content.

To display the Authors table of the Books database, drag the Authors node from the **Data Sources** window to the Form. Figure 20.31 presents the **Design** view after we performed this action and resized the Form and controls. The IDE generates two controls that appear on FrmDisplayTable—an AuthorsBindingNavigator and an AuthorsDataGridView. The IDE also generates several additional non-visual components that appear in the *component tray*—the gray region below the Form in **Design** view. We use the IDE's default names for these autogenerated components (and others throughout the chapter) to show exactly what the IDE creates. We briefly discuss the AuthorsBindingNavigator and AuthorsDataGridView controls here. The next section discusses all of the autogenerated components in detail and explains how the IDE uses these components to connect the GUI controls to the Authors table of the Books database.

A *DataGridView* displays data organized in rows and columns that correspond to the rows and columns of the underlying data source. In this case, the DataGridView displays the data of the Authors table, so the control has columns named AuthorID, FirstName and LastName. In **Design** view, the control does not display any rows of actual data below the column headers. The data is retrieved from the database and displayed in the DataGridView only at runtime. Execute the program. When the Form loads, the DataGridView contains four rows of data—one for each row of the Authors table (Fig. 20.32).

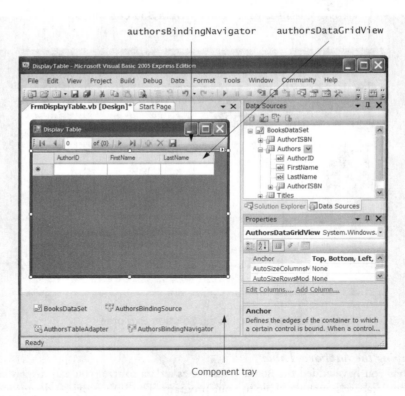

Fig. 20.31 | **Design** view after dragging the Authors data source node to the Form.

Fig. 20.32 | Displaying the Authors table in a DataGridView.

The strip of buttons below the title bar of the window is a ***BindingNavigator***, which enables users to browse and manipulate data displayed by another GUI control (in this case, a DataGridView) on the Form. A BindingNavigator's buttons resemble the controls on a CD or DVD player and allow you to move to the first row of data, the preceding row, the next row and the last row. The control also displays the currently selected row number in a text box. You can use this text box to enter the number of a row that you want to select. The AuthorsBindingNavigator in this example allows you to "navigate" the Authors table displayed in the AuthorsDataGridView. Clicking the buttons or entering a value in the text box causes the DataGridView to select the appropriate row. An arrow in the DataGridView's leftmost column indicates the currently selected row.

A BindingNavigator also has buttons that allow you to add a new row, delete a row and save changes back to the underlying data source (that is, the Authors table of the Books database). Clicking the button with the yellow plus icon (⊞) adds a new row to the DataGridView. However, simply typing values in the FirstName and LastName columns does not insert a new row in the Authors table. To add the new row to the database on disk, click the **Save** button (the button with the disk icon, 🖫). Clicking the button with the red **X** (✖) deletes the currently selected row from the DataGridView. Again, you must click the **Save** button to make the change in the database.

Changing the Database's Copy to Output Directory *Property*
By default, a new copy of the database file is used each time you run the application. Thus, any changes you make to the database when testing your application are lost. To allow changes to be made to the database file during testing, you must select Books.mdf in the **Solution Explorer**, then change its **Copy to Output Directory** property to **Copy if newer** in the **Properties** window. Now you can test BindingNavigator's buttons for adding and deleting records and see their results. Execute the program and add a new row, then save the changes and close the program. When you restart the program, you should see that the new row was saved to the database and appears in the DataGridView. Now delete the new row and click the **Save** button. Close and restart the program to see that the new row no longer exists in the database.

20.6.2 How Data Binding Works

The technique through which GUI controls are connected to data sources is known as *data binding*. The IDE allows controls, such as a DataGridView, to be bound to a data source, such as a DataSet that represents a table in a database. Any changes you make through the application to the underlying data source will automatically be reflected in the way the data is presented in the data-bound control (e.g., the DataGridView). Likewise, modifying the data in the data-bound control and saving the changes updates the underlying data source. In the current example, the DataGridView is bound to the DataTable of the BooksDataSet that represents the Authors table in the database. Dragging the Authors node from the **Data Sources** window to the Form caused the IDE to create this data binding for you, using several autogenerated components (i.e., objects) in the component tray. Figure 20.33 models these objects and their associations, which the following sections examine in detail to explain how data binding works.

BooksDataSet
As discussed in Section 20.6.1, adding the Books database to the project enabled the IDE to generate the BooksDataSet. Recall that a DataSet represents a cache of data that mimics the structure of a relational database. You can explore the structure of the BooksDataSet

Fig. 20.33 | Data binding architecture used to display the Authors table of the Books database in a GUI.

in the **Data Sources** window. A DataSet's structure can be determined at execution time or at design time. An *untyped DataSet*'s structure (i.e., the tables that comprise it and the relationships among them) is determined at execution time based on the result of a specific query. Tables and column values are accessed using indices into collections of DataTables and DataRows, respectively. The type of each piece of data in an untyped DataSet is unknown at design time. BooksDataSet, however, is created by the IDE at design time as a *strongly typed DataSet*. BooksDataSet (a derived class of DataSet) contains objects of classes derived from DataTable that represent the tables in the Books database. Books-DataSet provides properties corresponding to these objects. The property names match the names of the underlying tables. For example, BooksDataSet.Authors represents a cache of the data in the Authors table. Each DataTable contains a collection of DataRows. Each DataRow contains members whose names and types correspond to those of the columns of the underlying database table. Thus, BooksDataSet.Authors(0).AuthorID refers to the AuthorID of the first row of the Authors table in the Books database. Note that zero-based indices are used to access DataRows in a DataTable.

The BooksDataSet object in the component tray is an object of the BooksDataSet class. When you indicate that you want to display the contents of the Authors table on the Form, the IDE generates a BooksDataSet object to store the data that Form will display. This is the data to which the DataGridView will be bound. The DataGridView does not display data from the database directly. Instead, it displays the contents of a BooksDataSet object. As we discuss shortly, the AuthorsTableAdapter fills the BooksDataSet object with data retrieved from the database by executing a SQL query.

AuthorsTableAdapter

The AuthorsTableAdapter is the component that interacts with the Books database on disk (i.e., the Books.mdf file). When other components need to retrieve data from the database or write data to the database, they invoke the methods of the AuthorsTable-Adapter. Class AuthorsTableAdapter is generated by the IDE when you drag a table from the Books database onto the Form. The AuthorsTableAdapter object in the component tray is an object of this class. This object is responsible for filling the BooksDataSet with the Authors data from the database—this stores a copy of the Authors table in local memory. As you will soon see, the cached copy can be modified during program execution. The AuthorsTableAdapter is also responsible for updating the database when the data in the BooksDataSet changes.

Class AuthorsTableAdapter encapsulates a SqlDataAdapter object, which contains SqlCommand objects that specify how the SqlDataAdapter selects, inserts, updates and deletes data in the database. Recall from Section 20.5 that a SqlCommand object must have a SqlConnection object through which the SqlCommand can communicate with a database. In this example, the AuthorsTableAdapter sets the Connection property of each of the SqlDataAdapter's SqlCommand objects, based on the connection string that refers to the Books database.

To interact with the database, the AuthorsTableAdapter invokes the methods of its SqlDataAdapter, each of which executes the appropriate SqlCommand object. For example, to fill the BooksDataSet's Authors table, the AuthorsTableAdapter's Fill method invokes its SqlDataAdapter's Fill method, which executes a SqlCommand object representing the SELECT query

SELECT AuthorID, FirstName, LastName *FROM* Authors

This query selects all the rows and columns of the Authors table and places them in BooksDataSet.Authors. You will see an example of AuthorsTableAdapter's Fill method being invoked shortly.

AuthorsBindingSource *and* AuthorsDataGridView

The AuthorsBindingSource object (an object of class *BindingSource*) identifies a data source that a program can bind to a control and serves as an intermediary between a data-bound GUI control and its data source. In this example, the IDE uses a BindingSource object to connect the AuthorsDataGridView to BooksDataSet.Authors. To achieve this data binding, the IDE first sets AuthorsBindingSource's *DataSource* property to Books-DataSet. This property specifies the DataSet that contains the data to be bound. The IDE then sets the *DataMember* property to Authors. This property identifies a specific table within the DataSource. After configuring the AuthorsBindingSource object, the IDE assigns this object to AuthorsDataGridView's *DataSource* property to indicate what the DataGridView will display.

A BindingSource object also manages the interaction between a data-bound GUI control and its underlying data source. If you edit the data displayed in a DataGridView and want to save changes to the data source, your code must invoke the *EndEdit* method of the BindingSource object. This method applies the user's changes to the data (i.e., the pending changes) to the data source bound to that control. Note that this updates only the DataSet—an additional step is required to permanently update the database itself. You will see an example of this shortly, when we present the code generated by the IDE in the FrmDisplayTable.vb file.

AuthorsBindingNavigator

Recall that a BindingNavigator allows you to move through (i.e., navigate) and manipulate (i.e., add or delete rows) data bound to a control on a Form. A BindingNavigator communicates with a BindingSource (specified in the BindingNavigator's *BindingSource* property) to carry out these actions in the underlying data source (i.e., the DataSet). The BindingNavigator does not interact with the data-bound control. Instead, it invokes BindingSource methods that cause the data-bound control to update its presentation of the data. For example, when you click the BindingNavigator's button to add a new row, the BindingNavigator invokes a method of the BindingSource. The BindingSource then adds a new row to its associated DataSet. Once this DataSet is modified, the DataGrid-View displays the new row, because the DataGridView and the BindingNavigator are bound to the same BindingSource object (and thus the same DataSet).

Examining the Autogenerated Code for FrmDisplayTable

Figure 20.34 presents the code for FrmDisplayTable. You do not need to write any of this code—the IDE generates it when you drag and drop the Authors table from the **Data Sources** window onto the Form. We modified the autogenerated code to add comments and split long lines for display purposes. The IDE also generates a considerable amount of additional code, such as the code that defines classes BooksDataSet and AuthorsTable-Adapter, as well as the designer code that declares the autogenerated objects in the component tray. The additional IDE-generated code resides in files visible in the **Solution**

```
 1    ' Fig. 20.34: FrmDisplayTable.vb
 2    ' Displays data from a database table in a DataGridView.
 3    Public Class FrmDisplayTable
 4       ' Click event handler for the Save Button in the
 5       ' BindingNavigator saves the changes made to the data
 6       Private Sub AuthorsBindingNavigatorSaveItem_Click( _
 7          ByVal sender As System.Object, ByVal e As System.EventArgs) _
 8          Handles AuthorsBindingNavigatorSaveItem.Click
 9
10          Me.Validate()
11          Me.AuthorsBindingSource.EndEdit()
12          Me.AuthorsTableAdapter.Update(Me.BooksDataSet.Authors)
13       End Sub ' AuthorsBindingNavigatorSaveItem_Click
14
15       ' loads data into the BooksDataSet.Authors table,
16       ' which is then displayed in the DataGridView
17       Private Sub FrmDisplayTable_Load(ByVal sender As System.Object, _
18          ByVal e As System.EventArgs) Handles MyBase.Load
19          ' TODO: This line of code loads data into the 'BooksDataSet.Authors'
20          ' table. You can move, or remove it, as needed.
21          Me.AuthorsTableAdapter.Fill(Me.BooksDataSet.Authors)
22       End Sub ' FrmDisplayTable_Load
23    End Class ' FrmDisplayTable
```

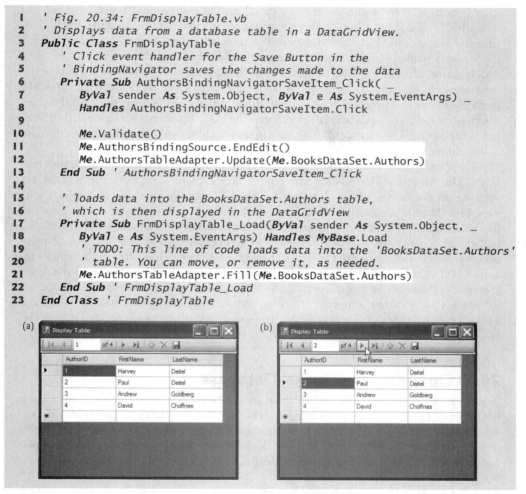

Fig. 20.34 | Auto-generated code for displaying data from a database table in a `DataGridView` control.

Explorer when you select **Show All Files**. We present only the code in FrmDisplay-Table.vb, because it is the only file you'll need to modify.

Lines 6–13 contain the Click event handler for the **Save** button in the AuthorsBind-ingNavigator. Recall that you click this button to save changes made to the data in the DataGridView in the underlying data source (i.e., the Authors table of the Books database). Saving the changes is a two-step process:

1. The DataSet associated with the DataGridView (indicated by its BindingSource) must be updated to include any changes made by the user.

2. The database on disk must be updated to match the new contents of the DataSet.

Before the event handler saves any changes, line 10 invokes Me.Validate() to validate the controls on the Form. If you implement Validating or Validated events for any of

Form's controls, these events enable you to validate user input and potentially indicate errors for invalid data. Line 11 invokes AuthorsBindingSource's *EndEdit* method to ensure that the object's associated data source (BooksDataSet.Authors) is updated with any changes made by the user to the currently selected row in the DataGridView (e.g., adding a row, changing a column value). Any changes to other rows were applied to the DataSet when you selected another row. Line 12 invokes AuthorsTableAdapter's *Update* method to write the modified version of the Authors table (in memory) to the SQL Server database on disk. The Update method executes the SQL statements (encapsulated in Sql-Command objects) necessary to make the data in the database's Authors table match the data in BooksDataSet.Authors.

The FrmDisplayTable_Load event handler (lines 17–22) executes when the program loads. This event handler fills the in-memory DataSet with data from the SQL Server database on disk. Once the DataSet is filled, the GUI control bound to it can display its data. Line 21 calls AuthorsTableAdapter's *Fill* method to retrieve information from the database, placing this information in the DataSet object provided as an argument. Recall that the IDE generated AuthorsTableAdapter to execute SqlCommands over the connection we created within the **Data Source Configuration Wizard**. Thus, the Fill method executes a SELECT statement to retrieve all the rows of the Authors table of the Books database, then places the result of this query in BooksDataSet.Authors. Recall that AuthorsData-GridView's DataSource property is set to AuthorsBindingSource (which references BooksDataSet.Authors). Thus, after this data source is loaded, the AuthorsDataGridView automatically displays the data retrieved from the database.

20.7 Querying the Books Database

Now that you have seen how to display an entire database table in a DataGridView, we demonstrate how to execute specific SQL SELECT queries on a database and display the results. Although this example only queries the data, the application could be modified easily to execute other SQL statements. Perform the following steps to build the example application, which executes custom queries against the Titles table of the Books database.

Step 1: Creating the Project
First, create a new Windows Application named DisplayQueryResult. Rename the Form FrmDisplayQueryResult and name its source file FrmDisplayQueryResult.vb, then set the Form's **Text** property to Display Query Result.

Step 2: Adding a Data Source to the Project
Perform the steps in Section 20.6.1 to include the Books database as a data source in the project and to create the BooksDataSet.

Step 3: Creating a DataGridView to Display the Titles Table
Drag the Titles node from the **Data Sources** window onto the Form to create a DataGridView that will display the entire contents of the Titles table.

Step 4: Adding Custom Queries to the TitlesTableAdapter
Recall that invoking a TableAdapter's Fill method populates the DataSet passed as an argument with the entire contents of the database table that corresponds to that Table-

Adapter. To populate a DataSet member (i.e., a DataTable) with only a portion of a table (e.g., books with copyright dates of 2006), you must add a method to the TableAdapter that fills the specified DataTable with the results of a custom query. The IDE provides the **TableAdapter Query Configuration Wizard** to perform this task. To open this wizard, right click the BooksDataSet.xsd node in the **Solution Explorer** and choose **View Designer**, or click the **Edit DataSet with Designer** icon (![icon]) in the **Data Sources** window. Either of these actions opens the **Dataset Designer** (Fig. 20.35), which displays a visual representation of the BooksDataSet (i.e., the tables AuthorISBN, Authors and Titles and the relationships among them). The **Dataset Designer** lists each table's columns and the autogenerated TableAdapter that accesses the table. Select the TitlesTableAdapter by clicking its name, then right click the name and select **Add Query...** to begin the **TableAdapter Query Configuration Wizard** (Fig. 20.36).

Step 5: Choosing How the TableAdapter Should Access the Database
On the first screen of the wizard (Fig. 20.36), keep the default option **Use SQL Statements** and click **Next**.

Step 6: Choosing a Query Type
On the next screen of the wizard (Fig. 20.37), keep the default option **SELECT which returns rows** and click **Next**.

Step 7: Specifying a SELECT Statement for the Query
The next screen (Fig. 20.38) asks you to enter a query that will be used to retrieve data from the Books database. Note that the default SELECT prefixes Titles with "dbo.". This prefix

Fig. 20.35 │ Viewing the BooksDataSet in the **Dataset Designer**.

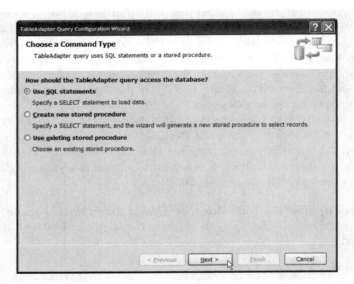

Fig. 20.36 | **TableAdapter Query Configuration Wizard** to add a query to a
`TableAdapter`.

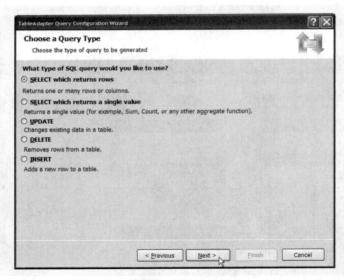

Fig. 20.37 | Choosing the type of query to be generated for the `TableAdapter`.

stands for "database owner" and indicates that the table `Titles` belongs to the database
owner (i.e., you). If you need to reference a table owned by another user of the system, this
prefix would be replaced by the owner's username. You can modify the SQL statement in
the text box here (using the SQL syntax discussed in Section 20.4), or you can click **Query
Builder…** to design and test the query using a visual tool.

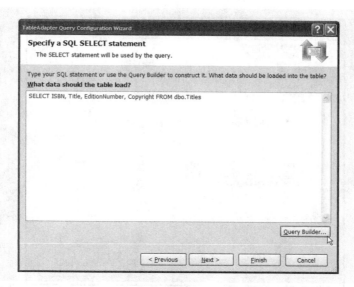

Fig. 20.38 | Specifying a SELECT statement for the query.

Step 8: Building a Query with Query Builder
Click the **Query Builder...** button to open the ***Query Builder*** (Fig. 20.39). The top portion
of the **Query Builder** window contains a box listing the columns of the **Titles** table. By
default, each column is checked (Fig. 20.39(a)), indicating that each column should be

Fig. 20.39 | **Query Builder** after adding a WHERE clause by entering a value in the **Filter**
column. (Part I of 2.)

(b)

Fig. 20.39 | **Query Builder** after adding a WHERE clause by entering a value in the **Filter** column. (Part 2 of 2.)

returned by the query. The middle portion of the window contains a table in which each row corresponds to a column in the Titles table. To the right of the column names are columns in which you can enter values or make selections that modify the query. For example, to create a query that selects only books that are copyright 2006, type 2006 in the **Filter** column of the Copyright row then press *Enter*. Note that the **Query Builder** modifies your input to be "= '2006'" and adds an appropriate WHERE clause to the SELECT statement displayed in the middle of Fig. 20.39(b). Click the **Execute Query** button to test the query and display the results in the bottom portion of the **Query Builder** window. For more **Query Builder** information, see msdn2.microsoft.com/library/ms172013.aspx.

Step 9: Closing the Query Builder
Click **OK** to close the **Query Builder** and return to the **TableAdapter Query Configuration Wizard** (Fig. 20.40), which now displays the SQL query created in the preceding step. Click **Next** to continue.

Step 10: Setting the Names of the Autogenerated Methods That Perform the Query
After you specify the SQL query, you must name the methods that the IDE will generate to perform the query (Fig. 20.41). Two methods are generated by default—a "Fill method" that fills a DataTable parameter with the query result and a "Get method" that returns a new DataTable filled with the query result. The text boxes to enter names for these methods are prepopulated with FillBy and GetDataBy, respectively. Modify these names to FillWithCopyright2006 and GetDataWithCopyright2006, as shown in Fig. 20.41. Finally, click **Finish** to complete the wizard and return to the **Dataset Designer** (Fig. 20.42). Note that these methods are now listed in the TitlesTableAdapter section of the box representing the Titles table.

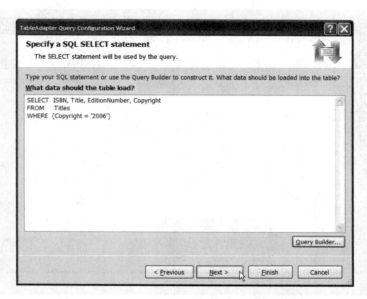

Fig. 20.40 | The SELECT statement created by the **Query Builder**.

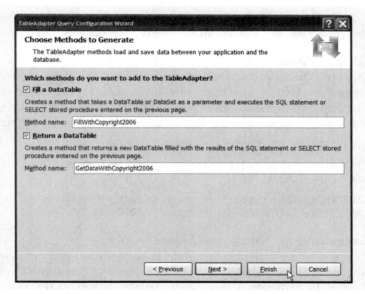

Fig. 20.41 | Specifying names for the methods to be added to the TitlesTableAdapter.

Step 11: Adding an Additional Query

Repeat *Steps 4–10* to add another query that selects all books whose titles end with the text "How to Program" and sorts the results by title in ascending order (see Section 20.4.3). In the **Query Builder**, enter LIKE '%How to Program' in the Title row's **Filter** column. To specify the sort order, select **Ascending** in the **Sort Type** column of the Title row. In the

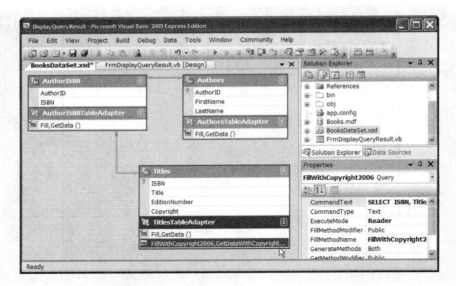

Fig. 20.42 | **Dataset Designer** after adding Fill and Get methods to the TitlesTableAdapter.

final step of the **TableAdapter Query Configuration Wizard**, name the Fill and Get methods FillWithHowToProgramBooks and GetDataForHowToProgramBooks, respectively.

Step 12: Adding a ComboBox to the Form
Return to the Form's **Design** view and add a ComboBox named cboQueries below the Data-GridView on the Form. Users will use this control to choose a SELECT query to execute. The results will be displayed in the DataGridView. Add three items to cboQueries—one to match each of the three queries that the TitlesTableAdapter can now perform:

> **SELECT** ISBN, Title, EditionNumber, Copyright **FROM** Titles
>
> **SELECT** ISBN, Title, EditionNumber, Copyright **FROM** Titles
> **WHERE** (Copyright = '2006')
>
> **SELECT** ISBN, Title, EditionNumber, Copyright **FROM** Titles
> **WHERE** (Title **LIKE** '%How to Program') **ORDER BY** Title

Step 13: Customizing the Form's Load Event Handler
Add a line of code to the autogenerated FrmDisplayQueryResult_Load event handler, which sets the initial SelectedIndex of the cboQueries to 0. Recall that the Load event handler calls the Fill method by default, which executes the first query (the item in index 0). Thus, setting the SelectedIndex to 0 causes the ComboBox to display the query that is initially performed when FrmDisplayQueryResult first loads.

Step 14: Programming an Event Handler for the ComboBox
Next you must write code that will execute the appropriate query each time the user chooses a different item from cboQueries. Double click cboQueries in **Design** view to generate a cboQueries_SelectedIndexChanged event handler (lines 30–43) in the FrmDisplay-

QueryResult.vb file (Fig. 20.43). In the event handler, add a Select Case statement (lines 34–42) to invoke the method of TitlesTableAdapter that executes the query associated with the ComboBox's current selection. Recall that method Fill (line 36) executes a SELECT query that selects all rows, method FillWithCopyright2006 (line 38) executes a SELECT query that selects all rows in which the copyright year is 2006 and method Fill-WithHowToProgramBooks (lines 40–41) executes a query that selects all rows that have "How to Program" at the end of their titles and sorts them in ascending order by title. Each method fills BooksDataSet.Titles with only those rows returned by the corresponding query. Thanks to the data binding relationships created by the IDE, refilling BooksDataSet.Titles causes the TitlesDataGridView to display the selected query's result with no additional code.

```vb
1    ' Fig. 20.43: FrmDisplayQueryResult.vb
2    ' Displays the result of a user-selected query in a DataGridView.
3    Public Class FrmDisplayQueryResult
4       ' Click event handler for the Save Button in the
5       ' BindingNavigator saves the changes made to the data
6       Private Sub TitlesBindingNavigatorSaveItem_Click( _
7          ByVal sender As System.Object, ByVal e As System.EventArgs) _
8          Handles TitlesBindingNavigatorSaveItem.Click
9
10         Me.Validate()
11         Me.TitlesBindingSource.EndEdit()
12         Me.TitlesTableAdapter.Update(Me.BooksDataSet.Titles)
13      End Sub ' TitlesBindingNavigatorSaveItem_Click
14
15      ' loads data into the BooksDataSet.Titles table,
16      ' which is then displayed in the DataGridView
17      Private Sub FrmDisplayQueryResult_Load(ByVal sender As System.Object, _
18         ByVal e As System.EventArgs) Handles MyBase.Load
19         ' TODO: This line of code loads data into the 'BooksDataSet.Titles'
20         ' table. You can move, or remove it, as needed.
21         Me.TitlesTableAdapter.Fill(Me.BooksDataSet.Titles)
22
23         ' set the ComboBox to show the default query that
24         ' selects all books from the Titles table
25         cboQueries.SelectedIndex = 0
26      End Sub ' FrmDisplayQueryResult_Load
27
28      ' loads data into the BooksDataSet.Titles table based on
29      ' user-selected query
30      Private Sub cboQueries_SelectedIndexChanged( _
31         ByVal sender As System.Object, ByVal e As System.EventArgs) _
32         Handles cboQueries.SelectedIndexChanged
33         ' fill the Titles DataTable with the result of the selected query
34         Select Case cboQueries.SelectedIndex
35            Case 0
36               TitlesTableAdapter.Fill(BooksDataSet.Titles)
37            Case 1 ' books with copyright year 2006
38               TitlesTableAdapter.FillWithCopyright2006(BooksDataSet.Titles)
```

Fig. 20.43 | Displaying the result of a user-selected query in a DataGridView. (Part 1 of 2.)

```
39            Case 2 ' How to Program books, sorted by Title
40              TitlesTableAdapter.FillWithHowToProgramBooks( _
41                BooksDataSet.Titles)
42          End Select
43      End Sub ' cboQueries_SelectedIndexChanged
44  End Class ' FrmDisplayQueryResult
```

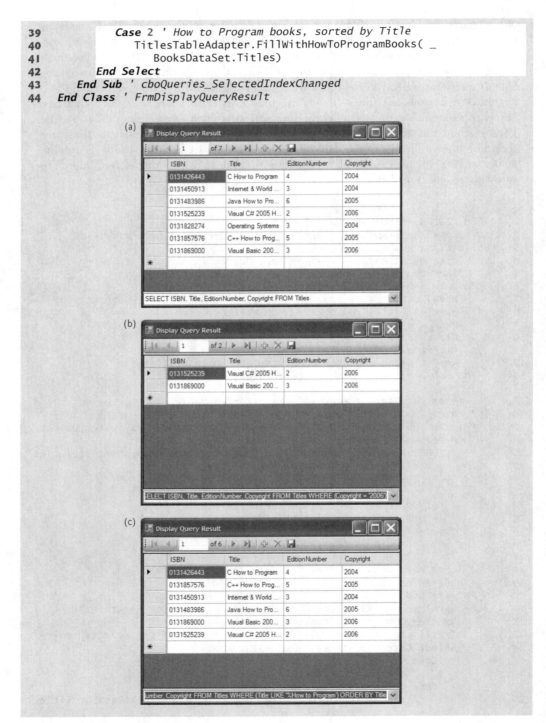

Fig. 20.43 | Displaying the result of a user-selected query in a `DataGridView`. (Part 2 of 2.)

Figure 20.43 also displays the output for `FrmDisplayQueryResult`. Figure 20.43(a) depicts the result of retrieving all rows from the `Titles` table. Figure 20.43(b) demonstrates the second query, which retrieves only rows for books with a 2006 copyright. Finally, Fig. 20.43(c) demonstrates the third query, which selects rows for How to Program books and sorts them in ascending order by title.

20.8 Programming with ADO.NET: Address Book Case Study

Our next example implements a simple address book application that enables users to insert rows into, locate rows from and update the SQL Server database `AddressBook.mdf`, which is included in the directory with this chapter's examples.

The `AddressBook` application (Fig. 20.44) provides a GUI through which users can execute SQL statements on the database. However, rather than displaying a database table in a `DataGridView`, this example presents data from a table one row at a time, using several `TextBox`es that display the values of each of the row's columns. A `BindingNavigator` allows you to control which row of the table is currently in view at any given time. The `BindingNavigator` also allows you to add new rows, delete rows, and save changes to the data. Note that lines 6–22 in Fig. 20.44 are similar to the corresponding lines of code in Figs. 20.34 and 20.43. We discuss the application's additional functionality and the code in lines 26–41 that supports it momentarily. We begin by showing you the steps to create this application.

```
 1   ' Fig. 20.44: FrmAddressBook.vb
 2   ' Allows users to manipulate an address book.
 3   Public Class FrmAddressBook
 4      ' Click event handler for the Save Button in the
 5      ' BindingNavigator saves the changes made to the data
 6      Private Sub AddressesBindingNavigatorSaveItem_Click( _
 7         ByVal sender As System.Object, ByVal e As System.EventArgs) _
 8         Handles AddressesBindingNavigatorSaveItem.Click
 9
10         Me.Validate()
11         Me.AddressesBindingSource.EndEdit()
12         Me.AddressesTableAdapter.Update(Me.AddressBookDataSet.Addresses)
13      End Sub ' AddressesBindingNavigatorSaveItem_Click
14
15      ' loads data into the AddressBookDataSet.Addresses table
16      Private Sub FrmAddressBook_Load(ByVal sender As System.Object, _
17         ByVal e As System.EventArgs) Handles MyBase.Load
18         ' TODO: This line of code loads data into the
19         ' 'AddressBookDataSet.Addresses' table. You can move, or remove
20         ' it, as needed.
21         Me.AddressesTableAdapter.Fill(Me.AddressBookDataSet.Addresses)
22      End Sub ' FrmAddressBook_Load
23
```

Fig. 20.44 | `AddressBook` application that allows you to manipulate entries in an address book database. (Part I of 2.)

```
24      ' loads data for the rows with the specified last name
25      ' into the AddressBookDataSet.Addresses table
26      Private Sub btnFind_Click(ByVal sender As System.Object, _
27        ByVal e As System.EventArgs) Handles btnFind.Click
28        ' fill the DataSet's DataTable with only rows
29        ' containing the user-specified last name
30        AddressesTableAdapter.FillByLastName( _
31          AddressBookDataSet.Addresses, txtFind.Text)
32      End Sub ' btnFind_Click
33
34      ' reloads AddressBookDataSet.Addresses with all rows
35      Private Sub btnBrowseAll_Click(ByVal sender As System.Object, _
36        ByVal e As System.EventArgs) Handles btnBrowseAll.Click
37        ' fill the DataSet's DataTable with all rows in the database
38        AddressesTableAdapter.Fill(AddressBookDataSet.Addresses)
39
40        txtFind.Text = "" ' clear Find TextBox
41      End Sub ' btnBrowseAll_Click
42    End Class ' FrmAddressBook
```

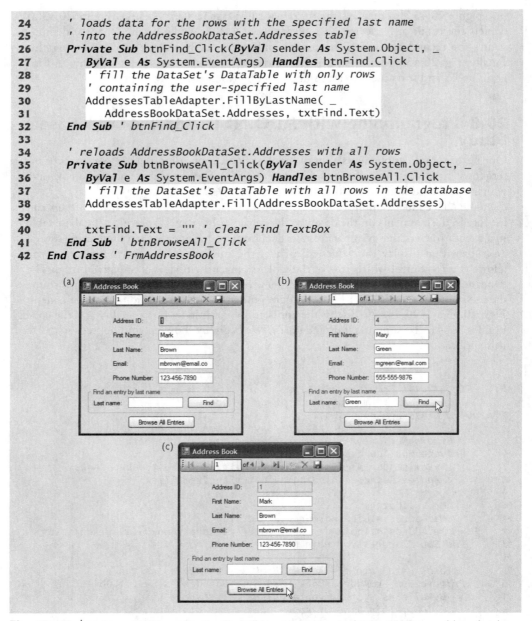

Fig. 20.44 | AddressBook application that allows you to manipulate entries in an address book database. (Part 2 of 2.)

Step 1: Creating the Project

Create a new Windows Application named AddressBook. Rename the Form FrmAddress-Book and name its source file FrmAddressBook.vb, then set the Form's **Text** property to Address Book.

Step 2: Adding the Database to the Project
As in Section 20.6.1, you must begin by adding the database to the project. After adding the AddressBook.mdf as a data source, the **Data Sources** window will list AddressBook-DataSet, which contains a table named Addresses.

Step 3: Indicating that the IDE Should Create a Set of Labels and TextBoxes to Display Each Row of Data
In the earlier sections, you dragged a node from the **Data Sources** window to the Form to create a DataGridView bound to the data source member represented by that node. The IDE allows you to specify the type of control(s) that it creates when you drag and drop a data source member onto a Form. In **Design** view, click the Addresses node in the **Data Sources** window (Fig. 20.45). Note that this node becomes a drop-down list when you select it. Click the down arrow to view the items in the list. The icon to the left of **Data-GridView** will initially be highlighted in blue, because the default control to be bound to a table is a DataGridView (as you saw in the earlier examples). Select the **Details** option in the drop-down list to indicate that the IDE should create a set of Label–TextBox pairs for each column name–column value pair when you drag and drop the Addresses table onto the Form. (You will see what this looks like in Fig. 20.46.) The drop-down list contains suggestions for controls to display the table's data, but you can also choose the **Customize...** option to select other controls that are capable of being bound to a table's data.

Step 4: Dragging the Addresses Data Source Node to the Form
Drag the Addresses node from the **Data Sources** window to the Form (Fig. 20.46). The IDE creates a series of Labels and TextBoxes because you selected **Details** in the preceding step. As in the earlier examples, the IDE also creates a BindingNavigator and the other components in the component tray. The IDE sets the text of each Label based on the

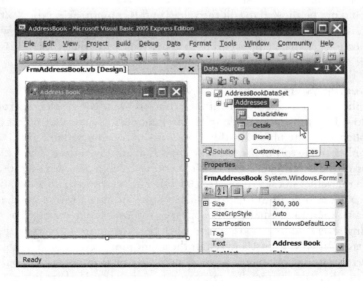

Fig. 20.45 | Selecting the control(s) to be created when dragging and dropping a data source member onto the Form.

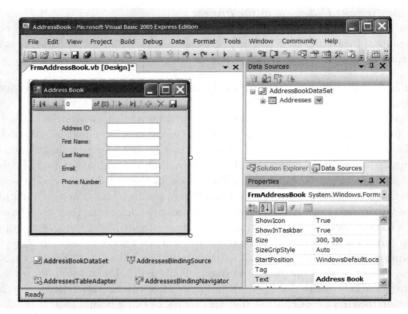

Fig. 20.46 | Displaying a table on a Form using a series of Labels and TextBoxes.

corresponding column name in the database table, and uses regular expressions to insert spaces into multiword column names to make the Labels more readable.

Step 5: Making the AddressID TextBox ReadOnly

The AddressID column of the Addresses table is an auto-incremented identity column, so users should not be allowed to edit the values in this column. Select the TextBox for the AddressID and set its ReadOnly property to True using the **Properties** window. Note that you may need to click in an empty part of the Form to deselect the other Labels and Text-Boxes before selecting the AddressID TextBox.

Step 6: Running the Application

Run the application and experiment with the controls in the BindingNavigator at the top of the window. Like the previous examples, this example fills a DataSet object (specifically an AddressBookDataSet object) with all the rows of a database table (i.e., Addresses). However, only a single row of the DataSet appears at any given time. The CD- or DVD-like buttons of the BindingNavigator allow you to change the currently displayed row (i.e., change the values in each of the TextBoxes). The buttons to add a row, delete a row and save changes also perform their designated tasks. Adding a row clears the TextBoxes and makes a new auto-incremented ID appear in the TextBox to the right of **Address ID**. After entering several address-book entries, click the **Save** button to record the new rows in the database. When you close and restart the application, your should be able to use the BindingNavigator controls to browse your entries. Recall from Section 20.6 that to allow changes to the database during changes, you must select the database in the **Solution Ex-plorer**, then change its **Copy to Output Directory** property to **Copy if newer** in the **Properties** window.

Step 7: Adding a Query to the AddressesTableAdapter

While the BindingNavigator allows you to browse the address book, it would be more convenient to be able to find a specific entry by last name. To add this functionality to the application, you must add a new query to the AddressesTableAdapter using the **Table-Adapter Query Configuration Wizard**. Click the **Edit DataSet with Designer** icon (🔛) in the **Data Sources** window. Select the box representing the AddressesTableAdapter. Right click the TableAdapter's name and select **Add Query...**. In the **TableAdapter Query Configuration Wizard**, keep the default option **Use SQL Statements** and click **Next**. On the next screen, keep the default option **SELECT which returns rows** and click **Next**. Rather than use the **Query Builder** to form your query (as we did in the preceding example), modify the query directly in the text box in the wizard. Append the clause

```
WHERE LastName = @lastName
```

to the end of the default query. Note that @lastName is a parameter that will be replaced by a value when the query executes. Click **Next**, then enter FillByLastName and GetDataByLastName as the names for the two methods that the wizard will generate. The query contains a parameter, so each of these methods will take a parameter to set the value of @lastName in the query. You will see how to call the FillByLastName method and specify a value for @lastName shortly. Click **Finish** to complete the wizard and return to the **Dataset Designer** (Fig. 20.47). Note that the new Fill and Get methods appear under the AddressesTableAdapter and that parameter @lastName is listed to the right of the method names.

Step 8: Adding Controls to Allow Users to Specify a Last Name to Locate

Now that you have created a query to locate rows with a specific last name, add controls to allow users to enter a last name and execute this query. Go to **Design** view (Fig. 20.48) and add to the Form a Label named lblFind, a TextBox named txtFind and a Button named btnFind. Place these controls in a GroupBox named grpFind, then set its Text

Fig. 20.47 | **Dataset Designer** for the AddressBookDataSet after adding a query to AddressesTableAdapter.

Fig. 20.48 | **Design** view after adding controls to locate a last name in the address book.

property to Find an entry by last name. Set the Text properties of the Label and Button as shown in Fig. 20.48.

Step 9: Programming an Event Handler That Locates the User-Specified Last Name
Double click btnFind to add a Click event handler for this Button. In the event handler, write the following lines of code (lines 30–31 of Fig. 20.44):

```
AddressesTableAdapter.FillByLastName( _
    AddressBookDataSet.Addresses, txtFind.Text)
```

The FillByLastName method replaces the current data in AddressBookDataSet.Addresses with data for only those rows with the last name entered in txtFind. Note that when invoking FillByLastName, you must pass the DataTable to be filled, as well as an argument specifying the last name to find. This argument becomes the value of the @lastName parameter in the SELECT statement created in *Step 7*. Start the application to test the new functionality. When you search for a specific entry (i.e., enter a last name and click Find), the BindingNavigator allows the user to browse only the rows containing the specified last name. This is because the data source bound to the Form's controls (i.e., AddressBookDataSet.Addresses) has changed and now contains only a limited number of rows. The database in this example is initially empty, so you'll need to add several records before testing the find capability.

Step 10: Allowing the User to Return to Browsing All Rows in the Database

To allow users to return to browsing all the rows after searching for specific rows, add a Button named btnBrowseAll below the grpFind. Set the Text property of btnBrowseAll to **Browse All Entries**. Double click btnBrowseAll in **Design** view to add a Click event handler to the code. Add a line of code that calls

```
AddressesTableAdapter.Fill(AddressBookDataSet.Addresses)
```

to refill the Addresses DataTable with all the rows from the table in the database (line 38 of Fig. 20.44). Also, add a line of code that clears the Text property of txtFind (line 40). Start the application. Find a specific last name as in the previous step, then click the btn-BrowseAll button to test the new functionality.

Data Binding in the AddressBook Application

Dragging and dropping the Addresses node from the **Data Sources** window onto the Form FrmAddressBook in this example caused the IDE to generate several components in the component tray. These serve the same purposes as those generated for the earlier examples that use the Books database. In this case, AddressBookDataSet is an object of a strongly typed DataSet, AddressBookDataSet, whose structure mimics that of the AddressBook database. AddressesBindingSource is a BindingSource object that refers to the Addresses table of the AddressBookDataSet. AddressesTableAdapter encapsulates a SqlDataAdapter object configured with SqlCommand objects that execute SQL statements against the AddressBook database. Finally, AddressesBindingNavigator is bound to the AddressesBindingSource object, which allows you to indirectly manipulate the Addresses table of the AddressBookDataSet.

In each of the earlier examples using a DataGridView to display all the rows of a database table, the DataGridView's BindingSource property was set to the corresponding BindingSource object. In this example, you selected **Details** from the drop-down list for the Addresses table in the **Data Sources** window, so the values from a single row of the table appear on the Form in a set of TextBoxes. In this example, the IDE binds each TextBox to a specific column of the Addresses DataTable in the AddressBookDataSet. To do this, the IDE sets the TextBox's ***DataBindings.Text*** property. You can view this property by clicking the plus sign next to **(DataBindings)** in the **Properties** window (Fig. 20.49). Clicking the drop-down list for this property allows you to choose a BindingSource object and a property (i.e., column) within the associated data source to bind to the TextBox.

Consider the TextBox that displays the FirstName value—named FirstNameTextBox by the IDE. This control's DataBindings.Text property is set to the FirstName property of the AddressesBindingSource (which refers to AddressBookDataSet.Addresses). Thus, FirstNameTextBox always displays the value of the FirstName column in the currently selected row of AddressBookDataSet.Addresses. Each IDE-created TextBox on the Form is configured in a similar manner. Browsing the address book with the AddressesBindingNavigator changes the current position in AddressBookDataSet.Addresses, and thus changes the values displayed in each TextBox. Regardless of changes to the contents of AddressBookDataSet.Addresses, the TextBoxes remain bound to the same properties of the DataTable and always display the appropriate data. The TextBoxes do not display any values if the cached version of Addresses is empty (i.e., if the DataTable is empty because the query that filled the DataTable returned no rows).

Fig. 20.49 | Viewing the `DataBindings.Text` property of a `TextBox` in the **Properties** window.

20.9 Using a DataSet to Read and Write XML

A powerful feature of ADO.NET is its ability to convert data stored in a data source to XML for exchanging data between applications in a portable format. Class `DataSet` of namespace `System.Data` provides methods *WriteXml*, *ReadXml* and *GetXml*, which enable developers to create XML documents from data sources and to convert data from XML into data sources.

Writing Data from a Data Source to an XML Document
The application of Fig. 20.50 populates a `DataSet` with statistics about baseball players, then writes the data to an XML document and displays the XML in a `TextBox`.

We created this GUI by adding the `Baseball.mdf` database (located in the chapter's examples directory) as a data source, then dragging the `Players` node from the **Data Sources** window to the `Form`. This action created the `BindingNavigator` and `DataGrid-View` seen in the output of Fig. 20.50. We then added the `Button btnWrite` and the `TextBox txtOutput`. The XML representation of the `Players` table should not be edited and will span more lines than the `TextBox` can display at once, so we set `txtOutput`'s `Read-Only` and `MultiLine` properties to `True` and its `ScrollBars` property to `Vertical`. Create the event handler for `btnWrite` by double clicking it in **Design** view.

The autogenerated `FrmXMLWriter_Load` event handler (lines 16–22) calls method `Fill` of class `PlayersTableAdapter` to populate `BaseballDataSet` with data from the `Players` table in the `Baseball` database. Note that the IDE binds the `DataGridView` to

BaseballDataSet.Players (through the PlayersBindingSource) to display the information to the user.

Lines 25–37 define the event handler for the **Write to XML** button. When the user clicks this button, line 29 sets BaseballDataSet's *Namespace* property to specify a namespace for the DataSet and any XML documents based on the DataSet (see Section 19.4 to learn about XML namespaces). Line 32 invokes DataSet method WriteXml, which generates an XML representation of the data contained in the DataSet, then writes the XML to the specified file. This file is created in the project's bin/Debug or bin/Release directory, depending on how you executed the program. Lines 35–36 then display this XML representation. Line 36 invokes DataSet method *GetXml*, which returns a String containing the XML.

```vb
1    ' Fig. 20.50: FrmXMLWriter.vb
2    ' Demonstrates generating XML from an ADO.NET DataSet.
3    Public Class FrmXMLWriter
4       ' Click event handler for the Save Button in the
5       ' BindingNavigator saves the changes made to the data
6       Private Sub PlayersBindingNavigatorSaveItem_Click( _
7          ByVal sender As System.Object, ByVal e As System.EventArgs) _
8          Handles PlayersBindingNavigatorSaveItem.Click
9
10         Me.Validate()
11         Me.PlayersBindingSource.EndEdit()
12         Me.PlayersTableAdapter.Update(Me.BaseballDataSet.Players)
13      End Sub ' PlayersBindingNavigatorSaveItem_Click
14
15      ' loads data into the BaseballDataSet.Players table
16      Private Sub FrmXMLWriter_Load(ByVal sender As System.Object, _
17         ByVal e As System.EventArgs) Handles MyBase.Load
18         ' TODO: This line of code loads data into the
19         ' 'BaseballDataSet.Players' table. You can move, or remove it,
20         ' as needed.
21         Me.PlayersTableAdapter.Fill(Me.BaseballDataSet.Players)
22      End Sub ' FrmXMLWriter_Load
23
24      ' write XML representation of DataSet when Button clicked
25      Private Sub btnWrite_Click(ByVal sender As System.Object, _
26         ByVal e As System.EventArgs) Handles btnWrite.Click
27         ' set the namespace for this DataSet
28         ' and the resulting XML document
29         BaseballDataSet.Namespace = "http://www.deitel.com/baseball"
30
31         ' write XML representation of DataSet to a file
32         BaseballDataSet.WriteXml("Players.xml")
33
34         ' display XML representation in TextBox
35         txtOutput.Text = "Writing the following XML:" & vbCrLf & _
36            BaseballDataSet.GetXml() + vbCrLf
37      End Sub ' btnWrite_Click
38   End Class ' FrmXMLWriter
```

Fig. 20.50 | Writing the XML representation of a DataSet to a file. (Part 1 of 2.)

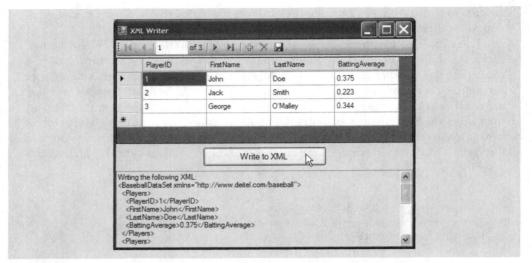

Fig. 20.50 | Writing the XML representation of a **DataSet** to a file. (Part 2 of 2.)

Examining an XML Document Generated By DataSet Method WriteXml
Figure 20.51 presents the Players.xml document generated by DataSet method WriteXml in Fig. 20.50. Note that the BaseballDataSet root element (line 2) declares the document's default namespace to be the namespace specified in line 29 of Fig. 20.50. Each Players element represents a record in the Players table. The PlayerID, FirstName, LastName and BattingAverage elements correspond to the columns with these names in the Players database table.

```
 1   <?xml version="1.0" standalone="yes"?>
 2   <BaseballDataSet xmlns="http://www.deitel.com/baseball">
 3     <Players>
 4       <PlayerID>1</PlayerID>
 5       <FirstName>John</FirstName>
 6       <LastName>Doe</LastName>
 7       <BattingAverage>0.375</BattingAverage>
 8     </Players>
 9     <Players>
10       <PlayerID>2</PlayerID>
11       <FirstName>Jack</FirstName>
12       <LastName>Smith</LastName>
13       <BattingAverage>0.223</BattingAverage>
14     </Players>
15     <Players>
16       <PlayerID>3</PlayerID>
17       <FirstName>George</FirstName>
18       <LastName>O'Malley</LastName>
19       <BattingAverage>0.344</BattingAverage>
20     </Players>
21   </BaseballDataSet>
```

Fig. 20.51 | XML document generated from BaseballDataSet in XMLWriter.

20.10 Wrap-Up

This chapter introduced relational databases, SQL, ADO.NET and the IDE's visual programming tools for working with databases. You examined the contents of a simple Books database and learned about the relationships among the tables in the database. You then learned basic SQL to retrieve data from, add new data to, and update data in a database.

We discussed the classes of namespaces System.Data and System.Data.SqlClient that allow programs to connect to a database, then access and manipulate its data. We also explained ADO.NET's disconnected model, which enables a program to store data from a database temporarily in local memory as a DataSet.

The second part of the chapter focused on using the IDE's tools and wizards to access and manipulate data sources like a database in GUI applications. You learned how to add data sources to projects and how to use the IDE's drag-and-drop capabilities to display database tables in applications. We discussed how the IDE hides from you the SQL used to interact with the database. You also learned how to add custom queries to GUI applications so that you can display only those rows of data that meet specific criteria. Finally, you learned how to write data from a data source to an XML file.

In the next chapter, we demonstrate how to build Web applications using Microsoft's ASP.NET technology. We also introduce the concept of a three-tier application, in which an application is divided into three pieces that can reside on the same computer or can be distributed among separate computers across a network such as the Internet. One of these tiers—the information tier—typically stores data in an RDBMS like SQL Server.

20.11 Web Resources

msdn.microsoft.com/sql/
The SQL Server Developer Center provides up-to-date product information, downloads, articles and community forums.

msdn.microsoft.com/vstudio/express/sql/default.aspx
The home page for SQL Server 2005 Express provides how-to articles, blogs, newsgroups and other valuable resources.

msdn2.microsoft.com/library/system.data.aspx
Microsoft's documentation for the System.Data namespace.

msdn.microsoft.com/SQL/sqlreldata/TSQL/default.aspx
Microsoft's SQL language reference guide.

msdn2.microsoft.com/library/ms172013.aspx
Microsoft's documentation for the **Query Builder** and other visual database tools.

www.w3schools.com/sql/default.asp
The W3C's SQL tutorial presents basic and advanced SQL features with examples.

www.sql.org
This SQL portal provides links to many resources, including SQL syntax, tips, tutorials, books, magazines, discussion groups, companies with SQL services, SQL consultants and free software.

www.oracle.com/database/index.html
The home page for Oracle's database management systems.

www.sybase.com
The home page for the Sybase database management system.

www-306.ibm.com/software/data/db2/
The home page for IBM's DB2 database management system.

www.postgresql.org
The home page for the PostgreSQL database management system.
www.mysql.com
The home page for the MySQL database server.

ASP.NET 2.0, Web Forms and Web Controls

If any man will draw up his case, and put his name at the foot of the first page, I will give him an immediate reply. Where he compels me to turn over the sheet, he must wait my leisure.
—Lord Sandwich

Rule One: Our client is always right
Rule Two: If you think our client is wrong, see Rule One.
—Anonymous

A fair question should be followed by a deed in silence.
—Dante Alighieri

You will come here and get books that will open your eyes, and your ears, and your curiosity, and turn you inside out or outside in.
—Ralph Waldo Emerson

OBJECTIVES

In this chapter you will learn:

- Web application development using Active Server Pages .NET (ASP.NET).
- To create Web Forms.
- To create ASP.NET applications consisting of multiple Web Forms.
- To maintain state information about a user with session tracking and cookies.
- To use the **Web Site Administration Tool** to modify Web application configuration settings.
- To control user access to Web applications using forms authentication and ASP.NET login controls.
- To use databases in ASP.NET applications.
- To design a master page and content pages to create a uniform look-and-feel for a Web site.

21.1 Introduction

In previous chapters, we used Windows Forms and controls to develop Windows applications. In this chapter, we introduce **Web application development** with Microsoft's **Active Server Pages .NET (ASP.NET) 2.0** technology. Web-based applications create Web content for Web browser clients. This Web content includes Extensible HyperText Markup Language (XHTML), client-side scripting, images and binary data. Readers not familiar with XHTML should first read Appendix F, Introduction to XHTML: Part 1, and Appendix G, Introduction to XHTML: Part 2, before studying this chapter.

We present several examples that demonstrate Web application development using **Web Forms**, **Web controls** (also called **ASP.NET server controls**) and Visual Basic programming. Web Form files have the filename extension **.aspx** and contain the Web page's GUI. You customize Web Forms by adding Web controls including labels, text boxes, images, buttons and other GUI components. The Web Form file represents the Web page that is sent to the client browser. From this point onward, we refer to Web Form files as *ASPX files*.

An ASPX file created in Visual Studio typically has a corresponding class written in a .NET language, such as Visual Basic. This class contains event handlers, initialization code, utility methods and other supporting code. The file that contains this class is called the *code-behind file* and provides the ASPX file's programmatic implementation.

To develop the code and GUIs in this chapter, we used Microsoft Visual Web Developer 2005 Express—an IDE designed for developing ASP.NET Web applications. Visual Web Developer and Visual Basic 2005 Express share many common features and visual programming tools that simplify building complex applications, such as those that access a database (presented in Sections 21.7 and 21.8). The full version of Visual Studio 2005 includes the functionality of Visual Web Developer, so the instructions we present for Visual Web Developer also apply to Visual Studio 2005. Note that you must install either Visual Web Developer 2005 Express (available from `msdn.microsoft.com/vstudio/express/vwd/default.aspx`) or a complete version of Visual Studio 2005 to implement the programs in this chapter and Chapter 22, Web Services.

21.2 Simple HTTP Transactions

Web application development requires a basic understanding of networking and the World Wide Web. In this section, we discuss the *Hypertext Transfer Protocol* (*HTTP*) and what occurs behind the scenes when a browser displays a Web page. HTTP specifies a set of *methods* and *headers* that allow clients and servers to interact and exchange information in a uniform and predictable manner.

In its simplest form, a Web page is nothing more than an XHTML document—a plain text file containing *markup* (i.e., *tags*) that indicate to a Web browser how to display and format the document's information. For example, the XHTML markup

```
<title>My Web Page</title>
```

indicates that the browser should display the text between the **`<title>`** *start tag* and the **`</title>`** *end tag* in the browser's title bar. XHTML documents also can contain *hypertext* data (usually called *hyperlinks*), which links to different pages or to other parts of the same page. When the user activates a hyperlink (usually by clicking it with the mouse), the requested Web page loads into the user's browser window.

Any XHTML document available for viewing over the Web has a corresponding Uniform Resource Locator (URL). A URL is an address indicating the location of an Internet resource, such as an XHTML document. The URL contains information that directs a browser to the resource that the user wishes to access. Computers that run *Web server* software make such resources available. When requesting ASP.NET Web applications, the Web server is usually Microsoft *Internet Information Services* (*IIS*). As we discuss shortly, it is also possible to test ASP.NET applications using the ASP.NET Development Server built into Visual Web Developer.

Let us examine the components of the URL

```
http://www.deitel.com/books/downloads.html
```

The `http://` indicates that the resource is to be obtained using the HTTP protocol. The middle portion, `www.deitel.com`, is the server's fully qualified *hostname*—the name of the computer on which the resource resides. This computer usually is referred to as the *host*, because it houses and maintains resources. The hostname www.deitel.com is translated into an *IP address* (68.236.123.125), which identifies the server in a manner similar to how a telephone number uniquely defines a particular phone line. The hostname is translated into an IP address by a *domain name system* (*DNS*) *server*—a computer that maintains a database of hostnames and their corresponding IP addresses. This translation operation is called a *DNS lookup*.

The remainder of the URL (i.e., /books/downloads.html) specifies both the name of the requested resource (the XHTML document downloads.html) and its path, or location (/books), on the Web server. The path could specify the location of an actual directory on the Web server's file system. However, for security reasons, the path often specifies the location of a *virtual directory*. In such systems, the server translates the virtual directory into a real location on the server (or on another computer on the server's network), thus hiding the true location of the resource. Some resources are created dynamically and do not reside anywhere on the server computer. The hostname in the URL for such a resource specifies the correct server, and the path and resource information identify the location of the resource with which to respond to the client's request.

When given a URL, a Web browser performs a simple HTTP transaction to retrieve and display the Web page found at that address. Figure 21.1 illustrates the transaction in detail. This transaction consists of interaction between the Web browser (the client side) and the Web server application (the server side).

In Fig. 21.1, the Web browser sends an HTTP request to the server. The request (in its simplest form) is

```
GET /books/downloads.html HTTP/1.1
```

The word *GET* is an HTTP method indicating that the client wishes to obtain a resource from the server. The remainder of the request provides the path name of the resource (an XHTML document) and the protocol's name and version number (HTTP/1.1).

Any server that understands HTTP version 1.1 can translate this request and respond appropriately. Figure 21.2 depicts the results of a successful request. The server first responds by sending a line of text that indicates the HTTP version, followed by a numeric code and a phrase describing the status of the transaction. For example,

(a) The **GET** request is sent from the client to the Web Server.

Web Server

(b) After it receives the request, the Web Server searches through its system for the resource.

Client

Internet

Fig. 21.1 | Client interacting with Web server. *Step 1:* The **GET** request.

Fig. 21.2 | Client interacting with Web server. *Step 2:* The HTTP response.

    HTTP/1.1 200 OK

indicates success, whereas

    HTTP/1.1 404 Not found

informs the client that the Web server could not locate the requested resource.

The server then sends one or more *HTTP headers,* which provide additional information about the data that will be sent. In this case, the server is sending an XHTML text document, so the HTTP header for this example reads:

    Content-type: text/html

The information provided in this header specifies the *Multipurpose Internet Mail Extensions* (*MIME*) type of the content that the server is transmitting to the browser. MIME is an Internet standard that specifies data formats so that programs can interpret data correctly. For example, the MIME type text/plain indicates that the sent information is text that can be displayed directly, without any interpretation of the content as XHTML markup. Similarly, the MIME type image/jpeg indicates that the content is a JPEG image. When the browser receives this MIME type, it attempts to display the image.

The header or set of headers is followed by a blank line, which indicates to the client that the server is finished sending HTTP headers. The server then sends the contents of the requested XHTML document (downloads.html). The server terminates the connection when the resource transfer is complete. At this point, the client-side browser parses the XHTML markup it has received and *renders* (or displays) the results.

21.3 Multitier Application Architecture

Web-based applications are *multitier applications* (sometimes referred to as *n-tier applications*). Multitier applications divide functionality into separate *tiers* (i.e., logical groupings of functionality). Although tiers can be located on the same computer, the tiers of Web-based applications typically reside on separate computers. Figure 21.3 presents the basic structure of a three-tier Web-based application.

The *information tier* (also called the *data tier* or the *bottom tier*) maintains data pertaining to the application. This tier typically stores data in a relational database management system (RDBMS). We discussed RDBMSs in Chapter 20. For example, a retail store

Fig. 21.3 | Three-tier architecture.

might have a database for storing product information, such as descriptions, prices and quantities in stock. The same database also might contain customer information, such as user names, billing addresses and credit card numbers. This tier can contain multiple databases, which together comprise the data needed for our application.

The *middle tier* implements *business logic, controller logic* and *presentation logic* to control interactions between the application's clients and the application's data. The middle tier acts as an intermediary between data in the information tier and the application's clients. The middle-tier controller logic processes client requests (such as requests to view a product catalog) and retrieves data from the database. The middle-tier presentation logic then processes data from the information tier and presents the content to the client. Web applications typically present data to clients as XHTML documents.

Business logic in the middle tier enforces *business rules* and ensures that data is reliable before the server application updates the database or presents the data to users. Business rules dictate how clients can and cannot access application data, and how applications process data. For example, a business rule in the middle tier of a retail store's Web-based application might ensure that all product quantities remain positive. A client request to set a negative quantity in the bottom tier's product information database would be rejected by the middle tier's business logic.

The *client tier*, or *top tier*, is the application's user interface, which gathers input and displays output. Users interact directly with the application through the user interface (typically viewed in a Web browser), keyboard and mouse. In response to user actions (e.g., clicking a hyperlink), the client tier interacts with the middle tier to make requests and to retrieve data from the information tier. The client tier then displays the data retrieved from the middle tier to the user. The client tier never directly interacts with the information tier.

21.4 Creating and Running a Simple Web-Form Example

Our first example displays the Web server's time of day in a browser window. When run, this program displays the text A Simple Web Form Example, followed by the Web server's time. As mentioned previously, the program consists of two related files—an ASPX file (Fig. 21.4) and a Visual Basic code-behind file (Fig. 21.5). We first display the markup, code and output, then we carefully guide you through the step-by-step process of creating this program. [*Note:* The markup in Fig. 21.4 and other ASPX file listings in this chapter

```
 1    <%-- Fig. 21.4: WebTime.aspx --%>
 2    <%-- A page that displays the current time in a Label. --%>
 3    <%@ Page Language="VB" AutoEventWireup="false" CodeFile="WebTime.aspx.vb"
 4       Inherits="WebTime" EnableSessionState="False" %>
 5
 6    <!DOCTYPE html PUBLIC "-//W3C//DTD XHTML 1.0 Transitional//EN"
 7       "http://www.w3.org/TR/xhtml1/DTD/xhtml1-transitional.dtd">
 8
 9    <html xmlns="http://www.w3.org/1999/xhtml" >
10    <head runat="server">
11       <title>A Simple Web Form Example</title>
12    </head>
13    <body>
14       <form id="form1" runat="server">
15       <div>
16          <h2>
17          Current time on the Web server:</h2>
18          <p>
19             <asp:Label ID="timeLabel" runat="server" BackColor="Black"
20                EnableViewState="False" Font-Size="XX-Large"
21                ForeColor="Yellow"></asp:Label>
22          </p>
23       </div>
24       </form>
25    </body>
26    </html>
```

Fig. 21.4 | ASPX file that displays the Web server's time.

is the same as the markup that appears in Visual Web Developer, but we have reformatted the markup for presentation purposes to make the code more readable.]

Visual Web Developer generates all the markup shown in Fig. 21.4 when you set the Web page's title, type text in the Web Form, drag a Label onto the Web Form and set the properties of the page's text and the Label. We discuss these steps in Section 21.4.6.

21.4.1 Examining an ASPX File

The ASPX file contains other information in addition to XHTML. Lines 1–2 are *ASP.NET comments* that indicate the figure number, the file name and the purpose of the file. ASP.NET comments begin with **<%--** and terminate with **--%>**. We added these comments to the file. Lines 3–4 use a *Page* directive (in an ASPX file a *directive* is delimited by **<%@** and **%>**) to specify information needed by ASP.NET to process this file. The **Language** attribute of the Page directive specifies the language of the code-behind file as Visual Basic ("VB"); the code-behind file (i.e., the **CodeFile**) is WebTime.aspx.vb. A code-behind file name usually consists of the full ASPX file name (e.g., WebTime.aspx) followed by the .vb extension.

The **AutoEventWireup** attribute (line 3) determines how Web Form events are handled. When AutoEventWireup is set to true, ASP.NET determines which methods in the class are called in response to an event generated by the Page. For example, ASP.NET will call methods Page_Init and Page_Load in the code-behind file to handle the Page's Init and Load events, respectively. (We discuss these events later in the chapter.)

The *Inherits* attribute (line 4) specifies the page's class name—in this case, WebTime. We say more about Inherits momentarily. [*Note:* We explicitly set the *EnableSession-State* attribute (line 4) to False. We explain the significance of this attribute later in the chapter. The IDE sometimes generates attribute values (e.g., true and false) and control names (as you will see later in the chapter) that do not adhere to our standard code capitalization conventions (i.e., True and False). Like Visual Basic, ASP.NET markup is not case-sensitive, so using a different case is not problematic. To remain consistent with the code generated by the IDE, we do not modify these values in our code listings or in our accompanying discussions.]

For this first ASPX file, we provide a brief discussion of the XHTML markup. We do not discuss the majority of the XHTML contained in subsequent ASPX files. Lines 6–7 contain the document type declaration, which specifies the document element name (HTML) and the PUBLIC Uniform Resource Identifier (URI) for the DTD that defines the XHTML vocabulary.

Lines 9–10 contain the <html> and <head> start tags, respectively. XHTML documents have the root element html and mark up information about the document in the head element. Also note that the html element specifies the XML namespace of the document using the xmlns attribute (see Section 19.4).

Notice the *runat* attribute in line 10, which is set to *"server"*. This attribute indicates that when a client requests this ASPX file, ASP.NET processes the head element and its nested elements on the server and generates the corresponding XHTML, which is then sent to the client. In this case, the XHTML sent to the client will be identical to the markup in the ASPX file. However, as you will see, ASP.NET can generate complex XHTML markup from simple elements in an ASPX file.

Line 11 sets the title of this Web page. We demonstrate how to set the title through a property in the IDE shortly. Line 13 contains the <body> start tag, which begins the body of the XHTML document; the body contains the main content that the browser displays. The form that contains our XHTML text and controls is defined in lines 14–24. Again, the runat attribute in the form element indicates that this element executes on the server, which generates equivalent XHTML and sends it to the client. Lines 15–23 contain a div element that groups the elements of the form in a block of markup.

Lines 16–17 are an XHTML h2 heading element that contains text indicating the purpose of the Web page. As we demonstrate shortly, the IDE generates this element in response to typing text directly in the Web Form and selecting the text as a second-level heading.

Lines 18–22 contain a p element to mark up a paragraph of content in the browser. Lines 19–21 mark up a label Web control. The properties that we set in the **Properties** window, such as Font-Size and BackColor (i.e., background color), are attributes here. The *ID* attribute (line 19) assigns a name to the control so that it can be manipulated programmatically in the code-behind file. We set the control's *EnableViewState* attribute (line 20) to False. We explain the significance of this attribute later in the chapter.

The *asp: tag prefix* in the declaration of the *Label* tag (line 19) indicates that the label is an ASP.NET Web control, not an XHTML element. Each Web control maps to a corresponding XHTML element (or group of elements)—when processing a Web control on the server, ASP.NET generates XHTML markup that will be sent to the client to represent that control in a Web browser.

Portability Tip 21.1

The same Web control can map to different XHTML elements, depending on the client browser and the Web control's property settings.

In this example, the asp:Label control maps to the XHTML *span* element (i.e., ASP.NET creates a span element to represent this control in the client's Web browser). A span element contains text that is displayed in a Web page. This particular element is used because span elements allow formatting styles to be applied to text. Several of the property values that were applied to our label are represented as part of the style attribute of the span element. You will soon see what the generated span element's markup looks like.

The Web control in this example contains the runat="server" attribute–value pair (line 19), because this control must be processed on the server so that the server can translate the control into XHTML that can be rendered in the client browser. If this attribute pair is not present, the asp:Label element is written as text to the client (i.e., the control is not converted into a span element and does not render properly).

21.4.2 Examining a Code-Behind File

Figure 21.5 presents the code-behind file. Recall that the ASPX file in Fig. 21.4 references this file in line 3.

Line 3 begins the declaration of class WebTime. Recall from Section 9.6 that a class declaration can span multiple source-code files and that the separate portions of the class declaration in each file are known as partial classes. The Partial modifier in line 3 indicates that the code-behind file is a partial class. We discuss the remainder of this class shortly.

```vb
1   ' Fig. 21.5: WebTime.aspx.vb
2   ' Code-behind file for a page that displays the current time.
3   Partial Class WebTime
4      Inherits System.Web.UI.Page
5
6      ' initializes the contents of the page
7      Protected Sub Page_Init(ByVal sender As Object, _
8         ByVal e As System.EventArgs) Handles Me.Init
9         ' display the server's current time in timeLabel
10        timeLabel.Text = DateTime.Now.ToString("hh:mm:ss")
11     End Sub ' Page_Init
12  End Class ' WebTime
```

A Simple Web Form Example - Microsoft Internet Expl...

File   Edit   View   Favorites   Tools   Help

Back · · ·   Search   »

Address http://localhost/WebTime/WebTime.aspx Go

Current time on the Web server:

13:16:05

Done   Local intranet

Fig. 21.5 | Code-behind file for a page that displays the Web server's time.

Line 4 indicates that WebTime inherits from class *Page* in namespace *System.Web.UI*. This namespace contains classes and controls that assist in building Web-based applications. Class Page provides event handlers and objects necessary for creating Web-based applications. In addition to class Page (from which all Web applications directly or indirectly inherit), System.Web.UI also includes class *Control*—the base class that provides common functionality for all Web controls.

Lines 7–11 define method *Page_Init*, which handles the page's *Init* event. This event indicates that the page is ready to be initialized. The only initialization required for this page is setting timeLabel's Text property to the time on the server (i.e., the computer on which this code executes). The statement in line 10 retrieves the current time and formats it as *hh:mm:ss*. For example, 9 AM is formatted as 09:00:00, and 2:30 PM is formatted as 14:30:00. Notice that the code-behind file can access timeLabel (the ID of the Label in the ASPX file) programmatically, even though the file does not contain a declaration for a variable named timeLabel. You will learn why momentarily.

21.4.3 Relationship Between an ASPX File and a Code-Behind File

How are the ASPX and code-behind files used to create the Web page that is sent to the client? First, recall that class WebTime is the base class specified in line 4 of the ASPX file (Fig. 21.4). This class (partially declared in the code-behind file) inherits from Page, which defines general Web page functionality. Partial class WebTime inherits this functionality and defines some of its own (i.e., displaying the current time). The code in the code-behind file displays the time, whereas the code in the ASPX file defines the GUI.

When a client requests an ASPX file, ASP.NET creates two partial classes behind the scenes. The code-behind file contains one partial class named WebTime and ASP.NET generate another partial class containing the remainder of class WebTime, based on the markup in the ASPX file. For example, WebTime.aspx contains a Label Web control with ID time-Label, so the generated partial class would contain a declaration for a variable named timeLabel of type System.Web.UI.WebControls.Label. Class Label represents a Web control defined in namespace *System.Web.UI.WebControls*, which contains various Web controls for designing a page's user interface. Web controls in this namespace derive from class *WebControl*. When compiled, the partial class that declares timeLabel combines with the code-behind file's partial class declaration to form the complete WebTime class. This explains why line 10 in Fig. 21.5 can access timeLabel, which is created in lines 19–21 of WebTime.aspx (Fig. 21.4)—method Page_Init and control timeLabel are actually members of the same class, but defined in separate partial classes.

The partial class generated by ASP.NET is based on the ASPX file that defines the page's visual representation. This partial class is combined with the one in Fig. 21.5, which defines the page's logic. The first time the Web page is requested, this class is compiled and an instance is created. This instance represents the page and creates the XHTML that is sent to the client. The assembly created from the compiled partial classes is placed in a subdirectory of

```
C:\WINDOWS\Microsoft.NET\Framework\VersionNumber\
    Temporary ASP.NET Files\WebTime
```

where *VersionNumber* is the version number of the .NET Framework (e.g., v2.0.50727) installed on your computer.

Once an instance of the Web page has been created, multiple clients can use it to access the page—no recompilation is necessary. The project will be recompiled only when you modify the application; changes are detected by the runtime environment, and the application is recompiled to reflect the altered content.

21.4.4 How the Code in an ASP.NET Web Page Executes

Let's look briefly at how the code for our Web page executes. When an instance of the page is created, the **PreInit** event occurs first, invoking method **Page_PreInit**. Method Page_PreInit can be used to set a page's theme and look-and-feel (and perform other tasks that are beyond this chapter's scope). The Init event occurs next, invoking method Page_Init. Method Page_Init is used to initialize objects and other aspects of the page. After Page_Init executes, the **Load** event occurs, and the **Page_Load** event handler executes. Although not present in this example, the PreInit and Load events are inherited from class Page. You will see examples of the Page_Load event handler later in the chapter. After the Load event handler finishes executing, the page processes events that are generated by the page's controls, such as user interactions with the GUI. When the Web Form object is ready for garbage collection, an **Unload** event occurs, which calls the **Page_Unload** event handler. This event, too, is inherited from class Page. Page_Unload typically contains code that releases resources used by the page. Other events occur as well, but are typically used only by ASP.NET controls to render themselves. You can learn more about a Page's event lifecycle at msdn2.microsoft.com/en-US/library/ms178472.aspx.

21.4.5 Examining the XHTML Generated by an ASP.NET Application

Figure 21.6 shows the XHTML generated by ASP.NET when a client browser requests WebTime.aspx (Fig. 21.4). To view this code, select **View > Source** in Internet Explorer. We added the comments in lines 1–2 and reformatted the XHTML for readability.

The markup in this page is similar to the ASPX file. Lines 7–9 define a document header comparable to that in Fig. 21.4. Lines 10–25 define the document's body. Line 11 begins the form, a mechanism for collecting user information and sending it to the Web server. In this particular program, the user does not submit data to the Web server for processing; however, processing user data is a crucial part of many applications that is facilitated by forms. We demonstrate how to submit form data to the server in later examples.

XHTML forms can contain visual and nonvisual components. Visual components include buttons and other GUI components with which users interact. Nonvisual components, called **hidden inputs**, store data, such as e-mail addresses, that the document author specifies. A hidden input is defined in lines 13–14. We discuss the precise meaning of this hidden input later in the chapter. Attribute **method** of the form element (line 11) specifies the method by which the Web browser submits the form to the server. The **action** attribute identifies the name and location of the resource that will be requested when this form is submitted—in this case, WebTime.aspx. Recall that the ASPX file's form element contained the runat="server" attribute–value pair (line 14 of Fig. 21.4). When the form is processed on the server, the runat attribute is removed. The method and action attributes are added, and the resulting XHTML form is sent to the client browser.

In the ASPX file, the form's Label (i.e., timeLabel) is a Web control. Here, we are viewing the XHTML created by our application, so the form contains a span element (lines 20–21 of Fig. 21.6) to represent the text in the label. In this particular case,

```
1   <!-- Fig. 21.6: WebTime.html -->
2   <!-- The XHTML generated when WebTime.aspx is loaded. -->
3   <!DOCTYPE html PUBLIC "-//W3C//DTD XHTML 1.1//EN"
4       "http://www.w3.org/TR/xhtml11/DTD/xhtml11.dtd">
5
6   <html xmlns="http://www.w3.org/1999/xhtml" >
7   <head>
8       <title>A Simple Web Form Example</title>
9   </head>
10  <body>
11      <form name="form1" method="post" action="WebTime.aspx" id="form1">
12          <div>
13              <input type="hidden" name="__VIEWSTATE" id="__VIEWSTATE" value=
14                  "/wEPDwUJODExMDE5NzY5ZGSzVbs789nqEeoNueQCnCJQEUgykw==" />
15          </div>
16
17          <div>
18              <h2>Current time on the Web server:</h2>
19              <p>
20                  <span id="timeLabel" style="color:Yellow;
21                      background-color:Black;font-size:XX-Large;">13:51:12</span>
22              </p>
23          </div>
24      </form>
25  </body>
26  </html>
```

Fig. 21.6 | XHTML response when the browser requests `WebTime.aspx`.

ASP.NET maps the *Label* Web control to an XHTML `span` element. The formatting options that were specified as properties of `timeLabel`, such as the font size and color of the text in the *Label*, are now specified in the `style` attribute of the `span` element.

Notice that only those elements in the ASPX file marked with the `runat="server"` attribute–value pair or specified as Web controls are modified or replaced when the file is processed by the server. The pure XHTML elements, such as the `h2` in line 18, are sent to the browser as they appear in the ASPX file.

21.4.6 Building an ASP.NET Web Application

Now that we have presented the ASPX file, the code-behind file and the resulting Web page sent to the Web browser, we show the steps we used to create this application in Visual Web Developer.

Step 1: Creating the Web Application Project

Select **File > New Web Site...** to display the **New Web Site** dialog (Fig. 21.7). In this dialog, select *ASP.NET Web Site* in the **Templates** pane. Below this pane, there are two fields in which you can specify the type and location of the Web application you are creating. If it is not already selected, select **HTTP** from the drop-down list closest to **Location**. This indicates that the Web application should be configured to run as an IIS application using HTTP (either on your computer or on a remote computer). We want our project to be located in `http://localhost`, which is the URL for IIS's root directory (this URL nor-

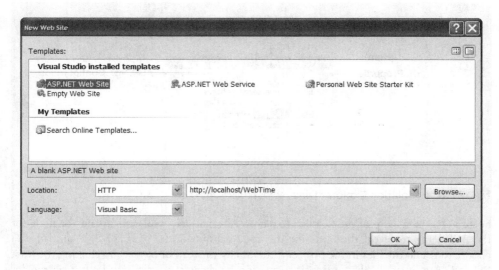

Fig. 21.7 | Creating an **ASP.NET Web Site** in Visual Web Developer.

mally corresponds to the `C:\InetPub\wwwroot` directory on your machine). The name *localhost* indicates that the server resides on local computer. If the Web server were located on a different computer, `localhost` would be replaced with the appropriate IP address or hostname. By default, Visual Web Developer sets the location where the Web site will be created to `http://localhost/WebSite`, which we change to `http://localhost/WebTime`.

If you do not have IIS on your computer or do not have permission to access it, you can select **File System** from the drop-down list next to **Location** to create the Web application in a folder on your computer. You will be able to test the application using Visual Web Developer's internal ASP.NET Development Server, but you will not be able to access the application remotely over the Internet.

The **Language** drop-down list in the **New Web Site** dialog allows you to specify the language (i.e., Visual Basic, Visual C# or Visual J#) in which you will write the code-behind file(s) for the Web application. Change the setting to Visual Basic. Click **OK** to create the Web application project. This creates the directory `C:\Inetpub\wwwroot\WebTime` (in IIS) and makes it accessible through the URL `http://localhost/WebTime`. This action also creates a `WebTime` directory in the directory `My Documents\Visual Studio 2005\Projects` in which the project's solution files (e.g., `WebTime.sln`) are stored.

Step 2: Examining the Solution Explorer of the Newly Created Project
The next several figures describe the new project's content, beginning with the **Solution Explorer** shown in Fig. 21.8. Like Visual Basic 2005 Express, Visual Web Developer creates several files when you create a new project. It creates an ASPX file (i.e., Web Form) named `Default.aspx` for each new **ASP.NET Web Site** project. This file is open by default in the Web Forms Designer in **Source** mode when the project first loads (we discuss this momentarily). As mentioned previously, a code-behind file is included as part of the project. Visual Web Developer creates a code-behind file named `Default.aspx.vb`. To open the ASPX file's code-behind file, right click the ASPX file and select **View Code** or click the **View Code**

Fig. 21.8 | **Solution Explorer** window for project `WebTime`.

button (⊡) at the top of the **Solution Explorer**. Alternatively, you can expand the node for the ASPX file to reveal the node for the code-behind file (see Fig. 21.8). You can also choose to list all the files in the project individually (instead of nested) by clicking the **Nest Related Files** button—this option is turned on by default, so clicking the button toggles the option off.

The **Properties** and **Refresh** buttons in Visual Web Developer's **Solution Explorer** behave like those in Visual Basic 2005 Express. Visual Web Developer's **Solution Explorer** also contains the buttons **View Designer**, **Copy Web Site** and **ASP.NET Configuration**. The **View Designer** button allows you to open the Web Form in **Design** mode, which we discuss shortly. The **Copy Web Site** button opens a dialog that allows you to move the files in this project to another location, such as a remote Web server. This is useful if you are developing the application on your local computer, but want to make it available to the public from a different location. Finally, the **ASP.NET Configuration** button takes you to a Web page called the **Web Site Administration Tool**, where you can manipulate various settings and security options for your application. We discuss this tool in greater detail in Section 21.8.

Step 3: Examining the Toolbox in Visual Web Developer
Figure 21.9 shows the **Toolbox** displayed in the IDE when the project loads. Figure 21.9(a) displays the beginning of the **Standard** list of Web controls, and Fig. 21.9(b) displays the remaining Web controls, and the list of **Data** controls used in ASP.NET. We discuss specific controls in Fig. 21.9 as they are used throughout the chapter. Notice that some controls in the **Toolbox** are similar to the Windows controls presented earlier in the book.

Step 4: Examining the Web Forms Designer
Figure 21.10 shows the Web Forms Designer in ***Source*** mode, which appears in the center of the IDE. When the project loads for the first time, the Web Forms Designer displays the auto-generated ASPX file (i.e., `Default.aspx`) in **Source** mode, which allows you to view and edit the markup that comprises the Web page. The markup listed in Fig. 21.10 was created by the IDE and serves as a template that we will modify shortly. Clicking the **Design** button in the lower-left corner of the Web Forms Designer switches to ***Design*** mode (Fig. 21.11), which allows you to drag and drop controls from the **Toolbox** on the

Fig. 21.9 | **Toolbox** in Visual Web Developer.

Web Form. You can also type at the current cursor location to add text to the Web page. We demonstrate this shortly. In response to such actions, the IDE generates the appropriate markup in the ASPX file. Notice that **Design** mode indicates the XHTML element where the cursor is currently located. Clicking the **Source** button returns the Web Forms Designer to **Source** mode, where you can see the generated markup.

Step 5: Examining the Code-Behind File in the IDE

The next figure (Fig. 21.12) displays Default.aspx.vb—the code-behind file generated by Visual Web Developer for Default.aspx. Right click the ASPX file in the **Solution Explorer** and select **View Code** to open the code-behind file. When it is first created, this file contains nothing more than a partial class declaration. We will add the Page_Init event handler to this code momentarily.

Step 6: Renaming the ASPX File

Now that you've seen the contents of the default ASPX and code-behind files, let's rename these files. Right click the ASPX file in the **Solution Explorer** and select **Rename**. Enter the new file name WebTime.aspx and press *Enter*. This updates the name of both the ASPX file and the code-behind file. The IDE also updates the Page directive's CodeFile attribute in WebTime.aspx.

Step 7: Renaming the Class in the Code-Behind File and Updating the ASPX File

Although renaming the ASPX file causes the name of the code-behind file to change, this action does not affect the name of the partial class declared in the code-behind file. Open

Fig. 21.10 | **Source** mode of the Web Forms Designer.

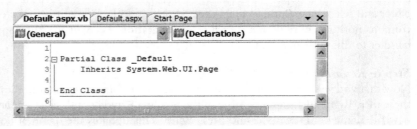

Fig. 21.11 | **Design** mode of the Web Forms Designer.

Fig. 21.12 | Code-behind file for `Default.aspx` generated by Visual Web Developer.

the code-behind file and change the class name from `_Default` (line 2 in Fig. 21.12) to `WebTime`, so the partial class declaration appears as in line 3 of Fig. 21.5. Recall that this class is also referenced by the `Page` directive in the ASPX file. Using the Web Forms Designer's **Source** mode, modify the `Inherits` attribute of the `Page` directive in `WebTime.aspx`, so it appears as in line 4 of Fig. 21.4. The value of the Inherits attribute and the class name in the code-behind file must be identical; otherwise, you'll get errors when you build the Web application.

Step 8: Changing the Title of the Page

Before designing the content of the Web Form, we change its title from the default Untitled Page (line 9 of Fig. 21.10) to A Simple Web Form Example. To do so, open the ASPX file in **Source** mode and modify the text in the title element—i.e., the text between the tags <title> and </title>). Alternatively, you can open the ASPX file in **Design** mode and modify the Web Form's *Title* property in the **Properties** window. To view the Web Form's properties, select DOCUMENT from the drop-down list in the **Properties** window; *DOCUMENT* represents the Web Form in the **Properties** window.

Step 9: Designing the Page

Designing a Web Form is as simple as designing a Windows Form. To add controls to the page, drag-and-drop them from the **Toolbox** onto the Web Form in **Design** mode. Like the Web Form itself, each control is an object that has properties, methods and events. You can set these properties and events visually using the **Properties** window or programmatically in the code-behind file. However, unlike working with a Windows Form, you can type text directly on a Web Form at the cursor location or insert XHTML elements using menu commands.

Controls and other elements are placed sequentially on a Web Form, much like how text and images are placed in a document using word processing software like Microsoft Word. Controls are placed one after another in the order in which you drag-and-drop them onto the Web Form. The cursor indicates the point at which text and XHTML elements will be inserted. If you want to position a control between existing text or controls, you can drop the control at a specific position within the existing elements. You can also rearrange existing controls using drag-and-drop actions. The positions of controls and other elements are relative to the Web Form's upper-left corner. This type of layout is known as *relative positioning*.

An alternate type of layout is known as *absolute positioning*, in which controls are located exactly where they are dropped on the Web Form. You can enable absolute positioning in **Design** mode by selecting **Layout > Position > Auto-position Options...**, then clicking the first checkbox in the **Positioning options** pane of the **Options** dialog that appears.

Portability Tip 21.2

Absolute positioning is discouraged, because pages designed in this manner may not render correctly on computers with different screen resolutions and font sizes. This could cause absolutely positioned elements to overlap each other or display off-screen, requiring the client to scroll to see the full page content.

In this example, we use one piece of text and one Label. To add the text to the Web Form, click the blank Web Form in **Design** mode and type Current time on the Web server:. Visual Web Developer is a *WYSIWYG* (*What You See Is What You Get*) editor—whenever you make a change to a Web Form in **Design** mode, the IDE creates the markup (visible in **Source** mode) necessary to achieve the desired visual effects seen in **Design** mode. After adding the text to the Web Form, switch to **Source** mode. You should see that the IDE added this text to the div element that appears in the ASPX file by default. Back in **Design** mode, highlight the text you added. From the **Block Format** drop-down list (see Fig. 21.13), choose **Heading 2** to format this text as a heading that will appear bold in a font slightly larger than the default. This action encloses the text in an h2 element. Finally, click to the right of the text and press the *Enter* key to start a new paragraph. This action generates a p (paragraph) element in the ASPX file's markup. The IDE should now look like Fig. 21.13.

You can place a Label on a Web Form either by dragging-and-dropping or by double clicking the **Toolbox**'s **Label** control. Ensure that the cursor is in the new paragraph, then add a Label that will be used to display the time. Using the **Properties** window, set the (ID) property of the Label to timeLabel. Delete timeLabel's text, because this text will be set programmatically in the code-behind file. When a Label does not contain text, its name is displayed in square brackets in the Web Forms Designer (Fig. 21.14) as a place-holder for design and layout purposes. This text is not displayed at execution time. We set timeLabel's BackColor, ForeColor and Font-Size properties to Black, Yellow and XX-Large, respectively. To change the Label's font properties, select the Label, expand the Font node in the **Properties** window and change each relevant property. As the Label's properties are set, Visual Web Developer updates the ASPX file's contents. Figure 21.14 shows the IDE after setting these properties.

Next, set the Label's EnableViewState property to False. Finally, select DOCUMENT from the drop-down list in the **Properties** window and set the Web Form's EnableSessionState property to False. We discuss both of these properties later in the chapter.

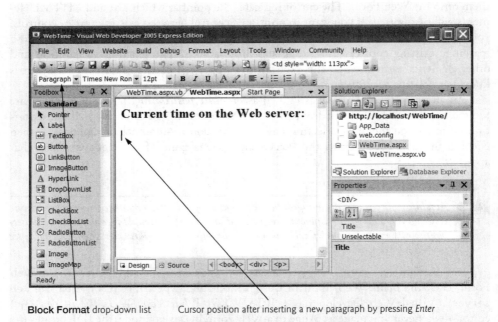

Block Format drop-down list   Cursor position after inserting a new paragraph by pressing *Enter*

Fig. 21.13 | WebTime.aspx after inserting text and a new paragraph.

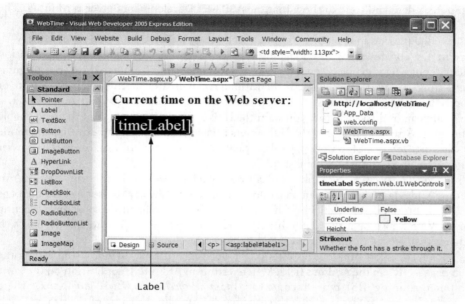

Label

Fig. 21.14 | WebTime.aspx after adding a Label and setting its properties.

Step 10: Adding Page Logic

Now that you've designed the user interface, you'll add Visual Basic code to the code-behind file to obtain the server's time. Open WebTime.aspx.vb by double clicking its node in the **Solution Explorer**. In this example, we add a Page_Init event handler (lines 16–21 of Fig. 21.5) to the code-behind file. Recall that Page_Init handles the Init event and contains code to initialize the page. The statement in lines 10–11 of Fig. 21.5 sets timeLabel's text to the server's current time.

Step 11: Running the Program

After creating the Web Form, you can view it several ways. First, you can select **Debug > Start Without Debugging**, which runs the application by opening it in a browser window. If you created the application on your local IIS server (as we did in this example), the URL shown in the browser will be http://localhost/WebTime/WebTime.aspx (Fig. 21.5), indicating that the Web page (the ASPX file) is located within the virtual directory WebTime on the local IIS Web server. IIS must be running to test the Web site in a browser. IIS can be started by executing inetmgr.exe from **Start > Run...**, right clicking **Default Web Site** and selecting **Start**. [*Note:* You might need to expand the node representing your computer to display the **Default Web Site**.]

If you created the ASP.NET application on the local file system, the URL shown in the browser will be http://localhost:*PortNumber*/WebTime/WebTime.aspx, where *PortNumber* is the number of the randomly assigned port on which Visual Web Developer's built-in test server runs. The IDE assigns the port number on a per solution basis. This URL indicates that the WebTime project folder is being accessed through the root directory of the test server running at localhost:*PortNumber*. When you select **Debug > Start Without Debugging**, a tray icon appears near the bottom-right of your screen next to the computer's date and time to show that the **ASP.NET Development Server** is running. The test server stops when you exit Visual Web Developer.

To debug your application, you can select **Debug > Start Debugging** to view the Web page in a Web browser with debugging enabled. You cannot debug a Web application unless debugging is explicitly enabled by the *Web.config* file—a file that stores configuration settings for an ASP.NET Web application. You will rarely need to manually create or modify Web.config. The first time you select **Debug > Start Debugging** in a project, a dialog appears and asks whether you want the IDE to modify the Web.config file to enable debugging. After you click **OK**, the IDE enters **Running** mode. You can exit **Running** mode by selecting **Debug > Stop Debugging** in Visual Web Developer or by closing the browser window in which the ASPX file is displayed.

To view a specific ASPX file, you can right click either the Web Forms Designer or the ASPX file name (in the **Solution Explorer**) and select *View In Browser* to load the page in a Web browser. Right clicking the ASPX file in the **Solution Explorer** and selecting **Browse With...** also opens the page in a browser, but first allows you to specify the Web browser that should display the page and its screen resolution.

Finally, you can run your application by opening a browser window and typing the Web page's URL in the **Address** field. When testing an ASP.NET application on the same computer running IIS, type `http://localhost/`*ProjectFolder*`/`*PageName*`.aspx`, where *ProjectFolder* is the folder in which the page resides (usually the name of the project), and *PageName* is the name of the ASP.NET page. If your application resides on the local file system, you must first start the **ASP.NET Development Server** by running the application using one of the methods described above. Then you can type the URL (including the *PortNumber* found in the test server's tray icon) in the browser to execute the application.

Note that all of these methods of running the application compile the project for you. In fact, ASP.NET compiles your Web page whenever it changes between HTTP requests. For example, suppose you browse the page, then modify the ASPX file or add code to the code-behind file. When you reload the page, ASP.NET recompiles the page on the server before returning the HTTP response to the browser. This important new behavior of ASP.NET 2.0 ensures that clients always see the latest version of the page. You can manually compile a Web page or an entire Web site by selecting *Build Page* or *Build Site*, respectively, from the **Build** menu in Visual Web Developer.

Windows Firewall Settings

If you would like to test your Web application over a network, you may need to change your Windows Firewall settings. For security reasons, Windows Firewall does not allow remote access to a Web server on your local computer by default. To change this, open the Windows Firewall utility in the Windows Control Panel. Click the **Advanced** tab and select your network connection from the **Network Connection Settings** list, then click **Settings....** On the **Services** tab of the **Advanced Settings** dialog, ensure that **Web Server (HTTP)** is checked.

21.5 Web Controls

This section introduces some of the Web controls located in the **Standard** section of the **Toolbox** (Fig. 21.9). Figure 21.15 summarizes some of the Web controls used in the chapter examples.

Web Control	Description
Label	Displays text that the user cannot edit.
TextBox	Gathers user input and displays text.
Button	Triggers an event when clicked.
HyperLink	Displays a hyperlink.
DropDownList	Displays a drop-down list of choices from which a user can select an item.
RadioButtonList	Groups radio buttons.
Image	Displays images (e.g., GIF and JPG).

Fig. 21.15 | Commonly used Web controls.

21.5.1 Text and Graphics Controls

Figure 21.16 depicts a simple form for gathering user input. This example uses all the controls listed in Fig. 21.15, except Label, which you used in Section 21.4. The code in Fig. 21.16 was generated by Visual Web Developer in response to dragging controls onto the page in **Design** mode. To begin, create an ASP.NET Web Site named WebControls. [*Note:* This example does not contain any functionality—i.e., no action occurs when the user clicks **Register**. In subsequent examples, we demonstrate how to add functionality to many of these Web controls.]

Before discussing the Web controls used in this ASPX file, we explain the XHTML that creates the layout seen in Fig. 21.16. The page contains an h3 heading element (line 16), followed by a series of additional XHTML blocks. We place most of the Web controls inside p elements (i.e., paragraphs), but we use an XHTML table element (lines 25–55) to organize the Image and TextBox controls in the user information section of the page. In the preceding section, we described how to add heading elements and paragraphs visually without manipulating any XHTML in the ASPX file directly. Visual Web Developer allows you to add a table in a similar manner.

Adding an XHTML Table to a Web Form

To create a table with two rows and two columns in **Design** mode, select the **Insert Table** command from the **Layout** menu. In the **Insert Table** dialog that appears, select the **Custom** radio button. In the **Layout** group box, change the values of **Rows** and **Columns** to 2. By default, the contents of a table cell are aligned vertically in the middle of the cell. We changed the vertical alignment of all cells in the table by clicking the **Cell Properties...** button, then selecting **top** from the **Vertical align** combo box in the resulting dialog. This causes the content of each table cell to align with the top of the cell. Click **OK** to close the **Cell Properties** dialog, then click **OK** to close the **Insert Table** dialog and create the table. Once a table is created, controls and text can be added to particular cells to create a neatly organized layout.

```
1   <%-- Fig. 21.16: WebControls.aspx --%>
2   <%-- Registration form that demonstrates Web controls. --%>
3   <%@ Page Language="VB" AutoEventWireup="false"
4      CodeFile="WebControls.aspx.vb" Inherits="WebControls" %>
5
6   <!DOCTYPE html PUBLIC "-//W3C//DTD XHTML 1.0 Transitional//EN"
7      "http://www.w3.org/TR/xhtml1/DTD/xhtml1-transitional.dtd">
8
9   <html xmlns="http://www.w3.org/1999/xhtml">
10  <head runat="server">
11     <title>Web Controls Demonstration</title>
12  </head>
13  <body>
14     <form id="form1" runat="server">
15     <div>
16        <h3>This is a sample registration form.</h3>
17        <p>
18           <em>Please fill in all fields and click Register.</em></p>
19        <p>
20           <asp:Image ID="userInformationImage" runat="server"
21              EnableViewState="False" ImageUrl="~/Images/user.png" />  
22           <span style="color: teal">
23              Please fill out the fields below.</span>
24        </p>
25        <table id="TABLE1">
26           <tr>
27              <td style="width: 230px; height: 21px" valign="top">
28                 <asp:Image ID="firstNameImage" runat="server"
29                    EnableViewState="False" ImageUrl="~/Images/fname.png" />
30                 <asp:TextBox ID="firstNameTextBox" runat="server"
31                    EnableViewState="False"></asp:TextBox>
32              </td>
33              <td style="width: 231px; height: 21px" valign="top">
34                 <asp:Image ID="lastNameImage" runat="server"
35                    EnableViewState="False" ImageUrl="~/Images/lname.png" />
36                 <asp:TextBox ID="lastNameTextBox" runat="server"
37                    EnableViewState="False"></asp:TextBox>
38              </td>
39           </tr>
40           <tr>
41              <td style="width: 230px" valign="top">
42                 <asp:Image ID="emailImage" runat="server"
43                    EnableViewState="False" ImageUrl="~/Images/email.png" />
44                 <asp:TextBox ID="emailTextBox" runat="server"
45                    EnableViewState="False"></asp:TextBox>
46              </td>
47              <td style="width: 231px" valign="top">
48                 <asp:Image ID="phoneImage" runat="server"
49                    EnableViewState="False" ImageUrl="~/Images/phone.png" />
50                 <asp:TextBox ID="phoneTextBox" runat="server"
51                    EnableViewState="False"></asp:TextBox>
52                 Must be in the form (555) 555-5555.
```

Fig. 21.16 | Web Form that demonstrates Web controls. (Part 1 of 3.)

```
 53                  </td>
 54              </tr>
 55          </table>
 56          <p>
 57              <asp:Image ID="publicationsImage" runat="server"
 58                  EnableViewState="False"
 59                  ImageUrl="~/Images/publications.png" />  
 60              <span style="color: teal">
 61                  Which book would you like information about?</span>
 62          </p>
 63          <p>
 64              <asp:DropDownList ID="booksDropDownList" runat="server"
 65                  EnableViewState="False">
 66              <asp:ListItem>Visual Basic 2005 How to Program 3e
 67                      </asp:ListItem>
 68              <asp:ListItem>Visual C# 2005 How to Program 2e
 69                      </asp:ListItem>
 70              <asp:ListItem>Java How to Program 6e</asp:ListItem>
 71              <asp:ListItem>C++ How to Program 5e</asp:ListItem>
 72              <asp:ListItem>XML How to Program 1e</asp:ListItem>
 73          </asp:DropDownList>
 74          </p>
 75          <p>
 76              <asp:HyperLink ID="booksHyperLink" runat="server"
 77                  EnableViewState="False" NavigateUrl="http://www.deitel.com"
 78                  Target="_blank">
 79                  Click here to view more information about our books
 80          </asp:HyperLink>
 81          </p>
 82          <p>
 83              <asp:Image ID="osImage" runat="server" EnableViewState="False"
 84                  ImageUrl="~/Images/os.png" />  
 85              <span style="color: teal">
 86                  Which operating system are you using?</span>
 87          </p>
 88          <p>
 89              <asp:RadioButtonList ID="operatingSystemRadioButtonList"
 90                  runat="server" EnableViewState="False">
 91              <asp:ListItem>Windows XP</asp:ListItem>
 92              <asp:ListItem>Windows 2000</asp:ListItem>
 93              <asp:ListItem>Windows NT</asp:ListItem>
 94              <asp:ListItem>Linux</asp:ListItem>
 95              <asp:ListItem>Other</asp:ListItem>
 96          </asp:RadioButtonList>
 97          </p>
 98          <p>
 99              <asp:Button ID="registerButton" runat="server"
100                  EnableViewState="False" Text="Register" />
101          </p>
102      </div>
103      </form>
104  </body>
105  </html>
```

Fig. 21.16 | Web Form that demonstrates Web controls. (Part 2 of 3.)

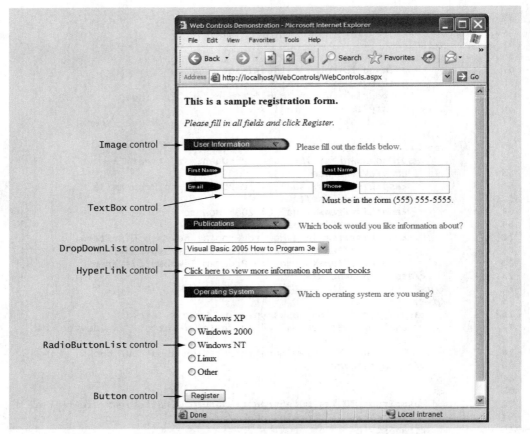

Fig. 21.16 | Web Form that demonstrates Web controls. (Part 3 of 3.)

Setting the Color of Text on a Web Form

Notice that some of the instructions to the user on the form appear in a teal color. To set the color of a specific piece of text, highlight the text and select **Format > Foreground color...**. In the **Color Picker** dialog, click the **Named Colors** tab and choose a color. Click **OK** to apply the color. Note that the IDE places the colored text in an XHTML span element (e.g., lines 22–23) and applies the color using the span's style attribute.

Examining Web Controls on a Sample Registration Form

Lines 20–21 of Fig. 21.16 define an *Image* control, which inserts an image into a Web page. The images used in this example are located in the chapter's examples directory. You can download the examples from www.deitel.com/books/vbforprogrammers2. Before an image can be displayed on a Web page using an Image Web control, the image must first be added to the project. We added an Images folder to this project (and to each example project in the chapter that uses images) by right clicking the location of the project in the **Solution Explorer**, selecting **New Folder** and entering the folder name Images. We then added each of the images used in the example to this folder by right clicking the folder, selecting **Add Existing Item...** and browsing for the files to add. You can also drag a folder full of images onto the project's location in the **Solution Explorer** to add the folder and all the images to the project.

The *ImageUrl* property (line 21) specifies the location of the image to display in the Image control. To select an image, click the ellipsis next to the ImageUrl property in the **Properties** window and use the **Select Image** dialog to browse for the desired image in the project's Images folder. When the IDE fills in the ImageUrl property based on your selection, it includes a tilde and forward slash (~/) at the beginning of the ImageUrl—this indicates that the Images folder is in the root directory of the project (i.e., http://localhost/WebControls, whose physical path is C:\Inetpub\wwwroot\WebControls).

Lines 25–55 contain the table element created by the steps discussed previously. Each td element contains an Image control and a *TextBox* control, which allows you to obtain text from the user and display text to the user. For example, lines 30–31 define a TextBox control used to collect the user's first name.

Lines 64–73 define a *DropDownList*. This control is similar to the Windows ComboBox control. When a user clicks the drop-down list, it expands and displays a list from which the user can make a selection. Each item in the drop-down list is defined by a *ListItem* element (lines 66–72). After dragging a DropDownList control onto a Web Form, you can add items to it using the **ListItem Collection Editor**. This process is similar to customizing a ListBox in a Windows application. In Visual Web Developer, you can access the **ListItem Collection Editor** by clicking the ellipsis next to the Items property of the DropDownList, or by using the **DropDownList Tasks** menu. You can open this menu by clicking the small arrowhead that appears in the upper-right corner of the control in **Design** mode (Fig. 21.17). This menu is called a *smart tag menu*. Visual Web Developer displays smart tag menus for many ASP.NET controls to facilitate common tasks. Clicking **Edit Items...** in the **DropDownList Tasks** menu opens the **ListItem Collection Editor**, which allows you to add ListItem elements to the DropDownList.

The *HyperLink* control (lines 76–80 of Fig. 21.16) adds a hyperlink to a Web page. The *NavigateUrl* property (line 77) of this control specifies the resource (i.e., http://www.deitel.com) that is requested when a user clicks the hyperlink. Setting the *Target* property to _blank specifies that the requested Web page should open in a new browser window. By default, HyperLink controls cause pages to open in the same browser window.

Lines 89–96 define a *RadioButtonList* control, which provides a series of radio buttons from which the user can select only one. Like options in a DropDownList, individual radio buttons are defined by ListItem elements. Note that, like the **DropDownList Tasks** smart tag menu, the **RadioButtonList Tasks** smart tag menu also provides an **Edit Items...** link to open the **ListItem Collection Editor**.

The final Web control in Fig. 21.16 is a *Button* (lines 99–100). A Button Web control represents a button that triggers an action when clicked. This control typically maps

Fig. 21.17 | **DropDownList Tasks** smart tag menu.

to an XHTML `input` element with attribute `type` set to `"button"`. As stated earlier, clicking the **Register** button in this example does not do anything.

21.5.2 AdRotator Control

Web pages often contain product or service advertisements, which usually consist of images. Although Web site authors want to include as many sponsors as possible, Web pages can display only a limited number of advertisements. To address this problem, ASP.NET provides the *AdRotator* Web control for displaying advertisements. Using advertisement data located in an XML file, an `AdRotator` randomly selects an image to display and generates a hyperlink to the Web page associated with that image. Browsers that do not support images display alternate text that is specified in the XML document. If a user clicks the image or substituted text, the browser loads the Web page associated with that image.

Demonstrating the AdRotator Web Control

Figure 21.18 demonstrates the `AdRotator` Web control. In this example, the "advertisements" that we rotate are the flags of 10 countries. When a user clicks the displayed flag image, the browser is redirected to a Web page containing information about the country that the flag represents. If a user refreshes the browser or requests the page again, one of the eleven flags is again chosen at random and displayed.

The ASPX file in Fig. 21.18 is similar to that in Fig. 21.4. However, instead of XHTML text and a `Label`, this page contains XHTML text (the `h3` element in line 17) and an `AdRotator` control named `countryRotator` (lines 18–19). This page also contains an `XmlDataSource` control (lines 20–22), which supplies the data to the `AdRotator` control. The `background` attribute of the page's body element (line 13) is set to the image `background.png`, located in the project's `Images` folder. To specify this file, click the ellipsis provided next to the `Background` property of `DOCUMENT` in the **Properties** window and use the resulting dialog to select `background.png` from the `Images` folder. The images and XML file used in this example are both located in the chapter's examples directory.

```
1   <%-- Fig. 21.18: FlagRotator.aspx --%>
2   <%-- A Web Form that displays flags using an AdRotator control. --%>
3   <%@ Page Language="VB" AutoEventWireup="false"
4      CodeFile="FlagRotator.aspx.vb" Inherits="FlagRotator" %>
5
6   <!DOCTYPE html PUBLIC "-//W3C//DTD XHTML 1.0 Transitional//EN"
7      "http://www.w3.org/TR/xhtml1/DTD/xhtml1-transitional.dtd">
8
9   <html xmlns="http://www.w3.org/1999/xhtml" >
10  <head runat="server">
11     <title>Flag Rotator</title>
12  </head>
13  <body background="Images/background.png">
14     <form id="form1" runat="server">
15     <div>
16        <h3>AdRotator Example</h3>
17        <p>
```

Fig. 21.18 | Web Form that demonstrates the `AdRotator` Web control. (Part 1 of 2.)

```
18            <asp:AdRotator ID="countryRotator" runat="server"
19               DataSourceID="adXmlDataSource" />
20            <asp:XmlDataSource ID="adXmlDataSource" runat="server"
21               DataFile="~/App_Data/AdRotatorInformation.xml">
22            </asp:XmlDataSource>
23         </p>
24      </div>
25      </form>
26   </body>
27   </html>
```

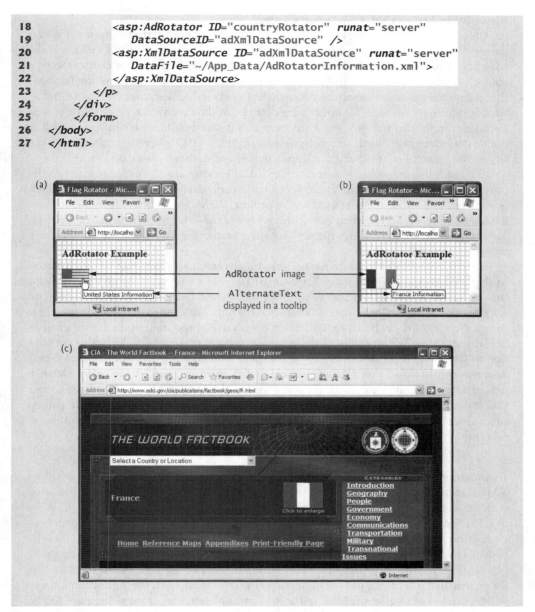

AdRotator image

AlternateText
displayed in a tooltip

Fig. 21.18 | Web Form that demonstrates the AdRotator Web control. (Part 2 of 2.)

You do not need to add any code to the code-behind file, because the AdRotator control "does all the work." The output depicts two different requests. Figure 21.18(a) shows the first time the page is requested, when the American flag is shown. In the second request, as shown in Fig. 21.18(b), the French flag is displayed. Figure 21.18(c) depicts the Web page that loads when the French flag is clicked.

Connecting Data to an AdRotator Control

An AdRotator control accesses an XML file (presented shortly) to determine what advertisement (i.e., flag) image, hyperlink URL and alternate text to display and include in the page. To connect the AdRotator control to the XML file, we create an *XmlDataSource* control—one of several ASP.NET data controls (found in the **Data** section of the **Toolbox**) that encapsulate data sources and make such data available for Web controls. An XmlDataSource references an XML file containing data that will be used in an ASP.NET application. Later in the chapter, you will learn more about data-bound Web controls, as well as the SqlDataSource control, which retrieves data from a SQL Server database, and the ObjectDataSource control, which encapsulates an object that makes data available.

To build this example, we first add the XML file AdRotatorInformation.xml to the project. Each project created in Visual Web Developer contains an App_Data folder, which is intended to store all the data used by the project. Right click this folder in the **Solution Explorer** and select **Add Existing Item...**, then browse for AdRotatorInformation.xml on your computer. We provide this file in the chapter's examples directory in the subdirectory named exampleXMLFiles.

After adding the XML file to the project, drag an AdRotator control from the **Toolbox** to the Web Form. The **AdRotator Tasks** smart tag menu will open automatically. From this menu, select **<New Data Source...>** from the **Choose Data Source** drop-down list to start the **Data Source Configuration Wizard**. Select **XML File** as the data-source type. This causes the wizard to create an XmlDataSource with the ID specified in the bottom half of the wizard dialog. We set the ID of the control to adXmlDataSource. Click **OK** in the **Data Source Configuration Wizard** dialog. The **Configure Data Source - adXmlDataSource** dialog appears next. In this dialog's **Data File** section, click **Browse...** and, in the **Select XML File** dialog, locate and select the XML file you added to the App_Data folder. Click **OK** to exit this dialog, then click **OK** to exit the **Configure Data Source - adXmlDataSource** dialog. After completing these steps, the AdRotator is configured to use the XML file to determine which advertisements to display.

Examining an XML File Containing Advertisement Information

XML document AdRotatorInformation.xml (Fig. 21.19)—or any XML document used with an AdRotator control—must contain one *Advertisements* root element (lines 4–94). Within that element can be several *Ad* elements (e.g., lines 5–12), each of which provides information about a different advertisement. Element *ImageUrl* (line 6) specifies the path (location) of the advertisement's image, and element *NavigateUrl* (lines 7–9) specifies the URL for the Web page that loads when a user clicks the advertisement. Note that we reformatted this file for presentation purposes. The actual XML file cannot contain any whitespace before or after the URL in the NavigateUrl element, or the whitespace will be considered part of the URL, and the page will not load properly.

The *AlternateText* element (line 10) nested in each Ad element contains text that displays in place of the image when the browser cannot locate or render the image for some reason (i.e., the file is missing, or the browser is not capable of displaying it), or to assist the visually impaired. The AlternateText element's text is also a tooltip that Internet Explorer displays when a user places the mouse pointer over the image (Fig. 21.18). The *Impressions* element (line 56) specifies how often a particular image appears, relative to the other images. An advertisement that has a higher Impressions value displays more frequently than an advertisement with a lower value. In our example, the advertisements display with equal probability, because the value of each Impressions element is set to 1.

```xml
1   <?xml version="1.0" encoding="utf-8"?>
2   <!-- Fig. 21.19: AdRotatorInformation.xml -->
3   <!-- XML file containing advertisement information. -->
4   <Advertisements>
5      <Ad>
6         <ImageUrl>Images/france.png</ImageUrl>
7         <NavigateUrl>
8            http://www.odci.gov/cia/publications/factbook/geos/fr.html
9         </NavigateUrl>
10        <AlternateText>France Information</AlternateText>
11        <Impressions>1</Impressions>
12     </Ad>
13
14     <Ad>
15        <ImageUrl>Images/germany.png</ImageUrl>
16        <NavigateUrl>
17           http://www.odci.gov/cia/publications/factbook/geos/gm.html
18        </NavigateUrl>
19        <AlternateText>Germany Information</AlternateText>
20        <Impressions>1</Impressions>
21     </Ad>
22
23     <Ad>
24        <ImageUrl>Images/italy.png</ImageUrl>
25        <NavigateUrl>
26           http://www.odci.gov/cia/publications/factbook/geos/it.html
27        </NavigateUrl>
28        <AlternateText>Italy Information</AlternateText>
29        <Impressions>1</Impressions>
30     </Ad>
31
32     <Ad>
33        <ImageUrl>Images/spain.png</ImageUrl>
34        <NavigateUrl>
35           http://www.odci.gov/cia/publications/factbook/geos/sp.html
36        </NavigateUrl>
37        <AlternateText>Spain Information</AlternateText>
38        <Impressions>1</Impressions>
39     </Ad>
40
41     <Ad>
42        <ImageUrl>Images/latvia.png</ImageUrl>
43        <NavigateUrl>
44           http://www.odci.gov/cia/publications/factbook/geos/lg.html
45        </NavigateUrl>
46        <AlternateText>Latvia Information</AlternateText>
47        <Impressions>1</Impressions>
48     </Ad>
```

Fig. 21.19 | XML file containing advertisement information used in AdRotator example. (Part 1 of 2.)

```
49
50     <Ad>
51        <ImageUrl>Images/peru.png</ImageUrl>
52        <NavigateUrl>
53           http://www.odci.gov/cia/publications/factbook/geos/pe.html
54        </NavigateUrl>
55        <AlternateText>Peru Information</AlternateText>
56        <Impressions>1</Impressions>
57     </Ad>
58
59     <Ad>
60        <ImageUrl>Images/senegal.png</ImageUrl>
61        <NavigateUrl>
62           http://www.odci.gov/cia/publications/factbook/geos/sg.html
63        </NavigateUrl>
64        <AlternateText>Senegal Information</AlternateText>
65        <Impressions>1</Impressions>
66     </Ad>
67
68     <Ad>
69        <ImageUrl>Images/sweden.png</ImageUrl>
70        <NavigateUrl>
71           http://www.odci.gov/cia/publications/factbook/geos/sw.html
72        </NavigateUrl>
73        <AlternateText>Sweden Information</AlternateText>
74        <Impressions>1</Impressions>
75     </Ad>
76
77     <Ad>
78        <ImageUrl>Images/thailand.png</ImageUrl>
79        <NavigateUrl>
80           http://www.odci.gov/cia/publications/factbook/geos/th.html
81        </NavigateUrl>
82        <AlternateText>Thailand Information</AlternateText>
83        <Impressions>1</Impressions>
84     </Ad>
85
86     <Ad>
87        <ImageUrl>Images/unitedstates.png</ImageUrl>
88        <NavigateUrl>
89           http://www.odci.gov/cia/publications/factbook/geos/us.html
90        </NavigateUrl>
91        <AlternateText>United States Information</AlternateText>
92        <Impressions>1</Impressions>
93     </Ad>
94  </Advertisements>
```

Fig. 21.19 | XML file containing advertisement information used in `AdRotator` example. (Part 2 of 2.)

21.5.3 Validation Controls

This section introduces a different type of Web control, called a *validation control* (or *validator)*, which determines whether the data in another Web control is in the proper format. For example, validators could determine whether a user has provided information in a required field or whether a ZIP-code field contains exactly five digits. Validators provide a mechanism for validating user input on the client. When the XHTML for our page is created, the validator is converted into *ECMAScript*[1] that performs the validation. ECMAScript is a scripting language that enhances the functionality and appearance of Web pages and is typically executed on the client. However, some clients do not support scripting or disable scripting. So, for security reasons, validation is always performed on the server—whether or not scripting is enabled on the client.

Validating Input in a Web Form

The example in this section prompts the user to enter a name, e-mail address and phone number. A Web site could use a form like this to collect contact information from site visitors. After the user enters any data, but before the data is sent to the Web server, validators ensure that the user entered a value in each field and that the e-mail address and phone number values are in an acceptable format. In this example, (555) 123-4567, 555-123-4567 and 123-4567 are all considered valid phone numbers. Once the data is submitted, the Web server responds by displaying an appropriate message and an XHTML table repeating the submitted information. Note that a real business application would typically store the submitted data in a database or in a file on the server. We simply send the data back to the form to demonstrate that the server received the data.

Figure 21.20 presents the ASPX file. Like the Web Form in Fig. 21.16, this Web Form uses a `table` to organize the page's contents. Lines 24–25, 36–37 and 58–59 define `TextBox`es for retrieving the user's name, e-mail address and phone number, respectively, and line 78 defines a **Submit** button. Lines 80–82 create a `Label` named `outputLabel` that displays the response from the server when the user successfully submits the form. Notice that `outputLabel`'s *Visible* property is initially set to `False` (line 81), so the `Label` does not appear in the client's browser when the page loads for the first time.

Using RequiredFieldValidator Controls

In this example, we use three *RequiredFieldValidator* controls (found in the **Validation** section of the **Toolbox**) to ensure that the name, e-mail address and phone number `TextBox`es are not empty when the form is submitted. A `RequiredFieldValidator` makes an input control a required field. If such a field is empty, validation fails. For example, lines 26–30 define `RequiredFieldValidator nameInputValidator`, which confirms that `nameTextBox` is not empty. Line 28 associates `nameTextBox` with `nameInputValidator` by setting the validator's *ControlToValidate* property to `nameTextBox`. This indicates that `nameInputValidator` verifies the `nameTextBox`'s contents. We set the value of this property (and the validator's other properties) by selecting the validator in **Design** mode and using the **Properties** window to specify property values. Property *ErrorMessage*'s text (line 29) is displayed on the Web Form if the validation fails. If the user does not input any data in `nameTextBox` and attempts to submit the form, the `ErrorMessage` text is displayed in

---

1. ECMAScript (commonly known as JavaScript) is a scripting standard developed by ECMA International. Both Netscape's JavaScript and Microsoft's JScript implement the ECMAScript standard, but each provides additional features beyond the specification. For information on the current ECMAScript standard, visit www.ecma-international.org/publications/standards/Ecma-262.htm. See www.mozilla.org/js for information on JavaScript and msdn.microsoft.com/library/en-us/script56/html/js56jsoriJScript.asp for information on JScript.

red. Because we set the validator's *Display* property to Dynamic (line 28), the validator is displayed on the Web Form only when validation fails. Space is allocated dynamically when validation fails, causing the controls below the validator to shift downward to accommodate the ErrorMessage, as seen in Fig. 21.20(a)–(c).

Using RegularExpressionValidator Controls

This example also uses *RegularExpressionValidator* controls to match the e-mail address and phone number entered by the user against regular expressions. (Regular expressions are introduced in Chapter 16.) These controls determine whether the e-mail address and phone number were each entered in a valid format. For example, lines 44–51 create a RegularExpressionValidator named emailFormatValidator. Line 46 sets property ControlToValidate to emailTextBox to indicate that emailFormatValidator verifies the emailTextBox's contents.

```
1   <%-- Fig. 21.20: Validation.aspx --%>
2   <%-- Form that demonstrates using validators to validate user input. --%>
3   <%@ Page Language="VB" AutoEventWireup="false"
4      CodeFile="Validation.aspx.vb" Inherits="Validation" %>
5
6   <!DOCTYPE html PUBLIC "-//W3C//DTD XHTML 1.0 Transitional//EN"
7      "http://www.w3.org/TR/xhtml1/DTD/xhtml1-transitional.dtd">
8
9   <html xmlns="http://www.w3.org/1999/xhtml" >
10  <head runat="server">
11     <title>Demonstrating Validation Controls</title>
12  </head>
13  <body>
14     <form id="form1" runat="server">
15     <div>
16        Please fill out the following form.<br /><em>All fields are
17        required and must contain valid information.</em><br />
18        <br />
19        <table>
20           <tr>
21              <td style="width: 100px" valign="top">
22                 Name:</td>
23              <td style="width: 450px" valign="top">
24                 <asp:TextBox ID="nameTextBox" runat="server">
25                 </asp:TextBox><br />
26                 <asp:RequiredFieldValidator
27                    ID="nameInputValidator" runat="server"
28                    ControlToValidate="nameTextBox" Display="Dynamic"
29                    ErrorMessage="Please enter your name.">
30                 </asp:RequiredFieldValidator>
31              </td>
32           </tr>
33           <tr>
34              <td style="width: 100px" valign="top">E-mail address:</td>
35              <td style="width: 450px" valign="top">
```

Fig. 21.20 | Validators used in a Web Form that retrieves user's contact information. (Part 1 of 4.)

```
36                    <asp:TextBox ID="emailTextBox" runat="server">
37                    </asp:TextBox>
38                     e.g., user@domain.com<br />
39                    <asp:RequiredFieldValidator
40                       ID="emailInputValidator" runat="server"
41                       ControlToValidate="emailTextBox" Display="Dynamic"
42                       ErrorMessage="Please enter your e-mail address.">
43                    </asp:RequiredFieldValidator>
44                    <asp:RegularExpressionValidator
45                       ID="emailFormatValidator" runat="server"
46                       ControlToValidate="emailTextBox" Display="Dynamic"
47                       ErrorMessage=
48                          "Please enter an e-mail address in a valid format."
49                       ValidationExpression=
50                          "\w+([-+.']\w+)*@\w+([-.]\w+)*\.\w+([-.]\w+)*">
51                    </asp:RegularExpressionValidator>
52                 </td>
53              </tr>
54              <tr>
55                 <td style="width: 100px; height: 21px" valign="top">
56                    Phone number:</td>
57                 <td style="width: 450px; height: 21px" valign="top">
58                    <asp:TextBox ID="phoneTextBox" runat="server">
59                    </asp:TextBox>
60                     e.g., (555) 555-1234<br />
61                    <asp:RequiredFieldValidator
62                       ID="phoneInputValidator" runat="server"
63                       ControlToValidate="phoneTextBox" Display="Dynamic"
64                       ErrorMessage="Please enter your phone number.">
65                    </asp:RequiredFieldValidator>
66                    <asp:RegularExpressionValidator
67                       ID="phoneFormatValidator" runat="server"
68                       ControlToValidate="phoneTextBox" Display="Dynamic"
69                       ErrorMessage=
70                          "Please enter a phone number in a valid format."
71                       ValidationExpression=
72                          "((\(\d{3}\) ?)|(\d{3}-))?\d{3}-\d{4}">
73                    </asp:RegularExpressionValidator>
74                 </td>
75              </tr>
76           </table>
77           <br />
78           <asp:Button ID="submitButton" runat="server" Text="Submit" /><br />
79           <br />
80           <asp:Label ID="outputLabel" runat="server"
81              Text="Thank you for your submission." Visible="False">
82           </asp:Label>
83        </div>
84     </form>
85  </body>
86  </html>
```

Fig. 21.20 | Validators used in a Web Form that retrieves user's contact information. (Part 2 of 4.)

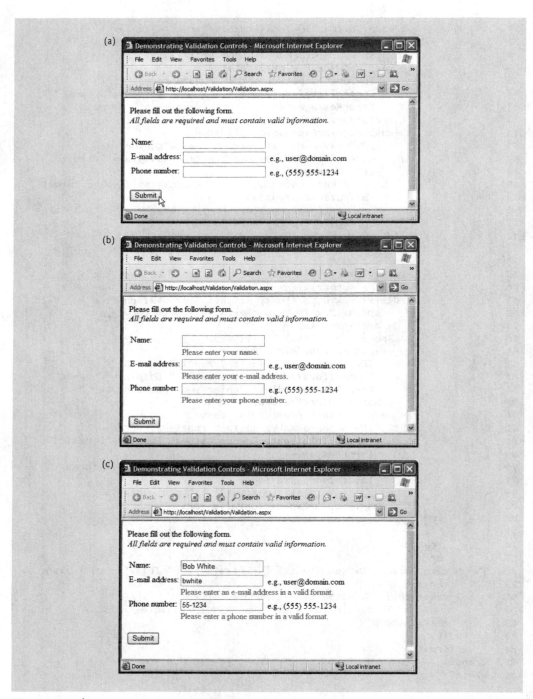

Fig. 21.20 | Validators used in a Web Form that retrieves user's contact information. (Part 3 of 4.)

Fig. 21.20 | Validators used in a Web Form that retrieves user's contact information. (Part 4 of 4.)

A RegularExpressionValidator's ***ValidationExpression*** property specifies the regular expression that validates the ControlToValidate's contents. Clicking the ellipsis next to property ValidationExpression in the **Properties** window displays the **Regular Expression Editor** dialog, which contains a list of **Standard expressions** for phone numbers, ZIP codes and other formatted information. You can also write your own custom expression. For the emailFormatValidator, we selected the standard expression **Internet e-mail address**, which uses the validation expression

```
\w+([-+.']\w+)*@\w+([-.]\w+)*\.\w+([-.]\w+)*
```

This regular expression indicates that an e-mail address is valid if the part of the address before the @ symbol contains one or more word characters (i.e., alphanumeric characters or underscores), followed by zero or more strings comprised of a hyphen, plus sign, period or apostrophe and additional word characters. After the @ symbol, a valid e-mail address must contain one or more groups of word characters potentially separated by hyphens or periods, followed by a required period and another group of one or more word characters potentially separated by hyphens or periods. For example, bob.white@email.com, bob-white@my-email.com and bob's-personal.email@white.email.com are all valid e-mail addresses. If the user enters text in the emailTextBox that does not have the correct format and either clicks in a different text box or attempts to submit the form, the ErrorMessage text is displayed in red.

We also use RegularExpressionValidator phoneFormatValidator (lines 66–73) to ensure that the phoneTextBox contains a valid phone number before the form is submitted. In the **Regular Expression Editor** dialog, we select **U.S. phone number**, which assigns

$$((\backslash(\backslash d\{3\}\backslash) \ ?)|(\backslash d\{3\}-))?\backslash d\{3\}-\backslash d\{4\}$$

to the ValidationExpression property. This expression indicates that a phone number can contain a three-digit area code either in parentheses and followed by an optional space or without parentheses and followed by required hyphen. After an optional area code, a phone number must contain three digits, a hyphen and another four digits. For example, (555) 123-4567, 555-123-4567 and 123-4567 are all valid phone numbers.

If all five validators are successful (i.e., each TextBox is filled in, and the e-mail address and phone number provided are valid), clicking the **Submit** button sends the form's data to the server. As shown in Fig. 21.20(d), the server then responds by displaying the submitted data in the outputLabel (lines 80–82).

Examining the Code-Behind File for a Web Form That Receives User Input
Figure 21.21 depicts the code-behind file for the ASPX file in Fig. 21.20. Notice that this code-behind file does not contain any implementation related to the validators. We say more about this soon.

Web programmers using ASP.NET often design their Web pages so that the current page reloads when the user submits the form; this enables the program to receive input, process it as necessary and display the results in the same page when it is loaded the second time. These pages usually contain a form that when submitted, sends the values of all the controls to the server and causes the current page to be requested again. This event is

```vb
1   ' Fig. 21.21: Validation.aspx.vb
2   ' Code-behind file for the form demonstrating validation controls.
3   Partial Class Validation
4      Inherits System.Web.UI.Page
5
6      ' Page_Load event handler executes when the page is loaded
7      Protected Sub Page_Load(ByVal sender As Object, _
8         ByVal e As System.EventArgs) Handles Me.Load
9         ' if this is not the first time the page is loading
10        ' (i.e., the user has already submitted form data)
11        If IsPostBack Then
12           ' retrieve the values submitted by the user
13           Dim name As String = Request.Form("nameTextBox")
14           Dim email As String = Request.Form("emailTextBox")
15           Dim phone As String = Request.Form("phoneTextBox")
16
17           ' create a table indicating the submitted values
18           outputLabel.Text &= _
19              "<br />We received the following information:" & _
20              "<table style=""background-color: yellow"">" & _
21              "<tr><td>Name: </td><td>" & name & "</td></tr>" & _
22              "<tr><td>E-mail address: </td><td>" & email & "</td></tr>" & _
23              "<tr><td>Phone number: </td><td>" & phone & "</td></tr>" & _
24              "<table>"
25           outputLabel.Visible = True ' display the output message
26        End If
27     End Sub ' Page_Load
28  End Class ' Validation
```

Fig. 21.21 | Code-behind file for a Web Form that obtains a user's contact information.

known as a *postback*. Line 11 uses the ***IsPostBack*** property of class Page to determine whether the page is being loaded due to a postback. The first time that the Web page is requested, IsPostBack is False, and the page displays only the form for user input. When the postback occurs (from the user clicking **Submit**), IsPostBack is True.

Lines 13–15 use the ***Request*** object to retrieve the values of nameTextBox, email-TextBox and phoneTextBox from the NameValueCollection ***Form***. When data is posted to the Web server, the XHTML form's data is accessible to the Web application through the Request object's Form array. Lines 18–24 append to outputLabel's Text a line break, an additional message and an XHTML table containing the submitted data so the user knows that the server received the data correctly. In a real business application, the data would be stored in a database or file at this point in the application. Line 25 sets the outputLabel's Visible property to True, so the user can see the thank you message and submitted data.

Examining the Client-Side XHTML for a Web Form with Validation

Figure 21.22 shows the XHTML and ECMAScript sent to the client browser when Validation.aspx loads after the postback. (We added the comments in lines 1–2.) To view this code, select **View > Source** in Internet Explorer. Lines 27–55, lines 126–190 and lines 196–212 contain the ECMAScript that provides the implementation for the validation controls and for performing the postback. ASP.NET generates this ECMAScript. You do not need to be able to create or even understand ECMAScript—the functionality defined for the controls in our application is converted to working ECMAScript for us.

```
 1   <!-- Fig. 21.22 -->
 2   <!-- The XHTML and ECMAScript generated for Validation.aspx -->
 3   <!DOCTYPE html PUBLIC "-//W3C//DTD XHTML 1.0 Transitional//EN"
 4      "http://www.w3.org/TR/xhtml1/DTD/xhtml1-transitional.dtd">
 5   <html xmlns="http://www.w3.org/1999/xhtml" >
 6   <head>
 7   <title>Demonstrating Validation Controls</title>
 8   </head>
 9   <body>
10   <form name="form1" method="post" action="Validation.aspx"
11      onsubmit="javascript:return WebForm_OnSubmit();" id="form1">
12      <div>
13         <input type="hidden" name="__EVENTTARGET" id="__EVENTTARGET"
14            value="" />
15         <input type="hidden" name="__EVENTARGUMENT" id="__EVENTARGUMENT"
16            value="" />
17         <input type="hidden" name="__VIEWSTATE" id="__VIEWSTATE"
18            value="/wEPDwUJMzg4NDI1NzgzD2QWAgIDD2QWAgITDw8WBB4EVGV4dAWVA1RoY
19            W5rIH1vdSBmb3IgeW91ciBzdWJtaXNzaW9uLjxiciAvPld1IHJ1Y2VpdmVkIHRoZ
20            SBmb2xsb3dpbmcgaW5mb3JtYXRpb246PHRrYmx1IHN0eWx1PSJiYWNrZ3JvdW5kL
21            WNvbG9yOiB5ZWxsb3ciPjx0cj48dGQ+TmFtZTogPC90ZD48dGQ+Qm9iIFdoaXR1P
22            C90ZD48L3RyPjx0cj48dGQ+RS1tYW1sIGFkZHJ1c3M6IDwvdGQ+PHRkPmJ3aG10Z
23            ZUB1bWFpbC5jb208L3RkPjwvdHI+PHRyPjx0ZD5QaG9uZSBudW1iZXI6IDwvdGQ+
24            PHRkPig1NTUpIDU1NS0xMjM0PC90ZD48L3RyPjx0YWJsZT4eB1Zpc21ibGVnZGRk
25            qbjgKg1/1LZfogqihtkd1C7nmSk=" />
26      </div>
```

Fig. 21.22 | XHTML and ECMAScript generated by ASP.NET and sent to the browser when Validation.aspx is requested. (Part 1 of 5.)

```
27    <script type="text/javascript">
28    <!--
29    var theForm = document.forms['form1'];
30    if (!theForm) {
31       theForm = document.form1;
32    }
33    function __doPostBack(eventTarget, eventArgument) {
34       if (!theForm.onsubmit || (theForm.onsubmit() != false)) {
35          theForm.__EVENTTARGET.value = eventTarget;
36          theForm.__EVENTARGUMENT.value = eventArgument;
37          theForm.submit();
38       }
39    }
40    // -->
41    </script>
42    <script src="/Validation/WebResource.axd?d=g4BXOwpt2-OjwFwNi7BCNQ2
43       &amp;t=632670465355304640" type="text/javascript"></script>
44    <script src="/Validation/WebResource.axd?d=ZlFGPYdcOpaOPqraRf9s2PN8QeuH
45       PzQxnkR5mPVtAVcl&amp;t=632670465355304640"
46       type="text/javascript"></script>
47    <script type="text/javascript">
48    <!--
49    function WebForm_OnSubmit() {
50       if (typeof(ValidatorOnSubmit) == "function" &&
51          ValidatorOnSubmit() == false) return false;
52       return true;
53    }
54    // -->
55    </script>
56    <div>
57       Please fill out the following form.<br />
58       <em>All fields are required and must contain valid information.
59       </em><br />
60       <br />
61       <table>
62          <tr>
63             <td style="width: 100px" valign="top"> Name:</td>
64             <td style="width: 450px" valign="top">
65                <input name="nameTextBox" type="text" value="Bob White"
66                   id="nameTextBox" />
67                <br />
68                <span id="nameInputValidator"
69                   style="color:Red;display:none;">
70                   Please enter your name.</span> </td>
71          </tr>
72          <tr>
73             <td style="width: 100px" valign="top">E-mail address:</td>
74             <td style="width: 450px" valign="top">
75                <input name="emailTextBox" type="text"
76                   value="bwhite@email.com" id="emailTextBox" />
77                 e.g., user@domain.com<br />
```

Fig. 21.22 | XHTML and ECMAScript generated by ASP.NET and sent to the browser when `Validation.aspx` is requested. (Part 2 of 5.)

```
78                    <span id="emailInputValidator"
79                        style="color:Red;display:none;">
80                        Please enter your e-mail address.</span>
81                    <span id="emailFormatValidator"
82                        style="color:Red;display:none;">Please enter an e-mail
83                        address in a valid format.</span> </td>
84            </tr>
85            <tr>
86                <td style="width: 100px; height: 21px" valign="top">
87                    Phone number:</td>
88                <td style="width: 450px; height: 21px" valign="top">
89                    <input name="phoneTextBox" type="text"
90                        value="(555) 555-1234" id="phoneTextBox" />
91                     e.g., (555) 555-1234<br />
92                    <span id="phoneInputValidator"
93                        style="color:Red;display:none;">
94                        Please enter your phone number.</span>
95                    <span id="phoneFormatValidator"
96                        style="color:Red;display:none;">Please enter a phone
97                        number in a valid format.</span> </td>
98            </tr>
99        </table>
100       <br />
101       <input type="submit" name="submitButton" value="Submit"
102           onclick="javascript:WebForm_DoPostBackWithOptions(
103               new WebForm_PostBackOptions(&quot;submitButton&quot;,
104               &quot;&quot;, true, &quot;&quot;, &quot;&quot;, false,
105               false))" id="submitButton" />
106       <br />
107       <br />
108       <span id="outputLabel">Thank you for your submission.<br />
109           We received the following information:
110           <table style="background-color: yellow">
111               <tr>
112                   <td>Name: </td>
113                   <td>Bob White</td>
114               </tr>
115               <tr>
116                   <td>E-mail address: </td>
117                   <td>bwhite@email.com</td>
118               </tr>
119               <tr>
120                   <td>Phone number: </td>
121                   <td>(555) 555-1234</td>
122               </tr>
123           <table>
124       </span>
125   </div>
126   <script type="text/javascript">
127   <!--
```

Fig. 21.22 | XHTML and ECMAScript generated by ASP.NET and sent to the browser when `Validation.aspx` is requested. (Part 3 of 5.)

```
128        var Page_Validators = new Array(
129            document.getElementById("nameInputValidator"),
130            document.getElementById("emailInputValidator"),
131            document.getElementById("emailFormatValidator"),
132            document.getElementById("phoneInputValidator"),
133            document.getElementById("phoneFormatValidator"));
134    // -->
135    </script>
136    <script type="text/javascript">
137    <!--
138        var nameInputValidator = document.all ?
139            document.all["nameInputValidator"] :
140            document.getElementById("nameInputValidator");
141        nameInputValidator.controltovalidate = "nameTextBox";
142        nameInputValidator.errormessage = "Please enter your name.";
143        nameInputValidator.display = "Dynamic";
144        nameInputValidator.evaluationfunction =
145            "RequiredFieldValidatorEvaluateIsValid";
146        nameInputValidator.initialvalue = "";
147        var emailInputValidator = document.all ?
148            document.all["emailInputValidator"] :
149            document.getElementById("emailInputValidator");
150        emailInputValidator.controltovalidate = "emailTextBox";
151        emailInputValidator.errormessage =
152            "Please enter your e-mail address.";
153        emailInputValidator.display = "Dynamic";
154        emailInputValidator.evaluationfunction =
155            "RequiredFieldValidatorEvaluateIsValid";
156        emailInputValidator.initialvalue = "";
157        var emailFormatValidator = document.all ?
158            document.all["emailFormatValidator"] :
159            document.getElementById("emailFormatValidator");
160        emailFormatValidator.controltovalidate = "emailTextBox";
161        emailFormatValidator.errormessage =
162            "Please enter an e-mail address in a valid format.";
163        emailFormatValidator.display = "Dynamic";
164        emailFormatValidator.evaluationfunction =
165            "RegularExpressionValidatorEvaluateIsValid";
166        emailFormatValidator.validationexpression =
167            "\\w+([-+.\\']\\w+)*@\\w+([-.]\\w+)*\\.\\w+([-.]\\w+)*";
168        var phoneInputValidator = document.all ?
169            document.all["phoneInputValidator"] :
170            document.getElementById("phoneInputValidator");
171        phoneInputValidator.controltovalidate = "phoneTextBox";
172        phoneInputValidator.errormessage =
173            "Please enter your phone number.";
174        phoneInputValidator.display = "Dynamic";
175        phoneInputValidator.evaluationfunction =
176            "RequiredFieldValidatorEvaluateIsValid";
177        phoneInputValidator.initialvalue = "";
```

Fig. 21.22 | XHTML and ECMAScript generated by ASP.NET and sent to the browser when `Validation.aspx` is requested. (Part 4 of 5.)

```
178        var phoneFormatValidator = document.all ?
179            document.all["phoneFormatValidator"] :
180            document.getElementById("phoneFormatValidator");
181        phoneFormatValidator.controltovalidate = "phoneTextBox";
182        phoneFormatValidator.errormessage =
183            "Please enter a phone number in a valid format.";
184        phoneFormatValidator.display = "Dynamic";
185        phoneFormatValidator.evaluationfunction =
186            "RegularExpressionValidatorEvaluateIsValid";
187        phoneFormatValidator.validationexpression =
188            "((\\(\\d{3}\\) ?)|(\\d{3}-))?\\d{3}-\\d{4}";
189    // -->
190    </script>
191    <div>
192        <input type="hidden" name="__EVENTVALIDATION" id="__EVENTVALIDATION"
193            value="/wEWBQL6jZCbCAKLsYSOBwKCkfPgDAKE8IO1CQKSuuDUCOeNO370TaQqZQ
194            OWPApDOKktGC5N" />
195    </div>
196    <script type="text/javascript">
197    <!--
198        var Page_ValidationActive = false;
199        if (typeof(ValidatorOnLoad) == "function") {
200            ValidatorOnLoad();
201        }
202
203        function ValidatorOnSubmit() {
204            if (Page_ValidationActive) {
205                return ValidatorCommonOnSubmit();
206            }
207            else {
208                return true;
209            }
210        }
211    // -->
212    </script>
213    </form>
214    </body>
215    </html>
```

Fig. 21.22 | XHTML and ECMAScript generated by ASP.NET and sent to the browser when Validation.aspx is requested. (Part 5 of 5.)

The EnableViewState attribute determines whether a Web control's value is retained when a postback occurs. Previously, we explicitly set this attribute to False. The default value, True, indicates that the control's value is retained. In Fig. 21.20(d), notice that the user input is retained after the postback occurs. A hidden input in the XHTML document (lines 17–25 of Fig. 21.22) contains the data of the controls on this page. This element is always named __*VIEWSTATE* and stores the controls' data as an encoded string.

Performance Tip 21.1

Setting EnableViewState to False reduces the amount of data passed to the Web server with each request.

21.6 Session Tracking

Originally, critics accused the Internet and e-business of failing to provide the kind of customized service typically experienced in "brick-and-mortar" stores. To address this problem, e-businesses began to establish mechanisms by which they could personalize users' browsing experiences, tailoring content to individual users while enabling them to bypass irrelevant information. Businesses achieve this level of service by tracking each customer's movement through the Internet and combining the collected data with information provided by the consumer, including billing information, personal preferences, interests and hobbies.

Personalization

Personalization makes it possible for e-businesses to communicate effectively with their customers and also improves users' ability to locate desired products and services. Companies that provide content of particular interest to users can establish relationships with customers and build on those relationships over time. Furthermore, by targeting consumers with personal offers, recommendations, advertisements, promotions and services, e-businesses create customer loyalty. Web sites can use sophisticated technology to allow visitors to customize home pages to suit their individual needs and preferences. Similarly, online shopping sites often store personal information for customers, tailoring notifications and special offers to their interests. Such services encourage customers to visit sites more frequently and make purchases more regularly.

Privacy

A trade-off exists, however, between personalized e-business service and protection of privacy. Some consumers embrace the idea of tailored content, but others fear the possible adverse consequences if the info they provide to e-businesses is released or collected by tracking technologies. Consumers and privacy advocates ask: What if the e-business to which we give personal data sells or gives that information to another organization without our knowledge? What if we do not want our actions on the Internet—a supposedly anonymous medium—to be tracked and recorded by unknown parties? What if unauthorized parties gain access to sensitive private data, such as credit-card numbers or medical history? All of these are questions that must be debated and addressed by programmers, consumers, e-businesses and lawmakers alike.

Recognizing Clients

To provide personalized services to consumers, e-businesses must be able to recognize clients when they request information from a site. As we have discussed, the request/response system on which the Web operates is facilitated by HTTP. Unfortunately, HTTP is a stateless protocol—it does not support persistent connections that would enable Web servers to maintain state information regarding particular clients. This means that Web servers cannot determine whether a request comes from a particular client or whether the same or different clients generate a series of requests. To circumvent this problem, sites can provide mechanisms by which they identify individual clients. A session represents a unique client on a Web site. If the client leaves a site and then returns later, the client will still be recognized as the same user. To help the server distinguish among clients, each client must identify itself to the server. Tracking individual clients, known as *session tracking*, can be achieved in a number of ways. One popular technique uses cookies (Section 21.6.1); another uses ASP.NET's HttpSessionState object (Section 21.6.2). Additional session-tracking techniques include the use of input form elements of type "hidden" and URL rewriting. Using "hidden" form elements, a Web Form can write session-tracking data into a form in the Web page that it returns to the client in response to a prior request. When the user submits the form in the new Web page, all the form data, including the "hidden" fields, is sent to the form handler on the Web server. When a Web site performs URL rewriting, the Web Form embeds session-tracking information directly in the URLs of hyperlinks that the user clicks to send subsequent requests to the Web server.

Note that our previous examples set the Web Form's EnableSessionState property to False. However, because we wish to use session tracking in the following examples, we keep this property's default setting—True.

21.6.1 Cookies

Cookies provide Web developers with a tool for personalizing Web pages. A cookie is a piece of data stored in a small text file on the user's computer. A cookie maintains information about the client during and between browser sessions. The first time a user visits the Web site, the user's computer might receive a cookie; this cookie is then reactivated each time the user revisits that site. The collected information is intended to be an anonymous record containing data that is used to personalize the user's future visits to the site. For example, cookies in a shopping application might store unique identifiers for users. When a user adds items to an online shopping cart or performs another task resulting in a request to the Web server, the server receives a cookie containing the user's unique identifier. The server then uses the unique identifier to locate the shopping cart and perform any necessary processing.

In addition to identifying users, cookies also can indicate users' shopping preferences. When a Web Form receives a request from a client, the Web Form can examine the cookie(s) it sent to the client during previous communications, identify the users's preferences and immediately display products of interest to the client.

Every HTTP-based interaction between a client and a server includes a header containing information either about the request (when the communication is from the client to the server) or about the response (when the communication is from the server to the client). When a Web Form receives a request, the header includes information such as the request type (e.g., Get) and any cookies that have been sent previously from the server to be stored on the client machine. When the server formulates its response, the header information contains any cookies the server wants to store on the client computer and other information, such as the MIME type of the response.

The *expiration date* of a cookie determines how long the cookie remains on the client's computer. If you do not set an expiration date for a cookie, the Web browser maintains the cookie for the duration of the browsing session. Otherwise, the Web browser maintains the cookie until the expiration date occurs. When the browser requests a resource from a Web server, cookies previously sent to the client by that Web server are returned to the Web server as part of the request formulated by the browser. Cookies are deleted when they *expire*.

Portability Tip 21.3

Users may disable cookies in their Web browsers to ensure that their privacy is protected. Such users will experience difficulty using Web applications that depend on cookies to maintain state information.

Using Cookies to Provide Book Recommendations

The next Web application demonstrates the use of cookies. The example contains two pages. In the first page (Figs. 21.23–21.24), users select a favorite programming language from a group of radio buttons and submit the XHTML form to the Web server for processing. The Web server responds by creating a cookie that stores a record of the chosen language, as well as the ISBN number for a book on that topic. The server then returns an XHTML document to the browser, allowing the user either to select another favorite programming language or to view the second page in our application (Figs. 21.25 and 21.26), which lists recommended books pertaining to the programming language that the user selected previously. When the user clicks the hyperlink, the cookies previously stored on the client are read and used to form the list of book recommendations.

The ASPX file in Fig. 21.23 contains five radio buttons (lines 20–26) with the values **Visual Basic 2005**, **Visual C# 2005**, **C**, **C++**, and **Java**. Recall that you can set the values of radio buttons via the **ListItem Collection Editor**, which you open either by clicking the RadioButtonList's **Items** property in the **Properties** window or by clicking the **Edit Items...** link in the **RadioButtonList Tasks** smart tag menu. The user selects a programming language by clicking one of the radio buttons. When the user clicks **Submit**, we'll create a cookie containing the selected language. Then, we'll add this cookie to the HTTP response header, so the cookie will be stored on the user's computer. Each time the user chooses a language and clicks **Submit**, a cookie is written to the client. Each time the client requests information from our Web application, the cookies are sent back to the server.

```
 1   <%-- Fig. 21.23: Options.aspx --%>
 2   <%-- Allows client to select programming languages and access --%>
 3   <%-- book recommendations. --%>
 4   <%@ Page Language="VB" AutoEventWireup="false"
 5      CodeFile="Options.aspx.vb" Inherits="Options" %>
 6
 7   <!DOCTYPE html PUBLIC "-//W3C//DTD XHTML 1.0 Transitional//EN"
 8      "http://www.w3.org/TR/xhtml1/DTD/xhtml1-transitional.dtd">
 9
10   <html xmlns="http://www.w3.org/1999/xhtml" >
11   <head runat="server">
12      <title>Cookies</title>
13   </head>
14   <body>
15    <form id="form1" runat="server">
16    <div>
17       <asp:Label ID="promptLabel" runat="server" Font-Bold="True"
18          Font-Size="Large" Text="Select a programming language:">
19       </asp:Label>
20       <asp:RadioButtonList ID="languageList" runat="server">
21          <asp:ListItem>Visual Basic 2005</asp:ListItem>
```

Fig. 21.23 | ASPX file that presents a list of programming languages. (Part 1 of 2.)

```
22            <asp:ListItem>Visual C# 2005</asp:ListItem>
23            <asp:ListItem>C</asp:ListItem>
24            <asp:ListItem>C++</asp:ListItem>
25            <asp:ListItem>Java</asp:ListItem>
26         </asp:RadioButtonList>
27         <asp:Button ID="submitButton" runat="server" Text="Submit" />
28         <asp:Label ID="responseLabel" runat="server" Font-Bold="True"
29            Font-Size="Large" Text="Welcome to cookies!" Visible="False">
30         </asp:Label><br />
31         <br />
32         <asp:HyperLink ID="languageLink" runat="server"
33            NavigateUrl="~/Options.aspx" Visible="False">
34            Click here to choose another language
35         </asp:HyperLink><br />
36         <br />
37         <asp:HyperLink ID="recommendationsLink" runat="server"
38            NavigateUrl="~/Recommendations.aspx" Visible="False">
39            Click here to get book recommendations
40         </asp:HyperLink>
41      </div>
42      </form>
43   </body>
44   </html>
```

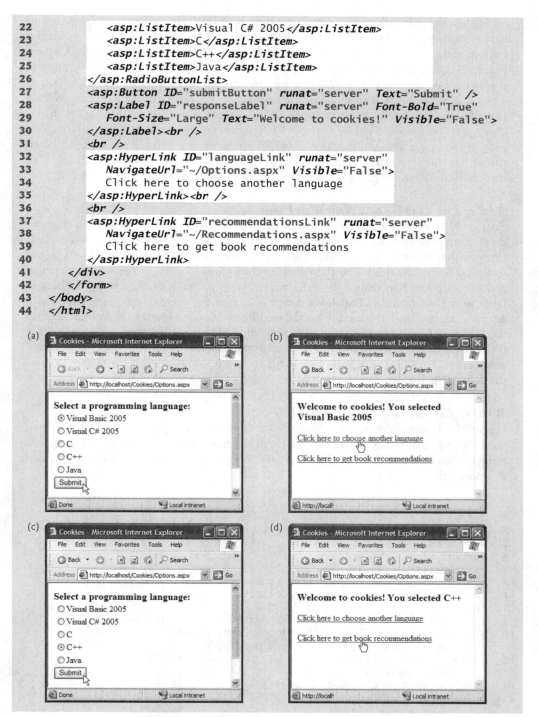

Fig. 21.23 | ASPX file that presents a list of programming languages. (Part 2 of 2.)

When the postback occurs, certain controls are hidden and others are displayed. The `Label`, `RadioButtonList` and `Button` used to select a language are hidden. Toward the bottom of the page, a `Label` and two `HyperLink`s are displayed. One link requests this page (lines 32–35), and the other requests `Recommendations.aspx` (lines 37–40). Clicking the first hyperlink (the one that requests the current page) does not cause a postback to occur. The file `Options.aspx` is specified in the `NavigateUrl` property of the hyperlink. When the hyperlink is clicked, a new request for this page occurs. Recall that earlier in the chapter, we set `NavigateUrl` to a remote Web site (`http://www.deitel.com`). To set this property to a page within the same ASP.NET application, click the ellipsis button next to the `NavigateUrl` property in the **Properties** window to open the **Select URL** dialog. Use this dialog to select a page within your project as the destination for the `HyperLink`.

Adding and Linking to a New Web Form

Setting the `NavigateUrl` property to a page in the current application requires that the destination page exist already. Thus, to set the `NavigateUrl` property of the second link (the one that requests the page with book recommendations) to `Recommendations.aspx`, you must first create this file by right clicking the project location in the **Solution Explorer** and selecting **Add New Item...** from the menu that appears. In the **Add New Item** dialog, select **Web Form** from the **Templates** pane and change the name of the file to `Recommendations.aspx`. Finally, check the box labeled **Place code in separate file** to indicate that the IDE should create a code-behind file for this ASPX file. Click **Add** to create the file. (We discuss the contents of this ASPX file and code-behind file shortly.) Once the `Recommendations.aspx` file exists, you can select it as the `NavigateUrl` value for a `HyperLink` in the **Select URL** dialog.

Writing Cookies in a Code-Behind File

Figure 21.24 presents the code-behind file for `Options.aspx` (Fig. 21.23). This file contains the code that writes a cookie to the client machine when the user selects a programming language. The code-behind file also modifies the appearance of the page in response to a postback.

```vb
1  ' Fig. 21.24: Options.aspx.vb
2  ' Processes user's selection of a programming language
3  ' by displaying links and writing a cookie to the user's machine.
4  Partial Class Options
5     Inherits System.Web.UI.Page
6        ' stores values to represent books as cookies
7        Private books As New System.Collections.Hashtable()
8
9        ' initializes the Hashtable of values to be stored as cookies
10       Protected Sub Page_Init(ByVal sender As Object, _
11          ByVal e As System.EventArgs) Handles Me.Init
12          books.Add("Visual Basic 2005", "0-13-186900-0")
13          books.Add("Visual C# 2005", "0-13-152523-9")
14          books.Add("C", "0-13-142644-3")
15          books.Add("C++", "0-13-185757-6")
```

Fig. 21.24 | Code-behind file that writes a cookie to the client. (Part 1 of 2.)

```
16          books.Add("Java", "0-13-148398-6")
17      End Sub ' Page_Init
18
19      ' if postback, hide form and display links to make additional
20      ' selections or view recommendations
21      Protected Sub Page_Load(ByVal sender As Object, _
22          ByVal e As System.EventArgs) Handles Me.Load
23
24          If IsPostBack Then
25              ' user has submitted information, so display message
26              ' and appropriate hyperlinks
27              responseLabel.Visible = True
28              languageLink.Visible = True
29              recommendationsLink.Visible = True
30
31              ' hide other controls used to make language selection
32              promptLabel.Visible = False
33              languageList.Visible = False
34              submitButton.Visible = False
35
36              ' if the user made a selection, display it in responseLabel
37              If languageList.SelectedItem IsNot Nothing Then
38                  responseLabel.Text &= " You selected " & _
39                      languageList.SelectedItem.Text.ToString()
40              Else
41                  responseLabel.Text &= " You did not select a language."
42              End If
43          End If
44      End Sub ' Page_Load
45
46      ' write a cookie to record the user's selection
47      Protected Sub submitButton_Click(ByVal sender As Object, _
48          ByVal e As System.EventArgs) Handles submitButton.Click
49          ' if the user made a selection
50          If languageList.SelectedItem IsNot Nothing Then
51              Dim language As String = languageList.SelectedItem.ToString()
52
53              ' get ISBN number of book for the given language
54              Dim ISBN As String = books(language).ToString()
55
56              ' create cookie using language-ISBN name-value pair
57              Dim cookie As New HttpCookie(language, ISBN)
58
59              ' add cookie to response to place it on the user's machine
60              Response.Cookies.Add(cookie)
61          End If
62      End Sub ' submitButton_Click
63  End Class ' Options
```

Fig. 21.24 | Code-behind file that writes a cookie to the client. (Part 2 of 2.)

Line 7 creates variable books as a *Hashtable* (namespace System.Collections)—a data structure that stores *key–value pairs*. A program uses the key to store and retrieve the associated value in the Hashtable. In this example, the keys are strings containing the programming languages' names, and the values are `strings` containing the ISBN numbers for the recommended books. Class `Hashtable` provides method **Add**, which takes as arguments a key and a value. A value that is added via method `Add` is placed in the `Hashtable` at a location determined by the key. The value for a specific `Hashtable` entry can be determined by indexing the `Hashtable` with that value's key. The expression

HashtableName(keyName)

returns the value in the key–value pair in which *keyName* is the key. For example, the expression `books(language)` in line 54 returns the value that corresponds to the key contained in `language`. Class `Hashtable` is discussed in detail in Section 26.4.3.

Clicking the **Submit** button creates a cookie if a language is selected and causes a postback to occur. In the `submitButton_Click` event handler (lines 47–62), a new cookie object (of type **HttpCookie**) is created to store the `language` and its corresponding ISBN number (line 57). This cookie is then `Added` to the **Cookies** collection sent as part of the HTTP response header (line 60). The postback causes the condition in the `If` statement of `Page_Load` (line 24) to evaluate to `True`, and lines 27–42 execute. Lines 27–29 reveal the initially hidden controls `responseLabel`, `languageLink` and `recommendationsLink`. Lines 32–34 hide the controls used to obtain the user's language selection. Line 37 determines whether the user selected a language. If so, that language is displayed in `response-Label` (lines 38–39). Otherwise, text indicating that a language was not selected is displayed in `responseLabel` (line 41).

Displaying Book Recommendations Based on Cookie Values
After the postback of `Options.aspx`, the user may request a book recommendation. The book recommendation hyperlink forwards the user to `Recommendations.aspx` (Fig. 21.25) to display the recommendations based on the user's language selections.

```
1   <%-- Fig. 21.25: Recommendations.aspx --%>
2   <%-- Displays book recommendations using cookies. --%>
3   <%@ Page Language="VB" AutoEventWireup="false"
4      CodeFile="Recommendations.aspx.vb" Inherits="Recommendations" %>
5
6   <!DOCTYPE html PUBLIC "-//W3C//DTD XHTML 1.0 Transitional//EN"
7      "http://www.w3.org/TR/xhtml1/DTD/xhtml1-transitional.dtd">
8
9   <html xmlns="http://www.w3.org/1999/xhtml" >
10  <head runat="server">
11     <title>Book Recommendations</title>
12  </head>
13  <body>
14     <form id="form1" runat="server">
15     <div>
16        <asp:Label ID="recommendationsLabel" runat="server"
17           Font-Bold="True" Font-Size="X-Large" Text="Recommendations">
18        </asp:Label><br />
19        <br />
20        <asp:ListBox ID="booksListBox" runat="server" Height="125px"
21           Width="450px"></asp:ListBox><br />
```

Fig. 21.25 | ASPX file that displays book recommendations based on cookies. (Part 1 of 2.)

```
22              <br />
23              <asp:HyperLink ID="languageLink" runat="server"
24                 NavigateUrl="~/Options.aspx">
25                 Click here to choose another language
26              </asp:HyperLink> </div>
27          </form>
28      </body>
29  </html>
```

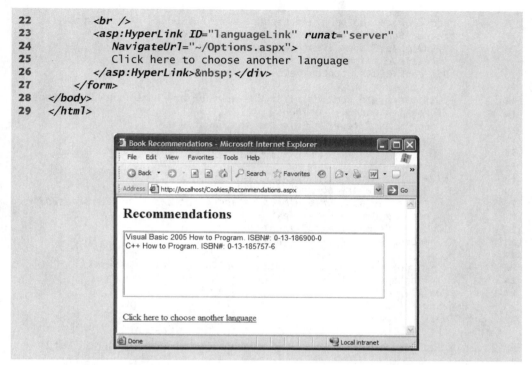

Fig. 21.25 | ASPX file that displays book recommendations based on cookies. (Part 2 of 2.)

Recommendations.aspx contains a Label (lines 16–18), a ListBox (lines 20–21) and a HyperLink (lines 23–26). The Label displays the text **Recommendations** if the user selects one or more languages; otherwise, it displays **No Recommendations**. The ListBox displays the recommendations specified by the code-behind file (Fig. 21.26). The Hyper-Link allows the user to return to Options.aspx to select additional languages.

Code-Behind File That Creates Book Recommendations From Cookies
In the code-behind file (Fig. 21.26), method Page_Init (lines 7–28) retrieves the cookies from the client, using the Request object's *Cookies* property (line 10). This returns a collection of type *HttpCookieCollection*, containing cookies that have previously been written to the client. Cookies can be read by an application only if they were created in the domain in which the application is running—a Web server can never access cookies created outside the domain associated with that server. For example, a cookie created by a Web server in the deitel.com domain cannot be read by a Web server in any other

```
1   ' Fig. 21.26: Recommendations.aspx.vb
2   ' Creates book recommendations based on cookies.
3   Partial Class Recommendations
4       Inherits System.Web.UI.Page
5
```

Fig. 21.26 | Reading cookies from a client to determine book recommendations. (Part 1 of 2.)

```
 6        ' read cookies and populate ListBox with any book recommendations
 7        Protected Sub Page_Init(ByVal sender As Object, _
 8           ByVal e As System.EventArgs) Handles Me.Init
 9           ' retrieve client's cookies
10           Dim cookies As HttpCookieCollection = Request.Cookies
11
12           ' if there are cookies, list the appropriate books and ISBN numbers
13           If cookies.Count <> 0 Then
14              For i As Integer = 0 To cookies.Count - 1
15                 booksListBox.Items.Add(cookies(i).Name & _
16                    " How to Program. ISBN#: " & cookies(i).Value)
17              Next
18           Else
19              ' if there are no cookies, then no language was chosen, so
20              ' display appropriate message and clear and hide booksListBox
21              recommendationsLabel.Text = "No Recommendations"
22              booksListBox.Items.Clear()
23              booksListBox.Visible = False
24
25              ' modify languageLink because no language was selected
26              languageLink.Text = "Click here to choose a language"
27           End If
28        End Sub ' Page_Init
29     End Class ' Recommendations
```

Fig. 21.26 | Reading cookies from a client to determine book recommendations. (Part 2 of 2.)

domain. [*Note:* Depending on the settings in web.config and whether other pages store cookies, other cookie values may be displayed by this Web application.]

Line 13 determines whether at least one cookie exists. Lines 14–17 add the information in the cookie(s) to the booksListBox. The loop retrieves the name and value of each cookie using i, the loop's control variable, to determine the current value in the cookie collection. The **Name** and **Value** properties of class HttpCookie, which contain the language and corresponding ISBN, respectively, are concatenated with " How to Program. ISBN# " and added to the ListBox. Lines 18–26 execute if no language was selected. We summarize some commonly used HttpCookie properties in Fig. 21.27.

Properties	Description
Domain	Returns a String containing the cookie's domain (i.e., the domain of the Web server running the application that wrote the cookie). This determines which Web servers can receive the cookie. By default, cookies are sent to the Web server that originally sent the cookie to the client. Changing the Domain property causes the cookie to be returned to a Web server other than the one that originally wrote it.
Expires	Returns a DateTime object indicating when the browser can delete the cookie.
Name	Returns a String containing the cookie's name.

Fig. 21.27 | HttpCookie properties. (Part 1 of 2.)

Properties	Description
Path	Returns a String containing the path to a directory on the server (i.e., the Domain) to which the cookie applies. Cookies can be "targeted" to specific directories on the Web server. By default, a cookie is returned only to applications operating in the same directory as the application that sent the cookie or a subdirectory of that directory. Changing the Path property causes the cookie to be returned to a directory other than the one from which it was originally written.
Secure	Returns a Boolean value indicating whether the cookie should be transmitted through a secure protocol. The value True causes a secure protocol to be used.
Value	Returns a String containing the cookie's value.

Fig. 21.27 | HttpCookie properties. (Part 2 of 2.)

21.6.2 Session Tracking with HttpSessionState

Session-tracking capabilities are provided by the FCL class ***HttpSessionState***. To demonstrate basic session-tracking techniques, we modified the example of Figs. 21.23–21.26 to use HttpSessionState objects. Figures 21.28–21.29 present the ASPX file and code-behind file for Options.aspx. Figures 21.31–21.32 present the ASPX file and code-behind file for Recommendations.aspx. Options.aspx is similar to the version presented in Fig. 21.23, but Fig. 21.28 contains two additional Labels (lines 32–33 and lines 35–36), which we discuss shortly.

Every Web Form includes an HttpSessionState object, which is accessible through property ***Session*** of class Page. Throughout this section, we use property Session to manipulate our page's HttpSessionState object. When the Web page is requested, an HttpSessionState object is created and assigned to the Page's Session property. As a result, we often refer to property Session as the Session object.

```
1    <%-- Fig. 21.28: Options.aspx --%>
2    <%-- Allows client to select programming languages and access --%>
3    <%-- book recommendations. --%>
4    <%@ Page Language="VB" AutoEventWireup="false"
5       CodeFile="Options.aspx.vb" Inherits="Options" %>
6
7    <!DOCTYPE html PUBLIC "-//W3C//DTD XHTML 1.0 Transitional//EN"
8       "http://www.w3.org/TR/xhtml1/DTD/xhtml1-transitional.dtd">
9
10   <html xmlns="http://www.w3.org/1999/xhtml" >
11   <head id="Head1" runat="server">
12      <title>Sessions</title>
13   </head>
14   <body>
15      <form id="form1" runat="server">
```

Fig. 21.28 | ASPX file that presents a list of programming languages. (Part 1 of 3.)

```
16    <div>
17       <asp:Label ID="promptLabel" runat="server" Font-Bold="True"
18          Font-Size="Large" Text="Select a programming language:">
19       </asp:Label>
20       <asp:RadioButtonList ID="languageList" runat="server">
21          <asp:ListItem>Visual Basic 2005</asp:ListItem>
22          <asp:ListItem>Visual C# 2005</asp:ListItem>
23          <asp:ListItem>C</asp:ListItem>
24          <asp:ListItem>C++</asp:ListItem>
25          <asp:ListItem>Java</asp:ListItem>
26       </asp:RadioButtonList>
27       <asp:Button ID="submitButton" runat="server" Text="Submit" />
28       <asp:Label ID="responseLabel" runat="server" Font-Bold="True"
29          Font-Size="Large" Text="Welcome to sessions!" Visible="False">
30       </asp:Label><br />
31       <br />
32       <asp:Label ID="idLabel" runat="server" Visible="False">
33       </asp:Label><br />
34       <br />
35       <asp:Label ID="timeoutLabel" runat="server" Visible="False">
36       </asp:Label><br />
37       <br />
38       <asp:HyperLink ID="languageLink" runat="server"
39          NavigateUrl="~/Options.aspx" Visible="False">
40          Click here to choose another language
41       </asp:HyperLink><br />
42       <br />
43       <asp:HyperLink ID="recommendationsLink" runat="server"
44          NavigateUrl="~/Recommendations.aspx" Visible="False">
45          Click here to get book recommendations
46       </asp:HyperLink>
47    </div>
48    </form>
49 </body>
50 </html>
```

(a)

Fig. 21.28 | ASPX file that presents a list of programming languages. (Part 2 of 3.)

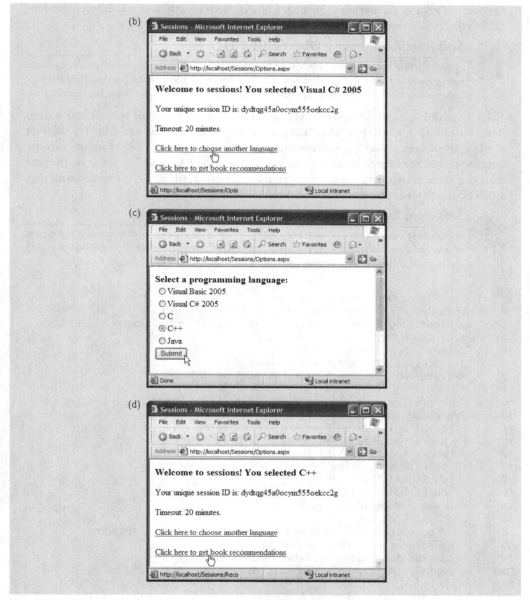

Fig. 21.28 | ASPX file that presents a list of programming languages. (Part 3 of 3.)

Adding Session Items

When the user presses **Submit** on the Web Form, submitButton_Click is invoked in the code-behind file (Fig. 21.29). Method submitButton_Click responds by adding a key–value pair to our Session object, specifying the language chosen and the ISBN number for a book on that language. These key–value pairs are often referred to as *session items*. Next, a postback occurs. Each time the user clicks **Submit**, submitButton_Click adds a new session item to the `HttpSessionState` object. Because much of this example is identical to the last example, we concentrate on the new features.

Software Engineering Observation 21.1

A Web Form should not use instance variables to maintain client state information, because each new request or postback is handled by a new instance of the page. Instead, maintain client state information in `HttpSessionState` objects, because such objects are specific to each client.

Like a cookie, an `HttpSessionState` object can store name–value pairs. These session items are placed in an `HttpSessionState` object by calling method **Add**. Line 64 calls `Add` to place the language and its corresponding recommended book's ISBN number in the `HttpSessionState` object. If the application calls method `Add` to add an attribute that has the same name as an attribute previously stored in a session, the object associated with that attribute is replaced.

Software Engineering Observation 21.2

A benefit of using `HttpSessionState` objects (rather than cookies) is that `HttpSessionState` objects can store any type of object (not just `Strings`) as attribute values. This provides you with increased flexibility in determining the type of state information to maintain for clients.

```vb
1    ' Fig. 21.29: Options.aspx.vb
2    ' Processes user's selection of a programming language
3    ' by displaying links and writing information in a Session object.
4    Partial Class Options
5       Inherits System.Web.UI.Page
6       ' stores values to represent books
7       Private books As New System.Collections.Hashtable()
8
9       ' initializes the Hashtable of values to be stored in a Session
10      Protected Sub Page_Init(ByVal sender As Object, _
11         ByVal e As System.EventArgs) Handles Me.Init
12         books.Add("Visual Basic 2005", "0-13-186900-0")
13         books.Add("Visual C# 2005", "0-13-152523-9")
14         books.Add("C", "0-13-142644-3")
15         books.Add("C++", "0-13-185757-6")
16         books.Add("Java", "0-13-148398-6")
17      End Sub ' Page_Init
18
19      ' if postback, hide form and display links to make additional
20      ' selections or view recommendations
21      Protected Sub Page_Load(ByVal sender As Object, _
22         ByVal e As System.EventArgs) Handles Me.Load
23
24         If IsPostBack Then
25            ' user has submitted information, so display message
26            ' and appropriate hyperlinks
27            responseLabel.Visible = True
28            idLabel.Visible = True
29            timeoutLabel.Visible = True
30            languageLink.Visible = True
```

Fig. 21.29 | Creates a session item for each programming language selected by the user on the ASPX page. (Part 1 of 2.)

```
31              recommendationsLink.Visible = True
32
33              ' hide other controls used to make language selection
34              promptLabel.Visible = False
35              languageList.Visible = False
36              submitButton.Visible = False
37
38              ' if the user made a selection, display it in responseLabel
39              If languageList.SelectedItem IsNot Nothing Then
40                 responseLabel.Text &= " You selected " & _
41                     languageList.SelectedItem.Text.ToString()
42              Else
43                 responseLabel.Text &= " You did not select a language."
44              End If
45
46              ' display session ID
47              idLabel.Text = "Your unique session ID is: " & Session.SessionID
48
49              ' display the timeout
50              timeoutLabel.Text = "Timeout: " & Session.Timeout & " minutes."
51          End If
52       End Sub ' Page_Load
53
54       ' record the user's selection in the Session
55       Protected Sub submitButton_Click(ByVal sender As Object, _
56          ByVal e As System.EventArgs) Handles submitButton.Click
57          ' if the user made a selection
58          If languageList.SelectedItem IsNot Nothing Then
59             Dim language As String = languageList.SelectedItem.ToString()
60
61             ' get ISBN number of book for the given language
62             Dim ISBN As String = books(language).ToString()
63
64             Session.Add(language, ISBN) ' add name/value pair to Session
65          End If
66       End Sub ' submitButton_Click
67    End Class ' Options
```

Fig. 21.29 | Creates a session item for each programming language selected by the user on the ASPX page. (Part 2 of 2.)

The application handles the postback event (lines 24–51) in method Page_Load. Here, we retrieve information about the current client's session from the Session object's properties and display this information in the Web page. The ASP.NET application contains information about the HttpSessionState object for the current client. Property **SessionID** (line 47) contains the *unique session ID*—a sequence of random letters and numbers. The first time a client connects to the Web server, a unique session ID is created for that client and a temporary cookie is written to the client so the server can identify the client on subsequent requests. When the client makes additional requests, the client's session ID from that temporary cookie is compared with the session IDs stored in the Web server's memory to retrieve the client's HttpSessionState object. Recall that clients may disable cookies in their Web browsers to ensure that their privacy is protected. Such clients will experience difficulty using Web applications that depend on `HttpSessionState` objects to maintain state information. Property **Timeout** (line 50) specifies the maximum amount of time that an `HttpSessionState` object can be inactive before it is discarded. Figure 21.30 lists some common `HttpSessionState` properties.

Displaying Recommendations Based on Session Values

As in the cookies example, this application provides a link to `Recommendations.aspx` (Fig. 21.31), which displays a list of book recommendations based on the user's language selections. Lines 20–21 define a `ListBox` Web control that is used to present the recommendations to the user.

Properties	Description
Count	Specifies the number of key–value pairs in the Session object.
IsNewSession	Indicates whether this is a new session (i.e., whether the session was created during loading of this page).
IsReadOnly	Indicates whether the Session object is read-only.
Keys	Returns a collection containing the Session object's keys.
SessionID	Returns the session's unique ID.
Timeout	Specifies the maximum number of minutes during which a session can be inactive (i.e., no requests are made) before the session expires. By default, this property is set to 20 minutes.

Fig. 21.30 | HttpSessionState properties.

```
 1   <%-- Fig. 21.31: Recommendations.aspx --%>
 2   <%-- Displays book recommendations using a Session object. --%>
 3   <%@ Page Language="VB" AutoEventWireup="false"
 4      CodeFile="Recommendations.aspx.vb" Inherits="Recommendations" %>
 5
 6   <!DOCTYPE html PUBLIC "-//W3C//DTD XHTML 1.0 Transitional//EN"
 7      "http://www.w3.org/TR/xhtml1/DTD/xhtml1-transitional.dtd">
 8
 9   <html xmlns="http://www.w3.org/1999/xhtml" >
10   <head id="Head1" runat="server">
11      <title>Book Recommendations</title>
12   </head>
13   <body>
14      <form id="form1" runat="server">
15      <div>
16         <asp:Label ID="recommendationsLabel" runat="server"
17            Font-Bold="True" Font-Size="X-Large" Text="Recommendations">
18         </asp:Label><br />
19         <br />
```

Fig. 21.31 | Session-based book recommendations displayed in a ListBox. (Part 1 of 2.)

```
20          <asp:ListBox ID="booksListBox" runat="server" Height="125px"
21             Width="450px"></asp:ListBox><br />
22          <br />
23          <asp:HyperLink ID="languageLink" runat="server"
24             NavigateUrl="~/Options.aspx">
25             Click here to choose another language
26          </asp:HyperLink> </div>
27       </form>
28    </body>
29    </html>
```

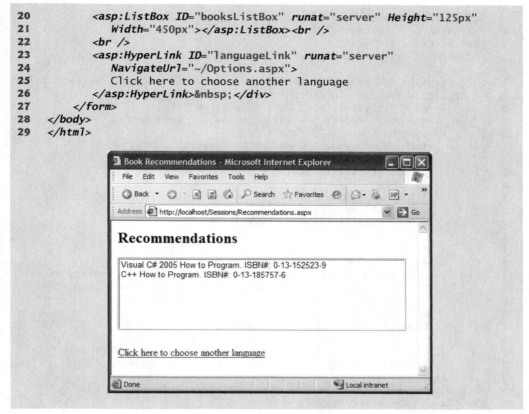

Fig. 21.31 | Session-based book recommendations displayed in a ListBox. (Part 2 of 2.)

Code-Behind File That Creates Book Recommendations from a Session

Figure 21.32 presents the code-behind file for Recommendations.aspx. Event handler Page_Init (lines 7–30) retrieves the session information. If a user has not selected a language on Options.aspx, our Session object's **Count** property will be 0. This property provides the number of session items contained in a Session object. If Session object's Count property is 0 (i.e., no language was selected), then we display the text **No Recommendations** and update the Text of the HyperLink back to Options.aspx.

If the user has chosen a language, the loop in lines 11–19 iterates through our Session object's session items, temporarily storing each key name (line 13). The value in a key–value pair is retrieved from the Session object by indexing the Session object with the key name, using the same process by which we retrieved a value from our Hashtable in the preceding section.

Line 13 accesses the **Keys** property of class HttpSessionState, which returns a collection containing all the keys in the session. Line 13 indexes this collection to retrieve the current key. Lines 16–18 concatenate keyName's value to the String " How to Program. ISBN#: " and the value from the Session object for which keyName is the key. This String is the recommendation that appears in the ListBox.

```
1    ' Fig. 21.32: Recommendations.aspx.vb
2    ' Creates book recommendations based on a Session object.
3    Partial Class Recommendations
4       Inherits System.Web.UI.Page
5
6       ' read Session items and populate ListBox with any book recommendations
7       Protected Sub Page_Init(ByVal sender As Object, _
8          ByVal e As System.EventArgs) Handles Me.Init
9          ' determine whether Session contains any information
10         If Session.Count <> 0 Then
11            For i As Integer = 0 To Session.Count - 1
12               ' get current key name from Session object
13               Dim keyName As String = Session.Keys(i)
14
15               ' use keyName to display one of Session's name-value pairs
16               booksListBox.Items.Add(keyName & _
17                  " How to Program. ISBN#: " & _
18                  Session(keyName).ToString())
19            Next
20         Else
21            ' if there are no session items, no language was chosen, so
22            ' display appropriate message and clear and hide booksListBox
23            recommendationsLabel.Text = "No Recommendations"
24            booksListBox.Items.Clear()
25            booksListBox.Visible = False
26
27            ' modify languageLink because no language was selected
28            languageLink.Text = "Click here to choose a language"
29         End If
30      End Sub ' Page_Init
31   End Class ' Recommendations
```

Fig. 21.32 | Session data used to provide book recommendations to the user.

21.7 Case Study: Connecting to a Database in ASP.NET

Many Web sites allow users to provide feedback about the Web site in a *guestbook*. Typically, users click a link on the Web site's home page to request the guestbook page. This page usually consists of an XHTML form that contains fields for the user's name, e-mail address, message/feedback and so on. Data submitted on the guestbook form is then stored in a database located on the Web server's machine.

In this section, we create a guestbook Web Form application. This example's GUI is slightly more complex than that of earlier examples. It contains a *GridView* ASP.NET data control, as shown in Fig. 21.33, which displays all the entries in the guestbook in tabular format. We explain how to create and configure this data control shortly. Note that the GridView displays **abc** in **Design** mode to indicate string data that will be retrieved from a data source at runtime.

The XHTML form consists of a name field, an e-mail address field and a message field. The form also contains a **Submit** button to send the data to the server and a **Clear** button to reset each of the fields on the form. The application stores the guestbook information in a SQL Server database called Guestbook.mdf located on the Web server. (We

Fig. 21.33 | Guestbook application GUI in **Design** mode.

provide this database in the examples directory for this chapter, which you can download from www.deitel.com/books/vbforprogrammers2.) Below the XHTML form, the Grid-View displays the data (i.e., guestbook entries) in the database's Messages table.

21.7.1 Building a Web Form That Displays Data from a Database

We now explain how to build this GUI and set up the data binding between the GridView control and the database. Many of these steps are similar to those performed in Chapter 20 to access and interact with a database in a Windows application. We present the ASPX file generated from the GUI later in the section, and we discuss the related code-behind file in the next section. To build the guestbook application, perform the following steps:

Step 1: Creating the Project
Create an **ASP.NET Web Site** named Guestbook and name the ASPX file Guestbook.aspx. Rename the class in the code-behind file Guestbook, and update the Page directive in the ASPX file accordingly.

Step 2: Creating the Form for User Input
In **Design** mode for the ASPX file, add the text Please leave a message in our guestbook: formatted as a navy blue h2 header. As discussed in Section 21.5.1, insert an XHTML table with two columns and four rows, configured so that the text in each cell aligns with the top of the cell. Place the appropriate text (see Fig. 21.33) in the top three cells in the table's left column. Then place TextBoxes named nameTextBox, emailTextBox and messageTextBox in the top three table cells in the right column. Set messageTextBox to be a multiline TextBox. Finally, add Buttons named submitButton and clearButton to the bottom-right table cell. Set the buttons' Text properties to Submit and Clear, respectively. We discuss the buttons' event handlers when we present the code-behind file.

Step 3: Adding a *GridView* Control to the Web Form

Add a GridView named messagesGridView that will display the guestbook entries. This control appears in the **Data** section of the **Toolbox**. The colors for the GridView are specified through the **Auto Format...** link in the **GridView Tasks** smart tag menu that opens when you place the GridView on the page. Clicking this link causes an **Auto Format** dialog to open with several choices. In this example, we chose **Simple**. We show how to set the GridView's data source (i.e., where it gets the data to display in its rows and columns) shortly.

Step 4: Adding a Database to an ASP.NET Web Application

To use a SQL Server 2005 Express database in an ASP.NET Web application, you must first add it to the project's App_Data folder. Right click this folder in the **Solution Explorer** and select **Add Existing Item...**. Locate the Guestbook.mdf file in the exampleDatabases subdirectory of the chapter's examples directory, then click **Add**.

Step 5: Binding the *GridView* to the *Messages* Table of the *Guestbook* Database

Now that the database is part of the project, we can configure the GridView to display its data. Open the **GridView Tasks** smart tag menu, then select **<New data source...>** from the **Choose Data Source** drop-down list. In the **Data Source Configuration Wizard** that appears, select **Database**. In this example, we use a *SqlDataSource* control that allows the application to interact with the Guestbook database. Set the ID of the data source to messagesSql-DataSource and click **OK** to begin the **Configure Data Source** wizard. In the **Choose Your Data Connection** screen, select Guestbook.mdf from the drop-down list (Fig. 21.34), then click **Next >** twice to continue to the **Configure the Select Statement** screen.

The **Configure the Select Statement** screen (Fig. 21.35) allows you to specify which data the SqlDataSource should retrieve from the database. Your choices on this page

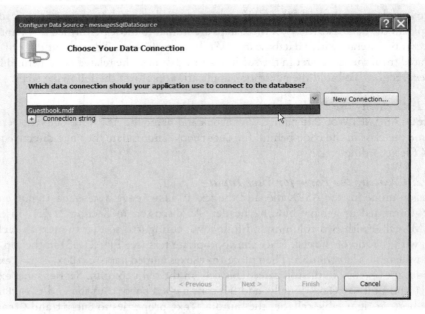

Fig. 21.34 | **Configure Data Source** dialog in Visual Web Developer.

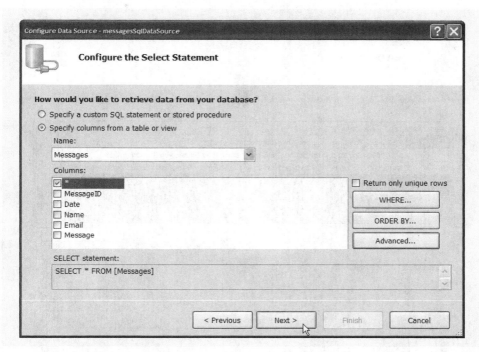

Fig. 21.35 | Configuring the SELECT statement used by the SqlDataSource to retrieve data.

design a SELECT statement, shown in the bottom pane of the dialog. The **Name** drop-down list identifies a table in the database. The Guestbook database contains only one table named Messages, which is selected by default. In the **Columns** pane, click the checkbox marked with an asterisk (*) to indicate that you want to retrieve the data from all the columns in the **Message** table. Click the **Advanced** button, then check the box next to **Generate UPDATE, INSERT and DELETE statements**. This configures the SqlDataSource control to allow us to change data in, insert new data into and delete data from the database. We discuss inserting new guestbook entries based on users' form submissions shortly. Click **OK**, then click **Next >** to continue the **Configure Data Source** wizard.

The next screen of the wizard allows you to test the query that you just designed. Click **Test Query** to preview the data that will be retrieved by the SqlDataSource (shown in Fig. 21.36).

Finally, click **Finish** to complete the wizard. Notice that a control named messages-SqlDataSource now appears on the Web Form directly below the GridView (Fig. 21.37). This control is represented in **Design** mode as a gray box containing its type and name. This control will *not* appear on the Web page—the gray box simply provides a way to manipulate the control visually through **Design** mode. Also notice that the GridView now has column headers that correspond to the columns in the Messages table and that the rows each contain either a number (which signifies an autoincremented column) or **abc** (which indicates string data). The actual data from the Guestbook database file will appear in these rows when the ASPX file is executed and viewed in a Web browser.

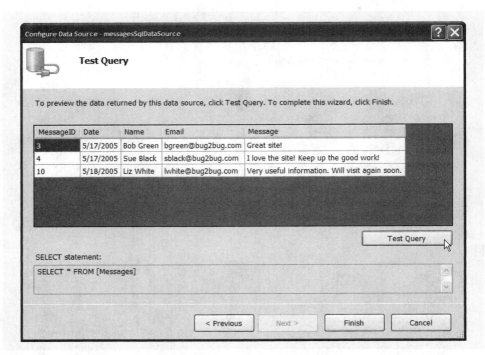

Fig. 21.36 | Previewing the data retrieved by the SqlDataSource.

Fig. 21.37 | **Design** mode displaying SqlDataSource control for a GridView.

***Step 6: Modifying the Columns of the Data Source Displayed in the* GridView**

It is not necessary for site visitors to see the MessageID column when viewing past guest-book entries—this column is merely a unique primary key required by the Messages table within the database. Thus, we modify the GridView so that this column does not display on the Web Form. In the **GridView Tasks** smart tag menu, click **Edit Columns**. In the resulting **Fields** dialog (Fig. 21.38), select **MessageID** in the **Selected fields** pane, then click the **X**. This removes the MessageID column from the GridView. Click **OK** to return to the main IDE window. The GridView should now appear as in Fig. 21.33.

Step 7: Modifying the Way the* SqlDataSource *Control Inserts Data

When you create a SqlDataSource in the manner described here, it is configured to permit INSERT SQL operations against the database table from which it gathers data. You must specify the values to insert either programmatically or through other controls on the Web Form. In this example, we wish to insert the data entered by the user in the nameTextBox, emailTextBox and messageTextBox controls. We also want to insert the current date—we will specify the date to insert programmatically in the code-behind file, which we present shortly.

To configure the SqlDataSource to allow such an insertion, select the messagesSql-DataSource control then click the ellipsis button next to the control's ***InsertQuery*** property of the messagesSqlDataSource control in the **Properties** window. The **Command and Parameter Editor** (Fig. 21.39) that appears displays the INSERT command used by the Sql-DataSource control. This command contains parameters @Date, @Name, @Email and @Message. You must provide values for these parameters before they are inserted into the database. Each parameter is listed in the **Parameters** section of the **Command and Parameter Editor**. Because we will set the **Date** parameter programmatically, we do not modify it here. For each of the remaining three parameters, select the parameter, then select **Control**

Fig. 21.38 | Removing the MessageID column from the GridView.

Fig. 21.39 | Setting up INSERT parameters based on control values.

from the **Parameter source** drop-down list. This indicates that the value of the parameter should be taken from a control. The **ControlID** drop-down list contains all the controls on the Web Form. Select the appropriate control for each parameter, then click **OK**. Now the SqlDataSource is configured to insert the user's name, e-mail address and message in the Messages table of the Guestbook database. We show how to set the date parameter and initiate the insert operation when the user clicks **Submit** shortly.

ASPX File for a Web Form That Interacts with a Database

The ASPX file generated by the guestbook GUI (and messagesSqlDataSource control) is shown in Fig. 21.40. This file contains a large amount of generated markup. We discuss only those parts that are new or noteworthy for the current example. Lines 19–58 contain the XHTML and ASP.NET elements that comprise the form that gathers user input. The GridView control appears in lines 60–85. The <asp:GridView> start tag (lines 60–63) contains properties that set various aspects of the GridView's appearance and behavior, such as whether grid lines should be displayed between rows and columns. The **DataSourceID** property identifies the data source that is used to fill the GridView with data at runtime.

Lines 66–75 define the Columns that appear in the GridView. Each column is represented as a **BoundField**, because the values in the columns are bound to values retrieved from the data source (i.e., the Messages table of the Guestbook database). The DataField property of each BoundField identifies the column in the data source to which the column in the GridView is bound. The HeaderText property indicates the text that appears as the column header. By default, this is the name of the column in the data source, but you can change this property as desired. Lines 76–84 contain nested elements that define the styles used to format the GridView's rows. The IDE configured these styles based on your selection of the **Simple** style in the **Auto Format** dialog for the GridView.

The messagesSqlDataSource is defined by the markup in lines 86–115 in Fig. 21.40. Line 87 contains a *ConnectionString* property, which indicates the connection through which the SqlDataSource control interacts with the database. The value of this property uses an *ASP.NET expression*, delimited by *<%$* and *%>*, to access the Guestbook-ConnectionString stored in the ConnectionStrings section of the application's Web.config configuration file. Recall that we created this connection string earlier in this section using the **Configure Data Source** wizard.

```
1    <%-- Fig. 21.40: Guestbook.aspx --%>
2    <%-- Guestbook Web application with a form for users to submit --%>
3    <%-- guestbook entires and a GridView to view existing entries. --%>
4    <%@ Page Language="VB" AutoEventWireup="false"
5       CodeFile="Guestbook.aspx.vb" Inherits="Guestbook" %>
6
7    <!DOCTYPE html PUBLIC "-//W3C//DTD XHTML 1.0 Transitional//EN"
8       "http://www.w3.org/TR/xhtml1/DTD/xhtml1-transitional.dtd">
9
10   <html xmlns="http://www.w3.org/1999/xhtml" >
11   <head runat="server">
12      <title>Guestbook</title>
13   </head>
14   <body>
15      <form id="form1" runat="server">
16      <div>
17         <h2>
18            Please leave a message in our guestbook:</h2>
19         <table>
20            <tr>
21               <td style="width: 130px; height: 21px" valign="top">
22                  Your name:<br />
23               </td>
24               <td style="width: 300px; height: 21px" valign="top">
25                  <asp:TextBox ID="nameTextBox" runat="server"
26                     Width="300px"></asp:TextBox>
27               </td>
28            </tr>
29            <tr>
30               <td style="width: 130px" valign="top">
31                  Your e-mail address:<br />
32               </td>
33               <td style="width: 300px" valign="top">
34                  <asp:TextBox ID="emailTextBox" runat="server"
35                     Width="300px"></asp:TextBox>
36               </td>
37            </tr>
38            <tr>
39               <td style="width: 130px" valign="top">
40                  Tell the world:<br />
41               </td>
```

Fig. 21.40 | ASPX file for the guestbook application. (Part 1 of 4.)

```
42            <td style="width: 300px" valign="top">
43                <asp:TextBox ID="messageTextBox" runat="server"
44                    Height="100px" Rows="8" Width="300px">
45                </asp:TextBox>
46            </td>
47        </tr>
48        <tr>
49            <td style="width: 130px" valign="top">
50            </td>
51            <td style="width: 300px" valign="top">
52                <asp:Button ID="submitButton" runat="server"
53                    Text="Submit" />
54                <asp:Button ID="clearButton" runat="server"
55                    Text="Clear" />
56            </td>
57        </tr>
58    </table>
59    <br />
60    <asp:GridView ID="messagesGridView" runat="server"
61        AutoGenerateColumns="False" CellPadding="4"
62        DataKeyNames="MessageID" DataSourceID="messagesSqlDataSource"
63        ForeColor="#333333" GridLines="None" Width="600px">
64        <FooterStyle BackColor="#1C5E55" Font-Bold="True"
65            ForeColor="White" />
66        <Columns>
67            <asp:BoundField DataField="Date" HeaderText="Date"
68                SortExpression="Date" />
69            <asp:BoundField DataField="Name" HeaderText="Name"
70                SortExpression="Name" />
71            <asp:BoundField DataField="Email" HeaderText="Email"
72                SortExpression="Email" />
73            <asp:BoundField DataField="Message" HeaderText="Message"
74                SortExpression="Message" />
75        </Columns>
76        <RowStyle BackColor="#E3EAEB" />
77        <EditRowStyle BackColor="#7C6F57" />
78        <SelectedRowStyle BackColor="#C5BBAF" Font-Bold="True"
79            ForeColor="#333333" />
80        <PagerStyle BackColor="#666666" ForeColor="White"
81            HorizontalAlign="Center" />
82        <HeaderStyle BackColor="#1C5E55" Font-Bold="True"
83            ForeColor="White" />
84        <AlternatingRowStyle BackColor="White" />
85    </asp:GridView>
86    <asp:SqlDataSource ID="messagesSqlDataSource" runat="server"
87        ConnectionString="<%$ ConnectionStrings:ConnectionString %>"
88        DeleteCommand="DELETE FROM [Messages] WHERE [MessageID] =
89            @MessageID" InsertCommand="INSERT INTO [Messages]
90            ([Date], [Name], [Email], [Message])
91            VALUES (@Date, @Name, @Email, @Message)"
92        SelectCommand="SELECT * FROM [Messages]" UpdateCommand=
93            "UPDATE [Messages] SET [Date] = @Date, [Name] = @Name,
```

Fig. 21.40 | ASPX file for the guestbook application. (Part 2 of 4.)

```
 94              [Email] = @Email, [Message] = @Message
 95              WHERE [MessageID] = @MessageID">
 96         <DeleteParameters>
 97            <asp:Parameter Name="MessageID" Type="Int32" />
 98         </DeleteParameters>
 99         <UpdateParameters>
100            <asp:Parameter Name="Date" Type="String" />
101            <asp:Parameter Name="Name" Type="String" />
102            <asp:Parameter Name="Email" Type="String" />
103            <asp:Parameter Name="Message" Type="String" />
104            <asp:Parameter Name="MessageID" Type="Int32" />
105         </UpdateParameters>
106         <InsertParameters>
107            <asp:Parameter Name="Date" Type="String" />
108            <asp:ControlParameter ControlID="nameTextBox" Name="Name"
109               PropertyName="Text" Type="String" />
110            <asp:ControlParameter ControlID="emailTextBox" Name="Email"
111               PropertyName="Text" Type="String" />
112            <asp:ControlParameter ControlID="messageTextBox"
113               Name="Message" PropertyName="Text" Type="String" />
114         </InsertParameters>
115      </asp:SqlDataSource>
116   </div>
117   </form>
118 </body>
119 </html>
```

(a)

Fig. 21.40 | ASPX file for the guestbook application. (Part 3 of 4.)

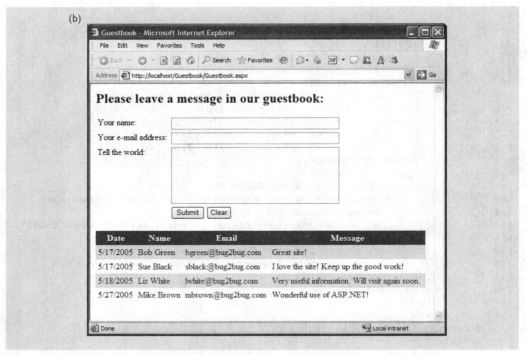

Fig. 21.40 | ASPX file for the guestbook application. (Part 4 of 4.)

As determined by our actions in the **Configure Data Source** wizard, this statement retrieves the data in all the columns in all the rows of the Messages table. Lines 88–95 define the *DeleteCommand*, *InsertCommand*, *SelectCommand* and *UpdateCommand* properties, which contain the DELETE, INSERT, SELECT and UPDATE SQL statements, respectively. These were generated by the **Configure Data Source** wizard. In this example, we use only the InsertCommand. We discuss invoking this command shortly.

Notice that the SQL commands used by the SqlDataSource contain several parameters (prefixed with @). Lines 96–114 contain elements that define the name, the type and, for some parameters, the source of the parameter. Parameters that are set programmatically are defined by *Parameter* elements containing Name and Type properties. For example, line 107 defines the Date parameter of Type String. This corresponds to the @Date parameter in the InsertCommand (line 91). Parameters that obtain their values from controls are defined by *ControlParameter* elements. Lines 108–113 contain markup that sets up the relationships between the INSERT parameters and the Web Form's TextBoxes. We established these relationships in the **Command and Parameter Editor** (Fig. 21.39). Each ControlParameter contains a ControlID property indicating the control from which the parameter gets its value. The PropertyName specifies the property that contains the actual value to be used as the parameter value. The IDE sets the PropertyName based on the type of control specified by the ControlID (indirectly via the **Command and Parameter Editor**). In this case, we use only TextBoxes, so the PropertyName of each ControlParameter is Text (e.g., the value of parameter @Name comes from nameTextBox.Text). However, if we were using a DropDownList, for example, the PropertyName would be SelectedValue.

21.7.2 Modifying the Code-Behind File for the Guestbook Application

After building the Web Form and configuring the data controls used in this example, double click the **Submit** and **Clear** buttons in **Design** view to create their corresponding `Click` event handlers in the `Guestbook.aspx.vb` code-behind file (Fig. 21.41). The IDE generates empty event handlers, so we must add the appropriate code to make these buttons work properly. The event handler for `clearButton` (lines 33–38) clears each `TextBox` by setting its `Text` property to an empty string. This resets the form for a new guestbook submission.

Lines 8–30 contain the event-handling code for `submitButton`, which adds the user's information to the `Messages` table of the `Guestbook` database. Recall that we configured

```vb
1   ' Fig. 21.41: Guestbook.aspx.vb
2   ' Code-behind file that defines event handlers for the guestbook.
3   Partial Class Guestbook
4      Inherits System.Web.UI.Page
5
6      ' Submit Button adds a new guestbook entry to the database,
7      ' clears the form and displays the updated list of guestbook entries
8      Protected Sub submitButton_Click(ByVal sender As Object, _
9         ByVal e As System.EventArgs) Handles submitButton.Click
10        ' create a date parameter to store the current date
11        Dim currentDate As New System.Web.UI.WebControls.Parameter( _
12           "Date", TypeCode.String, DateTime.Now.ToShortDateString())
13
14        ' set the @Date parameter to the date parameter
15        messagesSqlDataSource.InsertParameters.RemoveAt(0)
16        messagesSqlDataSource.InsertParameters.Add(currentDate)
17
18        ' execute an INSERT SQL statement to add a new row to the
19        ' Messages table in the Guestbook database that contains the
20        ' current date and the user's name, e-mail address and message
21        messagesSqlDataSource.Insert()
22
23        ' clear the TextBoxes
24        nameTextBox.Text = ""
25        emailTextBox.Text = ""
26        messageTextBox.Text = ""
27
28        ' update the GridView with the new database table contents
29        messagesGridView.DataBind()
30     End Sub ' submitButton_Click
31
32     ' Clear Button clears the Web Form's TextBoxes
33     Protected Sub clearButton_Click(ByVal sender As Object, _
34        ByVal e As System.EventArgs) Handles clearButton.Click
35        nameTextBox.Text = ""
36        emailTextBox.Text = ""
37        messageTextBox.Text = ""
38     End Sub ' clearButton_Click
39  End Class ' Guestbook
```

Fig. 21.41 | Code-behind file for the guestbook application.

messagesSqlDataSource's INSERT command to use the values of the TextBoxes on the Web Form as the parameter values inserted into the database. We have not yet specified the date value to be inserted, though. Lines 11–12 assign a String representation of the current date (e.g., "3/27/06") to a new object of type Parameter. This Parameter object is identified as "Date" and is given the current date as a default value. The SqlData-Source's InsertParameters collection contains an item named Date, which we Remove in line 15 and replace in line 16 by Adding our currentDate parameter. Invoking SqlData-Source method Insert in line 21 executes the INSERT command against the database, thus adding a row to the Messages table. After the data is inserted into the database, lines 24–26 clear the TextBoxes, and line 29 invokes messagesGridView's DataBind method to refresh the data that the GridView displays. This causes messagesSqlDataSource (the data source of the GridView) to execute its SELECT command to obtain the Messages table's newly updated data.

21.8 Case Study: Secure Books Database Application

This case study presents a Web application in which a user logs into a secure Web site to view a list of publications by an author of the user's choosing. The application consists of several ASPX files. Section 21.8.1 presents the application and explains the purpose of each of its Web pages. Section 21.8.2 provides step-by-step instructions to guide you through building the application and presents the markup in the ASPX files.

21.8.1 Examining the Completed Secure Books Database Application

This example uses a technique known as *forms authentication* to protect a page so that only users known to the Web site can access it. Such users are known as the site's members. Authentication is a crucial tool for sites that allow only members to enter the site or a portion of the site. In this application, Web site visitors must log in before they are allowed to view the publications in the Books database. The first page that a user would typically request is Login.aspx (Fig. 21.42). You will soon learn to create this page using a Login

Fig. 21.42 | Login.aspx page of the secure books database application.

control, one of several *ASP.NET login controls* that help create secure applications using authentication. These controls are found in the **Login** section of the **Toolbox**.

The Login.aspx page allows a site visitor to enter an existing user name and password to log into the Web site. A first-time visitor must click the link below the **Log In** button to create a new user before logging in. Doing so redirects the visitor to CreateNewUser.aspx (Fig. 21.43), which contains a CreateUserWizard control that presents the visitor with a user registration form. We discuss the CreateUserWizard control in detail in Section 21.8.2. In Fig. 21.43, we use the password pa$$word for testing purposes—as you will learn, the CreateUserWizard requires that the password contain special characters for security purposes. Clicking **Create User** establishes a new user account. After creating the account, the user is automatically logged in and shown a success message (Fig. 21.44).

Clicking the **Continue** button on the confirmation page sends the user to Books.aspx (Fig. 21.45), which provides a drop-down list of authors and a table containing the ISBNs, titles, edition numbers and copyright years of books in the database. By default, all the books by Harvey Deitel are displayed. Links appear at the bottom of the table that allow you to access additional pages of data. When the user chooses an author, a postback occurs, and the page is updated to display information about books written by the selected author (Fig. 21.46).

Note that once the user creates an account and is logged in, Books.aspx displays a welcome message customized for the particular logged-in user. As you will soon see, a Log-inName control provides this functionality. After you add this control to the page, ASP.NET handles the details of determining the user name.

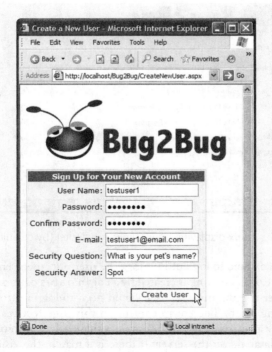

Fig. 21.43 | CreateNewUser.aspx page of the secure book database application.

Fig. 21.44 | Message displayed to indicate that a user account was created successfully.

Fig. 21.45 | Books.aspx displaying books by Harvey Deitel (by default).

Clicking the **Click here to log out** link logs the user out, then sends the user back to Login.aspx (Fig. 21.47). This link is created by a LoginStatus control, which handles the log out details. After logging out, the user would need to log in through Login.aspx to view the book listing again. The Login control on this page receives the user name and password entered by a visitor. ASP.NET compares these values with user names and passwords stored in a database on the server. If there is a match, the visitor is *authenticated* (i.e., the user's identity is confirmed). We explain the authentication process in detail in

Fig. 21.46 | `Books.aspx` displaying books by Andrew Goldberg.

Fig. 21.47 | Logging in using the `Login` control.

Section 21.8.2. When an existing user is successfully authenticated, `Login.aspx` redirects the user to `Books.aspx` (Fig. 21.45). If the user's login attempt fails, an appropriate error message is displayed (Fig. 21.48).

Notice that `Login.aspx`, `CreateNewUser.aspx` and `Books.aspx` share the same page header containing the logo image from the fictional company Bug2Bug. Instead of placing this image at the top of each page, we use a *master page* to achieve this. As we demonstrate shortly, a master page defines common GUI elements that are inherited by each page in a set of *content pages*. Just as Visual Basic classes can inherit instance variables and methods from existing classes, content pages inherit elements from master pages—this is known as *visual inheritance*.

Fig. 21.48 | Error message displayed for an unsuccessful login attempt using the Login control.

21.8.2 Creating the Secure Books Database Application

Now that you are familiar with how this application behaves, you'll learn how to create it from scratch. Thanks to the rich set of login and data controls provided by ASP.NET, you will not have to write *any* code to create this application. In fact, the application does not contain any code-behind files. All of the functionality is specified through properties of controls, many of which are set through wizards and other visual programming tools. ASP.NET hides the details of authenticating users against a database of user names and passwords, displaying appropriate success or error messages and redirecting the user to the correct page based on the authentication results. We now discuss the steps you must perform to create the secure books database application.

Step 1: Creating the Web Site
Create a new **ASP.NET Web Site** at http://localhost/Bug2Bug as described previously. We will explicitly create each of the ASPX files that we need in this application, so delete the IDE-generated Default.aspx file (and its corresponding code-behind file) by selecting Default.aspx in the **Solution Explorer** and pressing the *Delete* key. Click **OK** in the confirmation dialog to delete these files.

Step 2: Setting Up the Web Site's Folders
Before building any of the pages in the Web site, we create folders to organize its contents. First, create an Images folder by right clicking the location of the Web site in the **Solution Explorer** and selecting **New Folder**, then add the bug2bug.png file to it. This image can be found in the examples directory for this chapter. Next, add the Books.mdf database file (located in the exampleDatabases subdirectory examples directory) to the project's App_Data folder. We show how to retrieve data from this database later in the section.

Step 3: Configuring the Application's Security Settings

In this application, we want to ensure that only authenticated users are allowed to access Books.aspx (created in *Step 9* and *Step 10*) to view the information in the database. Previously, we created all of our ASPX pages in the Web application's root directory (e.g., http://localhost/*ProjectName*). By default, any Web site visitor (regardless of whether the visitor is authenticated) can view pages in the root directory. ASP.NET allows you to restrict access to particular folders of a Web site. We do not want to restrict access to the root of the Web site, however, because all users must be able to view Login.aspx and CreateNewUser.aspx to log in and create user accounts, respectively. Thus, if we want to restrict access to Books.aspx, it must reside in a directory other than the root directory. Create a folder named Secure. Later in the section, we will create Books.aspx in this folder. First, let's enable forms authentication in our application and configure the Secure folder to restrict access to authenticated users only.

Select **Website > ASP.NET Configuration** to open the **Web Site Administration Tool** in a Web browser (Fig. 21.49). This tool allows you to configure various options that determine how your application behaves. Click either the **Security** link or the **Security** tab to open a Web page in which you can set security options (Fig. 21.50), such as the type of authentication the application should use. In the **Users** column, click **Select authentication type**. On the resulting page (Fig. 21.51), select the radio button next to **From the internet** to indicate that users will log in via a form on the Web site in which the user can enter a username and password (i.e., the application will use forms authentication). The default setting—**From a local network**—relies on users' Windows user names and passwords for authentication purposes. Click the **Done** button to save this change.

Fig. 21.49 | Web Site Administration Tool for configuring a Web application.

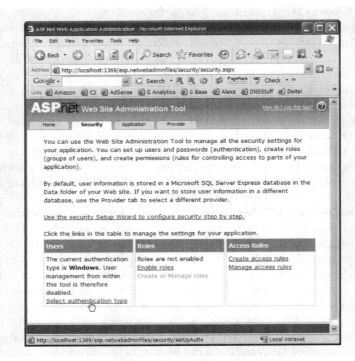

Fig. 21.50 | Security page of the **Web Site Administration Tool**.

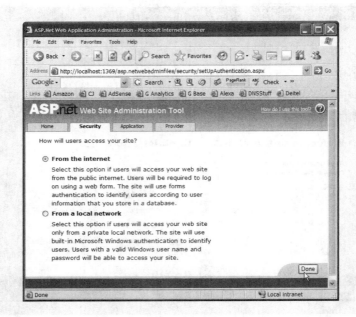

Fig. 21.51 | Choosing the type of authentication used by an ASP.NET Web application.

Now that forms authentication is enabled, the **Users** column on the main page of the **Web Site Administration Tool** (Fig. 21.52) provides links to create and manage users. As you saw in Section 21.8.1, our application provides the `CreateNewUser.aspx` page in which users can create their own accounts. Thus, while it is possible to create users through the **Web Site Administration Tool**, we do not do so here.

Even though no users exist at the moment, we configure the `Secure` folder to grant access only to authenticated users (i.e., deny access to all unauthenticated users). Click the **Create access rules** link in the **Access Rules** column of the **Web Site Administration Tool** (Fig. 21.52) to view the **Add New Access Rule** page (Fig. 21.53). This page is used to create an *access rule*—a rule that grants or denies access to a particular Web application directory for a specific user or group of users. Click the `Secure` directory in the left column of the page to identify the directory to which our access rule applies. In the middle column, select the radio button marked **Anonymous users** to specify that the rule applies to users who have not been authenticated. Finally, select **Deny** in the right column, labeled **Permission**, then click **OK**. This rule indicates that *anonymous users* (i.e., users who have not identified themselves by logging in) should be denied access to any pages in the `Secure` directory (e.g., `Books.aspx`). By default, anonymous users who attempt to load a page in the `Secure` directory are redirected to the `Login.aspx` page so that they can identify themselves. Note that because we did not set up any access rules for the `Bug2Bug` root directory, anonymous users may still access pages there (e.g., `Login.aspx`, `CreateNewUser.aspx`). We create these pages momentarily.

Fig. 21.52 | Main page of the **Web Site Administration Tool** after enabling forms authentication.

Fig. 21.53 | **Add New Access Rule** page used to configure directory access.

Step 4: Examining the Auto-Generated Web.config Files

We have now configured the application to use forms authentication and created an access rule to ensure that only authenticated users can access the Secure folder. Before creating the Web site's content, we examine how the changes made through the **Web Site Administration Tool** appear in the IDE. Recall that Web.config is an XML file used for application configuration, such as enabling debugging or storing database connection strings. Visual Web Developer generates two Web.config files in response to our actions using the **Web Site Administration Tool**—one in the application's root directory and one in the Secure folder. [*Note:* You may need to click the **Refresh** button in the **Solution Explorer** to see these files.] In an ASP.NET application, a page's configuration settings are determined by the current directory's Web.config file. The settings in this file take precedence over the settings in the root directory's Web.config file.

After setting the authentication type for the Web application, the IDE generates a Web.config file at http://localhost/Bug2Bug/Web.config, which contains an *authentication* element

```
<authentication mode="Forms" />
```

This element appears in the root directory's Web.config file, so the setting applies to the entire Web site. The value "Forms" of the *mode* attribute specifies that we want to use forms authentication. Had we left the authentication type set to **From a local network** in the **Web Site Administration Tool**, the mode attribute would be set to "Windows".

After creating the access rule for the Secure folder, the IDE generates a second Web.config file in that folder. This file contains an *authorization* element that indicates who is, and who is not, authorized to access this folder over the Web. In this application, we want to allow only authenticated users to access the contents of the Secure folder, so the authorization element appears as

```
<authorization>
    <deny users="?" />
</authorization>
```

Rather than grant permission to each individual authenticated user, we deny access to those who are not authenticated (i.e., those who have not logged in). The *deny* element inside the authorization element specifies the users to whom we wish to deny access. When the users attribute's value is set to "?", all anonymous (i.e., unauthenticated) users are denied access to the folder. Thus, an unauthenticated user will not be able to load http://localhost/Bug2Bug/Secure/Books.aspx. Instead, such a user will be redirected to the Login.aspx page—when a user is denied access to a part of a site, ASP.NET by default sends the user to a page named Login.aspx in the application's root directory.

Step 5: Creating a Master Page

Now that you have established the application's security settings, you can create the application's Web pages. We begin with the master page, which defines the elements we want to appear on each page. A master page is like a base class in a visual inheritance hierarchy, and content pages are like derived classes. The master page contains placeholders for custom content created in each content page. The content pages visually inherit the master page's content, then add content in place of the master page's placeholders.

For example, you might want to include a *navigation bar* (i.e., a series of buttons for navigating a Web site) on every page of a site. If the site encompasses a large number of pages, adding markup to create the navigation bar for each page can be time consuming. Moreover, if you subsequently modify the navigation bar, every page on the site that uses it must be updated. By creating a master page, you can specify the navigation bar markup in one file and have it appear on all the content pages, with only a few lines of markup. If the navigation bar changes, only the master page changes—any content pages that use it are updated the next time the page is requested.

In this example, we want the Bug2Bug logo to appear as a header at the top of every page, so we will place an Image control in the master page. Each subsequent page we create will be a content page based on this master page and thus will include the header. To create a master page, right click the location of the Web site in the **Solution Explorer** and select **Add New Item....** In the **Add New Item** dialog, select **Master Page** from the template list and specify Bug2Bug.master as the filename. Master pages have the filename extension .*master* and, like Web Forms, can optionally use a code-behind file to define additional functionality. In this example, we do not need to specify any code for the master page, so leave the box labeled **Place code in a separate file** unchecked. Click **Add** to create the page.

The IDE opens the master page in **Source** mode (Fig. 21.54) when the file is first created. [*Note:* We added a line break in the DOCTYPE element for presentation purposes.] The markup for a master page is almost identical to that of a Web Form. One difference is that a master page contains a *Master* directive (line 1 in Fig. 21.54), which specifies that this file defines a master page using the indicated Language for any code. Because we chose not to use a code-behind file, the master page also contains a *script* element (lines 6–8). Code that would usually be placed in a code-behind file can be placed in a script element.

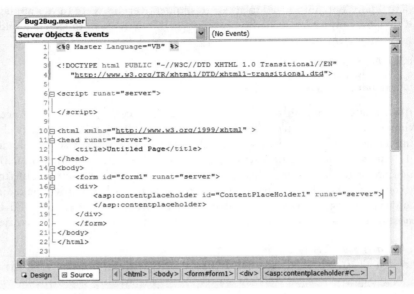

Fig. 21.54 | Master page in **Source** mode.

However, we remove the script element from this page, because we do not need to write any additional code. After deleting this block of markup, set the title of the page to Bug2Bug. Finally, notice that the master page contains a ***ContentPlaceHolder*** control (lines 17–18 of Fig. 21.54). This control serves as a placeholder for content that will be defined by a content page. You will see how to define content to replace the Content-PlaceHolder shortly.

At this point, you can edit the master page in **Design** mode (Fig. 21.55) as if it were an ASPX file. Notice that the ContentPlaceHolder control appears as a large rectangle with a gray bar indicating the control's type and ID. Using the **Properties** window, change the ID of this control to bodyContent.

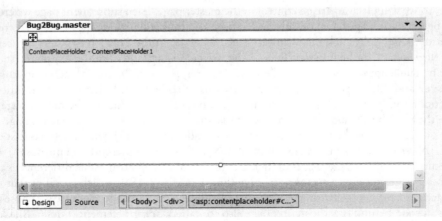

Fig. 21.55 | Master page in **Design** mode.

To create a header in the master page that will appear at the top of each content page, we insert a table into the master page. Place the cursor to the left of the ContentPlace-Holder and select **Layout > Insert Table**. In the **Insert Table** dialog, click the **Template** radio button, then select **Header** from the drop-down list of available table templates. Click **OK** to create a table that fills the page and contains two rows. Drag and drop the Content-PlaceHolder into the bottom table cell. Change the valign property of this cell to top, so the ContentPlaceHolder vertically aligns with the top of the cell. Next, set the Height of the top table cell to 130. Add to this cell an Image control named headerImage with its ImageUrl property set to the bug2bug.png file in the project's Images folder. (You can also simply drag the image from the **Solution Explorer** into the top cell.) Figure 21.56 shows the markup and **Design** view of the completed master page. As you will see in *Step 6*, a content page based on this master page displays the logo image defined here, as well as the content designed for that specific page (in place of the ContentPlaceHolder).

```
1   <%-- Fig. 21.56: Bug2bug.master --%>
2   <%-- Master page that defines common features of all pages in the --%>
3   <%-- secure book database application. --%>
4   <%@ Master Language="VB" %>
5
6   <!DOCTYPE html PUBLIC "-//W3C//DTD XHTML 1.0 Transitional//EN"
7      "http://www.w3.org/TR/xhtml1/DTD/xhtml1-transitional.dtd">
8
9   <html xmlns="http://www.w3.org/1999/xhtml" >
10  <head runat="server">
11     <title>Bug2Bug</title>
12  </head>
13  <body>
14     <form id="form1" runat="server">
15     <div>
16        <table border="0" cellpadding="0" cellspacing="0"
17           style="width: 100%; height: 100%">
18           <tr>
19              <td height="130" style="width: 887px">
20                 <asp:Image ID="headerImage" runat="server"
21                    ImageUrl="~/Images/bug2bug.png" />
22              </td>
23           </tr>
24           <tr>
25              <td style="width: 887px" valign="top">
26                 <asp:contentplaceholder id="bodyContent" runat="server">
27                 </asp:contentplaceholder>
28              </td>
29           </tr>
30        </table>
31         
32     </div>
33     </form>
34  </body>
35  </html>
```

Fig. 21.56 | Bug2Bug.master page that defines a logo image header for all pages in the secure book database application. (Part 1 of 2.)

Fig. 21.56 | `Bug2Bug.master` page that defines a logo image header for all pages in the secure book database application. (Part 2 of 2.)

Step 6: Creating a Content Page

We now create a content page based on `Bug2Bug.master`. We begin by building Create-NewUser.aspx. To create this file, right click the master page in the **Solution Explorer** and select **Add Content Page**. This action causes a `Default.aspx` file, configured to use the master page, to be added to the project. Rename this file `CreateNewUser.aspx`, then open it in **Source** mode (Fig. 21.57). Note that this file contains a `Page` directive with a Language property, a `MasterPageFile` property and a `Title` property. The `Page` directive indicates the ***MasterPageFile*** that is used as a starting point for this new page's design. In this case, the `MasterPageFile` property is set to `"~/Bug2Bug.master"` to indicate that the current file is based on the master page we just created. The ***Title*** property specifies the title that will be displayed in the Web browser's title bar when the content page is loaded. This value, which we set to `Create a New User`, replaces the value (i.e., `Bug2Bug`) set in the title element of the master page.

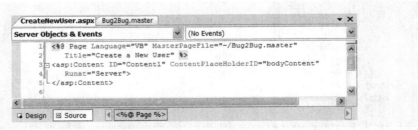

Fig. 21.57 | Content page `CreateNewUser.aspx` in **Source** mode.

Because `CreateNewUser.aspx`'s `Page` directive specifies `Bug2Bug.master` as the page's `MasterPageFile`, the content page implicitly contains the contents of the master page, such as the `DOCTYPE`, `html` and `body` elements. The content page file does not duplicate the XHTML elements found in the master page. Instead, the content page contains a ***Content*** control (lines 3–5 in Fig. 21.57), in which we will place page-specific content that will replace the master page's `ContentPlaceHolder` when the content page is requested. The `ContentPlaceHolderID` property of the `Content` control identifies the `ContentPlace-Holder` in the master page that the control should replace—in this case, `bodyContent`.

The relationship between a content page and its master page is more evident in **Design** mode (Fig. 21.58). The gray shaded region contains the contents of the master page `Bug2Bug.master` as they will appear in `CreateNewUser.aspx` when rendered in a Web browser. The only editable part of this page is the `Content` control, which appears in place of the master page's `ContentPlaceHolder`.

Step 7: Adding a CreateUserWizard Control to a Content Page
Recall from Section 21.8.1 that `CreateNewUser.aspx` is the page in our Web site that allows first-time visitors to create user accounts. To provide this functionality, we use a ***CreateUserWizard*** control. Place the cursor inside the `Content` control in **Design** mode and double click `CreateUserWizard` in the **Login** section of the **Toolbox** to add it to the page at the current cursor position. You can also drag-and-drop the control onto the page. To change the `CreateUserWizard`'s appearance, open the **CreateUserWizard Tasks** smart tag menu, and click **Auto Format**. Select the **Professional** color scheme.

As discussed previously, a `CreateUserWizard` provides a registration form that site visitors can use to create a user account. ASP.NET creates a SQL Server database (named `ASPNETDB.MDF` and located in the `App_Data` folder) to store the user names, passwords and other account information of the application's users. ASP.NET also enforces a default set of requirements for filling out the form. Each field on the form is required, the password must contain at least seven characters (including at least one non-alphanumeric character)

Fig. 21.58 | Content page `CreateNewUser.aspx` in **Design** mode.

and the two passwords entered must match. The form also asks for a security question and answer that can be used to identify a user in case the user needs to reset or recover the account's password.

After the user fills in the form's fields and clicks the **Create User** button to submit the account information, ASP.NET verifies that all the form's requirements were fulfilled and attempts to create the user account. If an error occurs (e.g., the user name already exists), the CreateUserWizard displays a message below the form. If the account is created successfully, the form is replaced by a confirmation message and a button that allows the user to continue. You can view this confirmation message in **Design** mode by selecting **Complete** from the **Step** drop-down list in the **CreateUserWizard Tasks** smart tag menu.

When a user account is created, ASP.NET automatically logs the user into the site (we say more about the login process shortly). At this point, the user is authenticated and allowed to access the Secure folder. After we create Books.aspx later in this section, we set the CreateUserWizard's ContinueDestinationPageUrl property to ~/Secure/Books.aspx to indicate that the user should be redirected to Books.aspx after clicking the **Continue** button on the confirmation page.

Figure 21.59 presents the completed CreateNewUser.aspx file (reformatted for readability). Inside the Content control, the CreateUserWizard control is defined by the markup in lines 7–36. The start tag (lines 7–10) contains several properties that specify formatting styles for the control, as well as the ContinueDestinationPageUrl property, which you will set later in the chapter. Lines 11–16 specify the wizard's two steps—CreateUserWizardStep and CompleteWizardStep—in a WizardSteps element. CreateUserWizardStep and CompleteWizardStep are classes that encapsulate the details of creating a user and issuing a confirmation message. Finally, lines 17–35 contain elements that define additional styles used to format specific parts of the control.

The sample outputs in Fig. 21.59(a) and Fig. 21.59(b) demonstrate successfully creating a user account with CreateNewUser.aspx. We use the password pa$$word for testing purposes. This password satisfies the minimum length and special character requirement imposed by ASP.NET, but in a real application, you should use a password that is more difficult for someone to guess. Figure 21.59(c) illustrates the error message that appears when you attempt to create a second user account with the same user name—ASP.NET requires that each user name be unique.

```
1   <%-- Fig. 21.59: CreateNewUser.aspx --%>
2   <%-- Content page using a CreateUserWizard control to register users. --%>
3   <%@ Page Language="VB" MasterPageFile="~/Bug2Bug.master"
4      Title="Create a New User" %>
5   <asp:Content ID="Content1" ContentPlaceHolderID="bodyContent"
6      Runat="Server">
7      <asp:CreateUserWizard ID="CreateUserWizard1" runat="server"
8         BackColor="#F7F6F3" BorderColor="#E6E2D8" BorderStyle="Solid"
9         BorderWidth="1px" Font-Names="Verdana" Font-Size="0.8em"
10        ContinueDestinationPageUrl="~/Secure/Books.aspx">
11        <WizardSteps>
12           <asp:CreateUserWizardStep runat="server">
```

Fig. 21.59 | CreateNewUser.aspx content page that provides a user registration form. (Part 1 of 3.)

```
13              </asp:CreateUserWizardStep>
14              <asp:CompleteWizardStep runat="server">
15              </asp:CompleteWizardStep>
16          </WizardSteps>
17          <SideBarStyle BackColor="#5D7B9D" BorderWidth="0px"
18              Font-Size="0.9em" VerticalAlign="Top" />
19          <TitleTextStyle BackColor="#5D7B9D" Font-Bold="True"
20              ForeColor="White" />
21          <SideBarButtonStyle BorderWidth="0px" Font-Names="Verdana"
22              ForeColor="White" />
23          <NavigationButtonStyle BackColor="#FFFBFF" BorderColor="#CCCCCC"
24              BorderStyle="Solid" BorderWidth="1px" Font-Names="Verdana"
25              ForeColor="#284775" />
26          <HeaderStyle BackColor="#5D7B9D" BorderStyle="Solid"
27              Font-Bold="True" Font-Size="0.9em"
28              ForeColor="White" HorizontalAlign="Center" />
29          <CreateUserButtonStyle BackColor="#FFFBFF" BorderColor="#CCCCCC"
30            BorderStyle="Solid" BorderWidth="1px" Font-Names="Verdana"
31            ForeColor="#284775" />
32          <ContinueButtonStyle BackColor="#FFFBFF" BorderColor="#CCCCCC"
33              BorderStyle="Solid" BorderWidth="1px" Font-Names="Verdana"
34              ForeColor="#284775" />
35          <StepStyle BorderWidth="0px" />
36      </asp:CreateUserWizard>
37  </asp:Content>
```

(a)

(b)
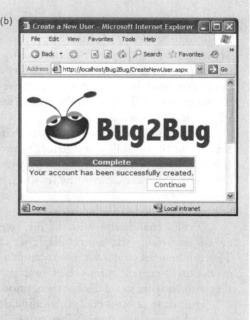

Fig. 21.59 | `CreateNewUser.aspx` content page that provides a user registration form. (Part 2 of 3.)

Fig. 21.59 | `CreateNewUser.aspx` content page that provides a user registration form. (Part 3 of 3.)

Step 8: Creating a Login Page

Recall from Section 21.8.1 that `Login.aspx` is the page in our Web site that allows returning visitors to log into their user accounts. To create this functionality, add another content page named `Login.aspx` and set its title to `Login`. In **Design** mode, drag a *Login* control (located in the **Login** section of the **Toolbox**) to the page's `Content` control. Open the **Auto Format** dialog from the **Login Tasks** smart tag menu and set the control's color scheme to **Professional**.

Next, configure the `Login` control to display a link to the page for creating new users. Set the `Login` control's `CreateUserUrl` property to `CreateNewUser.aspx` by clicking the ellipsis button to the right of this property in the **Properties** window and selecting the `CreateNewUser.aspx` file in the resulting dialog. Then set the `CreateUserText` property to `Click here to create a new user`. These property values cause a link to appear in the `Login` control.

Finally, change the value of the `Login` control's `DisplayRememberMe` property to `False`. By default, the control displays a checkbox and the text `Remember me next time`. This can be used to allow a user to remain authenticated beyond a single browser session on the user's current computer. However, we want to require that users log in each time they visit the site, so we disable this option.

The `Login` control encapsulates the details of logging a user into a Web application (i.e., authenticating a user). When a user enters a user name and password, then clicks the **Log In** button, ASP.NET determines whether the information provided match those of an account in the membership database (i.e., `ASPNETDB.MDF` created by ASP.NET). If they match, the user is authenticated (i.e., the user's identity is confirmed), and the browser is redirected to the page specified by the `Login` control's `DestinationPageUrl` property. We set this property to the `Books.aspx` page after creating it in the next section. If the user's identity cannot be confirmed (i.e., the user is not authenticated), the `Login` control displays an error message (see Fig. 21.60), and the user can attempt to log in again.

Figure 21.60 presents the completed `Login.aspx` file. Note that, as in `CreateNew-User.aspx`, the `Page` directive indicates that this content page inherits content from `Bug2Bug.master`. In the `Content` control that replaces the master page's `ContentPlace-Holder` with ID `bodyContent`, lines 6–18 create a `Login` control. Note the `CreateUser-Text` and `CreateUserUrl` properties (lines 8–9) that we set using the **Properties** window. Line 11 in the start tag for the `Login` control contains the `DestinationPageUrl` (you will

```
 1   <%-- Fig. 21.60: Login.aspx --%>
 2   <%-- Content page using a Login control that authenticates users. --%>
 3   <%@ Page Language="VB" MasterPageFile="~/Bug2Bug.master" Title="Login" %>
 4   <asp:Content ID="Content1" ContentPlaceHolderID="bodyContent"
 5      Runat="Server">
 6      <asp:Login ID="Login1" runat="server" BackColor="#F7F6F3"
 7         BorderColor="#E6E2D8" BorderPadding="4" BorderStyle="Solid"
 8         BorderWidth="1px" CreateUserText="Click here to create a new user"
 9         CreateUserUrl="~/CreateNewUser.aspx" DisplayRememberMe="False"
10         Font-Names="Verdana" Font-Size="0.8em" ForeColor="#333333"
11         DestinationPageUrl="~/Secure/Books.aspx">
12         <TitleTextStyle BackColor="#5D7B9D" Font-Bold="True"
13            Font-Size="0.9em" ForeColor="White" />
14         <InstructionTextStyle Font-Italic="True" ForeColor="Black" />
15         <TextBoxStyle Font-Size="0.8em" />
16         <LoginButtonStyle BackColor="#FFFBFF" BorderColor="#CCCCCC"
17            BorderStyle="Solid" BorderWidth="1px" Font-Names="Verdana"
18            Font-Size="0.8em" ForeColor="#284775" />
19      </asp:Login>
20   </asp:Content>
```

Fig. 21.60 | `Login.aspx` content page using a `Login` control.

set this property in the next step). The elements in lines 12–18 define various formatting styles applied to parts of the control. Note that all of the functionality related to actually logging the user in or displaying error messages is completely hidden from you.

When a user enters the user name and password of an existing user account, ASP.NET authenticates the user and writes to the client an *encrypted* cookie containing information about the authenticated user. Encrypted data is data translated into a code that only the sender and receiver can understand—thereby keeping it private. The encrypted cookie contains a String user name and a Boolean value that specifies whether this cookie should persist (i.e., remain on the client's computer) beyond the current session. Our application authenticates the user only for the current session.

Step 9: Creating a Content Page That Only Authenticated Users Can Access

A user who has been authenticated will be redirected to Books.aspx. We now create the Books.aspx file in the Secure folder—the folder for which we set an access rule denying access to anonymous users. If an unauthenticated user requests this file, the user will be redirected to Login.aspx. From there, the user can either log in or a create a new account, both of which will authenticate the user, thus allowing the user to return to Books.aspx.

To create Books.aspx, right click the Secure folder in the **Solution Explorer** and select **Add New Item...**. In the resulting dialog, select **Web Form** and specify the file name Books.aspx. Check the box **Select Master Page** to indicate that this Web Form should be created as a content page that references a master page, then click **Add**. In the **Select a Master Page** dialog, select Bug2Bug.master and click **OK**. The IDE creates the file and opens it in **Source** mode. Change the Title property of the Page directive to Book Information.

Step 10: Customizing the Secure Page

To customize the Books.aspx page for a particular user, we add a welcome message containing a *LoginName* control, which displays the current authenticated user name. Open Books.aspx in **Design** mode. In the Content control, type Welcome followed by a comma and a space. Then drag a LoginName control from the **Toolbox** onto the page. When this page executes on the server, the text [UserName] that appears in this control in **Design** mode will be replaced by the current user name. In **Source** mode, type an exclamation point (!) directly after the LoginName control (with no spaces in between). [*Note:* If you add the exclamation point in **Design** mode, the IDE may insert extra spaces or a line break between this character and the preceding control. Entering the ! in **Source** mode ensures that it appears adjacent to the user's name.]

Next, add a LoginStatus control, which will allow the user to log out of the Web site when finished viewing the listing of books in the database. A *LoginStatus* control renders on a Web page in one of two ways—by default, if the user is not authenticated, the control displays a hyperlink with the text Login; if the user is authenticated, the control displays a hyperlink with the text Logout. Each link performs the stated action. Add a LoginStatus control to the page by dragging it from the **Toolbox** onto the page. In this example, any user who reaches this page must already be authenticated, so the control will always render as a Logout link. The **LoginStatus Tasks** smart tag menu allows you switch between the control's **Views**. Select the **Logged In** view to see the Logout link. To change the actual text of this link, modify the control's LogoutText property to Click here to log out. Next, set the LogoutAction property to RedirectToLoginPage.

Step 11: Connecting the CreateUserWizard and Login Controls to the Secure Page
Now that we have created Books.aspx, we can specify that this is the page to which the CreateUserWizard and Login controls redirect users after they are authenticated. Open CreateNewUser.aspx in **Design** mode and set the CreateUserWizard control's Continue-DestinationPageUrl property to Books.aspx. Next, open Login.aspx and select Books.aspx as the DestinationPageUrl of the Login control.

At this point, you can run the Web application by selecting **Debug > Start Without Debugging**. First, create a user account on CreateNewUser.aspx, then notice how the LoginName and LoginStatus controls appear on Books.aspx. Next, log out of the site and log back in using Login.aspx.

Step 12: Generating a DataSet Based on the Books.mdf Database
Now, let's add the content (i.e., book information) to the secure page Books.aspx. This page will provide a DropDownList containing authors' names and a GridView displaying information about books written by the author selected in the DropDownList. A user will select an author from the DropDownList to cause the GridView to display information about only the books written by the selected author. As you will see, we create this functionality entirely in **Design** mode without writing any code.

To work with the Books database, we use an approach slightly different than in the preceding case study in which we accessed the Guestbook database using a SqlDataSource control. Here we use an ***ObjectDataSource*** control, which encapsulates an object that provides access to a data source. Recall that in Chapter 20, we accessed the Books database in a Windows application using TableAdapters configured to communicate with the database file. These TableAdapters placed a cached copy of the database's data in a DataSet, which the application then accessed. We use a similar approach in this example. An ObjectDataSource can encapsulate a TableAdapter and use its methods to access the data in the database. This helps separate the data-access logic from the presentation logic. As you will see shortly, the SQL statements used to retrieve data do not appear in the ASPX page when using an ObjectDataSource.

The first step in accessing data using an ObjectDataSource is to create a DataSet that contains the data from the Books database required by the application. In Visual Basic 2005 Express, this occurs automatically when you add a data source to a project. In Visual Web Developer, however, you must explicitly generate the DataSet. Right click the project's location in the **Solution Explorer** and select **Add New Item...**. In the resulting dialog, select **DataSet** and specify BooksDataSet.xsd as the file name, then click **Add**. A dialog will appear that asks you whether the DataSet should be placed in an App_Code folder—a folder whose contents are compiled and made available to all parts of the project. Click **Yes** for the IDE to create this folder to store BooksDataSet.xsd.

Step 13: Creating and Configuring an AuthorsTableAdapter
Once the DataSet is added, the **Dataset Designer** will appear, and the **TableAdapter Configuration Wizard** will open. Recall from Chapter 20 that this wizard allows you to configure a TableAdapter for filling a DataTable in a DataSet with data from a database. The Books.aspx page requires two sets of data—a list of authors that will be displayed in the page's DropDownList (created shortly) and a list of books written by a specific author. We focus on the first set of data here—the authors. Thus, we use the **TableAdapter Configura-**

tion Wizard first to configure an AuthorsTableAdapter. In the next step, we will configure a TitlesTableAdapter.

In the **TableAdapter Configuration Wizard**, select Books.mdf from the drop-down list. Then click **Next >** twice to save the connection string in the application's Web.config file and move to the **Choose a Command Type** screen.

In the wizard's **Choose a Command Type** screen, select **Use SQL statements** and click **Next >**. The next screen allows you to enter a SELECT statement for retrieving data from the database, which will then be placed in an Authors DataTable within the Books-DataSet. Enter the SQL statement

> *SELECT* AuthorID, FirstName + ' ' + LastName *AS* Name *FROM* Authors

in the text box on the **Enter a SQL Statement** screen. This query selects the AuthorID of each row. This query's result will also contain a column named Name that is created by con-catenating each row's FirstName and LastName, separated by a space. The *AS* SQL keyword allows you to generate a column in a query result—called an *alias*—that contains the result of a SQL expression (e.g., FirstName + ' ' + LastName). You will soon see how we use the result of this query to populate the DropDownList with items containing the authors' full names.

After entering the SQL statement, click the **Advanced Options...** button and uncheck **Generate Insert, Update and Delete statements**, since this application does not need to modify the database's contents. Click **OK** to close the **Advanced Options** dialog. Click **Next >** to advance to the **Choose Methods to Generate** screen. Leave the default names and click **Finish**. Notice that the **DataSet Designer** (Fig. 21.61) now displays a DataTable named Authors with AuthorID and Name members, and Fill and GetData methods.

Step 14: Creating and Configuring a TitlesTableAdapter

Books.aspx needs to access a list of books by a specific author and a list of authors. Thus we must create a TitlesTableAdapter that will retrieve the desired information from the database's Titles table. Right click the **Dataset Designer** and from the menu that appears, select **Add > TableAdapter...** to launch the **TableAdapter Configuration Wizard**. Make sure the BooksConnectionString is selected as the connection in the wizard's first screen, then click **Next >**. Choose **Use SQL statements** and click **Next >**.

In the **Enter a SQL Statement** screen, open the **Advanced Options** dialog and uncheck **Generate Insert, Update and Delete statements**, then click **OK**. Our application allows users to filter the books displayed by the author's name, so we need to build a query that takes an AuthorID as a parameter and returns the rows in the Titles table for books written by that author. To build this complex query, click the **Query Builder...** button.

Fig. 21.61 | Authors DataTable in the **Dataset Designer**.

In the **Add Table** dialog that appears, select **AuthorISBN** and click **Add**. Then **Add** the **Titles** table, too. Our query will require access to data in both of these tables. Click **Close** to exit the **Add Table** dialog. In the top pane of the **Query Builder** window (Fig. 21.62), check the box marked * **(All Columns)** in the **Titles** table. Next, in the middle pane, add a row with **Column** set to AuthorISBN.AuthorID. Uncheck the **Output** box, because we do not want the **AuthorID** to appear in our query result. Add an @authorID parameter in this row's **Filter** column. The SQL statement generated by these actions retrieves information about all books written by the author specified by parameter @authorID. The statement first merges the data from the AuthorISBN and Titles tables. The INNER JOIN clause specifies that the ISBN columns of each table are compared to determine which rows are merged. The INNER JOIN results in a temporary table containing the columns of both tables. The WHERE clause of the SQL statement restricts the book information from this temporary table to a specific author (i.e., all rows in which the AuthorID column is equal to @authorID).

Click **OK** to exit the **Query Builder**, then in the **TableAdapter Configuration Wizard**, click **Next >**. On the **Choose Methods to Generate** screen, enter FillByAuthorID and Get-DataByAuthorID as the names of the two methods to be generated for the TitlesTable-Adapter. Click **Finish** to exit the wizard. You should now see a Titles DataTable in the **Dataset Designer** (Fig. 21.63).

Step 15: Adding a DropDownList Containing Authors' First and Last Names
Now that we have created a BooksDataSet and configured the necessary TableAdapters, we add controls to Books.aspx that will display the data on the Web page. We first add

Fig. 21.62 | **Query Builder** for designing a query that selects books written by a particular author.

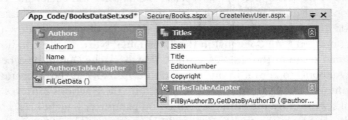

Fig. 21.63 | **Dataset Designer** after adding the `TitlesTableAdapter`.

the `DropDownList` from which users can select an author. Open `Books.aspx` in **Design** mode, then add the text `Author:` and a `DropDownList` control named `authorsDropDown-List` in the page's `Content` control, below the existing content. The `DropDownList` initially displays the text [Unbound]. We now bind the list to a data source, so the list displays the author information placed in the `BooksDataSet` by the `AuthorsTableAdapter`. In the **DropDownList Tasks** smart tag menu, click **Choose Data Source...** to start the **Data Source Configuration Wizard**. Select **<New data source...>** from the **Select a data source** drop-down list in the first screen of the wizard. Doing so opens the **Choose a Data Source Type** screen. Select **Object** and set the ID to `authorsObjectDataSource`, then click **OK**.

An `ObjectDataSource` accesses data through another object, often called a ***business object***. Recall from Section 21.3 that the middle tier of a three-tier application contains business logic that controls the way an application's top tier user interface (in this case, `Books.aspx`) accesses the bottom tier's data (in this case, the `Books.mdf` database file). Thus, a business object represents the middle tier of an application and mediates interactions between the other two tiers. In an ASP.NET Web application, a `TableAdapter` typically serves as the business object that retrieves the data from the bottom-tier database and makes it available to the top-tier user interface through a `DataSet`. In the **Choose a Business Object** screen of the **Configure Data Source** wizard (Fig. 21.64), select `BooksDataSet-TableAdapters.AuthorsTableAdapter`. [*Note:* You may need to save the project to see the `AuthorsTableAdapter`.] `BooksDataSetTableAdapters` is a namespace declared by the IDE when you create `BooksDataSet`. Click **Next >** to continue.

The **Define Data Methods** screen (Fig. 21.65) allows you to specify which method of the business object (in this case, `AuthorsTableAdapter`) should be used to obtain the data accessed through the `ObjectDataSource`. You can choose only methods that return data, so the only choice provided is the `GetData` method, which returns an `AuthorsDataTable`. Click **Finish** to close the **Configure Data Source** wizard and return to the **Data Source Configuration Wizard** for the `DropDownList` (Fig. 21.66). The newly created data source (i.e., `authorsObjectDataSource`) should be selected in the top drop-down list. The other two drop-down lists on this screen allow you to configure how the `DropDownList` control uses the data from the data source. Set `Name` as the data field to display and `AuthorID` as the data field to use as the value. Thus, when `authorsDropDownList` is rendered in a Web browser, the list items will display the names of the authors, but the underlying values associated with each item will be the `AuthorID`s of the authors. Finally, click **OK** to bind the `DropDownList` to the specified data.

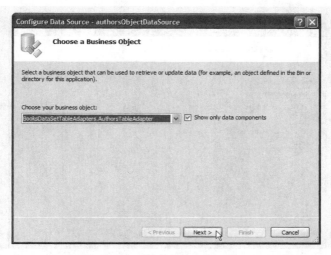

Fig. 21.64 | Choosing a business object for an `ObjectDataSource`.

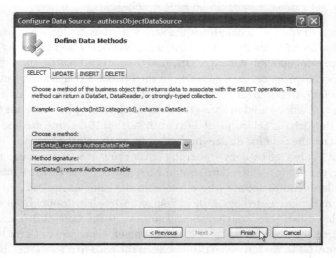

Fig. 21.65 | Choosing a data method of a business object for use with an `ObjectDataSource`.

The last step in configuring the `DropDownList` on `Books.aspx` is to set the control's ***AutoPostBack*** property to `True`. This property indicates that a postback occurs each time the user selects an item in the `DropDownList`. As you will see shortly, this causes the page's `GridView` (created in the next step) to display new data.

Step 16: Creating a GridView to Display the Selected Author's Books
We now add a `GridView` to `Books.aspx` for displaying the book information by the author selected in the `authorsDropDownList`. Add a `GridView` named `titlesGridView` below the other controls in the page's `Content` control.

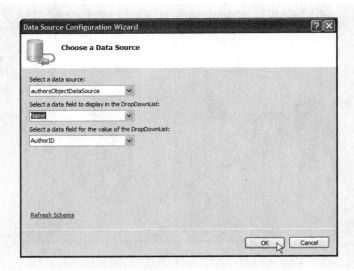

Fig. 21.66 | Choosing a data source for a `DropDownList`.

To bind the `GridView` to data from the `Books` database, select **<New data source...>** from the **Choose Data Source** drop-down list in the **GridView Tasks** smart tag menu. When the **Data Source Configuration Wizard** opens, select **Object** and set the ID of the data source to `titlesObjectDataSource`, then click **OK**. In the **Choose a Business Object** screen, select the `BooksDataSetTableAdapters.TitlesTableAdapter` from the drop-down list to indicate the object that will be used to access the data. Click **Next >**. In the **Define Data Methods** screen, leave the default selection of `GetDataByAuthorID` as the method that will be invoked to obtain the data for display in the `GridView`. Click **Next >**.

Recall that `TitlesTableAdapter` method `GetDataByAuthorID` requires a parameter to indicate the `AuthorID` for which data should be retrieved. The **Define Parameters** screen (Fig. 21.67) allows you to specify where to obtain the value of the `@authorID` parameter in the SQL statement executed by `GetDataByAuthorID`. Select **Control** from the **Parameter source** drop-down list. Select `authorsDropDownList` as the **ControlID** (i.e., the ID of the parameter source control). Next, enter 1 as the **DefaultValue**, so books by Harvey Deitel (who has `AuthorID` 1 in the database) display when the page first loads (i.e., before the user has made any selections using the `authorsDropDownList`). Finally, click **Finish** to exit the wizard. The `GridView` is now configured to display the data retrieved by `TitlesTable-Adapter.GetDataByAuthorID`, using the value of the current selection in `authorsDrop-DownList` as the parameter. Thus, when the user selects a new author and a postback occurs, the `GridView` displays a new set of data.

Now that the `GridView` is tied to a data source, we modify several of the control's properties to adjust its appearance and behavior. Set the `GridView`'s `CellPadding` property to 5, set the `BackColor` of the `AlternatingRowStyle` to `LightYellow`, and set the `Back-Color` of the `HeaderStyle` to `LightGreen`. Change the `Width` of the control to `600px` to accommodate long data values.

Next, in the **GridView Tasks** smart tag menu, check ***Enable Sorting***. This causes the column headings in the `GridView` to turn into hyperlinks that allow users to sort the data

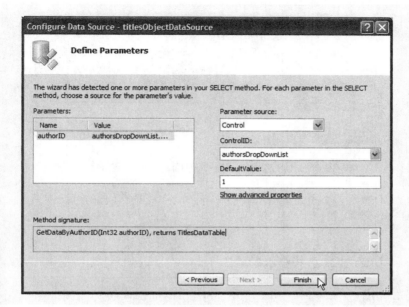

Fig. 21.67 | Choosing the data source for a parameter in a business object's data method.

in the GridView. For example, clicking the Titles heading in the Web browser will cause the displayed data to appear sorted in alphabetical order. Clicking this heading a second time will cause the data to be sorted in reverse alphabetical order. ASP.NET hides the details required to achieve this functionality.

Finally, in the **GridView Tasks** smart tag menu, check ***Enable Paging***. This causes the GridView to split across multiple pages. The user can click the numbered links at the bottom of the GridView control to display a different page of data. GridView's ***PageSize*** property determines the number of entries per page. Set the PageSize property to 4 using the **Properties** window so that the GridView displays only four books per page. This technique for displaying data makes the site more readable and enables pages to load more quickly (because less data is displayed at one time). Note that, as with sorting data in a GridView, you do not need to add any code to achieve paging functionality. Fig. 21.68 displays the completed Books.aspx file in **Design** mode.

Step 17: Examining the Markup in Books.aspx

Figure 21.69 presents the markup in Books.aspx (reformatted for readability). Aside from the exclamation point in line 8, which we added manually in **Source** mode, all the remaining markup was generated by the IDE in response to the actions we performed in **Design** mode. The Content control (lines 5–53) defines page-specific content that will replace the ContentPlaceHolder named bodyContent. Recall that this control is located in the master page specified in line 3. Line 8 creates the LoginName control, which displays the authenticated user's name when the page is requested and viewed in a browser. Lines 9–11 create the LoginStatus control. Recall that this control is configured to redirect the user to the login page after logging out (i.e., clicking the hyperlink with the LogoutText).

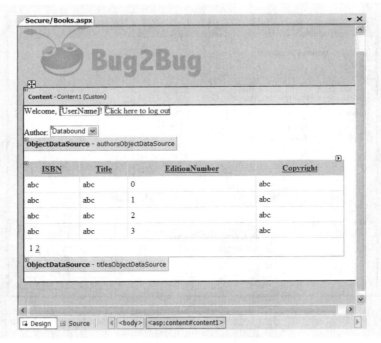

Fig. 21.68 | Completed Books.aspx in **Design** mode.

```
1   <%-- Fig. 21.69: Books.aspx --%>
2   <%-- Displays information from the Books database. --%>
3   <%@ Page Language="VB" MasterPageFile="~/Bug2Bug.master"
4       Title="Book Information" %>
5   <asp:Content ID="Content1" ContentPlaceHolderID="bodyContent"
6       Runat="Server">
7       Welcome,
8       <asp:LoginName ID="LoginName1" runat="server" />!
9       <asp:LoginStatus ID="LoginStatus1" runat="server"
10          LogoutAction="RedirectToLoginPage"
11          LogoutText="Click here to log out" />
12      <br />
13      <br />
14      Author:
15      <asp:DropDownList ID="authorsDropDownList" runat="server"
16          AutoPostBack="True" DataSourceID="authorsObjectDataSource"
17          DataTextField="Name" DataValueField="AuthorID">
18      </asp:DropDownList>
19      <asp:ObjectDataSource ID="authorsObjectDataSource"
20          runat="server" OldValuesParameterFormatString="original_{0}"
21          SelectMethod="GetData"
22          TypeName="BooksDataSetTableAdapters.AuthorsTableAdapter">
23      </asp:ObjectDataSource>
24      <br />
```

Fig. 21.69 | Markup for the completed Books.aspx file. (Part 1 of 3.)

```
25        <br />
26        <asp:GridView ID="titlesGridView" runat="server" AllowPaging="True"
27           AllowSorting="True" AutoGenerateColumns="False" CellPadding="5"
28           DataKeyNames="ISBN" DataSourceID="titlesObjectDataSource"
29           PageSize="4" Width="600px">
30           <Columns>
31              <asp:BoundField DataField="ISBN" HeaderText="ISBN"
32                 ReadOnly="True" SortExpression="ISBN" />
33              <asp:BoundField DataField="Title" HeaderText="Title"
34                 SortExpression="Title" />
35              <asp:BoundField DataField="EditionNumber"
36                 HeaderText="EditionNumber" SortExpression="EditionNumber" />
37              <asp:BoundField DataField="Copyright" HeaderText="Copyright"
38                 SortExpression="Copyright" />
39           </Columns>
40           <HeaderStyle BackColor="LightGreen" />
41           <AlternatingRowStyle BackColor="LightYellow" />
42        </asp:GridView>
43        <asp:ObjectDataSource ID="titlesObjectDataSource" runat="server"
44           OldValuesParameterFormatString="original_{0}"
45           SelectMethod="GetDataByAuthorID"
46           TypeName="BooksDataSetTableAdapters.TitlesTableAdapter">
47           <SelectParameters>
48              <asp:ControlParameter ControlID="authorsDropDownList"
49                 DefaultValue="1" Name="authorID"
50                 PropertyName="SelectedValue" Type="Int32" />
51           </SelectParameters>
52        </asp:ObjectDataSource>
53     </asp:Content>
```

(a)

Fig. 21.69 | Markup for the completed Books.aspx file. (Part 2 of 3.)

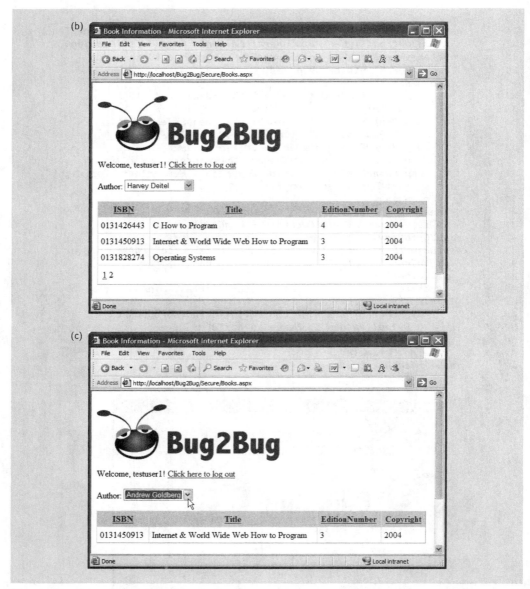

Fig. 21.69 | Markup for the completed Books.aspx file. (Part 3 of 3.)

Lines 15–18 define the DropDownList that displays the names of the authors in the Books database. Line 16 contains the control's AutoPostBack property, which indicates that changing the selected item in the list causes a postback to occur. The DataSourceID property in line 16 specifies that the DropDownList's items are created based on the data obtained through the authorsObjectDataSource (defined in lines 19–23). Line 21 specifies that this ObjectDataSource accesses the Books database by calling method GetData of the BooksDataSet's AuthorsTableAdapter (line 22).

Lines 26–42 create the `GridView` that displays information about the books written by the selected author. The start tag (lines 26–29) indicates that paging (with a page size of 4) and sorting are enabled in the `GridView`. The `AutoGenerateColumns` property indicates whether the columns in the `GridView` are generated at runtime based on the fields in the data source. This property is set to `False`, because the IDE-generated `Columns` element (lines 30–39) already specifies the columns for the `GridView` using `BoundFields`. Lines 43–52 define the `ObjectDataSource` used to fill the `GridView` with data. Recall that we configured `titlesObjectDataSource` to use method `GetDataByAuthorID` of the `Books-DataSet`'s `TitlesTableAdapter` for this purpose. The `ControlParameter` in lines 48–50 specifies that the value of method `GetDataByAuthorID`'s parameter comes from the `SelectedValue` property of the `authorsDropDownList`.

Figure 21.69(a) depicts the default appearance of `Books.aspx` in a Web browser. Because the `DefaultValue` property (line 49) of the `ControlParameter` for the `titles-ObjectDataSource` is set to 1, books by the author with `AuthorID` 1 (i.e., Harvey Deitel) are displayed when the page first loads. Note that the `GridView` displays paging links below the data, because the number of rows of data returned by `GetDataByAuthorID` is greater than the page size. Figure 21.69(b) shows the `GridView` after clicking the 2 link to view the second page of data. Figure 21.69(c) presents `Books.aspx` after the user selects a different author from the `authorsDropDownList`. The data fits on one page, so the `GridView` does not display paging links.

21.9 Wrap-Up

In this chapter, we introduced Web application development using ASP.NET and Visual Web Developer 2005 Express. We began by discussing the simple HTTP transactions that take place when you request and receive a Web page through a Web browser. You then learned about the three tiers (i.e., the client or top tier, the business logic or middle tier and the information or bottom tier) that comprise most Web applications.

Next, we explained the role of ASPX files (i.e., Web Form files) and code-behind files, and the relationship between them. We discussed how ASP.NET compiles and executes Web applications so that they can be displayed as XHTML in a Web browser. You also learned how to build an ASP.NET Web application using Visual Web Developer.

The chapter demonstrated several common ASP.NET Web controls used for displaying text and images on a Web Form. You learned how to use an `AdRotator` control to display randomly selected images. We also discussed validation controls, which allow you to ensure that user input on a Web page satisfies certain requirements.

We discussed the benefits of maintaining a user's state information across multiple pages of a Web site. We then demonstrated how you can include such functionality in a Web application using either cookies or session tracking with `HttpSessionState` objects.

Finally, we presented two case studies on building ASP.NET applications that interact with databases. First, we showed how to build a guestbook application that allows users to submit comments about a Web site. You learned how to save the user input in a SQL Server database and how to display past submissions on the Web page.

The second case study presented a secure Web application that requires users to log in before accessing information from the `Books` database (discussed in Chapter 20). You used the **Web Site Administration Tool** to configure the application to use forms authentication and prevent anonymous users from accessing the book information. This case study explained how to use the new ASP.NET 2.0 `Login`, `CreateUserWizard`, `LoginName` and `LoginStatus` controls to simplify user authentication. You also learned to create a uniform look-and-feel for a Web site using a master page and several content pages.

In the next chapter, we continue our coverage of ASP.NET technology with an introduction to Web services, which allow methods on one machine to call methods on other machines via common data formats and protocols, such as XML and HTTP. You will learn how Web services promote software reusability and interoperability across multiple computers on a network such as the Internet.

21.10 Web Resources

`asp.net`
This official Microsoft site overviews ASP.NET and provides a link for downloading Visual Web Developer. This site includes ASP.NET articles, links to useful ASP.NET resources and lists of books on Web development with ASP.NET.

`asp.net/QuickStartv20/aspnet/`
The ASP.NET QuickStart Tutorial from Microsoft provides code samples and discussion of fundamental ASP.NET topics.

`asp.net/guidedtour2/`
This guided tour of Visual Web Developer 2005 Express introduces key features in the IDE used to develop ASP.NET Web applications.

`www.15seconds.com`
This site offers ASP.NET news, articles, code samples, FAQs and links to valuable community resources, such as an ASP.NET message board and a mailing list.

`aspalliance.com`
This community site contains ASP.NET articles, tutorials and examples.

`aspadvice.com`
This site provides access to many e-mail lists where anyone can ask and respond to questions about ASP.NET and related technologies.

`www.asp101.com/aspdotnet/`
This site overviews ASP.NET and includes articles, code examples, a discussion board and links to ASP.NET resources. The code samples build on many of the techniques presented in the chapter, such as session tracking and connecting to a database.

`www.411asp.net`
This resource site provides programmers with ASP.NET tutorials and code samples. The community pages allow programmers to ask questions, answer questions and post messages.

`www.123aspx.com`
This site offers a directory of links to ASP.NET resources. The site also includes daily and weekly newsletters.

Web Services

A client is to me a mere unit,
a factor in a problem.
—Sir Arthur Conan Doyle

...if the simplest things of
nature have a message that
you understand, rejoice, for
your soul is alive.
—Eleonora Duse

Protocol is everything.
—Francoise Giuliani

They also serve who only
stand and wait.
—John Milton

OBJECTIVES

In this chapter you will learn:

- What a Web service is.
- How to create Web services.
- The important part that XML and the XML-based Simple Object Access Protocol play in enabling Web services.
- The elements that comprise Web services, such as service descriptions.
- How to create a client that uses a Web service.
- How to use Web services with Windows applications and Web applications.
- How to use session tracking in Web services to maintain state information for the client.
- How to pass user-defined types to a Web service.

22.1 Introduction

This chapter introduces Web services, which promote software reusability in distributed systems where applications execute across multiple computers on a network. A *Web service* is a class that allows its methods to be called by methods on other machines via common data formats and protocols, such as XML (see Chapter 19) and HTTP. In .NET, the over-the-network method calls are commonly implemented through the *Simple Object Access Protocol (SOAP)*, an XML-based protocol describing how to mark up requests and responses so that they can be transferred via protocols such as HTTP. Using SOAP, applications represent and transmit data in a standardized XML-based format.

Microsoft is encouraging software vendors and e-businesses to deploy Web services. As increasing numbers of organizations worldwide have connected to the Internet, the concept of applications that call methods across a network has become more practical. Web services represent the next step in object-oriented programming—rather than developing software from a small number of class libraries provided at one location, programmers can access Web service class libraries distributed worldwide.

Web services facilitate collaboration and allow businesses to grow. By purchasing Web services and using extensive free Web services that are relevant to their businesses, companies can spend less time developing new applications. E-businesses can use Web services to provide their customers with enhanced shopping experiences. Consider an online music store. The store's Web site provides links to information about various CDs, enabling users to purchase the CDs or to learn about the artists. Another company that sells concert tickets provides a Web service that displays upcoming concert dates for various artists, then allows users to buy tickets. By consuming the concert-ticket Web service on its site, the online music store can provide an additional service to its customers and increase its site traffic. The company that sells concert tickets also benefits from the business relationship by selling more tickets and possibly by receiving revenue from the online music store for the use of its Web service. Many Web services are provided at no charge. For example, Amazon and Google offer free Web services that you can use in your own applications to access the information they provide.

Visual Web Developer and the .NET Framework provide a simple, user-friendly way to create Web services. In this chapter, we show how to use these tools to create, deploy and use Web services. For each example, we provide the code for the Web service, then present an application that uses the Web service. Our first examples analyze Web services and how they work in Visual Web Developer. Then we demonstrate Web services that use more sophisticated features, such as session tracking (discussed in Chapter 21), database access and manipulating objects of user-defined types.

We distinguish between Visual Basic 2005 Express and Visual Web Developer 2005 Express in this chapter. We create Web services in Visual Web Developer 2005 Express, and we create client applications that use these Web services using both Visual Basic 2005 Express and Visual Web Developer 2005 Express. The full version of Visual Studio 2005 includes the functionality of both Express editions.

22.2 .NET Web Services Basics

A Web service is a software component stored on one machine that can be accessed by an application (or other software component) on another machine over a network. The machine on which the Web service resides is referred to as a *remote machine*. The application (i.e., the client) that accesses the Web service sends a method call over a network to the remote machine, which processes the call and returns a response over the network to the application. This kind of distributed computing benefits various systems. For example, an application without direct access to certain data on another system might be able to retrieve this data via a Web service. Similarly, an application lacking the processing power necessary to perform specific computations could use a Web service to take advantage of another system's superior resources.

A Web service is implemented as a class. In previous chapters, we included each class in a project either by defining the class in the project or by adding a reference to a DLL containing the compiled class. All the pieces of an application resided on one machine. When a client uses a Web service, the class (and its compiled DLL) is stored on a remote machine—a compiled version of the Web service class is not placed in the current application's directory. We discuss what happens shortly.

Requests to and responses from Web services created with Visual Web Developer are typically transmitted via Simple Object Access Protocol (SOAP). So any client capable of generating and processing SOAP messages can interact with a Web service, regardless of the language in which the Web service is written. We say more about SOAP in Section 22.3.

It is possible for Web services to limit access to authorized clients. See the Web Resources at the end of the chapter for links to information on standard mechanisms and protocols that address Web service security concerns.

Web services have important implications for *business-to-business* (*B2B*) *transactions*. They enable businesses to conduct transactions via standardized, widely available Web services rather than relying on proprietary applications. Web services and SOAP are platform and language independent, so companies can collaborate via Web services without worrying about the compatibility of their hardware, software and communications technologies. Companies such as Amazon, Google, eBay and many others are using Web services to their advantage. To read case studies of Web services used in business, visit msdn.microsoft.com/webservices/understanding/casestudies/default.aspx.

22.2.1 Creating a Web Service in Visual Web Developer

To create a Web service in Visual Web Developer, you first create a project of type *ASP.NET Web Service*. Visual Web Developer then generates files to contain the code that implements the Web service and an *ASMX file* (which provides access to the Web service). Figure 22.1 displays the files that comprise a Web service.

Visual Web Developer generates code files for the Web service class and any other code that is part of the Web service implementation. In the Web service class, you define the methods that your Web service makes available to client applications. Like ASP.NET Web applications, ASP.NET Web services can be tested using Visual Web Developer's built-in test server. However, to make an ASP.NET Web service publicly accessible to clients outside Visual Web Developer, you must deploy the Web service to a Web server such as an Internet Information Services (IIS) Web server.

Methods in a Web service are invoked through a *Remote Procedure Call* (*RPC*). These methods, which are marked with the **WebMethod** attribute, are often referred to as *Web service methods* or simply *Web methods*—we refer to them as Web methods from this point forward. Declaring a method with attribute WebMethod makes the method acces-

Fig. 22.1 | Web service components.

sible to other classes through RPCs and is known as *exposing* a Web method. We discuss the details of exposing Web methods in Section 22.4.

22.2.2 Determining a Web Service's Functionality

Once you select a Web service to use, you must determine the Web service's functionality and how to use it. For this purpose, Web services normally contain a *service description*. This is an XML document that conforms to the *Web Service Description Language* (*WSDL*)—an XML vocabulary that defines the methods a Web service makes available and how clients interact with them. The WSDL document also specifies lower-level information that clients might need, such as the required formats for requests and responses.

WSDL documents are not meant to be read by developers; rather, WSDL documents are meant to be read by applications, so they know how to interact with the Web services described in the documents. Visual Web Developer generates an ASMX file when a Web service is constructed. Files with the **.asmx** filename extension are ASP.NET Web service files and are executed by ASP.NET on a Web server (e.g., IIS). When viewed in a Web browser, an ASMX file presents Web method descriptions and links to test pages that allow users to execute sample calls to these methods. We explain these test pages in greater detail later in this section. The ASMX file also specifies the Web service's implementation class, and optionally the code-behind file in which the Web service is defined and the assemblies referenced by the Web service. When the Web server receives a request for the Web service, it accesses the ASMX file, which, in turn, invokes the Web service implementation. To view more technical information about the Web service, developers can access the WSDL file (which is generated by ASP.NET). We show how to do this shortly.

The ASMX page in Fig. 22.2 displays information about the `HugeInteger` Web service that we create in Section 22.4. This Web service is designed to perform calculations with integers that contain a maximum of 100 digits. Most programming languages cannot

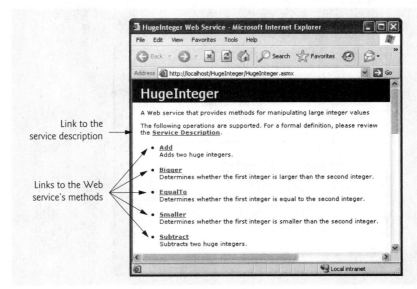

Fig. 22.2 | ASMX file rendered in a Web browser.

easily perform calculations using integers this large. The Web service provides client applications with methods that take two "huge integers" and determine their sum, their difference, which one is larger or smaller and whether the two numbers are equal. Note that the top of the page provides a link to the Web service's **Service Description**. ASP.NET generates the WSDL service description from the code you write to define the Web service. Client programs use a Web service's service description to validate Web method calls when the client programs are compiled.

ASP.NET generates WSDL information dynamically rather than creating an actual WSDL file. If a client requests the Web service's WSDL description (either by appending *?WSDL* to the ASMX file's URL or by clicking the **Service Description** link), ASP.NET generates the WSDL description, then returns it to the client for display in the Web browser. Generating the WSDL description dynamically ensures that clients receive the most current information about the Web service. It is common for an XML document (such as a WSDL description) to be created dynamically and not saved to disk.

When a user clicks the **Service Description** link at the top of the ASMX page in Fig. 22.2, the browser displays the generated WSDL document containing the service description for our `HugeInteger` Web service (Fig. 22.3).

22.2.3 Testing a Web Service's Methods

Below the **Service Description** link, the ASMX page shown in Fig. 22.2 lists the methods that the Web service offers. Clicking any method name requests a test page that describes the method (Fig. 22.4) and allows users to test the method by entering parameter values and clicking the **Invoke** button. (We discuss the process of testing a Web method shortly.)

Fig. 22.3 | Service description for our `HugeInteger` Web service.

Fig. 22.4 | Invoking a Web method from a Web browser.

Below the **Invoke** button, the page displays sample request-and-response messages using SOAP and HTTP POST. These protocols are two options for sending and receiving messages in Web services. The protocol that transmits request-and-response messages is also known as the Web service's *wire format* or *wire protocol*, because it defines how information is sent "along the wire." SOAP is the more commonly used wire format, because SOAP messages can be sent using several transport protocols, whereas HTTP POST must use HTTP. When you test a Web service via an ASMX page (as in Fig. 22.4), the ASMX page uses HTTP POST to test the Web service methods. Later in this chapter, when we use Web services in our Visual Basic programs, we employ SOAP—the default protocol for .NET Web services.

Figure 22.4 depicts the test page for the HugeInteger Web method Bigger. From this page, users can test the method by entering values in the **first:** and **second:** fields, then clicking **Invoke**. The method executes, and a new Web browser window opens, displaying an XML document that contains the result (Fig. 22.5).

Error-Prevention Tip 22.1

Using the ASMX page of a Web service to test and debug methods can help you make the Web service more reliable and robust.

Fig. 22.5 | Results of invoking a Web method from a Web browser.

22.2.4 Building a Client to Use a Web Service

Now that we have discussed the different files that comprise a .NET Web service, let's examine the parts of a .NET Web service client (Fig. 22.6). A .NET client can be any type of .NET application, such as a Windows application, a console application or a Web application. You can enable a client application to consume a Web service by *adding a Web reference* to the client. This process adds files to the client application that allow the client to access the Web service. This section discusses Visual Basic 2005 Express, but the discussion also applies to Visual Web Developer 2005 Express.

To add a Web reference, right click the project name in the **Solution Explorer** and select **Add Web Reference....** In the resulting dialog, specify the Web service to consume. The IDE then adds an appropriate Web reference to the client application. We demonstrate adding Web references in more detail in Section 22.4.

When you specify the Web service you want to consume, the IDE accesses the Web service's WSDL information and copies it into a WSDL file that is stored in the client project's Web References folder. This file is visible when you instruct Visual Basic 2005 to **Show All Files**. [*Note:* A copy of the WSDL file provides the client application with local access to the Web service's description. To ensure that the WSDL file is up-to-date, Visual Basic 2005 provides an **Update Web Reference** option (available by right clicking the Web

Fig. 22.6 | .NET Web service client after a Web reference has been added.

reference in the **Solution Explorer**), which updates the files in the Web References folder.] The WSDL information is used to create a *proxy class*, which handles all the "plumbing" required for Web method calls (i.e., the networking details and the formation of SOAP messages). Whenever the client application calls a Web method, the application actually calls a corresponding method in the proxy class. This method has the same name and parameters as the Web method that is being called, but formats the call to be sent as a request in a SOAP message. The Web service receives this request as a SOAP message, executes the method call and sends back the result as another SOAP message. When the client application receives the SOAP message containing the response, the proxy class deserializes it and returns the results as the return value of the Web method that was called. Figure 22.7 depicts the interactions among the client code, proxy class and Web service.

The .NET environment hides most of these details from you. Many aspects of Web service creation and consumption—such as generating WSDL files and proxy classes—are handled by Visual Web Developer, Visual Basic 2005 and ASP.NET. Although developers are relieved of the tedious process of creating these files, they can still modify the files if necessary. This is required only when developing advanced Web services—none of our examples require modifications to these files.

22.3 Simple Object Access Protocol (SOAP)

The *Simple Object Access Protocol* (*SOAP*) is a platform-independent protocol that uses XML to make remote procedure calls, typically over HTTP. Each request and response is packaged in a *SOAP message*—an XML message containing the information that a Web service requires to process the message. SOAP messages are written in XML so that they are human readable and platform independent. Most *firewalls*—security barriers that restrict communication among networks—do not restrict HTTP traffic. Thus, XML and HTTP enable computers on different platforms to send and receive SOAP messages with few limitations.

Web services also use SOAP for the extensive set of types it supports. The wire format used to transmit requests and responses must support all types passed between the applications. SOAP types include the primitive types (e.g., Integer), as well as DateTime, XmlNode and others. SOAP can also transmit arrays of all these types. In addition, DataSets can be serialized into SOAP. In Section 22.7, you will see that you can transmit user-defined types in SOAP messages.

When a program invokes a Web method, the request and all relevant information are packaged in a SOAP message and sent to the server on which the Web service resides. When the Web service receives this SOAP message, it begins to process the contents (con-

Fig. 22.7 | Interaction between a Web service client and a Web service.

tained in a *SOAP envelope*), which specify the method that the client wishes to execute and any arguments the client is passing to that method. This process of interpreting a SOAP message's contents is known as *parsing a SOAP message*. After the Web service receives and parses a request, the proper method is called with the specified arguments (if there are any), and the response is sent back to the client in another SOAP message. The client parses the response to retrieve the result of the method call.

The SOAP request in Fig. 22.8 was taken from the test page for the `HugeInteger` Web service's `Bigger` method (Fig. 22.4). Visual Basic 2005 creates such a message when a client wishes to execute the `HugeInteger` Web service's `Bigger` method. If the client is a Web application, Visual Web Developer creates the SOAP message. The message in Fig. 22.8 contains placeholders (`length` in line 4 and `string` in lines 16–17) representing values specific to a particular call to `Bigger`. If this were a real SOAP request, elements `first` and `second` (lines 16–17) would each contain an actual value passed from the client to the Web service, rather than the placeholder `string`. For example, if this envelope were transmitting the request from Fig. 22.4, element `first` and element `second` would contain the numbers displayed in the figure, and placeholder `length` (line 4) would contain the length of the SOAP message. Most programmers do not manipulate SOAP messages directly, but instead allow the .NET framework to handle the transmission details.

22.4 Publishing and Consuming Web Services

This section presents several examples of creating (also known as *publishing*) and using (also known as *consuming*) Web services. Recall that an application that consumes a Web service actually consists of two parts—a proxy class representing the Web service and a client application that accesses the Web service via an instance of the proxy class. The instance of the proxy class passes a Web method's arguments from the client application to

```
1   POST /HugeInteger/HugeInteger.asmx HTTP/1.1
2   Host: localhost
3   Content-Type: text/xml; charset=utf-8
4   Content-Length: length
5   SOAPAction: "http://www.deitel.com/Bigger"
6
7   <?xml version="1.0" encoding="utf-8"?>
8
9   <soap:Envelope
10     xmlns:xsi="http://www.w3.org/2001/XMLSchema-instance"
11     xmlns:xsd="http://www.w3.org/2001/XMLSchema"
12     xmlns:soap="http://schemas.xmlsoap.org/soap/envelope/">
13
14     <soap:Body>
15       <Bigger xmlns="http://www.deitel.com">
16         <first>string</first>
17         <second>string</second>
18       </Bigger>
19     </soap:Body>
20   </soap:Envelope>
```

Fig. 22.8 | SOAP request message for the `HugeInteger` Web service.

the Web service. When the Web method completes its task, the instance of the proxy class receives the result and parses it for the client application. Visual Basic 2005 and Visual Web Developer create these proxy classes for you. We demonstrate this momentarily.

22.4.1 Defining the HugeInteger Web Service

Figure 22.9 presents the code-behind file for the HugeInteger Web service that you will build in Section 22.4.2. When creating Web services in Visual Web Developer, you work almost exclusively in the code-behind file. As we mentioned earlier, this Web service is designed to perform calculations with integers that have a maximum of 100 digits. Long variables cannot handle integers of this size (i.e., an overflow occurs). The Web service provides methods that take two "huge integers" (represented as Strings) and determine their sum, their difference, which one is larger or smaller and whether the two numbers are equal. You can think of these methods as *services* available to programmers of other applications via the *Web* (hence the term Web services). Any programmer can access this Web service, use the methods and thus avoid writing 170 lines of code.

```vb
1    ' Fig. 22.9: HugeInteger.vb
2    ' HugeInteger Web service performs operations on large integers.
3    Imports System.Web
4    Imports System.Web.Services
5    Imports System.Web.Services.Protocols
6
7    <WebService(Namespace:="http://www.deitel.com/", _
8       Description:="A Web service that provides methods for" & _
9       " manipulating large integer values")> _
10   <WebServiceBinding(ConformsTo:=WsiProfiles.BasicProfile1_1)> _
11   <Global.Microsoft.VisualBasic.CompilerServices.DesignerGenerated()> _
12   Public Class HugeInteger
13      Inherits System.Web.Services.WebService
14
15      Private Const MAXIMUM As Integer = 100 ' maximum number of digits
16      Public number As Integer() ' array representing the huge integer
17
18      ' default constructor
19      Public Sub New()
20         number = New Integer(MAXIMUM - 1) {}
21      End Sub ' New
22
23      ' property that accepts an integer parameter
24      Public Property Digit(ByVal index As Integer) As Integer
25         Get
26            Return number(index)
27         End Get
28
29         Set(ByVal Value As Integer)
30            number(index) = Value
31         End Set
32      End Property ' Digit
33
```

Fig. 22.9 | HugeInteger Web service. (Part I of 4.)

```
34      ' returns String representation of HugeInteger
35      Public Overrides Function ToString() As String
36         Dim returnString As String = ""
37
38         For Each digit As Integer In number
39            returnString = digit & returnString
40         Next
41
42         Return returnString
43      End Function ' ToString
44
45      ' creates HugeInteger based on argument
46      Public Shared Function FromString(ByVal value As String) As HugeInteger
47         ' create temporary HugeInteger to be returned by the method
48         Dim parsedInteger As New HugeInteger()
49
50         For i As Integer = 0 To value.Length - 1
51            parsedInteger.Digit(i) = Int32.Parse( _
52               value.Chars(value.Length - i - 1).ToString())
53         Next
54
55         Return parsedInteger
56      End Function ' FromString
57
58      ' WebMethod that adds integers represented by the String arguments
59      <WebMethod(Description:="Adds two huge integers.")> _
60      Public Function Add(ByVal first As String, ByVal second As String) _
61         As String
62
63         Dim carry As Integer = 0
64         Dim operand1 As HugeInteger = HugeInteger.FromString(first)
65         Dim operand2 As HugeInteger = HugeInteger.FromString(second)
66         Dim result As New HugeInteger() ' stores result of addition
67
68         ' perform addition algorithm for each digit
69         For i As Integer = 0 To MAXIMUM - 1
70            ' add two digits in same column
71            ' result is their sum, plus carry from
72            ' previous operation modulo 10
73            result.Digit(i) = _
74               (operand1.Digit(i) + operand2.Digit(i) + carry) Mod 10
75
76            ' set carry to remainder of dividing sums of two digits by 10
77            carry = (operand1.Digit(i) + operand2.Digit(i) + carry) \ 10
78         Next
79
80         Return result.ToString()
81      End Function ' Add
82
83      ' WebMethod that subtracts integers represented by the String arguments
84      <WebMethod(Description:="Subtracts two huge integers.")> _
85      Public Function Subtract(ByVal first As String, _
86         ByVal second As String) As String
```

Fig. 22.9 | HugeInteger Web service. (Part 2 of 4.)

```vbnet
87
88        Dim operand1 As HugeInteger = HugeInteger.FromString(first)
89        Dim operand2 As HugeInteger = HugeInteger.FromString(second)
90        Dim result As New HugeInteger()
91
92        ' subtract bottom digit from top digit
93        For i As Integer = 0 To MAXIMUM - 1
94           ' if top digit is smaller than bottom digit we need to borrow
95           If operand1.Digit(i) < operand2.Digit(i) Then
96              Borrow(operand1, i)
97           End If
98
99            ' subtract bottom from top
100           result.Digit(i) = operand1.Digit(i) - operand2.Digit(i)
101     Next
102
103     Return result.ToString()
104  End Function ' Subtract
105
106  ' borrow 1 from next digit
107  Private Sub Borrow(ByVal hugeInteger As HugeInteger, _
108     ByVal place As Integer)
109
110      ' if no place to borrow from, signal problem
111      If place >= MAXIMUM - 1 Then
112         Throw New ArgumentException()
113
114          ' otherwise if next digit is zero, borrow from column to left
115      ElseIf hugeInteger.Digit(place + 1) = 0 Then
116          Borrow(hugeInteger, place + 1)
117      End If
118
119      ' add ten to current place because we borrowed and subtract one from
120      ' previous digit--this is the digit we borrowed from
121      hugeInteger.Digit(place) += 10
122      hugeInteger.Digit(place + 1) -= 1
123  End Sub ' Borrow
124
125  ' WebMethod that returns true if first integer is bigger than second
126  <WebMethod(Description:="Determines whether the first integer is " & _
127     "larger than the second integer.")> _
128  Public Function Bigger(ByVal first As String, _
129     ByVal second As String) As Boolean
130
131      Dim zeros() As Char = {"0"}
132
133      Try
134          ' if elimination of all zeros from result
135          ' of subtraction is an empty string,
136          ' numbers are equal, so return false, otherwise return true
137          If Subtract(first, second).Trim(zeros) = "" Then
138              Return False
```

Fig. 22.9 | HugeInteger Web service. (Part 3 of 4.)

```
139              Else
140                  Return True
141              End If
142          Catch exception As ArgumentException
143              Return False ' first number was smaller, so return False
144          End Try
145      End Function ' Bigger
146
147      ' WebMethod returns True if first integer is smaller than second
148      <WebMethod(Description:="Determines whether the first integer " & _
149          "is smaller than the second integer.")> _
150      Public Function Smaller(ByVal first As String, _
151          ByVal second As String) As Boolean
152          ' if second is bigger than first, then first is smaller than second
153          Return Bigger(second, first)
154      End Function ' Smaller
155
156      ' WebMethod that returns true if two integers are equal
157      <WebMethod(Description:="Determines whether the first integer " & _
158          "is equal to the second integer.")> _
159      Public Function EqualTo(ByVal first As String, _
160          ByVal second As String) As Boolean
161
162          ' if either first is bigger than second, or first is
163          ' smaller than second, they are not equal
164          If Bigger(first, second) OrElse Smaller(first, second) Then
165              Return False
166          Else
167              Return True
168          End If
169      End Function ' EqualTo
170  End Class ' HugeInteger
```

Fig. 22.9 | HugeInteger Web service. (Part 4 of 4.)

Lines 7–9 contain a *WebService* attribute. Attaching this attribute to a Web service class declaration allows you to specify the Web service's namespace and description. Like an XML namespace (see Section 19.4), a Web service's namespace is used by client applications to differentiate that Web service from others available on the Web. Line 7 assigns http://www.deitel.com as the Web service's namespace using the WebService attribute's *Namespace* property. Lines 8–9 use the WebService attribute's *Description* property to describe the Web service's purpose—this appears in the ASMX page (Fig. 22.2).

Visual Web Developer places line 10 in all newly created Web services. This line indicates that the Web service conforms to the *Basic Profile 1.1* (*BP 1.1*) developed by the *Web Services Interoperability Organization* (*WS-I*), a group dedicated to promoting interoperability among Web services developed on different platforms with different programming languages. BP 1.1 is a document that defines best practices for various aspects of Web service creation and consumption (www.WS-I.org). As we discussed in Section 22.2, the .NET environment hides many of these details from you. Setting the *WebServiceBinding* attribute's *ConformsTo* property to *WsiProfiles.BasicProfile1_1* instructs Visual Web Developer to perform its "behind-the-scenes" work, such as generating WSDL and ASMX files, in conformance with the guidelines laid out in BP 1.1. For more information on Web services interoperabilty and the Basic Profile 1.1, visit the WS-I Web site at www.ws-i.org.

By default, each new Web service class created in Visual Web Developer inherits from class `System.Web.Services.WebService` (line 13). Although a Web service need not derive from class `WebService`, this class provides members that are useful in determining information about the client and the Web service itself. Several methods in class `Huge-Integer` are tagged with the ***WebMethod attribute*** (lines 59, 84, 126, 148 and 157), which exposes a method so that it can be called remotely. When this attribute is absent, the method is not accessible to clients that consume the Web service. Note that this attribute, like the `WebService` attribute, contains a `Description` property that allows the ASMX page to display information about the method (see these descriptions shown in Fig. 22.2).

Common Programming Error 22.1

Failing to expose a method as a Web method by declaring it with the `WebMethod` *attribute prevents clients of the Web service from accessing the method.*

Portability Tip 22.1

Specify a namespace for each Web service so that it can be uniquely identified by clients. In general, you should use your company's domain name as the Web service's namespace, since company domain names are guaranteed to be unique.

Portability Tip 22.2

Specify descriptions for a Web service and its Web methods so that the Web service's clients can view information about the service in the service's ASMX page.

Common Programming Error 22.2

No method with the `WebMethod` *attribute can be declared* `Shared`*—for a client to access a Web method, an instance of that Web service must exist.*

Lines 24–32 define a `Digit` property, which provides access to any digit in a `Huge-Integer`. Lines 59–81 and 84–104 define Web methods `Add` and `Subtract`, which perform addition and subtraction, respectively. Method `Borrow` (lines 107–123) handles the case in which the digit that we are currently examining in the left operand is smaller than the corresponding digit in the right operand. For instance, when we subtract 19 from 32, we usually examine the numbers in the operands digit-by-digit, starting from the right. The number 2 is smaller than 9, so we add 10 to 2 (resulting in 12). After borrowing, we can subtract 9 from 12, resulting in 3 for the rightmost digit in the solution. We then subtract 1 from the 3 in 32—the next digit to the left (i.e., the digit we borrowed from). This leaves a 2 in the tens place. The corresponding digit in the other operand is now the 1 in 19. Subtracting 1 from 2 yields 1, making the corresponding digit in the result 1. The final result, when the digits are put together, is 13. Method `Borrow` is the method that adds 10 to the appropriate digits and subtracts 1 from the digits to the left. This is a utility method that is not intended to be called remotely, so it is not qualified with attribute `WebMethod`.

Recall that Fig. 22.2 presented a screen capture of the ASMX page `HugeInteger.asmx` for which the code-behind file `HugeInteger.vb` (Fig. 22.9) defines Web methods. A client application can invoke only the five methods listed in the screen capture in Fig. 22.2 (i.e., the methods qualified with the `WebMethod` attribute in Fig. 22.9).

22.4.2 Building a Web Service in Visual Web Developer

We now show you how to create the HugeInteger Web service. In the following steps, you will create an **ASP.NET Web Service** project that executes on your computer's local IIS Web server. To create the HugeInteger Web service in Visual Web Developer, perform the following steps:

Step 1: Creating the Project

To begin, you must create a project of type **ASP.NET Web Service.** Select **File > New Web Site...** to display the **New Web Site** dialog (Fig. 22.10). Select **ASP.NET Web Service** in the **Templates** pane. Select **HTTP** from the **Location** drop-down list to indicate that the files should be placed on a Web server. By default, Visual Web Developer indicates that it will place the files on the local machine's IIS Web server in a virtual directory named WebSite (http://localhost/WebSite). Replace the name WebSite with HugeInteger for this example. Next, select **Visual Basic** from the **Language** drop-down list to indicate that you will use Visual Basic to build this Web service. Visual Web Developer places the Web service project's solution file (.sln) in the My Documents\Visual Studio 2005\Projects folder. If you do not have access to an IIS Web server to build and test the examples in this chapter, you can select **File System** from the **Location** drop-down list. In this case, Visual Web Developer will place your Web service's files on your local hard disk. You will then be able to test the Web service using Visual Web Developer's built-in Web server.

Step 2: Examining the Newly Created Project

After you create the project, the code-behind file Service.vb, which contains code for a simple Web service (Fig. 22.11), is displayed by default. If the code-behind file is not

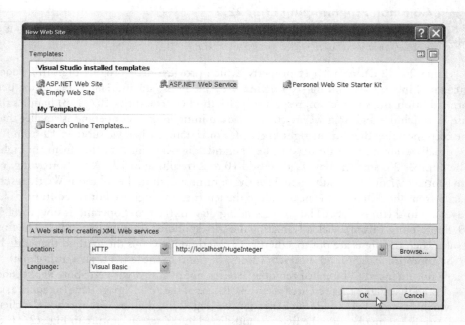

Fig. 22.10 | Creating an **ASP.NET Web Service** in Visual Web Developer.

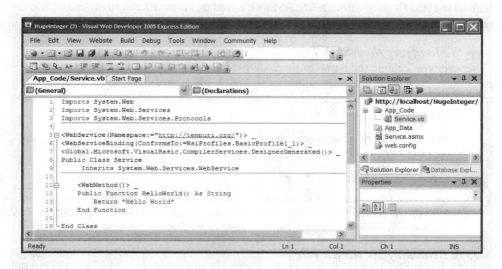

Fig. 22.11 | Code view of a Web service.

open, it can be opened by double clicking the file in the **App_Code** directory listed in the **Solution Explorer**. Visual Web Developer includes three Imports statements that are helpful for developing Web services (lines 1–3). By default, a new code-behind file defines a class named Service that is marked with the WebService and WebServiceBinding attributes (lines 5–6). The class contains a sample Web method named HelloWorld (lines 11–14). This method is a placeholder that you will replace with your own method(s).

Step 3: Modifying and Renaming the Code-Behind File
To create the HugeInteger Web service developed in this section, modify Service.vb by replacing all of the sample code provided by Visual Web Developer with all of the code from the HugeInteger code-behind file (Fig. 22.9). Then rename the file HugeInteger.vb (by right clicking the file in the **Solution Explorer** and choosing **Rename**). This code is provided in the examples directory for this chapter. You can download the examples from www.deitel.com/books/vbforprogrammers2/.

Step 4: Examining the ASMX File
The **Solution Explorer** lists a Service.asmx file in addition to the code-behind file. Recall from Fig. 22.2 that a Web service's ASMX page, when accessed through a Web browser, displays information about the Web service's methods and provides access to the Web service's WSDL information. However, if you open the ASMX file on disk, you will see that it actually contains only

```
<%@ WebService Language="vb" CodeBehind="~/App_Code/Service.vb"
    Class="Service" %>
```

to indicate the programming language in which the Web service's code-behind file is written, the code-behind file's location and the class that defines the Web service. When you request the ASMX page through IIS, ASP.NET uses this information to generate the content displayed in the Web browser (i.e., the list of Web methods and their descriptions).

Step 5: Modifying the ASMX File
Whenever you change the name of the code-behind file or the name of the class that defines the Web service, you must modify the ASMX file accordingly. Thus, after defining class `HugeInteger` in the code-behind file `HugeInteger.vb`, modify the ASMX file to contain the lines

```
<%@ WebService Language="vb" CodeBehind="~/App_Code/HugeInteger.vb"
    Class="HugeInteger" %>
```

Error-Prevention Tip 22.2

Update the Web service's ASMX file appropriately whenever the name of a Web service's code-behind file or the class name changes. Visual Web Developer creates the ASMX file, but does not automatically update it when you make changes to other files in the project.

Step 6: Renaming the ASMX File
The final step in creating the `HugeInteger` Web service is to rename the ASMX file `HugeInteger.asmx`.

22.4.3 Deploying the HugeInteger Web Service
The Web service is already deployed because we created the `HugeInteger` Web service directly on our computer's local IIS server. You can choose **Build Web Site** from the **Build** menu to ensure that the Web service compiles without errors. You can also test the Web service directly from Visual Web Developer by selecting **Start Without Debugging** from the **Debug** menu. This opens a browser window that contains the ASMX page shown in Fig. 22.2. Clicking the link for a particular `HugeInteger` Web service method displays a Web page like the one in Fig. 22.4 that allows you to test the method. Note that you can also access the Web service's ASMX page from your computer by typing the following URL in a Web browser

```
http://localhost/HugeInteger/HugeInteger.asmx
```

Accessing the HugeInteger Web Service's ASMX Page from Another Computer
Eventually, you will want other clients to be able to access and use your Web service. If you deploy the Web service on an IIS Web server, a client can connect to that server to access the Web service with a URL of the form

```
http://host/HugeInteger/HugeInteger.asmx
```

where *host* is the hostname or IP address of the Web server. To access the Web service from another computer in your company's or school's local area network, you can replace *host* with the actual name of the computer on which IIS is running.

   If you have the Windows XP Service Pack 2 operating system on the computer running IIS, that computer may not allow requests from other computers by default. If you wish to allow other computers to connect to your computer's Web server, perform the following steps:

1. Select **Start > Control Panel** to open your system's **Control Panel** window, then double click **Windows Firewall** to view the **Windows Firewall** settings dialog.

2. In the **Windows Firewall** settings dialog, click the **Advanced** tab, select **Local Area Connection** (or your network connection's name, if it is different) in the **Network Connection Settings** list box and click the **Settings...** button to display the **Advanced Settings** dialog.

3. In the **Advanced Settings** dialog, ensure that the checkbox for **Web Server (HTTP)** is checked to allow clients on other computers to submit requests to your computer's Web server.

4. Click **OK** in the **Advanced Settings** dialog, then click **OK** in the **Windows Firewall** settings dialog.

Accessing the HugeInteger Web Service's ASMX Page When the Web Service Executes in Visual Web Developer's Built-in Web Server

Recall from *Step 1* of Section 22.4.2 that if you do not have access to an IIS server to deploy and test your Web service, you can create the Web service on your computer's hard disk and use Visual Web Developer's built-in Web server to test the Web service. In this case, when you select **Start Without Debugging** from the **Debug** menu, Visual Web Developer executes its built-in Web server, then opens a Web browser containing the Web service's ASMX page so that you can test the Web service.

Web servers typically receive requests on port 80. To ensure that Visual Web Developer's built-in Web server does not conflict with another Web server running on your local computer, Visual Web Developer's Web server receives requests on a randomly selected port number. When a Web server receives requests on a port number other than port 80, the port number must be specified as part of the request. In this case, the URL to access the HugeInteger Web service's ASMX page would be of the form

```
http://host:portNumber/HugeInteger/HugeInteger.asmx
```

where *host* is the hostname or IP address of the computer on which Visual Web Developer's built-in Web server is running and *portNumber* is the specific port on which the Web server receives requests. You can see this port number in your Web browser's **Address** field when you test the Web service from Visual Web Developer. Unfortunately, Web services executed using Visual Web Developer's built-in server cannot be accessed over a network.

22.4.4 Creating a Client to Consume the HugeInteger Web Service

Now that you have defined and deployed the Web service, let's see how to consume it from a client application. In this section, you'll create a Windows application as the client using Visual Basic 2005. After creating the client application, you'll add a proxy class to the project that allows the client to access the Web service. Recall that the proxy class (or proxy) is generated from the Web service's WSDL file and enables the client to call Web methods over the Internet. The proxy class handles all the details of communicating with the Web service. The proxy class is hidden from you by default—you can view it in the **Solution Explorer** by clicking the **Show All Files** button. The proxy class's purpose is to make clients think that they are calling the Web methods directly.

This example demonstrates how to create a Web service client and generate a proxy class that allows the client to access the `HugeInteger` Web service. You will begin by creating a project and adding a Web reference to it. When you add the Web reference, the IDE will generate the appropriate proxy class. You will then create an instance of the proxy class and use it to call the Web service's methods. First, create a Windows application named `UsingHugeIntegerWebService` in Visual Basic 2005, then perform the following steps:

Step 1: Opening the Add Web Reference Dialog
Right click the project name in the **Solution Explorer** and select **Add Web Reference...** (Fig. 22.12).

Step 2: Locating Web Services on Your Computer
In the **Add Web Reference** dialog that appears (Fig. 22.13), click **Web services on the local machine** to locate Web references stored on the IIS Web server on your local computer (`http://localhost`). This server's files are located at `C:\Inetpub\wwwroot` by default. Note that the **Add Web Reference** dialog allows you to search for Web services in several different locations. Many companies that provide Web services simply distribute the exact URLs at which their Web services can be accessed. For this reason, the **Add Web Reference** dialog also allows you to enter the specific URL of a Web service in the **URL** field.

Step 3: Choosing the Web Service to Reference
Select the `HugeInteger` Web service from the list of available Web services (Fig. 22.14).

Step 4: Adding the Web Reference
Add the Web reference by clicking the **Add Reference** button (Fig. 22.15).

Fig. 22.12 | Adding a Web service reference to a project.

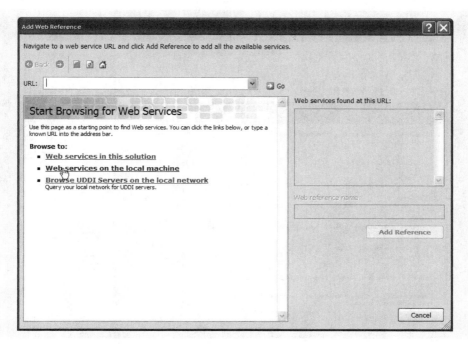

Fig. 22.13 | **Add Web Reference** dialog.

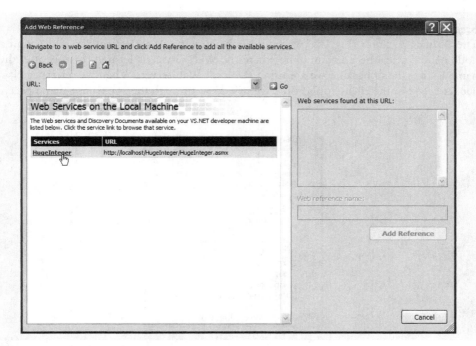

Fig. 22.14 | Web services located on `localhost`.

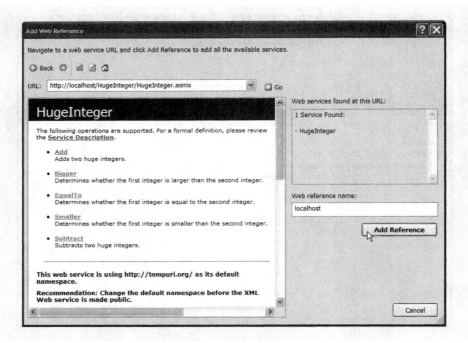

Fig. 22.15 | Web reference selection and description.

Step 5: Viewing the Web Reference in the Solution Explorer

The **Solution Explorer** (Fig. 22.16) should now contain a **Web References** folder with a node named after the domain name where the Web service is located. In this case, the name is localhost because we are using the local Web server. When we reference class HugeInteger in the client application, we will do so through the localhost namespace.

Fig. 22.16 | **Solution Explorer** after adding a Web reference to a project.

Notes on Creating a Client to Consume a Web Service

The steps we just presented also apply to adding Web references to Web applications created in Visual Web Developer. We present a Web application that consumes a Web service in Section 22.6.

When creating a client to consume a Web service, add the Web reference first so that Visual Basic 2005 (or Visual Web Developer) can recognize the Web service's class name. Once you add the Web reference to the client, it can access the Web service through an object of the proxy class. The proxy class (named `HugeInteger`) is located in namespace `localhost`, so you must use `localhost.HugeInteger` to reference this class. Although you must create an object of the proxy class to access the Web service, you do not need access to the proxy class's code. As we show in Section 22.4.5, you can invoke the proxy object's methods as if it were an object of the Web service class.

The steps that we just described work well if you know the appropriate Web service reference. However, what if you are trying to locate a new Web service? A technology to facilitate this process is *Universal Description, Discovery and Integration* (*UDDI*). UDDI is an ongoing project to develop a set of specifications that define how Web services should be published so that programmers searching for Web services can find them. You can learn more about UDDI by visiting www.uddi.org and uddi.microsoft.com. You can also visit Web services directory sites like www.xmethods.net, which list many available Web services.

22.4.5 Consuming the HugeInteger Web Service

The Windows Form in Fig. 22.17 uses the `HugeInteger` Web service to perform computations with positive integers up to 100 digits long. You are already familiar with Visual Basic applications that use `Labels`, `TextBoxes` and `Buttons`, so we focus our discussions on the Web services concepts in this chapter's applications.

```vb
1   ' Fig. 22.17: UsingHugeIntegerWebService.vb
2   ' Using the HugeInteger Web Service.
3   Imports System.Web.Services.Protocols
4
5   Public Class UsingHugeIntegerWebService
6      ' declare a reference to Web service
7      Private remoteInteger As localhost.HugeInteger
8
9      ' character to trim from strings
10     Private zeros As Char() = New Char() {"0"c}
11
12     ' instantiates object to interact with Web service
13     Private Sub UsingHugeIntegerWebService_Load(ByVal sender As Object, _
14        ByVal e As System.EventArgs) Handles Me.Load
15        ' instantiate remoteInteger
16        remoteInteger = New localhost.HugeInteger()
17     End Sub ' UsingHugeIntegerWebService_Load
```

Fig. 22.17 | Using the `HugeInteger` Web service. (Part 1 of 5.)

```
18
19        ' adds two numbers input by user
20        Private Sub btnAdd_Click(ByVal sender As System.Object, _
21           ByVal e As System.EventArgs) Handles btnAdd.Click
22           ' make sure numbers do not exceed 100 digits and that both
23           ' are not 100 digits long, which would result in overflow
24           If txtFirst.Text.Length > 100 Or txtSecond.Text.Length > 100 _
25              Or (txtFirst.Text.Length = 100 And _
26              txtSecond.Text.Length = 100) Then
27              MessageBox.Show( _
28                 "HugeIntegers must not be more than 100 digits" & _
29                 vbCrLf & "Both integers cannot be of length 100: " & _
30                 " this causes an overflow", "Error", _
31                 MessageBoxButtons.OK, MessageBoxIcon.Information)
32           Else
33              ' perform addition
34              lblResult.Text = remoteInteger.Add( _
35                 txtFirst.Text, txtSecond.Text).TrimStart(zeros)
36           End If
37        End Sub ' btnAdd_Click
38
39        ' subtracts two numbers input by user
40        Private Sub btnSubtract_Click(ByVal sender As System.Object, _
41           ByVal e As System.EventArgs) Handles btnSubtract.Click
42           ' ensure that HugeIntegers do not exceed 100 digits
43           If Not NumbersTooBig(txtFirst.Text, txtSecond.Text) Then
44              ' perform subtraction
45              Try
46                 Dim result As String = remoteInteger.Subtract( _
47                    txtFirst.Text, txtSecond.Text).TrimStart(zeros)
48
49                 If result = "" Then
50                    lblResult.Text = "0"
51                 Else
52                    lblResult.Text = result
53                 End If
54              Catch exception As SoapException
55                 ' if WebMethod throws an exception,
56                 ' then first argument was smaller than second
57                 MessageBox.Show( _
58                    "First argument was smaller than the second")
59              End Try
60           End If
61        End Sub ' btnSubtract_Click
62
63        ' determines whether first number input is larger than the second
64        Private Sub btnLarger_Click(ByVal sender As System.Object, _
65           ByVal e As System.EventArgs) Handles btnLarger.Click
66           ' ensure that HugeIntegers do not exceed 100 digits
67           If Not NumbersTooBig(txtFirst.Text, txtSecond.Text) Then
68              ' call Web-service method to determine whether
69              ' first integer is larger than the second
```

Fig. 22.17 | Using the HugeInteger Web service. (Part 2 of 5.)

```vb
70              If remoteInteger.Bigger(txtFirst.Text, txtSecond.Text) Then
71                  lblResult.Text = txtFirst.Text.TrimStart(zeros) & _
72                      " is larger than " & txtSecond.Text.TrimStart(zeros)
73              Else
74                  lblResult.Text = txtFirst.Text.TrimStart(zeros) & _
75                      " is not larger than " + txtSecond.Text.TrimStart(zeros)
76              End If
77          End If
78      End Sub ' btnLarger_Click
79
80      ' determines whether first number input is smaller than the second
81      Private Sub btnSmaller_Click(ByVal sender As System.Object, _
82          ByVal e As System.EventArgs) Handles btnSmaller.Click
83          ' make sure HugeIntegers do not exceed 100 digits
84          If Not NumbersTooBig(txtFirst.Text, txtSecond.Text) Then
85              ' call Web-service method to determine if
86              ' first integer is smaller than second
87              If remoteInteger.Smaller(txtFirst.Text, txtSecond.Text) Then
88                  lblResult.Text = txtFirst.Text.TrimStart(zeros) & _
89                      " is smaller than " + txtSecond.Text.TrimStart(zeros)
90              Else
91                  lblResult.Text = txtFirst.Text.TrimStart(zeros) & _
92                      " is not smaller than " & txtSecond.Text.TrimStart(zeros)
93              End If
94          End If
95      End Sub ' btnSmaller_Click
96
97      ' determines whether the two numbers input are equal
98      Private Sub btnEqual_Click(ByVal sender As System.Object, _
99          ByVal e As System.EventArgs) Handles btnEqual.Click
100         ' ensure that HugeIntegers do not exceed 100 digits
101         If Not NumbersTooBig(txtFirst.Text, txtSecond.Text) Then
102             ' call Web-service method to determine if integers are equal
103             If remoteInteger.EqualTo(txtFirst.Text, txtSecond.Text) Then
104                 lblResult.Text = txtFirst.Text.TrimStart(zeros) & _
105                     " is equal to " & txtSecond.Text.TrimStart(zeros)
106             Else
107                 lblResult.Text = txtFirst.Text.TrimStart(zeros) & _
108                     " is not equal to " & txtSecond.Text.TrimStart(zeros)
109             End If
110         End If
111     End Sub ' btnEqual_Click
112
113     ' determines whether numbers input by user are too big
114     Private Function NumbersTooBig(ByVal first As String, _
115         ByVal second As String) As Boolean
116         ' display an error message if either number has too many digits
117         If (first.Length > 100) Or (second.Length > 100) Then
118             MessageBox.Show("HugeIntegers must be less than 100 digits", _
119                 "Error", MessageBoxButtons.OK, MessageBoxIcon.Information)
120             Return True
121         End If
```

Fig. 22.17 | Using the HugeInteger Web service. (Part 3 of 5.)

```
122
123        Return False
124     End Function ' SizeCheck
125 End Class ' UsingHugeIntegerWebService
```

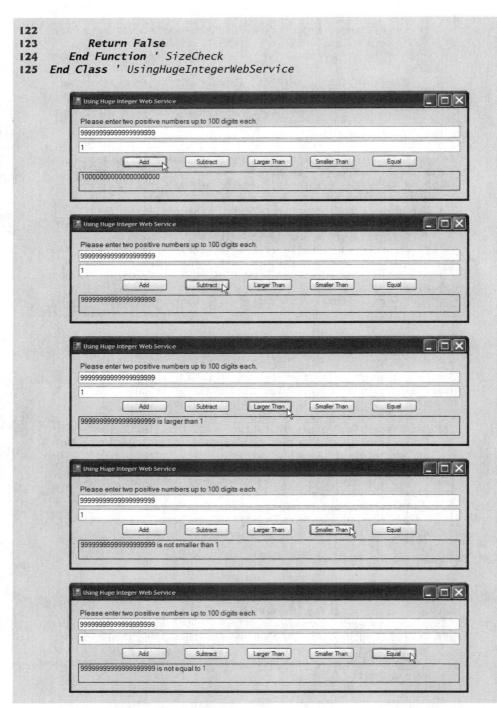

Fig. 22.17 | Using the HugeInteger Web service. (Part 4 of 5.)

Fig. 22.17 | Using the `HugeInteger` Web service. (Part 5 of 5.)

Line 7 declares variable `remoteInteger` of type `localhost.HugeInteger`. This variable is used in each of the application's event handlers to call methods of the `HugeInteger` Web service. The proxy object is created and assigned to this variable at line 16 in the Form's `Load` event handler. Lines 34–35, 46–47, 70, 87 and 103 in the various button event handlers invoke methods of the Web service. Note that each call is made on the local proxy object, which then communicates with the Web service on the client's behalf. If you downloaded the example from `www.deitel.com/books/vbforprogrammers2`, you might need to regenerate the proxy by removing the Web reference, then adding it again. To do so, right click **localhost** in the **Web References** folder in the **Solution Explorer** and select option **Delete**. Then follow the instructions in the preceding section to add the Web reference to the project.

The user inputs two integers, each up to 100 digits long. Clicking a button causes the application to invoke a Web method to perform the appropriate task and return the result. Note that client application `UsingHugeIntegerService` cannot perform operations using 100-digit numbers directly. Instead the application creates `String` representations of these numbers and passes them as arguments to Web methods that handle such tasks for the client. It then uses the return value of each operation to display an appropriate message.

Note that the application eliminates leading zeros in the numbers before displaying them by calling `String` method `TrimStart`. Like `String` method `Trim` (discussed in Chapter 16), `TrimStart` removes all occurrences of characters specified by a `Char` array (line 24) from the beginning of a `String`.

22.5 Session Tracking in Web Services

In Chapter 21, we described the advantages of maintaining information about users to personalize their experiences. In particular, we discussed session tracking using cookies and `HttpSessionState` objects. We will now incorporate session tracking into a Web service. Suppose a client application needs to call several methods from the same Web service, possibly several times each. In such a case, it can be beneficial for the Web service to maintain state information for the client. Session tracking eliminates the need for information about the client to be passed between the client and the Web service multiple times. For example, a Web service providing access to local restaurant reviews would benefit from storing the client user's street address. Once the user's address is stored in a session variable, Web methods can return personalized, localized results without requiring that the address be passed in each method call. This not only improves performance, but also requires less effort on the part of the programmer—less information is passed in each method call.

22.5.1 Creating a Blackjack Web Service

Storing session information can provide client programmers with a more intuitive Web service. Our next example is a Web service that assists programmers in developing a black-jack card game (Fig. 22.18). The Web service provides Web methods to deal a card and to evaluate a hand of cards. After presenting the Web service, we use it to serve as the dealer for a game of blackjack (Fig. 22.19). The blackjack Web service uses a session variable to maintain a unique deck of cards for each client application. Several clients can use the service at the same time, but Web method calls made by a specific client use only the deck stored in that client's session. Our example uses a simple subset of casino blackjack rules:

Two cards each are dealt to the dealer and the player. The player's cards are dealt face up. Only the first of the dealer's cards is dealt face up. Each card has a value. A card numbered 2 through 10 is worth its face value. Jacks, queens and kings each count as 10. Aces can count as 1 or 11—whichever value is more beneficial to the player (as we will soon see). If the sum of the player's two initial cards is 21 (i.e., the player was dealt a card valued at 10 and an ace, which counts as 11 in this situation), the player has "blackjack" and immediately wins the game. Otherwise, the player can begin taking additional cards one at a time. These cards are dealt face up, and the player decides when to stop taking cards. If the player "busts" (i.e., the sum of the player's cards exceeds 21), the game is over, and the player loses. When the player is satisfied with the current set of cards, the player "stays" (i.e., stops taking cards), and the dealer's hidden card is revealed. If the dealer's total is 16 or less, the dealer must take another card; otherwise, the dealer must stay. The dealer must continue to take cards until the sum of the dealer's cards is greater than or equal to 17. If the dealer exceeds 21, the player wins. Otherwise, the hand with the higher point total wins. If the dealer and the player have the same point total, the game is a "push" (i.e., a tie), and no one wins.

The Web service (Fig. 22.18) provides methods to deal a card and to determine the point value of a hand. We represent each card as a String consisting of a digit (e.g., 1–13) representing the card's face (e.g., ace through king), followed by a space and a digit (e.g., 0–3) representing the card's suit (e.g., clubs, diamonds, hearts or spades). For example, the jack of hearts is represented as "11 2", and the two of clubs is represented as "2 0". After deploying the Web service, we create a Windows application that uses the BlackjackWeb-Service's Web methods to implement a game of blackjack. To create and deploy this Web service follow the steps presented in Sections 22.4.2–22.4.3 for the HugeInteger service.

Lines 15–16 define method DealCard as a Web method. Setting property *EnableSession* to True indicates that session information should be maintained and should be accessible to this method. This is required only for methods that must access the session information. Doing so allows the Web service to use an HttpSessionState object (named Session by ASP.NET) to maintain the deck of cards for each client application that uses this Web service (line 22). We can use Session to store objects for a specific client between method calls. We discussed session state in detail in Chapter 21.

Method DealCard removes a card from the deck and sends it to the client. Without using a session variable, the deck of cards would need to be passed back and forth with each method call. Using session state makes the method easy to call (it requires no arguments), and avoids the overhead of sending the deck over the network multiple times.

At this point, our Web service contains methods that use session variables. However, the Web service still cannot determine which session variables belong to which user. If two clients successfully call the DealCard method, the same deck would be manipulated. To

```vb
 1   ' Fig. 22.18: BlackjackWebService.vb
 2   ' Blackjack Web Service deals and counts cards.
 3   Imports System.Web
 4   Imports System.Web.Services
 5   Imports System.Web.Services.Protocols
 6
 7   <WebService(Namespace:="http://www.deitel.com/", Description:= _
 8      "A Web service that deals and counts cards for the game Blackjack")> _
 9   <WebServiceBinding(ConformsTo:=WsiProfiles.BasicProfile1_1)> _
10   <Global.Microsoft.VisualBasic.CompilerServices.DesignerGenerated()> _
11   Public Class BlackjackWebService
12      Inherits System.Web.Services.WebService
13
14      ' deals card that has not yet been dealt
15      <WebMethod(EnableSession:=True, _
16         Description:="Deal a new card from the deck.")> _
17      Public Function DealCard() As String
18         ' get client's deck
19         Dim deck As ArrayList = CType(Session("deck"), ArrayList)
20         Dim card As String = Convert.ToString(deck(0))
21         deck.RemoveAt(0)
22         Return card
23      End Function ' DealCard
24
25      ' creates and shuffles a deck of cards
26      <WebMethod(EnableSession:=True, _
27         Description:="Create and shuffle a deck of cards.")> _
28      Public Sub Shuffle()
29         Dim temporary As Object ' holds card temporarily during swapping
30         Dim randomObject As New Random() ' generates random numbers
31         Dim newIndex As Integer ' index of randomly selected card
32         Dim deck As New ArrayList() ' stores deck of cards (strings)
33
34         ' generate all possible cards
35         For face As Integer = 1 To 13 ' loop through face values
36            For suit As Integer = 0 To 3 ' loop through suits
37               deck.Add(face & " " & suit) ' add card (string) to deck
38            Next
39         Next
40
41         ' shuffles deck by swapping each card with another card randomly
42         For i As Integer = 0 To deck.Count - 1
43            ' get random index
44            newIndex = randomObject.Next(deck.Count - 1)
45            temporary = deck(i) ' save current card in temporary variable
46            deck(i) = deck(newIndex) ' copy randomly selected card
47            deck(newIndex) = temporary ' copy current card back into deck
48         Next
49
50         Session.Add("deck", deck) ' add this deck to user's session state
51      End Sub ' Shuffle
52
```

Fig. 22.18 | Blackjack Web service. (Part 1 of 2.)

```vb
53      ' computes value of hand
54      <WebMethod(Description:= _
55         "Compute a numerical value for the current hand.")> _
56      Public Function GetHandValue(ByVal dealt As String) As Integer
57         ' split string containing all cards
58         Dim tab As Char() = New Char() {Convert.ToChar(vbTab)}
59         Dim cards As String() = dealt.Split(tab) ' get array of cards
60         Dim total As Integer = 0 ' total value of cards in hand
61         Dim face As integer ' face of the current card
62         Dim aceCount As Integer = 0 ' number of aces in hand
63
64         ' loop through the cards in the hand
65         For Each drawn As String In cards
66            ' get face of card
67            face = Int32.Parse(drawn.Substring(0, drawn.IndexOf(" ")))
68
69            Select Case face
70               Case 1 ' if ace, increment aceCount
71                  aceCount += 1
72               Case 11 To 13 ' if jack, queen or king add 10
73                  total += 10
74               Case Else ' otherwise, add value of face
75                  total += face
76            End Select
77         Next
78
79         ' if there are any aces, calculate optimum total
80         If aceCount > 0 Then
81            ' if it is possible to count one ace as 11, and the rest
82            ' as 1 each, do so otherwise, count all aces as 1 each
83            If (total + 11 + aceCount - 1 <= 21) Then
84               total += 11 + aceCount - 1
85            Else
86               total += aceCount
87            End If
88         End If
89
90         Return total
91      End Function ' GetHandValue
92   End Class ' BlackjackWebService
```

Fig. 22.18 | Blackjack Web service. (Part 2 of 2.)

avoid this problem, the Web service automatically creates a cookie to uniquely identify each client. A Web browser client that has cookie handling enabled stores cookies automatically. A non-browser client application that consumes this Web service must create a **CookieContainer** object to store cookies sent from the server. We discuss this in more detail in Section 22.5.2, when we examine the blackjack Web service's client.

Web method DealCard (lines 15–23) selects a card from the deck and sends it to the client. The method first obtains the current user's deck as an ArrayList from the Web service's Session object (line 19). After obtaining the user's deck, DealCard removes the top card from the deck (line 21) and returns the card's value as a String (line 22).

Method `Shuffle` (lines 26–51) generates an `ArrayList` representing a deck of cards, shuffles it and stores it cards in the client's `Session` object. Lines 35–39 generate `Strings` in the form *"face suit"* to represent each card in a deck. Lines 42–48 shuffle the deck by swapping each card with another randomly selected card. Line 50 adds the `ArrayList` to the `Session` object to maintain the deck between method calls from a particular client.

Method `GetHandValue` (lines 54–91) determines the total value of the cards in a hand by trying to attain the highest score possible without going over 21. Recall that an ace can be counted as either 1 or 11, and all face cards count as 10.

As you will see in Fig. 22.19, the client application maintains a hand of cards as a `String` in which each card is separated by a tab character. Line 59 tokenizes the hand of cards (represented by `dealt`) into individual cards by calling `String` method `Split` and passing to it an array that contains the delimiter characters (in this case, just a tab). `Split` uses the delimiter characters to separate tokens in the `String`. Lines 65–77 count the value of each card. Line 67 retrieves the first integer—the face—and uses that value in the `Select Case` statement (lines 69–76). If the card is an ace, the method increments variable `aceCount` (line 71). We discuss how this variable is used shortly. If the card is an 11, 12 or 13 (jack, queen or king), the method adds 10 to the total value of the hand (line 73). If the card is anything else, the method increases the total by that value (line 75).

Because an ace can have either of two values, additional logic is required to process aces. Lines 80–88 process the aces after all the other cards. If a hand contains several aces, only one ace can be counted as 11 (if two aces each are counted as 11, the hand would have a losing value of 22). The condition in line 83 determines whether counting one ace as 11 and the rest as 1 will result in a total that does not exceed 21. If this is possible, line 84 adjusts the total accordingly. Otherwise, line 86 adjusts the total, counting each ace as 1.

Method `GetHandValue` maximizes the value of the current cards without exceeding 21. Imagine, for example, that the dealer has a 7 and receives an ace. The new total could be either 8 or 18. However, `GetHandValue` always maximizes the value of the cards without going over 21, so the new total is 18.

22.5.2 Consuming the Blackjack Web Service

Now we use the blackjack Web service in a Windows application (Fig. 22.19). This application uses an instance of `BlackjackWeService` (declared in line 7 and created in line 30) to represent the dealer. The Web service keeps track of the player's and the dealer's cards (i.e., all the cards that have been dealt). As in Section 22.4.4, you must add a Web reference to your project so it can access the Web service. The code and images for this example are provided with the chapter's examples, which can be downloaded from our Web site: www.deitel.com/books/vbforprogrammers2.

Each player has 11 `PictureBoxes`—the maximum number of cards that can be dealt without automatically exceeding 21 (i.e., four aces, four twos and three threes). These `PictureBoxes` are placed in an `ArrayList` (lines 37–58), so we can index the `ArrayList` during the game to determine the `PictureBox` that will display a particular card image.

In Section 22.5.1, we mentioned that the client must provide a way to accept cookies created by the Web service to uniquely identify users. Line 33 in `BlackjackForm`'s Load event handler creates a new `CookieContainer` object for the dealer's `CookieContainer` property. A `CookieContainer` (namespace `System.Net`) stores the information from a cookie (created by the Web service) in a `Cookie` object in the `CookieContainer`. The

Cookie contains a unique identifier that the Web service can use to recognize the client when the client makes future requests. As part of each request, the cookie is automatically sent back to the server. If the client did not create a CookieContainer object, the Web service would create a new Session object for each request, and the user's state information would not persist across requests.

Method GameOver (lines 145–172) shows an appropriate message in the status PictureBox and displays the final point totals of both the dealer and the player. These values are obtained by calling the Web service's GetHandValue method in lines 164 and 166. Method GameOver receives as an argument a member of the GameStatus enumeration (defined in lines 19–24). The enumeration represents whether the player tied, lost or won the game; its four members are PUSH, LOSE, WIN and BLACKJACK.

When the player clicks the **Deal** button, the event handler (lines 175–226) clears all of the PictureBoxes and the Labels displaying the final point totals. Line 189 shuffles the deck by calling the Web Service's Shuffle method, then the player and dealer receive two cards each (returned by calls to the Web service's DealCard method in lines 192, 196, 201 and 203). Lines 212–213 evaluate both the dealer's and player's hands by calling the Web service's GetHandValue method. If the player and the dealer both obtain scores of 21, the program calls method GameOver, passing GameStatus.PUSH. If only the player has 21 after the first two cards are dealt, the program passes GameStatus.BLACKJACK to method GameOver. If only the dealer has 21, the program passes GameStatus.LOSE to method GameOver.

```vb
1    ' Fig. 22.19: FrmBlackjack.vb
2    ' Blackjack game that uses the Blackjack Web service.
3    Imports System.Net
4
5    Public Class FrmBlackjack
6       ' reference to Web service
7       Private dealer As localhost.BlackjackWebService
8
9       ' string representing the dealer's cards
10      Private dealersCards As String
11
12      ' string representing the player's cards
13      Private playersCards As String
14      Private cardBoxes As ArrayList ' list of PictureBoxes for card images
15      Private currentPlayerCard As Integer ' player's current card number
16      Private currentDealerCard As Integer ' dealer's current card number
17
18      ' enum representing the possible game outcomes
19      Public Enum GameStatus
20         PUSH ' game ends in a tie
21         LOSE ' player loses
22         WIN ' player wins
23         BLACKJACK ' player has blackjack
24      End Enum ' GameStatus
25
```

Fig. 22.19 | Blackjack game that uses the Blackjack Web service. (Part 1 of 8.)

```
26          ' sets up the game
27          Private Sub FrmBlackjack_Load(ByVal sender As Object, _
28              ByVal e As System.EventArgs) Handles Me.Load
29              ' instantiate object allowing communication with Web service
30              dealer = New localhost.BlackjackWebService()
31
32              ' allow session state
33              dealer.CookieContainer = New CookieContainer()
34              cardBoxes = New ArrayList()
35
36              ' put PictureBoxes into cardBoxes ArrayList
37              cardBoxes.Add(pictureBox1)
38              cardBoxes.Add(pictureBox2)
39              cardBoxes.Add(pictureBox3)
40              cardBoxes.Add(pictureBox4)
41              cardBoxes.Add(pictureBox5)
42              cardBoxes.Add(pictureBox6)
43              cardBoxes.Add(pictureBox7)
44              cardBoxes.Add(pictureBox8)
45              cardBoxes.Add(pictureBox9)
46              cardBoxes.Add(pictureBox10)
47              cardBoxes.Add(pictureBox11)
48              cardBoxes.Add(pictureBox12)
49              cardBoxes.Add(pictureBox13)
50              cardBoxes.Add(pictureBox14)
51              cardBoxes.Add(pictureBox15)
52              cardBoxes.Add(pictureBox16)
53              cardBoxes.Add(pictureBox17)
54              cardBoxes.Add(pictureBox18)
55              cardBoxes.Add(pictureBox19)
56              cardBoxes.Add(pictureBox20)
57              cardBoxes.Add(pictureBox21)
58              cardBoxes.Add(pictureBox22)
59          End Sub ' FrmBlackjack_Load
60
61          ' deals cards to dealer while dealer's total is less than 17,
62          ' then computes value of each hand and determines winner
63          Private Sub DealerPlay()
64              ' reveal dealer's second card
65              Dim tab As Char() = New Char() {Convert.ToChar(vbTab)}
66              Dim cards As String() = dealersCards.Split(tab)
67              DisplayCard(1, cards(1))
68
69              Dim nextCard As String
70
71              ' while value of dealer's hand is below 17,
72              ' dealer must take cards
73              While dealer.GetHandValue(dealersCards) < 17
74                  nextCard = dealer.DealCard() ' deal new card
75                  dealersCards &= vbTab & nextCard
76
77                  ' update GUI to show new card
78                  MessageBox.Show("Dealer takes a card")
```

Fig. 22.19 | Blackjack game that uses the Blackjack Web service. (Part 2 of 8.)

```vbnet
79              DisplayCard(currentDealerCard, nextCard)
80              currentDealerCard += 1
81          End While
82
83          Dim dealerTotal As Integer = dealer.GetHandValue(dealersCards)
84          Dim playerTotal As Integer = dealer.GetHandValue(playersCards)
85
86          ' if dealer busted, player wins
87          If dealerTotal > 21 Then
88              GameOver(GameStatus.WIN)
89          Else
90              ' if dealer and player have not exceeded 21,
91              ' higher score wins equal scores is a push.
92              If dealerTotal > playerTotal Then
93                  GameOver(GameStatus.LOSE)
94              ElseIf playerTotal > dealerTotal Then
95                  GameOver(GameStatus.WIN)
96              Else
97                  GameOver(GameStatus.PUSH)
98              End If
99          End If
100     End Sub ' DealerPlay
101
102     ' displays card represented by cardValue in specified PictureBox
103     Public Sub DisplayCard( _
104         ByVal card As Integer, ByVal cardValue As String)
105         ' retrieve appropriate PictureBox from ArrayList
106         Dim displayBox As PictureBox = CType(cardBoxes(card), PictureBox)
107
108         ' if string representing card is empty,
109         ' set displayBox to display back of card
110         If cardValue = "" Then
111             displayBox.Image = _
112                 Image.FromFile("blackjack_images/cardback.png")
113             Return
114         End If
115
116         ' retrieve face value of card from cardValue
117         Dim face As String = _
118             cardValue.Substring(0, cardValue.IndexOf(" "))
119
120         ' retrieve the suit of the card from cardValue
121         Dim suit As String = _
122             cardValue.Substring(cardValue.IndexOf(" ") + 1)
123
124         Dim suitLetter As Char ' suit letter used to form image file name
125
126         ' determine the suit letter of the card
127         Select Case Convert.ToInt32(suit)
128             Case 0 ' clubs
129                 suitLetter = "c"c
130             Case 1 ' diamonds
131                 suitLetter = "d"c
```

Fig. 22.19 | Blackjack game that uses the Blackjack Web service. (Part 3 of 8.)

```
132            Case 2 ' hearts
133                suitLetter = "h"c
134            Case Else ' spades
135                suitLetter = "s"c
136        End Select
137
138        ' set displayBox to display appropriate image
139        displayBox.Image = Image.FromFile( _
140            "blackjack_images/" & face & suitLetter & ".png")
141    End Sub ' DisplayCard
142
143    ' displays all player cards and shows
144    ' appropriate game status message
145    Public Sub GameOver(ByVal winner As GameStatus)
146        ' display appropriate status image
147        If winner = GameStatus.PUSH Then ' push
148            statusPictureBox.Image = _
149                Image.FromFile("blackjack_images/tie.png")
150        ElseIf winner = GameStatus.LOSE Then ' player loses
151            statusPictureBox.Image = _
152                Image.FromFile("blackjack_images/lose.png")
153        ElseIf winner = GameStatus.BLACKJACK Then
154            ' player has blackjack
155            statusPictureBox.Image = _
156                Image.FromFile("blackjack_images/blackjack.png")
157        Else ' player wins
158            statusPictureBox.Image = _
159                Image.FromFile("blackjack_images/win.png")
160        End If
161
162        ' display final totals for dealer and player
163        lblDealerTotal.Text = _
164            "Dealer: " & dealer.GetHandValue(dealersCards)
165        lblPlayerTotal.Text = _
166            "Player: " & dealer.GetHandValue(playersCards)
167
168        ' reset controls for new game
169        btnStay.Enabled = False
170        btnHit.Enabled = False
171        btnDeal.Enabled = True
172    End Sub ' GameOver
173
174    ' deal two cards each to dealer and player
175    Private Sub btnDeal_Click(ByVal sender As System.Object, _
176        ByVal e As System.EventArgs) Handles btnDeal.Click
177        Dim card As String ' stores a card temporarily until added to a hand
178
179        ' clear card images
180        For Each cardImage As PictureBox In cardBoxes
181            cardImage.Image = Nothing
182        Next
183
```

Fig. 22.19 | Blackjack game that uses the Blackjack Web service. (Part 4 of 8.)

```
184         statusPictureBox.Image = Nothing ' clear status image
185         lblDealerTotal.Text = "" ' clear final total for dealer
186         lblPlayerTotal.Text = "" ' clear final total for player
187
188         ' create a new, shuffled deck on the remote machine
189         dealer.Shuffle()
190
191         ' deal two cards to player
192         playersCards = dealer.DealCard() ' deal a card to player's hand
193
194         ' update GUI to display new card
195         DisplayCard(11, playersCards)
196         card = dealer.DealCard() ' deal a second card
197         DisplayCard(12, card) ' update GUI to display new card
198         playersCards &= vbTab & card ' add second card to player's hand
199
200         ' deal two cards to dealer, only display face of first card
201         dealersCards = dealer.DealCard() ' deal a card to dealer's hand
202         DisplayCard(0, dealersCards) ' update GUI to display new card
203         card = dealer.DealCard() ' deal a second card
204         DisplayCard(1, "") ' update GUI to show face-down card
205         dealersCards &= vbTab & card ' add second card to dealer's hand
206
207         btnStay.Enabled = True ' allow player to stay
208         btnHit.Enabled = True ' allow player to hit
209         btnDeal.Enabled = False ' disable Deal Button
210
211         ' determine the value of the two hands
212         Dim dealerTotal As Integer = dealer.GetHandValue(dealersCards)
213         Dim playerTotal As Integer = dealer.GetHandValue(playersCards)
214
215         ' if hands equal 21, it is a push
216         If dealerTotal = playerTotal And dealerTotal = 21 Then
217            GameOver(GameStatus.PUSH)
218         ElseIf dealerTotal = 21 Then ' if dealer has 21, dealer wins
219            GameOver(GameStatus.LOSE)
220         ElseIf playerTotal = 21 Then ' player has blackjack
221            GameOver(GameStatus.BLACKJACK)
222         End If
223
224         currentDealerCard = 2 ' next dealer card has index 2 in cardBoxes
225         currentPlayerCard = 13 ' next player card has index 13 in cardBoxes
226     End Sub ' btnDeal_Click
227
228     ' deal another card to player
229     Private Sub btnHit_Click(ByVal sender As System.Object, _
230         ByVal e As System.EventArgs) Handles btnHit.Click
231         ' get player another card
232         Dim card As String = dealer.DealCard() ' deal new card
233         playersCards &= vbTab & card ' add new card to player's hand
234
235         ' update GUI to show new card
236         DisplayCard(currentPlayerCard, card)
```

Fig. 22.19 | Blackjack game that uses the Blackjack Web service. (Part 5 of 8.)

```
237            currentPlayerCard += 1
238
239         ' determine the value of the player's hand
240         Dim total As Integer = dealer.GetHandValue(playersCards)
241
242         ' if player exceeds 21, house wins
243         If total > 21 Then
244            GameOver(GameStatus.LOSE)
245         End If
246
247         ' if player has 21,
248         ' they cannot take more cards, and dealer plays
249         If total = 21 Then
250            btnHit.Enabled = False
251            DealerPlay()
252         End If
253      End Sub ' btnHit_Click
254
255      ' play the dealer's hand after the play chooses to stay
256      Private Sub btnStay_Click(ByVal sender As System.Object, _
257         ByVal e As System.EventArgs) Handles btnStay.Click
258         btnStay.Enabled = False ' disable Stay Button
259         btnHit.Enabled = False ' display Hit Button
260         btnDeal.Enabled = True ' re-enable Deal Button
261         DealerPlay() ' player chose to stay, so play the dealer's hand
262      End Sub ' btnStay_Click
263   End Class ' FrmBlackjack
```

a) Initial cards dealt to the player and the dealer when the user pressed the **Deal** button.

Fig. 22.19 | Blackjack game that uses the `Blackjack` Web service. (Part 6 of 8.)

b) Cards after the player pressed the **Hit** button twice, then the **Stay** button. In this case, the player won the game with a higher total than the dealer.

c) Cards after the player pressed the **Hit** button once, then the **Stay** button. In this case, the player busted (exceeded 21) and the dealer won the game.

Fig. 22.19 | Blackjack game that uses the `Blackjack` Web service. (Part 7 of 8.)

d) Cards after the player pressed the **Deal** button. In this case, the player won with Blackjack because the first two cards were an ace and a card with a value of 10 (a jack in this case).

e) Cards after the player pressed the **Stay** button. In this case, the player and dealer push—they have the same card total.

Fig. 22.19 | Blackjack game that uses the `Blackjack` Web service. (Part 8 of 8.)

If `dealButton_Click` does not call `GameOver`, the player can take more cards by clicking the **Hit** button. The event handler for this button is in lines 229–253. Each time a player clicks **Hit**, the program deals the player one more card (line 232) and displays it in the GUI. Line 240 evaluates the player's hand. If the player exceeds 21, the game is over, and the player loses. If the player has exactly 21, the player is not allowed to take any more cards, and method `DealerPlay` (lines 63–100) is called, causing the dealer to keep taking cards until the dealer's hand has a value of 17 or more (lines 73–81). If the dealer exceeds 21, the player wins (line 88); otherwise, the values of the hands are compared, and `GameOver` is called with the appropriate argument (lines 92–98).

Clicking the **Stay** button indicates that a player does not want to be dealt another card. The event handler for this button (lines 256–262) disables the **Hit** and **Stay** buttons, then calls method `DealerPlay`.

Method `DisplayCard` (lines 103–141) updates the GUI to display a newly dealt card. The method takes as arguments an integer representing the index of the `PictureBox` in the `ArrayList` that must have its image set, and a `String` representing the card. An empty `String` indicates that we wish to display the card face down. If method `DisplayCard` receives a `String` that's not empty, the program extracts the face and suit from the `String` and uses this information to find the correct image. The `Select Case` statement (lines 127–136) converts the number representing the suit to an integer and assigns the appropriate character to `suitLetter` (c for clubs, d for diamonds, h for hearts and s for spades). The character in `suitLetter` is used to complete the image's file name (lines 139–140).

22.6 Using Web Forms and Web Services

Our prior examples accessed Web services from Windows applications. You can just as easily use Web services in Web applications. In fact, Web-based businesses are becoming increasingly prevalent, so it's common for Web applications to consume Web services. Figure 22.20 presents an airline reservation Web service that receives information regarding the type of seat a customer wishes to reserve and makes a reservation if such a seat is available. Later in this section, we present a Web application that allows a customer to specify a reservation request, then uses the airline reservation Web service to execute the request. The code and database used in this example are provided with the chapter's examples, which can be downloaded from www.deitel.com/books/vbforprogrammers2.

```
1   ' Fig. 22.20: ReservationWebService.vb
2   ' Airline reservation Web Service.Imports System.Web
3   Imports System.Web.Services
4   Imports System.Web.Services.Protocols
5
6   <WebService(Namespace:="http://www.deitel.com/")> _
7   <WebServiceBinding(ConformsTo:=WsiProfiles.BasicProfile1_1)> _
8   <Global.Microsoft.VisualBasic.CompilerServices.DesignerGenerated()> _
9   Public Class ReservationWebService
10      Inherits System.Web.Services.WebService
11      ' create TicketsDataSet object for caching data
12      ' from the Tickets database
13      Private ticketsDataSet As New TicketsDataSet()
```

Fig. 22.20 | Airline reservation Web service. (Part 1 of 2.)

```
14
15        ' create SeatsTableAdapter for interacting with the database
16        Private seatsTableAdapter As _
17           New TicketsDataSetTableAdapters.SeatsTableAdapter()
18
19        ' checks database to determine whether matching seat is available
20        <WebMethod(Description:="Method to reserve a seat.")> _
21        Public Function Reserve(ByVal seatType As String, _
22           ByVal classType As String) As Boolean
23           ' fill TicketsDataSet.Seats with rows that represent untaken
24           ' seats that match the specified seatType and classType
25           seatsTableAdapter.FillByTypeAndClass( _
26              ticketsDataSet.Seats, seatType, classType)
27
28           ' if the number of seats returned is nonzero,
29           ' obtain the first matching seat number and mark it as taken
30           If ticketsDataSet.Seats.Count <> 0 Then
31              Dim seatNumber As String = ticketsDataSet.Seats(0).Number
32
33              seatsTableAdapter.UpdateSeatAsTaken(seatNumber)
34              Return True ' seat was reserved
35           End If
36
37           Return False ' no seat was reserved
38        End Function ' Reserve
39     End Class ' ReservationWebService
```

Fig. 22.20 | Airline reservation Web service. (Part 2 of 2.)

The airline reservation Web service has a single Web method—Reserve (lines 20–38)—which searches a seat database (Tickets.mdf) to locate a seat matching a user's request. If it finds an appropriate seat, Reserve updates the database, makes the reservation and returns True; otherwise, no reservation is made, and the method returns False. Note that the statements at lines 25–26 and line 33, which query and update the database, use objects of classes TicketsDataSet and TicketsDataSetTableAdapters.SeatsTable-Adapter. Recall from Chapter 20 that DataSet and TableAdapter classes are created for you when you use the **DataSet Designer** to add a DataSet to a project. We discuss the steps for adding the TicketsDataSet in Section 22.6.1.

Reserve receives two parameters—a String representing the desired seat type (i.e., Window, Middle or Aisle) and a String representing the desired class type (i.e., Economy or First). Our database contains four columns—the seat number (i.e., 1–10), the seat type (i.e., Window, Middle or Aisle), the class type (i.e., Economy or First) and a column containing either 1 (true) or 0 (false) to indicate whether the seat is taken. Lines 25–26 retrieve the seat numbers of any available seats matching the requested seat and class type. This statement fills the Seats table in ticketsDataSet with the results of the query

```
SELECT Number
FROM Seats
WHERE (Taken = 0) AND (Type = @type) AND (Class = @class)
```

The parameters @type and @class in the query are replaced with values of the seatType and classType arguments to SeatsTableAdapter method FillByTypeAndClass. In line

30, if the number of rows in the Seats table (ticketsDataSet.Seats.Count) is not zero, there was at least one seat that matched the user's request. In this case, the Web service reserves the first matching seat number. We obtain the seat number in line 31 by accessing the Seats table's first element (i.e., Seats(0)—the first row in the table), then obtaining the value of that row's Number column. Line 33 invokes the SeatsTableAdapter method UpdateSeatAsTaken and passes to it seatNumber—the seat to reserve. The method uses the UPDATE statement

```
UPDATE Seats
SET Taken = 1
WHERE (Number = @number)
```

to mark the seat as taken in the database by replacing parameter @number with the value of seatNumber. Method Reserve returns True (line 34) to indicate that the reservation was successful. If there are no matching seats (line 30), Reserve returns False (line 37) to indicate that no seats matched the user's request.

22.6.1 Adding Data Components to a Web Service

Next, you'll use Visual Web Developer's tools to configure a DataSet that allows our Web service to interact with the Tickets.mdf SQL Server database file. You'll add a new DataSet to the project, then configure the DataSet's TableAdapter using the **TableAdapter Configuration Wizard**. The wizard allows you to select the data source (Tickets.mdf) and to create the SQL statements necessary to support the database operations discussed in Fig. 22.20's description. The following steps for configuring the DataSet and its corresponding TableAdapter are similar to those you saw in Chapters 20 and 21.

Step 1: Create ReservationWebService and Add a DataSet to the Project
Begin by creating an ASP.NET Web Service project named ReservationWebService. Rename the file Service.vb as ReservationWebService.vb and replace its code with the code in Fig. 22.20. Next, add a DataSet named TicketsDataSet to the project. Right click the **App_Code** folder in the **Solution Explorer** and select **Add New Item...** from the pop-up menu. In the **Add New Item** dialog, select **DataSet**, specify TicketsDataSet.xsd in the **Name** field and click **Add**. This displays the TicketsDataSet in design view and opens the **TableAdapter Configuration Wizard**. When you add a DataSet to a project, the IDE creates appropriate TableAdapter classes for interacting with the database tables.

Step 2: Select the Data Source and Create a Connection
You'll use the **TableAdapter Configuration Wizard** in the next several steps to configure a TableAdapter for manipulating the Seats table in the Tickets.mdf database. Now, you must select the database. In the **TableAdapter Configuration Wizard**, click the **New Connection...** button to display the **Add Connection** dialog. In this dialog, specify **Microsoft SQL Server Database File** as the **Data source**, then click the **Browse...** button to display the **Select SQL Server Database File** dialog. Locate Tickets.mdf on your computer, select it and click the **Open** button to return to the **Add Connection** dialog. Click the **Test Connection** button to test the database connection, then click **OK** to return to the **TableAdapter Configuration Wizard**. Click **Next >**, then click **Yes** when you are asked whether you would like to add the file to your project and modify the connection. Click **Next >** to save the connection string in the application configuration file.

Step 3: Open the Query Builder and Add the Seats Table from `Tickets.mdf`

You must specify how the `TableAdapter` will access the database. In this example, you'll use SQL statements, so choose **Use SQL Statements**, then click **Next >**. Click **Query Builder...** to display the **Query Builder** and **Add Table** dialogs. Before building a SQL query, you must specify the table(s) to use in the query. The `Tickets.mdf` database contains only one table, named `Seats`. Select this table from the **Tables** tab and click **Add**. Click **Close** to close the **Add Table** dialog.

Step 4: Configure a SELECT Query to Obtain Available Seats

Now let's create a query which selects seats that are not already reserved and that match a particular type and class. Select **Number** from the **Seats** table at the top of the **Query Builder** dialog. Next, specify the criteria for selecting seats. In the middle of the **Query Builder** dialog, click the cell below **Number** in the **Column** column and select **Taken**. In the **Filter** column of this row, type 0 (i.e., false) to indicate that we should select only seat numbers that are not taken. In the next row, select **Type** in the **Column** column and specify `@type` as the **Filter** to indicate that the filter value will be specified as an argument to the method that implements this query. In the next row, select **Class** in the **Column** column and specify `@class` as the **Filter** to indicate that this filter value also will be specified as a method argument. Uncheck the checkboxes in the **Output** column for the **Taken**, **Type** and **Class** rows. The **Query Builder** dialog should now appear as shown in Fig. 22.21. Click **OK** to close the **Query Builder** dialog. Click **Next >** to choose the methods to generate. Name the `Fill` and `Get` methods `FillByTypeAndClass` and `GetDataByTypeAndClass`, respectively. Click the **Finish** button to generate these methods.

Fig. 22.21 | **QueryBuilder** dialog specifying a SELECT query that selects seats that are not already reserved and that match a particular type and class.

Step 5: Add Another Query to the SeatsTableAdapter *for the* TicketsDataSet
Now, you'll create an UPDATE query that reserves a seat. In the design area for the Tick-etsDataSet, click **SeatsTableAdapter** to select it, then right click it and select **Add Query...** to display the **TableAdapter Query Configuration Wizard**. Select **Use SQL Statements** and click **Next >**. Select **Update** as the query type and click **Next >**. Delete the existing UPDATE query. Click **Query Builder...** to display the **Query Builder** and **Add Table** dialogs. Then add the Seats table as you did in *Step 3* and click **Close** to return to the **Query Builder** dialog.

Step 6: Configure an UPDATE Statement to Reserve a Seat
In the **Query Builder** dialog, select the **Taken** column from the **Seats** table at the top of the dialog. In the middle of the dialog, place the value 1 (i.e., true) in the **New Value** column for the **Taken** row. In the row below **Taken**, select **Number**, uncheck the checkbox in the **Set** column and specify @number as the **Filter** value to indicate that the seat number will be specified as an argument to the method that implements this query. The **Query Builder** dialog should now appear as shown in Fig. 22.22. Click **OK** to return to the **TableAdapter Query Configuration Wizard**. Then click **Next >** to choose the name of the update method. Name the method UpdateSeatAsTaken, then click **Finish** to close the **TableAdapter Query Configuration Wizard**. At this point, you can use the ReservationWebService.asmx page to test the Web service's Reserve method. To do so, select **Start Without Debugging** from the **Debug** menu. In Section 22.6.2, we build a Web form to consume this Web service.

22.6.2 Creating a Web Form to Interact with the Airline Reservation Web Service

Figure 22.23 presents the code for a Web Form through which users can select seat types. This page allows users to reserve a seat on the basis of its class (Economy or First) and location (Aisle, Middle or Window) in a row of seats. The page then uses the airline reserva-

Fig. 22.22 | QueryBuilder dialog specifying an UPDATE statement that reserves a seat.

```
 1   <%-- Fig. 22.23: ReservationClient.aspx              --%>
 2   <%-- Web Form that allows users to reserve seats on a plane. --%>
 3   <%@ Page Language="VB" AutoEventWireup="false"
 4      CodeFile="ReservationClient.aspx.vb" Inherits="ReservationClient" %>
 5
 6   <!DOCTYPE html PUBLIC "-//W3C//DTD XHTML 1.0 Transitional//EN"
 7      "http://www.w3.org/TR/xhtml1/DTD/xhtml1-transitional.dtd">
 8
 9   <html xmlns="http://www.w3.org/1999/xhtml" >
10   <head runat="server">
11      <title>Ticket Reservation</title>
12   </head>
13   <body>
14      <form id="form1" runat="server">
15      <div>
16         <asp:Label ID="instructionsLabel" runat="server"
17            Text="Please select the seat type and class to reserve:">
18         </asp:Label>
19         <br /><br />
20         <asp:DropDownList ID="seatList" runat="server"
21            Height="22px" Width="100px">
22            <asp:ListItem>Aisle</asp:ListItem>
23            <asp:ListItem>Middle</asp:ListItem>
24            <asp:ListItem>Window</asp:ListItem>
25         </asp:DropDownList>
26             
27         <asp:DropDownList ID="classList" runat="server" Width="100px">
28            <asp:ListItem>Economy</asp:ListItem>
29            <asp:ListItem>First</asp:ListItem>
30         </asp:DropDownList>
31             
32         <asp:Button ID="reserveButton" runat="server" Text="Reserve"
33            Width="102px" />
34         <br /><br />
35         <asp:Label ID="errorLabel" runat="server" ForeColor="#C00000"
36            Height="19px" Width="343px"></asp:Label>
37      </div>
38      </form>
39   </body>
40   </html>
```

Fig. 22.23 | ASPX file that takes reservation information.

tion Web service to carry out users' requests. If the database request is not successful, the user is instructed to modify the request and try again. When you create this ASP.NET application, remember to add a Web reference to the ReservationWebService of Fig. 22.20

This page defines two DropDownList objects and a Button. One DropDownList (lines 20–25) displays all the seat types from which users can select. The second (lines 27–30) provides choices for the class type. Users click the Button named reserveButton (lines 32–33) to submit requests after making selections from the DropDownLists. The page also defines an initially blank Label named errorLabel (lines 35–36), which displays an appropriate message if no seat matching the user's selection is available. Line 9 of the code-behind file (Fig. 22.24) attaches an event handler to reserveButton.

Line 6 of Fig. 22.24 creates a `ReservationWebService` object. When the user clicks **Reserve** (Fig. 22.25), the `reserveButton_Click` event handler (lines 8–26 of Fig. 22.24) executes, and the page reloads. The event handler calls the Web service's `Reserve` method and passes to it the selected seat and class type as arguments (lines 10–11). If `Reserve` returns `True`, the application hides the GUI controls and displays a message thanking the user for making a reservation (line 20); otherwise, the application notifies the user that the type of seat requested is not available and instructs the user to try again (lines 23–24). You can use the techniques presented in Chapter 21 to build this ASP.NET Web Form. Figure 22.25 shows several user interactions with this Web application.

```vb
 1  ' Fig. 22.24: ReservationClient.aspx.vb
 2  ' ReservationClient code behind file.
 3  Partial Class ReservationClient
 4     Inherits System.Web.UI.Page
 5        ' object of proxy type used to connect to Reservation Web service
 6        Private ticketAgent As New localhost.ReservationWebService()
 7
 8     Protected Sub reserveButton_Click(ByVal sender As Object, _
 9        ByVal e As System.EventArgs) Handles reserveButton.Click
10        If ticketAgent.Reserve(seatList.SelectedItem.Text, _
11           classList.SelectedItem.Text.ToString()) Then
12           ' hide other controls
13           instructionsLabel.Visible = False
14           seatList.Visible = False
15           classList.Visible = False
16           reserveButton.Visible = False
17           errorLabel.Visible = False
18
19           ' display message indicating success
20           Response.Write("Your reservation has been made. Thank you.")
21        Else ' WebMethod returned false, so signal failure
22           ' display message in the initially blank errorLabel
23           errorLabel.Text = "This type of seat is not available. " & _
24              "Please modify your request and try again."
25        End If
26     End Sub ' reserveButton_Click
27  End Class ' ReservationClient
```

Fig. 22.24 | Code-behind file for the reservation page.

a) Selecting a seat.

Fig. 22.25 | Ticket reservation Web Form sample execution. (Part 1 of 2.)

b) Seat reserved successfully.

c) Attempting to reserve another seat.

d) No seats match the requested type and class.

Fig. 22.25 | Ticket reservation Web Form sample execution. (Part 2 of 2.)

22.7 User-Defined Types in Web Services

The Web methods we have demonstrated so far all received and returned primitive-type values. It is also possible to process user-defined types—known as *custom types*—in a Web service. These types can be passed to or returned from Web methods. Web service clients also can use these user-defined types, because the proxy class created for the client contains the type definitions.

This section presents an EquationGenerator Web service that generates random arithmetic equations of type Equation. The client is a math-tutoring application that inputs information about the mathematical question that the user wishes to attempt (addition, subtraction or multiplication) and the skill level of the user (1 specifies equations using numbers from 1 to 10, 2 specifies equations involving numbers from 10 to 100, and

3 specifies equations containing numbers from 100 to 1000). The Web service then generates an equation consisting of random numbers in the proper range. The client application receives the Equation and displays the sample question to the user in a Windows Form.

Serialization of User-Defined Types

We mentioned earlier that all types passed to and from Web services must be supported by SOAP. How, then, can SOAP support a type that is not even created yet? Custom types that are sent to or from a Web service are serialized, enabling them to be passed in XML format. This process is referred to as *XML serialization*.

Requirements for User-Defined Types Used with Web Methods

Classes that are used to specify return types and parameter types for Web methods must meet several requirements:

1. They must provide a Public default or parameterless constructor. When a Web service or Web service consumer receives an XML serialized object, the .NET Framework must be able to call this constructor as part of the process of deserializing the object (i.e., converting it back to a Visual Basic object).

2. Properties and instance variables that should be serialized in XML format must be declared Public. (Note that the Public properties can be used to provide access to Private instance variables.)

3. Properties that should be serialized must provide both Get and Set accessors (even if they have empty bodies). Read-only properties are not serialized.

Any data that is not serialized simply receives its default value (or the value provided by the default or parameterless constructor) when an object of the class is deserialized.

Common Programming Error 22.3

Failure to define a default or parameterless Public constructor for a type being passed to or returned from a Web method is a runtime error.

Common Programming Error 22.4

Defining only the Get or Set accessor of a property for a user-defined type being passed to or returned from a Web method results in a property that is inaccessible to the client.

Software Engineering Observation 22.1

Clients of a Web service can access only the service's Public members. The programmer can provide Public properties to allow access to Private data.

Defining Class Equation

We define class Equation in Fig. 22.26. Lines 15–29 define a constructor that takes three arguments—two Integers representing the left and right operands and a String that represents the arithmetic operation to perform. The constructor sets the leftOperand, rightOperand and operationType instance variables, then calculates the appropriate result. The parameterless constructor (lines 10–12) calls the three-argument constructor (lines 15–29) and passes some default values. We do not use the parameterless constructor explicitly, but the XML serialization mechanism uses it when objects of this class are deserialized. Because we provide a constructor with parameters, we must explicitly define the parameterless constructor in this class so that objects of the class can be passed to or returned from Web methods.

```vb
1   ' Fig. 22.26: Equation.vb
2   ' Class Equation that contains information about an equation.
3   Public Class Equation
4      Private leftOperand As Integer ' number to the left of the operator
5      Private rightOperand As Integer ' number to the right of the operator
6      Private resultValue As Integer ' result of the operation
7      Private operationType As String ' type of the operation
8
9      ' required default constructor
10     Public Sub New()
11        MyClass.New(0, 0, "+")
12     End Sub ' parameterless New
13
14     ' three-argument constructor for class Equation
15     Public Sub New(ByVal leftValue As Integer, _
16        ByVal rightValue As Integer, ByVal type As String)
17        leftOperand = leftValue
18        rightOperand = rightValue
19        operationType = type
20
21        Select Case operationType ' perform appropriate operation
22           Case "+" ' addition
23              resultValue = leftOperand + rightOperand
24           Case "-" ' subtraction
25              resultValue = leftOperand - rightOperand
26           Case "*" ' multiplication
27              resultValue = leftOperand * rightOperand
28        End Select
29     End Sub ' three-parameter New
30
31     ' return string representation of the Equation object
32     Public Overrides Function ToString() As String
33        Return leftOperand.ToString() & " " & operationType & " " & _
34           rightOperand.ToString() & " = " & resultValue.ToString()
35     End Function ' ToString
36
37     ' property that returns a string representing left-hand side
38     Public Property LeftHandSide() As String
39        Get
40           Return leftOperand.ToString() & " " & operationType & " " & _
41              rightOperand.ToString()
42        End Get
43
44        Set(ByVal value As String) ' required set accessor
45           ' empty body
46        End Set
47     End Property ' LeftHandSide
```

Fig. 22.26 | Class that stores equation information. (Part 1 of 3.)

```
48
49        ' property that returns a string representing right-hand side
50        Public Property RightHandSide() As String
51           Get
52              Return resultValue.ToString()
53           End Get
54
55           Set(ByVal value As String) ' required set accessor
56              ' empty body
57           End Set
58        End Property ' RightHandSide
59
60        ' property to access the left operand
61        Public Property Left() As Integer
62           Get
63              Return leftOperand
64           End Get
65
66           Set(ByVal value As Integer)
67              leftOperand = value
68           End Set
69        End Property ' Left
70
71        ' property to access the right operand
72        Public Property Right() As Integer
73           Get
74              Return rightOperand
75           End Get
76
77           Set(ByVal value As Integer)
78              rightOperand = value
79           End Set
80        End Property ' Right
81
82        ' property to access the result of applying
83        ' an operation to the left and right operands
84        Public Property Result() As Integer
85           Get
86              Return resultValue
87           End Get
88
89           Set(ByVal value As Integer)
90              resultValue = value
91           End Set
92        End Property ' Result
93
94        ' property to access the operation
95        Public Property Operation() As String
96           Get
97              Return operationType
98           End Get
99
```

Fig. 22.26 | Class that stores equation information. (Part 2 of 3.)

```
100          Set(ByVal value As String)
101             operationType = value
102          End Set
103       End Property ' Operation
104 End Class ' Equation
```

Fig. 22.26 | Class that stores equation information. (Part 3 of 3.)

Class Equation defines properties LeftHandSide (lines 38–47), RightHandSide (lines 50–58), Left (lines 61–69), Right (lines 72–80), Result (lines 84–92) and Operation (lines 95–103). The client of the Web service does not need to modify the values of properties LeftHandSide and RightHandSide. However, recall that a property can be serialized only if it has both a Get and a Set accessor—this is true even if the Set accessor has an empty body. LeftHandSide (lines 38–47) returns a String representing everything to the left of the equals (=) sign in the equation, and RightHandSide (lines 50–58) returns a String representing everything to the right of the equals (=) sign. Left (lines 61–69) returns the Integer to the left of the operator (known as the left operand), and Right (lines 72–80) returns the Integer to the right of the operator (known as the right operand). Result (lines 84–92) returns the solution to the equation, and Operation (lines 95–103) returns the operator in the equation. The client in this case study does not use the RightHandSide property, but we included it in case future clients choose to use it. Method ToString (lines 32–35) returns a String representation of the equation.

Creating the EquationGenerator Web Service

Figure 22.27 presents the EquationGenerator Web service, which creates random, customized Equations. This Web service contains only method GenerateEquation (lines 16–32), which takes two parameters—a String representing the mathematical operation (addition, subtraction or multiplication) and an Integer representing the difficulty level.

```
1  ' Fig. 22.27: EquationGeneratorWebService.vb
2  ' Web Service to generate random equations based on a specified
3  ' operation and difficulty level.
4  Imports System.Web
5  Imports System.Web.Services
6  Imports System.Web.Services.Protocols
7
8  <WebService(Namespace:="http://www.deitel.com/")> _
9  <WebServiceBinding(ConformsTo:=WsiProfiles.BasicProfile1_1)> _
10 <Global.Microsoft.VisualBasic.CompilerServices.DesignerGenerated()> _
11 Public Class EquationGeneratorWebService
12    Inherits System.Web.Services.WebService
13    ' Method to generate a math equation
14    <WebMethod(Description:="Method to generate a math equation.")> _
15    Public Function GenerateEquation(ByVal operation As String, _
16       ByVal level As Integer) As Equation
17       ' calculate maximum and minimum number to be used
18       Dim maximum As Integer = Convert.ToInt32(Math.Pow(10, level))
19       Dim minimum As Integer = Convert.ToInt32(Math.Pow(10, level - 1))
```

Fig. 22.27 | Web service that generates random equations. (Part 1 of 2.)

```
20
21        Dim randomObject As New Random() ' used to generate random numbers
22
23        ' create Equation consisting of two random
24        ' numbers in the range minimum to maximum
25        Dim newEquation As New Equation( _
26            randomObject.Next(minimum, maximum), _
27            randomObject.Next(minimum, maximum), operation)
28
29        Return newEquation
30     End Function ' GenerateEquation
31  End Class ' EquationGeneratorWebService
```

Fig. 22.27 | Web service that generates random equations. (Part 2 of 2.)

Testing the EquationGenerator Web Service

Figure 22.28 shows the result of testing the EquationGenerator Web service. Note that the return value from our Web method is XML-encoded. However, this example differs from previous ones in that the XML specifies the values for all Public properties and data of the object that is being returned. The return object has been serialized in XML. The client's object class takes this XML and deserializes it into an object of class Equation, that can be used by the client.

Note that an Equation object is *not* being passed between the Web service and the client. Rather, the information in the object is being sent as XML-encoded data. Clients created using .NET will take the information and create a new Equation object. Clients created on other platforms, however, may use the information differently. Readers creating clients on other platforms should check the Web services documentation for the specific platform they are using, to see how their clients may process custom types.

a) Invoking the GenerateEquation method to create a subtraction equation with numbers in the range 10–100.

Fig. 22.28 | Returning an XML serialized object from a Web method. (Part 1 of 2.)

b) XML encoded results of invoking the `GenerateEquation` method to create a subtraction equation with numbers in the range 10–100.

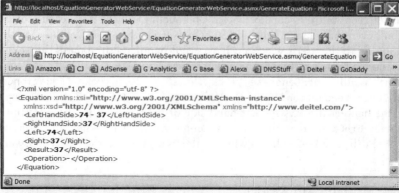

Fig. 22.28 | Returning an XML serialized object from a Web method. (Part 2 of 2.)

Let's examine Web method `GenerateEquation` more closely. Lines 18–19 of Fig. 22.27 define the upper and lower bounds for the random numbers that the method uses to generate an `Equation`. To set these limits, the program first calls `Shared` method `Pow` of class `Math`—this method raises its first argument to the power of its second argument. To calculate the value of `maximum` (the upper bound for any randomly generated numbers used to form an `Equation`), the program raises 10 to the power of the specified `level` argument (line 18). If `level` is 1, `maximum` is 10; if `level` is 2, `maximum` is 100; and if `level` is 3, `maximum` is 1000. Variable `minimum`'s value is determined by raising 10 to a power one less than `level` (line 19). This calculates the smallest number with `level` digits. If `level` is 1, `minimum` is 1; if `level` is 2, `minimum` is 10; and if `level` is 3, `minimum` is 100.

Lines 25–27 create a new `Equation` object. The program calls `Random` method `Next`, which returns an `Integer` that is greater than or equal to the specified lower bound, but less than the specified upper bound. This method generates a left operand value that is greater than or equal to `minimum` but less than `maximum` (i.e., a number with `level` digits). The right operand is another random number with the same characteristics. Line 27 passes the `String` operation received by `GenerateEquation` to the `Equation` constructor. Line 29 returns the new `Equation` object to the client.

Consuming the EquationGenerator Web Service

The `MathTutor` application (Fig. 22.29) calls the `EquationGenerator` Web service's `GenerateEquation` method to create an `Equation` object. The tutor then displays the left-hand side of the `Equation` and waits for user input. This example accesses classes `Generator` and `Equation` from the `localhost` namespace—both are placed in this namespace by default when the proxy is generated. We declare variables of these types at lines 6–7. Line 7 also creates the `Generator` proxy. (Remember to add a Web reference to the `EquationGeneratorWebService` when you create this application.

The math-tutoring application displays an equation and waits for the user to enter an answer. The default setting for the difficulty level is **1**, but the user can change this by choosing a level from the RadioButtons in the GroupBox labeled **Difficulty**. Clicking any of the levels invokes the corresponding RadioButton's CheckedChanged event handler (lines 69–87), which sets integer level to the level selected by the user. Although the default setting for the question type is **Addition**, the user also can change this by selecting one of the RadioButtons in the GroupBox labeled **Operation**. Doing so invokes the corresponding operation's event handlers in lines 45–66, which assigns to String operation the symbol corresponding to the user's selection. Each event handler also updates the Text property of the **Generate** button to match the newly selected operation.

Event handler btnGenerate_Click (lines 10–20) invokes EquationGenerator method GenerateEquation (line 13). After receiving an Equation object from the Web service, the handler displays the left-hand side of the equation in lblQuestion (line 16) and enables btnOK so that the user can enter an answer. When the user clicks **OK**, btnOK_Click (lines 23–42) checks whether the user provided the correct answer.

```vb
1   ' Fig. 22.29: FrmMathTutor.vb
2   ' Math tutoring program using Web service to generate random equations.
3   Public Class FrmMathTutor
4      Private operation As String = "+"
5      Private level As Integer = 1
6      Private currentEquation As localhost.Equation
7      Private generator As New localhost.EquationGeneratorWebService()
8
9      ' generates a new equation when user clicks button
10     Private Sub btnGenerate_Click(ByVal sender As System.Object, _
11        ByVal e As System.EventArgs) Handles btnGenerate.Click
12        ' generate equation using current operation and level
13        currentEquation = generator.GenerateEquation(operation, level)
14
15        ' display left-hand side of equation
16        lblQuestion.Text = currentEquation.LeftHandSide
17
18        btnOK.Enabled = True
19        txtAnswer.Enabled = True
20     End Sub ' btnGenerate_Click
21
22     ' check user's answer
23     Private Sub btnOK_Click(ByVal sender As System.Object, _
24        ByVal e As System.EventArgs) Handles btnOK.Click
25        ' determine correct result from Equation object
26        Dim answer As Integer = currentEquation.Result
27
28        If txtAnswer.Text <> "" Then
29           ' get user's answer
30           Dim userAnswer As Integer = Int32.Parse(txtAnswer.Text)
31
32           ' determine whether user's answer is correct
33           If answer = userAnswer Then
34              lblQuestion.Text = "" ' clear question
35              txtAnswer.Text = "" ' clear answer
```

Fig. 22.29 | Math-tutoring application. (Part I of 3.)

```vb
36              btnOK.Enabled = False ' disable OK button
37              MessageBox.Show("Correct! Good job!")
38          Else
39              MessageBox.Show("Incorrect. Try again.")
40          End If
41      End If
42   End Sub ' btnOK_Click
43
44   ' set the operation to addition
45   Private Sub radAddition_CheckedChanged( _
46      ByVal sender As System.Object, ByVal e As System.EventArgs) _
47      Handles radAddition.CheckedChanged
48      operation = "+"
49      btnGenerate.Text = "Generate " & radAddition.Text & " Example"
50   End Sub ' radAddition_CheckedChanged
51
52   ' set the operation to subtraction
53   Private Sub radSubtraction_CheckedChanged( _
54      ByVal sender As System.Object, ByVal e As System.EventArgs) _
55      Handles radSubtraction.CheckedChanged
56      operation = "-"
57      btnGenerate.Text = "Generate " & radSubtraction.Text & " Example"
58   End Sub ' radSubtraction_CheckedChanged
59
60   ' set the operation to multiplication
61   Private Sub radMultiplication_CheckedChanged( _
62      ByVal sender As System.Object, ByVal e As System.EventArgs) _
63      Handles radMultiplication.CheckedChanged
64      operation = "*"
65      btnGenerate.Text = "Generate " & radMultiplication.Text & " Example"
66   End Sub ' radMultiplication_CheckedChanged
67
68   ' set difficulty level to 1
69   Private Sub radLevelOne_CheckedChanged( _
70      ByVal sender As System.Object, ByVal e As System.EventArgs) _
71      Handles radLevelOne.CheckedChanged
72      level = 1
73   End Sub ' radLevelOne_CheckedChanged
74
75   ' set difficulty level to 2
76   Private Sub radLevelTwo_CheckedChanged( _
77      ByVal sender As System.Object, ByVal e As System.EventArgs) _
78      Handles radLevelTwo.CheckedChanged
79      level = 2
80   End Sub ' radLevelTwo_CheckedChanged
81
82   ' set difficulty level to 3
83   Private Sub radLevelThree_CheckedChanged( _
84      ByVal sender As System.Object, ByVal e As System.EventArgs) _
85      Handles radLevelThree.CheckedChanged
86      level = 3
87   End Sub ' radLevelThree_CheckedChanged
88 End Class ' FrmMathTutor
```

Fig. 22.29 | Math-tutoring application. (Part 2 of 3.)

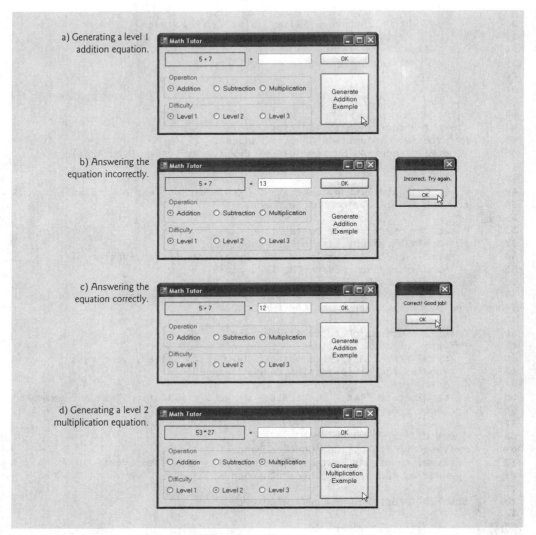

a) Generating a level 1 addition equation.

b) Answering the equation incorrectly.

c) Answering the equation correctly.

d) Generating a level 2 multiplication equation.

Fig. 22.29 | Math-tutoring application. (Part 3 of 3.)

22.8 Wrap-Up

This chapter introduced ASP.NET Web services—a technology that enables users to request and receive data via the Internet and promotes software reusability in distributed systems. You learned that a Web service is a class that allows client software to call the Web service's methods remotely via common data formats and protocols, such as XML, HTTP and SOAP. We discussed several benefits of this kind of distributed computing—e.g., clients can access certain data on remote machines, and clients lacking the processing power necessary to perform specific computations can leverage remote machines' resources.

We explained how Visual Basic 2005 Express, Visual Web Developer 2005 Express and the .NET Framework facilitate creating and consuming Web services. You learned how to define Web services and Web methods, as well as how to consume them from both Windows applications and ASP.NET Web applications. After explaining the mechanics of Web services through our `HugeInteger` example, we demonstrated more sophisticated Web services that use session tracking, database access and user-defined types.

In the next chapter, we discuss the low-level details of computer networking. We show how to implement servers and clients that communicate with one another, how to send and receive data via sockets (which make such transmissions as simple as writing to and reading from files, respectively), and how to create a multithreaded server for playing a networked version of the popular game Tic-Tac-Toe.

22.9 Web Resources

In addition to the Web resources shown here, you should also refer to the ASP.NET-related Web resources provided at the end of Chapter 21.

`msdn.microsoft.com/webservices`
The Microsoft Web Services Developer Center includes .NET Web services technology specifications and white papers as well as XML/SOAP articles, columns and links.

`www.webservices.org`
This site provides industry-related news, articles, resources and links on Web services.

`www-130.ibm.com/developerworks/webservices`
IBM's site for service-oriented architecture (SOA) and Web services includes articles, downloads, demos and discussion forums regarding Web services technology.

`www.w3.org/TR/wsdl`
This site provides extensive documentation on WSDL, including a thorough discussion of Web services–related technologies such as XML, SOAP, HTTP and MIME types in the context of WSDL.

`www.w3.org/TR/soap`
This site provides extensive documentation on SOAP messages, using SOAP with HTTP and SOAP security issues.

`www.uddi.com`
The Universal Description, Discovery and Integration site provides discussions, specifications, white papers and general information on UDDI.

`www.ws-i.org`
The Web Services Interoperability Organization's Web site provides detailed information regarding efforts to build Web services based on standards that promote interoperability and true platform independence.

`webservices.xml.com/security`
This site contains articles about Web services security issues and standard security protocols.

23

Networking: Streams-Based Sockets and Datagrams

If the presence of electricity can be made visible in any part of a circuit, I see no reason why intelligence may not be transmitted instantaneously by electricity.
—Samuel F. B. Morse

What networks of railroads, highways and canals were in another age, the networks of telecommunications, information and computerization ... are today.
—Bruno Kreisky

The port is near, the bells I hear, the people all exulting.
—Walt Whitman

Protocol is everything.
—Francois Giuliani

OBJECTIVES

In this chapter you will learn:

- To implement networking applications that use sockets and datagrams.

- To implement clients and servers that communicate with one another.

- To implement network-based collaborative applications.

- To construct a multithreaded server.

- To use the WebBrowser class to add Web browsing capabilities to any application.

- To use .NET remoting to enable an application executing on one computer to invoke methods from an application executing on a different computer.

23.1 Introduction

There is much excitement about the Internet and the Web. The Internet ties the information world together. The Web makes the Internet easy to use and gives it the flair and sizzle of multimedia. Organizations see the Internet and the Web as crucial to their information-systems strategies. The .NET FCL provides a number of built-in networking capabilities that make it easy to develop Internet- and Web-based applications. Programs can search the world for information and collaborate with programs running on other computers internationally, nationally or just within an organization.

In Chapter 21, ASP.NET 2.0, Web Forms and Web Controls, and Chapter 22, Web Services, we began our presentation of .NET's networking and distributed-computing capabilities. We discussed ASP.NET, Web Forms and Web services—high-level networking technologies that enable programmers to develop distributed applications. In this chapter, we focus on the underlying networking technologies that support .NET's ASP.NET and Web services capabilities.

The chapter begins with an overview of the communication techniques and technologies used to transmit data over the Internet. Next, we present the basic concepts of establishing a connection between two applications using streams of data that are similar to file I/O. This connection-oriented approach enables programs to communicate with one another as easily as writing to, and reading from, files on disk. Then we present a simple chat application that uses these techniques to send messages between a client and a server. The chapter continues with a presentation and an example of connectionless techniques for transmitting data between applications—this approach is less reliable than establishing a connection between the applications, but much more efficient. Such techniques are typically used in applications such as streaming audio and video over the Internet. Next we present an example of a client-server Tic-Tac-Toe game that demonstrates how to create a simple multithreaded server. Then we demonstrate the new WebBrowser class for adding Web browsing capabilities to any application. The chapter concludes with a brief introduction to .NET remoting, which, like Web services (Chapter 22), enables distributed computing over networks.

23.2 Connection-Oriented vs. Connectionless Communication

There are two primary approaches to communicating between applications—*connection oriented* and *connectionless*. Connection-oriented communications are similar to the telephone system, in which a connection is established and held for the length of the session. Connectionless services are similar to the postal service, in which two letters mailed at the same time from the same place and to the same destination may actually take two dramatically different paths through the system and even arrive at different times, or not at all.

In a connection-oriented approach, computers send each other control information—through a technique called *handshaking*—to initiate an end-to-end connection. The Internet is an *unreliable network*, which means that data sent across the Internet may be damaged or lost. Data is sent in *packets* that contain pieces of the data along with information that helps the Internet route the packets to the proper destination. The Internet does not guarantee anything about the packets sent; they could arrive corrupted or out of order, as duplicates or not at all. The Internet makes only a "best effort" to deliver packets. A connection-oriented approach ensures reliable communications on unreliable networks, guaranteeing that sent packets will arrive at the intended recipient undamaged and be reassembled in the correct sequence.

In a connectionless approach, the two computers do not handshake before transmission, and reliability is not guaranteed—data sent may never reach the intended recipient. A connectionless approach, however, avoids the overhead associated with handshaking and enforcing reliability—less information often needs to be passed between the hosts.

23.3 Protocols for Transporting Data

There are many protocols for communicating between applications. *Protocols* are sets of rules that govern how two entities interact. In this chapter, we focus on the Transmission Control Protocol (TCP) and the User Datagram Protocol (UDP). .NET's TCP and UDP networking capabilities are defined in the **System.Net.Sockets** namespace.

The *Transmission Control Protocol (TCP)* is a connection-oriented communication protocol which guarantees that sent packets will arrive at the intended recipient undamaged and in the correct sequence. TCP allows protocols like HTTP (Chapter 21) to send information across a network as simply and reliably as writing to a file on a local computer. If packets of information don't arrive at the recipient, TCP ensures that the packets are sent again. If the packets arrive out of order, TCP reassembles them in the correct order transparently to the receiving application. If duplicate packets arrive, TCP discards them.

Applications that don't require TCP's reliable end-to-end transmission guaranty typically use the connectionless *User Datagram Protocol (UDP)*. UDP incurs the minimum overhead necessary to communicate between applications. UDP makes no guarantees that packets, called *datagrams*, will reach their destination or arrive in their original order.

There are benefits to using UDP over TCP. UDP has little overhead because UDP datagrams do not need to carry the information that TCP packets carry to ensure reliability. UDP also reduces network traffic relative to TCP due to the absence of handshaking and retransmissions.

Unreliable communication is acceptable in many situations. First, reliability is not necessary for some applications, so the overhead imposed by a protocol that guarantees reliability can be avoided. Second, some applications, such as streaming audio and video, can tolerate occasional datagram loss. This usually results in a small pause (or "hiccup") in the audio or video being played. If the same application were run over TCP, a lost segment could cause a significant pause, since the protocol would wait until the lost segment was retransmitted and delivered correctly before continuing. Finally, applications that need to implement their own reliability mechanisms different from those provided by TCP can build such mechanisms over UDP.

23.4   Establishing a Simple TCP Server Using Stream Sockets

Typically, with TCP, a server "listens" (i.e., waits) for a connection request from a client. Often, the server program contains a control statement or block of code that executes continuously until the server receives a request. On receiving a request, the server establishes a connection to the client. The server then uses this connection—managed by a ***Socket*** object—to handle future requests from that client and to send data to the client. Since programs that communicate via TCP process the data they send and receive as streams of bytes, programmers sometimes refer to Sockets used with TCP as "stream Sockets."

Establishing a simple server with TCP and stream sockets requires five steps. First, create an object of class ***TcpListener*** of namespace System.Net.Sockets. This class represents a TCP stream socket through which a server can listen for requests. Creating a new TcpListener, as in

> ***Dim*** server ***As New*** TcpListener(*ipAddress*, *portNumber*)

binds (assigns) the server application to the specified *portNumber*. A ***port number*** is a numeric identifier that an application uses to identify itself at a given ***network address***, also known as an ***Internet Protocol Address (IP Address)***. IP addresses identify computers on the Internet. In fact, Web-site names, such as www.deitel.com, are aliases for IP addresses. An IP address is represented by an object of class ***IPAddress*** of namespace ***System.Net***. Any application that performs networking identifies itself via an *IP address/port number pair*—no two applications can have the same port number at a given IP address. In fact, a socket combines an IP address and a port number to uniquely identify a service. Explicitly binding a socket to a connection port (using method ***Bind*** of class Socket) is usually unnecessary, because class TcpListener and other classes discussed in this chapter do it automatically, along with other socket-initialization operations.

> **Software Engineering Observation 23.1**
>
> *Port numbers can have values between 0 and 65535. Many operating systems reserve port numbers below 1024 for system services (such as e-mail and Web servers). Applications must be granted special privileges to use the reserved port numbers.*

To receive requests, a TcpListener first must listen for them. The second step in the connection process is to call TcpListener's ***Start*** method, which causes the TcpListener object to begin listening for connection requests. The server listens indefinitely for a request—that is, the server-side application waits until a client attempts to connect with it. The server creates a connection to the client when it receives a connection request. An object of class Socket (namespace ***System.Net.Sockets***) manages a connection to a client.

Method *AcceptSocket* of class TcpListener accepts a connection request. This method returns a Socket object upon connection, as in the statement

```
Dim connection As Socket = server.AcceptSocket()
```

When the server receives a request, AcceptSocket calls method Accept of the TcpListener's underlying Socket to make the connection. This is an example of how networking complexity is hidden from the programmer. You simply place the preceding statement in a server-side program—the classes of namespace System.Net.Sockets handle the details of accepting requests and establishing connections.

The third step establishes the streams used for communication with the client. In this step, we create a NetworkStream object that uses the connection's Socket object to send and receive data. In our forthcoming example, we use this NetworkStream object to create a BinaryWriter and a BinaryReader that will be used to send information to and receive information from the client, respectively.

Step 4 is the processing phase, in which the server and client communicate using the connection established in step three. In this step, the client uses BinaryWriter method Write and BinaryReader method ReadString to communicate.

The fifth step is the connection-termination phase. When the client and server finish communicating, the server calls method Close of the BinaryReader, BinaryWriter, NetworkStream and Socket to terminate the connection. The server can then return to step two to wait for the next connection request. Note that the Socket class's documentation (msdn2.microsoft.com/en-us/library/system.net.sockets.socket.aspx) recommends that you call method Shutdown before method Close to ensure that all data is sent and received before the Socket closes.

One problem associated with the server scheme described in this section is that step four *blocks* other requests while processing the connected client's request, and thus no other client can connect with the server while the code that defines the processing phase is executing. The most common technique for addressing this problem is to use multithreaded servers (multithreading was discussed in Chapter 15), which place the processing-phase code in a separate thread. For each connection request the server receives, it creates a Thread to process the connection, leaving its TcpListener (or Socket) free to receive other connections. We demonstrate a multithreaded server in Section 23.8.

Software Engineering Observation 23.2

Multithreaded servers can efficiently manage simultaneous connections with multiple clients. This architecture is precisely what popular Linux and Windows network servers use.

Software Engineering Observation 23.3

You can implement a multithreaded server to create a thread that manages network I/O across a Socket object returned by method AcceptSocket. You can also implement a multithreaded server to maintain a pool of threads that manage network I/O across newly created Sockets.

Performance Tip 23.1

In high-performance systems with abundant memory, a multithreaded server can be implemented to create a pool of threads. These threads can be assigned quickly to handle network I/O across multiple Sockets. Thus, when a connection is received, the server does not incur the overhead of thread creation.

23.5 Establishing a Simple TCP Client Using Stream Sockets

There are four steps to creating a simple TCP client. First, we create an object of class **Tcp-Client** (namespace System.Net.Sockets) to connect to the server. The connection is established by calling TcpClient method **Connect**. One overloaded version of this method takes two arguments—the server's IP address and its port number—as in:

```
Dim client As New TcpClient()
client.Connect(serverAddress, serverPortNumber)
```

The *serverPortNumber* is an Integer that represents the port number to which the server application is bound to listen for connection requests. The *serverAddress* can be either an IPAddress instance that encapsulates the server's IP address or a String that specifies the server's hostname or IP address. Method Connect also has an overloaded version to which you can pass an **IPEndPoint** object that represents an IP address/port number pair. TcpClient method Connect calls Socket method Connect to establish the connection. If the connection is successful, TcpClient method Connect returns a positive integer; otherwise, it returns 0.

In Step 2, the TcpClient uses its **GetStream** method to get a **NetworkStream** so that it can write to and read from the server. We then use the NetworkStream object to create a BinaryWriter and a BinaryReader that will be used to send information to and receive information from the server, respectively.

The third step is the processing phase, in which the client and the server communicate. In this phase of our example, the client uses BinaryWriter method Write and BinaryReader method ReadString to perform the appropriate communications. Using a process similar to that used by servers, a client can employ threads to prevent blocking of communication with other servers while processing data from one connection.

After the transmission is complete, Step 4 requires the client to close the connection by calling method Close on each of BinaryReader, BinaryWriter, NetworkStream and TcpClient. This closes each of the streams and the TcpClient's Socket to terminate the connection with the server. At this point, a new connection can be established through method Connect, as we have described.

23.6 Client/Server Interaction with Stream-Socket Connections

Figures 23.1 and 23.2 use the classes and techniques discussed in the previous two sections to construct a simple *client/server chat application*. The server waits for a client's request to make a connection. When a client application connects to the server, the server application sends a String to the client, indicating that the connection was successful. The client then displays a message notifying the user that a connection has been established.

The client and server applications both contain TextBoxes that enable users to type messages and send them to the other application. When either the client or the server sends the message "TERMINATE," the connection between the client and the server terminates. The server then waits for another client to request a connection. Figure 23.1 and Fig. 23.2 provide the code for classes FrmChatServer and FrmChatClient, respectively. Figure 23.2 also contains screen captures displaying the execution between the client and the server.

FrmChatServer Class

In class FrmChatServer (Fig. 23.1), FrmChatServer_Load (lines 17–22) creates a Thread that will accept connections from clients (line 20). The ThreadStart delegate object that is passed as the Thread constructor's argument specifies which method the Thread executes. Line 21 starts the Thread, which uses the ThreadStart delegate to invoke method RunServer (lines 93–159). This method initializes the server to receive connection requests and process connections. Line 102 instantiates a TcpListener object to listen for a connection request from a client at port 50000 (Step 1). Line 105 then calls TcpListener method Start, which causes the TcpListener to begin waiting for requests (Step 2).

```vb
 1  ' Fig. 23.1: FrmChatServer.vb
 2  ' Set up a server that will receive a connection from a client, send a
 3  ' string to the client, chat with the client and close the connection.
 4  Imports System.Threading
 5  Imports System.Net
 6  Imports System.Net.Sockets
 7  Imports System.IO
 8
 9  Public Class FrmChatServer
10      Private connection As Socket ' Socket for accepting a connection
11      Private readThread As Thread ' Thread for processing incoming messages
12      Private socketStream As NetworkStream ' network data stream
13      Private writer As BinaryWriter ' facilitates writing to the stream
14      Private reader As BinaryReader ' facilitates reading from the stream
15
16      ' initialize thread for reading
17      Private Sub FrmChatServer_Load(ByVal sender As System.Object, _
18          ByVal e As System.EventArgs) Handles MyBase.Load
19
20          readThread = New Thread(New ThreadStart(AddressOf RunServer))
21          readThread.Start()
22      End Sub ' FrmChatServer_Load
23
24      ' close all threads associated with this application
25      Private Sub FrmChatServer_FormClosing(ByVal sender As System.Object, _
26          ByVal e As System.Windows.Forms.FormClosingEventArgs) _
27          Handles MyBase.FormClosing
28
29          System.Environment.Exit(System.Environment.ExitCode)
30      End Sub ' FrmChatServer_FormClosing
31
32      ' Delegate that allows method DisplayMessage to be called
33      ' in the thread that creates and maintains the GUI
34      Private Delegate Sub DisplayDelegate(ByVal message As String)
35
36      ' method DisplayMessage sets txtDisplay's Text property
37      ' in a thread-safe manner
38      Private Sub DisplayMessage(ByVal message As String)
39          ' if modifying txtDisplay is not thread safe
40          If txtDisplay.InvokeRequired Then
```

Fig. 23.1 | Server portion of a client/server stream-socket connection. (Part 1 of 4.)

```
41          ' use inherited method Invoke to execute DisplayMessage
42          ' via a Delegate
43          Invoke(New DisplayDelegate(AddressOf DisplayMessage), _
44             New Object() {message})
45       ' OK to modify txtDisplay in current thread
46       Else
47          txtDisplay.Text &= message
48       End If
49    End Sub ' DisplayMessage
50
51    ' Delegate that allows method DisableInput to be called
52    ' in the thread that creates and maintains the GUI
53    Private Delegate Sub DisableInputDelegate(ByVal value As Boolean)
54
55    ' method DisableInput sets txtInput's ReadOnly property
56    ' in a thread-safe manner
57    Private Sub DisableInput(ByVal value As Boolean)
58       ' if modifying txtInput is not thread safe
59       If txtInput.InvokeRequired Then
60          ' use inherited method Invoke to execute DisableInput
61          ' via a Delegate
62          Invoke(New DisableInputDelegate(AddressOf DisableInput), _
63             New Object() {value})
64       ' OK to modify txtInput in current thread
65       Else
66          txtInput.ReadOnly = value
67       End If
68    End Sub ' DisableInput
69
70    ' send the text typed at the server to the client
71    Private Sub txtInput_KeyDown(ByVal sender As System.Object, _
72       ByVal e As System.Windows.Forms.KeyEventArgs) _
73       Handles txtInput.KeyDown
74       ' send the text to the client
75       Try
76          If e.KeyCode = Keys.Enter And txtInput.ReadOnly = False Then
77             writer.Write("SERVER>>> " & txtInput.Text)
78             txtDisplay.Text &= vbCrLf & "SERVER>>> " & txtInput.Text
79
80             ' if the user at the server signaled termination
81             ' sever the connection to the client
82             If txtInput.Text = "TERMINATE" Then
83                connection.Close()
84             End If
85             txtInput.Clear() ' clear the user's input
86          End If
87       Catch ex As SocketException
88          txtDisplay.Text &= vbCrLf & "Error writing object"
89       End Try
90    End Sub ' txtInput_KeyDown
91
```

Fig. 23.1 | Server portion of a client/server stream-socket connection. (Part 2 of 4.)

```vb
 92      ' allows a client to connect; displays text the client sends
 93      Public Sub RunServer()
 94          Dim listener As TcpListener
 95          Dim counter As Integer = 1
 96
 97          ' wait for a client connection and display the text
 98          ' that the client sends
 99          Try
100              ' Step 1: create TcpListener
101              Dim local As IPAddress = IPAddress.Parse("localhost")
102              listener = New TcpListener(local, 50000)
103
104              ' Step 2: TcpListener waits for connection request
105              listener.Start()
106
107              ' Step 3: establish connection upon client request
108              While True
109                  DisplayMessage("Waiting for connection" & vbCrLf)
110
111                  ' accept an incoming connection
112                  connection = listener.AcceptSocket()
113
114                  ' create NetworkStream object associated with socket
115                  socketStream = New NetworkStream(connection)
116
117                  ' create objects for transferring data across stream
118                  writer = New BinaryWriter(socketStream)
119                  reader = New BinaryReader(socketStream)
120
121                  DisplayMessage( _
122                      "Connection " & counter & " received." & vbCrLf)
123
124                  ' inform client that connection was successfull
125                  writer.Write("SERVER>>> Connection successful")
126
127                  DisableInput(False) ' enable txtInput
128                  Dim theReply As String = ""
129
130                  ' Step 4: read string data sent from client
131                  Do
132                      Try
133                          ' read the string sent to the server
134                          theReply = reader.ReadString()
135
136                          ' display the message
137                          DisplayMessage(vbCrLf & theReply)
138                      Catch ex As Exception
139                          ' handle exception if error reading data
140                          Exit Do
141                      End Try
142                  Loop While theReply <> "CLIENT>>> TERMINATE" And _
143                      connection.Connected
```

Fig. 23.1 | Server portion of a client/server stream-socket connection. (Part 3 of 4.)

```
144
145                 DisplayMessage(vbCrLf & "User terminated connection" & vbCrLf)
146
147                 ' Step 5: close connection
148                 writer.Close()
149                 reader.Close()
150                 socketStream.Close()
151                 connection.Close()
152
153                 DisableInput(True) ' disable txtInput
154                 counter += 1
155             End While
156         Catch ex As Exception
157             MessageBox.Show(ex.ToString())
158         End Try
159     End Sub ' RunServer
160 End Class ' FrmChatServer_Load
```

Fig. 23.1 | Server portion of a client/server stream-socket connection. (Part 4 of 4.)

Accepting the Connection and Establishing the Streams

Lines 108–155 are an infinite loop that begins by establishing the connection requested by the client (Step 3). Line 112 calls method AcceptSocket of the TcpListener object, which returns a Socket upon successful connection. The thread in which method Accept-Socket is called blocks (i.e., stops executing) until a connection is established. The returned Socket object manages the connection. Line 115 passes this Socket object as an argument to the constructor of a NetworkStream object, which provides access to streams across a network. In this example, the NetworkStream object uses the streams of the specified Socket. Lines 118–119 create instances of the *BinaryWriter* and *BinaryReader* classes for writing and reading data. We pass the NetworkStream object as an argument to each constructor—BinaryWriter can write bytes to the NetworkStream, and BinaryReader can read bytes from NetworkStream. Line 121 calls DisplayMessage, indicating that a connection was received. Next, we send a message to the client indicating that the connection was received. BinaryWriter method *Write* has many overloaded versions that write data of various types to a stream. Line 125 uses method Write to send the client a String notifying the user of a successful connection. This completes Step 3.

Receiving Messages from the Client

We now begin the processing phase (Step 4). Lines 131–143 loop until the server receives the message CLIENT>>> TERMINATE, which indicates that the connection should be terminated. Line 134 uses BinaryReader method *ReadString* to read a String from the stream. Method ReadString blocks until a String is read. This is why we execute method Run-Server in a separate Thread (created in lines 20–21, when the Form loads). This Thread ensures that the application's user can continue to interact with the GUI to send messages to the client, even when this thread is blocked while awaiting a message from the client.

Modifying GUI Controls from Separate Threads

Windows Form controls are not thread safe—a control that is modified from multiple threads is not guaranteed to be modified correctly. The Visual Studio 2005 Documentation recommends that only the thread which created the GUI should modify the controls.[1] Class Control provides method *Invoke* to help ensure this. Invoke takes two arguments—a Delegate representing a method that will modify the GUI and an array of Objects representing the parameters of the method. (Delegates were introduced in Section 13.3.3.) At some point after Invoke is called, the thread that originally created the GUI will (when not executing any other code) execute the method represented by the Delegate, passing the contents of the Object array as the method's arguments.

Line 34 declares a Delegate type named DisplayDelegate, which represents methods that take a String argument and do not return a value. Method DisplayMessage (lines 38–49) meets these requirements—it receives a String parameter named message and does not return a value. The If statement in line 40 tests txtDisplay's *Invoke-Required* property (inherited from class Control), which returns True if the current thread is not allowed to modify this control directly and returns False otherwise. If the current thread executing method DisplayMessage is not the thread that created the GUI, the If condition evaluates to True and lines 43–44 call method Invoke, passing it a new DisplayDelegate representing the method DisplayMessage *itself* and a new Object array consisting of the String argument message. This causes the thread that created the GUI to call method DisplayMessage again at a later time with the same String argument as the original call. When that call occurs from the thread that created the GUI, the method *is* allowed to modify txtDisplay directly, so the Else body (line 47) executes and appends message to txtDisplay's Text property.

Lines 53–68 define the Delegate, DisableInputDelegate, and a method, DisableInput, to allow any thread to modify the ReadOnly property of txtInput using the same techniques. A thread calls DisableInput with a Boolean argument (True to disable; False to enable). If DisableInput is not allowed to modify the control from the current thread, DisableInput calls method Invoke. This causes the thread that created the GUI to call DisableInput at a later time to set txtInput.ReadOnly's value to the Boolean argument.

Terminating the Connection with the Client
When the chat is complete, lines 148–151 close the BinaryWriter, BinaryReader, NetworkStream and Socket (Step 5) by invoking their respective Close methods. The server then waits for another client connection request by returning to the beginning of the loop (line 108).

Sending Messages to the Client
When the server application's user enters a String in the TextBox and presses the *Enter* key, event handler txtInput_KeyDown (lines 71–90) reads the String and sends it via method Write of class BinaryWriter. If a user terminates the server application, line 83 calls method Close of the Socket object to close the connection.

Terminating the Server Application
Lines 25–30 define event handler FrmChatServer_FormClosing for the FormClosing event. The event closes the application and calls method Exit of class Environment with parameter ExitCode. Method Exit terminates all threads associated with the application.

---

1.   The MSDN article "How to: Make Thread-Safe Calls to Windows Forms Controls" can be found at msdn2.microsoft.com/en-us/library/ms171728.aspx.

FrmChatClient *Class*

Figure 23.2 lists the code for class `FrmChatClient`. Like the `FrmChatServer` object, the `FrmChatClient` object creates a `Thread` (lines 19–20) in its constructor to handle all incoming messages. `FrmChatClient` method `RunClient` (lines 86–133) connects to the `FrmChatServer`, receives data from the `FrmChatServer` and sends data to the `FrmChatServer`. Lines 94–95 instantiate a `TcpClient` object, then call its `Connect` method to establish a connection (Step 1). The first argument to method `Connect` is the name of the server—in our case, the server's name is `"localhost"`, meaning that the server is located on the local computer. The `localhost` is also known as the *loopback IP address* and is equivalent to the IP address `127.0.0.1`. This value sends the data transmission back to the sender's IP address. The second argument to method `Connect` is the server port number. This number must match the port number at which the server waits for connections. [*Note*: The host name `localhost` is commonly used to test networking applications on one computer. This is particularly useful if you don't have separate computers on which to execute the client and server. Normally, `localhost` would be replaced with the hostname or IP address of another computer.]

The `FrmChatClient` uses a `NetworkStream` to send data to and receive data from the server. The client obtains the `NetworkStream` in line 98 through a call to `TcpClient` method `GetStream` (Step 2). Lines 108–118 loop until the client receives the connection-termination message (`SERVER>>> TERMINATE`). Line 112 uses `BinaryReader` method `ReadString` to obtain the next message from the server (Step 3). Line 113 displays the message, and lines 121–124 close the `BinaryWriter`, `BinaryReader`, `NetworkStream` and `TcpClient` objects (Step 4).

Lines 33–67 declare `DisplayDelegate`, `DisplayMessage`, `DisableInputDelegate` and `DisableInput` just as in lines 34–68 of Fig. 23.1. These once again are used to ensure that the GUI is modified only by the thread that created the GUI controls.

When the user of the client application enters a `String` in the `TextBox` and presses the *Enter* key, event handler `txtInput_KeyDown` (lines 70–83) reads the `String` from the `TextBox` and sends it to the server via `BinaryWriter` method `Write`.

In this client/server chat program, the `FrmChatServer` receives a connection, processes it, closes it and waits for the next one. In a real-world application, a server would likely receive a connection, set up the connection to be processed as a separate thread of execution and wait for new connections. The separate threads that process existing connections could then continue to execute while the server concentrates on new connection requests.

```vb
 1  ' Fig. 23.2: FrmChatClient.vb
 2  ' Set up a client that will send information to and
 3  ' read information from a server.
 4  Imports System.Threading
 5  Imports System.Net.Sockets
 6  Imports System.IO
 7
 8  Public Class FrmChatClient
 9      Private output As NetworkStream ' stream for receiving data
10      Private writer As BinaryWriter ' facilitates writing to the stream
```

Fig. 23.2 | Client portion of a client/server stream-socket connection. (Part 1 of 5.)

```vbnet
11      Private reader As BinaryReader ' facilitates reading from the stream
12      Private readThread As Thread ' Thread for processing incoming messages
13      Private message As String = ""
14
15      ' initialize thread for reading
16      Private Sub FrmChatClient_Load(ByVal sender As System.Object, _
17         ByVal e As System.EventArgs) Handles MyBase.Load
18
19         readThread = New Thread(New ThreadStart(AddressOf RunClient))
20         readThread.Start()
21      End Sub ' FrmChatClient_Load
22
23      ' close all threads associated with this application
24      Private Sub FrmChatClient_FormClosing(ByVal sender As System.Object, _
25         ByVal e As System.Windows.Forms.FormClosingEventArgs) _
26         Handles MyBase.FormClosing
27
28         System.Environment.Exit(System.Environment.ExitCode)
29      End Sub ' FrmChatClient_FormClosing
30
31      ' Delegate that allows method DisplayMessage to be called
32      ' in the thread that creates and maintains the GUI
33      Private Delegate Sub DisplayDelegate(ByVal message As String)
34
35      ' method DisplayMessage sets txtDisplay's Text property
36      ' in a thread-safe manner
37      Private Sub DisplayMessage(ByVal message As String)
38         ' if modifying txtDisplay is not thread safe
39         If txtDisplay.InvokeRequired Then
40            ' use inherited method Invoke to execute DisplayMessage
41            ' via a Delegate
42            Invoke(New DisplayDelegate(AddressOf DisplayMessage), _
43               New Object() {message})
44         ' OK to modify txtDisplay in current thread
45         Else
46            txtDisplay.Text &= message
47         End If
48      End Sub ' DisplayMessage
49
50      ' Delegate that allows method DisableInput to be called
51      ' in the thread that creates and maintains the GUI
52      Private Delegate Sub DisableInputDelegate(ByVal value As Boolean)
53
54      ' method DisableInput sets txtInput's ReadOnly property
55      ' in a thread-safe manner
56      Private Sub DisableInput(ByVal value As Boolean)
57         ' if modifying txtInput is not thread safe
58         If txtInput.InvokeRequired Then
59            ' use inherited method Invoke to execute DisableInput
60            ' via a Delegate
61            Invoke(New DisableInputDelegate(AddressOf DisableInput), _
62               New Object() {value})
```

Fig. 23.2 | Client portion of a client/server stream-socket connection. (Part 2 of 5.)

```
63              ' OK to modify txtInput in current thread
64          Else
65              txtInput.ReadOnly = value
66          End If
67      End Sub ' DisableInput
68
69      ' sends text the user typed to server
70      Private Sub txtInput_KeyDown(ByVal sender As System.Object, _
71          ByVal e As System.Windows.Forms.KeyEventArgs) _
72          Handles txtInput.KeyDown
73
74          Try
75              If e.KeyCode = Keys.Enter And txtInput.ReadOnly = False Then
76                  writer.Write("CLIENT>>> " & txtInput.Text)
77                  txtDisplay.Text &= vbCrLf & "CLIENT>>> " & txtInput.Text
78                  txtInput.Clear()
79              End If
80          Catch ex As SocketException
81              txtDisplay.Text &= vbCrLf & "Error writing object"
82          End Try
83      End Sub ' txtInput_KeyDown
84
85      ' connect to server and display server-generated text
86      Public Sub RunClient()
87          Dim client As TcpClient
88
89          ' instantiate TcpClient for sending data to server
90          Try
91              DisplayMessage("Attempting connection" & vbCrLf)
92
93              ' Step 1: create TcpClient and connect to server
94              client = New TcpClient()
95              client.Connect("localhost", 50000)
96
97              ' Step 2: get NetworkStream associated with TcpClient
98              output = client.GetStream()
99
100             ' create objects for writing and reading across stream
101             writer = New BinaryWriter(output)
102             reader = New BinaryReader(output)
103
104             DisplayMessage(vbCrLf & "Got I/O streams" & vbCrLf)
105             DisableInput(False) ' enable txtInput
106
107             ' loop until server signals termination
108             Do
109                 ' Step 3: processing phase
110                 Try
111                     ' read message from server
112                     message = reader.ReadString()
113                     DisplayMessage(vbCrLf & message)
114                 Catch ex As Exception
```

Fig. 23.2 | Client portion of a client/server stream-socket connection. (Part 3 of 5.)

```
115                    ' handle exception if error in reading server data
116                    System.Environment.Exit(System.Environment.ExitCode)
117                End Try
118            Loop While message <> "SERVER>>> TERMINATE"
119
120                ' Step 4: close connection
121                writer.Close()
122                reader.Close()
123                output.Close()
124                client.Close()
125
126                Application.Exit()
127            Catch ex As Exception
128                ' handle exception if error in establishing connection
129                MessageBox.Show(ex.ToString(), "Connection Error", _
130                    MessageBoxButtons.OK, MessageBoxIcon.Error)
131                System.Environment.Exit(System.Environment.ExitCode)
132            End Try
133        End Sub ' RunClient
134 End Class ' FrmChatClient
```

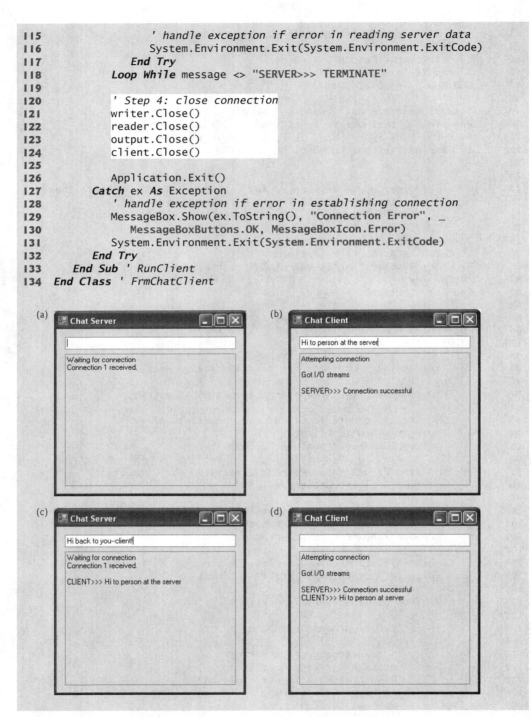

Fig. 23.2 | Client portion of a client/server stream-socket connection. (Part 4 of 5.)

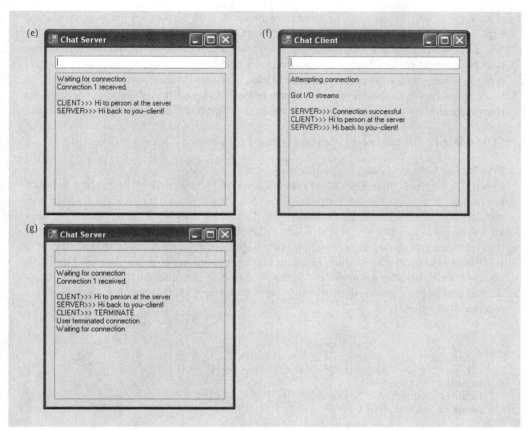

Fig. 23.2 | Client portion of a client/server stream-socket connection. (Part 5 of 5.)

23.7 Connectionless Client/Server Interaction with Datagrams

So far, we have discussed connection-oriented, streams-based transmissions using the TCP protocol to ensure that the packets of data are transmitted reliably. Now we consider connectionless transmission using datagrams and UDP.

Connectionless transmission via datagrams resembles the method by which the postal service carries and delivers mail. Information is bundled and sent in packets called datagrams, which can be thought of as similar to letters sent through the mail. If a large message will not fit in one envelope, it is broken into separate message pieces and placed in separate, sequentially numbered envelopes. All the envelopes are mailed at once. They may arrive in order, out of order or not at all. The person at the receiving end reassembles the message pieces in sequential order before attempting to interpret the message. If the message is small enough to fit in one envelope, the sequencing problem is eliminated, but it is still possible that the message will never arrive. (Unlike with postal mail, duplicate datagrams could reach receiving computers.) .NET provides the *UdpClient* class for connectionless transmission. Like TcpListener and TcpClient, UdpClient uses methods from class Socket. UdpClient method **Send** transmits data with Socket's SendTo method, and UdpClient method **Receive** reads data with Socket's ReceiveFrom method.

The programs in Fig. 23.3 and Fig. 23.4 use datagrams to send packets of information between client and server applications. In the PacketClient application, the user types a message into a TextBox and presses *Enter*. The client converts the message to a Byte array and sends it to the server. The server receives the packet and displays the packet's information, then *echoes*, or returns, the packet to the client. When the client receives the packet, the client displays the packet's information. In this example, classes FrmPacketClient and FrmPacketServer are implemented similarly.

FrmPacketServer Class

Figure 23.3 defines class FrmPacketServer. Line 16 in the Load event handler for class FrmPacketServer creates an instance of the UdpClient class that receives data at port number 50000. This initializes the underlying Socket for communications. Line 17 creates an instance of class IPEndPoint to hold the IP address and port number of the client(s) that transmit to FrmPacketServer. The first argument to the IPEndPoint constructor is an IPAddress object; the second argument is the port number of the endpoint. These values are both 0, because we need only instantiate an empty IPEndPoint object. The IP addresses and port numbers of clients are copied into the IPEndPoint when datagrams are received from clients.

```
1    ' Fig. 23.3: FrmPacketServer.vb
2    ' Set up a server that will receive packets from a
3    ' client and send the packets back to the client.
4    Imports System.Net
5    Imports System.Net.Sockets
6    Imports System.Threading
7
8    Public Class FrmPacketServer
9        Private client As UdpClient
10       Private receivePoint As IPEndPoint
11
12       ' initialize variables and thread for receiving packets
13       Private Sub FrmPacketServer_Load(ByVal sender As System.Object, _
14           ByVal e As System.EventArgs) Handles MyBase.Load
15
16           client = New UdpClient(50000)
17           receivePoint = New IPEndPoint(New IPAddress(0), 0)
18           Dim readThread As New Thread( _
19               New ThreadStart(AddressOf WaitForPackets))
20           readThread.Start()
21       End Sub ' FrmPacketServer_Load
22
23       ' shut down the server
24       Private Sub FrmPacketServer_FormClosing( _
25           ByVal sender As System.Object, _
26           ByVal e As System.Windows.Forms.FormClosingEventArgs) _
27           Handles MyBase.FormClosing
28
```

Fig. 23.3 | Server-side portion of connectionless client/server computing. (Part 1 of 2.)

```vbnet
29          System.Environment.Exit(System.Environment.ExitCode)
30       End Sub ' FrmPacketServer_FormClosing
31
32       ' Delegate that allows method DisplayMessage to be called
33       ' in the thread that creates and maintains the GUI
34       Private Delegate Sub DisplayDelegate(ByVal message As String)
35
36       ' method DisplayMessage sets txtDisplay's Text property
37       ' in a thread-safe manner
38       Private Sub DisplayMessage(ByVal message As String)
39          ' if modifying txtDisplay is not thread safe
40          If txtDisplay.InvokeRequired Then
41             ' use inherited method Invoke to execute DisplayMessage
42             ' via a Delegate
43             Invoke(New DisplayDelegate(AddressOf DisplayMessage), _
44                New Object() {message})
45          ' OK to modify txtDisplay in current thread
46          Else
47             txtDisplay.Text &= message
48          End If
49       End Sub ' DisplayMessage
50
51       ' wait for a packet to arrive
52       Public Sub WaitForPackets()
53          While True
54             ' set up packet
55             Dim data As Byte() = client.Receive(receivePoint)
56             DisplayMessage( _
57                vbCrLf & "Packet received:" & vbCrLf & "Length: " & _
58                data.Length & vbCrLf & "Contents: " & _
59                System.Text.Encoding.ASCII.GetString(data))
60
61             ' echo information from packet back to client
62             DisplayMessage(vbCrLf & vbCrLf & "Echo data back to client...")
63             client.Send(data, data.Length, receivePoint)
64             DisplayMessage(vbCrLf & "Packet sent" & vbCrLf)
65          End While
66       End Sub ' WaitForPackets
67    End Class ' FrmPacketServer
```

Fig. 23.3 | Server-side portion of connectionless client/server computing. (Part 2 of 2.)

Lines 34–49 define `DisplayDelegate` and `DisplayMessage`, allowing any thread to modify txtDisplay's Text property.

FrmPacketServer method `WaitForPackets` (lines 52–66) executes an infinite loop while waiting for data to arrive at the FrmPacketServer. When information arrives, Udp-Client method `Receive` (line 55) receives a Byte array from the client. We pass to `Receive` the IPEndPoint object created in the constructor—this provides the method with an IPEndPoint to which the program copies the client's IP address and port number.

Lines 56–59 display the packet's information and content in FrmPacketServer's TextBox. Line 63 echoes the data back to the client, using UdpClient method `Send`. This version of `Send` takes three arguments—the Byte array to send, the array's length and the IPEndPoint to which to send the data. We use array `data` returned by method `Receive` as the data, the length of array `data` as the length and the IPEndPoint passed to method `Receive` as the data's destination. The IP address and port number of the client that sent the data are stored in `receivePoint`, so passing `receivePoint` to Send allows FrmPacket-Server to respond to the client.

FrmPacketClient Class

Class `FrmPacketClient` (Fig. 23.4) works similarly to class FrmPacketServer, except that the client sends packets only when the user types a message in a TextBox and presses the *Enter* key. When this occurs, the program calls event handler `txtInput_KeyDown` (lines 51–69). Line 62 converts the String that the user entered in the TextBox to a Byte array. Line 65 calls UdpClient method `Send` to send the Byte array to the FrmPacketServer that is located on `localhost` (i.e., the same machine). We specify the port as 50000, which we know to be FrmPacketServer's port.

Lines 33–48 define `DisplayDelegate` and `DisplayMessage`, allowing any thread to modify txtDisplay's Text property.

```
1   ' Fig. 23.4: FrmPacketClient.vb
2   ' Set up a client that sends packets to a server and receives
3   ' packets from a server.
4   Imports System.Net
5   Imports System.Net.Sockets
6   Imports System.Threading
7
8   Public Class FrmPacketClient
9      Private client As UdpClient
10     Private receivePoint As IPEndPoint
11
12     ' initialize variables and thread for receiving packets
13     Private Sub FrmPacketClient_Load(ByVal sender As System.Object, _
14        ByVal e As System.EventArgs) Handles MyBase.Load
15
16        receivePoint = New IPEndPoint(New IPAddress(0), 0)
17        client = New UdpClient(50001)
18        Dim thread As New Thread(New ThreadStart(AddressOf WaitForPackets))
19        thread.Start()
20     End Sub ' FrmPacketClient_Load
21
```

Fig. 23.4 | Client portion of connectionless client/server computing. (Part 1 of 3.)

```vbnet
22      ' shut down the client
23      Private Sub FrmPacketClient_FormClosing( _
24         ByVal sender As System.Object, _
25         ByVal e As System.Windows.Forms.FormClosingEventArgs) _
26         Handles MyBase.FormClosing
27
28         System.Environment.Exit(System.Environment.ExitCode)
29      End Sub ' FrmPacketClient_FormClosing
30
31      ' Delegate that allows method DisplayMessage to be called
32      ' in the thread that creates and maintains the GUI
33      Private Delegate Sub DisplayDelegate(ByVal message As String)
34
35      ' method DisplayMessage sets txtDisplay's Text property
36      ' in a thread-safe manner
37      Private Sub DisplayMessage(ByVal message As String)
38         ' if modifying txtDisplay is not thread safe
39         If txtDisplay.InvokeRequired Then
40            ' use inherited method Invoke to execute DisplayMessage
41            ' via a Delegate
42            Invoke(New DisplayDelegate(AddressOf DisplayMessage), _
43               New Object() {message})
44         ' OK to modify txtDisplay in current thread
45         Else
46            txtDisplay.Text &= message
47         End If
48      End Sub ' DisplayMessage
49
50      ' send a packet
51      Private Sub txtInput_KeyDown(ByVal sender As System.Object, _
52         ByVal e As System.Windows.Forms.KeyEventArgs) _
53         Handles txtInput.KeyDown
54
55         If e.KeyCode = Keys.Enter Then
56            ' create packet (datagram) as string
57            Dim packet As String = txtInput.Text
58            txtDisplay.Text &= _
59               vbCrLf & "Sending packet containing: " & packet
60
61            ' convert packet to Byte array
62            Dim data As Byte() = System.Text.Encoding.ASCII.GetBytes(packet)
63
64            ' send packet to server on port 50000
65            client.Send(data, data.Length, "localhost", 50000)
66            txtDisplay.Text &= vbCrLf & "Packet sent" & vbCrLf
67            txtInput.Clear()
68         End If
69      End Sub ' txtInput_KeyDown
70
71      ' wait for packets to arrive
72      Public Sub WaitForPackets()
73         While True
```

Fig. 23.4 | Client portion of connectionless client/server computing. (Part 2 of 3.)

```
74              ' receive Byte array from server
75              Dim data As Byte() = client.Receive(receivePoint)
76
77              ' output packet data to TextBox
78              DisplayMessage( _
79                 vbCrLf & "Packet received:" & vbCrLf & "Length: " & _
80                 data.Length & vbCrLf & "Contents: " & _
81                 System.Text.Encoding.ASCII.GetString(data) & vbCrLf)
82          End While
83      End Sub ' WaitForPackets
84  End Class ' FrmPacketClient
```

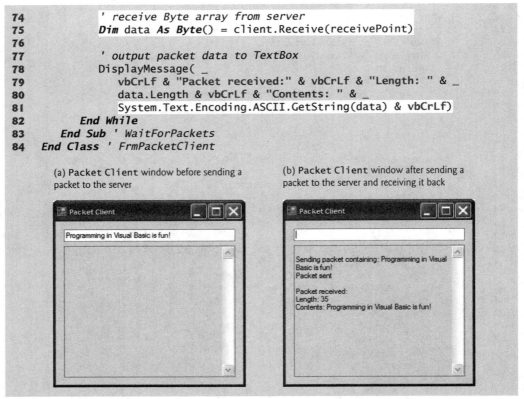

(a) **Packet Client** window before sending a packet to the server

(b) **Packet Client** window after sending a packet to the server and receiving it back

Fig. 23.4 | Client portion of connectionless client/server computing. (Part 3 of 3.)

Line 17 instantiates a UdpClient object to receive packets at port 50001—we choose port 50001 because the FrmPacketServer already occupies port 50000. Method WaitFor-Packets of class FrmPacketClient (lines 72–83) uses an infinite loop to wait for these packets. UdpClient method Receive blocks until a packet of data is received (line 75). The blocking performed by method Receive does not prevent class FrmPacketClient from performing other services (e.g., handling user input), because a separate thread (line 18) runs method WaitForPackets.

When a packet arrives, lines 78–81 display its contents in the TextBox. The user can type information in FrmPacketClient's TextBox and press the *Enter* key at any time, even while a packet is being received. The event handler for the TextBox processes the event and sends the data to the server.

23.8 Client/Server Tic-Tac-Toe Using a Multithreaded Server

We now present a networked version of the popular game Tic-Tac-Toe, implemented with stream sockets and client/server techniques. The program consists of a FrmTicTac-ToeServer application (Fig. 23.5) and a FrmTicTacToeClient application (Fig. 23.6). The FrmTicTacToeServer allows two FrmTicTacToeClients to connect to the server and play Tic-Tac-Toe against each other. Sample outputs appear in Fig. 23.6. When the server receives a client connection, lines 70–79 of Fig. 23.5 create instances of class `Player` to process each client in a separate thread of execution. This enables the server to handle requests from both clients. The server assigns value "X" to the first client that connects (player "X" makes the first move), then assigns value "O" to the second client. Throughout the game, the server maintains information regarding the status of the board so that it can validate players' requested moves. However, neither the server nor the client can establish whether a player has won the game—in this application, method `GameOver` (lines 134–137) always returns `False`. Each client maintains its own GUI version of the Tic-Tac-Toe board to display the game. The clients can place marks only in empty squares on the board. Class `Square` (Fig. 23.7) is used to define squares on the Tic-Tac-Toe board.

FrmTicTacToeServer Class

`FrmTicTacToeServer` (Fig. 23.5) uses its `Load` event handler (lines 19–30) to create a `Byte` array to store the moves the players have made (line 22). The program creates an array of two references to `Player` objects (line 23) and an array of two references to `Thread` objects (line 24). Each element in both arrays corresponds to a Tic-Tac-Toe player. Variable `currentPlayer` is set to 0 (line 25), which corresponds to player "X". In our program, player "X" makes the first move. Lines 28–29 create and start `Thread getPlayers`, which the `FrmTicTacToeServer` uses to accept connections so that the current `Thread` does not block while awaiting players.

```vb
1   ' Fig. 23.5: FrmTicTacToeServer.vb
2   ' This class maintains a game of Tic-Tac-Toe for two
3   ' client applications.
4   Imports System.Net
5   Imports System.Net.Sockets
6   Imports System.Threading
7   Imports System.IO
8
9   Public Class FrmTicTacToeServer
10      Private board() As Byte ' the local representation of the game board
11      Private players() As Player ' two Player objects
12      Private playerThreads() As Thread ' Threads for client interaction
13      Private listener As TcpListener ' listen for client connection
14      Private currentPlayer As Integer ' keep track of whose turn it is
15      Private getPlayers As Thread ' Thread for acquiring client connections
16      Friend disconnected As Boolean = False ' True if the server closes
17
18      ' initialize variables and thread for receiving clients
19      Private Sub FrmTicTacToeServer_Load(ByVal sender As System.Object, _
20          ByVal e As System.EventArgs) Handles MyBase.Load
21
22          board = New Byte(9) {}
23          players = New Player(2) {}
24          playerThreads = New Thread(2) {}
25          currentPlayer = 0
26
```

Fig. 23.5 | Server side of client/server Tic-Tac-Toe program. (Part 1 of 6.)

```vb
27      ' accept connections on a different thread
28      getPlayers = New Thread(New ThreadStart(AddressOf SetUp))
29      getPlayers.Start()
30   End Sub ' FrmTicTacToeServer_Load
31
32   ' notify Players to stop Running
33   Private Sub FrmTicTacToeServer_FormClosing( _
34      ByVal sender As System.Object, _
35      ByVal e As System.Windows.Forms.FormClosingEventArgs) _
36      Handles MyBase.FormClosing
37
38      disconnected = True
39      System.Environment.Exit(System.Environment.ExitCode)
40   End Sub ' FrmTicTacToeServer_FormClosing
41
42   ' Delegate that allows method DisplayMessage to be called
43   ' in the thread that creates and maintains the GUI
44   Private Delegate Sub DisplayDelegate(ByVal message As String)
45
46   ' method DisplayMessage sets txtDisplay's Text property
47   ' in a thread-safe manner
48   Friend Sub DisplayMessage(ByVal message As String)
49      ' if modifying txtDisplay is not thread safe
50      If txtDisplay.InvokeRequired Then
51         ' use inherited method Invoke to execute DisplayMessage
52         ' via a Delegate
53         Invoke(New DisplayDelegate(AddressOf DisplayMessage), _
54            New Object() {message})
55      ' OK to modify txtDisplay in current thread
56      Else
57         txtDisplay.Text &= message
58      End If
59   End Sub ' DisplayMessage
60
61   ' accepts connections from 2 players
62   Public Sub SetUp()
63      DisplayMessage("Waiting for players..." & vbCrLf)
64
65      ' set up Socket
66      listener = New TcpListener(IPAddress.Parse("localhost"), 50000)
67      listener.Start()
68
69      ' accept first player and start a player thread
70      players(0) = New Player(listener.AcceptSocket(), Me, 0)
71      playerThreads(0) = New Thread( _
72         New ThreadStart(AddressOf players(0).Run))
73      playerThreads(0).Start()
74
75      ' accept second player and start another player thread
76      players(1) = New Player(listener.AcceptSocket(), Me, 1)
77      playerThreads(1) = New Thread( _
78         New ThreadStart(AddressOf players(1).Run))
79      playerThreads(1).Start()
```

Fig. 23.5 | Server side of client/server Tic-Tac-Toe program. (Part 2 of 6.)

```
80
81            ' let the first player know that the other player has connected
82            SyncLock players(0)
83               players(0).threadSuspended = False
84               Monitor.Pulse(players(0))
85            End SyncLock
86         End Sub ' SetUp
87
88         ' determine if a move is valid
89         Public Function ValidMove(ByVal location As Integer, _
90            ByVal player As Integer) As Boolean
91            ' prevent another thread from making a move
92            SyncLock Me
93               ' while it is not the current player's turn, wait
94               While player <> currentPlayer
95                  Monitor.Wait(Me)
96               End While
97
98               ' if the desired square is not occupied
99               If Not IsOccupied(location) Then
100                  ' set the board to contain the current player's mark
101                  If currentPlayer = 0 Then
102                     board(location) = Convert.ToByte("X"c)
103                  Else
104                     board(location) = Convert.ToByte("O"c)
105                  End If
106
107                  ' set the currentPlayer to be the other player
108                  currentPlayer = (currentPlayer + 1) Mod 2
109
110                  ' notify the other player of the move
111                  players(currentPlayer).OtherPlayerMoved(location)
112
113                  ' alert the other player that it's time to move
114                  Monitor.Pulse(Me)
115                  Return True
116               Else
117                  Return False
118               End If
119            End SyncLock
120         End Function ' ValidMove
121
122         ' determines whether the specified square is occupied
123         Public Function IsOccupied(ByVal location As Integer) As Boolean
124            If board(location) = Convert.ToByte("X"c) Or _
125               board(location) = Convert.ToByte("O"c) Then
126
127               Return True
128            Else
129               Return False
130            End If
131         End Function ' IsOccupied
132
```

Fig. 23.5 | Server side of client/server Tic-Tac-Toe program. (Part 3 of 6.)

```
133        ' determines if the game is over
134        Public Function GameOver() As Boolean
135            ' place code here to test for a winner of the game
136            Return False
137        End Function ' GameOver
138    End Class ' FrmTicTacToeServer
139
140    ' class Player represents a tic-tac-toe player
141    Public Class Player
142        Friend connection As Socket ' Socket for accepting a connection
143        Private socketStream As NetworkStream ' network data stream
144        Private server As FrmTicTacToeServer ' reference to server
145        Private writer As BinaryWriter ' facilitates writing to the stream
146        Private reader As BinaryReader ' facilitates reading from the stream
147        Private number As Integer ' player number
148        Private mark As Char ' player's mark on the board
149        Friend threadSuspended As Boolean = True ' if waiting for other player
150
151        ' constructor requiring Socket, TicTacToeServerForm and Integer
152        ' objects as arguments
153        Public Sub New(ByVal socket As Socket, _
154            ByVal serverValue As FrmTicTacToeServer, ByVal newNumber As Integer)
155
156            If newNumber = 0 Then
157                mark = "X"c
158            Else
159                mark = "O"c
160            End If
161
162            connection = socket
163            server = serverValue
164            number = newNumber
165
166            ' create NetworkStream object for Socket
167            socketStream = New NetworkStream(connection)
168
169            ' create Streams for reading/writing bytes
170            writer = New BinaryWriter(socketStream)
171            reader = New BinaryReader(socketStream)
172        End Sub ' New
173
174        ' signal other player of move
175        Public Sub OtherPlayerMoved(ByVal location As Integer)
176            ' signal that opponent moved
177            writer.Write("Opponent moved.")
178            writer.Write(location) ' send location of move
179        End Sub ' OtherPlayerMoved
180
181        ' allows the players to make moves and receive moves
182        ' from the other player
183        Public Sub Run()
184            Dim done As Boolean = False
185
```

Fig. 23.5 | Server side of client/server Tic-Tac-Toe program. (Part 4 of 6.)

```vb
186        ' display on the server that a connection was made
187        If number = 0 Then
188           server.DisplayMessage("Player X connected" & vbCrLf)
189        Else
190           server.DisplayMessage("Player O connected" & vbCrLf)
191        End If
192
193        ' send the current player's mark to the client
194        writer.Write(mark)
195
196        ' if number equals 0 then this player is X,
197        ' otherwise O must wait for X's first move
198        If number = 0 Then
199           writer.Write("Player X connected.")
200        Else
201           writer.Write("Player O connected, please wait." & vbCrLf)
202        End If
203
204        ' X must wait for another player to arrive
205        If mark = "X"c Then
206           writer.Write("Waiting for another player.")
207
208           ' wait for notification from server that another
209           ' player has connected
210           SyncLock Me
211              While threadSuspended
212                 Monitor.Wait(Me)
213              End While
214           End SyncLock
215
216           writer.Write("Other player connected. Your move.")
217        End If
218
219        ' play game
220        While Not done
221           ' wait for data to become available
222           While connection.Available = 0
223              Thread.Sleep(1000)
224
225              If server.disconnected Then
226                 Return
227              End If
228           End While
229
230           ' receive data
231           Dim location As Integer = reader.ReadInt32()
232
233           ' if the move is valid, display the move on the
234           ' server and signal that the move is valid
235           If server.ValidMove(location, number) Then
236              server.DisplayMessage("loc: " & location & vbCrLf)
237              writer.Write("Valid move.")
```

Fig. 23.5 | Server side of client/server Tic-Tac-Toe program. (Part 5 of 6.)

```
238              ' signal that the move is invalid
239              Else
240                 writer.Write("Invalid move, try again.")
241              End If
242
243              ' if game is over, set done to True to exit while loop
244              If server.GameOver() Then
245                 done = True
246              End If
247           End While
248
249           ' close the socket connection
250           writer.Close()
251           reader.Close()
252           socketStream.Close()
253           connection.Close()
254        End Sub   ' Run
255     End Class ' Player
```

Fig. 23.5 | Server side of client/server Tic-Tac-Toe program. (Part 6 of 6.)

Lines 44–59 define DisplayDelegate and DisplayMessage, allowing any thread to modify txtDisplay's Text property. This time, the DisplayMessage method is declared as Friend, so it can be called inside a method of class Player through a FrmTicTac-ToeServer reference. Classes in the same project can access each other's Friend members.

Thread getPlayers executes method SetUp (lines 62–86), which creates a TcpListener object to listen for requests on port 50000 (lines 66–67). This object then listens for connection requests from the first and second players. Lines 70 and 76 instantiate Player objects representing the players, and lines 71–73 and 77–79 create two Threads that execute the Run methods of each Player object.

The Player constructor (Fig. 23.5, lines 153–172) receives as arguments a reference to the Socket object (i.e., the connection to the client), a reference to the FrmTicTac-ToeServer object and an Integer indicating the player number (from which the constructor infers the mark "X" or "O" used by that player). FrmTicTacToeServer calls method Run (lines 183–254) after instantiating a Player object. Lines 187–194 notify the server of a successful connection and send the client the Char that the client will place on the board when making a move. If Run is executing for Player "X", lines 205–217 execute, causing Player "X" to wait for a second player to connect. Lines 211–213 suspend the Player "X" Thread until the server signals that Player "O" has connected. The server notifies the Player of the connection by setting the Player's threadSuspended variable to False (line 83). When threadSuspended becomes False, Player exits the loop in lines 211–213.

Lines 220–247 in method Run enable the user to play the game. Each iteration of this statement waits for the client to send an Integer specifying where on the board to place the "X" or "O"—the Player then places the mark on the board if the specified mark location is valid (i.e., if that location does not already contain a mark). Note that the loop continues execution only if Boolean variable done is False. This variable is set to True by event handler FrmTicTacToeServer_FormClosing of class FrmTicTacToeServer, which is invoked when the server closes the connection.

Line 222 of Fig. 23.5 begins a loop that iterates until Socket property Available indicates that there is information to receive from the Socket (or until the server disconnects from the client). If there is none, the Thread sleeps for one second. On awakening, the Thread uses property Disconnected to check whether server variable disconnected is True (line 225). If so, the Thread exits the method (thus terminating the Thread); otherwise, the Thread loops again. However, if property Available indicates that there is data to receive, the loop in lines 222–228 terminates, enabling the information to be processed.

This information contains an Integer representing the location in which the client wants to place a mark. Line 231 calls method ReadInt32 of the BinaryReader object (which reads from the NetworkStream created with the Socket) to read this Integer. Line 235 then passes the Integer to FrmTicTacToeServer method ValidMove. If this method validates the move, the Player places the mark in the desired location.

Method ValidMove (lines 89–120) sends the client a message indicating whether the move was valid. Locations on the board correspond to numbers from 0 to 8 (0–2 for the top row, 3–5 for the middle and 6–8 for the bottom). All the statements in the method are enclosed in a SyncLock statement so that only one move can be attempted at a time. This prevents two players from modifying the game's state information simultaneously. If the Player attempting to validate a move is not the current player (i.e., the one allowed to make a move), that Player is placed in a *Wait* state until its turn. If the user attempts to place a mark on a location that already contains a mark, method ValidMove returns False. However, if the user has selected an unoccupied location (line 99), lines 101–105 place the mark on the local representation of the board. Line 111 notifies the other Player that a move has been made, and line 114 invokes the Pulse method so that the waiting Player can validate a move. The method then returns True to indicate that the move is valid.

When FrmTicTacToeClient (Fig. 23.6) executes, it creates a TextBox to display messages from the server and the Tic-Tac-Toe board representation. The board is created out of nine Square objects (Fig. 23.7) that contain Panels on which the user can click, indicating the position on the board in which to place a mark. FrmTicTacToeClient's Load event handler (lines 22–51) opens a connection to the server (line 43) and obtains a reference to the connection's associated NetworkStream object from TcpClient (line 44). Lines 49–50 start a thread to read messages sent from the server to the client. The server passes messages (e.g., whether each move is valid) to method ProcessMessage (lines 174–207). If the message indicates that a move is valid (line 178), the client sets its Mark to the current square (the square that the user clicked) and repaints the board. If the message indicates that a move is invalid (line 182), the client notifies the user to click a different square. If the message indicates that the opponent made a move (line 187), line 189 reads an Integer from the server specifying where on the board the client should place the opponent's Mark. FrmTicTacToeClient includes a Delegate/method pair for allowing threads to modify lblId's Text property (lines 92–107), as well as DisplayDelegate and DisplayMesage for modifying txtDisplay's Text property (lines 73–88).

```
1    ' Fig. 23.6: FrmTicTacToeClient.vb
2    ' Client for the TicTacToe program.
3    Imports System.Drawing
```

Fig. 23.6 | Client side of client/server Tic-Tac-Toe program. (Part 1 of 7.)

```vb
4  Imports System.Net.Sockets
5  Imports System.Threading
6  Imports System.IO
7
8  Public Class FrmTicTacToeClient
9     Private board(,) As Square ' local representation of the game board
10    Private currentSquareValue As Square ' Square that this player chose
11    Private outputThread As Thread ' Thread for receiving data from server
12    Private connection As TcpClient ' client to establish connection
13    Private stream As NetworkStream ' network data stream
14    Private writer As BinaryWriter ' facilitates writing to the stream
15    Private reader As BinaryReader ' facilitates reading from the stream
16    Private myMark As Char ' player's mark on the board
17    Private myTurn As Boolean ' is it this player's turn?
18    Private brush As SolidBrush ' brush for drawing X's and O's
19    Private done As Boolean = False ' True when game is over
20
21    ' initialize variables and thread for connecting to server
22    Private Sub FrmTicTacToeClient_Load(ByVal sender As System.Object, _
23       ByVal e As System.EventArgs) Handles MyBase.Load
24
25       board = New Square(3, 3) {}
26
27       ' create 9 Square objects and place them on the board
28       board(0, 0) = New Square(pnlBoard0, " "c, 0)
29       board(0, 1) = New Square(pnlBoard1, " "c, 1)
30       board(0, 2) = New Square(pnlBoard2, " "c, 2)
31       board(1, 0) = New Square(pnlBoard3, " "c, 3)
32       board(1, 1) = New Square(pnlBoard4, " "c, 4)
33       board(1, 2) = New Square(pnlBoard5, " "c, 5)
34       board(2, 0) = New Square(pnlBoard6, " "c, 6)
35       board(2, 1) = New Square(pnlBoard7, " "c, 7)
36       board(2, 2) = New Square(pnlBoard8, " "c, 8)
37
38       ' create a SolidBrush for writing on the Squares
39       brush = New SolidBrush(Color.Black)
40
41       ' make connection to server and get the associated
42       ' network stream
43       connection = New TcpClient("localhost", 50000)
44       stream = connection.GetStream()
45       writer = New BinaryWriter(stream)
46       reader = New BinaryReader(stream)
47
48       ' start a new thread for sending and receiving messages
49       outputThread = New Thread(New ThreadStart(AddressOf Run))
50       outputThread.Start()
51    End Sub ' FrmTicTacToeClient_Load
52
53    ' repaint the Squares
54    Private Sub FrmTicTacToeClient_Paint(ByVal sender As System.Object, _
55       ByVal e As System.Windows.Forms.PaintEventArgs) _
56       Handles MyBase.Paint
```

Fig. 23.6 | Client side of client/server Tic-Tac-Toe program. (Part 2 of 7.)

```vbnet
57
58          PaintSquares()
59      End Sub ' FrmTicTacToeClient_Paint
60
61      ' game is over
62      Private Sub FrmTicTacToeClient_FormClosing( _
63          ByVal sender As System.Object, _
64          ByVal e As System.Windows.Forms.FormClosingEventArgs) _
65          Handles MyBase.FormClosing
66
67          done = True
68          System.Environment.Exit(System.Environment.ExitCode)
69      End Sub ' FrmTicTacToeClient_FormClosing
70
71      ' Delegate that allows method DisplayMessage to be called
72      ' in the thread that creates and maintains the GUI
73      Private Delegate Sub DisplayDelegate(ByVal message As String)
74
75      ' method DisplayMessage sets txtDisplay's Text property
76      ' in a thread-safe manner
77      Private Sub DisplayMessage(ByVal message As String)
78          ' if modifying txtDisplay is not thread safe
79          If txtDisplay.InvokeRequired Then
80              ' use inherited method Invoke to execute DisplayMessage
81              ' via a Delegate
82              Invoke(New DisplayDelegate(AddressOf DisplayMessage), _
83                  New Object() {message})
84          ' OK to modify txtDisplay in current thread
85          Else
86              txtDisplay.Text &= message
87          End If
88      End Sub ' DisplayMessage
89
90      ' Delegate that allows method ChangeIdLabel to be called
91      ' in the thread that creates and maintains the GUI
92      Private Delegate Sub ChangeIdLabelDelegate(ByVal message As String)
93
94      ' method ChangeIdLabel sets txtDisplay's Text property
95      ' in a thread-safe manner
96      Private Sub ChangeIdLabel(ByVal label As String)
97          ' if modifying lblId is not thread safe
98          If lblId.InvokeRequired Then
99              ' use inherited method Invoke to execute ChangeIdLabel
100             ' via a Delegate
101             Invoke(New ChangeIdLabelDelegate(AddressOf ChangeIdLabel), _
102                 New Object() {label})
103         ' OK to modify lblId in current thread
104         Else
105             lblId.Text = label
106         End If
107     End Sub ' ChangeIdLabel
108
```

Fig. 23.6 | Client side of client/server Tic-Tac-Toe program. (Part 3 of 7.)

```vb
109     ' draws the mark of each square
110     Public Sub PaintSquares()
111        Dim g As Graphics
112
113        ' draw the appropriate mark on each panel
114        For row As Integer = 0 To 2
115
116           For column As Integer = 0 To 2
117              ' get the Graphics for each Panel
118              g = board(row, column).SquarePanel.CreateGraphics()
119
120              ' draw the appropriate letter on the panel
121              g.DrawString(board(row, column).Mark.ToString(), _
122                 pnlBoard0.Font, brush, 10, 8)
123           Next column
124
125        Next row
126     End Sub ' PaintSquares
127
128     ' send location of the clicked square to server
129     Private Sub square_MouseUp(ByVal sender As System.Object, _
130        ByVal e As System.Windows.Forms.MouseEventArgs) _
131        Handles pnlBoard0.MouseUp, pnlBoard5.MouseUp, pnlBoard4.MouseUp, _
132        pnlBoard3.MouseUp, pnlBoard2.MouseUp, pnlBoard1.MouseUp, _
133        pnlBoard8.MouseUp, pnlBoard7.MouseUp, pnlBoard6.MouseUp
134
135        ' for each square check if that square was clicked
136        For row As Integer = 0 To 2
137
138           For column As Integer = 0 To 2
139              If board(row, column).SquarePanel.Equals(sender) Then
140                 currentSquareValue = board(row, column)
141
142                 ' send the move to the server
143                 SendClickedSquare(board(row, column).Location)
144              End If
145           Next column
146        Next row
147     End Sub ' square_MouseUp
148
149     ' control thread that allows continuous update of the
150     ' TextBox display
151     Public Sub Run()
152        myMark = reader.ReadChar() ' first get players's mark (X or O)
153        ChangeIdLabel("You are player """ & myMark & """")
154
155        If myMark = "X"c Then
156           myTurn = True
157        Else
158           myTurn = False
159        End If
160
```

Fig. 23.6 | Client side of client/server Tic-Tac-Toe program. (Part 4 of 7.)

```vb
161        ' process incoming messages
162        Try
163            ' receive messages sent to client
164            While Not done
165                ProcessMessage(reader.ReadString())
166            End While
167        Catch ex As IOException
168            MessageBox.Show("Server is down, game over", "Error", _
169                MessageBoxButtons.OK, MessageBoxIcon.Error)
170        End Try
171    End Sub ' Run
172
173    ' process messages sent to client
174    Public Sub ProcessMessage(ByVal message As String)
175        ' if the move the player sent to the server is valid
176        ' update the display, set that square's mark to be
177        ' the mark of the current player and repaint the board
178        If message = "Valid move." Then
179            DisplayMessage("Valid move, please wait." & vbCrLf)
180            currentSquareValue.Mark = myMark
181            PaintSquares()
182        ElseIf message = "Invalid move, try again." Then
183            ' if the move is invalid, display that and it is now
184            ' this player's turn again
185            DisplayMessage(message & vbCrLf)
186            myTurn = True
187        ElseIf message = "Opponent moved." Then
188            ' if opponent moved, find location of their move
189            Dim location As Integer = reader.ReadInt32()
190
191            ' set that square to have the opponents mark and
192            ' repaint the board
193            If myMark = "X"c Then
194                board(location \ 3, location Mod 3).Mark = "O"c
195            Else
196                board(location \ 3, location Mod 3).Mark = "X"c
197            End If
198            PaintSquares()
199
200            DisplayMessage("Opponent moved.  Your turn." & vbCrLf)
201
202            ' it is now this player's turn
203            myTurn = True
204        Else
205            DisplayMessage(message & vbCrLf) ' display message
206        End If
207    End Sub ' ProcessMessage
208
209    ' sends the server the number of the clicked square
210    Public Sub SendClickedSquare(ByVal location As Integer)
211        ' if it is the current player's move right now
212        If myTurn Then
```

Fig. 23.6 | Client side of client/server Tic-Tac-Toe program. (Part 5 of 7.)

```
213              ' send the location of the move to the server
214              writer.Write(location)
215
216              ' it is now the other player's turn
217              myTurn = False
218          End If
219      End Sub ' SendClickedSquare
220
221      ' write-only property for the current square
222      Public WriteOnly Property CurrentSquare() As Square
223          Set(ByVal value As Square)
224              currentSquareValue = value
225          End Set
226      End Property ' CurrentSquare
227  End Class ' FrmTicTacToeClient
```

At the start of the game.

After Player X makes the first move.

Fig. 23.6 | Client side of client/server Tic-Tac-Toe program. (Part 6 of 7.)

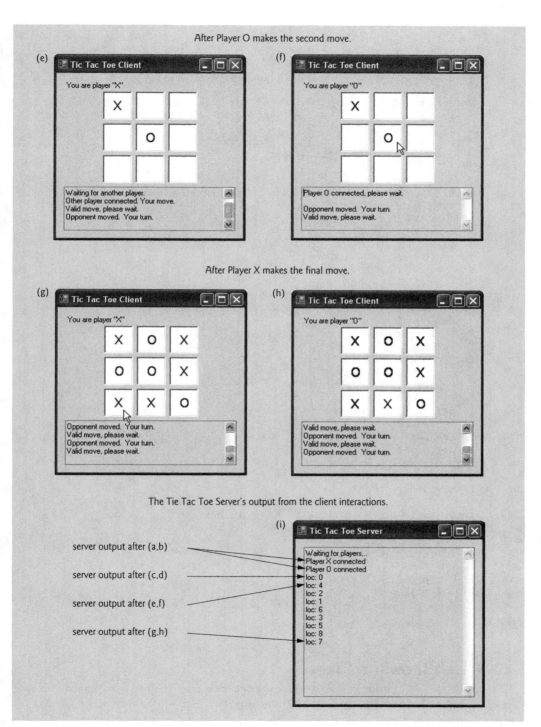

Fig. 23.6 | Client side of client/server Tic-Tac-Toe program. (Part 7 of 7.)

```
 1   ' Fig. 23.7: Square.vb
 2   ' A Square on the TicTacToe board.
 3
 4   ' the representation of a square in a tic-tac-toe grid
 5   Public Class Square
 6      Private panel As Panel ' GUI Panel that represents this Square
 7      Private markValue As Char ' player's markValue on this Square (if any)
 8
 9      ' locationValue on the board of this Square
10      Private locationValue As Integer
11
12      ' constructor
13      Public Sub New(ByVal newPanel As Panel, ByVal newMark As Char, _
14         ByVal newLocation As Integer)
15
16         panel = newPanel
17         markValue = newMark
18         locationValue = newLocation
19      End Sub ' New
20
21      ' property SquarePanel; the panel which the square represents
22      Public ReadOnly Property SquarePanel() As Panel
23         Get
24            Return panel
25         End Get
26      End Property ' SquarePanel
27
28      ' property Mark; the markValue on the square
29      Public Property Mark() As Char
30         Get
31            Return markValue
32         End Get
33         Set(ByVal value As Char)
34            markValue = value
35         End Set
36      End Property ' Mark
37
38      ' property Location; the square's locationValue on the board
39      Public ReadOnly Property Location() As Integer
40         Get
41            Return locationValue
42         End Get
43      End Property ' Location
44   End Class ' Square
```

Fig. 23.7 | Class Square.

23.9 WebBrowser Class

With FCL 2.0, Microsoft introduced the **WebBrowser class** (namespace System.Windows.Forms), which enables applications to incorporate Web browsing capabilities. The control provides methods for navigating Web pages and maintains its own history of Web sites visited. It also generates events as the user interacts with the content displayed in the control so that your application can respond to events such as the user clicking the links displayed in the content.

Figure 23.8 demonstrates the `WebBrowser` class's capabilities. Class `FrmBrowser` provides the basic functionality of a Web browser, allowing the user to navigate to a URL, move backward and forward through the history of visited sites, and reload the current Web page.

```
 1    ' Fig. 23.8: FrmBrowser.vb
 2    ' WebBrowser class example.
 3
 4    Public Class FrmBrowser
 5       ' navigate back one page
 6       Private Sub btnBack_Click(ByVal sender As System.Object, _
 7          ByVal e As System.EventArgs) Handles btnBack.Click
 8
 9          webBrowser.GoBack()
10       End Sub ' btnBack_Click
11
12       ' navigate forward one page
13       Private Sub btnForward_Click(ByVal sender As System.Object, _
14          ByVal e As System.EventArgs) Handles btnForward.Click
15
16          webBrowser.GoForward()
17       End Sub ' btnForward_Click
18
19       ' stop loading the current page
20       Private Sub btnStop_Click(ByVal sender As System.Object, _
21          ByVal e As System.EventArgs) Handles btnStop.Click
22
23          webBrowser.Stop()
24       End Sub ' btnStop_Click
25
26       ' reload the current page
27       Private Sub btnReload_Click(ByVal sender As System.Object, _
28          ByVal e As System.EventArgs) Handles btnReload.Click
29
30          webBrowser.Refresh()
31       End Sub ' btnReload_Click
32
33       ' navigate to the user's home page
34       Private Sub btnHome_Click(ByVal sender As System.Object, _
35          ByVal e As System.EventArgs) Handles btnHome.Click
36
37          webBrowser.GoHome()
38       End Sub ' btnHome_Click
39
40       ' if the user pressed enter, navigate to the specified URL
41       Private Sub txtNavigation_KeyDown(ByVal sender As System.Object, _
42          ByVal e As System.Windows.Forms.KeyEventArgs) _
43          Handles txtNavigation.KeyDown
44
```

Fig. 23.8 | WebBrowser class example. (Part 1 of 3.)

```
45          If e.KeyCode = Keys.Enter Then
46              webBrowser.Navigate(txtNavigation.Text)
47          End If
48      End Sub ' txtNavigation_KeyDown
49
50      ' enable btnStop while the current page is loading
51      Private Sub webBrowser_Navigating(ByVal sender As System.Object, _
52          ByVal e As System.Windows.Forms.WebBrowserNavigatingEventArgs) _
53          Handles webBrowser.Navigating
54
55          btnStop.Enabled = True
56      End Sub ' webBrowser_Navigating
57
58      ' update the status text
59      Private Sub webBrowser_StatusTextChanged( _
60          ByVal sender As System.Object, ByVal e As System.EventArgs) _
61          Handles webBrowser.StatusTextChanged
62
63          txtStatus.Text = webBrowser.StatusText
64      End Sub ' webBrowser_StatusTextChanged
65
66      ' update the ProgressBar for how much of the page has been loaded
67      Private Sub webBrowser_ProgressChanged( _
68          ByVal sender As System.Object, ByVal e As _
69          System.Windows.Forms.WebBrowserProgressChangedEventArgs) _
70          Handles webBrowser.ProgressChanged
71          ' Check if e.MaximumProgress is 0 or
72          ' if e.MaximumProgress is less than e.CurrentProgress
73          If e.MaximumProgress <> 0 And _
74              e.MaximumProgress >= e.CurrentProgress Then
75
76              prgPage.Value = Convert.ToInt32( _
77                  100 * e.CurrentProgress / e.MaximumProgress)
78          End If
79      End Sub ' webBrowser_ProgressChanged
80
81      ' update the web browser's controls appropriately
82      Private Sub webBrowser_DocumentCompleted( _
83          ByVal sender As System.Object, ByVal e As _
84          System.Windows.Forms.WebBrowserDocumentCompletedEventArgs) _
85          Handles webBrowser.DocumentCompleted
86          ' set the text in txtNavigation to the current page's URL
87          txtNavigation.Text = webBrowser.Url.ToString()
88
89          ' enable or disable btnBack and btnForward
90          btnBack.Enabled = webBrowser.CanGoBack
91          btnForward.Enabled = webBrowser.CanGoForward
92
93          ' disable btnStop
94          btnStop.Enabled = False
95
```

Fig. 23.8 | WebBrowser class example. (Part 2 of 3.)

```
96              ' clear the prgPage
97              prgPage.Value = 0
98      End Sub ' webBrowser_DocumentCompleted
99
100         ' update the title of the Browser
101     Private Sub webBrowser_DocumentTitleChanged( _
102         ByVal sender As System.Object, ByVal e As System.EventArgs) _
103         Handles webBrowser.DocumentTitleChanged
104
105         Me.Text = webBrowser.DocumentTitle & " - Browser"
106     End Sub ' webBrowser_DocumentTitleChanged
107 End Class ' FrmBrowser
```

Fig. 23.8 | WebBrowser class example. (Part 3 of 3.)

Lines 6–38 define five Click event handlers, one for each of the five navigation Buttons that appear at the top of the Form. Each event handler calls a corresponding WebBrowser method. WebBrowser method *GoBack* (line 9) navigates back to the previous page in the navigation history. Method *GoForward* (line 16) navigates forward to the next page in the navigation history. Method *Stop* (line 23) stops loading the current page. Method *Refresh* (line 30) reloads the current page. Method *GoHome* (line 37) navigates to the user's home page, as defined under Internet Explorer's settings (under **Tools > Internet Options…** in the **Home page** section).

The TextBox to the right of the navigation buttons allows the user to enter the URL of a Web site to browse. When the user types each keystroke in the TextBox, the event handler in lines 41–48 executes. If the key pressed was *Enter*, line 46 calls WebBrowser method *Navigate* to retrieve the document at the specified URL.

A WebBrowser object generates a *Navigating* event when it starts loading a new page. When this occurs, the event handler in lines 51–56 executes, and line 55 enables btnStop so that the user can cancel the loading of the Web page.

Typically, a user can see the status of a loading Web page at the bottom of the browser window. For this reason, we include a TextBox control (named txtStatus) and a ProgressBar control (named prgPage) at the bottom of our Form. A WebBrowser object generates a *StatusTextChanged* event when its *StatusText* property changes. The event handler for this event (lines 59–64) assigns the new contents of the WebBrowser's Status-

Text property to txtStatus's Text property (line 63) so that the user can monitor the WebBrowser's status messages. A WebBrowser object generates a ***ProgressChanged*** event when its page-loading progress is updated. The ProgressChanged event handler (lines 67–79) updates prgPage's Value (lines 76–77) to reflect how much of the current document has been loaded.

When the WebBrowser finishes loading a document, it generates a ***DocumentCompleted*** event. This executes the event handler in lines 82–98. Line 87 updates the contents of txtNavigation so that it shows the URL of the currently loaded page (WebBrowser property Url). This is particularly important if the user browses to another Web page by clicking a link in the existing page. Lines 90–91 use properties ***CanGoBack*** and ***CanGoForward*** to determine whether the back and forward buttons should be enabled or disabled. Since the document is now loaded, line 94 disables btnStop. Line 97 sets prgPage's Value to 0 to indicate that no content is currently being loaded.

Lines 101–106 define an event handler for the ***DocumentTitleChanged*** event, which occurs when a new document is loaded in the WebBrowser. Line 105 sets FrmBrowser's Text property (which is displayed in the Form's title bar) to the WebBrowser's current ***DocumentTitle***.

23.10 .NET Remoting

The .NET framework provides a distributed computing technology called *.NET remoting* that allows a program to invoke methods of objects located on other computers over a network, rather than communicate with streams of bytes (as demonstrated earlier in this chapter). .NET remoting is similar in concept to RMI (remote method invocation) in Java and RPC (remote procedure call) in procedural programming languages. .NET remoting is also similar to Web services (Chapter 22) with a few key differences. With Web services, a client application communicates with a Web service that is hosted by a Web server. The client and the Web service can be written in any language, as long as they can transmit messages in SOAP. With .NET remoting, a client application communicates with a server application, both of which must be written in .NET languages. Using .NET remoting, a client and a server can communicate via method calls, and objects can be transmitted between applications—a process known as *marshaling* the objects.

Channels

The client and the server are able to communicate with one another through *channels*. Channels typically use either the HTTP protocol or the TCP protocol to transmit messages. The advantage of an *HTTP channel* is that firewalls usually permit HTTP connections by default, while they normally block unfamiliar TCP connections. The advantage of a *TCP channel* is better performance than an HTTP channel. In a .NET remoting application, the client and the server each create a channel, and both channels must use the same protocol to communicate with one another. In our example, we use HTTP channels.

Marshaling

There are two ways to marshal an object—by value and by reference. *Marshal-by-value* requires that the object be *serializable*—that is, capable of being represented as a formatted message that can be sent between applications through a channel. The receiving end of the channel *deserializes* the object to obtain a copy of the original object. To enable an object to be serialized and deserialized, its class must be declared with the `<Serializable()>` attribute or must implement interface `ISerializable`.

Marshal-by-reference requires that the object's class extend class **`MarshalByRefObject`** of namespace `System`. An object that is marshaled by reference is referred to as a *remote object*, and its class is referred to as a *remote class*. When an object is marshaled by reference, the object itself is not transmitted. Instead, two *proxy* objects are created—a *transparent proxy* and a *real proxy*. The transparent proxy provides all the `Public` services of a remote object. Typically, a client calls the methods and properties of the transparent proxy as if it were the remote object. The transparent proxy then calls the `Invoke` method of the real proxy. This sends the appropriate message from the client channel to the server channel. The server receives this message and performs the specified method call or accesses the specified property on the actual object, which resides on the server. In our example, we marshal a remote object by reference.

Weather Information Application Using .NET Remoting

We now present a .NET remoting example that downloads the *Traveler's Forecast* weather information from the National Weather Service Web site:

```
http://iwin.nws.noaa.gov/iwin/us/traveler.html
```

[*Note:* As we developed this example, the National Weather Service indicated that the information provided on the *Traveler's Forecast* Web page would be provided via Web services in the near future. The information we use in this example depends directly on the format of the *Traveler's Forecast* Web page. If you have trouble running this example, please refer to the FAQ page for this book, which is accessible via www.deitel.com/faq.html. This potential problem demonstrates a benefit of using Web services or .NET remoting to implement distributed computing applications that may change in the future. Separating the server part of the application, which depends on the format of an outside data source, from the client part of the application allows the server implementation to be updated without requiring any changes to the client.]

Our .NET remoting application consists of five components:

1. Serializable class `CityWeather`, which represents the weather report for one city.

2. Interface `Report`, which declares a property `Reports` that a client application accesses via the marshaled object to obtain a collection of `CityWeather` objects.

3. Remote class `ReportInfo`, which extends class `MarshalByRefObject`, implements interface `Report` and will be instantiated only on the server.

4. A `WeatherServer` application that sets up a server channel and makes the `ReportInfo` class available at a particular URI (uniform resource identifier).

5. A `WeatherClient` application that sets up a client channel and requests a `ReportInfo` object from the `WeatherServer` to retrieve the day's weather report.

Class CityWeather

Class `CityWeather` (Fig. 23.9) contains weather information for one city. Class `CityWeather` will be published in the `Weather.dll` class library file that both the server application and the client application must reference. For this reason, you should place this class (and interface Report from Fig. 23.10) in a class library project. Class CityWeather is declared with attribute Serializable (line 4), which indicates that an object of class City-Weather can be marshaled by value. This is necessary because CityWeather objects will be returned by the ReportInfo object's Reports property, and the return values of the methods and properties declared by a remote class must themselves be marshaled by value from the server to the client. (The argument values in method calls will also be marshaled by value from the client to the server.) Thus when the client calls a Get accessor that returns CityWeather objects, the server channel will serialize the CityWeather objects in a message that the client channel can deserialize to create copies of the original CityWeather objects. Class CityWeather also implements interface IComparable (line 5) so that an ArrayList of CityWeather objects can be sorted alphabetically.

```
 1    ' Fig. 23.9: CityWeather.vb
 2    ' Class representing the weather information for one city.
 3
 4    <Serializable()> _
 5    Public Class CityWeather : Implements IComparable
 6       Private cityNameValue As String
 7       Private descriptionValue As String
 8       Private temperatureValue As String
 9
10       Public Sub New(ByVal city As String, ByVal information As String, _
11          ByVal degrees As String)
12
13          cityNameValue = city
14          descriptionValue = information
15          temperatureValue = degrees
16       End Sub ' New
17
18       ' read-only property that gets city's name
19       Public ReadOnly Property CityName() As String
20          Get
21             Return cityNameValue
22          End Get
23       End Property ' CityName
24
25       ' read-only property that gets city's weather description
26       Public ReadOnly Property Description() As String
27          Get
28             Return descriptionValue
29          End Get
30       End Property ' Description
31
32       ' read-only property that gets city's temperature
33       Public ReadOnly Property Temperature() As String
34          Get
35             Return temperatureValue
36          End Get
37       End Property ' Temperature
```

Fig. 23.9 | Class CityWeather. (Part 1 of 2.)

```
38
39          ' implementation of CompareTo method for alphabetizing
40          Public Function CompareTo(ByVal obj As Object) _
41             As Integer Implements System.IComparable.CompareTo
42
43             Return String.Compare(CityName, CType(obj, CityWeather).CityName)
44          End Function ' CompareTo
45
46          ' return string representation of this CityWeather object
47          ' (used to display the weather report on the server console)
48          Public Overrides Function ToString() As String
49             Return CityName & " | " & Temperature & " | " & Description
50          End Function ' ToString
51       End Class ' CityWeather
```

Fig. 23.9 | Class CityWeather. (Part 2 of 2.)

CityWeather contains three instance variables (lines 6–8) for storing the city's name (cityNameValue), the high/low temperature information (temperatureValue) and the description of the weather condition (descriptionValue). The CityWeather constructor (lines 10–16) initializes the three instance variables. Lines 19–37 declare three read-only properties that allow the values of the three instance variables to be retrieved. CityWeather implements IComparable, so it must declare a method called CompareTo that takes an Object reference and returns an Integer (lines 40–44). Also, we want to alphabetize CityWeather objects by their cityNames, so CompareTo calls String method Compare with the cityNames of the two CityWeather objects (line 43). Class CityWeather also overrides the ToString method to display information for this city (lines 48–50). Method ToString is used by the server application to display the weather information retrieved from the *Traveler's Forecast* Web page in the console.

Interface Report

Figure 23.10 shows the code for interface Report. Interface Report also will be included with class CityWeather in the Weather.dll class library file, so it can be used in both the client and server applications. Report declares a read-only property (line 7) that returns an ArrayList of CityWeather objects (ArrayList was introduced in the example in Section 17.8). The client application will use this property to retrieve the information in the weather report—each city's name, high/low temperature and weather condition.

```
1    ' Fig. 23.10: Report.vb
2    ' Interface that defines a property for getting
3    ' the information in a weather report.
4    Imports System.Collections
5
6    Public Interface Report
7       ReadOnly Property Reports() As ArrayList
8    End Interface ' Report
```

Fig. 23.10 | Interface Report in namespace Weather.

Class ReportInfo

Remote class ReportInfo (Fig. 23.11) implements interface Report (line 9) of namespace Weather (specified by the Imports statement in line 7). ReportInfo also extends base class

```vb
1   ' Fig. 23.11: ReportInfo.vb
2   ' Class that implements interface Report, retrieves
3   ' and returns data on weather
4   Imports System.Collections
5   Imports System.IO
6   Imports System.Net
7   Imports Weather
8
9   Public Class ReportInfo : Inherits MarshalByRefObject : Implements Report
10      Private cityList As ArrayList ' cities, temperatures, descriptions
11
12      Public Sub New()
13         cityList = New ArrayList()
14
15         ' create WebClient to get access to Web page
16         Dim myClient As New WebClient()
17
18         ' get StreamReader for response so we can read page
19         Dim input As New StreamReader(myClient.OpenRead( _
20            "http://iwin.nws.noaa.gov/iwin/us/traveler.html"))
21
22         ' indicates first batch of cities
23         Dim separator1 As String = "TAV12"
24         ' indicates second batch of cities
25         Dim separator2 As String = "TAV13"
26
27         ' locate separator1 in Web page
28         While Not input.ReadLine().StartsWith(separator1) ' do nothing
29         End While
30         ReadCities(input) ' read the first batch of cities
31
32         ' locate separator2 in Web page
33         While Not input.ReadLine().StartsWith(separator2) ' do nothing
34         End While
35         ReadCities(input) ' read the second batch of cities
36
37         cityList.Sort() ' sort list of cities by alphabetical order
38         input.Close() ' close StreamReader to NWS server
39
40         ' display the data on the server side
41         Console.WriteLine("Data from NWS Web site:")
42
43         For Each city As CityWeather In cityList
44            Console.WriteLine(city)
45         Next city ' end foreach
46      End Sub ' New
47
```

Fig. 23.11 | Class ReportInfo, which implements interface Report, is marshaled by reference. (Part 1 of 2.)

```
48      ' utility method that reads a batch of cities
49      Private Sub ReadCities(ByVal input As StreamReader)
50          ' day format and night format
51          Dim dayFormat As String = _
52              "CITY          WEA    HI/LO   WEA      HI/LO"
53          Dim nightFormat As String = _
54              "CITY          WEA    LO/HI   WEA      LO/HI"
55          Dim inputLine As String = ""
56
57          ' locate header that begins weather information
58          Do
59              inputLine = input.ReadLine()
60          Loop While Not inputLine.Equals(dayFormat) And Not _
61              inputLine.Equals(nightFormat)
62
63          inputLine = input.ReadLine() ' get first city's data
64
65          ' while there are more cities to read
66          While inputLine.Length > 28
67              ' create CityWeather object for city
68              Dim weather As New CityWeather(inputLine.Substring(0, 16), _
69                  inputLine.Substring(16, 7), inputLine.Substring(23, 7))
70
71              cityList.Add(weather) ' add to ArrayList
72              inputLine = input.ReadLine() ' get next city's data
73          End While ' end while
74      End Sub ' ReadCities
75
76      ' property for getting the cities' weather reports
77      Public ReadOnly Property Reports() As _
78          System.Collections.ArrayList Implements Weather.Report.Reports
79
80          Get
81              Return cityList
82          End Get
83      End Property ' Reports
84  End Class ' ReportInfo
```

Fig. 23.11 | Class ReportInfo, which implements interface Report, is marshaled by reference. (Part 2 of 2.)

MarshalByRefObject. Class ReportInfo is part of the remote WeatherServer application and will not be directly available to the client application.

Lines 12–46 declare the ReportInfo constructor. Line 16 creates a *WebClient* (namespace System.Net) object to interact with a data source that is specified by a URL— in this case, the URL for the NWS *Traveler's Forecast* page (http://iwin.nws.noaa.gov/ iwin/us/traveler.html). Lines 19–20 call WebClient method OpenRead, which returns a Stream that the program can use to read data containing the weather information from the specified URL. This Stream is used to create a StreamReader object so that the program can read the Web page's HTML markup line-by-line.

The section of the Web page in which we are interested consists of two batches of cities—Albany through Reno, and Salt Lake City through Washington, D.C. The first batch occurs in a section that starts with the string "TAV12" while the second batch occurs in a section that starts with the string "TAV13". We declare variables separator1 and separator2 to store these strings. Lines 28–29 read the HTML markup one line at a time until "TAV12" is encountered. Then the program calls utility method ReadCities to read a batch of cities into ArrayList cityList. Next, lines 33–34 read the HTML markup one line at a time until "TAV13" is encountered, and line 35 makes another call to method ReadCities to read the second batch of cities. Line 37 calls method *Sort* of class Array-List to sort the CityWeather objects into alphabetical order by city name. Line 38 closes the StreamReader connection to the Web site. Lines 43–45 output the weather information for each city to the server application's console display.

Lines 49–74 declare utility method ReadCities, which takes a StreamReader object and reads the information for each city, creates a CityWeather object for it and places the CityWeather object in cityList. The loop in lines 58–61 continues to read the page one line at a time until it finds the header line that begins the weather forecast table. This line starts with either dayFormat (lines 51–52), indicating the header for the daytime information, or nightFormat (lines 53–54), indicating the header for the nighttime information. Because the line could be in either format based on the time of day, the loop-continuation condition checks for both (lines 60–61). Line 59 reads the next line from the Web page, which is the first line containing temperature information.

The loop in lines 66–73 creates a new CityWeather object to represent the current city. It parses the string containing the current weather data, separating the city name, the weather condition and the temperature. The CityWeather object is added to cityList. Then the next line from the page is read and stored in inputLine for the next iteration. This process continues while the length of the string read from the Web page is greater than 28 (the lines containing weather data are all longer than 28 characters). The first line shorter than this signals the end of that forecast section in the Web page.

Read-only property Reports (lines 77–83) implements the Report interface's Reports property to return cityList. The client application will remotely call this property to retrieve the day's weather report.

Class WeatherServer

Figure 23.12 contains the server code. The Imports statements in lines 4–6 specify .NET remoting namespaces *System.Runtime.Remoting*, *System.Runtime.Remoting.Channels* and *System.Runtime.Remoting.Channels.Http*. The first two namespaces are required for .NET remoting, and the third is required for HTTP channels. Namespace System.Runtime.Remoting.Channels.Http requires the project to reference the System.Runtime.Remoting assembly, which can be found under the **.NET** tab in the **Add References** menu. The Imports statement at line 7 specifies namespace Weather, which contains interface Report. Remember to add a reference to Weather.dll in this project.

```
1    ' Fig. 23.12: WeatherServer.cs
2    ' Server application that uses .NET remoting to send
3    ' weather report information to a client
4    Imports System.Runtime.Remoting
5    Imports System.Runtime.Remoting.Channels
```

Fig. 23.12 | Class WeatherServer exposes remote class ReportInfo. (Part 1 of 2.)

```
 6    Imports System.Runtime.Remoting.Channels.Http
 7    Imports Weather
 8
 9    Module WeatherServer
10       Sub Main()
11          ' establish HTTP channel
12          Dim channel As New HttpChannel(50000)
13          ChannelServices.RegisterChannel(channel, False)
14
15          ' register ReportInfo class
16          RemotingConfiguration.RegisterWellKnownServiceType( _
17             GetType(ReportInfo), "Report", WellKnownObjectMode.Singleton)
18
19          Console.WriteLine("Press Enter to terminate server.")
20          Console.ReadLine()
21       End Sub ' Main
22    End Module ' WeatherServer
```

Fig. 23.12 | Class WeatherServer exposes remote class ReportInfo. (Part 2 of 2.)

Lines 12–13 in Main register an HTTP channel on the current machine at port 50000—the port number that clients will use to connect to the WeatherServer remotely. The argument False in line 13 indicates that we do not wish to enable security, which is beyond the scope of this introduction. Lines 16–17 register the ReportInfo class type at the "Report" URI as a Singleton remote class. If a remote class is registered as *Singleton*, only one remote object will be created when the first client requests that remote class, and that remote object will service all clients. The alternative mode is *SingleCall*, where one remote object is created for each individual remote method call to the remote class. [*Note:* A Singleton remote object will be garbage collected after being idle for 5 minutes. A new Singleton remote object will be created by the server if another client requests one later. The article msdn.microsoft.com/msdnmag/issues/03/12/LeaseManager/default.aspx provides more information on the lifetime of remote objects.] The ReportInfo remote class is now available to clients at the URI "http://*IPAddress*:5000/Report" where *IPAddress* is the IP address of the computer on which the server is running. The channel remains open as long as the server application continues running, so line 20 waits for the user running the server application to press **Enter** before terminating the application.

Class FrmWeatherClient

FrmWeatherClient (Fig. 23.13) is a Windows application that uses .NET remoting to retrieve weather information from the WeatherServer and displays the information in a graphical, easy-to-read manner. The GUI contains 43 Labels—each displays the weather information for one city in the *Traveler's Forecast*. The Labels are placed in a Panel with a vertical scroll bar. Lines 5–7 are Imports statements for the namespaces that are required to perform .NET remoting. For this project, you must add references to the assembly System.Runtime.Remoting and the Weather.dll file we created earlier.

Method FrmWeatherClient_Load (lines 12–85) retrieves the weather information when this Windows application loads. Line 15 creates an HTTP channel without specifying a port number. This causes the HttpChannel constructor to choose any available port number on the client computer. A specific port number is not necessary because this

```vb
1    ' Fig. 23.13: WeatherClient.vb
2    ' Client that uses .NET remoting to retrieve a weather report.
3    Imports System.Collections
4    Imports System.Drawing
5    Imports System.Runtime.Remoting
6    Imports System.Runtime.Remoting.Channels
7    Imports System.Runtime.Remoting.Channels.Http
8    Imports Weather
9
10   Public Class FrmWeatherClient
11      ' retrieve weather data
12      Private Sub FrmWeatherClient_Load(ByVal sender As System.Object, _
13         ByVal e As System.EventArgs) Handles MyBase.Load
14         ' setup HTTP channel, does not need to provide a port number
15         Dim channel As New HttpChannel()
16         ChannelServices.RegisterChannel(channel, False)
17
18         ' obtain a proxy for an object that implements interface Report
19         Dim info As Report = CType(RemotingServices.Connect( _
20            GetType(Report), "http://localhost:50000/Report"), Report)
21
22         ' retrieve an ArrayList of CityWeather objects
23         Dim cities As ArrayList = info.Reports
24
25         ' create array and populate it with every Label
26         Dim cityLabels(43) As Label
27         Dim labelCounter As Integer = 0
28
29         Dim control As Control
30         For Each control In pnlDisplay.Controls
31            If TypeOf control Is Label Then
32               cityLabels(labelCounter) = CType(control, Label)
33               labelCounter += 1 ' increment Label counter
34            End If
35         Next control
36
37         ' create Hashtable and populate with all weather conditions
38         Dim weather As New Hashtable()
39         weather.Add("SUNNY", "sunny")
40         weather.Add("PTCLDY", "pcloudy")
41         weather.Add("CLOUDY", "mcloudy")
42         weather.Add("MOCLDY", "mcloudy")
43         weather.Add("VRYCLD", "mcloudy")
44         weather.Add("TSTRMS", "rain")
45         weather.Add("RAIN", "rain")
46         weather.Add("FZRAIN", "rain")
47         weather.Add("SNOW", "snow")
48         weather.Add("VRYHOT", "vryhot")
49         weather.Add("FAIR", "fair")
50         weather.Add("RNSNOW", "rnsnow")
51         weather.Add("SHWRS", "showers")
```

Fig. 23.13 | Class `WeatherClient` accesses a `ReportInfo` object remotely and displays the weather report. (Part 1 of 2.)

```
52        weather.Add("WINDY", "windy")
53        weather.Add("NOINFO", "noinfo")
54        weather.Add("MISG", "noinfo")
55        weather.Add("DRZL", "rain")
56        weather.Add("HAZE", "noinfo")
57        weather.Add("SMOKE", "mcloudy")
58        weather.Add("SNOSHW", "snow")
59        weather.Add("FLRRYS", "snow")
60        weather.Add("FOG", "noinfo")
61
62        ' create the font for the text output
63        Dim font As New Font("Courier New", 8, FontStyle.Bold)
64
65        ' for every city
66        For i As Integer = 0 To cities.Count - 1
67            ' use array cityLabels to find the next Label
68            Dim currentCity As Label = cityLabels(i)
69
70            ' use ArrayList cities to find the next CityWeather object
71            Dim city As CityWeather = CType(cities(i), CityWeather)
72
73            ' set current Label's image to image
74            ' corresponding to the city's weather condition -
75            ' find correct image name in Hashtable weather
76            currentCity.Image = New Bitmap("images\" & _
77                weather(city.Description.Trim()).ToString() & ".png")
78            currentCity.Font = font ' set font of Label
79            currentCity.ForeColor = Color.White ' set text color of Label
80
81            ' set Label's text to city name and temperature
82            currentCity.Text = _
83                vbCrLf & " " & city.CityName & city.Temperature
84        Next
85    End Sub ' FrmWeatherClient_Load
86 End Class ' FrmWeatherClient
```

Fig. 23.13 | Class WeatherClient accesses a ReportInfo object remotely and displays the weather report. (Part 2 of 2.)

application does not have its own clients that need to know the port number in advance. Line 16 registers the channel on the client computer. This will allow the server to send information back to the client. Lines 19–20 declare a Report variable and assign to it a proxy for a Report object instantiated by the server. This proxy allows the client to remotely call ReportInfo's properties by redirecting method calls to the server. **Remoting-Services** method **Connect** connects to the server and returns a reference to the proxy for the Report object. For testing purposes, we execute the client and the server on the same computer, so we use localhost in the URL that represents the server application. To connect to a WeatherServer on a different computer, you must replace localhost with the name or IP address of the server computer. Line 23 retrieves the ArrayList of CityWeather objects generated by the ReportInfo constructor (lines 12–46 of Fig. 23.11). Variable cities now refers to an ArrayList of CityWeather objects that contains the information taken from the *Traveler's Forecast* Web page.

Because the application presents weather data for so many cities, we must establish a way to organize the information in the Labels and to ensure that each weather description is accompanied by an appropriate image. The program uses an array to store all the Labels, and a Hashtable (discussed further in Chapter 27, Collections) to store weather descriptions and the names of their corresponding images. A **Hashtable** stores key–value pairs, in which both the key and the value can be any type of object. Method **Add** adds key–value pairs to a Hashtable. The class also provides an indexer to return the values for particular keys in the Hashtable. Line 26 creates an array of Label references, and lines 30–35 place the Labels we created in the IDE's Form designer in the array so that they can be accessed programmatically to display weather information for individual cities. Line 38 creates Hashtable object weather to store pairs of weather conditions and the names for images associated with those conditions. Note that a given weather-description name does not necessarily correspond to the name of the PNG file containing the correct image. For example, both "TSTRMS" and "RAIN" weather conditions use the rain.png image file.

Lines 66–84 set each Label so that it contains a city name, the current temperature in the city and an image corresponding to the weather conditions for that city. Line 68 retrieves the Label that will display the weather information for the next city. Line 71 uses ArrayList cities to retrieve the CityWeather object that contains the weather information for the city. Lines 76–77 set the Label's image to the PNG image that corresponds to the city's weather conditions. This is done by eliminating any spaces in the description string by calling String method Trim and retrieving the name of the PNG image from the weather Hashtable. Lines 78–79 set Label's Font property to the Font object created at line 63, and the ForeColor property to white for readability against the black and blue background image on the Label. Lines 82–83 set the Text property to display the city's name and high/low temperatures. [*Note:* To preserve the layout of the client application's window, we set the MaximumSize and MinimumSize properties of the Windows Form to the same value so that the user cannot resize the window.]

Web Resources for .NET Remoting

This section provided a basic introduction to .NET remoting. There is much more to this powerful .NET framework capability. The following Web sites provide additional information. Searching for ".NET remoting" with most search engines yields many additional resources.

msdn.microsoft.com/library/en-us/cpguide/html/cpconaccessingobjectsinotherap-
plicationdomainsusingnetremoting.asp
The *.NET Framework Developer's Guide* on the MSDN Web site provides detailed information on
.NET remoting, including articles that include choosing between ASP.NET and .NET remoting,
an overview of .NET remoting, advanced .NET remoting techniques and .NET remoting examples.

msdn.microsoft.com/library/en-us/dndotnet/html/introremoting.asp
Offers a general overview of .NET remoting capabilties.

search.microsoft.com/search/results.aspx?qu=.net+remoting
Provides links to many .NET remoting articles and resources.

23.11 Wrap-Up

In this chapter, we presented both connection-oriented and connectionless networking
techniques. You learned that the Internet is an "unreliable" network that simply transmits
packets of data. We discussed two protocols for transmitting packets over the Internet—
the Transmission Control Protocol (TCP) and the User Datagram Protocol (UDP). You
learned that TCP is a connection-oriented communication protocol that guarantees sent
packets will arrive at the intended receiver undamaged and in the correct sequence. You
also learned that UDP is typically used in certain types of performance-oriented applications because it incurs minimum overhead for communicating between applications. We
presented some of .NET's capabilities for implementing communications with TCP and
UDP. We showed how to create a simple client/server chat application using stream sockets. We then showed how to send datagrams between a client and a server. You also saw a
multithreaded Tic-Tac-Toe server that allows two clients to connect simultaneously to the
server and play Tic-Tac-Toe against one another. We presented the new WebBrowser class,
which allows you to add Web browsing capabilities to your Windows applications. Finally, we demonstrated .NET remoting, a technology that allows a client application to remotely access the properties and methods of an object instantiated by a server application.
In Chapter 24, Data Structures, you will learn about dynamic data structures that can
grow or shrink at execution time.

24

Data Structures

OBJECTIVES

In this chapter you will learn:

- To form linked data structures using references, self-referential classes and recursion.

- How boxing and unboxing enable primitive-type values to be used where Objects are expected in a program.

- To create and manipulate dynamic data structures, such as linked lists, queues, stacks and binary trees.

- Various important applications of linked data structures.

- To create reusable data structures with classes, inheritance and composition.

Much that I bound,
I could not free;
Much that I freed
returned to me.
—Lee Wilson Dodd

"Will you walk a little
faster?" said a whiting
to a snail,
"There's a porpoise close
behind us, and he's treading
on my tail."
—Lewis Carroll

There is always room at the
top.
—Daniel Webster

Push on—keep moving.
—Thomas Morton

I think that I shall never see
A poem lovely as a tree.
—Joyce Kilmer

24.1 Introduction

This chapter begins our three-chapter data structures treatment. The *data structures* that we've studied thus far have had fixed sizes, such as one- and two-dimensional arrays. Here we introduce *dynamic data structures* that can grow and shrink at execution time. Linked lists are collections of data items "lined up in a row"—users can make insertions and deletions anywhere in a linked list. Stacks are important in compilers and operating systems; insertions and deletions are made at only one end—the *top* of the stack. Queues represent waiting lines; insertions are only made at the back (also referred to as the *tail*) of a queue, and deletions are made only from the front (also referred to as the *head*) of a queue. Binary trees facilitate high-speed searching and sorting of data, efficient elimination of duplicate data items, representation of file system directories and compilation of expressions into machine language. All these data structures have many other interesting applications as well.

We will discuss each of these data structures and implement programs that create and manipulate them. We use classes, inheritance and composition to create and package these data structures for reusability and maintainability. In Chapter 25, Generics, we introduce generics, which allow you to declare data structures that can be easily adapted to contain data of any type. In Chapter 26, Collections, we discuss the FCL's predefined classes that implement various data structures.

The chapter examples are practical programs that will be useful in more advanced courses and in industrial applications. The programs focus on reference manipulation.

24.2 Primitive-Type Structures; Boxing and Unboxing

The data structures we discuss in this chapter store Object references. As you'll soon see, these data structures can store both primitive- and reference-type values. This section discusses the mechanisms that enable primitive-type values to be manipulated as objects.

Primitive-Type Structures

Each primitive type (Appendix L, Primitive Types) has a corresponding Structure in namespace System that declares the primitive type. These Structures are called Boolean, Byte, SByte, Char, Decimal, Double, Single, Int16, UInt16, Int32, UInt32, Int64 and UInt64. Types declared with keyword Structure are implicitly value types.

Primitive types are actually aliases for their corresponding Structures, so a variable of a primitive type can be declared using the primitive type's keyword or the Structure name—e.g., Integer and Int32 are interchangeable. The methods related to a primitive type are located in the corresponding Structure (e.g., method Parse, which converts a String to an Integer value, is located in Structure Int32). Refer to the online documentation for each Structure type to see the methods for manipulating values of that type.

Boxing and Unboxing Conversions

All primitive-type Structures inherit from class *ValueType* (namespace System). Class ValueType inherits from class Object. Thus, any primitive-type value can be assigned to an Object variable; this is referred to as *boxing*. With boxing, a primitive-type value is copied into an object so that the primitive-type value can be manipulated as an Object. Boxing can be performed either explicitly or implicitly, as shown in the following statements:

```
Dim i As Integer = 5 ' create an Integer value
Dim object1 As Object = _
   CType(i, Object) ' explicitly box the Integer value
Dim object2 As Object = i ' implicitly box the Integer value
```

After executing the preceding code, both object1 and object2 refer to two different objects that contain a copy of the integer value in Integer variable i.

Unboxing can be used to explicitly convert an Object reference to a primitive value, as shown in the following statement:

```
' explicitly unbox the Integer value
Dim int1 As Integer = CType(object1, Integer)
```

Explicitly attempting to unbox an Object reference that does not refer to the correct primitive value type causes an *InvalidCastException*.

In Chapters 25 and 26, we discuss Visual Basic's generics and .NET's generic collections. As you will see, generics eliminate the overhead of boxing and unboxing by enabling us to create and use collections of specific value types.

24.3 Self-Referential Classes

A *self-referential class* contains a reference member that refers to an object of the same class type. For example, the class declaration in Fig. 24.1 defines the shell of a self-referential class named Node. This type has two Private instance variables—Integer dataValue and Node reference nextNodeReference. Member nextNodeReference references an object of type Node, an object of the same type as the one being declared here—thus the term "self-referential class." Member nextNodeReference is referred to as a *link* (i.e., nextNodeReference can be used to "tie" an object of type Node to another object of the same type). Class Node also has two properties—one for instance variable dataValue (named Data) and another for instance variable nextNodeReference (named NextNode).

Self-referential objects can be linked together to form useful data structures, such as lists, queues, stacks and trees. Figure 24.2 illustrates two self-referential objects linked together to form a linked list. A backslash (representing a Nothing reference) is placed in the link member of the second self-referential object to indicate that the link does not refer to another object. A Nothing reference normally indicates the end of a data structure.

```
 1   ' Fig. 24.01: Node.vb
 2   ' Self-referential Node class.
 3   Class Node
 4      Private dataValue As Integer
 5      Private nextNodeReference As Node
 6
 7      Public Sub New(ByVal value As Integer)
 8         ' constructor body
 9      End Sub ' New
10
11      ' Property Data
12      Public Property Data() As Integer
13         Get
14            ' get body
15         End Get
16         Set(ByVal value As Integer)
17            ' set body
18         End Set
19      End Property ' Data
20
21      ' Property NextNode
22      Public Property NextNode As Node
23         Get
24            ' get next node
25         End Get
26         Set(ByVal nodeReference As Node)
27            ' set next node
28         End Set
29      End Property ' NextNode
30   End Class 'Node
```

Fig. 24.1 | Self-referential **Node** class declaration skeleton.

Fig. 24.2 | Self-referential class objects linked together.

Creating and maintaining dynamic data structures requires ***dynamic memory allocation***—a program's ability to obtain more memory space at execution time to hold new nodes and to release space no longer needed. As you learned in Section 9.9, Visual Basic programs do not explicitly release dynamically allocated memory—rather, Visual Basic performs automatic garbage collection.

The New operator is essential to dynamic memory allocation. New takes as an operand the type of the object being dynamically allocated and returns a reference to an object of that type. For example, the statement

Dim nodeToAdd *As New* Node(10)

allocates the appropriate amount of memory to store a `Node` and stores a reference to this object in `nodeToAdd`. If no memory is available, `New` throws an `OutOfMemoryException`. The constructor argument 10 specifies the `Node` object's data.

The following sections discuss lists, stacks, queues and trees. These data structures are created and maintained with dynamic memory allocation and self-referential classes.

24.4 Linked Lists

A *linked list* is a linear collection (i.e., a sequence) of self-referential class objects called *nodes*, connected by reference links—thus the term "linked" list. A program accesses a linked list via a reference to the first node of the list. Each subsequent node is accessed via the link-reference member stored in the previous node. By convention, the link reference in the last node of a list is set to `Nothing` to mark the end of the list. Data is stored in a linked list dynamically—that is, each node is created as necessary. You can declare a node's class to store data of any type, including references to objects of other classes. Stacks and queues are also linear data structures—in fact, they are constrained versions of linked lists. Trees are non-linear data structures.

Lists of data can be stored in arrays, but linked lists provide several advantages. A linked list is appropriate when the number of data elements to be represented in the data structure is unpredictable. Unlike a linked list, the size of a conventional Visual Basic array cannot be altered, because the array size is fixed at creation time. Conventional arrays can become full, but linked lists become full only when the system has insufficient memory to satisfy dynamic memory allocation requests.

Performance Tip 24.1

An array can be declared to contain more elements than the number of items expected, possibly wasting memory. Linked lists provide better memory utilization in these situations, because they can grow and shrink at execution time.

Performance Tip 24.2

After locating the insertion point for a new item in a sorted linked list, inserting an element in the list is fast—only two references have to be modified. All existing nodes remain at their current locations in memory.

Programmers can maintain linked lists in sorted order simply by inserting each new element at the proper point in the list (locating the proper insertion point does take time). Existing list elements do not need to be moved.

Performance Tip 24.3

The elements of an array are stored contiguously in memory to allow immediate access to any array element—the address of any element can be calculated directly from its index. Linked lists do not afford such immediate access to their elements—an element can be accessed only by traversing the list from the front.

Performance Tip 24.4

Insertion and deletion in a sorted array can be time consuming—all the elements following the inserted or deleted element must be shifted appropriately.

Normally, linked-list nodes are not stored contiguously in memory. Rather, the nodes are said to be logically contiguous. Figure 24.3 illustrates a linked list with several nodes.

Fig. 24.3 | Linked list graphical representation.

Performance Tip 24.5

Using linked data structures and dynamic memory allocation (instead of arrays) for data structures that grow and shrink can save memory. Keep in mind, however, that reference links occupy space, and dynamic memory allocation incurs the overhead of method calls.

Linked List Implementation

The program in Figs. 24.4 and 24.5 uses an object of class List to manipulate a list of miscellaneous object types. The Main method of class ListTest (Fig. 24.5) creates a list of objects, inserts objects at the beginning of the list using List method InsertAtFront, inserts objects at the end of the list using List method InsertAtBack, deletes objects from the front of the list using List method RemoveFromFront and deletes objects from the end of the list using List method RemoveFromBack. After each insertion and deletion operation, the program invokes List method Print to display the current list contents. If an attempt is made to remove an item from an empty list, an EmptyListException is thrown. A detailed discussion of the program follows.

The program consists of four classes—ListNode (Fig. 24.4, lines 4–37), List (lines 40–153), EmptyListException (lines 156–160) and ListTest (Fig. 24.5). The classes in Fig. 24.4 create a linked-list library that can be reused throughout this chapter. You should place the code from Fig. 24.4 in its own class library project as described in Section 9.13. Name the project LinkedListLibrary.

Encapsulated in each List object is a linked list of ListNode objects. Class ListNode (Fig. 24.4, lines 4–37) contains instance variables dataValue and nextNodeReference. Member dataValue can refer to any object. [*Note:* Typically, a data structure will contain data of only one type, or data of any type derived from one base type.] In this example, we use data of various types derived from Object to demonstrate that our List class can store data of any type. Member nextNodeReference stores a reference to the next ListNode object in the linked list. The ListNode constructors (lines 10–12 and 16–19) enable us to initialize a ListNode that will be placed at the end of a List or before a specific ListNode in a List, respectively. A List accesses the ListNode member variables via properties NextNode (lines 22–29) and Data (lines 32–36), respectively.

```
1   ' Fig. 24.4: LinkedListLibrary.vb
2   ' Class ListNode and class List declarations.
3
```

Fig. 24.4 | ListNode, List and EmptyListException classes. (Part 1 of 4.)

```
 4    Public Class ListNode
 5        Private dataValue As Object ' stores data for this node
 6        Private nextNodeReference As ListNode ' stores reference to next node
 7
 8        ' constructor to create a ListNode that contains data
 9        ' and is the last node in the List
10        Public Sub New(ByVal data As Object)
11            MyClass.New(data, Nothing) ' invokes the other constructor
12        End Sub ' New
13
14        ' constructor to create a ListNode that contains data
15        ' and refers to the next ListNode in the List
16        Public Sub New(ByVal data As Object, ByVal nextNode As ListNode)
17            dataValue = data
18            nextNodeReference = nextNode
19        End Sub ' New
20
21        ' property NextNode
22        Public Property NextNode() As ListNode
23            Get
24                Return nextNodeReference
25            End Get
26            Set(ByVal value As ListNode)
27                nextNodeReference = value
28            End Set
29        End Property ' NextNode
30
31        ' property Data
32        Public ReadOnly Property Data() As Object
33            Get
34                Return dataValue
35            End Get
36        End Property ' Data
37    End Class ' ListNode
38
39    ' class List declaration
40    Public Class List
41        Private firstNode As ListNode
42        Private lastNode As ListNode
43        Private name As String ' string like "list" to display
44
45        ' construct empty List with "list" as its name
46        Public Sub New()
47            MyClass.New("list") ' invokes the other constructor
48        End Sub ' New
49
50        ' construct empty List with specified name
51        Public Sub New(ByVal listName As String)
52            name = listName
53            firstNode = Nothing
54            lastNode = Nothing
55        End Sub ' New
56
```

Fig. 24.4 | ListNode, List and EmptyListException classes. (Part 2 of 4.)

```
57    ' Insert object at front of List. If List is empty, firstNode and
58    ' lastNode will refer to same object. Otherwise, firstNode refers
59    ' to new node and the new node refers to the previous first node.
60    Public Sub InsertAtFront(ByVal insertItem As Object)
61       If IsEmpty() Then
62          lastNode = New ListNode(insertItem)
63          firstNode = lastNode
64       Else
65          firstNode = New ListNode(insertItem, firstNode)
66       End If
67    End Sub ' InsertAtFront
68
69    ' Insert object at end of List. If List is empty,
70    ' firstNode and lastNode will refer to same object.
71    ' Otherwise, lastNode's NextNode property refers to new node.
72    Public Sub InsertAtBack(ByVal insertItem As Object)
73       If IsEmpty() Then
74          lastNode = New ListNode(insertItem)
75          firstNode = lastNode
76       Else
77          lastNode.NextNode = New ListNode(insertItem)
78          lastNode = lastNode.NextNode
79       End If
80    End Sub ' InsertAtBack
81
82    ' remove first node from List
83    Public Function RemoveFromFront() As Object
84       If IsEmpty() Then
85          Throw New EmptyListException(name)
86       End If
87
88       Dim removeItem As Object = firstNode.Data ' retrieve data
89
90       ' reset firstNode and lastNode references
91       If firstNode.Equals(lastNode) Then
92          firstNode = Nothing
93          lastNode = Nothing
94       Else
95          firstNode = firstNode.NextNode
96       End If
97
98       Return removeItem ' return removed data
99    End Function ' RemoveFromFront
100
101   ' remove last node from List
102   Public Function RemoveFromBack() As Object
103      If IsEmpty() Then
104         Throw New EmptyListException(name)
105      End If
106
107      Dim removeItem As Object = lastNode.Data ' retrieve data
108
```

Fig. 24.4 | ListNode, List and EmptyListException classes. (Part 3 of 4.)

```
109         ' reset firstNode and lastNode references
110         If firstNode.Equals(lastNode) Then
111             firstNode = Nothing
112             lastNode = Nothing
113         Else
114             Dim current As ListNode = firstNode
115
116             ' loop while current node is not lastNode
117             While Not current.NextNode.Equals(lastNode)
118                 current = current.NextNode ' move to next node
119             End While
120
121             ' current is new lastNode
122             lastNode = current
123             current.NextNode = Nothing
124         End If
125
126         Return removeItem ' return removed data
127     End Function ' RemoveFromBack
128
129     ' return True if List is empty
130     Public Function IsEmpty() As Boolean
131         Return firstNode Is Nothing
132     End Function ' IsEmpty
133
134     ' output List contents
135     Public Sub Print()
136         If IsEmpty() Then
137             Console.WriteLine("Empty " & name)
138             Return
139         End If
140
141         Console.Write("The " & name & " is: ")
142
143         Dim current As ListNode = firstNode
144
145         ' output current node data while not at end of list
146         While Not (current Is Nothing)
147             Console.Write(current.Data & " ")
148             current = current.NextNode
149         End While
150
151         Console.WriteLine(vbCrLF)
152     End Sub ' Print
153 End Class ' List
154
155 ' class EmptyListException declaration
156 Public Class EmptyListException : Inherits ApplicationException
157     Public Sub New(ByVal name As String)
158         MyBase.New("The " & name & " is empty")
159     End Sub ' New
160 End Class ' EmptyListException
```

Fig. 24.4 | ListNode, List and EmptyListException classes. (Part 4 of 4.)

Class List (lines 40–153) contains Private instance variables firstNode (a reference to the first ListNode in a List) and lastNode (a reference to the last ListNode in a List). The constructors (lines 46–48 and 51–55) initialize both references to Nothing and enable us to specify the List's name for output purposes. InsertAtFront (lines 60–67), InsertAtBack (lines 72–80), RemoveFromFront (lines 83–99) and RemoveFromBack (lines 102–127) are the primary methods of class List. Method IsEmpty (lines 130–132) is a *predicate method* that determines whether the list is empty (i.e., the reference to the first node of the list is Nothing). Predicate methods typically test a condition and do not modify the object on which they are called. If the list is empty, method IsEmpty returns True; otherwise, it returns False. Method Print (lines 135–153) displays the list's contents.

Class EmptyListException (lines 156–160) defines an exception class that we use to indicate illegal operations on an empty List.

Class ListTest (Fig. 24.5) uses the linked-list library to create and manipulate a linked list. [*Note:* In the project containing Fig. 24.5, you must add a reference to the class library containing the classes in Fig. 24.4. If you use our existing example, you may need to update this reference.] Line 8 creates a new List object and assigns it to variable list.

```vb
1    ' Fig. 24.5: ListTest.vb
2    ' Testing class List.
3    Imports LinkedListLibrary
4
5    ' class to test List class functionality
6    Module LinkTest
7       Sub Main()
8          Dim list As New List() ' create List container
9
10         ' create data to store in List
11         Dim aBoolean As Boolean = True
12         Dim aCharacter As Char = "$"c
13         Dim anInteger As Integer = 34567
14         Dim aString As String = "hello"
15
16         ' use List insert methods
17         list.InsertAtFront(aBoolean)
18         list.Print()
19         list.InsertAtFront(aCharacter)
20         list.Print()
21         list.InsertAtBack(anInteger)
22         list.Print()
23         list.InsertAtBack(aString)
24         list.Print()
25
26         ' use List remove methods
27         Dim removedObject As Object
28
29         ' remove data from list and print after each removal
30         Try
31            removedObject = list.RemoveFromFront()
32            Console.WriteLine(removedObject & " removed")
```

Fig. 24.5 | Linked list demonstration. (Part 1 of 2.)

```
33              list.Print()
34
35              removedObject = list.RemoveFromFront()
36              Console.WriteLine(removedObject & " removed")
37              list.Print()
38
39              removedObject = list.RemoveFromBack()
40              Console.WriteLine(removedObject & " removed")
41              list.Print()
42
43              removedObject = list.RemoveFromBack()
44              Console.WriteLine(removedObject & " removed")
45              list.Print()
46        Catch exception As EmptyListException
47              Console.Error.WriteLine( _
48                 vbCrLf & exception.ToString())
49         End Try
50      End Sub ' Main
51    End Module ' LinkTest
```

```
The list is: True

The list is: $ True

The list is: $ True 34567

The list is: $ True 34567 hello

$ removed
The list is: True 34567 hello

True removed
The list is: 34567 hello

hello removed
The list is: 34567

34567 removed
Empty list
```

Fig. 24.5 | Linked list demonstration. (Part 2 of 2.)

Lines 11–14 create data of various types to add to the list. Lines 17–24 use the List insertion methods to insert these values and use List method Print to output the contents of the list object after each insertion. Note that the values of the primitive-type variables are implicitly boxed in lines 17, 19 and 21 where Object references are expected. The code inside the Try block (lines 30–45) removes objects via List deletion methods, outputs each removed object and displays the list after every deletion. If there is an attempt to remove an object from an empty list, the Catch at lines 46–48 catches the EmptyListException and displays an error message.

Method InsertAtFront

Over the next several pages, we discuss each of the methods of class List in detail. Method InsertAtFront (Fig. 24.4, lines 60–67) places a new node at the front of the list. The method consists of three steps:

1. Call `IsEmpty` to determine whether the list is empty (line 61).

2. If the list is empty, set both `firstNode` and `lastNode` to refer to a new `ListNode` initialized with `insertItem` (lines 62–63). The `ListNode` constructor in lines 10–12 of Fig. 24.4 calls the `ListNode` constructor in lines 16–19, which sets instance variable `dataValue` to refer to the `Object` passed as the first argument and sets `nextNodeReference` to `Nothing`.

3. If the list is not empty, the new node is "linked" into the list by setting `firstNode` to refer to a new `ListNode` object initialized with `insertItem` and `firstNode` (line 65). The `ListNode` constructor (lines 16–19) sets instance variable `dataValue` to refer to the `Object` passed as the first argument, and performs the insertion by setting `nextNodeReference` to the `ListNode` passed as the second argument.

In Fig. 24.6, part (a) shows a list and a new node during the `InsertAtFront` operation and before the new node is linked into the list. The dashed lines and arrows in part (b) illustrate *Step 3* of the `InsertAtFront` operation, which enables the node containing 12 to become the new list front.

Method `InsertAtBack`

Method `InsertAtBack` (Fig. 24.4, lines 72–80) places a new node at the back of the list. The method consists of three steps:

1. Call `IsEmpty` to determine whether the list is empty (line 73).

2. If the list is empty, set both `firstNode` and `lastNode` to refer to a new `ListNode` initialized with `insertItem` (lines 74–75). The `ListNode` constructor in lines 10–12 calls the `ListNode` constructor in lines 16–19, which sets instance variable `dataValue` to refer to the `Object` passed as the first argument and sets `nextNodeReference` to `Nothing`.

3. If the list is not empty, link the new node into the list by setting `lastNode` and `lastNode.NextNode` to refer to a new `ListNode` object initialized with `insertItem` (line 77). The `ListNode` constructor (lines 10–12) calls the constructor in lines 16–19, which sets instance variable `dataValue` to refer to the `Object` passed as an argument and sets the `nextNodeReference` reference to `Nothing`.

In Fig. 24.7, part (a) shows a list and a new node during the `InsertAtBack` operation and before the new node has been linked into the list. The dashed lines and arrows in part (b) illustrate *Step 3* of method `InsertAtBack`, which enables a new node to be added to the end of a list that is not empty.

Method `RemoveFromFront`

Method `RemoveFromFront` (Fig. 24.4, lines 83–99) removes the front node of the list and returns a reference to the removed data. The method throws an `EmptyListException` (line 85) if an attempt is made to remove a node from an empty list. Otherwise, the method returns a reference to the removed data. After determining that a `List` is not empty, the method consists of four steps to remove the first node:

1. Assign `firstNode.Data` (the data being removed from the list) to variable `removeItem` (line 88).

Fig. 24.6 | `InsertAtFront` operation.

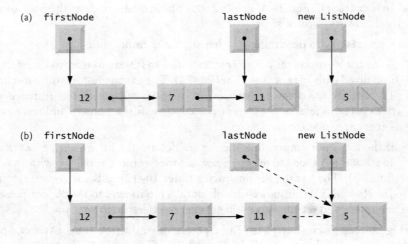

Fig. 24.7 | `InsertAtBack` operation.

2. If the objects to which `firstNode` and `lastNode` refer are the same object, the list has only one element, so the method sets `firstNode` and `lastNode` to `Nothing` (lines 92–93) to remove the node from the list (leaving the list empty).

3. If the list has more than one node, the method leaves reference `lastNode` as is and assigns `firstNode.NextNode` to `firstNode` (line 95). Thus, `firstNode` references the node that was previously the second node in the `List`.

4. Return the `removeItem` reference (line 98).

In Fig. 24.8, part (a) illustrates a list before a removal operation. The dashed lines and arrows in part (b) show the reference manipulations.

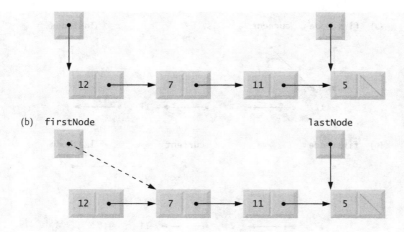

Fig. 24.8 | RemoveFromFront operation.

Method *RemoveFromBack*

Method RemoveFromBack (Fig. 24.4, lines 102–127) removes the last node of a list and returns a reference to the removed data. The method throws an EmptyListException (line 104) if the program attempts to remove a node from an empty list. The method consists of several steps:

1. Assign lastNode.Data (the data being removed from the list) to variable remove-Item (line 107).

2. If firstNode and lastNode refer to the same object (line 110), the list has only one element, so the method sets firstNode and lastNode to Nothing (lines 111–112) to remove that node from the list (leaving the list empty).

3. If the list has more than one node, create ListNode variable current and assign it firstNode (line 114).

4. Now "walk the list" with current until it references the node before the last node. The While loop (lines 117–119) assigns current.NextNode to current as long as current.NextNode is not equal to lastNode.

5. After locating the second-to-last node, assign current to lastNode (line 122) to update which node is last in the list.

6. Set current.NextNode to Nothing (line 123) to remove the last node from the list and terminate the list at the current node.

7. Return the removeItem reference (line 126).

In Fig. 24.9, part (a) illustrates a list before a removal operation. The dashed lines and arrows in part (b) show the reference manipulations.

Method *Print*

Method Print (Fig. 24.4, lines 135–152) first determines whether the list is empty (line 136). If so, Print displays a String consisting of "Empty " and the list's name, then termi-

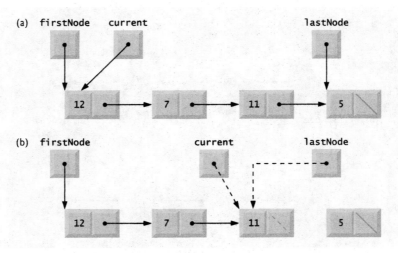

Fig. 24.9 | RemoveFromBack operation.

nates. Otherwise, Print outputs the data in the list. The method prints a String consisting of "The ", the list's name and " is: ". Then line 143 creates ListNode variable current and initializes it with firstNode. While current is not Nothing, there are more items in the list. Therefore, the method displays current.Data (line 147), then assigns current.NextNode to current (line 148) to move to the next node in the list.

Linear and Circular Singly Linked and Doubly Linked Lists

The kind of linked list we have been discussing is a *singly linked list*—the list begins with a reference to the first node, and each node contains a reference to the next node "in sequence." This list terminates with a node whose reference member has the value Nothing. A singly linked list may be traversed in only one direction.

A *circular, singly linked list* (Fig. 24.10) begins with a reference to the first node, and each node contains a reference to the next node. The "last node" does not contain a Nothing reference. Instead the reference in the last node points back to the first node, thus closing the "circle."

A *doubly linked list* (Fig. 24.11) allows traversals both forward and backward. Such a list is often implemented with two "start references"—one that refers to the first element

Fig. 24.10 | Circular, singly linked list.

Fig. 24.11 | Doubly linked list.

of the list to allow front-to-back traversal of the list, and one that refers to the last element to allow back-to-front traversal. Each node has both a forward reference to the next node in the list and a backward reference to the previous node in the list. If your list contains an alphabetized telephone directory, for example, a search for someone whose name begins with a letter near the front of the alphabet might begin from the front of the list. A search for someone whose name begins with a letter near the end of the alphabet might begin from the back of the list.

In a *circular, doubly linked list* (Fig. 24.12), the forward reference of the last node refers to the first node, and the backward reference of the first node refers to the last node, thus closing the "circle."

24.5 Stacks

A *stack* is a constrained version of a linked list—a stack receives new nodes and releases nodes only at the top. For this reason, a stack is referred to as a *last-in, first-out (LIFO)* data structure.

The primary operations to manipulate a stack are *push* and *pop*. Operation push adds a new node to the top of the stack. Operation pop removes a node from the top of the stack and returns the data item from the popped node.

Stacks have many interesting applications. For example, when a program calls a method, the called method must know how to return to its caller, so the return address is pushed onto the method call stack. If a series of method calls occurs, the successive return values are pushed onto the stack in last-in, first-out order so that each method can return to its caller. Stacks support recursive method calls in the same manner that they do conventional non-recursive method calls.

Fig. 24.12 | Circular, doubly linked list.

The System.Collections namespace contains class Stack for implementing and manipulating stacks that can grow and shrink during program execution. Chapters 25 and 26 both discuss class Stack.

In our next example, we take advantage of the close relationship between lists and stacks to implement a stack class by reusing a list class. We demonstrate two different forms of reusability. First, we implement the stack class by inheriting from class List of Fig. 24.4. Then we implement an identically performing stack class through composition by including a reference to a List object as a Private member of a stack class.

Stack Class That Inherits from List

The program of Figs. 24.13 and 24.14 creates a stack class by inheriting from class List of Fig. 24.4 (line 9). We want the stack to have methods Push, Pop, IsEmpty and Print. Essentially, these are the methods InsertAtFront, RemoveFromFront, IsEmpty and Print of class List. Of course, class List contains other methods (such as InsertAtBack and RemoveFromBack) that we would rather not make accessible through the Public interface of the stack. Remember that all methods in the Public interface of class List are inherited as Public methods of the derived class StackInheritance (Fig. 24.13).

The implementation of each StackInheritance method calls the appropriate List method—method Push calls InsertAtFront, method Pop calls RemoveFromFront. Class StackInheritance does not define methods IsEmpty and Print, because it inherits them from class List into StackInheritance's Public interface. Note that class StackInheritance uses namespace LinkedListLibrary (which is the name of the project you created in Fig. 24.4); thus, the class library that defines StackInheritance must have a reference to the LinkedListLibrary class library.

```vb
1   ' Fig. 24.13: StackInheritanceLibrary.vb
2   ' Implementing a stack by inheriting from class List.
3   Imports LinkedListLibrary
4
5   ' class StackInheritance inherits class List's capabilities
6   Public Class StackInheritance : Inherits List
7       ' pass name "stack" to List constructor
8       Public Sub New()
9           MyBase.New("stack")
10      End Sub ' New
11
12      ' place dataValue at top of stack by inserting
13      ' dataValue at front of linked list
14      Public Sub Push(ByVal dataValue As Object)
15          InsertAtFront(dataValue)
16      End Sub ' Push
17
18      ' remove item from top of stack by removing
19      ' item at front of linked list
20      Public Function Pop() As Object
21          Return RemoveFromFront()
22      End Function ' Pop
23  End Class ' StackInheritance
```

Fig. 24.13 | StackInheritance extends class List.

StackInheritanceTest's Main method (Fig. 24.14) uses class StackInheritance to create a stack of Objects called stack (line 8). Lines 11–14 define four values of various types to push onto and pop off the stack. The program pushes onto the stack (lines 17, 19, 21 and 23) a Boolean (True), a Char ('$'), an Integer (34567) and a String ("hello"). An infinite loop (lines 28–32) pops the elements from the stack. When the stack is empty, Pop throws an EmptyListException, and the program displays the exception's stack trace, which shows the program-execution stack at the time the exception occurred. The program uses method Print (inherited by StackInheritance from class List) to output the stack contents after each operation. Class StackInheritanceTest uses namespace LinkedListLibrary (Fig. 24.4) and namespace StackInheritanceLibrary (Fig. 24.13); thus, the solution for class StackInheritanceTest must have references to both class libraries.

```vb
 1    ' Fig. 24.14: StackInheritanceTest.vb
 2    ' Testing class StackInheritance.
 3    Imports StackInheritanceLibrary
 4    Imports LinkedListLibrary
 5
 6    Module StackInheritanceTest
 7       Sub Main()
 8          Dim stack As New StackInheritance()
 9
10          ' create objects to store in the stack
11          Dim aBoolean As Boolean = True
12          Dim aCharacter As Char = "$"c
13          Dim anInteger As Integer = 34567
14          Dim aString As String = "hello"
15
16          ' use method Push to add items to stack
17          stack.Push(aBoolean)
18          stack.Print()
19          stack.Push(aCharacter)
20          stack.Print()
21          stack.Push(anInteger)
22          stack.Print()
23          stack.Push(aString)
24          stack.Print()
25
26          ' remove items from stack
27          Try
28             While True
29                Dim removedObject As Object = stack.Pop()
30                Console.WriteLine(removedObject & " popped")
31                stack.Print()
32             End While
33          Catch exception As EmptyListException
34             ' if exception occurs, print stack trace
35             Console.Error.WriteLine(exception.StackTrace)
36          End Try
37       End Sub ' Main
38    End Module ' StackInheritanceTest
```

Fig. 24.14 | Using class StackInheritance. (Part 1 of 2.)

```
The stack is: True

The stack is: $ True

The stack is: 34567 $ True

The stack is: hello 34567 $ True

hello popped
The stack is: 34567 $ True

34567 popped
The stack is: $ True

$ popped
The stack is: True

True popped
Empty stack
   at LinkedListLibrary.List.RemoveFromFront()
   at StackInheritanceLibrary.StackInheritance.Pop()
   at StackInheritanceTest.StackInheritanceTest.Main(String[] args)
      in C:\examples\ch25\Fig25_14\StackInheritanceTest\
      StackInheritanceTest.cs:line 35
```

Fig. 24.14 | Using class `StackInheritance`. (Part 2 of 2.)

Stack Class That Contains a Reference to a List

Another way to implement a stack class is by reusing a list class through composition. The class in Fig. 24.15 uses a `Private` object of class `List` (line 6) in the declaration of class `StackComposition`. Composition enables us to hide the methods of class `List` that should not be in our stack's `Public` interface by providing `Public` interface methods only to the required `List` methods. This class implements each stack method by delegating its work to an appropriate `List` method. `StackComposition`'s methods call `List` methods `InsertAtFront`, `RemoveFromFront`, `IsEmpty` and `Print`. In this example, we do not show class `StackCompositionTest`, because the only difference (from `StackInheritanceTest`) in this example is that we change the name of the stack class from `StackInheritance` to `StackComposition`. If you download and execute the application, you will see that the output is identical.

```
1    ' Fig. 24.15: StackCompositionLibrary.vb
2    ' StackComposition declaration with composed List object.
3    Imports LinkedListLibrary
4
5    Public Class StackComposition
6       Private stack As List
7
8       ' construct empty stack
9       Public Sub New()
10          stack = New List("stack")
11       End Sub ' New
```

Fig. 24.15 | `StackComposition` class encapsulates functionality of class `List`. (Part 1 of 2.)

```
12
13              ' add object to stack
14              Public Sub Push(ByVal dataValue As Object)
15                  stack.InsertAtFront(dataValue)
16              End Sub ' Push
17
18              ' remove object from stack
19              Public Function Pop() As Object
20                  Return stack.RemoveFromFront()
21              End Function ' Pop
22
23              ' determine whether stack is empty
24              Public Function IsEmpty() As Boolean
25                  Return stack.IsEmpty()
26              End Function ' IsEmpty
27
28              ' output stack contents
29              Public Sub Print()
30                  stack.Print()
31              End Sub ' Print
32          End Class ' StackComposition
```

Fig. 24.15 | StackComposition class encapsulates functionality of class List. (Part 2 of 2.)

24.6 Queues

Another commonly used data structure is the queue. A queue is similar to a checkout line in a supermarket—the cashier services the person at the beginning of the line first. Other customers enter the line only at the end and wait for service. Queue nodes are removed only from the head (or front) of the queue and are inserted only at the tail (or end). For this reason, a queue is a *first-in, first-out* (*FIFO*) data structure. The insert and remove operations are known as *enqueue* and *dequeue*.

Queues have many uses in computer systems. Most computers have only a single processor, so only one application at a time can be serviced. The operating system places each application requiring processor time in a queue. The application at the front of the queue is the next to receive service. Each application gradually advances to the front as the applications before it receive service.

Queues are also used to support *print spooling*. For example, a single printer might be shared by all the users in a network. Many users can send print jobs to the printer, even when the printer is busy. The operating system places these print jobs in a queue until the printer becomes available. A program called a *spooler* manages the queue to ensure that as each print job completes, the next print job is sent to the printer.

Information packets also wait in queues in computer networks. Each time a packet arrives at a network node, it must be routed to the next node along the path to the packet's final destination. The routing node routes one packet at a time, so additional packets are enqueued until the router can route them.

A file server in a computer network handles file-access requests from many clients throughout the network. Servers have a limited capacity to service requests from clients. When that capacity is exceeded, client requests wait in queues.

Queue Class That Inherits from `List`

The program of Figs. 24.16 and 24.17 creates a queue class by inheriting from a list class. We want the `QueueInheritance` class (Fig. 24.16) to have methods `Enqueue`, `Dequeue`, `IsEmpty` and `Print`. Essentially, these are the methods `InsertAtBack`, `RemoveFromFront`, `IsEmpty` and `Print` of class `List`. Of course, the list class contains other methods (such as `InsertAtFront` and `RemoveFromBack`) that we would rather not make accessible through the `Public` interface to the queue class. Remember that all methods in the `Public` interface of the `List` class are also `Public` methods of the derived class `QueueInheritance`.

The implementation of each `QueueInheritance` method calls the appropriate `List` method—method `Enqueue` calls `InsertAtBack` (line 14), and method `Dequeue` calls `RemoveFromFront` (line 20). Calls to `IsEmpty` and `Print` invoke the base-class versions that were inherited from class `List` into `QueueInheritance`'s `Public` interface. Note that class `QueueInheritance` uses namespace `LinkedListLibrary` (Fig. 24.4); thus, the class library for `QueueInheritance` must have a reference to the `LinkedListLibrary` class library.

Class `QueueInheritanceTest`'s `Main` method (Fig. 24.17) creates a `QueueInheritance` object called queue (line 9). Lines 12–15 define four values that will be enqueued and dequeued. The program enqueues (lines 18, 20, 22 and 24) a `Boolean` containing `True`, a `Char` containing `'$'`, an `Integer` containing 34567 and a `String` containing "hello". Note that class `QueueInheritanceTest` uses namespace `LinkedListLibrary` and namespace `QueueInheritanceLibrary`; thus, the solution for class `StackInheritanceTest` must have references to both class libraries.

An infinite `While` loop (lines 32–36) dequeues the elements from the queue in FIFO order. When there are no objects left to dequeue, method `Dequeue` throws an `EmptyListException`, and the program displays the exception's stack trace, which shows the program execution stack at the time the exception occurred. The program uses method `Print` (inherited from class `List`) to output the contents of the queue after each operation. Note that class `QueueInheritanceTest` uses namespace `LinkedListLibrary` (Fig. 24.4) and namespace `QueueInheritanceLibrary` (Fig. 24.16); thus, the solution for class `QueueInheritanceTest` must have references to both class libraries.

```vb
 1   ' Fig. 24.16: QueueInheritanceLibrary.vb
 2   ' Implementing a queue by inheriting from class List.
 3   Imports LinkedListLibrary
 4
 5   Public Class QueueInheritance : Inherits List
 6      ' pass name "queue" to List constructor
 7      Public Sub New()
 8         MyBase.New("queue")
 9      End Sub ' New
10
11      ' place dataValue at end of queue by inserting
12      ' dataValue at end of linked list
13      Public Sub Enqueue(ByVal dataValue As Object)
14         InsertAtBack(dataValue)
15      End Sub ' Enqueue
16
```

Fig. 24.16 | QueueInheritance extends class List. (Part 1 of 2.)

```
17        ' remove item from front of queue by removing
18        ' item at front of linked list
19        Public Function Dequeue() As Object
20           Return RemoveFromFront()
21        End Function ' Dequeue
22     End Class ' QueueInheritance
```

Fig. 24.16 | QueueInheritance extends class List. (Part 2 of 2.)

```
1     ' Fig. 24.17: QueueTest.vb
2     ' Testing class QueueInheritance.
3     Imports QueueInheritanceLibrary
4     Imports LinkedListLibrary
5
6     ' demonstrate functionality of class QueueInheritance
7     Module QueueTest
8        Sub Main()
9           Dim queue As New QueueInheritance()
10
11          ' create objects to store in the stack
12          Dim aBoolean As Boolean = True
13          Dim aCharacter As Char = "$"c
14          Dim anInteger As Integer = 34567
15          Dim aString As String = "hello"
16
17          ' use method Enqueue to add items to queue
18          queue.Enqueue(aBoolean)
19          queue.Print()
20          queue.Enqueue(aCharacter)
21          queue.Print()
22          queue.Enqueue(anInteger)
23          queue.Print()
24          queue.Enqueue(aString)
25          queue.Print()
26
27          ' use method Dequeue to remove items from queue
28          Dim removedObject As Object = Nothing
29
30          ' remove items from queue
31          Try
32             While True
33                removedObject = queue.Dequeue()
34                Console.WriteLine(removedObject & " dequeued")
35                queue.Print()
36             End While
37          Catch exception As EmptyListException
38             ' if exception occurs, print stack trace
39             Console.Error.WriteLine(exception.StackTrace)
40          End Try
41       End Sub ' Main
42    End Module ' QueueTest
```

Fig. 24.17 | Queue created by inheritance. (Part 1 of 2.)

```
The queue is: True

The queue is: True $

The queue is: True $ 34567

The queue is: True $ 34567 hello

True dequeued
The queue is: $ 34567 hello

$ dequeued
The queue is: 34567 hello

34567 dequeued
The queue is: hello

hello dequeued
Empty queue
   at LinkedListLibrary.List.RemoveFromFront()
   at QueueInheritanceLibrary.QueueInheritance.Dequeue()
   at QueueTest.QueueTest.Main(String[] args)
      in C:\examples\ch25\Fig25_17\QueueTest.cs:line 38
```

Fig. 24.17 | Queue created by inheritance. (Part 2 of 2.)

24.7 Trees

Linked lists, stacks and queues are *linear data structures* (i.e., *sequences*). A *tree* is a non-linear, two-dimensional data structure with special properties. Tree nodes contain two or more links.

Basic Terminology

We now discuss *binary trees* (Fig. 24.18)—trees whose nodes all contain two links (none, one or both of which may be Nothing). The *root node* is the first node in a tree. Each link

Fig. 24.18 | Binary tree graphical representation.

in the root node refers to a *child*. The *left child* is the first node in the *left subtree*, and the *right child* is the first node in the *right subtree*. The children of a specific node are called *siblings*. A node with no children is called a *leaf node*. Computer scientists normally draw trees from the root node down—exactly the opposite of the way most trees grow in nature.

Binary Search Trees

In our binary tree example, we create a special binary tree called a *binary search tree*. A binary search tree (with no duplicate node values) has the characteristic that the values in any left subtree are less than the value in the subtree's *parent node*, and the values in any right subtree are greater than the value in the subtree's parent node. Figure 24.19 illustrates a binary search tree with nine integer values. Note that the shape of the binary search tree that corresponds to a set of data can depend on the order in which the values are inserted into the tree.

24.7.1 Binary Search Tree of Integer Values

The application of Figs. 24.20 and 24.21 creates a binary search tree of integers and traverses it (i.e., walks through all its nodes) in three ways—using recursive *inorder, preorder* and *postorder* traversals. The program generates 10 random numbers and inserts each into the tree. Figure 24.20 defines class Tree in namespace BinaryTreeLibrary for reuse purposes (the name of the project is automatically used as the library's namespace). Figure 24.21 defines class TreeTest to demonstrate class Tree's functionality. Method Main of class TreeTest instantiates an empty Tree object, then randomly generates 10 integers and inserts each value in the binary tree by calling Tree method InsertNode. The program then performs preorder, inorder and postorder traversals of the tree. We discuss these traversals shortly.

Class TreeNode (lines 4–65 of Fig. 24.20) is a self-referential class containing three Private data members—leftNodeReference and rightNodeReference of type TreeNode and dataValue of type Integer. Initially, every TreeNode is a leaf node, so the constructor (lines 10–14) initializes leftNodeReference and rightNodeReference to Nothing. Properties LeftNode (lines 17–24), Data (lines 27–34) and RightNode (lines 37–44) provide access to a ListNode's Private data members. We discuss TreeNode method Insert (lines 48–64) shortly.

Class Tree (lines 68–149 of Fig. 24.20) manipulates objects of class TreeNode. Class Tree has as Private data root (line 69)—a reference to the root node of the tree. The class contains Public method InsertNode (lines 79–85) to insert a new node in the tree and

Fig. 24.19 | Binary search tree containing nine values.

Public methods `PreorderTraversal` (lines 88–90), `InorderTraversal` (lines 109–111) and `PostorderTraversal` (lines 130–132) to begin traversals of the tree. Each of these methods calls a separate recursive utility method to perform the traversal operations on the internal representation of the tree. The `Tree` constructor (lines 72–74) initializes `root` to `Nothing` to indicate that the tree initially is empty.

```vb
1    ' Fig. 24.20: BinaryTreeLibrary.vb
2    ' Declaration of class TreeNode and class Tree.
3
4    Public Class TreeNode
5       Private leftNodeReference As TreeNode ' link to left child
6       Private dataValue As Integer ' dataValue stored in node
7       Private rightNodeReference As TreeNode ' link to right child
8
9       ' initialize dataValue and make this a leaf node
10      Public Sub New(ByVal nodeData As Integer)
11         dataValue = nodeData
12         leftNodeReference = Nothing
13         rightNodeReference = Nothing
14      End Sub ' New
15
16      ' LeftNode property
17      Public Property LeftNode() As TreeNode
18         Get
19            Return leftNodeReference
20         End Get
21         Set(ByVal value As TreeNode)
22            leftNodeReference = value
23         End Set
24      End Property ' LeftNode
25
26      ' Data property
27      Public Property Data() As Integer
28         Get
29            Return dataValue
30         End Get
31         Set(ByVal value As Integer)
32            dataValue = value
33         End Set
34      End Property ' Data
35
36      ' RightNode property
37      Public Property RightNode() As TreeNode
38         Get
39            Return rightNodeReference
40         End Get
41         Set(ByVal value As TreeNode)
42            rightNodeReference = value
43         End Set
44      End Property ' RightNode
45
```

Fig. 24.20 | TreeNode and Tree classes for a binary search tree. (Part 1 of 3.)

```vbnet
46        ' recursively insert TreeNode into Tree that contains nodes;
47        ' ignore duplicate values
48        Public Sub Insert(ByVal insertValue As Integer)
49           If insertValue < data Then ' insert in left subtree
50              ' insert new TreeNode
51              If LeftNode Is Nothing Then
52                 LeftNode = New TreeNode(insertValue)
53              Else ' continue traversing left subtree
54                 LeftNode.Insert(insertValue)
55              End If
56           ElseIf insertValue > data Then ' insert in right subtree
57              ' insert new TreeNode
58              If RightNode Is Nothing Then
59                 RightNode = New TreeNode(insertValue)
60              Else ' continue traversing right subtree
61                 RightNode.Insert(insertValue)
62              End If
63           End If
64        End Sub ' Insert
65     End Class ' TreeNode
66
67     ' class Tree declaration
68     Public Class Tree
69        Private root As TreeNode ' reference to root node of tree
70
71        ' construct an empty Tree of integers
72        Public Sub New()
73           root = Nothing
74        End Sub ' New
75
76        ' Insert a new node in the binary search tree.
77        ' If the root node is Nothing, create the root node here.
78        ' Otherwise, call the insert method of class TreeNode.
79        Public Sub InsertNode(ByVal insertValue As Integer)
80           If root Is Nothing Then
81              root = New TreeNode(insertValue)
82           Else
83              root.Insert(insertValue)
84           End If
85        End Sub ' InsertNode
86
87        ' begin preorder traversal
88        Public Sub PreorderTraversal()
89           PreorderHelper(root)
90        End Sub ' PreorderTraversal
91
92        ' recursive method to perform preorder traversal
93        Private Sub PreorderHelper(ByVal node As TreeNode)
94           If node Is Nothing Then
95              Return
96           End If
97
```

Fig. 24.20 | TreeNode and Tree classes for a binary search tree. (Part 2 of 3.)

```
 98              ' output node data
 99              Console.Write(node.Data & " ")
100
101              ' traverse left subtree
102              PreorderHelper(node.LeftNode)
103
104              ' traverse right subtree
105              PreorderHelper(node.RightNode)
106          End Sub ' PreorderHelper
107
108          ' begin inorder traversal
109          Public Sub InorderTraversal()
110              InorderHelper(root)
111          End Sub ' InorderTraversal
112
113          ' recursive method to perform inorder traversal
114          Private Sub InorderHelper(ByVal node As TreeNode)
115              If node Is Nothing Then
116                  Return
117              End If
118
119              ' traverse left subtree
120              InorderHelper(node.LeftNode)
121
122              ' output node data
123              Console.Write(node.Data & " ")
124
125              ' traverse right subtree
126              InorderHelper(node.RightNode)
127          End Sub ' InorderHelper
128
129          ' begin postorder traversal
130          Public Sub PostorderTraversal()
131              PostorderHelper(root)
132          End Sub ' PostorderTraversal
133
134          ' recursive method to perform postorder traversal
135          Private Sub PostorderHelper(ByVal node As TreeNode)
136              If node Is Nothing Then
137                  Return
138              End If
139
140              ' traverse left subtree
141              PostorderHelper(node.LeftNode)
142
143              ' traverse right subtree
144              PostorderHelper(node.RightNode)
145
146              ' output node data
147              Console.Write(node.Data & " ")
148          End Sub ' PostorderHelper
149      End Class ' Tree
```

Fig. 24.20 | TreeNode and Tree classes for a binary search tree. (Part 3 of 3.)

```vb
 1   ' Fig. 24.21: TreeTest.vb
 2   ' This program tests class Tree.
 3   Imports BinaryTreeLibrary
 4
 5   ' class TreeTest declaration
 6   Module TreeTest
 7      ' test class Tree
 8      Sub Main()
 9         Dim tree As New Tree()
10         Dim insertValue As Integer
11
12         Console.WriteLine("Inserting values: ")
13         Dim random As New Random()
14
15         ' insert 10 random integers from 0-99 in tree
16         Dim i As Integer
17         For i = 1 To 10
18            insertValue = random.Next(100)
19            Console.Write(insertValue & " ")
20
21            tree.InsertNode(insertValue)
22         Next i
23
24         ' perform preorder traversal of tree
25         Console.WriteLine(vbCrLf & vbCrLf & _
26            "Preorder traversal")
27         tree.PreorderTraversal()
28
29         ' perform inorder traversal of tree
30         Console.WriteLine(vbCrLf & vbCrLf & _
31            "Inorder traversal")
32         tree.InorderTraversal()
33
34         ' perform postorder traversal of tree
35         Console.WriteLine(vbCrLf & vbCrLf & _
36            "Postorder traversal")
37         tree.PostorderTraversal()
38      End Sub ' Main
39   End Module ' TreeTest
```

```
Inserting values:
39 69 94 47 50 72 55 41 97 73

Preorder traversal
39 69 47 41 50 55 94 72 73 97

Inorder traversal
39 41 47 50 55 69 72 73 94 97

Postorder traversal
41 55 50 47 73 72 97 94 69 39
```

Fig. 24.21 | Creating and traversing a binary tree.

Tree method `InsertNode` (lines 79–85) first determines whether the tree is empty. If so, line 81 allocates a new `TreeNode`, initializes the node with the integer being inserted in the tree and assigns the new node to `root`. If the tree is not empty, `InsertNode` calls `TreeNode` method `Insert` (lines 48–64), which recursively determines the location for the new node in the tree and inserts the node at that location. A node can be inserted only as a leaf node in a binary search tree.

`TreeNode` method `Insert` compares the value to insert with the `data` value in the root node. If the insert value is less than the root-node data, the program determines whether the left subtree is empty (line 51). If so, line 52 allocates a new `TreeNode`, initializes it with the integer being inserted and assigns the new node to reference `leftNode`. Otherwise, line 54 recursively calls `Insert` for the left subtree to insert the value into the left subtree. If the insert value is greater than the root-node data, the program determines whether the right subtree is empty (line 58). If so, line 59 allocates a new `TreeNode`, initializes it with the integer being inserted and assigns the new node to reference `rightNode`. Otherwise, line 61 recursively calls `Insert` for the right subtree to insert the value in the right subtree.

Methods `InorderTraversal`, `PreorderTraversal` and `PostorderTraversal` call the recursive helper methods `InorderHelper` (lines 114–127), `PreorderHelper` (lines 93–106) and `PostorderHelper` (lines 135–148), respectively, to traverse the tree and print the node values. The purpose of these helper methods in class `Tree` is to allow the programmer to start a traversal without needing to obtain a reference to the `root` node first, then call the recursive method with that reference. Methods `InorderTraversal`, `PreorderTraversal` and `PostorderTraversal` simply take `Private` variable `root` and pass it to the appropriate helper method to initiate a traversal of the tree. For the following discussion, we use the binary search tree shown in Fig. 24.22.

Inorder Traversal Algorithm

Method `InorderHelper` (lines 114–127) defines the steps for an inorder traversal. The steps are as follows:

1. If the argument is `Nothing`, return immediately.
2. Traverse the left subtree with a call to `InorderHelper` (line 120).
3. Process the value in the node (line 123).
4. Traverse the right subtree with a call to `InorderHelper` (line 126).

The inorder traversal does not process the value in a node until the values in the node's left subtree are processed. The inorder traversal of the tree in Fig. 24.22 is

    6 13 17 27 33 42 48

Fig. 24.22 | Binary search tree.

Note that the inorder traversal of a binary search tree prints the node values in ascending order. The process of creating a binary search tree actually sorts the data (when coupled with an inorder traversal)—thus, this process is called the *binary tree sort.*

Preorder Traversal Algorithm

Method `PreorderHelper` (lines 93–106) defines the steps for a preorder traversal. The steps are as follows:

1. If the argument is `Nothing`, return immediately.
2. Process the value in the node (line 99).
3. Traverse the left subtree with a call to `PreorderHelper` (line 102).
4. Traverse the right subtree with a call to `PreorderHelper` (line 105).

The preorder traversal processes the value in each node as the node is visited. After processing the value in a given node, the preorder traversal processes the values in the left subtree, then the values in the right subtree. The preorder traversal of the tree in Fig. 24.22 is

```
27 13 6 17 42 33 48
```

Postorder Traversal Algorithm

Method `PostorderHelper` (lines 135–148) defines the steps for a postorder traversal. The steps are as follows:

1. If the argument is `Nothing`, return immediately.
2. Traverse the left subtree with a call to `PostorderHelper` (line 141).
3. Traverse the right subtree with a call to `PostorderHelper` (line 144).
4. Process the value in the node (line 147).

The postorder traversal processes the value in each node after the values of all the node's children are processed. The postorder traversal of the tree in Fig. 24.22 is

```
6 17 13 33 48 42 27
```

Duplicate Elimination

The binary search tree facilitates *duplicate elimination.* While building a tree, the insertion operation recognizes attempts to insert a duplicate value, because a duplicate follows the same "go left" or "go right" decisions on each comparison as the original value did. Thus the insertion operation eventually compares the duplicate with a node containing the same value. At this point, the insertion operation might simply discard the duplicate value.

Searching a binary tree for a value that matches a key value is fast, especially for *tightly packed* binary trees. In a tightly packed binary tree, each level contains about twice as many elements as the previous level. Figure 24.22 is a tightly packed binary tree. A binary search tree with n elements has a minimum of $\log_2 n$ levels. Thus, at most $\log_2 n$ comparisons are required to either find a match or determine that no match exists. Searching a (tightly packed) 1,000-element binary search tree requires at most 10 comparisons, because $2^{10} > 1000$. Searching a (tightly packed) 1,000,000-element binary search tree requires at most 20 comparisons, because $2^{20} > 1,000,000$.

24.7.2 Binary Search Tree of IComparable Objects

The binary tree example in Section 24.7.1 works nicely when all the data is of type Integer. Suppose that you want to manipulate a binary tree of Double values. You could rewrite the TreeNode and Tree classes with different names and customize the classes to manipulate Double values. Similarly, for each data type you could create customized versions of classes TreeNode and Tree. This results in a proliferation of code, which can become difficult to manage and maintain.

Ideally, we would like to define the functionality of a binary tree once and reuse that functionality for many data types. Languages like Visual Basic, C# and Java provide polymorphic capabilities that enable all objects to be manipulated in a uniform manner. Using such capabilities enables us to design a more flexible data structure. The new version of Visual Basic provides these capabilities with generics (Chapter 25).

In our next example, we take advantage of Visual Basic's polymorphic capabilities by implementing TreeNode and Tree classes that manipulate objects of any type that implements interface *IComparable* (namespace System). It is imperative to compare objects stored in a binary search if we are to determine the path to the insertion point of a new node. Classes that implement IComparable define method *CompareTo*, which compares the object that invokes the method with the object that the method receives as an argument. The method returns an Integer value less than zero if the calling object is less than the argument object, zero if the objects are equal and a positive value if the calling object is greater than the argument object. Also, the invoking and argument objects must be of the same data type; otherwise, the method throws an ArgumentException.

The program of Figs. 24.23 and 24.24 enhances the program from Section 24.7.1 to manipulate IComparable objects. One restriction on the new versions TreeNode and Tree in Fig. 24.23 is that each Tree object can contain objects of only one data type (e.g., all Strings or all Doubles). If a program attempts to insert multiple data types in the same Tree object, ArgumentExceptions will occur. We modified only seven lines of code in class TreeNode (lines 7, 11, 28, 32, 49, 50 and 57) and one line of code in class Tree (line 80) to enable processing of IComparable objects. With the exception of lines 50 and 57, all the other changes simply replaced the type Integer with the type IComparable. Lines 50 and 57 previously used the < and > operators to compare the value being inserted with the value in a given node. These lines now compare IComparable objects via the interface's CompareTo method, then test the method's return value to determine whether it is less than zero (the invoking object is less than the argument object) or greater than zero (the invoking object is greater than the argument object), respectively. [*Note:* If this class were written using generics, the type of data, Integer or IComparable could be replaced at compile time by any other type that implements the necessary operators and methods.]

Class TreeTest (Fig. 24.24) creates three Tree objects to store Integer, Double and String values, all of which the .NET Framework defines as IComparable types. The program populates the trees with the values in arrays integerArray (line 9), doubleArray (lines 10–11) and stringArray (lines 12–13), respectively.

Method PopulateTree (lines 32–42) receives as arguments an Array containing the initializer values for the Tree, a Tree in which the array elements will be placed and a String representing the Tree name, then inserts each Array element into the Tree. Method TraverseTree (lines 45–60) receives as arguments a Tree and a String representing the Tree name, then outputs the preorder, inorder and postorder traversals of the

```vb
1    ' Fig. 24.23: BinaryTreeLibrary2.vb
2    ' Declaration of class TreeNode and class Tree for IComparable
3    ' objects.
4
5    Public Class TreeNode
6       Private leftNodeValue As TreeNode ' link to left child
7       Private dataValue As IComparable ' dataValue stored in node
8       Private rightNodeValue As TreeNode ' link to right subtree
9
10      ' initialize dataValue and make this a leaf node
11      Public Sub New(ByVal nodeData As IComparable)
12         dataValue = nodeData
13         leftNodeValue = Nothing
14         rightNodeValue = Nothing
15      End Sub ' New
16
17      ' LeftNode property
18      Public Property LeftNode() As TreeNode
19         Get
20            Return leftNodeValue
21         End Get
22         Set(ByVal value As TreeNode)
23            leftNodeValue = value
24         End Set
25      End Property ' LeftNode
26
27      ' Data property
28      Public Property Data() As IComparable
29         Get
30            Return dataValue
31         End Get
32         Set(ByVal value As IComparable)
33            dataValue = value
34         End Set
35      End Property ' Data
36
37      ' RightNode property
38      Public Property RightNode() As TreeNode
39         Get
40            Return rightNodeValue
41         End Get
42         Set(ByVal value As TreeNode)
43            rightNodeValue = value
44         End Set
45      End Property ' RightNode
46
47      ' insert TreeNode into Tree that contains nodes;
48      ' ignore duplicate values
49      Public Sub Insert(ByVal insertValue As IComparable)
50         If insertValue.CompareTo(data) < 0 Then
51            ' insert in left subtree
52            If LeftNode Is Nothing Then
53               LeftNode = New TreeNode(insertValue)
```

Fig. 24.23 | TreeNode and Tree classes for manipulating IComparable objects. (Part 1 of 3.)

```
54          Else ' continue traversing left subtree
55              LeftNode.Insert(insertValue)
56          End If
57      ElseIf insertValue.CompareTo(data) > 0 Then
58          ' insert in right subtree
59          If RightNode Is Nothing Then
60              RightNode = New TreeNode(insertValue)
61          Else ' continue traversing right subtree
62              RightNode.Insert(insertValue)
63          End If
64      End If
65   End Sub ' Insert
66 End Class ' TreeNode
67
68 ' class Tree declaration
69 Public Class Tree
70    Private root As TreeNode
71
72    ' construct an empty Tree of integers
73    Public Sub New()
74        root = Nothing
75    End Sub ' New
76
77    ' Insert a new node in the binary search tree.
78    ' If the root node is Nothing, create the root node here.
79    ' Otherwise, call the insert method of class TreeNode.
80    Public Sub InsertNode(ByVal insertValue As IComparable)
81        If root Is Nothing Then
82            root = New TreeNode(insertValue)
83        Else
84            root.Insert(insertValue)
85        End If
86    End Sub ' InsertNode
87
88    ' begin preorder traversal
89    Public Sub PreorderTraversal()
90        PreorderHelper(root)
91    End Sub ' PreorderTraversal
92
93    ' recursive method to perform preorder traversal
94    Private Sub PreorderHelper(ByVal node As TreeNode)
95        If node Is Nothing Then
96            Return
97        End If
98        ' output node data
99        Console.Write(Convert.ToString(node.Data) & " ")
100
101       ' traverse left subtree
102       PreorderHelper(node.LeftNode)
103
104       ' traverse right subtree
105       PreorderHelper(node.RightNode)
106   End Sub ' PreorderHelper
```

Fig. 24.23 | TreeNode and Tree classes for manipulating IComparable objects. (Part 2 of 3.)

```
107
108          ' begin inorder traversal
109          Public Sub InorderTraversal()
110             InorderHelper(root)
111          End Sub ' InorderTraversal
112
113          ' recursive method to perform inorder traversal
114          Private Sub InorderHelper(ByVal node As TreeNode)
115             If node Is Nothing Then
116                Return
117             End If
118             ' traverse left subtree
119             InorderHelper(node.LeftNode)
120
121             ' output node data
122             Console.Write(Convert.ToString(node.Data) & " ")
123
124             ' traverse right subtree
125             InorderHelper(node.RightNode)
126          End Sub ' InorderHelper
127
128          ' begin postorder traversal
129          Public Sub PostorderTraversal()
130             PostorderHelper(root)
131          End Sub ' PostorderTraversal
132
133          ' recursive method to perform postorder traversal
134          Private Sub PostorderHelper(ByVal node As TreeNode)
135             If node Is Nothing Then
136                Return
137             End If
138             ' traverse left subtree
139             PostorderHelper(node.LeftNode)
140
141             ' traverse right subtree
142             PostorderHelper(node.RightNode)
143
144             ' output node data
145             Console.Write(Convert.ToString(node.Data) & " ")
146          End Sub ' PostorderHelper
147       End Class ' Tree
```

Fig. 24.23 | TreeNode and Tree classes for manipulating IComparable objects. (Part 3 of 3.)

```
1       ' Fig. 24.24: TreeTest.vb
2       ' This program tests class Tree.
3       Imports BinaryTreeLibrary2
4
5       ' class TreeTest declaration
6       Module TreeTest
7          ' test class Tree
8          Sub Main()
```

Fig. 24.24 | Demonstrating class Tree with IComparable objects. (Part 1 of 3.)

```vb
 9          Dim integerArray As Integer() = {8, 2, 4, 3, 1, 7, 5, 6}
10          Dim doubleArray As Double() = _
11             {8.8, 2.2, 4.4, 3.3, 1.1, 7.7, 5.5, 6.6}
12          Dim stringArray As String() = _
13             {"eight", "two", "four", "three", "one", "seven", "five", "six"}
14
15          ' create Integer Tree
16          Dim integerTree As New Tree()
17          populateTree(integerArray, integerTree, "integerTree")
18          traverseTree(integerTree, "integerTree")
19
20          ' create Double Tree
21          Dim doubleTree As New Tree()
22          populateTree(doubleArray, doubleTree, "doubleTree")
23          traverseTree(doubleTree, "doubleTree")
24
25          ' create String Tree
26          Dim stringTree As New Tree()
27          populateTree(stringArray, stringTree, "stringTree")
28          traverseTree(stringTree, "stringTree")
29       End Sub ' Main
30
31       ' populate Tree with array elements
32       Sub populateTree(ByVal array As Array, _
33          ByVal tree As Tree, ByVal name As String)
34
35          Console.WriteLine(vbCrLf & vbCrLf & _
36             vbCrLf & "Inserting into " & name & ":")
37
38          For Each data As IComparable In array
39             Console.Write(Convert.ToString(data) & " ")
40             tree.InsertNode(data)
41          Next data
42       End Sub ' populateTree
43
44       ' insert perform traversals
45       Sub traverseTree(ByVal tree As Tree, ByVal treeType As String)
46          ' perform preorder traveral of tree
47          Console.WriteLine(vbCrLf & vbCrLf & _
48             "Preorder traversal of " & treeType)
49          tree.PreorderTraversal()
50
51          ' perform inorder traveral of tree
52          Console.WriteLine(vbCrLf & vbCrLf & _
53             "Inorder traversal of " & treeType)
54          tree.InorderTraversal()
55
56          ' perform postorder traveral of tree
57          Console.WriteLine(vbCrLf & vbCrLf & _
58             "Postorder traversal of " & treeType)
59          tree.PostorderTraversal()
60       End Sub ' traverseTree
61    End Module ' TreeTest
```

Fig. 24.24 | Demonstrating class Tree with IComparable objects. (Part 2 of 3.)

```
Inserting into intTree:
8 2 4 3 1 7 5 6

Preorder traversal of intTree
8 2 1 4 3 7 5 6

Inorder traversal of intTree
1 2 3 4 5 6 7 8

Postorder traversal of intTree
1 3 6 5 7 4 2 8


Inserting into doubleTree:
8.8 2.2 4.4 3.3 1.1 7.7 5.5 6.6

Preorder traversal of doubleTree
8.8 2.2 1.1 4.4 3.3 7.7 5.5 6.6

Inorder traversal of doubleTree
1.1 2.2 3.3 4.4 5.5 6.6 7.7 8.8

Postorder traversal of doubleTree
1.1 3.3 6.6 5.5 7.7 4.4 2.2 8.8


Inserting into stringTree:
eight two four three one seven five six

Preorder traversal of stringTree
eight two four five three one seven six

Inorder traversal of stringTree
eight five four one seven six three two

Postorder traversal of stringTree
five six seven one three four two eight
```

Fig. 24.24 | Demonstrating class Tree with IComparable objects. (Part 3 of 3.)

Tree. Note that the inorder traversal of each Tree outputs the data in sorted order regardless of the data type stored in the Tree. Our polymorphic implementation of class Tree invokes the appropriate data type's CompareTo method to determine the path to each value's insertion point by using the standard binary search tree insertion rules. Also note that the Tree of Strings appears in alphabetical order.

24.8 Wrap-Up

In this chapter, you learned that primitive types are value-type Structures, but can still be used anywhere Objects are expected in a program due to boxing and unboxing conversions. You learned that linked lists are collections of data items that are "linked together in a chain" and that a program can perform insertions and deletions anywhere in a linked list (though our implementation only performed insertions and deletions at the ends of the list). We demonstrated that the stack and queue data structures can be implemented as constrained versions of lists. For stacks, you saw that insertions and deletions are made only at the top—so stacks are known as last-in, first-out (LIFO) data structures. For queues, which represent waiting lines, you saw that insertions are made at the tail and deletions are made from the head—so queues are known as first-in, first-out (FIFO) data structures. We also presented the binary tree data structure. You saw a binary search tree that facilitated high-speed searching and sorting of data and efficient duplicate elimination. Finally, we presented a version of the binary tree data structure that processes IComparable objects and uses the CompareTo method to help determine where the object should be placed in the binary tree. In the next chapter, we introduce generics, a capability which allows you to declare a family of classes and methods that implement the same functionality on any type.

Generics

OBJECTIVES

In this chapter you will learn:

- To create generic methods that perform identical tasks on arguments of different types.

- To create a generic **Stack** class that can be used to store objects of any class or interface type.

- To understand how to overload generic methods with non-generic methods or with other generic methods.

- To understand the **New** constraint of a type parameter.

- To apply multiple constraints to a type parameter.

- The relationship between generics and inheritance.

25.1 Introduction

In Chapter 24, we presented data structures that store and manipulate Object references. You could store any Object in these data structures. One inconvenient aspect of storing Object references occurs when retrieving them from a collection. An application normally needs to process specific types of objects. As a result, the Object references obtained from a collection typically need to be downcast to an appropriate type to allow the application to process the objects correctly. In addition, data of value types (e.g., Integer and Double) must be boxed to be manipulated with Object references, which increases the overhead of processing such data. Also, processing all data as type Object limits the Visual Basic compiler's ability to perform type checking.

Though we can easily create data structures that manipulate any type of data as Objects (as we did in Chapter 24), it would be nice if we could detect type mismatches at compile time—this is known as *compile-time type safety*. For example, if a Stack should store only Integer values, attempting to push a String onto that Stack should cause a compile-time error. Similarly, a Sort method should be able to compare elements that are all guaranteed to have the same type. If we create type-specific versions of class Stack and method Sort, the Visual Basic compiler would certainly be able to ensure compile-time type safety. However, this would require that we create many copies of the same basic code.

This chapter discusses one of Visual Basic's newest features—*generics*—which provides the means to create the general models mentioned above. *Generic methods* enable you to specify a set of related methods with a single method declaration. *Generic classes* enable you to specify a set of related classes with a single class declaration. Similarly, *generic interfaces* enable you to specify a set of related interfaces with a single interface declaration. Generics provide compile-time type safety. [*Note:* You can also implement generic Structures and Delegates. For more information, see the Visual Basic language specification version 8.0, available at http://go.microsoft.com/fwlink/?LinkId=62990 .]

We can write a generic method for sorting an array of objects, then invoke the generic method separately with an Integer array, a Double array, a String array and so on, to sort each different type of array. The compiler performs *type checking* to ensure that the array passed to the sorting method contains only elements of the same type. We can write a single generic Stack class that manipulates a stack of objects, then instantiate Stack objects for a stack of Integers, a stack of Doubles, a stack of Strings and so on. The compiler performs type checking to ensure that the Stack stores only elements of the same type.

This chapter presents examples of generic methods and generic classes. It also considers the relationships between generics and other Visual Basic features, such as overloading and inheritance. Chapter 26, Collections, discusses the .NET Framework's generic and non-generic collections classes. A collection is a data structure that maintains a group of related objects or values. The .NET Framework collection classes use generics to allow you to specify the exact types of object that a particular collection will store.

25.2 Motivation for Generic Methods

Overloaded methods are often used to perform similar operations on different types of data. To motivate the concepte of generic methods, let's begin with an example (Fig. 25.1) that contains three overloaded PrintArray methods (lines 19–25, 28–34 and 37–43). These methods display the elements of an Integer array, a Double array and a Char array, respectively. In Section 25.3, we reimplement this program more concisely and elegantly using a single generic method.

```vb
 1   ' Fig. 25.1: OverloadedMethods.vb
 2   ' Using overloaded methods to print arrays of different types.
 3   Module OverloadedMethods
 4      Sub Main()
 5         ' create arrays of Integer, Double and Char types
 6         Dim integerArray As Integer() = {1, 2, 3, 4, 5, 6}
 7         Dim doubleArray As Double() = {1.1, 2.2, 3.3, 4.4, 5.5, 6.6, 7.7}
 8         Dim charArray As Char() = {"H"c, "E"c, "L"c, "L"c, "O"c}
 9
10         Console.WriteLine("Array integerArray contains:")
11         PrintArray(integerArray) ' pass an Integer array argument
12         Console.WriteLine("Array doubleArray contains:")
13         PrintArray(doubleArray) ' pass a Double array argument
14         Console.WriteLine("Array charArray contains:")
15         PrintArray(charArray) ' pass a Char array
16      End Sub ' Main
17
18      ' output Integer array
19      Sub PrintArray(ByVal inputArray() As Integer)
20         For Each element As Integer In inputArray
21            Console.Write(element.ToString() & " ")
22         Next element
23
24         Console.WriteLine(vbCrLf)
25      End Sub ' PrintArray
26
27      ' output Double array
28      Sub PrintArray(ByVal inputArray() As Double)
29         For Each element As Double In inputArray
30            Console.Write(element.ToString() & " ")
31         Next element
32
33         Console.WriteLine(vbCrLf)
34      End Sub ' PrintArray
```

Fig. 25.1 | Displaying arrays of different types using overloaded methods. (Part 1 of 2.)

```
35
36          ' output Char array
37          Sub PrintArray(ByVal inputArray() As Char)
38              For Each element As Char In inputArray
39                  Console.Write(element.ToString() & " ")
40              Next element
41
42              Console.WriteLine(vbCrLf)
43          End Sub ' PrintArray
44      End Module ' OverloadedMethods
```

```
Array integerArray contains:
1 2 3 4 5 6

Array doubleArray contains:
1.1 2.2 3.3 4.4 5.5 6.6 7.7

Array charArray contains:
H E L L O
```

Fig. 25.1 | Displaying arrays of different types using overloaded methods. (Part 2 of 2.)

The program begins by declaring and initializing three arrays—six-element Integer array integerArray (line 6), seven-element Double array doubleArray (line 7) and five-element Char array charArray (line 8). Then lines 10–15 output the arrays.

When the compiler encounters a method call, it attempts to locate a method declaration that has the same method name and parameters that match the argument types in the method call. In this example, each PrintArray call exactly matches one of the PrintArray method declarations. For example, line 11 calls PrintArray with integerArray as its argument. At compile time, the compiler determines argument integerArray's type (i.e., Integer()), attempts to locate a method named PrintArray that specifies a single Integer() parameter (which it finds in lines 19–25) and sets up a call to that method. Similarly, when the compiler encounters the PrintArray call in line 13, it determines argument doubleArray's type (i.e., Double()), then attempts to locate a method named PrintArray that specifies a single Double() parameter (which it finds in lines 28–34) and sets up a call to that method. Finally, when the compiler encounters the PrintArray call in line 15, it determines argument charArray's type (i.e., Char()), then attempts to locate a method named PrintArray that specifies a single Char() parameter (which it finds in lines 37–43) and sets up a call to that method.

Study each PrintArray method. Note that the array element type (Integer, Double or Char) appears in two locations in each method—the method header (lines 19, 28 and 37) and the For Each statement header (lines 20, 29 and 38). If we replace the element type in each method with a generic name—we chose E to represent the "element" type—then all three methods would look like the one in Fig. 25.2. It appears that if we can replace the array element type in each of the three methods with a single "generic type parameter," then we should be able to declare one PrintArray method that can display the elements of *any* array. The method in Fig. 25.2 will not compile because its syntax is not correct—we declare a generic PrintArray method with the proper syntax in Fig. 25.3.

```
 1    Public Sub PrintArray(ByVal inputArray() As E)
 2       For Each element As E In inputArray
 3          Console.Write(element.ToString() & " ")
 4       Next element
 5
 6       Console.WriteLine(vbCrLf)
 7    End Sub ' PrintArray
```

Fig. 25.2 | `PrintArray` method in which actual type names are replaced by convention with the generic name E (for "element"). [*Note:* This code will not compile.]

25.3 Generic Method Implementation

The overloaded methods of Fig. 25.1 can be more compactly and conveniently coded using a single generic method. You can write a single generic method declaration that can be called at different times with arguments of different types. Based on the types of the arguments passed to the generic method, the compiler handles each method call appropriately.

Figure 25.3 reimplements the application of Fig. 25.1 using a single generic Print-Array method (lines 19–25). Note that the PrintArray method calls in lines 11, 13 and 15 are identical to those in Fig. 25.1, the outputs of the two applications are identical and the code in Fig. 25.3 is 18 lines shorter than the code in Fig. 25.1. As illustrated in

```
 1    ' Fig. 25.3: GenericMethod.vb
 2    ' Using overloaded methods to print arrays of different types.
 3    Module GenericMethod
 4       Sub Main()
 5          ' create arrays of integer, double and char
 6          Dim integerArray As Integer() = {1, 2, 3, 4, 5, 6}
 7          Dim doubleArray As Double() = {1.1, 2.2, 3.3, 4.4, 5.5, 6.6, 7.7}
 8          Dim charArray As Char() = {"H"c, "E"c, "L"c, "L"c, "O"c}
 9
10          Console.WriteLine("Array integerArray contains:")
11          PrintArray(integerArray) ' pass an integer array argument
12          Console.WriteLine("Array doubleArray contains:")
13          PrintArray(doubleArray) ' pass a double array argument
14          Console.WriteLine("Array charArray contains:")
15          PrintArray(charArray) ' pass a char array argument
16       End Sub ' Main
17
18       ' output array of all types
19       Public Sub PrintArray(Of E)(ByVal inputArray() As E)
20          For Each element As E In inputArray
21             Console.Write(element.ToString() & " ")
22          Next element
23
24          Console.WriteLine(vbCrLf)
25       End Sub ' PrintArray
26    End Module ' GenericMethod
```

Fig. 25.3 | Printing array elements using generic method `PrintArray`. (Part I of 2.)

```
Array integerArray contains:
1 2 3 4 5 6

Array doubleArray contains:
1.1 2.2 3.3 4.4 5.5 6.6 7.7

Array charArray contains:
H E L L O
```

Fig. 25.3 | Printing array elements using generic method `PrintArray`. (Part 2 of 2.)

Fig. 25.3, generics enable us to create and test our code once, then reuse the code for many different types of data. This demonstrates the expressive power of generics.

Line 19 begins method `PrintArray`'s declaration. All generic method declarations have a *type parameter list* delimited by parentheses—(Of E) in this example—that follows the method's name. Each type parameter list begins with the keyword *Of* and contains one or more *type parameters* separated by commas. A type parameter is an identifier that is used in place of actual type names. The type parameters can be used to declare the return type, the parameter types and the local variable types in a generic method declaration; the type parameters act as placeholders for the types of the arguments passed to the generic method. A generic method's body is declared like that of any other method. Note that the type parameter names throughout the method declaration must match those declared in the type parameter list. For example, line 20 declares element in the For Each statement as type E, which matches the type parameter (E) declared in line 19. Also, a type parameter can be declared only once in the type parameter list but can appear more than once in the method's parameter list. Type parameter names need not be unique among different generic methods.

Common Programming Error 25.1

If you forget to include the type parameter list when declaring a generic method, the compiler will not recognize the type parameter names when they are encountered in the method. This results in compilation errors.

Method `PrintArray`'s type parameter list (line 19) declares type parameter E as the placeholder for the array element type that `PrintArray` will output. Note that E appears in the method's parameter list as the array element type (line 19). The For Each statement header (line 20) also uses E as the element type. These are the same two locations where the overloaded `PrintArray` methods of Fig. 25.1 specified Integer, Double or Char as the array element type. The remainder of `PrintArray` is identical to the version in Fig. 25.1.

Good Programming Practice 25.1

According to msdn.microsoft.com/library/en-us/dndotnet/html/BestPractices.asp, it is recommended that type parameters be specified as individual capital letters. Typically, a type parameter that represents the type of an element in an array (or other collection) is named E for "element" or T for "type."

As in Fig. 25.1, the program in Fig. 25.3 begins by declaring and initializing six-element Integer array integerArray (line 6), seven-element Double array doubleArray (line 7) and five-element Char array charArray (line 8). Then each array is output by calling

PrintArray (lines 11, 13 and 15)—once with argument integerArray, once with argument doubleArray and once with argument charArray.

When the compiler encounters a method call, such as line 11, it analyzes the set of methods (both non-generic and generic) that might match the method call, looking for a method that matches the call exactly. If there are no exact matches, the compiler picks the best match. If there are no matching methods, or if there is more than one best match, the compiler generates an error. The complete details of method-call resolution can be found in Section 11.8.1 of the Visual Basic Language Specification version 8.0, which can be downloaded from:

```
http://go.microsoft.com/fwlink/?LinkId=62990
```

For line 11, the compiler determines that an exact match occurs if the type parameter E in lines 19 and 20 of method PrintArray's declaration is replaced with the type of the elements in the method call's argument integerArray (i.e., Integer). Then the compiler sets up a call to PrintArray with Integer as the *type argument* for the type parameter E. This is known as the *type inferencing* process. The same process is repeated for the calls to method PrintArray in lines 13 and 15.

Common Programming Error 25.2

If the compiler cannot find a single non-generic or generic method declaration that is a best match for a method call, or if there are multiple best matches, a compilation error occurs.

You can also use *explicit type arguments* to indicate the exact type that should be used to call a generic function. For example, line 11 could be written as

```
PrintArray(Of Integer)(integerArray)  ' call Integer version
```

In the preceding method call, the first set of parentheses contains the explicit type argument Integer that should be used to replace type parameter E in lines 19 and 20 of method PrintArray's declaration.

The compiler also determines whether the operations performed on the method's type parameters can be applied to elements of the type stored in the array argument. The only operation performed on the array elements in this example is to output the String representation of the elements. Line 21 calls ToString on the current array element being processed. Since all objects have a ToString method, the compiler is satisfied that line 21 performs a valid operation for any array element.

By declaring PrintArray as a generic method in Fig. 25.3, we eliminated the need for the overloaded methods of Fig. 25.1, saving 18 lines of code and creating a reusable method that can output the string representations of the elements of *any* array, not just arrays of Integer, Double or Char elements.

25.4 Type Constraints

In this section, we present a generic Maximum method that determines and returns the largest of its three arguments (all of the same type). The generic method in this example uses the type parameter to declare both the method's return type and its parameters. Normally, when comparing values to determine which one is greater, you would use the > operator.

However, this operator is not overloaded for use with every type that is built into the FCL or that might be defined by extending the FCL types. Generic code is restricted to performing operations that are guaranteed to work for every possible type. Thus, an expression like variable1 < variable2 is not allowed unless the compiler can ensure that the operator < is provided for every type that will ever be used in the generic code. Similarly, you cannot call a method on a generic-type variable unless the compiler can ensure that all types that will ever be used in the generic code support that method.

IComparable(Of T) Interface

It is possible to compare two objects of the same type if that type implements the generic interface IComparable(Of T) from namespace System. A benefit of implementing this interface is that IComparable(Of T) objects can be used with the sorting and searching methods of classes in the System.Collections.Generic namespace—we discuss these methods in Chapter 26, Collections. The structures in the FCL that correspond to the primitive types (such as Int32 for primitive type Integer) all implement this interface. Types that implement IComparable(Of T) must declare a CompareTo method for comparing objects. For example, if we have two Integers, integer1 and integer2, they can be compared with the expression:

```
integer1.CompareTo(integer2)
```

Method CompareTo must return 0 if the objects are equal, a negative integer if integer1 is less than integer2 or a positive integer if integer1 is greater than integer2. It is the responsibility of the programmer who declares a type that implements IComparable(Of T) to declare method CompareTo such that it compares the contents of two objects of that type and returns the appropriate result.

Specifying Type Constraints

Even though IComparable objects can be compared, they cannot be used with generic code by default, because not all types implement interface IComparable(Of T). We can, however, restrict the types that can be used with a generic method or class to ensure that they meet certain requirements. This feature—known as a *type constraint*—limits the type arguments that can be supplied to a particular type parameter. Figure 25.4 declares method Maximum (lines 16–31) with a type constraint that requires each of the method's arguments to be of type IComparable(Of T). This restriction is important because not all objects can be compared. However, all IComparable(Of T) objects are guaranteed to have a CompareTo method that can be used in method Maximum to determine the largest of its three arguments.

Generic method Maximum uses type parameter T as the return type of the method (line 17), as the type of method parameters x, y and z (line 17), and as the type of local variable max (line 18). Generic method Maximum specifies the type constraint for type parameter T in its type parameter list in line 16. In this case, the type parameter list (Of T As IComparable(Of T)) indicates that this method requires the type arguments to implement interface IComparable(Of T). If no type constraint is specified, the default type constraint is Object.

Visual Basic provides several kinds of type constraints. A *class constraint* indicates that the type argument must be an object of a specific base class or one of its subclasses. An *interface constraint* indicates that the type argument's class must implement a specific interface. The type constraint in line 16 is an example of an interface constraint, because

```vb
1  ' Fig 25.4: MaximumTest.vb
2  ' Generic method maximum returns the largest of three objects.
3  Module MaximumTest
4     Sub Main()
5        Console.WriteLine("Maximum of {0}, {1} and {2} is {3}" & _
6           vbCrLf, 3, 4, 5, Maximum(3, 4, 5))
7        Console.WriteLine("Maximum of {0}, {1} and {2} is {3}" & _
8           vbCrLf, 6.6, 8.8, 7.7, Maximum(6.6, 8.8, 7.7))
9        Console.WriteLine("Maximum of {0}, {1} and {2} is {3}" & _
10          vbCrLf, "pear", "apple", "orange", _
11          Maximum("pear", "apple", "orange"))
12    End Sub ' Main
13
14    ' generic function determines the
15    ' largest of the IComparable objects
16    Public Function Maximum(Of T As IComparable(Of T)) _
17       (ByVal x As T, ByVal y As T, ByVal z As T) As T
18       Dim max As T = x ' assume x is initially the largest
19
20       ' compare y with max
21       If y.CompareTo(max) > 0 Then
22          max = y ' y is the largest so far
23       End If
24
25       ' compare z with max
26       If z.CompareTo(max) > 0 Then
27          max = z ' z is the largest
28       End If
29
30       Return max ' return largest object
31    End Function ' Maximum
32 End Module ' MaximumTest
```

```
Maximum of 3, 4 and 5 is 5

Maximum of 6.6, 8.8 and 7.7 is 8.8

Maximum of pear, apple and orange is pear
```

Fig. 25.4 | Generic method `Maximum` with a type constraint on its type parameter.

`IComparable(Of T)` is an interface. You can specify that the type argument must be a reference type or a value type by using the *reference type constraint* (**Class**) or the *value type constraint* (**Structure**), respectively. Finally, you can specify a **New** *constraint* to indicate that the generic code can use operator `New` to create new objects of the type represented by the type parameter. If a type parameter is specified with a `New` constraint, the type argument's class must be a concrete class. Also, the class must provide a `Public` parameterless or default constructor to ensure that objects of the class can be created without passing constructor arguments; otherwise, a compilation error occurs.

It is possible to apply *multiple constraints* to a type parameter. To do so, simply provide a comma-separated list of constraints in the type parameter list. If you have a class constraint, reference type constraint or value type constraint, it must be listed first—only one of these types of constraints can be used for each type parameter. Interface constraints (if any) are listed next. The New constraint is listed last (if there is one).

Analyzing the Code
Method Maximum assumes that its first argument (x) is the largest and assigns it to local variable max (line 18). Next, lines 21–23 determine whether y is greater than max. The condition invokes y's CompareTo method to compare y to max. If y is greater than max, then y is assigned to variable max (line 22). Similarly, lines 26–28 determine whether z is greater than max. If so, line 27 assigns z to max. Then line 30 returns max to the caller.

In Main (lines 4–12), line 6 calls Maximum with the integers 3, 4 and 5. Generic method Maximum is a match for this call, but its arguments must implement interface IComparable(Of T) to ensure that they can be compared. Type Integer is a synonym for Structure Int32, which implements interface IComparable(Of Integer). Thus, Integers (and other primitive types) are valid arguments to method Maximum.

Line 8 passes three Double arguments to Maximum. Again, this is allowed because primitive type Double is a synonym for the FCL's Double Structure, which implements IComparable(Of Double). Line 11 passes Maximum three Strings, which are also IComparable(Of String) objects. Note that we intentionally placed the largest value in a different position in each method call (lines 6, 8 and 11) to show that the generic method always finds the maximum value, regardless of its position in the argument list and regardless of the inferred type argument.

25.5 Overloading Generic Methods

Generic methods can be overloaded. A class can provide two or more generic methods with the same name but different method parameters. For example, we could provide a second version of generic method PrintArray (Fig. 25.3) with the additional parameters lowIndex and highIndex that specify the portion of the array to output. A generic method can also be overloaded by another generic method with the same method name and a different number of type parameters, or by a generic method with different numbers of type parameters and method parameters.

A generic method can be overloaded by non-generic methods that have the same method name and number of parameters. When the compiler encounters a method call, it searches for the method declaration that most precisely matches the method name and the argument types specified in the call. For example, generic method PrintArray of Fig. 25.3 could be overloaded with a version specific to Strings that outputs the Strings in neat, tabular format. If the compiler cannot match a method call to either a non-generic method or a generic method, or if there is ambiguity due to multiple possible matches, the compiler generates an error. Generic methods can also be overloaded by non-generic methods that have the same method name but a different number of method parameters.

25.6 Generic Classes

The concept of a data structure (e.g., a stack) that contains data elements can be understood independently of the element type it manipulates. A generic class provides a means for describing a class's capabilities in a type-independent manner. You can then instantiate type-specific objects of the generic class. This capability is an opportunity for software reusability.

Once you have a generic class, you can use a simple, concise notation to indicate the actual type(s) that should be used in place of the class's type parameter(s). At compilation time, the compiler ensures the type safety of your code, and the runtime system replaces type parameters with actual arguments to enable your client code to interact with the generic class.

One generic Stack class, for example, could be the basis for creating many Stack classes (e.g., "Stack of Double," "Stack of Integer," "Stack of Char," "Stack of Employee"). Figure 25.5 presents a generic Stack class declaration. A generic class declaration is similar to a non-generic class declaration, except that the class name is followed by a type parameter list (line 3). Type parameter E represents the element type the Stack will manipulate. As with generic methods, the type parameter list of a generic class can have one or more type parameters separated by commas. Type parameter E is used throughout the Stack class declaration (Fig. 25.5) to represent the element type. Class Stack declares variable elements as an array of type E (line 5). This array (created at line 15 or 17) will store the Stack's elements. [*Note:* This example implements a Stack as an array. As you have seen in Chapter 24, Data Structures, Stacks also are commonly implemented as linked lists.]

```vb
1    ' Fig. 25.5: Stack.vb
2    ' Generic class Stack
3    Public Class Stack(Of E)
4       Private top As Integer ' location of the top element
5       Private elements() As E ' array that stores Stack elements
6
7       ' parameterless constructor creates a Stack of the default size
8       Public Sub New()
9          MyClass.New(10) ' default stack size 10 elements
10      End Sub ' New
11
12      ' constructor creates a Stack of the specified number of elements
13      Public Sub New(ByVal stackSize As Integer)
14         If stackSize > 0 Then ' validate stackSize
15            elements = New E(stackSize - 1) {} ' create stackSize elements
16         Else
17            elements = New E(9) {} ' create 10 elements
18         End If
19
20         top = -1 ' Stack initially empty
21      End Sub ' New
22
23      ' push element onto the Stack; if successful, return true
24      ' otherwise, throw FullStackException
25      Public Sub Push(ByVal pushValue As E)
26         If top = elements.Length - 1 Then ' Stack is full
27            Throw New FullStackException(String.Format( _
28               "Stack is full, cannot push {0}", pushValue))
29         End If
```

Fig. 25.5 | Generic class Stack declaration. (Part 1 of 2.)

```
30
31            top += 1 ' increment top
32            elements(top) = pushValue ' place pushValue on Stack
33        End Sub ' Push
34
35        ' return the top element if not empty
36        ' else throw EmptyStackException
37        Public Function Pop() As E
38            If top = -1 Then ' Stack is empty
39                Throw New EmptyStackException("Stack is empty, cannot pop")
40            End If
41
42            top -= 1 ' decrement top
43            Return elements(top + 1) ' return top value
44        End Function ' Pop
45    End Class ' Stack
```

Fig. 25.5 | Generic class `Stack` declaration. (Part 2 of 2.)

Class `Stack` has two constructors. The parameterless constructor (lines 8–10) passes the default stack size (10) to the one-argument constructor (line 9) by invoking the constructor in lines 13–21. The one-argument constructor (lines 13–21) validates the stack-Size argument and creates an array of the specified `stackSize` if it is greater than 0 or an array of 10 elements otherwise.

Method `Push` (lines 25–33) first determines whether an attempt is being made to push an element onto a full `Stack`. If so, lines 27–28 throw a `FullStackException` (declared in Fig. 25.6). If the `Stack` is not full, line 31 increments the `top` counter to indicate the new top position, and line 32 places the argument in that location of array `elements`.

Method `Pop` (lines 37–44) first determines whether an attempt is being made to pop an element from an empty `Stack`. If so, line 39 throws an `EmptyStackException` (declared in Fig. 25.7). Otherwise, line 42 decrements the `top` counter to indicate the new top position, and line 43 returns the original top element of the `Stack`.

Classes `FullStackException` (Fig. 25.6) and `EmptyStackException` (Fig. 25.7) each provide a parameterless constructor and a one-argument constructor. The parameterless

```
1    ' Fig. 25.6: FullStackException.vb
2    ' Indicates a stack is full.
3    Public Class FullStackException : Inherits ApplicationException
4        ' parameterless constructor
5        Public Sub New()
6            MyBase.New("Stack is full")
7        End Sub ' New
8
9        ' one-parameter constructor
10       Public Sub New(ByVal exception As String)
11           MyBase.New(exception)
12       End Sub ' New
13   End Class ' FullStackException
```

Fig. 25.6 | `FullStackException` class declaration.

```
 1   ' Fig. 25.7: EmptyStackException.vb
 2   ' Indicates a stack is empty
 3   Public Class EmptyStackException : Inherits ApplicationException
 4      ' parameterless constructor
 5      Public Sub New()
 6         MyBase.New("Stack is empty")
 7      End Sub ' New
 8
 9      ' one-parameter constructor
10      Public Sub New(ByVal exception As String)
11         MyBase.New(exception)
12      End Sub ' New
13   End Class ' EmptyStackException
```

Fig. 25.7 | EmptyStackException class declaration.

constructor sets the default error message, and the one-argument constructor sets a custom error message.

As with generic methods, when a generic class is compiled, the compiler performs type checking on the class's type parameters to ensure that they can be used with the code in the generic class. The constraints determine the operations that can be performed on the type parameters. The runtime system replaces the type parameters with the actual types. For class Stack (Fig. 25.5), no type constraint is specified, so the default type constraint, Object, is used. The scope of a generic class's type parameter is the entire class.

Now let's consider an application (Fig. 25.8) that uses the Stack generic class. Lines 8–9 declare variables of type Stack(Of Double) (pronounced "Stack of Double") and Stack(Of Integer) (pronounced "Stack of Integer"). The types Double and Integer are the type arguments. The compiler replaces the type parameters in the generic class with the type arguments so that the compiler can perform type checking. Method Main instantiates objects doubleStack of size 5 (line 12) and integerStack of size 10 (line 13), then calls methods TestPushDouble (lines 22–38), TestPopDouble (lines 41–58), TestPushInteger (lines 61–77) and TestPopInteger (lines 80–97) to manipulate the two Stacks in this example.

Method TestPushDouble (lines 22–38) invokes method Push to place the Double values 1.1, 2.2, 3.3, 4.4 and 5.5 stored in array doubleElements onto doubleStack. The loop in lines 29–32 terminates when the test program attempts to Push a sixth value onto doubleStack (which is full, because doubleStack can store only five elements). In this case, the method throws a FullStackException (Fig. 25.6) to indicate that the Stack is full. Lines 33–36 catch this exception, and print the message and stack-trace information (see the output of Fig. 25.8). The stack trace indicates the exception that occurred and shows that Stack method Push generated the exception in line 27 of the file Stack.vb (Fig. 25.5). The trace also shows that method Push was called by StackTest method TestPushDouble in line 31 of StackTest.vb. This information enables you to determine the methods that were on the method call stack at the time that the exception occurred. The program catches the exception, so the Visual Basic runtime environment considers the exception to have been handled, and the program can continue executing.

Method TestPopDouble (lines 41–58) invokes Stack method Pop in an infinite loop to remove all the values from the stack. Note in the output that the values are popped in last-in, first-out (LIFO) order—this, of course, is the defining characteristic of stacks. The loop in lines 49–52 continues until the stack is empty. An EmptyStackException occurs when an attempt is made to pop from the empty stack. This causes the program to proceed to the Catch block (lines 53–56) and handle the exception, so that the program can continue executing. When the test program attempts to Pop a sixth value, the doubleStack is empty, so method Pop throws an EmptyStackException.

```vbnet
 1    ' Fig. 25.8: StackTest.vb
 2    ' Stack generic class test program.
 3    Module StackTest
 4       ' create arrays of doubles and integers
 5       Dim doubleElements() As Double = {1.1, 2.2, 3.3, 4.4, 5.5, 6.6}
 6       Dim integerElements() As Integer = {1, 2, 3, 4, 5, 6, 7, 8, 9, 10, 11}
 7
 8       Dim doubleStack As Stack(Of Double) ' stack stores double objects
 9       Dim integerStack As Stack(Of Integer) ' stack stores integer objects
10
11       Sub Main()
12          doubleStack = New Stack(Of Double)(5) ' Stack of doubles
13          integerStack = New Stack(Of Integer)(10) ' Stack of integers
14
15          TestPushDouble() ' push doubles onto doubleStack
16          TestPopDouble() ' pop doubles from doubleStack
17          TestPushInteger() ' push integers onto integerStack
18          TestPopInteger() ' pop integers from integerStack
19       End Sub ' Main
20
21       ' test Push method with doubleStack
22       Sub TestPushDouble()
23          ' push elements onto stack
24          Try
25             Console.WriteLine(vbCrLf & _
26                "Pushing elements onto doubleStack")
27
28             ' push elements onto stack
29             For Each element As Double In doubleElements
30                Console.Write("{0:F1} ", element)
31                doubleStack.Push(element) ' push onto doubleStack
32             Next element
33          Catch exception As FullStackException
34             Console.Error.WriteLine()
35             Console.Error.WriteLine("Message: " & exception.Message)
36             Console.Error.WriteLine(exception.StackTrace)
37          End Try
38       End Sub ' TestPushDouble
39
40       ' test Pop method with doubleStack
41       Sub TestPopDouble()
42          ' pop elements from stack
43          Try
44             Console.WriteLine(vbCrLf & _
45                "Popping elements from doubleStack")
```

Fig. 25.8 | Generic class Stack test program. (Part 1 of 3.)

```
46
47              Dim popValue As Double ' store element removed from stack
48              ' remove all elements from Stack
49              While True
50                  popValue = doubleStack.Pop() ' pop from doubleStack
51                  Console.Write("{0:F1} ", popValue)
52              End While
53          Catch exception As EmptyStackException
54              Console.Error.WriteLine()
55              Console.Error.WriteLine("Message: " & exception.Message)
56              Console.Error.WriteLine(exception.StackTrace)
57          End Try
58      End Sub ' TestPopDouble
59
60      ' test Push method with integerStack
61      Sub TestPushInteger()
62          ' push elements onto stack
63          Try
64              Console.WriteLine(vbCrLf & _
65                  "Pushing elements onto integerStack")
66
67              ' push elements onto stack
68              For Each element As Integer In integerElements
69                  Console.Write("{0} ", element)
70                  integerStack.Push(element) ' push onto integerStack
71              Next element
72          Catch exception As FullStackException
73              Console.Error.WriteLine()
74              Console.Error.WriteLine("Message: " & exception.Message)
75              Console.Error.WriteLine(exception.StackTrace)
76          End Try
77      End Sub ' TestPushInteger
78
79      ' test Pop method with integerStack
80      Sub TestPopInteger()
81          ' pop elements from stack
82          Try
83              Console.WriteLine(vbCrLf & _
84                  "Popping elements from integerStack")
85
86              Dim popValue As Integer ' store element removed from stack
87              ' remove all elements from Stack
88              While True
89                  popValue = integerStack.Pop() ' pop from integerStack
90                  Console.Write("{0} ", popValue)
91              End While
92          Catch exception As EmptyStackException
93              Console.Error.WriteLine()
94              Console.Error.WriteLine("Message: " & exception.Message)
95              Console.Error.WriteLine(exception.StackTrace)
96          End Try
97      End Sub ' TestPopInteger
98  End Module ' StackTest
```

Fig. 25.8 | Generic class Stack test program. (Part 2 of 3.)

```
Pushing elements onto doubleStack
1.1 2.2 3.3 4.4 5.5 6.6
Message: Stack is full, cannot push 6.6
   at Stack.Stack`1.Push(E pushValue) in
      C:\examples\ch25\Fig25_05-08\Stack\Stack.vb:line 27
   at Stack.StackTest.TestPushDouble() in
      C:\examples\ch25\Fig25_05-08\Stack\StackTest.vb:line 31

Popping elements from doubleStack
5.5 4.4 3.3 2.2 1.1
Message: Stack is empty, cannot pop
   at Stack.Stack`1.Pop() in
      C:\examples\ch25\Fig25_05-08\Stack\Stack.vb:line 39
   at Stack.StackTest.TestPopDouble() in
      C:\examples\ch25\Fig25_05-08\Stack\StackTest.vb:line 50

Pushing elements onto integerStack
1 2 3 4 5 6 7 8 9 10 11
Message: Stack is full, cannot push 11
   at Stack.Stack`1.Push(E pushValue) in
      C:\examples\ch25\Fig25_05-08\Stack\Stack.vb:line 27
   at Stack.StackTest.TestPushInteger() in
      C:\examples\ch25\Fig25_05-08\Stack\StackTest.vb:line 70

Popping elements from integerStack
10 9 8 7 6 5 4 3 2 1
Message: Stack is empty, cannot pop
   at Stack.Stack`1.Pop() in
      C:\examples\ch25\Fig25_05-08\Stack\Stack.vb:line 39
   at Stack.StackTest.TestPopInteger() in
      C:\examples\ch25\Fig25_05-08\Stack\StackTest.vb:line 89
```

Fig. 25.8 | Generic class Stack test program. (Part 3 of 3.)

Method TestPushInteger (lines 61–77) invokes Stack method Push to place values onto integerStack until it is full. Method TestPopInteger (lines 80–97) invokes Stack method Pop to remove values from integerStack until it is empty. Once again, note that the values pop off in last-in, first-out (LIFO) order.

Creating Generic Methods to Test Class Stack(Of E)

The code is almost identical in methods TestPushDouble and TestPushInteger for pushing values onto a Stack(Of Double) or a Stack(Of Integer), respectively. Similarly the code is almost identical in methods TestPopDouble and TestPopInteger for popping values from a Stack(Of Double) or a Stack(Of Integer), respectively. This presents another opportunity to use generic methods. Figure 25.9 declares generic method TestPush (lines 25–42) to perform the same tasks as TestPushDouble and TestPushInteger in Fig. 25.8—that is, Push values onto a Stack(Of E). Similarly, generic method TestPop (lines 44–62) performs the same tasks as TestPopDouble and TestPopInteger in Fig. 25.8—that is, Pop values off a Stack(Of E). Except for the slight differences in the stack traces, the output of Fig. 25.9 matches the output of Fig. 25.8.

Method Main (lines 11–23) creates the Stack(Of Double) and Stack(Of Integer) objects (lines 12–13) . Lines 16–22 invoke generic methods TestPush and TestPop to test the Stack objects.

```vb
1    ' Fig 25.9: StackTest.vb
2    ' Stack generic class test program.
3    Module StackTest
4       ' create arrays of doubles and integers
5       Dim doubleElements() As Double = {1.1, 2.2, 3.3, 4.4, 5.5, 6.6}
6       Dim integerElements() As Integer = {1, 2, 3, 4, 5, 6, 7, 8, 9, 10, 11}
7
8       Dim doubleStack As Stack(Of Double) ' stack stores double objects
9       Dim integerStack As Stack(Of Integer) ' stack stores integer objects
10
11      Sub Main()
12         doubleStack = New Stack(Of Double)(5) ' Stack of doubles
13         integerStack = New Stack(Of Integer)(10) ' Stack of integers
14
15         ' push doubles onto doubleStack
16         TestPush("doubleStack", doubleStack, doubleElements)
17         ' pop doubles from doubleStack
18         TestPop("doubleStack", doubleStack)
19         ' push integers onto integerStack
20         TestPush("integerStack", integerStack, integerElements)
21         ' pop integers from integerStack
22         TestPop("integerStack", integerStack)
23      End Sub ' Main
24
25      Sub TestPush(Of E)(ByVal name As String, ByVal stack As Stack(Of E), _
26         ByVal elements() As E)
27         ' push elements onto stack
28         Try
29            Console.WriteLine(vbCrLf & _
30               "Pushing elements onto " & name)
31
32            ' push elements onto stack
33            For Each element As E In elements
34               Console.Write("{0} ", element)
35               stack.Push(element) ' push onto stack
36            Next element
37         Catch exception As FullStackException
38            Console.Error.WriteLine()
39            Console.Error.WriteLine("Message: " & exception.Message)
40            Console.Error.WriteLine(exception.StackTrace)
41         End Try
42      End Sub ' TestPush
43
44      Sub TestPop(Of E)(ByVal name As String, ByVal stack As Stack(Of E))
45         ' pop elements off stack
46         Try
47            Console.WriteLine(vbCrLf & _
48               "Popping elements from " & name)
49
50            Dim popValue As E ' store element removed from stack
51
```

Fig. 25.9 | Passing a generic type Stack to a generic method. (Part 1 of 2.)

```
52              ' remove all elements from Stack
53              While True
54                  popValue = stack.Pop() ' pop from stack
55                  Console.Write("{0} ", popValue)
56              End While
57          Catch exception As EmptyStackException
58              Console.Error.WriteLine()
59              Console.Error.WriteLine("Message: " & exception.Message)
60              Console.Error.WriteLine(exception.StackTrace)
61          End Try
62      End Sub ' TestPop
63  End Module ' StackTest
```

```
Pushing elements onto doubleStack
1.1 2.2 3.3 4.4 5.5 6.6
Message: Stack is full, cannot push 6.6
   at Stack.Stack`1.Push(E pushValue) in
      C:\examples\ch25\Fig25_09\Stack\Stack.vb:line 27
   at Stack.StackTest.TestPush[E](String name, Stack`1 stack,
      IEnumerable`1 elements)
      in C:\examples\ch25\Fig25_09\Stack\StackTest.vb:line 35

Popping elements from doubleStack
5.5 4.4 3.3 2.2 1.1
Message: Stack is empty, cannot pop
   at Stack.Stack`1.Pop()
      in C:\examples\ch25\Fig25_09\Stack\Stack.vb:line 39
   at Stack.StackTest.TestPop[E](String name, Stack`1 stack)
      in C:\examples\ch25\Fig25_09\Stack\StackTest.vb:line 54

Pushing elements onto integerStack
1 2 3 4 5 6 7 8 9 10 11
Message: Stack is full, cannot push 11
   at Stack.Stack`1.Push(E pushValue)
      in C:\examples\ch25\Fig25_09\Stack\Stack.vb:line 27
   at Stack.StackTest.TestPush[E](String name, Stack`1 stack,
      IEnumerable`1 elements)
      in C:\examples\ch25\Fig25_09\Stack\StackTest.vb:line 35

Popping elements from integerStack
10 9 8 7 6 5 4 3 2 1
Message: Stack is empty, cannot pop
   at Stack.Stack`1.Pop()
      in C:\examples\ch25\Fig25_09\Stack\Stack.vb:line 39
   at Stack.StackTest.TestPop[E](String name, Stack`1 stack)
      in C:\examples\ch25\Fig25_09\Stack\StackTest.vb:line 54
```

Fig. 25.9 | Passing a generic type Stack to a generic method. (Part 2 of 2.)

Generic method TestPush (lines 25–42) uses type parameter E (specified in line 25) to represent the type stored in the Stack. The generic method takes three arguments—a String that represents the name of the Stack object for output purposes, an object of type Stack(Of E) and an array of type E that contains the elements that will be Pushed onto Stack(Of E). Note that the compiler enforces consistency between the type of the Stack and the elements that will be pushed onto the Stack when Push is invoked, which is the type argument of the generic method call. Generic method `TestPop` (lines 44–62) takes two arguments—a `String` that represents the name of the `Stack` object for output purposes and an object of type `Stack(Of E)`.

25.7 Notes on Generics and Inheritance

Generics can be used with inheritance in several ways:

- A generic class can be derived from a non-generic class. For example, class `Object` (which is not a generic class) is a direct or indirect base class of every generic class.

- A generic class can be derived from another generic class. Recall that in Chapter 24, the non-generic `Stack` class (Fig. 24.13) inherits from the non-generic `List` class (Fig. 24.6). You could also create a generic `Stack` class by inheriting from a generic `List` class.

- A non-generic class can be derived from a generic class with a specific type argument. For example, you can implement a non-generic `AddressList` class which inherits from a generic `List` class that stores `Address` objects.

25.8 Wrap-Up

This chapter introduced generics—one of Visual Basic's newest capabilities. We discussed how generics ensure compile-time type safety by checking for type mismatches at compile time. You learned that the compiler will allow generic code to compile only if all the operations performed on the type parameters in the generic code are supported for all the types that could be used with the generic code. You also learned how to declare generic methods and classes using type parameters. We demonstrated how to use a type constraint to specify the requirements for a type parameter—a key component of compile-time type safety. We discussed several kinds of type constraints, including reference type constraints, value type constraints, class constraints, interface constraints and `New` constraints. You learned that a `New` constraint indicates that the type argument's class must be concrete and must provide a `Public` parameterless or default constructor so that objects of that type can be created with `New`. We also discussed how to implement multiple type constraints for a type parameter. We showed how generics improve code reuse. Finally, we mentioned several ways to use generics in inheritance. In the next chapter, we demonstrate the FCL's collection classes, interfaces and algorithms. Collection classes are pre-built data structures that you can reuse in your applications, saving you time. We present both generic collections and the older, non-generic collections.

26

Collections

OBJECTIVES

In this chapter you will learn:

- The non-generic and generic collections that are provided by the .NET Framework.

- To use class `Array`'s `Shared` methods to manipulate arrays.

- To use enumerators to "walk through" a collection.

- To use the `For Each` statement with the .NET collections.

- To use non-generic collection classes `ArrayList`, `Stack` and `Hashtable`.

- To use generic collection classes `SortedDictionary` and `LinkedList`.

- To use synchronization wrappers to make collections safe in multithreaded applications.

The shapes a bright container can contain!
—Theodore Roethke

Not by age but by capacity is wisdom acquired.
—Titus Maccius Plautus

It is a riddle wrapped in a mystery inside an enigma.
—Winston Churchill

I think this is the most extraordinary collection of talent, of human knowledge, that has ever been gathered together at the White House—with the possible exception of when Thomas Jefferson dined alone.
—John F. Kennedy

26.1 Introduction

In Chapter 24, we discussed how to create and manipulate data structures. The discussion was "low level" in the sense that we painstakingly created each element of each data structure dynamically with New and modified the data structures by directly manipulating their elements and references to their elements. In this chapter, we consider the prepackaged data-structure classes provided by the .NET Framework. These classes are known as *collection classes*—they store collections of data. Each instance of one of these classes is a *collection* of items. Some examples of collections are the cards you hold in a card game, the songs stored in your computer, the real-estate records in your local registry of deeds (which map book numbers and page numbers to property owners), and the players on your favorite sports team.

Collection classes enable you to store sets of items by using existing data structures without concern for how they are implemented. This is a nice example of code reuse. You can code faster and expect excellent performance, maximizing execution speed and minimizing memory consumption. We discuss the collection interfaces that list the capabilities of each collection type, the implementation classes and the *enumerators* that "walk through" collections.

The .NET Framework provides three collections namespaces. The System.Collections namespace contains collections that store references to Objects. The *System.Collections.Generic* namespace (new to .NET 2.0) contains generic classes to store collections of specified types. (We introduced generic methods and classes in Chapter 25.) The *System.Collections.Specialized* namespace (also new to .NET 2.0) contains several collections that support specific types, such as Strings and bits. To learn more about the classes from this namespace, visit

msdn2.microsoft.com/en-us/library/system.collections.specialized.aspx

The collections in these namespaces provide standardized components that are written for broad reuse; you do not need to write your own collection classes.

26.2 Collections Overview

All the collection classes in the .NET Framework implement some combination of the collection interfaces. These interfaces declare the operations to be performed on various types of collections. Figure 26.1 lists some of the interfaces of the .NET Framework collections. All the interfaces in Fig. 26.1 are declared in namespace System.Collections and have generic analogues in namespace System.Collections.Generic. Implementations of these interfaces are provided within the framework. You may also create your own custom implementations.

Earlier versions of the .NET Framework provided the collection classes in the System.Collections and System.Collections.Specialized namespaces. These classes stored and manipulated Object references. You could store any Object in a collection. One inconvenient aspect of storing Object references occurs when retrieving them from a collection. An application normally needs to process specific types of objects, so the Object references obtained from a collection typically need to be downcast to an appropriate type.

The .NET Framework 2.0 now also includes the System.Collections.Generic namespace, which uses the generics capabilities we introduced in Chapter 25. Many of these new classes are simply generic counterparts of the classes in the System.Collections namespace. This means that you can specify the exact type that will be stored in a collection. You also receive the benefits of compile-time type checking—the compiler ensures that you are using appropriate types with your collection and, if not, issues compile-time error messages. Also, once you specify the type stored in a collection, any item you retrieve from the collection will have the correct type. This eliminates the need for explicit type casts that can

Interface	Description
ICollection	The root interface in the collections hierarchy from which interfaces IList and IDictionary inherit. Contains a Count property to determine the size of a collection and a CopyTo method for copying a collection's contents into a traditional array.
IList	An ordered collection that can be manipulated like an array. Provides an indexer for accessing elements with an Integer index. Also has methods for modifying and searching a collection, including Add, Remove, Contains and IndexOf.
IDictionary	A collection of values, indexed by an arbitrary "key" object. Provides an indexer for accessing elements with an Object index and methods for modifying the collection (e.g., Add, Remove). IDictionary property Keys contains the Objects used as indices, and property Values contains all the stored Objects.
IEnumerable	An object that can be enumerated. This interface contains exactly one method, GetEnumerator, which returns an IEnumerator object (discussed in Section 26.3). ICollection implements IEnumerable, so all collection classes implement IEnumerable directly or indirectly.

Fig. 26.1 | Some common collection interfaces.

throw InvalidCastExceptions at execution time if the referenced object is not of the appropriate type. This also eliminates the overhead of explicit casting, improving efficiency.

In this chapter, we demonstrate six collection classes—*Array*, *ArrayList*, *Stack*, *Hashtable*, generic *SortedDictionary* and generic *LinkedList*—plus built-in array capabilities. Namespace System.Collections provides several other data structures, including *BitArray* (a collection of true/false values), *Queue* and *SortedList* (a collection of key–value pairs that are sorted by key and can be accessed either by key or by index). Figure 26.2 summarizes many of the collection classes. We also discuss the IEnumerator interface. Collection classes can create enumerators that allow you to walk through the collections. Although these enumerators have different implementations, they all implement the IEnumerator interface so that they can be processed polymorphically. As we will soon see, the For Each statement is simply a convenient notation for using an enumerator. In the next section, we begin our discussion by examining enumerators and the collections capabilities for array manipulation.

Class	Implements	Description
System namespace:		
Array	IList	The base class of all conventional arrays. See Section 26.3.
System.Collections namespace:		
ArrayList	IList	Mimics a conventional array, but will grow or shrink as needed to accommodate the number of elements. See Section 26.4.1.
BitArray	ICollection	A memory-efficient array of Booleans.
Hashtable	IDictionary	An unordered collection of key–value pairs that can be accessed by key. See Section 26.4.3.
Queue	ICollection	A first-in, first-out (FIFO) collection. See Section 24.6.
SortedList	IDictionary	An ordered collection of key–value pairs that sorts data by keys and can be accessed either by key or by index.
Stack	ICollection	A last-in, first-out (LIFO) collection. See Section 26.4.2.
System.Collections.Generic namespace:		
Dictionary(Of K, E)	IDictionary(Of K, E)	A generic, unordered collection of key–value pairs that can be accessed by key.

Fig. 26.2 | Some collection classes of the .NET Framework. (Part 1 of 2.)

Class	Implements	Description
LinkedList(Of E)	ICollection(Of E)	A generic doubly linked list. See Section 26.5.2.
List(Of E)	IList(Of E)	A generic ArrayList.
Queue(Of E)	ICollection(Of E)	A generic Queue.
SortedDictionary _ (Of K, E)	IDictionary(Of K, E)	A generic Dictionary that sorts data by the keys in a binary tree. See Section 26.5.1.
SortedList(Of K, E)	IDictionary(Of K, E)	A generic SortedList.
Stack(Of E)	ICollection(Of E)	A generic Stack.

[*Note: All collection classes directly or indirectly implement* ICollection *and* IEnumerable *(or the equivalent generic interfaces* ICollection(Of E) *and* IEnumerable(Of E)*).*]

Fig. 26.2 | Some collection classes of the .NET Framework. (Part 2 of 2.)

26.3 Class Array and Enumerators

Chapter 8 presented basic array-processing capabilities. All arrays implicitly inherit from the MustInherit class Array (namespace System). Array property Length specifies the number of elements in the array. In addition, class Array provides Shared methods that provide algorithms for processing arrays. Typically, class Array overloads these methods—for example, Array method Reverse can reverse the order of the elements in an entire array or can reverse the elements in a specified range of elements in an array. For a complete list of class Array's Shared methods, visit:

> msdn2.microsoft.com/en-us/library/system.array.aspx

Figure 26.3 demonstrates several Shared methods of class Array.

```vb
1   ' Fig. 26.3: UsingArray.vb
2   ' Array class Shared methods for common array manipulations.
3   Imports System.Collections
4
5   Module UsingArray
6      Private integerValues As Integer() = {1, 2, 3, 4, 5, 6}
7      Private doubleValues As Double() = {8.4, 9.3, 0.2, 7.9, 3.4}
8      Private integerValuesCopy As Integer()
9
10     Sub Main()
11        ' defaults to zeroes
12        integerValuesCopy = New Integer(integerValues.Length - 1) {}
13
14        Console.WriteLine("Initial array values:" & vbCrLf)
15        PrintArrays() ' output initial array contents
```

Fig. 26.3 | Array class used to perform common array manipulations. (Part 1 of 3.)

```vb
16
17          ' sort doubleValues
18          Array.Sort(doubleValues)
19
20          ' copy integerValues into integerValuesCopy
21          Array.Copy(integerValues, integerValuesCopy, integerValues.Length)
22
23          Console.WriteLine(vbCrLf & _
24             "Array values after Sort and Copy:" & vbCrLf)
25          PrintArrays() ' output array contents
26          Console.WriteLine()
27
28          ' search for 5 in integerValues
29          Dim result As Integer = Array.BinarySearch(integerValues, 5)
30
31          If (result >= 0) Then
32             Console.WriteLine("5 found at element {0} in integerValues", _
33                result)
34          Else
35             Console.WriteLine("5 not found in integerValues")
36          End If
37
38          ' search for 8763 in integerValues
39          result = Array.BinarySearch(integerValues, 8763)
40
41          If (result >= 0) Then
42             Console.WriteLine("8763 found at element {0} in integerValues", _
43                 result)
44          Else
45             Console.WriteLine("8763 not found in integerValues")
46          End If
47       End Sub ' Main
48
49    ' output array content with enumerators
50    Private Sub PrintArrays()
51       Console.Write("doubleValues: ")
52
53       ' iterate through the Double array with an enumerator
54       Dim enumerator As IEnumerator = doubleValues.GetEnumerator()
55
56       While (enumerator.MoveNext())
57          Console.Write(enumerator.Current & " ")
58       End While
59
60       Console.Write(vbCrLf & "integerValues: ")
61
62       ' iterate through the integer array with an enumerator
63       enumerator = integerValues.GetEnumerator()
64
65       While (enumerator.MoveNext())
66          Console.Write(enumerator.Current & " ")
67       End While
68
```

Fig. 26.3 | Array class used to perform common array manipulations. (Part 2 of 3.)

```
69          Console.Write(vbCrLf & "integerValuesCopy: ")
70
71          ' iterate through the second integer array with a For Each statement
72          For Each element As Integer In integerValuesCopy
73             Console.Write(element & " ")
74          Next element
75
76          Console.WriteLine()
77       End Sub ' PrintArrays
78    End Module ' UsingArray
```

```
Initial array values:

doubleValues: 8.4 9.3 0.2 7.9 3.4
integerValues: 1 2 3 4 5 6
integerValuesCopy: 0 0 0 0 0 0

Array values after Sort and Copy:

doubleValues: 0.2 3.4 7.9 8.4 9.3
integerValues: 1 2 3 4 5 6
integerValuesCopy: 1 2 3 4 5 6

5 found at element 4 in integerValues
8763 not found in integerValues
```

Fig. 26.3 | Array class used to perform common array manipulations. (Part 3 of 3.)

The Imports statement in line 3 enables us to use the classes and interfaces of namespace System.Collections (such as interface IEnumerator, which we discuss shortly). A reference to the assembly for this namespace is implicitly included in every application, so we do not need to add any new references to the project file. Class Array is in namespace System, which is implicitly imported.

Our test class declares three array variables (lines 6–8). The first two lines initialize integerValues and doubleValues to an Integer and Double array, respectively. Variable integerValuesCopy is intended to demonstrate Array's Copy method, so it is declared, but does not yet refer to an array.

Line 12 initializes integerValuesCopy to an Integer array with the same length as array integerValues. Line 15 calls the PrintArrays method (lines 50–77) to output the initial contents of all three arrays. We discuss the PrintArrays method shortly. We can see from the output of Fig. 26.3 that each element of array integerValuesCopy is initialized to the default value 0.

Line 18 uses Shared Array method *Sort* to sort array doubleValues. When this method returns, the array contains its original elements sorted in ascending order.

Line 21 uses Shared Array method *Copy* to copy elements from array integerValues to array intValuesCopy. The first argument is the array to copy (integerValues), the second argument is the destination array (integerValuesCopy) and the third argument is an Integer representing the number of elements to copy (integerValues.Length specifies all elements).

Lines 29 and 39 invoke Shared Array method *BinarySearch* to perform binary searches on array integerValues. Method BinarySearch receives the *sorted* array to search and the key for which to search. The method returns the index in the array at which it finds the key (or a negative number otherwise). Note that BinarySearch assumes that it receives a sorted array.

Common Programming Error 26.1

Passing an unsorted array to BinarySearch is a logic error—the value returned is undefined.

The PrintArrays method (lines 50–77) uses class Array's methods to loop though each array. Recall that Array implements the **IEnumerable** interface. All arrays inherit implicitly from Array, so both the Integer() and Double() array types implement IEnumerable interface method **GetEnumerator**, which returns an enumerator that can iterate over the collection. In line 54, the GetEnumerator method obtains an enumerator for array doubleValues. Interface **IEnumerator** (which all enumerators implement) defines methods **MoveNext** and **Reset** and property **Current**. MoveNext moves the enumerator to the next element in the collection. The first call to MoveNext positions the enumerator at the first element of the collection. MoveNext returns True if there is at least one more element in the collection; otherwise, the method returns False. Method Reset positions the enumerator before the first element of the collection. Methods MoveNext and Reset throw an **InvalidOperationException** if the contents of the collection are modified in any way after the enumerator is created. Property Current returns the object at the current location in the collection.

Common Programming Error 26.2

If a collection is modified after an enumerator is created for it, the enumerator immediately becomes invalid—a method called with the enumerator after this point throws an Invalid-OperationException. For this reason, enumerators are said to be "fail fast."

When an enumerator is returned by the GetEnumerator method in line 54, it is initially positioned *before* the first element in Array doubleValues. Then, when line 56 calls MoveNext in the first iteration of the loop, the enumerator advances to the first element in doubleValues. The loop in lines 56–58 iterates over the elements until the enumerator passes the end of doubleValues and MoveNext returns False. Each iteration of the loop uses the enumerator's Current property to obtain and output the current array element. Lines 63–67 iterate over array integerValues.

Note that PrintArrays is called twice (lines 15 and 25), so GetEnumerator is called twice on doubleValues. The GetEnumerator method (lines 54 and 63) always returns an enumerator positioned before the first element. Also note that the IEnumerator property Current is read only. Enumerators cannot be used to modify the contents of collections, only to obtain the contents.

The For Each statement in lines 72–74 iterates over the collection elements. The For Each statement implicitly obtains an enumerator via the GetEnumerator method of a collection and uses the enumerator's MoveNext method and Current property to traverse the collection, just as we did explicitly in lines 54–58 and lines 63–67. For this reason, we can use the For Each statement to iterate over *any* collection that implements the IEnumerable interface—not just arrays. We demonstrate this functionality in the next section when we discuss class ArrayList.

Other Shared Array methods include **Clear** (to set a range of elements to 0 or Nothing), **CreateInstance** (to create a new array of a specified type), **IndexOf** (to locate the first occurrence of an object in an array or portion of an array), *LastIndexOf* (to locate the last occurrence of an object in an array or portion of an array) and *Reverse* (to reverse the contents of an array or portion of an array).

26.4 Non-Generic Collections

The System.Collections namespace in the .NET Framework Class Library is the primary source for non-generic collections. These classes provide standard implementations of many of the data structures discussed in Chapter 24 with collections that store references of type Object. In this section, we demonstrate classes ArrayList, Stack and Hashtable.

26.4.1 Class ArrayList

In most programming languages, conventional arrays have a fixed size—they cannot grow or shrink dynamically to conform to an application's execution-time memory requirements. In some applications, this fixed-size limitation presents a problem for programmers. They must choose between using fixed-size arrays that are large enough to store the maximum number of elements the application may require, and dynamic data structures that can grow and shrink the amount of memory required to store data in response to an application's changing requirements at execution time.

The .NET Framework's *ArrayList* collection class mimics the functionality of conventional arrays and provides dynamic resizing of the collection through the class's methods. At any time, an ArrayList contains a certain number of elements less than or equal to its *capacity*—the number of elements currently reserved for the ArrayList. An application can manipulate the capacity with ArrayList property Capacity. If an ArrayList needs to grow, by default it doubles its Capacity.

Performance Tip 26.1

As with linked lists, inserting additional elements into an ArrayList whose current size is less than its capacity is a fast operation.

Performance Tip 26.2

It is a slow operation to insert an element into an ArrayList that needs to grow larger to accommodate a new element. An ArrayList that is at its capacity must have its memory reallocated and the existing values copied into it.

Performance Tip 26.3

If storage is at a premium, use method TrimToSize of class ArrayList to trim an ArrayList to its exact size. This will optimize the ArrayList's memory use. Be careful—if the application needs to insert additional elements, the process will be slower because the ArrayList must grow dynamically (trimming leaves no room for growth).

Performance Tip 26.4

The default capacity increment, doubling the size of the ArrayList, may seem to waste storage, but doubling is an efficient way for an ArrayList to grow quickly to "about the right size." This is a much more efficient use of time than growing the ArrayList by one element at a time in response to insert operations.

ArrayLists store references to Objects. All classes derive from class Object, so an ArrayList can contain objects of any reference type and boxed primitive-type values. Figure 26.4 lists some useful methods and properties of class ArrayList.

Figure 26.5 demonstrates class ArrayList and several of its methods. Class Array-List belongs to the System.Collections namespace (line 3). Lines 6–8 declare two arrays of Strings (colors and removeColors) that we will use to fill two ArrayList objects. When the application begins execution, we create an ArrayList (named list) with an initial capacity of one element (line 11). The For Each statement in lines 15–17 adds the five elements of array colors to list via ArrayList's **Add** method, so list grows to accommodate these new elements. Line 21 uses ArrayList's overloaded constructor to create a new ArrayList (named removeList) initialized with the contents of array removeColors. This constructor can initialize the contents of an ArrayList with the elements of any ICollection passed to it. Many of the collection classes have such a constructor. Note that the constructor call in line 21 initializes ArrayList removeList in a manner similar to lines 15–17.

Method or property	Description
Add	Adds an Object to the ArrayList and returns an Integer specifying the index at which the Object was added.
Capacity	Property that gets and sets the number of elements for which space is currently reserved in the ArrayList.
Clear	Removes all the elements from the ArrayList.
Contains	Returns True if the specified Object is in the ArrayList; otherwise, returns False.
Count	Read-only property that gets the number of elements stored in the ArrayList.
IndexOf	Returns the index of the first occurrence of the specified Object in the ArrayList.
Insert	Inserts an Object at the specified index.
Remove	Removes the first occurrence of the specified Object.
RemoveAt	Removes an Object at the specified index.
RemoveRange	Removes a specified number of elements starting at a specified index in the ArrayList.
Sort	Sorts the ArrayList.
TrimToSize	Sets the Capacity of the ArrayList to the number of elements the ArrayList currently contains (Count).

Fig. 26.4 | Some methods and properties of class ArrayList.

```vb
1    ' Fig. 26.5: ArrayListTest.vb
2    ' Using class ArrayList.
3    Imports System.Collections
4
5    Module ArrayListTest
6       Private colors As String() = _
7          {"MAGENTA", "RED", "WHITE", "BLUE", "CYAN"}
8       Private removeColors As String() = {"RED", "WHITE", "BLUE"}
9
10      Sub Main()
11         Dim list As New ArrayList(1) ' initial capacity of 1
12
13         ' add the elements of the colors array
14         ' to the ArrayList list
15         For Each color As String In colors
16            list.Add(color) ' add color to the ArrayList list
17         Next color
18
19         ' add elements in the removeColors array to
20         ' the ArrayList removeList with the ArrayList constructor
21         Dim removeList As New ArrayList(removeColors)
22
23         Console.WriteLine("ArrayList: ")
24         DisplayInformation(list) ' output the list
25
26         ' remove from ArrayList list the colors in removeList
27         RemoveColorNames(list, removeList)
28
29         Console.WriteLine(vbCrLf & _
30            "ArrayList after calling RemoveColors: ")
31         DisplayInformation(list) ' output list contents
32      End Sub ' Main
33
34      ' displays information on the contents of an array list
35      Private Sub DisplayInformation(ByVal arrayList As ArrayList)
36         ' iterate through array list with a For Each statement
37         For Each element As Object In arrayList
38            Console.Write("{0} ", element) ' invokes ToString
39         Next element
40
41         ' display the size and capacity
42         Console.WriteLine(vbCrLf & "Size = {0}; Capacity = {1}", _
43            arrayList.Count, arrayList.Capacity)
44
45         Dim index As Integer = arrayList.IndexOf("BLUE")
46
47         If index <> -1 Then
48            Console.WriteLine("The array list contains BLUE at index {0}.", _
49               index)
50         Else
51            Console.WriteLine("The array list does not contain BLUE.")
52         End If
53      End Sub ' DisplayInformation
```

Fig. 26.5 | Using class ArrayList. (Part 1 of 2.)

```
54
55        ' remove colors specified in secondList from firstList
56        Private Sub RemoveColorNames(ByVal firstList As ArrayList, _
57          ByVal secondList As ArrayList)
58          ' iterate through second ArrayList like an array
59          For count As Integer = 0 To secondList.Count - 1
60            firstList.Remove(secondList(count))
61          Next count
62        End Sub ' RemoveColors
63      End Module ' ArrayListTest
```

```
ArrayList:
MAGENTA RED WHITE BLUE CYAN
Size = 5; Capacity = 8
The array list contains BLUE at index 3.

ArrayList after calling RemoveColors:
MAGENTA CYAN
Size = 2; Capacity = 8
The array list does not contain BLUE.
```

Fig. 26.5 | Using class `ArrayList`. (Part 2 of 2.)

Line 24 calls method `DisplayInformation` (lines 35–53) to output the contents of the `list`. This method uses a `For Each` statement to traverse the elements of an `ArrayList`. As we discussed in Section 26.3, the `For Each` statement is a convenient shorthand for calling `ArrayList`'s `GetEnumerator` method and using an enumerator to traverse the elements of the collection. Also, we use an iteration variable of type `Object` because class `ArrayList` stores references to `Objects`.

We use properties **Count** and **Capacity** in lines 42–43 to display the current number of elements and the maximum number of elements that can be stored without allocating more memory to the `ArrayList`. The output of Fig. 26.5 indicates that the `ArrayList` has capacity 8—recall that an `ArrayList` doubles its capacity whenever it needs more space.

In line 45, we invoke method **IndexOf** to determine the position of the `String` "BLUE" in `arrayList` and store the result in local variable `index`. `IndexOf` returns -1 if the element is not found. Lines 47–52 determine whether `arrayList` contains "BLUE". If it does (i.e., `index` is not equal to -1), we output the `index`. `ArrayList` also provides method **Contains**, which simply returns `True` if an object is in the `ArrayList`, and `False` otherwise. Method `Contains` is preferred if we do not need the index of the element.

Performance Tip 26.5

ArrayList methods IndexOf and Contains each perform a linear search, which is a costly operation for large ArrayLists. If the ArrayList is sorted, use ArrayList method BinarySearch to perform a more efficient search. Method BinarySearch returns the index of the element, or a negative number if the element is not found.

After `DisplayInformation` returns, we call method `RemoveColorNames` (lines 56–62) with the two `ArrayLists`. Lines 59–61 iterate through `secondList`. Line 60 uses an indexer to access an `ArrayList` element by following the `ArrayList` reference name with parentheses (`()`) containing the desired element's index. An `ArgumentOutOfRangeExcep-`

tion occurs if the specified index is not both greater than 0 and less than the number of elements currently stored in the ArrayList (specified by the ArrayList's Count property).

We use the indexer to obtain each of secondList's elements, then remove each one from firstList with the *Remove* method. This method deletes a specified item from an ArrayList by performing a linear search and removing (only) the first occurrence of the specified object. All subsequent elements shift toward the beginning of the ArrayList to fill the emptied position.

After the call to RemoveColorNames, line 31 again outputs the contents of list, confirming that the elements of removeList were, indeed, removed.

26.4.2 Class Stack

The Stack class implements a stack data structure and provides much of the functionality that we defined in our own implementation in Section 24.5. Refer to that section for a discussion of stack concepts. We created a test application in Fig. 24.14 to demonstrate our StackInheritance data structure. We adapt Fig. 24.14 in Fig. 26.6 to demonstrate the .NET Framework collection class Stack.

```vb
1    ' Fig. 26.6: StackTest.vb
2    ' Demonstrating class Stack.
3    Imports System.Collections
4
5    Module StackTest
6       Sub Main()
7          Dim stack As New Stack() ' default Capacity of 10
8
9          ' create objects to store in the stack
10         Dim aBoolean As Boolean = True
11         Dim aCharacter As Char = "$"c
12         Dim anInteger As Integer = 34567
13         Dim aString As String = "hello"
14
15         ' use method Push to add items to (the top of) the stack
16         stack.Push(aBoolean)
17         PrintStack(stack)
18         stack.Push(aCharacter)
19         PrintStack(stack)
20         stack.Push(anInteger)
21         PrintStack(stack)
22         stack.Push(aString)
23         PrintStack(stack)
24
25         ' check the top element of the stack
26         Console.WriteLine("The top element of the stack is {0}" & _
27            vbCrLf, stack.Peek())
28
29         ' remove items from stack
30         Try
31            While True
32               Dim removedObject As Object = stack.Pop()
```

Fig. 26.6 | Demonstrating class Stack. (Part 1 of 2.)

```
33                    Console.WriteLine(removedObject & " popped")
34                    PrintStack(stack)
35                End While
36           Catch exception As InvalidOperationException
37              ' if exception occurs, print stack trace
38              Console.Error.WriteLine(exception)
39           End Try
40      End Sub ' Main
41
42      ' print the contents of a stack
43      Private Sub PrintStack(ByVal stack As Stack)
44          If stack.Count = 0 Then
45              ' the stack is empty
46              Console.WriteLine("stack is empty" & vbCrLf)
47          Else
48              Console.Write("The stack is: ")
49
50              ' iterate through the stack with a For Each statement
51              For Each element As Object In stack
52                  Console.Write("{0} ", element) ' invokes ToString
53              Next element
54
55              Console.WriteLine(vbCrLf)
56          End If
57      End Sub ' PrintStack
58  End Module ' StackTest
```

```
The stack is: True

The stack is: $ True

The stack is: 34567 $ True

The stack is: hello 34567 $ True

The top element of the stack is hello

hello popped
The stack is: 34567 $ True

34567 popped
The stack is: $ True

$ popped
The stack is: True

True popped
stack is empty

System.InvalidOperationException: Stack empty.
   at System.Collections.Stack.Pop()
   at StackTest.StackTest.Main() in C:\examples\ch26\Fig26_06\StackTest\
      StackTest.vb:line 32
```

Fig. 26.6 | Demonstrating class Stack. (Part 2 of 2.)

Line 3 Imports class Stack. Line 7 creates a Stack with the default initial capacity (10 elements). Class Stack has methods Push and Pop to perform the basic stack operations.

Method Push takes an Object as an argument and inserts it at the top of the Stack. If the number of items on the Stack (the Count property) is equal to the capacity at the time of the Push operation, the Stack grows to accommodate more Objects. Lines 16, 18, 20 and 22 use method Push to add four elements (a Boolean, a Char, an Integer and a String) to the stack. After each Push, we invoke method PrintStack (lines 43–57) to output the contents of the stack. Note that this non-generic Stack class can store only references to Objects, so each of the value-type items—the Boolean, the Char and the Integer—are implicitly boxed before they are added to the Stack. (Namespace System.Collections.Generic provides a generic Stack class that has many of the same methods and properties used in Fig. 26.6.)

Method PrintStack (lines 43–57) uses Stack property Count to obtain the number of elements in Stack. If the stack is not empty (i.e., Count is not equal to 0), we use a For Each statement to iterate over the stack and output its contents by implicitly invoking the ToString method of each element. The For Each statement implicitly invokes Stack's GetEnumerator method, which we could have called explicitly to traverse the stack via an enumerator.

Method **Peek** returns the value of the top stack element, but does not remove the element from the Stack. We use Peek at line 27 to obtain the top object of the Stack, then output that object, implicitly invoking the object's ToString method. An InvalidOperationException occurs if the Stack is empty when the application calls Peek.

Method Pop takes no arguments—it removes and returns the object currently on top of the Stack. An infinite loop (lines 31–35) pops objects off the stack and outputs them until the stack is empty. When the application calls Pop on the empty stack, an InvalidOperationException is thrown. The Catch block (lines 36–38) outputs the exception, implicitly invoking the InvalidOperationException's ToString method to obtain its error message and stack trace.

Common Programming Error 26.3

Attempting to Peek or Pop an empty Stack (a Stack whose Count property is 0) causes an InvalidOperationException.

Although Fig. 26.6 does not demonstrate it, class Stack also has method Contains, which returns True if the Stack contains the specified object, and returns False otherwise.

26.4.3 Class Hashtable

When an application creates objects, it needs to manage those objects efficiently. This includes storing and retrieving objects. Storing and retrieving information with arrays is efficient if some aspect of your data directly matches the key value and if the keys are unique and tightly packed. If you have 100 employees with nine-digit Social Security numbers and you want to store and retrieve employee data by using the Social Security number as a key, it would nominally require an array with 999,999,999 elements, because there are 999,999,999 unique nine-digit numbers. If you have an array that large, you could get very high performance storing and retrieving employee records by simply using the Social Security number as the array index, but it would be a massive waste of memory.

Many applications have this problem—either the keys are of the wrong type (i.e., not non-negative integers), or they are of the right type, but they are sparsely spread over a large range.

What is needed is a high-speed scheme for converting keys such as Social Security numbers and inventory part numbers to unique array indices. Then, when an application needs to store something, the scheme could convert the application key rapidly to an index and the record of information could be stored at that location in the array. Retrieval occurs the same way—once the application has a key for which it wants to retrieve the data record, the application simply applies the conversion to the key, which produces the array subscript where the data resides in the array and retrieves the data.

The scheme we describe here is the basis of a technique called *hashing*, in which we store data in a data structure called a *hash table*. Why the name? Because, when we convert a key into an array subscript, we literally scramble the bits, making a "hash" of the number. The number actually has no real significance beyond its usefulness in storing and retrieving this particular data record.

A glitch in the scheme occurs when *collisions* occur (i.e., two different keys "hash into" the same cell, or element, in the array). Since we cannot store two different data records in the same space, we need to find an alternative home for all records beyond the first that hash to a particular array subscript. One scheme for doing this is to "hash again" (i.e., to reapply the hashing transformation to the key to provide a next candidate cell in the array). The hashing process is designed to be quite random, it is assumed is that an available cell will be found with just a few hashes.

Another scheme uses one hash to locate the first candidate cell. If the cell is occupied, successive cells are searched linearly until an available cell is found. Retrieval works the same way—the key is hashed once, and the resulting cell is checked to determine whether it contains the desired data. If it does, the search is complete. If it does not, successive cells are searched linearly until the desired data is found.

The most popular solution to hash-table collisions is to have each cell of the table be a hash "bucket"—typically, a linked list of all the key–value pairs that hash to that cell. This is the solution that the .NET Framework's *Hashtable* class implements.

The *load factor* affects the performance of hashing schemes. The load factor is the ratio of the number of objects stored in the hash table to the total number of cells of the hash table. As this ratio gets higher, the chance of collisions increases.

Performance Tip 26.6

*The load factor in a hash table is a classic example of a **space/time trade-off**: By increasing the load factor, we get better memory utilization, but the application runs slower due to increased hashing collisions. By decreasing the load factor, we get better application speed because of reduced hashing collisions, but we get poorer memory utilization because a larger portion of the hash table remains empty.*

The .NET Framework provides class Hashtable to enable you to easily employ hashing in applications. A *hash function* performs a calculation that determines where to place data in the hash table. The hash function is applied to the key in a key–value pair of objects. Class Hashtable can accept any Object as a key. For this reason, class Object defines method GetHashCode, which all classes inherit. Most classes that are candidates to be used as keys in a hash table override this method to provide one that performs efficient hash code calculations for a specific type. For example, a String has a hash code calculation that is based on the contents of the String. Figure 26.7 uses a Hashtable to count the number of occurrences of each word in a String.

Lines 4–5 contain Imports statements for the System.Text.RegularExpressions namespace (for class Regex, discussed in Chapter 16) and the System.Collections namespace (for class Hashtable). Class HashtableTest declares three methods. Method CollectWords (lines 17–40) inputs a String and returns a Hashtable in which each value stores the number of times that word appears in the String and the word is used as the key. Method DisplayHashtable (lines 43–54) displays in column format the Hashtable passed to it. The Main method (lines 8–14) invokes CollectWords (line 10), then passes the Hashtable returned by CollectWords to DisplayHashtable (line 13).

```vb
1   ' Fig. 26.7: HashtableTest.vb
2   ' Application counts the number of occurrences of each word in a String
3   ' and stores them in a hash table.
4   Imports System.Text.RegularExpressions
5   Imports System.Collections
6
7   Module HashtableTest
8      Sub Main()
9         ' create hash table based on user input
10        Dim table As Hashtable = CollectWords()
11
12        ' display hash table content
13        DisplayHashtable(table)
14     End Sub ' Main
15
16     ' create hash table from user input
17     Private Function CollectWords() As Hashtable
18        Dim table As New Hashtable() ' create a new hash table
19
20        Console.WriteLine("Enter a string: ") ' prompt for user input
21        Dim input As String = Console.ReadLine() ' get input
22
23        ' split input text into tokens
24        Dim words As String() = Regex.Split(input, "\s+")
25
26        ' processing input words
27        For Each word As String In words
28           Dim wordKey As String = word.ToLower() ' get word in lowercase
29
30           ' if the hash table contains the word
31           If table.ContainsKey(wordKey) Then
32              table(wordKey) = Convert.ToInt32(table(wordKey)) + 1
33           Else
34              ' add new word with a count of 1 to hash table
35              table.Add(wordKey, 1)
36           End If
37        Next
```

Fig. 26.7 | Application counts the number of occurrences of each word in a String and stores this information in a hash table. (Part 1 of 2.)

```
38
39          Return table
40       End Function ' CollectWords
41
42       ' display hash table content
43       Private Sub DisplayHashtable(ByVal table As Hashtable)
44          Console.WriteLine(vbCrLf & "Hashtable contains:" & _
45             vbCrLf & "{0,-12}{1,-12}", "Key:", "Value:")
46
47          ' generate output for each key in hash table
48          ' by iterating through the Keys property with a For Each statement
49          For Each key As Object In table.Keys
50             Console.WriteLine("{0,-12}{1,-12}", key, table(key))
51          Next
52
53          Console.WriteLine(vbCrLf & "size: {0}", table.Count)
54       End Sub ' DisplayHashtable
55    End Module ' HashtableTest
```

```
Enter a string:
As idle as a painted ship upon a painted ocean

Hashtable contains:
Key:        Value:
painted     2
a           2
upon        1
as          2
ship        1
idle        1
ocean       1

size: 7
```

Fig. 26.7 | Application counts the number of occurrences of each word in a String and stores this information in a hash table. (Part 2 of 2.)

Method CollectWords (lines 17–40) initializes local variable table with a new Hashtable (line 18) that has a default initial capacity of 0 elements and a default maximum load factor of 1.0. When the number of items in the Hashtable becomes greater than the number of cells times the load factor, the capacity is increased automatically. (This implementation detail is invisible to clients of the class.) Lines 20–21 prompt the user and input a String. We use Shared method Split of class Regex in line 24 to divide the String into words using whitespace characters as delimiters. This creates an array of "words," which we then store in local variable words.

The For Each statement in lines 27–37 iterates through the elements of array words. Each word is converted to lowercase with String method *ToLower*, then stored in variable wordKey (line 28). Line 31 calls Hashtable method *ContainsKey* to determine whether the word is in the hash table (and thus has occurred previously in the String). If the Hashtable does not contain an entry for the word, line 35 uses Hashtable method Add to create a new entry in the hash table, with the lowercase word as the key and an object containing

1 as the value. Note that autoboxing occurs when the application passes the Integer value 1 to method Add, because the hash table stores both the key and value as references to Objects.

Common Programming Error 26.4

Using the Add method to add a key that already exists in the hash table causes an ArgumentException.

If the word is already a key in the hash table, line 32 uses the Hashtable's indexer to obtain and set the key's associated value (the word count) in the hash table. We first downcast the value from an Object to an Integer. This unboxes the value so that we can increment it by 1. We then use the indexer to store the key's associated value. The incremented value is implicitly reboxed so that it can be stored in the hash table.

Invoking the Get accessor of a Hashtable indexer with a key that does not exist in the hash table returns a Nothing reference. Using the Set accessor with a key that does not exist in the hash table creates a new entry, as if you had used the Add method.

Line 39 returns the hash table to the Main method, which then passes it to method DisplayHashtable (lines 43–54), which displays all the entries. This method uses read-only property **Keys** (line 49) to get an ICollection that contains all the keys. Because ICollection extends IEnumerable, we can use this collection in the For Each statement in lines 49–51 to iterate over the keys of the hash table. This loop accesses and outputs each key and its value in a field width of -12. The negative field width indicates that the output should be left justified. Note that a hash table is not sorted, so the key–value pairs are not displayed in any particular order. Line 53 uses Hashtable property **Count** to get the number of key–value pairs in the Hashtable.

Lines 49–51 could also have used the For Each statement with the Hashtable object itself, rather than the Keys property. If you use a For Each statement with a Hashtable object, the iteration variable will be of type **DictionaryEntry**. The enumerator of a Hashtable (or any other class that implements **IDictionary**) uses the DictionaryEntry structure to store key–value pairs. This structure provides properties Key and Value for retrieving the key and value of the current element. If you do not need the key, class Hashtable also provides a read-only **Values** property that gets an ICollection of all the values stored in the Hashtable.

Problems with Non-Generic Collections

In the word-counting application in Fig. 26.7, our Hashtable stores its keys and data as Object references, even though we store only String keys and Integer values by convention. This results in some awkward code. For example, line 32 was forced to unbox and box the Integer data stored in the Hashtable every time it incremented the count for a particular key. This is inefficient. A similar problem occurs in lines 49 and 50—the iteration variable of the For Each statement is an Object reference. If we need to use any of its String-specific methods, we need an explicit downcast.

This can cause subtle bugs. Suppose we decide to improve the readability of Fig. 26.7 by using the indexer's Set accessor instead of the Add method to add a key–value pair in line 41, but accidentally type:

```
table(wordKey) = wordKey ' initialize to 1
```

This statement creates a new entry with a String key and String value instead of an Integer value of 1. Although the application will compile correctly, this is clearly incorrect. If a word appears twice, line 32 will try to downcast this String to an Integer, causing an InvalidCastException at execution time. The error that appears at execution time will indicate that the problem is in line 32, where the exception occurred, *not* in line 35. This makes the error more difficult to find and debug, especially in large software applications where the exception may occur in a different file—and even in a different assembly.

In Chapter 25, we introduced generics. In the next two sections, we demonstrate how to use generic collections, which can prevent the problem we just discussed.

26.5 Generic Collections

The System.Collections.Generic namespace in the FCL is a new addition for .NET 2.0. This namespace contains generic classes that allow us to create collections of specific types. As you saw in Fig. 26.2, many of the classes are simply generic versions of non-generic collections. A few classes implement new data structures. In this section, we demonstrate generic collections SortedDictionary and LinkedList.

26.5.1 Generic Class SortedDictionary

A *dictionary* is the general term for a collection of key–value pairs. A hash table is one way to implement a dictionary. The .NET Framework provides several implementations of dictionaries, both generic and non-generic (all of which implement the IDictionary interface in Fig. 26.1). The application in Fig. 26.8 is a modification of Fig. 26.7 that uses

```
1    ' Fig. 26.8: SortedDictionaryTest.vb
2    ' Application counts the number of occurrences of each word in a String
3    ' and stores them in a generic sorted dictionary.
4    Imports System.Text.RegularExpressions
5    Imports System.Collections.Generic
6
7    Module StoredDictionaryTest
8       Sub Main()
9          ' create sorted dictionary based on user input
10         Dim dictionary As SortedDictionary(Of String, Integer) = _
11            CollectWords()
12
13         ' display sorted dictionary content
14         DisplayDictionary(dictionary)
15      End Sub ' Main
16
17      ' create sorted dictionary from user input
18      Private Function CollectWords() As SortedDictionary(Of String, Integer)
19         ' create a new sorted dictionary
20         Dim dictionary As New SortedDictionary(Of String, Integer)()
21
22         Console.WriteLine("Enter a string: ") ' prompt for user input
```

Fig. 26.8 | Application counts the number of occurrences of each word in a String and stores them in a generic sorted dictionary. (Part 1 of 2.)

```
23          Dim input As String = Console.ReadLine() ' get input
24
25          ' split input text into tokens
26          Dim words As String() = Regex.Split(input, "\s+")
27
28          ' processing input words
29          For Each word As String In words
30             Dim wordKey As String = word.ToLower() ' get word in lowercase
31
32             ' if the dictionary contains the word
33             If dictionary.ContainsKey(wordKey) Then
34                dictionary(wordKey) += 1
35             Else
36                ' add new word with a count of 1 to the dictionary
37                dictionary.Add(wordKey, 1)
38             End If
39          Next
40
41          Return dictionary
42       End Function ' CollectWords
43
44       ' display dictionary content
45       Private Sub DisplayDictionary(Of K, V)( _
46          ByVal dictionary As SortedDictionary(Of K, V))
47
48          Console.WriteLine(vbCrLf & "Sorted dictionary contains:" _
49             & vbCrLf & "{0,-12}{1,-12}", "Key:", "Value:")
50
51          ' generate output for each key in the sorted dictionary
52          ' by iterating through the Keys property with a For Each statement
53          For Each key As K In dictionary.Keys
54             Console.WriteLine("{0,-12}{1,-12}", key, dictionary(key))
55          Next
56
57          Console.WriteLine(vbCrLf & "size: {0}", dictionary.Count)
58       End Sub ' DisplayDictionary
59    End Module ' StoredDictionaryTest
```

```
Enter a string:
We few, we happy few, we band of brothers

Sorted dictionary contains:
Key:        Value:
band        1
brothers    1
few,        2
happy       1
of          1
we          3

size: 6
```

Fig. 26.8 | Application counts the number of occurrences of each word in a `String` and stores them in a generic sorted dictionary. (Part 2 of 2.)

the generic class ***SortedDictionary***. Generic class SortedDictionary stores its key–value pairs in a binary search tree. We discuss binary trees in depth in Section 24.7. As the class name suggests, the entries in SortedDictionary are sorted in the tree by key. When the key implements generic interface IComparable, the SortedDictionary uses the results of IComparable method CompareTo to sort the keys. Note that despite these implementation details, we use the same Public methods, properties and indexers with classes Hashtable and SortedDictionary in the same ways. In fact, except for the generic-specific syntax, Fig. 26.8 looks remarkably similar to Fig. 26.7. That is the beauty of object-oriented programming.

Line 5 contains an Imports statement for the System.Collections.Generic namespace, which contains class SortedDictionary. The generic class SortedDictionary takes two type arguments—the first specifies the type of key (i.e., String), and the second specifies the type of value (i.e., Integer). We replaced the word Hashtable in lines 10, 18 and 20 with SortedDictionary(Of String, Integer) to create a dictionary of Integer values keyed with Strings. Now the compiler can check and notify us if we attempt to store an object of the wrong type in the dictionary. Also, because the compiler now knows that the data structure contains Integer values, there is no longer any need for the downcast in line 34. This allows line 34 to use the much more concise += notation.

Method DisplayDictionary (lines 45–58) has been modified to be completely generic. It takes type parameters K and V. These parameters are used in line 46 to indicate that DisplayDictionary takes a SortedDictionary with keys of type K and values of type V. We use type parameter K again in line 53 as the type of the iteration variable. This use of generics is a marvelous example of code reuse. If we decide to change the application to count the number of times each character appears in a String, method Display-Dictionary could receive an argument of type SortedDictionary(Of Char, Integer) without modification.

Common Programming Error 26.5

Invoking the Get accessor of a SortedDictionary indexer with a key that does not exist in the collection causes a KeyNotFoundException. This behavior is different from that of the Hashtable indexer's Get accessor, which would return Nothing.

26.5.2 Generic Class LinkedList

Chapter 24 began our discussion of data structures with the concept of a linked list. We end our discussion with the .NET Framework's generic ***LinkedList*** class. The LinkedList class is a doubly-linked list—we can navigate the list both backwards and forwards with nodes of generic class ***LinkedListNode***. Each node contains property ***Value*** and read-only properties ***Previous*** and ***Next***. The Value property's type matches LinkedList's single type parameter because it contains the data stored in the node. The Previous property gets a reference to the preceding node in the linked list (or Nothing if the node is the first in the list). Similarly, the Next property gets a reference to the subsequent reference in the linked list (or Nothing if the node is the last in the list). We demonstrate a few linked list manipulations in Fig. 26.9.

Line 3 Imports the LinkedList class. Lines 13–21 create LinkedLists list1 and list2 of Strings and fill them with the contents of arrays colors and colors2, respectively. Note that LinkedList is a generic class that has one type parameter for which we

```vb
 1    ' Fig. 26.9: LinkedListTest.vb
 2    ' Using LinkedLists.
 3    Imports System.Collections.Generic
 4
 5    Module LinkedListTest
 6       Private colors As String() = _
 7          {"black", "yellow", "green", "blue", "violet", "silver"}
 8       Private colors2 As String() = _
 9          {"gold", "white", "brown", "blue", "gray"}
10
11       ' set up and manipulate LinkedList objects
12       Sub Main()
13          Dim list1 As New LinkedList(Of String)()
14
15          ' add elements to first linked list
16          For Each color As String In colors
17             list1.AddLast(color)
18          Next
19
20          ' add elements to second linked list via constructor
21          Dim list2 As New LinkedList(Of String)(colors2)
22
23          Concatenate(list1, list2) ' concatenate list2 onto list1
24          PrintList(list1) ' print list1 elements
25
26          Console.WriteLine(vbCrLf & _
27             "Converting strings in list1 to uppercase" & vbCrLf)
28          ToUppercaseStrings(list1) ' convert to uppercase string
29          PrintList(list1) ' print list1 elements
30
31          Console.WriteLine(vbCrLf & _
32             "Deleting strings between BLACK and BROWN" & vbCrLf)
33          RemoveItemsBetween(list1, "BLACK", "BROWN")
34
35          PrintList(list1) ' print list1 elements
36          PrintReversedList(list1) ' print list in reverse order
37       End Sub ' Main
38
39       ' output list contents
40       Private Sub PrintList(Of E)(ByVal list As LinkedList(Of E))
41          Console.WriteLine("Linked list: ")
42
43          For Each value As E In list
44             Console.Write("{0} ", value)
45          Next value
46
47          Console.WriteLine()
48       End Sub ' PrintList
49
50       ' concatenate the second list on the end of the first list
51       Private Sub Concatenate(Of E)(ByVal list1 As LinkedList(Of E), _
52          ByVal list2 As LinkedList(Of E))
```

Fig. 26.9 | Using LinkedLists. (Part 1 of 3.)

```
53         ' concatenate lists by copying element values
54         ' in order from the second list to the first list
55         For Each value As E In list2
56            list1.AddLast(value) ' add new node
57         Next value
58      End Sub ' Concatenate
59
60      ' locate string objects and convert to uppercase
61      Private Sub ToUppercaseStrings(ByVal list As LinkedList(Of String))
62         ' iterate over the list by using the nodes
63         Dim currentNode As LinkedListNode(Of String) = list.First
64
65         While currentNode IsNot Nothing
66            currentNode.Value = _
67               currentNode.Value.ToUpper() ' convert to uppercase
68            currentNode = currentNode.Next ' get next node
69         End While
70      End Sub ' ToUppercaseStrings
71
72      ' delete list items between two given items
73      Private Sub RemoveItemsBetween(Of E)(ByVal list As LinkedList(Of E), _
74         ByVal startItem As E, ByVal endItem As E)
75         ' get the nodes corresponding to the start and end item
76         Dim currentNode As LinkedListNode(Of E) = list.Find(startItem)
77         Dim endNode As LinkedListNode(Of E) = list.Find(endItem)
78
79         ' remove items after the start item
80         ' until we find the last item or the end of the linked list
81         While currentNode.Next IsNot Nothing And _
82            Not currentNode.Next.Equals(endNode)
83            ' remove next node
84            list.Remove(currentNode.Next)
85         End While
86      End Sub ' RemoveItemsBetween
87
88      ' print reversed list
89      Private Sub PrintReversedList(Of E)(ByVal list As LinkedList(Of E))
90         Console.WriteLine("Reversed List:")
91
92         ' iterate over the list by using the nodes
93         Dim currentNode As LinkedListNode(Of E) = list.Last
94
95         While currentNode IsNot Nothing
96            Console.Write("{0} ", currentNode.Value)
97            currentNode = currentNode.Previous ' get previous node
98         End While
99
100        Console.WriteLine()
101     End Sub ' PrintReversedList
102  End Module ' LinkedListTest
```

Fig. 26.9 | Using LinkedLists. (Part 2 of 3.)

```
Linked list:
black yellow green blue violet silver gold white brown blue gray

Converting strings in list1 to uppercase

Linked list:
BLACK YELLOW GREEN BLUE VIOLET SILVER GOLD WHITE BROWN BLUE GRAY

Deleting strings between BLACK and BROWN

Linked list:
BLACK BROWN BLUE GRAY
Reversed List:
GRAY BLUE BROWN BLACK
```

Fig. 26.9 | Using LinkedLists. (Part 3 of 3.)

specify the type argument String in this example (lines 13 and 21). We demonstrate two ways to fill the lists. In lines 16–18, we use the For Each statement and method **AddLast** to fill list1. The AddLast method creates a new LinkedListNode and appends it to the end of the list. There is also an AddFirst method that inserts a node at the beginning of the list. Line 21 invokes the LinkedList constructor that takes a parameter of type IEnumerable(Of String). All arrays implicitly inherit from the generic interfaces IList and IEnumerable with the type of the array as the type argument, so the String array colors2 implements IEnumerable(Of String). The type parameter of this generic IEnumerable matches the type parameter of the generic LinkedList object. This constructor call (line 21) copies the contents of the array colors2 to list2.

Line 23 calls generic method Concatenate (lines 51–58) to append all elements of list2 to the end of list1. Line 24 calls method PrintList (lines 40–48) to output list1's contents. Line 28 calls method ToUppercaseStrings (lines 61–70) to convert each String element to uppercase, then line 29 calls PrintList again to display the modified Strings. Line 33 calls method RemoveItemsBetween (lines 73–86) to remove the elements between "BLACK" and "BROWN", but not including either. Line 35 outputs the list again, then line 36 invokes method PrintReversedList (lines 89–101) to print the list in reverse order.

Generic method Concatenate (lines 51–58) iterates over list2 with a For Each statement and calls method AddLast to append each value to the end of list1. The loop uses the LinkedList class's enumerator to obtain the values of the nodes. The loop creates a new node in list1 for each node in list2. One LinkedListNode cannot be a member of more than one LinkedList. Any attempt to add a node from one LinkedList to another generates an InvalidOperationException. If you want the same data to belong to more than one LinkedList, you must make a copy of the node for each list.

Generic method PrintList (lines 40–48) also uses a For Each statement to iterate over the values in a LinkedList and output them. Method ToUppercaseStrings (lines 61–70) takes a linked list of Strings and converts each String to uppercase. This method replaces the Strings stored in the list, so we cannot use an enumerator (via a For Each statement) as in the previous two methods. Recall that enumerators cannot be used to modify the values of elements in a collection. Instead, we obtain the first LinkedListNode via the First property (line 63), then loop through the list (lines 65–69). Each iteration of the loop obtains and updates the contents of currentNode via property Value, using

String method *ToUpper* to create an uppercase version of color. At the end of each iteration, we move the current node to the next node in the list by assigning to currentNode the node obtained by its own Next property (line 68). The Next property of the last node of the list returns Nothing, so when the loop iterates past the end of the list, the loop exits.

Note that it does not make sense to declare ToUppercaseStrings as a generic method, because it uses the String-specific methods of the values in the nodes. Methods Print-List (lines 40–48) and Concatenate (lines 51–58) do not need to use any String-specific methods, so they can be declared with generic type parameters to promote maximal code reuse.

Generic method RemoveItemsBetween (lines 73–86) removes a range of items between two nodes. Lines 76–77 obtain the two "boundary" nodes of the range by using method *Find*. This method performs a linear search, and returns the first node that contains a value equal to the passed argument. Method Find returns Nothing if the value is not found. We store the node preceding the range in local variable currentNode and the node following the range in endNode.

The loop in lines 81–85 removes all the elements between currentNode and endNode. On each iteration of the loop, we remove the node following currentNode by invoking method *Remove* (line 84). Method Remove takes a LinkedListNode, deletes that node from the LinkedList and fixes the references of the surrounding nodes. During the Remove call, currentNode's Next property is assigned the node *following* the removed node, and that node's Previous property is assigned currentNode. The loop continues until there are no nodes left between currentNode and endNode, or until currentNode is the last node in the list. (There is also an overloaded version of method Remove that performs a linear search for the specified value and removes the first node in the list that contains it.)

Method PrintReversedList (lines 89–101) prints the list backwards by navigating the nodes manually. Line 93 obtains the last element of the list via the *Last* property and stores it in currentNode. The loop in lines 95–98 iterates through the list backwards by moving the currentNode reference to the previous node at the end of each iteration, then exits when it moves past the beginning of the list. Note how similar this code is to lines 65–69, which iterated through the list from the beginning to the end.

26.6 Synchronized Collections

In Chapter 15, we discussed multithreading. Most of the non-generic collections are unsynchronized by default, so they can operate efficiently when multithreading is not required. Because they are unsynchronized, however, concurrent access to a collection by multiple threads could cause logic errors in your programs. To prevent potential threading problems, synchronization wrappers are provided for many of the collections that might be accessed by multiple threads. A *wrapper* object receives method calls, adds thread synchronization (to prevent concurrent access to the collection) and passes the calls to the wrapped collection object. Most of the non-generic collection classes in the .NET Framework provide Shared method *Synchronized*, which returns a synchronized wrapper object for the specified object. For example, the following code creates a synchronized ArrayList:

```
Dim unsafeList As New ArrayList()
Dim threadSafeList As ArrayList = ArrayList.Synchronized(unsafeList)
```

The collections in the .NET Framework do not all provide wrappers for thread safety. Some do not guarantee any thread safety at all. Many of the generic collections are inherently thread-safe for reading, but not for writing. To determine whether a particular class supports thread-safe processing, check its documentation in the .NET Framework class library reference (msdn2.microsoft.com/en-us/library/ms306608.aspx).

Also recall that when a collection is modified, any enumerator returned previously by the GetEnumerator method becomes invalid and will throw an exception if its methods are invoked. Other threads may change the collection, so using an enumerator is not thread safe—thus, the For Each statement is not thread safe either. If you use an enumerator or a For Each statement in a multithreaded application, you should use the SyncLock statement to prevent other threads from using the collection or use a Try statement to catch the InvalidOperationException.

26.7 Wrap-Up

This chapter introduced the .NET Framework collection classes. You learned the hierarchy of interfaces that many of the collection classes implement. You saw how to use class Array to perform array manipulations. You learned that the System.Collections and System.Collections.Generic namespaces contain many non-generic and generic collection classes, respectively. We presented the non-generic classes ArrayList, Stack and Hashtable as well as the generic classes SortedDictionary and LinkedList. In doing so, we discussed data structures in greater depth. We discussed dynamically expanding collections, hashing schemes, and two implementations of a dictionary. You saw the advantages of generic collections over their non-generic counterparts.

You also learned how to use enumerators to traverse these data structures and obtain their contents. We demonstrated the For Each statement with many of the classes of the FCL, and explained that this works by using enumerators "behind the scenes" to traverse the collections. Finally, we discussed some of the issues that you should consider when using collections in multithreaded applications.

Operator Precedence Chart

Operators are shown in decreasing order of precedence from top to bottom with each level of precedence separated by a horizontal line. Visual Basic operators associate from left to right.

Operator	Type
TypeOf	type comparison
^	exponentiation
+ -	unary plus unary minus
* /	multiplication division
\	integer division
Mod	modulus
+ -	addition subtraction
&	concatenation
<< >>	bitwise left shift bitwise right shift

Fig. A.1 | Operator precedence chart. (Part 1 of 2.)

Operator	Type
= <> < <= > >= Like Is	relational is equal to relational is not equal to relational less than relational less than or equal to relational greater than relational greater than or equal to pattern matching reference comparison
Not	logical negation
And AndAlso	logical AND without short-circuit evaluation logical AND with short-circuit evaluation
Or OrElse	logical inclusive OR without short-circuit evaluation logical inclusive OR with short-circuit evaluation
Xor	logical exclusive OR

Fig. A.1 | Operator precedence chart. (Part 2 of 2.)

B

Number Systems

Here are only numbers ratified.
—William Shakespeare

Nature has some sort of arithmetic-geometrical coordinate system, because nature has all kinds of models. What we experience of nature is in models, and all of nature's models are so beautiful.
It struck me that nature's system must be a real beauty, because in chemistry we find that the associations are always in beautiful whole numbers—there are no fractions.

—Richard Buckminster Fuller

OBJECTIVES

In this appendix you will learn:

- To understand basic number systems concepts, such as base, positional value and symbol value.

- To understand how to work with numbers represented in the binary, octal and hexadecimal number systems.

- To abbreviate binary numbers as octal numbers or hexadecimal numbers.

- To convert octal numbers and hexadecimal numbers to binary numbers.

- To convert back and forth between decimal numbers and their binary, octal and hexadecimal equivalents.

- To understand binary arithmetic and how negative binary numbers are represented using two's complement notation.

B.1 Introduction

In this appendix, we introduce the key number systems that programmers use, especially when they are working on software projects that require close interaction with machine-level hardware. Projects like this include operating systems, computer networking software, compilers, database systems and applications requiring high performance.

When we write an integer such as 227 or –63 in a program, the number is assumed to be in the decimal (base 10) number system. The digits in the decimal number system are 0, 1, 2, 3, 4, 5, 6, 7, 8 and 9. The lowest digit is 0 and the highest digit is 9—one less than the base of 10. Internally, computers use the binary (base 2) number system. The binary number system has only two digits, namely 0 and 1. Its lowest digit is 0 and its highest digit is 1—one less than the base of 2.

As you will see, binary numbers tend to be much longer than their decimal equivalents. Programmers who work in assembly languages and in high-level languages that enable programmers to reach down to the machine level, find it cumbersome to work with binary numbers. So two other number systems—the octal number system (base 8) and the hexadecimal number system (base 16)—are popular primarily because they make it convenient to abbreviate binary numbers.

In the octal number system, the digits range from 0 to 7. Because both the binary number system and the octal number system have fewer digits than the decimal number system, their digits are the same as the corresponding digits in decimal.

The hexadecimal number system poses a problem because it requires 16 digits—a lowest digit of 0 and a highest digit with a value equivalent to decimal 15 (one less than the base of 16). By convention, the letters A through F represent the hexadecimal digits corresponding to decimal values 10 through 15. Thus, in hexadecimal, you can have numbers like 876 consisting solely of decimal-like digits, numbers like 8A55F consisting of digits and letters and numbers like FFE consisting solely of letters. Occasionally, a hexadecimal number spells a common word such as FACE or FEED—this can appear strange to programmers accustomed to working with numbers. The digits of the binary, octal, decimal and hexadecimal number systems are summarized in Figs. B.1 and B.2.

Each of these number systems uses positional notation—each position in which a digit is written has a different positional value. For example, in the decimal number 937 (the 9, the 3 and the 7 are referred to as symbol values), we say that the 7 is written in the ones position, the 3 is written in the tens position and the 9 is written in the hundreds position. Note that each of these positions is a power of the base (base 10) and that these powers begin at 0 and increase by 1 as we move left in the number (Fig. B.3).

For longer decimal numbers, the next positions to the left would be the thousands position (10 to the 3rd power), the ten-thousands position (10 to the 4th power), the hun-

Binary digit	Octal digit	Decimal digit	Hexadecimal digit
0	0	0	0
1	1	1	1
	2	2	2
	3	3	3
	4	4	4
	5	5	5
	6	6	6
	7	7	7
		8	8
		9	9
			A (decimal value of 10)
			B (decimal value of 11)
			C (decimal value of 12)
			D (decimal value of 13)
			E (decimal value of 14)
			F (decimal value of 15)

Fig. B.1 | Digits of the binary, octal, decimal and hexadecimal number systems.

Attribute	Binary	Octal	Decimal	Hexadecimal
Base	2	8	10	16
Lowest digit	0	0	0	0
Highest digit	1	7	9	F

Fig. B.2 | Comparing the binary, octal, decimal and hexadecimal number systems.

Positional values in the decimal number system			
Decimal digit	9	3	7
Position name	Hundreds	Tens	Ones
Positional value	100	10	1
Positional value as a power of the base (10)	10^2	10^1	10^0

Fig. B.3 | Positional values in the decimal number system.

dred-thousands position (10 to the 5th power), the millions position (10 to the 6th power), the ten-millions position (10 to the 7th power) and so on.

In the binary number 101, the rightmost 1 is written in the ones position, the 0 is written in the twos position and the leftmost 1 is written in the fours position. Each position is a power of the base (base 2) and that these powers begin at 0 and increase by 1 as we move left in the number (Fig. B.4). So, $101 = 1 * 2^2 + 0 * 2^1 + 1 * 2^0 = 4 + 0 + 1 = 5$.

For longer binary numbers, the next positions to the left would be the eights position (2 to the 3rd power), the sixteens position (2 to the 4th power), the thirty-twos position (2 to the 5th power), the sixty-fours position (2 to the 6th power) and so on.

In the octal number 425, we say that the 5 is written in the ones position, the 2 is written in the eights position and the 4 is written in the sixty-fours position. Note that each of these positions is a power of the base (base 8) and that these powers begin at 0 and increase by 1 as we move left in the number (Fig. B.5).

For longer octal numbers, the next positions to the left would be the five-hundred-and-twelves position (8 to the 3rd power), the four-thousand-and-ninety-sixes position (8 to the 4th power), the thirty-two-thousand-seven-hundred-and-sixty-eights position (8 to the 5th power) and so on.

In the hexadecimal number 3DA, we say that the A is written in the ones position, the D is written in the sixteens position and the 3 is written in the two-hundred-and-fifty-sixes position. Note that each of these positions is a power of the base (base 16) and that these powers begin at 0 and increase by 1 as we move left in the number (Fig. B.6).

For longer hexadecimal numbers, the next positions to the left would be the four-thousand-and-ninety-sixes position (16 to the 3rd power), the sixty-five-thousand-five-hundred-and-thirty-sixes position (16 to the 4th power) and so on.

Positional values in the binary number system			
Binary digit	1	0	1
Position name	Fours	Twos	Ones
Positional value	4	2	1
Positional value as a power of the base (2)	2^2	2^1	2^0

Fig. B.4 | Positional values in the binary number system.

Positional values in the octal number system			
Decimal digit	4	2	5
Position name	Sixty-fours	Eights	Ones
Positional value	64	8	1
Positional value as a power of the base (8)	8^2	8^1	8^0

Fig. B.5 | Positional values in the octal number system.

Positional values in the hexadecimal number system			
Decimal digit	3	D	A
Position name	Two-hundred-and-fifty-sixes	Sixteens	Ones
Positional value	256	16	1
Positional value as a power of the base (16)	16^2	16^1	16^0

Fig. B.6 | Positional values in the hexadecimal number system.

B.2 Abbreviating Binary Numbers as Octal and Hexadecimal Numbers

The main use for octal and hexadecimal numbers in computing is for abbreviating lengthy binary representations. Figure B.7 highlights the fact that lengthy binary numbers can be expressed concisely in number systems with higher bases than the binary number system.

Decimal number	Binary representation	Octal representation	Hexadecimal representation
0	0	0	0
1	1	1	1
2	10	2	2
3	11	3	3
4	100	4	4
5	101	5	5
6	110	6	6
7	111	7	7
8	1000	10	8
9	1001	11	9
10	1010	12	A
11	1011	13	B
12	1100	14	C
13	1101	15	D
14	1110	16	E
15	1111	17	F
16	10000	20	10

Fig. B.7 | Decimal, binary, octal and hexadecimal equivalents.

A particularly important relationship that both the octal number system and the hexadecimal number system have to the binary system is that the bases of octal and hexadecimal (8 and 16 respectively) are powers of the base of the binary number system (base 2). Consider the following 12-digit binary number and its octal and hexadecimal equivalents. See if you can determine how this relationship makes it convenient to abbreviate binary numbers in octal or hexadecimal. The answer follows the numbers.

Binary number	Octal equivalent	Hexadecimal equivalent
100011010001	4321	8D1

To see how the binary number converts easily to octal, simply break the 12-digit binary number into groups of three consecutive bits each and write those groups over the corresponding digits of the octal number as follows:

100	011	010	001
4	3	2	1

Note that the octal digit you have written under each group of three bits corresponds precisely to the octal equivalent of that 3-digit binary number, as shown in Fig. B.7.

The same kind of relationship can be observed in converting from binary to hexadecimal. Break the 12-digit binary number into groups of four consecutive bits each and write those groups over the corresponding digits of the hexadecimal number as follows:

1000	1101	0001
8	D	1

Notice that the hexadecimal digit you wrote under each group of four bits corresponds precisely to the hexadecimal equivalent of that 4-digit binary number as shown in Fig. B.7.

B.3 Converting Octal and Hexadecimal Numbers to Binary Numbers

In the previous section, you learned how to convert binary numbers to their octal and hexadecimal equivalents by forming groups of binary digits and simply rewriting them as their equivalent octal digit values or hexadecimal digit values. This process may be used in reverse to produce the binary equivalent of a given octal or hexadecimal number.

For example, the octal number 653 is converted to binary simply by writing the 6 as its 3-digit binary equivalent 110, the 5 as its 3-digit binary equivalent 101 and the 3 as its 3-digit binary equivalent 011 to form the 9-digit binary number 110101011.

The hexadecimal number FAD5 is converted to binary simply by writing the F as its 4-digit binary equivalent 1111, the A as its 4-digit binary equivalent 1010, the D as its 4-digit binary equivalent 1101 and the 5 as its 4-digit binary equivalent 0101 to form the 16-digit 1111101011010101.

B.4 Converting from Binary, Octal or Hexadecimal to Decimal

We are accustomed to working in decimal, and therefore it is often convenient to convert a binary, octal, or hexadecimal number to decimal to get a sense of what the number is "really" worth. Our diagrams in Section B.1 express the positional values in decimal. To convert a number to decimal from another base, multiply the decimal equivalent of each digit by its positional value and sum these products. For example, the binary number 110101 is converted to decimal 53, as shown in Fig. B.8.

To convert octal 7614 to decimal 3980, we use the same technique, this time using appropriate octal positional values, as shown in Fig. B.9.

To convert hexadecimal AD3B to decimal 44347, we use the same technique, this time using appropriate hexadecimal positional values, as shown in Fig. B.10.

B.5 Converting from Decimal to Binary, Octal or Hexadecimal

The conversions in Section B.4 follow naturally from the positional notation conventions. Converting from decimal to binary, octal, or hexadecimal also follows these conventions.

Converting a binary number to decimal					
Postional values:	32	16	8	4	2	1
Symbol values:	1	1	0	1	0	1
Products:	1*32=32	1*16=16	0*8=0	1*4=4	0*2=0	1*1=1
Sum:	= 32 + 16 + 0 + 4 + 0s + 1 = 53					

Fig. B.8 | Converting a binary number to decimal.

Converting an octal number to decimal			
Positional values:	512	64	8	1
Symbol values:	7	6	1	4
Products	7*512=3584	6*64=384	1*8=8	4*1=4
Sum:	= 3584 + 384 + 8 + 4 = 3980			

Fig. B.9 | Converting an octal number to decimal.

Converting a hexadecimal number to decimal			
Postional values:	4096	256	16	1
Symbol values:	A	D	3	B
Products	A*4096=40960	D*256=3328	3*16=48	B*1=11
Sum:	= 40960 + 3328 + 48 + 11 = 44347			

Fig. B.10 | Converting a hexadecimal number to decimal.

Suppose we wish to convert decimal 57 to binary. We write the positional values of the columns right to left until we reach a column whose positional value is greater than the decimal number. We don't need that column, so we discard it. Thus, we first write:

Positional values: 64   32   16   8   4   2   1

Then we discard the column with positional value 64, leaving:

Positional values: 32   16   8   4   2   1

Next we work from the leftmost column to the right. We divide 32 into 57 and observe that there is one 32 in 57 with a remainder of 25, so we write 1 in the 32 column. We divide 16 into 25 and observe that there is one 16 in 25 with a remainder of 9 and write 1 in the 16 column. We divide 8 into 9 and observe that there is one 8 in 9 with a remainder of 1. The next two columns each produce quotients of 0 when their positional values are divided into 1, so we write 0s in the 4 and 2 columns. Finally, 1 into 1 is 1, so we write 1 in the 1 column. This yields:

Positional values:	32	16	8	4	2	1
Symbol values:	1	1	1	0	0	1

and thus decimal 57 is equivalent to binary 111001.

To convert decimal 103 to octal, we write the positional values of the columns until we reach a column whose positional value is greater than the decimal number. We do not need that column, so we discard it. Thus, we first write:

Positional values: 512   64   8   1

Then we discard the column with positional value 512, yielding:

Positional values: 64   8   1

Next we work from the leftmost column to the right. We divide 64 into 103 and observe that there is one 64 in 103 with a remainder of 39, so we write 1 in the 64 column. We divide 8 into 39 and observe that there are four 8s in 39 with a remainder of 7 and write 4 in the 8 column. Finally, we divide 1 into 7 and observe that there are seven 1s in 7 with no remainder, so we write 7 in the 1 column. This yields:

Positional values:	64	8	1
Symbol values:	1	4	7

and thus decimal 103 is equivalent to octal 147.

To convert decimal 375 to hexadecimal, we write the positional values of the columns until we reach a column whose positional value is greater than the decimal number. We do not need that column, so we discard it. Thus, we first write:

Positional values: 4096   256   16   1

Then we discard the column with positional value 4096, yielding:

Positional values: 256   16   1

Next we work from the leftmost column to the right. We divide 256 into 375 and observe that there is one 256 in 375 with a remainder of 119, so we write 1 in the 256 column. We divide 16 into 119 and observe that there are seven 16s in 119 with a remainder of 7 and write 7 in the 16 column. Finally, we divide 1 into 7 and observe that there are seven 1s in 7 with no remainder, so we write 7 in the 1 column. This yields:

```
Positional values:   256    16    1
Symbol values:        1      7     7
```

and thus decimal 375 is equivalent to hexadecimal 177.

B.6 Negative Binary Numbers: Two's Complement Notation

The discussion so far in this appendix has focused on positive numbers. In this section, we explain how computers represent negative numbers using *two's complement notation*. First we explain how the two's complement of a binary number is formed, then we show why it represents the negative value of the given binary number.

Consider a machine with 32-bit integers. Suppose

```
Dim value As Integer = 13
```

The 32-bit representation of value is

```
00000000 00000000 00000000 00001101
```

To form the negative of value we first form its *one's complement* by combining value with &H7FFFFFFF using Visual Basic's Xor operator, as in:

```
onesComplement = value Xor &H7FFFFFFF
```

Internally, onesComplement is now value with each of its bits reversed—ones become zeros and zeros become ones, as follows:

```
value:
00000000 00000000 00000000 00001101

onesComplement
11111111 11111111 11111111 11110010
```

To form the two's complement of value, we simply add 1 to value's one's complement, which produces

```
Two's complement of value:
11111111 11111111 11111111 11110011
```

Now if this is in fact equal to −13, we should be able to add it to binary 13 and obtain a result of 0. Let us try this:

```
  00000000 00000000 00000000 00001101
+ 11111111 11111111 11111111 11110011
-------------------------------------
  00000000 00000000 00000000 00000000
```

The carry bit coming out of the leftmost column is discarded and we indeed get 0 as a result. If we add the one's complement of a number to the number, the result would be all 1s. The key to getting a result of all zeros is that the twos complement is one more than the one's complement. The addition of 1 causes each column to add to 0 with a carry of 1. The carry keeps moving leftward until it is discarded from the leftmost bit, and thus the resulting number is all zeros.

Computers actually perform a subtraction, such as

```
x = a - value;
```

by adding the two's complement of value to a, as follows:

```
x = a + (onesComplement + 1);
```

Suppose a is 27 and value is 13 as before. If the two's complement of value is actually the negative of value, then adding the two's complement of value to a should produce the result 14. Let us try this:

```
a  (i.e., 27)                  00000000 00000000 00000000 00011011
+(onesComplement + 1)         +11111111 11111111 11111111 11110011
                              ------------------------------------
                               00000000 00000000 00000000 00001110
```

which is indeed equal to 14.

Using the Visual Studio 2005 Debugger

We are built to make mistakes, coded for error.
—Lewis Thomas

What we anticipate seldom occurs; what we least expect generally happens.
—Benjamin Disraeli

It is one thing to show a man that he is in error, and another to put him in possession of truth.
—John Locke

He can run but he can't hide.
—Joe Louis

And so shall I catch the fly.
—William Shakespeare

OBJECTIVES

In this appendix you will learn:

- To use the debugger to locate and correct logic errors in a program.
- To use breakpoints to pause program execution and allow you to examine the values of variables.
- To set, disable and remove breakpoints.
- To use the **Continue** command to continue execution from a breakpoint.
- To use the **Locals** window to view and modify variable values.
- To use the **Watch** window to evaluate expressions.
- To use the **Step Into**, **Step Out** and **Step Over** commands to execute a program line-by-line.
- To use the new Visual Studio 2005 debugging features Edit and Continue and Just My Code™ debugging.

C.1 Introduction

In Chapter 3, you learned that there are two types of errors—compilation errors and logic errors—and you learned how to eliminate compilation errors from your code. Logic errors, also called *bugs*, do not prevent a program from compiling successfully, but can cause a program to produce erroneous results, or terminate prematurely, when it runs. Most compiler vendors, like Microsoft, provide a tool called a *debugger*, which allows you to monitor the execution of your programs to locate and remove logic errors. A program must successfully compile before it can be used in the debugger—the debugger helps you analyze a program while it is running. The debugger allows you to suspend program execution, examine and set variable values and much more. In this appendix, we introduce the Visual Studio debugger, several of its debugging tools and new features added for Visual Studio 2005.

C.2 Breakpoints and the Continue Command

We begin by investigating *breakpoints*, which are markers that can be set at any executable line of code. When a running program reaches a breakpoint, execution pauses, allowing you to examine the values of variables to help determine whether logic errors exist. For example, you can examine the value of a variable that stores the result of a calculation to determine whether the calculation was performed correctly. You can also examine the value of an expression.

To illustrate the debugger features, we use the program in Figs. C.1 and C.2 that creates and manipulates an Account (Fig. C.1) object. This example is based on the concepts presented through Chapter 4, so it does not use features that are presented after that chapter. Execution begins in Main (lines 4–33 of Fig. C.2). Line 5 creates an Account object with an initial balance of $50.00. Account's constructor (lines 8–14 of Fig. C.1) accepts one argument, which specifies the Account's initial balance. Line 8 of Fig. C.2 outputs the initial account balance using Account property Balance. Lines 11–12 prompt the user for and input the withdrawalAmount. Lines 14–16 subtract the withdrawal amount from the Account's balanceValue using its Debit method. Lines 19–20 display the new balanceValue. Next, lines 23–32 perform similar steps to credit the account.

```vb
 1   ' Fig. C.01: Account.vb
 2   ' Account class with a constructor to initialize a customer's balance.
 3   Public Class Account
 4      ' instance variable that stores the balance
 5      Private balanceValue As Integer
 6
 7      ' constructor
 8      Public Sub New(ByVal initialBalance As Integer)
 9         ' if initialBalance is not greater than 0,
10         ' balance is still initialized to 0 by default
11         If initialBalance > 0 Then
12            Balance = initialBalance
13         End If
14      End Sub ' New
15
16      ' credit (increases) the account by amount
17      Public Sub Credit(ByVal amount As Integer)
18         Balance = Balance + amount ' add amount to balance
19      End Sub ' Credit
20
21      ' debits (decreases) the account by amount
22      Public Sub Debit(ByVal amount As Integer)
23         If amount > Balance Then
24            Console.WriteLine("Debit amount exceeded account balance.")
25         End If
26
27         If amount <= Balance Then
28            Balance = Balance - amount ' subtract amount to balance
29         End If
30      End Sub ' Debit
31
32      ' property makes balanceValue available to clients;
33      ' no validation required
34      Public Property Balance() As Integer
35         Get ' returns the account balance
36            Return balanceValue
37         End Get
38
39         Set(ByVal value As Integer) ' sets the balance value
40            balanceValue = value
41         End Set
42      End Property ' Balance
43   End Class ' Account
```

Fig. C.1 | Account class with a constructor to initialize variable balance.

```vb
 1   ' Fig. C.02 AccountTest.vb
 2   ' Create and manipulate an Account object.
 3   Module AccountTest
 4      Sub Main() ' begins execution
 5         Dim account1 As New Account(50) ' create Account object
```

Fig. C.2 | Creating and manipulating an Account object. (Part 1 of 2.)

```
6
7        ' display initial balance of each object
8        Console.WriteLine("account1 balance: " & account1.Balance)
9
10       ' obtain withdrawal input from Command Prompt
11       Console.Write("Enter withdrawal amount for account1: ")
12       Dim withdrawalAmount As Integer = Console.ReadLine()
13
14       Console.WriteLine(vbCrLf & "Subtracting " & withdrawalAmount & _
15          " from account1 balance")
16       account1.Debit(withdrawalAmount) ' subtract amount from account1
17
18       ' display balance
19       Console.WriteLine("account1 balance: " & account1.Balance)
20       Console.WriteLine()
21
22       ' obtain credit input from Command Prompt
23       Console.Write("Enter credit amount for account1: ")
24       Dim creditAmount As Integer = Console.ReadLine()
25
26       Console.WriteLine(vbCrLf & "Adding " & creditAmount & _
27          " to account1 balance")
28       account1.Credit(creditAmount) ' add amount to account1
29
30       ' display balance
31       Console.WriteLine("account1 balance: " & account1.Balance)
32       Console.WriteLine()
33    End Sub ' Main
34 End Module ' AccountTest
```

```
account1 balance: 50

Enter withdrawal amount for account1: 25

Subtracting 25 from account1 balance
account1 balance: 25

Enter credit amount for account1: 33

Adding 33 to account1 balance
account1 balance: 58
```

Fig. C.2 | Creating and manipulating an Account object. (Part 2 of 2.)

In the following steps, you will use breakpoints and various debugger commands to examine the value of the variable withdrawalAmount (declared in Fig. C.2) while the program executes.

1. *Inserting breakpoints in Visual Studio.* First, ensure that AccountTest.vb is open in the IDE's code editor. To insert a breakpoint, left click inside the *margin indicator bar* (the gray margin at the left of the code window in Fig. C.3) next to the line of code at which you wish to break, or right click that line of code and select Breakpoint > Insert Breakpoint. You can set as many breakpoints as you like.

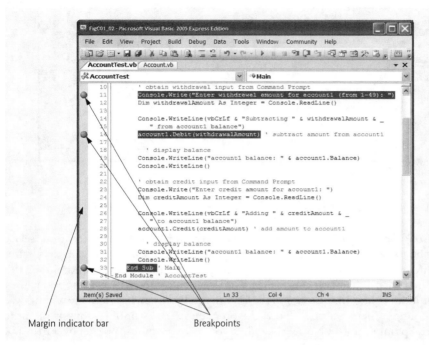

Fig. C.3 | Setting breakpoints.

Set breakpoints at lines 11, 16 and 33 of your code. A solid circle appears in the margin indicator bar where you clicked and the entire code statement is highlighted, indicating that breakpoints have been set (Fig. C.3). When the program runs, the debugger suspends execution at any line that contains a breakpoint. The program then enters ***break mode***. Breakpoints can be set before running a program, in break mode and during execution.

2. ***Beginning the debugging process.*** After setting breakpoints in the code editor, select **Build > Build Account** to compile the program, then select **Debug > Start Debugging** (or press the *F5* key) to begin the debugging process. While debugging a console application, the Command Prompt window appears (Fig. C.4), allowing program interaction (input and output).

3. ***Examining program execution.*** Program execution pauses at the first breakpoint (line 11), and the IDE becomes the active window (Fig. C.5). The *yellow arrow* to the left of line 11 indicates that this line contains the next statement to execute. The IDE also highlights the line as well.

Fig. C.4 | **Account** program running.

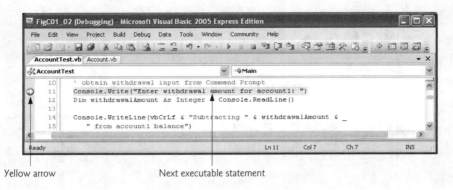

Fig. C.5 | Program execution suspended at the first breakpoint.

4. *Using the Continue command to resume execution.* To resume execution, select **Debug > Continue** (or press the *F5* key). The **Continue command** will execute the statements from the current point in the program to the next breakpoint or the end of Main, whichever comes first. The program continues executing and pauses for input at line 12. Enter 25 in the Command Prompt window as the withdrawal amount. When you press *Enter*, the program executes until it stops at the next breakpoint (line 16). Notice that when you place the mouse pointer over the variable name withdrawalAmount, its value is displayed in a *Quick Info box* (Fig. C.6). As you'll see, this can help you spot logic errors in your programs.

5. *Continuing program execution.* Use the **Debug > Continue** command to execute line 16. The program then asks for you to input a credit (deposit) amount. Enter 33, then press *Enter*. The program displays the result of its calculation (Fig. C.7).

6. *Disabling a breakpoint.* To *disable a breakpoint*, right click a line of code in which the breakpoint has been set and select **Breakpoint > Disable Breakpoint**. The disabled breakpoint is indicated by a hollow circle (Fig. C.8)—the breakpoint can be re-enabled by right clicking the line marked by the hollow circle and selecting **Breakpoint > Enable Breakpoint**.

Fig. C.6 | *QuickInfo* box displays value of variable depositAmount.

Fig. C.7 | Program output.

Fig. C.8 | Disabled breakpoint.

7. *Removing a breakpoint.* To remove a breakpoint that you no longer need, right click the line of code on which the breakpoint has been set and select **Breakpoint > Delete Breakpoint**. You also can remove a breakpoint by clicking the circle in the margin indicator bar.

8. *Finishing program execution.* Select **Debug > Continue** to execute the program to completion. Then delete all the breakpoints.

C.3 The Locals and Watch Windows

In the preceding section, you learned that the *Quick Info* feature allows you to examine the value of a variable. In this section, you will learn how to use the **Locals** *window* to assign new values to variables while your program is running. You will also use the **Watch** *window* to examine the values of expressions.

1. *Inserting breakpoints.* Set a breakpoint at line 16 (Fig. C.9) in the source code by left clicking in the margin indicator bar to the left of line 16. Use the same technique to set breakpoints at lines 19 and 20 as well.

2. *Starting debugging.* Select **Debug > Start Debugging**. Type 25 at the **Enter withdrawal amount for account1:** prompt (Fig. C.10) and press *Enter* so that the program reads the value you just entered. The program executes until the breakpoint at line 16.

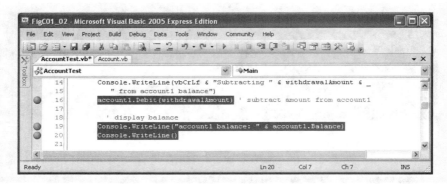

Fig. C.9 | Setting breakpoints at lines 16, 19 and 20.

Fig. C.10 | Entering the deposit amount before the breakpoint is reached.

3. *Suspending program execution.* When the program reaches line 16, Visual Studio suspends program execution and switches the program into break mode (Fig. C.11). At this point, the statement in line 12 (Fig. C.2) has input the withdrawalAmount that you entered (25), the statement in lines 14–15 has output that the program is subtracting that amount from the account1 balance and the statement in line 16 is the next statement that will execute.

4. *Examining data.* Once the program has entered break mode, you can explore the values of your local variables using the debugger's **Locals** window. To view the **Locals** window, select **Debug > Windows > Locals**. Click the plus box to the left of account1 in the **Name** column of the **Locals** window (Fig. C.12). This allows you

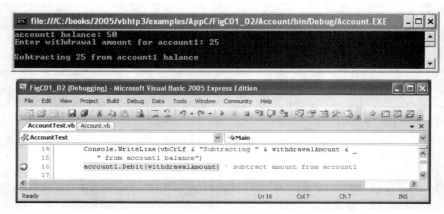

Fig. C.11 | Program execution pauses when debugger reaches the breakpoint at line 16.

Locals			
Name	Value		Type
⊟ ● account1	{Account.Account}		Account.A
🔧 Balance	50		Integer
🔧 balanceValue	50		Integer
● creditAmount	0		Integer
● withdrawalAmount	25		Integer

Fig. C.12 | Examining variable `depositAmount`.

to view each of `account1`'s instance variable values individually, including the value for `balanceValue` (50). Note that the **Locals** window displays properties of a class as data, which is why you see both the `Balance` property and the `balanceValue` instance variable in the **Locals** window. In addition, the current value of local variable `withdrawalAmount` (25) is also displayed.

5. ***Evaluating arithmetic and boolean expressions.*** You can evaluate arithmetic and boolean expressions using the **Watch** window. Select **Debug > Windows > Watch** to display the window (Fig. C.13). In the first row of the **Name** column (which should be blank initially), type `(withdrawalAmount + 10) * 5`, then press *Enter*. The value 175 is displayed (Fig. C.13). In the next row of the **Name** column in the **Watch** window, type `withdrawalAmount = 200`, then press *Enter*. This expression determines whether the value contained in `withdrawalAmount` is 200. Expressions containing the = symbol are `Boolean` expressions. The value returned is `False` (Fig. C.13), because `withdrawalAmount` does not currently contain the value 200.

6. ***Resuming execution.*** Select **Debug > Continue** to resume execution. Line 16 executes, subtracting the account with the withdrawal amount, and the program enters break mode again at line 19. Select **Debug > Windows > Locals**. The updated `balanceValue` instance variable and `Balance` property value are now displayed (Fig. C.14).

Evaluating an arithmetic expression

Watch			
Name	Value		Type
(withdrawalAmount + 10)*5	175		Integer
withdrawalAmount=200	False		Boolean

Evaluating a `Boolean` expression

Fig. C.13 | Examining the values of expressions.

Locals			
Name	Value		Type
⊟ ● account1	{Account.Account}		Account.A
🔧 Balance	25		Integer
🔧 balanceValue	25		Integer
● creditAmount			Integer
● withdrawalAmount	25		Integer

Updated value of the `balanceValue` variable

Fig. C.14 | Displaying the value of local variables.

7. *Modifying values.* Based on the value input by the user (25), the account balance output by the program should be 25. However, you can use the **Locals** window to change variable values during program execution. This can be valuable for experimenting with different values and for locating logic errors in programs. In the **Locals** window, click the **Value** field in the balanceValue row to select the value 25. Type 37, then press *Enter*. The debugger changes the value of balanceValue (and the Balance property as well), then displays its new value in red (Fig. C.15). Now select **Debug > Continue** to execute lines 19–20. Notice that the new value of balanceValue is displayed in the Command Prompt window.

8. *Stopping the debugging session.* Select **Debug > Stop Debugging**. Delete all breakpoints.

C.4 Controlling Execution Using the Step Into, Step Over, Step Out and Continue Commands

Sometimes you will need to execute a program line-by-line to find and fix logic errors. Stepping through a portion of your program this way can help you verify that a method's code executes correctly. The commands you learn in this section allow you to execute a method line-by-line, execute all the statements of a method or execute only the remaining statements of a method (if you have already executed some statements within the method).

1. *Setting a breakpoint.* Set a breakpoint at line 16 by left clicking in the margin indicator bar (Fig. C.16).

2. *Starting the debugger.* Select **Debug > Start Debugging**. Enter the value 25 at the **Enter withdrawal amount for account1:** prompt. Program execution halts when the program reaches the breakpoint at line 16.

3. *Using the Step Into command.* The **Step Into** *command* executes the next statement in the program (the yellow highlighted line of Fig. C.17) and immediately halts. If the statement to execute is a method call, control transfers to the called method. The **Step Into** command allows you to follow execution into a method and confirm its execution by individually executing each statement inside the method. Select **Debug > Step Into** (or press *F11*) to enter the Debit method (Fig. C.18).

Value modified in the debugger

Fig. C.15 | Modifying the value of a variable.

Fig. C.16 | Setting a breakpoint in the program.

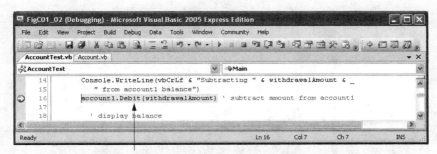

Next statement to execute is a method call

Fig. C.17 | The **Step Into** command will enter the Debit method.

Next statement to execute

Fig. C.18 | Stepping into the Debit method.

4. *Using the Step Over command.* Select **Debug > Step Over** to enter the Debit method's body and transfer control to line 23 (Fig. C.19). The ***Step Over command*** behaves like the **Step Into** command when the next statement to execute does not contain a method call or access a property. You will see how the **Step Over** command differs from the **Step Into** command in *Step 10*.

5. *Using the Step Out command.* Select **Debug > Step Out** to execute the remaining statements in the method and return control to the calling method. Often, in lengthy methods, you will want to look at a few key lines of code, then continue debugging the caller's code. The ***Step Out command*** executes the remainder of a method and returns to the caller.

6. *Setting a breakpoint.* Set a breakpoint (Fig. C.20) at line 20 of Fig. C.2. You will make use of this breakpoint in the next step.

7. *Using the Continue command.* Select **Debug > Continue** to execute until the next breakpoint is reached at line 20. This feature saves time when you do not want to step line-by-line through many lines of code to reach the next breakpoint.

Control is transferred to the next statement

Fig. C.19 | Stepping over a statement in the Credit method.

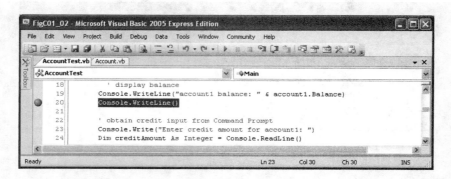

Fig. C.20 | Setting a second breakpoint in the program.

8. *Stopping the debugger.* Select **Debug > Stop Debugging** to end the debugging session.

9. *Starting the debugger.* Before we can demonstrate the next debugger feature, you must restart the debugger. Start it, as you did in *Step 2*, and enter the same value (25). The debugger pauses execution at line 16.

10. *Using the Step Over command.* Select **Debug > Step Over** (Fig. C.21). Recall that this command behaves like the **Step Into** command when the next statement to execute does not contain a method call. If the next statement to execute contains a method call, the called method executes in its entirety (without pausing execution at any statement inside the method—unless there is a breakpoint in the method), and the arrow advances to the next executable line (after the method call) in the current method. In this case, the debugger executes line 16 in Main (Fig. C.2), which calls the Debit method. Then, the debugger pauses execution at line 19, the next executable statement.

11. *Stopping the debugger.* Select **Debug > Stop Debugging**. Remove all remaining breakpoints.

C.5 Other Features

Visual Studio 2005 provides many new debugging features, that simplify the testing and debugging process. We discuss some of these features in this section.

C.5.1 Edit and Continue

The *Edit and Continue* feature allows you to make modifications or changes to your code in debug mode, then continue executing the program without having to recompile your code.

1. *Setting a breakpoint.* Set a breakpoint at line 11 in your example (Fig. C.22).

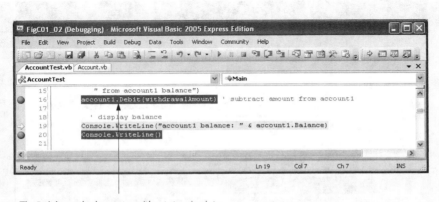

The Debit method executes without stepping into it when you select the **Step Over** command

Fig. C.21 | Using the debugger's **Step Over** command.

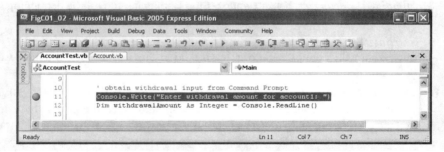

Fig. C.22 | Setting a breakpoint at line 11.

2. *Starting the debugger.* Select **Debug > Start Debugging**. When execution begins, the account1 balance is displayed. The debugger enters break mode when it reaches the breakpoint at line 11.

3. *Changing the input prompt text.* Suppose you wish to modify the input prompt text to provide the user with a range of values for variable withdrawalAmount. Rather than stopping the debugging process, add the text "(from 1-49):" to the end of "Enter withdrawal amount for account1" at line 11 in the code view window. Select **Debug > Continue**. The application prompts you for input using the updated text (Fig. C.23).

In this example, we wanted to make a change in the text for our input prompt before line 11 executes. However, if you want to make a change to a line that already executed, you must select a prior statement in your code from which to continue execution.

1. *Setting a breakpoint.* Set a breakpoint at line 14 (Fig. C.24).

Fig. C.23 | Application prompt displaying the updated text.

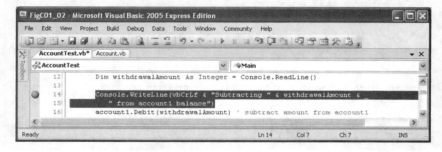

Fig. C.24 | Setting a breakpoint at line 14.

2. *Starting the debugger.* Delete the "(from 1-49)" text you just added in the previous steps. Select **Debug > Start Debugging**. When execution begins, the prompt **Enter withdrawal amount for account1:** appears. Enter the value 22 at the prompt (Fig. C.25). The debugger enters break mode at line 14 (Fig. C.25).

3. *Changing the input prompt text.* Let's say that you once again wish to modify the input prompt text to provide the user with a range of values for variable withdrawalAmount. Add the text "(from 1-49):" to the end of "Enter withdrawal amount for account1" in line 11 inside the code view window.

4. *Setting the next statement.* For the program to update the input prompt text correctly, you must set the execution point to a previous line of code. Right click in line 11 and select **Set Next Statement** from the menu that appears (Fig. C.26).

5. Select **Debug > Continue**. The application prompts you again for input using the updated text (Fig. C.27).

6. *Stopping the debugger.* Select **Debug > Stop Debugging**.

Certain types of change are not allowed with the Edit and Continue feature once the program begins execution. These include changing class names, adding or removing method parameters, adding public fields to a class and adding or removing methods. If a particular change that you make to your program is not allowed during the debugging process, Visual Studio displays a dialog box as shown in Fig. C.28.

C.5.2 Exception Assistant

Another new feature in Visual Studio 2005 is the Exception Assistant. You can run a program by selecting either **Debug > Start Debugging** or **Debug > Start Without Debugging**. If you select the option **Debug > Start Debugging** and the runtime environment detects uncaught exceptions, the application pauses, and a window called the **Exception Assistant** appears indicating where the exception occurred, the type of the exception and links to helpful information on handling the exception. We discuss the Exception Assistant in detail in Section 12.4.3.

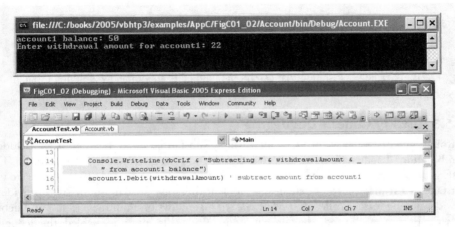

Fig. C.25 | Stopping execution at the breakpoint in line 14.

Fig. C.26 | Setting the next statement to execute.

Fig. C.27 | Program execution continues with updated prompt text.

Fig. C.28 | Dialog box stating that certain program edits are not allowed during program execution.

C.5.3 Just My Code™ Debugging

Throughout this book, we produce increasingly substantial programs that often include a combination of code written by the programmer and code generated by Visual Studio. The IDE-generated code can be difficult for novices (and even experienced programmers) to understand—fortunately, you rarely need to look at this code. Visual Studio 2005 provides a new debugging feature called *Just My Code*™, that allows programmers to test and debug only the portion of the code they have written. When this option is enabled, the debugger will always step over method calls to methods of classes that you did not write.

This feature is not available in Visual Basic 2005 Express. If you have the complete Visual Studio 2005, you can change this setting in the debugger options. Select **Tools > Options...**. In the **Options** dialog, select the **Debugging** category to view the available debugging tools and options. Then click the checkbox that appears next to the **Enable Just My Code (Managed only)** option (Fig. C.29) to enable or disable this feature.

C.5.4 Other New Debugger Features

The Visual Studio 2005 debugger offers additional new features, such as visualizers, trace-points and more, which you can learn about at msdn.microsoft.com/vstudio/express/vb/features/debug/default.aspx.

C.6 Wrap-Up

In this appendix, you learned how to enable the debugger and set breakpoints so that you can examine your code and results while a program executes. This capability enables you to locate and fix logic errors in your programs. You also learned how to continue execution after a program suspends execution at a breakpoint and how to disable and remove breakpoints.

We showed how to use the debugger's **Watch** and **Locals** windows to evaluate arithmetic and boolean expressions. We also demonstrated how to modify a variable's value during program execution so that you can see how changes in values affect your results.

You learned how to use the debugger's **Step Into** command to debug methods called during your program's execution. You saw how the **Step Over** command can be used to execute a method call without stopping the called method. You used the **Step Out** command to continue execution until the end of the current method. You also learned that the **Continue** command continues execution until another breakpoint is found or the program terminates.

Finally, we discussed new features of the Visual Studio 2005 debugger, including Edit and Continue, the Exception Assistant and Just My Code™ debugging.

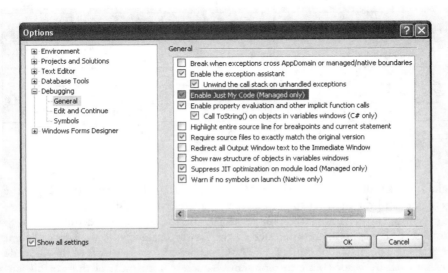

Fig. C.29 | Enabling the **Just My Code** debugging feature in Visual Studio.

ASCII Character Set

	0	1	2	3	4	5	6	7	8	9
ASCII character set										
0	nul	soh	stx	etx	eot	enq	ack	bel	bs	ht
1	lf	vt	ff	cr	so	si	dle	dc1	dc2	dc3
2	dc4	nak	syn	etb	can	em	sub	esc	fs	gs
3	rs	us	sp	!	"	#	$	%	&	'
4	(	)	*	+	,	-	.	/	0	1
5	2	3	4	5	6	7	8	9	:	;
6	<	=	>	?	@	A	B	C	D	E
7	F	G	H	I	J	K	L	M	N	O
8	P	Q	R	S	T	U	V	W	X	Y
9	Z	[	\	]	^	_	`	a	b	c
10	d	e	f	g	h	i	j	k	l	m
11	n	o	p	q	r	s	t	u	v	w
12	x	y	z	{	|	}	~	del		

Fig. D.1 | ASCII character set.

The digits at the left of the table are the left digits of the decimal equivalent (0–127) of the character code, and the digits at the top of the table are the right digits of the character code. For example, the character code for "F" is 70, and the character code for "&" is 38.

Most users of this book are interested in the ASCII character set used to represent English characters on many computers. The ASCII character set is a subset of the Unicode character set used by Visual Basic to represent characters from most of the world's languages. For more information on the Unicode character set, see Appendix E.

E

Unicode®

E.1 Introduction

The use of inconsistent character *encodings* (i.e., numeric values associated with characters) in the developing of global software products causes serious problems, because computers process information as numbers. For instance, the character "a" is converted to a numeric value so that a computer can manipulate that piece of data. Many countries and corporations have developed their own encoding systems that are incompatible with the encoding systems of other countries and corporations. For example, the Microsoft Windows operating system assigns the value 0xC0 to the character "A with a grave accent"; the Apple Macintosh operating system assigns that same value to an upside-down question mark. This results in the misrepresentation and possible corruption of data when data is not processed as intended.

In the absence of a widely-implemented universal character-encoding standard, global software developers had to *localize* their products extensively before distribution. Localization includes the language translation and cultural adaptation of content. The process of localization usually includes significant modifications to the source code (such as the conversion of numeric values and the underlying assumptions made by programmers), which results in increased costs and delays releasing the software. For example, some English-speaking programmers might design global software products assuming that a single character can be represented by one byte. However, when those products are localized for Asian markets, the programmer's assumptions are no longer valid; thus, the majority, if not the entirety, of the code needs to be rewritten. Localization is necessary with each release of a version. By the time a software product is localized for a particular market, a newer version, which needs to be localized as well, may be ready for distribution. As a result, it is cumbersome and costly to produce and distribute global software products in a market where there is no universal character-encoding standard.

In response to this situation, the *Unicode Standard*, an encoding standard that facilitates the production and distribution of software, was created. The Unicode Standard outlines a specification to produce consistent encoding of the world's characters and symbols. Software products that handle text encoded in the Unicode Standard need to be localized, but the localization process is simpler and more efficient because the numeric values need not be converted and the assumptions made by programmers about the character encoding are universal. The Unicode Standard is maintained by a nonprofit organization called the *Unicode Consortium*, whose members include Apple, IBM, Microsoft, Oracle, Sun Microsystems, Sybase and many others.

When the Consortium envisioned and developed the Unicode Standard, they wanted an encoding system that was *universal, efficient, uniform* and *unambiguous*. A universal encoding system encompasses all commonly used characters. An efficient encoding system allows text files to be parsed easily. A uniform encoding system assigns fixed values to all characters. An unambiguous encoding system represents a given character in a consistent manner. These four terms are referred to as the Unicode Standard *design basis*.

E.2 Unicode Transformation Formats

Although Unicode incorporates the limited ASCII character set (i.e., a collection of characters), it encompasses a more comprehensive character set. In ASCII each character is represented by a byte containing 0s and 1s. One byte is capable of storing the binary numbers from 0 to 255. Each character is assigned a number between 0 and 255; thus, ASCII-based systems can support only 256 characters, a tiny fraction of world's characters. Unicode extends the ASCII character set by encoding the vast majority of the world's characters. The Unicode Standard encodes all of those characters in a uniform numerical space from 0 to 10FFFF hexadecimal. An implementation will express these numbers in one of several transformation formats, choosing the one that best fits the particular application at hand.

Three such formats are in use, called *UTF-8, UTF-16* and *UTF-32*, depending on the size of the units—in bits—being used. UTF-8, a variable-width encoding form, requires one to four bytes to express each Unicode character. UTF-8 data consists of 8-bit bytes (sequences of one, two, three or four bytes depending on the character being encoded) and is well suited for ASCII-based systems, where there is a predominance of one-byte characters (ASCII represents characters as one byte). Currently, UTF-8 is widely implemented in UNIX systems and in databases.

The variable-width UTF-16 encoding form expresses Unicode characters in units of 16 bits (i.e., as two adjacent bytes, or a short integer in many machines). Most characters of Unicode are expressed in a single 16-bit unit. However, characters with values above FFFF hexadecimal are expressed with an ordered pair of 16-bit units called *surrogates*. Surrogates are 16-bit integers in the range D800 through DFFF, which are used solely for the purpose of "escaping" into higher numbered characters. Approximately one million characters can be expressed in this manner. Although a surrogate pair requires 32 bits to represent characters, it is space-efficient to use these 16-bit units. Surrogates are rare characters in current implementations. Many string-handling implementations are written in terms of UTF-16. [*Note:* Details and sample code for UTF-16 handling are available on the Unicode Consortium Web site at www.unicode.org.]

Implementations that require significant use of rare characters or entire scripts encoded above FFFF hexadecimal should use UTF-32, a 32-bit, fixed-width encoding form that usually requires twice as much memory as UTF-16 encoded characters. The major advantage of the fixed-width UTF-32 encoding form is that it expresses all characters uniformly, so it is easy to handle in arrays.

There are few guidelines that state when to use a particular encoding form. The best encoding form to use depends on computer systems and business protocols, not on the data itself. Typically, the UTF-8 encoding form should be used where computer systems and business protocols require data to be handled in 8-bit units, particularly in legacy systems being upgraded, because it often simplifies changes to existing programs. For this reason, UTF-8 has become the encoding form of choice on the Internet. Likewise, UTF-

16 is the encoding form of choice on Microsoft Windows applications. UTF-32 is likely to become more widely used in the future as more characters are encoded with values above FFFF hexadecimal. Also, UTF-32 requires less sophisticated handling than UTF-16 in the presence of surrogate pairs. Figure E.1 shows the different ways in which the three encoding forms handle character encoding.

E.3 Characters and Glyphs

The Unicode Standard consists of characters, written components (i.e., alphabetic letters, numerals, punctuation marks, accent marks, etc.) that can be represented by numeric values. Examples of characters include: U+0041 LATIN CAPITAL LETTER A. In the first character representation, U+*yyyy* is a *code value*, in which U+ refers to Unicode code values, as opposed to other hexadecimal values. The *yyyy* represents a four-digit hexadecimal number of an encoded character. Code values are bit combinations that represent encoded characters. Characters are represented with *glyphs*, various shapes, fonts and sizes for displaying characters. There are no code values for glyphs in the Unicode Standard. Examples of glyphs are shown in Fig. E.2.

The Unicode Standard encompasses the alphabets, ideographs, syllabaries, punctuation marks, *diacritics*, mathematical operators and so on. that compose the written languages and scripts of the world. A diacritic is a special mark added to a character to distinguish it from another letter or to indicate an accent (e.g., in Spanish, the tilde "~" above the character "n"). Currently, Unicode provides code values for 94,140 character representations, with more than 880,000 code values reserved for future expansion.

E.4 Advantages/Disadvantages of Unicode

The Unicode Standard has several significant advantages that promote its use. One is the impact it has on the performance of the international economy. Unicode standardizes the characters for the world's writing systems to a uniform model that promotes transferring

Character	UTF-8	UTF-16	UTF-32
Latin Capital Letter A	0x41	0x0041	0x00000041
Greek Capital Letter Alpha	0xCD 0x91	0x0391	0x00000391
CJK Unified Ideograph-4e95	0xE4 0xBA 0x95	0x4E95	0x00004E95
Old Italic Letter A	0xF0 0x80 0x83 0x80	0xDC00 0xDF00	0x00010300

Fig. E.1 | Correlation between the three encoding forms.

Fig. E.2 | Various glyphs of the character A.

and sharing data. Programs developed using such a schema maintain their accuracy because each character has a single definition (i.e., *a* is always U+0061, *%* is always U+0025). This enables corporations to manage the high demands of international markets by processing different writing systems at the same time. Also, all characters can be managed in an identical manner, thus avoiding any confusion caused by different character-code architectures. Moreover, managing data in a consistent manner eliminates data corruption, because data can be sorted, searched and manipulated via a consistent process.

Another advantage of the Unicode Standard is portability (i.e., the ability to execute software on disparate computers or with disparate operating systems). Most operating systems, databases, programming languages and Web browsers currently support, or are planning to support, Unicode. Additionally, Unicode includes more characters than any other character set in common use (although it does not yet include all of the world's characters).

A disadvantage of the Unicode Standard is the amount of memory required by UTF-16 and UTF-32. ASCII character sets are 8 bits in length, so they require less storage than the default 16-bit Unicode character set. However, the *double-byte character set (DBCS)* and the *multi-byte character set (MBCS)* that encode Asian characters (ideographs) require two to four bytes, respectively. In such instances, the UTF-16 or the UTF-32 encoding forms may be used with little hindrance on memory and performance.

E.5 Unicode Consortium's Web Site

If you would like to learn more about the Unicode Standard, visit www.unicode.org. This site provides a wealth of information about the Unicode Standard. Currently, the home page is organized into various sections: New to Unicode, General Information, The Consortium, The Unicode Standard, Work in Progress and For Members, Key Specifications and Technical Publications.

The *New to Unicode* section consists of four subsections: **What is Unicode?, How to Use this Site, FAQ** and **Glossary of Unicode Terms**. The first subsection provides a technical introduction to Unicode by describing design principles, character interpretations and assignments, text processing and Unicode conformance. This subsection is recommended reading for anyone new to Unicode. Also, this subsection provides a list of related links that provide the reader with additional information about Unicode. The **How to Use this Site** subsection contains information about using and navigating the site as well hyperlinks to additional resources.

The *General Information* section contains five subsections: **Where is my Character?, Display Problems?, Useful Resources, Unicode Enabled Products** and **Mail Lists**. The main areas covered in this section include a link to the Unicode code charts (a complete listing of code values) assembled by the Unicode Consortium as well as a detailed outline on how to locate an encoded character in the code chart. Also, the section contains advice on how to configure different operating systems and Web browsers so that the Unicode characters can be viewed properly. Moreover, from this section, the user can navigate to other sites that provide information on various topics, such as fonts, linguistics and such other standards as the *Armenian Standards Page* and the *Chinese GB 18030 Encoding Standard*.

The *Consortium* section consists of six subsections: **Who we are, Our Members, Job Postings, Press Info, Policies & Positions** and **Contact Us**. This section provides a list of the current Unicode Consortium members as well as information on how to become a member. Privileges for each member type—*full, associate, specialist* and *individual*—and the fees assessed to each member are listed here.

The *For Members* section consists of two subsections that are available only to consortium members: **Member Resources** and **Working Documents**.

The *Unicode Standard* section consists of five subsections: **Start Here**, **Latest Version**, **Code Charts**, **Unicode Character Database** and **Unihan Database**. This section describes the updates applied to the latest version of the Unicode Standard and categorizes all defined encoding. The user can learn how the latest version has been modified to encompass more features and capabilities. For instance, one enhancement of Version 3.1 is that it contains additional encoded characters.

The *Key Specifications* and *Technical Publications* sections provide all the Unicode technical documentation.

The *Work in Progress* section consists of seven subsections: **Calendar of Meetings**, **Proposals for Public Review**, **Unicode Technical Committee**, **UTC Meeting Minutes**, **Proposed Characters**, **Submitting Proposals** and **CLDR Technical Committee**. This section presents the user with a catalog of the recent characters included into the Unicode Standard scheme as well as those characters being considered for inclusion. If users determine that a character has been overlooked, then they can submit a written proposal for the inclusion of that character. The **Submitting Proposals** subsection contains strict guidelines that must be adhered to when submitting written proposals. In addition, this section provides information about upcoming and past technical committee meetings.

E.6 Using Unicode

Visual Studio uses Unicode UTF-16 encoding to represent all characters. Figure E.3 uses Visual Basic to display the text "Welcome to Unicode!" in eight different languages: English, French, German, Japanese, Portuguese, Russian, Spanish and Traditional Chinese.

```
 1   ' Fig. F.3: Unicode.vb
 2   ' Using Unicode encoding.
 3   Public Class FrmUnicodeDemo
 4      Private Sub FrmUnicodeDemo_Load(ByVal sender As System.Object, _
 5         ByVal e As System.EventArgs) Handles MyBase.Load
 6         'English
 7         lblEnglish.Text = ChrW(&H57) & ChrW(&H65) & ChrW(&H6C) & _
 8            ChrW(&H63) & ChrW(&H6F) & ChrW(&H6D) & ChrW(&H65) & _
 9            ChrW(&H20) & ChrW(&H74) & ChrW(&H6F) & ChrW(&H20) & _
10            "Unicode" & ChrW(&H21)
11
12         ' French
13         lblFrench.Text = ChrW(&H42) & ChrW(&H69) & ChrW(&H65) & _
14            ChrW(&H6E) & ChrW(&H76) & ChrW(&H65) & ChrW(&H6E) & _
15            ChrW(&H75) & ChrW(&H65) & ChrW(&H20) & ChrW(&H61) & _
16            ChrW(&H75) & ChrW(&H20) & "Unicode" & ChrW(&H21)
17
18         ' German
19         lblGerman.Text = ChrW(&H57) & ChrW(&H69) & ChrW(&H6C) & _
20            ChrW(&H6B) & ChrW(&H6F) & ChrW(&H6D) & ChrW(&H6D) & _
21            ChrW(&H65) & ChrW(&H6E) & ChrW(&H20) & ChrW(&H7A) & _
22            ChrW(&H75) & ChrW(&H20) & "Unicode" & ChrW(&H21)
```

Fig. E.3 | Windows application demonstrating Unicode encoding (Part 1 of 2.).

```
23
24          ' Japanese
25          lblJapanese.Text = "Unicode " & ChrW(&H3078) & _
26              ChrW(&H3087) & ChrW(&H3045) & ChrW(&H3053) & _
27              ChrW(&H305D) & ChrW(&H21)
28
29          ' Portuguese
30          lblPortuguese.Text = ChrW(&H53) & ChrW(&HE9) & ChrW(&H6A) & _
31              ChrW(&H61) & ChrW(&H20) & ChrW(&H42) & _
32              ChrW(&H65) & ChrW(&H6D) & ChrW(&H76) & _
33              ChrW(&H69) & ChrW(&H6E) & ChrW(&H64) & _
34              ChrW(&H6F) & ChrW(&H20) & "Unicode" & ChrW(&H21)
35
36          ' Russian
37          lblRussian.Text = ChrW(&H414) & ChrW(&H43E) & ChrW(&H431) & _
38              ChrW(&H440) & ChrW(&H43E) & ChrW(&H20) & _
39              ChrW(&H43F) & ChrW(&H43E) & ChrW(&H436) & _
40              ChrW(&H430) & ChrW(&H43B) & ChrW(&H43E) & _
41              ChrW(&H432) & ChrW(&H430) & ChrW(&H442) & _
42              ChrW(&H44A) & ChrW(&H20) & ChrW(&H432) & _
43              ChrW(&H20) & "Unicode" & ChrW(&H21)
44
45          ' Spanish
46          lblSpanish.Text = ChrW(&H42) & ChrW(&H69) & ChrW(&H65) & _
47              ChrW(&H6E) & ChrW(&H76) & ChrW(&H65) & _
48              ChrW(&H6E) & ChrW(&H69) & ChrW(&H64) & _
49              ChrW(&H61) & ChrW(&H20) & ChrW(&H61) & _
50              ChrW(&H20) & "Unicode" & ChrW(&H21)
51
52          ' Traditional Chinese
53          lblChinese.Text = ChrW(&H6B22) & ChrW(&H8FCE) & _
54              ChrW(&H4F7F) & ChrW(&H7528) & ChrW(&H20) & _
55              "Unicode" & ChrW(&H21)
56      End Sub ' FrmUnicodeDemo_Load
57  End Class ' FrmUnicodeDemo
```

Fig. E.3 | Windows application demonstrating Unicode encoding (Part 2 of 2.).

The first welcome message (lines 13–16) contains the hexadecimal codes for the English text. The **Code Charts** page on the Unicode Consortium Web site contains a document that lists the code values for the **Basic Latin** *block* (or category), which includes the English alphabet. The hexadecimal codes in lines 13–14 equate to "Welcome." When using Unicode characters in Visual Basic, the format &H*yyyy* is used, where *yyyy* represents the hexadecimal Unicode encoding. For example, the letter "W" (in "Welcome") is denoted by &H57. [*Note:* The actual code for the letter "W" is &H0057, but Visual Studio removes the two zeros.] Line 15 contains the hexadecimal for the *space* character (&H20). The hexadecimal value for the word "to" is on line 15 and the word "Unicode" is on line 14. "Unicode" is not encoded because it is a registered trademark and has no equivalent translation in most languages. Line 16 also contains the &H21 notation for the exclamation mark (!).

The remaining welcome messages (lines 18–61) contain the hexadecimal codes for the other seven languages. The code values used for the French, German, Portuguese and Spanish text are located in the **Basic Latin** block, the code values used for the Traditional Chinese text are located in the **CJK Unified Ideographs** block, the code values used for the Russian text are located in the **Cyrillic** block and the code values used for the Japanese text are located in the **Hiragana** block.

[*Note:* To render the Asian characters in a Windows application, you would need to install the proper language files on your computer. To do this, open the **Regional Options** dialog from the **Control Panel** (**Start > Settings > Control Panel**). At the bottom of the **General** tab is a list of languages. Check the **Japanese** and the **Traditional Chinese** checkboxes and press **Apply**. Follow the directions of the install wizard to install the languages. For additional assistance, visit www.unicode.org/help/display_problems.html.]

E.7 Character Ranges

The Unicode Standard assigns code values, which range from 0000 (**Basic Latin**) to E007F (**Tags**), to the written characters of the world. Currently, there are code values for 94,140 characters. To simplify the search for a character and its associated code value, the Unicode Standard generally groups code values by *script* and function (i.e., Latin characters are grouped in a block, mathematical operators are grouped in another block, etc.). As a rule, a script is a single writing system that is used for multiple languages (e.g., the Latin script is used for English, French, Spanish, etc.). The **Code Charts** page on the Unicode Consortium Web site lists all the defined blocks and their respective code values. Figure E.4 lists some blocks (scripts) from the Web site and their range of code values.

Script	Range of Code Values
Arabic	U+0600–U+06FF
Basic Latin	U+0000–U+007F
Bengali (India)	U+0980–U+09FF
Cherokee (Native America)	U+13A0–U+13FF
CJK Unified Ideographs (East Asia)	U+4E00–U+9FAF
Cyrillic (Russia and Eastern Europe)	U+0400–U+04FF
Ethiopic	U+1200–U+137F

Fig. E.4 | Some character ranges. (Part 1 of 2.)

Script	Range of Code Values
Greek	U+0370–U+03FF
Hangul Jamo (Korea)	U+1100–U+11FF
Hebrew	U+0590–U+05FF
Hiragana (Japan)	U+3040–U+309F
Khmer (Cambodia)	U+1780–U+17FF
Lao (Laos)	U+0E80–U+0EFF
Mongolian	U+1800–U+18AF
Myanmar	U+1000–U+109F
Ogham (Ireland)	U+1680–U+169F
Runic (Germany and Scandinavia)	U+16A0–U+16FF
Sinhala (Sri Lanka)	U+0D80–U+0DFF
Telugu (India)	U+0C00–U+0C7F
Thai	U+0E00–U+0E7F

Fig. E.4 | Some character ranges. (Part 2 of 2.)

Introduction to XHTML: Part 1

OBJECTIVES

In this appendix, you will learn:

- To understand important components of XHTML documents.
- To use XHTML to create Web pages.
- To be able to add images to Web pages.
- To understand how to create and use hyperlinks to navigate Web pages.
- To be able to mark up lists of information.

F.1 Introduction

Welcome to the world of opportunity created by the World Wide Web. The Internet is now three decades old, but it was not until the Web became popular in the 1990s that the explosion of opportunity that we are still experiencing began. Exciting new developments occur almost daily—the pace of innovation is unprecedented by any other technology. In this appendix, you will develop your own Web pages.

This appendix begins unlocking the power of Web-based application development with *XHTML*—the *Extensible HyperText Markup Language*. The next appendix introduces more sophisticated XHTML techniques, such as *tables*, which are particularly useful for structuring information from *databases* (i.e., software that stores structured sets of data).

Unlike procedural programming languages such as C, Fortran, Cobol and Pascal, XHTML is a *markup language* that specifies the format of the text that is displayed in a Web browser such as Microsoft's *Internet Explorer* or *Netscape*.

One key issue when using XHTML is the separation of the *presentation* of a document (i.e., the document's appearance when rendered by a browser) from the *structure* of the document's information. XHTML is based on HTML (HyperText Markup Language)—a legacy technology of the World Wide Web Consortium (W3C). In HTML, it was common to specify the document's content, structure and formatting. Formatting might specify where the browser placed an element in a Web page or the fonts and colors used to display an element. XHTML 1.1 (W3C's latest version of W3C XHTML Recommendation at the time of publication) allows only a document's content and structure to appear in a valid XHTML document, and not its formatting. Normally, such formatting is specified with Cascading Style Sheets. All our examples in this appendix are based upon the XHTML 1.1 Recommendation.

F.2 Editing XHTML

In this appendix, we write XHTML in its *source-code form*. We create *XHTML documents* by typing them in a text editor (e.g., *Notepad*, *Wordpad*, *vi*, *emacs*) and saving them with either an *.html* or an *.htm* file-name extension.

Good Programming Practice F.1

Assign documents file names that describe their functionality. This practice can help you identify documents faster. It also helps people who want to link to a page, by giving them an easy-to-remember name. For example, if you are writing an XHTML document that contains product information, you might want to call it products.html.

Machines running specialized software called **Web servers** store XHTML documents. Clients (e.g., Web browsers) request specific **resources** such as the XHTML documents from the Web server. For example, typing www.deitel.com/books/downloads.html into a Web browser's address field requests downloads.html from the Web server running at www.deitel.com. This document is located on the server in a directory named books. For now, we simply place the XHTML documents on our machine and open them using Internet Explorer.

F.3 First XHTML Example

In this appendix and the next, we present XHTML markup and provide screen captures that show how Internet Explorer renders (i.e., displays) the XHTML.[1] Every XHTML document we show has line numbers for the reader's convenience. These line numbers are not part of the XHTML documents.

Our first example (Fig. F.1) is an XHTML document named main.html that displays the message "Welcome to XHTML!" in the browser.

The key line in the program is line 14, which tells the browser to display "Welcome to XHTML!" Now let us consider each line of the program.

Lines 1–3 are required in XHTML documents to conform with proper XHTML syntax. For now, copy and paste these lines into each XHTML document you create. The meaning of these lines is discussed in detail in Chapter 19, Extensible Markup Language (XML).

```
 1   <?xml version = "1.0"?>
 2   <!DOCTYPE html PUBLIC "-//W3C//DTD XHTML 1.1//EN"
 3      "http://www.w3.org/TR/xhtml11/DTD/xhtml11.dtd">
 4
 5   <!-- Fig. F.1: main.html -->
 6   <!-- Our first Web page   -->
 7
 8   <html xmlns = "http://www.w3.org/1999/xhtml">
 9      <head>
10         <title>Internet and WWW How to Program - Welcome</title>
11      </head>
12
13      <body>
14         <p>Welcome to XHTML!</p>
15      </body>
16   </html>
```

Fig. F.1 | First XHTML example. (Part 1 of 2.)

---

1. This appendix's examples are available at www.deitel.com/books/vbforprogrammers2.

Fig. F.1 | First XHTML example. (Part 2 of 2.)

Lines 5–6 are *XHTML comments*. XHTML document creators insert comments to improve markup readability and describe the content of a document. Comments also help other people read and understand an XHTML document's markup and content. Comments do not cause the browser to perform any action when the user loads the XHTML document into the Web browser to view the document. XHTML comments always start with `<!--` and end with `-->`. Each of our XHTML examples includes comments that specify the figure number and file name, and provide a brief description of the example's purpose. Subsequent examples include comments in the markup, especially to highlight new features.

Good Programming Practice F.2

Place comments throughout your markup. Comments help other programmers understand the markup, assist in debugging and list useful information that you do not want the browser to render. Comments also help you understand your own markup when you revisit a document to modify or update it in the future.

XHTML markup contains text that represents the content of a document and *elements* that specify a document's structure. Some important elements of an XHTML document are the *html* element, the *head* element and the *body* element. The html element encloses the *head section* (represented by the head element) and the *body section* (represented by the body element). The head section contains information about the XHTML document, such as its *title*. The head section also can contain special document formatting instructions called *style sheets* and client-side programs called *scripts* for creating dynamic Web pages. The body section contains the page's content that the browser displays when the user visits the Web page.

XHTML documents delimit an element with *start* and *end* tags. A start tag consists of the element name in angle brackets (e.g., `<html>`). An end tag consists of the element name preceded by a / in angle brackets (e.g., `</html>`). In this example, lines 8 and 16 define the start and end of the html element. Note that the end tag in line 16 has the same name as the start tag, but is preceded by a / inside the angle brackets. Many start tags have *attributes* that provide additional information about an element. Browsers can use this additional information to determine how to process the element. Each attribute has a *name* and a *value* separated by an equals sign (=). Line 8 specifies a required attribute (`xmlns`) and value (`http://www.w3.org/1999/xhtml`) for the html element in an XHTML document. For now, simply copy and paste the html element start tag in line 8 into your XHTML documents. We discuss the details of the html element's xmlns attribute in Chapter 19, Extensible Markup Language (XML).

Common Programming Error F.1

Not enclosing attribute values in either single or double quotes is a syntax error. However, some Web browsers may still render the element correctly.

Common Programming Error F.2

Using uppercase letters in an XHTML element or attribute name is a syntax error. However, some Web browsers may still render the element correctly.

An XHTML document divides the html element into two sections—head and body. Lines 9–11 define the Web page's head section with a head element. Line 10 specifies a title element. This is called a *nested element* because it is enclosed in the head element's start and end tags. The head element is also a nested element because it is enclosed in the html element's start and end tags. The title element describes the Web page. Titles usually appear in the *title bar* at the top of the browser window and also as the text identifying a page when users add the page to their list of **Favorites** or **Bookmarks** that enables them to return to their favorite sites. Search engines (i.e., sites that allow users to search the Web) also use the title for cataloging purposes.

Good Programming Practice F.3

Indenting nested elements emphasizes a document's structure and promotes readability.

Common Programming Error F.3

XHTML does not permit tags to overlap—a nested element's end tag must appear in the document before the enclosing element's end tag. For example, the nested XHTML tags <head><title>hello</head></title> cause a syntax error, because the enclosing head element's ending </head> tag appears before the nested title element's ending </title> tag.

Good Programming Practice F.4

Use a consistent title-naming convention for all pages on a site. For example, if a site is named "Bailey's Web Site," then the title of the links page might be "Bailey's Web Site—Links." This practice can help users better understand the Web site's structure.

Line 13 opens the document's body element. The body section of an XHTML document specifies the document's content, which may include text and tags.

Some tags, such as the *paragraph tags* (**<p>** and **</p>**) in line 14, mark up text for display in a browser. All the text placed between the <p> and </p> tags forms one paragraph. When the browser renders a paragraph, a blank line usually precedes and follows paragraph text.

This document ends with two end tags (lines 15–16). These tags close the body and html elements, respectively. The </html> tag in an XHTML document informs the browser that the XHTML markup is complete.

To view this example in Internet Explorer, perform the following steps:

   1. Download the examples from www.deitel.com/books/vbforprogrammers2.

2. Launch Internet Explorer and select **Open...** from the **File** Menu. This displays the **Open** dialog.

3. Click the **Open** dialog's **Browse...** button to display the **Microsoft Internet Explorer** file dialog.

4. Navigate to the directory containing the examples for this appendix and select the file main.html, then click **Open**.

5. Click **OK** to have Internet Explorer render the document. Other examples are opened in a similar manner.

At this point your browser window should appear similar to the sample screen capture shown in Fig. F.1. (Note that we resized the browser window to save space in the book.)

F.4 W3C XHTML Validation Service

Programming Web-based applications can be complex, and XHTML documents must be written correctly to ensure that browsers process them properly. To promote correctly written documents, the World Wide Web Consortium (W3C) provides a *validation service* (validator.w3.org) for checking a document's syntax. Documents can be validated either from a URL that specifies the location of the file or by uploading a file to the site validator.w3.org/file-upload.html. Uploading a file copies the file from the user's computer to another computer on the Internet. Figure F.2 shows main.html (Fig. F.1) being uploaded for validation. The W3C's Web page indicates that the service name is **MarkUp Validation Service**, and the validation service is able to validate the syntax of XHTML documents. All the XHTML examples in this book have been validated successfully using validator.w3.org.

Fig. F.2 | Validating an XHTML document. (Courtesy of World Wide Web Consortium (W3C).)

By clicking **Browse...**, users can select files on their own computers for upload. After selecting a file, clicking the **Validate this file** button uploads and validates the file. Figure F.3 shows the results of validating `main.html`. This document does not contain any syntax errors. If a document does contain syntax errors, the validation service displays error messages describing the errors.

Error-Prevention Tip F.1

Most current browsers attempt to render XHTML documents even if they are invalid. This often leads to unexpected and possibly undesirable results. Use a validation service, such as the W3C MarkUp Validation Service, to confirm that an XHTML document is syntactically correct.

F.5 Headers

Some text in an XHTML document may be more important than other text. For example, the text in this section is considered more important than a footnote. XHTML provides six *headers*, called *header elements*, for specifying the relative importance of information. Figure F.4 demonstrates these elements (h1 through h6). Header element h1 (line 15) is considered the most significant header and is typically rendered in a larger font than the other five headers (lines 16–20). Each successive header element (i.e., h2, h3, etc.) is typically rendered in a progressively smaller font.

Portability Tip F.1

The text size used to display each header element can vary significantly between browsers.

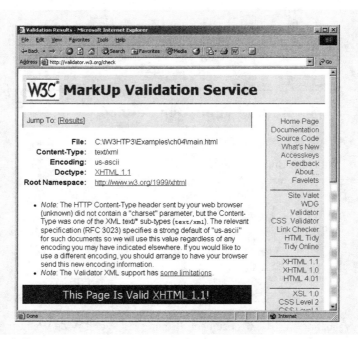

Fig. F.3 | XHTML validation results. (Courtesy of World Wide Web Consortium (W3C).)

```
 1   <?xml version = "1.0"?>
 2   <!DOCTYPE html PUBLIC "-//W3C//DTD XHTML 1.1//EN"
 3      "http://www.w3.org/TR/xhtml11/DTD/xhtml11.dtd">
 4
 5   <!-- Fig. F.4: header.html -->
 6   <!-- XHTML headers           -->
 7
 8   <html xmlns = "http://www.w3.org/1999/xhtml">
 9      <head>
10         <title>Internet and WWW How to Program - Headers</title>
11      </head>
12
13      <body>
14
15         <h1>Level 1 Header</h1>
16         <h2>Level 2 header</h2>
17         <h3>Level 3 header</h3>
18         <h4>Level 4 header</h4>
19         <h5>Level 5 header</h5>
20         <h6>Level 6 header</h6>
21
22      </body>
23   </html>
```

Fig. F.4 | Header elements h1 through h6.

Look-and-Feel Observation F.1

Placing a header at the top of every XHTML page helps viewers understand the purpose of each page.

Look-and-Feel Observation F.2

Use larger headers to emphasize more important sections of a Web page.

F.6 Linking

One of the most important XHTML features is the *hyperlink,* which references (or *links* to) other resources, such as XHTML documents and images. In XHTML, both text and images can act as hyperlinks. Web browsers typically underline text hyperlinks and color their text blue by default, so that users can distinguish hyperlinks from plain text. In Fig. F.5, we create text hyperlinks to four different Web sites.

Line 17 introduces the *strong* element. Browsers typically display such text in a bold font. Links are created using the *a (anchor) element.* Line 20 defines a hyperlink that links the text Deitel to the URL assigned to attribute *href*, which specifies the location of a linked resource, such as a Web page, a file or an e-mail address. This particular anchor element links to a Web page located at http://www.deitel.com. When a URL does not indicate a specific document on the Web site, the Web server returns a default Web page. This page is often called index.html; however, most Web servers can be configured to use any file as the default Web page for the site. (Open http://www.deitel.com in one browser window and http://www.deitel.com/index.html in a second browser window to confirm that they are identical.) If the Web server cannot locate a requested document, it returns an error indication to the Web browser, and the browser displays a Web page containing an error message to the user.

```
 1   <?xml version = "1.0"?>
 2   <!DOCTYPE html PUBLIC "-//W3C//DTD XHTML 1.1//EN"
 3      "http://www.w3.org/TR/xhtml11/DTD/xhtml11.dtd">
 4
 5   <!-- Fig. F.5: links.html        -->
 6   <!-- Introduction to hyperlinks -->
 7
 8   <html xmlns = "http://www.w3.org/1999/xhtml">
 9      <head>
10         <title>Internet and WWW How to Program - Links</title>
11      </head>
12
13      <body>
14
15         <h1>Here are my favorite sites</h1>
16
17         <p><strong>Click a name to go to that page.</strong></p>
18
19         <!-- Create four text hyperlinks -->
20         <p><a href = "http://www.deitel.com">Deitel</a></p>
21
22         <p><a href = "http://www.prenhall.com">Prentice Hall</a></p>
23
24         <p><a href = "http://www.yahoo.com">Yahoo!</a></p>
25
26         <p><a href = "http://www.usatoday.com">USA Today</a></p>
27
28      </body>
29   </html>
```

Fig. F.5 | Linking to other Web pages. (Part 1 of 2.)

Fig. F.5 | Linking to other Web pages. (Part 2 of 2.)

Anchors can link to e-mail addresses using a *mailto:* URL. When someone clicks this type of anchored link, most browsers launch the default e-mail program (e.g., Outlook Express) to enable the user to write an e-mail message to the linked address. Figure F.6 demonstrates this type of anchor. Lines 17–19 contain an e-mail link. The form of an e-mail anchor is `<a href = "mailto:emailaddress">...</a>`. In this case, we link to the e-mail address `deitel@deitel.com`.

```
1   <?xml version = "1.0"?>
2   <!DOCTYPE html PUBLIC "-//W3C//DTD XHTML 1.1//EN"
3      "http://www.w3.org/TR/xhtml11/DTD/xhtml11.dtd">
4
5   <!-- Fig. F.6: contact.html   -->
6   <!-- Adding email hyperlinks -->
7
8   <html xmlns = "http://www.w3.org/1999/xhtml">
9      <head>
```

Fig. F.6 | Linking to an e-mail address. (Part 1 of 2.)

```
10          <title>Internet and WWW How to Program - Contact Page</title>
11      </head>
12
13      <body>
14
15          <p>
16          My e-mail address is
17          <a href = "mailto:deitel@deitel.com">
18              deitel@deitel.com
19          </a>
20          . Click the address and your browser will
21          open an e-mail message and address it to me.
22          </p>
23      </body>
24  </html>
```

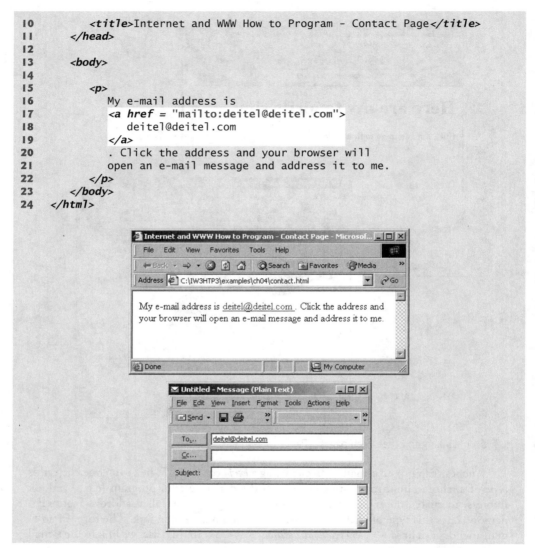

Fig. F.6 | Linking to an e-mail address. (Part 2 of 2.)

F.7 Images

The examples discussed so far demonstrate how to mark up documents that contain only text. However, most Web pages contain both text and images. In fact, images are an equal, if not essential, part of Web-page design. The three most popular image formats used by Web developers are Graphics Interchange Format (GIF), Joint Photographic Experts Group (JPEG) and Portable Network Graphics (PNG) images. Users can create images using specialized pieces of software, such as Adobe Photoshop Elements 2.0, Macromedia Fireworks (www.macromedia.com) and Jasc Paint Shop Pro (www.jasc.com). Images may also be acquired from various Web sites, such as the Yahoo! Picture Gallery (gallery.yahoo.com). Figure F.7 demonstrates how to incorporate images into Web pages.

Lines 16–17 use an *img* element to insert an image in the document. The image file's location is specified with the img element's ***src*** attribute. In this case, the image is located in the same directory as this XHTML document, so only the image's file name is required. Optional attributes ***width*** and ***height*** specify the image's width and height, respectively. The document author can scale an image by increasing or decreasing the values of the image width and height attributes. If these attributes are omitted, the browser uses the

```
1   <?xml version = "1.0"?>
2   <!DOCTYPE html PUBLIC "-//W3C//DTD XHTML 1.1//EN"
3      "http://www.w3.org/TR/xhtml11/DTD/xhtml11.dtd">
4
5   <!-- Fig. F.7: picture.html   -->
6   <!-- Adding images with XHTML -->
7
8   <html xmlns = "http://www.w3.org/1999/xhtml">
9      <head>
10        <title>Internet and WWW How to Program - Welcome</title>
11     </head>
12
13     <body>
14
15        <p>
16           <img src = "xmlhtp.jpg" height = "238" width = "183"
17              alt = "XML How to Program book cover" />
18           <img src = "jhtp.jpg" height = "238" width = "183"
19              alt = "Java How to Program book cover" />
20        </p>
21     </body>
22  </html>
```

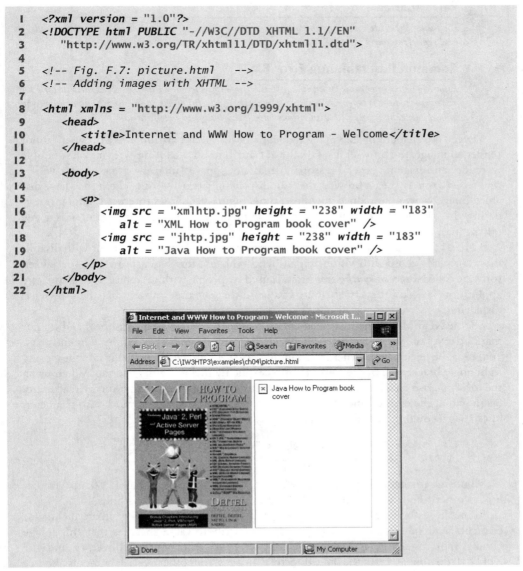

Fig. F.7 | Images in XHTML files.

image's actual width and height. Images are measured in *pixels* ("picture elements"), which represent dots of color on the screen. The image in Fig. F.7 is 183 pixels wide and 238 pixels high.

Good Programming Practice F.5

Always include the width and the height of an image inside the <img> tag. When the browser loads the XHTML file, it will know immediately from these attributes how much screen space to provide for the image and will lay out the page properly, even before it downloads the image.

Performance Tip F.1

Including the width and height attributes in an <img> tag can result in the browser loading and rendering pages faster.

Common Programming Error F.4

Entering new dimensions for an image that change its inherent width-to-height ratio distorts the appearance of the image. For example, if your image is 200 pixels wide and 100 pixels high, you should ensure that any new dimensions have a 2:1 width-to-height ratio.

Every img element in an XHTML document has an *alt* attribute. If a browser cannot render an image, the browser displays the alt attribute's value. A browser may not be able to render an image for several reasons. It may not support images—as is the case with a *text-based browser* (i.e., a browser that can display only text)—or the client may have disabled image viewing to reduce download time. Figure F.7 shows Internet Explorer 6 rendering the alt attribute's value when a document references a nonexistent image file (jhtp.jpg).

The alt attribute is important for creating *accessible* Web pages for users with disabilities, especially those with vision impairments who use text-based browsers. Specialized software called a *speech synthesizer* often is used by people with disabilities. This software application "speaks" the alt attribute's value so that the user knows what the browser is displaying.

Some XHTML elements (called *empty elements*) contain only attributes and do not mark up text (i.e., text is not placed between the start and end tags). Empty elements (e.g., img) must be terminated, either by using the *forward slash character* (/) inside the closing right angle bracket (>) of the start tag or by explicitly including the end tag. When using the forward slash character, we add a space before the forward slash to improve readability (as shown at the ends of lines 17 and 19). Rather than using the forward slash character, lines 18–19 could be written with a closing </img> tag as follows:

```
<img src = "jhtp.jpg" height = "238" width = "183"
    alt = "Java How to Program book cover"></img>
```

By using images as hyperlinks, Web developers can create graphical Web pages that link to other resources. In Fig. F.8, we create six different image hyperlinks.

Lines 17–20 create an *image hyperlink* by nesting an img element in an anchor (a) element. The value of the img element's src attribute value specifies that this image (links.jpg) resides in a directory named buttons. The buttons directory and the XHTML document are in the same directory. Images from other Web documents also can be referenced (after obtaining permission from the document's owner) by setting the src attribute to the name and location of the image. Clicking an image hyperlink takes a user to the Web page specified by the surrounding anchor element's `href` attribute.

```
 1   <?xml version = "1.0"?>
 2   <!DOCTYPE html PUBLIC "-//W3C//DTD XHTML 1.1//EN"
 3       "http://www.w3.org/TR/xhtml11/DTD/xhtml11.dtd">
 4
 5   <!-- Fig. F.8: nav.html           -->
 6   <!-- Using images as link anchors -->
 7
 8   <html xmlns = "http://www.w3.org/1999/xhtml">
 9      <head>
10         <title>Internet and WWW How to Program - Navigation Bar
11         </title>
12      </head>
13
14      <body>
15
16         <p>
17            <a href = "links.html">
18               <img src = "buttons/links.jpg" width = "65"
19                  height = "50" alt = "Links Page" />
20            </a><br />
21
22            <a href = "list.html">
23               <img src = "buttons/list.jpg" width = "65"
24                  height = "50" alt = "List Example Page" />
25            </a><br />
26
27            <a href = "contact.html">
28               <img src = "buttons/contact.jpg" width = "65"
29                  height = "50" alt = "Contact Page" />
30            </a><br />
31
32            <a href = "header.html">
33               <img src = "buttons/header.jpg" width = "65"
34                  height = "50" alt = "Header Page" />
35            </a><br />
36
37            <a href = "table1.html">
38               <img src = "buttons/table.jpg" width = "65"
39                  height = "50" alt = "Table Page" />
40            </a><br />
41
42            <a href = "form.html">
43               <img src = "buttons/form.jpg" width = "65"
44                  height = "50" alt = "Feedback Form" />
45            </a><br />
46         </p>
47
48      </body>
49   </html>
```

Fig. F.8 | Images as link anchors. (Part 1 of 2.)

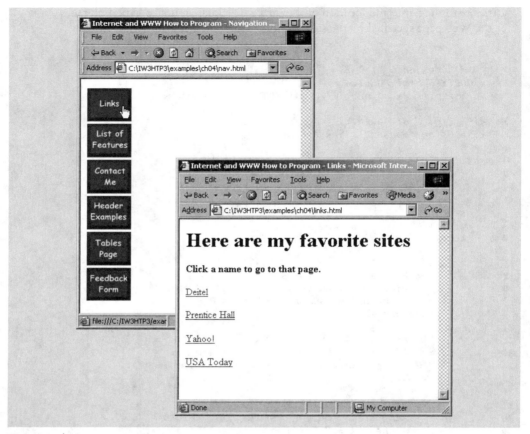

Fig. F.8 | Images as link anchors. (Part 2 of 2.)

In line 20, we introduce the ***br element***, which most browsers render as a ***line break***. Any markup or text following a br element is rendered on the next line. Like the img element, br is an example of an empty element terminated with a forward slash. We add a space before the forward slash to enhance readability. [*Note*: The last two image hyperlinks in Fig. F.8 link to XHTML documents (i.e., table1.html and form.html) presented as examples in Appendix G and included in the Appendix G examples directory. Clicking these links now will result in errors.]

F.8 Special Characters and More Line Breaks

When marking up text, certain characters or symbols (e.g., <) may be difficult to embed directly into an XHTML document. Some keyboards do not provide these symbols, or the presence of these symbols may cause syntax errors. For example, the markup

```
<p>if x < 10 then increment x by 1</p>
```

results in a syntax error because it uses the less-than character (<), which is reserved for start tags and end tags such as <p> and </p>. XHTML provides ***character entity references*** (in the form &*code*;) for representing special characters. We could correct the previous line by writing

        *<p>*if x *&lt*; 10 then increment x by 1*</p>*

which uses the character entity reference *<* for the less-than symbol.

    Figure F.9 demonstrates how to use special characters in an XHTML document. For a list of special characters, see Appendix H, XHTML Special Characters.

```
 1   <?xml version = "1.0"?>
 2   <!DOCTYPE html PUBLIC "-//W3C//DTD XHTML 1.1//EN"
 3      "http://www.w3.org/TR/xhtml11/DTD/xhtml11.dtd">
 4
 5   <!-- Fig. F.9: contact2.html       -->
 6   <!-- Inserting special characters -->
 7
 8   <html xmlns = "http://www.w3.org/1999/xhtml">
 9      <head>
10         <title>Internet and WWW How to Program - Contact Page
11         </title>
12      </head>
13
14      <body>
15
16         <!-- special characters are entered -->
17         <!-- using the form &code;           -->
18         <p>
19            Click
20            <a href = "mailto:deitel@deitel.com">here</a>
21            to open an e-mail message addressed to
22            deitel@deitel.com.
23         </p>
24
25         <hr /> <!-- inserts a horizontal rule -->
26
27         <p>All information on this site is <strong>&copy;</strong>
28            Deitel <strong>&amp;</strong> Associates, Inc. 2004.</p>
29
30         <!-- to strike through text use <del> tags    -->
31         <!-- to subscript text use <sub> tags         -->
32         <!-- to superscript text use <sup> tags       -->
33         <!-- these tags are nested inside other tags -->
34         <p><del>You may download 3.14 x 10<sup>2</sup>
35            characters worth of information from this site.</del>
36            Only <sub>one</sub> download per hour is permitted.</p>
37
38         <p>Note: <strong>&lt; &frac14;</strong> of the information
39            presented here is updated daily.</p>
40
41      </body>
42   </html>
```

Fig. F.9 | Special characters in XHTML. (Part 1 of 2.)

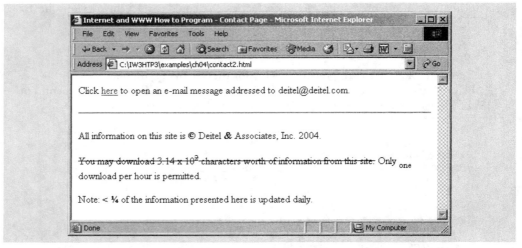

Fig. F.9 | Special characters in XHTML. (Part 2 of 2.)

Lines 27–28 contain other special characters, which can be expressed as either character entity references (i.e., word abbreviations such as amp for ampersand and copy for copyright) or *numeric character references*—decimal or *hexadecimal (hex)* values representing special characters. For example, the & character is represented in decimal and hexadecimal notation as & and &, respectively. Hexadecimal numbers are base 16 numbers—digits in a hexadecimal number have values from 0 to 15 (a total of 16 different values). The letters A–F represent the hexadecimal digits corresponding to decimal values 10–15. Thus in hexadecimal notation we can have numbers like 876 consisting solely of decimal-like digits, numbers like DA19F consisting of digits and letters and numbers like DCB consisting solely of letters. We discuss hexadecimal numbers in detail in Appendix B, Number Systems.

In lines 34–36, we introduce three new elements. Most browsers render the *del* element as strike-through text. With this format users can easily indicate document revisions. To *superscript* text (i.e., raise text on a line with a decreased font size) or *subscript* text (i.e., lower text on a line with a decreased font size), use the *sup* or *sub* element, respectively. We also use character entity reference < for a less-than sign and *¼* for the fraction 1/4 (line 38).

In addition to special characters, this document introduces a *horizontal rule*, indicated by the *<hr />* tag in line 25. Most browsers render a horizontal rule as a horizontal line. The <hr /> tag also inserts a line break above and below the horizontal line.

F.9 Unordered Lists

Up to this point, we have presented basic XHTML elements and attributes for linking to resources, creating headers, using special characters and incorporating images. In this section, we discuss how to organize information on a Web page using lists. In Appendix G, we introduce another feature for organizing information, called a table. Figure F.10 displays text in an *unordered list* (i.e., a list that does not order its items by letter or number). The unordered list element *ul* creates a list in which each item begins with a bullet symbol

```
 1   <?xml version = "1.0"?>
 2   <!DOCTYPE html PUBLIC "-//W3C//DTD XHTML 1.1//EN"
 3      "http://www.w3.org/TR/xhtml11/DTD/xhtml11.dtd">
 4
 5   <!-- Fig. F.10: links2.html              -->
 6   <!-- Unordered list containing hyperlinks -->
 7
 8   <html xmlns = "http://www.w3.org/1999/xhtml">
 9      <head>
10         <title>Internet and WWW How to Program - Links</title>
11      </head>
12
13      <body>
14
15         <h1>Here are my favorite sites</h1>
16
17         <p><strong>Click on a name to go to that page.</strong></p>
18
19         <!-- create an unordered list -->
20         <ul>
21
22            <!-- add four list items -->
23            <li><a href = "http://www.deitel.com">Deitel</a></li>
24
25            <li><a href = "http://www.w3.org">W3C</a></li>
26
27            <li><a href = "http://www.yahoo.com">Yahoo!</a></li>
28
29            <li><a href = "http://www.cnn.com">CNN</a></li>
30         </ul>
31      </body>
32   </html>
```

Fig. F.10 | Unordered lists in XHTML.

(called a *disc*). Each entry in an unordered list (element ul in line 20) is an *li* (*list item*) element (lines 23, 25, 27 and 29). Most Web browsers render these elements with a line break and a bullet symbol indented from the beginning of the new line.

F.10 Nested and Ordered Lists

Lists may be nested to represent hierarchical relationships, as in an outline format. Figure F.11 demonstrates nested lists and *ordered lists*. The ordered list element *ol* creates a list in which each item begins with a number.

A Web browser indents each nested list to indicate a hierarchical relationship. The first ordered list begins at line 33. Items in an ordered list are enumerated one, two, three and so on. Nested ordered lists are enumerated in the same manner. The items in the outermost unordered list (line 18) are preceded by discs. List items nested inside the unordered list of line 18 are preceded by *circles*. Although not demonstrated in this example, subsequent nested list items are preceded by *squares*.

```
 1    <?xml version = "1.0"?>
 2    <!DOCTYPE html PUBLIC "-//W3C//DTD XHTML 1.1//EN"
 3       "http://www.w3.org/TR/xhtml11/DTD/xhtml11.dtd">
 4
 5    <!-- Fig. F.11: list.html                    -->
 6    <!-- Advanced Lists: nested and ordered -->
 7
 8    <html xmlns = "http://www.w3.org/1999/xhtml">
 9       <head>
10          <title>Internet and WWW How to Program - Lists</title>
11       </head>
12
13       <body>
14
15          <h1>The Best Features of the Internet</h1>
16
17          <!-- create an unordered list -->
18          <ul>
19             <li>You can meet new people from countries around
20                the world.</li>
21             <li>
22                You have access to new media as it becomes public:
23
24                <!-- this starts a nested list, which uses a -->
25                <!-- modified bullet. The list ends when you -->
26                <!-- close the <ul> tag.                     -->
27                <ul>
28                   <li>New games</li>
29                   <li>
30                      New applications
31
32                      <!-- nested ordered list -->
33                      <ol>
34                         <li>For business</li>
```

Fig. F.11 | Nested and ordered lists in XHTML. (Part I of 2.)

```
35                              <li>For pleasure</li>
36                          </ol>
37                      </li>
38
39              <li>Around the clock news</li>
40              <li>Search engines</li>
41              <li>Shopping</li>
42              <li>
43                  Programming
44
45                  <!-- another nested ordered list -->
46                  <ol>
47                      <li>XML</li>
48                      <li>Java</li>
49                      <li>XHTML</li>
50                      <li>Scripts</li>
51                      <li>New languages</li>
52                  </ol>
53
54              </li>
55
56          </ul> <!-- ends the nested list of line 27 -->
57      </li>
58
59      <li>Links</li>
60      <li>Keeping in touch with old friends</li>
61      <li>It is the technology of the future!</li>
62
63  </ul>    <!-- ends the unordered list of line 18 -->
64
65  </body>
66  </html>
```

Fig. F.11 | Nested and ordered lists in XHTML. (Part 2 of 2.)

F.11 Web Resources

`www.w3.org/TR/xhtml11`

The *XHTML 1.1 Recommendation* contains XHTML 1.1 general information, compatibility issues, document type definition information, definitions, terminology and much more.

`www.xhtml.org`

XHTML.org provides XHTML development news and links to other XHTML resources, including books and articles.

`www.w3schools.com/xhtml/default.asp`

The *XHTML School* provides XHTML quizzes and references. This page also contains links to XHTML syntax, validation and document type definitions.

`validator.w3.org`

This is the W3C XHTML validation service site.

`hotwired.lycos.com/webmonkey/00/50/index2a.html`

This site provides an article about XHTML. Key sections of the article overview XHTML and discuss tags, attributes and anchors.

`wdvl.com/Authoring/Languages/XML/XHTML`

The *Web Developers Virtual Library* provides an introduction to XHTML. This site also contains articles, examples and links to other technologies.

`www.w3.org/TR/2001/REC-xhtml11-20010531`

The XHTML 1.1 DTD documentation site provides technical specifications of XHTML 1.1 syntax.

G

Introduction to XHTML: Part 2

*Yea, from the table of my
memory
I'll wipe away all trivial
fond records.*
—William Shakespeare

OBJECTIVES

In this appendix, you will learn:

- To be able to create tables with rows and columns of data.

- To be able to control table formatting.

- To be able to create and use forms.

- To be able to create and use image maps to aid in Web-page navigation.

- To be able to make Web pages accessible to search engines using `<meta>` tags.

- To be able to use the `frameset` element to display multiple Web pages in a single browser window.

G.1 Introduction

In the preceding appendix, we introduced XHTML. We built several complete Web pages featuring text, hyperlinks, images, horizontal rules and line breaks. In this appendix, we discuss more substantial XHTML features, including presentation of information in *tables* and incorporating *forms* for collecting information from a Web-page visitor. We also introduce *internal linking* and *image maps* for enhancing Web-page navigation, and *frames* for displaying multiple documents in the browser. By the end of this appendix, you will be familiar with the most commonly used XHTML features and will be able to create more complex Web documents.

G.2 Basic XHTML Tables

Tables are used to organize data in rows and columns. Our first example (Fig. G.1) creates a table with six rows and two columns to display price information for fruit.

Tables are defined with the ***table*** element (lines 16–66). Lines 16–18 specify the start tag for a `table` element that has several attributes. The ***border*** attribute specifies the table's border width in pixels. To create a table without a border, set `border` to "0". This example assigns attribute `width` the value "40%" to set the table's width to 40 percent of the browser's width. A developer can also set attribute `width` to a specified number of pixels. Try resizing the browser window to see how the width of the window affects the width of the table.

```
 1    <?xml version = "1.0"?>
 2    <!DOCTYPE html PUBLIC "-//W3C//DTD XHTML 1.1//EN"
 3       "http://www.w3.org/TR/xhtml11/DTD/xhtml11.dtd">
 4
 5    <!-- Fig. G.1: table1.html   -->
 6    <!-- Creating a basic table  -->
 7
 8    <html xmlns = "http://www.w3.org/1999/xhtml">
```

Fig. G.1 | XHTML table. (Part 1 of 3.)

```
 9    <head>
10       <title>A simple XHTML table</title>
11    </head>
12
13    <body>
14
15       <!-- the <table> tag opens a table -->
16       <table border = "1" width = "40%"
17          summary = "This table provides information about
18             the price of fruit">
19
20          <!-- the <caption> tag summarizes the table's   -->
21          <!-- contents (this helps the visually impaired) -->
22          <caption><strong>Price of Fruit</strong></caption>
23
24          <!-- the <thead> is the first section of a table -->
25          <!-- it formats the table header area            -->
26          <thead>
27             <tr>                  <!-- <tr> inserts a table row -->
28                <th>Fruit</th> <!-- insert a heading cell -->
29                <th>Price</th>
30             </tr>
31          </thead>
32
33          <!-- the <tfoot> is the last section of a table -->
34          <!-- it formats the table footer               -->
35          <tfoot>
36             <tr>
37                <th>Total</th>
38                <th>$3.75</th>
39             </tr>
40          </tfoot>
41
42          <!-- all table content is enclosed  -->
43          <!-- within the <tbody>            -->
44          <tbody>
45             <tr>
46                <td>Apple</td> <!-- insert a data cell -->
47                <td>$0.25</td>
48             </tr>
49
50             <tr>
51                <td>Orange</td>
52                <td>$0.50</td>
53             </tr>
54
55             <tr>
56                <td>Banana</td>
57                <td>$1.00</td>
58             </tr>
59
60             <tr>
61                <td>Pineapple</td>\
```

Fig. G.1 | XHTML table. (Part 2 of 3.)

```
62              <td>$2.00</td>
63          </tr>
64       </tbody>
65
66    </table>
67
68  </body>
69 </html>
```

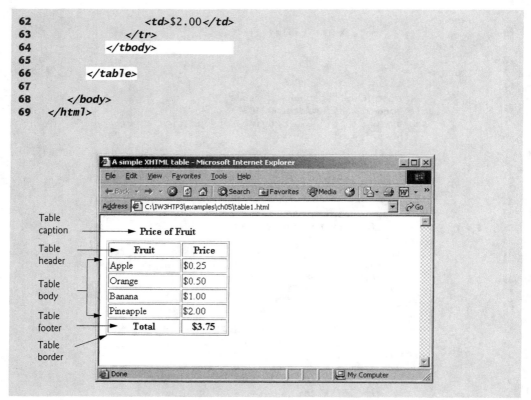

Fig. G.1 | XHTML table. (Part 3 of 3.)

As its name implies, attribute **summary** (lines 17–18) describes the table's contents. Speech devices use this attribute to make the table more accessible to users with visual impairments. The **caption** element (line 22) describes the table's content and helps text-based browsers interpret the table data. Text inside the <caption> tag is rendered above the table by most browsers. Attribute summary and element caption are two of the many XHTML features that make Web pages more accessible to users with disabilities.

A table has three distinct sections—*head*, *body* and *foot*. The head section (or header cell) is defined with a **thead** element (lines 26–31), which contains header information such as column names. Each **tr** element (lines 27–30) defines an individual *table row*. The columns in the head section are defined with **th** elements. Most browsers center text formatted by th (table header column) elements and display them in bold. Table header elements are nested inside table row elements.

The foot section (lines 35–40) is defined with a **tfoot** (table foot) element. The text placed in the footer commonly includes calculation results and footnotes. Like other sections, the foot section can contain table rows, and each row can contain columns.

The body section, or *table body*, contains the table's primary data. The table body (lines 44–64) is defined in a **tbody** element. In the body, each **tr** element specifies one row. *Data cells* contain individual pieces of data and are defined with **td** (*table data*) elements within each row.

G.3 Intermediate XHTML Tables and Formatting

In the preceding section, we explored the structure of a basic table. In Fig. G.2, we enhance our discussion of tables by introducing elements and attributes that allow the document author to build more complex tables.

The table begins in line 17. Element **colgroup** (lines 22–27) groups and formats columns. The col element (line 26) specifies two attributes in this example. The align attribute determines the alignment of text in the column. The **span** attribute determines how many columns the col element formats. In this case, we set align's value to "right" and span's value to "1" to right align text in the first column (the column containing the picture of the camel in the sample screen capture).

Table cells are sized to fit the data they contain. Document authors can create larger data cells by using the attributes **rowspan** and **colspan**. The values assigned to these attributes specify the number of rows or columns occupied by a cell. The th element at lines 36–39 uses the attribute rowspan = "2" to allow the cell containing the picture of the camel to use two vertically adjacent cells (thus the cell *spans* two rows). The th element in lines 42–45 uses the attribute colspan = "4" to widen the header cell (containing Camelid comparison and Approximate as of 9/2002) to span four cells.

Common Programming Error G.1

When using colspan and rowspan to adjust the size of table data cells, keep in mind that the modified cells will occupy more than one column or row. Other rows or columns of the table must compensate for the extra rows or columns spanned by individual cells. If they do not, the formatting of your table will be distorted and you may inadvertently create more columns and rows than you originally intended.

```
1   <?xml version = "1.0"?>
2   <!DOCTYPE html PUBLIC "-//W3C//DTD XHTML 1.1//EN"
3       "http://www.w3.org/TR/xhtml11/DTD/xhtml11.dtd">
4
5   <!-- Fig. G.2: table2.html      -->
6   <!-- Intermediate table design -->
7
8   <html xmlns = "http://www.w3.org/1999/xhtml">
9       <head>
10          <title>Internet and WWW How to Program - Tables</title>
11      </head>
12
13      <body>
14
15          <h1>Table Example Page</h1>
16
17          <table border = "1">
18              <caption>Here is a more complex sample table.</caption>
19
20              <!-- <colgroup> and <col> tags are used to -->
21              <!-- format entire columns                 -->
22              <colgroup>
23
```

Fig. G.2 | Complex XHTML table. (Part 1 of 3.)

```
24           <!-- span attribute determines how many columns -->
25           <!-- the <col> tag affects                       -->
26           <col align = "right" span = "1" />
27       </colgroup>
28
29       <thead>
30
31           <!-- rowspans and colspans merge the specified    -->
32           <!-- number of cells vertically or horizontally   -->
33           <tr>
34
35               <!-- merge two rows -->
36               <th rowspan = "2">
37                   <img src = "camel.gif" width = "205"
38                       height = "167" alt = "Picture of a camel" />
39               </th>
40
41               <!-- merge four columns -->
42               <th colspan = "4" valign = "top">
43                   <h1>Camelid comparison</h1><br />
44                   <p>Approximate as of 9/2002</p>
45               </th>
46           </tr>
47
48           <tr valign = "bottom">
49               <th># of Humps</th>
50               <th>Indigenous region</th>
51               <th>Spits?</th>
52               <th>Produces Wool?</th>
53           </tr>
54
55       </thead>
56
57       <tbody>
58
59           <tr>
60               <th>Camels (bactrian)</th>
61               <td>2</td>
62               <td>Africa/Asia</td>
63               <td>Yes</td>
64               <td>Yes</td>
65           </tr>
66
67           <tr>
68               <th>Llamas</th>
69               <td>1</td>
70               <td>Andes Mountains</td>
71               <td>Yes</td>
72               <td>Yes</td>
73           </tr>
74
75       </tbody>
76
```

Fig. G.2 | Complex XHTML table. (Part 2 of 3.)

```
77          </table>
78
79      </body>
80  </html>
```

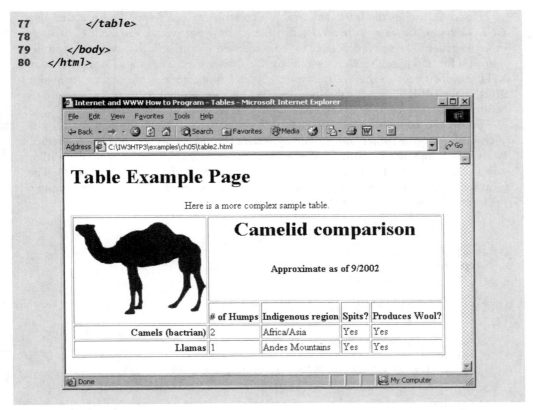

Fig. G.2 | Complex XHTML table. (Part 3 of 3.)

Line 42 introduces the attribute *valign*, which aligns data vertically and may be assigned one of four values—"top" aligns data with the top of the cell, "middle" vertically centers data (the default for all data and header cells), "bottom" aligns data with the bottom of the cell and "baseline" ignores the fonts used for the row data and sets the bottom of all text in the row on a common *baseline* (i.e., the horizontal line at which each character in a word is aligned).

G.4 Basic XHTML Forms

When browsing Web sites, users often need to provide such information as search keywords, e-mail addresses and zip codes. XHTML provides a mechanism, called a *form*, for collecting such data from a user.

Data that users enter on a Web page normally is sent to a Web server that provides access to a site's resources (e.g., XHTML documents, images). These resources are located either on the same machine as the Web server or on a machine that the Web server can access through the network. When a browser requests a Web page or file that is located on a server, the server processes the request and returns the requested resource. A request contains the name and path of the desired resource and the method of communication (called a *protocol*). XHTML documents use the Hypertext Transfer Protocol (HTTP).

Figure G.3 sends the form data to the Web server, which passes the form data to a *CGI* (*Common Gateway Interface*) script (i.e., a program) written in Perl, C or some other language. The script processes the data received from the Web server and typically returns information to the Web server. The Web server then sends the information as an XHTML document to the Web browser. [*Note:* This example demonstrates client-side functionality. If the form is submitted (by clicking **Submit Your Entries**) an error occurs because we have not yet configured the required server-side functionality.]

Forms can contain visual and nonvisual components. Visual components include clickable buttons and other graphical user interface components with which users interact. Nonvisual components, called *hidden inputs*, store any data that the document author specifies, such as e-mail addresses and XHTML document file names that act as links. The form is defined in lines 23–52 by a *form* element. Attribute *method* (line 23) specifies how the form's data is sent to the Web server.

```
1    <?xml version = "1.0"?>
2    <!DOCTYPE html PUBLIC "-//W3C//DTD XHTML 1.1//EN"
3       "http://www.w3.org/TR/xhtml11/DTD/xhtml11.dtd">
4
5    <!-- Fig. G.3: form.html    -->
6    <!-- Form Design Example 1 -->
7
8    <html xmlns = "http://www.w3.org/1999/xhtml">
9       <head>
10          <title>Internet and WWW How to Program - Forms</title>
11       </head>
12
13       <body>
14
15          <h1>Feedback Form</h1>
16
17          <p>Please fill out this form to help
18             us improve our site.</p>
19
20          <!-- this tag starts the form, gives the    -->
21          <!-- method of sending information and the -->
22          <!-- location of form scripts               -->
23          <form method = "post" action = "/cgi-bin/formmail">
24
25             <p>
26                <!-- hidden inputs contain non-visual -->
27                <!-- information                       -->
28                <input type = "hidden" name = "recipient"
29                   value = "deitel@deitel.com" />
30                <input type = "hidden" name = "subject"
31                   value = "Feedback Form" />
32                <input type = "hidden" name = "redirect"
33                   value = "main.html" />
34             </p>
35
```

Fig. G.3 | Form with hidden fields and a text box. (Part 1 of 2.)

```
36              <!-- <input type = "text"> inserts a text box -->
37              <p><label>Name:
38                  <input name = "name" type = "text" size = "25"
39                      maxlength = "30" />
40              </label></p>
41
42              <p>
43                  <!-- input types "submit" and "reset" insert  -->
44                  <!-- buttons for submitting and clearing the   -->
45                  <!-- form's contents                           -->
46                  <input type = "submit" value =
47                      "Submit Your Entries" />
48                  <input type = "reset" value =
49                      "Clear Your Entries" />
50              </p>
51
52          </form>
53
54      </body>
55  </html>
```

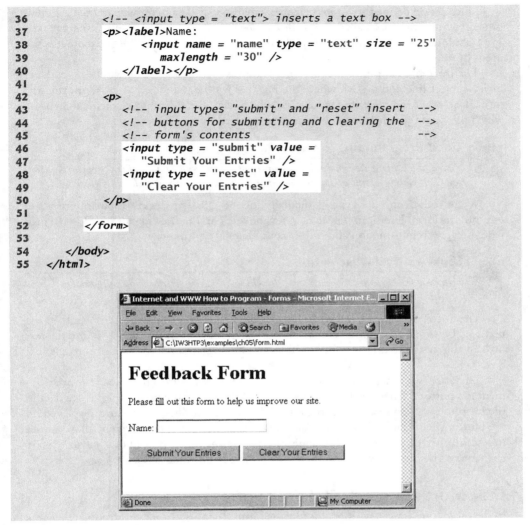

Fig. G.3 | Form with hidden fields and a text box. (Part 2 of 2.)

Using *method = "post"* appends form data to the browser request, which contains the protocol (i.e., HTTP) and the requested resource's URL. Scripts located on the Web server's computer (or on a computer accessible through the network) can access the form data sent as part of the request. For example, a script may take the form information and update an electronic mailing list. The other possible value, *method = "get"*, appends the form data directly to the end of the URL. For example, the URL /cgi-bin/formmail might have the form information name = bob appended to it.

The *action* attribute in the <form> tag specifies the URL of a script on the Web server; in this case, it specifies a script that e-mails form data to an address. Most Internet Service Providers (ISPs) have a script like this on their site; ask the Web site system administrator how to set up an XHTML document to use the script correctly.

Lines 28–33 define three *input* elements that specify data to provide to the script that processes the form (also called the *form handler*). These three input elements have the **type** attribute *"hidden"*, which allows the document author to send form data that is not input by a user.

The three hidden inputs are: an e-mail address to which the data will be sent, the e-mail's subject line and a URL where the browser will be redirected after submitting the form. Two other input attributes are *name*, which identifies the input element, and *value*, which provides the value that will be sent (or posted) to the Web server.

Good Programming Practice G.1

Place hidden input elements at the beginning of a form, immediately after the opening <form> tag. This placement allows document authors to locate hidden input elements quickly.

We introduce another type of input in lines 38–39. The *"text"* input inserts a *text box* into the form. Users can type data in text boxes. The **label** element (lines 37–40) provides users with information about the input element's purpose.

Look-and-Feel Observation G.1

Include a label element for each form element to help users determine the purpose of each form element.

The input element's **size** attribute specifies the number of characters visible in the text box. Optional attribute **maxlength** limits the number of characters input into the text box. In this case, the user is not permitted to type more than 30 characters into the text box.

There are two other types of input elements in lines 46–49. The *"submit"* input element is a button. When the user presses a "submit" button, the browser sends the data in the form to the Web server for processing. The **value** attribute sets the text displayed on the button (the default value is **Submit Query**). The *"reset"* input element allows a user to reset all form elements to their default values. The value attribute of the "reset" input element sets the text displayed on the button (the default value is **Reset**).

G.5 More Complex XHTML Forms

In the preceding section, we introduced basic forms. In this section, we introduce elements and attributes for creating more complex forms. Figure G.4 contains a form that solicits user feedback about a Web site.

```
1    <?xml version = "1.0"?>
2    <!DOCTYPE html PUBLIC "-//W3C//DTD XHTML 1.1//EN"
3        "http://www.w3.org/TR/xhtml11/DTD/xhtml11.dtd">
4
5    <!-- Fig. G.4: form2.html   -->
6    <!-- Form Design Example 2 -->
7
8    <html xmlns = "http://www.w3.org/1999/xhtml">
```

G.4 | Form with text areas, a password box and checkboxes. (Part 1 of 4.)

```
 9      <head>
10         <title>Internet and WWW How to Program - Forms</title>
11      </head>
12
13      <body>
14
15         <h1>Feedback Form</h1>
16
17         <p>Please fill out this form to help
18            us improve our site.</p>
19
20         <form method = "post" action = "/cgi-bin/formmail">
21
22            <p>
23               <input type = "hidden" name = "recipient"
24                  value = "deitel@deitel.com" />
25               <input type = "hidden" name = "subject"
26                  value = "Feedback Form" />
27               <input type = "hidden" name = "redirect"
28                  value = "main.html" />
29            </p>
30
31            <p><label>Name:
32               <input name = "name" type = "text" size = "25" />
33            </label></p>
34
35            <!-- <textarea> creates a multiline textbox -->
36            <p><label>Comments:<br />
37               <textarea name = "comments" rows = "4" cols = "36">
38   Enter your comments here.
39               </textarea>
40            </label></p>
41
42            <!-- <input type = "password"> inserts a    -->
43            <!-- textbox whose display is masked with   -->
44            <!-- asterisk characters                    -->
45            <p><label>E-mail Address:
46               <input name = "email" type = "password"
47                  size = "25" />
48            </label></p>
49
50            <p>
51               <strong>Things you liked:</strong><br />
52
53               <label>Site design
54               <input name = "thingsliked" type = "checkbox"
55                  value = "Design" /></label>
56
57               <label>Links
58               <input name = "thingsliked" type = "checkbox"
59                  value = "Links" /></label>
60
```

Fig. G.4 | Form with text areas, a password box and checkboxes. (Part 2 of 4.)

```
61              <label>Ease of use
62              <input name = "thingsliked" type = "checkbox"
63                 value = "Ease" /></label>
64
65              <label>Images
66              <input name = "thingsliked" type = "checkbox"
67                 value = "Images" /></label>
68
69              <label>Source code
70              <input name = "thingsliked" type = "checkbox"
71                 value = "Code" /></label>
72          </p>
73
74          <p>
75              <input type = "submit" value =
76                 "Submit Your Entries" />
77              <input type = "reset" value =
78                 "Clear Your Entries" />
79          </p>
80
81       </form>
82
83    </body>
84  </html>
```

Fig. G.4 | Form with text areas, a password box and checkboxes. (Part 3 of 4.)

Fig. G.4 | Form with text areas, a password box and checkboxes. (Part 4 of 4.)

The ***textarea*** element (lines 37–39) inserts a multiline text box, called a ***text area***, into the form. The <u>number of rows is specified with the **rows** attribute, and the number of columns (i.e., characters) is specified with the **cols** attribute</u>. In this example, the textarea is four rows high and 36 characters wide. To display default text in the text area, place the text between the **<textarea>** and **</textarea>** tags. Default text can be specified in other input types, such as text boxes, by using the value attribute

The *"password"* input in lines 46–47 inserts a password box with the specified size. A password box allows users to enter sensitive information, such as credit card numbers and passwords, by "masking" the information input with asterisks (*). The actual value input is sent to the Web server, not the characters that mask the input.

Lines 54–71 introduce the ***checkbox*** form element. Checkboxes enable users to select from a set of options. When a user selects a checkbox, a check mark appears in the check box. Otherwise, the checkbox remains empty. Each *"checkbox"* input creates a new checkbox. Checkboxes can be used individually or in groups. Checkboxes that belong to a group are assigned the same name (in this case, "thingsliked").

Common Programming Error G.2

When your form has several checkboxes with the same name, you must make sure that they have different values, or the scripts running on the Web server will not be able to distinguish them.

We continue our discussion of forms by presenting a third example that introduces several additional form elements from which users can make selections (Fig. G.5). In this

```
1    <?xml version = "1.0"?>
2    <!DOCTYPE html PUBLIC "-//W3C//DTD XHTML 1.1//EN"
3       "http://www.w3.org/TR/xhtml11/DTD/xhtml11.dtd">
4
5    <!-- Fig. G.5: form3.html  -->
6    <!-- Form Design Example 3 -->
7
8    <html xmlns = "http://www.w3.org/1999/xhtml">
9       <head>
10          <title>Internet and WWW How to Program - Forms</title>
11       </head>
12
13       <body>
14
15          <h1>Feedback Form</h1>
16
17          <p>Please fill out this form to help
18             us improve our site.</p>
19
20          <form method = "post" action = "/cgi-bin/formmail">
21
22             <p>
23                <input type = "hidden" name = "recipient"
24                   value = "deitel@deitel.com" />
25                <input type = "hidden" name = "subject"
26                   value = "Feedback Form" />
27                <input type = "hidden" name = "redirect"
28                   value = "main.html" />
29             </p>
30
31             <p><label>Name:
32                <input name = "name" type = "text" size = "25" />
33                </label></p>
34
35             <p><label>Comments:<br />
36                   <textarea name = "comments" rows = "4"
37                      cols = "36"></textarea>
38                </label></p>
39
40             <p><label>E-mail Address:
41                   <input name = "email" type = "password"
42                      size = "25" /></label></p>
43
44             <p>
45                <strong>Things you liked:</strong><br />
46
47                <label>Site design
48                   <input name = "thingsliked" type = "checkbox"
49                      value = "Design" /></label>
50
51                <label>Links
52                   <input name = "thingsliked" type = "checkbox"
53                      value = "Links" /></label>
```

Fig. G.5 | Form including radio buttons and a drop-down list. (Part 1 of 4.)

```
54
55          <label>Ease of use
56             <input name = "thingsliked" type = "checkbox"
57                value = "Ease" /></label>
58
59          <label>Images
60             <input name = "thingsliked" type = "checkbox"
61                value = "Images" /></label>
62
63          <label>Source code
64             <input name = "thingsliked" type = "checkbox"
65                value = "Code" /></label>
66      </p>
67
68      <!-- <input type = "radio" /> creates a radio      -->
69      <!-- button. The difference between radio buttons -->
70      <!-- and checkboxes is that only one radio button -->
71      <!-- in a group can be selected.                  -->
72      <p>
73         <strong>How did you get to our site?:</strong><br />
74
75          <label>Search engine
76             <input name = "howtosite" type = "radio"
77                value = "search engine" checked = "checked" />
78          </label>
79
80          <label>Links from another site
81             <input name = "howtosite" type = "radio"
82                value = "link" /></label>
83
84          <label>Deitel.com Web site
85             <input name = "howtosite" type = "radio"
86                value = "deitel.com" /></label>
87
88          <label>Reference in a book
89             <input name = "howtosite" type = "radio"
90                value = "book" /></label>
91
92          <label>Other
93             <input name = "howtosite" type = "radio"
94                value = "other" /></label>
95
96      </p>
97
98      <p>
99         <label>Rate our site:
100
101            <!-- the <select> tag presents a drop-down -->
102            <!-- list with choices indicated by the    -->
103            <!-- <option> tags                          -->
104         <select name = "rating">
105            <option selected = "selected">Amazing</option>
106            <option>10</option>
```

Fig. G.5 | Form including radio buttons and a drop-down list. (Part 2 of 4.)

```
107                         <option>9</option>
108                         <option>8</option>
109                         <option>7</option>
110                         <option>6</option>
111                         <option>5</option>
112                         <option>4</option>
113                         <option>3</option>
114                         <option>2</option>
115                         <option>1</option>
116                         <option>Awful</option>
117                      </select>
118
119               </label>
120          </p>
121
122          <p>
123             <input type = "submit" value =
124                "Submit Your Entries" />
125             <input type = "reset" value = "Clear Your Entries" />
126          </p>
127
128       </form>
129
130    </body>
131 </html>
```

Fig. G.5 | Form including radio buttons and a drop-down list. (Part 3 of 4.)

Fig. G.5 | Form including radio buttons and a drop-down list. (Part 4 of 4.)

example, we introduce two new input types. The first type is the *radio button* (lines 76–94) specified with type "radio". Radio buttons are similar to checkboxes, except that only one radio button in a group of radio buttons may be selected at any time. The radio buttons in a group all have the same name attributes and are distinguished by their different value attributes. The attribute-value pair checked = "checked" (line 77) indicates which radio button, if any, is selected initially. The checked attribute also applies to checkboxes.

Common Programming Error G.3

Not setting the name attributes of the radio buttons in a form to the same name is a logic error because it lets the user select all of them at the same time.

The *select* element (lines 104–117) provides a drop-down list of items from which the user can select an item. The name attribute identifies the drop-down list. The *option* element (lines 105–116) adds items to the drop-down list. The option element's *selected attribute* specifies which item initially is displayed as the selected item.

G.6 Internal Linking

In Appendix F, we discussed how to hyperlink one Web page to another. Figure G.6 introduces *internal linking*—a mechanism that enables the user to jump between locations in the same document. Internal linking is useful for long documents that contain many sections. Clicking an internal link enables users to find a section without scrolling through the entire document.

Line 16 contains a tag with the *id* attribute (called "features") for an internal hyperlink. To link to a tag with this attribute inside the same Web page, the href attribute of an anchor element includes the id attribute value preceded by a pound sign (as in #features). Lines 61–62 contain a hyperlink with the id features as its target. Selecting this hyperlink in a Web browser scrolls the browser window to the h1 tag in line 16.

```
1    <?xml version = "1.0"?>
2    <!DOCTYPE html PUBLIC "-//W3C//DTD XHTML 1.1//EN"
3       "http://www.w3.org/TR/xhtml11/DTD/xhtml11.dtd">
4
5    <!-- Fig. G.6: links.html -->
6    <!-- Internal Linking       -->
7
8    <html xmlns = "http://www.w3.org/1999/xhtml">
9       <head>
10         <title>Internet and WWW How to Program - List</title>
11      </head>
12
13      <body>
14
15         <!-- id attribute creates an internal hyperlink destination -->
16         <h1 id = "features">The Best Features of the Internet</h1>
17
18         <!-- an internal link's address is "#id" -->
19         <p><a href = "#bugs">Go to <em>Favorite Bugs</em></a></p>
20
21         <ul>
22            <li>You can meet people from countries
23               around the world.</li>
24
25            <li>You have access to new media as it becomes public:
26               <ul>
27                  <li>New games</li>
28                  <li>New applications
29                     <ul>
30                        <li>For Business</li>
31                        <li>For Pleasure</li>
32                     </ul>
33                  </li>
34
35                  <li>Around the clock news</li>
36                  <li>Search Engines</li>
37                  <li>Shopping</li>
38                  <li>Programming
39                     <ul>
40                        <li>XHTML</li>
41                        <li>Java</li>
42                        <li>Dynamic HTML</li>
43                        <li>Scripts</li>
```

Fig. G.6 | Internal hyperlinks to make pages more navigable. (Part 1 of 3.)

```
44                      <li>New languages</li>
45                  </ul>
46              </li>
47          </ul>
48      </li>
49
50      <li>Links</li>
51      <li>Keeping in touch with old friends</li>
52      <li>It is the technology of the future!</li>
53   </ul>
54
55   <!-- id attribute creates an internal hyperlink destination -->
56   <h1 id = "bugs">My 3 Favorite Bugs</h1>
57
58   <p>
59
60      <!-- internal hyperlink to features -->
61      <a href = "#features">Go to <em>Favorite Features</em>
62      </a></p>
63
64   <ol>
65      <li>Fire Fly</li>
66      <li>Gal Ant</li>
67      <li>Roman Tic</li>
68   </ol>
69
70   </body>
71 </html>
```

Fig. G.6 | Internal hyperlinks to make pages more navigable. (Part 2 of 3.)

Fig. G.6 | Internal hyperlinks to make pages more navigable. (Part 3 of 3.)

Look-and-Feel Observation G.2

Internal hyperlinks are useful in XHTML documents that contain large amounts of information. Internal links to different parts of the page makes it easier for users to navigate the page. They do not have to scroll to find the section they want.

Although not demonstrated in this example, a hyperlink can specify an internal link in another document by specifying the document name followed by a pound sign and the id value, as in:

    href = "*filename*.html#*id*"

For example, to link to a tag with the id attribute called booklist in books.html, href is assigned "books.html#booklist".

G.7 Creating and Using Image Maps

In Appendix F, we demonstrated how images can be used as hyperlinks to link to other resources on the Internet. In this section, we introduce another technique for image linking called *image maps*, which designates certain areas of an image (called *hotspots*) as links.[1] Figure G.7 introduces image maps and hotspots.

---

1. Some Web browsers do not support XHTML 1.1 image maps. For this reason we use XHTML 1.0 Transitional, an earlier W3C version of XHTML. In order to validate the code in Figure G.7 as XHTML 1.1, remove the # from the usemap attribute of the img tag (line 53).

```
 1    <?xml version = "1.0" ?>
 2    <!DOCTYPE html PUBLIC "-//W3C//DTD XHTML 1.0 Transitional//EN"
 3        "http://www.w3.org/TR/xhtml1/DTD/xhtml1-transitional.dtd">
 4
 5    <!-- Fig. G.7: picture.html          -->
 6    <!-- Creating and Using Image Maps -->
 7
 8    <html xmlns = "http://www.w3.org/1999/xhtml">
 9       <head>
10          <title>
11             Internet and WWW How to Program - Image Map
12          </title>
13       </head>
14
15       <body>
16
17          <p>
18
19          <!-- the <map> tag defines an image map -->
20          <map id = "picture">
21
22             <!-- shape = "rect" indicates a rectangular      -->
23             <!-- area, with coordinates for the upper-left -->
24             <!-- and lower-right corners                     -->
25             <area href = "form.html" shape = "rect"
26                coords = "2,123,54,143"
27                alt = "Go to the feedback form" />
28             <area href = "contact.html" shape = "rect"
29                coords = "126,122,198,143"
30                alt = "Go to the contact page" />
31             <area href = "main.html" shape = "rect"
32                coords = "3,7,61,25" alt = "Go to the homepage" />
33             <area href = "links.html" shape = "rect"
34                coords = "168,5,197,25"
35                alt = "Go to the links page" />
36
37             <!-- value "poly" creates a hotspot in the shape -->
38             <!-- of a polygon, defined by coords             -->
39             <area shape = "poly" alt = "E-mail the Deitels"
40                coords = "162,25,154,39,158,54,169,51,183,39,161,26"
41                href = "mailto:deitel@deitel.com" />
42
43             <!-- shape = "circle" indicates a circular -->
44             <!-- area with the given center and radius -->
45             <area href = "mailto:deitel@deitel.com"
46                shape = "circle" coords = "100,36,33"
47                alt = "E-mail the Deitels" />
48          </map>
49
50          <!-- <img src =... usemap = "#id"> indicates that the -->
51          <!-- specified image map is used with this image       -->
52          <img src = "deitel.gif" width = "200" height = "144"
53             alt = "Deitel logo" usemap = "#picture" />
```

Fig. G.7 | Image with links anchored to an image map. (Part 1 of 2.)

```
54        </p>
55     </body>
56  </html>
```

Fig. G.7 | Image with links anchored to an image map. (Part 2 of 2.)

Lines 20–48 define an image map by using a *map* element. Attribute *id* (line 20) identifies the image map. If id is omitted, the map cannot be referenced by an image (which we will see momentarily). Hotspots are defined with *area* elements (as shown in lines 25–27). Attribute href (line 25) specifies the link's target (i.e., the resource to which to link). Attributes *shape* (line 25) and *coords* (line 26) specify the hotspot's shape and coordinates, respectively. Attribute alt (line 27) provides alternative text for the link.

Common Programming Error G.4

Not specifying an id attribute for a map *element prevents an* img *element from using the* map's area *elements to define hotspots.*

The markup in lines 25–27 creates a *rectangular hotspot* (shape = "rect") for the *coordinates* specified in the coords attribute. A coordinate pair consists of two numbers representing the locations of a point on the *x*-axis and the *y*-axis, respectively. The *x*-axis extends horizontally and the *y*-axis extends vertically from the upper-left corner of the image. Every point on an image has a unique *x-y*-coordinate. For rectangular hotspots, the required coordinates are those of the upper-left and lower-right corners of the rectangle. In this case, the upper-left corner of the rectangle is located at 2 on the *x*-axis and 123 on the *y*-axis, annotated as *(2, 123)*. The lower-right corner of the rectangle is at *(54, 143)*. Coordinates are measured in pixels.

Common Programming Error G.5

Overlapping coordinates of an image map cause the browser to render the first hotspot it encounters for the area.

The map area at lines 39–41 assigns the shape attribute *"poly"* to create a hotspot in the shape of a polygon using the coordinates in attribute coords. These coordinates represent each *vertex*, or corner, of the polygon. The browser connects these points with lines to form the hotspot's area.

The map area at lines 45–47 assigns the shape attribute *"circle"* to create a *circular hotspot*. In this case, the coords attribute specifies the circle's center coordinates and the circle's radius, in pixels.

To use an image map with an img element, you must assign the img element's *usemap* attribute to the id of a map. Lines 52–53 reference the image map "#picture". The image map is located within the same document, so internal linking is used.

G.8 meta Elements

Search engines are used to find Web sites. They usually catalog sites by following links from page to page (known as spidering or crawling) and saving identification and classification information for each page. One way that search engines catalog pages is by reading the content in each page's *meta* elements, which specify information about a document.

Two important attributes of the meta element are *name*, which identifies the type of meta element, and *content*, which provides the information search engines use to catalog pages. Figure G.8 introduces the meta element.

```
1   <?xml version = "1.0"?>
2   <!DOCTYPE html PUBLIC "-//W3C//DTD XHTML 1.1//EN"
3      "http://www.w3.org/TR/xhtml11/DTD/xhtml11.dtd">
4
5   <!-- Fig. G.8: main.html -->
6   <!-- <meta> tag          -->
7
8   <html xmlns = "http://www.w3.org/1999/xhtml">
9      <head>
10        <title>Internet and WWW How to Program - Welcome</title>
11
12        <!-- <meta> tags provide search engines with -->
13        <!-- information used to catalog a site      -->
14        <meta name = "keywords" content = "Web page, design,
15           XHTML, tutorial, personal, help, index, form,
16           contact, feedback, list, links, frame, deitel" />
17
18        <meta name = "description" content = "This Web site will
19           help you learn the basics of XHTML and Web page design
20           through the use of interactive examples and
21           instruction." />
22
23     </head>
```

Fig. G.8 | meta tags provide keywords and a description of a page. (Part 1 of 2.)

```
24
25      <body>
26
27        <h1>Welcome to Our Web Site!</h1>
28
29        <p>We have designed this site to teach about the wonders
30        of <strong><em>XHTML</em></strong>. <em>XHTML</em> is
31        better equipped than <em>HTML</em> to represent complex
32        data on the Internet. <em>XHTML</em> takes advantage of
33        XML's strict syntax to ensure well-formedness. Soon you
34        will know about many of the great new features of
35        <em>XHTML.</em></p>
36
37        <p>Have Fun With the Site!</p>
38
39      </body>
40    </html>
```

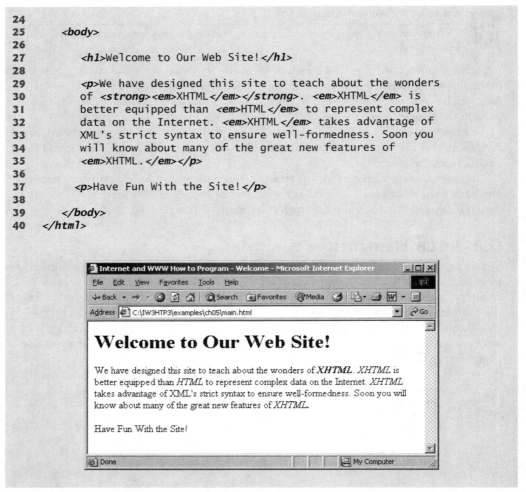

Fig. G.8 | meta tags provide keywords and a description of a page. (Part 2 of 2.)

Lines 14–16 demonstrate a *"keywords"* meta element. The content attribute of such a meta element provides search engines with a list of words that describe a page. These words are compared with words in search requests. Thus, including meta elements and their content information can draw more viewers to your site.

Lines 18–21 demonstrate a *"description"* meta element. The content attribute of such a meta element provides a three- to four-line description of a site, written in sentence form. Search engines also use this description to catalog your site and sometimes display this information as part of the search results.

Software Engineering Observation G.1

meta elements are not visible to users and must be placed inside the head *section of your XHTML document. If* meta *elements are not placed in this section, they will not be read by search engines.*

G.9 frameset Element

All of the Web pages we present in this book have the ability to link to other pages, but can display only one page at a time. *Frames* allow a Web developer to display more than one XHTML document in the browser simultaneously. Figure G.9 uses frames to display the documents in Fig. G.8 and Fig. G.10.

Most of our earlier examples adhere to the XHTML 1.1 document type, whereas these use the XHTML 1.0 document types.[1] These document types are specified in lines 2–3 and are required for documents that define framesets or use the target attribute to work with framesets.

A document that defines a frameset normally consists of an html element that contains a head element and a *frameset* element (lines 23–40). In Fig. G.9, the *<frameset>* tag (line 23) informs the browser that the page contains frames. Attribute *cols* specifies the frameset's column layout. The value of cols gives the width of each frame, either in pixels or as a percentage of the browser width. In this case, the attribute cols = "110,*" informs the browser that there are two vertical frames. The first frame extends 110 pixels from the left edge of the browser window, and the second frame fills the remainder of the browser width (as indicated by the asterisk). Similarly, frameset attribute *rows* can be used to specify the number of rows and the size of each row in a frameset.

```
1    <?xml version = "1.0"?>
2    <!DOCTYPE html PUBLIC "-//W3C//DTD XHTML 1.0 Frameset//EN"
3        "http://www.w3.org/TR/xhtml1/DTD/xhtml1-frameset.dtd">
4
5    <!-- Fig. G.9: index.html -->
6    <!-- XHTML Frames I        -->
7
8    <html xmlns = "http://www.w3.org/1999/xhtml">
9      <head>
10         <title>Internet and WWW How to Program - Main</title>
11         <meta name = "keywords" content = "Webpage, design,
12            XHTML, tutorial, personal, help, index, form,
13            contact, feedback, list, links, frame, deitel" />
14
15         <meta name = "description" content = "This Web site will
16            help you learn the basics of XHTML and Web page design
17            through the use of interactive examples
18            and instruction." />
19
20      </head>
21
22      <!-- the <frameset> tag sets the frame dimensions    -->
23      <frameset cols = "110,*">
```

Fig. G.9 | XHTML frames document with navigation and content. (Part I of 3.)

---

1. XHTML 1.1 no longer supports the use of frames. The W3C recommends using Cascading Style Sheets to achieve the same effect. Frames are still used by some Web sites and supported by most browsers, however. The frameset element and the target attribute are still supported in the XHTML 1.0 Frameset and the XHTML 1.0 Transitional document type definitions, respectively. Please refer to www.w3.org/TR/xhtml1/#dtds for more information.

```
24
25        <!-- frame elements specify which pages -->
26        <!-- are loaded into a given frame        -->
27        <frame name = "leftframe" src = "nav.html" />
28        <frame name = "main" src = "main.html" />
29
30        <noframes>
31           <body>
32              <p>This page uses frames, but your browser does not
33              support them.</p>
34
35              <p>Please, <a href = "nav.html">follow this link to
36              browse our site without frames</a>.</p>
37           </body>
38        </noframes>
39
40     </frameset>
41  </html>
```

Fig. G.9 | XHTML frames document with navigation and content. (Part 2 of 3.)

Fig. G.9 | XHTML frames document with navigation and content. (Part 3 of 3.)

The documents that will be loaded into the frameset are specified with **frame** elements (lines 27–28 in this example). Attribute src specifies the URL of the page to display in the frame. Each frame has name and src attributes. The first frame (which covers 110 pixels on the left side of the frameset), named leftframe, displays the page nav.html (Fig. G.10). The second frame, named main, displays the page main.html (Fig. G.8).

Attribute name identifies a frame, enabling hyperlinks in a frameset to specify the *target* frame in which a linked document should display when the user clicks the link. For example

```
<a href = "links.html" target = "main">
```

loads links.html in the frame whose name is "main".

Not all browsers support frames. XHTML provides the **noframes** element (lines 30–38) to enable XHTML document designers to specify alternative content for browsers that do not support frames.

Portability Tip G.1

Some browsers do not support frames. Use the noframes element inside a frameset to direct users to a nonframed version of your site.

Figure G.10 is the Web page displayed in the left frame of Fig. G.9. This XHTML document provides the navigation buttons that, when clicked, determine which document is displayed in the right frame.

Line 27 (Fig. G.9) displays the XHTML page in Fig. G.10. Anchor attribute `target` (line 18 in Fig. G.10) specifies that the linked documents are loaded in frame `main` (line 28 in Fig. G.9). A `target` can be set to a number of preset values: `"_blank"` loads the page into a new browser window, `"_self"` loads the page into the frame in which the anchor element appears and `"_top"` loads the page into the full browser window (i.e., removes the `frameset`).

```
1   <?xml version = "1.0"?>
2   <!DOCTYPE html PUBLIC "-//W3C//DTD XHTML 1.0 Transitional//EN"
3       "http://www.w3.org/TR/xhtml1/DTD/xhtml1-transitional.dtd">
4
5   <!-- Fig. G.10: nav.html          -->
6   <!-- Using images as link anchors -->
7
8   <html xmlns = "http://www.w3.org/1999/xhtml">
9
10     <head>
11        <title>Internet and WWW How to Program - Navigation Bar
12        </title>
13     </head>
14
15     <body>
16
17        <p>
18           <a href = "links.html" target = "main">
19              <img src = "buttons/links.jpg" width = "65"
20                 height = "50" alt = "Links Page" />
21           </a><br />
22
23           <a href = "list.html" target = "main">
24              <img src = "buttons/list.jpg" width = "65"
25                 height = "50" alt = "List Example Page" />
26           </a><br />
27
28           <a href = "contact.html" target = "main">
29              <img src = "buttons/contact.jpg" width = "65"
30                 height = "50" alt = "Contact Page" />
31           </a><br />
32
33           <a href = "header.html" target = "main">
34              <img src = "buttons/header.jpg" width = "65"
35                 height = "50" alt = "Header Page" />
36           </a><br />
37
38           <a href = "table1.html" target = "main">
39              <img src = "buttons/table.jpg" width = "65"
40                 height = "50" alt = "Table Page" />
41           </a><br />
```

Fig. G.10 | XHTML document displayed in the left frame of Fig. G.9. (Part 1 of 2.)

```
42
43              <a href = "form.html" target = "main">
44                  <img src = "buttons/form.jpg" width = "65"
45                      height = "50" alt = "Feedback Form" />
46              </a><br />
47          </p>
48
49      </body>
50  </html>
```

Fig. G.10 | XHTML document displayed in the left frame of Fig. G.9. (Part 2 of 2.)

G.10 Nested framesets

You can use the frameset element to create more complex layouts in a Web page by nesting framesets, as in Fig. G.11. The nested frameset in this example displays the XHTML documents in Fig. G.7, Fig. G.8 and Fig. G.10.

```
 1  <?xml version = "1.0"?>
 2  <!DOCTYPE html PUBLIC "-//W3C//DTD XHTML 1.0 Frameset//EN"
 3      "http://www.w3.org/TR/xhtml1/DTD/xhtml1-frameset.dtd">
 4
 5  <!-- Fig. G.11: index2.html -->
 6  <!-- XHTML Frames II          -->
 7
 8  <html xmlns = "http://www.w3.org/1999/xhtml">
 9      <head>
10          <title>Internet and WWW How to Program - Main</title>
11
12          <meta name = "keywords" content = "Webpage, design,
13              XHTML, tutorial, personal, help, index, form,
14              contact, feedback, list, links, frame, deitel" />
15
16          <meta name = "description" content = "This Web site will
17              help you learn the basics of XHTML and Web page design
18              through the use of interactive examples
19              and instruction." />
20
21      </head>
22
23  <frameset cols = "110,*">
24      <frame name = "leftframe" src = "nav.html" />
25
26      <!-- nested framesets are used to change the -->
27      <!-- formatting and layout of the frameset   -->
28      <frameset rows = "175,*">
29          <frame name = "picture" src = "picture.html" />
30          <frame name = "main" src = "main.html" />
31      </frameset>
32
```

Fig. G.11 | Framed Web site with a nested frameset. (Part 1 of 2.)

```
33          <noframes>
34            <body>
35              <p>This page uses frames, but your browser does not
36              support them.</p>
37
38              <p>Please, <a href = "nav.html">follow this link to
39              browse our site without frames</a>.</p>
40            </body>
41          </noframes>
42
43        </frameset>
44   </html>
```

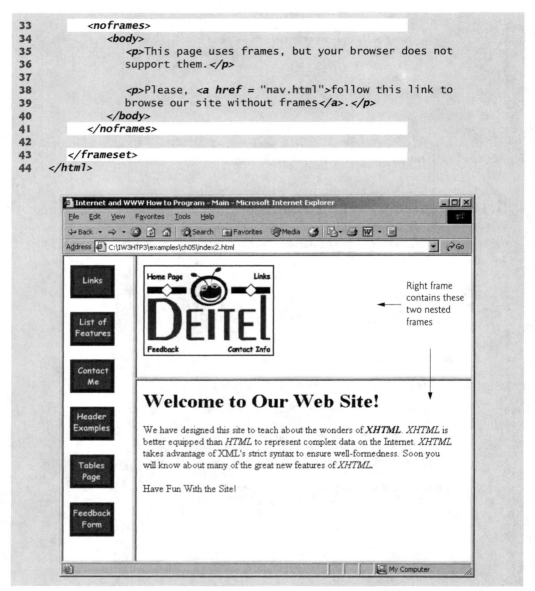

Fig. G.11 | Framed Web site with a nested frameset. (Part 2 of 2.)

The outer `frameset` element (lines 23–43) defines two columns. The left frame extends over the first 110 pixels from the left edge of the browser, and the right frame occupies the rest of the window's width. The `frame` element in line 24 specifies that the document `nav.html` (Fig. G.10) will be displayed in the left column.

Lines 28–31 define a nested `frameset` element for the second column of the outer frameset. This `frameset` defines two rows. The first row extends 175 pixels from the top of the browser window, as indicated by `rows = "175,*"`. The second row occupies the remainder of the browser window's height. The frame element at line 29 specifies that the first row of the nested frameset will display picture.html (Fig. G.7). The frame element in line 30 specifies that the second row of the nested frameset will display main.html (Fig. G.8).

Error-Prevention Tip G.1

When using nested frameset elements, indent every level of <frame> tag. This practice makes the page clearer and easier to debug.

G.11 Web Resources

www.vbxml.com/xhtml/articles/xhtml_tables
The *VBXML.com* Web site contains a tutorial on creating XHTML tables.

www.webreference.com/xml/reference/xhtml.html
This Web page contains a list of frequently used XHTML tags, such as header tags, table tags, frame tags and form tags. It also provides a description of each tag.

XHTML Special Characters

The table of Fig. H.1 shows many commonly used XHTML special characters—called *character entity references* by the World Wide Web Consortium. For a complete list of character entity references, see the site

www.w3.org/TR/REC-html40/sgml/entities.html

Character	XHTML encoding	Character	XHTML encoding
non-breaking space		ā	&#227;
§	&#167;	å	&#229;
©	&#169;	ç	&#231;
®	&#174;	è	&#232;
π	&#188;	é	&#233;
∫	&#189;	ê	&#234;
Ω	&#190;	ì	&#236;
à	&#224;	í	&#237;
á	&#225;	î	&#238;
â	&#226;	ñ	&#241;

Fig. H.1 | XHTML special characters. (Part 1 of 2.)

Character	XHTML encoding	Character	XHTML encoding
ò	`&#242;`	ù	`&#249;`
ó	`&#243;`	ú	`&#250;`
ô	`&#244;`	û	`&#251;`
õ	`&#245;`	•	`&#8226;`
÷	`&#247;`	™	`&#8482;`

Fig. H.1 | XHTML special characters. (Part 2 of 2.)

I

XHTML Colors

Colors may be specified by using a standard name (such as aqua) or a hexadecimal RGB value (such as #00FFFF for aqua). Of the six hexadecimal digits in an RGB value, the first two represent the amount of red in the color, the middle two represent the amount of green in the color, and the last two represent the amount of blue in the color. For example, black is the absence of color and is defined by #000000, whereas white is the maximum amount of red, green and blue and is defined by #FFFFFF. Pure red is #FF0000, pure green (which is called lime) is #00FF00 and pure blue is #0000FF. Note that green in the standard is defined as #008000. Figure I.1 contains the XHTML standard color set. Figure I.2 contains the XHTML extended color set.

Color name	Value	Color name	Value
aqua	#00FFFF	navy	#000080
black	#000000	olive	#808000
blue	#0000FF	purple	#800080
fuchsia	#FF00FF	red	#FF0000
gray	#808080	silver	#C0C0C0
green	#008000	teal	#008080
lime	#00FF00	yellow	#FFFF00
maroon	#800000	white	#FFFFFF

Fig. I.1 | XHTML standard colors and hexadecimal RGB values.

Color name	Value	Color name	Value
aliceblue	#F0F8FF	darkslategray	#2F4F4F
antiquewhite	#FAEBD7	darkturquoise	#00CED1
aquamarine	#7FFFD4	darkviolet	#9400D3
azure	#F0FFFF	deeppink	#FF1493
beige	#F5F5DC	deepskyblue	#00BFFF
bisque	#FFE4C4	dimgray	#696969
blanchedalmond	#FFEBCD	dodgerblue	#1E90FF
blueviolet	#8A2BE2	firebrick	#B22222
brown	#A52A2A	floralwhite	#FFFAF0
burlywood	#DEB887	forestgreen	#228B22
cadetblue	#5F9EA0	gainsboro	#DCDCDC
chartreuse	#7FFF00	ghostwhite	#F8F8FF
chocolate	#D2691E	gold	#FFD700
coral	#FF7F50	goldenrod	#DAA520
cornflowerblue	#6495ED	greenyellow	#ADFF2F
cornsilk	#FFF8DC	honeydew	#F0FFF0
crimson	#DC1436	hotpink	#FF69B4
cyan	#00FFFF	indianred	#CD5C5C
darkblue	#00008B	indigo	#4B0082
darkcyan	#008B8B	ivory	#FFFFF0
darkgoldenrod	#B8860B	khaki	#F0E68C
darkgray	#A9A9A9	lavender	#E6E6FA
darkgreen	#006400	lavenderblush	#FFF0F5
darkkhaki	#BDB76B	lawngreen	#7CFC00
darkmagenta	#8B008B	lemonchiffon	#FFFACD
darkolivegreen	#556B2F	lightblue	#ADD8E6
darkorange	#FF8C00	lightcoral	#F08080
darkorchid	#9932CC	lightcyan	#E0FFFF
darkred	#8B0000	lightgoldenrodyellow	#FAFAD2
darksalmon	#E9967A	lightgreen	#90EE90
darkseagreen	#8FBC8F	lightgrey	#D3D3D3
darkslateblue	#483D8B	lightpink	#FFB6C1

Fig. I.2 | XHTML extended colors and hexadecimal RGB values (Part 1 of 2.).

Color name	Value	Color name	Value
lightsalmon	#FFA07A	palevioletred	#DB7093
lightseagreen	#20B2AA	papayawhip	#FFEFD5
lightskyblue	#87CEFA	peachpuff	#FFDAB9
lightslategray	#778899	peru	#CD853F
lightsteelblue	#B0C4DE	pink	#FFC0CB
lightyellow	#FFFFE0	plum	#DDA0DD
limegreen	#32CD32	powderblue	#B0E0E6
mediumaquamarine	#66CDAA	rosybrown	#BC8F8F
mediumblue	#0000CD	royalblue	#4169E1
mediumorchid	#BA55D3	saddlebrown	#8B4513
mediumpurple	#9370DB	salmon	#FA8072
mediumseagreen	#3CB371	sandybrown	#F4A460
mediumslateblue	#7B68EE	seagreen	#2E8B57
mediumspringgreen	#00FA9A	seashell	#FFF5EE
mediumturquoise	#48D1CC	sienna	#A0522D
mediumvioletred	#C71585	skyblue	#87CEEB
midnightblue	#191970	slateblue	#6A5ACD
mintcream	#F5FFFA	slategray	#708090
mistyrose	#FFE4E1	snow	#FFFAFA
moccasin	#FFE4B5	springgreen	#00FF7F
navajowhite	#FFDEAD	steelblue	#4682B4
oldlace	#FDF5E6	tan	#D2B48C
olivedrab	#6B8E23	thistle	#D8BFD8
orange	#FFA500	tomato	#FF6347
orangered	#FF4500	turquoise	#40E0D0
orchid	#DA70D6	violet	#EE82EE
palegoldenrod	#EEE8AA	wheat	#F5DEB3
palegreen	#98FB98	whitesmoke	#F5F5F5
paleturquoise	#AFEEEE	yellowgreen	#9ACD32

Fig. I.2 | XHTML extended colors and hexadecimal RGB values (Part 2 of 2.).

ATM Case Study Code

J.1 ATM Case Study Implementation

This appendix contains the complete working implementation of the ATM system that we designed in the nine Software Engineering Case Study sections in Chapters 1, 3–9 and 11. The implementation comprises 597 lines of Visual Basic code. We consider the 11 classes in the order in which we identified them in Section 4.9 (with the exception of Transaction, which was introduced in Chapter 11 as the base class of classes Balance-Inquiry, Withdrawal and Deposit):

- ATM
- Screen
- Keypad
- CashDispenser
- DepositSlot
- Account
- BankDatabase
- Transaction
- BalanceInquiry
- Withdrawal
- Deposit

We apply the guidelines discussed in Section 9.14 and Section 11.8 to code these classes based on how we modeled them in the UML class diagrams of Fig. 11.19 and Fig. 11.20. To develop the bodies of class methods, we refer to the activity diagrams presented in Section 6.11 and the communication and sequence diagrams presented in Section 7.20. Note that our ATM design does not specify all the program logic and may not specify all the attributes and operations required to complete the ATM implementation. This is a normal part of the object-oriented design process. As we implement the system, we complete the program logic and add attributes and behaviors as necessary to construct the ATM system specified by the requirements document in Section 3.9.

We conclude the discussion by presenting a Visual Basic application (ATMCaseStudy in Section J.13) that creates an object of class ATM and starts it by calling its run method. Recall that we are developing a first version of the ATM system that runs on a personal computer and uses the keyboard and monitor to approximate the ATM's keypad and screen. Also, we simulate the actions of the ATM's cash dispenser and deposit slot. We attempt to implement the system, however, so that real hardware versions of these devices could be integrated without significant code changes.

J.2 Class ATM

Class ATM (Fig. J.1) represents the ATM as a whole. Lines 4–10 implement the class's attributes. We determine all but one of these attributes from the UML class diagrams of Fig. 11.19 and Fig. 11.20. Line 4 declares the Boolean attribute userAuthenticated from Fig. 11.21. Line 5 declares an attribute not found in our UML design—an Integer attribute currentAccountNumber that keeps track of the account number of the current authenticated user. We will soon see how the class uses this attribute. Lines 6–10 declare reference-type attributes corresponding to the ATM class's associations modeled in the class diagram of Fig. 11.19. These attributes allow the ATM to access its parts (i.e., its Screen, Keypad, CashDispenser and DepositSlot) and interact with the bank's account information database (i.e., a BankDatabase object).

```vb
1    ' ATM.vb
2    ' Represents an automated teller machine.
3    Public Class ATM
4       Private userAuthenticated As Boolean ' whether user is authenticated
5       Private currentAccountNumber As Integer ' user's account number
6       Private screenHandle As Screen ' ATM's screen
7       Private keypadHandle As Keypad ' ATM's keypad
8       Private cashDispenserHandle As CashDispenser ' ATM's cash dispenser
9       Private depositSlotHandle As DepositSlot ' ATM's deposit slot
10      Private bankDatabaseHandle As BankDatabase ' account database
11
12      ' enumeration constants represent main menu options
13      Private Enum MenuOption
14         BALANCE_INQUIRY = 1
15         WITHDRAWAL
16         DEPOSIT
17         EXIT_ATM
18      End Enum ' MenuOption
19
20      ' parameterless constructor initializes instance variables
21      Public Sub New()
22         userAuthenticated = False ' user is not authenticated to start
23         currentAccountNumber = 0 ' no current account number to start
24         screenHandle = New Screen() ' create screen
```

Fig. J.1 | Class ATM represents the ATM. (Part 1 of 3.)

```
25          keypadHandle = New Keypad() ' create keypad
26          cashDispenserHandle = New CashDispenser() ' create cash dispenser
27          depositSlotHandle = New DepositSlot() ' create deposit slot
28          bankDatabaseHandle = New BankDatabase() ' create database
29       End Sub ' New
30
31       ' start ATM
32       Public Sub Run()
33          ' welcome and authenticate users; perform transactions
34          While (True) ' infinite loop
35             ' loop while user is not yet authenticated
36             While (Not userAuthenticated)
37                screenHandle.DisplayMessageLine(vbCrLf & "Welcome!")
38                AuthenticateUser() ' authenticate user
39             End While
40
41             PerformTransactions() ' for authenticated user
42             userAuthenticated = False ' reset before next ATM session
43             currentAccountNumber = 0 ' reset before next ATM session
44             screenHandle.DisplayMessageLine(vbCrLf & "Thank you! Goodbye!")
45          End While
46       End Sub ' Run
47
48       ' attempt to authenticate user against database
49       Private Sub AuthenticateUser()
50          screenHandle.DisplayMessage(vbCrLf & _
51             "Please enter your account number: ")
52          Dim accountNumber As Integer = keypadHandle.GetInput()
53          screenHandle.DisplayMessage(vbCrLf & "Enter your PIN: ") ' prompt
54          Dim pin As Integer = keypadHandle.GetInput() ' get PIN
55
56          ' set userAuthenticated to Boolean value returned by database
57          userAuthenticated = _
58             bankDatabaseHandle.AuthenticateUser(accountNumber, pin)
59
60          ' check whether authentication succeeded
61          If userAuthenticated Then
62             currentAccountNumber = accountNumber ' save user's account #
63          Else
64             screenHandle.DisplayMessageLine( _
65                "Invalid account number or PIN. Please try again.")
66          End If
67       End Sub ' AuthenticateUser
68
69       ' display the main menu and perform transactions
70       Private Sub PerformTransactions()
71          Dim currentTransaction As Transaction ' transaction being processed
72          Dim userExited As Boolean = False ' user has not chosen to exit
73
74          ' loop while user has not chosen exit option
75          While (Not userExited)
76             ' show main menu and get user selection
77             Dim mainMenuSelection As Integer = DisplayMainMenu()
```

Fig. J.1 | Class ATM represents the ATM. (Part 2 of 3.)

```
78
79                ' decide how to proceed based on user's menu selection
80            Select Case (mainMenuSelection)
81                ' user chooses to perform one of three transaction types
82                Case MenuOption.BALANCE_INQUIRY, MenuOption.WITHDRAWAL, _
83                    MenuOption.DEPOSIT
84                    ' initialize as new object of chosen type
85                    currentTransaction = CreateTransaction(mainMenuSelection)
86                    currentTransaction.Execute() ' execute transaction
87                Case MenuOption.EXIT_ATM ' user chose to terminate session
88                    screenHandle.DisplayMessageLine( _
89                        vbCrLf & "Exiting the system...")
90                    userExited = True ' this ATM session should end
91                Case Else ' user did not enter an integer from 1-4
92                    screenHandle.DisplayMessageLine(vbCrLf & _
93                        "You did not enter a valid selection. Try again.")
94            End Select
95        End While
96    End Sub ' PerformTransactions
97
98    ' display the main menu and return an input selection
99    Private Function DisplayMainMenu() As Integer
100        screenHandle.DisplayMessageLine(vbCrLf & "Main menu:")
101        screenHandle.DisplayMessageLine("1 - View my balance")
102        screenHandle.DisplayMessageLine("2 - Withdraw cash")
103        screenHandle.DisplayMessageLine("3 - Deposit funds")
104        screenHandle.DisplayMessageLine("4 - Exit" & vbCrLf)
105        screenHandle.DisplayMessage("Enter a choice: ")
106        Return keypadHandle.GetInput() ' return user's selection
107    End Function ' DisplayMainMenu
108
109    ' return object of specified Transaction derived class
110    Private Function CreateTransaction(ByVal type As Integer) _
111        As Transaction
112        Dim temp As Transaction = Nothing ' temporary Transaction object
113
114        ' determine which type of Transaction to create
115        Select Case (type)
116            ' create new BalanceInquiry transaction
117            Case MenuOption.BALANCE_INQUIRY
118                temp = New BalanceInquiry( _
119                    currentAccountNumber, screenHandle, bankDatabaseHandle)
120            Case MenuOption.WITHDRAWAL ' create new Withdrawal transaction
121                temp = New Withdrawal(currentAccountNumber, screenHandle, _
122                    bankDatabaseHandle, keypadHandle, cashDispenserHandle)
123            Case MenuOption.DEPOSIT ' create new Deposit transaction
124                temp = New Deposit(currentAccountNumber, screenHandle, _
125                    bankDatabaseHandle, keypadHandle, depositSlotHandle)
126        End Select
127
128        Return temp
129    End Function ' CreateTransaction
130 End Class ' ATM
```

Fig. J.1 | Class ATM represents the ATM. (Part 3 of 3.)

Lines 13–18 declare an enumeration that corresponds to the four options in the ATM's main menu (i.e., balance inquiry, withdrawal, deposit and exit). Lines 21–29 declare class ATM's constructor, which initializes the class's attributes. When an ATM object is first created, no user is authenticated, so line 22 initializes userAuthenticated to False. Line 23 initializes currentAccountNumber to 0 because there is no current user yet. Lines 24–27 instantiate new objects to represent the parts of the ATM. Recall that class ATM has composition relationships with classes Screen, Keypad, CashDispenser and DepositSlot, so class ATM is responsible for their creation. Line 28 creates a new BankDatabase. As you will soon see, the BankDatabase creates two Account objects that can be used to test the ATM. [*Note:* If this were a real ATM system, the ATM class would receive a reference to an existing database object created by the bank. However, in this implementation we are only simulating the bank's database, so class ATM creates the BankDatabase object with which it interacts.]

Implementing the Operation

The class diagram of Fig. 11.20 does not list any operations for class ATM. We now implement one operation (i.e., Public method) in class ATM that allows an external client of the class (i.e., module ATMCaseStudy; Section J.13) to tell the ATM to run. ATM method Run (lines 32–46) uses an infinite loop (lines 34–45) to repeatedly welcome a user, attempt to authenticate the user and, if authentication succeeds, allow the user to perform transactions. After an authenticated user performs the desired transactions and chooses to exit, the ATM resets itself, displays a goodbye message to the user and restarts the process. We use an infinite loop here to simulate the fact that an ATM appears to run continuously until the bank turns it off (an action beyond the user's control). An ATM user has the option to exit the system, but does not have the ability to turn off the ATM completely.

Inside method Run's infinite loop, lines 36–39 cause the ATM to repeatedly welcome and attempt to authenticate the user as long as the user has not been authenticated (i.e., the condition Not userAuthenticated is True). Line 37 invokes method DisplayMessageLine of the ATM's screen to display a welcome message. Like Screen method DisplayMessage designed in the case study, method DisplayMessageLine (declared in lines 10–12 of Fig. J.2) displays a message to the user, but this method also outputs a newline after displaying the message. We add this method during implementation to give class Screen's clients more control over the placement of displayed messages. Line 38 invokes class ATM's Private utility method AuthenticateUser (declared in lines 49–67) to attempt to authenticate the user.

Authenticating the User

We refer to the requirements document to determine the steps necessary to authenticate the user before allowing transactions to occur. Lines 50–51 of method AuthenticateUser invoke method DisplayMessage of the ATM's screen to prompt the user to enter an account number. Line 52 invokes method GetInput of the ATM's keypad to obtain the user's input, then stores the integer value entered by the user in local variable accountNumber. Method AuthenticateUser next prompts the user to enter a PIN (line 53), and stores the PIN input by the user in local variable pin (line 54). Next, lines 57–58 attempt to authenticate the user by passing the accountNumber and pin entered by the user to the bank database's AuthenticateUser method. Class ATM sets its userAuthenticated attribute to the Boolean value returned by this method—userAuthenticated becomes True if authentication succeeds (i.e., accountNumber and pin match those of an existing Account in the bank database) and remains False otherwise. If userAuthenticated is True, line 62 saves the account number entered by the user (i.e., accountNumber) in the ATM attribute current-AccountNumber. The other methods of class ATM use this variable whenever an ATM session requires access to the user's account number. If userAuthenticated is False, lines 64–65 use the screenHandle's DisplayMessageLine method to indicate that an invalid account number and/or PIN was entered, so the user must try again. Note that we set current-AccountNumber only after authenticating the user's account number and the associated PIN—if the database could not authenticate the user, currentAccountNumber remains 0.

After method Run attempts to authenticate the user (line 38), if userAuthenticated is still False (line 36), the While loop body (lines 37–38) executes again. If userAuthenticated is now True, the loop terminates and control continues with line 41, which calls class ATM's Private utility method PerformTransactions.

Performing Transactions
Method PerformTransactions (lines 70–96) carries out an ATM session for an authenticated user. Line 71 declares local variable Transaction to which we assign a Balance-Inquiry, Withdrawal or Deposit object representing the ATM transaction currently being processed. Note that we use a Transaction variable here to allow us to take advantage of polymorphism. Also note that we name this variable after the role name included in the class diagram of Fig. 4.19—currentTransaction. Line 72 declares another local variable—a Boolean called userExited that keeps track of whether the user has chosen to exit. This variable controls a While loop (lines 75–95) that allows the user to execute an unlimited number of transactions before choosing to exit. Within this loop, line 77 displays the main menu and obtains the user's menu selection by calling ATM utility method DisplayMainMenu (declared in lines 99–107). This method displays the main menu by invoking methods of the ATM's screen and returns a menu selection obtained from the user through the ATM's keypad. Line 77 stores the user's selection returned by DisplayMainMenu in local variable mainMenuSelection.

After obtaining a main menu selection, method PerformTransactions uses a Select Case statement (lines 80–94) to respond to the selection appropriately. If mainMenu-Selection is equal to any of the three integer constants representing transaction types (i.e., if the user chose to perform a transaction), line 85 calls utility method CreateTransaction (declared in lines 110–129) to return a newly instantiated object of the type that corresponds to the selected transaction. Variable currentTransaction is assigned the reference returned by method CreateTransaction, then line 86 invokes method Execute of this transaction to execute it. We will discuss Transaction method Execute and the three Transaction derived classes shortly. Note that we assign to the Transaction variable currentTransaction an object of one of the three Transaction derived classes so that we can execute transactions polymorphically. For example, if the user chooses to perform a balance inquiry, mainMenuSelection equals MenuOption.BALANCE_INQUIRY, and CreateTransaction returns a BalanceInquiry object (line 85). Thus, currentTransaction refers to a BalanceInquiry and invoking currentTransaction.Execute() (line 86) results in BalanceInquiry's version of Execute being called.

Creating Transactions
Method CreateTransaction (lines 110–129) uses a Select Case statement (lines 115–126) to instantiate a new Transaction derived class object of the type indicated by the pa-

rameter type. Recall that method `PerformTransactions` passes `mainMenuSelection` to method `CreateTransaction` only when `mainMenuSelection` contains a value corresponding to one of the three transaction types. So parameter `type` (line 110) receives one of the values `MenuOption.BALANCE_INQUIRY`, `MenuOption.WITHDRAWAL` or `MenuOption.DEPOSIT`. Each `Case` in the `Select Case` statement instantiates a new object by calling the appropriate `Transaction` derived class constructor. Note that each constructor has a unique parameter list, based on the specific data required to initialize the derived class object. A `BalanceInquiry` (lines 118–119) requires only the account number of the current user and the ATM's `screenHandle` and `bankDatabaseHandle`. In addition to these parameters, a `Withdrawal` (lines 121–122) requires the ATM's `keypadHandle` and `cashDispenserHandle`, and a `Deposit` (lines 124–125) requires the ATM's `keypadHandle` and `depositSlotHandle`. We discuss the transaction classes in more detail in Sections J.9–J.12.

After executing a transaction (line 86 in method `PerformTransactions`), `userExited` remains `False` and the `While` loop in lines 75–95 repeats, returning the user to the main menu. However, if a user does not perform a transaction and instead selects the main menu option to exit, line 90 sets `userExited` to `True` causing the condition in line 75 of the `While` loop (`Not userExited`) to become `False`. This `While` is the final statement of method `PerformTransactions`, so control returns to line 42 of the calling method `Run`. If the user enters an invalid main menu selection (i.e., not an integer in the range 1–4), lines 92–93 display an appropriate error message, `userExited` (as set in line 72) remains `False` and the user returns to the main menu to try again.

When method `PerformTransactions` returns control to method `Run`, the user has chosen to exit the system, so lines 42–43 reset the ATM's attributes `userAuthenticated` and `currentAccountNumber` to `False` and 0, respectively, to prepare for the next ATM user. Line 44 displays a goodbye message to the current user before the ATM welcomes the next user.

J.3 Class Screen

Class `Screen` (Fig. J.2) represents the screen of the ATM and encapsulates all aspects of displaying output to the user. Class `Screen` simulates a real ATM's screen with the computer monitor and outputs text messages using standard console output methods `Console.Write` and `Console.WriteLine`. In the design portion of this case study, we endowed class `Screen` with one operation—`DisplayMessage`. For greater flexibility in displaying messages to the `Screen`, we now declare three `Screen` methods—`DisplayMessage`, `DisplayMessageLine` and `DisplayDollarAmount`.

```vb
1   ' Screen.vb
2   ' Represents the screen of the ATM
3   Public Class Screen
4      ' displays a message without a terminating carriage return
5      Public Sub DisplayMessage(ByVal message As String)
6         Console.Write(message)
7      End Sub ' DisplayMessage
8
```

Fig. J.2 | Class `Screen` represents the screen of the ATM. (Part 1 of 2.)

```
 9      ' display a message with a terminating carriage return
10      Public Sub DisplayMessageLine(ByVal message As String)
11          Console.WriteLine(message)
12      End Sub ' DisplayMessageLine
13
14      ' display a dollar amount
15      Public Sub DisplayDollarAmount(ByVal amount As Decimal)
16          Console.Write("{0:C}", amount)
17      End Sub ' DisplayDollarAmount
18  End Class ' Screen
```

Fig. J.2 | Class `Screen` represents the screen of the ATM. (Part 2 of 2.)

Method `DisplayMessage` (lines 5–7) takes a `String` as an argument and prints it to the screen using `Console.Write`. The cursor stays on the same line, making this method appropriate for displaying prompts to the user. Method `DisplayMessageLine` (lines 10–12) does the same using `Console.WriteLine`, which outputs a newline to move the cursor to the next line. Finally, method `DisplayDollarAmount` (lines 15–17) outputs a properly formatted dollar amount (e.g., `$1,234.56`). Line 16 uses method `Console.Write` to output a `Decimal` value formatted as currency with two decimal places and commas to increase the readability of large dollar amounts.

J.4 Class Keypad

Class `Keypad` (Fig. J.3) represents the keypad of the ATM and is responsible for receiving all user input. Recall that we are simulating this hardware, so we use the computer's keyboard to approximate the keypad. We use method `Console.ReadLine` to obtain keyboard input from the user. A computer keyboard contains many keys not found on the ATM's keypad. We assume that the user presses only the keys on the computer keyboard that also appear on the keypad—the keys numbered 0–9 and the *Enter* key.

Method `GetInput` (lines 5–7) invokes `Convert` method `ToInt32` to convert the input returned by `Console.ReadLine` (line 6) to an `Integer` value. [*Note:* Method `ToInt32` can throw a `FormatException` if the user enters non-integer input. Because the real ATM's keypad permits only integer input, we simply assume that no exceptions will occur. See Chapter 12, Exception Handling, for information on catching and processing exceptions.] Recall that `ReadLine` obtains all the input used by the ATM. Class `Keypad`'s `GetInput` method simply returns the integer input by the user. If a client of class `Keypad` requires

```
1  ' Keypad.vb
2  ' Represents the keypad of the ATM.
3  Public Class Keypad
4      ' return an integer value entered by user
5      Public Function GetInput() As Integer
6          Return Convert.ToInt32(Console.ReadLine())
7      End Function ' GetInput
8  End Class ' Keypad
```

Fig. J.3 | Class `Keypad` represents the ATM's keypad.

input that satisfies some particular criteria (i.e., a number corresponding to a valid menu option), the client must perform the appropriate error checking.

J.5 Class CashDispenser

Class CashDispenser (Fig. J.4) represents the cash dispenser of the ATM. Line 5 declares constant INITIAL_COUNT, which indicates the initial count of bills in the cash dispenser when the ATM starts (i.e., 500). Line 6 implements attribute billCount (modeled in Fig. 11.20), which keeps track of the number of bills remaining in the CashDispenser at any time. The constructor (lines 9–11) sets billCount to the initial count. [*Note:* We assume that the process of adding more bills to the CashDispenser and updating the billCount occur outside the ATM system.] Class CashDispenser has two Public methods—DispenseCash (lines 14–18) and IsSufficientCashAvailable (lines 21–31). The class trusts that a client (i.e., Withdrawal) calls method DispenseCash only after establishing that sufficient cash is available by calling method IsSufficientCashAvailable. Thus, DispenseCash simply simulates dispensing the requested amount without checking whether sufficient cash is available.

```vb
1   ' CashDispenser.vb
2   ' Represents the cash dispenser of the ATM
3   Public Class CashDispenser
4      ' the default initial number of bills in the case dispenser
5      Private Const INITIAL_COUNT As Integer = 500
6      Private billCount As Integer ' number of $20 bills remaining
7
8      ' parameterless constructor initializes billCount to INITIAL_COUNT
9      Public Sub New()
10        billCount = INITIAL_COUNT ' set billCount to INITIAL_COUNT
11     End Sub ' New
12
13     ' simulates dispensing of specified amount of cash
14     Public Sub DispenseCash(ByVal amount As Decimal)
15        ' number of $20 bills required
16        Dim billsRequired As Integer = (Convert.ToInt32(amount) \ 20)
17        billCount -= billsRequired
18     End Sub ' DispenseCash
19
20     ' indicates whether cash dispenser can dispense desired amount
21     Public Function IsSufficientCashAvailable(ByVal amount As Decimal) _
22        As Boolean
23        ' number of $20 bills required
24        Dim billsRequired As Integer = (Convert.ToInt32(amount) \ 20)
25
26        If (billCount >= billsRequired) Then
27           Return True ' enough bills available
28        Else
29           Return False ' not enough bills available
30        End If
31     End Function ' IsSufficientCashAvailable
32  End Class ' CashDispenser
```

Fig. J.4 | Class CashDispenser represents the ATM's cash dispenser.

Method `IsSufficientCashAvailable` (lines 21–31) has a parameter `amount` that specifies the amount of cash in question. Line 24 calculates the number of $20 bills required to dispense the specified `amount`. The ATM allows the user to choose only withdrawal amounts that are multiples of $20, so we convert `amount` to an integer value and divide it by 20 to obtain the number of `billsRequired`. Lines 26–30 return `True` if the `CashDispenser`'s `billCount` is greater than or equal to `billsRequired` (i.e., enough bills are available) and `False` otherwise (i.e., not enough bills). For example, if a user wishes to withdraw $80 (i.e., `billsRequired` is 4), but only three bills remain (i.e., `billCount` is 3), the method returns `False`.

Method `DispenseCash` (lines 14–18) simulates cash dispensing. If our system were hooked up to a real hardware cash dispenser, this method would interact with the hardware device to physically dispense cash. Our simulated version of the method simply decreases the `billCount` of bills remaining by the number required to dispense the specified `amount` (line 17). Note that it is the responsibility of the client of the class (i.e., `Withdrawal`) to inform the user that cash has been dispensed—`CashDispenser` does not interact directly with `Screen`.

J.6 Class DepositSlot

Class `DepositSlot` (Fig. J.5) represents the deposit slot of the ATM. Like the version of class `CashDispenser` presented here, this version of class `DepositSlot` merely simulates the functionality of a real hardware deposit slot. `DepositSlot` has no attributes and only one method—`IsDepositEnvelopeReceived` (lines 6–8)—that indicates whether a deposit envelope was received.

Recall from the requirements document that the ATM allows the user up to two minutes to insert an envelope. The current version of method `IsDepositEnvelopeReceived` simply returns `True` immediately (line 7), because this is only a software simulation, and we assume that the user inserts an envelope within the required time frame. If an actual hardware deposit slot were connected to our system, method `IsDepositEnvelopeReceived` would be implemented to wait for a maximum of two minutes to receive a signal from the hardware deposit slot indicating that the user has indeed inserted a deposit envelope. If `IsDepositEnvelopeReceived` were to receive such a signal within two minutes, the method would return `True`. If two minutes were to elapse and the method still had not received a signal, then the method would return `False`.

```vb
1   ' DepositSlot.vb
2   ' Represents the deposit slot of the ATM
3   Public Class DepositSlot
4      ' indicates whether envelope was received (always returns true,
5      ' because this is only a software simulation of a real deposit slot)
6      Public Function IsDepositEnvelopeReceived() As Boolean
7         Return True ' deposit envelope was received
8      End Function ' IsDepositEnvelopeReceived
9   End Class ' DepositSlot
```

Fig. J.5 | Class `DepositSlot` represents the ATM's deposit slot.

J.7 Class Account

Class Account (Fig. J.6) represents a bank account. Each Account has four attributes (modeled in Fig. 11.20)—accountNumber, pin, availableBalance and totalBalance. Lines 4–7 implement these attributes as Private instance variables. Note that when we provide a property to access an instance variable, we create the instance variable name by appending Value to the end of the attribute name that was listed in the model. We provide a property with the same name as the attribute name (but starting with a capital letter) to access the instance variable. For example, property AccountNumber corresponds to the accountNumber attribute modeled in Fig. 11.20. Since clients of this class do not need to modify the accountNumberValue instance variable, AccountNumber is a ReadOnly property (i.e., it provides only a Get accessory).

```vb
1   ' Account.vb
2   ' Represents a bank account.
3   Public Class Account
4       Private accountNumberValue As Integer ' account number
5       Private pin As Integer ' PIN for authentication
6       Private availableBalanceValue As Decimal ' available withdrawal amount
7       Private totalBalanceValue As Decimal ' funds available+pending deposit
8
9       ' constructor initializes attributes
10      Public Sub New(ByVal theAccountNumber As Integer, _
11          ByVal thePIN As Integer, ByVal theAvailableBalance As Decimal, _
12          ByVal theTotalBalance As Decimal)
13          accountNumberValue = theAccountNumber
14          pin = thePIN
15          availableBalanceValue = theAvailableBalance
16          totalBalanceValue = theTotalBalance
17      End Sub ' New
18
19      ' property AccountNumber
20      Public ReadOnly Property AccountNumber() As Integer
21          Get
22              Return accountNumberValue
23          End Get
24      End Property ' AccountNumber
25
26      ' property AvailableBalance
27      Public ReadOnly Property AvailableBalance() As Decimal
28          Get
29              Return availableBalanceValue
30          End Get
31      End Property ' AvailableBalance
32
33      ' property TotalBalance
34      Public ReadOnly Property TotalBalance() As Decimal
35          Get
36              Return totalBalanceValue
37          End Get
38      End Property ' TotalBalance
```

Fig. J.6 | Class Account represents a bank account. (Part 1 of 2.)

```
39
40        ' determines whether a user-specified PIN matches PIN in Account
41        Public Function ValidatePIN(ByVal userPIN As Integer) As Boolean
42           If userPIN = pin Then
43              Return True
44           Else
45              Return False
46           End If
47        End Function ' ValidatePIN
48
49        ' credits the account (funds have not yet cleared)
50        Public Sub Credit(ByVal amount As Decimal)
51           totalBalanceValue += amount ' add to total balance
52        End Sub ' Credit
53
54        ' debits the account
55        Public Sub Debit(ByVal amount As Decimal)
56           availableBalanceValue -= amount ' subtract from available balance
57           totalBalanceValue -= amount ' subtract from total balance
58        End Sub ' Debit
59     End Class ' Account
```

Fig. J.6 | Class Account represents a bank account. (Part 2 of 2.)

Class Account has a constructor (lines 10–17) that takes an account number, the PIN established for the account, the initial available balance and the initial total balance as arguments. Lines 13–16 assign these values to the class's attributes (i.e., instance variables). Note that Account objects would normally be created externally to the ATM system. However, in this simulation, the Account objects are created in the BankDatabase class (Fig. J.7).

Public ReadOnly Properties of Class Account

ReadOnly property AccountNumber (lines 20–24) provides access to an Account's accountNumberValue. We include this property in our implementation so that a client of the class (e.g., BankDatabase) can identify a particular Account. For example, BankDatabase contains many Account objects, and it can access this property on each of its Account objects to locate the one with a specific account number.

ReadOnly properties AvailableBalance (lines 27–31) and TotalBalance (lines 34–38) allow clients to retrieve the values of Private Decimal instance variables available-BalanceValue and totalBalanceValue, respectively. Property AvailableBalance represents the amount of funds available for withdrawal. Property TotalBalance represents the amount of funds available, plus the amount of deposited funds still pending confirmation (of cash in deposit envelopes) or clearance (of checks in deposit envelopes).

Public Methods of Class Account

Method ValidatePIN (lines 41–47) determines whether a user-specified PIN (i.e., parameter userPIN) matches the PIN associated with the account (i.e., attribute pin). Recall that we modeled this method's parameter userPIN in the UML class diagram of Fig. 7.26. If the two PINs match, the method returns True (line 43); otherwise, it returns False (line 45).

Method Credit (lines 50–52) adds an amount of money (i.e., parameter amount) to an Account as part of a deposit transaction. Note that this method adds the amount only to instance variable totalBalanceValue (line 45). The money credited to an account during a deposit does not become available immediately, so we modify only the total balance. We assume that the bank updates the available balance appropriately at a later time when the amount of cash in the deposit envelope has been verified and when the checks in the deposit envelope have cleared. Our implementation of class Account includes only methods required for carrying out ATM transactions. Therefore, we omit the methods that some other bank system would invoke to add to instance variable availableBalanceValue (to confirm a deposit) or subtract from attribute totalBalanceValue (to reject a deposit).

Method Debit (lines 55–58) subtracts an amount of money (i.e., parameter amount) from an Account as part of a withdrawal transaction. This method subtracts the amount from both instance variable availableBalanceValue (line 56) and instance variable totalBalanceValue (line 57), because a withdrawal affects both measures of an account balance.

J.8 Class BankDatabase

Class BankDatabase (Fig. J.7) models the bank's database with which the ATM interacts to access and modify a user's account information. We determine one reference-type attribute for class BankDatabase based on its composition relationship with class Account. Recall from Fig. 11.19 that a BankDatabase is composed of zero or more objects of class Account. Line 4 implements attribute accounts—an array that will store Account objects—to implement this composition relationship. Class BankDatabase has a parameterless constructor (lines 7–13) that initializes accounts with new Account objects. We create two new Account objects with test data and place them in the array (lines 11–12). Note that the Account constructor has four parameters—the account number, the PIN assigned to the account, the initial available balance and the initial total balance.

Recall that class BankDatabase serves as an intermediary between class ATM and the actual Account objects that contain users' account information. Thus, methods of class BankDatabase invoke the corresponding methods and properties of the Account object belonging to the current ATM user.

Private *Utility Method GetAccount*

We include Private utility method GetAccount (lines 16–25) to allow the BankDatabase to obtain a reference to a particular Account within the accounts ArrayList. To locate the user's Account, the BankDatabase compares the value returned by property AccountNumber for each element of accounts to a specified account number until it finds a match. Lines 18–22 traverse the accounts ArrayList. If currentAccount's account number equals the value of parameter accountNumber, the method returns currentAccount. If no account has the given account number, then line 24 returns Nothing.

Public *Methods*

Method AuthenticateUser (lines 29–40) proves or disproves the identity of an ATM user. This method takes a user-specified account number and a user-specified PIN as arguments and indicates whether they match the account number and PIN of an Account in

```vb
1    ' BankDatabase.vb
2    ' Represents the bank account information database
3    Public Class BankDatabase
4       Private accounts As Account() ' array of the bank's Accounts
5
6       ' parameterless BankDatabase constructor initializes accounts
7       Public Sub New()
8          ' create two Account objects for testing and
9          ' place them in the accounts array
10         accounts = New Account(0 To 1) {} ' create accounts array
11         accounts(0) = New Account(12345, 54321, 1000, 1200)
12         accounts(1) = New Account(98765, 56789, 200, 200)
13      End Sub ' New
14
15      ' retrieve Account object containing specified account number
16      Private Function GetAccount(ByVal accountNumber As Integer) As Account
17         ' loop through accounts searching for matching account number
18         For Each currentAccount As Account In accounts
19            If currentAccount.AccountNumber = accountNumber Then
20               Return currentAccount
21            End If
22         Next
23
24         Return Nothing
25      End Function ' GetAccount
26
27      ' determine whether user-specified account number and PIN match
28      ' those of an account in the database
29      Public Function AuthenticateUser(ByVal userAccountNumber As Integer, _
30         ByVal userPIN As Integer) As Boolean
31         ' attempt to retrieve the account with the account number
32         Dim userAccount As Account = GetAccount(userAccountNumber)
33
34         ' if account exists, return result of Account function ValidatePIN
35         If (userAccount IsNot Nothing) Then
36            Return userAccount.ValidatePIN(userPIN)
37         Else
38            Return False ' account number not found, so return false
39         End If
40      End Function ' AuthenticateUser
41
42      ' return available balance of Account with specified account number
43      Public Function GetAvailableBalance( _
44         ByVal userAccountNumber As Integer) As Decimal
45         Dim userAccount As Account = GetAccount(userAccountNumber)
46         Return userAccount.AvailableBalance
47      End Function ' GetAvailableBalance
48
49      ' return total balance of Account with specified account number
50      Public Function GetTotalBalance( _
51         ByVal userAccountNumber As Integer) As Decimal
52         Dim userAccount As Account = GetAccount(userAccountNumber)
```

Fig. J.7 | Class **BankDatabase** represents the bank's account information database. (Part 1 of 2.)

```
53          Return userAccount.TotalBalance
54       End Function ' GetTotalBalance
55
56       ' credit the Account with specified account number
57       Public Sub Credit(ByVal userAccountNumber As Integer, _
58          ByVal amount As Decimal)
59          Dim userAccount As Account = GetAccount(userAccountNumber)
60          userAccount.Credit(amount)
61       End Sub ' Credit
62
63       ' debit the Account with specified account number
64       Public Sub Debit(ByVal userAccountNumber As Integer, _
65          ByVal amount As Decimal)
66          Dim userAccount As Account = GetAccount(userAccountNumber)
67          userAccount.Debit(amount)
68       End Sub ' Debit
69    End Class ' BankDatabase
```

Fig. J.7 | Class BankDatabase represents the bank's account information database. (Part 2 of 2.)

the database. Line 32 calls method GetAccount, which returns either an Account with userAccountNumber as its account number or Nothing to indicate that userAccountNumber is invalid. If GetAccount returns an Account object, line 36 returns the Boolean value returned by that object's ValidatePIN method. Note that BankDatabase's AuthenticateUser method does not perform the PIN comparison itself—rather, it forwards userPIN to the Account object's ValidatePIN method to do so. The value returned by Account method ValidatePIN (line 36) indicates whether the user-specified PIN matches the PIN of the user's Account, so method AuthenticateUser simply returns this value (line 36) to the client of the class (i.e., ATM).

BankDatabase trusts the ATM to invoke method AuthenticateUser and receive a return value of True before allowing the user to perform transactions. BankDatabase also trusts that each Transaction object created by the ATM contains the valid account number of the current authenticated user and that this is the account number passed to the remaining BankDatabase methods as argument userAccountNumber. Methods GetAvailableBalance (lines 43–47), GetTotalBalance (lines 50–54), Credit (lines 57–61) and Debit (lines 64–68) therefore simply retrieve the user's Account object with utility method GetAccount, then invoke the appropriate Account method on that object. We know that the calls to GetAccount within these methods will never return Nothing, because userAccountNumber must refer to an existing Account. Note that GetAvailableBalance and GetTotalBalance return the values returned by the corresponding Account properties. Also note that methods Credit and Debit simply redirect parameter amount to the Account methods they invoke.

J.9 Class Transaction

Class Transaction (Fig. J.8) is an abstract base class that represents the notion of an ATM transaction. It contains the common features of derived classes BalanceInquiry, Withdrawal and Deposit. This class expands upon the "skeleton" code first developed in Section 11.8. Line 3 declares this class to be MustInherit (the Visual Basic equivalent of

```vb
1    ' Transaction.vb
2    ' MustInherit base class Transaction represents an ATM transaction.
3    Public MustInherit Class Transaction
4        Private accountNumberValue As Integer ' indicates account involved
5        Private screenHandle As Screen ' ATM's screen
6        Private bankDatabaseHandle As BankDatabase ' account info database
7
8        ' constructor invoked by derived classes using MyBase.New
9        Public Sub New(ByVal userAccount As Integer, _
10           ByVal userScreen As Screen, ByVal database As BankDatabase)
11           accountNumberValue = userAccount
12           screenHandle = userScreen
13           bankDatabaseHandle = database
14       End Sub ' New
15
16       ' property AccountNumber
17       Public ReadOnly Property AccountNumber() As Integer
18           Get
19               Return accountNumberValue
20           End Get
21       End Property ' AccountNumber
22
23       ' property ScreenReference
24       Public ReadOnly Property ScreenReference() As Screen
25           Get
26               Return screenHandle
27           End Get
28       End Property ' ScreenReference
29
30       ' property BankDatabaseReference
31       Public ReadOnly Property BankDatabaseReference() As BankDatabase
32           Get
33               Return bankDatabaseHandle
34           End Get
35       End Property ' BankDatabaseReference
36
37       ' perform the transaction (overridden by each derived class)
38       Public MustOverride Sub Execute()
39   End Class ' Transaction
```

Fig. J.8 | MustInherit base class Transaction represents an ATM transaction.

an abstract class). Lines 4–6 declare the class's Private instance variables. Recall from the class diagram of Fig. 11.20 that class Transaction contains an property AccountNumber that indicates the account involved in the Transaction. Line 4 implements the instance variable accountNumberValue to maintain the AccountNumber property's data. We derive attributes screen (implemented as instance variable screenHandle in line 7) and bank-Database (implemented as instance variable bankDatabaseHandle in line 8) from class Transaction's associations modeled in Fig. 11.19. All transactions require access to the ATM's screen and the bank's database.

Class Transaction has a constructor (lines 9–14) that takes the current user's account number and references to the ATM's screen and the bank's database as arguments. Because

Transaction is a MustInherit class (line 3), this constructor will never be called directly to instantiate Transaction objects. Instead, this constructor will be invoked by the constructors of the Transaction derived classes via MyBase.New.

Class Transaction has three Public ReadOnly properties—AccountNumber (lines 17–21), ScreenReference (lines 24–28) and BankDatabaseReference (lines 31–35). Derived classes of Transaction inherit these properties and use them to gain access to class Transaction's Private instance variables. Note that we use the word "Reference" in the names of the ScreenReference and BankDatabaseReference properties for clarity—we wanted to avoid property names that are the same as the class names Screen and BankDatabase, which can be confusing.

Class Transaction also declares a MustOverride method Execute (line 38). It does not make sense to provide an implementation for this method in class Transaction, because a generic transaction cannot be executed. Thus, we declare this method to be MustOverride, forcing each Transaction derived class to provide its own concrete implementation that executes the particular type of transaction.

J.10 Class BalanceInquiry

Class BalanceInquiry (Fig. J.9) inherits from Transaction (line 4) and represents an ATM balance inquiry transaction. BalanceInquiry does not have any attributes of its own, but it inherits Transaction attributes accountNumber, screen and bankDatabase, which are accessible through Transaction's Public ReadOnly properties. The BalanceInquiry constructor (lines 7–10) takes arguments corresponding to these attributes and simply forwards them to Transaction's constructor using MyBase.New (line 9).

```vb
 1    ' BalanceInquiry.vb
 2    ' Represents a balance inquiry ATM transaction
 3    Public Class BalanceInquiry
 4       Inherits Transaction
 5
 6       ' BalanceInquiry constructor initializes base class variables
 7       Public Sub New(ByVal userAccountNumber As Integer, _
 8          ByVal atmScreen As Screen, ByVal atmBankDatabase As BankDatabase)
 9          MyBase.New(userAccountNumber, atmScreen, atmBankDatabase)
10       End Sub ' New
11
12       ' performs transaction; overrides Transaction's MustOverride method
13       Public Overrides Sub Execute()
14          ' get the available balance for the current user's Account
15          Dim availableBalance As Decimal = _
16             BankDatabaseReference.GetAvailableBalance(AccountNumber)
17
18          ' get the total balance for the current user's Account
19          Dim totalBalance As Decimal = _
20             BankDatabaseReference.GetTotalBalance(AccountNumber)
21
22          ' display the balance information on the screen
23          ScreenReference.DisplayMessageLine(vbCrLf & "Balance Information:")
```

Fig. J.9 | Class BalanceInquiry represents a balance inquiry ATM transaction. (Part 1 of 2.)

```
24          ScreenReference.DisplayMessage(" - Available balance: ")
25          ScreenReference.DisplayDollarAmount(availableBalance)
26          ScreenReference.DisplayMessage(vbCrLf & " - Total balance: ")
27          ScreenReference.DisplayDollarAmount(totalBalance)
28          ScreenReference.DisplayMessageLine("")
29      End Sub ' Execute
30  End Class ' BalanceInquiry
```

Fig. J.9 | Class `BalanceInquiry` represents a balance inquiry ATM transaction. (Part 2 of 2.)

Class `BalanceInquiry` overrides `Transaction`'s `MustOverride` method `Execute` to provide a concrete implementation (lines 13–29) that performs the steps involved in a balance inquiry. Lines 15–16 obtain the specified `Account`'s available balance by invoking the inherited property `BankDatabaseReference`'s `GetAvailableBalance` method. Note that line 16 uses the inherited property `AccountNumber` is used to get the account number of the current user. Lines 19–24 retrieve the specified `Account`'s total balance. Lines 23–28 display the balance information on the ATM's screen using the inherited property `ScreenReference`. Recall that `DisplayDollarAmount` takes a `Decimal` argument and outputs it to the screen formatted as a dollar amount. For example, if a user's available balance is `1000.5`, line 25 outputs `$1,000.50`. Note that line 28 inserts a blank line of output to separate the balance information from subsequent output (i.e., the main menu repeated by class `ATM` after executing the `BalanceInquiry`).

J.11 Class **Withdrawal**

Class `Withdrawal` (Fig. J.10) extends `Transaction` and represents an ATM withdrawal transaction. This class expands upon the "skeleton" code for this class developed in Fig. 11.22. Recall from the class diagram of Fig. 11.19 that class `Withdrawal` has one attribute, `amount`, which line 6 implements as a `Decimal` instance variable. Fig. 11.19 models associations between class `Withdrawal` and classes `Keypad` and `CashDispenser`, for which lines 7–8 implement reference attributes `keypadHandle` and `dispenserHandle`, respectively. Line 11 declares a constant corresponding to the cancel menu option. We will soon discuss how the class uses this constant.

Class `Withdrawal`'s constructor (lines 14–23) has five parameters. It uses `MyBase.New` to pass parameters `userAccountNumber`, `atmScreen` and `atmBankDatabase` to base class `Transaction`'s constructor to set the attributes that `Withdrawal` inherits from `Transaction`. The constructor also takes references `atmKeypad` and `atmCashDispenser` as parameters and assigns them to variables `keypadHandle` and `dispenserHandle`.

Overriding **MustOverride** Method **Execute**

Class `Withdrawal` overrides `Transaction`'s `MustOverride` method `Execute` with a concrete implementation (lines 26–74) that performs the steps involved in a withdrawal. Line 27 declares and initializes a local `Boolean` variable `cashDispensed`. This variable indicates whether cash has been dispensed (i.e., whether the transaction has completed successfully) and is initially `False`. Line 30 declares and initializes to `False` a `Boolean` variable `transactionCanceled` to indicate that the transaction has not yet been canceled by the user.

```
1    ' Withdrawal.vb
2    ' Class Withdrawal represents an ATM withdrawal transaction.
3    Public Class Withdrawal
4       Inherits Transaction
5
6       Private amount As Decimal ' amount to withdraw
7       Private keypadHandle As Keypad ' reference to Keypad
8       Private dispenserHandle As CashDispenser ' reference to cash dispenser
9
10       ' constant that corresponds to menu option to cancel
11       Private Const CANCELED As Integer = 6
12
13       ' Withdrawal constructor
14       Public Sub New(ByVal userAccountNumber As Integer, _
15          ByVal atmScreen As Screen, ByVal atmBankDatabase As BankDatabase, _
16          ByVal atmKeypad As Keypad, ByVal atmCashDispenser As CashDispenser)
17          ' initialize base class variables
18          MyBase.New(userAccountNumber, atmScreen, atmBankDatabase)
19
20          ' initialize references to keypad and cash dispenser
21          keypadHandle = atmKeypad
22          dispenserHandle = atmCashDispenser
23       End Sub ' New
24
25       ' perform transaction
26       Public Overrides Sub Execute()
27          Dim cashDispensed As Boolean = False ' cash was not dispensed yet
28
29          ' transaction was not canceled yet
30          Dim transactionCanceled As Boolean = False
31
32          ' loop until cash is dispensed or the user cancels
33          Do
34             ' obtain the chosen withdrawal amount from the user
35             Dim selection As Integer = DisplayMenuOfAmounts()
36
37             ' check whether user chose a withdrawal amount or canceled
38             If (selection <> CANCELED) Then
39                amount = selection ' set amount to the selected dollar amount
40
41                ' get available balance of account involved
42                Dim availableBalance As Decimal = _
43                   BankDatabaseReference.GetAvailableBalance(AccountNumber)
44
45                ' check whether the user has enough money in the account
46                If (amount <= availableBalance) Then
47                   ' check whether the cash dispenser has enough money
48                   If (dispenserHandle.IsSufficientCashAvailable(amount)) Then
49                      ' update the account involved to reflect withdrawal
50                      BankDatabaseReference.Debit(AccountNumber, amount)
51
52                      dispenserHandle.DispenseCash(amount) ' dispense cash
53                      cashDispensed = True ' cash was dispensed
```

Fig. J.10 | Class Withdrawal represents an ATM withdrawal transaction. (Part 1 of 3.)

```
54
55                         ' instruct user to take cash
56                         ScreenReference.DisplayMessageLine(vbCrLf & _
57                             "Please take your cash from the cash dispenser.")
58                     Else ' cash dispenser does not have enough cash
59                         ScreenReference.DisplayMessageLine(vbCrLf & _
60                             "Insufficient cash available in the ATM." & _
61                             vbCrLf & vbCrLf & "Please choose a smaller amount.")
62                     End If
63                 Else ' not enough money available in user's account
64                     ScreenReference.DisplayMessageLine(vbCrLf & _
65                         "Insufficient cash available in your account." & _
66                         vbCrLf & vbCrLf & "Please choose a smaller amount.")
67                 End If
68             Else
69                 ScreenReference.DisplayMessageLine( _
70                     vbCrLf & "Canceling transaction...")
71                 transactionCanceled = True ' user canceled the transaction
72             End If
73         Loop While ((Not cashDispensed) And (Not transactionCanceled))
74     End Sub ' Execute
75
76     ' display a menu of withdrawal amounts and the option to cancel;
77     ' return the chosen amount or 0 if the user chooses to cancel
78     Private Function DisplayMenuOfAmounts() As Integer
79         Dim userChoice As Integer = 0 ' variable to store return value
80
81         ' array of amounts to correspond to menu numbers
82         Dim amounts As Integer() = New Integer() { _
83             0, 20, 40, 60, 100, 200}
84
85         ' loop while no valid choice has been made
86         While (userChoice = 0)
87             ' display the menu
88             ScreenReference.DisplayMessageLine( _
89                 vbCrLf & "Withdrawal options:")
90             ScreenReference.DisplayMessageLine("1 - $20")
91             ScreenReference.DisplayMessageLine("2 - $40")
92             ScreenReference.DisplayMessageLine("3 - $60")
93             ScreenReference.DisplayMessageLine("4 - $100")
94             ScreenReference.DisplayMessageLine("5 - $200")
95             ScreenReference.DisplayMessageLine("6 - Cancel transaction")
96             ScreenReference.DisplayMessage( _
97                 vbCrLf & "Choose a withdrawal option (1-6): ")
98
99             ' get user input through keypad
100            Dim input As Integer = keypadHandle.GetInput()
101
102            ' determine how to proceed based on the input value
103            Select Case (input)
104                ' if the user chose a withdrawal amount (i.e., option
105                ' 1, 2, 3, 4, or 5), return the corresponding amount
106                ' from the amounts array
```

Fig. J.10 | Class Withdrawal represents an ATM withdrawal transaction. (Part 2 of 3.)

```
107               Case 1 To 5
108                  userChoice = amounts(input) ' save user's choice
109               Case CANCELED ' the user chose to cancel
110                  userChoice = CANCELED ' save user's choice
111               Case Else
112                  ScreenReference.DisplayMessageLine( _
113                     vbCrLf & "Invalid selection. Try again.")
114            End Select
115         End While
116
117         Return userChoice
118      End Function ' DisplayMenuOfAmounts
119   End Class ' Withdrawal
```

Fig. J.10 | Class Withdrawal represents an ATM withdrawal transaction. (Part 3 of 3.)

Lines 33–73 contain a Do...Loop While statement that executes its body until cash is dispensed (i.e., until cashDispensed becomes True) or until the user chooses to cancel (i.e., until transactionCanceled becomes True). We use this loop to continuously return the user to the start of the transaction if an error occurs (i.e., the requested withdrawal amount is greater than the user's available balance or greater than the amount of cash in the cash dispenser). Line 35 displays a menu of withdrawal amounts and obtains a user selection by calling Private utility method DisplayMenuOfAmounts (declared in lines 78–118). This method displays the menu of amounts and returns either an Integer withdrawal amount or an Integer constant CANCELED to indicate that the user has chosen to cancel the transaction.

Displaying Options With Private Utility Method DisplayMenuOfAmounts
Method DisplayMenuOfAmounts (lines 81–121) first declares local variable userChoice (initially 0) to store the value that the method will return (line 82). Lines 82–83 declare an integer array of withdrawal amounts that correspond to the amounts displayed in the withdrawal menu. We ignore the first element in the array (index 0) because the menu has no option 0. The While statement at lines 86–115 repeats until userChoice takes on a value other than 0. We will see shortly that this occurs when the user makes a valid selection from the menu. Lines 88–97 display the withdrawal menu on the screen and prompt the user to enter a choice. Line 100 obtains integer input through the keypad. The Select Case statement at lines 103–114 determines how to proceed based on the user's input. If the user selects a number between 1 and 5, line 108 sets userChoice to the value of the element in the amounts array at index input. For example, if the user enters 3 to withdraw $60, line 108 sets userChoice to the value of amounts(3) (i.e., 60). Variable userChoice no longer equals 0, so the While at lines 86–115 terminates and line 117 returns userChoice. If the user selects the cancel menu option, line 110 executes, setting userChoice to CANCELED and causing the method to return this value. If the user does not enter a valid menu selection, lines 112–113 display an error message and the user is returned to the withdrawal menu.

The If statement at line 38 in method Execute determines whether the user has selected a withdrawal amount or chosen to cancel. If the user cancels, lines 69–70 display an appropriate message to the user before returning control to the calling method (i.e., ATM method `PerformTransactions`). If the user has chosen a withdrawal amount, lines 39 assigns local variable `selection` to instance variable `amount`. Lines 42–43 retrieve the available balance of the current user's `Account` and store it in a local `Decimal` variable `availableBalance`. Next, the `If` statement at line 46 determines whether the selected amount is less than or equal to the user's available balance. If it is not, lines 64–66 display an error message. Control then continues to the end of the `Do...Loop While`, and the loop repeats because both `cashDispensed` and `transactionCanceled` are still `False`. If the user's balance is high enough, the `If` statement at line 48 determines whether the cash dispenser has enough money to satisfy the withdrawal request by invoking the cash dispenser's `IsSufficientCashAvailable` method. If this method returns `False`, lines 59–61 display an error message and the `Do...Loop While` repeats. If sufficient cash is available, then the requirements for the withdrawal are satisfied, and line 50 debits the user's account in the database by `amount`. Lines 52–53 then instruct the cash dispenser to dispense the cash to the user and set `cashDispensed` to `True`. Finally, lines 56–57 display a message to the user to take the dispensed cash. Because `cashDispensed` is now `True`, control continues after the `Do...Loop While`. No additional statements appear below the loop, so the method returns control to class `ATM`.

J.12 Class `Deposit`

Class `Deposit` (Fig. J.11) inherits from `Transaction` and represents an ATM deposit transaction. Recall from the class diagram of Fig. 11.20 that class `Deposit` has one attribute, amount, which line 6 implements as a `Decimal` instance variable. Lines 7–8 create reference attributes `keypadHandle` and `depositSlotHandle` that implement the associations between class `Deposit` and classes `Keypad` and `DepositSlot` modeled in Fig. 11.19. Line 11 declares a constant `CANCELED` that corresponds to the value a user enters to cancel. We will soon discuss how the class uses this constant.

```
1    ' Deposit.vb
2    ' Represents a deposit ATM transaction.
3    Public Class Deposit
4       Inherits Transaction
5
6       Private amount As Decimal ' amount to deposit
7       Private keypadHandle As Keypad ' reference to Keypad
8       Private depositSlotHandle As DepositSlot ' reference to deposit slot
9
10      ' constant representing cancel option
11      Private Const CANCELED As Integer = 0
12
13      ' Deposit constructor initializes class's instance variables
14      Public Sub New(ByVal userAccountNumber As Integer, _
15         ByVal atmScreen As Screen, ByVal atmBankDatabase As BankDatabase, _
16         ByVal atmKeypad As Keypad, ByVal atmDepositSlot As DepositSlot)
17         ' initialize base class variables
18         MyBase.New(userAccountNumber, atmScreen, atmBankDatabase)
19
```

Fig. J.11 | Class `Deposit` represents an ATM deposit transaction. (Part 1 of 3.)

```
20          ' initialize references to keypad and deposit slot
21          keypadHandle = atmKeypad
22          depositSlotHandle = atmDepositSlot
23       End Sub ' New
24
25       ' perform transaction; overrides Transaction's MustOverride method
26       Public Overrides Sub Execute()
27          amount = PromptForDepositAmount() ' get deposit amount from user
28
29          ' check whether user entered a deposit amount or canceled
30          If (amount <> CANCELED) Then
31             ' request deposit envelope containing specified amount
32             ScreenReference.DisplayMessage(vbCrLf & _
33                "Please insert a deposit envelope containing ")
34             ScreenReference.DisplayDollarAmount(amount)
35             ScreenReference.DisplayMessageLine(" in the deposit slot.")
36
37             ' retrieve deposit envelope
38             Dim envelopeReceived As Boolean = _
39                depositSlotHandle.IsDepositEnvelopeReceived()
40
41             ' check whether deposit envelope was received
42             If envelopeReceived Then
43                ScreenReference.DisplayMessageLine(vbCrLf & _
44                   "Your envelope has been received." & vbCrLf & _
45                   "The money just deposited will not be available " & _
46                   "until we" & vbCrLf & "verify the amount of any " & _
47                   "enclosed cash, and any enclosed checks clear.")
48
49                ' credit account to reflect the deposit
50                BankDatabaseReference.Credit(AccountNumber, amount)
51             Else
52                ScreenReference.DisplayMessageLine(vbCrLf & _
53                   "You did not insert an envelope, so the ATM has " & _
54                   "canceled your transaction.")
55             End If
56          Else
57             ScreenReference.DisplayMessageLine( _
58                vbCrLf & "Canceling transaction...")
59          End If
60       End Sub ' Execute
61
62       ' prompt user to enter a deposit amount to credit
63       Private Function PromptForDepositAmount() As Decimal
64          ' display the prompt and receive input
65          ScreenReference.DisplayMessage(vbCrLf & _
66             "Please input a deposit amount in CENTS (or 0 to cancel): ")
67          Dim input As Integer = Convert.ToInt32(keypadHandle.GetInput())
68
69          ' check whether the user canceled or entered a valid amount
70          If (input = CANCELED) Then
71             Return CANCELED
```

Fig. J.11 | Class Deposit represents an ATM deposit transaction. (Part 2 of 3.)

```
72          Else
73              Return Convert.ToDecimal(input / 100)
74          End If
75      End Function ' PromptForDepositAmount
76  End Class ' Deposit
```

Fig. J.11 | Class `Deposit` represents an ATM deposit transaction. (Part 3 of 3.)

Like class `Withdrawal`, class `Deposit` contains a constructor (lines 14–23) that passes three parameters to base class `Transaction`'s constructor using `MyBase.New`. The constructor also has parameters `atmKeypad` and `atmDepositSlot`, which it assigns to corresponding reference attributes (lines 21–22).

Overriding `MustOverride` Method `Execute`

Method `Execute` (lines 26–60) overrides `MustOverride` method `Execute` in base class `Transaction` with a concrete implementation that performs the steps required in a deposit transaction. Line 27 prompts the user to enter a deposit amount by invoking `Private` utility method `PromptForDepositAmount` (declared in lines 63–75) and sets attribute `amount` to the value returned. Method `PromptForDepositAmount` asks the user to enter a deposit amount as an integer number of cents (because the ATM's keypad does not contain a decimal point; this is consistent with many real ATMs) and returns the `Decimal` value representing the dollar amount to be deposited.

Getting Deposit Amount With `Private` Utility Method `PromptForDepositAmount`

Lines 65–66 in method `PromptForDepositAmount` display a message on the screen asking the user to input a deposit amount as a number of cents or "0" to cancel the transaction. Line 67 receives the user's input from the keypad. The `If` statement at lines 70–74 determines whether the user has entered a real deposit amount or chosen to cancel. If the user chooses to cancel, line 71 returns the constant `CANCELED`. Otherwise, line 73 returns the deposit amount after converting from the number of cents to a dollar amount by dividing `input` by 100, then converting the result to a `Decimal`. For example, if the user enters 125 as the number of cents, line 73 returns 125 divided by 100, or 1.25—125 cents is $1.25.

Lines 30–59 in method `Execute` determine whether the user chose to cancel the transaction rather than enter a deposit amount. If the user cancels, lines 57–58 display an appropriate message and the method returns. If the user enters a deposit amount, lines 32–35 instruct the user to insert a deposit envelope with the correct amount. Recall that `Screen` method `DisplayDollarAmount` outputs a `Decimal` value formatted as a dollar amount.

Lines 38–39 sets a local `Boolean` variable to the value returned by the deposit slot's `IsDepositEnvelopeReceived` method, indicating whether a deposit envelope has been received. Recall that we coded method `IsDepositEnvelopeReceived` (lines 6–8 of Fig. J.5) to always return `True`, because we are simulating the functionality of the deposit slot and assume that the user always inserts an envelope. However, we code method `Execute` of class `Deposit` to test for the possibility that the user does not insert an envelope— good software engineering demands that programs account for all possible return values. Thus, class `Deposit` is prepared for future versions of `IsDepositEnvelopeReceived` that could return `False`. Lines 43–50 execute if the deposit slot receives an envelope. Lines 43–47 display an appropriate message to the user. Line 50 credits the user's account in the database with the deposit amount. Lines 52–54 execute if the deposit slot does not receive a deposit envelope. In this case, we display a message to the user stating that the ATM has canceled the transaction. The method then returns without modifying the user's account.

J.13 Module ATMCaseStudy

Module ATMCaseStudy (Fig. J.12) simply allows us to start, or "turn on," the ATM and test the implementation of our ATM system model. Module ATMCaseStudy's Main method (lines 4–7) does nothing more than instantiate a new ATM object named theATM (line 5) and invoke its Run method (line 6) to start the ATM.

J.14 Wrap-Up

Now that we have presented the complete ATM implementation, you can see that many issues arose during implementation for which we did not provide detailed UML diagrams. This is not uncommon in an object-oriented design and implementation experience. For example, many attributes listed in the class diagrams were implemented as Visual Basic properties so that clients of the classes could gain controlled access to the underlying Private instance variables. We did not make these properties during our design process, because there was nothing in the requirements document or our design process to indicate that certain attributes would eventually need to be accessed outside of their classes.

We also encountered various issues with simulating hardware. A real world ATM is a hardware device that does not have a complete computer keyboard. One problem with using a computer keyboard to simulate the keypad is that the user can enter non-digits as input. We did not spend much time dealing with such issues, because this problem is not possible in a real ATM, which has only a numeric keypad. However, having to think about issues like this is a good thing. Quite typically, software designs for complete systems involve simulating hardware devices like the cash dispenser and keypad. Despite the fact that some aspects of our ATM may seem contrived, in real world systems, hardware design and implementation often occurs in parallel with software design and implementation. In such cases, the software cannot be implemented in final form because the hardware is not yet ready. So, software developers must simulate the hardware as we have done in this case study with the keypad, cash dispenser and deposit slot.

Congratulations on completing the entire software engineering ATM case study! We hope you found this experience to be valuable and that it reinforced many of the concepts that you learned in Chapters 1–11. We would sincerely appreciate your comments, criticisms and suggestions. You can reach us at deitel@deitel.com. We will respond promptly.

```
1    ' ATMCaseStudy.vb
2    ' Module for testing the ATM case study.
3    Module ATMCaseStudy
4        Sub Main()
5            Dim theATM As New ATM()
6            theATM.Run()
7        End Sub ' Main
8    End Module ' ATMCaseStudy
```

Fig. J.12 | ATMCaseStudy.vb starts the ATM.

UML 2: Additional Diagram Types

K.1 Introduction

If you read the optional Software Engineering Case Study sections in Chapters 1 3–9 and 11, you should now have a comfortable grasp of the UML diagram types that we use to model our ATM system. The case study is intended for use in first- or second-semester courses, so we limit our discussion to a concise subset of the UML. The UML 2 provides 13 diagram types. The end of Section 3.9 summarizes the six diagram types that we use in the case study. This appendix lists and briefly defines the seven remaining diagram types.

K.2 Additional Diagram Types

The following are the seven diagram types that we have chosen not to use in our Software Engineering Case Study.

- *Object diagrams* model a "snapshot" of the system by modeling a system's objects and their relationships at a specific point in time. Each object represents an instance of a class from a class diagram, and several objects may be created from one class. For our ATM system, an object diagram could show several distinct Account objects side by side, illustrating that they are all part of the bank's account database.

- *Component diagrams* model the *artifacts* and *components*—resources (which include source files)—that make up the system.

- *Deployment diagrams* model the system's runtime requirements (such as the computer or computers on which the system will reside), memory requirements, or other devices the system requires during execution.

- *Package diagrams* model the hierarchical structure of *packages* (which are groups of classes) in the system at compile time and the relationships that exist between the packages.

- *Composite structure diagrams* model the internal structure of a complex object at runtime. New in UML 2, they allow system designers to hierarchically decompose a complex object into smaller parts. Composite structure diagrams are beyond the scope of our case study. They are more appropriate for larger industrial applications, which exhibit complex groupings of objects at execution time.

- *Interaction overview diagrams*, new in UML 2, provide a summary of control flow in the system by combining elements of several types of behavioral diagrams (e.g., activity diagrams, sequence diagrams).

- *Timing diagrams*, also new in UML 2, model the timing constraints imposed on stage changes and interactions between objects in a system.

To learn more about these diagrams and advanced UML topics, please visit www.uml.org and the Web resources listed at the ends of Section 1.9 and Section 3.9.

L

Primitive Types

Type	Size in bytes	Value range
SByte	1	−128 to 127, inclusive
Byte	1	0 to 255, inclusive
Boolean	2	True or False
Char	2	0 to 65,535, inclusive (representing the Unicode character set)
Short	2	−32,768 to 32,767, inclusive
UShort	2	0 to 65,535, inclusive
Integer	4	−2,147,483,648 to 2,147,483,647, inclusive
UInteger	4	0 to 4,294,967,295, inclusive
Single	4	negative range: −3.4028235E+38 to −1.401298E-45 positive range: 1.401298E−45 to 3.4028235E+38
Long	8	−9,223,372,036,854,775,808 to 9,223,372,036,854,775,807, inclusive
ULong	8	0 to 18,446,744,073,709,551,615, inclusive
Double	8	negative range: −1.79769313486231570E+308 to −4.94065645841246544E−324 positive range: 4.94065645841246544E−324 to 1.79769313486231570E+308
Date	8	0:00:00 on 1 January 0001 to 23:59:59 on 31 December 9999

Fig. L.1 | Primitive types. (Part 1 of 2.)

Type	Size in bytes	Value range
Decimal	16	Range with no decimal point: ±79,228,162,514,264,337,593,543,950,335 Range with 28 places to the right of the decimal point: ±7.9228162514264337593543950335 The smallest nonzero number is ±0.0000000000000000000000000001 (±1E–28)
String	Depends on platform	up to approximately 2 billion Unicode characters

Fig. L.1 | Primitive types. (Part 2 of 2.)

Additional Primitive Type Information

This appendix is based on information from Section 7.3 of *The Microsoft Visual Basic Language Specification* (available at `http://go.microsoft.com/fwlink/?LinkId=62990`) and additional information provided at the site

`msdn.microsoft.com/library/en-us/vblr7/html/vagrpDataType.asp`

Index

CD-ROM Warranty

This program was reproduced by Prentice Hall under special arrangement with Microsoft Corporation. For this reason, Prentice Hall is responsible for the product warranty. If your disk is defective, please return it to Prentice Hall, who will arrange for its replacement. PLEASE DO NOT RETURN IT TO OR CONTACT MICROSOFT CORPORATION FOR SOFTWARE SUPPORT. This product is provided for free, and no support is provided for by Prentice hall or Microsoft Corporation. To the extent of any inconsistencies between this statement and the end user license agreement which accompanies this program, this statement shall govern.

Prentice Hall PTR warrants the enclosed CD-ROM to be free of defects in materials and faulty workmanship under normal use for a period of ninety days after purchase (when purchased new). If a defect is discovered in the CD-ROM during this warranty period, a replacement CD-ROM can be obtained at no charge by sending the defective CD-ROM, postage prepaid, with proof of purchase to:

Disc Exchange
Prentice Hall PTR
Pearson Technology Group
75 Arlington Street, Suite 300
Boston, MA 02116
Email: AWPro@aw.com

Prentice Hall PTR makes no warranty or representation, either expressed or implied, with respect to this software, its quality, performance, merchantability, or fitness for a particular purpose. In no event will Prentice Hall PTR, its distributors, or dealers be liable for direct, indirect, special, incidental, or consequential damages arising out of the use or inability to use the software. The exclusion of implied warranties is not permitted in some states. Therefore, the above exclusion may not apply to you. This warranty provides you with specific legal rights. There may be other rights that you may have that vary from state to state. The contents of this CD-ROM are intended for personal use only.